BECKETT
WRESTLING
A L M A N A C

BECKETT - THE #1 AUTHORITY ON COLLECTIBLES

THE HOBBY'S MOST RELIABLE
AND RELIED UPON SOURCE ™

Founder: Dr. James Beckett III

Edited by Matt Bible and the Price Guide Staff of Beckett Collectibles LLC

BECKETT is a registered trademark of BECKETT COLLECTIBLES LLC, DALLAS, TEXAS
Manufactured in the United States of America | Published by Beckett Media LLC

Beckett Collectibles LLC
4635 McEwen Dr.
Dallas, TX 75244
972.991.6657
beckett.com

First Printing
ISBN: 978-1-936681-40-2

BECKETT WRESTLING ALMANAC

NUMBER 4
BECKETT - THE #1 AUTHORITY ON COLLECTIBLES

EDITORIAL
Mike Payne - Editorial Director

COVER DESIGN
Eric Knagg - Graphic Designer

ADVERTISING
Ted Barker - Advertising Director
972.448.9147, tbarker@beckett.com
Alex Soriano - Advertising Sales
Executive, 619.392.5299,
alex@beckett.com

COLLECTIBLES DATA PUBLISHING
Brian Fleischer
Manager, | Sr. Market Analyst
Daniel Moscoso - Digital Studio
Lloyd Almonguera, Matt Bible,
Jeff Camay, Steve Dalton, Justin
Grunert, Badz Mercader, Eric Norton,
Kristian Redulla, Sam Zimmer
Price Guide Staff

BECKETT GRADING SERVICES
Jeromy Murray
VP, Grading & Authentication
jmurray@beckett.com
4635 McEwen Road, Dallas, TX 75244
Grading Sales – 972-448-9188 |
grading@beckett.com

BECKETT GRADING SALES/ SHOW STAFF
DALLAS OFFICE
4635 McEwen, Dallas, TX 75244
Derek Ficken - Midwest/Southeast
Regional Sales Manager
dficken@beckett.com
972.448.9144

NEW YORK OFFICE
Charles Stabile - Northeast Regional
Sales Manager
484 White Plains Rd, 2nd Floor,
Eastchester, N.Y. 10709
cstabile@beckett.com
914.268.0533

ASIA OFFICE
Dongwoon Lee - Asia/Pacific Sales
Manager, Seoul, Korea
dongwoonl@beckett.com
Cell: +82.10.6826.6868

GRADING CUSTOMER SERVICE:
972-448-9188 or grading@beckett.com

OPERATIONS
Amit Sharma – Manager-Business Analytics
Alberto Chavez - Sr. Logistics &
Facilities Manager

EDITORIAL, PRODUCTION & SALES OFFICE
4635 McEwen Road,
Dallas TX 75244
972.991.6657
www.beckett.com

CUSTOMER SERVICE
Beckett Collectibles, LLC
4635 Mc Ewen Road.
Dallas, TX 75244
Subscriptions, Address Changes,
Renewals, Missing or Damaged Copies
866.287.9383 • 239.653.0225

FOREIGN INQUIRES
subscriptions@beckett.com
Back Issues: www.beckettmedia.com

BOOKS, MERCHANDISE, REPRINTS
239.280.2380
Dealer Sales & Production
dealers@beckett.com

BECKETT COLLECTIBLES, LLC
Jeromy Murray: President - Beckett
Collectibles LLC

COVER BACKGROUND: GETTY IMAGES

SUPERIOR SPORTS INVESTMENTS

SSI

Always Buying Unopened Boxes and Singles

 Call us at: 817-770-0804

 Text us pictures of your cards

 Check Out Our Website for Our Huge Inventory of Graded Cards!

We have purchased thousands of collections
THIS YEAR!

WE BUY WHAT OTHERS DON'T!

www.superiorsportsinvestments.com

CONTENTS

BECKETT WRESTLING ALMANAC - NUMBER 4

| IN MEMORIAM |

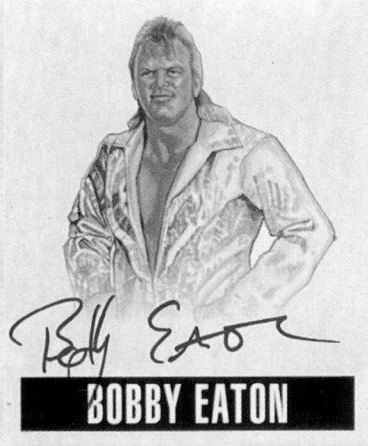

BOBBY EATON

THE NATURAL BUTCH REED

A LEG UP!

DAFFNEY

PAUL ORNDORFF

How-To-Use Guide and Glossary..........................18

Trading Cards...19-209

Action Figures & Figurines 210-272

ABOUT THE AUTHOR

     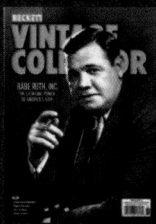

Based in Dallas, Beckett Collectibles LLC is the leading publisher of sports and specialty market collectible products in the U.S. Beckett operates Beckett.com and is the premier publisher of monthly sports and entertainment collectibles magazines.

The growth of Beckett Media's sports magazines, **Beckett Baseball, Beckett Sports Card Monthly, Beckett Basketball, Beckett Football, Beckett Hockey** and **Beckett Vintage Collector**, is another indication of the unprecedented popularity of sports cards. Founded in 1984 by Dr. James Beckett, Beckett sports magazines contain the most extensive and accepted Price Guide, collectible superstar covers, colorful feature articles, the Hot List, tips for beginners, information on errors and varieties, autograph collecting tips and profiles of the sport's hottest stars. Published 12 times a year, **Beckett Baseball** is the hobby's largest baseball periodical.

TOP 10
AEW WRESTLERS

1. "HANGMAN" ADAM PAGE

2. KENNY OMEGA

3. MJF

4. DARBY ALLIN

5. JON MOXLEY

6. BRITT BAKER

7. JUNGLE BOY

8. HIKARU SHIDA

9. SAMMY GUEVARA

10. REY FENIX

ALL-TIME TOP 10 WRESTLERS

1. HULK HOGAN

2. RIC FLAIR

3. UNDERTAKER

4. STONE COLD STEVE AUSTIN

5. JOHN CENA

6. THE ROCK

7. SHAWN MICHAELS

8. BRUNO SAMMARTINO

9. BRET "HIT MAN" HART

10. "MACHO MAN" RANDY SAVAGE

DOUBLE DOWN &
SAVE BIG

ALL-TIME TOP 10 WOMAN WRESTLERS

1. TRISH STRATUS

2. CHARLOTTE FLAIR

3. CHYNA

4. THE FABULOUS MOOLAH

5. AWESOME KONG (KHARMA)

6. LITA

7. BETH PHOENIX

8. BECKY LYNCH

9. ALUNDRA BLAYZE (MADUSA)

10. SENSATIONAL SHERRI

ALL-TIME TOP 10 BABYFACES

1. JOHN CENA

2. STING

3. HULK HOGAN

4. BRUNO SAMMARTINO

5. ANDRE THE GIANT

6. THE ROCK

7. BOB BACKLUND

8. DUSTY RHODES

9. RICKY "THE DRAGON" STEAMBOAT

10. REY MYSTERIO

ALL-TIME TOP 10 HEELS

1. TRIPLE H

2. RIC FLAIR

3. "HOLLYWOOD" HULK HOGAN

4. THE FABULOUS MOOLAH

5. BOBBY "THE BRAIN" HEENAN

6. MR. MCMAHON

7. "MR. PERFECT" CURT HENNIG

8. "THE MILLION DOLLAR MAN" TED DIBIASE

9. HARLEY RACE

10. CHRIS JERICHO

ALL-TIME TOP 10

VINTAGE ACTION FIGURES
(PRE-2000)

1. 1993 HASBRO WWF SERIES 7 KAMALA CRESCENT MOON BELLY

2. 1993 HASBRO WWF MAGAZINE SERIES UNDERTAKER

3. 1992 HASBRO WWF SERIES 3 BRUTUS THE BARBER BEEFCAKE ZEBRA TIGHTS

4. 1989 LJN WWF SUPERSTARS BLACK CARD RE-RELEASE MACHO MAN RANDY SAVAGE

5. 1987 LJN WWF WRESTLING SUPERSTARS SERIES 4 MISS ELIZABETH PURPLE SKIRT

6. 1991 HASBRO WWF SERIES 2 DUSTY RHODES

7. 1994 HASBRO WWF SERIES 11 1-2-3 KID

8. 1984 LJN WWF WRESTLING SUPERSTARS SERIES 1 HULK HOGAN

9. 1991 GALOOB WCW SUPERSTARS UK BIG JOSH

10. 1991 GALOOB WCW SUPERSTARS SERIES 1 STING ORANGE TIGHTS

ALL-TIME TOP 10

ACTION FIGURES
(2000-PRESENT)

1. 2004-08 JAKKS PACIFIC WWE
ULTIMATE WARRIOR EXCLUSIVES

2. 2006 JAKKS PACIFIC WWE EXCLUSIVES
HULK HOGAN/100* TOYFARE MAGAZINE

3. 2004 JAKKS PACIFIC WWE EMPLOYEE
GIFT EXCLUSIVES RIC FLAIR/25*

4. 2004 JAKKS PACIFIC WWE
EXCLUSIVES ROWDY RODDY PIPER/100*
TOYFARE MAGAZINE

5. 2006 JAKKS PACIFIC WWE
EXCLUSIVES BOBBY THE BRAIN HEENAN
WEASEL/100* TOY FAIR GIVEAWAY

6. 2008 JAKKS PACIFIC WWE
EXCLUSIVES EDDIE GUERRERO/100*
NYC TOY FAIR GIVEAWAY

7. 2007 JAKKS PACIFIC WWE
EXCLUSIVES ROWDY RODDY PIPER DELUXE
STYLE/100* NYC TOY FAIR GIVEAWAY

8. 2008 JAKKS PACIFIC WWE EXCLUSIVES
UNDERTAKER GITD/100*
TOYFARE MAGAZINE

9. 2009 JAKKS PACIFIC WWE
EXCLUSIVES REY MYSTERIO/100*
TOYFARE MAGAZINE

10. 2009 JAKKS PACIFIC WWE
EXCLUSIVES SUNNY/100*
TOYFARE MAGAZINE

ALL-TIME TOP 10
FUNKO POPS

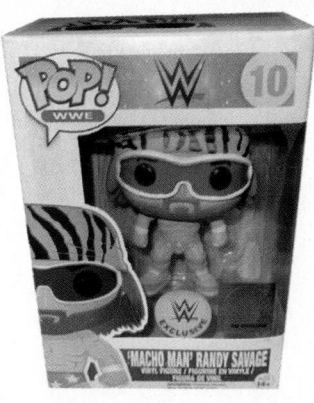

1. #10B MACHO MAN RANDY SAVAGE (PINK)#((2015 WWE.COM EXCLUSIVE)

2. #6C REY MYSTERIO (DARK)#((2014 SDCC EXCLUSIVE)

3. #1D JOHN CENA THE U (GREEN HAT)#((2014 WWE.COM EXCLUSIVE)

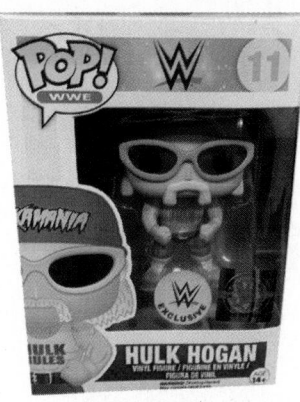

4. #11B HULK HOGAN HULK RULES#((2014 WWE.COM EXCLUSIVE)

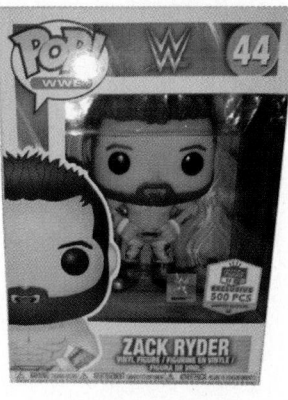

5. #44C ZACK RYDER (GREEN TIGHTS)/500*#((2017 FUNKO HQ EXCLUSIVE)

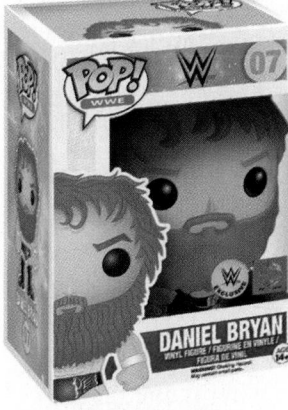

6. #7C DANIEL BRYAN (PATTERNED)#((2014 WWE.COM EXCLUSIVE)

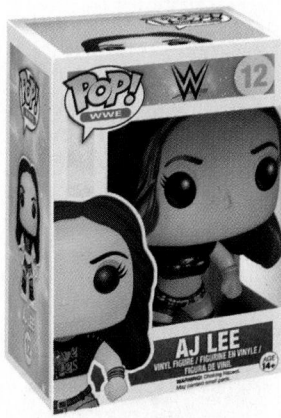

7. #12 AJ LEE#((2014 WWE.COM EXCLUSIVE)

8. #1B JOHN CENA (BLACK PANTS)#((2015 WWE.COM EXCLUSIVE)

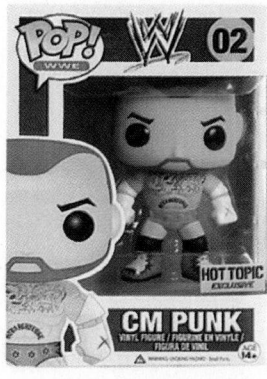

9. #2B CM PUNK (PINK TRUNKS)#((2014 HOT TOPIC EXCLUSIVE)

10. #6B REY MYSTERIO (BRIGHT BLUE)#((2014 7-11 EXCLUSIVE)

ALL-TIME TOP 10 AUTOGRAPH CARDS

1. 1998 DUOCARDS WWF AUTOGRAPHS
THE ROCK

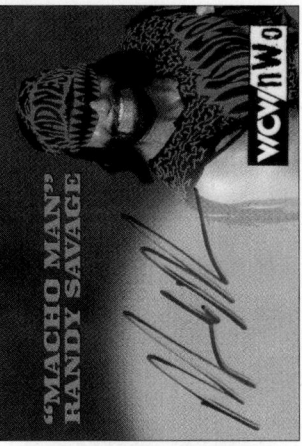

2. 1999 TOPPS WCW/NWO NITRO
AUTHENTIC SIGNATURES "MACHO MAN"
RANDY SAVAGE

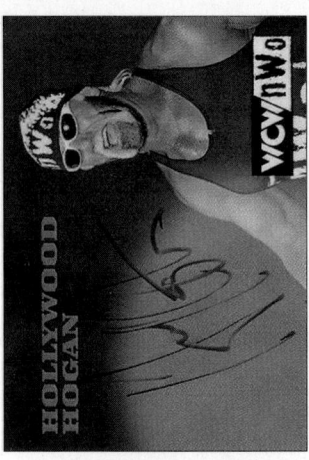

3. 1998 TOPPS WCW/NWO AUTHENTIC
SIGNATURES HULK HOGAN

4. 2001 FLEER WWF WRESTLEMANIA
SIGNATURE MOVES AUTOGRAPHS STONE
COLD STEVE AUSTIN

5. 2001 FLEER WWF ULTIMATE DIVA
COLLECTION SIGNED WITH A KISS
TRISH STRATUS

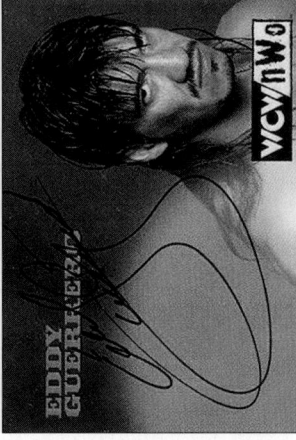

6. 1998 TOPPS WCW/NWO AUTHENTIC
SIGNATURES EDDIE GUERRERO

7. 2001 FLEER RAW IS WAR BOOTY
AUTOGRAPHS UNDERTAKER

8. 2019 TOPPS WWE TRANSCENDENT
VINCE MCMAHON

9. 1999 TOPPS WCW/NWO NITRO
AUTHENTIC SIGNATURES
MISS ELIZABETH

10. 2001 FLEER WWF CHAMPIONSHIP
CLASH DIVAS PRIVATE SIGNING
STEPHANIE MCMAHON-HELMSLEY

ALL-TIME TOP 10 CARD SETS

1. 1985 TOPPS WWF

2. 1979 RAX ROAST BEEF GULAS NWA MID AMERICA CHAMPIONSHIP WRESTLING

3. 1982 PWE WRESTLING ALL-STARS SERIES A

4. 1982 PWE WRESTLING ALL-STARS SERIES B

5. 1954-55 PARKHURST WRESTLING

6. 2019 TOPPS WWE TRANSCENDENT

7. 2015 TOPPS WWE UNDISPUTED

8. 2016 TOPPS WWE DIVAS REVOLUTION

9. 1987 TOPPS WWF

10. 2021 UPPER DECK AEW

Welcome to the Beckett® Wrestling Almanac. This 4th edition is an enhanced and expanded volume with the addition of new releases, updated prices, and changes to older listings. The Beckett® Wrestling Almanac will do what no other publication has done -- give you the most complete and comprehensive collectible listings possible. The prices were added to the checklists just prior to printing and reflect not the author's opinions or desires, but the going retail prices for each collectible, based on the marketplace such as conventions and shows, hobby shops, online trading, auction results and other first-hand reports of realized sales.

What is the best price guide available on the market today? Of course sellers will prefer the price guide with the highest prices, while buyers will naturally prefer the one with the lower prices. Accuracy, however, is the true test. Compared to other price guides, The Beckett® Wrestling Almanac may not always have the highest or lowest values, but the accuracy of both our checklists and pricing – produced with the utmost integrity – will make it the most widely used reference book in the hobby.

LISTINGS AND SECTIONS

Each collection is personal and reflects the individuality of its owner. There are no set rules on how to collect. Since collecting is a hobby or leisure pastime, what you collect, how much you collect, and how much time and money you spend collecting are entirely up to you. The funds you have available for collecting and your own personal taste should determine how you collect.

It is not possible to collect every card and action figure ever produced. Therefore, beginners, as well as intermediate and advanced collectors, usually specialize in some way. One of the reasons this hobby is popular is that individual collectors can define and tailor their collecting methods to match their own tastes.

Many collectors select complete sets from particular years or acquire only certain wrestlers/athletes, while some collectors are only interested in collecting certain figures or autographs.

WHAT'S LISTED

Products listed in the Price Guide typically:
- Are produced by licensed manufacturers
- Are widely available
- Have market activity on single items
- International releases

HOW IT'S LISTED

Unlike regular Beckett® Almanacs, the sort order of this publication is somewhat unique. Like the others, all listings are organized 1) alphabetically then 2) chronologically.

WHAT THE COLUMNS MEAN

The LO and HI columns reflect current retail selling ranges. The HI column on the right generally represents the full retail selling price. The LO column on the left generally represents the lowest price one would expect to find with extensive shopping.

GRADING

All cards in the price guide are based on NrMint to Mint condition. Damaged cards are generally sold for 25 to 75 percent of Mint value. Toy prices are based on Mint condition. Toys that are loose (out-of-package) are generally sold for 50 percent of the listed price, but may list for less/more depending on market sales.

CURRENCY

This price guide is intended to reflect the entire North American market. While not all of the cards are produced in the United States, they will reflect the market value in U.S. dollars.

GLOSSARY/LEGEND

Our glossary defines terms most frequently used in the collecting hobby. Some of these terms are common to other types of collecting while others may have several meanings depending on the use and context.

7-11	7-11 Exclusive
AMZ	Amazon Exclusive
ARGO	Argo's Exclusive
BJ	BJ's Exclusive
BL	Big Lots Exclusive
CAN	Issued in Canada
CH	Chase Figure
FB	Flashback
FCE	Fall Convention Exclusive
FHQ	Funko Headquarters Exclusive
FL	Foot Locker Exclusive
FP	First Piece in an Action Figure Line
FYE	fYe Exclusive
GITD	Glow-in-the-Dark
GS	GameStop Exclusive
HILLS	Hills Exclusive
HT	Hot Topic Exclusive
KB	Kay-Bee Toys Exclusive
KM	K-Mart Exclusive
LE	Limited Edition
MA	Mail-Away
MANIA TIX	WrestleMania Ticket Mail-In Exclusive
MEI	Meijer Exclusive
NYC TF	New York City Toy Fair Exclusive
NYCC	New York Comic Con
OL	Internet/Online Exclusive
PROFIG	Profigures.com Exclusive
RTWM21 TOUR	- Road to WrestleMania 21 Tour Giveaway Exclusive
RSC	Ringside Collectibles Exclusive
RSF	Ringside Fest Exclusive
SC	Sam's Club Exclusive
SCE	Summer Convention Exclusive
SDCC	San Diego Comic Con Exclusive
SE	Special Edition
TAR	Target Exclusive
TFM	Toyfare Magazine Exclusive
TRU	Toys R Us Exclusive
UK	Issued in United Kingdom
US	Issued in the United States
V	Vaulted (applies only to Funko products)
WG	Walgreens Exclusive
WM	Walmart Exclusive
WRMS	WrestleMania Shop Exclusive
WWE SZ	WWE Shopzone Exclusive

As with any new publication, we appreciate reader feedback. If you have any questions, concerns, corrections or suggestions, please contact us at: **nonsports@beckett.com**

Trading Cards

1994 Action Packed WWF

COMPLETE SET (42)	20.00	50.00
COMPLETE FACTORY SET (42)	25.00	60.00
UNOPENED BOX (24 PACKS)		
UNOPENED PACK (6 CARDS)		
COLOSSAL CRUSHERS (30-36)		
1 Bam Bam Bigelow	1.25	3.00
2 I.R.S.	.75	2.00
3 Doink the Clown	.40	1.00
4 Diesel	3.00	8.00
5 Razor Ramon	.25	.60
6 Ludvig Borga	.20	.50
7 Shawn Michaels	.40	1.00
8 Yokozuna	1.25	3.00
9 Head Shrinkers	.20	.50
10 Bushwhackers	.20	.50
11 Bob Backlund	.20	.50
12 Undertaker	5.00	12.00
13 Macho Man Randy Savage	.50	1.25
14 Adam Bomb	.20	.50
15 Bret Hit Man Hart	.60	1.50
16 Luna	.25	.60
17 1-2-3 Kid	.20	.50
18 Owen Hart	3.00	8.00
19 Lex Luger	.60	1.50
20 Bastion Booger	.20	.50
21 Quebecers	.20	.50
22 Marty Jannetty	.20	.50
23 Freddie Blassie	.25	.60
24 Stenier Brothers	.25	.60
25 Smoking Gunns	.20	.50
26 Andre the Giant	2.00	5.00
27 Paul Bearer	.30	.75
28 M.O.M.	.20	.50
29 Tatanka	.20	.50
30 Yokozuna CC	2.00	5.00
31 Diesel CC	2.00	5.00
32 Adam Bomb CC	.20	.50
33 Bastion Booger CC	.20	.50
34 Earthquake CC	.20	.50
35 Mabel CC	.20	.50
36 Ludvig Borga CC	.20	.50
37 Razor Ramon	2.50	6.00
38 Shawn Michaels	2.00	5.00
39 Macho Man Randy Savage	2.00	5.00
40 Bret Hit Man Hart	2.00	5.00
41 Steiner Brothers	.25	.60
42 Undertaker/Paul Bearer CC	4.00	10.00

1994 Action Packed WWF 24 Kt Gold Leaf

COMPLETE SET (6)	25.00	60.00
STATED ODDS 1:24		
1G Razor Ramon	15.00	40.00
2G Shawn Michaels	8.00	20.00
3G Macho Man Randy Savage	6.00	15.00
4G Bret Hit Man Hart	6.00	15.00
5G Steiner Brothers	5.00	12.00
6G Undertaker/Paul Bearer	10.00	25.00

1994 Action Packed WWF Autographed Prototypes

1 Macho Man Randy Savage	500.00	1000.00
2 Undertaker	300.00	600.00

1994 Action Packed WWF Prototypes

COMPLETE SET (2)	3.00	8.00
1 Macho Man Randy Savage	2.00	5.00
2 Undertaker	2.50	6.00

1995 Action Packed WWF

COMPLETE SET (42)	15.00	40.00
COMPLETE FACTORY SET (42)	15.00	40.00
UNOPENED BOX (24 PACKS)		
UNOPENED PACK (6 CARDS)		
1 Bret Hit Man Hart	.30	.75
2 Undertaker	.75	2.00
3 Razor Ramon	.40	1.00
4 Diesel	.20	.50
5 Heavenly Bodies	.20	.50
6 Doink the Clown	.20	.50
7 Lex Luger	.25	.60
8 Alundra Blayze	.50	1.25
9 Yokozuna	.20	.50
10 Bam Bam Bigelow	.25	.60
11 British Bulldog	.25	.60
12 Crush	.20	.50
13 King Kong Bundy	.25	.60
14 Nikolai Volkoff	.20	.50
15 Tatanka	.20	.50
16 Paul Bearer	.30	.75
17 Head Shrinkers	.20	.50
18 Duke the Dumpster	.20	.50
19 Dink	.20	.50
20 Bushwhackers	.20	.50
21 Diesel	.20	.50
22 Mabel	.20	.50
23 Smoking Gunns	.20	.50
24 Undertaker	1.25	3.00
25 Shawn Michaels DD	.75	2.00
26 Owen Hart DD	.50	1.25
27 Jim The Anvil Neidhart DD	.25	.60
28 Mr. Fuji DD	.20	.50
29 IRS DD	.60	1.50
30 Luna DD	.40	1.00
31 Well Dunn DD	.20	.50
32 Jerry The King Lawler DD	.40	1.00
33 Double J Jeff Jarrett DD	.25	.60
34 Mr. Bob Backlund DD	.20	.50
35 Bull Nakano DD	.20	.50
36 Million Dollar Man Ted DiBiase DD	.30	.75
37 1-2-3 Kid HFR	.20	.50
38 Shawn Michaels HFR	.40	1.00
39 Adam Bomb HFR	.20	.50
40 Bob Spark Plugg Holly HFR	.25	.60
41 Bret "Hit Man" Hart HFR	.40	1.00
42 Bam Bam Bigelow HFR	.25	.60

1995 Action Packed WWF 24 Kt Gold Leaf

COMPLETE SET (12)	30.00	75.00
STATED ODDS 1:96		
G1 Shawn Michaels	6.00	15.00
G2 Owen Hart	6.00	15.00
G3 Jim The Anvil Neidhart	4.00	10.00
G4 Mr. Fuji	4.00	10.00
G5 IRS	4.00	10.00
G6 Luna	5.00	12.00
G7 Well Dunn	3.00	8.00
G8 Jerry The King Lawler	5.00	12.00
G9 Double J Jeff Jarrett	4.00	10.00
G10 Mr. Bob Backlund	4.00	10.00
G11 Bull Nakano	3.00	8.00
G12 Ted Dibiase	5.00	12.00

1995 Action Packed WWF Promos

LT1 Lawrence Taylor WMXI	15.00	40.00
MM1 Diesel	6.00	15.00
MM2 Undertaker	10.00	25.00

1952 Al Haft's Stars of the Mat

COMPLETE SET (16)	
NNO Argentine Rocca	
NNO Big Bill Miller	
NNO Buddy Rogers	
NNO Don Arnold	
NNO Don Eagle	
NNO Edmund Francis	
NNO Frankie Talaber	
NNO Gene Stanlee (Mr. America)	
NNO Honest Johnny Valentine	
NNO Jackie Nichols	
NNO Joe Scarpello	
NNO Lou Thesz	
NNO Luther Lindsey	
NNO Marvin Mercer	
NNO Professor Roy Shire	
NNO Ruffy Silverstein	

1953 Al Haft's Stars of the Mat

COMPLETE SET (16)	
NNO Argentina Rocca	
NNO Bob Geigel	
NNO Buddy Nature Boy Rogers	
NNO Daffy Ed Francis	
NNO Don Arnold	
NNO Don Eagle	
NNO Don Lewin	
NNO Dr. Big Bill Miller	
NNO Frankie Talaber	
NNO Joe Scarpello	
NNO Lou Thesz	
NNO Luther Lindsey	
NNO Marvin Mercer	
NNO Roy Professor Shire	
NNO Ruffy Silverstein	
NNO Vern Gagne	

1954 Al Haft's Stars of the Mat

COMPLETE SET (12)	
NNO Al Kashey	
NNO Andre Drapp	
NNO Bob Geigel	
NNO Carol Cook	
NNO Don Eagle	
NNO Dr. Big Bill Miller	
NNO Frankie Talaber	
NNO Great Scott	
NNO Jack Pesek	
NNO June Byers	
NNO Mary Jane Mull	
NNO Nell Stewart	

2018 All In Series 1

COMPLETE SET (36)	50.00	100.00
1 All In	.60	1.50
2 Cody	4.00	10.00
3 Brandi	2.50	6.00
4 Kenny Omega	5.00	12.00
5 Matt Jackson	2.50	6.00
6 Nick Jackson	2.50	6.00
7 Nick Aldis	1.25	3.00
8 Stephen Amell	2.00	5.00
9 Joey Janela	2.00	5.00
10 Penelope Ford	3.00	8.00
11 Tessa Blanchard	2.50	6.00
12 Kazuchika Okada	2.00	5.00
13 Kota Ibushi	2.00	5.00
14 Penta El Zero M	2.50	6.00
15 Rey Fenix	3.00	8.00
16 El Bandido	.60	1.50
17 Flip Gordon	.60	1.50
18 MJF	25.00	60.00
19 Adam Page	4.00	10.00
20 Joey Ryan	3.00	8.00
21 Rey Mysterio	1.50	4.00
22 Jerry Lynn	.60	1.50
23 Jay Lethal	2.00	5.00
24 Burnard	.60	1.50
25 Briscoe Brothers	.75	2.00
26 Best Friends	2.00	5.00
27 Chelsea Green	5.00	12.00
28 Britt Baker	15.00	40.00
29 Madison Rayne	2.50	6.00
30 Marty Scurll	.60	1.50
31 SoCal Uncensored	2.00	5.00
32 BTE	.60	1.50
33 Masa	.60	1.50
34 Bury	.60	1.50
35 Cracker Barrel	.60	1.50
36 Checklist	.75	2.00

1926 Allen's Candy Wrestlers

COMPLETE SET (24)	
NNO Al Karasick	
(Combination Bar & Toe Hold)	

NNO Billy Edwards
NNO Billy Edwards
(Hammerlock & Leg Cradle Hold)
NNO Billy Meeske
NNO Billy Meeske
(Standing Reverse Wristlock)
NNO Clarence Weber
NNO John Kilonis
NNO John Kilonis
(Aeroplane Spin)
NNO John Kilonis
(Reverse Head and Armlock)
NNO Mike Yokel
NNO Mike Yokel
(Short Arm Scissors)
NNO Mike Yokel
(Standing Splits)
NNO Sam Clapham
NNO Sam Clapham
(Standing Wristlock)
NNO Sam Clapham
(Straight Arm Bar & Shoulder Twist)
NNO Sam Clapham vs. Mike Yokel
(Body Scissors & Armhold)
NNO Ted Thye
NNO Ted Thye
(Headlock)
NNO Ted Thye
(Reserve Wristlock)
NNO Ted Thye
(Standing Reverse Double Wristlock)
NNO Walter Miller
(Head & Armlock)
NNO Walter Miller
(Half Nelson)
NNO Walter Miller
(Head & Crotch Hold)
NNO Walter Miller
(Straight Arm Scissors)

1999 Artbox WWF MotionCardz

COMPLETE SET (40)		10.00	25.00
UNOPENED BOX (24 PACKS)			
UNOPENED PACK (8 CARDS)			
1	The Undertaker SM	.40	1.00
2	Stone Cold Steve Austin SM	.50	1.25
3	Kane SM	.40	1.00
4	Kane SM	.40	1.00
5	Road Dogg SM	.40	1.00
6	The Rock SM	.60	1.50
7	Stone Cold Steve Austin SM	.50	1.25
8	The Undertaker SM	.75	2.00
9	The Undertaker/Kane	.40	1.00
10	The Undertaker/Kane	.40	1.00
11	The Undertaker/Kane	.40	1.00
12	The Undertaker/Kane	.40	1.00
13	The Undertaker/Kane	.40	1.00
14	The Undertaker/Kane	.40	1.00
15	The Undertaker/Kane	.40	1.00
16	The Undertaker/Kane	.40	1.00
17	D-Generation X	.40	1.00
18	D-Generation X	.40	1.00
19	D-Generation X	.40	1.00
20	D-Generation X	.40	1.00
21	D-Generation X	.40	1.00
22	D-Generation X	.40	1.00
23	D-Generation X	.40	1.00
24	D-Generation X	.40	1.00

25	The Rock	.60	1.50
26	The Rock	.60	1.50
27	The Rock	.75	2.00
28	The Rock	.75	2.00
29	The Rock	.75	2.00
30	The Rock	.60	1.50
31	The Rock	.60	1.50
32	The Rock	2.00	5.00
33	Stone Cold Steve Austin	.50	1.25
34	Stone Cold Steve Austin	.50	1.25
35	Stone Cold Steve Austin	.50	1.25
36	Stone Cold Steve Austin	.50	1.25
37	Stone Cold Steve Austin	.50	1.25
38	Stone Cold Steve Austin	.50	1.25
39	Stone Cold Steve Austin	.50	1.25
40	Stone Cold Steve Austin	.50	1.25
R1	Sable Revealed	5.00	12.00

1999 Artbox WWF MotionCardz Attitudes

COMPLETE SET (4)		8.00	20.00
STATED ODDS 1:12			
AT1	Undertaker	6.00	15.00
AT2	No Holds Barred	1.50	4.00
AT3	Kane	1.25	3.00
AT4	D-Generation X	2.00	5.00

1999 Artbox WWF MotionCardz Temporary Tattooz

COMPLETE SET (8)		6.00	15.00
STATED ODDS 1:1			
WWF11	Stone Cold 3:16 Logo	1.25	3.00
WWF12	Kane	1.00	2.50
WWF13	Undertaker	1.25	3.00
WWF14	Stone Cold Skull Logo	1.25	3.00
WWF15	Stone Cold Skull Logo	1.25	3.00
WWF16	Stone Cold Skull Logo	1.25	3.00
WWF17	Raw Is War Logo	.75	2.00
WWF18	War Zone Logo	.75	2.00

1999 Artbox WWF MotionCardz Promos

P1	Val Venis/Taka Michinoku	4.00	10.00
P2	Undertaker/Road Dogg	5.00	12.00

2001 Artbox WWF Slams! MotionCardz

COMPLETE SET (45)		12.00	30.00
COMPLETE SET W/O SP (40)			
UNOPENED BOX (24 PACKS)			
UNOPENED PACK (4 CARDS)			
SP 41-44 STATED ODDS 1:12			
SP 45 STATED ODDS 1:240			
1	Test	.25	.60
2	Rikishi vs. Val Venis	.25	.60
3	The Undertaker vs. HHH FM	1.00	2.50
4	Bradshaw vs. Edge FM	.60	1.50
5	Trish Stratus FM	6.00	15.00
6	HHH vs. Chris Jericho	1.00	2.50
7	The Rock vs. Chris Benoit	1.00	2.50
8	Scotty 2 Hotty/Grandmaster Sexay FM	.25	.60
9	Road Dogg vs. Chris Jericho FM	.40	1.00
10	Bradshaw vs. Edge	.60	1.50
11	The Rock FM	2.50	6.00
12	D-Von & Buh-Buh Ray vs. Edge	.60	1.50
13	Buh-Buh Ray Dudley vs. Christian	.40	1.00
14	Trish vs. Lita FM	1.50	4.00

15	Rikishi vs. Val Venis	.25	.60
16	Steve Blackman	.15	.40
17	Steve Blackman vs. Crash Holly	.15	.40
18	Kurt Angle vs. The Undertaker	.75	2.00
19	The Undertaker vs. HHH	1.00	2.50
20	Lita vs. Test	1.00	2.50
21	Edge and Christian vs. Kane	.60	1.50
22	Bob Hardcore Holly vs. Kurt Angle	.60	1.50
23	Buh-Buh Ray vs. Road Dogg	.25	.60
24	X-Pac vs. Buh-Buh Ray Dudley	.25	.60
25	Commissioner Foley FM	.60	1.50
26	Faarooq vs. X-Pac	.25	.60
27	X-Pac vs. Faarooq	.25	.60
28	Chyna vs. Edge	.60	1.50
29	Buh-Buh Ray Dudley vs. Edge	.60	1.50
30	Hardyz vs. Dudley Boyz	.40	1.00
31	Steve Austin vs. Mr. Ass #1	1.00	2.50
32	The Rock	1.00	2.50
33	Stephanie vs. Buh-Buh Ray Dudley	.75	2.00
34	The Rock vs. Shane McMahon	2.50	6.00
35	Mankind vs. Prince Albert FM	.60	1.50
36	Grandmaster Sexay vs. Test FM	.25	.60
37	Rock & Mick Foley vs. Chris Benoit	1.00	2.50
38	Chris Benoit vs. Eddie Guerrero	.60	1.50
39	Edge vs. Buh-Buh Ray Dudley	.60	1.50
40	Val Venis vs. Rikishi	.25	.60
41	Kurt Angle/Hardcore Holly SP	1.00	2.50
42	Kane vs. Kurt Angle SP	1.00	2.50
43	Steve Blackman/Shano Mac SP	1.00	2.50
44	Matt Hardy SP	1.00	2.50
45	The Godfather SP		

1999 Candy Planet WWF Poster Puzzle Cards

COMPLETE SET (5)		
NNO	Kane	
NNO	The Rock	
NNO	Sable	
NNO	Stone Cold Steve Austin	
NNO	The Undertaker	

1997 Cardinal WWF Trivia Game Cards Series 1

COMPLETE SET (30)		200.00	400.00
1	Stone Cold Steve Austin	60.00	120.00
2	Justin Bradshaw	2.50	6.00
3	Brakus	2.00	5.00
4	British Bulldog	3.00	8.00
5	Crush	1.50	4.00
6	Diesel	2.00	5.00
7	Faarooq	1.50	4.00
8	Flash Funk	1.25	3.00
9	Doug Furnas	1.25	3.00
10	Henry Godwinn	1.25	3.00
11	Phineas Godwinn	1.25	3.00
12	The Goon	1.25	3.00
13	Bret Hit Man Hart	5.00	12.00
14	Owen Hart	3.00	8.00
15	Hunter Hearst-Helmsley	15.00	40.00
16	Bob Holly	2.00	5.00
17	Goldust	2.50	6.00
18	Ahmed Johnson	1.50	4.00
19	Philip LaFon	1.25	3.00
20	Jerry Lawler	2.00	5.00
21	Rocky Maivia	150.00	300.00
22	Mankind	4.00	10.00
23	Marc Mero	1.25	3.00

24	Shawn Michaels	3.00	8.00
25	Aldo Montoya	1.25	3.00
26	Papa Shango	1.25	3.00
27	Sycho Sid	2.00	5.00
28	The Sultan	1.25	3.00
29	Undertaker	10.00	25.00
30	Vader	2.00	5.00

2001 Cardinal WWF Trivia Game Cards Series 3

NNO	Al Snow	1.50	4.00
NNO	APA	1.50	4.00
NNO	The Big Show	2.00	5.00
NNO	Chris Benoit		
NNO	Chris Jericho		
NNO	Chyna	15.00	40.00
NNO	Debra		
NNO	Dudley Boyz	1.50	4.00
NNO	Edge & Christian	1.50	4.00
NNO	Hardy Boyz	3.00	8.00
NNO	Kane		
NNO	K-Kwik		
NNO	Kurt Angle	10.00	25.00
NNO	Lita	15.00	40.00
NNO	Perry Saturn w/Terri		
NNO	Rhyno		
NNO	Rikishi		
NNO	The Rock	20.00	50.00
NNO	RTC		
NNO	Steve Blackman	1.50	4.00
NNO	Stone Cold Steve Austin	10.00	25.00
NNO	Tazz		
NNO	Test		
NNO	Too Cool		
NNO	Triple H w/Stephanie McMahon-Helmsley		
NNO	Trish Stratus	25.00	60.00
NNO	Undertaker	8.00	20.00
NNO	Vince McMahon	4.00	10.00
NNO	William Regal	1.50	4.00
NNO	X-Pac	1.50	4.00

1995 CARDZ WCW Main Event

COMPLETE SET (100)		30.00	75.00
UNOPENED BOX (36 PACKS)		300.00	500.00
UNOPENED PACK (8 CARDS)		8.00	15.00
1	Wild Cat Willie	.20	.50
2	Hulk Hogan	2.00	5.00
3	Ric Flair	.30	.75
4	Sting	.25	.60
5	Macho Man Randy Savage	.20	.50
6	Frank Andersson	.10	.25
7	Marcus Bagwell	.20	.50
8	The Patriot	.10	.25
9	Paul Roma	.10	.25
10	Paul Orndorff	.12	.30
11	Blacktop Bully	.10	.25
12	Bobby Eaton	.10	.25
13	Diamond Dallas Page	.25	.60
14	Meng	.10	.25
15	Bunkhouse Buck	.10	.25
16	Booker T	.20	.50
17	Stevie Ray	.10	.25
18	Brad Armstrong	.10	.25
19	Arn Anderson	.12	.30
20	Lord Steven Regal	.12	.30
21	Johnny B. Badd	.10	.25
22	Flyin Brian	.30	.75
23	Big Bubba	.10	.25

24	Dustin Rhodes	.12	.30
25	Jerry Sags	.10	.25
26	Brian Knobs	.10	.25
27	Kevin Sullivan	.10	.25
28	Vader	.12	.30
29	Stunning Steve Austin	15.00	40.00
30	Alex Wright	.10	.25
31	Avalanche	.10	.25
32	Butcher	.10	.25
33	Hacksaw Jim Duggan	.20	.50
34	Dave Sullivan	.10	.25
35	Nasty Boys	.10	.25
36	Harlem Heat	.12	.30
37	Pretty Wonderful	.10	.25
38	Stars & Stripes	.10	.25
39	Monster Maniacs	.40	1.00
40	Jimmy Hart	.20	.50
41	Sister Sherri	.12	.30
42	Harley Race	.10	.25
43	Colonel Parker	.10	.25
44	Gary Cappetta	.10	.25
45	Mean Gene Okerlund	.60	1.50
46	Bobby Heenan	.20	.50
47	Tony Schiavone	.10	.25
48	Eric Bischoff	.40	1.00
49	Gordon Solie	.10	.25
50	Larry Zbyszko	.12	.30
51	Nick Bockwinkel	.10	.25
52	Diamond Doll	.60	1.50
53	Das Wunderkind Alex Wright	.10	.25
54	Harlem Heat	.12	.30
55	Dave Sullivan	.10	.25
56	Atomic Leg Drop	.40	1.00
57	Scorpion Death Lock	.25	.60
58	Power Bomb	.12	.30
59	Bulldog	.12	.30
60	Sleeper	.10	.25
61	Sunset Flip	.10	.25
62	Hollywood & Vine	5.00	12.00
63	Vadersault	.12	.30
64	Pit Stop	.10	.25
65	Flying Elbow	.20	.50
66	Figure Four Leglock	.30	.75
67	Headlock	.40	1.00
68	Hulk Hogan/Ric Flair	2.50	6.00
69	Hulk Hogan/Ric Flair	2.50	6.00
70	Hogan/Vader	.20	.50
71	Rhodes/Anderson	.20	.50
72	Macho Man Randy Savage	.40	1.00
73	Macho Man Randy Savage	.40	1.00
74	Macho Man Randy Savage	.40	1.00
75	Macho Man Randy Savage	.40	1.00
76	Ric Flair	.30	.75
77	Ric Flair	.30	.75
78	Ric Flair	.30	.75
79	Ric Flair	.30	.75
80	Sting	.30	.75
81	Sting	.30	.75
82	Sting	.30	.75
83	Hulk Hogan	2.00	5.00
84	Hulk Hogan	2.00	5.00
85	Hulk Hogan	2.00	5.00
86	Hulk Hogan	2.00	5.00
87	Hulk Hogan	2.00	5.00
88	Hulk Hogan	2.00	5.00
89A	Uncensored	.10	.25
89B	Spring Stampede	.10	.25
90	Starrcade 1994	.10	.25
91	Halloween Havoc 1994	.10	.25
92	Fall Brawl	.10	.25
93	Bash at the Beach	.10	.25
94	Slamboree 1994	.10	.25
95A	Superbrawl IV	.10	.25
95B	Superbrawl V	.10	.25
96	Arn Anderson	.12	.30
97	Harlem Heat	.10	.25
98	Vader	.12	.30
99	Hulk Hogan	2.00	5.00
100	Checklist	.10	.25

1995 CARDZ WCW Main Event Promos

P1	Hulk Hogan	1.50	4.00
P2	Sting	1.25	3.00
NNO	Hogan vs. Flair TEK	2.00	5.00
NNO	Clash of the Champions KKLZ		

1986 Carnation Major League Wrestling

	COMPLETE SET (6)	150.00	300.00
NNO	Kamala	15.00	40.00
NNO	The Koloffs	20.00	50.00
NNO	Ric Flair	75.00	150.00
NNO	Rick Martel	15.00	40.00
NNO	The Road Warriors	30.00	75.00
NNO	Sergeant Slaughter	25.00	60.00

1993 Catcher Quartett WWF Series 5

A1	Bret Hit Man Hart		
A2	Undertaker	6.00	15.00
A3	Hulk Hogan	6.00	15.00
A4	Crush	1.25	3.00
B1	Mr. Perfect	3.00	8.00
B2	Bam Bam Bigelow		
B3	Kamala	1.50	4.00
B4	Money Inc.		
C1	Doink	1.00	2.50
C2	Macho Man Randy Savage		
C3	Big Boss Man	1.00	2.50
C4	Tatanka	1.00	2.50
D1	Virgil	1.00	2.50
D2	Papa Shango	2.00	5.00
D3	Shawn Michaels	3.00	8.00
D4	Repo Man	1.00	2.50
E1	Hacksaw Jim Duggan	1.25	3.00
E2	Razor Ramon		
E3	Bushwhackers		
E4	Nasty Boys	1.00	2.50
F1	Giant Gonzalez	1.00	2.50
F2	Head Shrinkers	1.00	2.50
F3	Beverly Brothers	1.25	3.00
F4	Damian Demento		
G1	Bob Backlund	1.00	2.50
G2	Brutus The Barber Beefcake	1.50	4.00
G3	Lex Luger	2.00	5.00
G4	Steiner Brothers	2.50	6.00
H1	Yokozuna	6.00	15.00
H2	El Matador	1.00	2.50
H3	Paul Bearer		
H4	Billy of the Smoking Gunns	1.00	2.50

1993 Catcher Quartett WWF Series 7

A1	Bret Hit Man Hart		
A2	Undertaker	5.00	12.00
A3	Hulk Hogan		
A4	Crush		
B1	Mr. Perfect		
B2	Bam Bam Bigelow	1.50	4.00
B3	Kamala		
B4	Money Inc.	1.00	2.50
C1	Doink		
C2	Macho Man Randy Savage		
C3	Big Boss Man		
C4	Tatanka	1.00	2.50
D1	Virgil	1.00	2.50
D2	Papa Shango		
D3	Shawn Michaels		
D4	Repo Man		
E1	Hacksaw Jim Duggan		
E2	Razor Ramon	4.00	10.00
E3	Bushwhackers	1.00	2.50
E4	Knobbs of the Nasty Boys		
F1	Giant Gonzalez	1.00	2.50
F2	Head Shrinkers	1.00	2.50
F3	Beverly Brothers		
F4	Damian Demento		
G1	Bob Backlund	1.00	2.50
G2	Brutus The Barber Beefcake		
G3	Lex Luger	2.50	6.00
G4	Steiner Brothers	1.50	4.00
H1	Yokozuna		
H2	El Matador		
H3	Paul Bearer	1.00	2.50
H4	The Smoking Gunns	1.00	2.50

1993 Catcher Quartett WWF Series 8

A1	Bret Hit Man Hart		
A2	Undertaker		
A3	Hulk Hogan		
A4	Crush	1.00	2.50
B1	Mr. Perfect	2.50	6.00
B2	Bam Bam Bigelow	1.25	3.00
B3	Kamala		
B4	Money Inc.	1.00	2.50
C1	Doink	1.00	2.50
C2	Macho Man Randy Savage		8.00
C3	Big Boss Man		
C4	Tatanka		
D1	Virgil		
D2	Papa Shango	2.00	5.00
D3	Shawn Michaels	2.50	6.00
D4	Repo Man		
E1	Hacksaw Jim Duggan	1.25	3.00
E2	Razor Ramon	2.50	6.00
E3	Luke of the Bushwhackers	1.00	2.50
E4	Nasty Boys		
F1	Giant Gonzalez		
F2	Head Shrinkers		
F3	Beverly Brothers	1.25	3.00
F4	Damian Demento		
G1	Bob Backlund		
G2	Brutus The Barber Beefcake		
G3	Lex Luger		
G4	Steiner Brothers	3.00	8.00
H1	Yokozuna	8.00	20.00
H2	El Matador		
H3	Paul Bearer	1.00	2.50
H4	Billy of the Smoking Gunns		

1991 Championship Marketing WCW

COMPLETE SET (110)	12.00	30.00
UNOPENED BOX (36 PACKS)		
UNOPENED PACK (16 CARDS)		

1	Sting	.30	.75
2	Arn Anderson	.15	.40
3	Michael Hayes	.12	.30
4	Rick Steiner	.15	.40
5	The Fabulous Freebirds	.15	.40
6	The Steiner Brothers	.15	.40
7	Lex Luger	.15	.40
8	Ric Flair	.50	1.25
9	Tom Zenk	.12	.30
10	Sid Vicious	.12	.30
11	Brian Pillman	.12	.30
12	Ric Flair	.50	1.25
13	Sid Vicious	.12	.30
14	The Four Horsemen	.50	1.25
15	Jim Ross	.12	.30
16	Ron Simmons	.15	.40
17	Barry Windham	.12	.30
18	Sid Vicious	.12	.30
19	Sid Vicious	.12	.30
20	Sting and Ric	.50	1.25
21	Beautiful Bobby Punishes Opponent	.12	.30
22	New Champion/Sting	.30	.75
23	Paul E. with Mouth Open	.12	.30
24	Michael Hayes	.12	.30
25	Scott Steiner	.15	.40
26	Rick Steiner	.15	.40
27	World TV Champion/Arn Anderson	.15	.40
28	Barry Windham with Arms Raised	.12	.30
29	Tommy Rich	.12	.30
30	Ricky Morton	.12	.30
31	Horsemen Press Conference	.50	1.25
32	The Freebirds	.15	.40
33	Terry Taylor	.12	.30
34	Dirty Dutch Mantell	.15	.40
35	Nature Boy Ric Flair	.50	1.25
36	Lex Presses Ric	.50	1.25
37	Lex and Sting	.15	.40
38	Flyin' Brian	.12	.30
39	Ric Flair	.50	1.25
40	Sting and Lex	.30	.75
41	Missy Hyatt	.15	.40
42	Three Out of Four/Horsemen	.12	.30
43	Sid Vicious in Action	.12	.30
44	Terry Taylor vs. Z-Man	.12	.30
45	Southern Boys	.12	.30
46	Sting	.30	.75
47	What Did You Say?/Ric Flair	.50	1.25
48	Arn, Paul E. and Ric Flair	.50	1.25
49	Sting	.30	.75
50	Say Uncle/Sid Vicious	.12	.30
51	Paul E. Dangerously	.12	.30
52	Sting and Ric	.50	1.25
53	Sting, Jim and Lex	.30	.75
54	What a Belt!/Sting	.30	.75
55	Sting	.30	.75
56	Ric All In White	.50	1.25
57	Lex Presses Ric II	.50	1.25
58	El Gigante	.15	.40
59	Arn Says My Turn	.15	.40
60	Sid Vicious	.12	.30
61	Brian and Ric	.50	1.25
62	Flyin Brian	.12	.30
63	The Fabulous Freebirds	.15	.40
64	No Sid This High	.12	.30
65	El Gigante	.12	.30
66	Ric, Jim and Sting	.50	1.25
67	No It's Mine/Flair, JR & Sting	.50	1.25
68	Golden Nature Boy	.50	1.25

#	Card		
69	Missy and Scott	.15	.40
70	Ron Simmons	.15	.40
71	Telephone/Paul E. Dangerously	.12	.30
72	Jimmy Jam Garvin	.15	.40
73	Ric Flair in Pink Robe	.50	1.25
74	Beautiful Bobby	.12	.30
75	Lex Luger	.15	.40
76	Z-Man	.12	.30
77	Where's The Door?/Ric Flair	.50	1.25
78	El Gigante	.12	.30
79	What Do You Think?/Ric Flair	.50	1.25
80	6 Time World Champion/Ric Flair	.50	1.25
81	Missy Hyatt	.15	.40
82	The New Champion/Sting	.30	.75
83	Celebration/Sting	.30	.75
84	USA Sting	.30	.75
85	Sting Is Injured	.30	.75
86	Let's Get Busy/Sting	.30	.75
87	Courage of a Champion/Sting	.30	.75
88	No Hold the Anchovies Paul E. Dangerously	.12	.30
89	Lex Presses Ric III	.50	1.25
90	Barry Windham	.12	.30
91	Heads or Tails/Ric Flair & Lex Luger	.50	1.25
92	U.S. Heavyweight Champion/Lex Luger	.15	.40
93	Getting Ready For Battle/Lex Luger	.15	.40
94	Lex Wins the Title	.15	.40
95	Ric Goes Too Far	.50	1.25
96	El Gigante and the Champ/Sting	.30	.75
97	Z-Man	.12	.30
98	World Tag-Team Champions Doom with Teddy Long	.12	.30
99	Missy in Evening Gown	.15	.40
100	Missy Hyatt	.15	.40
101	Tony (Schiavone) in Front of Chicago Building	.12	.30
102	Ricky Morton	.12	.30
103	Flyin Brian	.12	.30
104	The Steiners Want Sting Revenge	.15	.40
105	Z-Man Tom Zenk	.12	.30
106	Southern Boys	.12	.30
107	Teddy R. Long	.12	.30
108	Arn Anderson in Action	.15	.40
109	Sting in Action	.30	.75
110	Doom	.12	.30

1991 Championship Marketing WCW Puzzle

COMPLETE SET (110)		6.00	15.00
STATED ODDS 1:1			
1	Puzzle Card	.12	.30
2	Puzzle Card	.12	.30
3	Puzzle Card	.12	.30
4	Puzzle Card	.12	.30
5	Puzzle Card	.12	.30
6	Puzzle Card	.12	.30
7	Puzzle Card	.12	.30
8	Puzzle Card	.12	.30
9	Puzzle Card	.12	.30
10	Puzzle Card	.12	.30
11	Puzzle Card	.12	.30
12	Puzzle Card	.12	.30
13	Puzzle Card	.12	.30
14	Puzzle Card	.12	.30
15	Puzzle Card	.12	.30
16	Puzzle Card	.12	.30
17	Puzzle Card	.12	.30
18	Puzzle Card	.12	.30
19	Puzzle Card	.12	.30
20	Puzzle Card	.12	.30
21	Puzzle Card	.12	.30
22	Puzzle Card	.12	.30
23	Puzzle Card	.12	.30
24	Puzzle Card	.12	.30
25	Puzzle Card	.12	.30
26	Puzzle Card	.12	.30
27	Puzzle Card	.12	.30
28	Puzzle Card	.12	.30
29	Puzzle Card	.12	.30
30	Puzzle Card	.12	.30
31	Puzzle Card	.12	.30
32	Puzzle Card	.12	.30
33	Puzzle Card	.12	.30
34	Puzzle Card	.12	.30
35	Puzzle Card	.12	.30
36	Puzzle Card	.12	.30
37	Puzzle Card	.12	.30
38	Puzzle Card	.12	.30
39	Puzzle Card	.12	.30
40	Puzzle Card	.12	.30
41	Puzzle Card	.12	.30
42	Puzzle Card	.12	.30
43	Puzzle Card	.12	.30
44	Puzzle Card	.12	.30
45	Puzzle Card	.12	.30
46	Puzzle Card	.12	.30
47	Puzzle Card	.12	.30
48	Puzzle Card	.12	.30
49	Puzzle Card	.12	.30
50	Puzzle Card	.12	.30
51	Puzzle Card	.12	.30
52	Puzzle Card	.12	.30
53	Puzzle Card	.12	.30
54	Puzzle Card	.12	.30
55	Puzzle Card	.12	.30
56	Puzzle Card	.12	.30
57	Puzzle Card	.12	.30
58	Puzzle Card	.12	.30
59	Puzzle Card	.12	.30
60	Puzzle Card	.12	.30
61	Puzzle Card	.12	.30
62	Puzzle Card	.12	.30
63	Puzzle Card	.12	.30
64	Puzzle Card	.12	.30
65	Puzzle Card	.12	.30
66	Puzzle Card	.12	.30
67	Puzzle Card	.12	.30
68	Puzzle Card	.12	.30
69	Puzzle Card	.12	.30
70	Puzzle Card	.12	.30
71	Puzzle Card	.12	.30
72	Puzzle Card	.12	.30
73	Puzzle Card	.12	.30
74	Puzzle Card	.12	.30
75	Puzzle Card	.12	.30
76	Puzzle Card	.12	.30
77	Puzzle Card	.12	.30
78	Puzzle Card	.12	.30
79	Puzzle Card	.12	.30
80	Puzzle Card	.12	.30
81	Puzzle Card	.12	.30
82	Puzzle Card	.12	.30
83	Puzzle Card	.12	.30
84	Puzzle Card	.12	.30
85	Puzzle Card	.12	.30
86	Puzzle Card	.12	.30
87	Puzzle Card	.12	.30
88	Puzzle Card	.12	.30
89	Puzzle Card	.12	.30
90	Puzzle Card	.12	.30
91	Puzzle Card	.12	.30
92	Puzzle Card	.12	.30
93	Puzzle Card	.12	.30
94	Puzzle Card	.12	.30
95	Puzzle Card	.12	.30
96	Puzzle Card	.12	.30
97	Puzzle Card	.12	.30
98	Puzzle Card	.12	.30
99	Puzzle Card	.12	.30
100	Puzzle Card	.12	.30
101	Puzzle Card	.12	.30
102	Puzzle Card	.12	.30
103	Puzzle Card	.12	.30
104	Puzzle Card	.12	.30
105	Puzzle Card	.12	.30
106	Puzzle Card	.12	.30
107	Puzzle Card	.12	.30
108	Puzzle Card	.12	.30
109	Puzzle Card	.12	.30
110	Puzzle Card	.12	.30

1987 Circle K Coca-Cola WWF Supermatch

COMPLETE SET (20)		30.00	75.00
1	Hulk Hogan	10.00	25.00
2	Hercules and Bobby Heenan	2.00	5.00
3	The Hart Foundation	2.50	6.00
4	Randy Macho Man Savage	3.00	8.00
5	Koko B. Ware	1.25	3.00
6	George The Animal Steele	1.25	3.00
7	Ricky The Dragon Steamboat	1.50	4.00
8	The Honky Tonk Man	2.00	5.00
9	Hacksaw Jim Duggan	1.25	3.00
10	Kamala and Kimchee	2.50	6.00
11	Billy Jack Haynes	1.25	3.00
12	Junk Yard Dog	1.50	4.00
13	Jake The Snake Roberts	4.00	10.00
14	The Killer Bees	1.25	3.00
15	Tito Santana	1.25	3.00
16	The Can-Am Connection	1.25	3.00
17	Andre the Giant	6.00	15.00
18	Elizabeth	3.00	8.00
19	The British Bulldogs	2.00	5.00
20	The Iron Sheik	1.25	3.00

1990 Classic WWF

COMPLETE FACTORY SET (145)		10.00	25.00
UNOPENED BOX (36 PACKS)			
UNOPENED PACK (15 CARDS)			
1	Hulk Hogan	.60	1.50
2	Big Boss Man	.10	.25
3	Ravishing Rick Rude	.15	.40
4	Macho Man Randy Savage	.40	1.00
5	The Ultimate Warrior	.25	.60
6	Demolition	.10	.25
7	Jake The Snake Roberts	.25	.60
8	Million Dollar Man Ted DiBiase	.15	.40
9	Hacksaw Jim Duggan	.15	.40
10	Andre the Giant	.40	1.00
11	Miss Elizabeth	.15	.40
12	Brutus The Barber Beefcake	.15	.40
13	Rowdy Roddy Piper	.75	2.00
14	Jimmy Superfly Snuka	.25	.60
15	Bushwhackers	.10	.25
16	Dusty Rhodes	.10	.25
17	Hercules	.10	.25
18	Sensational Queen Sherri	.15	.40
19	Mr. Perfect	.15	.40
20	Rick Martel	.60	1.50
21	Tito Santana	.10	.25
22	Mr. Fuji	.10	.25
23	Jimmy Hart	.15	.40
24	Brother Love	.10	.25
25	Akeem	.10	.25
26	Bad News Brown	.10	.25
27	Honky Tonk Man	.15	.40
28	The Rockers	.15	.40
29	Koko B. Ware	.15	.40
30	Bobby The Brain Heenan	.15	.40
31	Dino Bravo	.10	.25
32	The Genius	.10	.25
33	Greg The Hammer Valentine	.15	.40
34	Virgil	.10	.25
35	Haku	.10	.25
36	Rugged Ronnie Garvin	.10	.25
37	Bret Hit Man Hart	.15	.40
38	Hart Foundation	.15	.40
39	Red Rooster	.10	.25
40	Hillbilly Jim	.10	.25
41	Slick		
42	The Widow Maker	.10	.25
43	The Ultimate Warrior	.25	.60
44	Honky Tonk Man	.15	.40
45	Bret Hit Man Hart	.15	.40
46	Jim Neidhart	.15	.40
47	Bushwhackers	.10	.25
48	Paul Roma	.10	.25
49	Barry Horowitz	.10	.25
50	Brooklyn Brawler	.10	.25
51	Mean Gene Okerlund	.10	.25
52	Gorilla Monsoon	.10	.25
53	Jesse The Body Ventura	.40	1.00
54	Sean Mooney	.10	.25
55	Danny Davis	.10	.25
56	Jack Tunney	.10	.25
57	Hulk Hogan	.60	1.50
58	Big Boss Man	.10	.25
59	Ravishing Rick Rude	.15	.40
60	Macho Man Randy Savage	.40	1.00
61	The Ultimate Warrior	.25	.60
62	Demolition	.10	.25
63	Jake The Snake Roberts	.25	.60
64	Million Dollar Man Ted DiBiase	.15	.40
65	Hacksaw Jim Duggan	.15	.40
66	Andre the Giant	.40	1.00
67	Miss Elizabeth	.15	.40
68	Brutus The Barber Beefcake	.15	.40
69	Jimmy Superfly Snuka	.25	.60
70	Bushwhackers	.10	.25
71	Dusty Rhodes	.10	.25
72	Hercules	.10	.25
73	Sensational Queen Sherri	.15	.40
74	Mr. Perfect	.15	2.50
75	Jimmy Hart	.15	.40
76	Andre the Giant	.40	1.00
77	Brother Love	.10	.25
78	Akeem	.10	.25
79	Bad News Brown	.10	.25
80	Honky Tonk Man	.15	.40
81	The Rockers	.15	.40
82	Koko B. Ware	.15	.40

No.	Card		
83	Bobby The Brain Heenan	.15	.40
84	Dino Bravo	.10	.25
85	The Genius	.10	.25
86	Greg The Hammer Valentine	.15	.40
87	Virgil	.10	.25
88	Haku	.10	.25
89	Rugged Ronnie Garvin	.10	.25
90	Hulk Hogan	.60	1.50
91	Red Rooster	.10	.25
92	Hillbilly Jim	.10	.25
93	The Widow Maker	.10	.25
94	Freddie Blassie	.10	.25
95	Bret Hit Man Hart	.15	.40
96	Jim Neidhart	.15	.40
97	Demolition	.10	.25
98	Paul Roma	.10	.25
99	Barry Horowitz	.10	.25
100	Brooklyn Brawler	.10	.25
101	Danny Davis	.10	.25
102	Hulk Hogan	.60	1.50
103	Big Boss Man	.10	.25
104	Ravishing Rick Rude	.15	.40
105	Macho Man Randy Savage	.40	1.00
106	The Ultimate Warrior	.25	.60
107	Demolition	.10	.25
108	Jake The Snake Roberts	1.25	3.00
109	Million Dollar Man Ted DiBiase	.15	.40
110	Hacksaw Jim Duggan	.15	.40
111	Andre the Giant	.40	1.00
112	Miss Elizabeth	.15	.40
113	Brutus The Barber Beefcake	.15	.40
114	Jimmy Superfly Snuka	.25	.60
115	Tito Santana	.10	.25
116	Bushwhackers	.10	.25
117	Honky Tonk Man	.15	.40
118	The Rockers	.15	.40
119	Koko B. Ware	.15	.40
120	Haku	.10	.25
121	The Rockers	.15	.40
122	Red Rooster	.10	.25
123	Bret Hit Man Hart	2.50	6.00
124	Jim Neidhart	.75	2.00
125	Hulk Hogan	.60	1.50
126	Macho Man Randy Savage	1.50	4.00
127	The Ultimate Warrior	1.50	4.00
128	Demolition	1.25	3.00
129	Hulk Hogan	3.00	8.00
130	Andre the Giant	2.00	5.00
131	Jimmy Superfly Snuka	.25	.60
132	Bushwhackers	.10	.25
133	Honky Tonk Man	.15	.40
134	The Rockers	1.25	3.00
135	Haku	.10	.25
136	Miss Elizabeth	1.00	2.50
137	Macho Madness	.40	1.00
138	Honky Tonk Man	.15	.40
139	The Ultimate Warrior	1.50	4.00
140	Million Dollar Man Ted DiBiase	.15	.40
141	Simply Ravishing	.15	.40
142	Big Boss Man	.10	.25
143	Brutus The Barber Beefcake	.15	.40
144	Koko B. Ware	.15	.40
145	Hulk Hogan Rules	.60	1.50

1990 Classic WWF History of WrestleMania

COMPLETE SET (150)		10.00	25.00
COMPLETE FACTORY SET (150)			

UNOPENED BOX (36 PACKS)
UNOPENED PACK (15 CARDS)
*TRADEMARK: .6X TO 1.5X BASIC CARDS

No.	Card		
1	Greg The Hammer Valentine / Junk Yard Dog	.12	.30
2	Tito Santana / Masked Executioner	.10	.25
3	Hulk Hogan	.50	1.25
4	Dream Team / British Bulldogs	.10	.25
5	Battle Royal	.10	.25
6	Battle Royal	.10	.25
7	Battle Royal	.10	.25
8	Brutus The Barber Beefcake / British Bulldogs	.12	.30
9	Tito Santana / Junk Yard Dog/Funk Brothers	.12	.30
10	Greg The Hammer Valentine	.12	.30
11	Hulk Hogan / King Kong Bundy	.50	1.25
12	Macho Man Randy Savage / George The Animal Steele	.20	.50
13	Macho Man Randy Savage / George The Animal Steele	.20	.50
14	Hulk Hogan / King Kong Bundy	.50	1.25
15	Hulk Hogan / King Kong Bundy	.50	1.25
16	Andre the Giant	.40	1.00
17	Slick / Tito Santana	.10	.25
18	Rowdy Roddy Piper / Adrian Adonis	.20	.50
19	Andre the Giant / Hulk Hogan	.50	1.25
20	Jim Neidhart / Dynamite Kid	.10	.25
21	Davey Boy Smith / Danny Davis	.12	.30
22	Slick / Tito Santana	.10	.25
23	Stadium Scene	.10	.25
24	Honky Tonk Man / Jake The Snake Roberts	.15	.40
25	Brutus The Barber Beefcake / Adrian Adonis	.12	.30
26	Hulk Hogan / Andre the Giant	.50	1.25
27	Hulk Hogan / Andre the Giant	.50	1.25
28	Hulk Hogan / Andre the Giant	.50	1.25
29	Million Dollar Man / Macho Man Randy Savage	.20	.50
30	Million Dollar Man / Macho Man Randy Savage	.20	.50
31	Million Dollar Man / Macho Man Randy Savage	.20	.50
32	Hulk Hogan / Macho Man Randy Savage	.50	1.25
33	Hulk Hogan / Macho Man Randy Savage	.50	1.25
34	Hulk Hogan / Andre the Giant	.50	1.25
35	Hulk Hogan / Andre the Giant	.50	1.25
36	Hulk Hogan / Andre the Giant	.50	1.25
37	Hulk Hogan / Andre the Giant	.50	1.25
38	Hulk Hogan / Andre the Giant	.50	1.25
39	Hulk Hogan / Andre the Giant	.50	1.25
40	Hulk Hogan / Andre the Giant	.50	1.25
41	Hulk Hogan	.50	1.25
42	Brutus The Barber Beefcake	.12	.30
43	Brutus The Barber Beefcake / Honky Tonk Man	.12	.30
44	Honky Tonk Man / Brutus The Barber Beefcake	.12	.30
45	Rick Martel / Demolition	.10	.25
46	Demolition / Strike Force	.10	.25
47	Ravishing Rick Rude / Jake The Snake Roberts	.15	.40
48	Hercules / Ultimate Warrior	.12	.30
49	The Hammer / Macho Man Randy Savage	.20	.50
50	The Hammer / Macho Man Randy Savage	.20	.50
51	Hulk Hogan	.50	1.25
52	Million Dollar Man / Virgil/Andre the Giant	.40	1.00
53	Hulk Hogan / Macho Man Randy Savage	.50	1.25
54	Macho Man Randy Savage / Akeem	.20	.50
55	Ring Scene	.10	.25
56	Bobby The Brain Heenan / Koko B. Ware	.10	.25
57	Battle Royal	.10	.25
58	Million Dollar Man / Hacksaw Jim Duggan	.12	.30
59	Dino Bravo / Don Muraco	.10	.25
60	Jake The Snake Roberts / Rick Rude	.15	.40
61	Hercules / Ultimate Warrior	.12	.30
62	Jake The Snake Roberts / Rick Rude	.15	.40
63	Hercules / Ultimate Warrior	.12	.30
64	Hercules / Ultimate Warrior	.12	.30
65	Hercules / Ultimate Warrior	.12	.30
66	Mr. Fuji / Ax	.10	.25
67	Demolition / Tito Santana	.10	.25
68	Rick Martel / Smash	.10	.25
69	Honky Tonk Man / Brutus The Barber Beefcake	.12	.30
70	Bret Hit Man Hart / Bad News Brown	.12	.30
71	Bret Hit Man Hart / Bad News Brown	.12	.30
72	Bret Hit Man Hart / Bad News Brown	.12	.30
73	Bad News Brown	.10	.25
74	Power of Pain	.10	.25
	Demolition		
75	Million Dollar Man / Virgil	.12	.30
76	Mr. Fuji / Ax	.10	.25
77	Demolition	.10	.25
78	Andre the Giant / Jake The Snake Roberts	.40	1.00
79	Bret Hit Man Hart / Honky Tonk Man	.12	.30
80	Brooklyn Brawler	.10	.25
81	King Haku / Hercules	.10	.25
82	King Haku / Hercules	.10	.25
83	Million Dollar Man / Brutus The Barber Beefcake	.12	.30
84	Dino Bravo / Ronnie Garvin	.10	.25
85	Bad News Brown / Hacksaw Jim Duggan	.12	.30
86	Bad News Brown / Hacksaw Jim Duggan	.12	.30
87	Bret Hit Man Hart / Greg The Hammer Valentine	.12	.30
88	Bret Hit Man Hart / Honky Tonk Man	.12	.30
89	Mr. Perfect / Blue Blazer	.12	.30
90	Bobby The Brain Heenan	.12	.30
91	Bushwhackers / Rougeau Brothers	.10	.25
92	Bushwhackers / Rougeau Brothers	.10	.25
93	Dino Bravo / Ronnie Garvin	.10	.25
94	Hulk Hogan / Macho Man Randy Savage	.50	1.25
95	Hulk Hogan / Macho Man Randy Savage	.50	1.25
96	Hulk Hogan / Macho Man Randy Savage	.50	1.25
97	Akeem / Shawn Michaels	.15	.40
98	The Rockers / Akeem	.12	.30
99	Hulk Hogan / Macho Man Randy Savage	.50	1.25
100	Hulk Hogan / Macho Man Randy Savage	.50	1.25
101	Hulk Hogan / Macho Man Randy Savage	.50	1.25
102	Hulk Hogan / Macho Man Randy Savage	.50	1.25
103	Hulk Hogan / Macho Man Randy Savage	.50	1.25
104	Ravishing Rick Rude / Ultimate Warrior	.12	.30
105	Ravishing Rick Rude / Ultimate Warrior	.12	.30
106	The Ultimate Warrior	.12	.30
107	Hulk Hogan / Macho Man Randy Savage	.50	1.25
108	Marty Jannetty / Akeem	.10	.25
109	Brutus The Barber Beefcake / Virgil	.12	.30
110	Ravishing Rick Rude	.12	.30

Ultimate Warrior
| 111 Ravishing Rick Rude | .12 | .30 |

Ultimate Warrior
| 112 Ravishing Rick Rude | .12 | .30 |

Ultimate Warrior
| 113 Haku | .40 | 1.00 |

Andre the Giant
| 114 Million Dollar Man | .15 | .40 |

Jake The Snake Roberts
| 115 Barbarian | .10 | .25 |

Tito Santana
| 116 Rick Martel | .10 | .25 |

Koko B. Ware
| 117 Million Dollar Man Ted DiBiase | .12 | .30 |
| 118 Hacksaw Jim Duggan | .12 | .30 |

Bravo
| 119 Hacksaw Jim Duggan | .12 | .30 |

Bravo
| 120 Hacksaw Jim Duggan | .12 | .30 |

Bravo
| 121 Macho King | .10 | .25 |

Dusty Rhodes
| 122 American Dream | .15 | .40 |

Sapphire/Miss Elizabeth
123 Macho Man Randy Savage	.20	.50
124 Hart Foundation	.12	.30
125 Dusty Rhodes	.20	.50

Macho Man Randy Savage
| 126 American Dream | .12 | .30 |

Sapphire/Queen Sherri
| 127 Bad News | .20 | .50 |

Rowdy Roddy Piper
| 128 Brutus The Barber Beefcake | .12 | .30 |

Genius
| 129 Sato | .10 | .25 |

Tanaka/Marty Jannetty
| 130 Big Boss Man | .10 | .25 |

Akeem
| 131 Sato | .15 | .40 |

Shawn Michaels
| 132 Hulk Hogan | .50 | 1.25 |

Ultimate Warrior
| 133 Hulk Hogan | .50 | 1.25 |

Ultimate Warrior
| 134 Hulk Hogan | .50 | 1.25 |

Ultimate Warrior
| 135 Hulk Hogan | .50 | 1.25 |

Immortal One
136 The Ultimate Warrior	.12	.30
137 Rhythm and Blues	.10	.25
138 Ravishing Rick Rude	.15	.40

Superfly Jimmy Snuka
| 139 Rhythm and Blues | .12 | .30 |

Jimmy Hart
| 140 Demolition | .10 | .25 |
| 141 Andre the Giant | .40 | 1.00 |

Bobby Heenan
| 142 Haku | .10 | .25 |

Smash
| 143 Smash | .10 | .25 |

Haku/Ax
| 144 Brutus The Barber Beefcake | .12 | .30 |

Mr.Perfect
| 145 Hulk Hogan | .50 | 1.25 |

Ultimate Warrior
146 Brutus The Barber Beefcake	.12	.30
147 The Ultimate Warrior	.12	.30
148 Bushwackers	.10	.25

| 149 The Rockers | .12 | .30 |
| 150 Dusty Rhodes | .10 | .25 |

1991 Classic WWF Superstars

COMPLETE SET (150)	50.00	100.00
COMPLETE FACTORY SET (150)	100.00	200.00
UNOPENED BOX (36 PACKS)		
UNOPENED PACK (12 CARDS)		
*EUROPEAN: SAME VALUE		

1 Hulk Hogan	.50	1.25
2 Ultimate Warrior	.30	.75
3 Texas Tornado	.12	.30
4 Jake The Snake Roberts	.20	.50
5 Big Boss Man	.10	.25
6 Hacksaw Jim Duggan	.12	.30
7 Davey Boy Smith	.12	.30
8 The Model Rick Martel	.10	.25
9 Million Dollar Man Ted DiBiase	.12	.30
10 Bobby Heenan	.75	2.00
11 Rockers	.15	.40
12 Legion of Doom	.12	.30
13 Tugboat	.10	.25
14 Power & Glory	.10	.25
15 Bushwackers	.10	.25
16 Macho King Randy Savage	.30	.75
17 Koko B. Ware	.10	.25
18 Superfly Jimmy Snuka	.15	.40
19 Davey Boy Smith	.12	.30
20 Sensational Queen Sherri	.12	.30
21 Barbarian	.10	.25
22 Virgil	.10	.25
23 Nasty Boys	1.00	2.50
24 Million Dollar Man Ted DiBiase	.12	.30
25 Big Boss Man	.10	.25
26 Sgt. Slaughter	.15	.40
27 Barbarian	.10	.25
28 Nasty Boys	.10	.25
29 Mr. Perfect	.15	.40
30 Undertaker	6.00	15.00
31 Rowdy Roddy Piper	.40	1.00
32 The Mountie	.10	.25
33 Davey Boy Smith	.12	.30
34 General Adnan	.10	.25
35 Hulk Hogan	.50	1.25
36 Ultimate Warrior	.30	.75
37 Texas Tornado	.12	.30
38 Hacksaw Jim Duggan	.12	.30
39 Jake The Snake Roberts	.20	.50
40 Hulk Hogan	.50	1.25
41 The Model Rick Martel	.10	.25
42 Earthquake	.10	.25
43 Jimmy Hart	.15	.40
44 Rockers	.15	.40
45 Slick	.10	.25
46 Legion of Doom	.12	.30
47 Mr. Fuji	.10	.25
48 Tugboat	.10	.25
49 Power & Glory	.10	.25
50 Bushwackers	.10	.25
51 Macho King Randy Savage	.30	.75
52 Hulk Hogan	.50	1.25
53 Koko B. Ware	.10	.25
54 Superfly Jimmy Snuka	.15	.40
55 Haku	.10	.25
56 Sensational Queen Sherri	.12	.30
57 Nasty Boys	.10	.25
58 Virgil	.10	.25
59 Million Dollar Man Ted DiBiase	.12	.30

60 Big Boss Man	.10	.25
61 Sgt. Slaughter	.15	.40
62 Barbarian	.10	.25
63 Mr. Perfect	.15	.40
64 Undertaker	10.00	25.00
65 Rowdy Roddy Piper	.40	1.00
66 The Mountie	.10	.25
67 General Adnan	.10	.25
68 The Dragon Ricky Steamboat	.12	.30
69 Hulk Hogan	.50	1.25
70 Ultimate Warrior	.30	.75
71 Texas Tornado	.12	.30
72 Hacksaw Jim Duggan	.12	.30
73 Jake The Snake Roberts	.20	.50
74 The Model Rick Martel	.10	.25
75 Earthquake	.10	.25
76 Mr. Fuji	.10	.25
77 Jimmy Hart	.15	.40
78 Rockers	.15	.40
79 Legion of Doom	.12	.30
80 Tugboat	.10	.25
81 Paul Roma	.10	.25
82 Power & Glory	.10	.25
83 Bushwackers	.10	.25
84 Macho King Randy Savage	.30	.75
85 General Adnan	.10	.25
86 The Mountie	.10	.25
87 Rowdy Roddy Piper	.40	1.00
88 Undertaker	5.00	12.00
89 Mr. Perfect	.15	.40
90 Sgt. Slaughter	.15	.40
91 Hulk Hogan	.50	1.25
92 Earthquake	.10	.25
93 Paul Bearer	1.50	4.00
94 Koko B. Ware	.10	.25
95 Superfly Jimmy Snuka	.15	.40
96 Sensational Queen Sherri	.12	.30
97 Sgt. Slaughter	.15	.40
98 Rowdy Roddy Piper	.40	1.00
99 Hulk Hogan	.50	1.25
100 Ultimate Warrior	.30	.75
101 Texas Tornado	.12	.30
102 The Model Rick Martel	.10	.25
103 Earthquake	.10	.25
104 Legion of Doom	.12	.30
105 Bret Hart	.75	2.00
106 Undertaker	15.00	40.00
107 Mr. Perfect	.15	.40
108 Sgt. Slaughter w/General Adnan	.15	.40
109 Big Boss Man	.10	.25
110 Million Dollar Man Ted DiBiase	.12	.30
111 Hulk Hogan	.50	1.25
112 Legion Of Doom	.12	.30
113 Mr. Perfect	.15	.40
114 Ultimate Warrior	.30	.75
115 Big Boss Man	.10	.25
116 Hacksaw Jim Duggan	.12	.30
117 Power & Glory w/Slick	.10	.25
118 Macho King Randy Savage	.30	.75
119 Bushwackers	.10	.25
120 Tugboat	.10	.25
121 Mr. Perfect	.15	.40
122 Barbarian	.10	.25
123 Hulk Hogan	.50	1.25
124 Ultimate Warrior	3.00	8.00
125 Big Boss Man	1.00	2.50
126 Hacksaw Jim Duggan	1.50	4.00
127 Jake The Snake Roberts	2.50	6.00

128 The Model Rick Martel	.10	.25
129 The Dragon Ricky Steamboat	.12	.30
130 Mr. Perfect	1.50	4.00
131 Haku	.10	.25
132 Million Dollar Man Ted DiBiase	.12	.30
133 Texas Tornado	.12	.30
134 Macho King Randy Savage	.30	.75
135 Macho King Randy Savage	.30	.75
136 Legion of Doom	.12	.30
137 Rockers	.15	.40
138 Earthquake	.10	.25
139 Superfly Jimmy Snuka	.15	.40
140 Hulk Hogan	3.00	8.00
141 The Dragon Ricky Steamboat	1.50	4.00
142 Sgt. Slaughter	2.00	5.00
143 Texas Tornado	.12	.30
144 Million Dollar Man Ted DiBiase	.12	.30
145 Earthquake	.10	.25
146 Legion of Doom	.12	.30
147 Rockers	.15	.40
148 Macho King Randy Savage	2.00	5.00
149 Earthquake	.10	.25
150 The Model Rick Martel	.10	.25

1994 Coliseum Video WWF Akklaim Strategy Tips

COMPLETE SET (4)	5.00	12.00
NNO Doink	2.00	5.00
NNO Luna Vachon	2.00	5.00
NNO Shawn Michaels	2.50	6.00
NNO Yokozuna	2.00	5.00

1994 Coliseum Video WWF Bret Hart

COMPLETE SET (5)	2.50	6.00
1 Bret Hitman Hart	.75	2.00
2 Bret Hitman Hart	.75	2.00
3 Bret Hitman Hart	.75	2.00
4 Bret Hitman Hart	.75	2.00
5 Bret Hitman Hart	.75	2.00

1993 Coliseum Video WWF Collectors Cards

COMPLETE SET (9)	10.00	25.00
COLISEUM VIDEO RENTAL EXCLUSIVE		
1 Hulk Hogan/Mr. T	2.50	6.00
2 King Kong Bundy/Hulk Hogan	2.50	6.00
3 Andre the Giant/Hulk Hogan	2.00	5.00
4 Macho Man Randy Savage/Miss Elizabeth	2.00	5.00
5 Macho Man Randy Savage/Hulk Hogan	4.00	10.00
6 Ultimate Warrior	1.50	4.00
7 Sgt. Slaughter/Hulk Hogan	2.00	5.00
8 Macho Man Randy Savage	1.50	4.00
9 Wrestlemania IX	1.25	3.00

1993 Coliseum Video WWF Lenticular

COMPLETE SET (5)	10.00	25.00
NNO Bret Hit Man Hart	4.00	10.00
NNO Hulk Hogan	3.00	8.00
NNO Mr. Perfect	2.50	6.00
NNO Tatanka	1.50	4.00
NNO The Undertaker	5.00	12.00

2004 Comic Images WWE Raw Deal Armageddon

1 Flying Head Scissors TB C	.12	.25
2 Double Axe Handle TB C	.12	.25
3 Leg Drop TB U	.50	1.00

#	Card	Low	High
4	Splash TB U	.50	1.00
5	Flying Clothesline TB R	2.00	4.00
6	Moonsault TB R	2.00	4.00
7	Chump Punch C	.12	.25
8	Slap C	.12	.25
9	Super Punch C	.12	.25
10	Struck by a Kendo Stick TB C	.12	.25
11	Shoulder Thrust U	.50	1.00
12	Solarplex Knife Chop U	.50	1.00
13	Cold-Cocked U	.50	1.00
14	Ensugiri TB U	.50	1.00
15	Knee Lift TB R	2.00	4.00
16	Whirling Backhand R	2.00	4.00
17	European Uppercut R	2.00	4.00
18	Flurry of Strikes R	2.00	4.00
19	Throw C	.12	.25
20	Inverse Atomic Drop TB C	.12	.25
21	Rib Breaker TB C	.12	.25
22	Back Breaker TB C	.12	.25
23	Double Leg Takedown TB U	.50	1.00
24	Fireman's Carry TB U	.50	1.00
25	Toss U	.50	1.00
26	Leg Drag TB U	.50	1.00
27	Brainbuster TB R	2.00	4.00
28	Airplane Spin TB R	2.00	4.00
29	Power Slam TB R	2.00	4.00
30	Atomic Driver R	2.00	4.00
31	Short Arm Hammerlock TB C	.12	.25
32	Cranial Crunch C	.12	.25
33	Chin Lock TB C	.12	.25
34	Go-Behind C	.12	.25
35	Grab U	.50	1.00
36	Head Vise TB U	.50	1.00
37	Chicken Wing TB U	.50	1.00
38	Asphyxiater U	.50	1.00
39	Rest Hold R	2.00	4.00
40	Abdominal Stretch TB R	2.00	4.00
41	STF TB R	2.00	4.00
42	Figure Four Leg Lock TB R	2.00	4.00
43	Anything and Hate It C	.12	.25
44	I Gotta Say, Out of Play U	.50	1.00
45	Raw and Ready R	2.00	4.00
46	Ask Yourself... C	.12	.25
47	I Got That, Too C	.12	.25
48	Hmmmm Don't Think... TB C	.12	.25
49	Back in Style C	.12	.25
50	From the Middle Turnbuckle C	.12	.25
51	Throw Opponent Out... TB C	.12	.25
52	From the Top Rope TB C	.12	.25
53	I'm Desperate C	.12	.25
54	J.R. Style Action U	.50	1.00
55	Volley This U	.50	1.00
56	Flawless Execution U	.50	1.00
57	Great Power Brawl TB U	.50	1.00
58	The Rub U	.50	1.00
59	Egomaniacal U	.50	1.00
60	It's Not Always the Charisma U	.50	1.00
61	Throwback Represent U	.50	1.00
62	Calculated Revenge R	2.00	4.00
63	The Show Must Go On R	2.00	4.00
64	I'm Giving You a Chance R	2.00	4.00
65	Personal Vendetta R	2.00	4.00
66	I Won't Stop R	2.00	4.00
67	Defensive Style TB R	2.00	4.00
68	Take It Back R	2.00	4.00
69	The Switch R	2.00	4.00
70	Like a Bat Out of Hell R	2.00	4.00
71	Boston, Massachusetts C	.12	.25
72	I Want to Play the Game C	.12	.25
73	Old School Antics C	.12	.25
74	San Diego, California C	.12	.25
75	Unbreakable Chain C	.12	.25
76	All Alone in the Night U	.50	1.00
77	Managed by William Regal U	.50	1.00
78	New Orleans, Louisiana U	.50	1.00
79	Buried Alive Match U	.50	1.00
80	Washington, DC U	.50	1.00
81	Little Rock, Arkansas R	2.00	4.00
82	Managed by the Coach R	2.00	4.00
83	Evening Gown Match R	2.00	4.00
84	Singapore City, Singapore R	2.00	4.00
85	Clear the Way C	.12	.25
86	Old-Fashioned Lock-Up C	.12	.25
87	Pop You One C	.12	.25
88	Atomic Bear Hug C	.12	.25
89	Here Comes the Coach C	.12	.25
90	Out of Control U	.50	1.00
91	You'll Really Be Stunned U	.50	1.00
92	The Darkness Before the Dawn U	.50	1.00
93	Goodnight, Everybody U	.50	1.00
94	Sometimes You Need to... U	.50	1.00
95	Here Comes the Headache R	2.00	4.00
96	Suicide Plancha TB R	2.00	4.00
97	I'm Making This Up As I Go Along R	2.00	4.00
98	It's All For My Fans R	2.00	4.00
99	Anybody Can Be King... R	2.00	4.00
100	Babe of the Year EX		
101	Give Me a Little UR	7.50	15.00
102	Time to Catch My Breath UR	7.50	15.00
103	Babe Buster EX		
104	Tyson Interferes EX		
105	Keys to the City EX		
106	John Bradshaw Layfield EX		
107	Ten Gallon Hat UR	7.50	15.00
108	JBL's Limo UR	7.50	15.00
109	Work Harder, Work Smarter EX		
110	You Forgot About Orlando... EX		
111	JBL's Clothesline from Hell EX		
112	The Phenom EX		
113	The Urn UR	7.50	15.00
114	Takin' Care of Business UR	7.50	15.00
115	The Dead Will Rise Again EX		
116	There is No Forgiveness... EX		
117	The Deadman is Alive EX		
118	Randy Orton EX		
119	The Legend Killer UR	7.50	15.00
120	RKO UR	7.50	15.00
121	Youngest Champion in WWE... EX		
122	Third Generation Superstar EX		
123	Overdrive EX		
124	Shane O'Mac EX		
125	Mean Streets of Greenwich, CT UR	7.50	15.00
126	Coast to Coast UR	7.50	15.00
127	Mean Streets Silver Spoon EX		
128	Here's Where the Buck Stops EX		
129	Leap of Faith EX		
130	Shelton Benjamin EX		
131	World's Greatest Upset... UR	7.50	15.00
132	T-Bone Exploder Suplex UR	7.50	15.00
133	Ain't No Stopping Me Now EX		
134	Shelton's Spinning Heel Kick EX		
135	Shelton's Splash EX		
136	Eugene PR		
137	I'm Special UR	7.50	15.00
138	Eugening Up PR		
139	The Jacket's Coming Off PR		
140	The Pride of the Family PR		
141	The Dream Lives On PR		
142	Rene Dupree PR		
143	Rene's Elbow Drop UR	7.50	15.00
144	Managed by Fifi PR		
145	The French Tickler PR		
146	Fifi Interferes PR		
147	The French Neck Breaker PR		
148	Cerebral Spray PR		
149	Pago Pago, American Samoa PR		
150	Out of the Hellfire PR		
151	Don't You Wish You Were Me? PR		
152	For Real PR		
153	El Paso, Texas PR		
154	Angle's Leg Bar PR		
155	Dudleyville, USA PR		
156	You're Just a Puppet PR		
157	Captain Charisma Strikes PR		
158	I Can Slap a Tornado PR		
159	The Hog Log PR		
160	A Less Traveled Road PR		
161	Step Over Heel Kick PR		
162	I Ain't No Minor Leaguer PR		
163	People Like Us Are Just Born... PR		
164	The Best Thing Going Today PR		
165	Double Chop PR		
166	Superhero in Training PR		
167	Crossing Borders PR		
168	The Legend Lives On PR		
169	Throwback PR		
170	Taunt the Crowd PR		
171	Why Can't We Just Dance? UR	7.50	15.00
172	The Inmates Aren't Running... UR	7.50	15.00
173	It's Not a Wig UR	7.50	15.00
174	The Cena Throwback UR	7.50	15.00
175	A Welcome Distraction UR	7.50	15.00
176	Victoria's Secret UR	7.50	15.00
177	Drastic Times... UR	7.50	15.00
178	If You Want to Play... UR	7.50	15.00
179	Master Manipulator UR	7.50	15.00
180	Armageddon is Upon Us UR	7.50	15.00
181	Vinny Mac Attack UR	7.50	15.00

2004 Comic Images WWE Raw Deal Divas Overload

#	Card	Low	High
1	Show and Go C	.12	.25
2	Diving Bulldog U	.50	1.00
3	Suicide Dive R	2.00	4.00
4	Girly Punch C	.12	.25
5	Boot Lace C	.12	.25
6	Chop Block C	.12	.25
7	Elbow Smash C	.12	.25
8	Jab U	.50	1.00
9	Forearm Uppercut U	.50	1.00
10	Ax Kick U	.50	1.00
11	Spinning Clothesline U	.50	1.00
12	Chick Kick R	2.00	4.00
13	Double Clothesline Takedown R	2.00	4.00
14	Atomic Lariat R	2.00	4.00
15	Hurricane Clothesline R	2.00	4.00
16	Chest Lock Drop C	.12	.25
17	Wheelbarrow Slam C	.12	.25
18	Running Spinebuster U	.50	1.00
19	Gut Buster On Top Rope U	.50	1.00
20	Top Rope Toss R	2.00	4.00
21	Reverse Fall-away Slam R	2.00	4.00
22	Modified Clutch Onto Opponent C	.12	.25
23	Arm Breaker C	.12	.25
24	Unorthodox Wrist Lock U	.50	1.00
25	Modified Bow and Arrow U	.50	1.00
26	Front Chancery R	2.00	4.00
27	Lady's Grapevine R	2.00	4.00
28	Girl on Girl Action C	.12	.25
29	Some Gals Don't Get Any Action C	.12	.25
30	Overshot Your Mark U	.50	1.00
31	Reach for the Ropes U	.50	1.00
32	Too Many Rules... R	2.00	4.00
33	You Fight Like a Woman R	2.00	4.00
34	Let's Wrestle Already C	.12	.25
35	No Matching Tights C	.12	.25
36	Don't Be Shy C	.12	.25
37	It's Time I Made Some Changes C	.12	.25
38	Lousy Foot Work C	.12	.25
39	Recover Again C	.12	.25
40	Name of the Game... C	.12	.25
41	I've Got a Leg Up On You C	.12	.25
42	I've Got a Nice Bottom U	.50	1.00
43	I'll Take a Shot U	.50	1.00
44	The Hubbub Backstage U	.50	1.00
45	Get a Look at These U	.50	1.00
46	So Solly So Sorey U	.50	1.00
47	Sump'tin' Be Started U	.50	1.00
48	This Diva's Got Claws U	.50	1.00
49	Shake My Hand, Boy U	.50	1.00
50	My New Gimmick R	2.00	4.00
51	Puppy Love R	2.00	4.00
52	What Are You Gawking At? R	2.00	4.00
53	Where's the Payoff? R	2.00	4.00
54	Don't Cross the Boss R	2.00	4.00
55	Twisted Smile R	2.00	4.00
56	Tap Tap Tap, You Sonofa- R	2.00	4.00
57	If You're Not Cheating... R	2.00	4.00
58	Asset Retrieval C	.12	.25
59	Not Today, Cupcake C	.12	.25
60	I'm Always on Top C	.12	.25
61	Distractingly Divalicious C	.12	.25
62	You Should Cover Your Eyes C	.12	.25
63	Old School Psychology C	.12	.25
64	Back to Basics U	.50	1.00
65	Falls Count Anywhere Match U	.50	1.00
66	Skirt vs. Skirt Match U	.50	1.00
67	Dare to Take a Challenge U	.50	1.00
68	Perennial Fan Favorites U	.50	1.00
69	Run the Gauntlet U	.50	1.00
70	Backstage Interview with Terri R	2.00	4.00
71	I've Had More Championships... R	2.00	4.00
72	I'm Gonna Break You R	2.00	4.00
73	Rules Were Meant to be Broken R	2.00	4.00
74	Managed by Miss Jackie R	2.00	4.00
75	Managed by Theodore Long R	2.00	4.00
76	Took That on the Chin C	.12	.25
77	Skirt the Issue C	.12	.25
78	Get the Tables C	.12	.25
79	Teaser Mode C	.12	.25
80	Victory Roll C	.12	.25
81	I'm Trying Not to Lose... U	.50	1.00
82	Panic Assault U	.50	1.00
83	Panic Grab U	.50	1.00
84	Panic Throw U	.50	1.00
85	This Is Going Nowhere Fast U	.50	1.00
86	That's Gonna Leave a Mark R	2.00	4.00
87	It Doesn't Stop R	2.00	4.00
88	Divas Overload R	2.00	4.00
89	It's Over R	2.00	4.00
90	Reverse 180-Degree Chair Shot R	2.00	4.00
91	Goldberg EX		

#	Card		
92	Gooooooolllllldddddd-berg UR	7.50	15.00
93	Goldberg's Jackhammer UR	7.50	15.00
94	Who's Next? EX		
95	Believe the Hype EX		
96	Goldberg's Spear EX		
97	Stacy Keibler EX		
98	Straddle the Ropes UR	7.50	15.00
99	Superior Leg Work UR	7.50	15.00
100	Test or Freakzilla? EX		
101	Pump Me Up EX		
102	I Know How to Use Them EX		
103	Gail Kim and Molly Holly EX		
104	Change Reality UR	7.50	15.00
105	Gail's Hurricanrana UR	7.50	15.00
106	Wake Up EX		
107	Look Around EX		
108	Molly-Go-Round EX		
109	John Cena EX		
110	Yo Kill da Beat UR	7.50	15.00
111	F-U UR	7.50	15.00
112	You Can't See Me EX		
113	Word Life EX		
114	I'm Gonna Teach You... EX		
115	Sable EX		
116	Sable-licious UR	7.50	15.00
117	And the Men that Come... UR	7.50	15.00
118	APA or A-Train? EX		
119	For the Women that Want... EX		
120	Sable Bomb EX		
121	Torrie Wilson EX		
122	WWE Centerfold of the Year UR	7.50	15.00
123	Torrie's DDT UR	7.50	15.00
124	Does This Look Good on Me? EX		
125	Strike a Pose EX		
126	The Boise Beauty EX		
127	Victoria PR		
128	Widow's Peak UR	7.50	15.00
129	Managed by Stevie Richards PR		
130	All the Things She Said PR		
131	Yes, I've Lost My Mind PR		
132	Stevie Interferes PR		
133	Nidia PR		
134	The Special Kiss UR	7.50	15.00
135	Managed by Jamie Noble PR		
136	Trailer Park Slap PR		
137	Drop Dead Gorgeous PR		
138	Jamie Noble Interferes PR		
139	Do You Want a Hug? PR		
140	You're Gonna Pay PR		
141	The Peep's Champ PR		
142	A Beating You'll Never Forget PR		
143	Unmasked Vengeance PR		
144	Highlight Reel PR		
145	Rikishi's Superkick PR		
146	Wrestling with a Broken... PR		
147	Benoit's German Suplex PR		
148	Gory Special PR		
149	That One Thing PR		
150	Beatings from Dudleyville PR		
151	Side Effect PR		
152	Showdown PR		
153	Mr. Monday Night PR		
154	Houston Hangover PR		
155	The Goddess Returns PR		
156	Drinking Beer - Raising Hell... PR		
157	The Flair Flop PR		
158	Puppy Power PR		
159	Tough Enough Head Trainer PR		
160	Series of Kicks PR		
161	Gregory Helms, Ace Reporter PR		
162	You Will Never Forget... UR	7.50	15.00
163	Brock Block UR	7.50	15.00
164	Rey Rey's Flying Body Press UR	7.50	15.00
165	Nidia, Hook Up the Double Wide UR	7.50	15.00
166	Steiner Flatliner UR	7.50	15.00
167	I'm Just a Sexy Boy UR	7.50	15.00
168	The World's Greatest Suplex UR	7.50	15.00
169	Once You Go Test... UR	7.50	15.00
170	Unstoppable UR	7.50	15.00
171	RVD or Booker T? UR	7.50	15.00
172	Edge or Big Show? UR	7.50	15.00

2006 Comic Images WWE Raw Deal
Great American Bash

#	Card		
1	Blindside Elbow Drop C	.12	.25
2	BASH Drop Kick C	.12	.25
3	Technical Splash in the Corner U	.50	1.00
4	BASH Aerial Clothesline U	.50	1.00
5	Corkscrew Somersault R	2.00	4.00
6	Dynamic Flying Body Press R	2.00	4.00
7	BASH Punch C	.12	.25
8	Straight Head Butt C	.12	.25
9	Shoot Kicker Hold C	.12	.25
10	Sizzling Clotheslin C	.12	.25
11	Blindside Hook U	.50	1.00
12	BASH Kick U	.50	1.00
13	Shoot Forearm U	.50	1.00
14	The Olí Straight-Arm Shot U	.50	1.00
15	Thrust Knee Lift R	2.00	4.00
16	Technical Lunging Lariat R	2.00	4.00
17	Dynamic Gut Stomp R	2.00	4.00
18	Precision Haymaker R	2.00	4.00
19	BASH Suplex C	.12	.25
20	Blindside Drop Toe Hold C	.12	.25
21	Leaping DDT C	.12	.25
22	Technical Monkey Flip U	.50	1.00
23	BASH Slam U	.50	1.00
24	Quick Snap Suplex U	.50	1.00
25	Precision Reverse Neck Breaker R	2.00	4.00
26	BASH Drop Over the Ropes R	2.00	4.00
27	Dynamic Back Breaker R	2.00	4.00
28	BASH Headlock C	.12	.25
29	Diva Lock C	.12	.25
30	Shoot Double Arm Lock C	.12	.25
31	Stretch Opponent C	.12	.25
32	BASH Vise U	.50	1.00
33	Blindside Sleeper U	.50	1.00
34	Technical Bear Hug U	.50	1.00
35	Precision Figure Four U	.50	1.00
36	Shoot Lock-up R	2.00	4.00
37	Neck Torque R	2.00	4.00
38	BASH Pin Hold R	2.00	4.00
39	Dynamic Torture Rack R	2.00	4.00
40	BASH Evader C	.12	.25
41	Me Llamo... Armando... C	.12	.25
42	Get Back in the Ring U	.50	1.00
43	The Return BASHÖ U	.50	1.00
44	Booby Trap R	2.00	4.00
45	Volleyed Beyond the Edge R	2.00	4.00
46	Takiní a BASH C	.12	.25
47	Stay Away from Daivari C	.12	.25
48	Give me an S...Give me a P... C	.12	.25
49	Hide and Seek U	.50	1.00
50	Blindsided by the... U	.50	1.00
51	Shane OíMac Delivers the BASH U	.50	1.00
52	Give & Take R	2.00	4.00
53	Jillian: Foxy Fixer R	2.00	4.00
54	Kristal: Broadcast Beauty R	2.00	4.00
55	Donít BASH the Star C	.12	.25
56	Find Out How to Fight From Finlay C	.12	.25
57	Straight-Shootiní Interview C	.12	.25
58	The Luck of the Draw C	.12	.25
59	All Together Now U	.50	1.00
60	Itís Not My Fault Being... EX	.50	1.00
61	The Best Laid PlansÖ U	.50	1.00
62	Not On My Broadcast U	.50	1.00
63	A No Show R	2.00	4.00
64	First of All R	2.00	4.00
65	For the Love of The Game R	2.00	4.00
66	Managed by Shane OíMac R	2.00	4.00
67	My Name is Matt Striker... C	.12	.25
68	Cheaters Never Win C	.12	.25
69	Throw DownóDonít Kiss Up C	.12	.25
70	Trevor Murdoch Is Gonna... U	.50	1.00
71	Backfire U	.50	1.00
72	A Phoenix Rising U	.50	1.00
73	Can U Believe the Witte Retort? R	2.00	4.00
74	This Is Between You and Me R	2.00	4.00
75	BASH: Great American Style R	2.00	4.00
76	Andre íThe Giantí EX		
77	We Face Each Other... UR	7.50	15.00
78	The 8th Wonder of the World UR	7.50	15.00
79	Giant Head Butt EX		
80	Inspiration for a New... PR		
81	Obey EX		
82	Lashley EX		
83	The Elevator Lift UR	7.50	15.00
84	The Real Hard Dominator UR	7.50	15.00
85	Hard Hitting EX		
86	Soft Spoken EX		
87	lím the Real Deal EX		
88	Ken Kennedy EX		
89	Mr. Kennedyís Mic UR	7.50	15.00
90	The Kenton Bomb UR	7.50	15.00
91	Say It Loud; Say It Proud: EX		
92	Mmmmmisterrrrr KennedyyyyyÖ EX		
93	ÖKENóNEóDY! EX		
94	Mickie James EX		
95	You Think lím a Psycho? UR	7.50	15.00
96	Laree DDT UR	7.50	15.00
97	Do You Love Me Now? EX		
98	Mick Kick EX		
99	Itís Time for a Great... U		
100	Mr. Pay-Per-View EX		
101	Unscripted UR	7.50	15.00
102	The Fury of the Storm UR	7.50	15.00
103	Flying Higher Than Ever EX		
104	Still Ö One of a Kind EX		
105	Split-legged Moonsault EX		
106	The Ultimate Survivor EX		
107	You Couldnít Pay Me Enough UR	7.50	15.00
108	Stronger Than Death UR	7.50	15.00
109	The Matt Hardy Movement... EX		
110	The Shirt Is Off EX		
111	Indestructible Soul EX		
112	The Boogeyman PR		
113	The Bottomless Pit UR	7.50	15.00
114	The Tick Tock of the Clock PR		
115	Mouthful of Worms PR		
116	I Am The BoogeymanÖ PR		
117	ÖAnd lím Coming To Getcha! PR		
118	The Spirit Squad PR		
119	Johnny PR		
120	Kenny PR		
121	Mikey PR		
122	Mitch PR		
123	Nicky PR		
124	High Spirits UR	7.50	15.00
125	S-P-I-R-I-T-S-Q-U-A-D... PR		
126	The Johnny-Go-Round Kick PR		
127	Trampoline Leap PR		
128	Air Kenny PR		
129	The Condemned PR		
130	Look Into the Eyes... PR		
131	The King of Kings PR		
132	See No Evil PR		
133	Angleís Uppercut PR		
134	20 Years: From theÖ PR		
135	The Rated R Superstar PR		
136	You Wonít See It ComingÖ PR		
137	Sharmellís Shenanigans PR		
138	The Art of Persuasion PR		
139	Regal Readying PR		
140	Hulkamania: Always in Style PR		
141	16-Time HeavyweightÖ PR		
142	Diva of the Decade PR		
143	The Size Advantage PR		
144	Grapple With Your Faith PR		
145	Billion Dollar Princess PR		
146	The Chain Gang: Hustle... PR		
147	Chloe: Best in Show PR		
148	I Ainít the Lady to Mess With PR		
149	Zero Tolerance: Kiss MyÖ PR		
150	I Am Who I Say I Am PR		
151	Fully Evolved: PR		
152	McMahon-icide PR		
153	líve Seen the Light PR		
154	Inspiration for a New Generation PR		
155	Blindside Spinebuster UR	7.50	15.00
156	Seen the GloryóTold the Story UR	7.50	15.00
157	Never Bet Against Me, Playa UR	7.50	15.00
158	Ground & Pound UR	7.50	15.00
159	I Wish Monsoon Was Here UR	7.50	15.00
160	JYDís Chain UR	7.50	15.00
161	Cobra Clutch UR	7.50	15.00
162	United We Stand UR	7.50	15.00
163	Divided You Fall UR	7.50	15.00
164	Whoís Under the Paint? UR	7.50	15.00
165	Carlitoís Cool Caribbean... UR	7.50	15.00
166	The Snakeline UR	7.50	15.00
167	Backed by Virgil UR	7.50	15.00
168	The Three Amigos UR	7.50	15.00
169	Funakiís Ensugiri UR	7.50	15.00
170	Size Matters UR	7.50	15.00

2003 Comic Images WWE Raw Deal
Insurrextion

#	Card		
1	Flying Choke Hold C	.12	.25
2	Flying Takedown U	.50	1.00
3	Flying Lariat R	2.00	4.00
4	Poke C	.12	.25
5	Noggin Knocker U	.50	1.00
6	Series of Punches R	2.00	4.00
7	Shake C	.12	.25
8	Capture Suplex C	.12	.25
9	Tossed Between the Ropes C	.12	.25
10	Rolling Suplex U	.50	1.00
11	Inside Cradle U	.50	1.00
12	Inverted Snake Eyes U	.50	1.00
13	Snap Slam R	2.00	4.00
14	Hangman's Neck Breaker R	2.00	4.00
15	Faceplant R	2.00	4.00

26

16	Split Finger Lock C	.12	.25
17	Body Vise U	.50	1.00
18	Inverted Leg Lock R	2.00	4.00
19	Dude, Try Something Else C	.12	.25
20	Fall into the Corner U	.50	1.00
21	Don't Try This at Home R	2.00	4.00
22	Blind Tag C	.12	.25
23	The Devil's in the Detail C	.12	.25
24	Hey, Whatcha Doin'? C	.12	.25
25	Crowd Pleaser C	.12	.25
26	Pump Up the Crowd C	.12	.25
27	How Ya Like Me Now? C	.12	.25
28	Perplex Opponent C	.12	.25
29	Always U	.50	1.00
30	Add Insult to Injury U	.50	1.00
31	It's Your Own Fault U	.50	1.00
32	This is Gonna Get Ugly U	.50	1.00
33	What's Mine is Mine... U	.50	1.00
34	Beat You Raw U	.50	1.00
35	Forget the Smackdown... U	.50	1.00
36	No One Wants to Watch... R	2.00	4.00
37	I Can't Be Reading This Right R	2.00	4.00
38	Pass the Buck R	2.00	4.00
39	From the Mind of Eric Bischoff R	2.00	4.00
40	Stephanie McMahon Decrees R	2.00	4.00
41	The End Is Near R	2.00	4.00
42	Forceable Entry R	2.00	4.00
43	Give and Take C	.12	.25
44	I'm the Underdog C	.12	.25
45	Ring Psychology: Arm C	.12	.25
46	Ring Psychology: Leg C	.12	.25
47	Stun the Crowd C	.12	.25
48	Take Care of Number One C	.12	.25
49	Backstage Donnybrook U	.50	1.00
50	Dance, Coach, Dance U	.50	1.00
51	Man of 1000 Holds U	.50	1.00
52	Premiere Raw Superstar U	.50	1.00
53	Premiere Smackdown Superstar U	.50	1.00
54	Smackdown #1 Announcer Funaki U	.50	1.00
55	According to Linda and the Board of Executives R	2.00	4.00
56	Backstage Politics R	2.00	4.00
57	It's Hard Being This Original R	2.00	4.00
58	Mangled Intro by Lillian Garcia R	2.00	4.00
59	Raw Roulette Wheel R	2.00	4.00
60	Series of Stipulations R	2.00	4.00
61	The Ref Takes Control C	.12	.25
62	Power Struggle C	.12	.25
63	Chase Off Manager C	.12	.25
64	Cut the Ring in Half C	.12	.25
65	Really, That's Enough C	.12	.25
66	Mental Acumen C	.12	.25
67	Don't Cross a McMahon U	.50	1.00
68	Give You the Runaround U	.50	1.00
69	Electric Chair U	.50	1.00
70	Glad Someone Has My Back U	.50	1.00
71	You Make Me Sick U	.50	1.00
72	Do Something R	2.00	4.00
73	Show Me Something R	2.00	4.00
74	Chief Morley Says R	2.00	4.00
75	Real Predictable R	2.00	4.00
76	Outside Interference R	2.00	4.00
77	Big Poppa Pump EX		
78	Holla If Ya Hear Me UR	7.50	15.00
79	Genetic Freak Push-ups UR	7.50	15.00
80	Freakzilla Says... EX		
81	All I Care About Are My... EX		
82	The Big, Bad Booty Daddy... EX		

83	The Rattlesnake EX		
84	The Bionic Redneck UR	7.50	15.00
85	Gimme a Hell Yeah UR	7.50	15.00
86	Stomp a Mudhole EX		
87	Don't Trust Nobody EX		
88	Walk It Dry EX		
89	Shawn Michaels EX		
90	The Icon, The Showstoppa... UR	7.50	15.00
91	Sweet Chin Music UR	7.50	15.00
92	Don't Hunt What You Can't Kill EX		
93	Top Rope Elbow Drop EX		
94	The Heart Break Kid EX		
95	The Crippler EX		
96	There's No Holding Me Back UR	7.50	15.00
97	Toothless Aggression UR	7.50	15.00
98	Cripple Opponent EX		
99	Rabid Attack in the Corner EX		
100	Surprise Drop Kick EX		
101	Los Guerreros EX		
102	We Lie, We Cheat, We Steal UR	7.50	15.00
103	Chavo's Inverted Powerbomb UR	7.50	15.00
104	Cheat 2 Win EX		
105	Tu Locas, Ese You Crazy, Man EX		
106	Lasso from El Paso EX		
107	Team Angle EX		
108	Collegiate Champions UR	7.50	15.00
109	Leapfrog Stun Gun UR	7.50	15.00
110	Submit EX		
111	It's All About the Benjamins EX		
112	The Haas of Pain EX		
113	Test PR		
114	Test Drive UR	7.50	15.00
115	I Love My Testicles PR		
116	Stacy Keibler, Marketing... PR		
117	Test's Pump Handle Slam PR		
118	Test's Running Boot PR		
119	Rhyno PR		
120	GORE GORE GORE UR	7.50	15.00
121	Extreme Warfare PR		
122	Rhyno's Garbage Can PR		
123	The Manbeast PR		
124	Rhyno Stampede PR		
125	Big Evil - Red Devil PR		
126	Screw the Rules PR		
127	Get Ready... PR		
128	Big Freak'n Powerslam PR		
129	I'm the King of the World PR		
130	Makin' a Difference PR		
131	Dudleyz3 PR		
132	You're a Human Vacuum... PR		
133	I Ain't Not No Sucka Neitha PR		
134	Version 1.0 PR		
135	X-treme Sendoff PR		
136	You Can't Manhandle... PR		
137	Dude Whatever PR		
138	Yo Dawg, Respect... PR		
139	Proper Planning Prevents... PR		
140	I Live for My Hulkamaniacs UR	7.50	15.00
141	You're Going to Space Mountain UR	7.50	15.00
143	No Gimmicks Needed UR	7.50	15.00
144	Double Face Kick UR	7.50	15.00
145	Shining Wizard Kick UR	7.50	15.00
146	Electrifying UR	7.50	15.00
147	Here Comes the Pain UR	7.50	15.00
148	West Coast Bronco Buster UR	7.50	15.00
149	3 Minutes and We're Out UR	7.50	15.00
150	Nidia Interferes UR	7.50	15.00
142-A	X-treme Hedonism - A Image UR	7.50	15.00
142-B	X-treme Hedonism - B Image UR	7.50	15.00

2004 Comic Images WWE Raw Deal Lethal Library

1	Vince McMahon
2	Remember Who Pays Your Salary
3	Master of Promotion
4	I'm Vincent Kennedy McMahon...
5	First Family of Professional Wrestling
6	A Dynasty's Destiny
7	Shane O'Mac or Stephanie ?
8	King's Crown
9	White Wedding
10	Osaka, Japan
11	I Don't Care About the Heat
12	Change in Programming Lineup
13	The Road to Victory
14	Suicide Strike
15	Counterproductive Ambitions
16	How Important Is It?
17	Sucker Punch
18	Gut Punch Body Slam
19	Atomic Spine Buster
20	Leg Lock
21	McMahon Family Values
22	Explosion Raw Deal
23	Lethal Library
24	The Price We Pay

2006 Comic Images WWE Raw Deal No Way Out

1	Technical Stomp C	.12	.25
2	Shoot Aerial 360-Degree Kick U	.50	1.00
3	Precision Knee Drop R	2.00	4.00
4	Dynamic Punch C	.12	.25
5	Dynamic Hook C	.12	.25
6	Straight Clothesline C	.12	.25
7	Thrust Kick C	.12	.25
8	Shoot Punch U	.50	1.00
9	Dynamic Forearm U	.50	1.00
10	Technical Clothesline U	.50	1.00
11	Dynamic Knee Lift U	.50	1.00
12	Precision Kick U	.50	1.00
13	Blindside Tornado Strike R	2.00	4.00
14	Whirling Elbow R	2.00	4.00
15	Dynamic Lariat R	2.00	4.00
16	Punch After Punch R	2.00	4.00
17	Snap DDT C	.12	.25
18	Dynamic Throw C	.12	.25
19	Dynamic Drop C	.12	.25
20	Delayed Atomic Drop C	.12	.25
21	Blindside Beal Toss U	.50	1.00
22	Rolling Neck Breaker U	.50	1.00
23	Dynamic Takedown U	.50	1.00
24	Dynamic Slam U	.50	1.00
25	Precision Suplex U	.50	1.00
26	Dynamic Driver R	2.00	4.00
27	Technical Power Bomb R	2.00	4.00
28	Vertical Power Bomb R	2.00	4.00
29	Atomic Power Slam R	2.00	4.00
30	Dynamic Arm Bar C	.12	.25
31	Arm Twist C	.12	.25
32	Dynamic Headlock C	.12	.25
33	Blindside Abdominal Stretch C	.12	.25
34	Arm Wrench U	.50	1.00
35	Vise Lock U	.50	1.00
36	Dynamic Stretch U	.50	1.00
37	Dynamic Bear Hug U	.50	1.00
38	Precision Sleeper U	.50	1.00
39	Technical Crab R	2.00	4.00

40	Fujiwara Arm Bar R	2.00	4.00
41	Dynamic Figure Four R	2.00	4.00
42	Atomic Body Lock R	2.00	4.00
43	It's Great To Be Back Here In... C	.12	.25
44	Just What the Game Needs C	.12	.25
45	The Coach Says... U	.50	1.00
46	Once Again, Kissing Up... R	2.00	4.00
47	You Can't Cheat an Honest Man... R	2.00	4.00
48	Contrary to Popular Opinion C	.12	.25
49	Between the Ropes C	.12	.25
50	Over the Ropes C	.12	.25
51	Painfully Obvious Precision C	.12	.25
52	...And the Crowd Roars U	.50	1.00
53	By Any Means Necessary U	.50	1.00
54	Shoot Action R	2.00	4.00
55	Ashley: Pretty Punk R	2.00	4.00
56	Mickie: Fervent Fanatic R	2.00	4.00
57	Kick Out! R	2.00	4.00
58	Givin' Íem High Fives C	.12	.25
59	In The Interest Of Fairness C	.12	.25
60	Technically Sound & Brutal C	.12	.25
61	I Have A Major Announcement U	.50	1.00
62	You Will Witness History U	.50	1.00
63	There Is No Escape U	.50	1.00
64	Denville, New Jersey R	2.00	4.00
65	WWE Homecoming R	2.00	4.00
66	That's Value! R	2.00	4.00
67	Go For the Cover! C	.12	.25
68	Tormented Tomfoolery C	.12	.25
69	A Punch That'll Take... C	.12	.25
70	Precision Personified U	.50	1.00
71	Shoot Counter U	.50	1.00
72	Blindsided Rage U	.50	1.00
73	A Great Deal Of Confusion R	2.00	4.00
74	Overwhelming Crowd Support R	2.00	4.00
75	Volley Finisher R	2.00	4.00
76	Carlito EX		
77	Carlito's Apple UR	7.50	15.00
78	Carlito's Cabana UR	7.50	15.00
79	I Spit In the Face Of... EX		
80	...People Who Don't Want... EX		
81	Carlito's Way DDT EX		
82	Jake "the Snake" EX		
83	Lucifer UR	7.50	15.00
84	Mind Games EX		
85	The Snake Will Always.... EX		
86	The Snake Bite DDT EX		
87	The Million Dollar Man... EX		
88	The Million Dollar Title Belt UR	7.50	15.00
89	Everybody's Got a Price EX		
90	Everybody's Gonna Pay EX		
91	The Million Dollar Dream EX		
92	The Bookerman EX		
93	Managed by Sharmell UR	7.50	15.00
94	Sharmell Interferes UR	7.50	15.00
95	You Didn't Just Try That... EX		
96	Spinning Straight Elbow EX		
97	Distracted by Sharmell EX		
98	The Largest Athlete... EX		
99	Mine Is Bigger Than Yours UR	7.50	15.00
100	The Biggest Precision... UR	7.50	15.00
101	Colossal Clubbing EX		
102	Big Enough to Eat Somebody EX		
103	The Big & The Small of It EX		
104	X-treme Diva EX		
105	It Just Feels Right UR	7.50	15.00
106	Just the Way I Planned... UR	7.50	15.00
107	Girly Choke EX		

#	Card		
108	Don't Call Me A... EX		
109	Love... Fury... Passion... EX		
110	Chavo Guerrero PR		
111	One for One UR	7.50	15.00
112	My Life For You PR		
113	Guerreros por Siempre! PR		
114	A Family Tradition PR		
115	The Gory Bomb PR		
116	Funaki PR		
117	The Rising Sun UR	7.50	15.00
118	Japanese Flying Bulldog PR		
119	I'll Do Anything For the... PR		
120	...I Do Ask the Tough Questions PR		
121	Springboard Body Block PR		
122	Mexicools PR		
123	Lawn Maintenance... UR	7.50	15.00
124	Forget Your Stereotypes PR		
125	Crazy Moonsault PR		
126	Psychotic Guillotine Leg Drop PR		
127	Mexi-Leg-Lace Powerbomb PR		
128	Viscera PR		
129	The Sex Drive UR	7.50	15.00
130	A Big Man Has A Big... Appetite PR		
131	500 Pound Love Machine PR		
132	Take It Like a Man PR		
133	Flying Somersault Kick PR		
134	STUNNER! PR		
135	Death Waits for No Man PR		
136	Bring the Hammer Down PR		
137	This Is The Rock's Show PR		
138	Journey Into Darkness PR		
139	American By Birth... PR		
140	I'm Driven by Anger PR		
141	Liaison with Lita PR		
142	It's Us vs. Them PR		
143	Nobody Gets Higher PR		
144	Walking a Golden Mile PR		
145	24-inch Pythons PR		
146	Walk That Aisle PR		
147	Trish's Chick Kick PR		
148	Old School Luche Libre... PR		
149	Tuning Up the Band PR		
150	One Issue On My Mind PR		
151	The B!tch Is Back! PR		
152	You Want Some? Come Get Some! PR		
153	Too Hot For TV PR		
154	Is Chloe Your Favorite Puppy? PR		
155	Backed by Torrie & Candice PR		
156	It's Good For Business PR		
157	I Am a Wrestling God UR	7.50	15.00
158	The Ego Cutter UR	7.50	15.00
159	Hold On, Hotshot! UR	7.50	15.00
160	Shelton's Lunging Lariat UR	7.50	15.00
161	Dernier Slam UR	7.50	15.00
162	Unleashed Bomb UR	7.50	15.00
163	The Rowdy Sleeper UR	7.50	15.00
164	Listen Up, Playa! UR	7.50	15.00
165	No Fault Drop UR	7.50	15.00
166	Jillian Hall: The Fixer UR	7.50	15.00
167	The Brain UR	7.50	15.00
168	The Thump UR	7.50	15.00
169	At Ease, Soldier UR	7.50	15.00
170	The Intensity of Ten Cities UR	7.50	15.00
171	Should've Seen This Coming UR	7.50	15.00
172	Pails o' Fun UR	7.50	15.00

2006 Comic Images WWE Raw Deal Royal Rumble

COMPLETE SET (90)

#	Card		
1	Roundhouse Kick C	.12	.25
2	Big Splash in the Corner U	.50	1.00
3	Technical Tope R	2.00	4.00
4	Handcuffed C	.12	.25
5	Fisticuffs C	.12	.25
6	Armed & Dangerous U	.50	1.00
7	Technical Drop Kick U	.50	1.00
8	Ankle Breaker R	2.00	4.00
9	Running Clothesline R	2.00	4.00
10	Slingshot Into the Ring Post C	.12	.25
11	Slam C	.12	.25
12	Scoop Slam U	.50	1.00
13	Thunder Bulldog U	.50	1.00
14	Fall-away Suplex R	2.00	4.00
15	Technical Slam R	2.00	4.00
16	Hair Pull C	.12	.25
17	Entangle in the Ropes C	.12	.25
18	Key Lock U	.50	1.00
19	Take Your Own Medicine U	.50	1.00
20	Face Stretch R	2.00	4.00
21	Technical Body Lock R	2.00	4.00
22	How Many Do You Need? C	.12	.25
23	Always Have a Plan B U	.30	.75
24	Once is Enough R	2.00	4.00
25	Volley Call C	.12	.25
26	Everyone Wants to Watch... C	.12	.25
27	Everyone Wants to Watch... C	.12	.25
28	Chained Aggression C	.12	.25
29	No Pain, No Chain C	.12	.25
30	Feel the Fire U	.50	1.00
31	Sparks of Glory U	.50	1.00
32	Underestimated Prowess U	.50	1.00
33	Backed by Eric Bischoff U	.25	.50
34	Backed by Theodore Long U	.30	.60
35	Grab the Mic R	2.00	4.00
36	You Feeling Lucky? R	2.00	4.00
37	Face the Music R	2.00	4.00
38	Let the Heeling Begin R	2.00	4.00
39	I Waited Long Enough R	2.00	4.00
40	Chain Reaction C	.12	.25
41	Argue With Tony Chimel C	.15	.30
42	Product Endorsements C	.12	.25
43	Unrelenting Assault U	.50	1.00
44	Restart the Match U	.50	1.00
45	Sit Right Here and Bide My Time U	.50	1.00
46	It's Getting Hot in Here R	2.00	4.00
47	Let's Get It On! R	2.00	4.00
48	Managed by Lita R	2.00	4.00
49	A Technical Shoot C	.50	1.00
50	Quick Poke C	.12	.25
51	Small Concealed Foreign Object C	.12	.25
52	USA! USA! USA! C	.12	.25
53	Chain Barrier U	.50	1.00
54	Heat Barrier U	.50	1.00
55	Volley Barrier U	.50	1.00
56	Too Hot to Handle U	.50	1.00
57	Future Considerations R	2.00	4.00
58	The Sex, the Gods... R	2.00	4.00
59	Ready to Fight R	2.00	4.00
60	Break It Out, Break You... R	3.00	6.00
61	Hollywood Hulk Hogan PR	2.00	4.00
62	Whatcha Gonna Do, Brother? UR	7.50	15.00
63	When Hulkamania Runs... UR	7.50	15.00
64	I Live for My Hulkamaniacs... UR	7.50	15.00
65	Hulkin' Up UR	7.50	15.00
66	Original <WWE logo> Icon PR		
67	Hollywood's Big Boot PR		
68	Say Your Prayers... PR		
69	Hollywood Leg Drop PR		
70	Sgt. Slaughter PR		
71	Real American Cobra Clutch UR	7.50	15.00
72	The Motor Pool PR		
73	Boot Camp Match PR		
74	At-Ten-HUT! PR		
75	Gimme Ten, Maggot! PR		
76	The Home Team PR		
77	Because the Fans Demanded It UR	7.50	15.00
78	Flurry of Finishers UR	7.50	15.00
79	The Shhhhh Chop PR		
80	Never Back Down - Never Quit PR		
81	I Will Not Die PR		
82	The Whole Dam Show PR		
83	The Heat Seekers PR		
84	On Your Home Turf UR	7.50	15.00
85	Good Old-Fashioned Mugging UR	7.50	15.00
86	I Know Cool ... And You're... PR		
87	Kokubetsu PR		
88	The Proper Punch PR		
89	We're Not Mexicans... PR		
90	Violent Vendetta UR	7.50	15.00

2002 Comic Images WWE Raw Deal SummerSlam

#	Card		
1	Head Butt Drop C	.12	.25
2	Inverted Body Block U	.50	1.00
3	Back Splash R	2.00	4.00
4	Knife-Edge Chop C	.12	.25
5	Spinning Back Fist C	.12	.25
6	Atomic Back Body Drop C	.12	.25
7	Back Rake C	.12	.25
8	Brass Nuks Shot U	.50	1.00
9	Short Arm Clothesline U	.50	1.00
10	Kangaroo Kick U	.50	1.00
11	360-Degree Clothesline R	2.00	4.00
12	Up and At 'em C	.12	.25
13	Double Underhook Back Breaker C	.12	.25
14	Snap Suplex C	.12	.25
15	Bulldog Lariat C	.12	.25
16	Face-buster Suplex U	.50	1.00
17	Tilt-a-Whirl Powerslam U	.50	1.00
18	Back Breaker Torture Rack R	2.00	4.00
19	Arm Wringer C	.12	.25
20	Nerve Hold C	.12	.25
21	Knee Lock U	.50	1.00
22	Half Crab U	.50	1.00
23	Dragon Sleeper R	2.00	4.00
24	Booby Trap C	.12	.25
25	That's Enough Out of You C	.12	.25
26	There Are Two Things... U	.50	1.00
27	I Change the Questions R	2.00	4.00
28	Grab the Mic C	.12	.25
29	Use 'em or Lose 'em C	.12	.25
30	You Feeling Lucky? C	.12	.25
31	I'm Gonna Try That Again C	.12	.25
32	Battling the Voices C	.12	.25
33	Springboard C	.12	.25
34	Let's Pick Up the Pace C	.12	.25
35	Filthy, Disgusting, Brutal... U	.50	1.00
36	Energy Burst U	.50	1.00
37	Mind Games U	.50	1.00
38	Play the Game U	.50	1.00
39	Give It All I Got U	.50	1.00
40	Beating the Odds R	2.00	4.00
41	Smart Mark R	2.00	4.00
42	Hardcore 'Til the End R	2.00	4.00
43	Simply The Best R	2.00	4.00
44	Pencil-Necked Geek R	2.00	4.00
45	Go For the Cover R	2.00	4.00
46	Don't Hate da Playa, Hate da Game R	2.00	4.00
47	It's Showtime C	.12	.25
48	J.R. Style Clubberin' C	.12	.25
49	Pick Your Spots C	.12	.25
50	Glass Ceiling C	.12	.25
51	In the Interest of Fairness C	.12	.25
52	Do You Know What... U	.50	1.00
53	I'm The Biggest Dog on This Block U	.50	1.00
54	Just Who in the Blue Hell... U	.50	1.00
55	The Game Is Back... U	.50	1.00
56	I'm Better Than You U	.50	1.00
57	Bra and Panties Match R	2.00	4.00
58	Lethal nWo Poison R	2.00	4.00
59	Living Legend R	2.00	4.00
60	Managed by Stephanie... R	2.00	4.00
61	Managed by Torrie Wilson R	2.00	4.00
62	Managed by Stacy Keibler R	2.00	4.00
63	Managed by Terri Runnels R	2.00	4.00
64	I'm Not Outta It Yet C	.12	.25
65	Shove C	.12	.25
66	Business Is About to Pick Up C	.12	.25
67	Get What You're Expectin' C	.12	.25
68	Silent, But Violent C	.12	.25
69	My God He's Broken in Half C	.12	.25
70	Tag Out C	.12	.25
71	It's All in the Teamwork C	.12	.25
72	Save da Drama fo' yo' Mama U	.50	1.00
73	Turn Up the Heat U	.50	1.00
74	Greco-Roman Holiday U	.50	1.00
75	That's a Near Fall U	.50	1.00
76	You Suck You Suck U	.50	1.00
77	Ham-and-Egger U	.50	1.00
78	Not According to the Fine Print R	2.00	4.00
79	Squared Circle is No Place... R	2.00	4.00
80	Been There, Done That R	2.00	4.00
81	Human Highlight Reel R	2.00	4.00
82	To Be the Man... R	2.00	4.00
83	Ring General R	2.00	4.00
84	Hollywood Hogan EX		
85	Whatcha Gonna Do, Brother? UR	7.50	15.00
86	Hulkin' Up UR		
87	Hollywood's Big Boot EX		
88	Say Your Prayers and... EX		
89	Hollywood Leg Drop EX		
90	Ric Flair EX		
91	Stylin', Profilin', Limousine Ridin'... UR	7.50	15.00
92	Wooooooooo UR	7.50	15.00
93	Diamonds are Forever... EX		
94	Now You're Going to School EX		
95	The Dirtiest Player in the Game EX		
96	Hall and Nash EX		
97	Too Sweet UR	7.50	15.00
98	Jack-knife UR		
99	nWo Black and White EX		
100	4 Life EX		
101	Hall's Fall-Away Slam EX		
102	Trish Stratus EX		
103	The T and A Factor UR	7.50	15.00
104	100 Stratusfaction Guaranteed UR		
105	Stratusfaction Bulldog EX		
106	I've Been a Very Naughty Girl EX		
107	Perhaps I Need a Spanking? EX		

108 Billy and Chuck PU
109 Rico Enters UR 7.50 15.00
110 Oh, Baby, You Look So... PR
111 Chuck's Jungle Kick PR
112 Stretching is Good for the Groin PU
113 I've Had Many Partners... PU
114 Al Snow PU
115 Snow Plow UR 7.50 15.00
116 Head PR
117 What Does Everybody Need? PR
118 What Does Everybody Want? PU
119 Snow Slide PU
120 Tajiri PU
121 Kick of Death UR
122 Tarantula PR
123 Asian Mist PR
124 Tajiri's Handspring Elbow PU
125 Japanese Buzzsaw PU
126 Hurricane PU
127 Eye of the Hurricane UR
128 Stand Back There's a... PR
129 Caped Body Press PR
130 To the Hurricycle PU
131 Whassupwitdat??? PU
132 In the Presence of the Kanenites PR
133 I'm a Bad Man PR
134 Do YOU Live By the Three I's? PR
135 The Mood Is About to Change PR
136 The Best Technical Wrestler... PR
137 Whatchoo Talkin' 'bout, Ese? PR
138 Outsider Distraction PR
139 Brothers from Another Mother UR
140 Edge-acution UR
141 Temper Tantrum UR 7.50 15.00
142 Team X-Treme UR 7.50 15.00
143 Big All Over UR
144 Lita's Twist of Fate UR
145 Dude, Nice Hang Time UR
146 Tell Me You Didn't Just Say That UR7.50 15.00
147 Damn UR
148 Giant Killer UR
149 Listen Up, Sunshine UR
150 Raven's Shopping Cart UR 7.50 15.00
8/TR cUndisputed Heavyweight Title R 2.00 4.00
9/TR Women's Title Belt R 2.00 4.00

2003 Comic Images WWE Raw Deal Survivor Series 2

1 Spinning Crescent Kick (M) C .12 .25
2 Knee Smash (S) C .12 .25
3 Big Splash in the Corner (B) C .12 .25
4 Inverted Body Block (SS) U .50 1.00
5 Flying Body Press (PR) U .50 1.00
6 Flying Tope (M) U .50 1.00
7 Drive Opponent Thru... (B) U .50 1.00
8 Back Splash (SS) R 2.00 4.00
9 Superplex (F) R 2.00 4.00
10 Atomic Back Body Drop (SS) C .12 .25
11 Struck by a Kendo Stick (B) C .12 .25
12 Gut Punch (M) C .12 .25
13 Back Rake (SS) C .12 .25
14 Eye Rake (S) C .12 .25
15 Shoulder Block (S) U .50 1.00
16 Kick (S) U .50 1.00
17 Running Lariat (B) U .50 1.00
18 Discus Punch (P) U .50 1.00
19 Garbage Can Lid (B) U .50 1.00
20 Brass Nuks Shot (SS) U .50 1.00
21 Pump Kick (M) R 2.00 4.00
22 Superkick (S) R 2.00 4.00
23 European Uppercut (S) R 2.00 4.00
24 360-Degree Clothesline (SS) R 2.00 4.00
25 Running Clothesline (B) R 2.00 4.00
26 Chair Shot (S) R 2.00 4.00
27 Within Your Grasp (M) C .12 .25
28 Double Underhook... (SS) C .12 .25
29 Neck Breaker (B) C .12 .25
30 Headlock Takedown (S) U .50 1.00
31 Backslide (M) U .50 1.00
32 German Suplex (F) U .50 1.00
33 Spine Buster (B) U .50 1.00
34 Face-buster Suplex (SS) U .50 1.00
35 Tilt-a-Whirl Powerslam (SS) U .50 1.00
36 Samoan Drop (S) R 2.00 4.00
37 Fisherman's Suplex (S) R 2.00 4.00
38 DDT (S) R 2.00 4.00
39 Running Bulldog (M) R 2.00 4.00
40 Back Breaker Torture Rack (SS) R 2.00 4.00
41 Clutch onto Opponent (B) C .12 .25
42 Short Arm Hammerlock (M) C .12 .25
43 Nerve Hold (SS) C .12 .25
44 Ankle Lock (S) U .50 1.00
45 Standing Side Headlock (S) U .50 1.00
46 Strangle Hold (M) U .50 1.00
47 Apply Illegal Leverage (B) U .50 1.00
48 Half Crab (SS) U .50 1.00
49 Sleeper (S) R 2.00 4.00
50 Boston Crab (S) R 2.00 4.00
51 Claw (S) R 2.00 4.00
52 Sharpshooter (B) R 2.00 4.00
53 Step Aside (S) C .12 .25
54 Escape Move (S) C .12 .25
55 Break the Hold (S) C .12 .25
56 Roll Out of the Way (S) C .12 .25
57 Clumsy Opponent (B) C .12 .25
58 No Sell Maneuver (B) C .12 .25
59 Over Sell Maneuver (B) C .12 .25
60 All Talk, No Action (M) C .12 .25
61 Elbow to the Face (S) U .50 1.00
62 Knee to the Gut (S) U .50 1.00
63 Rolling Takedown (S) U .50 1.00
64 There Are Two Things... (SS) U .50 1.00
65 Clean Break (P) U .50 1.00
66 Just Bring It (S) U .50 1.00
67 Hebner Calls It (S) U .50 1.00
68 Kissing Up to the Stinkin'... (B) U .50 1.00
69 Partner Interference (S) U .50 1.00
70 Iron Will (M) R 2.00 4.00
71 Not Today, Pal (M) R 2.00 4.00
72 No Chance in Hell (S) R 2.00 4.00
73 I Change the Questions (SS) R 2.00 4.00
74 Manager Interferes (S) R 2.00 4.00
75 Tag in Partner (S) C .12 .25
76 You Feeling Lucky? (SS) C .12 .25
77 Great Technical Knowledge (B) C .12 .25
78 Jockeying for Position (S) C .12 .25
79 Turn the Match into a Pier... (B) C .12 .25
80 Irish Whip (S) C .12 .25
81 Throw Into the Corner... (S) C .12 .25
82 From the Top Rope (S) C .12 .25
83 Little She Devil (M) C .12 .25
84 Gut Wrench (M) C .12 .25
85 Amazing Display of Power (B) C .12 .25
86 Charismatic Style (B) C .12 .25
87 Cole Calls It Right (M) C .12 .25
88 Trailer Park Trash (M) C .12 .25
89 Where the Hell Are We? (PR) U .50 1.00
90 J.R. Style Slobber-knocker U .50 1.00
91 Roll Out of the Ring (S) U .50 1.00
92 Shake It Off (P) U .50 1.00
93 Defensive Posture (S) U .50 1.00
94 Energy Burst (SS) U .50 1.00
95 Table Table Table (FL) U .50 1.00
96 Backed by Stephanie... (S) U .50 1.00
97 Offer Handshake (S) U .50 1.00
98 Who Booked This Match? (F) U .50 1.00
99 Well Deserved Push (B) U .50 1.00
100 Get Crowd Support (S) U .50 1.00
101 Spit at Opponent (S) U .50 1.00
102 Beating the Odds (SS) R 2.00 4.00
103 Ego Boost (S) R 2.00 4.00
104 Lita to the Xtreme (B) R 2.00 4.00
105 Simply the Best (SS) R 2.00 4.00
106 Maintain Hold (S) R 2.00 4.00
107 Enter the Stratusphere (S) R 2.00 4.00
108 Puppies Puppies (S) R 2.00 4.00
109 Ring Steps (M) R 2.00 4.00
110 Diversion (P) R 2.00 4.00
111 Turn the Tide (S) R 2.00 4.00
112 Don't Hate da Playa... (SS) R 2.00 4.00
113 You're Not in My League (B) R 2.00 4.00
114 Awesome Pyro (B) C .12 .25
115 It's Showtime (SS) C .12 .25
116 J.R. Style Clubberin' (SS) C .12 .25
117 Pick Your Spots (SS) C .12 .25
118 Glass Ceiling (SS) C .12 .25
119 Givin' 'em High Fives (B) C .12 .25
120 Taunt the Fans (B) C .12 .25
121 Fans Love an Underdog (B) U .50 1.00
122 Chicago Street Fight (M) U .50 1.00
123 Trash Talkin' Interview (B) U .50 1.00
124 Snubbed by the Fans (M) U .50 1.00
125 Old School Wrestling Match (B) R 2.00 4.00
126 Underrated Superstar (B) R 2.00 4.00
127 Hell in a Cell Match (M) R 2.00 4.00
128 Indian Strap Match (M) R 2.00 4.00
129 Duchess of Queensbury Rules (M) R2.00 4.00
130 Handicap Match (M) R 2.00 4.00
131 Bra and Panties Match (SS) R 2.00 4.00
132 Managed by Stephanie... (SS) R 2.00 4.00
133 Managed by Torrie Wilson (SS) R 2.00 4.00
134 Managed by Terri Runnels (SS) R 2.00 4.00
135 Backlash (B) C .12 .25
136 Fortitude Surge (M) C .12 .25
137 Business Is About to Pick Up (SS) C.12 .25
138 Silent, But Violent (SS) C .12 .25
139 Fan Appreciation Day (M) C .12 .25
140 Dirty Low Blow (B) C .12 .25
141 Tag Out (SS) C .12 .25
142 When You Thought You Had... (B) U .50 1.00
143 Turn Up the Heat (SS) U .50 1.00
144 Over the Top Rope (M) U .50 1.00
145 Don't Mess with the Champ (B) R 2.00 4.00
146 Sustained Damage (M) R 2.00 4.00
147 Been There, Done That (SS) R 2.00 4.00
148 Fully Loaded (B) R 2.00 4.00
149 Ring General (SS) R 2.00 4.00
150 No Mercy (B) R 2.00 4.00
151 Dude Love Superstar Card R 2.00 4.00
152 Feel the Love (SS2) R 2.00 4.00
153 Psychedelic Dance Fever (SS2) R 2.00 4.00
154 Tree of Woe (SS2) R 2.00 4.00
156 Split Personalities... (SS2) UR 7.50 15.00
157 Get Softcore (S) UR 7.50 15.00
158 Three Faces of Foley (B) UR 7.50 15.00
159 Foley is Good (M) PR
160 Chris Jericho Superstar Card (S) R2.00 4.00
161 Lionsault (S) R 2.00 4.00
162 Y2J (S) R 2.00 4.00
163 Don't You Never Eeeever (S) R 2.00 4.00
164 Walls of Jericho (S) UR 7.50 15.00
165 Ayatollah of Rock 'n' Roll-a (S) UR 7.50 15.00
166 Springboard Drop Kick (S) UR 7.50 15.00
167 Superior Acrobatics (B) UR 7.50 15.00
168 Would You Please Shut... (M) PR
169 Eddie Guerrero... (F) R 2.00 4.00
170 Snap Senton Splash (F) R 2.00 4.00
171 Study for Your GED (F) R 2.00 4.00
172 Latino Heeeeeeeat (F) R 2.00 4.00
173 Guerrero Frog Splash (F) UR 7.50 15.00
174 Get Your GED (F) UR 7.50 15.00
175 Eddie's Roll Up (B) UR 7.50 15.00
176 Ultimo Rechazo (M) UR 7.50 15.00
177 Whatchoo Talkin' 'bout, Ese (SS) PR
178 Edge Superstar Card (B) R 2.00 4.00
179 Listen, You Reekazoid (B) R 2.00 4.00
180 Sodas Rule (B) R 2.00 4.00
181 Million Dollar Smile (B) R 2.00 4.00
182 Edge-O-Matic (B) UR 7.50 15.00
183 You Think You Know Me? (M) UR 7.50 15.00
184 Edge-acution (SS) UR 7.50 15.00
185 Big Slide in the Ring (B) PR
186 Christian Superstar Card (B) R 2.00 4.00
187 This is So Totally Unfair (B) R 2.00 4.00
188 Greetings to Our Fans... (B) R 2.00 4.00
189 Kazoo Theme Songs (B) R 2.00 4.00
190 Unprettier (B) UR 7.50 15.00
191 Temper Tantrum (SS) UR 7.50 15.00
192 Christian's Shades (B) PR
193 Matt Hardy Superstar Card (B) R 2.00 4.00
194 M.Hardy's Patented Leg Drop (B) R2.00 4.00
195 Put It All On the Line (B) R 2.00 4.00
196 Matt's Moonsault (B) R 2.00 4.00
197 Twist of Fate (B) UR 7.50 15.00
198 Live for the Moment (M) UR 7.50 15.00
199 Team X-Treme (SS) UR 7.50 15.00
200 Roar For the Fans (B) PR
201 Jeff Hardy Superstar Card (B) R 2.00 4.00
202 Whisper in the Wind (B) R 2.00 4.00
203 Incite the Fans (B) R 2.00 4.00
204 Ride the Barricade (B) R 2.00 4.00
205 Swanton Bomb (B) UR 7.50 15.00
206 No, Jeff, Don't Do It (B) PR
207 Big Show Superstar Card (M) R 2.00 4.00
208 Showstopper Chokeslam (M) R 2.00 4.00
209 Big Show Splash (M) R 2.00 4.00
210 500 lbs. of Raw Power (M) R 2.00 4.00
211 Final Cut (M) UR 7.50 15.00
212 Wellllll (M) UR 7.50 15.00
213 Big All Over (SS) UR 7.50 15.00
214 Lita Superstar Card (M) R 2.00 4.00
215 Lita-canrana (M) R 2.00 4.00
216 Lita Drop Kick (M) R 2.00 4.00
217 Crimson Goddess (M) R 2.00 4.00
218 Lita-sault (M) UR 7.50 15.00
219 X-Treme Thong (M) UR 7.50 15.00
220 Lita's Twist of Fate (SS) UR 7.50 15.00
221 Rob Van Dam Superstar Card (M) R2.00 4.00
222 Five Star Frog Splash (M) R 2.00 4.00
223 Extreme Monkey Flip (M) R 2.00 4.00
224 Rolling Thunder (M) R 2.00 4.00
225 Van Daminator (M) UR 7.50 15.00

#	Card	Low	High
226	R-V-D (M) UR	7.50	15.00
227	Dude, Nice Hang Time (SS) UR	7.50	15.00
228	Booker T Superstar Card (M) R	2.00	4.00
229	Can You Dig It, Sucka? (M) R	2.00	4.00
230	Booker's Scissor Kick (M) R	2.00	4.00
231	Spinning T Kick (M) R	2.00	4.00
232	Bookend (M) UR	7.50	15.00
233	Spinnerooni (M) UR	7.50	15.00
234	Tell Me You Didn't Just... (SS) UR	7.50	15.00
235	Trish Stratus... (SS) R	2.00	4.00
236	Stratusfaction Bulldog (SS) R	2.00	4.00
237	I've Been a Very Naughty Girl (SS) R	2.00	4.00
238	Perhaps I Need a Spanking? (SS) R	2.00	4.00
239	The TandA Factor (SS) UR	7.50	15.00
240	100 Stratusfaction... (SS) UR	7.50	15.00
241	Stone Cold Steve Austin... (S) PR		
242	Austin Elbow Smash (S) PR		
243	Double Digits (S) PR		
244	Lou Thesz Press (S) PR		
245	Stone Cold Stunner (S) UR	7.50	15.00
246	Open Up a Can of Whoop-A$ (S) UR	7.50	15.00
247	Patented Austin Kick to the Gut (F) UR	7.50	15.00
248	DTA (B) UR	7.50	15.00
249	What??? (M) PR		
250	Deadman Inc... (S) PR		
251	Bad Ass Chokeslam (S) PR		
252	Old School Clothesline (S) PR		
253	Dead Man Walking (S) PR		
254	The Last Ride (S) UR	7.50	15.00
255	This is My Yard (S) UR	7.50	15.00
256	I'll Make You Famous (S) UR	7.50	15.00
257	Brothers 'til the End (B) UR	7.50	15.00
258	You Will Respect Me (M) PR		
259	Triple H Superstar Card (S) PR		
260	Leaping Knee to the Face (S) PR		
261	Facebuster (S) PR		
262	I Am the Game (S) PR		
263	Pedigree (S) UR	7.50	15.00
264	I've Got Two Words for Ya (F) UR	7.50	15.00
265	Triple H's Reverse Neck... (S) UR	7.50	15.00
266	Sledgehammer Shot (B) UR	7.50	15.00
267	Cerebral Assassin (M) PR		
268	The Rock Superstar Card (S) PR		
269	Take That Move... PR		
270	Rock Bottom (S) PR		
271	Smackdown Hotel (S) PR		
272	The People's Eyebrow (S) UR	7.50	15.00
273	The People's Elbow (S) UR	7.50	15.00
274	Patented Rock Footstomp (F) UR	7.50	15.00
275	The Brahma Bull (B) UR	7.50	15.00
276	Shades of the Great One (M) PR		
277	Kane Superstar Card (S) PR		
278	Kane's Chokeslam (S) PR		
279	Kane's Flying Clothesline (S) PR		
280	Kane's Return (S) PR		
281	Kane's Tombstone...(S) UR	7.50	15.00
282	Hellfire and Brimstone (S) UR	7.50	15.00
283	Masked Vengeance (S) UR	7.50	15.00
284	Born of Hellfire (M) PR		
285	In the Presence of... (SS) PR		
286	Rikishi Superstar Card (F) PR		
287	Drive, Rikishi, Drive (F) PR		
288	Back That A$ Up (F) PR		
289	Stink Face (F) PR		
290	Rikishi Driver (F) UR	7.50	15.00
291	A$ Drop (F) UR	7.50	15.00
292	I Did It for You (B) UR	7.50	15.00
294	I'm a Bad Man (SS) PR		

#	Card	Low	High
295	Kurt Angle Superstar Card (S) PR		
296	Intensity (S) PR		
297	Integrity (S) PR		
298	Intelligence (S) PR		
299	Olympic Slam (S) UR	7.50	15.00
300	It's True, It's True (S) UR	7.50	15.00
301	Where Are Your Medals? (B) UR	7.50	15.00
302	Angle Lock (M) UR	7.50	15.00
303	Do YOU Live by... (SS) PR		
304	Tazz (S) PR		
305	T-Bone Tazzplex (S) PR		
306	Head-and-Arms Tazzplex (S) PR		
307	Northern Lights Tazzplex (S) PR		
308	Tazzmission (S) UR	7.50	15.00
309	Thug It - Dead (S) UR	7.50	15.00
310	Just Another Victim (B) UR	7.50	15.00
311	Tough Enough (M) UR	7.50	15.00
312	The Mood Is About... (SS) PR		
313	Chris Benoit Superstar Card (S) PR		
314	Kamikaze Headbutt (S) PR		
315	Series of Suplexes (S) PR		
316	Rabid Wolverine (S) PR		
317	Crippler Crossface (S) UR	7.50	15.00
318	Big Stupid Grin (S) UR	7.50	15.00
319	Prove Me Wrong (B) UR	7.50	15.00
320	First to Tap Out Match (M) UR	7.50	15.00
321	The Best Technical... (SS) PR		
322	Dudley Boyz Superstar Card (B) PR		
323	3D (B) UR	7.50	15.00
324	Wazzzzuuup??? (B) PR		
325	Buh-Buh Ray Dudley... (B) PR		
326	Buh-Buh Bomb (B) UR	7.50	15.00
327	Catatonic Stare (B) PR		
328	My Name Is (B) PR		
329	Buh-Buh Drop (B) PR		
330	Buh-Buh Punch (B) PR		
331	D-Von Dudley Superstar Card (B) PR		
332	Testify (B) UR	7.50	15.00
333	Spinning Elbow (B) PR		
334	Doin' the D-Von (B) PR		
335	Thou Shall Not... (B) PR		
336	D-Von Get the Table (B) PR		
337	Greetings from Dudleyville... (M) UR	7.50	15.00
338	Brothers from Another... (SS) UR	7.50	15.00
339	Spike Dudley Superstar Card (M) PR		
340	Dudley Dog (M) UR	7.50	15.00
341	150 lbs. Soaking Wet (M) PR		
342	Good Golly, Miss Molly... (M) PR		
343	Psychotic Bump (M) PR		
344	Brotherly Love (M) PR		
345	Giant Killer (SS) UR	7.50	15.00
346	William Regal... (M) PR		
347	Union Jack (M) PR		
348	I've Been Besmirched (M) PR		
349	Goodwill Ambassador (M) PR		
350	Regal Stretch (M) UR	7.50	15.00
351	Commissioner Regal's... (M) PR		
352	Listen Up, Sunshine (SS) UR	7.50	15.00
353	Hollywood Hulk Hogan... (SS) PR		
354	Hollywood's Big Boot (SS) PR		
355	Say Your Prayers... (SS) PR		
356	Hollywood Leg Drop (SS) PR		
357	Whatcha Gonna Do... (SS) UR	7.50	15.00
358	Hulkin' Up (SS) UR	7.50	15.00
359	Ric Flair Superstar Card (SS) PR		
360	Diamonds are Forever... (SS) PR		
361	Now You're Going... (SS) PR		
362	The Dirtiest Player... (SS) PR		

#	Card	Low	High
363	Stylin', Profilin'... (SS) UR	7.50	15.00
364	Wooooooooo (SS) UR	7.50	15.00
365	Rico Enters (SS) UR	7.50	15.00
366	Al Snow Superstar Card (SS) PR		
367	What Does Everybody... (SS) PR		
368	What Does Everybody... (SS) PR		
369	Snow Slide (SS) PR		
370	Snow Plow (SS) UR	7.50	15.00
371	Head (SS) PR		
372	Tajiri Superstar Card (SS) PR		
373	Asian Mist (SS) PR		
374	Tajiri's Handspring Elbow (SS) PR		
375	Japanese Buzzsaw (SS) PR		
376	Kick of Death (SS) UR	7.50	15.00
377	Tarantula (SS) PR		
378	Hurricane Superstar Card (SS) PR		
379	Caped Body Press (SS) PR		
380	To the Hurricycle (SS) PR		
381	Whassupwitdat??? (SS) PR		
382	Eye of the Hurricane (SS) UR	7.50	15.00
383	Stand Back... (SS) PR		
155A	The Love Handle (SS2) UR	7.50	15.00
155B	Sweet Shin Music (SS2) UR	7.50	15.00
293A	Gettin' Cheeky with It - A (M) UR	7.50	15.00
293B	Gettin' Cheeky with It - B (M) UR	7.50	15.00
293C	Gettin' Cheeky with It - C (M) UR	7.50	15.00

2005 Comic Images WWE Raw Deal Survivor Series 3

#	Card	Low	High
1	Diving Takedown C	.12	.25
2	Revolving Takedown TB U	.50	1.00
3	Flying Leg Scissors R	2.00	4.00
4	Suicide Dive R	2.00	4.00
5	Superplex TB R	2.00	4.00
6	Girly Punch C	.12	.25
7	Spinning Kick C	.12	.25
8	Right Cross Punch C	.12	.25
9	Left Cross Punch C	.12	.25
10	Atomic Back Body Drop C	.12	.25
11	Kick TB U	.50	1.00
12	Running Lariat U	.50	1.00
13	Lariat U	.50	1.00
14	Garbage Can Lid TB U	.50	1.00
15	Brass Nuks Shot U	.50	1.00
16	Steel Chain Shot TB U	.50	1.00
17	Superkick R	2.00	4.00
18	Lariat Takedown R	2.00	4.00
19	Short Arm Rib Breaker R	2.00	4.00
20	Atomic Lariat R	2.00	4.00
21	Blindside Kick R	2.00	4.00
22	360-Degree Clothesline R	2.00	4.00
23	Chair Shot R	2.00	4.00
24	Double Underhook Back Breaker C	.12	.25
25	Wheelbarrow Slam C	.12	.25
26	Snap Neckbreaker C	.12	.25
27	Face Driver C	.12	.25
28	Neck Breaker C	.12	.25
29	Vertical DDT Drop TB C	.12	.25
30	Shoot Slam U	.50	1.00
31	Judo Takedown U	.50	1.00
32	Quick Snap Body Slam U	.50	1.00
33	Double Underhook Power Bomb U	.50	1.00
34	Tilt-a-Whirl Powerslam U	.50	1.00
35	Blindside Slam U	.50	1.00
36	Suplex R	2.00	4.00
37	Rolling Headlock Vise R	2.00	4.00
38	Reverse Fall-away Slam R	2.00	4.00
39	Military Slam R	2.00	4.00

#	Card	Low	High
40	Takedown R	2.00	4.00
41	Death Valley Driver R	2.00	4.00
42	Back Breaker Torture Rack R	2.00	4.00
43	Faceplant TB R	2.00	4.00
44	Clutch onto Opponent C	.12	.25
45	Modified Clutch onto Opponent C	.12	.25
46	Triangle Choke C	.12	.25
47	Arm Breaker TB C	.12	.25
48	Body Lock C	.12	.25
49	Waist Lock TB U	.50	1.00
50	Shoot Headlock U	.50	1.00
51	Judo Choke TB U	.50	1.00
52	Wraparound Wrist Lock U	.50	1.00
53	Headlock U	.50	1.00
54	Strangle Hold TB U	.50	1.00
55	Apply Illegal Leverage U	.50	1.00
56	Front Chancery R	2.00	4.00
57	Apply Legal Leverage TB R	2.00	4.00
58	Blindside Choke R	2.00	4.00
59	Super Hold R	2.00	4.00
60	Inverted Leg Lock R	2.00	4.00
61	Sharpshooter TB R	2.00	4.00
62	Step Aside C	.12	.25
63	Escape Move C	.12	.25
64	No Sell Maneuver C	.12	.25
65	Over Sell Maneuver C	.12	.25
66	Clumsy Opponent C	.12	.25
67	I Already Warned You C	.12	.25
68	Quick Reflexes C	.12	.25
69	Unexpected Turn of Events C	.12	.25
70	Elbow to the Face U	.50	1.00
71	Hold the Phone U	.50	1.00
72	There Are Two Things... U	.50	1.00
73	Blindsided Ego TB U	.50	1.00
74	Overshot Your Mark U	.50	1.00
75	Leave Me Alone U	.50	1.00
76	Blindsided Control U	.50	1.00
77	Just Bring It U	.50	1.00
78	Reach for the Ropes U	.50	1.00
79	Iron Will TB R	2.00	4.00
80	Don't Try This at Home R	2.00	4.00
81	Too Many Rules... R	2.00	4.00
82	Headstrong R	2.00	4.00
83	Sloppy - Very Sloppy R	2.00	4.00
84	Manager Interferes R	2.00	4.00
85	Let's Wrestle Already C	.12	.25
86	Suplex into the Ring TB C	.12	.25
87	Chain Wrestling C	.12	.25
88	When Hell Freezes Over TB C	.12	.25
89	Commission-er Rules C	.12	.25
90	Battling the Voices TB C	.12	.25
91	Irish Whip C	.12	.25
92	Gut Wrench C	.12	.25
93	I've Got a Nice Bottom U	.50	1.00
94	Chained Heat U	.50	1.00
95	Roll Out of the Ring U	.50	1.00
96	Backed by Stephanie McMahon U	.50	1.00
97	Offer Handshake TB U	.50	1.00
98	Spit at Opponent U	.50	1.00
99	Ego Boost R	2.00	4.00
100	I Can't Be Reading This Right R	2.00	4.00
101	Why the Hell are We Back? R	2.00	4.00
102	Escape the Rules R	2.00	4.00
103	That's Broken R	2.00	4.00
104	Twisted Smile R	2.00	4.00
105	The End is Near R	2.00	4.00
106	Don't Hate da Playa... R	2.00	4.00
107	Enough with the Trash Talk TB R	2.00	4.00

No.	Name		
108	No Disqualification Match TB C	.12	.25
109	Spontaneous Combustion C	.12	.25
110	This is Gonna Be a Rocket Buster C	.12	.25
111	Old School Psychology C	.12	.25
112	Taunt the Fans C	.12	.25
113	Old School Beating C	.12	.25
114	Chicago Street Fight U	.50	1.00
115	Pay-Per-View Main Event U	.50	1.00
116	Raw or Smackdown... U	.50	1.00
117	Smackdown #1 Announcer... TB U	.50	1.00
118	Calgary, Alberta, Canada U	.50	1.00
119	The Title is on the Line U	.50	1.00
120	You Rang? U	.50	1.00
121	Old School Wrestling Match R	2.00	4.00
122	Underrated Superstar TB R	2.00	4.00
123	Managed by Theodore Long R	2.00	4.00
124	Houston, Texas R	2.00	4.00
125	Philadelphia, Pennsylvania R	2.00	4.00
126	Bitter Rivals R	2.00	4.00
127	Managed by Dawn Marie R	2.00	4.00
128	Backlash C	.12	.25
129	Fortitude Surge C	.12	.25
130	Took That on the Chin C	.12	.25
131	Hardcore Style TB C	.12	.25
132	Skirt the Issue C	.12	.25
133	Check This Out C	.12	.25
134	Really, That's Enough C	.12	.25
135	Fan Appreciation Day C	.12	.25
136	Victory Roll C	.12	.25
137	Dirty Low Blow C	.12	.25
138	Grab the Ref C	.12	.25
139	Turn Up the Heat U	.50	1.00
140	Panic Assault U	.50	1.00
141	Panic Grab U	.50	1.00
142	Panic Throw U	.50	1.00
143	Immune to Pain TB U	.50	1.00
144	You're as Graceful... U	.50	1.00
145	This is Going Nowhere Fast U	.50	1.00
146	Chain Finisher U	.50	1.00
147	Sustained Damage R	2.00	4.00
148	The King Interferes R	2.00	4.00
149	Unscrupulous S.O.B. R	2.00	4.00
150	Reverse 180-Degree Chair Shot R	2.00	4.00
151	Stone Cold Steve Austin RUM		
152	Rattlesnake RUM		
153	Austin Elbow Smash RUM		
154	Double Digits RUM		
155	Lou Thesz Press TB RUM		
156	Stone Cold Stunner UR	7.50	15.00
157	Open Up a Can... UR	7.50	15.00
158	Patented Austin... UR	7.50	15.00
159	Do You Know What... TB RUM		
160	DTA TB UR	7.50	15.00
161	Rattlesnake Rulz RUM		
162	Cause Stone Cold Said So RUM		
163	And That's the Bottom Line RUM		
164	What??? RUM		
165	The Bionic Redneck UR	7.50	15.00
166	Gimme a Hell Yeah UR	7.50	15.00
167	Stomp a Mudhole RUM		
168	Don't Trust Nobody RUM		
169	Walk it Dry RUM		
170	Do You Want a Hug? RUM		
171	Undertaker RUM		
172	Undertaker's Chokeslam RUM		
173	Undertaker's Flying... TB RUM		
174	Undertaker Sits Up RUM		
175	Undertaker's Tombstone... UR	7.50	15.00
176	Power of Darkness UR	7.50	15.00
177	Rest in Peace UR	7.50	15.00
178	Throttled Within an Inch... RUM		
179	Rollin' - Rollin' - Rollin' RUM		
180	I'm the Biggest Dog... TB RUM		
181	Bad to the Bone RUM		
182	Twelve Years of Terror RUM		
183	Brothers 'til the End UR	7.50	15.00
184	You Will Respect Me RUM		
185	Throwin' Big Ol' Soup... RUM		
186	Big Evil - Red Devil RUM		
187	Your'e Gonna Pay TB RUM		
188	Managed by Paul Bearer RUM		
189	HHH RUM		
190	The Game RUM		
191	Leaping Knee to the Face RUM		
192	Facebuster TB RUM		
193	I Am the Game TB RUM		
194	Ric Flair Interferes UR	7.50	15.00
195	Pedigree UR	7.50	15.00
196	I've Got Two Words for Ya UR	7.50	15.00
197	Triple H's Reverse... UR	7.50	15.00
198	Cause I am That Damn Good RUM		
199	Flip Over the Corner Ringpost RUM		
200	It's Time to Play the Game RUM		
201	Sledgehammer Shot UR	7.50	15.00
202	Cerebral Assassin RUM		
203	The Game is Back... TB RUM		
204	Game Over? UR	7.50	15.00
205	The Game's Sleeper RUM		
206	Lunging Choke Hold RUM		
207	You Don't Want to Play Me RUM		
208	It's All About Control RUM		
209	Screw the Rules RUM		
210	A Beating You'll Never Forget RUM		
211	The Rock RUM		
212	The People's Champion RUM		
213	Take That Move... RUM		
214	Rock Bottom TB RUM		
215	Smackdown Hotel RUM		
216	The People's Eyebrow UR	7.50	15.00
217	The People's Elbow UR	7.50	15.00
218	Patented Rock Footstomp TB UR	7.50	15.00
219	Do You Smell... RUM		
220	Your Brush with... TB RUM		
221	Rock's Spit Punch RUM		
222	The Brahma Bull UR	7.50	15.00
223	Who in the Blue Hell... TB RUM		
224	Shades of the Great One RUM		
225	The People's Kip-Up UR	7.50	15.00
226	Remove the People's... TB RUM		
227	It Doesn't Matter... RUM		
228	You Bring the A$... RUM		
229	The People's DDT RUM		
230	Get Ready... TB RUM		
231	The Peep's Champ RUM		
232	Know Your Role... RUM		
233	Kane RUM		
234	The Big Freak'n Machine RUM		
235	Kane's Chokeslam RUM		
236	Kane's Flying Clothesline TB RUM		
237	Kane's Return RUM		
238	Kane's Tombstone Piledriver UR	7.50	15.00
239	Hellfire and Brimstone UR	7.50	15.00
240	Help's on the Way UR	7.50	15.00
241	Masked Vengeance UR	7.50	15.00
242	Boot to the Face RUM		
243	Chains of Destruction RUM		
244	Born of Hellfire RUM		
245	In the Presence... RUM		
246	Freaks are Cool TB UR	7.50	15.00
247	The Fire Still Burns RUM		
248	Big Freak'n Uppercut RUM		
249	My Path is Chosen RUM		
250	Hellfire Chokeslam TB RUM		
251	Big Freak'n Powerslam RUM		
252	Unmasked Vengeance RUM		
253	Kane's Rage RUM		
254	Chris Jericho RUM		
255	Highlight of the Night TB RUM		
256	Lionsault RUM		
257	Y2J RUM		
258	Don't You Never - Eeeever RUM		
259	Walls of Jericho UR	7.50	15.00
260	Ayatollah of Rock 'n' Roll-a TB UR	7.50	15.00
261	Springboard Drop Kick TB UR	7.50	15.00
262	Jericholics TB RUM		
263	Superior Acrobatics UR	7.50	15.00
264	Would You Please... RUM		
265	Happy You're Here... TB RUM		
266	I'm Better Than You TB RUM		
267	The Breakdown RUM		
268	I'm the King of the World RUM		
269	Highlight Reel RUM		
270	You Sanctimonious... UR	7.50	15.00
271	Listen Up, Junior... UR	7.50	15.00
272	My Obscenely Expensive... RUM		
273	Roll the Footage, Monkeys RUM		
274	Jericho's Ensugiri RUM		
275	Kurt Angle TB RUM		
276	Your Freaking Hero RUM		
277	Intensity RUM		
278	Integrity RUM		
279	Intelligence RUM		
280	Olympic Slam UR	7.50	15.00
281	It's True, It's True UR	7.50	15.00
282	I'll Make You Tap RUM		
283	Where Are Your Medals? UR	7.50	15.00
284	Angle Lock UR	7.50	15.00
285	Do YOU Live by... RUM		
286	Just Hold On a Second... RUM		
287	Collegiate Champions UR	7.50	15.00
288	Submit RUM		
289	Wrestling with a... TB RUM		
290	The Straps are Down UR	7.50	15.00
291	Oh, It's True UR	7.50	15.00
292	Angle's German Suplex RUM		
293	Whoo RUM		
294	Angle's Moonsault RUM		
295	Chris Benoit TB RUM		
296	The Crippler RUM		
297	Kamikaze Headbutt RUM		
298	Series of Suplexes RUM		
299	Rabid Wolverine TB RUM		
300	Crippler Crossface UR	7.50	15.00
301	Big Stupid Grin UR	7.50	15.00
302	Prove Me Wrong UR	7.50	15.00
303	First to Tap Out Match TB UR	7.50	15.00
304	Best Technical Wrestler... RUM		
305	A Victim of the Crippler TB RUM		
306	There's No Holding Me Back UR	7.50	15.00
307	Toothless Aggression UR	7.50	15.00
308	Cripple Opponent RUM		
309	Rabid Attack in the Corner TB RUM		
310	Surprise Drop Kick RUM		
311	Benoit's German Suplex RUM		
312	Pain is Inevitable RUM		
313	Eddie Guerrero RUM		
314	Snap Senton Splash RUM		
315	Study for Your GED RUM		
316	Latino Heeeeeeeat RUM		
317	Guerrero Frog Splash UR	7.50	15.00
318	Get Your GED TB UR	7.50	15.00
319	Eddie's Roll Up TB UR	7.50	15.00
320	Ultimo Rechazo UR	7.50	15.00
321	Whatchoo Talkin' 'bout... RUM		
322	Yo, Ese, I Know Your... TB RUM		
323	Lasso from El Paso RUM		
324	Gory Special RUM		
325	Viva La Raza Low Rider TB RUM		
326	Dudley Boyz RUM		
327	3D TB UR	7.50	15.00
328	Wazzzzuuup??? RUM		
329	TLC Match TB UR	7.50	15.00
330	Dudler Tough RUM		
331	Dudleyz3 RUM		
332	Beatings from Dudleyville RUM		
333	Blood is Thicker than Wood RUM		
334	Buh-Buh Ray Dudley TB RUM		
335	Buh-Buh Bomb TB UR	7.50	15.00
336	Catatonic Stare RUM		
337	My Name Is TB RUM		
338	Buh-Buh Drop RUM		
339	Buh-Buh Punch RUM		
340	D-Von Dudley RUM		
341	Testify TB UR	7.50	15.00
342	Spinning Elbow TB RUM		
343	Doin' the D-Von TB RUM		
344	Thou Shall Not... TB RUM		
345	D-Von -- Get the Table RUM		
346	Greetings from Dudleyville... TB UR	7.50	15.00
347	Brothers from Another Mother UR	7.50	15.00
348	Edge RUM		
349	Leader of the Edge... TB RUM		
350	Listen, You Reekazoid RUM		
351	Soda's Rule RUM		
352	Million Dollar Smile RUM		
353	Edge-O-Matic UR	7.50	15.00
354	You Think You Know Me? UR	7.50	15.00
355	Edge's Spear TB RUM		
356	Edge-acution UR	7.50	15.00
357	Big Slide in the Ring RUM		
358	Never Gonna Stop Me RUM		
359	You're a Human Vacuum... RUM		
360	Edgeucation of Adam... UR	7.50	15.00
361	Downward Spiral UR	7.50	15.00
362	Edge Kick RUM		
363	Scream if You Want It RUM		
364	'Cause I Want More RUM		
365	Christian RUM		
366	This is so Totally Unfair RUM		
367	Greetings to Our Fans... RUM		
368	Kazoo Theme Song RUM		
369	Unprettier UR	7.50	15.00
370	Temper Tantrum UR	7.50	15.00
371	Christian's Shades TB RUM		
372	Impaler RUM		
373	I Ain't No Sucka Neitha RUM		
374	To All My Peeps... RUM		
375	Matt Hardy RUM		
376	M.Hardy's Patented Leg Drop RUM		
377	Put It All on the Line TB RUM		
378	Matt's Moonsault TB RUM		
379	Twist of Fate UR	7.50	15.00

#	Card		
380	Live for the Moment UR	7.50	15.00
381	Team X-Treme UR	7.50	15.00
382	Roar for the Fans RUM		
383	Mattitude Adjustment RUM		
384	Version 1.0 TB RUM		
385	Side Effect RUM		
386	Era Mattitude Has Arrived RUM		
387	Big Show RUM		
388	Showstopper Chokeslam RUM		
389	Bog Show Splash RUM		
390	500 lbs. of Raw Power RUM		
391	Final Cut UR		
392	Wellllll UR	7.50	15.00
393	Big All Over UR	7.50	15.00
394	Mountain of a Man UR	7.50	15.00
395	You Can't Manhandle... RUM		
396	Showdown RUM		
397	Lita RUM		
398	Lita-canrana RUM		
399	Lita Drop Kick RUM		
400	Crimson Goddess RUM		
401	Lita-sault UR	7.50	15.00
402	X-Treme Thong UR	7.50	15.00
403	Lita's Twist of Fate UR	7.50	15.00
404	If You've Got It, Flaunt It UR	7.50	15.00
405	X-Treme Hedonism UR	7.50	15.00
406	The Goddess Returns RUM		
407	Lita's DDT TB RUM		
408	Rob Van Dam RUM		
409	Five Star Frog Splash TB RUM		
410	Extreme Monkey Flip TB RUM		
411	Rolling Thunder RUM		
412	Van Daminator UR	7.50	15.00
413	R-V-D UR	7.50	15.00
414	Dude, Nice Hang Time TB UR	7.50	15.00
415	Everything's Cool When... UR	7.50	15.00
416	Dude Whatever RUM		
417	Mr. Monday Night RUM		
418	Van Terminator RUM		
419	Booker T RUM		
420	Can You Dig It, Sucka? RUM		
421	Booker's Scissor Kick TB RUM		
422	Spinning T Kick RUM		
423	Bookend UR	7.50	15.00
424	Spinnerooni UR	7.50	15.00
425	Tell Me You Didn't Just... UR	7.50	15.00
426	Five Time Five Time... UR	7.50	15.00
427	Yo Dawg... RUM		
428	Houston Hangover RUM		
429	How Many Times? RUM		
430	Spike Dudley RUM		
431	Dudley Dog UR	7.50	15.00
432	150 lbs. Soaking Wet RUM		
433	Get Him, Boyz RUM		
434	Psychotic Bump RUM		
435	Brotherly Love RUM		
436	Giant Killer UR	7.50	15.00
437	Pound 4 Pound UR	7.50	15.00
438	William Regal RUM		
439	Union Jack RUM		
440	I've Been Besmirched RUM		
441	Goodwill Ambassador TB RUM		
442	Regal Stretch UR	7.50	15.00
443	Commissioner Regal's... RUM		
444	Listen Up, Sunshine UR	7.50	15.00
445	Regal Upper Class Punch UR	7.50	15.00
446	Proper Planning Prevents... RUM		
447	Keep It Simple, Sir RUM		
448	Ric Flair RUM		
449	Summer of Slam TB RUM		
450	Diamonds are Forever... RUM		
451	Now You're Going to School RUM		
452	The Dirtiest Player... TB RUM		
453	Stylin', Profilin', Limousine Ridin' UR	7.50	15.00
454	Wooooooooo UR	7.50	15.00
455	The Game Interferes TB UR	7.50	15.00
456	You're Going to Space... TB UR	7.50	15.00
457	The Flair Flop RUM		
458	Trish Stratus RUM		
459	Stratusfaction Bulldog TB RUM		
460	I've Been a Very Naughty Girl RUM		
461	Perhaps I Need a Spanking? RUM		
462	The TandA Factor UR	7.50	15.00
463	100 Stratusfaction... UR	7.50	15.00
464	Puppy Power RUM		
465	The StratusFear RUM		
466	Tajiri RUM		
467	Asian Mist TB RUM		
468	Tajiri's Handspring Elbow TB RUM		
469	Japanese Buzzsaw TB RUM		
470	Kick of Death UR	7.50	15.00
471	Tarantula TB RUM		
472	Octopus UR	7.50	15.00
473	Double Face Kick UR	7.50	15.00
474	Series of Kicks RUM		
475	Managed by Kyo Dai TB RUM		
476	Hurricane RUM		
477	Caped Body Press TB RUM		
478	To the Hurricycle TB RUM		
479	Whassupwitdat??? TB RUM		
480	Eye of the Hurricane UR	7.50	15.00
481	Stand Back There's... RUM		
482	Hurrislam UR	7.50	15.00
483	Shining Wizard Kick UR	7.50	15.00
484	Gregory Helms... RUM		
485	I've Got Hurri-Powers RUM		
486	Rey Mysterio RUM		
487	Luche Libre Extravaganza UR	7.50	15.00
488	The West Coast Pop TB UR	7.50	15.00
489	Too Fast For You RUM		
490	The 619 RUM		
491	Rey-Rey's Tope RUM		
492	West Coast Bronco Buster UR	7.50	15.00
493	Flying Body Press UR	7.50	15.00
494	Who's That Jumpin'... TB RUM		
495	Shawn Michaels RUM		
496	The Icon, The Showstoppa... UR	7.50	15.00
497	Sweet Chin Music UR	7.50	15.00
498	Don't Hunt What You... RUM		
499	Top Rope Elbow Drop RUM		
500	The Heart Break Kid RUM		
501	I'm Just a Sexy Boy UR	7.50	15.00
502	All Things are Possible UR	7.50	15.00
503	Rhyno RUM		
504	Gore Gore Gore UR	7.50	15.00
505	Extreme Warfare RUM		
506	Rhyno's Garbage Can RUM		
507	The Manbeast TB RUM		
508	Rhyno Stampede RUM		
509	Unstoppable RUM		
510	Unleash the Beast UR	7.50	15.00
511	Stacy Keibler RUM		
512	Straddle the Ropes UR	7.50	15.00
513	Superior Leg Work TB UR	7.50	15.00
514	Test or Freakzilla? RUM		
515	Pump Me Up RUM		
516	I Know How to Use Them RUM		
517	I Should've Been in that Magazine UR	7.50	15.00
518	Gail Kim and Molly Holly RUM		
519	Change Reality UR	7.50	15.00
520	Gail's Hurricanrana UR	7.50	15.00
521	Wake Up RUM		
522	Look Around RUM		
523	Molly-Go-Round RUM		
524	Control Your World UR	7.50	15.00
525	Bald is Beautiful UR	7.50	15.00
526	John Cena RUM		
527	Yo Kill da Beat UR	7.50	15.00
528	F-U UR		
529	You Can't See Me TB RUM		
530	Word Life TB RUM		
531	I'm Gonna Teach You... RUM		
532	So You Think You're... UR	7.50	15.00
533	Torrie Wilson RUM		
534	WWE Centerfold of the Year UR	7.50	15.00
535	Torrie's DDT UR	7.50	15.00
536	Does This Look Good on Me? RUM		
537	Strike a Pose RUM		
538	The Boise Beauty RUM		
539	Golden Thong Award UR	7.50	15.00
540	Victoria RUM		
541	Widow's Peak UR	7.50	15.00
542	Managed by Stevie Richards RUM		
543	All the Things She Said RUM		
544	Yes, I've Lost My Mind TB RUM		
545	Stevie Interferes RUM		
546	This is Not Enough UR	7.50	15.00
547	Evolution RUM		
548	Evolution is a Mystery UR	7.50	15.00
549	Paid, Laid, and Made UR	7.50	15.00
550	Yesterday is So Long Ago RUM		
551	I See the Line in the Sand RUM		
552	Nothing Ever Stays the Same RUM		
553	Paul Heyman RUM		
554	Let the Bodies Hit the Floor UR	7.50	15.00
555	You're Dangerously Close RUM		
556	Coach, Cole, or Finkel? RUM		
557	Big Boys Club RUM		
558	Do You Know Who... RUM		
559	Raw GM Eric Bischoff RUM		
560	Smackdown GM RUM		
561	Chavo's Inverted Powerbomb UR	7.50	15.00
562	It's All About the Benjamins RUM		
563	Greco Roman Specialists UR	7.50	15.00
564	Stone Cold Steve Austin... RUM		
565	Chris Jericho, Kane... RUM		
566	Rock, Deadman... RUM		
567	Rikishi, Chris Benoit... RUM		
568	APA or A-Train? RUM		
569	RVD or Booker T? UR	7.50	15.00
570	Edge or Big Show? UR	7.50	15.00
571	The People's Champ... RUM		
572	Mankind / Cactus Jack... RUM		
573	Backed by Mr. McMahon TB RUM		
574	Calling You Out RUM		
575	Chain Lashing TB RUM		
576	Managed by Vince... TB RUM		
577	Managed by Paul Heyman RUM		
578	Overhand Chairshot RUM		
579	Suicide Lariat RUM		
580	Atomic Knee Drop RUM		
581	Banned from Ringside RUM		
582	Divas Divas Divas RUM		
583	Vince McMahon Interferes RUM		
584	That Won't Make the Cut RUM		
585	Testicular Fortitude RUM		
586	I'm Hardcore I'm Hardcore RUM		
587	Back to Basics RUM		
588	Arm Bar RUM		
589	Arm Bar Takedown RUM		
590	Arm Drag RUM		
591	Atomic Drop RUM		
592	Belly to Back Suplex RUM		
593	Belly to Belly Suplex RUM		
594	Body Slam RUM		
595	Chop RUM		
596	Clothesline RUM		
597	Collar and Elbow Lockup RUM		
598	Drop Kick RUM		
599	Haymaker RUM		
600	Head Butt RUM		
601	Hip Toss RUM		
602	Press Slam RUM		
603	Punch RUM		
604	Roundhouse Punch RUM		
605	Russian Leg Sweep RUM		
606	Snap Mare RUM		
607	Vertical Suplex RUM		
608	Wrist Lock RUM		
609	Backhand Slap RUM		
610	Drop Toe Hold RUM		
611	Elbow Drop RUM		
612	Foot Stomp RUM		
613	Hammerlock RUM		
614	Comeback TB RUM		
615	Dem Damn Dudleyz TB RUM		
616	Hurricanrana TB RUM		
617	Chop to the Chest TB RUM		
618	Single Arm DDT TB RUM		
619	Ladder in the Ring TB RUM		
620	Drawing Extra Heat TB RUM		
621	Knife-Edge Chop TB RUM		
622	Springboard TB RUM		
623	Gut Punch TB RUM		
624	Spine Buster TB RUM		
625	DDT TB RUM		
626	Ankle Lock TB RUM		
627	No Chance in Hell TB RUM		
628	Great Technical... TB RUM		
629	Throw Into the Corner... RUM		
630	Charismatic Style TB RUM		
631	Table Table Table TB RUM		
632	Who Booked This Match? TB RUM		
633	Maintain Hold TB RUM		
634	Enter the Stratusphere RUM		
635	Puppies Puppies TB RUM		
636	Diversion TB RUM		
637	Hell in a Cell Match RUM		
638	Indian Strap Match RUM		
639	Duchess of Queensbury... RUM		
640	Bulldog Takedown TB RUM		
641	Corkscrew DDT TB RUM		
642	Did I Just Say... TB RUM		
643	Don't Cross the Boss TB RUM		

2005 Comic Images WWE Raw Deal Unforgiven

#	Card		
1	Counter Slash C	.12	.25
2	Corkscrew Elbow C	.12	.25
3	Body Block C	.12	.25
4	Spinning Leg Drop C	.12	.25
5	Missile Dropkick TB U	.50	1.00

#	Card	Low	High
6	Shooting Star Press TB U	.50	1.00
7	Girly Slap C	.12	.25
8	Shoulder Block TB C	.12	.25
9	Running Elbow Smash TB C	.12	.25
10	Kidney Punch C	.12	.25
11	Standing Drop Kick TB C	.12	.25
12	Knee Breaker TB U	.50	1.00
13	Back Fist TB U	.50	1.00
14	Back Body Drop TB U	.50	1.00
15	Reverse Clothesline U	.50	1.00
16	Everything and the Kitchen Sink U	.50	1.00
17	Ap Chaki Kick R	2.00	4.00
18	Precision Clothesline R	2.00	4.00
19	Baseball Slide TB R	2.00	4.00
20	Lock, Stock, and Barrel R	2.00	4.00
21	Rolling Hip Toss C	.12	.25
22	Japanese Arm Drag TB C	.12	.25
23	Sidewalk Slam TB C	.12	.25
24	Flip C	.12	.25
25	Running Spinebuster TB C	.12	.25
26	Shoot Suplex C	.12	.25
27	Snap Suplex TB U	.50	1.00
28	Headlock Takedown TB U	.50	1.00
29	Small Package TB U	.50	1.00
30	Swinging Neck Breaker U	.50	1.00
31	Pendulum Back Breaker U	.50	1.00
32	Powerbomb TB U	.50	1.00
33	Full Nelson Slam TB R	2.00	4.00
34	Shoot Russian Leg Sweep R	2.00	4.00
35	German Suplex TB R	2.00	4.00
36	Sit Out Powerbomb TB R	2.00	4.00
37	Tornado DDT TB R	2.00	4.00
38	Workin' on the Knee TB R	2.00	4.00
39	Precision Power Slam R	2.00	4.00
40	Side Headlock C	.12	.25
41	Bear Hug TB C	.12	.25
42	Full Nelson TB C	.12	.25
43	Bow and Arrow TB C	.12	.25
44	Guillotine Stretch TB C	.12	.25
45	Wrist Breaker U	.50	1.00
46	Arm Stretch U	.50	1.00
47	Sleeper TB U	.50	1.00
48	Side Chinlock U	.50	1.00
49	Camel Clutch TB U	.50	1.00
50	Spinning Toe Hold R	2.00	4.00
51	Boston Crab TB R	2.00	4.00
52	Precision Leg Lock R	2.00	4.00
53	Torture Rack TB R	2.00	4.00
54	Choke Hold TB R	2.00	4.00
55	Lift a Boot TB C	.12	.25
56	Spot Adjustment U	.50	1.00
57	A Revolution of the Mind R	2.00	4.00
58	Build Momentum C	.12	.25
59	Viva Las Divas C	.12	.25
60	Shake It Off TB C	.12	.25
61	Listen Loud and Clear C	.12	.25
62	Hardcore Timekeeper's Bell C	.12	.25
63	Not Yet TB C	.12	.25
64	Afterburn U	.50	1.00
65	Stagger TB U	.50	1.00
66	Kickin' It Old School U	.50	1.00
67	That's It U	.50	1.00
68	Marking Out TB U	.50	1.00
69	Grab WWE Timekeeper... U	.50	1.00
70	Sharmell: Sizzling Spouse R	2.00	4.00
71	Maria: Ideal Interviewer R	2.00	4.00
72	Christy: Curvy Cutie R	2.00	4.00
73	Melina: Naughty Manager R	2.00	4.00
74	Lilian: Amazing Announcer R	2.00	4.00
75	Candice: Internet Icon R	2.00	4.00
76	Hello, Ladies C	.12	.25
77	Rochester, New York C	.12	.25
78	Trash Talkin' Interview TB C	.12	.25
79	Who's Cooler... C	.12	.25
80	Blindsided Precision U	.50	1.00
81	Backstage Shenanigans U	.50	1.00
82	Pyrotechnic Volley U	.50	1.00
83	You Can't Spell... U	.50	1.00
84	Fans Love an Underdog R	2.00	4.00
85	Frankie Takes Hollywood R	2.00	4.00
86	Inferno Match TB R	2.00	4.00
87	The Old Switcheroo R	2.00	4.00
88	Not in Front of the Kids C	.12	.25
89	The GM of Stevie Night Heat C	.12	.25
90	This is Just the Beginning C	.12	.25
91	You Knew it Would End This Way C	.12	.25
92	Here I Stand: the Champion U	.50	1.00
93	WWE Divas: the Next Generation U	.50	1.00
94	Eviscerated by Viscera U	.50	1.00
95	WWE Divas Rule U	.50	1.00
96	I'm Just Hitting My Stride R	2.00	4.00
97	In This Ring, I Just Might Be R	2.00	4.00
98	Introduce Your Brain... R	2.00	4.00
99	One More Time... R	2.00	4.00
100	Batista EX		
101	The Destroyer UR	7.50	15.00
102	Batista Bomb UR	7.50	15.00
103	The Animal EX		
104	Physically Dominant Force EX		
105	Batista's Spinebuster EX		
106	Leader of the Peepulation EX		
107	Managed by Tyson Tomko UR	7.50	15.00
108	Just Close Your Eyes UR	7.50	15.00
109	That's How I Roll EX		
110	The Christian Coalition EX		
111	Tomakazi DDT EX		
112	Christy EX		
113	Temecula, California UR	7.50	15.00
114	2004 Diva Search Winner UR	7.50	15.00
115	Ain't It Fair? EX		
116	Christy's Twist EX		
117	Redheaded Sparkplug EX		
118	Immortal One EX		
119	Feathered Boa UR	7.50	15.00
120	I am a Real American UR	7.50	15.00
121	Hogan's Patented... EX		
122	Fight For the Rights... EX		
123	In My Day, a Maneuver... EX		
124	Rowdy Roddy Piper EX		
125	Bagpipe Introduction UR	7.50	15.00
126	Piper's Pit UR	7.50	15.00
127	Over Sell: Hot Rod Style EX		
128	Hot Rod EX		
129	Cowboy Bob Orton Interferes EX		
130	Smackdown GM... EX		
131	Haterade UR	7.50	15.00
132	Holla Holla Holla UR	7.50	15.00
133	Your Freaking Hero... EX		
134	Thuggin' and Buggin' EX		
135	The Mack Militant EX		
136	Heidenreich PR		
137	Disasterpiece UR	7.50	15.00
138	Heidenreich's Elbow Drop PR		
139	Who Wants to be My... PR		
140	A Friendly Boot PR		
141	Running Shoulder Block PR		
142	Gene Snitsky PR		
143	Baby Carriage UR	7.50	15.00
144	You Have Tasty Toes PR		
145	It's Not My Fault PR		
146	No Fault Clothesline PR		
147	No Fault Pump Handle... PR		
148	MNM PR		
149	The Snapshot UR	7.50	15.00
150	Managed by Melina PR		
151	There's Nothing Sweeter PR		
152	A-List Attack PR		
153	Melina Interferes PR		
154	Hurri-Friends PR		
155	The Hurri-Friends Armory UR	7.50	15.00
156	Super Masks... PR		
157	Super Storm Front PR		
158	Greetings, Citizen PR		
159	Stacy's Roundhouse Kick PR		
160	Unleash Hell PR		
161	Nobody's Safe PR		
162	Making the Game PR		
163	Finally The Rock... PR		
164	Another Big Freak'n... PR		
165	Chris Jericho PR		
166	Wolverine's Sharpshooter PR		
167	Addicted to the Heat PR		
168	Kurt Angle Invitational PR		
169	Edge's Running Spear PR		
170	Big Show's F5 PR		
171	When I Get You Alone PR		
172	The Hidden Dragon... PR		
173	Booker's Thrust Kick PR		
174	The Power of the Punch PR		
175	Flair's Chop Block PR		
176	The MaTrish Move PR		
177	Educated Hands PR		
178	Restricted Use in This Area PR		
179	Forever PR		
180	Flying Forearm PR		
181	Uncle Eric's Karate Kick PR		
182	Daddy's Little Girl TB PR		
183	Five Knuckle Shuffle PR		
184	Managed by Stacy Keibler PR		
185	Want to Take My Test? PR		
186	Spider Web Moonsault PR		
187	Girly Grab PR		
188	When You Run... PR		
189	Never Forgive... PR		
190	McMahon-us Interrupt-us UR	7.50	15.00
191	Gentlemen's Establishment UR	7.50	15.00
192	Hardcore Originator of ECW UR	7.50	15.00
193	Orlando Jordan... UR	7.50	15.00
194	Destiny UR	7.50	15.00
195	Here Comes the Money TB UR	7.50	15.00
196	Incredible Athleticism UR	7.50	15.00
197	Hello, My Name is Eugene UR	7.50	15.00
198	Le Bonsoir UR	7.50	15.00

2003 Comic Images WWE Raw Deal Velocity

#	Card	Low	High
1	Flying Mare C	.12	.25
2	Diving Takedown C	.12	.25
3	Quick Follow Through U	.50	1.00
4	Shoot Aerial 360-Degree Kick U	.50	1.00
5	Missile Shoulder Block R	2.00	4.00
6	Roll Up R	2.00	4.00
7	Standing Drop Kick C	.12	.25
8	Abdominal Rake C	.12	.25
9	Shoot Punch U	.50	1.00
10	Rapid-Fire Punches U	.50	1.00
11	Lariat Takedown R	2.00	4.00
12	Bionic Elbow R	2.00	4.00
13	Lock-up C	.12	.25
14	Oklahoma Roll C	.12	.25
15	Fall-Away Suplex C	.12	.25
16	Single Leg Takedown U	.50	1.00
17	Shoot Slam U	.50	1.00
18	Corkscrew DDT U	.50	1.00
19	Bulldog Takedown R	2.00	4.00
20	Rolling Headlock Vise R	2.00	4.00
21	Slam Bomb R	2.00	4.00
22	Body Scissors C	.12	.25
23	Breather Hold C	.12	.25
24	Waist Lock U	.50	1.00
25	Shoot Headlock U	.50	1.00
26	Sleeper Bomb R	2.00	4.00
27	Flying Body Lock R	2.00	4.00
28	Cartwheel C	.12	.25
29	Hold the Phone U	.50	1.00
30	Get the F Out R	2.00	4.00
31	He's as Crazy as a Pet Raccoon C	.12	.25
32	I'm Sorry, But You're Boring Me C	.12	.25
33	Measure Him C	.12	.25
34	Not on My Broadcast C	.12	.25
35	Wanna Know What I'm Gonna Do? C	.12	.25
36	Hot Tag [Tag Team Only Symbol] C	.12	.25
37	Back-and-Forth Action U	.50	1.00
38	Fire Extinguisher U	.50	1.00
39	Caught Red-handed U	.50	1.00
40	Gettin' Beat Like a... U	.50	1.00
41	Good Things Sometimes Happen U	.50	1.00
42	It Pays to be Evil U	.50	1.00
43	Here's a Ratings Booster R	2.00	4.00
44	Did I Just Say Three Minutes? R	2.00	4.00
45	One of a Kind R	2.00	4.00
46	Defensive Stance R	2.00	4.00
47	He's Runnin' Like a Scalded Dawg R	2.00	4.00
48	Singapore Cane R	2.00	4.00
49	Don't You Usually Wrestle... C	.12	.25
50	Educated Feet C	.12	.25
51	Ring Psychology: Back C	.12	.25
52	Ring Psychology: Neck C	.12	.25
53	Unorthodox Style of Wrestling C	.12	.25
54	Lumberjack Match U	.50	1.00
55	Pay-Per-View Main Event U	.50	1.00
56	Raw or Smackdown... U	.50	1.00
57	Velocity U	.50	1.00
58	Proper Conditioning U	.50	1.00
59	I Aims ta be Startin' Sump'tin' R	2.00	4.00
60	Managed by Eric Bischoff R	2.00	4.00
61	Managed by Shane O'Mac R	2.00	4.00
62	I'm the Champ... R	2.00	4.00
63	My Sacrifice R	2.00	4.00
64	You Can't Spell Furniture... C	.12	.25
65	Check This Out C	.12	.25
66	Desire C	.12	.25
67	Dragged to the Center of the Ring C	.12	.25
68	See How It Feels C	.12	.25
69	Reap the Rewards U	.50	1.00
70	The Ref Got in the Way U	.50	1.00
71	Hold On It's Not Time... U	.50	1.00
72	Human Suplex Machine U	.50	1.00
73	Beg For Mercy U	.50	1.00
74	Justice for All R	2.00	4.00
75	The King Interferes R	2.00	4.00
76	That's J.R.'s Animal Hat Trick... R	2.00	4.00

#	Card		
77	Title Belt Clubberin' R	2.00	4.00
78	The Big Freak'n Machine EX		
79	Freaks Are Cool UR	7.50	15.00
80	The Fire Still Burns PR		
81	Big Freak'n Uppercut EX		
82	My Path is Chosen EX		
83	Hellfire Chokeslam EX		
84	The Game EX		
85	Game Over? UR	7.50	15.00
86	The Game's Sleeper PR		
87	Lunging Choke Hold EX		
88	You Don't Want to Play Me EX		
89	It's All About Control EX		
90	Goldust EX		
91	Shattered Dreams Production UR	7.50	15.00
92	Shattered Dreams UR	7.50	15.00
93	<inhale> Goooooooooooldust EX		
94	Butt Bump EX		
95	Director's Cut EX		
96	Brock Lesnar EX		
97	Backstage Warm-up Routine UR	7.50	15.00
98	F-5 UR	7.50	15.00
99	An Irresistible Force... EX		
100	The Next Big Thing EX		
101	Series of Back Breakers EX		
102	The People's Champion EX		
103	The People's Kip-up UR	7.50	15.00
104	Remove the People's... PR		
105	It Doesn't Matter... EX		
106	You Bring the A$... EX		
107	The People's DDT EX		
108	Rey Mysterio EX		
109	Luche Libre Extravaganza UR	7.50	15.00
110	The West Coast Pop UR	7.50	15.00
111	Too Fast For You EX		
112	The 619 EX		
113	Rey-Rey's Tope EX		
114	3 Minute Warning PR		
115	Jamal's Top Rope Splash UR	7.50	15.00
116	Your Three Minutes Are Up PR		
117	Jamal's Atomic Samoan Drop PR		
118	Victim of the Revolving... PR		
119	Double Elbow Drop PR		
120	Jamie Noble PR		
121	The Trailer Hitch UR	7.50	15.00
122	Managed by Nidia PR		
123	Now I'm Gonna Get... PR		
124	I'm Jamie Noble, Boy PR		
125	Go On - Give 'im Some Sugar PR		
126	Throwin' Big Ol' Soup Bones... PR		
127	The Breakdown PR		
128	Raisin' the Roof PR		
129	Just Hold On a Second, Mister PR		
130	Red Hook's Premiere... PR		
131	A Victim of the Crippler PR		
132	Yo, Ese, I Know You, Homes PR		
133	Dudley Tough PR		
134	Never Gonna Stop Me PR		
135	Impaler PR		
136	Mattitude Adjustment PR		
137	That's Suicide PR		
138	Mountain of a Man UR	7.50	15.00
139	If You've Got It, Flaunt It UR	7.50	15.00
140	Everything's Cool When You're UR	7.50	15.00
141	Five Time Five Time... UR	7.50	15.00
142	Pound 4 Pound UR	7.50	15.00
143	Regal Upper Class Punch UR	7.50	15.00
144	Raven's Playground UR	7.50	15.00

#	Card		
145	When Hulkamania Runs... UR	7.50	15.00
146	The Game Interferes UR	7.50	15.00
147	We're Sorry But This Has... UR	7.50	15.00
148	eM pleH UR	7.50	15.00
149	Octopus UR	7.50	15.00
150	Hurrislam UR	7.50	15.00
10/TR	World Heavyweight Title Belt R	2.00	4.00
11/TR	Cruiserweight Title Belt R	2.00	4.00

2004 Comic Images WWE Raw Deal Vengeance

#	Card		
1	Leaping Neck Snap C	.12	.25
2	Revolving Takedown U	.50	1.00
3	Flying Leg Scissors R	2.00	4.00
4	Spinning Kick C	.12	.25
5	Right Cross Punch C	.12	.25
6	Left Cross Punch C	.12	.25
7	Judo Thrust U	.50	1.00
8	Lariat U	.50	1.00
9	Steel Chain Shot U	.50	1.00
10	Short Arm Rib Breaker R	2.00	4.00
11	Blindside Kick R	2.00	4.00
12	Struck by an Unknown... R	2.00	4.00
13	Snap Neckbreaker C	.12	.25
14	Pretzel Jerk C	.12	.25
15	Face Driver C	.12	.25
16	Vertical DDT Drop C	.12	.25
17	Judo Takedown U	.50	1.00
18	Quick Snap Body Slam U	.50	1.00
19	Double Underhook Power Bomb U	.50	1.00
20	Blindside Slam U	.50	1.00
21	Suplex R	2.00	4.00
22	Military Slam R	2.00	4.00
23	Takedown R	2.00	4.00
24	Death Valley Driver R	2.00	4.00
25	Ankle Torque C	.12	.25
26	Triangle Choke C	.12	.25
27	Body Lock C	.12	.25
28	Judo Choke U	.50	1.00
29	Wraparound Wrist Lock U	.50	1.00
30	Headlock U	.50	1.00
31	Apply Legal Leverage R	2.00	4.00
32	Blindside Choke R	2.00	4.00
33	Super Hold R	2.00	4.00
34	I Already Warned You C	.12	.25
35	Quick Reflexes C	.12	.25
36	Unexpected Turn of Events C	.12	.25
37	Blindsided Ego U	.50	1.00
38	Leave Me Alone U	.50	1.00
39	Blindsided Control U	.50	1.00
40	Two R	2.00	4.00
41	Headstrong R	2.00	4.00
42	SloppyVery Sloppy R	2.00	4.00
43	Suplex into the Ring C	.12	.25
44	Chain Wrestling C	.12	.25
45	When Hell Freezes Over C	.12	.25
46	Minute Hold C	.12	.25
47	Throw Into the Ring C	.12	.25
48	J.R. Style Donnybrook C	.12	.25
49	Chained Heat U	.50	1.00
50	Down and Out U	.50	1.00
51	According to the Contract Table U	.50	1.00
52	Last Chance U	.50	1.00
53	J.R. Style Authentic BBQ Sauce U	.50	1.00
54	For the Love of God - Why, King, Why? U		.50 1.00
55	Escape the Rules R	2.00	4.00
56	That's Broken R	2.00	4.00

#	Card		
57	He's Playing Possum? R	2.00	4.00
58	J.R. Style Push R	2.00	4.00
59	Now or Never R	2.00	4.00
60	Enough With the Trash Talk R	2.00	4.00
61	Anaheim, California C	.12	.25
62	Atlanta, Georgia C	.12	.25
63	Newcastle, England C	.12	.25
64	Omaha, Nebraska C	.12	.25
65	Calgary, Alberta, Canada U	.50	1.00
66	Las Vegas, Nevada U	.50	1.00
67	New York, New York U	.50	1.00
68	Saskatoon, Saskatchewan... U	.50	1.00
69	Houston, Texas R	2.00	4.00
70	Philadelphia, Pennsylvania R	2.00	4.00
71	Raleigh, North Carolina R	2.00	4.00
72	Springfield, Illinois R	2.00	4.00
73	A Chorus of Boos C	.12	.25
74	Spontaneous Combustion C	.12	.25
75	This is Gonna Be a Rocket Buster C	.12	.25
76	Old School Beating C	.12	.25
77	First Blood Match U	.50	1.00
78	The Title is on the Line U	.50	1.00
79	You Rang? U	.50	1.00
80	You, Me, and Whoever? U	.50	1.00
81	Bad Blood R	2.00	4.00
82	Bitter Rivals R	2.00	4.00
83	It's All About the Game R	2.00	4.00
84	Managed by Dawn Marie R	2.00	4.00
85	Hardcore Style C	.12	.25
86	Immune to Pain C	.12	.25
87	Number One Contender C	.12	.25
88	The Beautiful People C	.12	.25
89	Grab the Ref C	.12	.25
90	Desperate Tag U	.50	1.00
91	Ringside Assistance U	.50	1.00
92	You're as Graceful... U	.50	1.00
93	Revolutionizing the Business U	.50	1.00
94	Chain Finisher U	.50	1.00
95	All Thatand Nothing? R	2.00	4.00
96	Divas Revealed R	2.00	4.00
97	To the Rescue R	2.00	4.00
98	Unscrupulous S.O.B. R	2.00	4.00
99	Cheap Accolades R	2.00	4.00
100	Evolution EX		
101	Evolution is a Mystery UR	7.50	15.00
102	Paid, Laid, and Made UR	7.50	15.00
103	Yesterday is So Long Ago EX		
104	I See the Line in the Sand EX		
105	Nothing Ever Stays the Same EX		
106	The Highlight of the Night EX		
107	You Sanctimounious... UR	7.50	15.00
108	Listen Up, Junior... UR	7.50	15.00
109	My Obscenely Expensive... EX		
110	Roll the Footage, Monkeys EX		
111	Jericho's Ensugiri EX		
112	The Mystery Wrestler EX		
113	You Don't Want to Go... UR	7.50	15.00
114	Mankind / Cactus Jack... EX		
115	Testicular Fortitude EX		
116	I'm Hardcore I'm Hardcore EX		
117	Leader of the Edge Army EX		
118	Edgeucation of Adam... UR	7.50	15.00
119	Downward Spiral UR	7.50	15.00
120	Edge Kick EX		
121	Scream If You Want It EX		
122	Cause I Want More EX		
123	Paul Heyman EX		
124	Let the Bodies Hit the Floor UR	7.50	15.00

#	Card		
125	You're Dangerously Close PR		
126	Coach, Cole, or Finkel? EX		
127	Big Boys Club EX		
128	Do You Know Who... EX		
129	Your Freaking Hero EX		
130	The Straps are Down UR	7.50	15.00
131	Oh, It's True UR	7.50	15.00
132	Angle's German Suplex EX		
133	Wooooo EX		
134	Angle's Moonsault EX		
135	FBI PR		
136	It's a Numbers Game UR	7.50	15.00
137	FBI Hit List PR		
138	The Arrivederci PR		
139	The Whack PR		
140	The Fuhgeddaboutit PR		
141	The A-Train PR		
142	Snot Rocket UR	7.50	15.00
143	Who Do You Think You Are? PR		
144	Chugga-chugga... PR		
145	Derailer PR		
146	Train Wreck PR		
147	Managed by Paul Bearer PR		
148	Know Your Role... PR		
149	Kane's Rage PR		
150	Rikishi's Hip Toss PR		
151	Pain is Inevitable PR		
152	Viva La Raza Low Rider PR		
153	WWE Commentators PR		
154	The Best Surprises... PR		
155	Blood is Thicker Than Wood PR		
156	To All My Peeps... PR		
157	Era of Mattitude Has Arrived PR		
158	Lita's DDT PR		
159	Van Terminator PR		
160	How Many Times? PR		
161	Keep It Simple, Sir PR		
162	The StratusFear PR		
163	Managed by Kyo Dai PR		
164	I've Got Hurri-Powers PR		
165	Who's That Jumpin'... PR		
166	Noble Bomb PR		
167	Didn't I Already Fire You? PR		
168	The People's Champ... PR		
169	Belly-to-Belly Steinerplex UR	7.50	15.00
170	All Things Are Possible UR	7.50	15.00
171	Greco Roman Specialists UR	7.50	15.00
172	Test's Top Rope... UR	7.50	15.00
173	Unleash the Beast UR	7.50	15.00
174	I Should've Been in That Magazine UR	7.50	15.00
175	Control Your World UR	7.50	15.00
176	Bald is Beautiful UR	7.50	15.00
177	So You Think You're... UR	7.50	15.00
178	The Boss's Main Squeeze UR	7.50	15.00
179	Golden Thong Award UR	7.50	15.00
180	This is Not Enough UR	7.50	15.00
181	Nidia's Mink Coat UR	7.50	15.00

2000 Comic Images WWF Raw Deal

#	Card		
1	Chop C	.12	.25
2	Punch C	.12	.25
3	Head Butt C	.12	.25
4	Roundhouse Punch C	.12	.25
5	Haymaker C	.12	.25
6	Back Body Drop C	.12	.25
7	Big Boot C	.12	.25
8	Shoulder Block U	.50	1.00
9	Kick U	.50	1.00

#	Card	Rarity	Low	High
10	Cross Body Block U		.50	1.00
11	Cheap Shot From the Corner U		.50	1.00
12	Ensugiri U		.50	1.00
13	Running Elbow Smash U		.50	1.00
14	Drop Kick U		.50	1.00
15	Discus Punch U		.50	1.00
16	Superkick R		2.00	4.00
17	Spinning Heel Kick R		2.00	4.00
18	Spear R		2.00	4.00
19	Clothesline R		2.00	4.00
20	Chair Shot R		2.00	4.00
21	Hurricanrana R		2.00	4.00
22	Arm Bar Takedown C		.12	.25
23	Hip Toss C		.12	.25
24	Arm Drag C		.12	.25
25	Russian Leg Sweep C		.12	.25
26	Snap Mare C		.12	.25
27	Gut Buster C		.12	.25
28	Body Slam C		.12	.25
29	Back Breaker C		.12	.25
30	Double Leg Takedown U		.50	1.00
31	Fireman's Carry U		.50	1.00
32	Headlock Takedown U		.50	1.00
33	Belly to Belly Suplex U		.50	1.00
34	Atomic Facebuster U		.50	1.00
35	Atomic Drop U		.50	1.00
36	Inverse Atomic Drop U		.50	1.00
37	Vertical Suplex U		.50	1.00
38	Belly to Back Suplex U		.50	1.00
39	Pump Handle Slam U		.50	1.00
40	Reverse DDT U		.50	1.00
41	Samoan Drop R		2.00	4.00
42	Sit Out Powerbomb R		2.00	4.00
43	Bulldog R		2.00	4.00
44	Fisherman's Suplex R		2.00	4.00
45	DDT R		2.00	4.00
46	Power Slam R		2.00	4.00
47	Powerbomb R		2.00	4.00
48	Press Slam R		2.00	4.00
49	Collar and Elbow Lockup C		.12	.25
50	Wrist Lock C		.12	.25
51	Arm Bar C		.12	.25
52	Chin Lock C		.12	.25
53	Bear Hug C		.12	.25
54	Full Nelson C		.12	.25
55	Choke Hold C		.12	.25
56	Step Over Toe Hold C		.12	.25
57	Ankle Lock U		.50	1.00
58	Standing Side Headlock U		.50	1.00
59	Cobra Clutch U		.50	1.00
60	Bow and Arrow U		.50	1.00
61	Chicken Wing U		.50	1.00
62	Sleeper R		2.00	4.00
63	Camel Clutch R		2.00	4.00
64	Boston Crab R		2.00	4.00
65	Guillotine Stretch R		2.00	4.00
66	Abdominal Stretch R		.75	1.50
67	Torture Rack R		2.00	4.00
68	Figure Four Leg Lock R		2.00	4.00
69	Combination Attack R		2.00	4.00
70	Step Aside C		.12	.25
71	Escape Move C		.12	.25
72	Break the Hold C		.12	.25
73	Trip C		.12	.25
74	Rolling Takedown U		.50	1.00
75	Knee to the Gut U		.50	1.00
76	Elbow to the Face U		.50	1.00
77	Clean Break U		.50	1.00

#	Card	Rarity	Low	High
78	Partner Interference R		2.00	4.00
79	Manager Interferes R		2.00	4.00
80	Disqualification R		2.00	4.00
81	No Chance in Hell R		2.00	4.00
82	Hmmm C		.12	.25
83	Don't Think Too Hard C		.12	.25
84	Tag in Partner C		.12	.25
85	Whaddya Got? C		.12	.25
86	Not Yet C		.12	.25
87	Jockeying for Position C		.12	.25
88	Irish Whip C		.12	.25
89	Flash in the Pan C		.12	.25
90	View of Villainy C		.12	.25
91	Shake It Off U		.50	1.00
92	Offer Handshake U		.50	1.00
93	Roll Out of the Ring U		.50	1.00
94	Distract the Ref U		.50	1.00
95	Recovery U		.50	1.00
96	Spit At Opponent U		.50	1.00
97	Double Team U		.50	1.00
98	Get Crowd Support U		.50	1.00
99	Comeback R		2.00	4.00
100	Ego Boost R		2.00	4.00
101	Deluding Yourself R		2.00	4.00
102	Stagger R		2.00	4.00
103	Diversion R		2.00	4.00
104	Marking Out R		2.00	4.00
105	Puppies Puppies R		2.00	4.00
106	Shane O'Mac R		2.00	4.00
107	Maintain Hold R		2.00	4.00
108	Pat and Gerry R		2.00	4.00
109	Stone Cold Stunner UR		7.50	15.00
110	Open Up a Can of Whoop-A$ UR		7.50	15.00
111	Undertaker's Tombstone... UR		7.50	15.00
112	Power of Darkness UR		7.50	15.00
113	Mandible Claw UR		7.50	15.00
114	Mr. Socko UR		7.50	15.00
115	Pedigree UR		7.50	15.00
116	Chyna Interferes UR		7.50	15.00
117	The People's Eyebrow UR		7.50	15.00
118	The People's Elbow UR		7.50	15.00
119	Kane's Tombstone Piledriver UR		7.50	15.00
120	Hellfire and Brimstone UR		7.50	15.00
121	Walls of Jericho UR		7.50	15.00
122	Ayatollah of Rock 'n' Roll-a UR		7.50	15.00
123	STONE COLD STEVE AUSTIN EX			
124	Austin Elbow Smash EX			
125	Lou Thesz Press EX			
126	Double Digits EX			
127	THE UNDERTAKER EX			
128	Undertaker's Chokeslam EX			
129	Undertaker's Flying Clothesline EX			
130	Undertaker Sits Up EX			
131	MANKIND EX			
132	Have a Nice Day EX			
133	Double Arm DDT EX			
134	Tree of Woe EX			
135	HHH EX			
136	Leaping Knee to the Face EX			
137	Facebuster EX			
138	I Am the Game. EX			
139	THE ROCK EX			
140	Smackdown Hotel EX			
141	Take That Move EX			
142	Rock Bottom EX			
143	KANE EX			
144	Kane's Chokeslam EX			
145	Kane's Flying Clothesline EX			

#	Card	Rarity	Low	High
146	Kane's Return EX			
147	CHRIS JERICHO EX			
148	Lionsault EX			
149	Y2J EX			
150	Don't You Never EVER EX			
1TR	WWF Heavyweight Title Belt			
2TR	WWF Intercontinental Title Belt			
3TR	WWF European Title Belt			

2001 Comic Images WWF Raw Deal Backlash

#	Card	Rarity	Low	High
1	Flying Head Scissors C		.12	.25
2	Big Splash in the Corner C		.12	.25
3	Flying Clothesline U		.50	1.00
4	Drive Opponent Thru Announcer's Table U		.50	1.00
5	Crucifix Rollup R		2.00	4.00
6	Chop to the Chest C		.12	.25
7	Slap the Taste Out of Your Mouth C		.12	.25
8	Leg Sweep C		.12	.25
9	Struck by a Kendo Stick C		.12	.25
10	Pop the Guy On the Apron U		.50	1.00
11	Running Lariat U		.50	1.00
12	Garbage Can Lid U		.50	1.00
13	Stun Gun R		2.00	4.00
14	Hung Out to Dry R		2.00	4.00
15	Running Clothesline R		2.00	4.00
16	Scoop Slam C		.12	.25
17	Leg Drag C		.12	.25
18	Neck Breaker C		.12	.25
19	Rib Breaker C		.12	.25
20	Tiger Bomb C		.12	.25
21	Single Arm DDT U		.50	1.00
22	Tandem Atomic Drop U		.50	1.00
23	Brainbuster U		.50	1.00
24	Spine Buster U		.50	1.00
25	Workin' on the Knee R		2.00	4.00
26	Half Hour Suplex R		2.00	4.00
27	Clutch onto Opponent C		.12	.25
28	Captive Tag Out C		.12	.25
29	Arm Wrench C		.12	.25
30	Entangle In the Ropes C		.12	.25
31	Apply Illegal Leverage U		.50	1.00
32	Texas Cloverleaf U		.50	1.00
33	Microphone Cord R		2.00	4.00
34	Sharpshooter R		2.00	4.00
35	Clumsy Opponent C		.12	.25
36	No Sell Maneuver C		.12	.25
37	Over Sell Maneuver C		.12	.25
38	Kissing Up to the Stinkin' Fans U		.50	1.00
39	Hey That's Cheap Heat U		.50	1.00
40	Blown Spot R		2.00	4.00
41	Charismatic Style C		.12	.25
42	Set Him Up C		.12	.25
43	Great Technical Knowledge C		.12	.25
44	Turn the Match... C		.12	.25
45	Amazing Display of Power C		.12	.25
46	Adrenaline Rush C		.12	.25
47	Let's Take it Home C		.12	.25
48	Drawing Extra Heat U		.50	1.00
49	Well-Deserved Push U		.50	1.00
50	Propel Partner U		.50	1.00
51	Ladder In the Ring U		.50	1.00
52	Giving Away the Business U		.50	1.00
53	Heel Turn R		2.00	4.00
54	Lita to the Xtreme R		2.00	4.00
55	You're Not in My League R		2.00	4.00
56	Busted Wide Open R		2.00	4.00
57	Seeing Stars R		2.00	4.00

#	Card	Rarity	Low	High
58	Announcer's Table R		2.00	4.00
59	I'm Gonna Put You... R		2.00	4.00
60	Watching My Back R		2.00	4.00
61	Study the Tapes C		.12	.25
62	Student of the Sport C		.12	.25
63	Awesome Pyro C		.12	.25
64	Givin' 'em High Fives C		.12	.25
65	Taunt the Fans C		.12	.25
66	Fans Love an Underdog U		.50	1.00
67	Trash Talkin' Interview U		.50	1.00
68	Jump the Bell U		.50	1.00
69	Old School Wrestling Match R		2.00	4.00
70	Here a Mark, There a Mark... R		2.00	4.00
71	Premiere WWF (logo) Superstar R		2.00	4.00
72	Underrated Superstar R		2.00	4.00
73	Backlash C		.12	.25
74	Dirty Low Blow C		.12	.25
75	Small Concealed Foreign Object C		.12	.25
76	Armageddon (WWF Logo) Style C		.12	.25
77	Per Order of the Chairman U		.50	1.00
78	Spectacular Ring Entrance U		.50	1.00
79	When You Thought You... U		.50	1.00
80	Referee Finally Catches... U		.50	1.00
81	Don't Mess with the Champ R		2.00	4.00
82	Fully Loaded R		2.00	4.00
83	Again With This Crap?? R		2.00	4.00
84	No Mercy R		2.00	4.00
85	Dudley Boyz EX			
86	3D UR		7.50	15.00
87	Wazzzzuuup??? EX			
88	Buh-Buh Ray Dudley U		.50	1.00
89	Buh-Buh Bomb UR		7.50	15.00
90	Catatonic Stare R		2.00	4.00
91	My Name Is U		.50	1.00
92	Buh-Buh Drop EX			
93	Buh-Buh Punch R		2.00	4.00
94	D-Von Dudley U		.50	1.00
95	Testify UR		7.50	15.00
96	Spinning Elbow R		2.00	4.00
97	Doin' the D-Von U		.50	1.00
98	Thou Shall Not ####... EX			
99	D-Von Get the Table R		2.00	4.00
100	Edge and Christian EX			
101	Con-Chair-To UR		7.50	15.00
102	For the Benefit of Those... EX			
103	Edge U		.50	1.00
104	Edge-O-Matic UR		7.50	15.00
105	Million Dollar Smile R		2.00	4.00
106	Big Slide Into the Ring U		.50	1.00
107	Listen, You Reekazoid EX			
108	Sodas Rule R		2.00	4.00
109	Christian U		.50	1.00
110	Unprettier UR		7.50	15.00
111	Kazoo Theme Songs R		2.00	4.00
112	Christian's Shades U		.50	1.00
113	This Is So Totally Unfair EX			
114	Greetings to Our Fans... R		2.00	4.00
115	Hardy Boyz EX			
116	Poetry in Motion UR		7.50	15.00
117	Spin Cycle EX			
118	Matt Hardy U		.50	1.00
119	Twist of Fate UR		7.50	15.00
120	Matt's Moonsault R		2.00	4.00
121	Roar for the Fans U		.50	1.00
122	Matt Hardy's Patented Leg Drop EX			
123	Put It All On the Line R		2.00	4.00
124	Jeff Hardy U		.50	1.00
125	Swanton Bomb UR		7.50	15.00

#	Card		
126	Ride the Barricade R	2.00	4.00
127	No, Jeff, Don't Do It U	.50	1.00
128	Whisper in the Wind EX		
129	Incite the Fans R	2.00	4.00
130	Right to Censor EX		
131	Right to (Censor) Interfere UR	7.50	15.00
132	We're Doing This For... R	2.00	4.00
133	What's Wrong with You People? R	2.00	4.00
134	We're Here to Clean Up... EX		
135	This is Unacceptable Behavior EX		
136	Censored EX		
137	DTA UR	7.50	15.00
138	Brothers 'til the End UR	7.50	15.00
139	Three Faces of Foley UR	7.50	15.00
140	The Brahma Bull UR	7.50	15.00
141	Sledge Hammer Shot UR	7.50	15.00
142	Superior Acrobatics UR	7.50	15.00
143	I Did It For You UR	7.50	15.00
144	Where Are Your Medals? UR	7.50	15.00
145	Ovicular Fortitude UR	7.50	15.00
146	Just Another Victim UR	7.50	15.00
147	Prove Me Wrong UR	7.50	15.00
148	Eddie's Roll Up UR	7.50	15.00
149	Pac's Back UR	7.50	15.00
150	The One Billy Gunn UR	7.50	15.00

2001 Comic Images WWF Raw Deal
Fully Loaded

#	Card		
1	Falling Fist C	.12	.25
2	Knee Smash C	.12	.25
3	Elbow Drop C	.12	.25
4	Foot Stomp C	.12	.25
5	Splash U	.50	1.00
6	Leg Drop U	.50	1.00
7	Double Axe Handle U	.50	1.00
8	Shooting Star Press U	.50	1.00
9	Missile Dropkick R	2.00	4.00
10	Suicide Plancha R	2.00	4.00
11	Superplex R	2.00	4.00
12	Moonsault R	2.00	4.00
13	Backhand Slap C	.12	.25
14	Turnbuckle Smash C	.12	.25
15	Eye Rake C	.12	.25
16	Knee Lift U	.50	1.00
17	Baseball Slide U	.50	1.00
18	Surprise Hit U	.50	1.00
19	European Uppercut R	2.00	4.00
20	Trash Can R	2.00	4.00
21	Double Clothesline R	2.00	4.00
22	Jaw Jammer C	.12	.25
23	Japanese Arm Drag C	.12	.25
24	Jackhammer C	.12	.25
25	Drop Toe Hold C	.12	.25
26	Shoulder Breaker C	.12	.25
27	Small Package C	.12	.25
28	Monkey Flip U	.50	1.00
29	Knee Breaker U	.50	1.00
30	Full Nelson Slam U	.50	1.00
31	German Suplex U	.50	1.00
32	Airplane Spin U	.50	1.00
33	Swinging Neck Breaker U	.50	1.00
34	Fall-Away Slam R	2.00	4.00
35	Double Underhook Suplex R	2.00	4.00
36	Sidewalk Slam R	2.00	4.00
37	Giant Swing R	2.00	4.00
38	Northern Lights Suplex R	2.00	4.00
39	Hair Pull C	.12	.25
40	Front Face Lock C	.12	.25
41	Hammerlock C	.12	.25
42	Head Vise U	.50	1.00
43	Surfboard U	.50	1.00
44	Stump Puller U	.50	1.00
45	Claw R	2.00	4.00
46	STF R	2.00	4.00
47	Roll Out of the Way C	.12	.25
48	Borrring Borrring C	.12	.25
49	Shove Off the Top Rope C	.12	.25
50	Tornado DDT C	.12	.25
51	Just Bring It U	.50	1.00
52	Hebner Calls It U	.50	1.00
53	Lift a Boot U	.50	1.00
54	That's Gonna Cost You Reversa		
55	Ref KO'd R	2.00	4.00
56	Attitude Adjustment R	2.00	4.00
57	In This Very Ring C	.12	.25
58	Defensive Cover C	.12	.25
59	Ho Train C	.12	.25
60	Playing With Fire C	.12	.25
61	Stare Down Opponent C	.12	.25
62	Moongoose In the House C	.12	.25
63	Commission-er Rules C	.12	.25
64	McMahon-Helmsley Era C	.12	.25
65	Throw Into the Corner Turnbuckle C	.12	.25
66	From the Top Rope C	.12	.25
67	Hardyz' Ambush C	.12	.25
68	American Bad A$ C	.12	.25
69	Do You Like Pie? C	.12	.25
70	Doing the Job C	.12	.25
71	Go for the Cheap Pop U	.50	1.00
72	Predictable Opponent U	.50	1.00
73	Who Booked This Match? U	.50	1.00
74	JR Style Slobberknocker U	.50	1.00
75	Bait Opponent U	.50	1.00
76	Defensive Posture U	.50	1.00
77	Table Table Table U	.50	1.00
78	Backed by Stephanie McMahon U	.50	1.00
79	Here Kitty, Kitty U	.50	1.00
80	Throw Opponent Out of the Ring U	.50	1.00
81	Quick Count Ref U	.50	1.00
82	Turn the Tide R	2.00	4.00
83	Time Keeper's Bell R	2.00	4.00
84	Inferno Match R	2.00	4.00
85	Call to the Crowd R	2.00	4.00
86	Dem Damn Dudleyz R	2.00	4.00
87	Reeking of Awesomeness Action		
88	Enter the Stratus-phere R	2.00	4.00
89	Kick Out R	2.00	4.00
90	Acolyte Protection Agency R	2.00	4.00
91	Rikishi Driver UR	7.50	15.00
92	A$ Drop UR	7.50	15.00
93	Rikishi EX		
94	Drive, Rikishi, Drive EX		
95	Back That A$ Up EX		
96	Stink Face EX		
97	Olympic Slam UR	7.50	15.00
98	It's True, It's True UR	7.50	15.00
99	Kurt Angle EX		
100	Intensity EX		
101	Integrity EX		
102	Intelligence EX		
103	Chyna's Pedigree UR	7.50	15.00
104	The 9th Wonder of the World UR	7.50	15.00
105	Chyna EX		
106	Handspring Elbow EX		
107	I'd Rather Be In Chyna EX		
108	Chyna's Patented Low Blow EX		
109	Tazzmission UR	7.50	15.00
110	Thug It - Dead UR	7.50	15.00
111	Tazz EX		
112	T-Bone Tazzplex EX		
113	Head-and-Arms Tazzplex EX		
114	Northern Lights Tazzplex EX		
115	Crippler Crossface UR	7.50	15.00
116	Big Stupid Grin UR	7.50	15.00
117	Chris Benoit EX		
118	Kamikaze Headbutt EX		
119	Series of Suplexes EX		
120	Rabid Wolverine EX		
121	Guerrero Frog Splash... UR	7.50	15.00
122	Get Your GED UR	7.50	15.00
123	Eddie Guerrero EX		
124	Snap Senton Splash EX		
125	Study for Your GED EX		
126	Latino Heeeeeeeat EX		
127	Doggy Pump Handle Slam UR	7.50	15.00
128	Road Dogg EX		
129	Kickin' The Shizt-nit... EX		
130	Juke N Jive EX		
131	Let's Make Some Noise EX		
132	X-Factor UR	7.50	15.00
133	X-Pac EX		
134	Leaping Spin Kick EX		
135	Bronco Buster EX		
136	Huge Bump Out of the Ring EX		
137	Fame-A$-er UR	7.50	15.00
138	B. A. Billy Gunn EX		
139	I'm an A$ Man EX		
140	B.A.'s Military Press Slam EX		
141	The Federation's Purest Athlete EX		
142	I've Got Two Words For Ya... UR	7.50	15.00
143	Tori Enters the Fray UR	7.50	15.00
144	Patented Rock Footstomp UR	7.50	15.00
145	Patented Austin Kick... UR	7.50	15.00
146	Rest In Peace UR	7.50	15.00
147	Get Hardcore UR	7.50	15.00
148	Triple H's Reverse... UR	7.50	15.00
149	Masked Vengence UR	7.50	15.00
150	Springboard Drop Kick UR	7.50	15.00

2002 Comic Images WWF Raw Deal
Mania

#	Card		
1	Spinning Crescent Kick C	.12	.25
2	Flying Reverse Elbow C	.12	.25
3	Flying TopÈ U	.50	1.00
4	Stackplex U	.50	1.00
5	Asai Moonsault R	2.00	4.00
6	Forearm Shot C	.12	.25
7	Feign Strike C	.12	.25
8	Gut Punch C	.12	.25
9	Step on Opponent's Noggin U	.50	1.00
10	Into the Barricade U	.50	1.00
11	Pump Kick R	2.00	4.00
12	Catapult C	.12	.25
13	Within Your Grasp C	.12	.25
14	Butterfly Suplex C	.12	.25
15	Beal Toss C	.12	.25
16	Backslide U	.50	1.00
17	Tandem Flapjack U	.50	1.00
18	Running Bulldog R	2.00	4.00
19	Short Arm Hammerlock C	.12	.25
20	Knee Bar C	.12	.25
21	Strangle Hold U	.50	1.00
22	Arm Grapevine U	.50	1.00
23	Indian Deathlock R	2.00	4.00
24	All Talk, No Action C	.12	.25
25	Iron Will R	2.00	4.00
26	Not Today, Pal R	2.00	4.00
27	Out Think the Fink C	.12	.25
28	Stratusfied C	.12	.25
29	Got Wood? C	.12	.25
30	Playing by the Rules C	.12	.25
31	Kay-Fabe C	.12	.25
32	Totally Bogus C	.12	.25
33	Little She Devil C	.12	.25
34	Gut Wrench C	.12	.25
35	X-treme Measures C	.12	.25
36	Cole Calls It Right C	.12	.25
37	Trailer Park Trash C	.12	.25
38	Veteran Referee: Tim White U	.50	1.00
39	Daddy's Little Girl U	.50	1.00
40	Messing With the Champ U	.50	1.00
41	Everybody Wants... U	.50	1.00
42	Wooden Palette U	.50	1.00
43	Judgment Day U	.50	1.00
44	Mania U	.50	1.00
45	Torrie Wilson, On It R	2.00	4.00
46	Keibler's Cookies R	2.00	4.00
47	V.K.M.'s Patented Big Gulp R	2.00	4.00
48	Money Talks, BS Walks R	2.00	4.00
49	Ring Rats R	2.00	4.00
50	Billion Dollar Princess R	2.00	4.00
51	Unforgiven R	2.00	4.00
52	Ring Steps R	2.00	4.00
53	No Way Out R	2.00	4.00
54	Superior Training C	.12	.25
55	Slandered Online C	.12	.25
56	Product Endorsements C	.12	.25
57	Backstage Ambush Attempt C	.12	.25
58	No Disqualification Match C	.12	.25
59	Personal Appearance U	.50	1.00
60	Snubbed by the Fans U	.50	1.00
61	Not Done with Any Flair U	.50	1.00
62	Chicago Street Fight U	.50	1.00
63	Four Corners Match U	.50	1.00
64	Hell in a Cell Match R	2.00	4.00
65	Indian Strap Match R	2.00	4.00
66	Duchess of Queensbury Rules R	2.00	4.00
67	Handicap Match R	2.00	4.00
68	Signed Contract with Linda McMahon R	2.00	4.00
69	Fortitude Surge C	.12	.25
70	Fan Appreciation Day C	.12	.25
71	Here Comes the Money C	.12	.25
72	Remove Corner Turnbuckle C	.12	.25
73	Over the Barricade C	.12	.25
74	Touch Turnbuckle #1 U	.50	1.00
75	Touch Turnbuckle #2 U	.50	1.00
76	Touch Turnbuckle #3 U	.50	1.00
77	Touch Turnbuckle #4 U	.50	1.00
78	Over the Top Rope U	.50	1.00
79	Second Wind R	2.00	4.00
80	Sustained Damage R	2.00	4.00
81	Happy You're Here... R	2.00	4.00
82	Test of Strength R	2.00	4.00
83	Debilitating Injury: Concussion R	2.00	4.00
84	Big Show EX		
85	Final Cut UR	7.50	15.00
86	Wellllllllllll UR	7.50	15.00
87	Showstopper Chokeslam EX		
88	Big Show Splash EX		
89	500lbs. of Raw Power EX		
90	Lita EX		
91	Lita-sault UR	7.50	15.00

92 X-treme Thong UR	7.50	15.00
93 Lita-canrana EX		
94 Lita's Drop Kick EX		
95 Crimson Goddess EX		
96 Rob Van Dam EX		
97 Van Daminator UR	7.50	15.00
98 R - V - D UR	7.50	15.00
99 Five Star Frog Splash EX		
100 Extreme Monkey Flip EX		
101 Rolling Thunder EX		
102 Booker T EX		
103 Bookend UR	7.50	15.00
104 Spinnerooni UR	7.50	15.00
105 Can You Dig It, Sucka? EX		
106 Booker's Scissor Kick EX		
107 Spinning T Kick EX		
108 APA PU		
109 Beer, Cards, and More Beer UR	7.50	15.00
110 Dominator PR		
111 Clothesline from Hell PR		
112 Faarooq's Spike Spine Buster PU		
113 Bradshaw's Fall Away Slam PU		
114 Spike Dudley PU		
115 Dudley Dog UR	7.50	15.00
116 150 lbs. Soaking Wet PR		
117 Good Golly, Miss Molly Holly PR		
118 Psychotic Bump PU		
119 Brotherly Love PU		
120 William Regal PU		
121 Regal Stretch UR	7.50	15.00
122 Commissioner Regal's Decree PR		
123 Union Jack PR		
124 I've Been Besmirched PU		
125 Goodwill Ambassador PU		
126 Raven PU		
127 Raven Effect DDT UR	7.50	15.00
128 From the Bowery PR		
129 What About Me? PR		
130 Quoth the Raven Nevermore PU		
131 I Feel Your Pain PU		
132 What??? PR		
133 You Will Respect Me PR		
134 Foley is Good PR		
135 Shades of the Great One PR		
136 Cerebral Assassin PR		
137 Born of Hellfire PR		
138 Would You Please... PR		
139 Gettin' Cheeky with It UR	7.50	15.00
140 Angle Lock UR	7.50	15.00
141 Tough Enough UR	7.50	15.00
142 First to Tap Out Match UR	7.50	15.00
143 /timo Rechazo UR	7.50	15.00
144 Pac's Pack UR	7.50	15.00
145 The One and Only UR	7.50	15.00
146 Greetings from Dudleyville... UR	7.50	15.00
147 You Think You Know Me? UR	7.50	15.00
148 Live for the Moment UR	7.50	15.00
149 TLC Match UR	7.50	15.00
150 Censorship Match UR	7.50	15.00
6/TR WCW Title Belt R	2.00	4.00
7/TR WWF Light Heavyweight Title R	2.00	4.00

2000 Comic Images WWF Axxess Fan Fest

1 Big Show	4.00	10.00
2 Triple H	6.00	15.00
3 The Rock	10.00	25.00

2000 Comic Images WWF The Divas Promos

COMPLETE SET (8)	12.00	30.00
P1 Chyna	3.00	8.00
P2 Debra	2.50	6.00
P3 Ivory	2.00	5.00
P4 Jacqueline	2.00	5.00
P5 The Kat	2.00	5.00
P6 Terri	3.00	8.00
P7 Tori	2.00	5.00
P8 Trish	4.00	10.00

2000 Comic Images WWF No Mercy

COMPLETE SET (81)	8.00	20.00
UNOPENED BOX (36 PACKS)		
UNOPENED PACK (7 CARDS)		
1 Mankind	.50	1.25
2 Cactus Jack	.50	1.25
3 Stone Cold Steve Austin	.75	2.00
4 Hardcore Holly	.20	.50
5 Al Snow	.20	.50
6 Road Dogg	.12	.30
7 Big Boss Man	.20	.50
8 The Undertaker	.60	1.50
9 Kane	.50	1.25
10 The Rock	.75	2.00
11 Vince McMahon	.50	1.25
12 Shane McMahon	.30	.75
13 Edge/Christian	.50	1.25
14 The Hardy Boyz	.30	.75
15 The Dudley Boyz	.20	.50
16 The Acolytes	.30	.75
17 Faarooq	.12	.30
18 Bradshaw	.30	.75
19 X-Pac	.20	.50
20 The Big Show	.30	.75
21 Viscera	.12	.30
22 Prince Albert	.12	.30
23 Test	.20	.50
24 Mr. Ass	.12	.30
25 Triple H	.75	2.00
26 Chyna	.50	1.25
27 Ken Shamrock	.20	.50
28 Godfather	.12	.30
29 Chris Jericho	.30	.75
30 Tazz	.20	.50
31 Hardcore Belt	.12	.30
32 D-Generation X	.30	.75
33 Gangrel	.12	.30
34 The Headbangers	.12	.30
35 British Bulldog	.20	.50
36 D'Lo Brown	.12	.30
37 Mark Henry	.12	.30
38 Kurt Angle	.50	1.25
39 Mean Street Posse	.12	.30
40 Rikishi Phatu	.20	.50
41 Too Cool	.12	.30
42 Mick Foley	.50	1.25
43 Shawn Michaels	.50	1.25
44 The Undertaker	.60	1.50
45 Stone Cold Steve Austin	.75	2.00
46 Legion Of Doom	.40	1.00
47 Wild Samoans	.20	.50
48 Sgt. Slaughter	.30	.75
49 Mankind/The Rock	.75	2.00
50 Mankind/The Rock	.75	2.00
51 Mankind/The Undertaker	.60	1.50

52 Mankind/Triple H	.75	2.00
53 Mankind/Ken Shamrock	.50	1.25
54 The Rock/Triple H	.75	2.00
55 The Undertaker/Shawn Michaels	.60	1.50
56 The Hardy Boyz/Edge/Christian	.50	1.25
57 The Undertaker/Kane	.60	1.50
58 Undertaker/Kane/Austin	.75	2.00
59 Kane/Vince McMahon/Undertaker	.60	1.50
60 Steve Austin/Kane	.75	2.00
61 Steve Austin/Dude Love	.75	2.00
62 Steve Austin/Undertaker	.75	2.00
63 Steve Austin/Undertaker	.75	2.00
64 Steve Austin/Vince McMahon	.75	2.00
65 Steve Austin/Shane & Vince McMahon	.75	2.00
66 Shane McMahon/Test	.30	.75
67 Al Snow/Big Boss Man	.20	.50
68 Al Snow/Hardcore Holly	.20	.50
69 Al Snow/Minis	.20	.50
70 Ivory/Luna	.50	1.25
71 Ken Shamrock/Steve Blackman	.20	.50
72 Mr. Ass/Hardcore Holly	.20	.50
73 The Acolytes	.30	.75
74 New Age Outlaws/Mankind/Kane	.50	1.25
75 Vince McMahon/Mankind	.50	1.25
76 Sgt. Slaughter/Triple H	.75	2.00
77 Shawn Michaels/The Undertaker	.60	1.50
78 The Rock/Mankind	.75	2.00
79 Triple H/Cactus Jack	.75	2.00
80 The Hardy Boyz/The Dudley Boyz	.30	.75
81 Checklist	.12	.30

2000 Comic Images WWF No Mercy Hardcore Champions Holofoil

COMPLETE SET (8)	3.00	8.00
RANDOMLY INSERTED INTO PACKS		
C1 Mankind	1.25	3.00
C2 Big Bossman	.50	1.25
C3 Road Dogg	.50	1.25
C4 Hardcore Holly	.50	1.25
C5 Al Snow	.50	1.25
C6 Mr. Ass	.50	1.25
C7 British Bulldog	.50	1.25
C8 Test	.50	1.25

2000 Comic Images WWF No Mercy Piece of the Ring Relics

COMPLETE SET (4)	12.00	30.00
RANDOMLY INSERTED INTO PACKS		
P1 Ring Mat	6.00	15.00
P2 Road Dogg Hat	4.00	10.00
P3 Chris Jericho Shirt	8.00	20.00
P4 D-Generation X Shirt	5.00	12.00

2000 Comic Images WWF No Mercy Promos

COMPLETE SET (3)	1.50	4.00
RANDOMLY INSERTED INTO PACKS		
P1 Mankind/The Rock	.75	2.00
P2 The Undertaker/Kane	.75	2.00
P3 Vince McMahon	.75	2.00

2000 Comic Images WWF Rock Solid

COMPLETE SET (72)	10.00	25.00
UNOPENED BOX (36 PACKS)	100.00	150.00
UNOPENED PACK (7 CARDS)	3.00	4.00
1 Title Card	.30	.75
2 Reeling 'Em In	.30	.75

3 Catching Up	.30	.75
4 The People's Threads	.30	.75
5 Sweet Ride	.30	.75
6 The Rock's Roots	.30	.75
7 Shirt Off His Back	.30	.75
8 Electrifying Threads	.30	.75
9 In For A Trim	.30	.75
10 Laying It Down In Miami	.30	.75
11 Electrifying Author	.30	.75
12 The Little People's Champ	.30	.75
13 A Class Act	.30	.75
14 The Fans Bring It	.30	.75
15 They Smell It	.30	.75
16 Another Happy Customer	.30	.75
17 Author, Author	.30	.75
18 Who's The Champ	.15	.75
19 Rocky Rocky Rocky	.30	.75
20 Action, Rock	.30	.75
21 The People's Host	.30	.75
22 Hot, Hot, Hot	.30	.75
23 Getting Cheffy With It	.30	.75
24 The Best-Selling Author	.30	.75
25 The People's Show	.30	.75
26 Check Right In	.30	.75
27 Stretch 'Em Out, Rock	.30	.75
28 Electrifying	.30	.75
29 Rough Landing	.30	.75
30 Goin' Down	.30	.75
31 Off With The Pad	.30	.75
32 Table For One	.30	.75
33 Rock Bottom	.30	.75
34 Over The Top	.30	.75
35 His Own Medicine	.30	.75
36 Not A Friendly Hug	.30	.75
37 Who's The Game	.30	.75
38 The End In Near	.30	.75
39 Say Cheese	.30	.75
40 Respect	.30	.75
41 Taker Takes One	.30	.75
42 Some Pain For Kane	.30	.75
43 Big Blow To The Big Show	.30	.75
44 One Giant Hit For Mankind	.30	.75
45 Crippling The Crippler	.30	.75
46 Take That, Boss	.30	.75
47 Shane Can Smell It	.30	.75
48 Double Trouble	.30	.75
49 Olympic Zero	.30	.75
50 Turn That Camera Sideways And	.30	.75
51 Raw Is Who	.30	.75
52 Rock vs. Brooklyn Brawler	.30	.75
53 Rock vs. Faarooq	.30	.75
54 Rock vs. Triple H	.30	.75
55 Rock vs. Ken Shamrock & Mankind	.30	.75
56 Rock vs. Mr. Ass	.30	.75
57 Rock vs. Steve Austin	.30	.75
58 Rock vs. Mankind	.30	.75
59 Rock vs. Mankind	.30	.75
60 Rock vs. Chris Benoit	.30	.75
61 Rock vs. Triple H	.30	.75
62 Rock vs. Vince McMahon	.30	.75
63 Rock vs. Triple H	.30	.75
64 Rock vs. Mankind	.30	.75
65 Rock 'N' Sock Wins First Title	.30	.75
66 Rock 'N' Sock Wins Third Title	.30	.75
67 CL Rock on runway	.30	.75
68 CL Rock in crowd	.30	.75
69 CL Rock w/Mick Foley	.30	.75
70 CL Rock w/Kane	.30	.75

2000 Comic Images WWF Rock Solid Holofoil

71 CL Rock w/Steve Austin	.30	.75
72 CL Rock w/Stevie Richards	.30	.75
COMPLETE SET (6)	8.00	20.00
STATED ODDS 1:18		
C1 Rock Bottom	2.50	6.00
C2 Lethal Style	2.50	6.00
C3 The People's Champ	2.50	6.00
C4 The People's Elbow	2.50	6.00
C5 Kickin' Back	2.50	6.00
C6 Lights, Camera, Rock	2.50	6.00

2000 Comic Images WWF Rock Solid Promos

P1 Rock w/Sunglasses	1.50	4.00
P2 Rock on Ropes	1.50	4.00
P3 Rock Lounging	1.50	4.00

1999 Comic Images WWF SmackDown

COMPLETE SET (72)	6.00	15.00
UNOPENED BOX (36 PACKS)		
UNOPENED PACK (7 CARDS)		
*CHROMIUM: .5X TO 1.2X BASIC CARDS		
1 Title Card	.10	.25
2 Stone Cold Steve Austin	.60	1.50
3 The Rock	.60	1.50
4 The Big Show	.15	.40
5 Mankind	.30	.75
6 The Undertaker	.40	.75
7 X-Pac	.15	.40
8 Triple H	.50	1.25
9 The Road Dogg	.15	.40
10 Mr. Ass	.15	.40
11 Al Snow	.15	.40
12 Big Boss Man	.15	.40
13 Kane	.20	.50
14 D'Lo Brown	.10	.25
15 Droz	.10	.25
16 Edge	.50	1.25
17 Gangrel	.10	.25
18 Christian	.15	.40
19 Godfather	.15	.40
20 Prince Albert	.10	.25
21 Mark Henry	.10	.40
22 Jeff Jarrett	.15	.40
23 Chyna	.50	1.25
24 Mideon	.10	.25
25 Hardcore Holly	.15	.40
26 Test	.10	.25
27 Val Venis	.10	.25
28 Viscera	.10	.25
29 Too Cool	.10	.25
30 The Hardy Boyz	.20	.50
31 Debra	.20	.50
32 Tori	.20	.50
33 P.M.S.	.20	.50
34 Ken Shamrock	.20	.50
35 Jerry The King Lawler	.15	.40
36 Meat	.10	.25
37 Steve Blackman	.10	.25
38 Paul Bearer	.15	.40
39 Ivory	.20	.50
40 Shane McMahon	.15	.40
41 Vince McMahon	.30	.75

42 Stone Cold Steve Austin	.60	1.50
43 The Undertaker	.40	1.00
44 The Big Show	.15	.40
45 The Rock	.60	1.50
46 Mankind	.30	.75
47 Triple H/Chyna	.50	1.25
48 X-Pac	.15	.40
49 Kane	.20	.50
50 Ken Shamrock	.20	.50
51 Mean Street Posse	.10	.25
52 Test	.10	.25
53 Steve Austin/Undertaker	.40	1.00
54 The Rock/Triple H	.40	1.00
55 S.McMahon/The Rock/V.McMahon	.40	1.00
56 The Undertaker/Kane	.30	.75
57 Vince McMahon	.20	.60
58 The Rock/Mick Foley	.40	1.00
59 The Big Show	.15	.40
60 Stone Cold Steve Austin/The Rock	.40	1.00
61 Vince McMahon	.20	.50
62 Mankind/Vince McMahon	.30	.75
63 The Big Show	.20	.50
64 X-Pac/Shane McMahon	.10	.25
65 Mr. Ass	.10	.25
66 Vince McMahon/Shane McMahon	.20	.50
67 Stone Cold Steve Austin	.30	.75
68 The Rock	.40	1.00
69 The Brood	.30	.75
70 X-Pac/Road Dogg	.15	.40
71 Jeff Jarrett/Debra	.15	.40
72 Checklist	.10	.25

1999 Comic Images WWF SmackDown Chromium

COMPLETE SET (90)	6.00	15.00
1 Title Card	.12	.30
2 Stone Cold Steve Austin	.75	2.00
3 The Rock	.75	2.00
4 The Big Show	.20	.50
5 Mankind	.30	.75
6 The Undertaker	.40	1.00
7 X-Pac	.20	.50
8 Triple H	.60	1.50
9 The Road Dogg	.20	.50
10 Mr. Ass	.12	.30
11 Al Snow	.20	.50
12 Big Boss Man	.20	.50
13 Kane	.25	.60
14 D'Lo Brown	.12	.30
15 Droz	.12	.30
16 Edge	.60	1.50
17 Gangrel	.12	.30
18 Christian	.20	.50
19 Godfather	.20	.50
20 Prince Albert	.12	.30
21 Mark Henry	.12	.30
22 Jeff Jarrett	.20	.50
23 Chyna	.25	.60
24 Mideon	.12	.30
25 Hardcore Holly	.20	.50
26 Test	.12	.30
27 Val Venis	.12	.30
28 Viscera	.12	.30
29 Shawn Michaels	.40	1.00
30 The Hardy Boyz	.30	.75
31 Debra	.30	.75
32 Tori	.30	.75
33 P.M.S.	.30	.75

34 Ken Shamrock	.12	.30
35 Jerry The King Lawler	.20	.50
36 Meat	.12	.30
37 Steve Blackman	.12	.30
38 Paul Bearer	.20	.50
39 Ivory	.30	.75
40 Shane McMahon	.20	.50
41 Vince McMahon	.40	1.00
42 Stone Cold Steve Austin	.75	2.00
43 The Undertaker	.40	1.00
44 The Big Show	.20	.50
45 The Rock	.75	2.00
46 Mankind	.30	.75
47 Triple H/Chyna	.60	1.50
48 X-Pac	.20	.50
49 Kane	.25	.60
50 Ken Shamrock	.12	.30
51 Mean Street Posse	.12	.30
52 Test	.12	.30
53 Steve Austin/Undertaker	.50	1.25
54 The Rock/Triple H	.50	1.25
55 S.McMahon/The Rock/V.McMahon	.50	1.25
56 The Undertaker/Kane	.40	1.00
57 Vince McMahon	.30	.75
58 The Rock/Mick Foley	.30	.75
59 The Big Show	.25	.60
60 Stone Cold Steve Austin/The Rock	.50	1.25
61 Vince McMahon	.30	.75
62 Mankind/Vince McMahon	.30	.75
63 The Big Show	.25	.60
64 X-Pac/Shane McMahon	.20	.50
65 Mr. Ass	.12	.30
66 Vince McMahon/Shane McMahon	.25	.60
67 Stone Cold Steve Austin	.50	1.25
68 The Rock	.50	1.25
69 The Brood	.30	.75
70 X-Pac/Road Dogg	.20	.50
71 Jeff Jarrett/Debra	.20	.50
72 The Undertaker/Big Boss Man	.25	.60
73 Four-Way Match	.20	.50
74 Triple Threat Match	.20	.50
75 Shane McMahon/X-Pac	.20	.50
76 Triple H/Kane	.50	1.25
77 Stone Cold Steve Austin	.75	2.00
78 Mr. Ass	.20	.50
79 Road Dogg/Chyna	.20	.50
80 Road Dogg/X-Pac	.20	.50
81 Shane/Vince McMahon	.30	.75
82 Kane/The Big Show	.30	.75
83 X-Pac/Hardcore Holly	.20	.50
84 Triple H/The Rock	.60	1.50
85 Undertaker/Steve Austin	.60	1.50
86 Jeff Jarrett/Edge	.50	1.25
87 D'Lo Brown/Mideon	.12	.30
88 Big Boss Man/Al Snow	.20	.50
89 Acolytes/Hardy Boyz	.30	.75
90 Checklist	.12	.30

1999 Comic Images WWF SmackDown 22KT Gold Signatures

COMPLETE SET (6)	50.00	100.00
STATED ODDS 1:80		
1 Stone Cold Steve Austin	12.00	30.00
2 The Undertaker	10.00	25.00
3 The Rock	20.00	50.00
4 Triple H	12.00	30.00
5 The Big Show	12.00	30.00
6 Mankind	8.00	20.00
SE Stone Cold Steve Austin Special Edition		

1999 Comic Images WWF SmackDown Autographs

COMPLETE SET (8)		
STATED ODDS 1:80		
NNO Al Snow	6.00	15.00
NNO Big Boss Man	15.00	40.00
NNO D'Lo Brown	6.00	15.00
NNO Godfather	6.00	15.00
NNO The Hardy Boyz	15.00	40.00
NNO Hardcore Holly	6.00	15.00
NNO Ivory	12.00	30.00
NNO Tori	6.00	15.00

1999 Comic Images WWF SmackDown Chrome Inserts

COMPLETE SET (6)	5.00	12.00
STATED ODDS 1:18		
C1 Stone Cold Steve Austin	1.50	4.00
C2 The Corporate Ministry	1.00	2.50
C3 X-Pac/Kane	.60	1.50
C4 The Brood	1.00	2.50
C5 Mankind	1.00	2.50
C6 The Rock	1.50	4.00

1999 Comic Images WWF SmackDown Promos

P1 Stone Cold Steve Austin	1.50	4.00
(Non-Sport Update Exclusive)		
P2 The Rock	2.00	5.00
P3 Mankind	1.00	2.50

1999-05 Danbury Mint WWF/WWE 22kt Gold

COMPLETE SET (124)	250.00	500.00
1 Andre The Giant	3.00	8.00
2 Ken Shamrock	2.00	5.00
3 Stone Cold Steve Austin	4.00	10.00
3 Bob Backlund	2.00	5.00
4 The Rock	4.00	10.00
5 B.A. Billy Gunn	1.50	4.00
6 Road Dogg	1.50	4.00
7 Gorilla Monsoon	1.50	4.00
8 Val Venis	1.00	2.50
9 Al Snow	1.25	3.00
10 Kane	2.00	5.00
11 Jesse The Body Ventura	2.50	6.00
12 Undertaker	5.00	12.00
13 Shawn Michaels	6.00	15.00
14 Jerry The King Lawler	4.00	10.00
15 Lita	3.00	8.00
16 Fabulous Moolah	2.50	6.00
17 Rikishi Fatu	1.25	3.00
18 Big Boss Man	1.00	2.50
19 Jim Ross	4.00	10.00
20 The Iron Sheik	1.25	3.00
21 Hardy Boyz	3.00	8.00
22 Trish Stratus	6.00	15.00
23 Chris Jericho	4.00	10.00
24 Sgt. Slaughter	1.50	4.00
25 Triple H	2.50	6.00
26 Stephanie McMahon-Helmsley	2.00	5.00
27 Chris Benoit	8.00	20.00
28 Captain Lou Albano	2.50	6.00
29 George The Animal Steele	2.00	5.00

#	Name	Low	High
30	X-Pac	1.25	3.00
31	Vince McMahon	2.00	5.00
32	Shane O Mac	2.50	6.00
33	Stone Cold Steve Austin	3.00	8.00
33	Bob Backlund	2.00	5.00
34	Chyna	3.00	8.00
35	Dudley Boyz	2.50	6.00
36	British Bulldog	2.50	6.00
37	Jimmy Superfly Snuka	1.50	4.00
38	Mankind	4.00	10.00
39	Tazz	2.00	5.00
40	Big Show	1.50	4.00
41	Kurt Angle	2.50	6.00
42	Eddie Guerrero	4.00	10.00
43	Debra	2.00	5.00
44	Mr. Fuji	1.25	3.00
45	The Godfather	2.50	6.00
46	Edge/Christian	2.50	6.00
47	Too Cool	1.25	3.00
48	Test	1.25	3.00
49	The Acolytes	1.50	4.00
50	Steve Blackman	2.50	6.00
51	William Regal	2.00	5.00
52	Ric Flair	5.00	12.00
53	Tajiri	2.00	5.00
54	Rhyno	1.25	3.00
55	Stacy Keibler	6.00	15.00
56	K-Kwik	1.25	3.00
57	Crash Holly	1.25	3.00
58	Molly Holly	1.50	4.00
59	Albert	1.50	4.00
60	Perry Saturn	2.00	5.00
61	Booker T	2.50	6.00
62	Kaientai	1.25	3.00
63	Jacqueline	1.25	3.00
64	Steven Richards	1.25	3.00
65	Raven	1.50	4.00
66	Rob Van Dam	2.00	5.00
67	Earl Hebner	2.50	6.00
68	Spike Dudley	1.25	3.00
69	Hardcore Holly	3.00	8.00
70	Linda McMahon	1.50	4.00
71	Hollywood Hulk Hogan	12.00	30.00
72	Nidia	2.50	6.00
73	Garrison Cade	4.00	10.00
74	Luther Reigns	4.00	10.00
75	Eric Bischoff	3.00	8.00
76	Gail Kim	8.00	20.00
77	Matt Hardy	2.50	6.00
78	Scott Steiner	8.00	20.00
79	Tyson Tomko	6.00	15.00
80	Miss Jackie	3.00	8.00
81	Ivory	4.00	10.00
82	Billy/Chuck	2.00	5.00
83	Chavo Guerrero	3.00	8.00
84	Jamie Noble	2.00	5.00
85	Mark Henry	3.00	8.00
86	Tommy Dreamer	2.50	6.00
87	Diamond Dallas Page	2.00	5.00
88	Mark Jindrak	2.50	6.00
89	Victoria	2.50	6.00
90	Kevin Nash	3.00	8.00
91	Eugene	3.00	8.00
92	John Cena	6.00	15.00
93	Rey Mysterio	4.00	10.00
94	Muhammad Hassan	5.00	12.00
95	The Hurricane	2.00	5.00
96	Matt Morgan	2.50	6.00

#	Name	Low	High
97	Sable	5.00	12.00
98	Rene/Kenzo	2.50	6.00
99	Billy Kidman	2.00	5.00
100	Goldust	2.00	5.00
101	Theodore Long	2.50	6.00
102	JBL	6.00	15.00
103	Lance Storm	2.00	5.00
104	Zach Gowen	3.00	8.00
105	FBI	1.25	3.00
106	Edge	6.00	15.00
107	Randy Orton	2.50	6.00
108	Maven	1.50	4.00
109	La Resistance	2.00	5.00
110	Chavo Guerrero	3.00	8.00
111	Basham Brothers	2.50	6.00
112	Bubba Ray Dudley	2.50	6.00
113	The Coach	4.00	10.00
114	Heidenreich	5.00	12.00
115	Benjamin/Haas	2.50	6.00
116	Jazz	2.50	6.00
117	Batista	2.50	6.00
118	Goldberg	6.00	15.00
119	Torrie Wilson	4.00	10.00
120	Brock Lesnar	3.00	8.00
B1	Mankind Bonus	15.00	40.00
B2	Cactus Jack Bonus	15.00	40.00

1991 Diamond WWF SuperStars Stickers

#	Name	Low	High
	COMPLETE SET (150)	12.00	30.00
1	Hulk Hogan	.60	1.50
2	Hulk Hogan (Puzzle)	.60	1.50
3	Hulk Hogan (Puzzle)	.60	1.50
4	Hulk Hogan (Puzzle)	.60	1.50
5	Hulk Hogan (Puzzle)	.60	1.50
6	Nasty Boys	.12	.30
7	Nasty Boys	.12	.30
8	Earthquake	.12	.30
9	Earthquake	.12	.30
10	Earthquake	.12	.30
11	Jimmy Hart	.20	.50
12	Dino Bravo	.12	.30
13	Dino Bravo (Puzzle)	.12	.30
14	Dino Bravo (Puzzle)	.12	.30
15	British Bulldog (Puzzle)	.15	.40
16	British Bulldog (Puzzle)	.15	.40
17	British Bulldog (Puzzle)	.15	.40
18	British Bulldog (Puzzle)	.15	.40
19	British Bulldog	.15	.40
20	British Bulldog	.15	.40
21	Bobby The Brain Heenan	.15	.40
22	Mr. Perfect	.20	.50
23	Mr. Perfect (Puzzle)	.20	.50
24	Mr. Perfect (Puzzle)	.20	.50
25	Texas Tornado	.15	.40
26	Texas Tornado (Puzzle)	.15	.40
27	Texas Tornado (Puzzle)	.15	.40
28	Tugboat	.12	.30
29	Tugboat (Puzzle)	.12	.30
30	Tugboat (Puzzle)	.12	.30
31	Hacksaw Jim Duggan (Puzzle)	.15	.40
32	Hacksaw Jim Duggan (Puzzle)	.15	.40
33	Hacksaw Jim Duggan (Puzzle)	.15	.40
34	Hacksaw Jim Duggan (Puzzle)	.15	.40
35	Hacksaw Jim Duggan	.15	.40
36	Big Boss Man (Puzzle)	.12	.30
37	Big Boss Man (Puzzle)	.12	.30
38	Big Boss Man	.12	.30

#	Name	Low	High
39	Big Boss Man	.12	.30
40	Power & Glory (Puzzle)	.12	.30
41	Power & Glory (Puzzle)	.12	.30
42	Power & Glory (Puzzle)	.12	.30
43	Power & Glory (Puzzle)	.12	.30
44	Hercules	.12	.30
45	Paul Roma	.12	.30
46	Slick	.12	.30
47	Ultimate Warrior (Puzzle)	.40	1.00
48	Ultimate Warrior (Puzzle)	.40	1.00
49	Ultimate Warrior (Puzzle)	.40	1.00
50	Ultimate Warrior (Puzzle)	.40	1.00
51	Ultimate Warrior (Puzzle)	.40	1.00
52	Ultimate Warrior (Puzzle)	.40	1.00
53	Ultimate Warrior	.40	1.00
54	Ultimate Warrior (Puzzle)	.40	1.00
55	Ultimate Warrior (Puzzle)	.40	1.00
56	Ultimate Warrior (Puzzle)	.40	1.00
57	Ultimate Warrior (Puzzle)	.40	1.00
58	Rockers (Puzzle)	.20	.50
59	Rockers (Puzzle)	.20	.50
60	Rockers (Puzzle)	.20	.50
61	Rockers (Puzzle)	.20	.50
62	Marty Jannetty	.12	.30
63	Shawn Michaels	.20	.50
64	Rockers	.20	.50
65	Rockers	.20	.50
66	The Model Rick Martel (Puzzle)	.12	.30
67	The Model Rick Martel (Puzzle)	.12	.30
68	The Model Rick Martel (Puzzle)	.12	.30
69	The Model Rick Martel (Puzzle)	.12	.30
70	The Model Rick Martel	.12	.30
71	The Model Rick Martel	.12	.30
72	The Model Rick Martel	.12	.30
73	Hulk Hogan	.60	1.50
74	Hulk Hogan (Puzzle)	.60	1.50
75	Hulk Hogan (Puzzle)	.60	1.50
76	Hulk Hogan (Puzzle)	.60	1.50
77	Hulk Hogan (Puzzle)	.60	1.50
78	Hulk Hogan	.60	1.50
79	Hulk Hogan	.60	1.50
80	Hulk Hogan (Puzzle)	.60	1.50
81	Hulk Hogan (Puzzle)	.60	1.50
82	Hulk Hogan (Puzzle)	.60	1.50
83	Hulk Hogan (Puzzle)	.60	1.50
84	Warlord	.12	.30
85	Warlord	.12	.30
86	Barbarian	.12	.30
87	Barbarian	.12	.30
88	Orient Express	.12	.30
89	Orient Express	.12	.30
90	Mr. Fuji	.12	.30
91	Superfly Jimmy Snuka (Puzzle)	.20	.50
92	Superfly Jimmy Snuka (Puzzle)	.20	.50
93	Superfly Jimmy Snuka	.20	.50
94	Superfly Jimmy Snuka	.20	.50
95	Bushwackers (Puzzle)	.12	.30
96	Bushwackers (Puzzle)	.12	.30
97	Bushwackers (Puzzle)	.12	.30
98	Bushwackers (Puzzle)	.12	.30
99	Bushwackers	.12	.30
100	Macho Man	.40	1.00
101	Macho Man (Puzzle)	.40	1.00
102	Macho Man (Puzzle)	.40	1.00
103	Macho Man & Queen Sherri	.40	1.00
104	Sensational Queen Sherri	.15	.40
105	Sensational Queen Sherri	.15	.40
106	Million Dollar Man (Puzzle)	.15	.40

#	Name	Low	High
107	Million Dollar Man (Puzzle)	.15	.40
108	Million Dollar Man (Puzzle)	.15	.40
109	Million Dollar Man (Puzzle)	.15	.40
110	Million Dollar Man Ted DiBiase	.15	.40
111	Million Dollar Man Ted DiBiase	.15	.40
112	Rowdy Roddy Piper (Puzzle)	.50	1.25
113	Rowdy Roddy Piper (Puzzle)	.50	1.25
114	Rowdy Roddy Piper	.50	1.25
115	Legion of Doom	.20	.50
116	Animal	.20	.50
117	Legion of Doom	.20	.50
118	Legion of Doom	.20	.50
119	Legion of Doom (Puzzle)	.20	.50
120	Legion of Doom (Puzzle)	.20	.50
121	Legion of Doom (Puzzle)	.20	.50
122	Legion of Doom (Puzzle)	.20	.50
123	Haku (Puzzle)	.12	.30
124	Haku (Puzzle)	.12	.30
125	Haku	.12	.30
126	Virgil (Puzzle)	.12	.30
127	Virgil (Puzzle)	.12	.30
128	Sgt. Slaughter (Puzzle)	.20	.50
129	Sgt. Slaughter (Puzzle)	.20	.50
130	Sgt. Slaughter (Puzzle)	.20	.50
131	Sgt. Slaughter (Puzzle)	.20	.50
132	Sgt. Slaughter	.20	.50
133	Sgt. Slaughter	.20	.50
134	Sgt. Slaughter	.20	.50
135	Jake The Snake Roberts (Puzzle)	.25	.60
136	Jake The Snake Roberts (Puzzle)	.25	.60
137	Jake The Snake Roberts	.25	.60
138	Jake The Snake Roberts (Puzzle)	.25	.60
139	Jake The Snake Roberts (Puzzle)	.25	.60
140	Jake The Snake Roberts (Puzzle)	.25	.60
141	Jake The Snake Roberts (Puzzle)	.25	.60
142	Koko B. Ware	.12	.30
143	Koko B. Ware	.12	.30
144	The Undertaker (Puzzle)	.50	1.25
145	The Undertaker (Puzzle)	.50	1.25
146	Undertaker/Paul Bearer (Puzzle)	.50	1.25
147	Undertaker/Paul Bearer (Puzzle)	.50	1.25
148	Undertaker/Paul Bearer (Puzzle)	.50	1.25
149	Undertaker/Paul Bearer (Puzzle)	.50	1.25
150	Paul Bearer	.15	.40

2002 Doritos WWF Super Stars

#	Name	Low	High
	COMPLETE SET (12)	5.00	12.00
1	The Rock	.75	2.00
2	Stone Cold Steve Austin	.75	2.00
3	Kurt Angle	.50	1.25
4	Booker T	.25	.60
5	Triple H	.75	2.00
6	Edge	.50	1.25
7	Rob Van Dam	.25	.60
8	Chris Jericho	.40	1.00
9	Undertaker	.50	1.25
10	Jeff Hardy	.40	1.00
11	Lita	.75	2.00
12	Trish Stratus	1.25	3.00

1998 DuoCards WWF

#	Name	Low	High
	COMPLETE SET (72)	50.00	100.00
	UNOPENED BOX (30 PACKS)		
	UNOPENED PACK (7 CARDS)		
1	WWF Attitude	.10	.25
2	Mr. Vince McMahon	.30	.75
3	Commissioner Slaughter	.20	.50
4	Mr. Pat Patterson	.10	.25

5 Mr. Gerald Brisco	.15	.40
6 WWF Champion	.60	1.50
7 WWF Tag Team Champions	.20	.50
8 WWF IC Champ/The Rock	15.00	40.00
9 WWF European Champion	.10	.25
10 WWF Light Heavyweight Champion	.10	.25
11 Stone Cold Steve Austin	3.00	8.00
12 Undertaker	3.00	8.00
13 Shawn Michaels	2.50	6.00
14 Ken Shamrock	2.00	5.00
15 The Rock	15.00	40.00
16 Triple H	.20	.50
17 Kane	.20	.50
18 Owen Hart	.30	1.00
19 Mankind	.30	.75
20 Dude Love	.30	.75
21 Cactus Jack	1.50	4.00
22 Sable	.30	.75
23 X-Pac	.20	.50
24 D'Lo Brown	.10	.25
25 Mark Henry	.10	.25
26 Bradshaw	.20	.50
27 The Godfather	.10	.25
28 Double J	.10	.25
29 Dustin Runnels	.10	.25
30 Marvelous Marc Mero	.10	.25
31 Lethal Weapon Steve Blackman	.10	.25
32 Al Snow and Head	.15	.40
33 Taka Michinoku	.10	.25
34 Badd Ass Billy Gunn	.20	.50
35 Savio Vega	.10	.25
36 Dr. Death Steve Williams	.10	.25
37 Steven Regal	.15	.40
38 Faarooq	.15	.40
39 Scorpio	.10	.25
40 Kurrgan	.10	.25
41 Luna	.10	.25
42 Dan The Beast Severn	.15	.40
43 Golga	.10	.25
44 Giant Silva	.10	.25
45 Road Dog Jesse James	.20	.50
46 Edge RWT	.40	1.00
47 Darren Droz Drozdov RWT	.10	.25
48 Val Venis RWT	.15	.40
49 Papi Chulo RWT	.10	.25
50 Tiger Ali Singh RWT	.15	.40
51 D-Generation X FW	.20	.50
52 The Nation FW	.20	.60
53 Kaientai FW	.10	.25
54 Kane w/Mankind DD	.20	.60
55 New Age Outlaws DD	.20	.50
56 Headbangers DD	.10	.25
57 D.O.A. DD	.10	.25
58 L.O.D. 2000 DD	.15	.40
59 Southern Justice DD	.10	.25
60 Too Much DD	.10	.25
61 Los Boricuas DD	.10	.25
62 Paul Bearer BBB	.10	.25
63 Chyna BBB	2.50	6.00
64 Jackyl BBB	.10	.25
65 Jim Cornette BBB	.15	.40
66 Yamaguchi-San BBB	.10	.25
67 Jacqueline BBB	.15	.40
68 Paul Ellering BBB	.10	.25
69 Jim Ross MTR	.15	.40
70 Jerry The King Lawler MTR	1.50	4.00
71 Raw is War	.10	.25
72 Checklist	.10	.25

1998 DuoCards WWF Autographs

STATED ODDS 1:100

NNO Billy Gunn	10.00	25.00
NNO Chyna	60.00	120.00
NNO Hawk	150.00	300.00
NNO Jacqueline	5.00	12.00
NNO Mankind	25.00	60.00
NNO Owen Hart	400.00	800.00
NNO Paul Bearer	50.00	100.00
NNO Road Dog Jesse James	12.00	30.00
NNO Sable	15.00	40.00
NNO Sable - Unsigned	6.00	15.00
NNO Steve Blackman	10.00	25.00
NNO The Rock	1500.00	3000.00
NNO Redemption Card	2.00	5.00

1998 DuoCards WWF Stone Cold's Greatest Hitz

COMPLETE SET (8)	15.00	30.00
STATED ODDS 1:20		
OMNI1 1996 King of the Ring	2.00	5.00
OMNI2 WM 13 Submission Match	2.00	5.00
OMNI3 1998 Royal Rumble	2.00	5.00
OMNI4 Wrestlemania XIV	2.00	5.00
OMNI5 King of the Ring	2.00	5.00
OMNI6 Raw is War	2.00	5.00
BONUS1 D-X In Your House	2.00	5.00
BONUS2 Arrest That Hyperlink	2.00	5.00

1998 DuoCards WWF Promos

1 Stone Cold Steve Austin	3.00	8.00
2 Sable	1.25	3.00
3 D-Generation X	2.00	5.00
4 Dude Love/Steve Austin	2.00	5.00

1999 Eastman Kodak WWF Collectible Motion

COMPLETE SET (6)	15.00	40.00
NNO Mankind	3.00	8.00
NNO The Rock	6.00	15.00
NNO Stone Cold Hell Yeah	6.00	15.00
NNO Stone Cold Stuns McMahon	6.00	15.00
NNO The Undertaker	5.00	12.00

2004 Edibas WWE Lamincards

COMPLETE SET (120)	15.00	40.00
UNOPENED BOX (24 PACKS)		
UNOPENED PACK (4 CARDS)		
1 Chris Benoit	.75	2.00
2 Randy Orton	.75	2.00
3 Kane	1.25	3.00
4 Chris Jericho	.75	2.00
5 Ric Flair	1.50	4.00
6 Rob Conway	.30	.75
7 Val Venis	.50	1.25
8 Chuck Palumbo	.50	1.25
9 Rosey	.30	.75
10 Tyson Tomko	.50	1.25
11 Shawn Michaels	2.00	5.00
12 The Rock	2.00	5.00
13 Shelton Benjamin	.30	.75
14 Christian	1.00	2.50
15 Mark Henry	.50	1.25
16 Test	.50	1.25
17 A-Train	.30	.75
18 Eric Bischoff	.50	1.25
19 Jonathan Coachman	.30	.75

20 Jerry The King Lawler	.75	2.00
21 Jim Ross	.50	1.25
22 Gail Kim	1.25	3.00
23 Ivory	1.25	3.00
24 Jazz	.75	2.00
25 Lita	2.00	5.00
26 Molly	1.50	4.00
27 Nidia	.75	2.00
28 Stacy Keibler	3.00	8.00
29 Trish Stratus	3.00	8.00
30 Victoria	1.50	4.00
31 Undertaker	1.50	4.00
32 JBL	.75	2.00
33 Eddie Guerrero	1.50	4.00
34 Booker T	1.25	3.00
35 Kurt Angle	1.25	3.00
36 John Cena	2.00	5.00
37 Rob Van Dam	1.25	3.00
38 Rene Dupree	.50	1.25
39 Rey Mysterio	.75	2.00
40 Paul Heyman	.30	.75
41 Hardcore Holly	.50	1.25
42 Paul London	.30	.75
43 Charlie Haas	.30	.75
44 Bubba Ray	.50	1.25
45 Billy Kidman	.30	.75
46 D-Von Dudley	.50	1.25
47 Chavo Guerrero	.50	1.25
48 Nunzio	.30	.75
49 Scotty 2 Hotty	.50	1.25
50 Johnny Stamboli	.30	.75
51 Danny Basham	.30	.75
52 Luther Reigns	.30	.75
53 Orlando Jordan	.30	.75
54 Akio	.30	.75
55 Big Show	1.25	3.00
56 Rico	.30	.75
57 Tazz	.50	1.25
58 Kenzo Suzuki	.30	.75
59 Theodore Long	.30	.75
60 Jon Heidenreich	.30	.75
61 Funaki	.50	1.25
62 Spike Dudley	.50	1.25
63 Hiroko	.30	.75
64 Dawn Marie	.75	2.00
65 Miss Jackie	1.25	3.00
66 Torrie Wilson	3.00	8.00
67 Chris Benoit LOGO	.75	2.00
68 Randy Orton LOGO	.75	2.00
69 Triple H LOGO	2.00	5.00
70 Batista LOGO	1.25	3.00
71 Kane LOGO	1.25	3.00
72 Chris Jericho LOGO	.75	2.00
73 Ric Flair LOGO	1.50	4.00
74 Shawn Michaels LOGO	2.00	5.00
75 Rob Conway LOGO	.30	.75
76 Stacy Keibler LOGO	3.00	8.00
77 Ivory LOGO	1.25	3.00
78 Molly Holly LOGO	1.50	4.00
79 Eddie Guerrero LOGO	1.50	4.00
80 Undertaker LOGO	1.50	4.00
81 Booker T LOGO	1.25	3.00
82 Kurt Angle LOGO	1.25	3.00
83 Rob Van Dam LOGO	1.25	3.00
84 Rey Mysterio LOGO	.75	2.00
85 Hardcore Holly LOGO	.50	1.25
86 Paul London LOGO	.30	.75
87 Billy Kidman LOGO	.30	.75

88 Dawn Marie LOGO	.75	2.00
89 Miss Jackie LOGO	1.25	3.00
90 Torrie Wilson LOGO	3.00	8.00
91 Chavo Guerrero LOGO	.50	1.25
92 Chuck Palumbo LOGO	.50	1.25
93 Mark Henry LOGO	.50	1.25
94 Orlando Jordan LOGO	.30	.75
95 Rico LOGO	.30	.75
96 The Rock LOGO	2.00	5.00
97 Scotty 2 Hotty LOGO	.50	1.25
98 Lita LOGO	2.00	5.00
99 Victoria LOGO	1.50	4.00
100 Gail Kim LOGO	1.25	3.00
101 Benoit vs. Flair IA	1.50	4.00
102 Jericho vs. Michaels IA	2.00	5.00
103 Hurricane vs. The Rock IA	2.00	5.00
104 Orton vs. Benoit IA	.75	2.00
105 Kane vs. Jericho IA	1.25	3.00
106 Test vs. Richards IA	.50	1.25
107 HHH vs. Benoit IA	2.00	5.00
108 Benjamin vs. Orton IA	.75	2.00
109 Conway vs. Hurricane IA	.30	.75
110 Jericho vs. Edge IA	1.25	3.00
111 Guerrero vs. Angle IA	1.50	4.00
112 Orton vs. The Rock IA	2.00	5.00
113 Akio vs. Moore IA	.30	.75
114 Big Show vs. RVD IA	1.25	3.00
115 Dudleys vs. La Resistance IA	.40	1.00
116 Cena vs. Big Show IA	2.00	5.00
117 JBL vs. Mysterio IA	.75	2.00
118 Nunzio vs. Chavo IA	.50	1.25
119 Booker T vs. Guerrero IA	1.50	4.00
120 Undertaker vs. Cena IA	2.00	5.00

2005 Edibas WWE Lamincards

COMPLETE SET (150)	15.00	40.00
UNOPENED BOX (24 PACKS)		
UNOPENED PACK (4 CARDS)		
1 Al Snow	.30	.75
2 Batista	.75	2.00
3 Booker T	.50	1.25
4 Candice	2.00	5.00
5 Chris Benoit	1.25	3.00
6 Christian	1.00	2.50
7 Doug Basham	.30	.75
8 Eddie Guerrero	1.50	4.00
9 Funaki	.30	.75
10 Hardcore Holly	.50	1.25
11 Heidenreich	.30	.75
12 John Bradshaw Layfield	.50	1.25
13 Joey Mercury	.30	.75
14 Johnny Nitro	.30	.75
15 Melina	1.50	4.00
16 Michelle McCool	1.50	4.00
17 Nunzio	.30	.75
18 Orlando Jordan	.30	.75
19 Paul London	.30	.75
20 Randy Orton	.75	2.00
21 Rey Mysterio	1.00	2.50
22 Scotty 2 Hotty	.50	1.25
23 Sylvain Grenier	.30	.75
24 Torrie Wilson	3.00	8.00
25 Undertaker	1.50	4.00
26 William Regal	.50	1.25
27 Antonio	.30	.75
28 Big Show	1.25	3.00
29 Carlito	.30	.75
30 Chris Jericho	1.00	2.50

#	Card		
31	Christy Hemme	3.00	8.00
32	Danny Basham	.30	.75
33	Edge	1.00	2.50
34	Eugene	.75	2.00
35	Gene Snitzky	.30	.75
36	Jerry The King Lawler	.75	2.00
37	John Cena	2.00	5.00
38	Kane	1.00	2.50
39	Kerwin White	.30	.75
40	Kurt Angle	1.25	3.00
41	Lita	2.00	5.00
42	Rene Dupree	.30	.75
43	Ric Flair	1.50	4.00
44	Rob Van Dam	1.00	2.50
45	Romeo	.30	.75
46	Rosey	.30	.75
47	Shawn Michaels	1.50	4.00
48	Shelton Benjamin	.30	.75
49	Stacy Keibler	3.00	8.00
50	Tajiri	.30	.75
51	The Hurricane	.30	.75
52	The Rock	2.00	5.00
53	Triple H	1.50	4.00
54	Trish Stratus	3.00	8.00
55	Tyson Tomko	.30	.75
56	Val Venis	.50	1.25
57	Victoria	2.00	5.00
58	Viscera	.30	.75
59	Sicilian Slide	.30	.75
60	The Worm	.50	1.25
61	Clothesline from Hell	.50	1.25
62	Tombstone Piledriver	1.50	4.00
63	Frog Splash	1.50	4.00
64	Crippler Crossface	1.25	3.00
65	ChokeSlam	1.50	4.00
66	Scissors Kick	.50	1.25
67	619	1.50	4.00
68	Flying Headbutt	1.25	3.00
69	Book-End	.50	1.25
70	The Walls of Jericho	1.00	2.50
71	Moonsault	2.00	5.00
72	Gory Bomb	.40	1.00
73	FU	2.00	5.00
74	Rock Bottom	2.00	5.00
75	Super Splash	.30	.75
76	Sweet Chin Music	1.50	4.00
77	Show Stopper	1.25	3.00
78	Ankle Lock	1.25	3.00
79	Twist of Fate	3.00	8.00
80	Chick Kick	3.00	8.00
81	Five Star Frog Splash	1.00	2.50
82	Bear Hug	.30	.75
83	Clothesline	.20	.50
84	Head Lock	.30	.75
85	Boston Crab	1.50	4.00
86	Chinlock	.20	.50
87	Jumping Foot Stomp	.20	.50
88	Shoulder Block	.30	.75
89	Right Hand	.20	.50
90	Hip Toss	2.00	5.00
91	Sleeper Hold	.30	.75
92	Hard Kick	.20	.50
93	Leap Frog	.20	.50
94	Head Lock	1.00	2.50
95	Pescado	1.00	2.50
96	Chinlock	.30	.75
97	Spinebuster	2.00	5.00
98	Chinlock	.20	.50
99	Vertical Suplex	.20	.50
100	Moonsault	1.00	2.50
101	One Leg Boston Crab	1.25	3.00
102	One Leg Boston Crab	.30	.75
103	Rope Walk	1.50	4.00
104	Bulldog	.20	.50
105	Drop Kick	1.00	2.50
106	Clothesline	.30	.75
107	Back Kick	1.00	2.50
108	Clothesline	.30	.75
109	Forearm	1.25	3.00
110	Face Slam	.20	.50
111	Head Lock	.20	.50
112	Belly to Back Suplex	1.50	4.00
113	Shoulder Tackle	2.00	5.00
114	Armbar	1.50	4.00
115	Big Boot	1.50	4.00
116	Armbar	1.50	4.00
117	Sharpshooter	2.00	5.00
118	Gorilla Press Slam	1.25	3.00
119	Double Flying Clothesline	.20	.50
120	Batista	.75	2.00
121	Booker T	.50	1.25
122	Chris Benoit	1.25	3.00
123	Christian	1.00	2.50
124	Eddie Guerrero	1.50	4.00
125	John Bradshaw Layfield	.50	1.25
126	Randy Orton	.30	.75
127	Rey Mysterio	1.00	2.50
128	Undertaker	1.50	4.00
129	Big Show	1.25	3.00
130	Carlito	.30	.75
131	John Cena	2.00	5.00
132	Kane	1.00	2.50
133	Kurt Angle	1.25	3.00
134	Shawn Michaels	1.50	4.00
135	The Hurricane	.30	.75
136	Triple H	1.50	4.00
137	Val Venis	.50	1.25
138	The Rock	2.00	5.00
139	Hulk Hogan	2.00	5.00
140	Sgt. Slaughter	.75	2.00
141	The Iron Sheik	.75	2.00
142	WWE Champion	.20	.50
143	WWE Intercontinental Champion	.20	.50
144	WWE Tag Team Champion	.20	.50
145	WWE Champion	.20	.50
146	WWE Tag Team Champion	.20	.50
147	WWE U.S. Champion	.20	.50
148	WWE Heavyweight Champion	.20	.50
149	WWE Cruiserweight Champion	.20	.50
150	WWE Women's Champion	.20	.50

2007 eTopps WWE

	COMPLETE SET W/O AU (6)	50.00	100.00
	STATED PRINT RUN 999 SERIAL #'d SETS		
	WILSON AU STATED PRINT RUN TO 867*		
1	Batista	2.00	5.00
2	John Cena	3.00	8.00
3	Shawn Michaels	8.00	20.00
4	The Rock	125.00	250.00
5	Undertaker	10.00	25.00
6	Rowdy Roddy Piper	2.50	6.00
7	Torrie Wilson AU/867	50.00	100.00

1991 Euroflash WWF SuperStars Stickers

COMPLETE SET (150)
UNOPENED BOX (98 PACKS)
UNOPENED PACK (6 STICKERS)

#	Sticker		
1	Hulk Hogan	.75	2.00
2	Hulk Hogan (Puzzle)	.75	2.00
3	Hulk Hogan (Puzzle)	.75	2.00
4	Hulk Hogan (Puzzle)	.75	2.00
5	Hulk Hogan (Puzzle)	.75	2.00
6	Nasty Boys	.15	.40
7	Nasty Boys	.15	.40
8	Earthquake	.15	.40
9	Earthquake	.15	.40
10	Earthquake	.15	.40
11	Jimmy Hart	.25	.60
12	Dino Bravo	.15	.40
13	Dino Bravo (Puzzle)	.15	.40
14	Dino Bravo (Puzzle)	.15	.40
15	British Bulldog (Puzzle)	.20	.50
16	British Bulldog (Puzzle)	.20	.50
17	British Bulldog (Puzzle)	.20	.50
18	British Bulldog (Puzzle)	.20	.50
19	British Bulldog	.20	.50
20	British Bulldog	.20	.50
21	Bobby The Brain Heenan	.20	.50
22	Mr. Perfect	.25	.60
23	Mr. Perfect (Puzzle)	.25	.60
24	Mr. Perfect (Puzzle)	.25	.60
25	Texas Tornado	.20	.50
26	Texas Tornado (Puzzle)	.20	.50
27	Texas Tornado (Puzzle)	.20	.50
28	Tugboat	.15	.40
29	Tugboat (Puzzle)	.15	.40
30	Tugboat (Puzzle)	.15	.40
31	Hacksaw Jim Duggan (Puzzle)	.20	.50
32	Hacksaw Jim Duggan (Puzzle)	.20	.50
33	Hacksaw Jim Duggan (Puzzle)	.20	.50
34	Hacksaw Jim Duggan (Puzzle)	.20	.50
35	Hacksaw Jim Duggan	.20	.50
36	Big Boss Man (Puzzle)	.15	.40
37	Big Boss Man (Puzzle)	.15	.40
38	Big Boss Man	.15	.40
39	Big Boss Man	.15	.40
40	Power & Glory (Puzzle)	.15	.40
41	Power & Glory (Puzzle)	.15	.40
42	Power & Glory (Puzzle)	.15	.40
43	Power & Glory (Puzzle)	.15	.40
44	Hercules	.15	.40
45	Paul Roma	.15	.40
46	Slick	.15	.40
47	Ultimate Warrior (Puzzle)	.50	1.25
48	Ultimate Warrior (Puzzle)	.50	1.25
49	Ultimate Warrior (Puzzle)	.50	1.25
50	Ultimate Warrior (Puzzle)	.50	1.25
51	Ultimate Warrior (Puzzle)	.50	1.25
52	Ultimate Warrior (Puzzle)	.50	1.25
53	Ultimate Warrior	.50	1.25
54	Ultimate Warrior (Puzzle)	.50	1.25
55	Ultimate Warrior (Puzzle)	.50	1.25
56	Ultimate Warrior (Puzzle)	.50	1.25
57	Ultimate Warrior (Puzzle)	.50	1.25
58	Rockers (Puzzle)	.25	.60
59	Rockers (Puzzle)	.25	.60
60	Rockers (Puzzle)	.25	.60
61	Rockers (Puzzle)	.25	.60
62	Marty Jannetty	.15	.40
63	Shawn Michaels	.25	.60
64	Rockers	.25	.60
65	Rockers	.25	.60
66	The Model Rick Martel (Puzzle)	.15	.40
67	The Model Rick Martel (Puzzle)	.15	.40
68	The Model Rick Martel (Puzzle)	.15	.40
69	The Model Rick Martel (Puzzle)	.15	.40
70	The Model Rick Martel	.15	.40
71	The Model Rick Martel	.15	.40
72	The Model Rick Martel	.15	.40
73	Hulk Hogan	.75	2.00
74	Hulk Hogan (Puzzle)	.75	2.00
75	Hulk Hogan (Puzzle)	.75	2.00
76	Hulk Hogan (Puzzle)	.75	2.00
77	Hulk Hogan (Puzzle)	.75	2.00
78	Hulk Hogan	.75	2.00
79	Hulk Hogan	.75	2.00
80	Hulk Hogan (Puzzle)	.75	2.00
81	Hulk Hogan (Puzzle)	.75	2.00
82	Hulk Hogan (Puzzle)	.75	2.00
83	Hulk Hogan (Puzzle)	.75	2.00
84	Warlord	.15	.40
85	Warlord	.15	.40
86	Barbarian	.15	.40
87	Barbarian	.15	.40
88	Orient Express	.15	.40
89	Orient Express	.15	.40
90	Mr. Fuji	.15	.40
91	Superfly Jimmy Snuka (Puzzle)	.25	.60
92	Superfly Jimmy Snuka (Puzzle)	.25	.60
93	Superfly Jimmy Snuka	.25	.60
94	Superfly Jimmy Snuka	.25	.60
95	Bushwackers (Puzzle)	.15	.40
96	Bushwackers (Puzzle)	.15	.40
97	Bushwackers (Puzzle)	.15	.40
98	Bushwackers (Puzzle)	.15	.40
99	Bushwackers	.15	.40
100	Macho Man	.50	1.25
101	Macho Man (Puzzle)	.50	1.25
102	Macho Man (Puzzle)	.50	1.25
103	Macho Man & Queen Sherri	.50	1.25
104	Sensational Queen Sherri	.20	.50
105	Sensational Queen Sherri	.20	.50
106	Million Dollar Man (Puzzle)	.20	.50
107	Million Dollar Man (Puzzle)	.20	.50
108	Million Dollar Man (Puzzle)	.20	.50
109	Million Dollar Man (Puzzle)	.20	.50
110	Million Dollar Man Ted DiBiase	.20	.50
111	Million Dollar Man Ted DiBiase	.20	.50
112	Rowdy Roddy Piper (Puzzle)	.60	1.50
113	Rowdy Roddy Piper (Puzzle)	.60	1.50
114	Rowdy Roddy Piper	.60	1.50
115	Legion of Doom	.25	.60
116	Animal	.25	.60
117	Legion of Doom	.25	.60
118	Legion of Doom	.25	.60
119	Legion of Doom (Puzzle)	.25	.60
120	Legion of Doom (Puzzle)	.25	.60
121	Legion of Doom (Puzzle)	.25	.60
122	Legion of Doom (Puzzle)	.25	.60
123	Haku (Puzzle)	.15	.40
124	Haku (Puzzle)	.15	.40
125	Haku	.15	.40
126	Virgil (Puzzle)	.15	.40
127	Virgil (Puzzle)	.15	.40
128	Sgt. Slaughter (Puzzle)	.25	.60
129	Sgt. Slaughter (Puzzle)	.25	.60
130	Sgt. Slaughter (Puzzle)	.25	.60
131	Sgt. Slaughter (Puzzle)	.25	.60
132	Sgt. Slaughter	.25	.60
133	Sgt. Slaughter (Puzzle)	.25	.60
134	Sgt. Slaughter (Puzzle)	.25	.60
135	Jake The Snake Roberts (Puzzle)	.30	.75

#	Card	Lo	Hi
136	Jake The Snake Roberts (Puzzle)	.30	.75
137	Jake The Snake Roberts (Puzzle)	.30	.75
138	Jake The Snake Roberts (Puzzle)	.30	.75
139	Jake The Snake Roberts (Puzzle)	.30	.75
140	Jake The Snake Roberts (Puzzle)	.30	.75
141	Jake The Snake Roberts (Puzzle)	.30	.75
142	Koko B. Ware	.15	.40
143	Koko B. Ware	.15	.40
144	The Undertaker (Puzzle)	.60	1.50
145	The Undertaker (Puzzle)	.60	1.50
146	Undertaker/Paul Bearer (Puzzle)	.60	1.50
147	Undertaker/Paul Bearer (Puzzle)	.60	1.50
148	Undertaker/Paul Bearer (Puzzle)	.60	1.50
149	Undertaker/Paul Bearer (Puzzle)	.60	1.50
150	Paul Bearer	.20	.50

1964 Exhibit

#	Card	Lo	Hi
	COMPLETE SET (16)	50.00	100.00
NNO	Andre Drapp	5.00	12.00
NNO	Antonio Rocca	3.00	8.00
NNO	Bruno Sammartino	15.00	40.00
NNO	Buddy Rogers	8.00	20.00
NNO	Count Billy Vargo	3.00	8.00
NNO	Cowboy Bob Ellis	3.00	8.00
NNO	Don Leo Jonathan	3.00	8.00
NNO	Enrique Torres	3.00	8.00
NNO	Hard Boiled Haggerty	3.00	8.00
NNO	Haystacks Calhoun	6.00	15.00
NNO	Jerry Graham	3.00	8.00
NNO	Lou Thesz	8.00	20.00
NNO	Pat O'Connor	3.00	8.00
NNO	Pepper Gomez	3.00	8.00
NNO	Roy Heffernan	3.00	8.00
NNO	Sailor Art Thomas	3.00	8.00

2010 FCW Summer Slamarama

#	Card	Lo	Hi
NNO	Bo Rotunda	12.00	30.00
NNO	Darren Young	10.00	25.00
NNO	Duke Rotunda		
NNO	Heath Slater	8.00	20.00
NNO	Joe Hennig	12.00	30.00
NNO	Justin Angel	8.00	20.00
NNO	Kaval	10.00	25.00
NNO	Naomi Knight	30.00	75.00
NNO	Savannah	10.00	25.00
NNO	Skip Sheffield (Ryback)	8.00	20.00
NNO	Tyler Reks	8.00	20.00
NNO	Wade Barrett	10.00	25.00

2011 FCW Summer Slamarama

#	Card	Lo	Hi
NNO	AJ	100.00	200.00
NNO	Aksana	6.00	15.00
NNO	Bo Rotundo	6.00	15.00
NNO	Brad Maddox	4.00	10.00
NNO	Briley Pierce	3.00	8.00
NNO	Brodus Clay	5.00	12.00
NNO	Calvin Raines	2.50	6.00
NNO	Conor O'Brian	2.50	6.00
NNO	Damien Sandow	8.00	20.00
NNO	Dean Ambrose	20.00	50.00
NNO	Hunico	3.00	8.00
NNO	Husky Harris	75.00	150.00
NNO	Jinder Mahal	8.00	20.00
NNO	Kenneth Cameron	2.50	6.00
NNO	Leo Kruger	4.00	10.00
NNO	Mason Ryan	3.00	8.00
NNO	Peter Orlov	2.50	6.00
NNO	Raquel Diaz	3.00	8.00

#	Card	Lo	Hi
NNO	Richie Steamboat	6.00	15.00
NNO	Roman Leakee	100.00	200.00
NNO	Seth Rollins	75.00	150.00
NNO	Titus O'Neill	5.00	12.00
NNO	Xavier Woods	6.00	15.00

2012 FCW Summer Slamarama

#	Card	Lo	Hi
NNO	Bo Dallas	3.00	8.00
NNO	Brad Maddox	2.00	5.00
NNO	Briley Pierce	2.00	5.00
NNO	Caylee Turner	1.50	4.00
NNO	CJ Parker	1.50	4.00
NNO	Jake Carter	1.50	4.00
NNO	Mike Dalton	6.00	15.00
NNO	Paige	125.00	250.00
NNO	Raquel Diaz	3.00	8.00
NNO	Richie Steamboat	2.00	5.00
NNO	Rick Victor	1.50	4.00
NNO	Sofia Cortez	2.50	6.00
NNO	Summer Rae	30.00	75.00

2020 Finest WWE

#	Card	Lo	Hi
	COMPLETE SET W/O SP (100)	25.00	60.00
	COMMON SP (101-125)		
	*REFRACTOR: .5X TO 1.2X BASIC CARDS		
	*X-FRACTOR: .6X TO 1.5X BASIC CARDS		
	*BLUE/150: .75X TO 2X BASIC CARDS		
	*GREEN/99: 1X TO 2.5X BASIC CARDS		
	*ORANGE/50: 1.2X TO 3X BASIC CARDS		
	*BLACK/25: 4X TO 10X BASIC CARDS		
	*GOLD/10: UNPRICED DUE TO SCARCITY		
	*RED/5: UNPRICED DUE TO SCARCITY		
	*SUPERFR/1: UNPRICED DUE TO SCARCITY		
	SP STATED ODDS (101-125) 1:80		
1	Angel Garza	.60	1.50
2	Akam	.60	1.50
3	Aleister Black	1.00	2.50
4	Andrade	.75	2.00
5	Angelo Dawkins	.50	1.25
6	Asuka	2.00	5.00
7	Austin Theory	.75	2.00
8	Becky Lynch	2.00	5.00
9	Bianca Belair	1.25	3.00
10	Bobby Lashley	1.00	2.50
11	Murphy	.60	1.50
12	Charlotte Flair	2.00	5.00
13	Drew McIntyre	1.00	2.50
14	Edge	1.00	2.50
15	Erik	.50	1.25
16	Humberto Carrillo	.75	2.00
17	Ivar	.50	1.25
18	Kairi Sane	1.00	2.50
19	Kevin Owens	.60	1.50
20	Lana	1.25	3.00
21	Liv Morgan	1.25	3.00
22	Montez Ford	.50	1.25
23	Nia Jax	.75	2.00
24	R-Truth	.50	1.25
25	Randy Orton	1.25	3.00
26	Rezar	.50	1.25
27	Ricochet	.75	2.00
28	Riddick Moss	.50	1.25
29	Ruby Riott	.75	2.00
30	Samoa Joe	.75	2.00
31	Seth Rollins	1.00	2.50
32	Shayna Baszler	1.50	4.00
33	Zelina Vega	1.00	2.50
34	AJ Styles	1.50	4.00

#	Card	Lo	Hi
35	Alexa Bliss	3.00	8.00
36	Bayley	1.00	2.50
37	Big E	.50	1.25
38	Braun Strowman	1.25	3.00
39	The Fiend Bray Wyatt	1.50	4.00
40	Carmella	1.25	3.00
41	Cesaro	.50	1.25
42	Daniel Bryan	1.50	4.00
43	Dolph Ziggler	.50	1.25
44	Elias	1.00	2.50
45	Jeff Hardy	1.25	3.00
46	Jey Uso	.50	1.25
47	Jimmy Uso	.50	1.25
48	John Morrison	.50	1.25
49	King Corbin	.60	1.50
50	Kofi Kingston	.75	2.00
51	Lacey Evans	1.25	3.00
52	Mandy Rose	2.50	6.00
53	Matt Riddle	1.00	2.50
54	Mojo Rawley	.50	1.25
55	Mustafa Ali	.75	2.00
56	Naomi	1.00	2.50
57	Nikki Cross	1.00	2.50
58	Otis	.75	2.00
59	Robert Roode	.50	1.25
60	Roman Reigns	1.25	3.00
61	Sami Zayn	.60	1.50
62	Sasha Banks	2.50	6.00
63	Sheamus	.60	1.50
64	Shinsuke Nakamura	1.00	2.50
65	Shorty G	.50	1.25
66	Sonya Deville	1.25	3.00
67	Tamina	.60	1.50
68	The Miz	.75	2.00
69	Tucker	.50	1.25
70	Xavier Woods	.50	1.25
71	Adam Cole	1.25	3.00
72	Bobby Fish	.50	1.25
73	Cameron Grimes	.50	1.25
74	Candice LeRae	1.50	4.00
75	Chelsea Green	2.50	6.00
76	Dakota Kai	1.00	2.50
77	Damian Priest	.50	1.25
78	Dominik Dijakovic	.50	1.25
79	Finn Balor	1.25	3.00
80	Io Shirai	.75	2.00
81	Isaiah Swerve Scott	.60	1.50
82	Johnny Gargano	1.00	2.50
83	Kacy Catanzaro	1.00	2.50
84	Karrion Kross	1.00	2.50
85	Keith Lee	.50	1.25
86	Kushida	.60	1.50
87	Kyle O'Reilly	.60	1.50
88	Mia Yim	1.00	2.50
89	Pete Dunne	.50	1.25
90	Rhea Ripley	2.00	5.00
91	Roderick Strong	1.00	2.50
92	Scarlett	2.00	5.00
93	Shotzi Blackheart	1.50	4.00
94	Tegan Nox	1.25	3.00
95	Tommaso Ciampa	1.00	2.50
96	Tyler Breeze	.60	1.50
97	Velveteen Dream	.60	1.50
98	Kay Lee Ray	.75	2.00
99	Toni Storm	1.25	3.00
100	WALTER	1.00	2.50
101	Big Show SP		
102	Jinder Mahal SP		

#	Card	Lo	Hi
103	Natalya SP		
104	Ember Moon SP		
105	Dana Brooke SP		
106	Jaxson Ryker SP		
107	Kalisto SP		
108	Kane SP		
109	Aliyah SP		
110	Bronson Reed SP		
111	Robert Stone SP		
112	Santos Escobar SP		
113	Jordan Devlin SP		
114	Mercedes Martinez SP		
115	John Cena SP		
116	Rob Gronkowski SP		
117	Ronda Rousey SP		
118	The Rock SP		
119	Triple H SP		
120	Undertaker SP		
121	Batista SP		
122	Bret Hit Man Hart SP		
123	Goldberg SP		
124	Shawn Michaels SP		
125	Stone Cold Steve Austin SP		

2020 Finest WWE Autographs

#	Card	Lo	Hi
	*GREEN/99: .6X TO 1.2X BASIC AUTOS		
	*ORANGE/50 .6X TO 1.5X BASIC AUTOS		
	*BLACK/25: UNPRICED DUE TO SCARCITY		
	*GOLD/10: UNPRICED DUE TO SCARCITY		
	*RED/5: UNPRICED DUE TO SCARCITY		
	*SUPERFR/1: UNPRICED DUE TO SCARCITY		
	STATED ODDS 1:17		
AAB	Aleister Black	8.00	20.00
AAC	Adam Cole	10.00	25.00
AAD	Angelo Dawkins	5.00	12.00
AAG	Angel Garza	12.00	30.00
AAJ	AJ Styles	15.00	40.00
AAN	Andrade	5.00	12.00
AAS	Asuka	30.00	75.00
ABA	Bayley	25.00	60.00
ABB	Bianca Belair	15.00	40.00
ABD	Roman Reigns	15.00	40.00
ABE	Big E	6.00	15.00
ABM	Murphy	5.00	12.00
ABO	Bobby Lashley	8.00	20.00
ABW	The Fiend Bray Wyatt	30.00	75.00
ACG	Cameron Grimes	10.00	25.00
ACS	Cesaro	6.00	15.00
ADD	Dominik Dijakovic	5.00	12.00
ADK	Dakota Kai	20.00	50.00
ADM	Drew McIntyre	15.00	40.00
ADZ	Dolph Ziggler	6.00	15.00
AEK	Erik	5.00	12.00
AFB	Finn Balor	10.00	25.00
AIO	Io Shirai	30.00	75.00
AIS	Isaiah Swerve Scott	8.00	20.00
AJE	Jey Uso	6.00	15.00
AJG	Johnny Gargano	5.00	12.00
AJH	Jeff Hardy	12.00	30.00
AKC	King Corbin	6.00	15.00
AKL	Keith Lee	10.00	25.00
AKU	Kushida	5.00	12.00
ALM	Liv Morgan	20.00	50.00
AMA	Mandy Rose	25.00	60.00
AMF	Montez Ford	6.00	15.00
AMY	Mia Yim	10.00	25.00
ANC	Nikki Cross	10.00	25.00
AOT	Otis	8.00	20.00

AQS	Shayna Baszler	10.00	25.00
ARC	Ricochet	10.00	25.00
ARH	Rhea Ripley	50.00	100.00
ARR	Ruby Riott	15.00	40.00
ART	R-Truth	8.00	20.00
ASB	Sasha Banks	50.00	100.00
ASG	Shorty G	5.00	12.00
ASH	Sheamus	6.00	15.00
ASJ	Samoa Joe	5.00	12.00
ASN	Shinsuke Nakamura	8.00	20.00
ASR	Seth Rollins	10.00	25.00
ATB	Tyler Breeze	5.00	12.00
ATC	Tucker	6.00	15.00
ATN	Tegan Nox	30.00	75.00
ATO	Tommaso Ciampa	10.00	25.00
AVD	Velveteen Dream	5.00	12.00
AZV	Zelina Vega	15.00	40.00

2020 Finest WWE Decade's Finest Debuts

COMPLETE SET (9) 6.00 15.00
*GOLD/50: .6X TO 1.5X BASIC CARDS
*RED/5: UNPRICED DUE TO SCARCITY
*SUPERFR/1: UNPRICED DUE TO SCARCITY
STATED ODDS 1:11

D1	Daniel Bryan	2.00	5.00
D2	Roman Reigns	1.50	4.00
D3	Seth Rollins	1.25	3.00
D4	Kevin Owens	.75	2.00
D5	Samoa Joe	1.00	2.50
D6	Braun Strowman	1.50	4.00
D7	AJ Styles	2.00	5.00
D8	Shinsuke Nakamura	1.25	3.00
D9	Adam Cole	1.50	4.00
D10	Ronda Rousey		

2020 Finest WWE Decade's Finest Debuts Autographs

*GOLD/50: .5X TO 1.2X BASIC AUTOS
*RED/5: UNPRICED DUE TO SCARCITY
*SUPERFR/1: UNPRICED DUE TO SCARCITY
STATED ODDS 1:124

DAC	Adam Cole	12.00	30.00
DAJ	AJ Styles	12.00	30.00
DKO	Kevin Owens	6.00	15.00
DSJ	Samoa Joe	6.00	15.00
DSN	Shinsuke Nakamura	8.00	20.00

2020 Finest WWE Decade's Finest Returns

COMPLETE SET (17) 12.00 30.00
*GOLD/50: .6X TO 1.5X BASIC CARDS
*RED/5: UNPRICED DUE TO SCARCITY
*SUPERFR/1: UNPRICED DUE TO SCARCITY
STATED ODDS 1:7

R1	Bret Hit Man Hart	1.50	4.00
R2	Booker T	1.25	3.00
R3	Diesel	1.00	2.50
R4	The Rock	3.00	8.00
R5	Kane	.75	2.00
R6	Undertaker	2.50	6.00
R7	Ultimate Warrior	1.50	4.00
R9	Shane McMahon	1.00	2.50
R10	Seth Rollins	1.25	3.00
R11	Goldberg	2.50	6.00
R12	Paige	1.50	4.00
R13	Daniel Bryan	2.00	5.00
R14	Bobby Lashley	1.25	3.00
R15	Roman Reigns	1.50	4.00
R16	Trish Stratus	3.00	8.00
R17	Batista	1.00	2.50
R18	Sasha Banks	3.00	8.00

2020 Finest WWE Decade's Finest Returns Autographs

*GOLD/50: .5X TO 1.2X BASIC AUTOS
*RED/5: UNPRICED DUE TO SCARCITY
*SUPERFR/1: UNPRICED DUE TO SCARCITY
STATED ODDS 1:106

RBL	Bobby Lashley	8.00	20.00
RRR	Roman Reigns	20.00	50.00
RSB	Sasha Banks	50.00	100.00
RSR	Seth Rollins	8.00	20.00

2020 Finest WWE Decade's Finest Superstars

COMPLETE SET (10) 10.00 25.00
*GOLD/50: .6X TO 1.5X BASIC CARDS
*RED/5: UNPRICED DUE TO SCARCITY
*SUPERFR/1: UNPRICED DUE TO SCARCITY
STATED ODDS 1:11

S1	Becky Lynch	2.50	6.00
S2	Charlotte Flair	2.50	6.00
S3	Daniel Bryan	2.00	5.00
S4	John Cena	2.50	6.00
S5	Kofi Kingston	1.00	2.50
S6	Randy Orton	1.50	4.00
S7	Roman Reigns	1.50	4.00
S8	Seth Rollins	1.25	3.00
S9	Sheamus	.75	2.00
S10	The Miz	1.00	2.50

2020 Finest WWE Decade's Finest Superstars Autographs

*GOLD/50: .5X TO 1.2X BASIC AUTOS
*RED/5: UNPRICED DUE TO SCARCITY
*SUPERFR/1: UNPRICED DUE TO SCARCITY
STATED ODDS 1:123

SKK	Kofi Kingston	6.00	15.00
SRR	Roman Reigns	15.00	40.00
SSR	Seth Rollins	12.00	30.00

2020 Finest WWE Finest Careers Die-Cuts

COMPLETE SET (10) 30.00 75.00
*GOLD/50: .6X TO 1.5X BASIC CARDS
*RED/5: UNPRICED DUE TO SCARCITY
*SUPERFR/1: UNPRICED DUE TO SCARCITY
STATED ODDS 1:48

C1	Austin 3:16 Is Born	6.00	15.00
C2	Stunner Heard Around World	6.00	15.00
C3	First WWE Championship	6.00	15.00
C4	Zamboni Mayhem	6.00	15.00
C5	Cementing the Boss' Car	6.00	15.00
C6	Raining on Corporation's Parade	6.00	15.00
C7	Stone Cold's Final Match	6.00	15.00
C8	Chasing Down Mr. McMahon	6.00	15.00
C9	Mr. McMahon Inducts Austin	6.00	15.00
C10	Celebrating Raw's 25th Anniversary	6.00	15.00

2020 Finest WWE Finest Tag Teams

COMPLETE SET (17) 12.00 30.00
*GOLD/50: .6X TO 1.5X BASIC CARDS
*RED/5: UNPRICED DUE TO SCARCITY
*SUPERFR/1: UNPRICED DUE TO SCARCITY
STATED ODDS 1:7

TT1	Akam/Rezar	1.00	2.50
TT2	Montez Ford/Angelo Dawkins	.75	2.00
TT3	Kairi Sane/Asuka	3.00	8.00
TT4	Billie Kay/Peyton Royce	1.50	4.00
TT5	Ivar/Erik	.75	2.00
TT6	Alexa Bliss/Nikki Cross	5.00	12.00
TT7	Sasha Banks/Bayley	4.00	10.00
TT8	Big E/Kofi Kingston	1.25	3.00
TT9	John Morrison/The Miz	1.25	3.00
TT10	Jimmy Uso/Jey Uso	.75	2.00
TT11	Tucker/Otis	1.25	3.00
TT12	Bobby Fish/Kyle OiReilly	1.00	2.50
TT13	Pete Dunne/Matt Riddle	1.50	4.00
TT14	Wesley Blake/Steve Cutler	1.00	2.50
TT15	Wolfgang/Mark Coffey	1.00	2.50
TT16	James Drake/Zack Gibson	1.00	2.50
TT17	Marcel Barthel/Fabian Aichner	.75	2.00

2020 Finest WWE Finest Tag Teams Autographs

*GOLD REF/25: UNPRICED DUE TO SCARCITY
*RED REF/5: UNPRICED DUE TO SCARCITY
*SUPERFR/1: UNPRICED DUE TO SCARCITY
STATED ODDS 1:74

TTBC	Alexa Bliss/Nikki Cross	75.00	150.00
TTBH	Sasha Banks/Bayley	100.00	200.00
TTHM	Tucker/Otis	20.00	50.00
TTII	Billie Kay/Peyton Royce	60.00	120.00
TTIM	Marcel Barthel/Fabian Aichner	10.00	25.00
TTMM	John Morrison/The Miz	30.00	75.00
TTSP	Angelo Dawkins/Montez Ford	15.00	40.00
TTUE	Bobby Fish/Kyle O'Reilly	15.00	40.00
TTVR	Ivar/Erik	10.00	25.00

2002 Fleer WWE Absolute Divas

COMPLETE SET (100) 15.00 40.00
UNOPENED BOX (24 PACKS)
UNOPENED PACK (8 CARDS)
*DIVA GEM: .75X TO 2X BASIC CARDS

1	Trish Stratus	1.25	3.00
2	Terri	.60	1.50
3	Ivory	.50	1.25
4	Lita	.75	2.00
5	Jackie	.50	1.25
6	Stacy Keibler	1.25	3.00
7	Torrie Wilson	1.25	3.00
8	Jacqueline	.30	.75
9	Molly	.30	.75
10	Jazz	.30	.75
11	Stephanie McMahon	.60	1.50
12	Nidia	.30	.75
13	Dawn Marie	.30	.75
14	Victoria	.60	1.50
15	Linda	.30	.75
16	Trish Stratus	1.25	3.00
17	Terri	.60	1.50
18	Ivory	.50	1.25
19	Lita	.75	2.00
20	Jazz	.30	.75
21	Stacy Keibler	1.25	3.00
22	Torrie Wilson	1.25	3.00
23	Jacqueline	.30	.75
24	Molly	.30	.75
25	Stephanie McMahon	.60	1.50
26	Trish Stratus	1.25	3.00
27	Terri	.60	1.50
28	Ivory	.50	1.25
29	Lita	.75	2.00
30	Jackie	.50	1.25
31	Stacy Keibler	1.25	3.00
32	Torrie Wilson	1.25	3.00
33	Jacqueline	.30	.75
34	Molly	.30	.75
35	Jazz	.30	.75
36	Trish Stratus	1.25	3.00
37	Terri	.60	1.50
38	Ivory	.50	1.25
39	Lita	.75	2.00
40	Stacy Keibler	1.25	3.00
41	Torrie Wilson	1.25	3.00
42	Jacqueline	.30	.75
43	Molly	.30	.75
44	Jazz	.30	.75
45	Lita PS	.75	2.00
46	Bubba Ray PS	.20	.50
47	Jamie Noble PS	.20	.50
48	Matt Hardy PS	.30	.75
49	Brock Lesnar with Paul Heyman PS	1.25	3.00
50	William Regal PS	.20	.50
51	Triple H PS	.75	2.00
52	Vince McMahon PS	.50	1.25
53	Booker T PS	.50	1.25
54	Tajiri PS	.20	.50
55	Steven Richards PS	.20	.50
56	Chris Jericho PS	.30	.75
57	D-Von Dudley PS	.20	.50
58	Rob Van Dam PS	.50	1.25
59	The Rock PS	.75	2.00
60	Ric Flair PS	.60	1.50
61	Bradshaw PS	.30	.75
62	Hollywood Hulk Hogan PS	1.25	3.00
63	Hurricane PS	.20	.50
64	Jeff Hardy PS	.30	.75
65	Kurt Angle PS	.50	1.25
66	Jazz DM	.30	.75
67	Trish Stratus DM	1.25	3.00
68	Molly DM	.30	.75
69	Lita DM	.75	2.00
70	Stacy Keibler DM	1.25	3.00
71	Torrie Wilson DM	1.25	3.00
72	Trish Stratus DM	1.25	3.00
73	Jacqueline DM	.30	.75
74	Ivory DM	.50	1.25
75	Trish Stratus DM	1.25	3.00
76	Lita DM	.75	2.00
77	Terri DM	.60	1.50
78	Jacqueline DM	.30	.75
79	Molly DM	.30	.75
80	Dawn Marie DM	.30	.75
81	Lita GOF	.75	2.00
82	Jacqueline GOF	.30	.75
83	Molly GOF	.30	.75
84	Stacy Keibler GOF	1.25	3.00
85	Ivory GOF	.50	1.25
86	Trish Stratus GOF	1.25	3.00
87	Torrie Wilson GOF	1.25	3.00
88	Terri GOF	.60	1.50
89	Victoria GOF	.60	1.50
90	Jazz GOF	.30	.75
91	Trish Stratus GOF	1.25	3.00
92	Torrie Wilson GOF	1.25	3.00
93	Ivory GOF	.50	1.25
94	Lita GOF	.75	2.00

#	Card	Lo	Hi
95	Dawn Marie GOF	.30	.75
96	Terri GOF	.60	1.50
97	Linda GOF	.30	.75
98	Stacy Keibler GOF	1.25	3.00
99	Molly GOF	.30	.75
100	Jackie GOF	.50	1.25

2002 Fleer WWE Absolute Divas Cover Shots

COMPLETE SET (10) 12.00 30.00
STATED ODDS 1:12 HOBBY

#	Card	Lo	Hi
1	Ivory	1.25	3.00
2	Jacqueline	.75	2.00
3	Lita	2.50	6.00
4	Dawn Marie	.75	2.00
5	Stacy Keibler (w/Dudley Boyz)	5.00	12.00
6	Terri	1.50	4.00
7	Torrie Wilson	3.00	8.00
8	Trish Stratus	5.00	12.00
9	Stephanie McMahon	6.00	15.00
10	Stacy & Torrie	4.00	10.00

2002 Fleer WWE Absolute Divas Diva Ink

STATED ODDS 1:198 HOBBY
CARDS AVAILABLE BY EXCH ONLY

	Card	Lo	Hi
NNO	Dawn Marie	20.00	50.00
NNO	Jackie	15.00	40.00
NNO	Linda	10.00	25.00
NNO	Stacy Keibler	125.00	250.00
NNO	Torrie Wilson	100.00	200.00

2002 Fleer WWE Absolute Divas Diva Ink Redemption

COMPLETE SET (5)
RANDOMLY INSERTED INTO PACKS

NNO Dawn Marie
NNO Jackie
NNO Linda
NNO Stacy Keibler
NNO Torrie Wilson

2002 Fleer WWE Absolute Divas Inter-Actions

COMPLETE SET (20) 10.00 25.00
STATED ODDS 1:6 HOBBY

#	Card	Lo	Hi
1	Swimsuit Competition	1.50	4.00
2	Terri Wins The Hardcore Championship	.75	2.00
3	Six-Person Intergender Match	1.50	4.00
4	Bra And Panties Paddle On A Pole Match	.75	2.00
5	Mixed Tag Team Match	1.50	4.00
6	Tag Team	1.50	4.00
7	Bikini Match	1.50	4.00
8	Table Match	.40	1.00
9	Mixed Tag Team Match	1.50	4.00
10	Tag Team Hardcore Women's Title Match	1.50	4.00
11	Tag Team	1.50	4.00
12	Judgment Day Match	1.50	4.00
13	Gravy Bowl Match	1.50	4.00
14	Tag Team Match	1.50	4.00
15	Wrestlemania X-8 Triple Threat	1.00	2.50
16	Tag Team	.40	1.00
17	Swimsuit Competition	.40	1.00
18	Women's Title Match-KOTR	1.50	4.00
19	Bra And Panties Match (Women's Title)	1.50	4.00
20	Lingerie Match	1.50	4.00

2002 Fleer WWE Absolute Divas Lip Service

STATED PRINT RUN 50 SER. #'d SETS
CARDS AVAILABLE BY EXCH ONLY

	Card	Lo	Hi
NNO	Dawn Marie	50.00	100.00
NNO	Jackie	20.00	50.00
NNO	Linda	6.00	15.00
NNO	Stacy Keibler	200.00	400.00
NNO	Torrie Wilson	150.00	300.00

2002 Fleer WWE Absolute Divas Lip Service Redemption

COMPLETE SET (5)
RANDOMLY INSERTED INTO PACKS

NNO Dawn Marie
NNO Jackie
NNO Linda
NNO Stacy Keibler
NNO Torrie Wilson

2002 Fleer WWE Absolute Divas Material Girls

STATED ODDS 1:36 HOBBY

	Card	Lo	Hi
NNO	Dawn Marie	4.00	10.00
	Skirt		
NNO	Ivory	2.00	5.00
	Mat		
NNO	Jazz	2.00	5.00
	Mat		
NNO	Lita	3.00	8.00
	Mat		
NNO	Lita	6.00	15.00
	Top		
NNO	Molly	4.00	10.00
	Top		
NNO	Nidia	4.00	10.00
	Shorts		
NNO	Stacy Keibler	30.00	75.00
NNO	Stacy Keibler	15.00	40.00
NNO	Terri	6.00	15.00
	Outfit		
NNO	Torrie Wilson	8.00	20.00
	Bikini		
NNO	Trish Stratus	10.00	25.00
NNO	Trish Stratus	20.00	50.00
NNO	Victoria	6.00	15.00
	Shorts		

2002 Fleer WWE Absolute Divas Mini-Posters

COMPLETE SET (30) 8.00 20.00
STATED ODDS 1:1 HOBBY

	Card	Lo	Hi
NNO	Booker T	.40	1.00
NNO	Brock Lesnar/Paul Heyman	1.00	2.50
NNO	Chris Jericho	.25	.60
NNO	Dawn Marie	.25	.60
NNO	Hollywood Hulk Hogan	1.00	2.50
NNO	Ivory	.40	1.00
NNO	Jackie (orange border)	.40	1.00
NNO	Jackie (yellow border)	.40	1.00
NNO	Jacqueline	.25	.60
NNO	Jazz	.25	.60
NNO	Jeff Hardy	.25	.60
NNO	Kurt Angle	.40	1.00
NNO	Lita (blue border)	.60	1.50
NNO	Lita (purple border)	.60	1.50

	Card	Lo	Hi
NNO	Matt Hardy	.25	.60
NNO	Molly	.25	.60
NNO	Nidia	.25	.60
NNO	Rob Van Dam	.40	1.00
NNO	The Rock	.60	1.50
NNO	Stacy Keibler (purple border)	1.00	2.50
NNO	Stacy Keibler (red border)	1.00	2.50
NNO	Stephanie McMahon	.50	1.25
NNO	Terri (orange border)	.50	1.25
NNO	Terri (purple border)	.50	1.25
NNO	Torrie Wilson (black outfit)	1.00	2.50
NNO	Torrie Wilson (blue outfit)	1.00	2.50
NNO	Triple H	.60	1.50
NNO	Trish Stratus (red border)	1.00	2.50
NNO	Trish Stratus (yellow border)	1.00	2.50
NNO	Victoria	.50	1.25

2002 Fleer WWE Absolute Divas Signed with a Kiss

STATED PRINT RUN 50 SER. #'d SETS
AVAILABLE BY EXCH ONLY

	Card	Lo	Hi
NNO	Dawn Marie	60.00	120.00
NNO	Ivory	20.00	50.00
NNO	Jackie	25.00	60.00
NNO	Linda	15.00	40.00
NNO	Lita	50.00	100.00
NNO	Stacy Keibler	500.00	1000.00
NNO	Torrie Wilson	200.00	400.00

2002 Fleer WWE Absolute Divas Signed with a Kiss Redemption

COMPLETE SET (7)
RANDOMLY INSERTED INTO PACKS

NNO Dawn Marie
NNO Ivory
NNO Jackie
NNO Linda
NNO Lita
NNO Stacy Keibler
NNO Torrie Wilson

2002 Fleer WWE Absolute Divas Tropical Pleasures

COMPLETE SET (10) 12.00 30.00
STATED ODDS 1:12 HOBBY

#	Card	Lo	Hi
1	Ivory	1.25	3.00
2	Trish Stratus	3.00	8.00
3	Lita	2.00	5.00
4	Lita and Trish Stratus	3.00	8.00
5	Stacy Keibler	3.00	8.00
6	Terri	1.50	4.00
7	Torrie Wilson	3.00	8.00
8	Jacqueline	.75	2.00
9	Molly Holly	.75	2.00
10	Victoria	1.50	4.00

2002 Fleer WWE Absolute Divas Wardrobe Closet

STATED ODDS 1:23 HOBBY

	Card	Lo	Hi
NNO	Lita	6.00	15.00
	Jacket		
NNO	Molly	4.00	10.00
	Top		
NNO	Nidia	3.00	8.00
	Shorts		
NNO	Stacy Keibler	15.00	40.00
NNO	Torrie Wilson	12.00	30.00

	Card	Lo	Hi
NNO	Torrie Wilson	12.00	30.00
NNO	Trish Stratus	20.00	50.00
NNO	Victoria	5.00	12.00

2003 Fleer WWE Aggression

COMPLETE SET (89) 10.00 25.00
UNOPENED BOX (24 PACKS)
UNOPENED PACK (5 CARDS)

#	Card	Lo	Hi
1	Goldberg	.75	2.00
2	Batista	.50	1.25
3	Booker T	.50	1.25
4	Bradshaw	.30	.75
5	Bubba Ray Dudley	.20	.50
6	Chief Morley	.20	.50
7	Chris Jericho	.30	.75
8	Chris Nowinski	.12	.30
9	Christian	.30	.75
10	D-Von Dudley	.20	.50
11	Eric Bischoff	.20	.50
12	Goldust	.12	.30
13	Ivory	.50	1.25
14	Jacqueline	.30	.75
15	Jazz	.20	.50
16	Jamal	.20	.50
17	Charlie Haas	.12	.30
18	Kane	.50	1.25
19	Kevin Nash	.60	1.50
20	Lance Storm	.12	.30
21	Al Snow	.12	.30
22	Lita	.75	2.00
23	Maven	.12	.30
24	Molly	.60	1.50
25	Randy Orton	.30	.75
26	Ric Flair	.60	1.50
27	Rico	.12	.30
28	Rob Van Dam	.50	1.25
29	Rosey	.12	.30
30	Scott Steiner	.60	1.50
31	Shawn Michaels	.75	2.00
32	Spike Dudley	.20	.50
33	Stacy Keibler	1.25	3.00
34	Steven Richards	.20	.50
35	Stone Cold Steve Austin	.75	2.00
36	Terri	.60	1.50
37	Test	.20	.50
38	The Hurricane	.12	.30
39	Tommy Dreamer	.12	.30
40	Trish Stratus	1.25	3.00
41	Triple H	.75	2.00
42	Victoria	.60	1.50
43	William Regal	.30	.75
44	Big Show	.50	1.25
45	Bill DeMott	.12	.30
46	Billy Kidman	.12	.30
47	Brock Lesnar	1.25	3.00
48	Chavo Guerrero	.20	.50
49	Chuck Palumbo	.20	.50
50	Chris Benoit	.30	.75
51	Crash	.12	.30
52	Dawn Marie	.60	1.50
53	Edge	.50	1.25
54	Eddie Guerrero	.60	1.50
55	Funaki	.20	.50
56	Sable	.75	2.00
57	Hulk Hogan	.75	2.00
58	Jamie Noble	.12	.30
59	John Cena	.75	2.00
60	Johnny Stamboli	.12	.30

61 Kurt Angle	.50	1.25
62 Mark Henry	.20	.50
63 Matt Hardy	.30	.75
64 Nathan Jones	.12	.30
65 Nidia	.30	.75
66 Nunzio	.12	.30
67 Rey Mysterio	.30	.75
68 Rhyno	.50	1.25
69 Rikishi	.30	.75
70 Shannon Moore	.12	.30
71 The Rock	.75	2.00
72 Tajiri	.12	.30
73 Torrie Wilson	1.25	3.00
74 Tazz	.20	.50
75 Undertaker	.60	1.50
76 A-Train	.12	.30
77 Paul Heyman	.12	.30
78 Brian Kendrick	.20	.50
79 Torrie Wilson DL	1.25	3.00
80 Sable DL	.75	2.00
81 Lita DL	.75	2.00
82 Ivory DL	.50	1.25
83 Jacqueline DL	.30	.75
84 Jazz DL	.20	.50
85 Molly DL	.60	1.50
86 Stacy Keibler DL	1.25	3.00
87 Terri DL	.60	1.50
88 Trish Stratus DL	1.25	3.00
89 Nidia DL	.30	.75

2003 Fleer WWE Aggression Matitude

COMPLETE SET (10)	10.00	25.00
STATED ODDS 1:12 HOBBY		
1 Triple H	2.00	5.00
2 The Rock	2.00	5.00
3 Brock Lesnar	3.00	8.00
4 Stone Cold Steve Austin	2.00	5.00
5 Kurt Angle	1.25	3.00
6 Chris Jericho	.75	2.00
7 Hulk Hogan	2.00	5.00
8 Scott Steiner	1.50	4.00
9 Rob Van Dam	1.25	3.00
10 Undertaker	1.50	4.00

2003 Fleer WWE Aggression Matitude Event Used

MR The Rock	4.00	10.00
MU Undertaker	3.00	8.00
MBL Brock Lesnar	3.00	8.00
MCJ Chris Jericho	2.50	6.00
MHH Hollywood Hulk Hogan	6.00	15.00
MKA Kurt Angle	4.00	10.00
MSA Stone Cold Steve Austin	3.00	8.00
MSS Scott Steiner	2.00	5.00
MTR Triple H	3.00	8.00
MRVD Rob Van Dam	2.00	5.00

2003 Fleer WWE Aggression Matitude Event Used Jumbo Images

STATED PRINT RUN 50 SER.#'d SETS		
MR The Rock	15.00	40.00
MU Undertaker	15.00	40.00
MBL Brock Lesnar	20.00	50.00
MCJ Chris Jericho	10.00	25.00
MHH Hollywood Hulk Hogan	25.00	60.00
MKA Kurt Angle	12.00	30.00
MSA Stone Cold Steve Austin	15.00	40.00
MSS Scott Steiner	12.00	30.00
MTH Triple H	15.00	40.00
MRVD Rob Van Dam	10.00	25.00

2003 Fleer WWE Aggression Queens of the Ring

COMPLETE SET (10)	25.00	60.00
STATED ODDS 1:8 HOBBY		
1 Lita	3.00	8.00
2 Ivory	2.00	5.00
3 Jacqueline	1.25	3.00
4 Jazz	.75	2.00
5 Molly	2.50	6.00
6 Stacy Keibler	5.00	12.00
7 Terri	2.50	6.00
8 Trish Stratus	5.00	12.00
9 Nidia	1.25	3.00
10 Torrie Wilson	5.00	12.00

2003 Fleer WWE Aggression Queens of the Ring Autographs

STATED PRINT RUN 50 SER.#'d SETS		
SK AVAILABLE AT NATIONAL ONLY		
SK STATED PRINT RUN 1500 CARDS		
NNO Ivory/50	30.00	75.00
NNO Molly Holly/50	50.00	75.00
NNO Stacy Keibler/50	125.00	250.00
NNO Stacy Keibler NSCC	30.00	75.00
NNO Terri/50	60.00	125.00
NNO Trish Stratus/50	125.00	250.00

2003 Fleer WWE Aggression Queens of the Ring Event Used

STATED ODDS 1:115 HOBBY		
QRI Ivory	10.00	25.00
QRJ Jacqueline	8.00	20.00
QRL Lita	12.00	30.00
QRN Nidia	8.00	20.00
QRT Terri	12.00	30.00
QRJA Jazz	8.00	20.00
QRMH Molly Holly	8.00	20.00
QRSK Stacy Keibler	20.00	50.00
QRTS Trish Stratus	15.00	40.00
QRTW Torrie Wilson	20.00	50.00

2003 Fleer WWE Aggression Ring Leaders

COMPLETE SET (15)	8.00	20.00
STATED ODDS 1:4 HOBBY		
1 Triple H	1.25	3.00
2 The Rock	1.25	3.00
3 Brock Lesnar	2.00	5.00
4 Stone Cold Steve Austin	1.25	3.00
5 The Hurricane	.20	.50
6 Undertaker	1.00	2.50
7 Kane	.75	2.00
8 Chris Jericho	.50	1.25
9 Hulk Hogan	1.25	3.00
10 Scott Steiner	1.00	2.50
11 Rob Van Dam	.75	2.00
12 Shawn Michaels	1.25	3.00
13 Chris Benoit	.50	1.25
14 Edge	.75	2.00
15 Booker T	.75	2.00

2003 Fleer WWE Aggression Ring Leaders Event Used

STATED ODDS 1:29 HOBBY		
RLE Edge	6.00	15.00
RLH The Hurricane	3.00	8.00
RLK Kane	4.00	10.00
RLR The Rock	8.00	20.00
RLU Undertaker	6.00	15.00
RLBL Brock Lesnar	8.00	20.00
RLBT Booker T	3.00	8.00
RLCB Chris Benoit	4.00	10.00
RLCJ Chris Jericho	4.00	10.00
RLHH Hollywood Hulk Hogan	8.00	20.00
RLSA Stone Cold Steve Austin	8.00	20.00
RLSM Shawn Michaels	4.00	10.00
RLSS Scott Steiner	4.00	10.00
RLTH Triple H	6.00	15.00
RLRVD Rob Van Dam	4.00	10.00

2004 Fleer WWE Chaos

COMPLETE SET (95)	10.00	25.00
UNOPENED BOX (24 PACKS)		
UNOPENED PACK (5 CARDS)		
*GOLD: 1X TO 2.5X BASIC CARDS		
1 Stone Cold Steve Austin	1.25	3.00
2 Test	.30	.75
3 Jazz	.50	1.25
4 Kurt Angle	.75	2.00
5 Batista	.75	2.00
6 The Hurricane		
7 Rey Mysterio	.50	1.25
8 Steven Richards	.30	.75
9 Goldberg	1.50	4.00
10 Chris Benoit	.50	1.25
11 Doug Basham	.20	.50
12 Torrie Wilson	2.00	5.00
13 Booker T	.75	2.00
14 Lance Storm	.20	.50
15 Rhyno	.75	2.00
16 Matt Hardy	.50	1.25
17 Maven	.20	.50
18 Rico	.20	.50
19 Rodney Mack	.20	.50
20 Jacqueline	.60	1.50
21 Rosey	.20	.50
22 Rikishi	.50	1.25
23 Scotty 2 Hotty	.30	.75
24 Mark Jindrak	.20	.50
25 Spike Dudley	.30	.75
26 Shawn Michaels	1.25	3.00
27 Paul Heyman	.20	.50
28 Val Venis	.30	.75
29 Shannon Moore	.20	.50
30 Triple H	1.25	3.00
31 Rob Conway	.20	.50
32 Edge	.75	2.00
33 A-Train	.20	.50
34 Big Show	.75	2.00
35 Theodore Long	.20	.50
36 Shelton Benjamin	.20	.50
37 Billy Gunn	.25	.60
38 Billy Kidman	.20	.50
39 Bradshaw	.50	1.25
40 Kane	.75	2.00
41 Charlie Haas	.20	.50
42 Chavo Guerrero	.30	.75
43 The Rock	1.25	3.00
44 Danny Basham	.20	.50
45 Chuck Palumbo	.30	.75
46 D-Von Dudley	.30	.75
47 Eddie Guerrero	1.00	2.50
48 Rene Dupree	.30	.75
49 Tajiri	.20	.50
50 Undertaker	1.00	2.50
51 Rob Van Dam	.75	2.00
52 Ric Flair	1.00	2.50
53 Matt Morgan	.25	.60
54 Eric Bischoff	.30	.75
55 Garrison Cade	.20	.50
56 Funaki	.30	.75
57 Brock Lesnar	2.00	5.00
58 Chris Jericho	.50	1.25
59 Hardcore Holly	.30	.75
60 Ultimo Dragon	.20	.50
61 Jamie Noble	.20	.50
62 Scott Steiner	1.00	2.50
63 John Cena	1.25	3.00
64 Randy Orton	.50	1.25
65 Johnny Stamboli	.20	.50
66 Nunzio	.20	.50
67 Bubba Ray Dudley	.30	.75
68 Mark Henry	.30	.75
69 Christian	.60	1.50
70 Jazz SI	.50	1.25
71 Torrie Wilson SI	2.00	5.00
72 Trish Stratus SI	2.00	5.00
73 Dawn Marie SI	.50	1.25
74 Stacy Keibler SI	2.00	5.00
75 Nidia SI	.50	1.25
76 Shaniqua SI	.50	1.25
77 Lita SI	1.25	3.00
78 Jacqueline SI	.60	1.50
79 Victoria SI	1.00	2.50
80 Terri SI	1.00	2.50
81 Ivory SI	.75	2.00
82 Gail Kim SI	.75	2.00
83 Miss Jackie SI	.75	2.00
84 Molly SI	1.00	2.50
85 Sable SI	1.25	3.00
86 Brock Lesnar PI	2.00	5.00
87 Triple H PI	1.25	3.00
88 Kurt Angle PI	.75	2.00
89 Batista PI	.75	2.00
90 Test PI	.30	.75
91 Randy Orton PI	.50	1.25
92 Scott Steiner PI	1.00	2.50
93 Booker T PI	.75	2.00
94 The Rock PI	1.25	3.00
95 Goldberg PI	1.50	4.00

2004 Fleer WWE Chaos Controlled Chaos

COMPLETE SET (15)	8.00	20.00
STATED ODDS 1:6 HOBBY AND RETAIL		
1 Brock Lesnar	2.00	5.00
2 Chris Benoit	.50	1.25
3 Triple H	1.25	3.00
4 Kurt Angle	.75	2.00
5 Kane	.75	2.00
6 Shawn Michaels	1.25	3.00
7 Edge	.75	2.00
8 Chris Jericho	.50	1.25
9 Stone Cold	1.25	3.00
10 Big Poppa Pump	1.00	2.50
11 Undertaker	1.00	2.50

12 Rob Van Dam	.75	2.00
13 Ric Flair	1.00	2.50
14 The Rock	1.25	3.00
15 Goldberg	1.50	4.00

2004 Fleer WWE Chaos Showing Off

COMPLETE SET (16)	12.50	30.00
STATED ODDS 1:4 HOBBY AND RETAIL		
1 Lita	1.50	4.00
2 Jacqueline	.75	2.00
3 Ivory	1.00	2.50
4 Dawn Marie	.60	1.50
5 Stacy Keibler	2.50	6.00
6 Nidia	.60	1.50
7 Molly Holly	1.25	3.00
8 Jazz	.60	1.50
9 Torrie Wilson	2.50	6.00
10 Victoria	1.25	3.00
11 Terri	1.25	3.00
12 Trish Stratus	2.50	6.00
13 Sable	1.50	4.00
14 Miss Jackie	1.00	2.50
15 Shaniqua	.60	1.50
16 Gail Kim	1.00	2.50

2004 Fleer WWE Chaos Showing Off Autographs

STATED PRINT RUN 25 SER.#'d SETS		
NNO Dawn Marie	50.00	100.00
NNO Gail Kim	60.00	125.00
NNO Ivory	60.00	125.00
NNO Jacqueline	30.00	75.00
NNO Jazz	50.00	100.00
NNO Lita	75.00	150.00
NNO Molly	50.00	100.00
NNO Miss Jackie	60.00	125.00
NNO Nidia	30.00	75.00
NNO Sable	75.00	150.00
NNO Shaniqua	30.00	75.00
NNO Stacy Keibler	100.00	200.00
NNO Terri	100.00	200.00
NNO Torrie Wilson	60.00	120.00
NNO Trish Stratus	125.00	250.00
NNO Victoria	30.00	75.00

2004 Fleer WWE Chaos Showing Off Memorabilia

STATED ODDS 1:36 HOBBY; 1:72 RETAIL		
SOI Ivory	5.00	12.00
SOJ Jacqueline	4.00	10.00
SOJ Jazz	4.00	10.00
SOL Lita	6.00	15.00
SOM Molly	5.00	12.00
SON Nidia	4.00	10.00
SOS Sable	6.00	15.00
SOS Shaniqua	4.00	10.00
SOT Terri	6.00	15.00
SOV Victoria	5.00	12.00
SODM Dawn Marie	5.00	12.00
SOGK Gail Kim	6.00	15.00
SOMJ Miss Jackie	6.00	15.00
SOSK Stacy Keibler	10.00	25.00
SOTS Trish Stratus	10.00	25.00
SOTW Torrie Wilson	10.00	25.00

2004 Fleer WWE Chaos Tuff Guys

COMPLETE SET (12)	12.00	30.00
STATED ODDS 1:12 HOBBY AND RETAIL		
1 The Rock	2.50	6.00
2 Eddie Guerrero	2.00	5.00
3 Triple H	2.50	6.00
4 Kurt Angle	1.50	4.00
5 Undertaker	2.00	5.00
6 Shawn Michaels	2.50	6.00
7 Rob Van Dam	1.50	4.00
8 Stone Cold Steve Austin	2.50	6.00
9 Chris Benoit	1.00	2.50
10 Brock Lesnar	4.00	10.00
11 Chris Jericho	1.00	2.50
12 Kane	1.50	4.00

2004 Fleer WWE Chaos Tuff Guys Event Used Mat

STATED ODDS 1:8 RETAIL		
TGK Kane	2.00	5.00
TGU Undertaker	2.50	6.00
TGBL Brock Lesnar	6.00	15.00
TGCB Chris Benoit	1.50	4.00
TGCJ Chris Jericho	1.50	4.00
TGEG Eddie Guerrero	1.50	4.00
TGKA Kurt Angle	2.00	5.00
TGRV Rob Van Dam	1.50	4.00
TGSA Stone Cold Steve Austin	3.00	8.00
TGSM Shawn Michaels	2.50	6.00
TGTH Triple H	2.50	6.00
TGTR The Rock	3.00	8.00

2004 Fleer WWE Chaos Tuff Guys Event Worn Memorabilia

STATED ODDS 1:12 HOBBY EXCLUSIVE		
TGK Kane	3.00	8.00
TGU Undertaker	4.00	10.00
TGBL Brock Lesnar	5.00	12.00
TGCB Chris Benoit	5.00	15.00
TGCJ Chris Jericho	2.50	6.00
TGEG Eddie Guerrero	3.00	8.00
TGKA Kurt Angle	4.00	10.00
TGRV Rob Van Dam	2.50	6.00
TGSA Stone Cold Steve Austin	5.00	12.00
TGSM Shawn Michaels	3.00	8.00
TGTH Triple H	4.00	10.00
TGTR The Rock	5.00	12.00

2003 Fleer WWE Divine Divas

COMPLETE SET (90)	10.00	25.00
UNOPENED BOX (24 PACKS)		
UNOPENED PACK (5 CARDS)		
1 Lita	.60	1.50
2 Jacqueline	.25	.60
3 Ivory	.40	1.00
4 Dawn Marie	.50	1.25
5 Stacy Keibler	1.00	2.50
6 Nidia	.25	.60
7 Molly	.50	1.25
8 Jazz	.15	.40
9 Torrie Wilson	1.00	2.50
10 Victoria	.50	1.25
11 Terri	.50	1.25
12 Trish Stratus	1.00	2.50
13 Sable	.60	1.50
14 Lita	.60	1.50
15 Jacqueline	.25	.60
16 Ivory	.40	1.00
17 Dawn Marie	.50	1.25
18 Stacy Keibler	1.00	2.50
19 Nidia	.25	.60
20 Molly	.50	1.25
21 Jazz	.15	.40
22 Torrie Wilson	1.00	2.50
23 Victoria	.50	1.25
24 Terri	.50	1.25
25 Trish Stratus	1.00	2.50
26 Sable	.60	1.50
27 Lita	.60	1.50
28 Jacqueline	.25	.60
29 Ivory	.40	1.00
30 Dawn Marie	.50	1.25
31 Stacy Keibler	1.00	2.50
32 Nidia	.25	.60
33 Molly	.50	1.25
34 Jazz	.15	.40
35 Torrie Wilson	1.00	2.50
36 Victoria	.50	1.25
37 Terri	.50	1.25
38 Trish Stratus	1.00	2.50
39 Sable	.60	1.50
40 Lita	.60	1.50
41 Jacqueline	.25	.60
42 Ivory	.40	1.00
43 Dawn Marie	.50	1.25
44 Stacy Keibler	1.00	2.50
45 Nidia	.25	.60
46 Molly	.50	1.25
47 Jazz	.15	.40
48 Torrie Wilson	1.00	2.50
49 Victoria	.50	1.25
50 Terri	.50	1.25
51 Trish Stratus	1.00	2.50
52 Sable	.60	1.50
53 Lita	.60	1.50
54 Jacqueline	.25	.60
55 Ivory	.40	1.00
56 Dawn Marie	.50	1.25
57 Stacy Keibler	1.00	2.50
58 Nidia	.25	.60
59 Molly	.50	1.25
60 Jazz	.15	.40
61 Torrie Wilson	1.00	2.50
62 Victoria	.50	1.25
63 Terri	.50	1.25
64 Trish Stratus	1.00	2.50
65 Sable	.60	1.50
66 Lita	.60	1.50
67 Jacqueline	.25	.60
68 Ivory	.40	1.00
69 Dawn Marie	.50	1.25
70 Stacy Keibler	1.00	2.50
71 Nidia	.25	.60
72 Molly	.50	1.25
73 Jazz	.15	.40
74 Torrie Wilson	1.00	2.50
75 Victoria	.50	1.25
76 Terri	.50	1.25
77 Trish Stratus	1.00	2.50
78 Sable	.60	1.50
79 Triple H/Victoria DT	.60	1.50
80 Trish Stratus/The Rock DT	1.00	2.50
81 Sable/Brock Lesnar DT	1.00	2.50
82 Lita/Edge DT	.60	1.50
83 Stacy Keibler/Scott Steiner DT	1.00	2.50
84 Terri/Stone Cold Steve Austin DT	.60	1.50
85 Chris Jericho/Ivory DT	.25	.60
86 Kurt Angle/Torrie Wilson DT	1.00	2.50
87 Booker T/Jazz DT	.40	1.00
88 Gail Kim/Kane DT	.40	1.00
89 Nidia/Jamie Noble DT	.25	.60
90 Zach Gowen/Stephanie DT	.50	1.25

2003 Fleer WWE Divine Divas Dress Code Memorabilia

STATED ODDS 1:288 HOBBY		
NNO Dawn Marie	10.00	25.00
NNO Ivory	30.00	75.00
NNO Molly	12.00	30.00
NNO Nidia	12.00	30.00
NNO Sable	20.00	50.00
NNO Stacy Keibler	50.00	100.00
NNO Trish Stratus	25.00	60.00
NNO Victoria	10.00	25.00

2003 Fleer WWE Divine Divas Hugs and Kisses

COMPLETE SET (14)	15.00	40.00
STATED ODDS 1:8		
NNO Dawn Marie	1.50	4.00
NNO Gail Kim	1.25	3.00
NNO Ivory	1.25	3.00
NNO Lita	2.00	5.00
NNO Miss Jackie	1.25	3.00
NNO Molly	1.50	4.00
NNO Nidia	.75	2.00
NNO Sable	2.00	5.00
NNO Shaniqua	.75	2.00
NNO Stacy Keibler	3.00	8.00
NNO Terri	1.50	4.00
NNO Torrie Wilson	3.00	8.00
NNO Trish Stratus	3.00	8.00
NNO Victoria	1.50	4.00

2003 Fleer WWE Divine Divas Hugs and Kisses Autographs

STATED PRINT RUN 25 SER #'d SETS		
NNO Dawn Marie	50.00	100.00
NNO Gail Kim	60.00	125.00
NNO Ivory	30.00	75.00
NNO Jazz	30.00	75.00
NNO Miss Jackie	60.00	125.00
NNO Lita	75.00	150.00
NNO Molly	50.00	100.00
NNO Nidia	30.00	75.00
NNO Sable	125.00	250.00
NNO Shaniqua	30.00	75.00
NNO Stacy Keibler	200.00	350.00
NNO Terri	100.00	200.00
NNO Trish Stratus	125.00	250.00
NNO Victoria	60.00	125.00
NNO Torrie Wilson	125.00	250.00

2003 Fleer WWE Divine Divas On Location

COMPLETE SET (16)	20.00	50.00
STATED ODDS 1:12 HOBBY AND RETAIL		
1 Jacqueline	1.00	2.50
2 Jazz	.60	1.50
3 Nidia	1.00	2.50
4 Dawn Marie	2.00	5.00
5 Torrie Wilson	4.00	10.00

6	Lita	2.50	6.00
7	Sable	2.50	6.00
8	Ivory	1.50	4.00
9	Stacy Keibler	4.00	10.00
10	Trish Stratus	4.00	10.00
11	Terri	2.00	5.00
12	Victoria	2.00	5.00
13	Molly	2.00	5.00
14	Miss Jackie	1.50	4.00
15	Shaniqua	1.00	2.50
16	Gail Kim	1.50	4.00

2003 Fleer WWE Divine Divas On Location Memorabilia

STATED ODDS 1:24 HOBBY: 1:96 RETAIL

NNO	Dawn Marie	5.00	12.00
NNO	Ivory	6.00	15.00
NNO	Miss Jackie	6.00	15.00
NNO	Molly	5.00	12.00
NNO	Nidia	4.00	10.00
NNO	Sable	8.00	20.00
NNO	Shaniqua	4.00	10.00
NNO	Victoria	6.00	15.00

2003 Fleer WWE Divine Divas With Love

1	Lita	1.25	3.00
2	Jacqueline	.50	1.25
3	Ivory	.75	2.00
4	Dawn Marie	1.00	2.50
5	Stacy Keibler	2.00	5.00
6	Nidia	.50	1.25
7	Molly	1.00	2.50
8	Jazz	.30	.75
9	Torrie Wilson	2.00	5.00
10	Victoria	1.00	2.50
11	Terri	1.00	2.50
12	Trish Stratus	2.00	5.00
13	Sable	1.25	3.00
14	Shaniqua	.50	1.25
15	Gail Kim	.75	2.00
16	Miss Jackie	.75	2.00

2003 Fleer WWE Divine Divas With Love Autographs

STATED PRINT RUN 100 SER.#'d SETS

NNO	Dawn Marie	12.00	30.00
NNO	Gail Kim	15.00	40.00
NNO	Ivory	20.00	50.00
NNO	Jacqueline	12.00	30.00
NNO	Jazz	12.00	30.00
NNO	Miss Jackie	15.00	40.00
NNO	Molly	15.00	40.00
NNO	Nidia	12.00	30.00
NNO	Sable	100.00	200.00
NNO	Shaniqua	12.00	30.00
NNO	Stacy Keibler	75.00	150.00
NNO	Trish Stratus	50.00	100.00
NNO	Victoria	15.00	40.00

2003 Fleer WWE Divine Divas With Love Memorabilia

NNO	Dawn Marie	4.00	10.00
NNO	Gail Kim	6.00	15.00
NNO	Ivory	6.00	15.00
NNO	Jacqueline	3.00	8.00
NNO	Miss Jackie	5.00	12.00

NNO	Molly	4.00	10.00
NNO	Nidia	3.00	8.00
NNO	Sable	15.00	40.00
NNO	Shaniqua	3.00	8.00
NNO	Stacy Keibler	20.00	50.00
NNO	Trish Stratus	8.00	20.00
NNO	Victoria	4.00	10.00

2003 Fleer WWE Divine Divas Promo

5	Stacy Keibler	1.50	4.00

2004 Fleer WWE Divine Divas 2005

COMPLETE SET (80)		10.00	25.00
UNOPENED BOX			
UNOPENED PACK			
1	Lita	.50	1.25
2	Ivory	.30	.75
3	Dawn Marie	.20	.50
4	Stacy Keibler	.75	2.00
5	Nidia	.20	.50
6	Molly Holly	.40	1.00
7	Jazz	.20	.50
8	Torrie Wilson	.75	2.00
9	Victoria	.40	1.00
10	Trish Stratus	.75	2.00
11	Sable	.50	1.25
12	Miss Jackie	.30	.75
13	Gail Kim	.30	.75
14	Lita	.50	1.25
15	Ivory	.30	.75
16	Dawn Marie	.20	.50
17	Stacy Keibler	.75	2.00
18	Nidia	.20	.50
19	Molly Holly	.40	1.00
20	Jazz	.20	.50
21	Torrie Wilson	.75	2.00
22	Victoria	.40	1.00
23	Trish Stratus	.75	2.00
24	Sable	.50	1.25
25	Miss Jackie	.30	.75
26	Gail Kim	.30	.75
27	Lita	.50	1.25
28	Ivory	.30	.75
29	Dawn Marie	.20	.50
30	Stacy Keibler	.75	2.00
31	Torrie Wilson	.20	.50
32	Molly Holly	.40	1.00
33	Jazz	.20	.50
34	Torrie Wilson	.75	2.00
35	Victoria	.40	1.00
36	Trish Stratus	.75	2.00
37	Sable	.50	1.25
38	Miss Jackie	.30	.75
39	Gail Kim	.30	.75
40	Lita	.50	1.25
41	Ivory	.30	.75
42	Dawn Marie	.20	.50
43	Stacy Keibler	.75	2.00
44	Stacy Keibler	.75	2.00
45	Molly Holly	.40	1.00
46	Jazz	.20	.50
47	Torrie Wilson	.75	2.00
48	Victoria	.40	1.00
49	Trish Stratus	.75	2.00
50	Sable	.50	1.25
51	Miss Jackie	.30	.75
52	Gail Kim	.30	.75
53	Trish/Victoria CF	.75	2.00

54	Jazz & Gail Kim CF	.30	.75
55	Victoria & Molly Holly CF	.40	1.00
56	Sable/Torri/Stacy/Jackie CF	.75	2.00
57	Gail Kim & Lita CF	.50	1.25
58	Molly Holly & Gail Kim CF	.40	1.00
59	Jazz & Trish Stratus CF	.75	2.00
60	Lita & Trish Stratus CF	.75	2.00
61	Stacy Keibler & Miss Jackie CF	.75	2.00
62	Victoria & Gail Kim CF	.40	1.00
63	Molly Holly & Trish Stratus CF	.75	2.00
64	Sable & Torrie Wilson CF	.75	2.00
65	Victoria & Jazz CF	.40	1.00
66	Triple H OS	.50	1.25
67	Chris Jericho OS	.20	.50
68	Kurt Angle OS	.30	.75
69	Christian OS	.25	.60
70	Eric Bischoff OS	.12	.30
71	Shawn Michaels OS	.50	1.25
72	Eddie Guerrero OS	.40	1.00
73	Undertaker OS	.40	1.00
74	Booker T OS	.30	.75
75	Tyson Tomko OS	.12	.30
76	Chris Benoit OS	.20	.50
77	Eugene OS	.12	.30
78	Randy Orton OS	.20	.50
79	Edge OS	.30	.75
80	Babe of the Year Trish Stratus	.75	2.00

2004 Fleer WWE Divine Divas 2005 Body and Soul

COMPLETE SET (10)		8.00	20.00
STATED ODDS 1:8 HOBBY			
1	Dawn Marie	.60	1.50
2	Stacy Keibler	2.50	6.00
3	Torrie Wilson	2.50	6.00
4	Trish Stratus	2.50	6.00
5	Victoria	1.25	3.00
6	Miss Jackie	1.00	2.50
7	Lita	1.50	4.00
8	Ivory	1.00	2.50
9	Nidia	.60	1.50
10	Sable	1.50	4.00

2004 Fleer WWE Divine Divas 2005 Body and Soul Memorabilia

STATED ODDS 1:288 HOBBY

BSDM	Dawn Marie	4.00	10.00
BSIV	Ivory	6.00	15.00
BSLI	Lita	8.00	20.00
BSMJ	Miss Jackie	5.00	12.00
BSNI	Nidia	4.00	10.00
BSSA	Sable	8.00	20.00
BSSK	Stacy Keibler	10.00	25.00
BSTS	Trish Stratus	10.00	25.00
BSTW	Torrie Wilson	8.00	20.00
BSVI	Victoria	6.00	15.00

2004 Fleer WWE Divine Divas 2005 Divas Uncensored

COMPLETE SET (13)		15.00	40.00
STATED ODDS 1:12 HOBBY			
1	Dawn Marie	1.25	3.00
2	Jazz	1.25	3.00
3	Sable	3.00	8.00
4	Nidia	1.25	3.00
5	Victoria	2.50	6.00
6	Gail Kim	2.00	5.00

7	Ivory	2.00	5.00
8	Molly Holly	2.50	6.00
9	Trish Stratus	5.00	12.00
10	Lita	3.00	8.00
11	Stacy Keibler	5.00	12.00
12	Torrie Wilson	5.00	12.00
13	Miss Jackie	2.00	5.00

2004 Fleer WWE Divine Divas 2005 Divas Uncensored Memorabilia

STATED ODDS 1:24 HOBBY

DUL	Lita	6.00	15.00
DUDM	Dawn Marie	4.00	10.00
DUGK	Gail Kim	4.00	10.00
DUIV	Ivory	5.00	12.00
DUJA	Jazz	3.00	8.00
DUMH	Molly Holly	4.00	10.00
DUMJ	Miss Jackie	5.00	12.00
DUNI	Nidia	3.00	8.00
DUSA	Sable	6.00	15.00
DUSK	Stacy Keibler	12.00	30.00
DUTS	Trish Stratus	8.00	20.00
DUTW	Torrie Wilson	12.00	30.00
DUVI	Victoria	4.00	10.00

2004 Fleer WWE Divine Divas 2005 Femme Physique

COMPLETE SET (13)		8.00	20.00
STATED ODDS 1:4 HOBBY			
1	Lita	1.25	3.00
2	Ivory	.75	2.00
3	Dawn Marie	.50	1.25
4	Stacy Keibler	2.00	5.00
5	Nidia	.50	1.25
6	Molly Holly	1.00	2.50
7	Jazz	.50	1.25
8	Torrie Wilson	2.00	5.00
9	Victoria	1.00	2.50
10	Trish Stratus	2.00	5.00
11	Sable	1.25	3.00
12	Miss Jackie	.75	2.00
13	Gail Kim	.75	2.00

2004 Fleer WWE Divine Divas 2005 Femme Physique Memorabilia

STATED ODDS 1:28 HOBBY

FPL	Lita	6.00	15.00
FPDM	Dawn Marie	3.00	8.00
FPGK	Gail Kim	3.00	8.00
FPIV	Ivory	4.00	10.00
FPJA	Jazz	3.00	8.00
FPMH	Molly Holly	4.00	10.00
FPMJ	Miss Jackie	5.00	12.00
FPNI	Nidia	3.00	8.00
FPSA	Sable	6.00	15.00
FPSK	Stacy Keibler	8.00	20.00
FPTS	Trish Stratus	8.00	20.00
FPTW	Torrie Wilson	8.00	20.00
FPVI	Victoria	4.00	10.00

2004 Fleer WWE Divine Divas 2005 Hugs and Kisses Autographs

STATED PRINT RUN 15 SER.#'d SETS

HKDM	Dawn Marie	50.00	100.00
HKIV	Ivory	60.00	125.00
HKLI	Lita	150.00	300.00
HKMJ	Miss Jackie	60.00	125.00

HKNI Nidia	50.00	100.00
HKSA Sable	250.00	500.00
HKSK Stacy Keibler	250.00	500.00
HKTM Torrie Wilson	125.00	250.00
HKTS Trish Stratus	200.00	400.00
HKVI Victoria	60.00	125.00

2004 Fleer WWE Divine Divas 2005 With Love Wardrobe Autographs

WLDM Dawn Marie
WLIV Ivory
WLLI Lita
WLMJ Miss Jackie
WLNI Nidia
WLSA Sable
WLSK Stacy Keibler
WLTS Trish Stratus
WLTW Torrie Wilson
WLVI Victoria

2002 Fleer WWE KB Toys SmackDown! Shut Your Mouth

1 Kurt Angle	2.00	5.00
2 The Rock	5.00	12.00
3 Undertaker	2.50	6.00
4 Trish Stratus	4.00	10.00
5 Stacy Keibler	4.00	10.00
6 Triple H	2.50	6.00
7 Chris Jericho	2.00	5.00
8 Booker T	1.25	3.00
9 Rob Van Dam	1.25	3.00
10 Hollywood Hulk Hogan	4.00	10.00

2002 Fleer WWE Raw vs. SmackDown

COMPLETE SET (90)	12.00	30.00
UNOPENED BOX (24 PACKS)		
UNOPENED PACK (8 CARDS)		
1 The Rock	.75	2.00
2 Undertaker	.60	1.50
3 Kurt Angle	.50	1.25
4 Kevin Nash	.60	1.50
5 Jim Ross	.20	.50
6 X-Pac	.20	.50
7 Chris Benoit	.30	.75
8 Kane	.50	1.25
9 Hollywood Hulk Hogan	1.25	3.00
10 Rob Van Dam	.50	1.25
11 Billy Gunn	.20	.50
12 Chuck Palumbo	.20	.50
13 Booker T	.50	1.25
14 Edge	.50	1.25
15 Big Show	.50	1.25
16 Rikishi	.30	.75
17 Bubba Ray Dudley	.20	.50
18 D-Von Dudley	.20	.50
19 Brock Lesnar	6.00	15.00
20 Mark Henry	.20	.50
21 William Regal	.20	.50
22 Maven	.12	.30
23 Lita	.75	2.00
24 Billy Kidman	.12	.30
25 Bradshaw	.30	.75
26 Tajiri	.20	.50
27 Steven Richards	.20	.50
28 Chris Jericho	.30	.75
29 Matt Hardy	.30	.75
30 Ivory	.50	1.25
31 Raven	.20	.50
32 Albert	.12	.30
33 Jeff Hardy	.30	.75
34 The Hurricane	.20	.50
35 Jerry Lawler	.30	.75
36 Al Snow	.20	.50
37 D'Lo Brown	.12	.30
38 Diamond Dallas Page	.20	.50
39 Shawn Stasiak	.12	.30
40 Torrie Wilson	1.25	3.00
41 Terri	.60	1.50
42 Scotty 2 Hotty	.20	.50
43 Jacqueline	.30	.75
44 Stacy Keibler	1.25	3.00
45 Goldust	.12	.30
46 Christian	.30	.75
47 Trish Stratus	1.25	3.00
48 Test	.20	.50
49 Justin Credible	.12	.30
50 Faarooq	.12	.30
51 Boss Man	.12	.30
52 Tazz	.20	.50
53 Tommy Dreamer	.12	.30
54 Hardcore Holly	.20	.50
55 Crash	.12	.30
56 The Big Valbowski	.20	.50
57 Molly Holly	.30	.75
58 Perry Saturn	.12	.30
59 Spike Dudley	.20	.50
60 Lance Storm	.12	.30
61 Triple H	.75	2.00
62 Vince McMahon	.50	1.25
63 Ric Flair	.60	1.50
64 nWo	.20	.50
65 Rico	.12	.30
66 Debra QR	.30	.75
67 Jazz QR	.30	.75
68 Lita QR	.75	2.00
69 Ivory QR	.50	1.25
70 Terri QR	.60	1.50
71 Torrie Wilson QR	1.25	3.00
72 Jacqueline QR	.30	.75
73 Stacy Keibler QR	1.25	3.00
74 Trish Stratus QR	1.25	3.00
75 Molly Holly QR	.30	.75
76 Rob Van Dam/Kurt Angle RVS	.50	1.25
77 Big Show/Rikishi RVS	.50	1.25
78 Undertaker/DDP RVS	.60	1.50
79 Stone Cold/The Rock RVS	2.00	5.00
80 William Regal/Chris Jericho RVS	.50	1.25
81 Bubba Ray Dudley/D-Von Dudley RVS	.20	.50
82 Trish Stratus/Torrie Wilson RVS	1.25	3.00
83 Lita/Stacy Keibler RVS	1.25	3.00
84 Jacqueline/Ivory RVS	.50	1.25
85 Raven/Tajiri RVS	.20	.50
86 Brock Lesnar/The Rock RVS	5.00	12.00
87 Booker T/Edge RVS	.50	1.25
88 Goldust/The Hurricane RVS	.20	.50
89 Bradshaw/Faarooq RVS	.30	.75
90 Kane/Hulk Hogan RVS	1.25	3.00

2002 Fleer WWE Raw vs. SmackDown Catch Phrases

COMPLETE SET (15)	6.00	15.00
STATED ODDS 1:4 HOBBY		
CP1 The Rock	1.25	3.00
CP2 Ric Flair	1.00	2.50
CP3 Kurt Angle	.75	2.00
CP4 Stone Cold Steve Austin	1.25	3.00
CP5 Tazz	.30	.75
CP6 Raven	.30	.75
CP7 Trish Stratus	2.00	5.00
CP8 Triple H	1.25	3.00
CP9 The Big Valbowski	.30	.75
CP10 Booker T	.75	2.00
CP11 Chris Jericho	.50	1.25
CP12 Hollywood Hulk Hogan	2.00	5.00
CP13 nWo	.30	.75
CP14 Jim Ross	.30	.75
CP15 Chris Benoit	.50	1.25

2002 Fleer WWE Raw vs. SmackDown Exposure

COMPLETE SET (10)	8.00	20.00
STATED ODDS 1:8 HOBBY		
XP1 Debra	.60	1.50
XP2 Ivory	1.00	2.50
XP3 Jacqueline	.60	1.50
XP4 Jazz	.60	1.50
XP5 Lita	1.50	4.00
XP6 Molly Holly	.60	1.50
XP7 Stacy Keibler	2.50	6.00
XP8 Terri	1.25	3.00
XP9 Torrie Wilson	2.50	6.00
XP10 Trish Stratus	2.50	6.00

2002 Fleer WWE Raw vs. SmackDown Pay-Per-View Relics

COMPLETE SET (5)	30.00	75.00
STATED ODDS 1:33 HOBBY		
NNO Kurt Angle/Kane	6.00	15.00
NNO Ric Flair/Undertaker	10.00	25.00
NNO The Rock/Hulk Hogan	20.00	50.00
NNO Scott Hall/Steve Austin	10.00	25.00
NNO William Regal/Rob Van Dam	6.00	15.00

2002 Fleer WWE Raw vs. SmackDown Pop-Ups

COMPLETE SET (10)	20.00	50.00
STATED ODDS 1:HOBBY BOX		
NNO Chris Jericho	1.25	3.00
NNO Hollywood Hulk Hogan	5.00	12.00
NNO Kurt Angle	2.00	5.00
NNO Lita	3.00	8.00
NNO The Rock	3.00	8.00
NNO Stacy Keibler	5.00	12.00
NNO Stone Cold Steve Austin	3.00	8.00
NNO Triple H	3.00	8.00
NNO Trish Stratus	5.00	12.00
NNO Undertaker	2.50	6.00

2002 Fleer WWE Raw vs. SmackDown Raw Certified

STATED ODDS 1:72		
NNO Kevin Nash	10.00	25.00
NNO Rob Van Dam	8.00	20.00
NNO Spike Dudley	8.00	20.00
NNO William Regal	8.00	20.00
NNO X-Pac	8.00	20.00

2002 Fleer WWE Raw vs. SmackDown SmackDown Authentics

STATED ODDS 1:36 HOBBY		
NNO Billy Gunn Headband	4.00	10.00
NNO Chuck Palumbo Headband	4.00	10.00
NNO DDP Pants	5.00	12.00
NNO Edge Shirt	6.00	15.00
NNO Hollywood Hulk Hogan Shirt	8.00	20.00
NNO Triple H Shirt	6.00	15.00
NNO Undertaker Shirt	6.00	15.00

2002 Fleer WWE Raw vs. SmackDown Triple Exposure

NNO Lita/Debra/Molly	25.00	60.00
NNO Molly/Stacy Keibler/Debra	30.00	75.00
NNO Terri/Torrie/Stacy	75.00	150.00

2002 Fleer WWE Raw vs. SmackDown Ultimate Exposure

STATED ODDS 1:96 HOBBY		
NNO Debra Jacket	8.00	20.00
NNO Lita Top	10.00	25.00
NNO Molly Holly Swimsuit	6.00	15.00
NNO Molly Holly Top	6.00	15.00
NNO Stacy Keibler Shirt	12.00	30.00
NNO Terri Dress	10.00	25.00
NNO Torrie Wilson Stocking	12.00	30.00

2002 Fleer WWE Royal Rumble

COMPLETE SET W/CENA (90)	125.00	250.00
COMPLETE SET W/O CENA (89)	50.00	100.00
UNOPENED PACK (8 CARDS)		
UNOPENED BOX (24 PACKS)		
1 Big Show	.50	1.25
2 Booker T	.50	1.25
3 Bradshaw	.30	.75
4 Brock Lesnar	25.00	50.00
5 Bubba Ray Dudley	.20	.50
6 Chris Nowinski	.12	.30
7 John Cena	100.00	200.00
8 D'Lo Brown	.12	.30
9 Eddie Guerrero	.60	1.50
10 Goldust	.12	.30
11 Jacqueline	.30	.75
12 Jazz	.30	.75
13 Jeff Hardy	.30	.75
14 Randy Orton	12.00	30.00
15 Kane	.50	1.25
16 Kevin Nash	.60	1.50
17 Lita	.75	2.00
18 Mark Henry	.20	.50
19 Matt Hardy	.30	.75
20 Molly	.30	.75
21 Rob Van Dam	.50	1.25
22 Raven	.20	.50
23 Shawn Michaels	.75	2.00
24 Shawn Stasiak	.12	.30

25	Spike Dudley	.20	.50
26	Steven Richards	.20	.50
27	Terri	.60	1.50
28	Ric Flair	.60	1.50
29	William Regal	.20	.50
30	X-Pac	.20	.50
31	Al Snow	.20	.50
32	Billy	.20	.50
33	Billy Kidman	.12	.30
34	Chris Benoit	.30	.75
35	Christian	.30	.75
36	Chuck	.20	.50
37	D-Von	.20	.50
38	Paul Heyman	.12	.30
39	Edge	.50	1.25
40	Faarooq	.12	.30
41	Funaki	.20	.50
42	Chris Jericho	.30	.75
43	Hollywood Hulk Hogan	1.25	3.00
44	The Hurricane	.20	.50
45	Ivory	.50	1.25
46	Kurt Angle	.50	1.25
47	Maven	.12	.30
48	Nidia	.30	.75
49	Rico	.12	.30
50	The Rock	.75	2.00
51	Tajiri	.20	.50
52	Torrie Wilson	1.25	3.00
53	Triple H	.75	2.00
54	Scotty 2 Hotty	.20	.50
55	Stacy Keibler	1.25	3.00
56	Lance Storm	.12	.30
57	Tazz	.20	.50
58	Test	.20	.50
59	Eric Bischoff	.12	.30
60	Jackie	.50	1.25
61	Victoria	.60	1.50
62	Stephanie	.60	1.50
63	Vince McMahon	.50	1.25
64	Rikishi	.30	.75
65	Jerry Lawler	.30	.75
66	Jim Ross	.20	.50
67	Deacon Batista	12.00	30.00
68	Shane McMahon	.30	.75
69	Albert	.12	.30
70	Trish Stratus	1.25	3.00
71	Undertaker	.60	1.50
72	Dawn Marie	.30	.75
73	Chavo Guerrero	.20	.50
74	Rey Mysterio	.30	.75
75	Tommy Dreamer	.12	.30
76	Eddie Guerrero AKA	.60	1.50
77	Brock Lesnar AKA	6.00	15.00
78	Chris Benoit AKA	.30	.75
79	Triple H AKA	.75	2.00
80	Undertaker AKA	.60	1.50
81	The Rock AKA	.75	2.00
82	Jim Ross AKA	.20	.50
83	Jerry Lawler AKA	.30	.75
84	Ric Flair AKA	.60	1.50
85	Shawn Stasiak AKA	.12	.30
86	Kurt Angle AKA	.50	1.25
87	Shawn Michaels AKA	.75	2.00
88	Hulk Hogan AKA	1.25	3.00
89	Rob Van Dam AKA	.50	1.25
90	J.Hardy/M.Hardy/Lita AKA	.75	2.00

2002 Fleer WWE Royal Rumble AKA Memorabilia

STATED ODDS 1:24 HOBBY

NNO	Triple H Ring Mat	4.00	10.00
NNO	Undertaker Ring Mat	4.00	10.00

2002 Fleer WWE Royal Rumble Divastating

COMPLETE SET (15)		10.00	25.00
STATED ODDS 1:8 HOBBY			
D1	Ivory	1.00	2.50
D2	Torrie Wilson	2.50	6.00
D3	Terri	1.25	3.00
D4	Stacy Keibler	2.50	6.00
D5	Trish Stratus	2.50	6.00
D6	Molly	.60	1.50
D7	Stephanie McMahon	4.00	10.00
D8	Jazz	.60	1.50
D9	Jacqueline	.60	1.50
D10	Lita	1.50	4.00
D11	Dawn Marie	.60	1.50
D12	Nidia	.60	1.50
D13	Linda	.60	1.50
D14	Jackie	1.00	2.50
D15	Victoria	1.25	3.00

2002 Fleer WWE Royal Rumble Divastating Autographs

PRINT RUN 100 SER. #'d SETS

NNO	Lita	50.00	100.00
NNO	Stacy Keibler	75.00	150.00
NNO	Terri	25.00	60.00
NNO	Torrie Wilson	60.00	120.00

2002 Fleer WWE Royal Rumble Divastating Memorabilia

STATED ODDS 1:48 HOBBY

NNO	Dawn Marie	8.00	20.00
NNO	Ivory Undergarment	6.00	15.00
NNO	Jazz Ring Mat	4.00	10.00
NNO	Stacy Keibler Shirt	10.00	25.00
NNO	Torrie Wilson Skirt	10.00	25.00
NNO	Trish Stratus	15.00	40.00

2002 Fleer WWE Royal Rumble Factions

COMPLETE SET (5)		20.00	50.00
STATED ODDS 1:120			
F1	The Nation of Domination	6.00	15.00
F2	The Corporation	6.00	15.00
F3	The Radicalz	6.00	15.00
F4	D-Generation X	6.00	15.00
F5	New World Order	6.00	15.00

2002 Fleer WWE Royal Rumble Factions Memorabilia

STATED ODDS 1:48 HOBBY

NNO	The Rock Shirt	8.00	20.00
NNO	Shawn Michaels	6.00	15.00

	D-X Shirt		
NNO	Shawn Michaels	6.00	15.00
	nWo Shirt		
NNO	X-Pac Shirt	4.00	10.00

2002 Fleer WWE Royal Rumble Gimmick Matches

COMPLETE SET (10)		6.00	15.00
STATED ODDS 1:4 HOBBY			
GM1	Triple H/Chris Jericho	1.25	3.00
GM2	Undertaker/Jeff Hardy	1.00	2.50
GM3	Rob Van Dam/Eddie Guerrero	1.00	2.50
GM4	Kurt Angle/Edge	.75	2.00
GM5	Rob Van Dam/Jeff Hardy	.75	2.00
GM6	Stacy Keibler/Trish Stratus	2.00	5.00
GM7	The Rock/Trish Stratus	2.00	5.00
GM8	Kurt Angle/Shane McMahon	.75	2.00
GM9	Chris Jericho/Kane	.75	2.00
GM10	Kurt Angle/Edge	.75	2.00

2002 Fleer WWE Royal Rumble Gimmick Matches Dual Memorabilia

STATED PRINT RUN 25 SER. #'d SETS

NNO	The Rock/Trish Stratus	15.00	40.00
NNO	Stacy Keibler/Trish Stratus	20.00	50.00
NNO	Triple H/Chris Jericho	20.00	50.00
NNO	Undertaker/Jeff Hardy	50.00	100.00

2002 Fleer WWE Royal Rumble Gimmick Matches Memorabilia

STATED ODDS 1:24 HOBBY

NNO	Chris Jericho Shirt (Hell in a Cell)	6.00	15.00
NNO	Chris Jericho Shirt (Last Man Standing)	6.00	15.00
NNO	Edge Shirt (Cage Match)	8.00	20.00
NNO	Edge Shirt (Hair vs Hair)	8.00	20.00
NNO	Jeff Hardy Shirt (Ladder Match)	8.00	20.00
NNO	Jeff Hardy Tank Top (Hardcore Match)	8.00	20.00
NNO	Stacy Keibler Shirt (Gravy Bowl Match)	10.00	25.00
NNO	Triple H Shirt (Hell in a Cell)	8.00	20.00
NNO	Trish Stratus Pants (Gender Match)	10.00	25.00
NNO	Trish Stratus Shirt (Gender Match)	10.00	25.00
NNO	Trish Stratus Shirt (Gravy Bowl Match)	10.00	25.00
NNO	Undertaker Shirt (Ladder Match)	8.00	20.00

2002 Fleer WWE Royal Rumble Memorabilia

STATED ODDS 1:24 HOBBY

NNO	Brock Lesnar	30.00	75.00
NNO	Chris Benoit	6.00	15.00
NNO	Edge Ring Mat	6.00	15.00
NNO	Funaki Shirt	3.00	8.00
NNO	Hollywood Hulk Hogan	15.00	40.00

NNO	The Hurricane Ring Mat	3.00	8.00
NNO	Kane Ring Mat	5.00	12.00
NNO	Kurt Angle Ring Mat	5.00	12.00
NNO	Maven T-Shirt	3.00	8.00
NNO	Rey Mysterio	10.00	25.00
NNO	Rob Van Dam Ring Mat	4.00	10.00
NNO	The Rock	10.00	25.00
NNO	Scotty 2 Hotty Jeans	4.00	10.00
NNO	Shawn Michaels Shirt	5.00	12.00
NNO	Tazz Sweat Pants	3.00	8.00

2002 Fleer WWE Royal Rumble Recap

COMPLETE SET (10)		15.00	40.00
STATED ODDS 1:24 HOBBY			
RR1	Kane	1.50	4.00
RR2	Kane vs The Undertaker	2.00	5.00
RR3	Triple H vs Cactus Jack	2.50	6.00
RR4	Vince McMahon	1.50	4.00
RR5	Stone Cold	2.50	6.00
RR6	Hollywood Hulk Hogan	4.00	10.00
RR7	Ric Flair	2.00	5.00
RR8	The Rock vs Mankind	2.50	6.00
RR9	Shawn Michaels	2.50	6.00
RR10	Mae Young	1.00	2.50

2003 Fleer WWE WrestleMania XIX

COMPLETE SET (90)		12.50	30.00
UNOPENED BOX (24 PACKS)			
UNOPENED PACK (5 CARDS)			
1	Scott Steiner	.60	1.50
2	Scotty 2 Hotty	.20	.50
3	Albert	.12	.30
4	Kurt Angle	.50	1.25
5	Batista	.50	1.25
6	Chris Benoit	.30	.75
7	Big Show	.50	1.25
8	Billy	.20	.50
9	Eric Bischoff	.20	.50
10	Bradshaw	.30	.75
11	D'Lo Brown	.20	.50
12	John Cena	.75	2.00
13	Christian	.30	.75
14	Chuck	.20	.50
15	Tommy Dreamer	.12	.30
16	Bubba Ray Dudley	.20	.50
17	Spike Dudley	.20	.50
18	D-Von	.20	.50
19	Edge	.50	1.25
20	Ron Simmons	.20	.50
21	Ric Flair	.60	1.50
22	Funaki	.20	.50
23	Goldust	.12	.30
24	Crash	.12	.30
25	Eddie Guerrero	.60	1.50
26	Triple H	.75	2.00
27	Jeff Hardy	.30	.75
28	Matt Hardy	.30	.75
29	Hollywood Hulk Hogan	.75	2.00

30	The Hurricane	.12	.30
31	Chris Jericho	.30	.75
32	Kane	.50	1.25
33	Billy Kidman	.12	.30
34	Jerry Lawler	.30	.75
35	Brock Lesnar	1.25	3.00
36	Mark Henry	.20	.50
37	Maven	.12	.30
38	Godfather	.12	.30
39	Johnny Stamboli	.12	.30
40	Shawn Michaels	.75	2.00
41	Rey Mysterio	.30	.75
42	Kevin Nash	.60	1.50
43	Chris Nowinski	.12	.30
44	Randy Orton	.30	.75
45	Raven	.30	.75
46	William Regal	.30	.75
47	Steven Richards	.20	.50
48	Rico	.12	.30
49	Rikishi	.30	.75
50	The Rock	.75	2.00
51	Jim Ross	.20	.50
52	Al Snow	.12	.30
53	Jamie Noble	.12	.30
54	Lance Storm	.12	.30
55	Booker T	.50	1.25
56	Tajiri	.12	.30
57	Tazz	.20	.50
58	Test	.20	.50
59	Undertaker	.60	1.50
60	Rob Van Dam	.50	1.25
61	Lilian Garcia	1.00	2.50
62	Dawn Marie	.60	1.50
63	Trish Stratus	1.25	3.00
64	Jackie	.50	1.25
65	Victoria	.60	1.50
66	Stephanie	.60	1.50
67	Torrie Wilson	1.25	3.00
68	Stacy Keibler	1.25	3.00
69	Nidia	.30	.75
70	Ivory	.50	1.25
71	Terri	.60	1.50
72	Jacqueline	.30	.75
73	Jazz	.20	.50
74	Lita	.75	2.00
75	Molly	.60	1.50
76	Undertaker MM	.60	1.50
77	Kane MM	.50	1.25
78	Hollywood Hulk Hogan MM	.75	2.00
79	The Rock MM	.75	2.00
80	Triple H MM	.75	2.00
81	Kurt Angle MM	.50	1.25
82	Chris Jericho MM	.30	.75
83	Trish Stratus MM	1.25	3.00
84	Shawn Michaels MM	.75	2.00
85	Ivory MM	.50	1.25
86	Lita MM	.75	2.00
87	Jeff Hardy MM	.30	.75
88	Ric Flair MM	.60	1.50
89	Rikishi MM	.30	.75
90	Stone Cold Steve Austin MM	.75	2.00

2003 Fleer WWE WrestleMania XIX
Diva Las Vegas

COMPLETE SET (2)			
NNO	Dawn Marie/1350	8.00	20.00
NNO	Torrie Wilson/150	20.00	50.00

2003 Fleer WWE WrestleMania XIX
Flashbacks

COMPLETE SET (6)		30.00	60.00
STATED ODDS 1:48 HOBBY			
NNO	Chris Jericho	4.00	10.00
NNO	Hollywood Hulk Hogan	12.00	30.00
NNO	Kurt Angle	6.00	15.00
NNO	Stone Cold Steve Austin	6.00	15.00
NNO	Triple H	10.00	25.00
NNO	Undertaker	10.00	25.00

2003 Fleer WWE WrestleMania XIX
Mat Finish

COMPLETE SET (10)		40.00	80.00
STATED ODDS 1:24 HOBBY			
NNO	Brock Lesnar	6.00	15.00
NNO	Edge	5.00	12.00
NNO	The Hurricane	4.00	10.00
NNO	Kurt Angle	5.00	12.00
NNO	Rob Van Dam	4.00	10.00
NNO	The Rock	6.00	15.00
NNO	Stone Cold Steve Austin	6.00	15.00
NNO	Triple H	5.00	12.00
NNO	Trish Stratus	6.00	15.00
NNO	Undertaker	5.00	12.00

2003 Fleer WWE WrestleMania XIX
Title Shots

COMPLETE SET (7)		50.00	100.00
STATED ODDS 1:48 HOBBY			
NNO	Brock Lesnar	10.00	25.00
NNO	Kane	6.00	15.00
NNO	Kurt Angle	8.00	20.00
NNO	Rob Van Dam	6.00	15.00
NNO	The Rock	12.00	30.00
NNO	Triple H	8.00	20.00
NNO	Undertaker	8.00	20.00

2004 Fleer WWE WrestleMania XX

COMPLETE SET (84)		10.00	25.00
UNOPENED BOX (24 PACKS)			
UNOPENED PACK (5 CARDS)			
*GOLD: .75X TO 2X BASIC CARDS			
1	Batista	.50	1.25
2	A-Train	.12	.30
3	Chris Jericho	.30	.75
4	Bill DeMott	.12	.30
5	Goldberg	1.00	2.50
6	Undertaker	.60	1.50
7	Kevin Nash	.60	1.50
8	Eddie Guerrero	.60	1.50
9	Mark Henry	.20	.50
10	John Cena	.75	2.00
11	Ric Flair	.60	1.50
12	Shannon Moore	.12	.30
13	Scott Steiner	.60	1.50
14	Brock Lesnar	1.25	3.00
15	Shawn Michaels	.75	2.00
16	Basham Brothers	.12	.30
17	Mark Jindrak & Garrison Cade	.12	.30
18	Chavo Guerrero	.20	.50
19	Eric Bischoff	.20	.50
20	Ultimo Dragon	.12	.30
21	Triple H	.75	2.00
22	The World's Greatest Tag Team	.12	.30
23	La Resistance	.12	.30
24	Rhyno	.50	1.25

25	Rico	.12	.30
26	Edge	.50	1.25
27	Steven Richards	.20	.50
28	Jerry The King Lawler	.30	.75
29	Vince McMahon	.50	1.25
30	Linda McMahon	.20	.50
31	Stephanie McMahon	.60	1.50
32	Shane McMahon	.30	.75
33	Jim Ross	.20	.50
34	Chris Nowinski	.12	.30
35	Tazz	.20	.50
36	Maven	.12	.30
37	Sean O'Haire	.12	.30
38	Dudley Boyz	.20	.50
39	The Hurricane		
40	Rey Mysterio	.30	.75
41	Test	.20	.50
42	Tajiri	.12	.30
43	Stone Cold Steve Austin	.75	2.00
44	Chris Benoit	.30	.75
45	The Rock	.75	2.00
46	APA	.30	.75
47	Rosey	.12	.30
48	Rodney Mack	.12	.30
49	Matt Hardy	.30	.75
50	Randy Orton	.30	.75
51	Kurt Angle	.50	1.25
52	Lance Storm	.12	.30
53	FBI		
54	Kane	.50	1.25
55	Billy Kidman	.12	.30
56	Christian	.40	1.00
57	Big Show	.50	1.25
58	Booker T	.50	1.25
59	Sable RD	.75	2.00
60	Lita RD	.75	2.00
61	Ivory RD	.50	1.25
62	Stacy Keibler RD	1.25	3.00
63	Molly RD	.60	1.50
64	Torrie Wilson RD	1.25	3.00
65	Terri RD	.60	1.50
66	Shaniqua RD	.30	.75
67	Gail Kim	.50	1.25
68	Miss Jackie RD	.50	1.25
69	Victoria RD	.60	1.50
70	Jazz RD	.30	.75
71	Nidia RD	.30	.75
72	Dawn Marie RD	.30	.75
73	Jacqueline RD	.40	1.00
74	Trish Stratus RD	1.25	3.00
75	Ric Flair MM	.60	1.50
76	Shawn Michaels MM	.75	2.00
77	Shawn Michaels MM	.75	2.00
78	Undertaker MM	.60	1.50
79	Stone Cold Steve Austin MM	.75	2.00
80	The Rock MM	.75	2.00
81	Triple H MM	.75	2.00
82	Steve Austin & The Rock MM	.75	2.00
83	Triple H MM	.75	2.00
84	Brock Lesnar MM	1.25	3.00

2004 Fleer WWE WrestleMania XX
Champions and Contenders

COMPLETE SET (17)		8.00	20.00
STATED ODDS 1:4 HOBBY AND RETAIL			
1	Kurt Angle	1.50	4.00
	Brock Lesnar		
2	Steve Austin	2.00	5.00

2004 Fleer WWE WrestleMania XX
The Rock
3	Trish Stratus	1.50	4.00
	Jazz		
4	Triple H	1.00	2.50
	Booker T		
5	Kane	.60	1.50
	Big Show		
6	Eddie Guerrero	.75	2.00
	Test		
7	Undertaker	.75	2.00
	Ric Flair		
8	Edge & Christian	.60	1.50
	Dudley Boyz		
9	Jazz	1.00	2.50
	Lita		
10	Triple H	1.00	2.50
	The Rock		
11	Shane McMahon	.60	1.50
	Vince McMahon		
12	Chris Benoit	.40	1.00
	Chris Jericho		
13	Rob Van Dam	.60	1.50
	William Regal		
14	Trish Stratus	1.50	4.00
	Victoria		
15	Matt Hardy	.40	1.00
	Rey Mysterio		
16	Steve Austin	1.00	2.50
	Shawn Michaels		
17	Triple H	1.00	2.50
	Chris Jericho		

2004 Fleer WWE WrestleMania XX
Champions and Contenders Dual Memorabilia

STATED ODDS 1:144 HOBBY			
CCDJ/L	Jazz	6.00	12.00
	Lita		
CCDK/BS	Kane	6.00	12.00
	Big Show		
CCDSA/R	Steve Austin	10.00	20.00
	The Rock		
CCDTS/J	Trish Stratus	10.00	20.00
	Jazz		
CCDCB/CJ	Chris Benoit	5.00	10.00
	Chris Jericho		
CCDKA/BL	Kurt Angle	7.50	15.00
	Brock Lesnar		
CCDMH/RM	Matt Hardy	6.00	12.00
	Rey Mysterio		
CCDSA/SM	Steve Austin	7.50	15.00
	Shawn Michaels		
CCDTH/BT	Triple H	6.00	12.00
	Booker T		
CCDTH/CJ	Triple H	6.00	12.00
	Chris Jericho		

2004 Fleer WWE WrestleMania XX
Champions and Contenders Memorabilia

STATED ODDS 1:18 HOBBY			
CCSJ	Jazz	3.00	8.00
CCSK	Kane	4.00	10.00
CCSL	Lita	5.00	12.00
CCSR	The Rock	6.00	15.00
CCST	Test	3.00	8.00
CCSU	Undertaker	5.00	12.00

CCSBL Brock Lesnar	6.00	15.00
CCSBT Booker T	3.00	8.00
CCSCB Chris Benoit	3.00	8.00
CCSCJ Chris Jericho	3.00	8.00
CCSKA Kurt Angle	4.00	10.00
CCSMH Matt Hardy	5.00	12.00
CCSSA Stone Cold Steve Austin	6.00	15.00
CCSSM Shawn Michaels	5.00	12.00
CCSTH Triple H	5.00	12.00
CCSTS Trish Stratus	6.00	15.00
CCSRVD Rob Van Dam	3.00	8.00

2004 Fleer WWE WrestleMania XX Road to WrestleMania

COMPLETE SET (10) 20.00 50.00
STATED ODDS 1:24 HOBBY AND RETAIL

1 Shawn Michaels	3.00	8.00
2 Trish Stratus	5.00	12.00
3 Brock Lesnar	5.00	12.00
4 Stone Cold Steve Austin	3.00	8.00
5 Undertaker	2.50	6.00
6 Scott Steiner	2.50	6.00
7 Lita	3.00	8.00
8 Triple H	3.00	8.00
9 The Rock	3.00	8.00
10 Kurt Angle	2.00	5.00

2004 Fleer WWE WrestleMania XX To the Mat Memorabilia

STATED ODDS 1:48 HOBBY

1 Lita	6.00	15.00
2 Stacy Keibler	8.00	20.00
3 Molly	4.00	10.00
4 Torrie Wilson	8.00	20.00
5 Gail Kim	4.00	10.00
6 Victoria	5.00	12.00
7 Miss Jackie	5.00	12.00
8 Trish Stratus	8.00	20.00
9 Sable	6.00	15.00
10 Ivory	5.00	12.00

2004 Fleer WWE WrestleMania XX To the Mat Memorabilia Autographs

STATED PRINT RUN 50 SER.#'d SETS

TTML Lita	50.00	100.00
TTMS Sable	30.00	75.00
TTMSK Stacy Keibler	60.00	120.00
TTMTS Trish Stratus	75.00	150.00
TTMTW Torrie Wilson	30.00	75.00

2002 Fleer WWF All Access

COMPLETE SET (100) 8.00 20.00
UNOPENED BOX (24 PACKS)
UNOPENED PACK (8 CARDS)

16 The Rock	2.00	5.00
1 Justin Credible	.12	.30
2 Shane McMahon	.30	.75
3 Tajiri	.20	.50
4 Jerry Lynn	.12	.30
5 Christian	.30	.75
6 Haku	.12	.30
7 Kurt Angle	.50	1.25
8 Albert	.12	.30
9 Chris Jericho	.30	.75
10 Jeff Hardy	.30	.75
11 Triple H	.75	2.00
12 The One Billy Gunn	.20	.50
13 Booker T	.50	1.25
14 Funaki	.20	.50
15 Chris Benoit	.30	.75
17 Bradshaw	.30	.75
18 Stephanie McMahon-Helmsley	2.00	5.00
19 Crash Holly	.12	.30
20 Rhyno	.30	.75
21 Faarooq	.12	.30
22 Al Snow	.20	.50
23 Hardcore Holly	.20	.50
24 Rikishi	.30	.75
25 Rob Van Dam	.50	1.25
26 X-Pac	.20	.50
27 D-Von Dudley	.20	.50
28 Kane	.50	1.25
29 Spike Dudley	.20	.50
30 William Regal	.20	.50
31 Taka Michinoku	.12	.30
32 Mick Foley	.50	1.25
33 Undertaker	.60	1.50
34 Edge	.50	1.25
35 Stone Cold Steve Austin	.75	2.00
36 Jim Ross	.20	.50
37 Bubba Ray Dudley	.20	.50
38 Steve Blackman	.12	.30
39 Test	.20	.50
40 Molly Holly	.30	.75
41 Vince Mcmahon	.50	1.25
42 Stacy Keibler	1.25	3.00
43 Torrie Wilson	1.25	3.00
44 Perry Saturn	.12	.30
45 Raven	.20	.50
46 Scotty 2 Hotty	.20	.50
47 Big Show	.50	1.25
48 Matt Hardy	.30	.75
49 Tazz	.20	.50
50 The Hurricane	.20	.50
51 Kane OTM	.50	1.25
52 Mick Foley OTM	.50	1.25
53 Lita OTM	.75	2.00
54 Justin Credible OTM	.12	.30
55 Big Show OTM	.50	1.25
56 Chris Benoit OTM	.30	.75
57 Stone Cold OTM	.75	2.00
58 Edge OTM	.50	1.25
59 Trish Stratus OTM	2.50	6.00
60 Faarooq OTM	.12	.30
61 Linda McMahon OTM	.20	.50
62 Matt Hardy OTM	.30	.75
63 Diamond Dallas Page OTM	.20	.50
64 The Hurricane OTM	.20	.50
65 Kurt Angle OTM	.50	1.25
66 Ric Flair OTM	.60	1.50
67 Undertaker OTM	.60	1.50
68 Tajiri OTM	.20	.50
69 Vince McMahon OTM	.50	1.25
70 Chris Jericho OTM	.30	.75
71 Triple H OTM	.75	2.00
72 Tazz OTM	.20	.50
73 Rob Van Dam OTM	.50	1.25
74 Sgt. Slaughter OTM	.30	.75
75 The Rock OTM	.75	2.00
76 Jim Ross OTM	.20	.50
77 Bradshaw OTM	.30	.75
78 Matt Hardy OTM	.30	.75
79 Perry Saturn OTM	.12	.30
80 X-Pac OTM	.20	.50
81 Maven RR	.12	.30
82 Molly Holly RR	.30	.75
83 Big Show RR	.50	1.25
84 Edge RR	.50	1.25
85 Stone Cold Steve Austin RR	.75	2.00
86 Vince McMahon RR	.50	1.25
87 Jeff Hardy RR	.30	.75
88 Kane RR	.50	1.25
89 Lita RR	.75	2.00
90 Ivory RR	.50	1.25
91 Kurt Angle RR	.50	1.25
92 Triple H RR	.75	2.00
93 Rob Van Dam RR	.50	1.25
94 Trish Stratus RR	1.25	3.00
95 Nidia RR	.30	.75
96 Matt Hardy RR	.30	.75
97 Christian RR	.30	.75
98 Mick Foley RR	.50	1.25
99 The Rock RR	.75	2.00
100 Undertaker RR	.60	1.50

2002 Fleer WWF All Access All Access Memorabilia

STATED ODDS 1:15

AAMF Funaki	3.00	8.00
AAMH The Hurricane SP		
AAMK Kane	12.00	30.00
AAMU Undertaker	20.00	50.00
AAMA Stone Cold Steve Austin	12.00	30.00
AAMJH Jeff Hardy	5.00	12.00
AAMKA Kurt Angle		
AAMMH Molly Holly	5.00	12.00
AAMSH Scotty 2 Hotty	4.00	10.00
AAMSK Stacy Keibler	15.00	40.00
AAMT1 Tajiri	3.00	8.00
AAMT2 Tazz	3.00	8.00
AAMTH Triple H	6.00	15.00
AAMTW Torrie Wilson	8.00	20.00
AAMDVD D-Von Dudley	5.00	12.00
AAMRVD Rob Van Dam	4.00	10.00

2002 Fleer WWF All Access Famous Rides

COMPLETE SET (12) 5.00 12.00
STATED ODDS 1:6

FR1 Diamond Dallas Page's Pink Cadillac	.30	.75
FR2 Stone Cold's Truck	1.25	3.00
FR3 The Rock's Limo	1.25	3.00
FR4 D-Generation X's Tank Jeep	.30	.75
FR5 Stone Cold Destroys Vince's Vette	1.25	3.00
FR6 Vince McMahon's Jet	.75	2.00
FR7 Big Show's Purple Car	.75	2.00
FR8 Kurt Angle's Scooter	.75	2.00
FR9 Jeff Hardy's Motorcycle	.50	1.25
FR10 Stone Cold's 18-Wheeler	1.25	3.00
FR11 D-Generation X's Bus	.30	.75
FR12 Al Snow's Lil' Racecar	.30	.75

2002 Fleer WWF All Access Match Makers

COMPLETE SET (15) 6.00 15.00
STATED ODDS 1:6

MM1 Triple H & Stephanie	1.00	2.50
MM2 Kane & Undertaker	.75	2.00
MM3 Debra & Stone Cold	1.00	2.50
MM4 Dudley Boyz	.25	.60
MM5 The Rock & Mick Foley	1.00	2.50
MM6 Edge & Christian	.60	1.50
MM7 Stephanie & Chris Jericho	.75	2.00
MM8 Kurt Angle & Triple H	1.00	2.50
MM9 The Rock & Stone Cold	1.00	2.50
MM10 Kaientai	.25	.60
MM11 Benoit & Jericho	.40	1.00
MM12 Stone Cold & Undertaker	1.00	2.50
MM13 Kurt Angle & The Rock	1.00	2.50
MM14 Matt Hardy, Lita & Jeff Hardy	1.00	2.50
MM15 Mr. McMahon & Stone Cold	1.00	2.50

2002 Fleer WWF All Access Match Makers Memorabilia

STATED ODDS 1:95

MMDB Dudley Boyz	15.00	40.00
MMEC Edge & Christian	12.00	30.00
MMKU Kane & Undertaker	10.00	25.00
MMRKA Kurt Angle & The Rock	12.00	30.00
MMRMF The Rock & Mick Foley	12.00	30.00
MMRSA The Rock & Stone Cold	15.00	40.00
MMSAU Stone Cold & Undertaker	12.00	30.00

2002 Fleer WWF All Access Off the Mat Autographs

RANDOMLY INSERTED INTO PACKS

NNO The Hurricane	12.00	30.00
NNO Jim Ross	30.00	75.00
NNO Lita	50.00	100.00
NNO Rob Van Dam	25.00	60.00
NNO Stacy Keibler	100.00	200.00
NNO Torrie Wilson	30.00	80.00
NNO Triple H	250.00	500.00
NNO Trish Stratus	60.00	120.00

2002 Fleer WWF All Access Pay-Per-View Posters

COMPLETE SET (8) 15.00 40.00
STATED ODDS 1:33

PPV1 Backlash	3.00	8.00
PPV2 Invasion	2.00	5.00
PPV3 Judgment Day	3.00	8.00
PPV4 No Mercy	2.00	5.00
PPV5 No Way Out	2.00	5.00
PPV6 SummerSlam	3.00	8.00
PPV7 Unforgiven	3.00	8.00
PPV8 Vengeance	3.00	8.00
PPV9 WrestleMania X-7	3.00	8.00
PPV10 Survivor Series	5.00	12.00

2001 Fleer WWF Championship Clash

COMPLETE SET (80) 8.00 20.00
UNOPENED BOX (24 PACKS)
UNOPENED PACK (5 CARDS)

1 The Rock	4.00	10.00
2 K-Kwik	.12	.30
3 Steve Blackman	.12	.30
4 Eddie Guerrero	.50	1.25
5 Jerry Lynn	.12	.30
6 Christian	.30	.75
7 Kane	.50	1.25
8 Tazz	.20	.50
9 Stone Cold Steve Austin	.75	2.00
10 Crash Holly	.12	.30
11 Matt Hardy	.30	.75
12 Undertaker	.60	1.50
13 Al Snow	.20	.50
14 Tajiri	.12	.30

15 Scotty 2 Hotty	.20	.50
16 Dean Malenko	.20	.50
17 Raven	.12	.30
18 Big Show	.50	1.25
19 Jeff Hardy	.30	.75
20 Spike Dudley	.20	.50
21 Chris Jericho	.30	.75
22 Kurt Angle	.50	1.25
23 Test	.20	.50
24 Chris Benoit	.30	.75
25 William Regal	.20	.50
26 Rikishi	.20	.50
27 D-Von Dudley	.20	.50
28 Mick Foley	.50	1.25
29 Triple H	.75	2.00
30 Albert	.12	.30
31 Haku	.12	.30
32 Perry Saturn	.12	.30
33 The One Billy Gunn	.12	.30
34 Hardcore Holly	.20	.50
35 Shane McMahon	.30	.75
36 Edge	.50	1.25
37 Rhyno	.20	.50
38 Bubba Ray Dudley	.20	.50
39 Justin Credible	.12	.30
40 X-Pac	.20	.50
41 The Rock PC	2.50	6.00
42 K-Kwik PC	.12	.30
43 Steve Blackman PC	.12	.30
44 Eddie Guerrero PC	.50	1.25
45 Jerry Lynn PC	.12	.30
46 Christian PC	.30	.75
47 Kane PC	.50	1.25
48 Tazz PC	.20	.50
49 Stone Cold Steve Austin PC	.75	2.00
50 Crash Holly PC	.12	.30
51 Matt Hardy PC	.30	.75
52 Undertaker PC	.60	1.50
53 Al Snow PC	.20	.50
54 Tajiri PC	.12	.30
55 Scotty 2 Hotty PC	.20	.50
56 Dean Malenko PC	.20	.50
57 Raven PC	.12	.30
58 Big Show PC	.50	1.25
59 Jeff Hardy PC	.30	.75
60 Spike Dudley PC	.20	.50
61 Chris Jericho PC	.30	.75
62 Kurt Angle PC	.50	1.25
63 Test PC	.20	.50
64 Chris Benoit PC	.30	.75
65 William Regal PC	.20	.50
66 Rikishi PC	.20	.50
67 D-Von Dudley PC	.20	.50
68 Mick Foley PC	.50	1.25
69 Triple H PC	.75	2.00
70 Albert PC	.12	.30
71 Haku PC	.12	.30
72 Perry Saturn PC	.12	.30
73 The One Billy Gunn PC	.12	.30
74 Hardcore Holly PC	.20	.50
75 Shane McMahon PC	.30	.75
76 Edge PC	.50	1.25
77 Rhyno PC	.20	.50
78 Bubba Ray Dudley PC	.20	.50
79 Justin Credible PC	.12	.30
80 X-Pac PC	.20	.50

2001 Fleer WWF Championship Clash Divas Private Collection

STATED ODDS 1:30 HOBBY; 1:576 RETAIL

DPDE Debra	10.00	25.00
DPTO Tori	6.00	15.00
DPCIV Ivory	8.00	20.00
DPCMH Molly Holly	4.00	10.00
Halter Top		
DPCTE Terri	7.50	15.00
Dress		
DPCLBT Lita	25.00	50.00
Bikini Top		
DPCLTS Lita	10.00	25.00

2001 Fleer WWF Championship Clash Divas Private Signing

COMPLETE SET (8)	175.00	350.00
STATED ODDS 1:120		
CARDS 1-4 AVAIL.IN CHAMP.CLASH		
CARDS 5-8 AVAIL.IN ULT DIVA COL.		
HOBBY EXCLUSIVE		
DPSD Debra	100.00	200.00
DPSI Ivory	30.00	75.00
DPSJ Jacqueline	20.00	40.00
DPSL Lita	25.00	50.00
DPSMH Molly Holly	75.00	150.00
DPSSM Stephanie McMahon-Helmsley	200.00	400.00
DPSTE Terri	25.00	50.00
DPSTS Trish Stratus	150.00	300.00

2001 Fleer WWF Championship Clash Females

COMPLETE SET (9)	12.00	30.00
STATED ODDS 1:4 HOBBY; 1:7 RETAIL		
WF1 Ivory	.75	2.00
WF2 Trish Stratus	6.00	15.00
WF3 Lita	1.25	3.00
WF4 Molly Holly	4.00	10.00
WF5 Debra	3.00	8.00
WF6 Stephanie McMahon	5.00	12.00
WF7 Terri	1.00	2.50
WF8 Jacqueline	.75	2.00
WF9 Tori	1.00	2.50

2001 Fleer WWF Championship Clash Main Event Memorabilia

COMPLETE SET (9)	25.00	60.00
STATED ODDS 1:24 HOBBY; 1:144 RETAIL		
SA Steve Austin	5.00	12.00
Ring Skirt		
BKR Big Show vs. Kane vs. Raven	3.00	8.00
Ring Mat		
EGT Test vs. Eddie Guerrero	2.50	6.00
Ring Mat		
CBCJ Chris Benoit vs. Chris Jericho	12.00	30.00
CJWR William Regal vs. Chris Jericho	3.00	8.00
KATH Triple H vs. Kurt Angle	6.00	15.00
SATR Steve Austin vs. The Rock	5.00	12.00
Ring Mat		
SMKA Shane McMahon vs. Kurt Angle	3.00	8.00
Garbage Can SP		
SAKACJ Kurt Angle vs. Chris		
Jericho vs. Steve Austin	4.00	10.00
Steel Chair SP		

2001 Fleer WWF Championship Clash Piece of the Champion

STATED ODDS 1:24 HOBBY; 1:576 RETAIL

PCB Bradshaw	10.00	20.00
T-Shirt		
PCCJ Chris Jericho	12.00	30.00
PCER Essa Rios	6.00	12.00
Pants		
PCFA Faarooq (spelled Faaroog)		
Knee Brace UER SP		
PCFN Funaki	6.00	12.00
T-Shirt		
PCJH Jeff Hardy	15.00	40.00
PCKA K. Angle	125.00	250.00
Gold Medal Strap SP		
PCKA2 Kurt Angle	15.00	30.00
T-Shirt		
PCMH Matt Hardy	15.00	30.00
T-Shirt		
PCSA Steve Austin	15.00	30.00
T-Shirt		
PCSH Scotty 2 Hotty	10.00	25.00
PCTM Taka Michinoku	6.00	12.00
T-Shirt		
PCXP X- Pac	10.00	20.00
Bandana		

2001 Fleer WWF Diva Magazine Set 1

1 Chyna	
2 Chyna	
3 Chyna	
4 Jacqueline	
5 Jacqueline	
6 Jacqueline	
7 The Kat	
8 The Kat	
9 The Kat	

2001 Fleer WWF Diva Magazine Set 2

1 Lita	
2 Lita	
3 Lita	
4 Terri	
5 Terri	
6 Terri	
7 Tori	
8 Tori	
9 Tori	

2001 Fleer WWF Diva Magazine Set 3

1 Trish Stratus	
2 Trish Stratus	
3 Trish Stratus	
4 Debra	
5 Debra	
6 Debra	
7 Molly Holly	
8 Molly Holly	
9 Molly Holly	

2002 Fleer WWF Divas Magazine Series 1

1 Lita	.40	1.00
2 Lita	.40	1.00
3 Lita	.40	1.00
4 Jacqueline	.20	.50
5 Jacqueline	.20	.50
6 Jacqueline	.20	.50
7 Torrie	.60	1.50
8 Torrie	.60	1.50
9 Torrie	.60	1.50

2002 Fleer WWF Divas Magazine Series 2

1 Trish	.60	1.50
2 Trish	.60	1.50
3 Trish	.60	1.50
4 Ivory	.20	.50
5 Ivory	.20	.50
6 Ivory	.20	.50
7 Terri	.30	.75
8 Terri	.30	.75
9 Terri	.30	.75

2002 Fleer WWF Divas Magazine Series 3

1 Stacy	.60	1.50
2 Stacy	.60	1.50
3 Stacy	.60	1.50
4 Sharmell	.20	.50
5 Sharmell	.20	.50
6 Sharmell	.20	.50
7 Molly	.20	.50
8 Molly	.20	.50
9 Molly	.20	.50

2001 Fleer WWF KB Toys Get Real

COMPLETE SET (18)	12.00	30.00
UNOPENED PACK (3 CARDS)	1.50	2.00
1 The Rock	2.50	6.00
2 Undertaker	2.50	6.00
3 Kane	1.25	3.00
4 Stone Cold Steve Austin	2.00	5.00
5 Kurt Angle	.75	2.00
6 Triple H	.75	2.00
7 Albert	.50	1.25
8 The Dudley Boyz	1.25	3.00
9 The Hardy Boyz	1.50	4.00
10 Lita	3.00	8.00
11 Edge	1.50	4.00
12 Christian	.60	1.50
13 Tazz	.50	1.25
14 Raven	.75	2.00
15 Chris Jericho	2.00	5.00
16 Jacqueline	.75	2.00
17 Ivory	.75	2.00
18 Trish Stratus	2.50	6.00

2001 Fleer WWF Raw Is War

COMPLETE SET (100)	8.00	20.00
UNOPENED BOX (24 PACKS)		
UNOPENED PACK (8 CARDS)		
1 Stone Cold Steve Austin	.75	2.00
2 Triple H	.75	2.00
3 Mick Foley	.50	1.25
4 Dean Malenko	.20	.50
5 Chris Jericho	.30	.75
6 Lita	6.00	15.00
7 Bubba Ray Dudley	.20	.50
8 JR	.20	.50
9 Bull Buchanan	.12	.30

10	Kane	.50	1.25
11	Gerald Brisco	.20	.50
12	The Goodfather	.20	.50
13	Matt Hardy	.30	.75
14	Rikishi	.20	.50
15	Vince McMahon	.50	1.25
16	Ivory	.50	1.25
17	Trish Stratus	3.00	8.00
18	Test	.20	.50
19	Raven	.12	.30
20	Albert	.12	.30
21	Val Venis	.20	.50
22	Tazz	.20	.50
23	Chyna	.50	1.25
24	Molly Holly	.50	1.25
25	Christian	.30	.75
26	Edge	.50	1.25
27	William Regal	.20	.50
28	Crash Holly	.12	.30
29	Jeff Hardy	.30	.75
30	Kurt Angle	.50	1.25
31	K-Kwik	.12	.30
32	Bradshaw	.30	.75
33	Terri	.60	1.50
34	Bob Hardcore Holly	.20	.50
35	Grandmaster Sexay		
36	Perry Saturn	.12	.30
37	D-Von Dudley	.20	.50
38	The One Billy Gunn	.12	.30
39	The Rock	2.50	6.00
40	Eddie Guererro	.50	1.25
41	Steven Richards	.20	.50
42	Pat Patterson	.20	.50
43	Chris Benoit	.30	.75
44	Big Show	.50	1.25
45	Faarooq	.12	.30
46	Steve Blackman	.12	.30
47	Undertaker	.60	1.50
48	Jacqueline	.50	1.25
49	Scotty Too Hotty	.20	.50
50	Chris Jericho WZ	.30	.75
51	APA WZ	.30	.75
52	Billy Gunn vs. Val Venis WZ	.20	.50
53	Taka Michinoku WZ	.12	.30
54	Triple H vs.The Rock WZ	.75	2.00
55	Edge & Christian WZ	.50	1.25
56	Big Show WZ	.50	1.25
57	Hardy Boyz vs. Edge & Christian WZ	.50	1.25
58	Debra WZ	.60	1.50
59	Kurt Angle WZ	.50	1.25
60	Kaientai WZ	.12	.30
61	Rock & Undertaker vs. Edge & Christian WZ	.75	2.00
62	Right to Censor WZ	.50	1.25
63	Undertaker WZ	.60	1.50
64	Billy Gunn with Chyna WZ	.50	1.25
65	Dudleyz vs. Edge & Christian WZ	.50	1.25
66	Lita vs. Trish Stratus WZ	1.25	3.00
67	The Rock WZ	2.50	6.00
68	Stephanie McMahon-Helmsley WZ	3.00	8.00
69	Dudley Boyz WZ	.20	.50
70	Triple H WZ	.75	2.00
71	Steve Austin vs. Vince McMahon WZ	2.50	6.00
72	Shane McMahon WZ	.30	.75
73	Perry Saturn with Terri WZ	.60	1.50
74	Too Cool WZ	.20	.50
75	Triple H WZ	.50	1.25
76	Hardy Boyz WZ	2.00	5.00
77	Stone Cold Steve Austin WZ	2.50	6.00
78	Undertaker vs. Kane WZ	.60	1.50
79	Hardcore/Molly/Crash Holly WZ	.50	1.25
80	William Regal WZ	.20	.50
81	Steve Austin vs. Kurt Angle WZ	.75	2.00
82	Vince McMahon WZ	.50	1.25
83	Right to Censor vs. Hardy Boyz WZ	.30	.75
84	Kane WZ	.50	1.25
85	The Rock vs. Undertaker SE	.60	1.50
86	Steve Austin vs. William Regal SE	.60	1.50
87	Steve Austin vs. Chris Benoit SE	.60	1.50
88	Steve Austin vs. Rikishi vs. Angle SE	.60	1.50
89	Chris Jericho vs. The Rock SE	.60	1.50
90	Steve Austin vs. Kurt Angle SE	.60	1.50
91	Steve Austin vs. Edge & Christian & Angle SE	.60	1.50
92	Triple H vs. Kurt Angle SE	.60	1.50
93	Undertaker vs. The Rock SE	.60	1.50
94	Chris Jericho vs. Benoit SE	.30	.75
95	Rock vs. HHH vs. Kurt Angle SE	.60	1.50
96	Shane McMahon vs. The Rock SE	.60	1.50
97	Triple H vs. The Rock SE	.60	1.50
98	The Rock vs. Kane SE	.60	1.50
99	Lita vs. Stephanie SE	.60	1.50
100	The Rock vs. Benoit SE	.60	1.50

2001 Fleer WWF Raw Is War Booty

STATED ODDS 1:26 HOBBY; 1:134 RETAIL

NNO	Chris Benoit	10.00	25.00
	Ring Skirt		
NNO	Chris Jericho	10.00	25.00
	Ring Skirt		
NNO	Dudley Boyz	8.00	20.00
	Ring Skirt		
NNO	Edge & Christian	10.00	25.00
	Ring Skirt		
NNO	Hardy Boyz	10.00	25.00
	Ring Mat		
NNO	Kane	6.00	15.00
	Ring Skirt		
NNO	Kurt Angle	12.00	30.00
	T-Shirt		
NNO	Mick Foley	10.00	25.00
	Ring Mat		
NNO	The One Billy Gunn	12.00	30.00
	Ring Trunks		
NNO	The Rock	20.00	50.00
	Ring Mat		
NNO	Stone Cold Steve Austin	20.00	50.00
	Ring Mat		
NNO	Triple H	10.00	25.00
	Ring Mat		
NNO	Undertaker	10.00	25.00
	Ring Mat		
NNO	Vince McMahon	8.00	20.00
	Ring Mat		
NNO	William Regal	6.00	15.00
	Ring Skirt		

2001 Fleer WWF Raw Is War Booty Autographs

STATED ODDS 1:354
EXCH.EXPIRATION: 07/01/2002

NNO	Christian	20.00	50.00
NNO	Edge	30.00	75.00
NNO	Triple H		
NNO	Undertaker	400.00	800.00

2001 Fleer WWF Raw Is War Famous Nicknames

COMPLETE SET (14) 25.00 60.00
STATED ODDS 1:15 HOBBY; 1:20 RETAIL

FN1	Chyna	3.00	8.00
FN2	Steve Austin	4.00	10.00
FN3	Kurt Angle	3.00	8.00
FN4	Billy Gunn	1.50	4.00
FN5	Triple H	3.00	8.00
FN6	Lita	5.00	12.00
FN7	Steve Blackman	1.50	4.00
FN8	The Rock	4.00	10.00
FN9	Shawn Michaels	3.00	8.00
FN10	Chris Jericho	3.00	8.00
FN11	Chris Benoit	2.50	6.00
FN12	Undertaker	3.00	8.00
FN13	Jim Ross	1.25	3.00
FN14	Eddie Guerrero	1.50	4.00

2001 Fleer WWF Raw Is War Femme Fatale

COMPLETE SET (20) 10.00 25.00
STATED ODDS 1:2 HOBBY AND RETAIL

FF1	Trish Stratus	2.50	6.00
FF2	Molly Holly	.25	.60
FF3	Terri	.40	1.00
FF4	Lita	2.00	5.00
FF5	Tori	.30	.75
FF6	Trish Stratus	2.50	6.00
FF7	Molly Holly	.25	.60
FF8	Terri	.40	1.00
FF9	Lita	2.00	5.00
FF10	Tori	.30	.75
FF11	Trish Stratus	2.50	6.00
FF12	Molly Holly	.25	.60
FF13	Terri	.40	1.00
FF14	Lita	2.00	5.00
FF15	Tori	.30	.75
FF16	Trish Stratus	2.50	6.00
FF17	Molly Holly	.25	.60
FF18	Terri	.40	1.00
FF19	Lita	2.00	5.00
FF20	Tori	.30	.75

2001 Fleer WWF Raw Is War Raw Is Jericho

COMPLETE SET (15) 4.00 10.00
STATED ODDS 1:2 HOBBY AND RETAIL

RJ1	The Rock	.40	1.00
RJ2	Stone Cold Steve Austin	.40	1.00
RJ3	Chris Benoit	.40	1.00
RJ4	Kurt Angle	.40	1.00
RJ5	Edge and Christian	.40	1.00
RJ6	Kane	.40	1.00
RJ7	Undertaker	.40	1.00
RJ8	Chyna	.40	1.00
RJ9	Triple H	.40	1.00
RJ10	McMahon Family	.40	1.00
RJ11	Dudley Boyz	.40	1.00
RJ12	Hardy Boyz	.40	1.00
RJ13	Divas	.40	1.00
RJ14	Mick Foley	.40	1.00
RJ15	Chris Jericho	.40	1.00

2001 Fleer WWF Raw Is War TLC

COMPLETE SET (15) 10.00 25.00
STATED ODDS 1:5 HOBBY; 1:10 RETAIL

TLC1	Hardy Boyz vs. Dudley Boyz vs. Edge & Christian	.60	1.50
TLC2	Hardy Boyz	1.25	3.00
TLC3	Dudley Boyz	1.25	3.00
TLC4	Edge & Christian	1.25	3.00
TLC5	Rock/Dudleyz vs. Angle/Edge/Christian	.60	1.50
TLC6	Jericho/Dudleyz vs. Angle/Edge/Christian	.60	1.50
TLC7	Bob Holly vs. Steve Blackman	.60	1.50
TLC8	Triple H	1.25	3.00
TLC9	Stone Cold Steve Austin	1.50	4.00
TLC10	Kane	1.00	2.50
TLC11	Chris Jericho	1.25	3.00
TLC12	Kurt Angle	1.25	3.00
TLC13	Big Show	1.00	2.50
TLC14	Undertaker	1.25	3.00
TLC15	The Rock	1.50	4.00

2001 Fleer WWF The Ultimate Diva Collection

COMPLETE SET (100) 20.00 50.00
COMPLETE SET W/O SP (85) 10.00 25.00
UNOPENED BOX (24 PACKS)
UNOPENED PACK (8 CARDS)
*GOLD (1-85): 1X TO 2.5X BASIC CARDS
*GOLD SP (86-100): 2X TO 5X BASIC CARDS
HEDONISM STATED ODDS 1:4

1	Trish Stratus	.60	1.50
2	Debra	.30	.75
3	Ivory	.25	.60
4	Jacqueline	.25	.60
5	Lita	.40	1.00
6	Molly Holly	.25	.60
7	Terri	.30	.75
8	Trish Stratus	.60	1.50
9	Debra	.30	.75
10	Ivory	.25	.60
11	Jacqueline	.25	.60
12	Lita	.40	1.00
13	Molly Holly	.25	.60
14	Debra	.30	.75
15	Trish Stratus	.60	1.50
16	Debra	.30	.75
17	Ivory	.25	.60
18	Jacqueline	.25	.60
19	Lita	.40	1.00
20	Molly Holly	.25	.60
21	Terri	.30	.75
22	Trish Stratus	.60	1.50
23	Debra	.30	.75
24	Ivory	.25	.60
25	Jacqueline	.25	.60
26	Lita	.40	1.00
27	Molly Holly	.25	.60
28	Terri	.30	.75
29	Trish Stratus	.60	1.50
30	Debra	.30	.75
31	Ivory	.25	.60
32	Jacqueline	.25	.60
33	Lita	.40	1.00
34	Molly Holly	.25	.60
35	Terri	.30	.75
36	Trish Stratus	.60	1.50
37	Debra	.30	.75
38	Ivory	.25	.60
39	Jacqueline	.25	.60
40	Lita	.40	1.00

#	Card		
41	Molly Holly	.25	.60
42	Terri	.30	.75
43	Trish Stratus	.60	1.50
44	Debra	.30	.75
45	Ivory	.25	.60
46	Jacqueline	.25	.60
47	Lita	.40	1.00
48	Molly Holly	.25	.60
49	Terri	.30	.75
50	Trish Stratus	.60	1.50
51	Debra	.30	.75
52	Ivory	.25	.60
53	Jacqueline	.25	.60
54	Lita	.40	1.00
55	Molly Holly	.25	.60
56	The Rock RP	.60	1.50
57	Stone Cold Steve Austin RP	.60	1.50
58	Triple H RP	.60	1.50
59	Undertaker RP	.50	1.25
60	APA RP	.25	.60
61	The Hardy Boyz RP	.25	.60
62	Dudley Boyz RP	.15	.40
63	Chris Jericho RP	.25	.60
64	Kurt Angle RP	.40	1.00
65	Kane RP	.40	1.00
66	Debra ITR	.30	.75
67	Jacqueline ITR	.25	.60
68	Lita ITR	.40	1.00
69	Trish Stratus ITR	.60	1.50
70	Lita ITR	.40	1.00
71	Molly Holly ITR	.25	.60
72	Jacqueline ITR	.25	.60
73	Terri ITR	.30	.75
74	Ivory ITR	.25	.60
75	Debra ITR	.30	.75
76	Molly Holly ITR	.25	.60
77	Lita ITR	.40	1.00
78	Ivory ITR	.25	.60
79	Terri ITR	.30	.75
80	Trish Stratus ITR	.60	1.50
81	M.Holly/T.Stratus ITR	.60	1.50
82	M.Holly/Jacqueline ITR	.25	.60
83	Lita/T.Stratus ITR	.60	1.50
84	M.Holly/Lita ITR	.40	1.00
85	Terri/T.Stratus ITR	.60	1.50
86	Debra HED SP	.75	2.00
87	Terri HED SP	.75	2.00
88	Lita HED SP	1.00	2.50
89	Trish Stratus HED SP	1.50	4.00
90	Jacqueline HED SP	.60	1.50
91	Debra HED SP	.75	2.00
92	Terri HED SP	.75	2.00
93	Lita HED SP	1.00	2.50
94	Trish Stratus HED SP	1.50	4.00
95	Jacqueline HED SP	.60	1.50
96	Debra HED SP	.75	2.00
97	Terri HED SP	.75	2.00
98	Lita HED SP	1.00	2.50
99	Trish Stratus HED SP	1.50	4.00
100	Jacqueline HED SP	.60	1.50

2001 Fleer WWF The Ultimate Diva Collection The Bad and The Beautiful

COMPLETE SET (15) 10.00 20.00
STATED ODDS 1:4 HOBBY; 1:8 RETAIL

#	Card		
1	Trish Stratus	1.25	3.00
2	Jacqueline	.50	1.25
3	Ivory	.50	1.25
4	Molly Holly	.50	1.25
5	Lita	.75	2.00
6	Terri	.60	1.50
7	Trish Stratus	1.25	3.00
8	Jacqueline	.50	1.25
9	Debra	.60	1.50
10	Ivory	.50	1.25
11	Molly Holly	.50	1.25
12	Debra	.60	1.50
13	Terri	.60	1.50
14	Lita	.75	2.00
15	Trish Stratus	1.25	3.00

2001 Fleer WWF The Ultimate Diva Collection Diva Ink

COMPLETE SET (2) 150.00 300.00
STATED ODDS 1:104 HOBBY; 1:1,787 RETAIL
EXCH.EXPIRATION: 1/1/2003

Card		
NNO Debra	20.00	40.00
NNO Ivory	30.00	60.00
NNO Jacqueline	20.00	40.00
NNO Lita	30.00	60.00
NNO Molly Holly	20.00	40.00
NNO Terri	30.00	60.00
NNO Trish Stratus	40.00	80.00

2001 Fleer WWF The Ultimate Diva Collection Kiss and Tell

COMPLETE SET (12) 15.00 30.00
STATED ODDS 1:12 HOBBY; 1:20 RETAIL

#	Card		
1	Vince McMahon / Trish Stratus	3.00	8.00
2	Kurt Angle / Stephanie McMahon-Helmsley	1.50	4.00
3	Chris Jericho / Terri	1.50	4.00
4	Stone Cold Steve Austin / Debra	2.00	5.00
5	Triple H / Stephanie McMahon-Helmsley	2.00	5.00
6	APA / Jacqueline	1.25	3.00
7	Perry Saturn / Terri	1.50	4.00
8	Undertaker / Ivory	1.50	4.00
9	The Hardy Boyz / Lita	2.00	5.00
10	The Rock / Trish Stratus	3.00	8.00
11	Dudley Boyz / Molly Holly	1.25	3.00
12	Kane / Ivory	1.25	3.00

2001 Fleer WWF The Ultimate Diva Collection Matching Set

COMPLETE SET (8) 25.00 60.00
COMMON CARD (1-8) 4.00 10.00
SEMISTARS 5.00 12.00
UNLISTED STARS 6.00 15.00

Card		
NNO Debra/Stone Cold	8.00	20.00
NNO Jacqueline/APA	4.00	10.00
NNO Jacqueline/Bradshaw	5.00	12.00
NNO Lita/Jeff Hardy	6.00	15.00
NNO Lita/Matt Hardy	8.00	20.00
NNO Molly Holly/Spike Dudley	5.00	12.00
NNO Terri/Perry Saturn	6.00	15.00
NNO Trish Stratus/Big Show	6.00	15.00

2001 Fleer WWF The Ultimate Diva Collection National Assets

COMPLETE SET (15) 15.00 30.00
STATED ODDS 1:12 HOBBY; 1:20 RETAIL

#	Card		
1	Lita	1.50	4.00
2	Debra	1.25	3.00
3	Ivory	1.00	2.50
4	Terri	1.25	3.00
5	Trish Stratus	2.50	6.00
6	Terri	1.25	3.00
7	Molly Holly	1.00	2.50
8	Jacqueline	1.00	2.50
9	Debra	1.25	3.00
10	Molly Holly	1.00	2.50
11	Trish Stratus	2.50	6.00
12	Terri	1.25	3.00
13	Ivory	1.00	2.50
14	Jacqueline	1.00	2.50
15	Lita	1.50	4.00

2001 Fleer WWF The Ultimate Diva Collection Ring Accessories

COMPLETE SET (7) 20.00 50.00
COMMON CARD (1-7) 4.00 8.00
SEMISTARS 4.00 10.00
UNLISTED STARS 5.00 12.00

Card		
NNO Debra	4.00	8.00
NNO Ivory	5.00	12.00
NNO Jacqueline	4.00	10.00
NNO Lita	7.50	15.00
NNO Molly Holly	5.00	10.00
NNO Terri	5.00	12.00
NNO Trish Stratus	15.00	40.00

2001 Fleer WWF The Ultimate Diva Collection Signed with a Kiss

RANDOMLY INSERTED INTO PACKS
STATED PRINT RUN 50 SERIAL #'d SETS
EXCH.EXPIRATION: 1/1/2003

Card		
NNO Debra	30.00	75.00
NNO Ivory	20.00	50.00
NNO Jacqueline	15.00	40.00
NNO Lita	75.00	150.00
NNO Molly Holly	75.00	150.00
NNO Terri Runnels	15.00	40.00
NNO Trish Stratus	600.00	1200.00

2001 Fleer WWF WrestleMania

COMPLETE SET (100) 8.00 20.00
UNOPENED BOX (28 PACKS)
UNOPENED PACK (7 CARDS)
*CH GOLD: 1.2X TO 3X BASIC CARDS

#	Card		
1	The Rock	2.00	5.00
2	D-Von Dudley	.20	.50
3	Matt Hardy	.30	.75
4	Test	.20	.50
5	Raven	.12	.30
6	Chris Benoit	.30	.75
7	Jeff Hardy	.30	.75
8	Shane McMahon	.30	.75
9	Brooklyn Brawler	.12	.30
10	Gerald Brisco	.20	.50
11	Linda McMahon	.20	.50
12	Albert	.12	.30
13	Eddie Guerrero	.50	1.25
14	Mick Foley	.50	1.25
15	The Goodfather	.20	.50
16	Buh-Buh Ray Dudley	.20	.50
17	Grandmaster Sexay	.20	.50
18	Scotty 2 Hotty	.20	.50
19	William Regal	.20	.50
20	Big Boss Man	.20	.50
21	Edge	.50	1.25
22	Mideon	.12	.30
23	Al Snow	.20	.50
24	Stephanie McMahon-Helmsley	8.00	20.00
25	Dean Malenko	.20	.50
26	Tazz	.20	.50
27	Bull Buchanan	.12	.30
28	Hardcore Holly	.20	.50
29	Sgt. Slaughter	.30	.75
30	X-Pac	.20	.50
31	Christian	.30	.75
32	Jim JR Ross	.20	.50
33	Steve Blackman	.12	.30
34	Fabulous Moolah	.20	.50
35	Gangrel	.12	.30
36	Rikishi	.20	.50
37	Vince McMahon	.50	1.25
38	Essa Rios	.12	.30
39	Pat Patterson	.20	.50
40	Triple H	.75	2.00
41	K-Kwik	.12	.30
42	Crash Holly	.12	.30
43	Kane	.50	1.25
44	Steven Richards	.20	.50
45	Joey Abs	.12	.30
46	The One Billy Gunn	.12	.30
47	Faarooq	.12	.30
48	Undertaker	.60	1.50
49	Tiger Ali Singh	.12	.30
50	D'Lo Brown	.12	.30
51	Kurt Angle	.50	1.25
52	Stone Cold Steve Austin	.75	2.00
53	Chaz	.12	.30
54	Chris Jericho	.30	.75
55	Jerry The King Lawler	.20	.50
56	Mae Young	.20	.50
57	Bradshaw	.30	.75
58	Funaki	.12	.30
59	Perry Saturn	.12	.30
60	Val Venis	.20	.50
61	Tori DIVAS	.60	1.50
62	Debra DIVAS	.60	1.50
63	Chyna DIVAS	.50	1.25
64	Ivory DIVAS	.50	1.25
65	Jacqueline DIVAS	.50	1.25
66	The Kat DIVAS	.15	.40
67	Lita DIVAS	2.50	6.00
68	Trish Stratus DIVAS	3.00	8.00
69	Molly Holly DIVAS	.50	1.25
70	Terri DIVAS	.60	1.50
71	Edge & Christian TT	.50	1.25
72	Hardy Boyz TT	.30	.75
73	Dudley Boyz TT	.20	.50
74	T & A TT	.20	.50
75	Right to Censor TT	.20	.50
76	The Radicalz TT	.50	1.25
77	The Hollys TT	.20	.50
78	K-Kwik & Road Dogg TT	.12	.30
79	Lo Down TT	.12	.30
80	Too Cool TT	.20	.50

#	Card		
81	I Pity the Fool WR	.20	.50
82	Hulkamania Runs Wild WR	.60	1.50
83	Rage in the Cage WR	.60	1.50
84	A New Attendance Record WR	.12	.30
85	The Proud Chairman WR	.50	1.25
86	Brain Awakens Sleeping Giant WR	.40	1.00
87	Stars and Stripes Challenge WR	.12	.30
88	Don't Do It, Roddy WR	.30	.75
89	When in Rome WR	.20	.50
90	Megabucks vs. Megamaniacs WR	1.50	4.00
91	Good Friends, Better Enemies WR	.15	.40
92	Enter the Rattlesnake WR	.75	2.00
93	Dark Days Cometh WR	.60	1.50
94	Rock/Rikishi Early Years WR	.75	2.00
95	Hardcore Highlight WR	.12	.30
96	Rough Night for Charlie Hustle WR	.12	.30
97	The Stone Cold Age Begins WR	.75	2.00
98	Strike Two for the Hit King WR	.20	.50
99	The Rattlesnake Reigns Supreme WR	.75	2.00
100	Tag Team Daredevils WR	.12	.30

2001 Fleer WWF WrestleMania Foreign Objects

COMPLETE SET (9)		150.00	300.00
UNLISTED STARS		20.00	50.00
STATED ODDS 1:63 HOBBY EXCLUSIVE			
NNO	Chris Jericho Jersey	10.00	25.00
NNO	Dudley Boyz	75.00	150.00
NNO	The Rock T-Shirt	15.00	40.00
NNO	Stone Cold Steve Austin	12.00	30.00
NNO	Triple H Jeans	10.00	25.00
NNO	Triple H T-Shirt	10.00	25.00
NNO	Trish Stratus Shirt	20.00	50.00
NNO	Trish Stratus	30.00	75.00
NNO	Undertaker T-Shirt	10.00	25.00

2001 Fleer WWF WrestleMania Lip Service

STATED PRINT RUN 50 SERIAL #'d SETS			
EXCH.EXPIRATION: 04/01/2002			
HOBBY EXCLUSIVE			
NNO	Chyna	200.00	400.00
NNO	Ivory	50.00	100.00
NNO	Jacqueline	25.00	60.00
NNO	Lita	175.00	350.00
NNO	Molly Holly	75.00	150.00
NNO	Terri	50.00	100.00
NNO	Tori	30.00	75.00
NNO	Trish Stratus	250.00	500.00

2001 Fleer WWF WrestleMania The People's Champion

COMPLETE SET (15)		2.00	5.00
STATED ODDS 1:2			
PC1	The People's Elbow	.20	.50
PC2	The Rock on the Mic	.20	.50
PC3	The People's Eyebrow	.20	.50
PC4	Blood From a Rock	.20	.50
PC5	Football Career	.20	.50
PC6	The Rock, The Author	.20	.50
PC7	The Great One	.20	.50
PC8	The Brahma Bull	.20	.50

PC9	Layeth the Smackdown	.20	.50
PC10	The Rock Bottom	.20	.50
PC11	Can You Smell?	.20	.50
PC12	Just Bring It Jabroni	.20	.50
PC13	Five-Time WWF Champion	.20	.50
PC14	The Millions And Millions	.20	.50
PC15	Not Just a WWF Superstar	.20	.50

2001 Fleer WWF WrestleMania Signature Moves

COMPLETE SET (15)		40.00	80.00
STATED ODDS 1:24 HOBBY EXCLUSIVE			
SM1	The Rock	6.00	12.00
SM2	Stone Cold Steve Austin	6.00	12.00
SM3	Kurt Angle	5.00	10.00
SM4	Triple H	5.00	10.00
SM5	Chris Jericho	5.00	10.00
SM6	Chris Benoit	4.00	8.00
SM7	Undertaker	5.00	10.00
SM8	Kane	4.00	8.00
SM9	Too Cool	4.00	8.00
SM10	Hardy Boyz	5.00	10.00
SM11	Dudley Boyz	5.00	10.00
SM12	Tazz	5.00	10.00
SM13	Eddie Guerrero	2.00	5.00
SM14	The One Billy Gunn	2.00	5.00
SM15	Lita	7.50	15.00

2001 Fleer WWF WrestleMania Signature Moves Autographs

COMPLETE SET (4)			
RANDOM INSERTS IN PACKS			
STATED PRINT RUN 500 SERIAL #'d SETS			
STRATUS PROMO ONLY AVAILABLE AT '01 NSCC			
NNO	Bubba Ray Dudley	20.00	50.00
NNO	D-Von Dudley	15.00	40.00
NNO	Kurt Angle	50.00	100.00
NNO	Stone Cold Steve Austin	400.00	750.00
NNO	Trish Stratus (NSCC Exclusive)	75.00	150.00

2001 Fleer WWF WrestleMania Stone Cold Said So

COMPLETE SET (15)		5.00	12.00
STATED ODDS 1:2			
SC1	The Rock	2.50	6.00
SC2	Kurt Angle	.50	1.25
SC3	Rikishi	.30	.75
SC4	Chris Benoit	.40	1.00
SC5	Chris Jericho	.50	1.25
SC6	Triple H	.50	1.25
SC7	Vince McMahon	.40	1.00
SC8	Undertaker	.50	4.00
SC9	Kane	.40	1.00
SC10	Stephanie McMahon-Helmsley	1.50	4.00
SC11	X-Pac	.30	.75
SC12	Mick Foley	.50	1.25
SC13	Tazz	.50	1.25
SC14	Shane McMahon	.40	1.00
SC15	The One Billy Gunn	.30	.75

2015 Frame By Frame WWE Flip Madness Collection

UNOPENED BOX (24 PACKS)			
UNOPENED PACK (1 FLIPBOOK)			
COMMON GOLD SP (21-30)		1.25	3.00
COMMON TITANIUM SP (31-36)		2.00	5.00

#			
1	Batista	1.50	4.00
2	Big Show	1.50	4.00
3	Brock Lesnar	2.50	6.00
4	Cesaro	.60	1.50
5	Roman Reigns	1.50	4.00
6	Daniel Bryan	2.50	6.00
7	Dean Ambrose	1.50	4.00
8	Dolph Ziggler	1.00	2.50
9	Goldust	.60	1.50
10	John Cena	3.00	8.00
11	Kofi Kingston	.60	1.50
12	Mark Henry	1.00	2.50
13	Randy Orton	2.50	6.00
14	Ryback	.60	1.50
15	Seth Rollins	1.00	2.50
16	Sheamus	1.50	4.00
17	The Miz	1.00	2.50
18	King Barrett	.60	1.50
19	Triple H	2.50	6.00
20	Undertaker	2.50	6.00
21	Big Show SP	3.00	8.00
22	Brock Lesnar SP	5.00	12.00
23	Cesaro SP	1.25	3.00
24	Dolph Ziggler SP	2.00	5.00
25	Goldust SP	1.25	3.00
26	Roman Reigns SP	3.00	8.00
27	Ryback SP	1.25	3.00
28	Sheamus SP	3.00	8.00
29	Triple H SP	5.00	12.00
30	Undertaker SP	5.00	12.00
31	Daniel Bryan SP	8.00	20.00
32	Dean Ambrose SP	5.00	12.00
33	John Cena SP	10.00	25.00
34	Randy Orton SP	8.00	20.00
35	Seth Rollins SP	3.00	8.00
36	King Barrett SP	2.00	5.00

1988 Gold Bond WWF

COMPLETE SET (12)		15.00	40.00
NNO	Andre The Giant	5.00	12.00
NNO	Bobby The Brain Heenan	4.00	10.00
NNO	Elizabeth	3.00	8.00
NNO	George The Animal Steele	2.50	6.00
NNO	Hillbilly Jim	2.00	5.00
NNO	Honky Tonk Man	2.00	5.00
NNO	Hulk Hogan	5.00	12.00
NNO	Koko B. Ware	1.50	4.00
NNO	The Million Dollar Man Ted DiBiase	3.00	8.00
NNO	Randy Macho Man Savage	3.00	8.00
NNO	Ricky The Dragon Steamboat	1.50	4.00
NNO	Strike Force	1.50	4.00

1989 Gold Bond WWF

COMPLETE SET (12)			
NNO	Andre the Giant	3.00	8.00
NNO	Bobby The Brain Heenan		
NNO	Brutus The Barber Beefcake	1.50	4.00
NNO	Demolition (Ax & Smash)		
NNO	Hacksaw Jim Duggan	2.50	6.00
NNO	Hercules		
NNO	Hulk Hogan	6.00	15.00
NNO	Jake The Snake Roberts	3.00	8.00
NNO	Macho Man Randy Savage	4.00	10.00
NNO	Million Dollar Man Ted DiBiase	1.50	4.00
NNO	Miss Elizabeth	3.00	8.00
NNO	Ultimate Warrior		

1990 Gold Bond WWF

COMPLETE SET (12)		12.00	30.00
NNO	Andre the Giant	2.50	6.00
NNO	Bobby The Brain Heenan	2.00	5.00
NNO	Brutus The Barber Beefcake	1.50	4.00
NNO	Demolition	1.50	4.00
NNO	Hulk Hogan	3.00	8.00
NNO	Hulk Hogan No Holds Barred	4.00	10.00
NNO	Macho Man Randy Savage	3.00	8.00
NNO	Million Dollar Man Ted DiBiase	1.50	4.00
NNO	Ravishing Rick Rude	1.50	4.00
NNO	Rowdy Roddy Piper	3.00	8.00
NNO	Ultimate Warrior	3.00	8.00
NNO	Wrestlemania III	1.00	2.50

1991 Gold Bond WWF

NNO	Big Boss Man		
NNO	Honky Tonk Man		
NNO	Hulk Hogan	3.00	8.00
NNO	Jake The Snake Roberts	2.00	5.00
NNO	Macho King Randy Savage	3.00	8.00
NNO	Million Dollar Man Ted Dibiase	5.00	12.00
NNO	Mr. Perfect	4.00	10.00
NNO	Rowdy Roddy Piper	3.00	8.00
NNO	Sensational Queen Sherri	10.00	25.00
NNO	Sgt. Slaughter	2.50	6.00
NNO	Superfly Jimmy Snuka		
NNO	Ultimate Warrior		

1992 Good Humor WWF

COMPLETE SET (12)			
NNO	Big Boss Man		
NNO	Bret Hit Man Hart	6.00	15.00
NNO	Elizabeth	3.00	8.00
NNO	Hulk Hogan	12.00	30.00
NNO	Legion of Doom		
NNO	Macho Man Randy Savage	5.00	12.00
NNO	Million Dollar Man Ted Dibiase	3.00	8.00
NNO	Mr. Perfect		
NNO	Rowdy Roddy Piper	5.00	12.00
NNO	Sid Justice		
NNO	The Nasty Boys		
NNO	The Undertaker	6.00	15.00

2002 Good Humor WWF

COMPLETE SET (10)		15.00	40.00
NNO	Chris Jericho	1.50	4.00
NNO	Dudley Boyz	1.50	4.00
NNO	Edge & Christian	2.50	6.00
NNO	Hardy Boyz	1.50	4.00
NNO	Kane	2.50	6.00
NNO	Kurt Angle	2.50	6.00
NNO	The Rock	4.00	10.00
NNO	Stone Cold Steve Austin	4.00	10.00
NNO	Triple H	4.00	10.00
NNO	The Undertaker	3.00	8.00

1990 Hasbro WWF Flips Trading Cards

NNO	Big Boss Man	1.25	3.00
NNO	Brutus The Barber Beefcake	1.50	4.00
NNO	The Bushwhackers		
NNO	Hacksaw Jim Duggan	4.00	10.00
NNO	Hulk Hogan	6.00	15.00
NNO	Jake The Snake Roberts		
NNO	Macho King Randy Savage	5.00	12.00

NNO Million Dollar Man Ted Dibiase
NNO The Rockers
NNO Ultimate Warrior

1988 Hostess WWF WrestleMania IV Stickers

COMPLETE SET (34)

1 Jake The Snake Roberts		
2 Billy Jack Haynes		
3 Brutus The Barber Beefcake	.40	1.00
4 Randy Macho Man Savage and Elizabeth		
5 Koko B. Ware	.40	1.00
6 George The Animal Steele		
7 Hulk Hogan	4.00	10.00
8 Junkyard Dog		
9 Magnificent Muraco	.40	1.00
10 Bam Bam Bigelow	.75	2.00
11 Elizabeth		
12 The Honky Tonk Man	.75	2.00
13 Ted DiBiase	.40	1.00
14 The Natural Butch Reed	.40	1.00
15 Ravishing Rick Rude		
16 Killer Khan		
17 Bobby The Brain Heenan		
18 Jimmy Hart		
19 Slick The Doctor of Style		
20 Hulk Hogan	8.00	20.00
21 Mr. Fuji		
22 Oliver Humperdink		
23 Strike Force		
24 The British Bulldogs		
25 The Killer Bees		
26 Demolition Ax and Smash		
27 The Islanders		
28 Ken Patera		
29 The Rougeau Brothers		
30 The Hart Foundation		
31 Strike Force		
32 Jesse The Body Ventura		
33 Hillbilly Jim		
34 Randy Macho Man Savage		

1987 Hostess Munchies WWF Stickers

COMPLETE SET (20) 10.00 20.00

NNO British Bulldogs	.20	.50
NNO Don Muraco	.15	.40
NNO George The Animal Steele	.40	1.00
NNO Hillbilly Jim	.20	.50
NNO Honky Tonk Man	.20	.50
NNO Hulk Hogan	3.00	8.00
NNO Hulk Hogan	3.00	8.00
NNO Iron Sheik and Nikoli Volkoff	.25	.60
NNO Jake The Snake Roberts	.50	1.25
NNO Junkyard Dog	.20	.50
NNO Kamala	.15	.40
NNO King Kong Bundy	.20	.50
NNO Koko B. Ware	.15	.40
NNO Outback Jack	.15	.40
NNO Paul Mr. Wonderful Orndorff	.20	.50
NNO Randy Savage and Elizabeth	1.50	4.00
NNO Ricky The Dragon Steamboat	.20	.50
NNO Rowdy Roddy Piper	1.25	3.00
NNO Sika	.40	1.00
NNO Tito Santana	.15	.40

1999 Hot Shots WWF Stickers

COMPLETE SET (212) 12.00 30.00

1 Stone Cold Steve Austin	.75	2.00
2 Stone Cold Steve Austin	.75	2.00
3 Stone Cold Steve Austin	.75	2.00
4 Stone Cold Steve Austin	.75	2.00
5 Stone Cold Steve Austin	.75	2.00
6 Stone Cold Steve Austin	.75	2.00
7 Stone Cold Steve Austin	.75	2.00
8 Stone Cold Steve Austin	.75	2.00
9 Stone Cold Steve Austin	.75	2.00
10 Stone Cold Steve Austin	.75	2.00
11 Stone Cold Steve Austin	.75	2.00
12 Stone Cold Steve Austin	.75	2.00
13 Stone Cold Steve Austin	.75	2.00
14 Stone Cold Steve Austin	.75	2.00
15 Stone Cold Steve Austin	.75	2.00
16 Stone Cold Steve Austin	.75	2.00
17 Stone Cold Steve Austin	.75	2.00
18 Stone Cold Steve Austin	.75	2.00
19 The Rock	.75	2.00
20 The Rock	.75	2.00
21 The Rock	.75	2.00
22 The Rock	.75	2.00
23 The Rock	.75	2.00
24 The Rock	.75	2.00
25 The Rock	.75	2.00
26 The Rock	.75	2.00
27 The Rock	.75	2.00
28 The Rock	.75	2.00
29 The Rock	.75	2.00
30 The Rock	.75	2.00
31 The Rock	.75	2.00
32 The Rock	.75	2.00
33 The Rock	.75	2.00
34 The Rock	.75	2.00
35 The Rock	.75	2.00
36 The Rock	.75	2.00
37 Big Show	.25	.60
38 Big Show	.25	.60
39 Big Show	.25	.60
40 Big Show	.25	.60
41 Big Show	.25	.60
42 Big Show	.25	.60
43 Undertaker	.60	1.50
44 Undertaker	.60	1.50
45 Undertaker	.60	1.50
46 Undertaker	.60	1.50
47 Undertaker	.60	1.50
48 Undertaker	.60	1.50
49 Undertaker	.60	1.50
50 Undertaker	.60	1.50
51 Undertaker	.60	1.50
52 Undertaker	.60	1.50
53 Undertaker	.60	1.50
54 Undertaker	.60	1.50
55 Undertaker	.60	1.50
56 Undertaker	.60	1.50
57 Undertaker	.60	1.50
58 Undertaker	.60	1.50
59 Undertaker	.60	1.50
60 Undertaker	.60	1.50
61 Acolytes	.12	.30
62 Corporate Ministry	.12	.30
63 Viscera	.12	.30
64 Chyna	.20	.50
65 Chyna	.20	.50
66 Big Boss Man	.12	.30
67 Big Boss Man	.12	.30
68 Viscera	.12	.30
69 Corporate Ministry	.12	.30
70 Big Boss Man	.12	.30
71 Acolytes	.12	.30
72 Paul Bearer	.15	.40
73 Ken Shamrock	.15	.40
74 Ken Shamrock	.15	.40
75 Ken Shamrock	.15	.40
76 Ken Shamrock	.15	.40
77 Ken Shamrock	.15	.40
78 Ken Shamrock	.15	.40
79 Mankind	.30	.75
80 Mankind	.30	.75
81 Mankind	.30	.75
82 Mankind	.30	.75
83 Mankind	.30	.75
84 Mankind	.30	.75
85 Mankind	.30	.75
86 Mankind	.30	.75
87 Mankind	.30	.75
88 Mankind	.30	.75
89 Mankind	.30	.75
90 Mankind	.30	.75
91 Vince McMahon	.20	.50
92 Vince McMahon	.20	.50
93 Vince McMahon	.20	.50
94 Vince McMahon	.20	.50
95 Vince McMahon	.20	.50
96 Vince McMahon	.20	.50
97 Shane McMahon	.20	.50
98 Shane McMahon	.20	.50
99 Shane McMahon	.20	.50
100 Shane McMahon	.20	.50
101 Shane McMahon	.20	.50
102 Shane McMahon	.20	.50
103 Triple H	.30	.75
104 Triple H	.30	.75
105 Triple H	.30	.75
106 Triple H	.30	.75
107 Triple H	.30	.75
108 Triple H	.30	.75
109 Jeff Jarrett	.25	.60
110 Jeff Jarrett	.25	.60
111 Jeff Jarrett	.25	.60
112 Jeff Jarrett	.25	.60
113 Jeff Jarrett	.25	.60
114 Jeff Jarrett	.25	.60
115 Debra	.30	.75
116 Debra	.30	.75
117 Debra	.30	.75
118 Debra	.30	.75
119 Debra	.30	.75
120 Debra	.30	.75
121 Kane	.25	.60
122 Kane	.25	.60
123 Kane	.25	.60
124 Kane	.25	.60
125 Kane	.25	.60
126 Kane	.25	.60
127 Kane	.25	.60
128 Kane	.25	.60
129 Kane	.25	.60
130 Kane	.25	.60
131 Kane	.25	.60
132 Kane	.25	.60
133 X-Pac	.25	.60
134 X-Pac	.25	.60
135 X-Pac	.25	.60
136 X-Pac	.25	.60
137 X-Pac	.25	.60
138 X-Pac	.25	.60
139 Road Dogg	.25	.60
140 Road Dogg	.25	.60
141 Road Dogg	.25	.60
142 Road Dogg	.25	.60
143 Road Dogg	.25	.60
144 Road Dogg	.25	.60
145 Billy Gunn	.25	.60
146 Billy Gunn	.25	.60
147 Billy Gunn	.25	.60
148 Billy Gunn	.25	.60
149 Billy Gunn	.25	.60
150 Billy Gunn	.25	.60
151 Al Snow	.15	.40
152 Al Snow	.15	.40
153 Al Snow	.15	.40
154 Al Snow	.15	.40
155 Al Snow	.15	.40
156 Al Snow	.15	.40
157 Val Venis	.15	.40
158 Val Venis	.15	.40
159 Val Venis	.15	.40
160 Val Venis	.15	.40
161 Val Venis	.15	.40
162 Val Venis	.15	.40
163 The Brood	.30	.75
164 Edge	.30	.75
165 The Brood	.30	.75
166 Christian	.25	.60
167 Edge	.30	.75
168 Christian	.25	.60
169 Gangrel	.12	.30
170 Gangrel	.12	.30
171 Gangrel	.12	.30
172 Gangrel	.12	.30
173 Gangrel	.12	.30
174 Gangrel	.12	.30
175 D-Lo Brown	.12	.30
176 D-Lo Brown	.12	.30
177 D-Lo Brown	.12	.30
178 D-Lo Brown	.12	.30
179 Mark Henry	.15	.40
180 Mark Henry	.15	.40
181 Goldust	.25	.60
182 Goldust	.25	.60
183 Goldust	.25	.60
184 Goldust	.25	.60
185 Goldust	.25	.60
186 Goldust	.25	.60
187 Godfather	.20	.50
188 Godfather	.20	.50
189 Godfather	.20	.50
190 Godfather	.20	.50
191 Godfather	.20	.50
192 Godfather	.20	.50
193 PMS	.15	.40
194 PMS	.15	.40
195 PMS	.15	.40
196 PMS	.15	.40
197 PMS	.15	.40
198 PMS	.15	.40
199 Nicole Bass	.12	.30
200 Droz	.12	.30
201 Shawn Michaels	.40	1.00
202 Ivory	.20	.50

203 Droz	.12	.30
204 Hardcore Holly	.12	.30
205 Test	.12	.30
206 Tiger Ali Singh	.12	.30
207 Tiger Ali Singh	.12	.30
208 Kurrgan	.12	.30
209 Test	.12	.30
210 Shawn Michaels	.40	1.00
211 Test	.12	.30
212 Raw Is War	.12	.30

1991 Imagine Wrestling Legends

COMPLETE SET (60)	25.00	60.00
1 Bruno Sammartino	1.25	3.00
2 Buddy Rogers	.75	2.00
3 Ivan Koloff	.75	2.00
4 Lou Albano	.40	1.00
5 Billy Graham	1.00	2.50
6 Killer Kowalski	1.00	2.50
7 Lou Thesz	1.25	3.00
8 Domenic DeNucci	.40	1.00
9 Bruno Sammartino	1.25	3.00
10 Buddy Rogers	.75	2.00
11 Ivan Koloff	.75	2.00
12 Lou Albano	.40	1.00
13 Billy Graham	1.00	2.50
14 Killer Kowalski	1.00	2.50
15 Lou Thesz	1.25	3.00
16 Bill Miller	.40	1.00
17 Domenic DeNucci	.40	1.00
18 Bruno Sammartino	1.25	3.00
19 Antonio Rocca	.40	1.00
20 Buddy Rogers	.75	2.00
21 Ivan Koloff	.75	2.00
22 Primo Carnerra	.75	2.00
23 Lou Albano	.40	1.00
24 Bruno Sammartino	1.25	3.00
25 Crusher Lisowski	.75	2.00
26 Billy Graham	1.00	2.50
27 Killer Kowalski	1.00	2.50
28 Domenic DeNucci	.40	1.00
29 Rocca & Perez	.75	2.00
30 Bill Watts	.40	1.00
31 BoBo Brazil	.75	2.00
32 Lou Thesz	1.25	3.00
33 Pedro Morales	1.00	2.50
34 Johnny Valentine	.75	2.00
35 Argentine Apollo	.40	1.00
36 Billy Graham	1.00	2.50
37 Haystacks Calhoun	.40	1.00
38 Bruno Sammartino	1.25	3.00
39 The Destroyer	.75	2.00
40 Buddy Rogers	.75	2.00
41 Ray Stevens	.75	2.00
42 Lou Albano	.40	1.00
43 Edouard Carpentier	.40	1.00
44 Killer Kowalski	1.00	2.50
45 Bob Backlund	1.00	2.50
46 Killer Kowalski	1.00	2.50
47 Mil Mascaras	1.00	2.50
48 Domenic DeNucci	.40	1.00
49 Smasher Sloan	.40	1.00
50 Ivan Koloff	.75	2.00
51 Lou Albano	.40	1.00
52 Lou Thesz	1.25	3.00
53 Harly Race UER	1.25	3.00
54 Billy Graham	1.00	2.50
55 Domenic DeNucci	.40	1.00

56 Hawk & Hansen	.75	2.00
57 Lou Thesz	1.25	3.00
58 Ivan Koloff	.75	2.00
59 Buddy Rogers	.75	2.00
60 Bruno Sammartino	1.25	3.00
61 Bruno Sammartino AU	50.00	100.00
62 Buddy Rogers AU	25.00	60.00
63 Lou Thesz AU	25.00	60.00
64 Billy Graham AU	15.00	40.00
65 Ivan Koloff AU	15.00	40.00
66 Killer Kowalski AU	30.00	75.00
67 Lou Albano AU	20.00	50.00
68 Domenic DeNucci AU	12.00	30.00

2021 Impact Wrestling Complete Series

COMPLETE SET (40)	60.00	120.00
COMPLETE S1 SET (10)		
COMPLETE S2 SET (10)		
COMPLETE S3 SET (10)		
COMPLETE S4 SET (10)		
1 Mike Tenay	1.50	3.00
2 Abyss	1.25	3.00
3 Bobby Roode	1.50	4.00
4 Christian Cage	2.50	6.00
5 Gail Kim	4.00	10.00
6 Madison Rayne	5.00	12.00
7 Scott D'Amore	1.25	3.00
8 Chris Sabin	1.25	3.00
9 Matt Cardona	6.00	15.00
10 Matthew Rehwoldt		
11 Brian Myers	6.00	15.00
12 Deonna Purrazzo	10.00	25.00
13 Moose	8.00	20.00
14 Big LG	2.50	6.00
15 Karl Anderson	3.00	8.00
16 Eric Young	2.50	6.00
17 Rich Swann	2.00	5.00
18 Sami Callihan		
19 Suicide	5.00	12.00
20 Rosemary		
21 Tasha Steelz		
22 Ace Austin	6.00	15.00
23 Chris Bey	1.50	4.00
24 Eddie Edwards	3.00	8.00
25 Heath	3.00	8.00
26 Havok	1.25	3.00
27 Jordynne Grace	6.00	15.00
28 Josh Alexander		
29 Willie Mack	2.00	5.00
30 Crazzy Steve	1.25	3.00
31 VBD		
32 Hernandez	1.25	3.00
33 Jake Something	1.25	3.00
34 Johnny Swinger	3.00	8.00
35 Tenille Dashwood	4.00	10.00
36 Taylor Wilde	3.00	8.00
37 Trey Miguel	2.00	5.00
38 Rohit Raju		
39 Petey Williams	1.25	3.00
40 Steve Maclin	1.25	3.00

2021 Impact Wrestling Complete Series Autographs

M3 Moose	20.00	50.00
AA2 Ace Austin	15.00	40.00
BM1 Brian Myers		
CS1 Chris Sabin	15.00	40.00

DP2 Deonna Purrazzo	50.00	100.00
JG3 Jordynne Grace	25.00	60.00
JS1 Johnny Swinger	10.00	25.00
LG1 Big LG	12.00	30.00
MC2 Matt Cardona	30.00	75.00
TD2 Tenille Dashwood	20.00	50.00
TM3 Trey Miguel	15.00	40.00
TS3 Tasha Steelz	30.00	75.00

1991 Impel WCW

COMPLETE SET (162)	6.00	15.00
UNOPENED BOX (36 PACKS)		
UNOPENED PACK (12 CARDS)		
1 Sting	.20	.50
2 Sting	.20	.50
3 Sting	.20	.50
4 Sting	.20	.50
5 Sting	.20	.50
6 Sting	.20	.50
7 Sting	.20	.50
8 Sting	.20	.50
9 Sting	.20	.50
10 Sting	.20	.50
11 Sting	.20	.50
12 Sting	.20	.50
13 Sting	2.00	5.00
14 Lex Luger	.10	.25
15 Lex Luger	.10	.25
16 Lex Luger	.10	.25
17 Lex Luger	.10	.25
18 Lex Luger	.10	.25
19 Lex Luger	.10	.25
20 Lex Luger	.10	.25
21 Lex Luger	.10	.25
22 Lex Luger	.10	.25
23 Lex Luger	.10	.25
24 Sid Vicious	.07	.20
25 Sid Vicious	.07	.20
26 Sid Vicious	.07	.20
27 Sid Vicious	.07	.20
28 Sid Vicious	.07	.20
29 Sid Vicious	.07	.20
30 Sid Vicious	.07	.20
31 Sid Vicious	.07	.20
32 Sid Vicious	.07	.20
33 Sid Vicious	.07	.20
34 Sid Vicious	.07	.20
35 Sid Vicious	.07	.20
36 Ric Flair	.30	.75
37 Ric Flair	.30	.75
38 Ric Flair	.30	.75
39 Ric Flair	.30	.75
40 Ric Flair	.30	.75
41 Ric Flair	.30	.75
42 Ric Flair	.30	.75
43 Ric Flair	.30	.75
44 Ric Flair	.30	.75
45 Ric Flair	.30	.75
46 Ric Flair	.30	.75
47 Ric Flair	2.00	5.00
48 Arn Anderson	.10	.25
49 Arn Anderson	.10	.25
50 Arn Anderson	.10	.25
51 Arn Anderson	.10	.25
52 Arn Anderson	.10	.25
53 Arn Anderson	.10	.25
54 Arn Anderson	.10	.25
55 Flyin Brian	.07	.20

56 Flyin Brian	.07	.20
57 Flyin Brian	.07	.20
58 Flyin Brian	.07	.20
59 Flyin Brian	.07	.20
60 Flyin Brian	.07	.20
61 Flyin Brian	.07	.20
62 Flyin Brian	.07	.20
63 Flyin Brian	.07	.20
64 Flyin Brian	.07	.20
65 Z-Man	.07	.20
66 Z-Man	.07	.20
67 Z-Man	.07	.20
68 Terry Taylor	.07	.20
69 Terry Taylor	.07	.20
70 Terry Taylor	.07	.20
71 Terry Taylor	.07	.20
72 Terry Taylor	.07	.20
73 Terry Taylor	.07	.20
74 Terry Taylor	.07	.20
75 Terry Taylor	.07	.20
76 Dutch Mantell	.10	.25
77 Dutch Mantell	.10	.25
78 Dutch Mantell	.10	.25
79 Dutch Mantell	.10	.25
80 Dutch Mantell	.10	.25
81 Dutch Mantell	.10	.25
82 Mr. Wall Street	.07	.20
83 Mr. Wall Street	.07	.20
84 Mr. Wall Street	.07	.20
85 El Gigante	.07	.20
86 El Gigante	.07	.20
87 El Gigante	.07	.20
88 El Gigante	.07	.20
89 El Gigante	.07	.20
90 El Gigante	.07	.20
91 El Gigante	.07	.20
92 El Gigante	.07	.20
93 Tommy Rich	.07	.20
94 Tommy Rich	.07	.20
95 Tommy Rich	.07	.20
96 Tommy Rich	.07	.20
97 Ricky Morton	.07	.20
98 Ricky Morton	.07	.20
99 Ricky Morton	.07	.20
100 Ricky Morton	.07	.20
101 Ricky Morton	.07	.20
102 Ricky Morton	.07	.20
103 Steiner Brothers	.10	.25
104 Steiner Brothers	.10	.25
105 Steiner Brothers	.10	.25
106 Steiner Brothers	.10	.25
107 Steiner Brothers	.10	.25
108 Steiner Brothers	.10	.25
109 Steiner Brothers	.10	.25
110 Steiner Brothers	.10	.25
111 Steiner Brothers	.10	.25
112 Steiner Brothers	.10	.25
113 Steiner Brothers	.10	.25
114 Steiner Brothers	.10	.25
115 Steiner Brothers	.10	.25
116 Steiner Brothers	.10	.25
117 Fabulous Freebirds	.10	.25
118 Fabulous Freebirds	.10	.25
119 Fabulous Freebirds	.10	.25
120 Fabulous Freebirds	.10	.25
121 Fabulous Freebirds	.10	.25
122 Fabulous Freebirds	.10	.25
123 Fabulous Freebirds	.10	.25

124	Fabulous Freebirds	.10	.25
125	Fabulous Freebirds	.10	.25
126	Fabulous Freebirds	.10	.25
127	Fabulous Freebirds	.10	.25
128	Fabulous Freebirds	.10	.25
129	Southern Boys	.07	.20
130	Southern Boys	.07	.20
131	Southern Boys	.07	.20
132	Southern Boys	.07	.20
133	Southern Boys	.07	.20
134	Southern Boys	.07	.20
135	Southern Boys	.07	.20
136	Southern Boys	.07	.20
137	Southern Boys	.07	.20
138	Southern Boys	.07	.20
139	Doom	.10	.25
140	Doom	.10	.25
141	Doom	.10	.25
142	Doom	.10	.25
143	Doom	.10	.25
144	Doom	.10	.25
145	Doom	.10	.25
146	Doom	.10	.25
147	Doom	.10	.25
148	Doom	.10	.25
149	Doom	.10	.25
150	Doom	.10	.25
151	Teddy Long	.07	.20
152	Teddy Long	.07	.20
153	Teddy Long	.07	.20
154	Jim Ross	.07	.20
155	Jim Ross	.07	.20
156	Jim Ross	.07	.20
157	Missy Hyatt	.10	.25
158	Missy Hyatt	.10	.25
159	Missy Hyatt	.10	.25
160	Missy Hyatt	.10	.25
161	Checklist	.07	.20
162	Checklist	.07	.20
NNO	Sting HOLO	8.00	20.00

1988 Jay's Potato Chips WWF Tag Teams of the Year

NNO	Billy Jack Haynes		
NNO	The British Bulldogs		
NNO	George The Animal Steele		
NNO	The Honky Tonk Man		
NNO	Hulk Hogan	2.50	6.00
NNO	Jake The Snake Roberts		
NNO	Ken Patera		
NNO	The Killer Bees		
NNO	Randy Savage and Elizabeth		
NNO	Slick		
NNO	Smash and Ax - Demolition		
NNO	Strike Force		

2018 Leaf Legends of Wrestling Autographs

*GREEN/15: UNPRICED DUE TO SCARCITY
*GOLD/10: UNPRICED DUE TO SCARCITY
*PURPLE/5: UNPRICED DUE TO SCARCITY
*RED/1: UNPRICED DUE TO SCARCITY

LWC1	Christian	5.00	12.00
LWE1	Edge	8.00	20.00
LWK1	Konnan	4.00	10.00
LWR1	Ricochet	15.00	40.00
LWS1	Slick	5.00	12.00
LW2CS	2 Cold Scorpio	4.00	10.00

LWAS1	Alexis Smirnoff	12.00	30.00
LWBF1	Bad Luck Fale	6.00	15.00
LWBH1	Bret Hart	8.00	20.00
LWBL1	Bobby Lashley	6.00	15.00
LWBVR	Baron Von Raschke	10.00	25.00
LWBW1	Barry Windham	5.00	12.00
LWCJ1	Chris Jericho	8.00	20.00
LWCK1	Corporal Kirchner	5.00	12.00
LWCR1	Cody Rhodes	15.00	40.00
LWDK1	Dynamite Kid	12.00	30.00
LWGS1	The Great Sasuke	6.00	15.00
LWGV1	Greg Valentine	5.00	12.00
LWHT1	Hiroshi Tanahashi	6.00	15.00
LWJB1	Jim Brunzell	4.00	10.00
LWJH1	Jimmy Hart	5.00	12.00
LWJR1	Jacques Rougeau	4.00	10.00
LWJR2	Jake Roberts	6.00	15.00
LWJR3	Jim Ross	6.00	15.00
LWJV1	Jesse Ventura	20.00	50.00
LWJV2	Jesse Ventura	20.00	50.00
LWKF1	Kazuyuki Fujita	8.00	20.00
LWKI1	Kota Ibushi	10.00	25.00
LWKK1	Kendo Kashin	4.00	10.00
LWKN1	Kevin Nash	6.00	15.00
LWKO1	Kazuchika Okada	12.00	30.00
LWKO2	Kenny Omega	25.00	60.00
LWKS1	Katsuyori Shibata	8.00	20.00
LWLH1	Larry Hennig	12.00	30.00
LWMS1	Minoru Suzuki	8.00	20.00
LWMW1	Mikey Whipwreck	4.00	10.00
LWPE1	Penta El Zero M	10.00	25.00
LWPO1	Pierre Ouellet	6.00	15.00
LWRF1	Ric Flair	15.00	40.00
LWRR1	Rocky Romero	4.00	10.00
LWSD1	Shane Douglas	4.00	10.00
LWSH1	Sam Houston	5.00	12.00
LWTI1	Tomohiro Ishii	12.00	30.00
LWTL1	Tanga Loa	12.00	30.00
LWTN1	Tetsuya Naito	12.00	30.00
LWTT1	Tama Tonga	10.00	25.00
LWWO1	Will Ospreay	12.00	30.00

2018 Leaf Legends of Wrestling Dual Autographs

LWD1	Edge /Christian	12.00	30.00
LWD2	C.Jericho/Christian	10.00	25.00
LWD3	K.Ibushi/B.L.Fale	8.00	20.00
LWD4	B.Hart/K.Nash		
LWD5	K.Nash/Konnan	10.00	25.00
LWD6	Konnan/S.Douglas		
LWD7	S.Douglas/2 Cold Scorpio	8.00	20.00
LWD8	J.Rougeau/P.Ouellet		
LWD9	2 Cold Scorpio/M.Whipwreck		
LWD10	B.L.Fale/T.Loa	12.00	30.00
LWD11	B.Windham/2 Cold Scorpio	8.00	20.00
LWD12	C.Rhodes/Christian		
LWD13	G.Valentine/J.Roberts	8.00	20.00
LWD14	L.Hennig/B.Von Raschke		
LWD15	Minoru Suzuki	15.00	40.00
	Tomohiro Ishii		

2018 Leaf Legends of Wrestling Originals Update Autographs

E1	Edge (2014)	6.00	15.00
S3	Sunny (2014)	8.00	20.00
BW1	The Bushwackers (2014)	15.00	40.00
DB1	Dick Beyer (2017)	8.00	20.00
FE1	Fedor Emelianenko (2016)	12.00	30.00

JB1	Jim Brunzell (2017)	6.00	15.00
KS1	Kazuzki Sakuraba (2016)	8.00	20.00
MTA	Magnum T.A. (2017)	6.00	15.00
PP1	Pat Patterson (2014)	6.00	15.00
PVZ	Paige VanZant (2016)	10.00	25.00
RG1	Royce Gracie (2016)	12.00	30.00
RMJ	Rey Mysterio Jr. (2017)	10.00	25.00
RS1	Ricky Steamboat (2017)	8.00	20.00
RS2	Ryan Shamrock (2017)	5.00	12.00
SL1	Stan Lane (2014)	5.00	12.00
SR2	Stevie Richards (2014)	5.00	12.00

2012 Leaf Originals Wrestling

*YELLOW/99: .5X TO 1.2X BASIC AUTOS
*BLUE/25: .6X TO 1.5X BASIC AUTOS
*RED/10: UNPRICED DUE TO SCARCITY
*BLACK/1: UNPRICED DUE TO SCARCITY
*P.P.BLACK/1: UNPRICED DUE TO SCARCITY
*P.P.CYAN/1: UNPRICED DUE TO SCARCITY
*P.P.MAGENTA/1: UNPRICED DUE TO SCARCITY
*P.P.YELLOW/1: UNPRICED DUE TO SCARCITY
*A.A.: SAME VALUE AS BASIC AUTOS
*A.A.YELLOW/25: .6X TO 1.5X BASIC AUTOS
*A.A.BLUE/10: UNPRICED DUE TO SCARCITY
*A.A.RED/5: UNPRICED DUE TO SCARCITY
*A.A.BLACK/1: UNPRICED DUE TO SCARCITY
*A.A.P.P.BLACK/1: UNPRICED DUE TO SCARCITY
*A.A.P.P.CYAN/1: UNPRICED DUE TO SCARCITY
*A.A.P.P.MAGENTA/1: UNPRICED DUE TO SCARCITY
*A.A.P.P.YELLOW/1: UNPRICED DUE TO SCARCITY

ATB	Abdullah the Butcher	10.00	25.00
BB1	Bob Backlund	10.00	25.00
BB2	Brutus Beefcake	8.00	20.00
BB3	Buff Bagwell	8.00	20.00
BH1	Bobby Heenan	12.00	30.00
BH2	Bret Hart	40.00	80.00
BO1	Cowboy Bob Orton Jr.	8.00	20.00
BS1	Bruno Sammartino	15.00	40.00
DDP	Diamond Dallas Page	8.00	20.00
DS1	Dan Severn	6.00	15.00
GJG	Jimmy Garvin	6.00	15.00
GS1	George Steele	10.00	25.00
GV1	Greg Valentine	8.00	20.00
HH1	Hulk Hogan	60.00	120.00
HJ1	Hillbilly Jim	10.00	25.00
HTM	The Honky Tonk Man	10.00	25.00
IK1	Ivan Koloff	8.00	20.00
IP1	The Polish Hammer Ivan Putski	8.00	20.00
JD1	Hacksaw Jim Duggan	12.00	30.00
JH1	Jimmy Hart	10.00	25.00
JN1	Jim Neidhart	8.00	20.00
JR1	Jake Roberts	12.00	30.00
KA1	Kamala	8.00	20.00
KBW	Koko B. Ware	8.00	20.00
KN1	Kevin Nash	15.00	40.00
KS1	Ken Shamrock	8.00	20.00
LL1	Lex Luger	10.00	25.00
LP1	Lanny Poffo	6.00	15.00
LZ1	Larry Zbyszko	6.00	15.00
MH1	Missy Hyatt	6.00	15.00
MJ1	Marty Jannetty	6.00	15.00
NK1	Nikita Koloff	8.00	20.00
NV1	Nikolai Volkoff	8.00	20.00
OMG	One Man Gang	8.00	20.00
PO1	Paul Orndorff	25.00	60.00
PR1	Pete Rose	12.00	30.00
RM1	Rick Martel	6.00	15.00
RRP	Rowdy Roddy Piper	75.00	150.00

RS1	Rick Steiner	6.00	15.00
SBG	Billy Graham	25.00	50.00
SH1	Scott Hall	12.00	30.00
SID	Sid	8.00	20.00
SS1	Scott Steiner	8.00	20.00
TA1	Tony Atlas	6.00	15.00
TAT	Tatanka	8.00	20.00
TDB	Ted DiBiase	10.00	25.00
TIS	The Iron Sheik	15.00	40.00
TNB	Ric Flair	30.00	75.00
TS1	Tito Santana	8.00	20.00
VAD	Vader	25.00	60.00
WR1	Wendi Richter	8.00	20.00
PARWA	Road Warrior Animal LOS	30.00	75.00

2014 Leaf Originals Wrestling

*YELLOW/99: SAME VALUE AS BASIC AUTOS
*BLUE/25: .5X TO 1.2X BASIC AUTOS
*RED/10: UNPRICED DUE TO SCARCITY
*BLACK/1: UNPRICED DUE TO SCARCITY
*P.P.BLACK/1: UNPRICED DUE TO SCARCITY
*P.P.CYAN/1: UNPRICED DUE TO SCARCITY
*P.P.MAGENTA/1: UNPRICED DUE TO SCARCITY
*P.P.YELLOW/1: UNPRICED DUE TO SCARCITY
*ALT.ART./ .5X TO 1.2X BASIC AUTOS
*A.A.YELLOW/25: .6X TO 1.5X BASIC AUTOS
*A.A.BLUE/10: UNPRICED DUE TO SCARCITY
*A.A.RED/5: UNPRICED DUE TO SCARCITY
*A.A.BLACK/1: UNPRICED DUE TO SCARCITY
*A.A.P.P.BLACK/1: UNPRICED DUE TO SCARCITY
*A.A.P.P.CYAN/1: UNPRICED DUE TO SCARCITY
*A.A.P.P.MAGENTA/1: UNPRICED DUE TO SCARCITY
*A.A.P.P.YELLOW/1: UNPRICED DUE TO SCARCITY

AF1	Francine	5.00	12.00
AG1	Gangrel SP	6.00	15.00
AG2	Godfather	5.00	12.00
AG3	Goldberg	50.00	100.00
AM1	Maryse	6.00	15.00
AR1	Raven	5.00	12.00
AS1	Sabu	12.00	30.00
AS2	Samu	5.00	12.00
AS2	Sting	25.00	60.00
AS3	Sandman	5.00	12.00
AW1	Warlord	5.00	12.00
AZ1	Zeus	5.00	12.00
A2CS	2 Cold Scorpio SP	5.00	12.00
AAB1	Adam Bomb	5.00	12.00
AAS1	Al Snow	5.00	12.00
ABH1	Bob Holly	5.00	12.00
ABH1	Bobby Heenan SP	12.00	30.00
ABM1	Balls Mahoney	5.00	12.00
ABM1	Blue Meanie	5.00	12.00
ACM1	Candice Michelle SP	10.00	25.00
ADA1	Demolition Ax	5.00	12.00
ADK1	Dynamite Kid SP	12.00	30.00
ADM1	Don Muraco	5.00	12.00
ADR1	Dennis Rodman SP	15.00	40.00
ADS1	Demolition Smash	5.00	12.00
AGB1	Gerald Brisco	5.00	12.00
AHH1	Hulk Hogan SP	75.00	150.00
AIS1	Iron Sheik	6.00	15.00
AJD1	J.J. Dillon	5.00	12.00
AJH1	Jeff Hardy SP	10.00	25.00
AJR2	Jake Roberts SP	10.00	25.00
AKK1	Kelly Kelly	6.00	15.00
AKKB	King Kong Bundy	15.00	40.00
AKN1	Kevin Nash	8.00	20.00
AKP1	Ken Patera	5.00	12.00
AKVE	Kevin Von Erich	6.00	15.00

ALS1	Lance Storm	5.00	12.00
AMK1	Maria Kanellis	6.00	15.00
AMT1	Mike Tyson SP	80.00	150.00
AOA1	Ole Anderson	25.00	60.00
ARF1	Ric Flair SP	75.00	150.00
ARF2	Rikishi Fatu	10.00	25.00
ARG1	Robert Gibson	5.00	12.00
ARM1	Ricky Morton	5.00	12.00
ARP1	Roddy Piper SP	50.00	100.00
ARS1	Ron Simmons	6.00	15.00
ASH1	Scott Hall	15.00	40.00
ASR1	Stevie Ray SP	6.00	15.00
ATB1	The Barbarian	5.00	12.00
ATD1	Tommy Dreamer	5.00	12.00
ATF1	Terry Funk	25.00	60.00
ATNB	The Nasty Boys	8.00	20.00
ATS1	Trish Stratus	20.00	50.00
AVV1	Val Venis	5.00	12.00

2014 Leaf Originals Wrestling Flair's Epic Battles

*YELLOW/25: X TO X BASIC AUTO
*BLUE/10: UNPRICED DUE TO SCARCITY
*RED/5: UNPRICED DUE TO SCARCITY
*BLACK/1: UNPRICED DUE TO SCARCITY
*P.P.BLACK/1: UNPRICED DUE TO SCARCITY
*P.P.CYAN/1: UNPRICED DUE TO SCARCITY
*P.P.MAGENTA/1: UNPRICED DUE TO SCARCITY
*P.P.YELLOW/1: UNPRICED DUE TO SCARCITY

RFBH1	Ric Flair	80.00	150.00
	Bret Hart		
RFHH1	Ric Flair/Hulk Hogan	120.00	250.00
RFRM1	Ric Flair/Ricky Morton	20.00	50.00
RFRP1	Ric Flair/Roddy Piper	80.00	150.00

2017 Leaf Originals Wrestling Autographs

*YELLOW/99: .6X TO 1.5X BASIC AUTOS
*BLUE/25: .75X TO 2X BASIC AUTOS
*RED/10: 1X TO 2.5X BASIC CARDS
*BLACK/1: UNPRICED DUE TO SCARCITY
*ALT.ART: SAME VALUE AS BASIC AUTOS
*ALT.YELLOW/25: .75X TO 2X BASIC AUTOS
*ALT.BLUE/10: 1X TO 2.5X BASIC AUTOS
*ALT.RED/5: UNPRICED DUE TO SCARCITY
*ALT.BLACK/1: UNPRICED DUE TO SCARCITY

K1	Konnan	8.00	20.00
V2	Victoria	5.00	12.00
BB1	B. Brian Blair	5.00	12.00
BL1	Bobby Lashley	5.00	12.00
BW1	Barry Windham	6.00	15.00
DFJ	Dory Funk Jr.	6.00	15.00
DLB	D'Lo Brown	5.00	12.00
DM2	Dutch Mantel	5.00	12.00
JR1	Jacques Rougeau	5.00	12.00
JR2	Jim Ross	8.00	20.00
LK1	Leilani Kai	5.00	12.00
MF1	Manny Fernandez	5.00	12.00
MM1	Marc Mero	5.00	12.00
MVP	MVP	6.00	15.00
SB1	Shelton Benjamin	6.00	15.00
SD1	Shane Douglas	5.00	12.00
TW1	Torrie Wilson	8.00	20.00

2017 Leaf Originals Wrestling '14 Design Autographs

*YELLOW/50-99: .6X TO 1.5X BASIC AUTOS
*BLUE/25: .75X TO 2X BASIC AUTOS

---

*RED/10: 1X TO 2.5X BASIC AUTOS
*BLACK/1: UNPRICED DUE TO SCARCITY
*P.P.BLACK/1: UNPRICED DUE TO SCARCITY
*P.P.CYAN/1: UNPRICED DUE TO SCARCITY
*P.P.MAGENTA/1: UNPRICED DUE TO SCARCITY
*P.P.YELLOW/1: UNPRICED DUE TO SCARCITY
*ALT.ART: SAME VALUE AS BASIC AUTOS
*ALT.YELLOW/25: .75X TO 2X BASIC AUTOS
*ALT.BLUE/10: 1X TO 2.5X BASIC AUTOS
*ALT.RED/5: UNPRICED DUE TO SCARCITY
*ALT.BLACK/1: UNPRICED DUE TO SCARCITY
*ALT.P.P.BLACK/1: UNPRICED DUE TO SCARCITY
*ALT.P.P.CYAN/1: UNPRICED DUE TO SCARCITY
*ALT.P.P.MAGENTA/1: UNPRICED DUE TO SCARCITY
*ALT.P.P.YELLOW/1: UNPRICED DUE TO SCARCITY

C1	Chyna	20.00	50.00
H1	Haku	6.00	15.00
S1	Slick	5.00	12.00
BE1	Bobby Eaton	5.00	12.00
BG1	Billy Gunn	5.00	12.00
BH2	Bret Hart	15.00	40.00
BR1	Butch Reed	5.00	12.00
BT1	Booker T	8.00	20.00
CH1	Christy Hemme	6.00	15.00
CJ1	Chris Jericho	8.00	20.00
DC1	Dennis Condrey	5.00	12.00
DH1	Danny Hodge	6.00	15.00
EB1	Eric Bischoff	5.00	12.00
JC1	Jim Cornette	6.00	15.00
JJ1	Jeff Jarrett	6.00	15.00
JL1	Jushin Liger	8.00	20.00
KS1	Kevin Sullivan	5.00	12.00
MF1	Mick Foley	8.00	20.00
MH1	Matt Hardy	5.00	12.00
RVD	Rob Van Dam	5.00	12.00
TB1	Tully Blanchard	5.00	12.00
TR1	Terri Runnels	6.00	15.00
WS1	Wild Samoans	8.00	20.00
XP1	X-Pac	6.00	15.00

2017 Leaf Originals Wrestling '16 Design Autographs

*YELLOW/50: .6X TO 1.5X BASIC AUTOS
*BLUE/25: .75X TO 2X BASIC AUTOS
*RED/10: 1X TO 2.5X BASIC AUTOS
*BLACK/1: UNPRICED DUE TO SCARCITY
*ALT.ART: SAME VALUE AS BASIC AUTOS
*ALT.YELLOW/25: .75X TO 2X BASIC AUTOS
*ALT.BLUE/10: 1X TO 2.5X BASIC AUTOS
*ALT.RED/5: UNPRICED DUE TO SCARCITY
*ALT.BLACK/1: UNPRICED DUE TO SCARCITY

HH1	Hulk Hogan	20.00	50.00
KS1	Kazushi Sakuraba	12.00	30.00

2016 Leaf Signature Series Wrestling

*BLUE/7-50: UNPRICED DUE TO SCARCITY
*GREEN/5-25: UNPRICED DUE TO SCARCITY
*RED/3-10: UNPRICED DUE TO SCARCITY
*BLACK/2-5: UNPRICED DUE TO SCARCITY
*PURPLE/1: UNPRICED DUE TO SCARCITY
*P.P.BLACK/1: UNPRICED DUE TO SCARCITY
*P.P.CYAN/1: UNPRICED DUE TO SCARCITY
*P.P.MAGENTA/1: UNPRICED DUE TO SCARCITY
*P.P.BLACK/1: UNPRICED DUE TO SCARCITY

1	6-Pac	8.00	20.00
2	Adam Bomb	8.00	20.00

3	Adam Pearce	8.00	20.00
4	Al Snow	6.00	15.00
5	Balls Mahoney	10.00	25.00
6	The Barbarian	8.00	20.00
7	Barry Windham	10.00	25.00
8	Goldberg	25.00	60.00
9	Blue Meanie	8.00	20.00
10	Bob Holly	6.00	15.00
11	Bobby Heenan	30.00	75.00
12	Bolo Mongol/Ax	10.00	25.00
13	Brutus Beefcake	8.00	20.00
14	Bushwacker Luke	8.00	20.00
15	Carlito	6.00	15.00
16	Carlos Colon	10.00	25.00
17	Chris Masters	6.00	15.00
18	Christopher Daniels	6.00	15.00
19	Christy Hemme	12.00	30.00
20	Debra McMichael	10.00	25.00
21	Dennis Condrey	6.00	15.00
22	Dennis Rodman	15.00	40.00
23	Dynamite Kid	10.00	25.00
24	Ezekiel Jackson	6.00	15.00
25	Fifi/Wendy Barlow	10.00	25.00
26	Francine	10.00	25.00
27	Frankie Kazarian	6.00	15.00
28	Gangrel	6.00	15.00
29	Greg Valentine	10.00	25.00
30	Harley Race	12.00	30.00
31	Headshrinker Fatu	8.00	20.00
32	Hulk Hogan	30.00	80.00
33	Jeff Jarrett	10.00	25.00
34	Gerald Brisco	6.00	15.00
35	Jesus	6.00	15.00
36	Jimmy Garvin	6.00	15.00
37	Jimmy Hart	8.00	20.00
38	J.J. Dillon	8.00	20.00
39	Jushin Liger	15.00	40.00
40	Kama	6.00	15.00
	Kama Mustafa		
41	Kamala	8.00	20.00
42	Kelly Kelly	15.00	40.00
43	Ken Patera	8.00	20.00
44	Kevin Nash	10.00	25.00
45	Kevin Sullivan	10.00	25.00
46	King Kong Bundy	10.00	25.00
47	King Mo	6.00	15.00
48	Lanny Poffo	6.00	15.00
49	Larry Zbyszko	8.00	20.00
50	Lita	15.00	40.00
51	Maria Kanellis	10.00	25.00
52	Marlena	12.00	30.00
53	Masato Tanaka	8.00	20.00
54	Matt Hardy	8.00	20.00
55	Matt Striker	6.00	15.00
56	Mike Tyson	50.00	100.00
57	Mil Mascaras	30.00	80.00
58	Nick Bockwinkel	30.00	75.00
59	Nikita Koloff	8.00	20.00
60	Nikolai Volkoff	8.00	20.00
61	Ole Anderson	10.00	25.00
62	Papa Shango	8.00	20.00
63	Pat Tanaka	6.00	15.00
64	Pete Rose	15.00	40.00
65	Reby Sky	8.00	20.00
66	Repo Man	12.00	30.00
67	Ric Flair	20.00	50.00
68	Rick Steiner	10.00	25.00
69	Ricky Morton	8.00	20.00

70	Robert Gibson	8.00	20.00
71	Ron Simmons	8.00	20.00
72	Sabu	8.00	20.00
73	Samu	6.00	15.00
74	Scott Hall	15.00	40.00
75	Scott Norton	6.00	15.00
76	Sid Vicious	10.00	25.00
77	Steve Corino	6.00	15.00
78	Stevie Ray	8.00	20.00
79	Sunny	12.00	30.00
80	Terri Runnels	10.00	25.00
81	The Godfather	6.00	15.00
82	Iron Sheik	12.00	30.00
83	Tito Santana	10.00	25.00
84	Tommy Dreamer	8.00	20.00
85	Tully Blanchard	10.00	25.00
86	Val Venis	6.00	15.00
87	Warlord	6.00	15.00
88	Wendi Richter	15.00	40.00
89	Wrath	8.00	20.00
90	X-Pac	8.00	20.00
91	Zeus	12.00	30.00
92	Zodiac	8.00	20.00

2016 Leaf Signature Series Wrestling Adversaries

*BLUE/15-25: UNPRICED DUE TO SCARCITY
*GREEN/10: UNPRICED DUE TO SCARCITY
*RED/5: UNPRICED DUE TO SCARCITY
*BLACK/3: UNPRICED DUE TO SCARCITY
*PURPLE/1: UNPRICED DUE TO SCARCITY
*P.P.BLACK/1: UNPRICED DUE TO SCARCITY
*P.P.CYAN/1: UNPRICED DUE TO SCARCITY
*P.P.MAGENTA/1: UNPRICED DUE TO SCARCITY
*P.P.YELLOW/1: UNPRICED DUE TO SCARCITY
RANDOMLY INSERTED INTO PACKS

ADV01	S.Corino/T.Funk	15.00	40.00
ADV02	R.Flair/J.Garvin	20.00	50.00
ADV03	123 Kid/S.Hall	12.00	30.00
ADV05	B.Windham/B.Beefcake	12.00	30.00
ADV06	B.Eaton/R.Morton	12.00	30.00
ADV07	Carlito/Sabu	10.00	25.00
ADV09	S.Douglas/C.Daniels	10.00	25.00
ADV10	C.Hemme/V.Sky	20.00	50.00
ADV11	T.Dreamer/Francine	15.00	40.00
ADV12	Raven /F.Kazarian	10.00	25.00
ADV13	Animal/K.Sullivan	12.00	30.00
ADV14	Sandman/M.Striker	10.00	25.00
ADV15	Bushwacker Luke/P.Tanaka	12.00	30.00
ADV16	T.Dreamer/Sabu	15.00	40.00
ADV17	Zeus/H.Hogan	60.00	120.00

2016 Leaf Signature Series Wrestling Hall of Fame

*BLUE/15-50: UNPRICED DUE TO SCARCITY
*GREEN/10-25: UNPRICED DUE TO SCARCITY
*RED/5-10: UNPRICED DUE TO SCARCITY
*BLACK/3-5: UNPRICED DUE TO SCARCITY
*PURPLE/1: UNPRICED DUE TO SCARCITY
*P.P.BLACK/1: UNPRICED DUE TO SCARCITY
*P.P.CYAN/1: UNPRICED DUE TO SCARCITY
*P.P.MAGENTA/1: UNPRICED DUE TO SCARCITY
*P.P.YELLOW/1: UNPRICED DUE TO SCARCITY
RANDOMLY INSERTED INTO PACKS

HOF01	Bobby Heenan	20.00	50.00
HOF02	Carlos Colon	10.00	25.00
HOF03	Iron Sheik	10.00	25.00

HOF04	Wendi Richter	10.00	25.00
HOF05	Ron Simmons	10.00	25.00
HOF06	Nick Bockwinkel	50.00	100.00
HOF07	Ric Flair	25.00	60.00
HOF08	Mil Mascaras	30.00	80.00
HOF09	Harley Race	12.00	30.00
HOF10	Pete Rose	15.00	40.00
HOF11	Mike Tyson	50.00	100.00

2016 Leaf Signature Series Wrestling Ring Showdowns

*BLUE/7-50: UNPRICED DUE TO SCARCITY
*GREEN/5-10: UNPRICED DUE TO SCARCITY
*RED/3-5: UNPRICED DUE TO SCARCITY
*BLACK/2-3: UNPRICED DUE TO SCARCITY
*PURPLE/1: UNPRICED DUE TO SCARCITY
*P.P.BLACK/1: UNPRICED DUE TO SCARCITY
*P.P.CYAN/1: UNPRICED DUE TO SCARCITY
*P.P.MAGENTA/1: UNPRICED DUE TO SCARCITY
*P.P.YELLOW/1: UNPRICED DUE TO SCARCITY
RANDOMLY INSERTED INTO PACKS

RS201	Steve Corino/Greg Valentine	12.00	30.00
RS202	B.Bagwell/S.Norton	10.00	25.00
RS203	X-Pac /V.Venis	10.00	25.00
RS204	123 Kid/P.Tanaka	10.00	25.00
RS206	A.Bomb/Virgil	8.00	20.00
RS207	A.Snow/Raven	10.00	25.00
RS208	B.Mahoney/Sabu	15.00	40.00
RS209	Gangrel/Blue Meanie	10.00	25.00
RS210	H.Hogan/B.Beefcake	25.00	60.00
RS211	B.Beefcake/Masked Superstar	20.00	50.00
RS213	X-Pac /Gangrel	8.00	20.00
RS214	Gangrel /Godfather	8.00	20.00
RS215	K.Patera/T.Atlas	12.00	30.00
RS216	M.Bennett/S.Richards	8.00	20.00
RS217	M.Hardy/M.Bennett	12.00	30.00
RS218	R.Steiner/Vincent	8.00	20.00
RS219	K.Nash/R.Steiner	15.00	40.00
RS220	K.Nash/S.Vicious	15.00	40.00
RS222	T.Runnels/S.Richards	10.00	25.00
RS224	H.Hogan/D.Rodman	50.00	100.00

2016 Leaf Signature Series Wrestling Team Effort

*BLUE/7-50: UNPRICED DUE TO SCARCITY
*GREEN/5-25: UNPRICED DUE TO SCARCITY
*RED/3-10: UNPRICED DUE TO SCARCITY
*BLACK/2-5: UNPRICED DUE TO SCARCITY
*PURPLE/1: UNPRICED DUE TO SCARCITY
*P.P.BLACK/1: UNPRICED DUE TO SCARCITY
*P.P.CYAN/1: UNPRICED DUE TO SCARCITY
*P.P.MAGENTA/1: UNPRICED DUE TO SCARCITY
*P.P.YELLOW/1: UNPRICED DUE TO SCARCITY
RANDOMLY INSERTED INTO PACKS

TE01	S.Corino/A.Pearce	12.00	30.00
TE02	K.Patera/S.Norton	10.00	25.00
TE03	Konnan/S.Norton	20.00	50.00
TE05	J.Garvin/Precious	15.00	40.00
TE06	Ax/Smash	20.00	50.00
TE08	B.Eaton/D.Condrey	12.00	30.00
TE09	S.Lane/B.Eaton	12.00	30.00
TE10	S.Too Hotty/B.Christopher	15.00	40.00
TE11	B.Knobbs/J.Sags	12.00	30.00
TE13	J.Cornette/D.Condrey	10.00	25.00
TE14	Kama/Tatanka	10.00	25.00
TE15	C.Michelle/K.Kelly	12.00	30.00
TE16	N.Koloff/K.Kruschev	15.00	40.00

TE18	T.Runnels/V.Venis	15.00	40.00
TE19	N.Jackson/M.Jackson	8.00	20.00
TE20	M.Kanellis/M.Bennett	15.00	40.00
TE21	R.Steiner/S.Steiner	20.00	50.00
TE22	R.Morton/R.Gibson	12.00	30.00
TE23	Rikishi Fatu	8.00	20.00
	Samu		
TE24	Tori/X-Pac	12.00	30.00

2020 Leaf Ultimate Wrestling Ultimate Stars Autographs

*PLATINUM/25>: UNPRICED DUE TO SCARCITY
*RED/10>: UNPRICED DUE TO SCARCITY
*EMERALD/5>: UNPRICED DUE TO SCARCITY
*SILVER/3>: UNPRICED DUE TO SCARCITY
*GOLD/1: UNPRICED DUE TO SCARCITY
*P.P.BLACK/1: UNPRICED DUE TO SCARCITY
*P.P.CYAN/1: UNPRICED DUE TO SCARCITY
*P.P.MAGENTA/1: UNPRICED DUE TO SCARCITY
*P.P.YELLOW/1: UNPRICED DUE TO SCARCITY

USE1	Edge	12.00	30.00
USG1	Goldberg	25.00	60.00
USK1	Kamala	10.00	25.00
UST1	Tugboat/Typhoon/Shockmaster	20.00	50.00
USW1	Warlord	8.00	20.00
USAA1	Arn Anderson	12.00	30.00
USAP1	Adam Page	15.00	40.00
USBB1	Britt Baker	12.00	30.00
USBB1	Brutus Beefcake	6.00	15.00
USBH1	Bret Hart	15.00	40.00
USBL1	Brother Love	8.00	20.00
USBOJ	Bob Orton Jr.	6.00	15.00
USBP1	Brian Pillman Jr.	6.00	15.00
USBV1	Baron Von Raschke	10.00	25.00
USBW1	Barry Windham	10.00	25.00
USCC1	Colt Cabana	6.00	15.00
USCM1	Cima	5.00	12.00
USCR1	Cody Rhodes	15.00	40.00
USDA1	Demolition Ax	8.00	20.00
USDF1	Don Frye	6.00	15.00
USDS1	Demolition Smash	12.00	30.00
USEB1	Eric Bischoff	10.00	25.00
USED1	El Hijo del Fantasma	6.00	15.00
USFG1	Flip Gordon	5.00	12.00
USFL1	Flamita	5.00	12.00
USFU1	Funaki	6.00	15.00
USGM1	The Great Muta	15.00	40.00
USHH1	Hulk Hogan	60.00	120.00
USHT1	Hiroshi Tanahashi	8.00	20.00
USHTM	The Honky Tonk Man	10.00	25.00
USJB1	Josh Barnett	10.00	25.00
USJH1	Jimmy Hart	8.00	20.00
USJL1	Jushin Liger	15.00	40.00
USKBW	Koko B. Ware	10.00	25.00
USKI1	Kota Ibushi	15.00	40.00
USKO1	Kenny Omega	15.00	40.00
USKS1	Ken Shamrock	15.00	40.00
USLH1	Larry Hennig	10.00	25.00
USMF1	Manny Fernandez	6.00	15.00
USMF1	Mick Foley	15.00	40.00
USMS1	Minoru Suzuki	10.00	25.00
USPE1	Penta El Zero M	10.00	25.00
USPF1	Penelope Ford	10.00	25.00
USPS1	Perry Saturn	5.00	12.00
USRF1	Ric Flair	25.00	60.00
USRS1	Ricky Steamboat	10.00	25.00
USSS1	Sumie Sakai	5.00	12.00
USSV1	Sid Vicious	6.00	15.00

USTA1	Tony Atlas	6.00	15.00
USTB1	The Barbarian	6.00	15.00
USTB1	Tully Blanchard	10.00	25.00
USTD1	Ted DiBiase	10.00	25.00
USTF1	Terry Funk	15.00	40.00
USTS1	Tito Santana	8.00	20.00
USTZ1	Tazz	8.00	20.00
USVP1	Vampiro	8.00	20.00
USYH1	Yoshi-Hashi	6.00	15.00

2020 Leaf Ultimate Wrestling Clearly Dominant Autographs

*PINK/10-15: UNPRICED DUE TO SCARCITY
*PLATINUM/10: UNPRICED DUE TO SCARCITY
*GREEN/4-6: UNPRICED DUE TO SCARCITY
*RED/3-5: UNPRICED DUE TO SCARCITY
*SILVER/2-3: UNPRICED DUE TO SCARCITY
*GOLD/1: UNPRICED DUE TO SCARCITY
STATED PRINT RUN 25 SER.#'d SETS

CDG1	Goldberg	20.00	50.00
CDAA1	Arn Anderson	15.00	40.00
CDBH1	Bret Hart	20.00	50.00
CDCJ1	Chris Jericho	15.00	40.00
CDGM1	The Great Muta	30.00	75.00
CDHH1	Hulk Hogan	75.00	150.00
CDHT1	Hiroshi Tanahashi	12.00	30.00
CDJL1	Jushin Liger	20.00	50.00
CDJV1	Jesse Ventura		
CDKK1	Kenta Kobashi	25.00	60.00
CDKN1	Kevin Nash	12.00	30.00
CDKO1	Kenny Omega	25.00	60.00
CDMF1	Mick Foley	15.00	40.00
CDRF1	Ric Flair	50.00	100.00

2020 Leaf Ultimate Wrestling Enshrined Autographs

*PURPLE/35>: UNPRICED DUE TO SCARCITY
*PLATINUM/10-15: UNPRICED DUE TO SCARCITY
*RED/7-10: UNPRICED DUE TO SCARCITY
*EMERALD/5: UNPRICED DUE TO SCARCITY
*SILVER/3: UNPRICED DUE TO SCARCITY
*GOLD/1: UNPRICED DUE TO SCARCITY
*P.P.BLACK/1: UNPRICED DUE TO SCARCITY
*P.P.CYAN/1: UNPRICED DUE TO SCARCITY
*P.P.MAGENTA/1: UNPRICED DUE TO SCARCITY
*P.P.YELLOW/1: UNPRICED DUE TO SCARCITY
RANDOMLY INSERTED INTO PACKS

EBB1	Brutus Beefcake	6.00	15.00
EBH1	Bret Hart	15.00	40.00
EBOJ	Bob Orton Jr.	8.00	20.00
EHH1	Hulk Hogan	50.00	100.00
EJH1	Jimmy Hart	6.00	15.00
EKBW	Koko B. Ware	6.00	15.00
EKN1	Kevin Nash	10.00	25.00
ERS1	Ricky Steamboat	12.00	30.00
ETA1	Tony Atlas	6.00	15.00

2020 Leaf Ultimate Wrestling Ultimate Ring Queens Autographs

*PURPLE/6-25: UNPRICED DUE TO SCARCITY
*PLATINUM/5-10: UNPRICED DUE TO SCARCITY
*RED/4-7: UNPRICED DUE TO SCARCITY
*EMERALD/3-5: UNPRICED DUE TO SCARCITY
*SILVER/2-3: UNPRICED DUE TO SCARCITY
*GOLD/1: UNPRICED DUE TO SCARCITY
*P.P.BLACK/1: UNPRICED DUE TO SCARCITY
*P.P.CYAN/1: UNPRICED DUE TO SCARCITY

2020 Leaf Ultimate Wrestling Ultimate Signatures 2

*PLATINUM/25>: UNPRICED DUE TO SCARCITY
*RED/15>: UNPRICED DUE TO SCARCITY
*EMERALD/5>: UNPRICED DUE TO SCARCITY
*SILVER/2-3: UNPRICED DUE TO SCARCITY
*GOLD/1: UNPRICED DUE TO SCARCITY
*P.P.BLACK/1: UNPRICED DUE TO SCARCITY
*P.P.CYAN/1: UNPRICED DUE TO SCARCITY
*P.P.MAGENTA/1: UNPRICED DUE TO SCARCITY
*P.P.YELLOW/1: UNPRICED DUE TO SCARCITY
RANDOMLY INSERTED INTO PACKS

US201	Ax/Smash	20.00	50.00
US202	Barbarian/Warlord	15.00	40.00
US203	B.Baker/P.Ford	25.00	60.00
US204	B.Beefcake/H.Hogan	60.00	120.00
US205	C.Cabana/T.Yano	15.00	40.00
US206	K.Omega/Cima	20.00	50.00
US207	E.Bischoff/T.Funk	20.00	50.00
US208	Honky Tonk Man/J.B. Badd	10.00	25.00
US209	T.DiBiase/J.Hart	12.00	30.00
US210	K.B. Ware/Bushwacker Luke	12.00	30.00
US211	S.Vicious/Vampiro	12.00	30.00
US212	Tazz/Funaki	12.00	30.00
US213	Tully & Tessa Blanchard	25.00	60.00
US214	T.Santana/T.DiBiase	15.00	40.00
US215	K.B. Ware/Warlord	10.00	25.00
US216	M.Foley/Edge	20.00	50.00
US217	Kat/Victoria	10.00	25.00
US218	Victoria/B.Reed	10.00	25.00
US219	T.Tonga/T.Loa	12.00	30.00
US220	A.Page/Y.Takahashi	15.00	40.00
US221	H.Hogan/D.Rodman	100.00	200.00

2020 Leaf Ultimate Wrestling Ultimate Signatures 4

*PURPLE/10-25: UNPRICED DUE TO SCARCITY
*PLATINUM/7-10: UNPRICED DUE TO SCARCITY
*RED/6-7: UNPRICED DUE TO SCARCITY
*EMERALD/4-5: UNPRICED DUE TO SCARCITY
*SILVER/3: UNPRICED DUE TO SCARCITY
*GOLD/1: UNPRICED DUE TO SCARCITY
*P.P.BLACK/1: UNPRICED DUE TO SCARCITY
*P.P.CYAN/1: UNPRICED DUE TO SCARCITY
*P.P.MAGENTA/1: UNPRICED DUE TO SCARCITY
*P.P.YELLOW/1: UNPRICED DUE TO SCARCITY
RANDOMLY INSERTED INTO PACKS

US401	Anderson/Blanchard/Flair/Windham		
US402	Barbarian/Warlord/Ax/Smash	60.00	120.00

*P.P.MAGENTA/1: UNPRICED DUE TO SCARCITY
*P.P.YELLOW/1: UNPRICED DUE TO SCARCITY
RANDOMLY INSERTED INTO PACKS

RQBB1	Britt Baker	25.00	60.00
RQBR1	Brandi Rhodes	15.00	40.00
RQIV1	Ivelisse	8.00	20.00
RQJH1	Jackie Haas	8.00	20.00
RQPF1	Penelope Ford	12.00	30.00
RQRS1	Ryan Shamrock		
RQSB1	Scarlett Bordeaux	25.00	60.00
RQTB1	Tessa Blanchard	15.00	40.00
RQVI1	Victoria	6.00	15.00

1999 Little Caesar's WCW/nWo Lenticular

	COMPLETE SET (4)	3.00	8.00
NNO	Diamond Dallas Page	1.25	3.00

NNO	Goldberg	2.50	6.00
NNO	Hollywood Hogan	2.00	5.00
NNO	Sting	2.50	6.00

1991 Mello Smello WWF Stickers

COMPLETE SET (6)		15.00	40.00
1	Hulk Hogan	10.00	25.00
2	The Bushwhackers	3.00	8.00
3	Big Boss Man	3.00	8.00
4	The Ultimate Warrior	6.00	15.00
5	The Legion of Doom	6.00	15.00
6	Jake The Snake Roberts	4.00	10.00

2008 Merlin WWE Heroes Stickers

COMPLETE SET (230)		50.00	100.00
1	RAW Logo	.15	.40
2	SmackDown Logo	.15	.40
3	ECW Logo	.15	.40
4	Randy Orton	.40	1.00
5	Randy Orton	.40	1.00
6	Randy Orton	.40	1.00
7	Randy Orton	.40	1.00
8	Randy Orton	.40	1.00
9	Randy Orton	.40	1.00
10	Randy Orton	.40	1.00
11	Randy Orton	.40	1.00
12	Randy Orton	.40	1.00
13	Randy Orton	.40	1.00
14	Randy Orton	.40	1.00
15	Undertaker	.75	2.00
16	Undertaker	.75	2.00
17	Undertaker	.75	2.00
18	Undertaker	.75	2.00
19	Undertaker	.75	2.00
20	Undertaker	.75	2.00
21	Undertaker	.75	2.00
22	Undertaker	.75	2.00
23	Undertaker	.75	2.00
24	Undertaker	.75	2.00
25	Undertaker	.75	2.00
26	Shawn Michaels	1.00	2.50
27	Shawn Michaels	1.00	2.50
28	Shawn Michaels	1.00	2.50
29	Shawn Michaels	1.00	2.50
30	Shawn Michaels	1.00	2.50
31	Shawn Michaels	1.00	2.50
32	Shawn Michaels	1.00	2.50
33	Shawn Michaels	1.00	2.50
34	Shawn Michaels	1.00	2.50
35	Shawn Michaels	1.00	2.50
36	Shawn Michaels	1.00	2.50
37	MVP	.25	.60
38	MVP	.25	.60
39	MVP	.25	.60
40	MVP	.25	.60
41	MVP	.25	.60
42	MVP	.25	.60
43	Michelle McCool	.75	2.00
44	Michelle McCool	.75	2.00
45	Michelle McCool	.75	2.00
46	Michelle McCool	.75	2.00
47	Michelle McCool	.75	2.00
48	Triple H	1.00	2.50
49	Triple H	1.00	2.50
50	Triple H	1.00	2.50
51	Triple H	1.00	2.50
52	Triple H	1.00	2.50
53	Triple H	1.00	2.50
54	Triple H	1.00	2.50
55	Triple H	1.00	2.50
56	Triple H	1.00	2.50
57	Triple H	1.00	2.50
58	Triple H	1.00	2.50
59	Batista	.60	1.50
60	Batista	.60	1.50
61	Batista	.60	1.50
62	Batista	.60	1.50
63	Batista	.60	1.50
64	Batista	.60	1.50
65	Batista	.60	1.50
66	Batista	.60	1.50
67	Batista	.60	1.50
68	Batista	.60	1.50
69	Batista	.60	1.50
70	Umaga	.25	.60
71	Umaga	.25	.60
72	Umaga	.25	.60
73	Umaga	.25	.60
74	Umaga	.25	.60
75	Umaga	.25	.60
76	Hornswoggle	.25	.60
77	Hornswoggle	.25	.60
78	Hornswoggle	.25	.60
79	Hornswoggle	.25	.60
80	Hornswoggle	.25	.60
81	Matt Hardy	.60	1.50
82	Matt Hardy	.60	1.50
83	Matt Hardy	.60	1.50
84	Matt Hardy	.60	1.50
85	Matt Hardy	.60	1.50
86	Matt Hardy	.60	1.50
87	Matt Hardy	.60	1.50
88	Matt Hardy	.60	1.50
89	Matt Hardy	.60	1.50
90	Matt Hardy	.60	1.50
91	Matt Hardy	.60	1.50
92	CM Punk	.15	.40
93	CM Punk	.15	.40
94	CM Punk	.15	.40
95	CM Punk	.15	.40
96	CM Punk	.15	.40
97	CM Punk	.15	.40
98	The Miz	.25	.60
99	The Miz	.25	.60
100	The Miz	.25	.60
101	The Miz	.25	.60
102	The Miz	.25	.60
103	Ken Kennedy	.40	1.00
104	Ken Kennedy	.40	1.00
105	Ken Kennedy	.40	1.00
106	Ken Kennedy	.40	1.00
107	Ken Kennedy	.40	1.00
108	Ken Kennedy	.40	1.00
109	Melina	.60	1.50
110	Melina	.60	1.50
111	Melina	.60	1.50
112	Melina	.60	1.50
113	Melina	.60	1.50
114	John Morrison	.15	.40
115	John Morrison	.15	.40
116	John Morrison	.15	.40
117	John Morrison	.15	.40
118	John Morrison	.15	.40
119	Elijah Burke	.15	.40
120	Elijah Burke	.15	.40
121	Elijah Burke	.15	.40
122	Elijah Burke	.15	.40
123	Elijah Burke	.15	.40
124	Elijah Burke	.15	.40
125	Kane	.60	1.50
126	Kane	.60	1.50
127	Kane	.60	1.50
128	Kane	.60	1.50
129	Kane	.60	1.50
130	Kane	.60	1.50
131	Kane	.60	1.50
132	Kane	.60	1.50
133	Kane	.60	1.50
134	Kane	.60	1.50
135	Kane	.60	1.50
136	John Cena	1.00	2.50
137	John Cena	1.00	2.50
138	John Cena	1.00	2.50
139	John Cena	1.00	2.50
140	John Cena	1.00	2.50
141	John Cena	1.00	2.50
142	John Cena	1.00	2.50
143	John Cena	1.00	2.50
144	John Cena	1.00	2.50
145	John Cena	1.00	2.50
146	John Cena	1.00	2.50
147	Rey Mysterio	.40	1.00
148	Rey Mysterio	.40	1.00
149	Rey Mysterio	.40	1.00
150	Rey Mysterio	.40	1.00
151	Rey Mysterio	.40	1.00
152	Rey Mysterio	.40	1.00
153	Rey Mysterio	.40	1.00
154	Rey Mysterio	.40	1.00
155	Rey Mysterio	.40	1.00
156	Rey Mysterio	.40	1.00
157	Rey Mysterio	.40	1.00
158	Chris Jericho	.40	1.00
159	Chris Jericho	.40	1.00
160	Chris Jericho	.40	1.00
161	Chris Jericho	.40	1.00
162	Chris Jericho	.40	1.00
163	Chris Jericho	.40	1.00
164	Beth Phoenix	.75	2.00
165	Beth Phoenix	.75	2.00
166	Beth Phoenix	.75	2.00
167	Beth Phoenix	.75	2.00
168	Beth Phoenix	.75	2.00
169	Chavo Guerrero	.25	.60
170	Chavo Guerrero	.25	.60
171	Chavo Guerrero	.25	.60
172	Chavo Guerrero	.25	.60
173	Chavo Guerrero	.25	.60
174	The Great Khali	.15	.40
175	The Great Khali	.15	.40
176	The Great Khali	.15	.40
177	The Great Khali	.15	.40
178	The Great Khali	.15	.40
179	The Great Khali	.15	.40
180	Shelton Benjamin	.15	.40
181	Shelton Benjamin	.15	.40
182	Shelton Benjamin	.15	.40
183	Shelton Benjamin	.15	.40
184	Shelton Benjamin	.15	.40
185	Boogeyman	.25	.60
186	Boogeyman	.25	.60
187	Boogeyman	.25	.60
188	Boogeyman	.25	.60
189	Boogeyman	.25	.60
190	Boogeyman	.25	.60
191	Edge	.60	1.50
192	Edge	.60	1.50
193	Edge	.60	1.50
194	Edge	.60	1.50
195	Edge	.60	1.50
196	Edge	.60	1.50
197	Edge	.60	1.50
198	Edge	.60	1.50
199	Edge	.60	1.50
200	Edge	.60	1.50
201	Edge	.60	1.50
202	Jeff Hardy	.60	1.50
203	Jeff Hardy	.60	1.50
204	Jeff Hardy	.60	1.50
205	Jeff Hardy	.60	1.50
206	Jeff Hardy	.60	1.50
207	Jeff Hardy	.60	1.50
208	Jeff Hardy	.60	1.50
209	Jeff Hardy	.60	1.50
210	Jeff Hardy	.60	1.50
211	Jeff Hardy	.60	1.50
212	Jeff Hardy	.60	1.50
213	Undertaker/Mark Henry	.75	2.00
214	CM Punk/Miz	.25	.60
215	Carlito/Mr. Anderson	.40	1.00
P1	Undertaker	.75	2.00
P2	World Title	.15	.40
P3	Randy Orton	.40	1.00
P4	Batista	.60	1.50
P5	Rey Mysterio	.40	1.00
P6	Triple H	1.00	2.50
P7	WWE Title	.15	.40
P8	John Cena	1.00	2.50
P9	Randy Orton	.40	1.00
P10	Edge	.60	1.50
P11	JBL	.15	.40
P12	Beth Phoenix	.75	2.00
P13	WWE Women's Title	.15	.40
P14	Melina	.60	1.50
P15	Mickie James	1.00	2.50

1993 Merlin WWF SuperStars Stickers

COMPLETE SET (300)			
1	WWF Logo FOIL	.10	.25
2	Battle Royal (Puzzle)	.10	.25
3	Battle Royal (Puzzle)	.10	.25
4	Battle Royal (Puzzle)	.10	.25
5	Lex Luger Logo FOIL	.10	.25
6	Lex Luger	.10	.25
7	Lex Luger	.10	.25
8	Lex Luger (Puzzle)	.10	.25
9	Lex Luger (Puzzle)	.10	.25
10	Lex Luger	.10	.25
11	Lex Luger (Puzzle)	.10	.25
12	Lex Luger (Puzzle)	.10	.25
13	Lex Luger FOIL	.10	.25
14	Lex Luger	.10	.25
15	Bob Backlund	.10	.25
16	Bob Backlund Logo FOIL	.10	.25
17	Bob Backlund	.10	.25
18	Bob Backlund	.10	.25
19	Bob Backlund FOIL	.10	.25
20	Bob Backlund (Puzzle)	.10	.25
21	Bob Backlund (Puzzle)	.10	.25
22	Bob Backlund	.10	.25
23	The Undertaker Logo FOIL	.10	.25

#	Card	.10	.25
24	The Undertaker	.10	.25
25	The Undertaker	.10	.25
26	The Undertaker	.10	.25
27	The Undertaker FOIL	.10	.25
28	The Undertaker	.10	.25
29	The Undertaker (Puzzle)	.10	.25
30	The Undertaker (Puzzle)	.10	.25
31	The Undertaker (Puzzle)	.10	.25
32	The Undertaker (Puzzle)	.10	.25
33	Paul Bearer (Puzzle)	.10	.25
34	Paul Bearer (Puzzle)	.10	.25
35	Paul Bearer	.10	.25
36	Paul Bearer (Puzzle)	.10	.25
37	Paul Bearer (Puzzle)	.10	.25
38	The Model Rick Martel Logo FOIL	.10	.25
39	The Model Rick Martel (Puzzle)	.10	.25
40	The Model Rick Martel (Puzzle)	.10	.25
41	The Model Rick Martel (Puzzle)	.10	.25
42	The Model Rick Martel (Puzzle)	.10	.25
43	Bret Hit Man Hart Logo FOIL	.10	.25
44	Bret Hit Man Hart	.10	.25
45	Bret Hit Man Hart	.10	.25
46	Bret Hit Man Hart (Puzzle)	.10	.25
47	Bret Hit Man Hart (Puzzle)	.10	.25
48	Bret Hit Man Hart	.10	.25
49	Bret Hit Man Hart	.10	.25
50	Bret Hit Man Hart (Puzzle)	.10	.25
51	Bret Hit Man Hart (Puzzle)	.10	.25
52	Bret Hit Man Hart	.10	.25
53	Diesel (Puzzle)	.10	.25
54	Diesel (Puzzle)	.10	.25
55	Diesel	.10	.25
56	Diesel (Puzzle)	.10	.25
57	Diesel (Puzzle)	.10	.25
58	Diesel (Puzzle)	.10	.25
59	Diesel (Puzzle)	.10	.25
60	Diesel	.10	.25
61	Hulk Hogan Logo FOIL	.10	.25
62	Hulk Hogan (Puzzle)	.10	.25
63	Hulk Hogan (Puzzle)	.10	.25
64	Hulk Hogan	.10	.25
65	Hulk Hogan FOIL	.10	.25
66	Hulk Hogan	.10	.25
67	Hulk Hogan	.10	.25
68	Hulk Hogan	.10	.25
69	Hulk Hogan (Puzzle)	.10	.25
70	Hulk Hogan (Puzzle)	.10	.25
71	Irwin R. Schyster	.10	.25
72	Irwin R. Schyster Logo FOIL	.10	.25
73	Irwin R. Schyster	.10	.25
74	Irwin R. Schyster (Puzzle)	.10	.25
75	Irwin R. Schyster (Puzzle)	.10	.25
76	Irwin R. Schyster	.10	.25
77	Irwin R. Schyster	.10	.25
78	Irwin R. Schyster FOIL	.10	.25
79	Irwin R. Schyster	.10	.25
80	Yokozuna Logo FOIL	.10	.25
81	Yokozuna (Puzzle)	.10	.25
82	Yokozuna (Puzzle)	.10	.25
83	Yokozuna	.10	.25
84	Yokozuna FOIL	.10	.25
85	Yokozuna	.10	.25
86	Yokozuna (Puzzle)	.10	.25
87	Yokozuna (Puzzle)	.10	.25
88	Yokozuna	.10	.25
89	Yokozuna	.10	.25
90	Mr. Fuji	.10	.25
91	Mr. Fuji FOIL	.10	.25
92	Mr. Fuji	.10	.25
93	Mr. Fuji (Puzzle)	.10	.25
94	Mr. Fuji (Puzzle)	.10	.25
95	Shawn Michaels Logo FOIL	.10	.25
96	Shawn Michaels (Puzzle)	.10	.25
97	Shawn Michaels (Puzzle)	.10	.25
98	Shawn Michaels	.10	.25
99	Shawn Michaels	.10	.25
100	Adam Bomb FOIL	.10	.25
101	Adam Bomb	.10	.25
102	Adam Bomb	.10	.25
103	Adam Bomb (Puzzle)	.10	.25
104	Adam Bomb (Puzzle)	.10	.25
105	Adam Bomb (Puzzle)	.10	.25
106	Adam Bomb (Puzzle)	.10	.25
107	Adam Bomb (Puzzle)	.10	.25
108	Adam Bomb (Puzzle)	.10	.25
109	Adam Bomb FOIL	.10	.25
110	Randy Savage Logo FOIL	.10	.25
111	Randy Savage (Puzzle)	.10	.25
112	Randy Savage (Puzzle)	.10	.25
113	Randy Savage	.10	.25
114	Randy Savage	.10	.25
115	Randy Savage (Puzzle)	.10	.25
116	Randy Savage (Puzzle)	.10	.25
117	Randy Savage	.10	.25
118	Randy Savage	.10	.25
119	Randy Savage FOIL	.10	.25
120	Marty Jannetty	.10	.25
121	Marty Jannetty	.10	.25
122	Marty Jannetty (Puzzle)	.10	.25
123	Marty Jannetty (Puzzle)	.10	.25
124	Marty Jannetty Logo FOIL	.10	.25
125	Marty Jannetty (Puzzle)	.10	.25
126	Marty Jannetty (Puzzle)	.10	.25
127	Marty Jannetty (Puzzle)	.10	.25
128	Marty Jannetty (Puzzle)	.10	.25
129	Tatanka Logo FOIL	.10	.25
130	Tatanka (Puzzle)	.10	.25
131	Tatanka (Puzzle)	.10	.25
132	Tatanka FOIL	.10	.25
133	Tatanka (Puzzle)	.10	.25
134	Tatanka (Puzzle)	.10	.25
135	Tatanka	.10	.25
136	Tatanka (Puzzle)	.10	.25
137	Tatanka (Puzzle)	.10	.25
138	Tatanka	.10	.25
139	Ludvig Borga Logo FOIL	.10	.25
140	Ludvig Borga (Puzzle)	.10	.25
141	Ludvig Borga (Puzzle)	.10	.25
142	Ludvig Borga	.10	.25
143	Ludvig Borga (Puzzle)	.10	.25
144	Ludvig Borga (Puzzle)	.10	.25
145	Ludvig Borga FOIL	.10	.25
146	Ludvig Borga	.10	.25
147	Ludvig Borga	.10	.25
148	King of the Ring Logo FOIL	.10	.25
149	Summer Slam Logo FOIL	.10	.25
150	Survivor Series Logo FOIL	.10	.25
151	Royal Rumble Logo FOIL	.10	.25
152	WrestleMania Logo FOIL	.10	.25
153	123 Kid Logo FOIL	.10	.25
154	123 Kid (Puzzle)	.10	.25
155	123 Kid (Puzzle)	.10	.25
156	123 Kid	.10	.25
157	123 Kid	.10	.25
158	123 Kid	.10	.25
159	123 Kid (Puzzle)	.10	.25
160	123 Kid (Puzzle)	.10	.25
161	123 Kid (Puzzle)	.10	.25
162	123 Kid (Puzzle)	.10	.25
163	Razor Ramon Logo FOIL	.10	.25
164	Razor Ramon	.10	.25
165	Razor Ramon	.10	.25
166	Razor Ramon (Puzzle)	.10	.25
167	Razor Ramon (Puzzle)	.10	.25
168	Razor Ramon (Puzzle)	.10	.25
169	Razor Ramon (Puzzle)	.10	.25
170	Razor Ramon FOIL	.10	.25
171	Razor Ramon (Puzzle)	.10	.25
172	Razor Ramon (Puzzle)	.10	.25
173	Bam Bam Bigelow Logo FOIL	.10	.25
174	Bam Bam Bigelow	.10	.25
175	Bam Bam Bigelow	.10	.25
176	Bam Bam Bigelow (Puzzle)	.10	.25
177	Bam Bam Bigelow (Puzzle)	.10	.25
178	Bam Bam Bigelow (Puzzle)	.10	.25
179	Bam Bam Bigelow (Puzzle)	.10	.25
180	Bam Bam Bigelow	.10	.25
181	Bam Bam Bigelow FOIL	.10	.25
182	Bam Bam Bigelow	.10	.25
183	Luna Vachon	.10	.25
184	Luna Vachon Logo FOIL	.10	.25
185	Luna Vachon	.10	.25
186	Luna Vachon	.10	.25
187	Luna Vachon	.10	.25
188	Luna Vachon	.10	.25
189	Luna Vachon FOIL	.10	.25
190	Luna Vachon (Puzzle)	.10	.25
191	Luna Vachon (Puzzle)	.10	.25
192	Bastion Booger (Puzzle)	.10	.25
193	Bastion Booger (Puzzle)	.10	.25
194	Bastion Booger	.10	.25
195	Bastion Booger	.10	.25
196	Bastion Booger (Puzzle)	.10	.25
197	Bastion Booger (Puzzle)	.10	.25
198	Bastion Booger	.10	.25
199	Bastion Booger (Puzzle)	.10	.25
200	Bastion Booger (Puzzle)	.10	.25
201	Crush FOIL	.10	.25
202	Crush (Puzzle)	.10	.25
203	Crush (Puzzle)	.10	.25
204	Crush Logo FOIL	.10	.25
205	Crush	.10	.25
206	MVP	.10	.25
207	MVP (Puzzle)	.10	.25
208	MVP (Puzzle)	.10	.25
209	MVP (Puzzle)	.10	.25
210	MVP (Puzzle)	.10	.25
211	Harvey Wippleman	.10	.25
212	Harvey Wippleman	.10	.25
213	Harvey Wippleman (Puzzle)	.10	.25
214	Harvey Wippleman (Puzzle)	.10	.25
215	Bobby Heenan (Puzzle)	.10	.25
216	Bobby Heenan (Puzzle)	.10	.25
217	Bobby Heenan Logo FOIL	.10	.25
218	Doink Logo FOIL	.10	.25
219	Doink	.10	.25
220	Doink (Puzzle)	.10	.25
221	Doink (Puzzle)	.10	.25
222	Doink	.10	.25
223	Doink FOIL	.10	.25
224	Doink	.10	.25
225	Doink (Puzzle)	.10	.25
226	Doink (Puzzle)	.10	.25
227	Doink	.10	.25
228	Rick of the Steiner Brother	.10	.25
229	The Steiner Brothers FOIL	.10	.25
230	The Steiner Brothers (Puzzle)	.10	.25
231	The Steiner Brothers (Puzzle)	.10	.25
232	Scott of the Steiner Brother	.10	.25
233	The Steiner Brothers (Puzzle)	.10	.25
234	The Steiner Brothers (Puzzle)	.10	.25
235	The Steiner Brothers Logo FOIL	.10	.25
236	The Steiner Brothers (Puzzle)	.10	.25
237	The Steiner Brothers (Puzzle)	.10	.25
238	Men On A Mission (Puzzle)	.10	.25
239	Men On A Mission (Puzzle)	.10	.25
240	Men On A Mission FOIL	.10	.25
241	Mabel of Men On A Mission	.10	.25
242	Men On A Mission (Puzzle)	.10	.25
243	Men On A Mission (Puzzle)	.10	.25
244	Mo of Men On A Mission	.10	.25
245	Men On A Mission Logo FOIL	.10	.25
246	Men On A Mission (Puzzle)	.10	.25
247	Men On A Mission (Puzzle)	.10	.25
248	Well Dunn Logo FOIL	.10	.25
249	Well Dunn (Puzzle)	.10	.25
250	Well Dunn (Puzzle)	.10	.25
251	Well Dunn (Puzzle)	.10	.25
252	Well Dunn (Puzzle)	.10	.25
253	Quebecers (Puzzle)	.10	.25
254	Quebecers (Puzzle)	.10	.25
255	Quebecers	.10	.25
256	Quebecers Logo FOIL	.10	.25
257	Jacques of the Quebecers	.10	.25
258	Head Shrinkers Logo FOIL	.10	.25
259	Head Shrinkers	.10	.25
260	Head Shrinkers (Puzzle)	.10	.25
261	Head Shrinkers (Puzzle)	.10	.25
262	Fatu of the Head Shrinkers	.10	.25
263	Head Shrinkers (Puzzle)	.10	.25
264	Head Shrinkers (Puzzle)	.10	.25
265	Head Shrinkers	.10	.25
266	Head Shrinkers and Afa (Puzzle)	.10	.25
267	Head Shrinkers and Afa (Puzzle)	.10	.25
268	Tom Prichard of Heavenly Bodies	.10	.25
269	Heavenly Bodies (Puzzle)	.10	.25
270	Heavenly Bodies (Puzzle)	.10	.25
271	Jimmy Del Ray of Heavenly Bodies	.10	.25
272	Heavenly Bodies/J.Cornette (Puzzle)	.10	.25
273	Heavenly Bodies/J.Cornette (Puzzle)	.10	.25
274	Jim Cornette	.10	.25
275	Heavenly Bodies/J.Cornette (Puzzle)	.10	.25
276	Heavenly Bodies/J.Cornette (Puzzle)	.10	.25
277	Jim Cornette	.10	.25
278	Smoking Gunns Logo FOIL	.10	.25
279	Smoking Gunns (Puzzle)	.10	.25
280	Smoking Gunns (Puzzle)	.10	.25
281	Bart of Smoking Gunns	.10	.25
282	Billy of Smoking Gunns	.10	.25
283	Smoking Gunns (Puzzle)	.10	.25
284	Smoking Gunns (Puzzle)	.10	.25
285	Smoking Gunns FOIL	.10	.25
286	Smoking Gunns (Puzzle)	.10	.25
287	Smoking Gunns (Puzzle)	.10	.25
288	The Bushwackers Logo FOIL	.10	.25
289	The Bushwackers (Puzzle)	.10	.25
290	The Bushwackers (Puzzle)	.10	.25
291	Luke of The Bushwackers	.10	.25
292	The Bushwackers (Puzzle)	.10	.25
293	The Bushwackers (Puzzle)	.10	.25
294	Butch of The Bushwackers	.10	.25
295	The Bushwackers FOIL	.10	.25

296	The Bushwhackers (Puzzle)	.10	.25
297	The Bushwhackers (Puzzle)	.10	.25
298	WWF Title Belt FOIL	.10	.25
299	WWF Intercontinental Belt FOIL	.10	.25
300	WWF Tag Team Title Belt FOIL	.10	.25

1986 Monty Gum Wrestling

	COMPLETE SET (100)	75.00	150.00
	UNOPENED BOX (50 PACKS)		
	UNOPENED PACK		
1	Rip Rogers	.40	1.00
2	Chris Adams	.25	.75
3	Black Bart	.20	.50
4	Steve Regal	.60	1.50
5	Gino Hernandez	.40	1.00
6	Ricky Steamboat	.75	2.00
7	The Road Warriors	1.00	2.50
8	Joe LeDuc	.60	1.50
9	Fritz Von Erich	.60	1.50
10	Kevin Von Erich	.60	1.50
11	Kerry Von Erich	.60	1.50
12	Baron Von Raschke UER	.20	.50
13	Sgt. Slaughter	.75	2.00
14	Magnificent Don Muraco	.40	1.00
15	Bobby Jaggers	.20	.50
16	Wahoo McDaniel	2.00	5.00
17	The Great Kabuki & Sunshine	1.00	2.50
18	The Iron Sheik	.30	.75
19	Greg Valentine	.50	1.25
20	Rick Martel	.40	1.00
21	The Road Warriors	1.00	2.50
22	Hulk Hogan	4.00	10.00
23	Kerry Von Erich	1.00	2.50
24	David Schultz	1.25	3.00
25	The Road Warriors	1.25	3.00
26	Nikita Koloff	.25	.60
27	Baron Von Raschke	.20	.50
28	Hercules Hernandez	.50	1.25
29	The RPM's	.30	.75
30	Buzz Sawyer	1.00	2.50
31	Junkyard Dog UER	.40	1.00
32	Nikita Koloff	.40	1.00
33	Krusher Khruschev & Ivan Koloff	.20	.50
34	Kevin Von Erich (Ric Flair) UER	.75	2.00
35	Kerry Von Erich	.75	2.00
36	Bobby Fulton & Tommy Rogers	.75	2.00
37	Magnificent Don Muraco	.20	.50
38	Rick Martel	.40	1.00
39	Rick Martel	.20	.50
40	Rick Martel	.75	2.00
41	Gino Hernandez	.20	.50
42	Terry Taylor	.50	1.25
43	Rock 'N Roll Express	.75	2.00
44	Billy Jack Haynes & Rick Rude	.50	1.25
45	Billy Jack Haynes & Rick Rude	.50	1.25
46	Arn Anderson & Brett Sawyer	.40	1.00
47	Kerry Von Erich	.75	2.00
48	Rick Martel & Nick Bockwinkel	.20	.50
49	Hulk Hogan (w/Joan Rivers)	8.00	20.00
50	Hulk Hogan & Cyndi Lauper	4.00	10.00
51	Hulk Hogan & Muhammed Ali	8.00	20.00
52	Hulk Hogan & M.Ali (Stallone) UER	4.00	10.00
53	Tully Blanchard	1.25	3.00
54	Bruno Sammartino/Nikolai Volkoff	.75	2.00
55	Bruno Sammartino	1.25	3.00
56	B.Sammartino & Killer Kowalski	.50	1.25
57	B.Sammartino & Johnny Valentine	.75	2.00
58	Ric Flair & Kerry Von Erich	1.00	2.50
59	Ric Flair	5.00	12.00
60	Ric Flair & Dusty Rhodes	4.00	10.00
61	Hulk Hogan & Nick Bockwinkel	5.00	12.00
62	Hulk Hogan	8.00	20.00
63	Hulk Hogan & Ken Patera	3.00	8.00
64	Dusty Rhodes & Manny Fernandez	.30	.75
65	Dusty Rhodes	3.00	8.00
66	Dusty Rhodes & King Curtis	.75	2.00
67	The Missing Link	.75	2.00
68	The Road Warriors	1.00	2.50
69	Precious Paul Ellering	.20	.50
70	Fabulous Free-Birds: Terry Gordy	.75	2.00
71	Fabulous Freebirds: Michael Hayes	1.25	3.00
72	Jim Cornette UER	.75	2.00
73	Jesse Barr	.25	.60
74	Rip Rogers & Bugsy McGraw	.30	.75
75	Konga, the Barbarian	.40	1.00
76	Eric Embry	.20	.50
77	Magnum T.A. Terry Allen	1.50	4.00
78	Magnum T.A. Terry Allen	1.25	3.00
79	Greg Allen (Valentine) UER	.30	.75
80	Tully Blanchard	.40	1.00
81	The Sheepherders	.75	2.00
82	Tito Santana	.40	1.00
83	The One Man Gang	.75	2.00
84	Gary Hart	.20	.50
85	Brett Sawyer	.20	.50
86	Ron Bass	.20	.50
87	Hulk Hogan	6.00	15.00
88	Rick Flair UER	2.00	5.00
89	Rick Flair & Sgt. Slaughter UER	1.50	4.00
90	Rick Flair UER	6.00	15.00
91	Sgt. Slaughter	.75	2.00
92	Rick Steamboat	1.25	3.00
93	King Kong Brody	.50	1.25
94	Randy Savage	12.00	30.00
95	Dusty Rhodes	1.00	2.50
96	King Kong Bundy	.50	1.25
97	Nikita Koloff	.75	2.00
98	Nikita Koloff & Dusty Rhodes	.50	1.25
99	Butch Reed	.40	1.00
100	Konga, the Barbarian	.75	2.00

2005 NBC Universal WWE RAW Ringside Sweepstakes

	COMPLETE SET (4)	4.00	10.00
NNO	Carlito	1.25	3.00
NNO	John Cena	2.00	5.00
NNO	Torrie Wilson	1.50	4.00
NNO	Triple H	1.25	3.00

1985 O'Quinn Wrestling All-Stars

	COMPLETE SET (54)	150.00	300.00
	ONLY AVAILABLE IN WRESTLING ALL STARS MAGAZINE		
1	Hulk Hogan	30.00	75.00
2	Ric Flair	20.00	50.00
3	Rick Martel	2.50	6.00
4	Sergeant Slaughter	3.00	8.00
5	The Iron Sheik	6.00	15.00
6	Kamala	3.00	8.00
7	Dusty Rhodes	3.00	8.00
8	Paul Orndorff	2.50	6.00
9	The Fabulous Freebirds	3.00	8.00
10	Big John Studd	2.50	6.00
11	Kerry Von Erich	2.50	6.00
12	Jimmy Valiant	2.50	6.00
13	Baron Von Raschke	6.00	15.00
14	Missing Link	2.50	6.00
15	Roddy Piper	12.00	30.00
16	Terry Taylor	2.50	6.00
17	Superstar Billy Graham	3.00	8.00
18	Carlos Colon	2.50	6.00
19	Kevin Sullivan	3.00	8.00
20	Tommy Rich	2.50	6.00
21	(Jesse) The Body Ventura	8.00	20.00
22	Kevin Von Erich	2.50	6.00
23	King Kong Bundy	4.00	10.00
24	Wahoo McDaniel	3.00	8.00
25	Greg Valentine	3.00	8.00
26	Ken Patera	2.50	6.00
27	Terry Allen	2.50	6.00
28	Rock n Roll Express	4.00	10.00
29	Jerry Lawler	6.00	15.00
30	Junkyard Dog	3.00	8.00
31	Barry Windham	3.00	8.00
32	The Youngbloods	2.50	6.00
33	Ricky Steamboat	4.00	10.00
34	Superfly Snuka	3.00	8.00
35	The Road Warriors	12.00	30.00
36	Bob Orton	5.00	12.00
37	Mil Mascaras	3.00	8.00
38	Ivan Putski	2.50	6.00
39	Jimmy Garvin	2.50	6.00
40	Mike Von Erich	2.50	6.00
41	Chris Adams	2.50	6.00
42	Brad Armstrong	2.50	6.00
43	Gino Hernandez	4.00	10.00
44	Tully Blanchard	4.00	10.00
45	The Sheepherders	2.50	6.00
46	Andre The Giant	25.00	60.00
47	The Fabulous Ones	2.50	6.00
48	The Tonga Kid	2.50	6.00
49	Masked Superstar	3.00	8.00
50	Billy Haynes	3.00	8.00
51	Adrian Street	2.50	6.00
52	Pedro Morales	3.00	8.00
53	David Sammartino	3.00	8.00
54	Bruno Sammartino	5.00	12.00

1985 O-Pee-Chee WWF

	COMPLETE SET W/HOGAN (66)	200.00	400.00
	COMPLETE SET W/O HOGAN (60)	30.00	75.00
	UNOPENED BOX (36 PACKS)		
	UNOPENED PACK (9 CARDS+1 STICKER)		
	RINGSIDE ACTION (22-56)		
	SUPERSTARS SPEAK (57-66)		
1	Hulk Hogan	75.00	150.00
2	The Iron Sheik	1.00	2.50
3	Captain Lou Albano	.75	2.00
4	Junk Yard Dog	1.00	2.50
5	Paul Mr. Wonderful Orndorff	.60	1.50
6	Jimmy Superfly Snuka	.60	1.50
7	Rowdy Roddy Piper	6.00	15.00
8	Wendi Richter	.75	2.00
9	Greg The Hammer Valentine	1.00	2.50
10	Brutus Beefcake	1.00	2.50
11	Jesse The Body Ventura	3.00	8.00
12	Big John Studd	.60	1.50
13	Fabulous Moolah	1.25	3.00
14	Tito Santana	1.25	3.00
15	Hillbilly Jim	1.00	2.50
16	Hulk Hogan	100.00	200.00
17	Mr. Fuji	.75	2.00
18	Rotundo & Windham	.75	2.00
19	Moondog Spot	.50	1.25
20	Chief Jay Strongbow	.50	1.25
21	George The Animal Steele	1.25	3.00
22	Let Go of My Toe! RA	.50	1.25
23	Lock 'Em Up! RA	.50	1.25
24	Scalp 'Em! RA	.50	1.25
25	Going for the Midsection! RA	.75	2.00
26	Up in the Air! RA	.60	1.50
27	All Tied Up! RA	1.50	4.00
28	Here She Comes! RA	.50	1.25
29	Stretched to the Limit! RA	3.00	8.00
30	Over He Goes! RA	1.00	2.50
31	An Appetite for Mayhem! RA	.60	1.50
32	Putting on Pressure! RA	.50	1.25
33	Smashed on a Knee! RA	.75	2.00
34	A Fist Comes Flying! RA	.50	1.25
35	Lemme' Out of This! RA	.50	1.25
36	No Fair Chokin'! RA	.50	1.25
37	Attacked by an Animal!! RA	.50	1.25
38	One Angry Man! RA	1.25	3.00
39	Someone's Going Down! RA	1.25	3.00
40	Strangle Hold! RA	2.00	5.00
41	Bending an Arm! RA	.50	1.25
42	Ready for a Pile Driver! RA	.75	2.00
43	Face to the Canvas! RA	.50	1.25
44	Paul Wants It All! RA	.75	2.00
45	Kick to the Face! RA	3.00	8.00
46	Ready for Action! RA	.50	1.25
47	Putting on the Squeeze! RA	.60	1.50
48	Giants in Action! RA	1.50	4.00
49	Camel Clutch! RA	.60	1.50
50	Pile Up! RA	2.00	5.00
51	Can't Get Away! RA	.60	1.50
52	Going for the Pin! RA	.50	1.25
53	Ready to Fly! RA	2.00	5.00
54	Crusher in a Crusher! RA	.50	1.25
55	Fury of the Animal! RA	.75	2.00
56	Wrong Kind of Music! RA	6.00	15.00
57	Who's your next challenger? SS	2.50	6.00
58	This dog has got a mean bite! SS	.75	2.00
59	I don't think I'll ask... SS	1.25	3.00
60	You Hulkster fans... SS	8.00	20.00
61	This ain't my idea... SS	1.00	2.50
62	You mean Freddie Blassie... SS	1.25	3.00
63	Mppgh Ecch Oong. SS	1.00	2.50
64	Rock n' wrestling connection SS	.75	2.00
65	Arrrggghhhh! SS	.60	1.50
66	They took my reindeer! SS	.60	1.50

1985 O-Pee-Chee WWF Stickers

	COMPLETE SET W/HOGAN (22)	50.00	100.00
	COMPLETE SET W/O HOGAN (17)	12.00	30.00
	STATED ODDS 1:1		
1	Hulk Hogan	15.00	40.00
2	Captain Lou Albano	.75	2.00
3	Brutus Beefcake	1.25	3.00
4	Jesse Ventura	2.00	5.00
5	The Iron Sheik	1.50	4.00
6	Wendi Richter	1.25	3.00
7	Jimmy Snuka	.75	2.00
8	Ivan Putski	1.00	2.50
9	Hulk Hogan	4.00	10.00
10	Junk Yard Dog	1.25	3.00
11	Hulk Hogan	6.00	15.00
12	Captain Lou Albano	.75	2.00
13	Captain Lou Albano	.75	2.00
14	Freddy Blassie & Iron Sheik	.75	2.00
15	Jimmy Snuka	.75	2.00

16	Hulk Hogan	10.00	25.00
17	Iron Sheik	1.50	4.00
18	Rene Goulet & S.D. Jones	1.25	3.00
19	Junk Yard Dog	.75	2.00
20	Wendi Richter	1.25	3.00
21	Le gÉant FerrÈ	3.00	8.00
22	Hulk Hogan	8.00	20.00

1985-86 O-Pee-Chee WWF Series 2

COMPLETE SET (75)		60.00	120.00
UNOPENED BOX (36 PACKS)			
UNOPENED PACK (10 CARDS)			
1	Nikolai Volkoff	4.00	10.00
2	The Magnificent Muraco	1.25	3.00
3	Tony Atlas	.40	1.00
4	Jim The Anvil Neidhart	.40	1.00
5	Ricky Steamboat	.75	2.00
6	The British Bulldogs	1.50	4.00
7	King Kong Bundy	3.00	8.00
8	Bobby The Brain Heenan	1.25	3.00
9	Lei Lani Kai	.40	1.00
10	Snaky Squeeze!	.75	2.00
11	Savage Attack!	15.00	40.00
12	Cowboy Bob Orton	.50	1.25
13	Showing the Flag	1.25	3.00
14	Showboating!	1.50	4.00
15	Terry Funk	1.25	3.00
16	Martial Artist!	1.25	3.00
17	Don't Call Me Beach Bum	.75	2.00
18	Up and Over!	.30	1.00
19	Brewing Up Trouble!	.40	1.00
20	A Leg Up!	.75	2.00
21	About To Explode	.40	1.00
22	Twister!	.50	1.25
23	Headed For the Turnbuckle	5.00	12.00
24	Hercules Hernandez	2.50	6.00
25	Leggo' My Head!	.40	1.00
26	The Dragon Has Struck!	.40	1.00
27	Top Dog	1.00	2.50
28	Watch Out For Me	1.25	3.00
29	It's Time For A Little Road Work!	.60	1.50
30	Karate Chop!	.60	1.50
31	Crafty Fuji	.75	2.00
32	Bulldog Grip!	.60	1.50
33	Jake The Snake	4.00	10.00
34	Siva Afi	.60	1.50
35	This Is Gonna' Hurt!	1.25	3.00
36	Military Press!	.60	1.50
37	Tower Of Strength!	.40	1.00
38	Bulldog Grip!	.40	1.00
39	Piggyback!	2.00	5.00
40	Shove Off!	.40	1.00
41	Jimmy Mouth of the South Hart	1.25	3.00
42	Fliperoo!	.50	1.25
43	Ring Toss!	.50	1.25
44	Uncle Elmer	.50	1.25
45	Iran and Russia - Number One?	1.25	3.00
46	The Killer Bees	.50	1.25
47	Secret Plans	.50	1.25
48	Davey Boy Smith	1.50	4.00
49	Aerial Escape!	.40	1.00
50	Caught by Kong!	.60	1.50
51	Banging Away!	1.50	4.00
52	All American Boy!	.40	1.00
53	Fiji Fury!	.40	1.00
54	What d'ya mean...	1.00	2.50
55	Do you know any way...	.40	1.00
56	Those are the biggest feet...	.40	1.00
57	I make sukiyaki...	1.25	3.00
58	This guy really looks sick.	.40	1.00
59	Nikolai, he sings...	.40	1.00
60	The Animal In Love!	.40	1.00
61	Hoss Funk	.75	2.00
62	Can I autograph your cast?	.60	1.50
63	Randy Savage & Elizabeth	12.00	30.00
64	I don't know...	.40	1.00
65	If anybody calls you...	.40	1.00
66	It's rock and wrestling - forever!	2.00	5.00
67	Wrestlers vs. Football Greats	1.25	3.00
68	Big Men Battle	.50	1.25
69	Help Coming	.40	1.00
70	The Body Struts His Stuff	.40	1.00
71	In the Corner	1.25	3.00
72	Plenty of Beef	.75	2.00
73	Battle Royal Winner	.50	1.25
74	Working for a Position	.40	1.00
75	Ready for a War!	1.50	4.00

1987 O-Pee-Chee WWF

COMPLETE SET (75)		60.00	120.00
UNOPENED BOX (36 PACKS)			
UNOPENED PACK (10 CARDS)			
1	Bret "Hit Man" Hart	25.00	60.00
2	Andre the Giant	6.00	15.00
3	Hulk Hogan	5.00	12.00
4	Frankie	.75	2.00
5	Koko B. Ware	.75	2.00
6	Tito Santana	.60	1.50
7	Randy Savage & Elizabeth	10.00	25.00
8	Billy Jack Haynes	.40	1.00
9	Hercules & Bobby Heenan	.40	1.00
10	King Harley Race	.60	1.50
11	Kimchee & Kamala	.40	1.00
12	Bravo/Johnny V/Valentine	.50	1.25
13	Honky Tonk Man	1.00	2.50
14	Outback Jack	.40	1.00
15	King Kong Bundy	1.25	3.00
16	The Magnificent Muraco	.40	1.00
17	Mr. Fuji and Killer Khan	.75	2.00
18	The Natural Butch Reed	.60	1.50
19	Davey Boy Smith	.75	2.00
20	The Dynamite Kid	.40	1.00
21	Ricky The Dragon Steamboat	1.50	4.00
22	Two-Man Clothesline RA	.40	1.00
23	Ref Turned Wrestler RA	.75	2.00
24	Ready to Strike RA	.60	1.50
25	In the Outback RA	.40	1.00
26	The Hulkster Explodes RA	2.00	5.00
27	Double Whammy RA	.40	1.00
28	Spoiling for a Fight RA	.40	1.00
29	Flip Flop RA	.40	1.00
30	Islanders Attack RA	.40	1.00
31	King Harley Parades RA	.40	1.00
32	Backbreaker RA	.40	1.00
33	Double Dropkick RA	.40	1.00
34	The Loser Must Bow RA	.40	1.00
35	American-Made RA	2.50	6.00
36	A Challenge Answered RA	2.00	5.00
37	Champ in the Ring RA	4.00	10.00
38	Listening to Hulkamania RA	2.00	5.00
39	Heading for the Ring RA	.40	1.00
40	Out to Destroy RA	.40	1.00
41	Tama Takes a Beating RA	.40	1.00
42	Bundy in Mid-Air RA	.40	1.00
43	Karate Stance RA	.40	1.00
44	Her Eyes on Randy RA	2.50	6.00
45	The Olympian Returns RA	.40	1.00
46	Reed Is Riled RA	.40	1.00
47	Flying Bodypress RA	.40	1.00
48	Hooking the Leg RA	.40	1.00
49	A Belly Buster WMIII	.40	1.00
50	Revenge on Randy WMIII	.75	2.00
51	Fighting the Full Nelson WMIII	.40	1.00
52	Honky Tonk Goes Down WMIII	.40	1.00
53	Over the Top WMIII	.40	1.00
54	The Giant Is Slammed WMIII	1.25	3.00
55	Out of the Ring WMIII	.75	2.00
56	And Still Champion WMIII	1.50	4.00
57	Harts Hit Concrete WMIII	.40	1.00
58	The Challenge RA	1.25	3.00
59	Bearhug RA	.40	1.00
60	Fantastic Bodypress RA	.40	1.00
61	Aerial Maneuvers RA	.40	1.00
62	Ready to Sting! RA	.40	1.00
63	Showing Off RA	.40	1.00
64	Scare Tactics RA	.40	1.00
65	Taking a Bow RA	.60	1.50
66	Out to Eat a Turnbuckle RA	.40	1.00
67	Nice guys finish last! SS	.40	1.00
68	Here's how we keep... SS	.40	1.00
69	Urrggh. Nice! SS	.40	1.00
70	No Kamala...him not dinner! SS	.40	1.00
71	We are the original destroyers. SS	.40	1.00
72	I think the fans are mad at me. SS	.40	1.00
73	You ain't nothin'... SS	.40	1.00
74	I'm gonna take a big bit... SS	.40	1.00
75	Good! SS	.40	1.00

2004 Pacific TNA

COMPLETE SET (75)		10.00	25.00
UNOPENED BOX (24 PACKS)		85.00	100.00
UNOPENED PACK (5 CARDS)		4.00	5.00
*RED: .6X TO 1.5X BASIC CARDS			
1	April	.20	.50
2	Chelsea	.12	.30
3	Goldylocks	.75	2.00
4	Lollipop	.30	.75
5	Athena	.20	.50
6	Abyss	.30	.75
7	Jeremy Borash	.12	.30
8	Traci	.50	1.25
9	D'Lo Brown	.20	.50
10	Christopher Daniels	.12	.30
11	Delirious	.12	.30
12	Simon Diamond	.12	.30
13	Julio Dinero	.12	.30
14	Shane Douglas	.12	.30
15	Sonjay Dutt	.12	.30
16	Ekmo Fatu	.20	.50
17	Glenn Gilberti	.12	.30
18	Juventud Guerrera	.12	.30
19	Chris Harris	.12	.30
20	Don Harris	.12	.30
21	Ron Harris	.12	.30
22	Chris Hero	.12	.30
23	BG James	.20	.50
24	Jeff Jarrett	.60	1.50
25	Kid Kash	.12	.30
26	Frankie Kazarian	.12	.30
27	Ron Killings	.20	.50
28	Konnan	.12	.30
29	Lazz	.12	.30
30	Jerry Lynn	.12	.30
31	Father James Mitchell	.12	.30
32	Kevin Northcutt	.12	.30
33	Nosawa	.12	.30
34	CM Punk	20.00	50.00
35	Raven	.50	1.25
36	Dusty Rhodes	.30	.75
37	Vince Russo	.12	.30
38	Chris Sabin	.12	.30
39	Sandman	.20	.50
40	Rick Santel	.12	.30
41	Michael Shane	.12	.30
42	Shark Boy	.12	.30
43	Sonny Siaki	.12	.30
44	Sinn	.12	.30
45	Slash	.12	.30
46	James Storm	.20	.50
47	AJ Styles	12.00	30.00
48	Johnny Swinger	.12	.30
49	Terry Taylor	.12	.30
50	Trinity	.20	.50
51	Chris Vaughn	.12	.30
52	Ryan Wilson	.12	.30
53	David Young	.12	.30
54	Scott Hudson	.12	.30
55	Mike Tenay	.12	.30
56	Don West	.12	.30
57	Don Callis	.12	.30
58	Erik Watts	.12	.30
59	Rudy Charles	.12	.30
60	Mike Posey	.12	.30
61	Andrew Thomas	.12	.30
62	3Live Kru	.20	.50
63	America's Most Wanted	.20	.50
64	D'Lo Brown	.20	.50
65	Simon Diamond	.12	.30
66	Jeff Jarrett	.60	1.50
67	Raven	.50	1.25
68	Dusty Rhodes	.30	.75
69	Chris Sabin	.12	.30
70	Sonny Siaki	.12	.30
71	AJ Styles	6.00	15.00
72	Chris Vaughn	.12	.30
73	Trinity	.20	.50
74	Goldylocks	.75	2.00
75	Lollipop	.30	.75

2004 Pacific TNA Red

1	April	.30	.75
2	Chelsea	.20	.50
3	Goldylocks	1.25	3.00
4	Lollipop	.50	1.25
5	Athena	.30	.75
6	Abyss	.50	1.25
7	Jeremy Borash	.20	.50
8	Traci	.75	2.00
9	D'Lo Brown	.30	.75
10	Christopher Daniels	.20	.50
11	Delirious	.20	.50
12	Simon Diamond	.20	.50
13	Julio Dinero	.20	.50
14	Shane Douglas	.20	.50
15	Sonjay Dutt	.20	.50
16	Ekmo Fatu	.30	.75
17	Glenn Gilberti	.20	.50
18	Juventud Guerrera	.20	.50
19	Chris Harris	.20	.50
20	Don Harris	.20	.50
21	Ron Harris	.20	.50
22	Chris Hero	.20	.50

#	Player		
23	BG James	.30	.75
24	Jeff Jarrett	1.00	2.50
25	Kid Kash	.20	.50
26	Frankie Kazarian	.20	.50
27	Ron Killings	.30	.75
28	Konnan	.20	.50
29	Lazz	.20	.50
30	Jerry Lynn	.20	.50
31	Father James Mitchell	.20	.50
32	Kevin Northcutt	.20	.50
33	Nosawa	.20	.50
34	CM Punk	30.00	75.00
35	Raven	.75	2.00
36	Dusty Rhodes	.50	1.25
37	Vince Russo	.20	.50
38	Chris Sabin	.20	.50
39	Sandman	.30	.75
40	Rick Santel	.20	.50
41	Michael Shane	.20	.50
42	Shark Boy	.20	.50
43	Sonny Siaki	.20	.50
44	Sinn	.20	.50
45	Slash	.20	.50
46	James Storm	.30	.75
47	AJ Styles	20.00	50.00
48	Johnny Swinger	.20	.50
49	Terry Taylor	.20	.50
50	Trinity	.30	.75
51	Chris Vaughn	.20	.50
52	Ryan Wilson	.20	.50
53	David Young	.20	.50
54	Scott Hudson	.20	.50
55	Mike Tenay	.20	.50
56	Don West	.20	.50
57	Don Callis	.20	.50
58	Erik Watts	.20	.50
59	Rudy Charles	.20	.50
60	Mike Posey	.20	.50
61	Andrew Thomas	.20	.50
62	3Live Kru	.30	.75
63	America's Most Wanted	.30	.75
64	D'Lo Brown	.30	.75
65	Simon Diamond	.20	.50
66	Jeff Jarrett	1.00	2.50
67	Raven	.75	2.00
68	Dusty Rhodes	.50	1.25
69	Chris Sabin	.20	.50
70	Sonny Siaki	.20	.50
71	AJ Styles	8.00	20.00
72	Chris Vaughn	.20	.50
73	Trinity	.30	.75
74	Goldylocks	1.25	3.00
75	Lollipop	.50	1.25

2004 Pacific TNA Event-Used

STATED PRINT RUN 1,525 SER.#'d SETS

#	Player		
1	America's Most Wanted	4.00	8.00
2	AJ Styles	5.00	10.00
3	D'Lo Brown	4.00	8.00
4	Raven	4.00	8.00
5	BG James	4.00	8.00

2004 Pacific TNA Event-Used Limited Edition

NOT AVAILABLE IN PACKS

#	Player		
1	TNA Babes	15.00	40.00
2	America's Most Wanted	15.00	40.00

2004 Pacific TNA Legends and Superstars Autographs

COMPLETE SET (6)
STATED ODDS 1:24 HOBBY

#	Player		
1	Rowdy Roddy Piper	75.00	150.00
3	Jeff Jarrett	10.00	25.00
4	Terry Taylor	5.00	12.00
5	Dusty Rhodes	100.00	200.00
6	Harley Race	30.00	75.00
7	Raven	5.00	12.00

2004 Pacific TNA Main Event Autographs

STATED ODDS 1:24 HOBBY

#	Player		
NNO	AJ Styles Red Border SP	15.00	40.00
NNO	AJ Styles Gold Border SP	15.00	40.00
NNO	AMW DUAL AU	6.00	15.00
NNO	April	4.00	10.00
NNO	Goldylocks	4.00	10.00
NNO	Lollipop	5.00	12.00
NNO	Chris Vaughn	4.00	10.00
NNO	Trinity	4.00	10.00

2004 Pacific TNA Tag Teams

COMPLETE SET (8)		2.00	5.00

STATED ODDS 1:5 HOBBY

#	Team		
1	Diamond/Swinger	.30	.75
2	The Naturals	.30	.75
3	3Live Kru	.50	1.25
4	The Gathering	2.00	5.00
5	Red Shirt Security	.30	.75
6	Black Shirt Security	.30	.75
7	Gilberti/Young	.30	.75
8	America's Most Wanted	.50	1.25

2004 Pacific TNA Tattoos

COMPLETE SET (28)		3.00	8.00

STATED ODDS 1:1 HOBBY

#	Tattoo		
1	TNA Logo 1	.12	.30
2	TNA Logo 2	.12	.30
3	TNA Logo 3	.12	.30
4	Total Non-Stop Action	.12	.30
5	PTC Logo 1	.12	.30
6	PTC Logo 2	.12	.30
7	PTC Logo 3	.12	.30
8	Raven	.50	1.25
9	AJ Styles	.30	.75
10	Jeff Jarrett	.60	1.50
11	D'Lo Brown	.20	.50
12	Chris Harris	.12	.30
13	James Storm	.20	.50
14	Shark Boy	.20	.50
15	Ron Killings	.20	.50
16	Konnan	.12	.30
17	BG James	.20	.50
18	Chris Sabin	.12	.30
19	Michael Shane	.12	.30
20	Sonny Siaki	.12	.30
21	Chris Vaughn	.12	.30
22	Trinity	.20	.50
23	America's Most Wanted	.20	.50
24	3Live Kru	.20	.50
25	Red Shirt Security	.12	.30
26	Black Shirt Security	.12	.30
27	Lollipop	.30	.75
28	Goldylocks	.75	2.00

1998 Panini WCW/nWo Photocards

COMPLETE SET (108)		15.00	40.00
UNOPENED BOX (24 PACKS)			
UNOPENED PACK (6 CARDS)			

#	Card		
1	Goldberg	.50	1.25
2	Goldberg	.50	1.25
3	Goldberg	.50	1.25
4	Goldberg	.50	1.25
5	Goldberg	.50	1.25
6	Goldberg	.50	1.25
7	Goldberg	.50	1.25
8	Goldberg	.50	1.25
9	Goldberg	.50	1.25
10	Goldberg	.50	1.25
11	Goldberg Logo	.50	1.25
12	Goldberg	.50	1.25
13	Goldberg	.50	1.25
14	Goldberg	.50	1.25
15	Goldberg vs. Konnan	.50	1.25
16	Disco Inferno	.12	.30
17	Sting	.50	1.25
18	Sting	.50	1.25
19	Sting	.50	1.25
20	Sting	.50	1.25
21	Sting	.50	1.25
22	Sting Logo	.75	2.00
23	Sting	.50	1.25
24	Sting	.50	1.25
25	Hollywood Hogan	.60	1.50
26	Hollywood Hogan	.60	1.50
27	Hollywood Hogan	.60	1.50
28	Hollywood Hogan Logo	.60	1.50
29	Hollywood Hogan	.60	1.50
30	Hogan vs. Luger	.60	1.50
31	Hollywood Hogan	.60	1.50
32	Ric Flair	.40	1.00
33	Diamond Dallas Page	.30	.75
34	Diamond Dallas Page	.30	.75
35	Dallas Page Logo	.30	.75
36	Diamond Dallas Page	.30	.75
37	Scott Hall	.30	.75
38	Hall vs. Piper	.30	.75
39	Scott Hall	.30	.75
40	Scott Hall	.30	.75
41	Kevin Nash	.25	.60
42	Kevin Nash	.25	.60
43	Kevin Nash Logo	.25	.60
44	Kevin Nash	.25	.60
45	Macho Man	.40	1.00
46	Macho Man Logo	.40	1.00
47	Macho Man	.40	1.00
48	Macho Man vs. Hart	.40	1.00
49	Public Enemy	.12	.30
50	Public Enemy	.12	.30
51	Lex Luger	.20	.50
52	Lex Luger	.20	.50
53	Luger vs. Hogan	.30	.75
54	Lex Luger	.20	.50
55	Lex Luger Logo	.20	.50
56	Lex Luger	.20	.50
57	Buff Bagwell	.12	.30
58	Bagwell vs. Booker T	.15	.40
59	Buff Bagwell	.12	.30
60	Anvil	.15	.40
61	Rick Steiner	.15	.40
62	Rick Steiner	.15	.40
63	Scott Steiner	.15	.40
64	Scott Steiner	.15	.40
65	Raven	.15	.40
66	Raven Logo	.15	.40
67	Raven	.15	.40
68	Glacier	.12	.30
69	Roddy Piper	.40	1.00
70	Piper vs. Hogan	.50	1.25
71	Roddy Piper	.40	1.00
72	Scott Norton	.12	.30
73	Rey Mysterio	.30	.75
74	Rey Mysterio Logo	.30	.75
75	Chris Benoit	.25	.60
76	Benoit vs. Malenko	.25	.60
77	Alex Wright	.12	.30
78	Alex Wright	.12	.30
79	Brian Adams	.12	.30
80	Brian Adams	.12	.30
81	Guerrero vs Konnan	.12	.30
82	Eddie Guerrero	.40	1.00
83	Guerrero vs Malenko	.40	1.00
84	Wrath	.15	.40
85	Chris Jericho	.40	1.00
86	Chris Jericho	.40	1.00
87	Jericho vs. Wright	.40	1.00
88	Chris Jericho	.40	1.00
89	Dean Malenko	.15	.40
90	Malenko vs. Benoit	.15	.40
91	Dean Malenko Logo	.15	.40
92	Dean Malenko	.15	.40
93	Dragon vs Wright	.15	.40
94	Dragon vs Mysterio	.25	.60
95	Konnan	.20	.50
96	Konnan	.20	.50
97	Bret Hart	.40	1.00
98	Bret Hart	.40	1.00
99	Bret Hart	.40	1.00
100	British Bulldog	.30	.75
101	Juventud vs Kidman	.15	.40
102	Juventud vs Kidman	.15	.40
103	Juventud vs Kidman	.15	.40
104	Curt Hennig	.25	.60
105	Saturn	.12	.30
106	Saturn	.12	.30
107	Saturn	.12	.30
108	Nitro Girls	.75	2.00

1999 Panini WCW/nWo Stickers

COMPLETE SET (120)		20.00	50.00
UNOPENED BOX (100 PACKS)			
UNOPENED PACK			

#	Sticker		
1	Bill Goldberg	.60	1.50
2	Kevin Nash	.30	.75
3	Diamond Dallas Page	.30	.75
4	Hollywood Hogan	.60	1.50
5	Ric Flair	.50	1.25
6	Nash & Luger Rule!	.30	.75
7	Kevin Nash	.30	.75
8	Kevin Nash	.30	.75
9	Goldberg-Nash Bash!!!	.75	2.00
10	Kevin Nash	.30	.75
11	Kevin Nash	.25	.60
12	Kevin Nash	.30	.75
13	Kevin Nash	.30	.75
14	Kevin Nash	.30	.75
15	Red & Black Attack	.25	.60
16	Who's Next?	.40	1.00
17	Bill Goldberg	.60	1.50
18	Bill Goldberg	.60	1.50
19	Bill Goldberg	.60	1.50

#	Card		
20	Raven's Wings Are Clipped!	.40	1.00
21	A Crushing Headlock On Konnan	.40	1.00
22	Goldberg Tattoo	.75	2.00
23	Bill Goldberg	.60	1.50
24	Bill Goldberg	.60	1.50
25	Bill Goldberg	.60	1.50
26	Hogan Hands Out A Beating!	.60	1.50
27	Hollywood Hogan	.60	1.50
28	Hollywood Hogan	.60	1.50
29	Hollywood Hogan	.60	1.50
30	Hollywood Hogan	.60	1.50
31	Hogan And His Buddy Bischoff!	.60	1.50
32	No Mercy!	.25	.60
33	Hollywood Hogan	.60	1.50
34	Hollywood Hogan	.60	1.50
35	Hollywood Hogan	.60	1.50
36	Ric Flair Struts His Stuff!	.50	1.25
37	Horsemen/Arn Anderson	.40	1.00
38	Chris Benoit	.25	.60
39	Dean Makenko	.15	.40
40	Steve McMichael	.12	.30
41	Malenko Mauls Benoit!	.20	.50
42	Ric Flair Tells It Like It Is...	.60	1.50
43	WOOOOOOOOO!!!	.50	1.25
44	Ric Flair In Action...	.40	1.00
45	Four Horsemen	.25	.60
46	Eddie Guerrero	.40	1.00
47	Juventud Guerrera	.15	.40
48	Rey Mysterio	.40	1.00
49	Juventud Jumps Kidman!	.15	.40
50	Guerrero Airborne!	.40	1.00
51	Eddie Guerrero	.40	1.00
52	Hector Garza	.12	.30
53	La Parka	.12	.30
54	Damian	.12	.30
55	Psychosis	.12	.30
56	Che, Fyre, and Spice	.40	1.00
57	Tigress	.40	1.00
58	The Happy Loving Couple...	.60	1.50
59	AC Jazz	.40	1.00
60	Whisper	.40	1.00
61	Alex Wright...	.12	.30
62	Kidman Gets Drop...	.15	.40
63	Kidman	.15	.40
64	Wrath's Guillotine Drop!	.12	.30
65	Kidman Hangs Tough!	.15	.40
66	Konnan Krushes Eddie Guerrero!	.30	.75
67	Konnan	.20	.50
68	Whisper	.40	1.00
69	British Bulldog	.30	.75
70	Disco Inferno	.12	.30
71	Van Hammer Slams Alex Wright!	.12	.30
72	Booker T.	.25	.60
73	Saturn	.12	.30
74	Ernest Miller Wrestling...	.15	.40
75	Chavo and Pepe	.15	.40
76	Diamond Dallas Page	.30	.75
77	Diamond Dallas Page	.30	.75
78	DDP Has Hart!	.40	1.00
79	DDP Gets The Drop On Sting!	.40	1.00
80	Diamond Dallas Page	.30	.75
81	Bret Hart	.40	1.00
82	Hart Gets A Leg up!	.40	1.00
83	Hart Puts The Hurt On DDP!	.40	1.00
84	DDP Gets Hit By The Hitman!	.40	1.00
85	Your Seat Is Ready!	.40	1.00
86	Scott Hall	.30	.75
87	The Pac In The House!	.30	.75

#	Card		
88	Scott Hall	.30	.75
89	Scott Hall	.30	.75
90	Scott Hall	.30	.75
91	Luger Lights It Up!	.20	.50
92	Luger's Got A Flair For Winning!	.20	.50
93	Lex Luger	.20	.50
94	Lex Luger	.20	.50
95	Lex Luger	.20	.50
96	Big Poppa Pump Pumps It Up!	.15	.40
97	Big Poppa Pump Pummels XXX!	.15	.40
98	NWO Bad Boy Buff Bagwell!	.12	.30
99	Big Poppa Pump Makes His Point!	.15	.40
100	Steiner's Super Bod!	.15	.40
101	Hollywood Hogan Gets Stung!	.40	1.00
102	Sting	.50	1.25
103	Scorpion	.50	1.25
104	Sting	.50	1.25
105	Sting	.50	1.25
106	Alex Wright	.12	.30
107	Chris Jericho	.40	1.00
108	Eric Bischoff	.25	.60
109	Scott Norton	.12	.30
110	Glacier	.12	.30
111	Rick Steiner	.15	.40
112	Public Enemy	.12	.30
113	Brian Adams	.12	.30
114	Bagwell Bags Rick Steiner!	.15	.40
115	The Announcers	.12	.30
116	Kendall Windham Slam...	.12	.30
117	Where The Big Boys Play!	.25	.60
118	Raven At Rest!	.15	.40
119	Wright Or Wrong?	.12	.30
120	Anvil!!! (Bam Bam Bigelow)	.20	.50

1954-55 Parkhurst Wrestling

#	Card		
	COMPLETE SET (75)	350.00	600.00
	*PREMIUM BACKS: SAME VALUE		
1	Lou Thesz	10.00	25.00
2	Sky Hi Lee	4.00	10.00
3	Whipper Billy Watson	4.00	10.00
4	Johnny Barend	4.00	10.00
5	Antonio Argentina Rocca	6.00	15.00
6	Dirty Dick Raines	4.00	10.00
7	Frank Valois	4.00	10.00
8	Hombre Montana	4.00	10.00
9	Lou Plummer	4.00	10.00
10	Chief Big Heart	4.00	10.00
11	Man Mountain Dean Jr.	4.00	10.00
12	Primo Carnera	10.00	25.00
13	Paul Baillargeon	4.00	10.00
14	Nick Roberts	4.00	10.00
15	Tim Geohagen	4.00	10.00
16	The Togo Brothers	4.00	10.00
17	Verne Gagne	12.00	30.00
18	Maurice Tillet	4.00	10.00
19	Yukon Eric	4.00	10.00
20	Toar Morgan	4.00	10.00
21	Mighty Schultz	4.00	10.00
22	Bill Stack	4.00	10.00
23	Argentina Rocca	6.00	15.00
24	Big Ben Morgan	4.00	10.00
25	Lou Pitoscia	4.00	10.00
26	Earl McCready & Billy Watson	4.00	10.00
27	Hans Schmidt	4.00	10.00
28	Lu Kim	4.00	10.00
29	Roy McLarity	4.00	10.00
30	Lord Jan Blears	4.00	10.00
31	Lee Henning & Fred Atkins	4.00	10.00

#	Card		
32	Jim Goon Henry	4.00	10.00
33	Wee Willie Davis	4.00	10.00
34	Yvon Robert	4.00	10.00
35	Joe Killer Christie	4.00	10.00
36	Bo Bo Brazil	8.00	20.00
37	The Sharpe Brothers	4.00	10.00
38	Larry Moquin	4.00	10.00
39	Nanjo Singh	4.00	10.00
40	Wladek Kowalski	10.00	25.00
41	Frank Sexton	4.00	10.00
42	George Bollas	4.00	10.00
43	Ray Villmer	4.00	10.00
44	Steve Stanlee	4.00	10.00
45	Tuffy McCrae & Little Beaver	4.00	10.00
46	Johnny Rougeau	4.00	10.00
47	Harry Lewis	4.00	10.00
48	Pat Flanagan	4.00	10.00
49	Ovila Asselin	4.00	10.00
50	Sammy Berg	4.00	10.00
51	The Mighty Ursus	4.00	10.00
52	Lou Newman	4.00	10.00
53	George Scott	4.00	10.00
54	Hans Hermann	4.00	10.00
55	Bob Wagner	4.00	10.00
56	Little Beaver/Salassi	4.00	10.00
57	Sandor Kovacs	4.00	10.00
58	The Mills Brothers	4.00	10.00
59	Roberto Pico	4.00	10.00
60	Fred Atkins	4.00	10.00
61	Wild Bill Longson	4.00	10.00
62	Bobby Managoff	4.00	10.00
63	Athol Layton	4.00	10.00
64	Warren Bockwinkle	4.00	10.00
65	The Mighty Atlas	4.00	10.00
66	Mike Sharpe	4.00	10.00
67	Ernie Dusek	4.00	10.00
68	Danno O'Shocker	4.00	10.00
69	Gorgeous George	20.00	50.00
70	The Great Togo	4.00	10.00
71	Bob Langevin	4.00	10.00
72	Emil Dusek	4.00	10.00
73	Chief Sunni War Cloud	4.00	10.00
74	Pat O'Connor	4.00	10.00
75	Baron Leone	5.00	12.00

1955-56 Parkhurst Wrestling

#	Card		
	COMPLETE SET (121)	450.00	800.00
1	Frank Valois	6.00	15.00
2	Johnny Barend	4.00	10.00
3	Sky Hi Lee	4.00	10.00
4	Hans Schmidt	4.00	10.00
5	Hans Hermann	4.00	10.00
6	Bo Bo Brazil	8.00	20.00
7	Chief Sunni War Cloud	4.00	10.00
8	The Mills Brothers	4.00	10.00
9	Roy McLarity	4.00	10.00
10	Danno O'Shocker	4.00	10.00
11	Chief Big Heart	4.00	10.00
12	Bob Wagner	4.00	10.00
13	Lou Pitoscia	4.00	10.00
14	Ernie Dusek	4.00	10.00
15	Whipper Watson	4.00	10.00
16	Johnny Rougeau	4.00	10.00
17	Ovila Asselin	4.00	10.00
18	Bill Stack	4.00	10.00
19	Ken Kenneth	4.00	10.00
20	Lou Newman	4.00	10.00
21	Warren Bockwinkle	4.00	10.00

#	Card		
22	The Sharpe Brothers	4.00	10.00
23	Bobby Managoff	4.00	10.00
24	Nick Roberts	4.00	10.00
25	Lee Henning	4.00	10.00
26	Joe Christie	4.00	10.00
27	Larry Moquin	4.00	10.00
28	Jim Goon Henry	4.00	10.00
29	Bob Langevin	4.00	10.00
30	Roberto Pico	4.00	10.00
31	Sammy Berg	4.00	10.00
32	Mighty Atlas	4.00	10.00
33	Baron Leone	4.00	10.00
34	Hassen Bay	4.00	10.00
35	Allen Garfield	4.00	10.00
36	Don Evans	4.00	10.00
37	Dory Funk	8.00	20.00
38	Art Neilson	4.00	10.00
39	Don Lee Jonathan	4.00	10.00
40	Argentina Rocca	6.00	15.00
41	Tex McKenzie	4.00	10.00
42	Pat Flanagan	4.00	10.00
43	Verne Gagne	8.00	20.00
44	Selassi & Little Beaver	4.00	10.00
45	Steve Stanlee	4.00	10.00
46	Frank Sexton	4.00	10.00
47	Pat O'Connor	4.00	10.00
48	Nanjo Singh	4.00	10.00
49	Toar Morgan	4.00	10.00
50	Harry Lewis	4.00	10.00
51	Doug Hepburn	4.00	10.00
52	Reggie Lisowski	4.00	10.00
53	Kenny Ackles	4.00	10.00
54	Argentina Rocca	6.00	15.00
55	Herb Parks	4.00	10.00
56	Bearcat Wright	4.00	10.00
57	Yvon Robert	4.00	10.00
58	Waldo Von Sieber	4.00	10.00
59	Harold Nelson	4.00	10.00
60	Sumo Wrestlers	4.00	10.00
61	Golden Hawk	4.00	10.00
62	Wee Willie Davis	4.00	10.00
63	Mike Sharpe	4.00	10.00
64	Sandor Kovacs	4.00	10.00
65	Lord Blears	4.00	10.00
66	Tim Goehagen	4.00	10.00
67	Jack Laskin	4.00	10.00
68	Emil Dusek	4.00	10.00
69	Ben Morgan	4.00	10.00
70	Lu Kim	4.00	10.00
71	Frank Marconi	4.00	10.00
72	Prince Maiava	4.00	10.00
73	Larry Kasaboski	4.00	10.00
74	Frank Thompson	4.00	10.00
75	Yukon Eric	4.00	10.00
76	Lou Thesz	6.00	15.00
77	Bill Longson	4.00	10.00
78	Fred Atkins	4.00	10.00
79	Lord Layton	4.00	10.00
80	Dusek Brothers	4.00	10.00
81	Zorra	4.00	10.00
82	Lou Thesz	10.00	25.00
83	Luther Lindsey	4.00	10.00
84	Jack Bence	4.00	10.00
85	Primo Carnera	8.00	20.00
86	Kalmikoff Brothers	4.00	10.00
87	The Great Togo	4.00	10.00
88	Lou Plummer	4.00	10.00
89	Bates Ford	4.00	10.00

90	Ursus and Montana	4.00	10.00
91	Paul Baillargeon	4.00	10.00
92	Bill McDaniels	4.00	10.00
93	Ray Villmer	4.00	10.00
94	Yvon Robert	4.00	10.00
95	Gorgeous George	15.00	40.00
96	Scott Brothers	4.00	10.00
97	Bronko Nagurski	50.00	100.00
98	Pete Managoff	4.00	10.00
99	The Togo Brothers	4.00	10.00
100	Don Lee	4.00	10.00
101	Steve Patrick	4.00	10.00
102	George Gordienko	4.00	10.00
103	Vic Holbrook	4.00	10.00
104	Gil Mains	4.00	10.00
105	Firpo Zbyszko	4.00	10.00
106	Mike Paidousis	4.00	10.00
107	Al Oeming	4.00	10.00
108	Matt Murphy	4.00	10.00
109	Martin Hutzler	4.00	10.00
110	Tommy O'Toole	4.00	10.00
111	Steve Gob	4.00	10.00
112	Riot Call Wright	4.00	10.00
113	Leo Newman	4.00	10.00
114	Frank Hurley	4.00	10.00
115	Jack Claybourne	4.00	10.00
116	Ken Colley	4.00	10.00
117	Whipper Watson	4.00	10.00
118	Steve McGill	4.00	10.00
119	Buddy Rogers	4.00	10.00
120	Gino Garibaldi	4.00	10.00
121	Ed Gardenia	5.00	12.00

2006 Popeye's WWE Mania Moments

	COMPLETE SET (21)	15.00	40.00
1	Andre the Giant	1.50	4.00
2	Rowdy Roddy Piper	1.50	4.00
3	Hulk Hogan	2.00	5.00
4	Ted Dibiase	1.25	3.00
5	Jake The Snake Roberts	1.50	4.00
6	Skydome	.60	1.50
7	Sgt. Slaughter	2.00	5.00
8	Ric Flair	1.50	4.00
9	Bobby Heenan	.75	2.00
10	Mr. Perfect	1.00	2.50
11	Bam Bam Bigelow	1.00	2.50
12	Shawn Michaels	2.00	5.00
13	Undertaker	1.50	4.00
14	Stone Cold Steve Austin	2.00	5.00
15	The Rock	2.00	5.00
16	Mick Foley	1.00	2.50
17	Kurt Angle	1.25	3.00
18	Triple H	2.00	5.00
19	Rey Mysterio	1.25	3.00
20	Chris Benoit	1.25	3.00
21	Batista / John Cena	2.00	5.00

1982 PWE Wrestling All-Stars Series A

	COMPLETE SET (36)	1000.00	2000.00
	CARDS PRICED IN NR-MT CONDITION		
1	Andre the Giant	150.00	300.00
2	Hulk Hogan	300.00	600.00
3	Mil Mascaras	25.00	60.00
4	Ted DiBiase	50.00	100.00
5	The Junkyard Dog	30.00	75.00
6	Dusty Rhodes	50.00	100.00

7	Jack Brisco	10.00	25.00
8	Harley Race	25.00	60.00
9	Dory Funk Jr.	10.00	25.00
10	Terry Funk	50.00	100.00
11	Nick Bockwinkel	12.00	30.00
12	Bob Backlund	20.00	50.00
13	Bruno Sammartino	20.00	50.00
14	Pedro Morales	10.00	25.00
15	Don Muraco	20.00	50.00
16	Bill Dundee	15.00	40.00
17	Steve Olsonoski	6.00	15.00
18	Tommy Rich	15.00	40.00
19	Angelo Mosca	12.00	30.00
20	Bruiser Brody	75.00	150.00
21	The Fabulous Moolah	20.00	50.00
22	Wahoo McDaniel	12.00	30.00
23	Billy Robinson	6.00	15.00
24	Ivan Koloff	15.00	40.00
25	Tony Atlas	20.00	50.00
26	Pat Patterson	20.00	50.00
27	Ric Flair	400.00	800.00
28	Ivan Putski	12.00	30.00
29	Dick Murdoch	8.00	20.00
30	The Crusher	8.00	20.00
31	Ken Patera	15.00	40.00
32	Ernie Ladd	12.00	30.00
33	Dick the Bruiser	10.00	25.00
34	Jerry Lawler	75.00	150.00
35	Cowboy Bill Watts	12.00	30.00
36	The Destroyer	10.00	25.00

1983 PWE Wrestling All-Stars Series A

	COMPLETE SET (36)	250.00	500.00
	CARDS PRICED IN NR-MT CONDITION		
1	Superstar (Billy) Graham	15.00	40.00
2	Tiger Mask	8.00	20.00
3	Sheik El Kaissey	6.00	15.00
4	Sgt. Jacque Goulet	5.00	12.00
5	Curt Hennig	30.00	75.00
6	Tully Blanchard	12.00	30.00
7	Jimmy Superfly Snuka	15.00	40.00
8	Gino Hernandez	8.00	20.00
9	Lou Thesz	6.00	15.00
10	Hacksaw (Jim) Duggan	25.00	60.00
11	Mr. Olympia	6.00	15.00
12	Iron Mike Sharpe	12.00	30.00
13	Jimmy Hart	20.00	50.00
14	Spike Huber	6.00	15.00
15	Steve Regal	6.00	15.00
16	Buddy Rogers	8.00	20.00
17	Jules Strongbow	10.00	25.00
18	Salvatore Bellomo	8.00	20.00
19	Bob Sweetan	6.00	15.00
20	Scott Casey	3.00	8.00
21	The Grappler	5.00	12.00
22	Big John Studd	10.00	25.00
23	Buddy Rose	5.00	12.00
24	Rocky Johnson	25.00	60.00
25	Jake Roberts	50.00	100.00
26	The Super Destroyer	3.00	8.00
27	Antonio Inoki	12.00	30.00
28	Dick Slater	6.00	15.00
29	Ken Lucas	2.00	8.00
30	Ricky Morton	15.00	40.00
31	Fred Blassie	12.00	30.00
32	Lou Albano	12.00	30.00
33	The Grand Wizard	4.00	10.00

34	Candi Divine	5.00	12.00
35	Austin Idol	4.00	10.00
36	Matt Borne	3.00	8.00

1982 PWE Wrestling All-Stars Series B

	COMPLETE SET (36)	400.00	800.00
	CARDS PRICED IN NR-MT CONDITION		
1	Rick Martel	10.00	25.00
2	Tony Garea	8.00	20.00
3	Bob Roop	8.00	20.00
4	Greg Gagne	12.00	30.00
5	Jim Brunzell	6.00	15.00
6	Jay Strongbow	10.00	25.00
7	Kerry Von Erich	60.00	120.00
8	S.D. Jones	6.00	15.00
9	Brad Rheingans	6.00	15.00
10	Killer Khan	15.00	40.00
11	Ricky Steamboat	50.00	100.00
12	Paul Orndorff	15.00	40.00
13	Tito Santana	25.00	60.00
14	Sergeant Slaughter	50.00	100.00
15	Verne Gagne	10.00	25.00
16	Bobby Heenan	15.00	40.00
17	Jerry Blackwell	8.00	20.00
18	Les Thornton	4.00	10.00
19	Adrian Adonis	10.00	25.00
20	Jesse Ventura	30.00	75.00
21	Buck Zum Hofe	4.00	10.00
22	Jimmy Valiant	8.00	20.00
23	Steve Keirn	5.00	12.00
24	Ray Stevens	6.00	15.00
25	The Iron Sheik	50.00	100.00
26	Mr. Wrestling II	12.00	30.00
27	Col. Buck Robley	4.00	10.00
28	Bobby Duncum	5.00	12.00
29	Mike George	4.00	10.00
30	Dino Bravo	6.00	15.00
31	Baron Von Raschke	12.00	30.00
32	Bobo Brazil	6.00	15.00
33	Greg Valentine	15.00	40.00
34	Joyce Grable	6.00	15.00
35	Sweet Brown Sugar	4.00	10.00
36	Dutch Mantell	10.00	25.00

1979 Rax Roast Beef Gulas NWA Mid America Championship Wrestling

NNO	Cover Card		
NNO	Bobby Eaton		
NNO	Chief Thundercloud		
NNO	David Shultz		
NNO	Dennis Condry		
NNO	Donna Bower		
NNO	George Gulas		
NNO	Hans Shroeder		
NNO	Jerry Barber		
NNO	Ken Lucas		
NNO	Len Rossi		
NNO	Mike St. John		
NNO	Nick Gulas		
NNO	Pat Smith		
NNO	Prince Tonga		
NNO	The Red Terror		
NNO	Ricky Gibson		
NNO	Robert Gibson		
NNO	Tojo Yamamoto		
NNO	Tom Renesto, Jr.		
NNO	Tom Renesto, Sr.		

NNO	Tommy Kerkeles		
NNO	Tommy Sloan		

1986 Scanlens WWF Australian

	COMPLETE SET (66)	20.00	50.00
	UNOPENED BOX		
	UNOPENED PACK		
	RINGSIDE ACTION (22-56)		
	SUPERSTARS SPEAK (57-66)		
1	Hulk Hogan	100.00	200.00
2	The Iron Sheik	.20	.50
3	Captain Lou Albano	.20	.50
4	Junk Yard Dog	.20	.50
5	Paul Mr. Wonderful Orndorff	.15	.40
6	Jimmy Superfly Snuka	.15	.40
7	Rowdy Roddy Piper	2.00	5.00
8	Wendi Richter	.20	.50
9	Greg The Hammer Valentine	.15	.40
10	Brutus Beefcake	.12	.30
11	Jesse The Body Ventura	1.50	4.00
12	Big John Studd	.15	.40
13	Fabulous Moolah	.15	.40
14	Tito Santana	.12	.30
15	Hillbilly Jim	.15	.40
16	Hulk Hogan	125.00	250.00
17	Mr. Fuji	.12	.30
18	Rotundo & Windham	.12	.30
19	Moondog Spot	.12	.30
20	Chief Jay Strongbow	.12	.30
21	George "The Animal" Steele	.15	.40
22	Let Go of My Toe! RA	.15	.40
23	Lock 'Em Up! RA	.15	.40
24	Scalp 'Em! RA	.20	.50
25	Going for the Midsection! RA	.20	.50
26	Up in the Air! RA	.12	.30
27	All Tied Up! RA	.40	1.00
28	Here She Comes! RA	.12	.30
29	Stretched to the Limit! RA	2.00	5.00
30	Over He Goes! RA	.15	.40
31	An Appetite for Mayhem! RA	.15	.40
32	Putting on Pressure! RA	.20	.50
33	Smashed on a Knee! RA	.15	.40
34	A Fist Comes Flying! RA	.12	.30
35	Lemme' Out of This! RA	.12	.30
36	No Fair Chokin'! RA	.15	.40
37	Attacked by an Animal! RA	.15	.40
38	One Angry Man! RA	.40	1.00
39	Someone's Going Down! RA	.40	1.00
40	Strangle Hold! RA	.40	1.00
41	Bending an Arm! RA	.12	.30
42	Ready for a Pile Driver! RA	.15	.40
43	Face to the Canvas! RA	.12	.30
44	Paul Wants It All! RA	.15	.40
45	Kick to the Face! RA	.75	2.00
46	Ready for Action! RA	.12	.30
47	Putting on the Squeeze! RA	.20	.50
48	Giants in Action! RA	.40	1.00
49	Camel Clutch! RA	.20	.50
50	Pile Up! RA	.75	2.00
51	Can't Get Away! RA	.20	.50
52	Going for the Pin! RA	.12	.30
53	Ready to Fly! RA	.40	1.00
54	Crusher in a Crusher! RA	.20	.50
55	Fury of the Animal! RA	.15	.40
56	Wrong Kind of Music! RA	2.00	5.00
57	Who's your next challenger? SS	2.00	5.00
58	This dog has got a mean bite! SS	.20	.50
59	I don't think I'll ask... SS	.40	1.00

60	You Hulkster fans... SS	2.00	5.00
61	This ain't my idea... SS	.40	1.00
62	You mean Freddie Blassie... SS	.40	1.00
63	Mppgh Ecch Oong. SS	.20	.50
64	Rock n' wrestling... SS	.20	.50
65	Arrrgggghhhh! SS	.15	.40
66	They took my reindeer! SS	.20	.50

2006 7-11 WWE Slam Philippines

COMPLETE SET (36)		20.00	50.00
1	Finlay	.75	2.00
2	William Regal	.75	2.00
3	Batista	1.25	3.00
4	Matt Hardy	.75	2.00
5	Lashley	.75	2.00
6	Rey Mysterio	1.25	3.00
7	Brian Kendrick	.30	.75
8	Paul London	.30	.75
9	Vito	.30	.75
10	Michelle McCool	1.50	4.00
11	Mr. Kennedy	.75	2.00
12	Booker T	.75	2.00
13	Undertaker	1.50	4.00
14	Ashley	1.25	3.00
15	Big Show	1.25	3.00
16	Rob Van Dam	.75	2.00
17	Nitro	.50	1.25
18	Hulk Hogan	2.00	5.00
19	Edge	1.25	3.00
20	Ric Flair	1.50	4.00
21	Carlito	1.25	3.00
22	Umaga	.50	1.25
23	Torrie Wilson	3.00	8.00
24	John Cena	2.00	5.00
25	Randy Orton	.75	2.00
26	Kane	1.25	3.00
27	Candice Michelle	2.00	5.00
28	Mickie James	2.00	5.00
29	Triple H	2.00	5.00
30	Shawn Michaels	2.00	5.00
31	Undertaker	1.50	4.00
32	Rey Mysterio	1.25	3.00
33	Batista	1.25	3.00
34	Triple H	2.00	5.00
35	John Cena	2.00	5.00
36	Shawn Michaels	2.00	5.00

1997 Stridex WWF

COMPLETE SET (7)		8.00	20.00
NNO	Header Card	.75	2.00
NNO	Ahmed Johnson	.75	2.00
NNO	Bret Hit Man Hart	2.00	5.00
NNO	Shawn Michaels	2.00	5.00
NNO	Stone Cold Steve Austin	3.00	8.00
NNO	Sycho Sid	1.25	3.00
NNO	Undertaker	3.00	8.00

1987 Stuart WWF Canadian

COMPLETE SET (16)		15.00	40.00
*CUT: X TO X BASIC CARDS			
1	Brutus The Barber Beefcake	1.25	3.00
2	Les Freres Rougeau Brothers	1.00	2.50
3	Strike Force	1.25	3.00
4	The Honky Tonk Man	1.25	3.00
5	Randy Savage with Elizabeth	4.00	10.00
6	Hulk Hogan	6.00	15.00
7	Demolition	1.25	3.00

8	Koko B. Ware	1.00	2.50
9	Ted DiBiase UER	1.50	4.00
10	Slick The Doctor of Style	1.25	3.00
11	British Bulldogs	1.25	3.00
12	Bobby The Brain Heenan	1.50	4.00
13	Jimmy Hart	1.25	3.00
14	George The Animal Steele	1.50	4.00
15	Jake The Snake Roberts	2.00	5.00
16	The Junk Yard Dog	1.25	3.00

1991 Swanson WWF Wrestling Canadian

COMPLETE SET (12)		30.00	75.00
NNO	Big Boss Man	3.00	8.00
NNO	Bret Hitman Hart	5.00	12.00
NNO	The Bushwhackers	4.00	10.00
NNO	Hulk Hogan	8.00	20.00
NNO	Jake The Snake Roberts	2.50	6.00
NNO	Legion of Doom	5.00	12.00
NNO	Macho Man Randy Savage	6.00	15.00
NNO	Million Dollar Man Ted DiBiase	3.00	8.00
NNO	The Mountie	2.50	6.00
NNO	Rockers Marty and Shawn	5.00	12.00
NNO	Texas Tornado	2.50	6.00
NNO	Ultimate Warrior	6.00	15.00

1994 Titan Sports WWF Vending Hologram Stickers

COMPLETE SET (10)		8.00	20.00
NNO	Adam Bomb	1.00	2.50
NNO	Bret Hitman Hart	2.00	5.00
NNO	Doink	1.00	2.50
NNO	Lex Luger	1.50	4.00
NNO	Ludvig Borga	1.00	2.50
NNO	Macho Man Randy Savage	2.00	5.00
NNO	Razor Ramon	1.25	3.00
NNO	Tatanka	1.00	2.50
NNO	Undertaker	3.00	8.00
NNO	Yokozuna	1.25	3.00

2013 Topps Best of WWE

COMPLETE SET (110)		8.00	20.00
UNOPENED BOX (24 PACKS)			
UNOPENED PACK (7 CARDS)			
*BLUE: .6X TO 1.5X BASIC CARDS			
*BRONZE: .6X TO 1.5X BASIC CARDS			
*SILVER: 2.5X TO 6X BASIC CARDS			
*GOLD/10: 5X TO 12X BASIC CARDS			
*P.P.BLACK/1: UNPRICED DUE TO SCARCITY			
*P.P.CYAN/1: UNPRICED DUE TO SCARCITY			
*P.P.MAGENTA/1: UNPRICED DUE TO SCARCITY			
*P.P.YELLOW/1: UNPRICED DUE TO SCARCITY			
1	The Rock	.75	2.00
2	Brock Lesnar/John Cena	.75	2.00
3	Daniel Bryan/AJ Lee	.75	2.00
4	Dusty Rhodes/Cody Rhodes	.25	.60
5	AJ Lee/Kaitlyn	.75	2.00
6	Layla/Nikki Bella	.30	.75
7	Cody Rhodes	.15	.40
8	CM Punk/Chris Jericho	.60	1.50
9	John Cena/Brock Lesnar	.75	2.00
10	Brock Lesnar/Triple H	.60	1.50
11	Kofi Kingston/R-Truth	.15	.40
12	Damien Sandow	.15	.40
13	John Laurinaitis/Big Show	.30	.75
14	Christian/Cody Rhodes	.15	.40
15	John Laurinaitis/John Cena	.75	2.00

16	AJ Lee/Kane	.75	2.00
17	Big Show/Mr. McMahon	.30	.75
18	CM Punk/Kane	.60	1.50
19	John Cena/John Laurinaitis	.75	2.00
20	Dolph Ziggler/Jack Swagger	.25	.60
21	AJ Lee	.75	2.00
22	Zack Ryder	.15	.40
23	AJ Lee/CM Punk	.75	2.00
24	Dolph Ziggler	.25	.60
25	John Cena	.75	2.00
26	AJ Lee/Daniel Bryan	.75	2.00
27	D-Generation X	.60	1.50
28	Dude Love/Brodus Clay	.60	1.50
29	Trish Stratus/Triple H	.75	2.00
30	AJ Lee/Daniel Bryan	.75	2.00
31	The Miz/Christian	.25	.60
32	APA/Heath Slater	.15	.40
33	Undertaker/Kane	.60	1.50
34	John Cena/Big Show	.75	2.00
35	CM Punk/The Rock	.75	2.00
36	Daniel Bryan	.40	1.00
37	Mr.McMahon/Booker T	.25	.60
38	Daniel Bryan	.40	1.00
39	Brock Lesnar/Shawn Michaels	.60	1.50
40	Antonio Cesaro/Santino Marella	.15	.40
41	Daniel Bryan/Kane	.40	1.00
42	Brock Lesnar/Triple H	.60	1.50
43	Dolph Ziggler/Chris Jericho	.60	1.50
44	Daniel Bryan/Kane	.40	1.00
45	CM Punk/Jerry Lawler	.60	1.50
46	Kane/Daniel Bryan	.40	1.00
47	CM Punk/Paul Heyman	.60	1.50
48	Kaitlyn	.30	.75
49	Kane/Bryan/Truth	.40	1.00
50	Eve	.60	1.50
51	CM Punk/John Cena	.75	2.00
52	CM Punk/Mr. McMahon	.60	1.50
53	Kofi Kingston/The Miz	.25	.60
54	AJ Lee/Vickie Guerrero	.75	2.00
55	Big Show/Sheamus	.30	.75
56	Brad Maddox/Ryback	.15	.40
57	Vickie Guerrero/John Cena	.75	2.00
58	Big Show/Sheamus	.30	.75
59	Randy Orton/Alberto Del Rio	.50	1.25
60	CM Punk/Jerry Lawler	.60	1.50
61	Ryback/Brad Maddox	.15	.40
62	Team Ziggler/Team Foley	.25	.60
63	Shield/Cena/Ryback	.75	2.00
64	John Cena/AJ Lee	.75	2.00
65	John Cena/Dolph Ziggler	.75	2.00
66	Vicki/AJ Lee/Maddox	.75	2.00
67	Cody Rhodes	.15	.40
68	Reigns/Bryan/Ambrose	.40	1.00
69	AJ Lee/Cena/Ziggler	.75	2.00
70	Big E Langston/John Cena	.75	2.00
71	8 Divas	.60	1.50
72	John Cena/Alberto Del Rio	.75	2.00
73	Great Khali	.15	.40
74	Wade Barrett/Kofi Kingston	.15	.40
75	Dolph Ziggler/AJ Lee	.75	2.00
76	Antonio Cesaro/Great Khali	.15	.40
77	CM Punk/Ryback	.60	1.50
78	The Rock/CM Punk	.75	2.00
79	Alberto Del Rio/Big Show	.30	.75
80	Kaitlyn/Eve	.60	1.50
81	Kane/Daniel Bryan	.40	1.00
82	Chris Jericho	.60	1.50
83	Bo Dallas	.15	.40
84	John Cena	.75	2.00

85	The Rock/CM Punk	.75	2.00
86	Brock Lesnar/Mr. McMahon	.60	1.50
87	Jack Swagger	.25	.60
88	Roman Reigns/Ryback	.25	.60
89	The Rock/CM Punk	.75	2.00
90	Vickie Guerrero/Brad Maddox	.25	.60
91	The Rock	.75	2.00
92	Heyman/McMahon/Brock/HHH	.60	1.50
93	John Cena/CM Punk	.75	2.00
94	The Deadman	.60	1.50
95	Ted Dibiase	.25	.60
96	Outlaws/Primo/Epico	.15	.40
97	CM Punk/Randy Orton	.60	1.50
98	Undertaker	.60	1.50
99	Brie Bella/Nikki Bella	.60	1.50
100	CM Punk/Undertaker	.60	1.50
101	Mick Foley/Chris Jericho	.60	1.50
102	Trish Stratus	.75	2.00
103	Booker T	.25	.60
104	Bob Backlund	.40	1.00
105	Bruno Sammartino	.40	1.00
106	The Miz/Wade Barrett	.25	.60
107	Fandango/Chris Jericho	.60	1.50
108	Undertaker/CM Punk	.60	1.50
109	Triple H/Brock Lesnar	.60	1.50
110	John Cena/The Rock	.75	2.00

2013 Topps Best of WWE Autographs

STATED ODDS 1:48 HOBBY AND RETAIL

NNO	American Dream Dusty Rhodes	200.00	400.00
NNO	Big E Langston	30.00	75.00
NNO	Bob Backlund	15.00	40.00
NNO	Brie Bella	15.00	40.00
NNO	Bruno Sammartino	75.00	150.00
NNO	Cactus Jack	15.00	40.00
NNO	Damien Sandow	10.00	25.00
NNO	Dean Ambrose	30.00	75.00
NNO	Dude Love	150.00	300.00
NNO	JBL	10.00	25.00
NNO	Lilian Garcia	20.00	50.00
NNO	Mankind	50.00	100.00
NNO	Mick Foley	20.00	50.00
NNO	Nikki Bella	15.00	40.00
NNO	Paul Heyman	30.00	75.00
NNO	Roman Reigns	150.00	300.00
NNO	Seth Rollins	100.00	200.00
NNO	Trish Stratus	30.00	75.00
NNO	Vickie Guerrero	10.00	25.00

2013 Topps Best of WWE Dual Autographs

STATED PRINT RUN 10 SER. #'d SETS

NNO	Brie Bella/Nikki Bella	75.00	150.00
NNO	B.Sammartino/B.Backlund		
NNO	D.Sandow/Big E	25.00	60.00
NNO	D.Ambrose/P.Heyman	60.00	120.00
NNO	J.Swagger/V.Guerrero	25.00	60.00
NNO	JBL/L.Garcia	50.00	100.00
NNO	M.Foley/T.Stratus	50.00	100.00
NNO	R.Dogg/B.Gunn	75.00	150.00
NNO	S.Rollins/R.Reigns	200.00	400.00
NNO	S.Michaels/X-Pac	100.00	200.00

2013 Topps Best of WWE Jerry Lawler Portraits

COMPLETE SET (10)		30.00	80.00
*P.P.BLACK/1: UNPRICED DUE TO SCARCITY			
*P.P.CYAN/1: UNPRICED DUE TO SCARCITY			

*P.P.MAGENTA/1: UNPRICED DUE TO SCARCITY
*P.P.YELLOW/1: UNPRICED DUE TO SCARCITY
RANDOMLY INSERTED INTO RETAIL PACKS

1 CM Punk	6.00	15.00
2 R-Truth	1.50	4.00
3 Undertaker	6.00	15.00
4 Kane	3.00	8.00
5 Paul Bearer	2.50	6.00
6 Vickie Guerrero	2.50	6.00
7 Stone Cold Steve Austin	6.00	15.00
8 Sgt. Slaughter	2.50	6.00
9 Vader	1.50	4.00
10 Doink the Clown	1.50	4.00

2013 Topps Best of WWE Swatch Relics

STATED ODDS 1:24 HOBBY EXCLUSIVE

NNO AJ Lee/Shirt	20.00	50.00
NNO AJ Lee/Teddy Bear	60.00	120.00
NNO Brodus Clay/Shirt	4.00	10.00
NNO CM Punk/Shirt	6.00	15.00
NNO Damien Sandow Shirt	4.00	10.00
NNO Daniel Bryan/Shirt	5.00	12.00
NNO Dean Ambrose/Shirt	5.00	12.00
NNO Dolph Ziggler/Shirt	5.00	12.00
NNO Great Khali/Referee Shirt	4.00	10.00
NNO John Cena/Hat	40.00	80.00
NNO John Cena/Headband		
NNO John Cena/Shirt	6.00	15.00
NNO John Cena/Wristband	40.00	80.00
NNO Miz/Shirt	4.00	10.00
NNO Randy Orton/Shirt	5.00	12.00
NNO Roman Reigns/Shirt	5.00	12.00
NNO Ryback/Shirt	4.00	10.00
NNO Seth Rollins/Shirt	6.00	15.00
NNO Sheamus/Shirt	4.00	10.00
NNO Wade Barrett/Shirt	4.00	10.00

2013 Topps Best of WWE Top 10 Catchphrases

COMPLETE SET (10)	4.00	10.00
*P.P.BLACK/1: UNPRICED DUE TO SCARCITY		
*P.P.CYAN/1: UNPRICED DUE TO SCARCITY		
*P.P.MAGENTA/1: UNPRICED DUE TO SCARCITY		
*P.P.YELLOW/1: UNPRICED DUE TO SCARCITY		
STATED ODDS OVERALL 3:1 HOBBY AND RETAIL		
1 The Rock/If Ya Smell	3.00	8.00
2 Undertaker/Rest in Peace	1.50	4.00
3 John Cena/You Can't See Me!	1.25	3.00
4 Booker T/Can You Dig It, Sucka?	.30	.75
5 The Miz/Because I'm the Miz...	.30	.75
6 Daniel Bryan/Yes!	.50	1.25
7 CM Punk/Best in the World	.75	2.00
8 Zack Ryder/Woo Woo Woo	.20	.50
9 Damien Sandow/You're Welcome!	.20	.50
10 Vickie Guerrero/Excuse Me!	.30	.75

2013 Topps Best of WWE Top 10 Finishers

COMPLETE SET (10)	5.00	12.00
*P.P.BLACK/1: UNPRICED DUE TO SCARCITY		
*P.P.CYAN/1: UNPRICED DUE TO SCARCITY		
*P.P.MAGENTA/1: UNPRICED DUE TO SCARCITY		
*P.P.YELLOW/1: UNPRICED DUE TO SCARCITY		
STATED ODDS OVERALL 3:1 HOBBY AND RETAIL		
1 Undertaker/Tombstone	2.50	6.00

2 Stone Cold Steve Austin/Stunner	1.50	4.00
3 Randy Orton/RKO	.75	2.00
4 Shawn Michaels/Sweet Chin Music	.75	2.00
5 Triple H/Pedigree	.75	2.00
6 The Rock/Rock Bottom	1.00	2.50
7 John Cena/Attitude Adjustment	1.00	2.50
8 CM Punk/GTS	.75	2.00
9 Rey Mysterio/619	.50	1.25
10 Eddie Guerrero/Frog Splash	.20	.50

2013 Topps Best of WWE Top 10 Greatest WWE Moments

COMPLETE SET (10)	5.00	12.00
*P.P.BLACK/1: UNPRICED DUE TO SCARCITY		
*P.P.CYAN/1: UNPRICED DUE TO SCARCITY		
*P.P.MAGENTA/1: UNPRICED DUE TO SCARCITY		
*P.P.YELLOW/1: UNPRICED DUE TO SCARCITY		
STATED ODDS OVERALL 3:1 HOBBY AND RETAIL		
1 Undertaker/Shawn Michaels	2.50	6.00
2 Triple H	1.50	4.00
3 John Cena	1.25	3.00
4 The Rock/John Cena	1.00	2.50
5 Eddie Guerrero/Brock Lesnar	.75	2.00
6 The Rock/Hollywood Hogan	1.00	2.50
7 John Cena/JBL	1.00	2.50
8 CM Punk	.75	2.00
9 CM Punk/John Cena	1.00	2.50
10 Mr. McMahon	.20	.50

2013 Topps Best of WWE Top 10 Intercontinental Champions

COMPLETE SET (10)	3.00	8.00
*P.P.BLACK/1: UNPRICED DUE TO SCARCITY		
*P.P.CYAN/1: UNPRICED DUE TO SCARCITY		
*P.P.MAGENTA/1: UNPRICED DUE TO SCARCITY		
*P.P.YELLOW/1: UNPRICED DUE TO SCARCITY		
STATED ODDS OVERALL 3:1 HOBBY AND RETAIL		
1 Randy Orton	2.00	5.00
2 Rey Mysterio	1.00	2.50
3 Christian	.25	.60
4 Kofi Kingston	.20	.50
5 Cody Rhodes	.20	.50
6 Wade Barrett	.20	.50
7 Dolph Ziggler	.30	.75
8 William Regal	.25	.60
9 Santino Marella	.20	.50
10 Ezekiel Jackson	.20	.50

2013 Topps Best of WWE Top 10 Rivalries

COMPLETE SET (10)	5.00	12.00
*P.P.BLACK/1: UNPRICED DUE TO SCARCITY		
*P.P.CYAN/1: UNPRICED DUE TO SCARCITY		
*P.P.MAGENTA/1: UNPRICED DUE TO SCARCITY		
*P.P.YELLOW/1: UNPRICED DUE TO SCARCITY		
STATED ODDS OVERALL 3:1 HOBBY AND RETAIL		
1 Shawn Michaels/Undertaker	2.50	6.00
2 Undertaker/Triple H	1.50	4.00
3 John Cena/The Rock	1.25	3.00
4 Undertaker/Kane	.75	2.00
5 CM Punk/John Cena	1.00	2.50
6 Triple H/Shawn Michaels	.75	2.00
7 Triple H/Randy Orton	.75	2.00
8 John Cena/Brock Lesnar	1.00	2.50
9 Triple H/Batista	.75	2.00
10 Rey Mysterio/Eddie Guerrero	.50	1.25

2013 Topps Best of WWE Top 10 Trash Talkers

COMPLETE SET (10)	5.00	12.00
*P.P.BLACK/1: UNPRICED DUE TO SCARCITY		
*P.P.CYAN/1: UNPRICED DUE TO SCARCITY		
*P.P.MAGENTA/1: UNPRICED DUE TO SCARCITY		
*P.P.YELLOW/1: UNPRICED DUE TO SCARCITY		
STATED ODDS OVERALL 3:1 HOBBY AND RETAIL		
1 Stone Cold Steve Austin	2.50	6.00
2 The Rock	2.00	5.00
3 CM Punk	1.00	2.50
4 Triple H	.75	2.00
5 Rowdy Roddy Piper	.50	1.25
6 John Cena	1.00	2.50
7 The Miz	.30	.75
8 Shawn Michaels	.75	2.00
9 Paul Heyman	.20	.50
10 AJ Lee	1.00	2.50

2013 Topps Best of WWE Top 10 2K14

COMPLETE SET (10)	60.00	120.00
RANDOMLY INSERTED INTO PACKS		
1 John Cena	15.00	40.00
2 Triple H	8.00	20.00
3 The Rock	20.00	50.00
4 Undertaker	10.00	25.00
5 CM Punk		
6 Sheamus		
7 Brock Lesnar	8.00	20.00
8 Eddie Guerrero	8.00	20.00
9 The Miz	6.00	15.00
10 JBL	6.00	15.00

2013 Topps Best of WWE Top 10 Undertaker Matches

COMPLETE SET (10)	5.00	12.00
*P.P.BLACK/1: UNPRICED DUE TO SCARCITY		
*P.P.CYAN/1: UNPRICED DUE TO SCARCITY		
*P.P.MAGENTA/1: UNPRICED DUE TO SCARCITY		
*P.P.YELLOW/1: UNPRICED DUE TO SCARCITY		
STATED ODDS OVERALL 3:1 HOBBY AND RETAIL		
1 Vs. Triple H	2.50	6.00
2 Vs. Shawn Michaels	1.50	4.00
3 Vs. Shawn Michaels	1.00	2.50
4 Vs. Triple H	.75	2.00
5 Vs. Stone Cold Steve Austin	.75	2.00
6 Wins Royal Rumble	.75	2.00
7 Vs. Batista	.75	2.00
8 Vs. Kane	.75	2.00
9 Vs. Randy Orton	.75	2.00
10 Vs. CM Punk	.75	2.00

2013 Topps Best of WWE Top 10 World Heavyweight Champions

COMPLETE SET (10)	4.00	10.00
*P.P.BLACK/1: UNPRICED DUE TO SCARCITY		
*P.P.CYAN/1: UNPRICED DUE TO SCARCITY		
*P.P.MAGENTA/1: UNPRICED DUE TO SCARCITY		
*P.P.YELLOW/1: UNPRICED DUE TO SCARCITY		
STATED ODDS OVERALL 3:1 HOBBY AND RETAIL		
1 Undertaker	2.50	6.00
2 Triple H	1.50	4.00
3 Randy Orton	.75	2.00
4 Batista	.50	1.25
5 Sheamus	.40	1.00

6 Rey Mysterio	.50	1.25
7 Kane	.40	1.00
8 CM Punk	.75	2.00
9 Booker T	.30	.75
10 Daniel Bryan	.50	1.25

2013 Topps Best of WWE Top 10 WWE Champions

COMPLETE SET (10)	5.00	12.00
*P.P.BLACK/1: UNPRICED DUE TO SCARCITY		
*P.P.CYAN/1: UNPRICED DUE TO SCARCITY		
*P.P.MAGENTA/1: UNPRICED DUE TO SCARCITY		
*P.P.YELLOW/1: UNPRICED DUE TO SCARCITY		
STATED ODDS OVERALL 3:1 HOBBY AND RETAIL		
1 John Cena	3.00	8.00
2 Triple H	1.50	4.00
3 The Rock	1.25	3.00
4 Undertaker	.75	2.00
5 CM Punk	.75	2.00
6 Sheamus	.40	1.00
7 Brock Lesnar	.75	2.00
8 Eddie Guerrero	.20	.50
9 The Miz	.30	.75
10 JBL	.30	.75

2013 Topps Best of WWE Top 10 WWE Tag Team Champions

COMPLETE SET (10)	3.00	8.00
*P.P.BLACK/1: UNPRICED DUE TO SCARCITY		
*P.P.CYAN/1: UNPRICED DUE TO SCARCITY		
*P.P.MAGENTA/1: UNPRICED DUE TO SCARCITY		
*P.P.YELLOW/1: UNPRICED DUE TO SCARCITY		
STATED ODDS OVERALL 3:1 HOBBY AND RETAIL		
1 D-Generation X	2.50	6.00
2 Team Hell No	1.00	2.50
3 Rey Mysterio/Eddie Guerrero	.60	1.50
4 Big Show/Kane	.40	1.00
5 Kofi Kingston/R-Truth	.20	.50
6 Air Boom	.20	.50
7 ShoMiz	.40	1.00
8 Ted DiBiase/Cody Rhodes	.25	.60
9 Curt Hawkins/Zack Ryder	.20	.50
10 Primo & Epico	.20	.50

2013 Topps Best of WWE WrestleMania 29 Mat Relics

STATED ODDS 1:48 HOBBY AND RETAIL

NNO Alberto Del Rio	4.00	10.00
NNO Big E Langston	4.00	10.00
NNO Big Show	4.00	10.00
NNO Brock Lesnar	5.00	12.00
NNO Chris Jericho	5.00	12.00
NNO CM Punk	12.00	30.00
NNO Daniel Bryan	5.00	12.00
NNO Dolph Ziggler	4.00	10.00
NNO Fandango	6.00	15.00
NNO Jack Swagger	4.00	10.00
NNO John Cena	6.00	20.00
NNO Kane	5.00	12.00
NNO Mark Henry	4.00	10.00
NNO Randy Orton	6.00	15.00
NNO Ryback	5.00	12.00
NNO Sheamus	4.00	10.00
NNO The Shield	6.00	15.00
NNO Triple H	5.00	12.00
NNO Undertaker	8.00	20.00
NNO The Rock	15.00	40.00

2014 Topps Chrome WWE

COMPLETE SET (110)	8.00	20.00
UNOPENED BOX (24 PACKS)		
UNOPENED PACK (4 CARDS)		
*REF.: .4X TO 1.2X BASIC CARDS		
*ATOMIC REF.: .6X TO 1.5X BASIC CARDS		
*XFRACTOR: .6X TO 1.5X BASIC CARDS		
*GOLD REF./50: 2X TO 5X BASIC CARDS		
*SUPERFR./1: UNPRICED DUE TO SCARCITY		
*P.P.BLACK/1: UNPRICE DUE TO SCARCITY		
*P.P.CYAN/1: UNPRICE DUE TO SCARCITY		
*P.P.MAGENTA/1: UNPRICE DUE TO SCARCITY		
*P.P.YELLOW/1: UNPRICE DUE TO SCARCITY		
1 AJ Lee	1.50	4.00
2 Alex Riley	.30	.75
3 Big E Langston	.30	.75
4 Bo Dallas	.30	.75
5 Brad Maddox	.30	.75
6 Bray Wyatt	.75	2.00
7 Brie Bella	1.00	2.50
8 Brock Lesnar	1.25	3.00
9 Brodus Clay	.30	.75
10 Cameron	.50	1.25
11 Chris Jericho	.75	2.00
12 CM Punk	1.25	3.00
13 Curtis Axel	.30	.75
14 Daniel Bryan	.50	1.25
15 David Otunga	.30	.75
16 Dean Ambrose	.75	2.00
17 Diego	.30	.75
18 Dolph Ziggler	.50	1.25
19 Erick Rowan	.50	1.25
20 Eva Marie	1.25	3.00
21 Fandango	.50	1.25
22 Fernando	.30	.75
23 Jack Swagger	.50	1.25
24 Jerry The King Lawler	.75	2.00
25 John Cena	1.50	4.00
26 JoJo	.50	1.25
27 Justin Roberts	.30	.75
28 Kane	.75	2.00
29 Kofi Kingston	.30	.75
30 Luke Harper	.50	1.25
31 El Torito	.30	.75
32 Michael Cole	.30	.75
33 The Miz	.50	1.25
34 Naomi	.50	1.25
35 Nikki Bella	1.00	2.50
36 Paul Heyman	.30	.75
37 R-Truth	.30	.75
38 Randy Orton	1.25	3.00
39 Rey Mysterio	.75	2.00
40 The Rock	1.50	4.00
41 Rob Van Dam	.75	2.00
42 Roman Reigns	.75	2.00
43 Ryback	.30	.75
44 Santino Marella	.50	1.25
45 Scott Stanford	.30	.75
46 Seth Rollins	.30	.75
47 Stephanie McMahon	.50	1.25
48 Summer Rae	1.25	3.00
49 Tamina Snuka	.50	1.25
50 Tensai	.30	.75
51 Triple H	1.25	3.00
52 Zack Ryder	.30	.75
53 Zeb Colter	.50	1.25
54 Aksana	.75	2.00
55 Alberto Del Rio	.75	2.00
56 Alicia Fox	.50	1.25
57 Antonio Cesaro	.30	.75
58 Big Show	.75	2.00
59 Booker T	.50	1.25
60 Camacho	.30	.75
61 Christian	.30	.75
62 Cody Rhodes	.30	.75
63 Curt Hawkins	.30	.75
64 Damien Sandow	.30	.75
65 Darren Young	.30	.75
66 Drew McIntyre	.30	.75
67 Ezekiel Jackson	.50	1.25
68 The Great Khali	.30	.75
69 Heath Slater	.30	.75
70 Hornswoggle	.50	1.25
71 Hunico	.30	.75
72 JBL	.50	1.25
73 Jey Uso	.30	.75
74 Jimmy Uso	.30	.75
75 Jinder Mahal	.30	.75
76 Josh Mathews	.30	.75
77 Justin Gabriel	.30	.75
78 Goldust	.30	.75
79 Layla	.75	2.00
80 Lilian Garcia	.75	2.00
81 Mark Henry	.50	1.25
82 Natalya	1.00	2.50
83 Renee Young	1.25	3.00
84 Ricardo Rodriguez	.30	.75
85 Rosa Mendes	.50	1.25
86 Sheamus	.75	2.00
87 Sin Cara	.75	2.00
88 Theodore Long	.30	.75
89 Titus O'Neil	.30	.75
90 Tony Chimel	.30	.75
91 Tyson Kidd	.30	.75
92 Undertaker	1.25	3.00
93 Vickie Guerrero	.50	1.25
94 Bad News Barrett	.30	.75
95 William Regal	.50	1.25
96 Andre the Giant L	1.25	3.00
97 Billy Gunn L	.50	1.25
98 Bob Backlund L	.50	1.25
99 Diamond Dallas Page L	.50	1.25
100 Eddie Guerrero L	.50	1.25
101 Honky Tonk Man L	.50	1.25
102 Jim Ross L	.50	1.25
103 Junkyard Dog L	.50	1.25
104 Kevin Nash L	.75	2.00
105 Larry Zbyszko L	.50	1.25
106 Mick Foley L	.75	2.00
107 Paul Bearer L	.50	1.25
108 Road Dogg L	.50	1.25
109 Shawn Michaels L	1.25	3.00
110 X-Pac L	.30	.75

2014 Topps Chrome WWE Autographs

*REFRACTOR/50: .5X TO 1.2X BASIC AUTOS		
*RED REF./25: .75X TO 2X BASIC AUTOS		
*GOLD REF./10: UNPRICED DUE TO SCARCITY		
*SUPERFR./1: UNPRICE DUE TO SCARCITY		
NNO Aksana	15.00	40.00
NNO Alicia Fox	5.00	12.00
NNO Diamond Dallas Page	12.00	30.00
NNO Dolph Ziggler	10.00	25.00
NNO Fandango	6.00	15.00
NNO Honky Tonk Man	8.00	20.00
NNO Kane	20.00	50.00
NNO Natalya	12.00	30.00
NNO Roman Reigns	100.00	200.00
NNO Sin Cara	5.00	12.00

2014 Topps Chrome WWE Championship Plates

*SUPERFR./1: UNPRICED DUE TO SCARCITY		
SP CARDS ARE SER.#'d TO 25		
NNO AJ Lee SP	75.00	150.00
NNO Alicia Fox	12.00	30.00
NNO Batista	15.00	40.00
NNO Brie Bella	15.00	40.00
NNO Chris Jericho SP	20.00	50.00
NNO Cody Rhodes	8.00	20.00
NNO Cody Rhodes and Goldust	8.00	20.00
NNO Daniel Bryan	12.00	30.00
World Title		
NNO Daniel Bryan	12.00	30.00
WWE Title		
NNO Dolph Ziggler	12.00	30.00
NNO Edge and Christian	15.00	40.00
NNO Greg The Hammer Valentine	8.00	20.00
NNO Honky Tonk Man	12.00	30.00
NNO John Cena SP	20.00	50.00
NNO Natalya	15.00	40.00
NNO Nikki Bella	15.00	40.00
NNO Randy Orton	20.00	50.00
NNO Ravishing Rick Rude	8.00	20.00
NNO Rey Mysterio	12.00	30.00
NNO Ricky The Dragon Steamboat	8.00	20.00
NNO RVD and Rey Mysterio	12.00	30.00
NNO Sgt. Slaughter	25.00	60.00
NNO Shawn Michaels	20.00	50.00
World Title		
NNO Shawn Michaels	20.00	50.00
WWE Title		
NNO Sheamus	12.00	30.00
NNO The Shield SP	120.00	200.00
NNO ShoMiz	12.00	30.00
NNO Stone Cold Steve Austin SP	25.00	60.00
NNO Triple H	20.00	50.00
NNO Undertaker SP	25.00	60.00

2014 Topps Chrome WWE Champions Tribute Batista

COMPLETE SET (5)	5.00	12.00
*P.P.BLACK/1: UNPRICED DUE TO SCARCITY		
*P.P.CYAN/1: UNPRICED DUE TO SCARCITY		
*P.P.MAGENTA/1: UNPRICED DUE TO SCARCITY		
*P.P.YELLOW/1: UNPRICED DUE TO SCARCITY		
STATED OVERALL ODDS 1:6		
1 Batista	1.50	4.00
2 Batista	1.50	4.00
3 Batista	1.50	4.00
4 Batista	1.50	4.00
5 Batista	1.50	4.00

2014 Topps Chrome WWE Champions Tribute Eddie Guerrero

COMPLETE SET (5)	2.50	6.00
*P.P.BLACK/1: UNPRICED DUE TO SCARCITY		
*P.P.CYAN/1: UNPRICED DUE TO SCARCITY		
*P.P.MAGENTA/1: UNPRICED DUE TO SCARCITY		
*P.P.YELLOW/1: UNPRICED DUE TO SCARCITY		
STATED OVERALL ODDS 1:6		
1 Eddie Guerrero	.75	2.00
2 Eddie Guerrero	.75	2.00
3 Eddie Guerrero	.75	2.00
4 Eddie Guerrero	.75	2.00
5 Eddie Guerrero	.75	2.00

2014 Topps Chrome WWE Champions Tribute Edge

COMPLETE SET (5)	4.00	10.00
*P.P.BLACK/1: UNPRICED DUE TO SCARCITY		
*P.P.CYAN/1: UNPRICED DUE TO SCARCITY		
*P.P.MAGENTA/1: UNPRICED DUE TO SCARCITY		
*P.P.YELLOW/1: UNPRICED DUE TO SCARCITY		
STATED OVERALL ODDS 1:6		
1 Edge	1.25	3.00
2 Edge	1.25	3.00
3 Edge	1.25	3.00
4 Edge	1.25	3.00
5 Edge	1.25	3.00

2014 Topps Chrome WWE Champions Tribute Iron Sheik

COMPLETE SET (5)		
*P.P.CYAN/1: UNPRICED DUE TO SCARCITY		
*P.P.MAGENTA/1: UNPRICED DUE TO SCARCITY		
*P.P.YELLOW/1: UNPRICED DUE TO SCARCITY		
STATED OVERALL ODDS 1:6		
1 Iron Sheik	.75	2.00
2 Iron Sheik	.75	2.00
3 Iron Sheik	.75	2.00
4 Iron Sheik	.75	2.00
5 Iron Sheik	.75	2.00

2014 Topps Chrome WWE Champions Tribute JBL

COMPLETE SET (5)	2.50	6.00
*P.P.BLACK/1: UNPRICED DUE TO SCARCITY		
*P.P.CYAN/1: UNPRICED DUE TO SCARCITY		
*P.P.MAGENTA/1: UNPRICED DUE TO SCARCITY		
*P.P.YELLOW/1: UNPRICED DUE TO SCARCITY		
STATED OVERALL ODDS 1:6		
1 JBL	.75	2.00
2 JBL	.75	2.00
3 JBL	.75	2.00
4 JBL	.75	2.00
5 JBL	.75	2.00

2014 Topps Chrome WWE Champions Tribute Kevin Nash

COMPLETE SET (5)	4.00	10.00
*P.P.BLACK/1: UNPRICED DUE TO SCARCITY		
*P.P.CYAN/1: UNPRICED DUE TO SCARCITY		
*P.P.MAGENTA/1: UNPRICED DUE TO SCARCITY		
*P.P.YELLOW/1: UNPRICED DUE TO SCARCITY		
STATED OVERALL ODDS 1:6		
1 Kevin Nash	1.25	3.00
2 Kevin Nash	1.25	3.00
3 Kevin Nash	1.25	3.00
4 Kevin Nash	1.25	3.00
5 Kevin Nash	1.25	3.00

2014 Topps Chrome WWE Champions Tribute Mick Foley

COMPLETE SET (5)	4.00	10.00
*P.P.BLACK/1: UNPRICED DUE TO SCARCITY	
*P.P.CYAN/1: UNPRICED DUE TO SCARCITY	
*P.P.MAGENTA/1: UNPRICED DUE TO SCARCITY	
*P.P.YELLOW/1: UNPRICED DUE TO SCARCITY	

Other Eddie Guerrero entries

2 Eddie Guerrero	.75	2.00
3 Eddie Guerrero	.75	2.00
4 Eddie Guerrero	.75	2.00
5 Eddie Guerrero	.75	2.00

1 Mick Foley	1.25	3.00
2 Mick Foley	1.25	3.00
3 Mick Foley	1.25	3.00
4 Mick Foley	1.25	3.00
5 Mick Foley	1.25	3.00

2014 Topps Chrome WWE Champions Tribute Sgt. Slaughter

COMPLETE SET (5)	4.00	10.00
*P.P.BLACK/1: UNPRICED DUE TO SCARCITY		
*P.P.CYAN/1: UNPRICED DUE TO SCARCITY		
*P.P.MAGENTA/1: UNPRICED DUE TO SCARCITY		
*P.P.YELLOW/1: UNPRICED DUE TO SCARCITY		
STATED OVERALL ODDS 1:6		
1 Sgt. Slaughter	1.25	3.00
2 Sgt. Slaughter	1.25	3.00
3 Sgt. Slaughter	1.25	3.00
4 Sgt. Slaughter	1.25	3.00
5 Sgt. Slaughter	1.25	3.00

2014 Topps Chrome WWE Champions Tribute Shawn Michaels

COMPLETE SET (5)	6.00	15.00
*P.P.BLACK/1: UNPRICED DUE TO SCARCITY		
*P.P.CYAN/1: UNPRICED DUE TO SCARCITY		
*P.P.MAGENTA/1: UNPRICED DUE TO SCARCITY		
*P.P.YELLOW/1: UNPRICED DUE TO SCARCITY		
STATED OVERALL ODDS 1:6		
1 Shawn Michaels	2.00	5.00
2 Shawn Michaels	2.00	5.00
3 Shawn Michaels	2.00	5.00
4 Shawn Michaels	2.00	5.00
5 Shawn Michaels	2.00	5.00

2014 Topps Chrome WWE Champions Tribute Yokozuna

COMPLETE SET (5)	2.50	6.00
*P.P.BLACK/1: UNPRICED DUE TO SCARCITY		
*P.P.CYAN/1: UNPRICED DUE TO SCARCITY		
*P.P.MAGENTA/1: UNPRICED DUE TO SCARCITY		
*P.P.YELLOW/1: UNPRICED DUE TO SCARCITY		
STATED OVERALL ODDS 1:6		
1 Yokozuna	.75	2.00
2 Yokozuna	.75	2.00
3 Yokozuna	.75	2.00
4 Yokozuna	.75	2.00
5 Yokozuna	.75	2.00

2014 Topps Chrome WWE Dual Autographs

STATED PRINT RUN 5 SER.#'d SETS		
NNO D.Bryan/B.Wyatt	150.00	300.00
NNO D.Rhodes/J.Swagger	100.00	200.00
NNO J.Cena/R.Orton	150.00	300.00
NNO L.Harper/E.Rowan	100.00	200.00

2014 Topps Chrome WWE Jerry Lawler's Tributes

COMPLETE SET (10)	10.00	25.00
*P.P.BLACK/1: UNPRICED DUE TO SCARCITY		
*P.P.CYAN/1: UNPRICED DUE TO SCARCITY		
*P.P.MAGENTA/1: UNPRICED DUE TO SCARCITY		
*P.P.YELLOW/1: UNPRICED DUE TO SCARCITY		
STATED ODDS 1:12 HOBBY AND RETAIL		
1 The Iron Sheik	1.00	2.50

2 Sgt. Slaughter	1.50	4.00
3 Yokozuna	1.00	2.50
4 Kevin Nash	1.50	4.00
5 Shawn Michaels	2.50	6.00
6 Mick Foley	1.50	4.00
7 Eddie Guerrero	1.00	2.50
8 JBL	1.00	2.50
9 Batista	2.00	5.00
10 Edge	1.50	4.00

2014 Topps Chrome WWE Kiss

NNO AJ Lee	50.00	100.00
NNO Aksana	20.00	50.00
NNO Alicia Fox	20.00	50.00
NNO Cameron	30.00	60.00
NNO Eva Marie	30.00	80.00
NNO Naomi	30.00	60.00
NNO Tamina Snuka	12.00	30.00
NNO Vickie Guerrero	12.00	30.00

2014 Topps Chrome WWE Kiss Autographs

NNO AJ Lee	250.00	400.00
NNO Aksana	30.00	75.00
NNO Cameron	30.00	75.00
NNO Tamina Snuka	30.00	75.00
NNO Vickie Guerrero	75.00	150.00

2014 Topps Chrome WWE NXT Prospects

COMPLETE SET (20)	30.00	75.00
*P.P.BLACK/1: UNPRICED DUE TO SCARCITY		
*P.P.CYAN/1: UNPRICED DUE TO SCARCITY		
*P.P.MAGENTA/1: UNPRICED DUE TO SCARCITY		
*P.P.YELLOW/1: UNPRICED DUE TO SCARCITY		
STATED ODDS 1:3 HOBBY AND RETAIL		
1 Adrian Neville	1.25	3.00
2 Alexander Rusev	1.50	4.00
3 Baron Corbin	.60	1.50
4 Bayley	5.00	12.00
5 Charlotte	12.00	30.00
6 CJ Parker	.60	1.50
7 Konnor O'Brian	.60	1.50
8 Corey Graves	.60	1.50
9 Emma	2.00	5.00
10 Enzo Amore	1.25	3.00
11 Jason Jordan	.60	1.50
12 Leo Kruger	.60	1.50
13 Mojo Rawley	.60	1.50
14 Paige	8.00	20.00
15 Rick Viktor	.60	1.50
16 Sami Zayn	1.25	3.00
17 Sasha Banks	10.00	25.00
18 Sylvester Lefort	.60	1.50
19 Tyler Breeze	.60	1.50
20 Xavier Woods	.60	1.50

2014 Topps Chrome WWE Royal Rumble Mat Relics

*SUPERFR/1: UNPRICED DUE TO SCARCITY		
STATED ODDS		
NNO Alberto Del Rio	4.00	10.00
NNO Alexander Rusev	6.00	15.00
NNO Batista	10.00	25.00
NNO Big E	3.00	8.00
NNO Billy Gunn	5.00	12.00
NNO Bray Wyatt	8.00	20.00

NNO Brock Lesnar	8.00	20.00
NNO Cody Rhodes	3.00	8.00
NNO Daniel Bryan	8.00	20.00
NNO El Torito	3.00	8.00
NNO Goldust	3.00	8.00
NNO JBL	5.00	12.00
NNO John Cena	10.00	25.00
NNO Kane	6.00	15.00
NNO Kevin Nash	8.00	20.00
NNO Randy Orton	8.00	20.00
NNO Rey Mysterio	8.00	20.00
NNO Road Dogg	5.00	12.00
NNO Roman Reigns	10.00	25.00
NNO Sheamus	6.00	15.00

2014 Topps Chrome WWE Swatch Relics

NNO Alberto Del Rio	6.00	15.00
NNO Bray Wyatt	12.00	30.00
NNO Curtis Axel	3.00	8.00
NNO Damien Sandow	3.00	8.00
NNO Daniel Bryan	8.00	20.00
NNO Diego	3.00	8.00
NNO Dolph Ziggler	5.00	12.00
NNO Fernando	3.00	8.00
NNO Goldust	3.00	8.00
NNO Jack Swagger	6.00	15.00
NNO John Cena	12.00	30.00
NNO Kofi Kingston	3.00	8.00
NNO Mark Henry	5.00	12.00
NNO The Miz	5.00	12.00
NNO Rey Mysterio	8.00	20.00
NNO Undertaker	15.00	40.00

2014 Topps Chrome WWE WrestleMania DVD Promo

P1 John Cena		

2015 Topps Chrome WWE

COMPLETE SET (100)	8.00	20.00
UNOPENED BOX (24 PACKS)	60.00	80.00
UNOPENED PACK (4 CARDS)	3.50	4.00
*REF.: .4X TO 1.2X BASIC CARDS		
*ATOMIC: .6X TO 1.5X BASIC CARDS		
*XFRACTOR: .6X TO 1.5X BASIC CARDS		
*PULSAR/75: 1.5X TO 4X BASIC CARDS		
*GOLD/50: 2X TO 5X BASIC CARDS		
*SILVER WAVE/20: 3X TO 8X BASIC CARDS		
*SHIMMER/10: 5X TO 12X BASIC CARDS		
*RED/5: UNPRICED DUE TO SCARCITY		
*SUPERFR./1: UNPRICED DUE TO SCARCITY		
*P.P.BLACK/1: UNPRICED DUE TO SCARCITY		
*P.P.CYAN/1: UNPRICED DUE TO SCARCITY		
*P.P.MAGENTA/1: UNPRICED DUE TO SCARCITY		
*P.P.YELLOW/1: UNPRICED DUE TO SCARCITY		
1 Adam Rose	.30	.75
2 AJ Lee	1.25	3.00
3 Alicia Fox	.50	1.25
4 Bad News Barrett	.25	.60
5 Batista	.60	1.50
6 Big E	.40	1.00
7 Big Show	.60	1.50
8 Bo Dallas	.25	.60
9 Booker T	.40	1.00
10 Bray Wyatt	1.00	2.50
11 Brie Bella	.75	2.00
12 Brock Lesnar	1.00	2.50
13 Cameron	.40	1.00

14 Cesaro	.25	.60
15 Chris Jericho	.60	1.50
16 Christian	.25	.60
17 Curtis Axel	.25	.60
18 Damien Mizdow	.40	1.00
19 Daniel Bryan	1.00	2.50
20 Darren Young	.25	.60
21 David Otunga	.25	.60
22 Dean Ambrose	.60	1.50
23 Diego	.25	.60
24 Dolph Ziggler	.40	1.00
25 Eden	.40	1.00
26 Emma	.40	1.00
27 Erick Rowan	.40	1.00
28 Eva Marie	1.00	2.50
29 Fandango	.25	.60
30 Fernando	.25	.60
31 Goldust	.25	.60
32 Heath Slater	.25	.60
33 Hornswoggle	.40	1.00
34 Jack Swagger	.40	1.00
35 Jerry The King Lawler	.40	1.00
36 Jey Uso	.25	.60
37 Jimmy Uso	.25	.60
38 John Cena	1.25	3.00
39 Justin Gabriel	.25	.60
40 Kane	.60	1.50
41 Kofi Kingston	.25	.60
42 Lana	1.00	2.50
43 Layla	.60	1.50
44 Lilian Garcia	.60	1.50
45 Luke Harper	.40	1.00
46 Mark Henry	.40	1.00
47 The Miz	.40	1.00
48 Naomi	.40	1.00
49 Natalya	.75	2.00
50 Nikki Bella	.75	2.00
51 Paige	1.25	3.00
52 Paul Heyman	.25	.60
53 R-Truth	.25	.60
54 Randy Orton	2.00	5.00
55 Renee Young	1.00	2.50
56 Rey Mysterio	.60	1.50
57 The Rock	1.25	3.00
58 Rob Van Dam	.60	1.50
59 Roman Reigns	.60	1.50
60 Rosa Mendes	.40	1.00
61 Rusev	.60	1.50
62 Ryback	.25	.60
63 Seth Rollins	.40	1.00
64 Sheamus	.60	1.50
65 Sin Cara	.40	1.00
66 Stardust	.25	.60
67 Stephanie McMahon	.40	1.00
68 Summer Rae	1.00	2.50
69 Tamina Snuka	.40	1.00
70 Titus O'Neil	.25	.60
71 El Torito	.25	.60
72 Triple H	1.00	2.50
73 Tyson Kidd	.25	.60
74 Undertaker	1.00	2.50
75 William Regal	.40	1.00
76 Xavier Woods	.40	1.00
77 Zack Ryder	.25	.60
78 Zeb Colter	.40	1.00
79 Bret Hit Man Hart	.75	2.00
80 Bruno Sammartino	.60	1.50
81 George The Animal Steele	.30	.75

82	Gerald Brisco	.40	1.00
83	Hulk Hogan	1.25	3.00
84	Larry Zbyszko	.40	1.00
85	Mouth of the South Jimmy Hart	.30	.75
86	Pat Patterson	.25	.60
87	Ric Flair	1.25	3.00
88	Rowdy Roddy Piper	.75	2.00
89	Sting	.60	1.50
90	Ultimate Warrior	.75	2.00
91	Aiden English NXT	.30	.75
92	Alexa Bliss NXT	12.00	30.00
93	Angelo Dawkins NXT	.30	.75
94	Bull Dempsey NXT	.40	1.00
95	Colin Cassady NXT	.40	1.00
96	Hideo Itami NXT	.25	.60
97	Kalisto NXT	.40	1.00
98	Marcus Louis NXT	.40	1.00
99	Sawyer Fulton NXT	.40	1.00
100	Tye Dillinger NXT	.40	1.00

2015 Topps Chrome WWE Autographs

*PULSAR/75: .5X TO 1.2X BASIC AUTOS
*GOLD/10: .75X TO 2X BASIC AUTOS
*RED/5: UNPRICED DUE TO SCARCITY

NNO	Adam Rose	6.00	15.00
NNO	Brie Bella	12.00	30.00
NNO	Bruno Sammartino	15.00	40.00
NNO	Eva Marie	20.00	50.00
NNO	Hulk Hogan	200.00	400.00
NNO	Lana	25.00	60.00
NNO	Lita	20.00	50.00
NNO	Nikki Bella	25.00	60.00
NNO	Renee Young	12.00	30.00
NNO	Roman Reigns	100.00	200.00

2015 Topps Chrome WWE Commemorative Championship Plates

*PULSAR/75: .6X TO 1.5X BASIC PLATES
*RED/5: UNPRICED DUE TO SCARCITY

NNO	Adrian Neville NXT Champion	6.00	15.00
NNO	Adrian Neville NXT Tag Champion	6.00	15.00
NNO	Big E	5.00	12.00
NNO	Bo Dallas	3.00	8.00
NNO	Charlotte	10.00	25.00
NNO	Corey Graves	6.00	15.00
NNO	Erick Rowan	5.00	12.00
NNO	Kalisto	5.00	12.00
NNO	Konnor	8.00	20.00
NNO	Luke Harper	5.00	12.00
NNO	Paige	15.00	40.00
NNO	Seth Rollins	6.00	15.00
NNO	Sin Cara	5.00	12.00
NNO	Viktor	8.00	20.00

2015 Topps Chrome WWE Diva Kiss

RANDOMLY INSERTED INTO PACKS

NNO	Brie Bella	20.00	50.00
NNO	Cameron	10.00	25.00
NNO	Eden	10.00	25.00
NNO	Emma	30.00	60.00
NNO	Naomi	20.00	40.00
NNO	Natalya	20.00	50.00
NNO	Nikki Bella	40.00	80.00
NNO	Renee Young	25.00	60.00
NNO	Summer Rae	25.00	60.00
NNO	Tamina Snuka	10.00	25.00

2015 Topps Chrome WWE Diva Kiss Autographs

*RED REF./5: UNPRICED DUE TO SCARCITY
*SUPERFR./1: UNPRICED DUE TO SCARCITY
STATED PRINT RUN 25 SER.#'d SETS

NNO	Brie Bella	50.00	100.00
NNO	Cameron	12.00	30.00
NNO	Eden	15.00	40.00
NNO	Emma	25.00	60.00
NNO	Naomi	15.00	50.00
NNO	Natalya	20.00	50.00
NNO	Nikki Bella	50.00	100.00
NNO	Renee Young	75.00	150.00
NNO	Summer Rae	30.00	75.00
NNO	Tamina Snuka	15.00	40.00

2015 Topps Chrome WWE Dual Autographs

STATED PRINT RUN 5 SER. #'d SETS
UNPRICED DUE TO SCARCITY

1 AJ Lee/Paige
2 D.Ambrose/S.Rollins
3 Emma/Eden
4 J.Cena/B.Wyatt

2015 Topps Chrome WWE King of the Ring Sign Relics

*RED/5: UNPRICED DUE TO SCARCITY
*SUPERFR./1: UNPRICED DUE TO SCARCITY
STATED ODDS 1:1,156 HOBBY

NNO	Billy Gunn	5.00	12.00
NNO	Bret Hit Man Hart	12.00	30.00
NNO	Brock Lesnar	15.00	40.00
NNO	Don Muraco	5.00	12.00
NNO	Edge	8.00	20.00
NNO	Harley Race	5.00	12.00
NNO	King Booker	5.00	12.00
NNO	Million Dollar Man Ted DiBiase	5.00	12.00
NNO	Sheamus	8.00	20.00
NNO	Stone Cold Steve Austin	10.00	25.00
NNO	Tito Santana	5.00	12.00
NNO	Triple H	8.00	20.00
NNO	William Regal	5.00	12.00

2015 Topps Chrome WWE Night of Champions Mat Relics

RANDOMLY INSERTED INTO PACKS
*PULSAR/75: .6X TO 1.5X BASIC RELICS

1	AJ Lee	12.00	30.00
2	Brock Lesnar	10.00	25.00
3	Cesaro	2.50	6.00
4	Chris Jericho	6.00	15.00
5	Dean Ambrose	6.00	15.00
6	Dolph Ziggler	4.00	10.00
7	John Cena	12.00	30.00
8	Mark Henry	4.00	10.00
9	The Miz	4.00	10.00
10	Nikki Bella	8.00	20.00
11	Paige	12.00	30.00
12	Randy Orton	10.00	25.00
13	Rusev	6.00	15.00
14	Seth Rollins	4.00	10.00
15	Sheamus	6.00	15.00

2015 Topps Chrome WWE Night of Champions Turnbuckle Relics

*SUPERFR./1: UNPRICED DUE TO SCARCITY
STATED PRINT RUN 33 SER.#'d SETS

NNO	AJ Lee	80.00	150.00
NNO	Brock Lesnar	15.00	40.00
NNO	Chris Jericho	12.00	30.00
NNO	Dean Ambrose	25.00	50.00
NNO	John Cena	25.00	60.00
NNO	Nikki Bella	15.00	40.00
NNO	Paige	25.00	60.00
NNO	Randy Orton	15.00	40.00
NNO	Seth Rollins	8.00	20.00

2015 Topps Chrome WWE NXT Autographs

*GOLD/10: .75X TO 2X BASIC AUTOS
*ATOMIC/5: UNPRICED DUE TO SCARCITY
*RED/5: UNPRICED DUE TO SCARCITY
*SUPERFR./1: UNPRICED DUE TO SCARCITY
RANDOMLY INSERTED INTO PACKS

NNO	Aiden English	6.00	15.00
NNO	Alexa Bliss	200.00	350.00
NNO	Charlotte	30.00	80.00
NNO	Colin Cassady	12.00	30.00
NNO	Sawyer Fulton	5.00	12.00

2015 Topps Chrome WWE Swatch Relics

RANDOMLY INSERTED INTO PACKS
*PULSAR/75: .1X TO 2.5X BASIC RELICS

NNO	Cesaro	1.50	4.00
NNO	Curtis Axel	1.50	4.00
NNO	Damien Mizdow	2.50	6.00
NNO	Daniel Bryan	6.00	15.00
NNO	Darren Young	1.50	4.00
NNO	Diego	1.50	4.00
NNO	Jack Swagger	2.50	6.00
NNO	Jerry The King Lawler	2.50	6.00
NNO	Jimmy Uso	1.50	4.00
NNO	John Cena	8.00	20.00
NNO	Kofi Kingston	1.50	4.00
NNO	Mark Henry	2.50	6.00
NNO	Paige	8.00	20.00
NNO	Randy Orton	6.00	15.00
NNO	Sheamus	4.00	10.00
NNO	Titus O'Neil	1.50	4.00
NNO	Tyson Kidd	1.50	4.00
NNO	Zack Ryder	1.50	4.00

2015 Topps Chrome WWE Ultimate Warrior Commemorative Face Paint Plate

*PULSAR REF/75: 1.2X TO 3X BASIC MEM
RANDOMLY INSERTED INTO PACKS

NNO	Ultimate Warrior	5.00	12.00

2020 Topps Chrome WWE

COMPLETE SET (100)   15.00   40.00
*REF: .5X TO 1.2X BASIC CARDS
*XFRAC: .6X TO 1.5X BASIC CARDS
*GREEN/99: 1.2X TO 3X BASIC CARDS
*GOLD/50: 2X TO 5X BASIC CARDS
*ORANGE/25: UNPRICED DUE TO SCARCITY
*BLACK/10: UNPRICED DUE TO SCARCITY
*RED/5: UNPRICED DUE TO SCARCITY
*SUPER/1: UNPRICED DUE TO SCARCITY

1	AJ Styles	1.25	3.00
2	Aleister Black	.75	2.00
3	Alexa Bliss	2.50	6.00
4	Mustafa Ali	.60	1.50
5	Andrade	.60	1.50
6	Asuka	1.50	4.00
7	King Corbin	.50	1.25
8	Bayley	.75	2.00
9	Becky Lynch	1.50	4.00
10	Big E	.40	1.00
11	Big Show	.50	1.25
12	Billie Kay	.75	2.00
13	Bobby Lashley	.75	2.00
14	Braun Strowman	1.00	2.50
15	The Fiend Bray Wyatt	1.25	3.00
16	Brock Lesnar	1.50	4.00
17	Murphy	.50	1.25
18	Carmella	1.00	2.50
19	Cesaro	.40	1.00
20	Charlotte Flair	1.50	4.00
21	Daniel Bryan	1.25	3.00
22	Drake Maverick	.40	1.00
23	Drew McIntyre	.75	2.00
24	Elias	.40	1.00
25	Erik	.40	1.00
26	Ember Moon	.75	2.00
27	Finn Balor	1.00	2.50
28	Humberto Carrillo	.60	1.50
29	Ivar	.40	1.00
30	Jeff Hardy	1.00	2.50
31	Jey Uso	.40	1.00
32	Jimmy Uso	.40	1.00
33	John Cena	1.50	4.00
34	Kairi Sane	.75	2.00
35	Kane	.50	1.25
36	Karl Anderson	.40	1.00
37	Kevin Owens	.50	1.25
38	Kofi Kingston	.60	1.50
39	Lana	1.00	2.50
40	Lacey Evans	1.00	2.50
41	Luke Gallows	.40	1.00
42	Mandy Rose	2.00	5.00
43	Naomi	.75	2.00
44	Natalya	.60	1.50
45	Nia Jax	.60	1.50
46	Nikki Cross	.75	2.00
47	Peyton Royce	.75	2.00
48	Randy Orton	1.00	2.50
49	Ricochet	.60	1.50
50	Roman Reigns	1.00	2.50
51	Ronda Rousey	2.00	5.00
52	R-Truth	.40	1.00
53	Ruby Riott	.60	1.50
54	Rusev	.50	1.25
55	Sami Zayn	.50	1.25
56	Samoa Joe	.60	1.50
57	Sasha Banks	2.00	5.00
58	Seth Rollins	.75	2.00
59	Sheamus	.50	1.25
60	Shinsuke Nakamura	.75	2.00
61	Shorty G	.40	1.00
62	Sonya Deville	1.00	2.50
63	The Miz	.60	1.50
64	The Rock	2.00	5.00
65	Triple H	1.00	2.50
66	Undertaker	1.50	4.00
67	Xavier Woods	.40	1.00
68	Zelina Vega	.75	2.00

69	Adam Cole	1.00	2.50
70	Angel Garza	.50	1.25
71	Angelo Dawkins	.40	1.00
72	Bianca Belair	1.00	2.50
73	Boa	.40	1.00
74	Bobby Fish	.40	1.00
75	Bronson Reed	.40	1.00
76	Cameron Grimes	.40	1.00
77	Candice LeRae	1.25	3.00
78	Damian Priest	.40	1.00
79	Dexter Lumis	.40	1.00
80	Io Shirai	.60	1.50
81	Isaiah Swerve Scott	.50	1.25
82	Joaquin Wilde	.40	1.00
83	Johnny Gargano	.75	2.00
84	Kushida	.50	1.25
85	Kyle O'Reilly	.50	1.25
86	Lio Rush	.40	1.00
87	Matt Riddle	.75	2.00
88	Mia Yim	.75	2.00
89	Montez Ford	.40	1.00
90	Roderick Strong	.75	2.00
91	Shayna Baszler	1.25	3.00
92	Velveteen Dream	.50	1.25
93	Alexander Wolfe	.40	1.00
94	Fabian Aichner	.40	1.00
95	Marcel Barthel	.40	1.00
96	Pete Dunne	.40	1.00
97	Rhea Ripley	1.50	4.00
98	Toni Storm	1.00	2.50
99	Travis Banks	.40	1.00
100	Walter	.75	2.00

2020 Topps Chrome WWE Autographs

*GREEN/99: .5X TO 1.2X BASIC AUTOS
*GOLD/50: .6X TO 1.5X BASIC AUTOS
*ORANGE/25: UNPRICED DUE TO SCARCITY
*BLACK/10: UNPRICED DUE TO SCARCITY
*RED/5: UNPRICED DUE TO SCARCITY
*SUPER/1: UNPRICED DUE TO SCARCITY
RANDOMLY INSERTED INTO PACKS

AAB	Aleister Black	8.00	20.00
AAC	Adam Cole	10.00	25.00
AAL	Alexa Bliss	60.00	120.00
AAN	Andrade	8.00	20.00
AAS	AJ Styles	12.00	30.00
ABY	Bayley	20.00	50.00
ACF	Charlotte Flair	20.00	50.00
ADB	Daniel Bryan	8.00	20.00
ADM	Drew McIntyre	12.00	30.00
AFB	Finn Balor	12.00	30.00
AHC	Humberto Carrillo	6.00	15.00
AIS	Io Shirai	30.00	75.00
AKC	King Corbin	6.00	15.00
AKK	Kofi Kingston	6.00	15.00
AKU	Kushida	8.00	20.00
ALE	Lacey Evans	15.00	40.00
AMA	Mustafa Ali	8.00	20.00
ARH	Rhea Ripley	30.00	75.00
ASB	Shayna Baszler	10.00	25.00
ASD	Johnny Gargano	6.00	15.00
ASJ	Samoa Joe	6.00	15.00
ASN	Shinsuke Nakamura	12.00	30.00
ASR	Seth Rollins	8.00	20.00
ATM	The Miz	8.00	20.00

2020 Topps Chrome WWE Big Legends

COMPLETE SET (25)		12.00	30.00

*GREEN/99: .75X TO 2X BASIC CARDS
*GOLD/50: 1.2X TO 3X BASIC CARDS
*ORANGE/25: UNPRICED DUE TO SCARCITY
*BLACK/10: UNPRICED DUE TO SCARCITY
*RED/5: UNPRICED DUE TO SCARCITY
*SUPER/1: UNPRICED DUE TO SCARCITY
RANDOMLY INSERTED INTO PACKS

BL1	Alundra Blayze	1.00	2.50
BL2	Boogeyman	.60	1.50
BL3	Booker T	1.25	3.00
BL4	Brutus The Barber Beefcake	.60	1.50
BL5	Christian	.75	2.00
BL6	Eve	1.25	3.00
BL7	Gerald Brisco	.60	1.50
BL8	The Godfather	.60	1.50
BL9	The Hurricane	.60	1.50
BL10	Jerry The King Lawler	1.50	4.00
BL11	Kerry Von Erich	1.00	2.50
BL12	Kevin Nash	1.00	2.50
BL13	Kurt Angle	1.50	4.00
BL14	Mick Foley	1.25	3.00
BL15	Molly Holly	.75	2.00
BL16	Pat Patterson	.60	1.50
BL17	Razor Ramon	1.00	2.50
BL18	Ric Flair	2.50	6.00
BL19	Rikishi	.60	1.50
BL20	Road Dogg Jesse James	.75	2.00
BL21	Ron Simmons	1.00	2.50
BL22	Sgt. Slaughter	1.25	3.00
BL23	The Million Dollar Man Ted DiBiase	1.25	3.00
BL24	Wendi Richter	.75	2.00
BL25	X-Pac	.60	1.50

2020 Topps Chrome WWE Big Legends Autographs

*GREEN/99: .5X TO 1.2X BASIC CARDS
*GOLD/50: .6X TO 1.5X BASIC CARDS
*ORANGE/25: UNPRICED DUE TO SCARCITY
*BLACK/10: UNPRICED DUE TO SCARCITY
*RED/5: UNPRICED DUE TO SCARCITY
*SUPER/1: UNPRICED DUE TO SCARCITY
RANDOMLY INSERTED INTO PACKS

BLJJ	Road Dogg Jesse James	10.00	25.00
BLJL	Jerry The King Lawler	12.00	30.00
BLHBK	Shawn Michaels		

2020 Topps Chrome WWE Fantasy Matches

COMPLETE SET (22)		15.00	40.00

*GREEN/99: .6X TO 1.5X BASIC CARDS
*GOLD/50: .75X TO 2X BASIC CARDS
*ORANGE/25: UNPRICED DUE TO SCARCITY
*BLACK/10: UNPRICED DUE TO SCARCITY
*RED/5: UNPRICED DUE TO SCARCITY
*SUPER/1: UNPRICED DUE TO SCARCITY
RANDOMLY INSERTED INTO PACKS

FM1	Samoa Joe/John Cena	2.50	6.00
FM2	Beth Phoenix/Chyna	1.50	4.00
FM3	Batista/Ultimate Warrior	1.50	4.00
FM4	AJ Styles/Mr. Perfect	2.00	5.00
FM5	Drew McIntyre/Booker T	1.25	3.00
FM6	The Miz/Rowdy Roddy Piper	1.50	4.00
FM7	Roman Reigns/The Rock	3.00	8.00
FM8	Randy Orton/DDP	1.50	4.00
FM9	Bret Hit Man Hart/Daniel Bryan	2.00	5.00
FM10	Alexa Bliss/Trish Stratus	4.00	10.00
FM11	Charlotte Flair/Lita	2.50	6.00
FM12	The Fiend/Jake The Snake Roberts	2.00	5.00
FM13	Seth Rollins/Shawn Michaels	1.50	4.00
FM14	Kurt Angle/Ken Shamrock	1.50	4.00
FM15	Mankind/Jeff Hardy	1.50	4.00
FM16	Braun Strowman/Goldberg	2.50	6.00
FM17	Finn Balor/Undertaker	2.50	6.00
FM18	Rick Rude/Robert Roode	.75	2.00
FM19	KO/Stone Cold Steve Austin	3.00	8.00
FM20	Big Show/Vader	1.00	2.50
FM21	Randy Savage/Kofi Kingston	2.00	5.00
FM22	Andrade/Eddie Guerrero	1.50	4.00

2020 Topps Chrome WWE Fantasy Matches Autographs

*BLACK/10: UNPRICED DUE TO SCARCITY
*RED/5: UNPRICED DUE TO SCARCITY
*SUPER/1: UNPRICED DUE TO SCARCITY
STATED PRINT RUN 25 SER.#'d SETS

FMKK	Jeff Hardy/Mankind	75.00	150.00
FMLC	Charlotte Flair/Lita	125.00	250.00
FMSA	Seth Rollins/Shawn Michaels	75.00	150.00
FMTA	Alexa Bliss/Trish Stratus	250.00	500.00

2020 Topps Chrome WWE Image Variations

COMPLETE SET (25)			

*GREEN/99: .5X TO 1.2X BASIC CARDS
*GOLD/50: .6X TO 1.5X BASIC CARDS
*ORANGE/25: UNPRICED DUE TO SCARCITY
*BLACK/10: UNPRICED DUE TO SCARCITY
*RED/5: UNPRICED DUE TO SCARCITY
*SUPER/1: UNPRICED DUE TO SCARCITY
RANDOMLY INSERTED INTO PACKS

IV1	AJ Styles	2.00	5.00
IV2	Alexa Bliss	5.00	12.00
IV3	Mustafa Ali	1.50	4.00
IV4	Asuka	3.00	8.00
IV5	Bayley	1.50	4.00
IV6	Becky Lynch	6.00	15.00
IV7	Bianca Belair	2.50	6.00
IV8	The Fiend Bray Wyatt	4.00	10.00
IV9	Carmella	4.00	10.00
IV10	Charlotte Flair	5.00	12.00
IV11	Ember Moon	1.50	4.00
IV12	Finn Balor	2.00	5.00
IV13	Jeff Hardy	2.50	6.00
IV14	Kairi Sane	3.00	8.00
IV15	Kofi Kingston	1.50	4.00
IV16	Lacey Evans	3.00	8.00
IV17	Matt Riddle	2.50	6.00
IV18	Naomi	2.50	6.00
IV19	Nikki Cross	3.00	8.00
IV20	Ricochet	2.00	5.00
IV21	Samoa Joe	2.00	5.00
IV22	Seth Rollins	2.00	5.00
IV23	Sonya Deville	2.50	6.00
IV24	Velveteen Dream	2.00	5.00
IV25	King Corbin	1.50	4.00

2020 Topps Chrome WWE Shocking Wins

COMPLETE SET (25)		12.00	30.00

*GREEN/99: .5X TO 1.2X BASIC CARDS
*GOLD/50: .6X TO 1.5X BASIC CARDS

*ORANGE/25: UNPRICED DUE TO SCARCITY
*BLACK/10: UNPRICED DUE TO SCARCITY
*RED/5: UNPRICED DUE TO SCARCITY
*SUPER/1: UNPRICED DUE TO SCARCITY
RANDOMLY INSERTED INTO PACKS

SW1	Ron Simmons	1.00	2.50
SW2	The 1-2-3 Kid	.60	1.50
SW3	Yokozuna	1.00	2.50
SW4	Shawn Michaels	1.50	4.00
SW5	Kevin Nash	1.00	2.50
SW6	Mankind	1.25	3.00
SW7	Jeff Hardy	1.50	4.00
SW8	Brock Lesnar	2.50	6.00
SW9	The Hurricane	.60	1.50
SW10	Eddie Guerrero	1.50	4.00
SW11	Shelton Benjamin	.75	2.00
SW12	Bobby Lashley	1.25	3.00
SW13	Sheamus	.75	2.00
SW14	The Miz	1.00	2.50
SW15	Sheamus	.75	2.00
SW16	Lord Tensai	.60	1.50
SW17	Bo Dallas	.60	1.50
SW18	Fandango	.60	1.50
SW19	Brock Lesnar	2.50	6.00
SW20	Paige	1.50	4.00
SW21	Charlotte Flair	2.50	6.00
SW22	Heath Slater	.60	1.50
SW23	Kevin Owens	.75	2.00
SW24	Finn Balor	1.50	4.00
SW25	Jinder Mahal	.60	1.50

2020 Topps Chrome WWE Shocking Wins Autographs

*GREEN/99: .5X TO 1.2X BASIC AUTOS
*GOLD/50: .6X TO 1.5X BASIC AUTOS
*ORANGE/25: UNPRICED DUE TO SCARCITY
*BLACK/10: UNPRICED DUE TO SCARCITY
*RED/5: UNPRICED DUE TO SCARCITY
*SUPER/1: UNPRICED DUE TO SCARCITY
RANDOMLY INSERTED INTO PACKS

SWABD	Bo Dallas	5.00	12.00
SWACF	Charlotte Flair	15.00	40.00
SWAFB	Finn Balor	12.00	30.00
SWAJH	Jeff Hardy	10.00	25.00
SWAJL	Jerry The King Lawler		
SWAJM	Jinder Mahal		
SWAKO	Kevin Owens	6.00	15.00
SWALA	Bobby Lashley	5.00	12.00
SWALT	Lord Tensai	5.00	12.00
SWAMA	Mustafa Ali	5.00	12.00
SWAMK	Mankind		
SWASB	Shelton Benjamin	6.00	15.00
SWASH	Sheamus		
SWASM	Sheamus	8.00	20.00
SWATM	The Miz	8.00	20.00
SWAZR	Zack Ryder		

2021 Topps Chrome WWE

*REFRACTOR: .5X TO 1.2X BASIC CARDS
*AQUA/150: .75X TO 2X BASIC CARDS
*GREEN/99: 1X TO 2.5X BASIC CARDS
*GOLD/50: 1.5X TO 4X BASIC CARDS
*ORANGE/25: UNPRICED DUE TO SCARCITY
*BLACK/10: UNPRICED DUE TO SCARCITY
*RED/5: UNPRICED DUE TO SCARCITY
*SUPERFR/1: UNPRICED DUE TO SCARCITY

1	AJ Styles	1.25	3.00

2	Akira Tozawa	.50	1.25
3	Alexa Bliss	2.50	6.00
4	Andrade	.60	1.50
5	Angel Garza	.50	1.25
6	Arturo Ruas	.40	1.00
7	Asuka	1.50	4.00
8	Becky Lynch	1.50	4.00
9	Bobby Lashley	1.00	2.50
10	Braun Strowman	1.00	2.50
11	The Fiend Bray Wyatt	1.50	4.00
12	Charlotte Flair	2.00	5.00
13	Charly Caruso	1.00	2.50
14	Dabba-Kato	.40	1.00
15	Drew Gulak	.50	1.25
16	Drew McIntyre	1.00	2.50
17	Gran Metalik	.40	1.00
18	John Morrison	.75	2.00
19	Edge	1.50	4.00
20	Erik	.40	1.00
21	Ivar	.40	1.00
22	Jeff Hardy	1.00	2.50
23	Keith Lee	.75	2.00
24	King Corbin	.40	1.00
25	Kofi Kingston	1.00	2.50
26	Lacey Evans	1.50	4.00
27	Lince Dorado	.40	1.00
28	Mandy Rose	2.00	5.00
29	Riddle	1.00	2.50
30	Naomi	.50	1.25
31	Nikki Cross	.75	2.00
32	Mustafa Ali	.50	1.25
33	MVP	.40	1.00
34	Nia Jax	.75	2.00
35	Peyton Royce	.75	2.00
36	R-Truth	.50	1.25
37	Randy Orton	1.25	3.00
38	Riddick Moss	.50	1.25
39	Samoa Joe	.75	2.00
40	Shayna Baszler	1.00	2.50
41	Sheamus	.60	1.50
42	Shelton Benjamin	.60	1.50
43	Dominik Dijakovic	.50	1.25
44	The Miz	.60	1.50
45	Xavier Woods	.40	1.00
46	Aleister Black	1.00	2.50
47	Angelo Dawkins	.50	1.25
48	Apollo Crews	.50	1.25
49	Bayley	1.00	2.50
50	Bianca Belair	1.00	2.50
51	Big E	1.00	2.50
52	Billie Kay	.75	2.00
53	Cesaro	.40	1.00
54	Daniel Bryan	1.50	4.00
55	Dolph Ziggler	.75	2.00
56	Kalisto	.50	1.25
57	Kayla Braxton	.75	2.00
58	Kevin Owens	.75	2.00
59	Liv Morgan	1.50	4.00
60	Montez Ford	.40	1.00
61	Murphy	.50	1.25
62	Natalya	.60	1.50
63	Otis	.50	1.25
64	Roman Reigns	2.00	5.00
65	Ruby Riott	.75	2.00
66	Sasha Banks	2.00	5.00
67	Sami Zayn	.60	1.50
68	Seth Rollins	1.00	2.50
69	Shinsuke Nakamura	1.00	2.50

70	Chad Gable	.40	1.00
71	Sonya Deville	1.00	2.50
72	Adam Cole	1.25	3.00
73	Aliyah	.75	2.00
74	Austin Theory	.75	2.00
75	Bobby Fish	.50	1.25
76	Bronson Reed	.50	1.25
77	Cameron Grimes	.75	2.00
78	Candice LeRae	1.50	4.00
79	Dakota Kai	.75	2.00
80	Damian Priest	.60	1.50
81	Dexter Lumis	.40	1.00
82	Finn Balor	1.00	2.50
83	Io Shirai	.75	2.00
84	Isaiah Swerve Scott	.60	1.50
85	Johnny Gargano	.75	2.00
86	Karrion Kross	1.50	4.00
87	Kyle O'Reilly	.60	1.50
88	Kushida	.60	1.50
89	Raquel Gonzalez	1.50	4.00
90	Rhea Ripley	1.50	4.00
91	Ridge Holland	.40	1.00
92	Robert Stone	.50	1.25
93	Roderick Strong	.75	2.00
94	Santos Escobar	.75	2.00
95	Scarlett	2.00	5.00
96	Shotzi Blackheart	2.00	5.00
97	Tegan Nox	1.00	2.50
98	Timothy Thatcher	.40	1.00
99	Tommaso Ciampa	1.00	2.50
100	Velveteen Dream	.50	1.25

2021 Topps Chrome WWE 5 Timers Club

COMPLETE SET (20)		20.00	50.00

*GREEN/99: .5X TO 1.2X BASIC CARDS
*GOLD/50: .6X TO 1.5X BASIC CARDS
*ORANGE/25: UNPRICED DUE TO SCARCITY
*BLACK/10: UNPRICED DUE TO SCARCITY
*RED/5: UNPRICED DUE TO SCARCITY
*SUPERFR/1: UNPRICED DUE TO SCARCITY
RANDOMLY INSERTED INTO PACKS

5T1	Booker T	1.25	3.00
5T2	Bret Hit Man Hart	1.50	4.00
5T3	Charlotte Flair	3.00	8.00
5T4	Dolph Ziggler	1.25	3.00
5T5	Edge	2.50	6.00
5T6	John Cena	3.00	8.00
5T7	Kevin Nash	1.00	2.50
5T8	Kofi Kingston	1.50	4.00
5T9	Lex Luger	.75	2.00
5T10	Randy Orton	2.00	5.00
5T11	Rey Mysterio	1.50	4.00
5T12	Ric Flair	2.50	6.00
5T13	R-Truth	.75	2.00
5T14	Sasha Banks	3.00	8.00
5T15	Stone Cold Steve Austin	3.00	8.00
5T16	The Miz	1.00	2.50
5T17	The Rock	4.00	10.00
5T18	Triple H	2.00	5.00
5T19	Trish Stratus	3.00	8.00
5T20	William Regal	1.00	2.50

2021 Topps Chrome WWE 5 Timers Club Autographs

*GOLD/50: .5X TO 1.2X BASIC AUTOS
*ORANGE/25: .6X TO 1.5X BASIC AUTOS
*BLACK/10: UNPRICED DUE TO SCARCITY
*RED/5: UNPRICED DUE TO SCARCITY
*SUPERFR/1: UNPRICED DUE TO SCARCITY
*P.P.BLACK/1: UNPRICED DUE TO SCARCITY
*P.P.CYAN/1: UNPRICED DUE TO SCARCITY
*P.P.MAGENTA/1: UNPRICED DUE TO SCARCITY
*P.P.YELLOW/1: UNPRICED DUE TO SCARCITY
STATED PRINT RUN 99 SER.#'d SETS

5TABT	Booker T	15.00	40.00
5TACF	Charlotte Flair	75.00	150.00
5TAKK	Kofi Kingston	12.00	30.00
5TARM	Rey Mysterio	50.00	100.00
5TASB	Sasha Banks	75.00	150.00
5TATM	The Miz	12.00	30.00
5TATS	Trish Stratus	75.00	150.00
5TAWR	William Regal	15.00	40.00

2021 Topps Chrome WWE Autographs

*GREEN/99: .5X TO 1.2X BASIC AUTOS
*GOLD/50: .6X TO 1.5X BASIC AUTOS
*ORANGE/25: UNPRICED DUE TO SCARCITY
*BLACK/10: UNPRICED DUE TO SCARCITY
*RED/5: UNPRICED DUE TO SCARCITY
*SUPERFR/1: UNPRICED DUE TO SCARCITY
*P.P.BLACK/1: UNPRICED DUE TO SCARCITY
*P.P.CYAN/1: UNPRICED DUE TO SCARCITY
*P.P.MAGENTA/1: UNPRICED DUE TO SCARCITY
*P.P.YELLOW/1: UNPRICED DUE TO SCARCITY
RANDOMLY INSERTED INTO PACKS

AAA	Aliyah	12.00	30.00
AAB	Alexa Bliss	75.00	150.00
AAC	Apollo Crews	5.00	12.00
AAD	Angelo Dawkins	6.00	15.00
AAJ	AJ Styles	12.00	30.00
AAS	Asuka	15.00	40.00
ABA	Bayley	20.00	50.00
ABB	Bianca Belair	15.00	40.00
ABE	Big E	6.00	15.00
ABH	Shotzi Blackheart	25.00	60.00
ABK	Billie Kay	15.00	40.00
ABL	Bobby Lashley	10.00	25.00
ABR	Bronson Reed	5.00	12.00
ACL	Candice LeRae	12.00	30.00
ACS	Cesaro	6.00	15.00
ADL	Dexter Lumis	6.00	15.00
ADP	Damian Priest	8.00	20.00
AFB	Finn Balor	12.00	30.00
AGM	Gran Metalik	6.00	15.00
AIS	Io Shirai	15.00	40.00
AJG	Johnny Gargano	5.00	12.00
AJM	John Morrison	8.00	20.00
AKC	King Corbin	6.00	15.00
AKO	Kevin Owens	12.00	30.00
AKR	Karrion Kross	15.00	40.00
AKY	Kyle O'Reilly	6.00	15.00
ALM	Liv Morgan	30.00	75.00
AMA	Mustafa Ali	5.00	12.00
AMF	Montez Ford	6.00	15.00
AMR	Mandy Rose	20.00	50.00
ANC	Nikki Cross	10.00	25.00
ANJ	Nia Jax	8.00	20.00
AOT	Otis	5.00	12.00
APR	Peyton Royce	15.00	40.00
ARB	Ruby Riott	15.00	40.00
ARG	Raquel Gonzalez	20.00	50.00
ARP	Rhea Ripley	20.00	50.00
ARS	Robert Stone	5.00	12.00
ASB	Shayna Baszler	10.00	25.00
ASC	Scarlett	50.00	100.00
ASD	Sonya Deville	15.00	40.00
ASG	Chad Gable	5.00	12.00
ASM	Sheamus	6.00	15.00
ASN	Shinsuke Nakamura	10.00	25.00
ASR	Seth Rollins	10.00	25.00
ASS	Isaiah Swerve Scott	6.00	15.00
AST	Roderick Strong	6.00	15.00
ATC	Tommaso Ciampa	8.00	20.00
ATK	Dakota Kai	12.00	30.00
ATT	Timothy Thatcher	6.00	15.00
AXW	Xavier Woods	6.00	15.00
ABAY	Adam Cole	25.00	60.00
ABRO	Riddle	15.00	40.00
ADMC	Drew McIntyre		
ALEE	Keith Lee	8.00	20.00
AMVP	MVP	6.00	15.00

2021 Topps Chrome WWE Best of In Your House

COMPLETE SET (25)		25.00	60.00

*GREEN/99: .5X TO 1.2X BASIC CARDS
*GOLD/50: .6X TO 1.5X BASIC CARDS
*ORANGE/25: UNPRICED DUE TO SCARCITY
*BLACK/10: UNPRICED DUE TO SCARCITY
*RED/5: UNPRICED DUE TO SCARCITY
*SUPERFR/1: UNPRICED DUE TO SCARCITY
RANDOMLY INSERTED INTO PACKS

IYH1	Shawn Michaels	2.50	6.00
IYH2	Razor Ramon	1.00	2.50
IYH3	Hunter Hearst Helmsley	2.00	5.00
IYH4	Undertaker	3.00	8.00
IYH5	Razor Ramon	1.00	2.50
IYH6	Shawn Michaels	2.50	6.00
IYH7	Mark Henry	.60	1.50
IYH8	HBK	2.50	6.00
IYH9	Stone Cold Steve Austin	3.00	8.00
IYH10	Undertaker	3.00	8.00
IYH11	Ken Shamrock	.75	2.00
IYH12	Shawn Michaels/Undertaker	3.00	8.00
IYH13	Shawn Michaels	2.50	6.00
IYH14	Kane	1.00	2.50
IYH15	Triple H	2.00	5.00
IYH16	Shawn Michaels	2.50	6.00
IYH17	Undertaker	3.00	8.00
IYH18	Stone Cold Steve Austin	3.00	8.00
IYH19	Steve Austin/Undertaker	3.00	8.00
IYH20	Christian	.75	2.00
IYH21	Ken Shamrock	.75	2.00
IYH22	Stone Cold Steve Austin	3.00	8.00
IYH23	Finn Balor	1.50	4.00
IYH24	Keith Lee	1.25	3.00
IYH25	Io Shirai	1.25	3.00

2021 Topps Chrome WWE Cruiserweight Greats

COMPLETE SET (10)		4.00	10.00

*GREEN/99: .5X TO 1.2X BASIC CARDS
*GOLD/50: .6X TO 1.5X BASIC CARDS
*ORANGE/25: UNPRICED DUE TO SCARCITY
*BLACK/10: UNPRICED DUE TO SCARCITY
*RED/5: UNPRICED DUE TO SCARCITY
*SUPERFR/1: UNPRICED DUE TO SCARCITY
FAT PACK EXCLUSIVES

CG1	Akira Tozawa	.60	1.50
CG2	Angel Garza	.60	1.50
CG3	Cedric Alexander	.50	1.25

CG4 Drew Gulak	.60	1.50
CG5 Jordan Devlin	.50	1.25
CG6 Kalisto	.60	1.50
CG7 Murphy	.60	1.50
CG8 Santos Escobar	1.00	2.50
CG9 The Brian Kendrick	.50	1.25
CG10 Tony Nese	.50	1.25

2021 Topps Chrome WWE Cruiserweight Greats Autographs

*ORANGE/25: .5X TO 1.2X BASIC AUTOS
*BLACK/10: UNPRICED DUE TO SCARCITY
*RED/5: UNPRICED DUE TO SCARCITY
*SUPERFR/1: UNPRICED DUE TO SCARCITY
FAT PACK EXCLUSIVES
STATED PRINT RUN 50 SER.#'d SETS

CGAAG Angel Garza	5.00	15.00
CGAAT Akira Tozawa	6.00	15.00
CGACA Cedric Alexander	8.00	20.00
CGAKL Kalisto	6.00	15.00
CGAMP Murphy	6.00	15.00
CGASE Santos Escobar	10.00	25.00
CGATN Tony Nese	8.00	20.00

2021 Topps Chrome WWE Great Feats of Strength

COMPLETE SET (10)	6.00	15.00

*GREEN/99: .5X TO 1.2X BASIC CARDS
*GOLD/50: .6X TO 1.5X BASIC CARDS
*ORANGE/25: UNPRICED DUE TO SCARCITY
*BLACK/10: UNPRICED DUE TO SCARCITY
*RED/5: UNPRICED DUE TO SCARCITY
*SUPERFR/1: UNPRICED DUE TO SCARCITY
BLASTER BOX EXCLUSIVES

GF1 Beth Phoenix	1.00	2.50
GF2 Mark Henry	.50	1.25
GF3 Mark Henry	.50	1.25
GF4 Titus O'Neil	.50	1.25
GF5 Braun Strowman	1.25	3.00
GF6 Ronda Rousey	2.50	6.00
GF7 Bobby Lashley	1.25	3.00
GF8 Cesaro	.50	1.25
GF9 Tyler Bate	.60	1.50
GF10 Bianca Belair	1.25	3.00

2021 Topps Chrome WWE Great Feats of Strength Autographs

*BLACK/10: UNPRICED DUE TO SCARCITY
*RED/5: UNPRICED DUE TO SCARCITY
*SUPERFR/1: UNPRICED DUE TO SCARCITY
BLASTER BOX EXCLUSIVES

GFABB Bianca Belair
GFABE Big E
GFABP Beth Phoenix
GFACS Cesaro
GFARR Ronda Rousey
GFATO Titus O'Neil
GFATY Tyler Bate
GFAWS Mark Henry

2021 Topps Chrome WWE Image Variations

*GREEN/99: 1X TO 2.5X BASIC CARDS
*GOLD/50: 1.5X TO 4X BASIC CARDS
*ORANGE/25: UNPRICED DUE TO SCARCITY
*BLACK/10: UNPRICED DUE TO SCARCITY
*RED/5: UNPRICED DUE TO SCARCITY

*SUPERFR/1: UNPRICED DUE TO SCARCITY
RANDOMLY INSERTED INTO PACKS

IV1 AJ Styles	3.00	8.00
IV2 Angel Garza	1.25	3.00
IV3 Asuka	6.00	15.00
IV4 Bray Wyatt	3.00	8.00
IV5 Erik	1.25	3.00
IV6 Gran Metalik	1.25	3.00
IV7 Keith Lee	2.00	5.00
IV8 King Corbin	2.00	5.00
IV9 Lince Dorado	1.50	4.00
IV10 Mandy Rose	8.00	20.00
IV11 Riddle	2.00	5.00
IV12 MVP	1.25	3.00
IV13 Naomi	1.25	3.00
IV14 Samoa Joe	1.25	3.00
IV15 Shayna Baszler	1.50	4.00
IV16 Sheamus	1.25	3.00
IV17 The Miz	1.25	3.00
IV18 Bianca Belair	2.50	6.00
IV19 Seth Rollins	1.50	4.00
IV20 Bayley	2.00	5.00
IV21 Big E	1.50	4.00
IV22 Cesaro	1.25	3.00
IV23 Dolph Ziggler	1.25	3.00
IV24 Kalisto	1.25	3.00
IV25 Kayla Braxton	2.50	6.00
IV26 Sasha Banks	6.00	15.00
IV27 Shinsuke Nakamura	2.00	5.00
IV28 Santos Escobar	1.25	3.00
IV29 Shotzi Blackheart	5.00	12.00
IV30 Velveteen Dream	1.25	3.00

2021 Topps Chrome WWE Slam Attax

COMPLETE SET (200)	125.00	250.00

*REF.: .5X TO 1.2X BASIC CARDS
*SPECKLE: .6X TO 1.5X BASIC CARDS
*YELLOW/99: .75X TO 2X BASIC CARDS
*GREEN/50: 1.2X TO 3X BASIC CARDS
*ORANGE/25: UNPRICED DUE TO SCARCITY
*BLACK/10: UNPRICED DUE TO SCARCITY
*RED WAVE/5: UNPRICED DUE TO SCARCITY
*SUPERFR/1: UNPRICED DUE TO SCARCITY

1 Adam Cole	1.00	2.50
2 AJ Styles	1.00	2.50
3 Akira Tozawa	.40	1.00
4 Danny Burch	.40	1.00
5 Alexa Bliss	2.00	5.00
6 Angel Garza	.40	1.00
7 Angelo Dawkins	.40	1.00
8 Apollo Crews	.40	1.00
9 Asuka	1.25	3.00
10 Austin Theory	.60	1.50
11 Bayley	.75	2.00
12 Becky Lynch	1.25	3.00
13 Bianca Belair	.75	2.00
14 Big E	.75	2.00
15 Doudrop	.50	1.25
16 Bobby Lashley	.75	2.00
17 Fabian Aichner	.40	1.00
18 Jimmy Uso	.30	.75
19 Cameron Grimes	.60	1.50
20 Candice LeRae	1.25	3.00
21 Carmella	.75	2.00
22 Cedric Alexander	.30	.75
23 Cesaro	.30	.75
24 Chad Gable	.30	.75
25 Charlotte Flair	1.50	4.00

26 Dakota Kai	.60	1.50
27 Damian Priest	.50	1.25
28 Dana Brooke	.30	.75
29 Flash Morgan Webster	.40	1.00
30 Dexter Lumis	.30	.75
31 Dolph Ziggler	.60	1.50
32 Dominik Mysterio	.40	1.00
33 Drew McIntyre	.75	2.00
34 Edge	1.25	3.00
35 Elias	.30	.75
36 Ember Moon	.40	1.00
37 Dominik Mysterio	.40	1.00
38 Finn Balor	.75	2.00
39 Indi Hartwell	1.00	2.50
40 Io Shirai	.60	1.50
41 Isaiah "Swerve" Scott	.50	1.25
42 Ivar	.30	.75
43 James Drake	.30	.75
44 Jeff Hardy	.75	2.00
45 Jey Uso	.30	.75
46 John Morrison	.60	1.50
47 Johnny Gargano	.60	1.50
48 Jordan Devlin	.30	.75
49 Kacy Catanzaro	.60	1.50
50 Karrion Kross	1.25	3.00
51 Kay Lee Ray	.75	2.00
52 Keith Lee	.60	1.50
53 Kevin Owens	.60	1.50
54 Lince Dorado	.30	.75
55 Baron Corbin	.30	.75
56 Kofi Kingston	.75	2.00
57 Jinder Mahal	.40	1.00
58 Kushida	.50	1.25
59 Kyle O'Reilly	.50	1.25
60 Lacey Evans	1.25	3.00
61 Gran Metalik	.30	.75
62 Reggie	.30	.75
63 Liv Morgan	1.25	3.00
64 Mace	.30	.75
65 Mandy Rose	1.50	4.00
66 Marcel Barthel	.40	1.00
67 Mark Andrews	.30	.75
68 Zelina Vega	.60	1.50
69 Montez Ford	.30	.75
70 Humberto Carrillo	.30	.75
71 Mustafa Ali	.40	1.00
72 Naomi	.40	1.00
73 Nash Carter	.30	.75
74 Natalya	.50	1.25
75 Nia Jax	.60	1.50
76 Nikki A.S.H.	.60	1.50
77 Oney Lorcan	.30	.75
78 Otis	.40	1.00
79 Pete Dunne	.75	2.00
80 R-Truth	.40	1.00
81 Randy Orton	1.00	2.50
82 Raquel Gonzalez	1.25	3.00
83 Rey Mysterio	.75	2.00
84 Rhea Ripley	1.25	3.00
85 Ricochet	.50	1.25
86 Riddle	.75	2.00
87 Robert Roode	.40	1.00
88 Roderick Strong	.60	1.50
89 Roman Reigns	1.50	4.00
90 MVP	.30	.75
91 Sami Zayn	.50	1.25
92 Santos Escobar	.60	1.50
93 Sasha Banks	1.50	4.00

94 Scarlett	1.50	4.00
95 Seth Rollins	.75	2.00
96 Shayna Baszler	.75	2.00
97 Sheamus	.50	1.25
98 Shelton Benjamin	.50	1.25
99 Shinsuke Nakamura	.75	2.00
100 Shotzi	1.50	4.00
101 T-Bar	.40	1.00
102 Tamina	.30	.75
103 Tegan Nox	.75	2.00
104 Omos	.30	.75
105 The Miz	.50	1.25
106 Timothy Thatcher	.30	.75
107 Tommaso Ciampa	.75	2.00
108 Toni Storm	1.25	3.00
109 Trent Seven	.40	1.00
110 Tyler Bate	.40	1.00
111 Ilja Dragunov	.30	.75
112 Walter	1.00	2.50
113 Wes Lee	.30	.75
114 Xavier Woods	.30	.75
115 Zack Gibson	.30	.75
116 Mankind 25th ANN	.50	1.25
117 îStone Coldî Steve Austin 25th ANN	1.50	4.00
118 Hulk Hogan 25th ANN	1.50	4.00
119 The Rock 25th ANN	2.00	5.00
120 The Undertaker TYT	1.50	4.00
121 The Undertaker TYT	1.50	4.00
122 The Undertaker TYT	1.50	4.00
123 The Undertaker TYT	1.50	4.00
124 The Undertaker TYT	1.50	4.00
125 Apollo Crews BS	.40	1.00
126 Bianca Belair BS	.75	2.00
127 Big E BS	.75	2.00
128 Cesaro BS	.30	.75
129 Damian Priest BS	.50	1.25
130 Jey Uso BS	.30	.75
131 Liv Morgan BS	1.25	3.00
132 Rhea Ripley BS	1.25	3.00
133 Riddle BS	.75	2.00
134 Andre the Giant L	4.00	10.00
135 Batista L	.60	1.50
136 Bret îHit Manî Hart L	.75	2.00
137 Hulk Hogan L	1.50	4.00
138 îMacho Manî Randy Savage L	2.00	5.00
139 Mankind L	.50	1.25
140 Shawn Michaels L	1.25	3.00
141 îStone Coldî Steve Austin L	1.50	4.00
142 Trish Stratus L	1.50	4.00
143 Ultimate Warrior L	2.00	5.00
144 Apollo Crews BL	.40	1.00
145 Bayley BL	.75	2.00
146 Sasha Banks BL	1.50	4.00
147 Sheamus BL	.50	1.25
148 Asuka ER	1.25	3.00
149 Cesaro ER	.30	.75
150 Kevin Owens ER	.60	1.50
151 Seth Rollins ER	.75	2.00
152 Drew McIntyre SS	.75	2.00
153 Mandy Rose SS	1.50	4.00
154 Montez Ford SS	.30	.75
155 Roman Reigns SS	1.50	4.00
156 Dominik Mysterio PB	.40	1.00
157 Keith Lee PB	.60	1.50
158 Riddle PB	.75	2.00
159 Shayna Baszler PB	.75	2.00
160 Angelo Dawkins COC	.40	1.00
161 Bobby Lashley COC	.75	2.00

#	Card		
162	Sami Zayn COC	.50	1.25
163	Shinsuke Nakamura COC	.75	2.00
164	AJ Styles SRS	1.00	2.50
165	Lacey Evans SRS	1.25	3.00
166	Nia Jax SRS	.60	1.50
167	The Miz SRS	.50	1.25
168	Big E TLC	.75	2.00
169	Cedric Alexander TLC	.30	.75
170	Otis TLC	.40	1.00
171	Randy Orton TLC	1.00	2.50
172	Bianca Belair RR	.75	2.00
173	Edge RR	1.25	3.00
174	Rhea Ripley RR	1.25	3.00
175	Asuka ICONS	1.25	3.00
176	Bayley ICONS	.75	2.00
177	Becky Lynch ICONS	1.25	3.00
178	Charlotte Flair ICONS	1.50	4.00
179	John Cena ICONS	1.50	4.00
180	Kofi Kingston ICONS	.75	2.00
181	Randy Orton ICONS	1.00	2.50
182	Seth Rollins ICONS	.75	2.00
183	Alexa Bliss 100	2.00	5.00
184	Bianca Belair 100	.75	2.00
185	Drew McIntyre 100	.75	2.00
186	Bobby Lashley 100	.75	2.00
187	Sasha Banks 100	1.50	4.00
188	Big E 100	.75	2.00
189	Edge 100	1.25	3.00
190	Hollywood Hulk Hogan nWo SR	1.50	4.00
191	Roman Reigns 100	1.50	4.00
192	AJ Styles F	1.00	2.50
193	Bobby Lashley F	.75	2.00
194	Drew McIntyre F	.75	2.00
195	Io Shirai F	.60	1.50
196	Jey Uso F	.30	.75
197	Randy Orton F	1.00	2.50
198	Rhea Ripley F	1.25	3.00
199	Roman Reigns F	1.50	4.00
200	John Cena nWo UR	6.00	15.00

2021 Topps Chrome WWE Slam Attax Autographs

*ORANGE/25: UNPRICED DUE TO SCARCITY
*RED WAVE/5: UNPRICED DUE TO SCARCITY
*SUPERFR./1: UNPRICED DUE TO SCARCITY
STATED ODDS 1:54

AB	Big E		
AR	Reckoning		
AAB	Alexa Bliss		
AAC	Adam Cole		
AAJ	AJ Styles		
ABB	Bianca Belair		
ABH	Bret îHit Manî Hart		
ABL	Becky Lynch		
ACF	Charlotte Flair		
ACL	Candice LeRae		
ADM	Drew McIntyre		
AED	Edge		
AFA	Fabian Aichner		
AFB	Finn Balor		
AGM	Gran Metalik		
AHH	Hulk Hogan		
AIS	Io Shirai		
AJC	John Cena		
AJR	Jaxson Ryker		
AKR	Kay Lee Ray		
AKU	Kushida		
AKY	Kyle OíReilly		

AMA	Ali		
AMF	Mick Foley		
AMY	Mia Yim		
ANC	Nikki A.S.H.		
ANM	Naomi		
ANT	Natalya		
ARC	Ricochet		
ARR	Rhea Ripley		
ARR	Roman Reigns		
ARS	Roderick Strong		
ASB	Sasha Banks		
ASH	Shelton Benjamin		
ASN	Shinsuke Nakamura		
AT7	Trent Seven		
ATC	Tommaso Ciampa		
ATM	The Miz		
ATS	Toni Storm		
ATY	Tyler Bate		
AWT	Walter		
AXW	Xavier Woods		
AZV	Zelina Vega		
AHHH	Triple H		

2006 Topps Heritage Chrome WWE

COMPLETE SET (90)		10.00	25.00
UNOPENED BOX (24 PACKS)			
UNOPENED PACK (5 CARDS)			

*REFRACTORS: .75X TO 2X BASIC CARDS
*X-FRACTORS: 1.5X TO 4X BASIC CARDS
*SUPERFR./25: 10X TO 25X BASIC CARDS

#	Card		
1	John Cena	4.00	10.00
2	Batista	.75	2.00
3	Carlito	.75	2.00
4	Orlando Jordan	.20	.50
5	Paul London	.20	.50
6	Johnny Nitro	.30	.75
7	Joey Mercury	.20	.50
8	The Hurricane	.20	.50
9	Rosey	.20	.50
10	The Rock	10.00	25.00
11	Stone Cold Steve Austin	1.25	3.00
12	Hulk Hogan	1.25	3.00
13	Big Show	.75	2.00
14	The Boogeyman	.30	.75
15	Danny Basham	.20	.50
16	Edge	.75	2.00
17	Finlay	.50	1.25
18	Eugene	.20	.50
19	Joey Styles	.20	.50
20	Jonathan Coachman	.20	.50
21	Kane	.75	2.00
22	Kid Kash	.20	.50
23	Kurt Angle	.75	2.00
24	Rene Dupree	.30	.75
25	Ric Flair	1.00	2.50
26	Rob Van Dam	.50	1.25
27	Shawn Michaels	1.25	3.00
28	Triple H	1.25	3.00
29	Chavo Guerrero	.30	.75
30	Val Venis	.30	.75
31	Viscera	.30	.75
32	Steven Richards	.30	.75
33	Booker T	.50	1.25
34	Chris Benoit	.75	2.00
35	Ken Kennedy	.50	1.25
36	Doug Basham	.30	.75
37	Lashley	.50	1.25
38	Funaki	.30	.75

#	Card		
39	Hardcore Holly	.30	.75
40	JBL	.50	1.25
41	Paul Burchill	.20	.50
42	Psicosis	.20	.50
43	Super Crazy	.30	.75
44	Shelton Benjamin	.20	.50
45	Chris Masters	.30	.75
46	Nunzio	.20	.50
47	Randy Orton	.50	1.25
48	Rey Mysterio	.75	2.00
49	Scotty 2 Hotty	.30	.75
50	Tazz	.30	.75
51	Theodore Long	.20	.50
52	Undertaker	1.00	2.50
53	William Regal	.50	1.25
54	Antonio	.20	.50
55	Romeo	.20	.50
56	Snitsky	.30	.75
57	Robert Conway	.30	.75
58	Mickie James DV	1.25	3.00
59	Sharmell DV	.75	2.00
60	Trish Stratus DV	2.00	5.00
61	Torrie Wilson DV	2.00	5.00
62	Ashley DV	.75	2.00
63	Lita DV	1.25	3.00
64	Lilian Garcia DV	1.00	2.50
65	Maria DV	.75	2.00
66	Stacy Keibler DV	2.00	5.00
67	Victoria DV	1.25	3.00
68	Candice Michelle DV	1.25	3.00
69	Michelle McCool DV	1.00	2.50
70	Melina DV	.75	2.00
71	The British Bulldog L	.75	2.00
72	Chief Jay Strongbow L	.30	.75
73	Classy Freddie Blassie L	.30	.75
74	Cowboy Bob Orton L	.50	1.25
75	Bobby The Brain Heenan L	.50	1.25
76	Gorilla Monsoon L	.30	.75
77	Hillbilly Jim L	.30	.75
78	Iron Sheik L	.75	2.00
79	Jake The Snake Roberts L	.60	1.50
80	Jerry The King Lawler L	.60	1.50
81	Junkyard Dog L	.60	1.50
82	Mouth of the South Jimmy Hart L	.75	2.00
83	Mr. Wonderful Paul Orndorff L	.75	2.00
84	Nikolai Volkoff L	.50	1.25
85	Rowdy Roddy Piper L	1.00	2.50
86	Sgt. Slaughter L	.75	2.00
87	Superstar Billy Graham L	.30	.75
88	Million-Dollar Man Ted DiBiase L	.75	2.00
89	Godfather L	.30	.75
90	Checklist	.20	.50

2006 Topps Heritage Chrome WWE Refractors

STATED ODDS 1:6 HOBBY AND RETAIL

#	Card		
1	John Cena	25.00	60.00
10	The Rock	60.00	120.00

2006 Topps Heritage Chrome WWE X-Fractors

STATED ODDS 1:12 HOBBY AND RETAIL

#	Card		
1	John Cena	60.00	120.00
10	The Rock	150.00	300.00

2006 Topps Heritage Chrome WWE Autographs

GROUP A ODDS: 1:404 HOBBY
GROUP B ODDS: 1:719 HOBBY
GROUP C ODDS: 1:167 HOBBY
GROUP D ODDS: 1:31 HOBBY

NNO	Ashley D	12.00	30.00
NNO	Big Show D	12.00	30.00
NNO	Bobby The Brain Heenan D	125.00	250.00
NNO	Boogeyman D	10.00	25.00
NNO	Booker T A	8.00	20.00
NNO	Carlito C	6.00	15.00
NNO	Chavo Guerrero D	6.00	15.00
NNO	Chief Jay Strongbow D	12.00	30.00
NNO	Chris Benoit D	300.00	600.00
NNO	Hillbilly Jim D	30.00	75.00
NNO	JBL A	25.00	60.00
NNO	Jerry The King Lawler D	15.00	40.00
NNO	John Cena D	75.00	150.00
NNO	Kane B	12.00	30.00
NNO	Ken Kennedy D	6.00	15.00
NNO	Kurt Angle C	10.00	25.00
NNO	Lashley D	15.00	40.00
NNO	Lilian Garcia D	12.00	30.00
NNO	Lita D	15.00	40.00
NNO	Mickie James D	15.00	40.00
NNO	Rey Mysterio D	20.00	50.00
NNO	Sgt. Slaughter D	20.00	50.00
NNO	Shawn Michaels D	75.00	150.00
NNO	Tazz C	15.00	40.00
NNO	Torrie Wilson D	15.00	40.00
NNO	Trish Stratus C	25.00	60.00
NNO	Victoria D	12.00	30.00

2006 Topps Heritage Chrome WWE Ringside Relics

COMPLETE SET (2)		10.00	25.00
RETAIL EXCLUSIVE			
NNO	JBL/Batista	6.00	15.00
NNO	Melina/T.Wilson	8.00	20.00

2007 Topps Heritage II Chrome WWE

COMPLETE SET (100)		10.00	25.00
UNOPENED BOX (24 PACKS)			
UNOPENED PACK (5 CARDS)			

*REFRACTORS: .8X TO 2X BASIC CARDS
*X-FRACTORS: 1.5X TO 4X BASIC CARDS
*SUPERFR/25: 10X TO 25X BASIC CARDS

#	Card		
1	John Cena	1.25	3.00
2	Batista	.75	2.00
3	Carlito	.75	2.00
4	Tatanka	.20	.50
5	Highlanders	.30	.75
6	Johnny Nitro	.30	.75
7	The Great Khali	.30	.75
8	Gregory Helms	.20	.50
9	Jeff Hardy	.50	1.25
10	The Rock	1.50	4.00
11	Stone Cold Steve Austin	1.25	3.00
12	Matt Striker	.20	.50
13	Montel Vontavious Porter	.30	.75
14	The Boogeyman	.30	.75
15	Mark Henry	.30	.75
16	Edge	.75	2.00
17	Finlay	.50	1.25
18	Eugene	.20	.50
19	Sandman	.30	.75

#	Card		
20	Sabu	.20	.50
21	Kane	.75	2.00
22	Brian Kendrick/Paul London	.50	1.25
23	Rene Dupree	.30	.75
24	Ric Flair	.75	2.00
25	Rob Van Dam	.75	2.00
26	Shawn Michaels	1.25	3.00
27	Triple H	1.25	3.00
28	Chavo Guerrero	.30	.75
29	Vito	.20	.50
30	Viscera	.50	1.25
31	King Booker	.75	2.00
32	Chris Benoit	.50	1.25
33	Ken Kennedy	.50	1.25
34	Bobby Lashley	.75	2.00
35	Funaki	.30	.75
36	Matt Hardy	.50	1.25
37	JBL	.50	1.25
38	Paul Burchill	.20	.50
39	CM Punk	.30	.75
40	Super Crazy	.30	.75
41	Shelton Benjamin	.20	.50
42	Chris Masters	.75	2.00
43	Little Guido Maritato	.20	.50
44	Randy Orton	.75	2.00
45	Rey Mysterio	.50	1.25
46	Scotty 2 Hotty	.30	.75
47	Kenny Dykstra	.30	.75
48	Undertaker	1.00	2.50
49	William Regal	.50	1.25
50	Charlie Haas	.20	.50
51	Umaga	.30	.75
52	Snitsky	.30	.75
53	Rob Conway	.20	.50
54	Mr. McMahon	.75	2.00
55	Shane McMahon	.50	1.25
56	Stephanie McMahon	1.00	2.50
57	Linda McMahon	.30	.75
58	Mickie James DV	1.00	2.50
59	Sharmell DV	.50	1.25
60	Torrie Wilson DV	1.50	4.00
61	Ashley DV	.75	2.00
62	Michelle McCool DV	1.00	2.50
63	Layla DV	.75	2.00
64	Maria DV	.75	2.00
65	Kristal DV	.75	2.00
66	Victoria DV	1.00	2.50
67	Candice Michelle DV	1.00	2.50
68	Jillian Hall DV	1.00	2.50
69	Melina DV	.75	2.00
70	Mean Gene Okerlund L	.50	1.25
71	Don Muraco L	.30	.75
72	Paul Bearer L	.30	.75
73	One Man Gang L	.30	.75
74	Dusty Rhodes L	.50	1.25
75	Bushwhackers L	.20	.50
76	The Wild Samoans L	.30	.75
77	Bam Bam Bigelow L	.50	1.25
78	Mr. Perfect Curt Hennig L	.50	1.25
79	The British Bulldog L	.75	2.00
80	Earthquake L	.30	.75
81	Rocky Johnson L	.30	.75
82	Papa Shango L	.25	.60
83	Jerry The King Lawler L	.50	1.25
84	High Chief Peter Maivia L	.20	.50
85	Arn Anderson L	.20	.50
86	Mick Foley L	.75	2.00
87	Ravishing Rick Rude L	.50	1.25
88	Doink L	.20	.50
89	Andre The Giant L	.75	2.00
90	Batista TR	.75	2.00
91	Triple H TR	1.25	3.00
92	Carlito TR	.75	2.00
93	John Cena TR	1.25	3.00
94	Rey Mysterio TR	.50	1.25
95	Andre The Giant TR	.75	2.00
96	Iron Sheik TR	.75	2.00
97	Jerry The King Lawler TR	.50	1.25
98	Rowdy Roddy Piper TR	.75	2.00
99	Superstar Billy Graham TR	.30	.75
100	Cena/Booker/Ashley/Mysterio CL	1.25	3.00

2007 Topps Heritage II Chrome WWE Autographs

STATED ODDS 1:24 HOBBY EXCLUSIVE

NNO	Ashley	12.00	30.00
NNO	Jeff Hardy	15.00	40.00
NNO	John Cena	25.00	60.00
NNO	Ken Kennedy	8.00	20.00
NNO	Layla	10.00	25.00
NNO	Melina	10.00	25.00
NNO	Michelle McCool	10.00	25.00
NNO	Mickie James	15.00	40.00
NNO	Sabu	10.00	25.00
NNO	Sandman	15.00	40.00
NNO	Sharmell	6.00	15.00
NNO	Torrie Wilson	15.00	40.00
NNO	William Regal	10.00	25.00

2007 Topps Heritage II Chrome WWE Mini

1 John Cena
2 Rey Mysterio
3 Andre The Giant
4 Hulk Hogan
5 Batista

2007 Topps Heritage II Chrome WWE Ringside Relics

STATED ODDS 1:24 RETAIL EXCLUSIVE

NNO	Jeff Hardy/Carlito	4.00	10.00
NNO	Kane/Umaga	4.00	10.00
NNO	Lita/Mickie James	6.00	15.00

2008 Topps Heritage III Chrome WWE

COMPLETE SET (90) 8.00 20.00
UNOPENED BOX (24 PACKS)
UNOPEND PACK (5 CARDS)
*REFRACTORS: .8X TO 2X BASIC CARDS
*X-FRACTORS: 1.5X TO 4X BASIC CARDS
*SUPERFR./25: 10X TO 25X BASIC CARDS

#	Card		
1	John Cena	1.25	3.00
2	Batista	.75	2.00
3	Rey Mysterio	.50	1.25
4	Stone Cold	1.25	3.00
5	The Great Khali	.20	.50
6	Chris Jericho	.50	1.25
7	Edge	.75	2.00
8	Hard Core Holly	.30	.75
9	Umaga	.30	.75
10	Montel Vontavious Porter	.30	.75
11	Stevie Richards	.30	.75
12	Deuce	.20	.50
13	Lance Cade	.20	.50
14	Super Crazy	.30	.75
15	Chuck Palumbo	.30	.75
16	Domino	.20	.50
17	Trevor Murdoch	.20	.50
18	Zack Ryder	.20	.50
19	Festus	.20	.50
20	Mark Henry	.30	.75
21	Boogeyman	.30	.75
22	Brian Kendrick	.30	.75
23	Tommy Dreamer	.20	.50
24	Charlie Haas	.20	.50
25	JBL	.20	.50
26	Armando Estrada	.20	.50
27	CM Punk	.20	.50
28	Triple H	1.25	3.00
29	Shannon Moore	.20	.50
30	Hacksaw Jim Duggan	.50	1.25
31	Jeff Hardy	.75	2.00
32	Kane	.75	2.00
33	Ron Simmons	.20	.50
34	Finlay	.30	.75
35	The Miz	.30	.75
36	Kenny Dykstra	.30	.75
37	Snitsky	.30	.75
38	Jesse	.20	.50
39	Santino Marella	.20	.50
40	Cody Rhodes	.20	.50
41	Shelton Benjamin	.20	.50
42	Hornswoggle	.30	.75
43	Big Daddy V	.30	.75
44	Matt Striker	.20	.50
45	Curt Hawkins	.20	.50
46	William Regal	.50	1.25
47	Jimmy Wang Yang	.20	.50
48	Elijah Burke	.20	.50
49	Chavo Guerrero	.30	.75
50	Paul London	.20	.50
51	Mr. Kennedy	.50	1.25
52	John Morrison	.20	.50
53	Matt Hardy	.75	2.00
54	Shawn Michaels	1.25	3.00
55	Randy Orton	.50	1.25
56	Ric Flair	.75	2.00
57	Undertaker	1.00	2.50
58	Torrie Wilson DV	1.50	4.00
59	Candice DV	1.00	2.50
60	Michelle McCool DV	1.00	2.50
61	Melina DV	.75	2.00
62	Cherry DV	.75	2.00
63	Jillian DV	.75	2.00
64	Ashley DV	.75	2.00
65	Maria DV	.75	2.00
66	Kelly Kelly DV	.75	2.00
67	Mickie James DV	1.25	3.00
68	Maryse DV	.75	2.00
69	Victoria DV	1.00	2.50
70	Anderson/Blanchard L	.30	.75
71	Brian Pillman L	.30	.75
72	Dean Malenko L	.50	1.25
73	Funk Brothers L	.30	.75
74	Dusty Rhodes L	.50	1.25
75	The Freebirds L	.30	.75
76	Jimmy Superfly Snuka L	.50	1.25
77	Jimmy Garvin L	.30	.75
78	Papa Shango L	.20	.50
79	Pat Patterson L	.20	.50
80	Bam Bam Bigelow L	.50	1.25
81	Gorilla Monsoon L	.50	1.25
82	Ted Dibiase L	.50	1.25
83	Rocky Johnson L	.30	.75
84	Bruiser Brody L	.30	.75
85	Kamala L	.30	.75
86	Earthquake L	.30	.75
87	Vader L	.30	.75
88	Jack and Gerry Brisco L	.30	.75
89	Cowboy Bob Orton L	.50	1.25
100	Checklist	.20	.50

2008 Topps Heritage III Chrome WWE Allen and Ginter Superstars

COMPLETE SET (10) 6.00 15.00
*REFRACTORS: .8X TO 2X BASIC CARDS
*X-FRACTORS: 1.5X TO 4X BASIC CARDS
*SUPERFR/25: 10X TO 25X BASIC CARDS

#	Card		
1	John Cena	1.25	3.00
2	Batista	.75	2.00
3	Rey Mysterio	.50	1.25
4	Triple H	1.25	3.00
5	Shawn Michaels	1.25	3.00
6	Undertaker	1.00	2.50
7	Rowdy Roddy Piper	.75	2.00
8	Chief Jay Strongbow	.50	1.25
9	Sgt. Slaughter	.50	1.25
10	Iron Sheik	.75	2.00

2008 Topps Heritage III Chrome WWE Autographs

STATED ODDS 1:24 HOBBY EXCLUSIVE

NNO	Ashley	25.00	60.00
NNO	Carlito	6.00	15.00
NNO	Cherry	8.00	20.00
NNO	Chuck Palumbo	6.00	15.00
NNO	Festus	6.00	15.00
NNO	Jeff Hardy	15.00	40.00
NNO	Jesse	8.00	20.00
NNO	Kane	25.00	60.00
NNO	Layla	8.00	20.00
NNO	Montel Vontavious Porter	6.00	15.00
NNO	Tommy Dreamer	6.00	15.00
NNO	Trevor Murdoch	6.00	15.00

2008 Topps Heritage III Chrome WWE Mini-Cards

1 Stone Cold Steve Austin
2 John Cena
3 Edge
4 Umaga
5 The Great Khali

2008 Topps Heritage III Chrome WWE Ringside Relics

STATED ODDS 1:24 RETAIL EXCLUSIVE

NNO	Hardcore Holly vs. Carlito	4.00	10.00
NNO	Mickie James vs. Beth Phoenix	4.00	10.00
NNO	Mr. Kennedy vs. Shawn Michaels	5.00	12.00

2006 Topps Heritage II WWE

COMPLETE SET (90) 8.00 20.00
UNOPENED BOX (24 PACKS)
UNOPENED PACK (5 CARDS)

#	Card		
1	John Cena	.75	2.00
2	Batista	.40	1.00
3	Carlito	.30	.75
4	Tatanka	.12	.30
5	Paul London/Brian Kendrick	.30	.75
6	Johnny Nitro	.12	.30

#	Card	Lo	Hi
7	The Great Khali	.12	.30
8	Gregory Helms	.12	.30
9	Gunnar Scott	.30	.75
10	The Rock	.75	2.00
11	Stone Cold Steve Austin	.75	2.00
12	Hulk Hogan	.75	2.00
13	Big Show	.40	1.00
14	The Boogeyman	.20	.50
15	Mark Henry	.30	.75
16	Edge	.40	1.00
17	Finlay	.30	.75
18	Eugene	.12	.30
19	Matt Striker	.12	.30
20	Jake and Jesse Gymini	.20	.50
21	Kane	.50	1.25
22	Kid Kash	.20	.50
23	Kurt Angle	.75	2.00
24	Rene Dupree	.12	.30
25	Ric Flair	.60	1.50
26	Rob Van Dam	.50	1.25
27	Shawn Michaels	.60	1.50
28	Triple H	.75	2.00
29	Chavo Guerrero	.30	.75
30	Vito	.12	.30
31	Viscera	.20	.50
32	Steven Richards	.20	.50
33	Booker T	.30	.75
34	Chris Benoit	.30	.75
35	Ken Kennedy	.30	.75
36	Goldust	.30	.75
37	Bobby Lashley	.30	.75
38	Funaki	.20	.50
39	Matt Hardy	.20	.50
40	JBL	.40	1.00
41	Paul Burchill	.12	.30
42	Psicosis	.12	.30
43	Super Crazy	.20	.50
44	Shelton Benjamin	.12	.30
45	Chris Masters	.40	1.00
46	Little Guido Maritato	.12	.30
47	Randy Orton	.40	1.00
48	Rey Mysterio	.30	.75
49	Scotty 2 Hotty	.20	.50
50	Tazz	.20	.50
51	Spirit Squad	.20	.50
52	Undertaker	.60	1.50
53	William Regal	.30	.75
54	Charlie Haas	.12	.30
55	Umaga	.20	.50
56	Snitsky	.20	.50
57	Rob Conway	.12	.30
58	Mickie James DV	.75	2.00
59	Sharmell DV	.40	1.00
60	Torrie Wilson DV	.75	2.00
61	Ashley DV	.40	1.00
62	Lita DV	.60	1.50
63	Beth Phoenix DV	.40	1.00
64	Maria DV	.50	1.25
65	Kristal DV	.40	1.00
66	Victoria DV	.60	1.50
67	Candice Michelle DV	.60	1.50
68	Jillian Hall DV	.50	1.25
69	Melina DV	.50	1.25
70	Mean Gene Okerlund L	.30	.75
71	Don Muraco L	.20	.50
72	Paul Bearer L	.20	.50
73	One Man Gang L	.20	.50
74	Dusty Rhodes L	.30	.75
75	Bushwhackers L	.20	.50
76	The Wild Samoans L	.30	.75
77	Bam Bam Bigelow L	.20	.50
78	Mr. Perfect Curt Hennig L	.30	.75
79	The British Bulldog L	.50	1.25
80	Earthquake L	.20	.50
81	Kamala L	.30	.75
82	Koko B Ware L	.20	.50
83	Jerry The King Lawler L	.30	.75
84	High Chief Peter Maivia L	.12	.30
85	Arn Anderson L	.12	.30
86	Mick Foley L	.50	1.25
87	Ravishing Rick Rude L	.30	.75
88	Vader L	.30	.75
89	Andre The Giant L	.50	1.25
90	Checklist	.12	.30

2006 Topps Heritage II WWE Autographs

		Lo	Hi
SEMISTARS		8.00	20.00
UNLISTED STARS		10.00	25.00
STATED ODDS 1:24 HOBBY EXCLUSIVE			
NNO	Ashley	10.00	25.00
NNO	Bobby Lashley	8.00	20.00
NNO	Booker T	15.00	40.00
NNO	Brian Kendrick	8.00	20.00
NNO	Carlito	8.00	20.00
NNO	Charlie Haas	6.00	15.00
NNO	Chavo Guerrero	6.00	15.00
NNO	Edge	20.00	50.00
NNO	Gene Snitsky	6.00	15.00
NNO	Jamie Noble	6.00	15.00
NNO	Jillian Hall	10.00	25.00
NNO	John Cena	60.00	120.00
NNO	Johnny Nitro	8.00	20.00
NNO	Kane	12.00	30.00
NNO	Ken Kennedy	8.00	20.00
NNO	Kurt Angle	12.00	30.00
NNO	Melina	10.00	25.00
NNO	Michelle McCool	15.00	40.00
NNO	Mickie James	15.00	40.00
NNO	The Miz	8.00	20.00
NNO	Paul London	6.00	15.00
NNO	Randy Orton	30.00	75.00
NNO	Sharmell	8.00	20.00
NNO	Shawn Michaels	75.00	150.00
NNO	Umaga	15.00	40.00
NNO	Vito	6.00	15.00

2006 Topps Heritage II WWE Magazine Promos

		Lo	Hi
COMPLETE SET (9)		4.00	10.00
WWE MAGAZINE EXCLUSIVE			
W1	John Cena	1.00	2.50
W2	Triple H	1.00	2.50
W3	Edge	.75	2.00
W4	Batista	.60	1.50
W5	Undertaker	.60	1.50
W6	Rey Mysterio	.60	1.50
W7	Hulk Hogan	1.00	2.50
W8	Rowdy Roddy Piper	.75	2.00
W9	Sgt. Slaughter	.75	2.00

2006 Topps Heritage II WWE Magnets

		Lo	Hi
COMPLETE SET (9)		6.00	15.00
STATED ODDS 1:4 RETAIL EXCLUSIVE			
1	John Cena	1.50	4.00
2	Batista	1.00	2.50
3	Carlito	.60	1.50
4	Shawn Michaels	1.50	4.00
5	Triple H	1.50	4.00
6	Rey Mysterio	.60	1.50
7	Edge	1.00	2.50
8	Hulk Hogan	1.50	4.00
9	Torrie Wilson	2.00	5.00

2006 Topps Heritage II WWE Raw vs. Smackdown

		Lo	Hi
COMPLETE SET (2)		.75	2.00
V1	John Cena	.60	1.50
V2	Rey Mysterio	.40	1.00

2006 Topps Heritage II WWE Ringside Relics

		Lo	Hi
COMPLETE SET (8)			
STATED ODDS 1:24 HOBBY			
NNO	Big Show	8.00	20.00
NNO	Carlito	5.00	12.00
NNO	Hulk Hogan	10.00	25.00
NNO	John Cena	30.00	75.00
Hat			
NNO	John Cena	10.00	25.00
Shirt			
NNO	Psicosis	5.00	12.00
NNO	Shawn Michaels	12.00	30.00
NNO	Triple H	8.00	20.00

2006 Topps Heritage II WWE Ringside Relics Doubles

		Lo	Hi
NNO	Gregory Helms	5.00	12.00
	Super Crazy		
NNO	Ken Kennedy	5.00	12.00
	Gunner Scott		
NNO	Bobby Lashley	5.00	12.00
	King Booker		

2006 Topps Heritage II WWE Tin Inserts

		Lo	Hi
COMPLETE SET (6)		6.00	15.00
STATED ODDS 1:RETAIL TIN			
TLB1	John Cena	2.50	6.00
TLB2	Hulk Hogan	2.00	5.00
TLB3	Edge	1.50	4.00
TLB4	Triple H	2.00	5.00
TLB5	Rey Mysterio	1.00	2.50
TLB6	Andre The Giant	1.50	4.00

2006 Topps Heritage II WWE Toppers

		Lo	Hi
COMPLETE SET (12)		4.00	10.00
B1-B3 STATED ODDS 1:HOBBY BOX			
B4-B9 STATED ODDS 1:RETAIL TIN			
B10-B12 STATED ODDS 1:2 RETAIL BLISTER			
B1	D-Generation X	1.00	2.50
B2	Edge & Lita	.75	2.00
B3	Armando Alejandro Estrada/Umaga	.30	.75
B4	Booker T & Sharmell	.60	1.50
B5	Johnny Nitro & Melina	.60	1.50
B6	Spirit Squad	.30	.75
B7	D-Generation X	1.00	2.50
B8	Edge & Lita	.75	2.00
B9	Armando Alejandro Estrada/Umaga	.30	.75
B10	The Great Khali/Daivari	.30	.75
B11	Highlanders	.30	.75
B12	Brian Kendrick/Paul London	.60	1.50

2006 Topps Heritage II WWE Turkey Red Legends

		Lo	Hi
COMPLETE SET (12)		6.00	15.00
STATED ODDS 1:6 HOBBY EXCLUSIVE			
1	Rowdy Roddy Piper	1.00	2.50
2	Jake The Snake Roberts	.60	1.50
3	Sgt. Slaughter	.75	2.00
4	Chief Jay Strongbow	.30	.75
5	Jerry The King Lawler	.60	1.50
6	Gorilla Monsoon	.30	.75
7	Iron Sheik	.75	2.00
8	Junkyard Dog	.75	2.00
9	Superstar Billy Graham	.30	.75
10	Classy Freddie Blassie	.30	.75
11	Bobby The Brain Heenan	.50	1.25
12	Andre The Giant	1.00	2.50

2006 Topps Heritage II WWE Turkey Red Superstars

		Lo	Hi
COMPLETE SET (12)		10.00	20.00
STATED ODDS 1:6 RETAIL EXCLUSIVE			
1	John Cena	1.50	4.00
2	Batista	1.00	2.50
3	Carlito	.60	1.50
4	Big Show	1.00	2.50
5	Shawn Michaels	1.50	4.00
6	Rey Mysterio	.60	1.50
7	Kurt Angle	1.00	2.50
8	Edge	1.00	2.50
9	Rob Van Dam	.60	1.50
10	Triple H	1.50	4.00
11	Hulk Hogan	1.50	4.00
12	Ric Flair	1.25	3.00

2007 Topps Heritage III WWE

		Lo	Hi
COMPLETE SET (90)		8.00	20.00
UNOPENED BOX (24 PACKS)			
UNOPENED PACK (5 CARDS)			
1	John Cena	1.00	2.50
2	Batista	.60	1.50
3	Rey Mysterio	.40	1.00
4	Stone Cold Steve Austin	1.00	2.50
5	The Great Khali	.25	.60
6	Carlito	.60	1.50
7	Edge	.60	1.50
8	Hardcore Holly	.40	1.00
9	Umaga	.25	.60
10	Montel Vontavious Porter	.25	.60
11	Stevie Richards	.25	.60
12	Deuce	.15	.40
13	Lance Cade	.15	.40
14	Super Crazy	.25	.60
15	Chuck Palumbo	.15	.40
16	Domino	.15	.40
17	Trevor Murdoch	.15	.40
18	Val Venis	.40	1.00
19	Bobby Lashley	.60	1.50
20	Mark Henry	.25	.60
21	Boogeyman	.25	.60
22	Brian Kendrick	.25	.60
23	Tommy Dreamer	.20	.50
24	Charlie Haas	.15	.40
25	JBL	.40	1.00
26	Armando Estrada	.15	.40
27	CM Punk	.25	.60
28	Triple H	1.00	2.50
29	Shannon Moore	.15	.40

30 Hacksaw Jim Duggan	.25	.60
31 Jeff Hardy	.40	1.00
32 Kane	.60	1.50
33 Ron Simmons	.25	.60
34 Finlay	.40	1.00
35 The Miz	.30	.75
36 Kenny Dykstra	.25	.60
37 Snitsky	.25	.60
38 Chris Masters	.60	1.50
39 Santino Marella	.20	.50
40 Cody Rhodes	.25	.60
41 Shelton Benjamin	.15	.40
42 Hornswoggle	.20	.50
43 Big Daddy V	.40	1.00
44 Matt Striker	.15	.40
45 Jamie Noble	.15	.40
46 William Regal	.40	1.00
47 Jimmy Wang Yang	.15	.40
48 Elijah Burke	.15	.40
49 Chavo Guerrero	.25	.60
50 Paul London	.40	1.00
51 Mr. Kennedy	.40	1.00
52 John Morrison	.25	.60
53 Matt Hardy	.40	1.00
54 Shawn Michaels	1.00	2.50
55 Randy Orton	.60	1.50
56 Ric Flair	.60	1.50
57 Undertaker	.75	2.00
58 Torrie Wilson DV	1.25	3.00
59 Candice DV	.75	2.00
60 Michelle McCool DV	.75	2.00
61 Melina DV	.60	1.50
62 Cherry DV	.15	.40
63 Jillian DV	.75	2.00
64 Ashley DV	.60	1.50
65 Maria DV	.60	1.50
66 Kelly Kelly DV	.40	1.00
67 Mickie James DV	.75	2.00
68 Maryse DV	.30	.75
69 Victoria DV	.75	2.00
70 Anderson/Blanchard L	.15	.40
71 Brian Pillman L	.15	.40
72 Dean Malenko L	.15	.40
73 Funk Brothers Dory & Terry L	.15	.40
74 Dusty Rhodes L	.40	1.00
75 The Freebirds L	.15	.40
76 Jimmy Superfly Snuka L	.25	.60
77 Jimmy Garvin L	.15	.40
78 Papa Shango L	.20	.50
79 Pat Patterson L	.15	.40
80 Bam Bam Bigelow L	.40	1.00
81 Gorilla Monsoon L	.30	.75
82 Ted DiBiase L	.30	.75
83 Rocky Johson L	.25	.60
84 Bruiser Brody L	.15	.40
85 Kamala L	.20	.50
86 Earthquake L	.25	.60
87 Vader L	.25	.60
88 Jack and Gerry Brisco L	.15	.40
89 Cowboy Bob Orton L	.20	.50
90 John Cena CL	1.00	2.50

2007 Topps Heritage III WWE Allen and Ginter Legends

COMPLETE SET (12)	6.00	15.00

STATED ODDS 1:6 HOBBY EXCLUSIVE

1 Rowdy Roddy Piper	1.00	2.50
2 Chief Jay Strongbow	.30	.75
3 Sgt. Slaughter	.60	1.50

4 Iron Sheik	.60	1.50
5 Don Muraco	.20	.50
6 Ravishing Rick Rude	.60	1.50
7 Classy Freddie Blassie	.30	.75
8 Bobby The Brain Heenan	.60	1.50
9 The British Bulldog	.60	1.50
10 Jake The Snake Roberts	.60	1.50
11 Nikolai Volkoff	.60	1.50
12 Junkyard Dog	1.00	2.50

2007 Topps Heritage III WWE Allen and Ginter Superstars

COMPLETE SET (12)	10.00	25.00

STATED ODDS 1:6 RETAIL EXCLUSIVE

1 John Cena	1.50	4.00
2 Batista	.75	2.00
3 Rey Mysterio	.60	1.50
4 Carlito	.60	1.50
5 Edge	.75	2.00
6 Bobby Lashley	.60	1.50
7 Mr. Kennedy	.75	2.00
8 Triple H	1.50	4.00
9 Shawn Michaels	1.25	3.00
10 Undertaker	1.25	3.00
11 Ric Flair	1.25	3.00
12 Booker T	.75	2.00

2007 Topps Heritage III WWE Allen and Ginter Tin Inserts

STATED ODDS 1:1 TIN EXCLUSIVES

1 John Cena
2 Batista
3 Ric Flair
4 Undertaker
5 Edge
6 Shawn Michaels

2007 Topps Heritage III WWE Autographs

STATED ODDS 1:24 HOBBY EXCLUSIVE

NNO Candice	8.00	20.00
NNO Carlito	6.00	15.00
NNO Cherry	6.00	15.00
NNO Chuck Palumbo	6.00	15.00
NNO CM Punk	75.00	150.00
NNO Deuce	6.00	15.00
NNO Domino	6.00	15.00
NNO Hacksaw Jim Duggan	15.00	40.00
NNO Jeff Hardy	20.00	50.00
NNO John Cena	75.00	150.00
NNO Kane	12.00	30.00
NNO Kelly Kelly	20.00	50.00
NNO Lance Cade	6.00	15.00
NNO Maria	12.00	30.00
NNO Miz	12.00	30.00
NNO Montel Vontavious Porter	8.00	20.00
NNO Randy Orton	25.00	60.00
NNO Stevie Richards	6.00	15.00
NNO Super Crazy	6.00	15.00
NNO Torrie Wilson	10.00	25.00
NNO Trevor Murdoch	6.00	15.00
NNO Victoria	12.00	30.00

2007 Topps Heritage III WWE Event-Used Mat Ringside Relics

STATED ODDS 1:24 RETAIL EXCLUSIVE

NNO John Cena/Randy Orton	4.00	10.00

NNO Rey Mysterio/Chavo Guerrero	3.00	8.00
NNO Triple H/King Booker	4.00	10.00

2007 Topps Heritage III WWE Ringside Relics

STATED ODDS 1:24 HOBBY EXCLUSIVE

NNO Bobby Lashley	5.00	10.00
NNO Carlito	5.00	10.00
NNO John Cena	6.00	12.00
NNO Matt Hardy	5.00	10.00
NNO Mr. Kennedy	5.00	10.00

2007 Topps Heritage III WWE Magnets

COMPLETE SET (9)	6.00	15.00

STATED ODDS 1:4 RETAIL

1 John Cena	1.50	4.00
2 Batista	1.00	2.50
3 Rey Mysterio	.60	1.50
4 Carlito	1.00	2.50
5 Edge	1.00	2.50
6 Bobby Lashley	1.00	2.50
7 Mr. Kennedy	.60	1.50
8 Triple H	1.50	4.00
9 Ric Flair	1.00	2.50

2007 Topps Heritage III WWE Ringside Bonus

COMPLETE SET (16)	25.00	60.00

STATED ODDS 4:1 WAL-MART BLASTER

R1 John Cena	5.00	12.00
R2 Carlito	2.50	6.00
R3 CM Punk	2.50	6.00
R4 Randy Orton	4.00	10.00
R5 Hornswoggle	1.50	4.00
R6 Jamie Noble	1.50	4.00
R7 Super Crazy	1.50	4.00
R8 Great Khali	2.50	6.00
R9 Jeff Hardy	3.00	8.00
R10 Matt Hardy	3.00	8.00
R11 Chavo Guerrero	1.50	4.00
R12 Finlay	1.50	4.00
R13 Kane	3.00	8.00
R14 Hardcore Holly	2.50	6.00
R15 Rey Mysterio	3.00	8.00
R16 Jimmy Wang Yang	1.50	4.00

2007 Topps Heritage III WWE Ringside Rookie Bonus

COMPLETE SET (4)	10.00	25.00

STATED ODDS 1:1 WAL-MART BLASTER

RK1 Cody Rhodes	4.00	10.00
RK2 Santino Marella	4.00	10.00
RK3 Deuce	3.00	8.00
RK4 Domino	3.00	8.00

2007 Topps Heritage III WWE Superstar Team

1 Brian Kendrick/Paul London	.20	.50
2 C.Haas/S.Benjamin	.12	.30
3 Lance Cade/Trevor Murdoch	.12	.30

2007 Topps Heritage III WWE Superstar Team Oversized

STATED ODDS 1:1 HOBBY EXCLUSIVES

1 Brian Kendrick/Paul London

2 Charlie Haas/Shelton Benjamin	
3 Lance Cade/Trevor Murdoch	

2007 Topps Heritage III WWE Tin Inserts

STATED ODDS 1:1 TIN EXCLUSIVES

B1 John Cena
B2 Batista
B3 Ric Flair
B4 Undertaker
B5 Edge
B6 Shawn Michaels

2008 Topps Heritage IV WWE

COMPLETE SET (90)	8.00	20.00
UNOPENED BOX (24 PACKS)		
UNOPENED PACK (5 CARDS)		
1 Armando Estrada	.12	.30
2 Ricky Ortiz	.12	.30
3 Bam Neely	.12	.30
4 Batista	.50	1.25
5 Big Show	.30	.75
6 Brian Kendrick	.20	.50
7 Carlito	.30	.75
8 Chavo Guerrero	.20	.50
9 Chris Jericho	.30	.75
10 CM Punk	.12	.30
11 Cody Rhodes	.12	.30
12 Undertaker	.60	1.50
13 Curt Hawkins	.12	.30
14 D-Lo Brown	.20	.50
15 Edge	.50	1.25
16 Evan Bourne	.12	.30
17 Ezekiel	.20	.50
18 Festus	.12	.30
19 Finlay	.20	.50
20 The Great Khali	.12	.30
21 Hardcore Holly	.20	.50
22 Hornswoggle	.20	.50
23 Jamie Noble	.12	.30
24 John Bradshaw Layfield	.12	.30
25 Jeff Hardy	.50	1.25
26 Jesse	.12	.30
27 John Cena	.75	2.00
28 John Morrison	.12	.30
29 JTG	.12	.30
30 Kane	.50	1.25
31 Kofi Kingston	.20	.50
32 Lance Cade	.12	.30
33 Mark Henry	.20	.50
34 Matt Hardy	.50	1.25
35 Primo Colon	.12	.30
36 Mike Knox	.12	.30
37 The Miz	.20	.50
38 Mr. Kennedy	.30	.75
39 MVP	.20	.50
40 Paul Burchill	.12	.30
41 Randy Orton	.30	.75
42 Rey Mysterio	.30	.75
43 Santino Marella	.12	.30
44 Shad	.12	.30
45 Shawn Michaels	.75	2.00
46 Shelton Benjamin	.12	.30
47 Snitsky	.20	.50
48 Super Crazy	.20	.50
49 Ted DiBiase Jr.	.30	.75
50 Tommy Dreamer	.12	.30

51	Tony Atlas	.12	.30
52	Triple H	.75	2.00
53	Umaga	.20	.50
54	Vladimir Kozlov	.20	.50
55	Zack Ryder	.12	.30
56	Tiffany DV	.60	1.50
57	Beth Phoenix DV	.60	1.50
58	Candice DV	.60	1.50
59	Eve DV	.50	1.25
60	Jillian DV	.50	1.25
61	Katie Lea Burchill DV	.50	1.25
62	Kelly Kelly DV	.50	1.25
63	Layla DV	.50	1.25
64	Lilian Garcia DV	.50	1.25
65	Maria DV	.50	1.25
66	Maryse DV	.50	1.25
67	Melina DV	.50	1.25
68	Michelle McCool DV	.60	1.50
69	Mickie James DV	.75	2.00
70	Natalya DV	.50	1.25
71	Victoria DV	.60	1.50
72	Tazz/Jim Ross A	.12	.30
73	Jerry Lawler/Michael Cole A	.12	.30
74	Matt Striker/Todd Grisham A	.12	.30
75	Bobby The Brain Heenan	.50	1.25
76	Brian Pillman L	.20	.50
77	Gerald Brisco L	.20	.50
78	Jack Brisco L	.20	.50
79	Mr. Perfect Curt Hennig	.30	.75
80	Mr. Wonderful Paul Orndorff	.30	.75
81	Rowdy Roddy Piper	.50	1.25
82	Superfly Jimmy Snuka	.30	.75
83	British Bulldog L	.30	.75
84	Hillbilly Jim L	.30	.75
85	Junkyard Dog L	.30	.75
86	Mean Gene Okerlund	.30	.75
87	Million-Dollar Man Ted DiBiase	.30	.75
88	Tully Blanchard L	.20	.50
89	Dusty Rhodes L	.30	.75
90	Checklist	.12	.30

2008 Topps Heritage IV WWE Allen and Ginter Legends

COMPLETE SET (12)		6.00	15.00
STATED ODDS 1:6 HOBBY			
1	Bobby The Brain Heenan	.60	1.50
2	Junkyard Dog	1.00	2.50
3	Hillbilly Jim	.60	1.50
4	British Bulldog	.60	1.50
5	Mean Gene Okerlund	.60	1.50
6	Mr. Perfect Curt Hennig	.40	1.00
7	Rowdy Roddy Piper	1.00	2.50
8	Jimmy Superfly Snuka	.60	1.50
9	Mr. Wonderful Paul Orndorff	.40	1.00
10	Million-Dollar Man Ted DiBiase	.60	1.50
11	Tully Blanchard	.40	1.00
12	Brian Pillman	.40	1.00

2008 Topps Heritage IV WWE Allen and Ginter Superstars

COMPLETE SET (12)		10.00	25.00
STATED ODDS 1:6 RETAIL EXCLUSIVE			
1	Batista	2.00	5.00
2	John Cena	3.00	8.00
3	Chavo Guerrero	1.25	3.00
4	Chris Jericho	1.25	3.00
5	Edge	2.00	5.00
6	Triple H	3.00	8.00
7	Jeff Hardy	2.00	5.00
8	Matt Hardy	2.00	5.00
9	Mr. Kennedy	1.25	3.00
10	CM Punk	1.25	3.00
11	Rey Mysterio	1.25	3.00
12	Undertaker	2.50	6.00

2008 Topps Heritage IV WWE Autographs

RANDOM INSERTS IN PACKS
STATED ODDS 1:24 HOBBY/TARGET/WALMART

NNO	Beth Phoenix	12.00	30.00
NNO	Carlito	25.00	60.00
NNO	Chavo Guerrero	8.00	20.00
NNO	Cody Rhodes	15.00	40.00
NNO	Deuce	6.00	15.00
NNO	John Cena	75.00	150.00
NNO	Kofi Kingston	12.00	30.00
NNO	Layla	15.00	40.00
NNO	Matt Hardy	12.00	30.00
NNO	Mickie James	75.00	150.00
NNO	Natalya	12.00	30.00
NNO	Tazz	6.00	15.00
NNO	Ted DiBiase Jr.	12.00	30.00

2008 Topps Heritage IV WWE Blister Bonus

COMPLETE SET (3)
RANDOMLY INSERTED INTO PACKS
RETAIL EXCLUSIVE

1 Edge
2 John Cena
3 Matt Hardy

2008 Topps Heritage IV WWE Magnets

COMPLETE SET (9)		12.00	30.00
STATED ODDS 1:4 RETAIL EXCLUSIVE			
1	John Cena	3.00	8.00
2	Mr. Kennedy	1.25	3.00
3	CM Punk	2.50	6.00
4	Chris Jericho	1.25	3.00
5	Batista	2.00	5.00
6	Triple H	3.00	8.00
7	Edge	2.00	5.00
8	Mickie James	3.00	8.00
9	Melina	2.00	5.00

2008 Topps Heritage IV WWE Mat Relics

STATED ODDS 1:24 RETAIL EXCLUSIVES

NNO	Batista vs. Paul Burchill	3.00	8.00
NNO	John Cena vs. Cody Rhodes	5.00	12.00
NNO	John Cena vs. Ted DiBiase	5.00	12.00

2008 Topps Heritage IV WWE Ringside Rookies

COMPLETE SET (4)		15.00	40.00
STATED ODDS 1:WALMART BLASTER			
RK1	Ted DiBiase Jr.	8.00	20.00
RK2	Vladimir Kozlov	4.00	10.00
RK3	Evan Bourne	5.00	12.00
RK4	Natalya	8.00	20.00

2008 Topps Heritage IV WWE Ringside Superstars

COMPLETE SET (16)		30.00	80.00
STATED ODDS 4:1 WALMART BLASTER			
R1	John Cena	6.00	15.00
R2	Batista	4.00	10.00
R3	CM Punk	2.00	5.00
R4	Rey Mysterio	2.50	6.00
R5	Triple H	6.00	15.00
R6	Undertaker	5.00	12.00
R7	MVP	2.00	5.00
R8	Jeff Hardy	4.00	10.00
R9	Matt Hardy	4.00	10.00
R10	Tommy Dreamer	2.00	5.00
R11	Mark Henry	2.00	5.00
R12	John Morrison	2.00	5.00
R13	Mickie James	6.00	15.00
R14	Beth Phoenix	5.00	12.00
R15	Candice	5.00	12.00
R16	Michelle McCool	5.00	12.00

2008 Topps Heritage IV WWE Shirt Relics

STATED ODDS

NNO	Jeff Hardy	7.50	15.00
NNO	MVP	6.00	12.00
NNO	Rey Mysterio	6.00	12.00

2008 Topps Heritage IV WWE Tin Inserts

COMPLETE SET (6)		12.00	30.00
STATED ODDS 1:TIN RETAIL EXCLUSIVE			
1	John Cena	4.00	10.00
2	Rey Mysterio	2.50	6.00
3	Shawn Michaels	4.00	10.00
4	Edge	2.50	6.00
5	Randy Orton	2.50	6.00
6	Triple H	4.00	10.00

2005 Topps Heritage WWE

COMPLETE SET (90)		8.00	20.00
UNOPENED BOX (24 PACKS)			
UNOPENED PACK (5 CARDS)			
1	John Cena	1.25	3.00
2	Batista	.50	1.25
3	Carlito	.20	.50
4	Orlando Jordan	.20	.50
5	Paul London	.20	.50
6	Johnny Nitro	.20	.50
7	Joey Mercury	.20	.50
8	Hurricane	.20	.50
9	Rosey	.20	.50
10	The Rock	1.25	3.00
11	Stone Cold Steve Austin	1.25	3.00
12	Hulk Hogan	1.25	3.00
13	Big Show	.75	2.00
14	Chris Jericho	.60	1.50
15	Danny Basham	.20	.50
16	Edge	.60	1.50
17	Eric Bischoff	.30	.75
18	Eugene	.50	1.25
19	Jim Ross	.30	.75
20	Jonathan Coachman	.20	.50
21	Kane	.60	1.50
22	Heidenreich	.20	.50
23	Kurt Angle	.75	2.00
24	Rene Dupree	.20	.50
25	Ric Flair	1.00	2.50
26	Rob Van Dam	.60	1.50
27	Shawn Michaels	1.00	2.50
28	Tajiri	.20	.50
29	Triple H	1.00	2.50
30	Kerwin White	.20	.50
31	Val Venis	.30	.75
32	Viscera	.20	.50
33	Steven Richards	.20	.50
34	Booker T	.30	.75
35	Chris Benoit	.75	2.00
36	Christian	.60	1.50
37	Doug Basham	.20	.50
38	Eddie Guerrero	1.00	2.50
39	Funaki	.20	.50
40	Hardcore Holly	.30	.75
41	JBL	.30	.75
42	Juventud	.20	.50
43	Psicosis	.20	.50
44	Super Crazy	.20	.50
45	Shelton Benjamin	.20	.50
46	Chris Masters	.20	.50
47	Nunzio	.20	.50
48	Randy Orton	.20	.50
49	Rey Mysterio	.60	1.50
50	Scotty 2 Hotty	.30	.75
51	Tazz	.20	.50
52	Theodore Long	.20	.50
53	Undertaker	1.00	2.50
54	William Regal	.30	.75
55	Antonio	.20	.50
56	Romeo	.20	.50
57	Snitsky	.20	.50
58	Robert Conway	.20	.50
59	Sharmell DV	1.00	2.50
60	Trish Stratus DV	2.00	5.00
61	Torrie Wilson DV	2.00	5.00
62	Christy Hemme DV	2.00	5.00
63	Lita DV	1.25	3.00
64	Lilian Garcia DV	1.00	2.50
65	Maria DV	1.25	3.00
66	Stacy Keibler DV	2.00	5.00
67	Victoria DV	1.25	3.00
68	Candice Michelle DV	1.25	3.00
69	Michelle McCool DV	1.00	2.50
70	Melina DV	1.00	2.50
71	The British Bulldog L	.30	.75
72	Chief Jay Strongbow L	.20	.50
73	Classy Freddie Blassie L	.20	.50
74	Cowboy Bob Orton L	.30	.75
75	Bobby The Brain Heenan L	.30	.75
76	Gorilla Monsoon L	.20	.50
77	Hillbilly Jim L	.30	.75
78	Iron Sheik L	.50	1.25
79	Jake The Snake Roberts L	.50	1.25
80	Jerry The King Lawler L	.50	1.25
81	Junkyard Dog L	.50	1.25
82	Mouth of the South Jimmy Hart L	.60	1.50
83	Mr. Wonderful Paul Orndorff L	.60	1.50
84	Nikolai Volkoff L	.30	.75
85	Rowdy Roddy Piper L	1.00	2.50
86	Sgt. Slaughter L	.50	1.25
87	Superstar Billy Graham L	.30	.75
88	The Million Dollar Man Ted DiBiase L	.60	1.50
89	Godfather L	.20	.50
90	Hogan/Cena/Batista CL	1.25	3.00

2005 Topps Heritage WWE Autographs

OVERALL STATED ODDS 1:36
HEMME ODDS 1:1574 H
ANGLE, HOGAN, SHIEK ODDS 1:530 H
MICHAELS, SLAUGHTER, WILSON ODDS 1:520 H
CENA, KANE, KIEBLER, LAWLER, PIPER, STRATUS, STRONBOW ODDS 1:510
HILLBILLY, HEENAN ODDS 1:473 RETAIL

NNO	Bobby The Brain Heenan RET	75.00	150.00
NNO	Chief Jay Strongbow	20.00	50.00
NNO	Christy Hemme	50.00	100.00
NNO	Hillbilly Jim RET	25.00	60.00
NNO	Hulk Hogan	300.00	600.00
NNO	Iron Sheik	15.00	40.00
NNO	Jerry The King Lawler	15.00	40.00
NNO	John Cena	200.00	400.00
NNO	Kane	25.00	60.00
NNO	Kurt Angle	25.00	60.00
NNO	Lita	30.00	75.00
NNO	Rowdy Roddy Piper	200.00	400.00
NNO	Sgt. Slaughter	15.00	40.00
NNO	Shawn Michaels	125.00	250.00
NNO	Stacy Keibler	75.00	150.00
NNO	Torrie Wilson	30.00	75.00
NNO	Trish Stratus	50.00	100.00

2005 Topps Heritage WWE Event-Used Mat Ringside Relics

STATED ODDS 1:12 RETAIL EXCLUSIVES

NNO	Booker T/Christian
NNO	Rey Mysterio/Eddie Guerrero
NNO	JBL/Batista

2005 Topps Heritage WWE Event-Worn Ringside Relics

OVERALL STATED ODDS 1:17
EUGENE ODDS 1:214
MICHAELS ODDS 1:196
ANGLE ODDS 1:185
JERICHO ODDS 1:158
TRIPLE H ODDS 1:104
CENA ODDS 1:89
HOGAN ODDS 1:70

NNO	Chris Jericho	6.00	15.00
NNO	Eugene	8.00	20.00
NNO	Hulk Hogan	10.00	25.00
NNO	John Cena	10.00	30.00
NNO	Kurt Angle	8.00	20.00
NNO	Shawn Michaels	10.00	25.00
NNO	Triple H	10.00	25.00

2005 Topps Heritage WWE Stickers

COMPLETE SET (10) 12.50 30.00
STATED ODDS 1:4 HOBBY

1	Hulk Hogan	2.00	5.00
2	The Rock	2.00	5.00
3	Batista	.75	2.00
4	Shawn Michaels	1.50	4.00
5	Carlito	.30	.75
6	Kurt Angle	1.25	3.00
7	Triple H	1.50	4.00
8	John Cena	2.00	5.00
9	Torrie Wilson	3.00	8.00
10	Christy Hemme	3.00	8.00

2005 Topps Heritage WWE World's Greatest Wrestling Managers DVD Promos

COMPLETE SET (4) 3.00 8.00
STATED ODDS 1:SET PER DVD

V1	Bobby The Brain Heenan	1.25	3.00
V2	Classy Freddie Blassie	.60	1.50
V3	Mouth of the South Jimmy Hart	.75	2.00
V4	Paul Bearer	1.25	3.00

2005 Topps Heritage WWE Promo

NNO	John Cena	1.50	4.00

2012 Topps Heritage WWE

COMPLETE SET (110) 10.00 25.00
UNOPENED BOX (24 PACKS)
UNOPENED PACK (9 CARDS)
*SILVER: .75X TO 2X BASIC CARDS
*BLACK: 5X TO 12X BASIC CARDS
*GOLD/10: UNPRICED DUE TO SCARCITY

1	AJ Lee	.75	2.00
2	Aksana	.40	1.00
3	Alberto Del Rio	.40	1.00
4	Alicia Fox	.25	.60
5	Beth Phoenix	.40	1.00
6	Big Show	.40	1.00
7	Brock Lesnar	.60	1.50
8	Brodus Clay	.15	.40
9	Cameron	.25	.60
10	Chris Jericho	.60	1.50
11	Christian	.15	.40
12	CM Punk	.60	1.50
13	Cody Rhodes	.15	.40
14	Damien Sandow	.15	.40
15	Daniel Bryan	.15	.40
16	Dolph Ziggler	.25	.60
17	Eve	.60	1.50
18	Jack Swagger	.25	.60
19	John Cena	.75	2.00
20	Kaitlyn	.40	1.00
21	Kane	.40	1.00
22	Ryback	.15	.40
23	Kofi Kingston	.15	.40
24	Layla	.40	1.00
25	Lilian Garcia	.40	1.00
26	Mark Henry	.25	.60
27	The Miz	.25	.60
28	Naomi	.25	.60
29	Natalya	.60	1.50
30	R-Truth	.15	.40
31	Randy Orton	.60	1.50
32	Rey Mysterio	.40	1.00
33	The Rock	.75	2.00
34	Rosa Mendes	.25	.60
35	Santino Marella	.25	.60
36	Sheamus	.40	1.00
37	Kama Mustafa	.15	.40
38	Tamina Snuka	.25	.60
39	Tensai	.15	.40
40	Triple H	.60	1.50
41	Tyson Kidd	.15	.40
42	Undertaker	.60	1.50
43	Zack Ryder	.15	.40
44	Batista	.25	.60
45	Booker T	.25	.60
46	Cactus Jack	.60	1.50
47	Dude Love	.60	1.50
48	Jerry The King Lawler	.40	1.00
49	Jim Ross	.15	.40
50	Kevin Nash	.25	.60
51	Mankind	.60	1.50
52	Mick Foley	.60	1.50
53	Shawn Michaels	.60	1.50
54	Stone Cold Steve Austin	.75	2.00
55	Trish Stratus	.75	2.00
56	Akeem	.15	.40
57	The American Dream Dusty Rhodes	.25	.60
58	Andre The Giant	.75	2.00
59	Arn Anderson	.25	.60
60	Barry Windham	.25	.60
61	Big Boss Man	.15	.40
62	Big John Studd	.25	.60
63	Bobby The Brain Heenan	.25	.60
64	Brian Pillman	.25	.60
65	The British Bulldog	.25	.60
66	Bushwhacker Butch	.15	.40
67	Bushwhacker Luke	.15	.40
68	Chief Jay Strongbow	.25	.60
69	Classy Freddie Blassie	.25	.60
70	Cowboy Bob Orton	.25	.60
71	Dean Malenko	.25	.60
72	Doink The Clown	.25	.60
73	Don Muraco	.25	.60
74	The Godfather	.15	.40
75	Gorilla Monsoon	.25	.60
76	Greg The Hammer Valentine	.25	.60
77	Hacksaw Jim Duggan	.25	.60
78	Harley Race	.25	.60
79	Hillbilly Jim	.25	.60
80	Howard Finkel	.25	.60
81	The Iron Sheik	.25	.60
82	Irwin R. Schyster	.15	.40
83	Jake The Snake Roberts	.25	.60
84	Jimmy Superfly Snuka	.25	.60
85	Junkyard Dog	.25	.60
86	Sin Cara	.40	1.00
87	Kamala	.25	.60
88	Koko B. Ware	.25	.60
89	Mean Gene Okerlund	.25	.60
90	Michael PS Hayes	.15	.40
91	Million Dollar Man Ted DiBiase	.25	.60
92	Mr. Perfect	.25	.60
93	Mr. Wonderful Paul Orndorff	.25	.60
94	Nikolai Volkoff	.25	.60
95	One Man Gang	.15	.40
96	Papa Shango	.15	.40
97	Paul Bearer	.15	.40
98	Ravishing Rick Rude	.25	.60
99	Ricky The Dragon Steamboat	.25	.60
100	Road Warrior Animal	.25	.60
101	Road Warrior Hawk	.25	.60
102	Rocky Johnson	.25	.60
103	Rowdy Roddy Piper	.40	1.00
104	Sgt. Slaughter	.25	.60
105	Terry Funk	.25	.60
106	Tito Santana	.25	.60
107	Tom Prichard	.15	.40
108	Tully Blanchard	.25	.60
109	Vader	.25	.60
110	Yokozuna	.25	.60

2012 Topps Heritage WWE Allen and Ginter

COMPLETE SET (30) 30.00 75.00
STATED ODDS 1:6 HOBBY AND RETAIL

1	Brock Lesnar	3.00	8.00
2	Christian	.75	2.00
3	CM Punk	3.00	8.00
4	Daniel Bryan	.75	2.00
5	John Cena	4.00	10.00
6	Kelly Kelly	3.00	8.00
7	Kofi Kingston	.75	2.00
8	Layla	2.00	5.00
9	Randy Orton	3.00	8.00
10	Sheamus	2.00	5.00
11	Booker T	1.25	3.00
12	Diesel	1.25	3.00
13	Mankind	3.00	8.00
14	Stone Cold Steve Austin	4.00	10.00
15	Trish Stratus	4.00	10.00
16	The American Dream Dusty Rhodes	1.25	3.00
17	Andre The Giant	4.00	10.00
18	Big Boss Man	.75	2.00
19	Big John Studd	1.25	3.00
20	Cowboy Bob Orton	1.25	3.00
21	Doink The Clown	1.25	3.00
22	Hacksaw Jim Duggan	1.25	3.00
23	Kamala	1.25	3.00
24	Koko B. Ware	1.25	3.00
25	Papa Shango	.75	2.00
26	Paul Bearer	.75	2.00
27	Ricky The Dragon Steamboat	1.25	3.00
28	Terry Funk	1.25	3.00
29	Vader	1.25	3.00
30	Yokozuna	1.25	3.00

2012 Topps Heritage WWE Andre the Giant Tribute

COMPLETE SET (10) 8.00 20.00
*SILVER/85: 1X TO 2.5X BASIC CARDS
*GOLD/10: UNPRICED DUE TO SCARCITY
STATED ODDS 1:8 HOBBY AND RETAIL

1	Andre the Giant	1.25	3.00
2	Andre the Giant	1.25	3.00
3	Andre the Giant	1.25	3.00
4	Andre the Giant	1.25	3.00
5	Andre the Giant	1.25	3.00
6	Andre the Giant	1.25	3.00
7	Andre the Giant	1.25	3.00
8	Andre the Giant	1.25	3.00
9	Andre the Giant	1.25	3.00
10	Andre the Giant	1.25	3.00

2012 Topps Heritage WWE Autographs

STATED ODDS HOBBY EXCLUSIVE 1:44
STATED ODDS RETAIL EXCLUSIVE 1:120

NNO	Akeem	25.00	60.00
NNO	Cameron	15.00	40.00
NNO	CM Punk	50.00	100.00
NNO	Doink The Clown	100.00	200.00
NNO	The Godfather	25.00	60.00
NNO	Howard Finkel	20.00	50.00
NNO	Irwin R. Schyster	25.00	60.00
NNO	Jake The Snake Roberts	20.00	50.00
NNO	John Cena	75.00	150.00
NNO	Kama Mustafa	10.00	25.00
NNO	Kamala	15.00	40.00
NNO	Layla	10.00	25.00
NNO	Mean Gene Okerlund	15.00	40.00
NNO	Michael PS Hayes	10.00	25.00
NNO	Naomi	15.00	40.00

NNO Natalya	12.00	30.00
NNO One Man Gang	25.00	60.00
NNO Papa Shango	20.00	50.00
NNO Paul Bearer	75.00	150.00
NNO Vader	30.00	75.00

2012 Topps Heritage WWE Fabled Tag Teams

COMPLETE SET (10) 6.00 15.00
STATED ODDS 1:12 HOBBY AND RETAIL

1 Nikolai Volkoff/Iron Sheik	.75	2.00
2 The Brain Busters	.75	2.00
3 Big Boss Man/Akeem	.50	1.25
4 The Road Warriors	.75	2.00
5 The Bushwhackers	.50	1.25
6 Money Inc	.75	2.00
7 The Rock N Sock Connection	2.50	6.00
8 The Brothers of Destruction	2.00	5.00
9 The Two-Man Power Trip	2.50	6.00
10 D-Generation X	2.00	5.00

2012 Topps Heritage WWE Family History

COMPLETE SET (10) 6.00 15.00
STATED ODDS 1:8 HOBBY AND RETAIL

1 B.Orton/R.Orton	2.00	5.00
2 T.DiBiase Sr./T.DiBiase Jr.	.75	2.00
3 J.Snuka/T.Snuka	.75	2.00
4 R.Johnson/The Rock	2.50	6.00
5 Yokozuna	.75	2.00
The Usos		
6 B.Bulldog/Natalya	2.00	5.00
7 D.Rhodes/C.Rhodes	.75	2.00
8 Animal/J.Laurinaitis	.50	1.25
9 Mr. Perfect/M.McGillicutty	.75	2.00
10 P.Bearer/Kane	1.25	3.00

2012 Topps Heritage WWE Jerry the King Lawler Portraits

COMPLETE SET (10) 12.00 30.00
STATED ODDS 1:24 HOBBY AND RETAIL

1 Big Show	2.50	6.00
2 Brodus Clay	1.00	2.50
3 CM Punk	4.00	10.00
4 Hornswoggle	1.50	4.00
5 Kelly Kelly	4.00	10.00
6 Rey Mysterio	2.50	6.00
7 Santino Marella	1.50	4.00
8 Sheamus	2.50	6.00
9 The Miz	1.50	4.00
10 Undertaker	4.00	10.00

2012 Topps Heritage WWE Ringside Action

COMPLETE SET (55) 10.00 25.00
STATED ODDS 1:1 HOBBY AND RETAIL

1 Superfly Splash	.60	1.50
Jimmy Superfly Snuka		
2 Double A Spinebuster	.60	1.50
3 Stone Cold Stunner	2.00	5.00
4 Perfect-Plex	.60	1.50
5 Cobra Clutch	.60	1.50
6 DDT	.60	1.50
7 Flying Fist Drop	1.00	2.50
8 Figure Four Leglock	.60	1.50
9 Mandible Claw	1.50	4.00
10 Jackknife Powerbomb	.60	1.50
11 Superplex	.60	1.50
12 Running Powerslam	.60	1.50
13 Doomsday Device	.60	1.50
14 Bionic Elbow	.60	1.50
15 Camel Clutch	.60	1.50
16 Flying Cross-body Press	.60	1.50
17 Three Point Stance Clothesline	.60	1.50
18 Scissor Kick	.60	1.50
19 Rude Awakening	.60	1.50
20 Chokeslam	1.00	2.50
21 Lariat	.60	1.50
22 Texas Cloverleaf	.60	1.50
23 Flying Splash	.60	1.50
24 Million Dollar Dream	.60	1.50
25 Rock Bottom	2.00	5.00
26 F-5	1.50	4.00
27 Battering Ram	.40	1.00
28 The Write-Off	.40	1.00
29 Killswitch	.40	1.00
30 Sidewalk Slam	.40	1.00
31 Flying Forearm	.60	1.50
32 Pimp Drop	.40	1.00
The Godfather		
33 The Whoopie Cushion		
34 Diving Headbutt	.60	1.50
35 STF	.40	1.00
36 619	1.00	2.50
37 G.T.S. (Go to Sleep)	1.50	4.00
38 World's Strongest Slam	.60	1.50
39 RKO	1.50	4.00
40 Moonsault Side Slam	1.00	2.50
41 Vader Bomb	.60	1.50
42 Air Pillman	.60	1.50
43 The Claw	.40	1.00
44 Banzai Drop	.60	1.50
45 Wasteland	.40	1.00
46 Brogue Kick	1.00	2.50
47 Attitude Adjustment	2.00	5.00
48 Reverse Piledriver	.60	1.50
49 Knockout Punch	.60	1.50
50 The Walls of Jericho	1.50	4.00
51 Sweet Chin Music	1.50	4.00
52 Batista Bomb	.60	1.50
53 Pedigree	1.50	4.00
54 Yes! Lock	.40	1.00
86 Dream Street	.60	1.50

2012 Topps Heritage WWE Shirt Relics

TWO AUTO OR MEM PER HOBBY BOX
STATED ODDS 1:97 RETAIL

NNO Alberto Del Rio/Scarf	6.00	15.00
NNO Batista	6.00	15.00
NNO CM Punk	6.00	15.00
NNO Cody Rhodes	5.00	12.00
NNO Daniel Bryan	5.00	12.00
NNO Dolph Ziggler	6.00	15.00
NNO John Cena	8.00	20.00
NNO Kofi Kingston	5.00	12.00
NNO Mark Henry	5.00	12.00
NNO The Miz	5.00	12.00
NNO Randy Orton	6.00	15.00
NNO Rey Mysterio	6.00	15.00
NNO R-Truth	5.00	12.00
NNO Santino Marella	5.00	12.00
NNO Sheamus	5.00	12.00
NNO Stone Cold Steve Austin	8.00	20.00
NNO Wade Barrett	5.00	12.00
NNO Zack Ryder	5.00	12.00

2012 Topps Heritage WWE Stickers

COMPLETE SET (18) 10.00 25.00
STATED ODDS 1:4 HOBBY AND RETAIL

1 Ricky The Dragon Steamboat	.75	2.00
2 Rey Mysterio	1.25	3.00
3 Trish Stratus	2.50	6.00
4 Undertaker	2.00	5.00
5 Mankind	2.00	5.00
6 Ravishing Rick Rude	.75	2.00
7 Sin Cara	1.25	3.00
8 Vader	.75	2.00
9 Dude Love	2.00	5.00
10 Jake The Snake Roberts	.75	2.00
11 Gorilla Monsoon	.75	2.00
12 Greg The Hammer Valentine	.75	2.00
13 Rowdy Roddy Piper	1.25	3.00
14 Doink The Clown	.75	2.00
15 Booker T	.75	2.00
16 Koko B. Ware	.75	2.00
17 Kamala	.75	2.00
18 Kane	1.25	3.00

2012 Topps Heritage WWE The Superstars Speak

COMPLETE SET (20) 8.00 20.00
STATED ODDS 1:4 HOBBY AND RETAIL

1 Stone Cold Steve Austin	2.00	5.00
2 Cactus Jack	1.50	4.00
3 Booker T	.60	1.50
4 Road Warrior Hawk	.60	1.50
5 Gorilla Monsoon	.60	1.50
6 Rowdy Roddy Piper	1.00	2.50
7 The American Dream Dusty Rhodes	.60	1.50
8 Classy Freddie Blassie	.60	1.50
9 The Iron Sheik	.60	1.50
10 Trish Stratus	2.00	5.00
11 The Rock	2.00	5.00
12 Mr. Perfect	.60	1.50
13 Kevin Nash	.60	1.50
14 Mankind	1.50	4.00
15 Hacksaw Jim Duggan	.60	1.50
16 Jim Ross	.40	1.00
17 Vader	.60	1.50
18 Million Dollar Man Ted DiBiase	.60	1.50
19 Yokozuna	.40	1.00
20 Sgt. Slaughter	.60	1.50

2012 Topps Heritage WWE Wrestlemania XXVII Mat Relics

TWO AUTO OR MEM PER HOBBY BOX
STATED ODDS 1:97 RETAIL

NNO Alberto Del Rio	6.00	15.00
NNO Big Show	6.00	15.00
NNO Booker T	4.00	10.00
NNO Christian	4.00	10.00
NNO CM Punk	6.00	15.00
NNO Cody Rhodes	5.00	12.00
NNO Dolph Ziggler	4.00	10.00
NNO Ezekiel Jackson	4.00	10.00
NNO Heath Slater	4.00	10.00
NNO Jerry The King Lawler	5.00	12.00
NNO John Cena	6.00	15.00
NNO Justin Gabriel	5.00	12.00
NNO Kane	5.00	12.00
NNO Kofi Kingston	5.00	12.00
NNO Layla	6.00	15.00
NNO Michael Cole	4.00	10.00
NNO The Miz	4.00	10.00
NNO Randy Orton	6.00	15.00
NNO The Rock	8.00	20.00
NNO Santino Marella	5.00	12.00
NNO Stone Cold Steve Austin	8.00	20.00
NNO Triple H	6.00	15.00
NNO Trish Stratus	8.00	20.00
NNO Undertaker	6.00	15.00
NNO Wade Barrett	5.00	12.00

2015 Topps Heritage WWE

COMPLETE SET (110) 12.00 30.00
UNOPENED BOX (24 PACKS)
UNOPENED PACK (9 CARDS)
*BLACK: .75X TO 2X BASIC CARDS
*SILVER: 5X TO 12X BASIC CARDS
*GOLD/10: 8X TO 20X BASIC CARDS
*RED/1: UNPRICED DUE TO SCARCITY
*P.P.BLACK/1: UNPRICED DUE TO SCARCITY
*P.P.CYAN/1: UNPRICED DUE TO SCARCITY
*P.P.MAGENTA/1: UNPRICED DUE TO SCARCITY
*P.P.YELLOW/1: UNPRICED DUE TO SCARCITY

1 The American Dream Dusty Rhodes	.25	.60
2 The Acolytes	.25	.60
3 Bob Backlund	.15	.40
4 Bam Bam Bigelow	.20	.50
5 Booker T	.25	.60
6 Bret Hit Man Hart	.50	1.25
7 The British Bulldog	.25	.60
8 Bruno Sammartino	.40	1.00
9 The Bushwhackers	.15	.40
10 Cowboy Bob Orton	.15	.40
11 D-Generation X	.60	1.50
12 Diamond Dallas Page	.30	.75
13 Doink the Clown	.15	.40
14 Earthquake	.15	.40
15 Edge	.40	1.00
16 The Foreign Legion	.25	.60
17 The Four Horsemen	.50	1.25
18 The Funks	.20	.50
19 Eddie Guerrero	.40	1.00
20 George The Animal Steele	.20	.50
21 Papa Shango	.15	.40
22 Hacksaw Jim Duggan	.25	.60
23 Hillbilly Jim	.25	.60
24 Rob Van Dam	.40	1.00
25 Jake The Snake Roberts	.25	.60
26 Jerry The King Lawler	.25	.60
27 Jim Ross	.25	.60
28 Junkyard Dog	.20	.50
29 Kamala	.20	.50
30 The King Harley Race	.25	.60
31 Koko B. Ware	.20	.50
32 Money Inc.	.25	.60
33 Mr. Perfect Curt Hennig	.25	.60
34 Mr. Wonderful Paul Orndorff	.25	.60
35 The Nasty Boys	.25	.60
36 The Outsiders	.40	1.00
37 Ravishing Rick Rude	.25	.60
38 Ricky The Dragon Steamboat	.25	.60
39 Rocky Johnson	.25	.60
40 Rowdy Roddy Piper	.50	1.25
41 Rhythm & Blues	.25	.60
42 Sgt. Slaughter	.25	.60
43 Lex Luger & Sting	.40	1.00
44 Stone Cold Steve Austin	.75	2.00
45 Tito Santana	.25	.60
46 The Twin Towers	.20	.50

47	Ultimate Warrior	.50	1.25
48	Vader	.20	.50
49	Virgil	.15	.40
50	Yokozuna	.25	.60
51	Eve	.30	.75
52	Lita	.60	1.50
53	Trish Stratus	.75	2.00
54	Alicia Fox	.30	.75
55	The Bella Twins	.50	1.25
56	Emma	.25	.60
57	Lana	.60	1.50
58	Naomi	.25	.60
59	Natalya	.50	1.25
60	Paige	.75	2.00
61	King Barrett	.15	.40
62	Batista	.40	1.00
63	Big Show	.40	1.00
64	Bo Dallas	.15	.40
65	Bray Wyatt	.60	1.50
66	Brock Lesnar	.60	1.50
67	Chris Jericho	.40	1.00
68	Christian	.15	.40
69	Damien Sandow	.15	.40
70	Daniel Bryan	.60	1.50
71	Dean Ambrose	.40	1.00
72	Dolph Ziggler	.25	.60
73	Goldust	.15	.40
74	J & J Security	.15	.40
75	John Cena	.75	2.00
76	Kalisto	.25	.60
77	Kane	.40	1.00
78	Luke Harper	.25	.60
79	Mark Henry	.25	.60
80	The Miz	.25	.60
81	Neville	.30	.75
82	The New Day	.25	.60
83	The Prime Time Players	.15	.40
84	R-Truth	.15	.40
85	Randy Orton	.60	1.50
86	The Rock	.75	2.00
87	Fandango	.15	.40
88	Roman Reigns	.40	1.00
89	Rusev	.40	1.00
90	Ryback	.15	.40
91	Santino Marella	.15	.40
92	Seth Rollins	.25	.60
93	Sheamus	.40	1.00
94	Sin Cara	.25	.60
95	Stardust	.15	.40
96	Cesaro	.15	.40
97	Undertaker	.60	1.50
98	The Usos	.15	.40
99	William Regal	.25	.60
100	Zack Ryder	.15	.40
101	Alexa Bliss	4.00	10.00
102	Baron Corbin	.25	.60
103	Bull Dempsey	.25	.60
104	Charlotte	.50	1.25
105	Finn Balor	.50	1.25
106	Hideo Itami	.15	.40
107	Kevin Owens	.50	1.25
108	Sami Zayn	.25	.60
109	Sasha Banks	.30	.75
110	Tyler Breeze	.15	.40
111	Steve Austin 2K16 SP		
111B	Steve Austin 2K16 SP Black		
111C	Steve Austin 2K16 SP Blue		
111D	Steve Austin 2K16 SP Yellow		

2015 Topps Heritage WWE 2K16

COMPLETE SET (8)		10.00	25.00

*BLACK/50: 1.2X TO 3X BASIC CARDS
*P.P.BLACK/1: UNPRICED DUE TO SCARCITY
*P.P.CYAN/1: UNPRICED DUE TO SCARCITY
*P.P.MAGENTA/1: UNPRICED DUE TO SCARCITY
*P.P.YELLOW/1: UNPRICED DUE TO SCARCITY

1	Stone Cold Steve Austin	4.00	10.00
2	Daniel Bryan	3.00	8.00
3	Finn Balor	2.50	6.00
4	King Barrett	.75	2.00
5	Paige	4.00	10.00
6	Paul Heyman	.75	2.00
7	Seth Rollins	1.25	3.00
8	Stone Cold Steve Austin	4.00	10.00

2015 Topps Heritage WWE Autographs

*BLACK/50: .5X TO 1.2X BASIC AUTOS
*SILVER/25: .75X TO 2X BASIC AUTOS
*GOLD/10: UNPRICED DUE TO SCARCITY
*RED/1: UNPRICED DUE TO SCARCITY

NNO	Alundra Blayze	8.00	20.00
NNO	Daniel Bryan	12.00	30.00
NNO	Dean Ambrose	15.00	40.00
NNO	Dolph Ziggler	10.00	25.00
NNO	Eva Marie	15.00	40.00
NNO	Finn Balor	20.00	50.00
NNO	Hideo Itami	10.00	25.00
NNO	John Cena	30.00	75.00
NNO	Neville	10.00	25.00
NNO	Pat Patterson	10.00	25.00
NNO	Roman Reigns	60.00	120.00
NNO	Sasha Banks	125.00	250.00
NNO	Seth Rollins	15.00	40.00

2015 Topps Heritage WWE Money in the Bank Relics

*BLACK/50: .5X TO 1.2X BASIC MEM
*SILVER/25: .75X TO 2X BASIC MEM
*GOLD/10: UNPRICED DUE TO SCARCITY
*RED/1: UNPRICED DUE TO SCARCITY

NNO	Big E	3.00	8.00
NNO	Big Show	5.00	12.00
NNO	Darren Young	2.00	5.00
NNO	Dean Ambrose	5.00	12.00
NNO	Dolph Ziggler	3.00	8.00
NNO	John Cena	10.00	25.00
NNO	Kane	5.00	12.00
NNO	Kevin Owens	6.00	15.00
NNO	King Barrett	2.00	5.00
NNO	Kofi Kingston	2.00	5.00
NNO	Neville	4.00	10.00
NNO	Nikki Bella	6.00	15.00
NNO	Paige	10.00	25.00
NNO	Randy Orton	8.00	20.00
NNO	Roman Reigns	5.00	12.00
NNO	R-Truth	2.00	5.00
NNO	Ryback	2.00	5.00
NNO	Seth Rollins	3.00	8.00
NNO	Sheamus	5.00	12.00
NNO	Titus O'Neil	2.00	5.00
NNO	Xavier Woods	3.00	8.00

2015 Topps Heritage WWE nWo Autographs

RANDOMLY INSERTED INTO PACKS

NNO	Big Show	20.00	50.00

2015 Topps Heritage WWE nWo Tribute

COMPLETE SET (10)		10.00	25.00

RANDOMLY INSERTED INTO PACKS

NNO	Booker T	12.00	30.00
NNO	Bret Hit Man Hart	25.00	60.00
NNO	Kevin Nash	20.00	50.00
NNO	Lex Luger	12.00	30.00
NNO	Shawn Michaels	60.00	120.00
NNO	X-Pac	15.00	40.00

31	Scott Hall	2.50	6.00
32	Kevin Nash	2.50	6.00
33	The Giant	2.50	6.00
34	Syxx	2.00	5.00
35	Miss Elizabeth	2.00	5.00
36	Mr. Wallstreet	1.00	2.50
37	Big Bubba Rogers	1.00	2.50
38	Curt Hennig	1.50	4.00
39	Bret Hit Man Hart	3.00	8.00
40	Stevie Ray	1.00	2.50

2015 Topps Heritage WWE NXT Called Up

COMPLETE SET (30)		8.00	20.00

*P.P.BLACK/1: UNPRICED DUE TO SCARCITY
*P.P.CYAN/1: UNPRICED DUE TO SCARCITY
*P.P.MAGENTA/1: UNPRICED DUE TO SCARCITY
*P.P.YELLOW/1: UNPRICED DUE TO SCARCITY
STATED ODDS 1:1

1	Bad News Barrett	.30	.75
2	David Otunga	.30	.75
3	Heath Slater	.30	.75
4	Darren Young	.30	.75
5	Daniel Bryan	1.25	3.00
6	Ryback	.30	.75
7	Alex Riley	.30	.75
8	Curtis Axel	.30	.75
9	Naomi	.50	1.25
10	Titus O'Neil	.30	.75
11	Dean Ambrose	.75	2.00
12	Roman Reigns	.75	2.00
13	Seth Rollins	.50	1.25
14	Big E	.50	1.25
15	Bo Dallas	.30	.75
16	Bray Wyatt	1.25	3.00
17	Luke Harper	.50	1.25
18	Erick Rowan	.50	1.25
19	Adam Rose	.40	1.00
20	Summer Rae	1.25	3.00
21	Xavier Woods	.50	1.25
22	Emma	.50	1.25
23	Byron Saxton	.30	.75
24	Rusev	.75	2.00
25	Lana	1.25	3.00
26	Paige	1.50	4.00
27	Konnor	.40	1.00
28	Viktor	.30	.75
29	Kalisto	.50	1.25
30	Neville	.60	1.50

2015 Topps Heritage WWE Rookie of the Year

COMPLETE SET (30)		10.00	25.00

*P.P.BLACK/1: UNPRICED DUE TO SCARCITY
*P.P.CYAN/1: UNPRICED DUE TO SCARCITY
*P.P.MAGENTA/1: UNPRICED DUE TO SCARCITY
*P.P.YELLOW/1: UNPRICED DUE TO SCARCITY
STATED ODDS 1:1

1	Mr. Wonderful Paul Orndorff	.50	1.25
2	Rowdy Roddy Piper	1.00	2.50
3	Davey Boy Smith	.50	1.25
4	Jake The Snake Roberts	.50	1.25
5	Ultimate Warrior	1.00	2.50
6	Shawn Michaels	1.25	3.00
7	Earthquake	.30	.75
8	Undertaker	1.25	3.00
9	I.R.S.	.30	.75
10	Razor Ramon	.75	2.00
11	Diesel	.75	2.00
12	Kama	.30	.75
13	Hunter Hearst Helmsley	1.25	3.00
14	Mark Henry	.50	1.25
15	Kane	.75	2.00
16	Edge	.75	2.00
17	Chris Jericho	.75	2.00
18	Lita	1.25	3.00
19	Brock Lesnar	1.25	3.00
20	Joey Mercury	.30	.75
21	The Miz	.50	1.25
22	Santino Marella	.30	.75
23	Dolph Ziggler	.50	1.25
24	Sheamus	.75	2.00
25	Daniel Bryan	1.25	3.00
26	Sin Cara	.50	1.25
27	Dean Ambrose	.75	2.00
28	Bray Wyatt	1.25	3.00
29	Rusev	.75	2.00
30	Neville	.60	1.50

2015 Topps Heritage WWE Swatch Relics

*BLACK/50: .5X TO 1.2 BASIC MEM
*GOLD/10: UNPRICED DUE TO SCARCITY
*RED/1: UNPRICED DUE TO SCARCITY

NNO	Aiden English	3.00	8.00
NNO	Baron Corbin	4.00	10.00
NNO	Bayley	5.00	12.00
NNO	Becky Lynch	5.00	12.00
NNO	Big E	4.00	10.00
NNO	Big Show	6.00	15.00
NNO	Bo Dallas	2.50	6.00
NNO	Bray Wyatt	10.00	25.00
NNO	Cesaro	2.50	6.00
NNO	Charlotte	8.00	20.00
NNO	Colin Cassady	4.00	10.00
NNO	Curtis Axel	2.50	6.00
NNO	Damien Sandow	2.50	6.00
NNO	Daniel Bryan	10.00	25.00
NNO	Darren Young	2.50	6.00
NNO	Dean Ambrose	6.00	15.00
NNO	Dolph Ziggler	4.00	10.00
NNO	Enzo Amore	2.50	6.00
NNO	Finn Balor	8.00	20.00
NNO	Goldust	2.50	6.00
NNO	Jack Swagger	4.00	10.00
NNO	Jimmy Uso	2.50	6.00
NNO	John Cena	12.00	30.00
NNO	Kalisto	4.00	10.00
NNO	Kevin Owens	8.00	20.00
NNO	King Barrett	2.50	6.00
NNO	Kofi Kingston	2.50	6.00
NNO	Konnor	3.00	8.00
NNO	Luke Harper	4.00	10.00
NNO	Luke Harper	4.00	10.00

NNO Mojo Rawley 2.50 6.00
NNO Natalya 8.00 20.00
NNO Neville 5.00 12.00
NNO Randy Orton 10.00 25.00
NNO Roman Reigns 6.00 15.00
NNO Rusev 6.00 15.00
NNO Ryback 2.50 6.00
NNO Samoa Joe 6.00 15.00
NNO Sasha Banks 5.00 12.00
NNO Seth Rollins 4.00 10.00
NNO Sheamus 6.00 15.00
NNO Simon Gotch 2.50 6.00
NNO Sin Cara 4.00 10.00
NNO Tamina 4.00 10.00
NNO The Miz 4.00 10.00
NNO Titus O'Neil 2.50 6.00
NNO Tyler Breeze 2.50 6.00
NNO Viktor 2.50 6.00
NNO Xavier Woods 4.00 10.00
NNO Zack Ryder 2.50 6.00

2015 Topps Heritage WWE Then and Now

COMPLETE SET (30) 10.00 25.00
*P.P.BLACK/1: UNPRICED DUE TO SCARCITY
*P.P.CYAN/1: UNPRICED DUE TO SCARCITY
*P.P.MAGENTA/1: UNPRICED DUE TO SCARCITY
*P.P.YELLOW/1: UNPRICED DUE TO SCARCITY
STATED ODDS 1:1

1 Batista .75 2.00
2 Big Show .75 2.00
3 Booker T .50 1.25
4 Brock Lesnar 1.25 3.00
5 Chris Jericho .75 2.00
6 Christian .30 .75
7 Daniel Bryan 1.25 3.00
8 Damien Sandow .30 .75
9 Darren Young .30 .75
10 Dean Ambrose .75 2.00
11 Edge .75 2.00
12 Goldust .30 .75
13 Hornswoggle .50 1.25
14 Jamie Noble .30 .75
15 JBL .30 .75
16 Joey Mercury .30 .75
17 John Cena 1.50 4.00
18 Kane .75 2.00
19 Mark Henry .50 1.25
20 The Miz .50 1.25
21 Randy Orton 1.25 3.00
22 Ryback .30 .75
23 Seth Rollins .50 1.25
24 Sting .75 2.00
25 Stone Cold Steve Austin 1.50 4.00
26 Triple H 1.25 3.00
27 Trish Stratus 1.50 4.00
28 Undertaker 1.25 3.00
29 William Regal .50 1.25
30 Zack Ryder .30 .75

2016 Topps Heritage WWE

COMPLETE SET (110) 10.00 25.00
UNOPENED BOX (24 PACKS)
UNOPENED PACKS (9 CARDS)
*BRONZE/99: .75X TO 2X BASIC CARDS
*SILVER/50: 1.2X TO 3X BASIC CARDS
*BLUE/25: 2X TO 5X BASIC CARDS
*GOLD/10: 4X TO 10X BASIC CARDS
*RED/1: UNPRICED DUE TO SCARCITY
*P.P.BLACK/1: UNPRICED DUE TO SCARCITY
*P.P.CYAN/1: UNPRICED DUE TO SCARCITY
*P.P.MAGENTA/1: UNPRICED DUE TO SCARCITY
*P.P.YELLOW/1: UNPRICED DUE TO SCARCITY

1 AJ Styles 1.00 2.50
2 Alberto Del Rio .40 1.00
3 Big E .25 .60
4 Big Show .50 1.25
5 Braun Strowman .30 .75
6 Bray Wyatt 1.00 2.50
7 Brock Lesnar 1.25 3.00
8 Bubba Ray Dudley .50 1.25
9 Cesaro .50 1.25
10 Chris Jericho .60 1.50
11 D-Von Dudley .40 1.00
12 Dean Ambrose .75 2.00
13 Dolph Ziggler .30 .75
14 Erick Rowan .25 .60
15 Goldust .40 1.00
16 Jack Swagger .25 .60
17 Jey Uso .25 .60
18 Jimmy Uso .25 .60
19 John Cena 1.25 3.00
20 Kalisto .60 1.50
21 Kane .40 1.00
22 Kevin Owens .60 1.50
23 Karl Anderson .25 .60
24 Kofi Kingston .25 .60
25 Luke Harper .25 .60
26 Neville .60 1.50
27 Randy Orton .60 1.50
28 The Rock 1.25 3.00
29 Roman Reigns .75 2.00
30 Rusev .60 1.50
31 Luke Gallows .30 .75
32 Seth Rollins .40 1.00
33 Sheamus .60 1.50
34 Sin Cara .30 .75
35 Zack Ryder .25 .60
36 Sting .60 1.50
37 Triple H 1.00 2.50
38 Tyson Kidd .25 .60
39 Undertaker 1.00 2.50
40 Xavier Woods .25 .60
41 Alicia Fox .40 1.00
42 Becky Lynch .75 2.00
43 Brie Bella .50 1.25
44 Charlotte .75 2.00
45 Eva Marie .50 1.25
46 Lana 1.00 2.50
47 Mandy Rose 6.00 15.00
48 Naomi .40 1.00
49 Natalya .40 1.00
50 Nikki Bella .75 2.00
51 Paige .75 2.00
52 Rosa Mendes .25 .60
53 Sasha Banks .75 2.00
54 Summer Rae .60 1.50
55 Tamina .30 .75
56 Aiden English .25 .60
57 Angelo Dawkins .25 .60
58 Apollo Crews .25 .60
59 Asuka 1.00 2.50
60 Bayley .60 1.50
61 Baron Corbin .30 .75
62 Carmella .60 1.50
63 Colin Cassady .50 1.25
64 Enzo Amore .50 1.25
65 Finn Balor .75 2.00
66 Hideo Itami .30 .75
67 Nia Jax .40 1.00
68 Sami Zayn .40 1.00
69 Samoa Joe .60 1.50
70 Simon Gotch .40 1.00
71 Alundra Blayze L .40 1.00
72 American Dream Dusty Rhodes L .25 .60
73 Andre The Giant L .75 2.00
74 Bam Bam Bigelow L .30 .75
75 Bret Hit Man Hart L .60 1.50
76 The British Bulldog L .30 .75
77 Bruno Sammartino L .30 .75
78 Daniel Bryan L 1.00 2.50
79 Diamond Dallas Page L .40 1.00
80 Eddie Guerrero L .60 1.50
81 Edge L .60 1.50
82 Eve L .50 1.25
83 The Honky Tonk Man L .25 .60
84 Irwin R. Schyster L .25 .60
85 Jake The Snake Roberts L .50 1.25
86 Jim The Anvil Neidhart L .25 .60
87 Kevin Nash L .60 1.50
88 Lex Luger L .40 1.00
89 Lita L .75 2.00
90 Macho Man Randy Savage L .60 1.50
91 Million Dollar Man Ted DiBiase L .30 .75
92 Miss Elizabeth L .25 .60
93 Mr. Perfect Curt Hennig L .60 1.50
94 Ravishing Rick Rude L .40 1.00
95 Ric Flair L 1.00 2.50
96 Ricky The Dragon Steamboat L .30 .75
97 Rikishi L .30 .75
98 Road Dogg L .40 1.00
99 Rob Van Dam L .50 1.25
100 Ron Simmons L .60 1.50
101 Rowdy Roddy Piper L .75 2.00
102 Scott Hall L .60 1.50
103 Sensational Sherri L .40 1.00
104 Shawn Michaels L 1.00 2.50
105 The Iron Sheik L .25 .60
106 Stone Cold Steve Austin L 1.25 3.00
107 Tatanka L .25 .60
108 Trish Stratus L 1.25 3.00
109 Ultimate Warrior L .60 1.50
110 X-Pac L .40 1.00
113 Macho Man Randy Savage SP

2016 Topps Heritage WWE All-Star Patches

*BRONZE/99: .5X TO 1.2X BASIC MEM
*SILVER/50: .6X TO 1.5X BASIC MEM
*BLUE/25: .75X TO 2X BASIC MEM
*GOLD/10: UNPRICED DUE TO SCARCITY
*P.P.BLACK/1: UNPRICED DUE TO SCARCITY
*P.P.CYAN/1: UNPRICED DUE TO SCARCITY
*P.P.MAGENTA/1: UNPRICED DUE TO SCARCITY
*P.P.YELLOW/1: UNPRICED DUE TO SCARCITY
RANDOMLY INSERTED INTO PACKS

NNO Andre the Giant 6.00 15.00
NNO Bam Bam Bigelow 2.50 6.00
NNO Bayley 5.00 12.00
NNO Big Van Vader 4.00 10.00
NNO Booker T 4.00 10.00
NNO Bret Hit Man Hart 5.00 12.00
NNO Brock Lesnar 10.00 25.00
NNO Bubba Ray Dudley 4.00 10.00
NNO Curt Hennig 5.00 12.00
NNO D-Von Dudley 3.00 8.00
NNO Finn Balor 6.00 15.00
NNO The Giant 4.00 10.00
NNO Hideo Itami 2.50 6.00
NNO John Cena 10.00 25.00
NNO Kevin Nash 5.00 12.00
NNO Lex Luger 3.00 8.00
NNO Macho Man Randy Savage 5.00 12.00
NNO Ric Flair 8.00 20.00
NNO Rob Van Dam 4.00 10.00
NNO The Rock 10.00 25.00
NNO Sami Zayn 3.00 8.00
NNO Samoa Joe 5.00 12.00
NNO Scott Hall 5.00 12.00
NNO Sting 5.00 12.00
NNO Stone Cold Steve Austin 10.00 25.00
NNO Syxx 3.00 8.00
NNO Terry Funk 2.00 5.00
NNO Triple H 8.00 20.00
NNO Ultimate Warrior 5.00 12.00
NNO Undertaker 8.00 20.00

2016 Topps Heritage WWE Autographs

*SILVER/50: .5X TO 1.2X BASIC AUTOS
*BLUE/25: .6X TO 1.5X BASIC AUTOS
*GOLD/10: 1X TO 2.5X BASIC AUTOS
*P.P.BLACK/1: UNPRICED DUE TO SCARCITY
*P.P.CYAN/1: UNPRICED DUE TO SCARCITY
*P.P.MAGENTA/1: UNPRICED DUE TO SCARCITY
*P.P.YELLOW/1: UNPRICED DUE TO SCARCITY
RANDOMLY INSERTED INTO PACKS

NNO Asuka 20.00 50.00
NNO Bayley 15.00 40.00
NNO Becky Lynch 30.00 75.00
NNO Big E 6.00 15.00
NNO Brian Knobbs 6.00 15.00
NNO Brie Bella 10.00 25.00
NNO Brock Lesnar 60.00 120.00
NNO Dean Ambrose 12.00 30.00
NNO Finn Balor 15.00 40.00
NNO Hideo Itami 10.00 25.00
NNO Jake The Snake Roberts 15.00 40.00
NNO Jerry Sags 6.00 15.00
NNO Jim The Anvil Neidhart 5.00 12.00
NNO John Cena 20.00 50.00
NNO Kevin Owens 10.00 25.00
NNO Kofi Kingston 6.00 15.00
NNO Nia Jax 8.00 20.00
NNO Nikki Bella 10.00 25.00
NNO Roman Reigns 30.00 75.00
NNO Sami Zayn 10.00 25.00
NNO Samoa Joe 12.00 30.00
NNO Sasha Banks 25.00 60.00
NNO Sting 25.00 60.00
NNO Tatanka 5.00 12.00
NNO Tyler Breeze 6.00 15.00
NNO Typhoon 5.00 12.00
NNO Xavier Woods 6.00 15.00

2016 Topps Heritage WWE Diva Kiss

GOLD/10: UNPRICED DUE TO SCARCITY
RANDOMLY INSERTED INTO PACKS

NNO Asuka 125.00 250.00
NNO Billie Kay 20.00 50.00
NNO Charlotte 25.00 60.00

NNO	Dasha Fuentes	30.00	75.00
NNO	Mandy Rose	60.00	120.00
NNO	Naomi	12.00	30.00
NNO	Nia Jax	20.00	50.00
NNO	Peyton Royce	30.00	75.00

2016 Topps Heritage WWE Diva Kiss Autographs

*GOLD/10: UNPRICED DUE TO SCARCITY
*P.P.BLACK/1: UNPRICED DUE TO SCARCITY
*P.P.CYAN/1: UNPRICED DUE TO SCARCITY
*P.P.MAGENTA/1: UNPRICED DUE TO SCARCITY
*P.P.YELLOW/1: UNPRICED DUE TO SCARCITY
RANDOMLY INSERTED INTO PACKS

NNO	Asuka	200.00	350.00
NNO	Billie Kay	50.00	100.00
NNO	Charlotte	100.00	200.00
NNO	Dasha Fuentes	30.00	80.00
NNO	Mandy Rose	50.00	100.00
NNO	Naomi	20.00	50.00
NNO	Nia Jax	60.00	120.00
NNO	Peyton Royce	80.00	150.00

2016 Topps Heritage WWE Dual Autographs

STATED PRINT RUN 11 SER.#'d SETS

NNO	Asuka/N.Jax	50.00	100.00
NNO	B.Knobbs/J.Sags	25.00	60.00
NNO	Charlotte/B.Lynch	125.00	250.00
NNO	F.Balor/S.Joe	80.00	150.00
NNO	J.Roberts/J.Neidhart	50.00	100.00
NNO	J.Cena/Sting	100.00	200.00
NNO	K.Owens/D.Ziggler	60.00	120.00
NNO	N.Bella/B.Bella	60.00	120.00
NNO	R.Reigns/D.Ambrose	50.00	100.00
NNO	S.Zayn/H.Itami	25.00	60.00
NNO	S.Banks/Bayley	125.00	250.00
NNO	Tatanka	25.00	60.00
Typhoon			

2016 Topps Heritage WWE NXT University of Central Florida Mat Relics

*BRONZE/99: .5X TO 1.2X BASIC MEM
GOLD/10: UNPRICED DUE TO SCARCITY
STATED PRINT RUN 99 SER.#'d SETS

NNO	Alex Riley	2.50	6.00
NNO	Asuka	10.00	25.00
NNO	Bayley	6.00	15.00
NNO	Carmella	6.00	15.00
NNO	Colin Cassady	5.00	12.00
NNO	Enzo Amore	5.00	12.00
NNO	Nia Jax	4.00	10.00
NNO	Sami Zayn	4.00	10.00
NNO	Samoa Joe	6.00	15.00
NNO	Tye Dillinger	3.00	8.00

2016 Topps Heritage WWE Record Breakers

COMPLETE SET (30)		12.00	30.00
*P.P.BLACK/1: UNPRICED DUE TO SCARCITY			
*P.P.CYAN/1: UNPRICED DUE TO SCARCITY			
*P.P.MAGENTA/1: UNPRICED DUE TO SCARCITY			
*P.P.YELLOW/1: UNPRICED DUE TO SCARCITY			
1	Bruno Sammartino	.40	1.00
2	John Cena	1.50	4.00
3	Brock Lesnar	1.50	4.00

4	Andre the Giant	1.00	2.50
5	Ric Flair	1.25	3.00
6	Triple H	1.25	3.00
7	Randy Orton	1.00	2.50
8	Edge	1.00	2.50
9	Honky Tonk Man	.40	1.00
10	Chris Jericho	1.00	2.50
11	Lex Luger	.60	1.50
12	Ric Flair	1.50	4.00
13	Nikki Bella	1.25	3.00
14	Eve Torres	.75	2.00
15	The Dudley Boyz	.75	2.00
16	Edge	1.00	2.50
17	Finn Balor	1.25	3.00
18	Paige	1.25	3.00
19	The Ascension	.40	1.00
20	Neville	1.00	2.50
21	The British Bulldog	.50	1.25
22	Big Boss Man	.60	1.50
23	Harlem Heat	.75	2.00
24	Undertaker	1.50	4.00
25	Stone Cold Steve Austin	2.00	5.00
26	Roman Reigns	1.25	3.00
27	Kane	.60	1.50
28	Triple H	1.50	4.00
29	Kane	.60	1.50
30	Bret Hit Man Hart	1.00	2.50

2016 Topps Heritage WWE Survivor Series 2015 Mat Relics

*BRONZE/99: SAME VALUE AS BASIC MEM
*SILVER/50: .5X TO 1.2X BASIC MEM
*BLUE/25: .6X TO 1.5X BASIC MEM
*GOLD/10: UNPRICED DUE TO SCARCITY
*P.P.BLACK/1: UNPRICED DUE TO SCARCITY
*P.P.CYAN/1: UNPRICED DUE TO SCARCITY
*P.P.MAGENTA/1: UNPRICED DUE TO SCARCITY
*P.P.YELLOW/1: UNPRICED DUE TO SCARCITY
RANDOMLY INSERTED INTO PACKS

NNO	Alberto Del Rio	4.00	10.00
NNO	Bray Wyatt	10.00	25.00
NNO	Bubba Ray Dudley	5.00	12.00
NNO	Charlotte	8.00	20.00
NNO	D-Von Dudley	4.00	10.00
NNO	Dean Ambrose	8.00	20.00
NNO	Dolph Ziggler	3.00	8.00
NNO	Goldust	4.00	10.00
NNO	Jey Uso	2.50	6.00
NNO	Jimmy Uso	2.50	6.00
NNO	Kalisto	6.00	15.00
NNO	Kane	4.00	10.00
NNO	Kevin Owens	6.00	15.00
NNO	Luke Harper	2.50	6.00
NNO	Paige	8.00	20.00
NNO	Roman Reigns	8.00	20.00
NNO	Sheamus	6.00	15.00
NNO	Titus O'Neil	2.50	6.00
NNO	Tyler Breeze	2.50	6.00
NNO	Undertaker	10.00	25.00

2016 Topps Heritage WWE Swatch Relics

*BRONZE/150: SAME VALUE AS BASIC MEM
*SILVER/50: .5X TO 1.2X BASIC MEM
*BLUE/25: .6X TO 1.5X BASIC MEM
*GOLD/10: UNPRICED DUE TO SCARCITY
*P.P.BLACK/1: UNPRICED DUE TO SCARCITY
*P.P.CYAN/1: UNPRICED DUE TO SCARCITY

*P.P.MAGENTA/1: UNPRICED DUE TO SCARCITY			
*P.P.YELLOW/1: UNPRICED DUE TO SCARCITY			
RANDOMLY INSERTED INTO PACKS			
1	Aiden English	2.50	6.00
2	Alberto Del Rio	4.00	10.00
3	Asuka	10.00	25.00
4	Bayley	6.00	15.00
5	Big E	2.50	6.00
6	Bray Wyatt	10.00	25.00
7	Brock Lesnar	12.00	30.00
8	Bubba Ray Dudley	5.00	12.00
9	Cesaro	5.00	12.00
10	Charlotte	8.00	20.00
11	D-Von Dudley	4.00	10.00
12	Dean Ambrose	8.00	20.00
13	Dolph Ziggler	3.00	8.00
14	Finn Balor	8.00	20.00
15	Jey Uso	2.50	6.00
16	Jimmy Uso	2.50	6.00
17	John Cena	12.00	30.00
18	Kevin Owens	6.00	15.00
19	Kofi Kingston	2.50	6.00
20	Paige	8.00	20.00
21	Roman Reigns	8.00	20.00
22	Samoa Joe	6.00	15.00
23	Sheamus	6.00	15.00
24	Simon Gotch	4.00	10.00
25	Xavier Woods	2.50	6.00
26	Zack Ryder	2.50	6.00

2016 Topps Heritage WWE Turn Back the Clock

COMPLETE SET (15)		10.00	25.00
*P.P.BLACK/1: UNPRICED DUE TO SCARCITY			
*P.P.CYAN/1: UNPRICED DUE TO SCARCITY			
*P.P.MAGENTA/1: UNPRICED DUE TO SCARCITY			
*P.P.YELLOW/1: UNPRICED DUE TO SCARCITY			
RANDOMLY INSERTED INTO PACKS			
1	The Iron Sheik	.50	1.25
2	Andre the Giant	1.50	4.00
3	Ricky The Dragon Steamboat	.60	1.50
4	Jake The Snake Roberts	1.00	2.50
5	Texas Tornado	.75	2.00
6	Big Boss Man	.75	2.00
7	Hacksaw Jim Duggan	.50	1.25
8	Rowdy Roddy Piper	1.50	4.00
9	Tatanka	.50	1.25
10	Undertaker	2.00	5.00
11	Macho Man Randy Savage	1.25	3.00
12	Sgt. Slaughter	.60	1.50
13	Shawn Michaels	2.00	5.00
14	Bret Hit Man Hart	1.25	3.00
15	The British Bulldog	.60	1.50

2016 Topps Heritage WWE WCW/nWo All-Stars

COMPLETE SET (40)		20.00	50.00
*P.P.BLACK/1: UNPRICED DUE TO SCARCITY			
*P.P.CYAN/1: UNPRICED DUE TO SCARCITY			
*P.P.MAGENTA/1: UNPRICED DUE TO SCARCITY			
*P.P.YELLOW/1: UNPRICED DUE TO SCARCITY			
1	Scott Hall	1.50	4.00
2	Kevin Nash	1.50	4.00
3	Trillionaire Ted DiBiase	.75	2.00
4	The Giant	1.25	3.00
5	Syxx	1.00	2.50
6	Vincent	.60	1.50

7	Miss Elizabeth	.60	1.50
8	Mr. Wallstreet	.60	1.50
9	Big Bubba Rogers	1.00	2.50
10	Macho Man Randy Savage	1.50	4.00
11	Curt Hennig	1.50	4.00
12	Rick Rude	1.00	2.50
13	Dusty Rhodes	.60	1.50
14	Bret Hit Man Hart	1.50	4.00
15	Stevie Ray	.60	1.50
16	Lex Luger	1.00	2.50
17	Sting	1.50	4.00
18	Shawn Michaels	2.50	6.00
19	Booker T	1.25	3.00
20	Ric Flair	2.50	6.00
21	Arn Anderson	.60	1.50
22	Diamond Dallas Page	1.00	2.50
23	Rowdy Roddy Piper	2.00	5.00
24	Ultimate Warrior	1.50	4.00
25	The British Bulldog	.75	2.00
26	Jim The Anvil Neidhart	.60	1.50
27	Hacksaw Jim Duggan	.60	1.50
28	Chris Jericho	1.50	4.00
29	Eddie Guerrero	1.50	4.00
30	Dean Malenko	.60	1.50
31	Mr. Wonderful Paul Orndorff	.60	1.50
32	Terry Funk	.60	1.50
33	Larry Zbyszko	.60	1.50
34	John Tenta	.60	1.50
35	Bam Bam Bigelow	.75	2.00
36	Brian Pillman	.75	2.00
37	Steven Regal	.60	1.50
38	Brian Knobbs	.60	1.50
39	Jerry Sags	.75	2.00
40	Madusa	.75	2.00

2017 Topps Heritage WWE

COMPLETE SET (100)		10.00	25.00
UNOPENED BOX (24 PACKS)			
UNOPENED PACK (9 CARDS)			
*BRONZE: .5X TO 1.2X BASIC CARDS			
*BLUE/99: .75X TO 2X BASIC CARDS			
*SILVER/25: 1.2X TO 3X BASIC CARDS			
*GOLD/10: 2X TO 5X BASIC CARDS			
*RED/1: UNPRICED DUE TO SCARCITY			
*P.P.BLACK/1: UNPRICED DUE TO SCARCITY			
*P.P.CYAN/1: UNPRICED DUE TO SCARCITY			
*P.P.MAGENTA/1: UNPRICED DUE TO SCARCITY			
*P.P.YELLOW/1: UNPRICED DUE TO SCARCITY			
1	Asuka	1.25	3.00
2	Bobby Roode	1.00	2.50
3	Ember Moon	1.00	2.50
4	Eric Young	.75	2.00
5	Hideo Itami	.60	1.50
6	Johnny Gargano	.40	1.00
7	Liv Morgan	.60	1.50
8	Tommaso Ciampa	.40	1.00
9	The Rock	2.00	5.00
10	Alicia Fox	.60	1.50
11	Austin Aries	.75	2.00
12	Bayley	1.25	3.00
13	Big Cass	.50	1.25
14	Big E	.50	1.25
15	Bob Backlund	.40	1.00
16	The Brian Kendrick	.40	1.00
17	Brock Lesnar	2.00	5.00
18	Cesaro	.75	2.00
19	Charlotte Flair	1.50	4.00
20	Chris Jericho	1.00	2.50

21	Enzo Amore	1.25	3.00
22	Finn Balor	1.50	4.00
23	Goldberg	1.50	4.00
24	Karl Anderson	.40	1.00
25	Kevin Owens	1.00	2.50
26	Kofi Kingston	.50	1.25
27	Lana	1.25	3.00
28	Luke Gallows	.60	1.50
29	Mick Foley	1.00	2.50
30	Roman Reigns	1.25	3.00
31	Rusev	.75	2.00
32	Sami Zayn	.50	1.25
33	Samoa Joe	1.25	3.00
34	Sasha Banks	1.25	3.00
35	Seth Rollins	1.25	3.00
36	Sheamus	.75	2.00
37	Triple H	1.00	2.50
38	Xavier Woods	.50	1.25
39	AJ Styles	2.00	5.00
40	Alexa Bliss	2.00	5.00
41	Baron Corbin	.60	1.50
42	Becky Lynch	1.25	3.00
43	Bray Wyatt	1.00	2.50
44	Carmella	1.00	2.50
45	Chad Gable	.50	1.25
46	Daniel Bryan	1.50	4.00
47	Dean Ambrose	1.25	3.00
48	Dolph Ziggler	.60	1.50
49	Heath Slater	.40	1.00
50	Jason Jordan	.50	1.25
51	Jey Uso	.50	1.25
52	Jimmy Uso	.50	1.25
53	John Cena	2.00	5.00
54	Kalisto	.60	1.50
55	Kane	.50	1.25
56	Luke Harper	.40	1.00
57	Maryse	.75	2.00
58	The Miz	.75	2.00
59	Mojo Rawley	.50	1.25
60	Naomi	.75	2.00
61	Natalya	.75	2.00
62	Nikki Bella	1.00	2.50
63	Randy Orton	1.00	2.50
64	Rhyno	.40	1.00
65	Shinsuke Nakamura	1.00	2.50
66	Undertaker	1.50	4.00
67	Zack Ryder	.40	1.00
68	Alundra Blayze L	.50	1.25
69	Andre the Giant L	.75	2.00
70	Batista L	.75	2.00
71	Bret Hit Man Hart L	.75	2.00
72	British Bulldog L	.40	1.00
73	Brutus The Barber Beefcake L	.40	1.00
74	Diamond Dallas Page L	.50	1.25
75	Dusty Rhodes L	.50	1.25
76	Edge L	1.00	2.50
77	Fit Finlay L	.40	1.00
78	Jake The Snake Roberts L	.50	1.25
79	Jim The Anvil Neidhart L	.40	1.00
80	Ken Shamrock L	.40	1.00
81	Kevin Nash L	.60	1.50
82	Lex Luger L	.50	1.25
83	Terri Runnels L	.40	1.00
84	Macho Man Randy Savage L	.75	2.00
85	Million Dollar Man Ted DiBiase L	.50	1.25
86	Mr. Perfect L	.75	2.00
87	Ravishing Rick Rude L	.60	1.50
88	Ric Flair L	1.00	2.50

89	Rob Van Dam L	.75	2.00
90	Ron Simmons L	.50	1.25
91	Rowdy Roddy Piper L	.75	2.00
92	Scott Hall L	.50	1.25
93	Sgt. Slaughter L	.50	1.25
94	Shawn Michaels L	1.00	2.50
95	Sid Vicious L	.50	1.25
96	Sting L	1.25	3.00
97	Stone Cold Steve Austin L	1.50	4.00
98	Trish Stratus L	1.50	4.00
99	Ultimate Warrior L	.75	2.00
100	Wendi Richter L	.50	1.25

2017 Topps Heritage WWE Thirty Years of SummerSlam

COMPLETE SET (50)		5.00	12.00
*P.P.BLACK/1: UNPRICED DUE TO SCARCITY			
*P.P.CYAN/1: UNPRICED DUE TO SCARCITY			
*P.P.MAGENTA/1: UNPRICED DUE TO SCARCITY			
*P.P.YELLOW/1: UNPRICED DUE TO SCARCITY			
STATED ODDS 2:1			
1	Ultimate Warrior	.50	1.25
2	The Mega Powers	.50	1.25
3	Ultimate Warrior	.50	1.25
4	Texas Tornado	.25	.60
5	Hart Foundation	.50	1.25
6	Ultimate Warrior	.50	1.25
7	Bret Hit Man Hart	.50	1.25
8	Virgil	.25	.60
9	Ultimate Warrior	.50	1.25
10	British Bulldog	.25	.60
11	Lex Luger	.30	.75
12	Alundra Blayze	.30	.75
13	Razor Ramon	.30	.75
14	Shawn Michaels	.60	1.50
15	Diesel	.40	1.00
16	Mankind	.60	1.50
17	Shawn Michaels	.60	1.50
18	Mankind	.60	1.50
19	Bret Hit Man Hart	.50	1.25
20	Triple H	.60	1.50
21	Stond Cold Steve Austin	1.00	2.50
22	Unholy Alliance	1.00	2.50
23	Mankind	.60	1.50
24	X-Pac	.25	.60
25	X-Pac	.25	.60
26	The Rock	1.25	3.00
27	Shawn Michaels	.60	1.50
28	Brock Lesnar	1.25	3.00
29	Kane	.30	.75
30	Kurt Angle	.50	1.25
31	JBL	.30	.75
32	John Cena	1.25	3.00
33	Edge	.60	1.50
34	John Cena	1.25	3.00
35	Undertaker	1.00	2.50
36	Randy Orton	.60	1.50
37	Randy Orton	.60	1.50
38	Team WWE	1.00	2.50
39	Randy Orton	.60	1.50
40	Brock Lesnar	1.25	3.00
41	Daniel Bryan	1.00	2.50
42	Randy Orton	.60	1.50
43	Roman Reigns	.75	2.00
44	Brock Lesnar	1.25	3.00
45	Seth Rollins	.75	2.00
46	Undertaker	1.00	2.50
47	Charlotte	1.00	2.50

48	AJ Styles	1.25	3.00
49	Finn Balor	1.00	2.50
50	Brock Lesnar	1.25	3.00

2017 Topps Heritage WWE Autographed NXT TakeOver Toronto 2016 Mat Relics

STATED ODDS 1:9,056
STATED PRINT RUN 10 SER.#'d SETS
UNPRICED DUE TO SCARCITY

NNO Asuka
NNO Booby Roode
NNO Johnny Gargano
NNO Mickie James
NNO Samoa Joe
NNO Shinsuke Nakamura
NNO Tommaso Ciampa

2017 Topps Heritage WWE Autographed Survivor Series 2016 Mat Relics

STATED ODDS 1:3,544
STATED PRINT RUN 10 SER.#'d SETS
UNPRICED DUE TO SCARCITY

NNO AJ Styles
NNO Alexa Bliss
NNO Alicia Fox
NNO Bayley
NNO Becky Lynch
NNO Braun Strowman
NNO Bray Wyatt
NNO Brock Lesnar
NNO Carmella
NNO Charlotte Flair
NNO Chris Jericho
NNO Goldberg
NNO Kevin Owens
NNO Natalya
NNO Randy Orton
NNO Roman Reigns
NNO Sasha Banks
NNO Seth Rollins

2017 Topps Heritage WWE Autographs

*BLUE/50: .5X TO 1.2X BASIC AUTOS
*SILVER/25: .6X TO 1.5X BASIC AUTOS
*GOLD/10: UNPRICED DUE TO SCARCITY
*RED/1: UNPRICED DUE TO SCARCITY
*P.P.BLACK/1: UNPRICED DUE TO SCARCITY
*P.P.CYAN/1: UNPRICED DUE TO SCARCITY
*P.P.MAGENTA/1: UNPRICED DUE TO SCARCITY
*P.P.YELLOW/1: UNPRICED DUE TO SCARCITY
STATED ODDS 1:24

NNO	AJ Styles	15.00	40.00
NNO	Alexa Bliss	60.00	120.00
NNO	Asuka	25.00	60.00
NNO	Bayley	15.00	40.00
NNO	Becky Lynch	50.00	100.00
NNO	Bobby Roode	12.00	30.00
NNO	Bray Wyatt	12.00	30.00
NNO	Bret Hit Man Hart	20.00	50.00
NNO	Brutus The Barber Beefcake	12.00	30.00
NNO	Charlotte Flair	20.00	50.00
NNO	Chris Jericho	10.00	25.00
NNO	Dean Ambrose	8.00	20.00
NNO	Ember Moon	6.00	15.00

NNO	Eric Young	6.00	15.00
NNO	Finn Balor	15.00	40.00
NNO	Fit Finlay	10.00	25.00
NNO	Goldberg	30.00	80.00
NNO	Kevin Owens	8.00	20.00
NNO	Sasha Banks	20.00	50.00
NNO	Shinsuke Nakamura	15.00	40.00
NNO	Sting	20.00	50.00

2017 Topps Heritage WWE Autographs Blue

STATED ODDS 1:93
STATED PRINT RUN 50 SER.#'d SETS

NNO	Undertaker	120.00	250.00

2017 Topps Heritage WWE Autographs Silver

NNO	Brock Lesnar	30.00	75.00

2017 Topps Heritage WWE Bizarre SummerSlam Matches

COMPLETE SET (10)		3.00	8.00
*P.P.BLACK/1: UNPRICED DUE TO SCARCITY			
*P.P.CYAN/1: UNPRICED DUE TO SCARCITY			
*P.P.MAGENTA/1: UNPRICED DUE TO SCARCITY			
*P.P.YELLOW/1: UNPRICED DUE TO SCARCITY			
STATED ODDS 1:3			
1	Big Boss Man	.40	1.00
2	Undertaker	1.25	3.00
3	Mankind	.75	2.00
4	British Bulldog	.30	.75
5	X-Pac	.30	.75
6	Ken Shamrock	.30	.75
7	Kane	.40	1.00
8	Ric Flair	.75	2.00
9	Bray Wyatt	.75	2.00
10	Rusev	.60	1.50

2017 Topps Heritage WWE Commemorative Patches

*BRONZE/99: .5X TO 1.2X BASIC MEM
*BLUE/50: .6X TO 1.5X BASIC MEM
*SILVER/25: .75X TO 2X BASIC MEM
*GOLD/10: UNPRICED DUE TO SCARCITY
*RED/1: UNPRICED DUE TO SCARCITY
*P.P.BLACK/1: UNPRICED DUE TO SCARCITY
*P.P.CYAN/1: UNPRICED DUE TO SCARCITY
*P.P.MAGENTA/1: UNPRICED DUE TO SCARCITY
*P.P.YELLOW/1: UNPRICED DUE TO SCARCITY
STATED ODDS 1:115

NNO	AJ Styles	6.00	15.00
NNO	Asuka	4.00	10.00
NNO	Bobby Roode	3.00	8.00
NNO	Charlotte Flair	5.00	12.00
NNO	Chris Jericho	3.00	8.00
NNO	Dean Ambrose	4.00	10.00
NNO	Dolph Ziggler	2.00	5.00
NNO	Ember Moon	3.00	8.00
NNO	Eric Young	2.50	6.00
NNO	Hideo Itami	2.00	5.00
NNO	John Cena	6.00	15.00
NNO	Kevin Owens	3.00	8.00
NNO	The Miz	2.50	6.00
NNO	Ric Flair	3.00	8.00
NNO	Roman Reigns	4.00	10.00
NNO	Rowdy Roddy Piper	2.50	6.00
NNO	Seth Rollins	4.00	10.00

NNO	Shawn Michaels	3.00	8.00
NNO	Sting	4.00	10.00
NNO	Trish Stratus	5.00	12.00

2017 Topps Heritage WWE Dual Autographs

STATED ODDS 1:2,264
STATED PRINT RUN 10 SER.#'d SETS
RANDOMLY INSERTED INTO PACKS

NNO	Big E/K.Kingston/10	30.00	75.00
NNO	B.Sammartino/L.Zbyszko/9	100.00	200.00
NNO	J.Lawler/M.Cole/10	50.00	100.00
NNO	Primo/Epico/10	25.00	60.00
NNO	S.Rollins/R.Reigns/10	60.00	120.00

2017 Topps Heritage WWE Kiss

*GOLD/10: UNPRICED DUE TO SCARCITY
*RED/1: UNPRICED DUE TO SCARCITY
STATED ODDS 1:685

NNO	Alexa Bliss	150.00	300.00
NNO	Asuka	25.00	60.00
NNO	Carmella	60.00	120.00
NNO	Charlotte Flair	100.00	200.00
NNO	Dana Brooke	30.00	75.00
NNO	Ember Moon	20.00	50.00
NNO	Liv Morgan	75.00	150.00

2017 Topps Heritage WWE Kiss Autographs

*GOLD/10: UNPRICED DUE TO SCARCITY
*RED/1: UNPRICED DUE TO SCARCITY
STATED ODDS 1:2,717

NNO	Alexa Bliss	500.00	1000.00
NNO	Asuka	75.00	150.00
NNO	Carmella	60.00	120.00
NNO	Charlotte Flair	60.00	120.00
NNO	Dana Brooke	75.00	150.00
NNO	Ember Moon	50.00	100.00
NNO	Liv Morgan	50.00	100.00

2017 Topps Heritage WWE NXT TakeOver Toronto 2016 Mat Relics

*BRONZE/99: .5X TO 1.2X BASIC MEM
*BLUE/50: .6X TO 1.5X BASIC MEM
*SILVER/25: .75X TO 2X BASIC MEM
*GOLD/10: UNPRICED DUE TO SCARCITY
*RED/1: UNPRICED DUE TO SCARCITY
*P.P.BLACK/1: UNPRICED DUE TO SCARCITY
*P.P.CYAN/1: UNPRICED DUE TO SCARCITY
*P.P.MAGENTA/1: UNPRICED DUE TO SCARCITY
*P.P.YELLOW/1: UNPRICED DUE TO SCARCITY
RANDOMLY INSERTED INTO PACKS

NNO	Akam	1.50	4.00
NNO	Asuka	5.00	12.00
NNO	Bobby Roode	4.00	10.00
NNO	Johnny Gargano	1.50	4.00
NNO	Mickie James	2.50	6.00
NNO	Rezar	1.50	4.00
NNO	Samoa Joe	5.00	12.00
NNO	Shinsuke Nakamura	4.00	10.00
NNO	Tommaso Ciampa	1.50	4.00
NNO	Tye Dillinger	1.50	4.00

2017 Topps Heritage WWE Roster Updates

COMPLETE SET (10) 12.00 30.00
*P.P.BLACK/1: UNPRICED DUE TO SCARCITY

*P.P.CYAN/1: UNPRICED DUE TO SCARCITY
*P.P.MAGENTA/1: UNPRICED DUE TO SCARCITY
*P.P.YELLOW/1: UNPRICED DUE TO SCARCITY
RANDOMLY INSERTED INTO PACKS

R1	Alexander Wolfe	2.00	5.00
R2	Kassius Ohno	1.50	4.00
R3	Nikki Cross	3.00	8.00
R4	Roderick Strong	2.00	5.00
R5	Tye Dillinger	1.50	4.00
R6	Cedric Alexander	2.50	6.00
R7	Gentleman Jack Gallagher	3.00	8.00
R8	Neville	2.50	6.00
R9	Rich Swann	1.50	4.00
R10	TJ Perkins	1.50	4.00

2017 Topps Heritage WWE Shirt Relics

*BLUE/50: .5X TO 1.2X BASIC MEM
*SILVER/25: .6X TO 1.5X BASIC MEM
*GOLD/10: UNPRICED DUE TO SCARCITY
*RED/1: UNPRICED DUE TO SCARCITY

RC	Carmella	5.00	12.00
RN	Naomi	4.00	10.00
RS	Sheamus	4.00	10.00
RAA	Andrade Cien Almas	2.00	5.00
RAC	Apollo Crews	2.50	6.00
RAE	Aiden English	2.00	5.00
RAF	Alicia Fox	3.00	8.00
RBK	Becky Lynch	6.00	15.00
RBL	Brock Lesnar	10.00	25.00
RBR	Bobby Roode	5.00	12.00
RCA	Curtis Axel	2.00	5.00
RCF	Charlotte Flair	8.00	20.00
RDY	Darren Young	2.00	5.00
RHI	Hideo Itami	3.00	8.00
RJC	John Cena	10.00	25.00
RJG	Johnny Gargano	2.00	5.00
RJJ	JoJo	3.00	8.00
RKA	Karl Anderson	2.00	5.00
RLH	Luke Harper	2.00	5.00
RNJ	No Way Jose	2.00	5.00
RNN	Natalya	4.00	10.00
RRO	Randy Orton	5.00	12.00
RSB	Sasha Banks	6.00	15.00
RSN	Shinsuke Nakamura	5.00	12.00
RSR	Seth Rollins	6.00	15.00
RSU	Summer Rae	5.00	12.00
RTC	Tommaso Ciampa	2.00	5.00
RZR	Zack Ryder	2.00	5.00

2017 Topps Heritage WWE SummerSlam All-Stars

COMPLETE SET (30) 6.00 15.00
*P.P.BLACK/1: UNPRICED DUE TO SCARCITY
*P.P.CYAN/1: UNPRICED DUE TO SCARCITY
*P.P.MAGENTA/1: UNPRICED DUE TO SCARCITY
*P.P.YELLOW/1: UNPRICED DUE TO SCARCITY
STATED ODDS 1:1

1	Undertaker	1.50	4.00
2	Edge	1.00	2.50
3	Triple H	1.00	2.50
4	Bret Hit Man Hart	.75	2.00
5	Shawn Michaels	1.00	2.50
6	Randy Orton	1.00	2.50
7	Kane	.50	1.25
8	Ultimate Warrior	.75	2.00
9	Rob Van Dam	.75	2.00

10	Brock Lesnar	2.00	5.00
11	Big Show	.50	1.25
12	Chris Jericho	1.00	2.50
13	Kurt Angle	.75	2.00
14	John Cena	2.00	5.00
15	Tatanka	.40	1.00
16	Jerry The King Lawler	.50	1.25
17	Earthquake	.40	1.00
18	Irwin R. Schyster	.40	1.00
19	British Bulldog	.30	.75
20	Stone Cold Steve Austin	1.50	4.00
21	Daniel Bryan	1.50	4.00
22	Mick Foley	1.00	2.50
23	The Rock	1.50	4.00
24	Sheamus	.75	2.00
25	Kofi Kingston	.50	1.25
26	X-Pac	.40	1.00
27	Dolph Ziggler	.60	1.50
28	Ric Flair	1.00	2.50
29	Texas Tornado	.40	1.00
30	Typhoon	.40	1.00

2017 Topps Heritage WWE Survivor Series 2016 Mat Relics

*BRONZE/99: .5X TO 1.2X BASIC MEM
*BLUE/50: .6X TO 1.5X BASIC MEM
*SILVER/25: .75X TO 2X BASIC MEM
*GOLD/10: UNPRICED DUE TO SCARCITY
*RED/1: UNPRICED DUE TO SCARCITY
*P.P.BLACK/1: UNPRICED DUE TO SCARCITY
*P.P.CYAN/1: UNPRICED DUE TO SCARCITY
*P.P.MAGENTA/1: UNPRICED DUE TO SCARCITY
*P.P.YELLOW/1: UNPRICED DUE TO SCARCITY
STATED ODDS 1:175

NNO	AJ Styles	6.00	15.00
NNO	Alexa Bliss	15.00	40.00
NNO	Alicia Fox	5.00	12.00
NNO	Bayley	6.00	15.00
NNO	Becky Lynch	6.00	15.00
NNO	Braun Strowman	5.00	12.00
NNO	Bray Wyatt	6.00	15.00
NNO	Brock Lesnar	8.00	20.00
NNO	Carmella	5.00	12.00
NNO	Charlotte Flair	6.00	15.00
NNO	Chris Jericho	6.00	15.00
NNO	Dean Ambrose	4.00	10.00
NNO	Goldberg	6.00	15.00
NNO	Kevin Owens	6.00	15.00
NNO	Natalya	4.00	10.00
NNO	Randy Orton	5.00	12.00
NNO	Roman Reigns	5.00	12.00
NNO	Sasha Banks	8.00	20.00
NNO	Seth Rollins	5.00	12.00
NNO	Shane McMahon	6.00	15.00

2018 Topps Heritage WWE

COMPLETE SET W/O SP (110) 10.00 25.00
UNOPENED BOX (24 PACKS)
UNOPENED PACK (6 CARDS)
*BRONZE: .6X TO 1.5X BASIC CARDS
*BLUE/99: .75X TO 2X BASIC CARDS
*SILVER/25: 2X TO 5X BASIC CARDS
*GOLD/10: UNPRICED DUE TO SCARCITY
*RED/1: UNPRICED DUE TO SCARCITY
*P.P.BLACK/1: UNPRICED DUE TO SCARCITY
*P.P.CYAN/1: UNPRICED DUE TO SCARCITY
*P.P.MAGENTA/1: UNPRICED DUE TO SCARCITY
*P.P.YELLOW/1: UNPRICED DUE TO SCARCITY

1	AJ Styles	1.00	2.50
2	Akira Tozawa	.40	1.00
3	Alexa Bliss	1.25	3.00
4	Alicia Fox	.40	1.00
5	Apollo Crews	.25	.60
6	Ariya Daivari	.25	.60
7	Asuka	.75	2.00
8	Baron Corbin	.40	1.00
9	Bayley	.40	1.00
10	Becky Lynch	.60	1.50
11	Big Cass	.30	.75
12	Big E	.30	.75
13	Big Show	.25	.60
14	Bobby Roode	.40	1.00
15	Braun Strowman	.60	1.50
16	Bray Wyatt	.60	1.50
17	Brie Bella	.50	1.25
18	Carmella	.50	1.25
19	Cedric Alexander	.25	.60
20	Cesaro	.50	1.25
21	Chad Gable	.25	.60
22	Charlotte Flair	.75	2.00
23	Chris Jericho	.60	1.50
24	Dean Ambrose	.50	1.25
25	Drew Gulak	.25	.60
26	Elias	.60	1.50
27	Fandango	.25	.60
28	Finn Balor	.60	1.50
29	Gentleman Jack Gallagher	.30	.75
30	Goldust	.50	1.25
31	Jason Jordan	.25	.60
32	Jeff Hardy	.50	1.25
33	Jey Uso	.25	.60
34	Jimmy Uso	.25	.60
35	Jinder Mahal	.30	.75
36	John Cena	1.00	2.50
37	Kalisto	.25	.60
38	Kane	.40	1.00
39	Karl Anderson	.25	.60
40	Kevin Owens	.60	1.50
41	Kofi Kingston	.30	.75
42	Kurt Angle	.60	1.50
43	Lana	.60	1.50
44	Liv Morgan	.50	1.25
45	Luke Gallows	.30	.75
46	Mandy Rose	.60	1.50
47	Maria Kanellis	.60	1.50
48	Maryse	.50	1.25
49	Woken Matt Hardy	.60	1.50
50	Mickie James	.50	1.25
51	Mojo Rawley	.25	.60
52	Mustafa Ali	.25	.60
53	Naomi	.30	.75
54	Natalya	.30	.75
55	Nia Jax	.40	1.00
56	Nikki Bella	.50	1.25
57	Noam Dar	.25	.60
58	Paige	.60	1.50
59	Pete Dunne	.25	.60
60	R-Truth	.30	.75
61	Randy Orton	.60	1.50
62	Rhyno	.25	.60
63	Roman Reigns	.60	1.50
64	Ruby Riott	.40	1.00
65	Rusev	.40	1.00
66	Sami Zayn	.25	.60
67	Samoa Joe	.50	1.25
68	Sarah Logan	.25	.60
69	Sasha Banks	.75	2.00
70	Seth Rollins	.60	1.50

71	Shane McMahon	.50	1.25
72	Sheamus	.50	1.25
73	Shelton Benjamin	.30	.75
74	Shinsuke Nakamura	.60	1.50
75	Sin Cara	.30	.75
76	Sonya Deville	.50	1.25
77	Stephanie McMahon	.50	1.25
78	Tamina	.25	.60
79	The Brian Kendrick	.40	1.00
80	The Miz	.50	1.25
81	The Rock	1.25	3.00
82	Titus O'Neil	.25	.60
83	Tony Nese	.25	.60
84	Triple H	.60	1.50
85	Tye Dillinger	.25	.60
86	Tyler Bate	.25	.60
87	Tyler Breeze	.25	.60
88	Undertaker	1.00	2.50
89	Xavier Woods	.30	.75
90	Zack Ryder	.25	.60
91	Adam Cole	.30	.75
92	Aleister Black	.30	.75
93	Alexander Wolfe	.25	.60
94	Andrade Cien Almas	.40	1.00
95	Billie Kay	.50	1.25
96	Bobby Fish	.25	.60
97	Drew McIntyre	.40	1.00
98	Ember Moon	.50	1.25
99	Eric Young	.30	.75
100	Johnny Gargano	.25	.60
101	Kairi Sane	.60	1.50
102	Kassius Ohno	.25	.60
103	Killian Dain	.30	.75
104	Kyle O'Reilly	.30	.75
105	Nikki Cross	.40	1.00
106	Oney Lorcan	.30	.75
107	Peyton Royce	.60	1.50
108	Roderick Strong	.25	.60
109	Tommaso Ciampa	.25	.60
110	Velveteen Dream	.25	.60
111	Aiden English SP	1.25	3.00
112	Ariya Daivari SP	1.25	3.00
113	Dash Wilder SP	1.50	4.00
114	Harper SP	2.00	5.00
115	Konnor SP	1.25	3.00
116	R-Truth SP	1.50	4.00
117	Rowan SP	2.00	5.00
118	Scott Dawson SP	1.50	4.00
119	Viktor SP	1.25	3.00

2018 Topps Heritage WWE Autographed NXT TakeOver War Games 2017 Mat Relics

STATED PRINT RUN 10 SER.#'d SETS
UNPRICED DUE TO SCARCITY

NXTAAC	Adam Cole		
NXTABF	Bobby Fish		
NXTADM	Drew McIntyre		
NXTAEM	Ember Moon		
NXTAKD	Killian Dain		
NXTAKO	Kyle O'Reilly		
NXTARS	Roderick Strong		

2018 Topps Heritage WWE Autographed Survivor Series 2017 Mat Relics

STATED PRINT RUN 10 SER.#'d SETS
UNPRICED DUE TO SCARCITY

SSAAJ	AJ Styles		
SSAAS	Asuka		
SSABR	Booby Roode		
SSABS	Braun Strowman		
SSAKA	Kurt Angle		
SSANJ	Nia Jax		
SSARO	Randy Orton		
SSASB	Sasha Banks		
SSASJ	Samoa Joe		
SSASN	Shinsuke Nakamura		
SSATH	Triple H		

2018 Topps Heritage WWE Autographed TLC 2017 Mat Relics

STATED PRINT RUN 10 SER.#'d SETS
UNPRICED DUE TO SCARCITY

TLCAAJ	AJ Styles		
TLCABS	Braun Strowman		
TLCAKA	Kurt Angle		
TLCASH	Sheamus		
TLCATM	The Miz		

2018 Topps Heritage WWE Autographed TLC Commemorative Medallion Relics

STATED PRINT RUN 10 SER.#'d SETS
UNPRICED DUE TO SCARCITY

CTMAAJ	AJ Styles		
CTMABC	Baron Corbin		
CTMABS	Braun Strowman		
CTMADZ	Dolph Ziggler		
CTMAKA	Kane		
CTMAKA	Kurt Angle		
CTMAMZ	The Miz		
CTMASA	Sheamus		
CTMASH	Sheamus		
CTMATM	The Miz		

2018 Topps Heritage WWE Autographs

*BLUE/50: .5X TO 1.2X BASIC AUTOS
*SILVER/25: .6X TO 1.5X BASIC AUTOS
*GOLD/10: UNPRICED DUE TO SCARCITY
*RED/1: UNPRICED DUE TO SCARCITY
STATED PRINT RUN 99 SER.#'d SETS

AAB	Alexa Bliss	50.00	100.00
AAC	Adam Cole	15.00	40.00
AAS	AJ Styles	15.00	40.00
AAS	Asuka	12.00	30.00
ABA	Bayley	12.00	30.00
ABE	Big E	5.00	12.00
ABL	Becky Lynch	15.00	40.00
ABS	Braun Strowman	12.00	30.00
ACF	Charlotte Flair	15.00	40.00
AFB	Finn Balor	12.00	30.00
AJH	Jeff Hardy	12.00	30.00
AKA	Kurt Angle	10.00	25.00
AKK	Kofi Kingston	6.00	15.00
AKO	Kevin Owens	6.00	15.00
ALM	Liv Morgan	10.00	25.00
AMH	Matt Hardy	10.00	25.00
AMR	Mandy Rose	15.00	40.00
ASB	Sasha Banks	12.00	30.00
ASN	Shinsuke Nakamura	10.00	25.00
AXW	Xavier Woods	5.00	12.00
AALB	Aleister Black	6.00	15.00

2018 Topps Heritage WWE Autographs Silver

ACA	Carmella	12.00	30.00
ASM	Stephanie McMahon	75.00	150.00
ATH	Triple H	150.00	300.00
AUN	Undertaker	125.00	250.00

2018 Topps Heritage WWE Big Legends

COMPLETE SET (50)		12.00	30.00
*BRONZE/99: .75X TO 2X BASIC CARDS			
*BLUE/50: 1.2X TO 3X BASIC CARDS			
*SILVER/25: 1.5X TO 4X BASIC CARDS			
*GOLD/10: UNPRICED DUE TO SCARCITY			
*RED/1: UNPRICED DUE TO SCARCITY			
*P.P.BLACK/1: UNPRICED DUE TO SCARCITY			
*P.P.CYAN/1: UNPRICED DUE TO SCARCITY			
*P.P.MAGENTA/1: UNPRICED DUE TO SCARCITY			
*P.P.YELLOW/1: UNPRICED DUE TO SCARCITY			
STATED ODDS 2:1; 4:1 FAT PACK			
BL1	Alundra Blayze	.30	.75
BL2	Andre the Giant	.60	1.50
BL3	Bam Bam Bigelow	.50	1.25
BL4	Bob Backlund	.30	.75
BL5	Booker T	.50	1.25
BL6	Bret Hit Man Hart	.75	2.00
BL7	British Bulldog	.60	1.50
BL8	Bruno Sammartino	.50	1.25
BL9	Brutus The Barber Beefcake	.30	.75
BL10	Cowboy Bob Orton	.30	.75
BL11	Dean Malenko	.30	.75
BL12	Diamond Dallas Page	.50	1.25
BL13	Dusty Rhodes	.60	1.50
BL14	Eddie Guerrero	.75	2.00
BL15	Edge	.75	2.00
BL16	George The Animal Steele	.40	1.00
BL17	Greg The Hammer Valentine	.30	.75
BL18	Hacksaw Jim Duggan	.30	.75
BL19	Harley Race	.30	.75
BL20	The Honky Tonk Man	.30	.75
BL21	Iron Sheik	.30	.75
BL22	Irwin R. Schyster	.30	.75
BL23	Jake The Snake Roberts	.40	1.00
BL24	Jerry The King Lawler	.60	1.50
BL25	Jim The Anvil Neidhart	.50	1.25
BL26	Kerry Von Erich	.30	.75
BL27	Kevin Nash	.60	1.50
BL28	Kevin Von Erich	.50	1.25
BL29	Larry Zbyszko	.30	.75
BL30	Lex Luger	.40	1.00
BL31	Lita	.75	2.00
BL32	Macho Man Randy Savage	1.00	2.50
BL33	Michael P.S. Hayes	.30	.75
BL34	Mick Foley	.60	1.50
BL35	Million Dollar Man Ted DiBiase	.40	1.00
BL36	Mr. Perfect	.40	1.00
BL37	Mr. Wonderful Paul Orndorff	.30	.75
BL38	Nikolai Volkoff	.30	.75
BL39	Ravishing Rick Rude	.40	1.00
BL40	Ric Flair	1.00	2.50
BL41	Ricky The Dragon Steamboat	.50	1.25
BL42	Ron Simmons	.40	1.00
BL43	Rowdy Roddy Piper	.75	2.00
BL44	Scott Hall	.60	1.50
BL45	Sgt. Slaughter	.40	1.00
BL46	Sid Vicious	.30	.75
BL47	Sting	.75	2.00
BL48	Stone Cold Steve Austin	1.50	4.00
BL49	Trish Stratus	1.25	3.00
BL50	Ultimate Warrior	1.25	3.00

2018 Topps Heritage WWE Big Legends Autographs

*SILVER/25: UNPRICED DUE TO SCARCITY
*GOLD/10: UNPRICED DUE TO SCARCITY
*RED/1: UNPRICED DUE TO SCARCITY

BLAAB	Alundra Blayze	6.00	15.00
BLABB	Brutus The Barber Beefcake	6.00	15.00
BLABH	Bret Hit Man Hart	25.00	60.00
BLAIS	Irwin R. Schyster	10.00	25.00
BLAJD	Hacksaw Jim Duggan	8.00	20.00
BLAJR	Jake The Snake Roberts	15.00	40.00
BLAST	Sting	25.00	60.00
BLATD	Million Dollar Man Ted DiBiase	12.00	30.00
BLATS	Trish Stratus	30.00	75.00
BLADDP	Diamond Dallas Page	10.00	25.00

2018 Topps Heritage WWE Dual Autographs

STATED PRINT RUN 10 SER.#'d SETS
UNPRICED DUE TO SCARCITY

DACC	Epico/Primo/9		
DAKR	B.Kay/P.Royce/10		
DALC	M.Cole/J.Lawler/10		
DATM	S.McMahon/Triple H/10		
DAUT	Triple H/Undertaker/10		

2018 Topps Heritage WWE Kiss

*GOLD/10: UNPRICED DUE TO SCARCITY
*RED/1: UNPRICED DUE TO SCARCITY

KCAB	Alexa Bliss	60.00	120.00
KCAF	Alicia Fox	15.00	40.00
KCAS	Asuka	30.00	75.00
KCCC	Charly Caruso	50.00	100.00
KCDB	Dana Brooke	20.00	50.00
KCDF	Dasha Fuentes	15.00	40.00
KCMR	Mandy Rose	50.00	100.00
KCNA	Natalya	15.00	40.00
KCNA	Naomi	15.00	40.00
KCRY	Renee Young	20.00	50.00

2018 Topps Heritage WWE Kiss Autographs

*GOLD/10: UNPRICED DUE TO SCARCITY
*RED/1: UNPRICED DUE TO SCARCITY
STATED PRINT RUN 25 SER.#'d SETS

KAAB	Alexa Bliss	150.00	300.00
KAAF	Alicia Fox	50.00	100.00
KAAS	Asuka	60.00	120.00
KACC	Charly Caruso	30.00	75.00
KADB	Dana Brooke	50.00	100.00
KADF	Dasha Fuentes	30.00	75.00
KAMR	Mandy Rose	75.00	150.00
KANA	Natalya	25.00	60.00
KARY	Renee Young	30.00	75.00

2018 Topps Heritage WWE Manufactured Coins

1	John Cena	8.00	20.00
2	Brock Lesnar	6.00	15.00
3	AJ Styles	5.00	12.00
4	Roman Reigns	5.00	12.00
5	Seth Rollins	5.00	12.00
6	Dean Ambrose	4.00	10.00

7 Braun Strowman	4.00	10.00
8 Samoa Joe	4.00	10.00
9 Shinsuke Nakamura	5.00	12.00
10 Kevin Owens	4.00	10.00

2018 Topps Heritage WWE NXT TakeOver War Games 2017 Mat Relics

*BRONZE/99: .5X TO 1.2X BASIC MEM
*BLUE/50: .6X TO 1.5X BASIC MEM
*SILVER/25: .75X TO 2X BASIC MEM
*GOLD/10: UNPRICED DUE TO SCARCITY
*RED/1: UNPRICED DUE TO SCARCITY
STATED PRINT RUN 299 SER.#'d SETS

NXTAA Andrade Cien Almas	2.50	6.00
NXTAC Adam Cole	8.00	20.00
NXTAW Alexander Wolfe	2.50	6.00
NXTBF Bobby Fish	4.00	10.00
NXTDM Drew McIntyre	2.50	6.00
NXTEM Ember Moon	3.00	8.00
NXTEY Eric Young	3.00	8.00
NXTKD Killian Dain	3.00	8.00
NXTKO Kyle O'Reilly	3.00	8.00
NXTRS Roderick Strong	2.50	6.00

2018 Topps Heritage WWE Shirt Relics

*BLUE/50: .5X TO 1.2X BASIC MEM
*SILVER/25: .6X TO 1.5X BASIC MEM
*GOLD/10: UNPRICED DUE TO SCARCITY
*RED/1: UNPRICED DUE TO SCARCITY
STATED PRINT RUN 99 SER.#'d SETS

SRAB Alexa Bliss	12.00	30.00
SRAE Aiden English	4.00	10.00
SRAF Alicia Fox	3.00	8.00
SRAK Akam	3.00	8.00
SRAW Alexander Wolfe	3.00	8.00
SRBE Becky Lynch	5.00	12.00
SRBL Brock Lesnar	6.00	15.00
SRCA Carmella	5.00	12.00
SRDW Dash Wilder	3.00	8.00
SREM Ember Moon	5.00	12.00
SREY Eric Young	3.00	8.00
SRGD Goldust	3.00	8.00
SRJC John Cena	6.00	15.00
SRJJ JoJo	5.00	12.00
SRNC Nikki Cross	5.00	12.00
SRRE Rezar	3.00	8.00
SRRR Roman Reigns	8.00	20.00
SRRY Renee Young	5.00	12.00
SRSD Scott Dawson	3.00	8.00
SRSR Seth Rollins	5.00	12.00

2018 Topps Heritage WWE Survivor Series 2017 Mat Relics

*BRONZE/99: .5X TO 1.2X BASIC MEM
*BLUE/50: .6X TO 1.5X BASIC MEM
*SILVER/25: .75X TO 2X BASIC MEM
*GOLD/10: UNPRICED DUE TO SCARCITY
*RED/1: UNPRICED DUE TO SCARCITY
STATED PRINT RUN 299 SER.#'d SETS

SSAB Alexa Bliss	10.00	25.00
SSAJ AJ Styles	3.00	8.00
SSAS Asuka	5.00	12.00
SSBA Bayley	3.00	8.00
SSBL Brock Lesnar	4.00	10.00
SSBR Bobby Roode	3.00	8.00
SSBS Braun Strowman	4.00	10.00

SSCF Charlotte Flair	5.00	12.00
SSDA Dean Ambrose	2.50	6.00
SSFB Finn Balor	3.00	8.00
SSJC John Cena	4.00	10.00
SSKA Kurt Angle	2.50	6.00
SSNJ Nia Jax	2.50	6.00
SSRO Randy Orton	2.50	6.00
SSRR Roman Reigns	3.00	8.00
SSSB Sasha Banks	6.00	15.00
SSSJ Samoa Joe	4.00	10.00
SSSN Shinsuke Nakamura	3.00	8.00
SSSR Seth Rollins	3.00	8.00
SSTH Triple H	4.00	10.00

2018 Topps Heritage WWE Tag Teams and Stables

COMPLETE SET (20)	6.00	15.00

*BRONZE/99: .5X TO 1.2X BASIC CARDS
*BLUE/50: .6X TO 1.5X BASIC CARDS
*SILVER/25: 1.2X TO 3X BASIC CARDS
*GOLD/10: UNPRICED DUE TO SCARCITY
*RED/1: UNPRICED DUE TO SCARCITY
STATED ODDS 1:2; 2:1 FAT PACK

TT1 Cesaro & Sheamus	.75	2.00
TT2 The Shield	1.00	2.50
TT3 The Hardy Boyz	1.00	2.50
TT4 Heath Slater & Rhyno	.40	1.00
TT5 Luke Gallows & Karl Anderson	.50	1.25
TT6 The Miz & The Miztourage	.75	2.00
TT7 The Revival	.50	1.25
TT8 Bludgeon Brothers	.60	1.50
TT9 Breezango	.40	1.00
TT10 Shelton Benjamin & Chad Gable	.50	1.25
TT11 Kevin Owens & Sami Zayn	1.00	2.50
TT12 The Hype Bros	.40	1.00
TT13 Jinder Mahal & The Singh Brothers	.50	1.25
TT14 The New Day	.60	1.50
TT15 The Authors of Pain	.40	1.00
TT16 Heavy Machinery	.40	1.00
TT17 The IIconics	1.00	2.50
TT18 SAnitY	.60	1.50
TT19 The Street Profits	.40	1.00
TT20 Undisputed ERA	.50	1.25

2018 Topps Heritage WWE TLC 2017 Mat Relics

*BRONZE/99: .5X TO 1.2X BASIC MEM
*BLUE/50: .6X TO 1.5X BASIC MEM
*SILVER/25: .75X TO 2X BASIC MEM
*GOLD/10: UNPRICED DUE TO SCARCITY
*RED/1: UNPRICED DUE TO SCARCITY
STATED PRINT RUN 299 SER.#'d SETS

TLCAJ AJ Styles	4.00	10.00
TLCBS Braun Strowman	2.00	5.00
TLCCE Cesaro	2.00	5.00
TLCDA Dean Ambrose	3.00	8.00
TLCFB Finn Balor	4.00	10.00
TLCKA Kurt Angle	4.00	10.00
TLCKN Kane	3.00	8.00
TLCSH Sheamus	2.00	5.00
TLCSR Seth Rollins	5.00	12.00
TLCTM The Miz	2.00	5.00

2018 Topps Heritage WWE TLC Commemorative Medallion Relics

*BRONZE/99: .5X TO 1.2X BASIC MEM
*BLUE/50: .6X TO 1.5X BASIC MEM
*SILVER/25: .75X TO 2X BASIC MEM

*GOLD/10: UNPRICED DUE TO SCARCITY
*RED/1: UNPRICED DUE TO SCARCITY
STATED PRINT RUN 199 SER.#'d SETS

CTMAB Alexa Bliss	10.00	25.00
CTMAJ AJ Styles	5.00	12.00
CTMBC Baron Corbin	4.00	10.00
CTMBL Becky Lynch	6.00	15.00
CTMBS Braun Strowman	5.00	12.00
CTMCE Cesaro	3.00	8.00
CTMDA Dean Ambrose	3.00	8.00
CTMDE Dean Ambrose	3.00	8.00
CTMDZ Dolph Ziggler	3.00	8.00
CTMJC John Cena	5.00	12.00
CTMKA Kurt Angle	3.00	8.00
CTMKA Kane	3.00	8.00
CTMKL Kalisto	3.00	8.00
CTMMZ The Miz	3.00	8.00
CTMRL Seth Rollins	4.00	10.00
CTMRR Roman Reigns	5.00	12.00
CTMSA Sheamus	3.00	8.00
CTMSH Sheamus	3.00	8.00
CTMSR Seth Rollins	3.00	8.00
CTMTM The Miz	3.00	8.00

2018 Topps Heritage WWE Top 10 Rookies

COMPLETE SET (10)	4.00	10.00

*BRONZE/99: .5X TO 1.2X BASIC CARDS
*BLUE/50: .6X TO 1.5X BASIC CARDS
*SILVER/25: .75X TO 2X BASIC CARDS
*GOLD/10: UNPRICED DUE TO SCARCITY
*RED/1: UNPRICED DUE TO SCARCITY
*P.P.BLACK/1: UNPRICED DUE TO SCARCITY
*P.P.CYAN/1: UNPRICED DUE TO SCARCITY
*P.P.MAGENTA/1: UNPRICED DUE TO SCARCITY
*P.P.YELLOW/1: UNPRICED DUE TO SCARCITY
STATED ODDS 1:3; 1:1 FAT PACK

TR1 Asuka	1.25	3.00
TR2 Shinsuke Nakamura	1.00	2.50
TR3 Bobby Roode	.60	1.50
TR4 Samoa Joe	.75	2.00
TR5 Tyler Bate	.40	1.00
TR6 Pete Dunne	.40	1.00
TR7 Dash Wilder	.50	1.25
TR8 Scott Dawson	.50	1.25
TR9 Elias	1.00	2.50
TR10 Tye Dillinger	.40	1.00

2018 Topps Heritage WWE Top 10 Rookies Autographs

*SILVER/25: .5X TO 1.2X BASIC AUTOS
*GOLD/10: UNPRICED DUE TO SCARCITY
*RED/1: UNPRICED DUE TO SCARCITY
STATED PRINT RUN 50 SER.#'d SETS

TTRAAS Asuka	15.00	40.00
TTRABR Bobby Roode	10.00	25.00
TTRADW Dash Wilder	5.00	12.00
TTRAEL Elias	25.00	60.00
TTRASD Scott Dawson	5.00	12.00
TTRASJ Samoa Joe	10.00	25.00
TTRASN Shinsuke Nakamura	12.00	30.00
TTRATD Tye Dillinger	6.00	15.00

2018 Topps Heritage WWE Triple Mat Relics

*SILVER/25: .5X TO 1.2X BASIC MEM
*GOLD/10: UNPRICED DUE TO SCARCITY

*RED/1: UNPRICED DUE TO SCARCITY
STATED PRINT RUN 50 SER.#'d SETS

TMBL Brock Lesnar	8.00	20.00
TMCF Charlotte Flair	12.00	30.00
TMDA Dean Ambrose	10.00	25.00
TMJC John Cena	10.00	25.00
TMKO Kevin Owens	8.00	20.00
TMTH Triple H	8.00	20.00
TMTM The Miz	8.00	20.00
TMUD Undertaker	15.00	40.00

2021 Topps Heritage WWE

COMPLETE SET (100)	10.00	25.00

*FOIL: .6X TO 1.5X BASIC CARDS
*GREEN/99: .75X TO 2X BASIC CARDS
*BLUE/25: 1.5X TO 4X BASIC CARDS
*RED/10: UNPRICED DUE TO SCARCITY
*FOILFRACTOR/1: UNPRICED DUE TO SCARCITY

1 AJ Styles	1.00	2.50
2 Akira Tozawa	.40	1.00
3 Alexa Bliss	2.00	5.00
4 Angel Garza	.40	1.00
5 Asuka	1.25	3.00
6 Bobby Lashley	.75	2.00
7 Cedric Alexander	.30	.75
8 Charlotte Flair	1.50	4.00
8 Charlotte Flair SP (peacock)	30.00	75.00
9 Damian Priest	.50	1.25
10 Dana Brooke	.30	.75
11 Drew McIntyre	.75	2.00
12 Doudrop	.50	1.25
13 Elias	.30	.75
14 Erik	.30	.75
15 Eva Marie	.75	2.00
16 Gran Metalik	.30	.75
17 Humberto Carrillo	.30	.75
18 Ivar	.30	.75
19 Jeff Hardy	.75	2.00
20 John Morrison	.60	1.50
21 Keith Lee	.60	1.50
22 Kofi Kingston	.75	2.00
23 Lacey Evans	1.25	3.00
24 Lince Dorado	.30	.75
25 MACE	.30	.75
26 Mandy Rose	1.50	4.00
26 Mandy Rose SP (roses)	30.00	75.00
27 Mustafa Ali	.40	1.00
28 MVP	.30	.75
29 Naomi	.40	1.00
30 Nia Jax	.60	1.50
31 Nikki ASH	.60	1.50
32 Omos	.30	.75
33 Randy Orton	1.00	2.50
33 Randy Orton SP (viper)	15.00	40.00
34 Rhea Ripley	1.25	3.00
35 Ricochet	.50	1.25
36 Riddick Moss	.40	1.00
37 Riddle	.75	2.00
38 R-Truth	.40	1.00
39 Shayna Baszler	.75	2.00
40 Sheamus	.50	1.25
40 Sheamus SP (great white shark)	12.00	30.00
41 Shelton Benjamin	.50	1.25
42 T-BAR	.40	1.00

43	The Fiend Bray Wyatt	1.25	3.00
44	The Miz	.50	1.25
45	Titus O'Neil	.30	.75
46	Xavier Woods	.30	.75
47	Angelo Dawkins	.40	1.00
48	Apollo Crews	.40	1.00
49	Baron Corbin	.30	.75
49	Baron Corbin SP (wolf)	8.00	20.00
50	Bayley	.75	2.00
51	Bianca Belair	.75	2.00
52	Big E	.75	2.00
53	Carmella	.75	2.00
54	Cesaro	.30	.75
55	Chad Gable	.30	.75
56	Commander Azeez	.40	1.00
57	Dolph Ziggler	.60	1.50
58	Dominik Mysterio	.40	1.00
59	Edge	1.25	3.00
60	Jey Uso	.30	.75
61	Jimmy Uso	.30	.75
62	Kevin Owens	.60	1.50
63	Liv Morgan	1.25	3.00
64	Mia Yim	.40	1.00
65	Montez Ford	.30	.75
66	Natalya	.50	1.25
67	Otis	.40	1.00
67	Otis SP (worm)	15.00	40.00
68	Rey Mysterio	.75	2.00
69	Robert Roode	.40	1.00
70	Roman Reigns	1.50	4.00
70	Roman Reigns SP (dog)	30.00	75.00
71	Sami Zayn	.50	1.25
72	Sasha Banks	1.50	4.00
72	Sasha Banks SP (stacks of cash)	25.00	60.00
73	Seth Rollins	.75	2.00
74	Shinsuke Nakamura	.75	2.00
74	Shinsuke Nakamura SP (king's crown)	10.00	25.00
75	Tamina	.30	.75
76	Zelina Vega	.60	1.50
77	Adam Cole	1.00	2.50
78	Boa	.30	.75
79	Cameron Grimes	.60	1.50
80	Candice LeRae	1.25	3.00
81	Dakota Kai	.60	1.50
82	Ember Moon	.40	1.00
83	Finn Balor	.75	2.00
84	Io Shirai	.60	1.50
85	Indi Hartwell	1.00	2.50
86	Johnny Gargano	.60	1.50
87	Karrion Kross	1.25	3.00
88	Kushida	.50	1.25
89	Kyle O'Reilly	.50	1.25
90	Santos Escobar	.60	1.50
91	Samoa Joe	.60	1.50
92	Scarlett	1.50	4.00
93	Shotzi	1.50	4.00
94	Timothy Thatcher	.30	.75
95	Tommaso Ciampa	.75	2.00
96	Toni Storm	1.25	3.00
97	Xia Li	.60	1.50
98	Becky Lynch	1.25	3.00
99	John Cena	1.50	4.00
100	Triple H	1.00	2.50

2021 Topps Heritage WWE Allen and Ginter

COMPLETE SET (30)		12.00	30.00
RANDOMLY INSERTED INTO PACKS			
AG1	AJ Styles	1.00	2.50
AG2	Alexa Bliss	2.00	5.00
AG3	Asuka	1.25	3.00
AG4	Bayley	.75	2.00
AG5	Becky Lynch	1.25	3.00
AG6	Big E	.75	2.00
AG7	Charlotte Flair	1.50	4.00
AG8	Diesel	.50	1.25
AG9	Drew McIntyre	.75	2.00
AG10	Eddie Guerrero	1.50	4.00
AG11	Kane	.50	1.25
AG12	Kevin Owens	.60	1.50
AG13	Mr. Perfect	1.00	2.50
AG14	Macho Man Randy Savage	2.00	5.00
AG15	Million Dollar Man Ted DiBiase	.60	1.50
AG16	Razor Ramon	.50	1.25
AG17	Rikishi	.40	1.00
AG18	Roman Reigns	1.50	4.00
AG19	Sasha Banks	1.50	4.00
AG20	Seth Rollins	.75	2.00
AG21	Shinsuke Nakamura	.75	2.00
AG22	Typhoon	.30	.75
AG23	Sycho Sid	.50	1.25
AG24	The 1-2-3 Kid	.40	1.00
AG25	The Fiend Bray Wyatt	1.25	3.00
AG26	The Miz	.50	1.25
AG27	The Rock	2.00	5.00
AG28	Ultimate Warrior	2.00	5.00
AG29	Vader	.50	1.25
AG30	The Godfather	.40	1.00

2021 Topps Heritage WWE Autographs

*GREEN/99: .5X TO 1.2X BASIC AUTOS
*PURPLE/50: .6X TO 1.5X BASIC AUTOS
*BLUE/25: 1.2X TO 3X BASIC AUTOS
*RED/10: UNPRICED DUE TO SCARCITY
*GOLD/1: UNPRICED DUE TO SCARCITY
STATED ODDS 1:264
STATED PRINT RUN 199 SER.#'d SETS

AS	Sasha Banks	60.00	120.00
AAB	Alexa Bliss	75.00	150.00
AAC	Apollo Crews	6.00	15.00
AAJ	AJ Styles	10.00	25.00
AAS	Asuka	15.00	40.00
ABE	Big E	6.00	15.00
ABL	Bobby Lashley	8.00	20.00
ACI	Tommaso Ciampa	6.00	15.00
ACM	Carmella	8.00	20.00
ACS	Cesaro	6.00	15.00
ADM	Drew McIntyre	8.00	20.00
ADZ	Dolph Ziggler	6.00	15.00
AEM	Ember Moon	5.00	12.00
AFB	Finn Balor	10.00	25.00
AIS	Io Shirai	10.00	25.00
AJC	John Cena		
AJM	John Morrison	8.00	20.00
AKA	Karrion Kross	10.00	25.00
AKO	Kevin Owens	6.00	15.00
AKU	Kushida	5.00	12.00
ALD	Lince Dorado	6.00	15.00
ALM	Liv Morgan	25.00	60.00
AMA	Mustafa Ali	5.00	12.00
ANJ	Nia Jax	5.00	12.00
ARH	Rhea Ripley	15.00	40.00
ART	R-Truth	5.00	12.00
ASB	Shayna Baszler	5.00	12.00
ASE	Santos Escobar	6.00	15.00
ASH	Shotzi Blackheart	25.00	60.00
ASL	Scarlett	20.00	50.00
ASN	Shinsuke Nakamura	8.00	20.00
ASR	Seth Rollins	10.00	25.00
ASZ	Sami Zayn	8.00	20.00
ATT	Timothy Thatcher	6.00	15.00
ABRO	Riddle	12.00	30.00
AJEY	Jey Uso	5.00	12.00
AKOR	Kyle O'Reilly	8.00	20.00
AMVP	MVP	5.00	12.00
AREY	Rey Mysterio	15.00	40.00

2021 Topps Heritage WWE Dual Autographs

*BLUE/25: .5X TO 1.2X BASIC AUTOS
*RED/10: UNPRICED DUE TO SCARCITY
*GOLD/1: UNPRICED DUE TO SCARCITY
STATED ODDS 1:3,796
STATED PRINT RUN 50 SER.#'d SETS

DAJB	S.Baszler/N.Jax	25.00	60.00
DAND	K.Kingston/X.Woods	20.00	50.00
DART	Mace/T-Bar	15.00	40.00
DASP	M.Ford/A.Dawkins	20.00	50.00
DAVR	Ivar/Erik	12.00	30.00
DAGYV	J.Drake/Z.Gibson	12.00	30.00
DALHP	G.Metalik/L.Dorado	20.00	50.00

2021 Topps Heritage WWE The Miz Superstar Tribute

COMPLETE SET (20)		6.00	15.00
STATED ODDS 1:3			
TM1	The Miz	.60	1.50
TM2	The Miz	.60	1.50
TM3	The Miz	.60	1.50
TM4	The Miz	.60	1.50
TM5	The Miz	.60	1.50
TM6	The Miz	.60	1.50
TM7	The Miz	.60	1.50
TM8	The Miz	.60	1.50
TM9	The Miz	.60	1.50
TM10	The Miz	.60	1.50
TM11	The Miz	.60	1.50
TM12	The Miz	.60	1.50
TM13	The Miz	.60	1.50
TM14	The Miz	.60	1.50
TM15	The Miz	.60	1.50
TM16	The Miz	.60	1.50
TM17	The Miz	.60	1.50
TM18	The Miz	.60	1.50
TM19	The Miz	.60	1.50
TM20	The Miz	.60	1.50

2021 Topps Heritage WWE The Miz Superstar Tribute Autographs

*RED/10: UNPRICED DUE TO SCARCITY
STATED ODDS 1:4,181
STATED PRINT RUN 25 SER.#'d SETS

AMZ6	The Miz	5.00	12.00
AMZ9	The Miz		
AMZ11	The Miz		
AMZ15	The Miz		
AMZ19	The Miz		

2021 Topps Heritage WWE Sketch Card Reproduction

COMPLETE SET (10)		
STATED ODDS 1:24		
SCR1	Eddie Guerrero	
SCR2	Edge	
SCR3	John Cena	
SCR4	Randy Orton	
SCR5	Triple H	
SCR6	Undertaker	
SCR7	Jeff Hardy	
SCR8	Kane	
SCR9	MVP	
SCR10	Rey Mysterio	

2021 Topps Heritage WWE Superstar Stickers

COMPLETE SET (18)		12.00	30.00
STATED ODDS 1:4			
S1	AJ Styles	1.25	3.00
S2	Alexa Bliss	2.50	6.00
S3	Bayley	1.00	2.50
S4	Becky Lynch	1.50	4.00
S5	Charlotte Flair	2.00	5.00
S6	D-Generation X	1.50	4.00
S7	Finn Balor	1.00	2.50
S8	Jeff Hardy	1.00	2.50
S9	John Cena	2.00	5.00
S10	Randy Orton	1.25	3.00
S11	Asuka	1.50	4.00
S12	Rey Mysterio	1.00	2.50
S13	Roman Reigns	2.00	5.00
S14	Sasha Banks	2.00	5.00
S15	Seth Rollins	1.00	2.50
S16	Shinsuke Nakamura	1.00	2.50
S17	The Miz	.60	1.50
S18	The New Day	1.00	2.50

2021 Topps Heritage WWE Superstars Speak

COMPLETE SET (10)		8.00	20.00
STATED ODDS 1:12			
SS1	Batista	.75	2.00
SS2	Booker T	.75	2.00
SS3	Goldberg	1.50	4.00
SS4	John Cena	2.00	5.00
SS5	Macho Man Randy Savage	2.50	6.00
SS6	Ric Flair	1.50	4.00
SS7	The Fiend Bray Wyatt	1.50	4.00
SS8	The Miz	.60	1.50
SS9	Undertaker	2.00	5.00
SS10	Ron Simmons	.60	1.50

2011 Topps Jim Ross JR's BarBQ Sauce Autograph Exclusive

NNO	Jim Ross	

2017 Topps Legends of WWE

COMPLETE SET (100)   8.00   20.00
UNOPENED BOX (12 PACKS)
UNOPENED PACK (5 CARDS)
*BRONZE: .6X TO 1.5X BASIC CARDS
*SILVER/99: .75X TO 2X BASIC CARDS
*BLUE/50: 1.2X TO 3X BASIC CARDS
*GOLD/10: UNPRICED DUE TO SCARCITY
*RED/1: UNPRICED DUE TO SCARCITY

1	Brock Lesnar	1.25	3.00
2	Goldberg	1.00	2.50
3	The Rock	1.25	3.00
4	Hunter Hearst Helmsley	.60	1.50
5	Undertaker	1.00	2.50
6	Afa	.25	.60
7	Alundra Blayze	.30	.75
8	Andre the Giant	.50	1.25
9	Bam Bam Bigelow	.40	1.00
10	The Berzerker	.25	.60
11	Big Boss Man	.30	.75
12	Big John Studd	.30	.75
13	Bob Backlund	.25	.60
14	Bobby The Brain Heenan	.40	1.00
15	The Boogeyman	.25	.60
16	Booker T	.30	.75
17	Bret Hit Man Hart	.50	1.25
18	Brian Knobbs	.25	.60
19	British Bulldog	.25	.60
20	Bruno Sammartino	.40	1.00
21	Brutus The Barber Beefcake	.25	.60
22	Cowboy Bob Orton	.40	1.00
23	D'Lo Brown	.25	.60
24	Daniel Bryan	1.00	2.50
25	Dean Malenko	.30	.75
26	Diamond Dallas Page	.30	.75
27	Don Muraco	.25	.60
28	Dory Funk Jr.	.25	.60
29	Dusty Rhodes	.30	.75
30	Earthquake	.25	.60
31	Eddie Guerrero	.50	1.25
32	Edge	.60	1.50
33	Eve Torres	.40	1.00
34	Fit Finlay	.25	.60
35	General Adnan	.25	.60
36	George The Animal Steele	.40	1.00
37	Gerald Brisco	.25	.60
38	The Goon	.25	.60
39	Greg The Hammer Valentine	.30	.75
40	Hacksaw Jim Duggan	.40	1.00
41	Haku	.25	.60
42	Harley Race	.30	.75
43	The Honky Tonk Man	.30	.75
44	Iron Sheik	.30	.75
45	Irwin R. Schyster	.25	.60
46	Jake The Snake Roberts	.30	.75
47	The Godfather	.25	.60
48	Jerry The King Lawler	.30	.75
49	Jerry Sags	.25	.60
50	Jim The Anvil Neidhart	.25	.60
51	Junkyard Dog	.30	.75
52	Mike Rotunda	.25	.60
53	Ken Shamrock	.25	.60
54	Kerry Von Erich	.25	.60
55	Kevin Nash	.40	1.00
56	Kevin Von Erich	.40	1.00
57	Larry Zbyszko	.30	.75
58	Lex Luger	.30	.75
59	Macho Man Randy Savage	.50	1.25
60	Magnum T.A.	.25	.60
61	Michael P.S. Hayes	.30	.75
62	Mick Foley	.60	1.50
63	Million Dollar Man Ted DiBiase	.30	.75
64	Miss Elizabeth	.40	1.00
65	Mr. Perfect	.50	1.25
66	Mr. Wonderful Paul Orndorff	.30	.75
67	Nikolai Volkoff	.30	.75
68	Norman Smiley	.30	.75
69	Papa Shango	.25	.60
70	Pat Patterson	.25	.60
71	Ravishing Rick Rude	.40	1.00
72	Ric Flair	.60	1.50
73	Ricky The Dragon Steamboat	.50	1.25
74	Road Dogg	.40	1.00
75	Rob Van Dam	.50	1.25
76	Rocky Johnson	.25	.60
77	Ron Simmons	.30	.75
78	Rowdy Roddy Piper	.50	1.25
79	Scott Hall	.30	.75
80	Sgt. Slaughter	.30	.75
81	Sensational Sherri	.30	.75
82	Sid Vicious	.30	.75
83	Sika	.25	.60
84	Stevie Ray	.25	.60
85	Sting	.75	2.00
86	Stone Cold Steve Austin	1.00	2.50
87	Tatanka	.25	.60
88	Tatsumi Fujinami	.25	.60
89	Terri Runnels	.25	.60
90	Terry Taylor	.25	.60
91	Trish Stratus	1.00	2.50
92	Tully Blanchard	.30	.75
93	Typhoon	.25	.60
94	Ultimate Warrior	.50	1.25
95	Umaga	.25	.60
96	Virgil	.25	.60
97	The Warlord	.25	.60
98	Wendi Richter	.30	.75
99	X-Pac	.25	.60
100	Yokozuna	.40	1.00

2017 Topps Legends of WWE Autographed Retired Championship Belt Relics

*GOLD/10: UNPRICED DUE TO SCARCITY
*BLACK/5: UNPRICED DUE TO SCARCITY
*RED/1: UNPRICED DUE TO SCARCITY
RANDOMLY INSERTED INTO PACKS

ARCAB	Alundra Blayze	8.00	20.00
ARCBH	Bret Hit Man Hart	15.00	40.00
ARCBP	Beth Phoenix	8.00	20.00
ARCBR	Bret Hit Man Hart	15.00	40.00
ARCBS	Big Show	10.00	25.00
ARCBT	Booker T	15.00	40.00
ARCCF	Charlotte Flair	15.00	40.00
ARCCH	Chris Jericho	20.00	50.00
ARCCJ	Chris Jericho	20.00	50.00
ARCDM	Dean Malenko	6.00	15.00
ARCET	Eve Torres	12.00	30.00
ARCGO	Goldberg	30.00	75.00
ARCIV	Ivory	8.00	20.00
ARCJA	Jim The Anvil Neidhart	6.00	15.00
ARCJB	JBL	8.00	20.00
ARCMA	Maryse	12.00	30.00
ARCMD	Alundra Blayze	6.00	15.00
ARCRD	Road Dogg	6.00	15.00
ARCRF	Ric Flair	60.00	120.00
ARCST	Sting	30.00	75.00
ARCTD	Ted DiBiase	10.00	25.00
ARCTS	Trish Stratus	25.00	60.00
ARCWR	Wendi Richter	10.00	25.00

2017 Topps Legends of WWE Autographed Shirt Relics

*GOLD/10: UNPRICED DUE TO SCARCITY
*BLACK/5: UNPRICED DUE TO SCARCITY
*RED/1: UNPRICED DUE TO SCARCITY

STATED ODDS

ARBH Bret Hit Man Hart
ARBS Big Show
ARDP Diamond Dallas Page
ARED Edge
ARIR The Iron Sheik
ARKN Kevin Nash
ARLL Lex Luger
ARMA Mankind
ARMF Mick Foley
ARRD Road Dogg
ARRS Ricky The Dragon Steamboat
ARSM Shawn Michaels
ARST Sting
ARTB Tully Blanchard
ARTD Million Dollar Man Ted DiBiase

2017 Topps Legends of WWE Autographs

*BRONZE/99: .5X TO 1.2X BASIC AUTOS
*SILVER/50: .6X TO 1.5X BASIC AUTOS
*BLUE/25: .75X TO 2X BASIC AUTOS
*GOLD/10: UNPRICED DUE TO SCARCITY
*BLACK/5: UNPRICED DUE TO SCARCITY
*RED/1: UNPRICED DUE TO SCARCITY
STATED PRINT RUN 199 SER.#'d SETS

LAAB	Alundra Blayze	8.00	20.00
LAAL	Albert	6.00	15.00
LABF	Brutus The Barber Beefcake	12.00	30.00
LABM	Bret Hit Man Hart	30.00	75.00
LABT	Booker T	6.00	15.00
LADP	Diamond Dallas Page	12.00	30.00
LAED	Edge	12.00	30.00
LAET	Eve Torres	10.00	25.00
LAFF	Fit Finlay	6.00	15.00
LAGD	Goldust	8.00	20.00
LAGV	Greg The Hammer Valentine	6.00	15.00
LAHA	Hacksaw Jim Duggan	12.00	30.00
LAIR	Irwin R. Schyster	5.00	12.00
LAJA	Jim The Anvil Neidhart	20.00	50.00
LAKE	Kane	10.00	25.00
LAKN	Kevin Nash	12.00	30.00
LAKS	Ken Shamrock	10.00	25.00
LALL	Lex Luger	12.00	30.00
LAMF	Mick Foley	20.00	50.00
LAMP	Michael P.S. Hayes	6.00	15.00
LANS	Norman Smiley	5.00	12.00
LAPE	Paul Ellering	10.00	25.00
LARS	Ricky The Dragon Steamboat	15.00	40.00
LASM	Shawn Michaels	15.00	40.00
LASS	Sgt. Slaughter	10.00	25.00
LAST	Sting	25.00	60.00
LASV	Sid Vicious	6.00	15.00
LATA	Tatanka	10.00	25.00
LATD	Million Dollar Man Ted DiBiase	15.00	40.00
LATH	The Boogeyman	6.00	15.00
LAWE	Wendi Richter	6.00	15.00
LAWR	William Regal	6.00	15.00

2017 Topps Legends of WWE Autographs Bronze

*BRONZE: .5X TO 1.2X BASIC AUTOS

LAGO	Goldberg	20.00	50.00

2017 Topps Legends of WWE Autographs Silver

STATED PRINT RUN 50 SER.#'d SETS

LAUN	Undertaker	150.00	300.00

2017 Topps Legends of WWE Dual Autographs

STATED PRINT RUN 10 SER.#'d SETS
RANDOMLY INSERTED INTO PACKS

DADS	T.DiBiase/IRS	50.00	100.00
DAFB	R.Flair/T.Blanchard	50.00	100.00
DAHN	J.Neidhart/B.Hart	75.00	150.00
DARB	A.Blayze/W.Richter	30.00	60.00
DASV	I.Sheik/N.Volkoff	30.00	75.00
DASZ	L.Zbyszko/B.Sammartino	30.00	75.00
DATM	HHH/S.McMahon	500.00	1000.00
DAUK	Kane/Undertaker	300.00	500.00
DAUS	Sting/Undertaker	300.00	600.00
DASTL	L.Luger	100.00	200.00
	Sting		

2017 Topps Legends of WWE Legendary Bouts

COMPLETE SET (20)		6.00	15.00

RANDOMLY INSERTED INTO PACKS

1	Undertaker/Shawn Michaels	1.25	3.00
2	Bret Hart/Steve Austin	1.25	3.00
3	Randy Savage/Ricky Steamboat	.60	1.50
4	Ultimate Warrior/Randy Savage	.60	1.50
5	Bret Hart/The British Bulldog	.30	.75
6	Bret Hart/Shawn Michaels	.75	2.00
7	The Rock/Steve Austin	1.50	4.00
8	Undertaker/Shawn Michaels	1.25	3.00
9	John Cena/Brock Lesnar	1.50	4.00
10	Mr. Perfect/Bret Hart	.60	1.50
11	Razor Ramon/Shawn Michaels	.75	2.00
12	Ric Flair/Mr. Perfect	.60	1.50
13	Randy Orton/Cactus Jack	.75	2.00
14	Ric Flair Wins 1992 Royal Rumble	.75	2.00
15	Undertaker/Triple H	1.25	3.00
16	Ric Flair/Randy Savage	.75	2.00
17	Chris Jericho/Shawn Michaels	.75	2.00
18	Triple H/Cactus Jack	.75	2.00
19	Sting's Squad./Dangerous Alliance	1.00	2.50
20	Edge/John Cena	1.50	4.00

2017 Topps Legends of WWE Retired Titles

COMPLETE SET (22)		5.00	12.00

RANDOMLY INSERTED INTO PACKS

1	Bret Hit Man Hart	.75	2.00
2	Ric Flair	1.00	2.50
3	Terry Funk	.40	1.00
4	Triple H	1.00	2.50
5	Money Inc.	.50	1.25
6	The Outsiders	.60	1.50
7	Terry Taylor & Greg Valentine	.50	1.25
8	The Glamour Girls	.40	1.00
9	Trish Stratus	1.50	4.00
10	Nikki Bella	1.00	2.50
11	Ted DiBiase	.50	1.25
12	Tatsumi Fujinami	.40	1.00
13	British Bulldog	.40	1.00
14	Ricky Steamboat	.75	2.00
15	Rob Van Dam	.75	2.00
16	Chris Jericho	1.00	2.50
17	Dean Malenko	.50	1.25
18	Tatsumi Fujinami	.40	1.00
19	Brian Pillman	.40	1.00
20	Bradshaw	.50	1.25
21	Norman Smiley	.50	1.25
22	Virgil	.40	1.00

2017 Topps Legends of WWE Shirt Relics

STATED PRINT RUN 299 SER.#'d SETS

ARBH	Bret Hit Man Hart	5.00	12.00
ARBL	Brock Lesnar	4.00	10.00
ARBS	Big Show	3.00	8.00
ARDP	Diamond Dallas Page	3.00	8.00
ARED	Edge	3.00	8.00
ARIR	The Iron Sheik	2.50	6.00
ARKN	Kevin Nash	2.50	6.00
ARLL	Lex Luger	2.50	6.00
ARMA	Mankind	2.50	6.00
ARMF	Mick Foley	3.00	8.00
ARRD	Road Dogg	2.50	6.00
ARRS	Ricky The Dragon Steamboat	3.00	8.00
ARSM	Shawn Michaels	6.00	15.00
ARST	Sting	6.00	15.00
ARTB	Tully Blanchard	2.50	6.00
ARTD	Million Dollar Man Ted DiBiase	3.00	8.00

2017 Topps Legends of WWE Triple Autographs

TAFSG	Flair/Sting/Goldberg	150.00	300.00
TAHNH	Neidhart/J.Hart/B.Hart	125.00	250.00
TALJM	D.Love/Cactus Jack/Mankind	100.00	250.00
TANSL	Luger/Nash/Sting	100.00	200.00

2018 Topps Legends of WWE

COMPLETE SET (100)
UNOPENED BOX (12 PACKS)
UNOPENED PACK (5 CARDS)
*BRONZE: .6X TO 1.5X BASIC CARDS
*SILVER/50: 1X TO 2.5X BASIC CARDS
*BLUE/25: 1.5X TO 4X BASIC CARDS
*GOLD/10: UNPRICED DUE TO SCARCITY
*BLACK/5: UNPRICED DUE TO SCARCITY
*RED/1: UNPRICED DUE TO SCARCITY
*P.P.BLACK/1: UNPRICED DUE TO SCARCITY
*P.P.CYAN/1: UNPRICED DUE TO SCARCITY
*P.P.MAGENTA/1: UNPRICED DUE TO SCARCITY
*P.P.YELLOW/1: UNPRICED DUE TO SCARCITY

1	Andre the Giant	.60	1.50
2	Bam Bam Bigelow	.50	1.25
3	Batista	.50	1.25
4	Big John Studd	.30	.75
5	Bob Backlund	.30	.75
6	Bobby The Brain Heenan	.50	1.25
7	Booker T	.50	1.25
8	Bret Hit Man Hart	.75	2.00
9	Chief Jay Strongbow	.50	1.25
10	Classy Freddie Blassie	.30	.75
11	Cowboy Bob Orton	.30	.75
12	D'Lo Brown	.30	.75
13	Diamond Dallas Page	.50	1.25
14	Don Muraco	.30	.75
15	Dusty Rhodes	.60	1.50
16	Eddie Guerrero	.75	2.00
17	Edge	.75	2.00
18	Fit Finlay	.30	.75
19	George The Animal Steele	.40	1.00
20	Gorilla Monsoon	.60	1.50
21	Hacksaw Jim Duggan	.30	.75
22	Harley Race	.30	.75
23	Honky Tonk Man	.30	.75
24	Jake The Snake Roberts	.40	1.00
25	Jim Ross	.50	1.25
26	Jerry The King Lawler	.60	1.50

27	Jim The Anvil Neidhart	.50	1.25
28	Junkyard Dog	.30	.75
29	Ken Shamrock	.40	1.00
30	Kevin Nash	.60	1.50
31	Kevin Von Erich	.50	1.25
32	Kurt Angle	.75	2.00
33	Lex Luger	.40	1.00
34	Mark Henry	.40	1.00
35	Million Dollar Man Ted DiBiase	.40	1.00
36	Mr. Perfect	.40	1.00
37	Mr. Wonderful Paul Orndorff	.30	.75
38	Papa Shango	.30	.75
39	Pat Patterson	.30	.75
40	Ravishing Rick Rude	.40	1.00
41	Ric Flair	1.00	2.50
42	Ricky The Dragon Steamboat	.50	1.25
43	Rowdy Roddy Piper	.75	2.00
44	Sgt. Slaughter	.40	1.00
45	Shawn Michaels	1.00	2.50
46	Sid Vicious	.30	.75
47	Stevie Ray	.30	.75
48	Sting	.75	2.00
49	Stone Cold Steve Austin	1.50	4.00
50	Tatanka	.30	.75
51	Tatsumi Fujinami	.30	.75
52	Ultimate Warrior	1.25	3.00
53	Vader	.40	1.00
54	William Regal	.50	1.25
55	Yokozuna	.40	1.00
56	Big Show	.30	.75
57	Bobby Lashley	.60	1.50
58	The Brian Kendrick	.50	1.25
59	Daniel Bryan	.75	2.00
60	Dolph Ziggler	.40	1.00
61	Jeff Hardy	.60	1.50
62	Goldust	.60	1.50
63	John Cena	1.25	3.00
64	Kane	.50	1.25
65	Woken Matt Hardy	.75	2.00
66	Randy Orton	.75	2.00
67	The Rock	1.50	4.00
68	Shelton Benjamin	.40	1.00
69	Undertaker	1.25	3.00
70	Triple H	.75	2.00
IC1	X-Pac/1-2-3 Kid	.40	1.00
IC2	Albert/Tensai	.30	.75
IC3	Big Bubba Rogers/Big Boss Man	.30	.75
IC4	Brutus Beefcake/The Zodiac	.30	.75
IC5	The Booty Man/The Disciple	.30	.75
IC6	Earthquake/The Shark	.30	.75
IC7	Kama Mustafa/Kama	.30	.75
IC8	The Godfather/Goodfather	.30	.75
IC9	Trillionaire/Million Dollar Man	.40	1.00
WD1	Alundra Blayze	.30	.75
WD2	Beth Phoenix	.60	1.50
WD3	Eve Torres	.60	1.50
WD4	Lita	.75	2.00
WD5	Miss Elizabeth	.75	2.00
WD6	Sherri Martel	.60	1.50
WD7	Stephanie McMahon	.60	1.50
WD8	Terri Runnels	.40	1.00
WD9	Trish Stratus	1.25	3.00
IC10	Colonel Mustafa/Iron Sheik	.30	.75
IC11	Michael Wallstreet/IRS	.30	.75
IC12	Umaga/Jamal	.30	.75
IC13	Road Dogg/Jesse James	.30	.75
IC14	Macho Man/Macho King R.Savage	1.00	2.50
IC15	Dok Hendrix/Michael P.S. Hayes	.30	.75

IC16	Scott Hall/Razor Ramon	.60	1.50
IC17	Faarooq/Ron Simmons	.40	1.00
IC18	Terry Taylor/Red Rooster	.30	.75
IC19	Tugboat/Typhoon	.30	.75
IC20	Virgil/Vincent	.30	.75
WD10	Wendi Richter	.30	.75

2018 Topps Legends of WWE Autographed Commemorative Hall of Fame Rings

*SILVER/50: .5X TO 1.2X BASIC AUTOS
*BLUE/25: .6X TO 1.5X BASIC AUTOS
*GOLD/10: UNPRICED DUE TO SCARCITY
*BLACK/5: UNPRICED DUE TO SCARCITY
*RED/1: UNPRICED DUE TO SCARCITY
STATED PRINT RUN 99 SER.#'d SETS

HOFAB	Alundra Blayze	10.00	25.00
HOFBH	Bret Hit Man Hart	15.00	40.00
HOFBP	Beth Phoenix	12.00	30.00
HOFBT	Booker T	15.00	40.00
HOFDP	Diamond Dallas Page	10.00	25.00
HOFEG	Edge	10.00	25.00
HOFHR	Harley Race	15.00	40.00
HOFJD	Hacksaw Jim Duggan	10.00	25.00
HOFJL	Jerry The King Lawler	20.00	50.00
HOFJR	Jake The Snake Roberts	12.00	30.00
HOFKA	Kurt Angle	12.00	30.00
HOFKN	Kevin Nash	12.00	30.00
HOFLT	Lita	20.00	50.00
HOFMH	Mark Henry	10.00	25.00
HOFPO	Mr. Wonderful Paul Orndorff	12.00	30.00
HOFRD	Ricky The Dragon Steamboat	10.00	25.00
HOFRF	Ric Flair/84	30.00	75.00
HOFRR	Razor Ramon	15.00	40.00
HOFSS	Sgt. Slaughter	12.00	30.00
HOFST	Sting	25.00	60.00
HOFWR	Wendi Richter	10.00	25.00

2018 Topps Legends of WWE Autographed Dual Relics

*GOLD/10: UNPRICED DUE TO SCARCITY
*BLACK/5: UNPRICED DUE TO SCARCITY
*RED/1: UNPRICED DUE TO SCARCITY
STATED PRINT RUN 25 SER.#'d SETS

ADRGD	Goldust	12.00	30.00
ADRJH	Jeff Hardy	15.00	40.00
ADRMH	Woken Matt Hardy	20.00	50.00

2018 Topps Legends of WWE Autographed Shirt Relics

*SILVER/50: .5X TO 1.2X BASIC AUTOS
*BLUE/25: .6X TO 1.5X BASIC AUTOS
*GOLD/10: UNPRICED DUE TO SCARCITY
*BLACK/5: UNPRICED DUE TO SCARCITY
*RED/1: UNPRICED DUE TO SCARCITY
STATED PRINT RUN 99 SER.#'d SETS

ASRDP	Diamond Dallas Page	10.00	25.00
ASREG	Edge	12.00	30.00
ASRIS	The Iron Sheik	10.00	25.00
ASRKN	Kevin Nash	15.00	40.00
ASRLL	Lex Luger	10.00	25.00
ASRMH	Woken Matt Hardy	8.00	20.00
ASRRD	Road Dogg		
ASRRS	Ricky The Dragon Steamboat	8.00	20.00
ASRST	Sting	15.00	40.00

2018 Topps Legends of WWE Autographs

*BRONZE/99: SAME VALUE AS BASIC AUTOS
*SILVER/50: .5X TO 1.2X BASIC AUTOS
*BLUE/25: .6X TO 1.5X BASIC AUTOS
*GOLD/10: UNPRICED DUE TO SCARCITY
*BLACK/5: UNPRICED DUE TO SCARCITY
*RED/1: UNPRICED DUE TO SCARCITY
*P.P.BLACK/1: UNPRICED DUE TO SCARCITY
*P.P.CYAN/1: UNPRICED DUE TO SCARCITY
*P.P.MAGENTA/1: UNPRICED DUE TO SCARCITY
*P.P.YELLOW/1: UNPRICED DUE TO SCARCITY
STATED ODDS

AAB	Alundra Blayze	6.00	15.00
AAF	Afa	5.00	12.00
ABE	Brutus The Barber Beefcake	8.00	20.00
ABH	Bret Hit Man Hart	12.00	30.00
ABN	Brian Knobbs	6.00	15.00
ABS	Big Show	8.00	20.00
ABT	Booker T	8.00	20.00
ACB	Cowboy Bob Orton	5.00	12.00
ACJ	Chris Jericho	12.00	30.00
ADB	Daniel Bryan	10.00	25.00
ADP	Diamond Dallas Page	6.00	15.00
AED	Edge	12.00	30.00
AFA	Faarooq	5.00	12.00
AFF	Fit Finlay	6.00	15.00
AGD	Goldust	6.00	15.00
AGO	The Goon	10.00	25.00
AHA	Haku	8.00	20.00
AHR	Harley Race	8.00	20.00
AHT	Honky Tonk Man	6.00	15.00
AIR	Irwin R. Schyster	5.00	12.00
AJD	Hacksaw Jim Duggan	10.00	25.00
AJH	Jimmy Hart	6.00	15.00
AJJ	JJ Dillon	6.00	15.00
AJL	Jerry The King Lawler	8.00	20.00
AJS	Jake The Snake Roberts	10.00	25.00
AKA	Kurt Angle	12.00	30.00
AKE	Kane	6.00	15.00
AKN	Kevin Nash	6.00	15.00
ALL	Lex Luger	8.00	20.00
ALT	Lita	12.00	30.00
AMA	Mankind	6.00	15.00
AMC	Michael Cole	5.00	12.00
AMD	Million Dollar Man Ted DiBiase	8.00	20.00
ANB	Jerry Sags	5.00	12.00
ANS	Norman Smiley	6.00	15.00
APE	Paul Ellering	8.00	20.00
APS	Michael P.S. Hayes	6.00	15.00
ARH	Rhyno	5.00	12.00
ARO	Randy Orton	10.00	25.00
ARS	Ricky The Dragon Steamboat	10.00	25.00
ASI	Sika	6.00	15.00
ASR	Stevie Ray	6.00	15.00
ASS	Sgt. Slaughter	6.00	15.00
AST	Sting	15.00	40.00
ASV	Sid Vicious	6.00	15.00
ATA	Magnum T.A.	6.00	15.00
ATG	The Godfather	6.00	15.00
ATK	Tatanka	5.00	12.00
ATS	Trish Stratus	20.00	50.00
ATT	Terry Taylor	5.00	12.00
ATW	The Warlord	5.00	12.00
AWD	Wendi Richter	6.00	15.00
AWR	William Regal	8.00	20.00

2018 Topps Legends of WWE Autographs Silver

STATED PRINT RUN 50 SER.#'d SETS

ASM	Stephanie McMahon	75.00	150.00
ATH	Triple H	125.00	250.00
AUD	Undertaker	100.00	200.00

2018 Topps Legends of WWE Dual Autographs

DABW	Bushwhackers
DADX	HHH/HBK
DAGG	J.Martin/L.Kai
DAHF	P.Orndorff/H.Race
DAHH	Booker T/S.Ray

2018 Topps Legends of WWE Relics

RANDOMLY INSERTED INTO PACKS

SRBH	Bret Hit Man Hart	5.00	12.00
SRDP	Diamond Dallas Page	3.00	8.00
SREG	Edge	3.00	8.00
SRGD	Goldust	2.50	6.00
SRIS	The Iron Sheik	2.50	6.00
SRJC	John Cena	5.00	12.00
SRKN	Kevin Nash	3.00	8.00
SRLL	Lex Luger	2.50	6.00
SRMH	Woken Matt Hardy	2.00	5.00
SRRD	Road Dogg	2.00	5.00
SRRS	Ricky The Dragon Steamboat	2.00	5.00
SRST	Sting	3.00	8.00
SRTD	Million Dollar Man Ted DiBiase	2.00	5.00

2018 Topps Legends of WWE Triple Autographs

STATED PRINT RUN 10 SER.#'d SETS
UNPRICED DUE TO SCARCITY

TAMHF	K.Angle/HHH/S.McMahon
TAMOD	Faarooq/Edge/Undertaker
TATCM	HHH/Undertaker/Faarooq

2021 Topps Living WWE

1	Stone Cold Steve Austin/5,521*	8.00	20.00
2	Trish Stratus/3,546*	8.00	20.00
3	The Miz/1,582*	2.50	6.00
4	Maryse/1,592*	2.50	6.00
5	Erik/1,116*	1.50	4.00
6	Ivar/1,135*	1.50	4.00
7	Bobby Lashley/1,031*	4.00	10.00
8	MVP/1,024*	1.50	4.00
9	Jeff Hardy/1,699*	4.00	10.00
10	Undertaker/3,231*	8.00	20.00
11	Shinsuke Nakamura/962*	4.00	10.00
12	Akira Tozawa/968*	2.00	5.00
13	Jey Uso/800*	1.50	4.00
14	Jimmy Uso/785*	1.50	4.00
15	Mia Yim/792*	2.00	5.00
16	Keith Lee/786*	3.00	8.00
17	Sami Zayn/825*	2.50	6.00
18	Edge/1,022*	6.00	15.00
19	Sheamus/758*	2.50	6.00
20	Cesaro/744*	1.50	4.00
21	Titus O'Neil/696*	1.50	4.00
22	Roman Reigns/1,105*	8.00	20.00
23	Braun Strowman/839	4.00	10.00
24	Alexa Bliss/1,601*	10.00	25.00
25	Drew McIntyre/674*	4.00	10.00
26	Jinder Mahal/718*	2.00	5.00
27	Carmella/683*	4.00	10.00
28	R-Truth/619*	2.00	5.00
29	Aleister Black/606*	4.00	10.00
30	Ricochet/565*	2.50	6.00
31	Eddie Guerrero/925*	8.00	20.00
32	Sasha Banks/1,242*	8.00	20.00
33	Nikki Cross/541*	3.00	8.00
34	Finn Balor/570*	4.00	10.00
35	Angelo Dawkins/529*	2.00	5.00
36	Montez Ford/529*	1.50	4.00
37	Dolph Ziggler/551*	3.00	8.00
38	Robert Roode/512*	2.00	5.00
39	Karrion Kross/686*	6.00	15.00
40	Scarlett/936*	8.00	20.00
41	Bianca Belair/671*	4.00	10.00
42	Naomi/621*	2.00	5.00
43	Kayden Carter/483*	3.00	8.00
44	Kacy Catanzaro/554*	3.00	8.00
45	Mr. America (Hulk Hogan)/1,216*	8.00	20.00
46	Lex Luger/713*	2.00	5.00
47	Rey Mysterio/676*	4.00	10.00
48	Dominik Mysterio/563*	2.00	5.00
49	Miss Elizabeth/1,142*	3.00	8.00
50	Macho Man Randy Savage/1,866*	10.00	25.00
51	Beth Phoenix/1,142*	3.00	8.00
52	Lacey Evans/564*	6.00	15.00
53	Bobby "The Brain" Heenan/701*	2.50	6.00
54	Razor Ramon/769*	2.50	6.00
55	AJ Styles//574*	5.00	12.00
56	Omos/544*	1.50	4.00
57	Kane/658*	2.50	6.00
58	Rob Van Dam/527*	3.00	8.00
59	Seth Rollins/643*	4.00	10.00
60	Becky Lynch/932*	6.00	15.00
61	British Bulldog/646*	2.50	6.00
62	Bret Hart/1,013*	4.00	10.00
63	Cedric Alexander/430*	1.50	4.00
64	Shelton Benjamin/431*	2.50	6.00
65	Dakota Kai/490*	3.00	8.00
66	Raquel Gonzalez/572*	6.00	15.00
67	John Morrison/426*	3.00	8.00
68	Franky Monet/483*	3.00	8.00
69	Natalya/442*	2.50	6.00
70	Tamina/404*	1.50	4.00
71	Rikishi/485*	2.00	5.00
72	Yokozuna/506*	2.50	6.00
73	Asuka/767*	6.00	15.00
74	Io Shirai/663*	3.00	8.00
75	Apollo Crews/412*	2.00	5.00
76	Commander Azeez/412*	2.00	5.00
77	Papa Shango/648*	2.00	5.00
78	Ultimate Warrior/1,267*	10.00	25.00
79	Riddle/509*	4.00	10.00
80	Randy Orton/601*	5.00	12.00
81	Rocky Johnson/827*	3.00	8.00
82	The Rock/3,671*	10.00	25.00
83	Gobbledy Gooker/565*	1.50	4.00
84	Big E/485*	4.00	10.00
85	Kofi Kingston/424*	4.00	10.00
86	Xavier Woods/419*	1.50	4.00
87	Shotzi Blackheart/769*	8.00	20.00
88	Charlotte Flair/796*	8.00	20.00
89	Billy Gunn/491*	2.00	5.00
90	Road Dogg/496*	2.00	5.00
91	Chyna/596*	3.00	8.00
92	X-Pac/516*	2.00	5.00
93	John Cena/		
94	Mick Foley/		
95	Shawn Michaels/		
96	Triple H/		

2021 Topps Living WWE Rainbow Foil

STATED PRINT RUN 50 SER.#'d SETS
VIP PARTY EXCLUSIVE

1	Stone Cold Steve Austin	100.00	200.00

2016-18 Topps Now WWE

1	Brock Lesnar/132*	6.00	15.00
2	Finn Balor/221*	5.00	12.00
3	Dean Ambrose/114*	6.00	15.00
4	Charlotte/124*	6.00	15.00
5	AJ Styles/127*	8.00	20.00
6	AJ Styles/191*	6.00	15.00
7	Becky Lynch/212*	8.00	20.00
8	Heath Slater and Rhyno/104*	4.00	10.00
9	Kane/81*	12.00	30.00
10	The Miz/85*	6.00	15.00
11	Kevin Owens/68*	5.00	12.00
12	The New Day/61*	15.00	40.00
13	Charlotte/88*	5.00	12.00
14	Roman Reigns/61*	8.00	20.00
15	Chris Jericho/62*	10.00	25.00
16	AJ Styles/73*	5.00	12.00
17	Naomi/70*	8.00	20.00
18	Heath Slater & Rhyno/65*	8.00	20.00
19	Dolph Ziggler/73*	5.00	12.00
20	Bray Wyatt/86*	5.00	12.00
21	Nikki Bella/87*	5.00	12.00
22	Goldberg/249*	6.00	15.00
23	Kevin Owens/98*	8.00	20.00
24	Charlotte Flair/151*	6.00	15.00
25	Roman Reigns/69*	5.00	12.00
26	New Day/70*	5.00	12.00
27	Brian Kendrick/72*	5.00	12.00
28	The Miz/59*	5.00	12.00
29	Edge/58*	5.00	12.00
30	Undertaker/126*	8.00	20.00
31	Goldberg/125*	6.00	15.00
32	Team Smackdown Live Men/62*	5.00	12.00
33	Team Raw Women/88*	4.00	10.00
34	Team Raw Tag Team/60*	5.00	12.00
35	The Brian Kendrick/59*	5.00	12.00
36	The Miz/60*	5.00	12.00
37	AJ Styles/122*	4.00	10.00
38	Alexa Bliss/180*	15.00	40.00
39	The Miz/82*	4.00	10.00
40	Nikki Bella/93*	6.00	15.00
41	Baron Corbin/91*	4.00	10.00
42	Randy Orton & Bray Wyatt/115*	5.00	12.00
43A	Kevin Owens/65*	4.00	10.00
44	Cesaro & Sheamus/65*	4.00	10.00
45	Sami Zayn/68*	4.00	10.00
46	Seth Rollins/63*	4.00	10.00
47	Rich Swann/65*	4.00	10.00
48A	Charlotte Flair/108*	6.00	15.00
49	Naomi/Nikki Bella/Becky Lynch/88*	4.00	10.00
50	Luke Gallows & Karl Anderson/64*	4.00	10.00
51	Charlotte Flair/100*	4.00	10.00
52	Kevin Owens/62*	6.00	15.00
53	Neville/61*	5.00	12.00
54A	John Cena/82*	6.00	15.00
55	Goldberg/Undertaker/73*	6.00	15.00
56A	Randy Orton/85*	5.00	12.00
57	Nia Jax/83*	6.00	15.00
58	Bray Wyatt/102*	5.00	12.00
59	Naomi/82*	6.00	15.00
60	Randy Orton/54*	6.00	15.00
61	Nikki Bella & Natalya/74*	6.00	15.00
62	American Alpha/39*	4.00	10.00
63	Becky Lynch/73*	6.00	15.00
64	Bayley/288*	6.00	15.00
65	Goldberg/223*	8.00	20.00
66	Bayley/153*	5.00	12.00
67	Roman Reigns/64*	5.00	12.00
68	Neville/73*	5.00	12.00
69	Sasha Banks/141*	5.00	12.00
70	Luke Gallows & Karl Anderson/74*	5.00	12.00
71	Samoa Joe/81*	5.00	12.00
72	Undertaker/172*	6.00	15.00
73	Naomi/72*	5.00	12.00
74	Goldberg/64*	8.00	20.00
75	Randy Orton/69*	5.00	12.00
76	John Cena/Nikki Bella/91*	5.00	12.00
77	Hardy Boyz/114*	8.00	20.00
78	Bayley/97*	5.00	12.00
79	Kevin Owens/71*	5.00	12.00
80	Shinsuke Nakamura/78*	8.00	20.00
82	Tye Dillinger/37*	10.00	25.00
81	Finn Balor/46*	10.00	25.00
83	The Revival/46*	5.00	12.00
84	Dean Ambrose/Miz/Maryse/40*	5.00	12.00
85	Alexa Bliss/123*	10.00	25.00
86	Kevin Owens/49*	5.00	12.00
87	Charlotte Flair/57*	8.00	20.00
88	Braun Strowman/55*	5.00	12.00
89	Bray Wyatt/49*	5.00	12.00
90	Seth Rollins/50*	5.00	12.00
91	Alexa Bliss/223*	10.00	25.00
92	The Hardy Boyz/65*	5.00	12.00
93	Chris Jericho/56*	5.00	12.00
94	Shinsuka Nakamura/96*	5.00	12.00
95	The Usos/		
96	Sami Zayn/41*	5.00	12.00
97	Natalya Carmella Tamina/49*	5.00	12.00
98	Kevin Owens/44*	5.00	12.00
99	Jinder Mahal/69*	5.00	12.00
100	The Miz/60*	5.00	12.00
101	Sasha Banks/Rich Swann/78*	6.00	15.00
102	Alexa Bliss/264*	8.00	20.00
103	Cesaro & Sheamus/53*	4.00	10.00
104	Neville/53*	4.00	10.00
105	Samoa Joe/56*	4.00	10.00
106	Carmella/112*	6.00	15.00
107	The Usos/41*	5.00	12.00
108	Naomi/49*	5.00	12.00
109	Jinder Mahal/41*	4.00	10.00
110	Baron Corbin/60*	4.00	10.00
111	Brock Lesnar/61*	6.00	15.00
112	Braun Strowman/39*	4.00	10.00
113	The Miz/33*	4.00	10.00
114	Sasha Banks/103*	5.00	12.00
115	Cesaro & Sheamus/33*	4.00	10.00
116	Big Cass/32*	4.00	10.00
117	Bray Wyatt/37*	4.00	10.00
118	Neville/32*	4.00	10.00
119	Jinder Mahal/50*	4.00	10.00
120	The New Day/49*	4.00	10.00
121	John Cena/59*	5.00	12.00
122	Kevin Owens/44*	4.00	10.00
123	Natalya/44*	4.00	10.00
124	Baron Corbin/38*	4.00	10.00
125	HHH & Stephanie/Connor's Cure/216*	4.00	10.00
126	Natalya/62*	4.00	10.00
127	Sasha Banks/114*	6.00	15.00
128	Dean Ambrose & Seth Rollins/80*	5.00	12.00

129	AJ Styles/63*	5.00	12.00
130	Jinder Mahal/38*	5.00	12.00
131	Brock Lesnar/50*	5.00	12.00
132	Brock Lesnar/51*	5.00	12.00
133	Enzo Amore/48*	5.00	12.00
134	Roman Reigns/46*	5.00	12.00
135	Alexa Bliss/138*	10.00	25.00
136	Ambrose/Rollins/38*	5.00	12.00
137	Finn Balor/40*	5.00	12.00
138	Kevin Owens/39*	5.00	12.00
139	Bobby Roode/32*	5.00	12.00
140	Jinder Mahal/29*	5.00	12.00
141	Natalya/53*	5.00	12.00
142	Baron Corbin/30*	5.00	12.00
143	The Usos/32*	5.00	12.00
144	Angle/Rollins/Ambrose/75*	5.00	12.00
145	Alexa Bliss/191*	8.00	20.00
146	The Demon Finn Balor/94*	5.00	12.00
147	Asuka/146*	6.00	15.00
148	Enzo Amore/55*	4.00	10.00
149	Sasha Banks/100*	5.00	12.00
150	The Shield/50*	4.00	10.00
151	Team Raw Women/35*	4.00	10.00
152	Charlotte Flair/102*	6.00	15.00
153	Team Raw Men/	4.00	10.00
154	AJ Styles/65*	4.00	10.00
155	Kevin Owens & Sami Zayn/34*	4.00	10.00
156	Charlotte Flair/63*	6.00	15.00
157	The Usos/33*	4.00	10.00
158	Dolph Ziggler/33*	4.00	10.00
159	Scott Hall/89*	4.00	10.00
160	Undertaker/147*	6.00	15.00
161	The Miz/88*	4.00	10.00
162	John Cena/91*	6.00	15.00
163	Stone Cold Steve Austin/153*	8.00	20.00

2016-18 Topps Now WWE Relics

STATED PRINT RUN 25 SER.#'d SETS

43B	Kevin Owens	20.00	50.00
48B	Charlotte Flair	60.00	120.00
54B	John Cena	50.00	100.00
56B	Randy Orton	25.00	60.00
72A	Undertaker	80.00	150.00
74A	Goldberg	15.00	40.00
75A	Randy Orton	20.00	50.00
76A	John Cena/Nikki Bella	30.00	75.00
127A	Sasha Banks	60.00	120.00
128A	Dean Ambrose & Seth Rollins	30.00	75.00
131A	Brock Lesnar	30.00	75.00
144A	Kurt Angle	30.00	75.00
147A	Asuka	50.00	100.00
163A	Stone Cold Steve Austin	60.00	120.00

2018 Topps Now WWE

COMPLETE SET (72)		300.00	600.00
1	AJ Styles/99*	6.00	15.00
2	Shinsuke Nakamura/127*	5.00	12.00
3	Cesaro & Sheamus/82*	5.00	12.00
4	Lita/102*	6.00	15.00
5	Trish Stratus/186*	8.00	20.00
6	Asuka/145*	6.00	15.00
7	Alexa Bliss/171*	10.00	25.00
8	Asuka/140*	6.00	15.00
9	Woken Matt Hardy/56*	6.00	15.00
10	Roman Reigns/59*	6.00	15.00
11	AJ Styles/53*	5.00	12.00
12	Asuka/103*	6.00	15.00
13	Charlotte Flair/101*	6.00	15.00

14	Randy Orton/67*	5.00	12.00
15	Shinsuke Nakamura/50*	5.00	12.00
16	Daniel Bryan/125*	6.00	15.00
17	Woken Matt Hardy/76*	8.00	20.00
18	Cedric Alexander/74*	8.00	20.00
19	Naomi/87*	8.00	20.00
20	Seth Rollins/77*	8.00	20.00
21	Charlotte Flair/261*	8.00	20.00
22	Jinder Mahal/64*	5.00	12.00
23	The Bludgeon Brothers/67*	5.00	12.00
24	The Undertaker/145*	8.00	20.00
25	Daniel Bryan/93*	8.00	20.00
26	Nia Jax/115*	5.00	12.00
27	AJ Styles/85*	5.00	12.00
28	Braun Strowman/67*	5.00	12.00
29	Brock Lesnar/44*	5.00	12.00
30	Ronda Rousey/1342*	12.00	30.00
31	Braun Strowman/66*	5.00	12.00
32	Daniel Bryan/52*	6.00	15.00
33	Undertaker/62*	8.00	20.00
34	AJ Styles/52*	6.00	15.00
35	John Cena/66*	5.00	12.00
36	Seth Rollins/37*	6.00	15.00
37	Daniel Bryan/30*	12.00	30.00
38	Roman Reigns/33*	8.00	20.00
39	Alexa Bliss/301*	8.00	20.00
40	AJ Styles/101*	6.00	15.00
41	Alexa Bliss/304*	10.00	25.00
42	Braun Strowman/101*	5.00	12.00
43	Bobby Lashley/47*	8.00	20.00
44	Alexa Bliss/175*	10.00	25.00
45	AJ Styles/58*	8.00	20.00
46	Dolph Ziggler/48*	6.00	15.00
47	Seth Rollins/80*	6.00	15.00
48	Charlotte Flair/191*	8.00	20.00
49	Ronda Rousey/970*	8.00	20.00
50	Roman Reigns/79*	12.00	30.00
51	Becky Lynch/172*	5.00	12.00
52	Dolph Ziggler/Drew McIntyre/73*	5.00	12.00
53	AJ Styles/74*	5.00	12.00
54	Ronda Rousey/299*	6.00	15.00
55	John Cena/64*	5.00	12.00
56	Ilconics/146*	5.00	12.00
57	AJ Styles/64*	4.00	10.00
58	Ronda Rousey/Bellas/166*	6.00	15.00
59	Triple H/72*	4.00	10.00
60	Buddy Murphy/64*	10.00	25.00
61	Trish Stratus & Lita/212*	6.00	15.00
62	Nia Jax/139*	12.00	30.00
63	Toni Storm/239*	8.00	20.00
64	Shayna Baszler/149*	6.00	15.00
65	Becky Lynch/325*	5.00	12.00
66	Ronda Rousey/324*	5.00	12.00
67	Seth Rollins/63*	10.00	25.00
68	Charlotte Flair/143*	8.00	20.00
69	Brock Lesnar/63*	10.00	25.00
70	Asuka/270*	4.00	10.00
71	Daniel Bryan/70*	6.00	15.00
72	Ronda Rousey/295*	5.00	12.00

2018 Topps Now WWE Relics

*GOLD/1: UNPRICED/SCARCITY

2A	Shinsuke Nakamura	25.00	60.00
6A	Asuka	75.00	150.00
24A	The Undertaker	25.00	60.00
25A	Daniel Bryan	30.00	75.00
29A	Brock Lesnar	60.00	120.00
30A	Ronda Rousey	150.00	300.00

48A	Charlotte Flair	30.00	75.00
49A	Ronda Rousey	100.00	200.00
50A	Roman Reigns		
68A	Charlotte Flair	50.00	100.00
69A	Brock Lesnar		

2019 Topps Now WWE

1	Women's Royal Rumble/166*	8.00	20.00
2	Men's Royal Rumble/75*	5.00	12.00
3	Asuka/186*	6.00	15.00
4	Ronda Rousey/268*	6.00	15.00
5	Daniel Bryan/90*	5.00	12.00
6	Brock Lesnar/91*	6.00	15.00
7	Becky Lynch/279*	6.00	15.00
8	Seth Rollins/113*	5.00	12.00
9	WM35 Men's Preview/100*	4.00	10.00
10	WM35 Women's Preview/215*	5.00	12.00
11	Seth Rollins/157*	4.00	10.00
12	Roman Reigns/119*	4.00	10.00
13	Kurt Angle/127*	6.00	15.00
14	Kofi Kingston/217*	4.00	10.00
15	The Ilconics/211*	3.00	8.00
16	Triple H/95*	3.00	8.00
17	John Cena/136*	4.00	10.00
18	Becky Lynch/710*	6.00	15.00
19	Seth Rollins/58*	6.00	15.00
20	Kofi Kingston/49*	5.00	12.00
21	Rey Mysterio/48*	8.00	20.00
22	Bayley/164*	5.00	12.00
23	Charlotte Flair/140*	6.00	15.00
24	Becky Lynch/163*	5.00	12.00
25	Bayley/138*	5.00	12.00
26	Brock Lesnar/49*	5.00	12.00
27	Mansoor/29*	12.00	30.00
28	Randy Orton/26*	6.00	15.00
29	Undertaker/31*	6.00	15.00
30	Drew Gulak/45*	5.00	12.00
31	Becky Lynch/109*	6.00	15.00
32	Ricochet/48*	5.00	12.00
33	Bayley/81*	8.00	20.00
34	Seth Rollins w/Becky Lynch/111*	6.00	15.00
35	Undertaker & Roman Reigns/58*	6.00	15.00
36	AJ Styles/57*	5.00	12.00
37	Bayley/81*	5.00	12.00
38	Seth Rollins & Becky Lynch/91*	5.00	12.00
39	Brock Lesnar/55*	5.00	12.00
40	Becky Lynch vs. Natalya/58*	6.00	15.00
41	Kofi Kingston vs. Randy Orton/29*	4.00	10.00
42	Brock Lesnar vs. Seth Rollins/29*	8.00	20.00
43	Becky Lynch/159*	8.00	20.00
44	AJ Styles/67*	4.00	10.00
45	Charlotte Flair/171*	6.00	15.00
46	The Fiend Bray Wyatt/	8.00	20.00
47	Seth Rollins//96*	4.00	10.00
48	Bayley//96*	5.00	12.00
49	Samoa Joe/26*	6.00	15.00
50	Cedric Alexander/26*	3.00	8.00
51	Elias/29*	3.00	8.00
52	Andrade/28*	5.00	12.00
53	Ricochet/31*	4.00	10.00
54	Baron Corbin/31*	4.00	10.00
55	Ali/20*		
56	Chad Gable/56*	6.00	15.00
57	Baron Corbin/21*		
58	Samoa Joe and Ricochet/21*		
59	Elias/21*		
60	Chad Gable/20*		
61	Baron Corbin/30*		

62	Chad Gable/31*	6.00	15.00
63	Bayley/101*		
64	Sasha Banks/172*	5.00	12.00
65	Kofi Kingston/55*		
66	Erick Rowan/55*		
67	Seth Rollins/66*		
68	Baron Corbin/		
69	Rock & Becky Lynch/118*	6.00	15.00
70	Becky & Charlotte/81*	6.00	15.00
71	Kevin Owens/41*	5.00	12.00
72	Roman Reigns/38*		
73	Roman Reigns & Daniel Bryan/44*		
74	Kabuki Warriors/74*	5.00	12.00
75	Charlotte Flair/75*	6.00	15.00
76	Becky Lynch/110*	4.00	10.00
77	The Fiend Bray Wyatt/182*	8.00	20.00
78	Team Hogan/36*	5.00	12.00
79	Natalya/Lacey Evans/104*		
80	AJ Styles/34*		
81	Mansoor/34*		
82	The OC/34*	5.00	12.00
83	Brock Lesnar/34*	6.00	15.00
84	Team NXT Women/79*	6.00	15.00
85	Roderick Strong/43*	6.00	15.00
86	Adam Cole/43*	6.00	15.00
87	The Fiend Bray Wyatt/80*	8.00	20.00
88	Team SmackDown Men/38*	8.00	20.00
89	Brock Lesnar/43*	5.00	12.00
90	Shayna Baszler/61*	8.00	20.00
91	The New Day/29*		
92	Aleister Black/29*		
93	King Corbin/24*		
94	Bray Wyatt/50*	6.00	15.00
95	The Kabuki Warriors/70*	5.00	12.00

2020 Topps Now WWE

1	Roman Reigns/51*	6.00	15.00
2	Charlotte Flair/170*	6.00	15.00
3	Bayley/77*	3.00	8.00
4	The Fiend/85*	5.00	12.00
5	Becky Lynch/152*	6.00	15.00
6	Drew McIntyre/*76	3.00	8.00
7	Undertaker/77*	6.00	15.00
8	The Miz & John Morrison/40*		
9	Roman Reigns/41*	6.00	15.00
10	Bayley/83*	3.00	8.00
11	Goldberg/67*	6.00	15.00
12	Alexa Bliss & Nikki Cross/160*	10.00	25.00
13	Becky Lynch/162*	6.00	15.00
14	Sami Zayn/66*	3.00	8.00
15	John Morrison/56*	4.00	10.00
16	Kevin Owens/61*	3.00	8.00
17	Braun Strowman/75*	6.00	15.00
18	Undertaker/141*	6.00	15.00
19	Rob Gronkowski/393*	2.50	6.00
20	Charlotte Flair/153*	6.00	15.00
21	Aleister Black/55*		
22	Edge/96*	4.00	10.00
23	Street Profits/71*	4.00	10.00
24	Bayley/105*	8.00	20.00
25	The Fiend Bray Wyatt/107*	6.00	15.00
26	Drew McIntyre/105*	3.00	8.00
27	The New Day/45*		
28	Bayley/75*	3.00	8.00
29	Braun Strowman/55*		
30	Drew McIntyre/59*		
31	Asuka/155*	6.00	15.00
32	Otis/78*	2.50	6.00

33 Bayley & Sasha Banks/148*	8.00	20.00
34 Sheamus/38*		
35 Braun Strowman/40*		
36 Drew McIntyre/41*		
37 Randy Orton/84*	4.00	10.00
38 Cesaro & Nakamura/38*		
39 Seth Rollins/31*		
40 Drew McIntyre/36*		
41 Bayley/73*	3.00	8.00
42 The Fiend Bray Wyatt/116*	5.00	12.00
43 Drew McIntyre/79*	3.00	8.00
44 Asuka/209*	6.00	15.00
45 Seth Rollins/57*		
46 Mandy Rose/93*	8.00	20.00
47 Bayley/128*	3.00	8.00
48 Roman Reigns/86*	4.00	10.00
49 Roman Reigns/73*	4.00	10.00
50 Rey & Dominik Mysterio/97*	3.00	8.00
51 Shayna Baszler & Nia Jax/72*	5.00	12.00
52 Bobby Lashley/45*		
53 Roman Reigns/62*	4.00	10.00
54 Drew McIntyre/52*		
55 Asuka/102*	6.00	15.00
56 Sami Zayn/52*		
57 Roman Reigns/61*	4.00	10.00
58 The Miz/39*		
59 Sasha Banks/163*	8.00	20.00
60 Randy Orton/73*	4.00	10.00
61 Team RAW (men)/68*	5.00	12.00
62 Street Profits/55*		
63 Bobby Lashley/65*	3.00	8.00
64 Sasha Banks/261*	8.00	20.00
65 Team RAW (women)/129*	4.00	10.00
66 Roman Reigns/65*	4.00	10.00
67 Undertaker/736*	6.00	15.00
68 Drew McIntyre		
69 Sasha Banks	8.00	20.00
70 The Hurt Business		
71 Asuka & Charlotte Flair	6.00	15.00
72 Roman Reigns		
73 Randy Orton		

2020 Topps Now WWE Autographs

*RED/10: UNPRICED DUE TO SCARCITY
*GOLD/1: UNPRICED DUE TO SCARCITY
STATED PRINT RUN 25 SER.#'d SETS

31A Asuka	75.00	150.00
32A Otis	30.00	75.00
DMA Dominik Mysterio	60.00	120.00

2020 Topps Now WWE Relics

1A Drew McIntyre	30.00	75.00
2A Charlotte Flair	50.00	100.00

2021 Topps Now WWE

1 Drew McIntyre/181*	3.00	8.00
2 Sasha Banks/426*	6.00	15.00
3 Bianca Belair/342*	3.00	8.00
4 Roman Reigns/160*	6.00	15.00
5 Edge/224*	5.00	12.00
6 Bobby Lashley/132*	3.00	8.00
7 Alexa Bliss/679*	8.00	20.00
8 The Fiend Bray Wyatt/487*	8.00	20.00
9 Bobby Lashley/118*	3.00	8.00
10 Cesaro/130*	1.25	3.00
11 AJ Styles & Omos/141*	4.00	10.00
12 Braun Strowman/153*	3.00	8.00
13 Bianca Belair/286*	3.00	8.00
14 Randy Orton/		
15 Kevin Owens/116*	2.50	6.00
16 Sheamus/144*	3.00	8.00
17 Apollo Crews/118*	1.50	4.00
18 Shayna Baszler & Nia Jax/135*	3.00	8.00
19 Rhea Ripley/475*	5.00	12.00
20 Roman Reigns/193*	6.00	15.00
21 John Cena/293*	6.00	15.00
22 RK-Bro/197*	4.00	10.00
23 Becky Lynch/437*	5.00	12.00
24 Roman Reigns/189*	6.00	15.00
25 Damian Priest/201*	2.00	5.00
26 Edge/207*	5.00	12.00
27 Charlotte Flair/285*	6.00	15.00
28 Bobby Lashley/120*	3.00	8.00
29 Big E/		

2021 Topps Now WWE Autographs

STATED PRINT RUN 25 SER.#'d SETS

6A Bobby Lashley
29A Big E

2021 Topps Now WWE Mat Relics

STATED PRINT RUN 25 SER.#'d SETS

13A Bianca Belair		
20A Roman Reigns		
23A Becky Lynch	50.00	100.00
24A Roman Reigns		
27A Charlotte Flair	30.00	75.00
SS1A Goldberg		
SS2A John Cena		

2017 Topps Now WWE Countdown to NXT TakeOver Orlando

1 Asuka vs. Ember Moon	5.00	12.00
2 Bobby Roode vs. Nakamura	5.00	12.00
3 AOP vs. Revival vs. #DIY	5.00	12.00
4 Aleister Black vs. Andrade	5.00	12.00
5 Dillinger/Strong/Jose/Ruby vs. Sanity	5.00	12.00

2017 Topps Now WWE Countdown to WrestleMania

1 Goldberg vs. Brock Lesnar	5.00	12.00
2 Bray Wyatt vs. Randy Orton	5.00	12.00
3 Chris Jericho vs. Kevin Owens	6.00	15.00
4 Undertaker vs. Roman Reigns	8.00	20.00
5 Bayley/Charlotte/Sasha/Nia	8.00	20.00
6 SD Women's Title Match	12.00	30.00
7 Cena & Nikki vs. Miz & Maryse	5.00	12.00
8 Seth Rollins vs. HHH	5.00	12.00
9 AJ Styles vs. Shane McMahon	5.00	12.00
10 Dean Ambrose vs. Baron Corbin	5.00	12.00
11 Neville vs. Austin Aries	5.00	12.00

2017 Topps Now WWE SummerSlam

STATED PRINT RUN 36 SER.#'d SETS
UNPRICED DUE TO SCARCITY

1 Lesnar/Reigns/Samoa Joe/Strowman
2 Jinder Mahal vs. Nakamura
3 Alexa Bliss vs. Sasha Banks
4 Naomi vs. Natalya
5 AJ Styles vs. Kevin Owens
6 Akira Tozawa vs. Neville
7 Cesaro/Sheamus vs. Ambrose/Rollins
8 New Day vs. Usos
9 John Cena vs. Baron Corbin
10 Randy Orton vs. Rusev
11 The Demon Finn Balor vs. Bray Wyatt
12 Big Show vs. Big Cass

2021 Topps Now WWE Turn Back the Clock

COMPLETE SET (9)

1 Ron Simmons/149*
2 King Booker/113*
3 Alicia Fox/109*
4 Mark Henry/107*
5 Big E/104*
6 Sasha Banks/257*
7 Naomi/110*
8 Ember Moon/108*
9 Kofi Kingston/146*

2016-18 Topps Now WWE NXT

1 Samoa Joe/43*		
2 Asuka/77*	20.00	50.00
3 DIY/58*		
4 Authors of Pain/44*		
5 Bobby Roode/40*		
7 Eric Young/50*	6.00	15.00
8 Roderick Strong/71*	6.00	15.00
9 The Authors of Pain/49*	5.00	12.00
10 Asuka/87*	5.00	12.00
11 Bobby Roode/56*	6.00	15.00
12 Seth Rollins/62*	6.00	15.00
13 Bobby Roode/74*	5.00	12.00
14 Asuka/117*	5.00	12.00
15 Roderick Strong/27*	4.00	10.00
16 Asuka/74*	4.00	10.00
17 Bobby Roode/25*	4.00	10.00
18 The Authors of Pain/27*	4.00	10.00
19 Tommaso Ciampa/43*	4.00	10.00
20 Sanity/47*	5.00	12.00
21 Asuka/86*	5.00	12.00
22 Drew McIntyre/46*	5.00	12.00
23 Adam Cole/104*	5.00	12.00
24 Undisputed Era/57*	5.00	12.00
25 Andrade Cien Almas/46*	5.00	12.00
26 Ember Moon/63*	5.00	12.00

2016-18 Topps Now WWE NXT Relics

4B Asuka	30.00	75.00
5B Bobby Roode	8.00	20.00

2018 Topps Now WWE NXT

1 The Undisputed Era/38*	5.00	12.00
2 Ember Moon/56*	5.00	12.00
3 Aleister Black/54*	5.00	12.00
4 Andrade Cien Almas/31*	5.00	12.00
5 Adam Cole/80*	8.00	20.00
6 Shayna Baszler/80*	8.00	20.00
7 The Undisputed Era/50*	8.00	20.00
8 Aleister Black/56*	8.00	20.00
9 Johnny Gargano/51*	8.00	20.00
10 Kairi Sane/196*		
11 Tommaso Ciampa/66*		

2019 Topps Now WWE NXT

1 War Raiders/67*	6.00	15.00
2 Johnny Gargano/77*	3.00	8.00
3 Shayna Baszler/71*	6.00	15.00
4 Tommaso Ciampa/65*	4.00	10.00
5 War Raiders/91*	4.00	10.00
6 Johnny Gargano/131*	4.00	10.00
7 Shayna Baszler/104*	5.00	12.00
8 Velveteen Dream/93*	6.00	15.00
9 Matt Riddle/36*	4.00	10.00
10 Street Profits/34*	5.00	12.00
11 Velveteen Dream/36*	5.00	12.00
12 Shayna Baszler/36*	5.00	12.00
13 Adam Cole/56*	5.00	12.00
14 The Street Profits/64*	4.00	10.00
15 Io Shirai/93*	5.00	12.00
16 The Velveteen Dream/65*	4.00	10.00
17 Shayna Baszler/80*	5.00	12.00
18 Adam Cole/86*	4.00	10.00
19 Candice LeRae/110*	8.00	20.00
20 Roderick Strong/31*	6.00	15.00
21 Team Ripley/79*		
22 Pete Dunne/46*		
23 Finn Balor/38*		
25 The Undisputed Era/22*		
26 Tyler Bate/24*		
27 Kay Lee Ray/45*		
28 Gallus/36*		

2020 Topps Now WWE NXT

1 Jordan Devlin/48*	6.00	15.00
2 #DIY/		
3 Rhea Ripley/131*	5.00	12.00
4 Imperium/37*	8.00	20.00
5 Adam Cole/35*	5.00	12.00
6 The Broserweights/38*	6.00	15.00
7 Rhea Ripley/81*	5.00	12.00
8 Finn Balor/29*	8.00	20.00
9 Dakota Kai/88*	4.00	10.00
10 Keith Lee/34*	5.00	12.00
11 Finn Balor/42*		
12 Keith Lee/48*		
13 Adam Cole/64*		
14 Karrion Kross/88*		
15 Io Shirai/314*		
16 Io Shirai/94*		
17 Dexter Lumis/67*		
18 Tegan Nox/227*		
19 Candice LeRae/85*		
20 Keith Lee/125*		
21A Karrion Kross/		
21B Damian Priest/35*		
22A Io Shirai/		
22B Kushida/57*		
23A Damian Priest/		
23B Santos Escobar/47*		
24 Io Shirai/110*		
25 Finn Balor/*40		
26 Johnny Gargano/28*		
27 Dexter Lumis/36*		
28 Rhea Ripley/83*		
29 Io Shirai/96*		
30 Team Candice/95*	15.00	40.00
31 Johnny Gargano/42*		
32 The Undisputed Era/61*		
LR Leon Ruff/148*	5.00	12.00

2020 Topps Now WWE NXT Autograph

LRA Leon Ruff	30.00	75.00

2017 Topps Now WWE NXT TakeOver Brooklyn III

1 Bobby Roode vs. Drew McIntyre	6.00	15.00
2 Asuka vs. Ember Moon	8.00	20.00
3 AOP vs. SAnitY	6.00	15.00

4	Aleister Black vs. Hideo Itami	6.00	15.00
5	Andrade vs. Johnny Gargano	6.00	15.00

2021 Topps On-Demand WWE Best of British

COMPLETE SET (30)
*GREEN/99: X TO X BASIC CARDS
*BLUE/49: X TO X BASIC CARDS
*PURPLE/25: X TO X BASIC CARDS
*RED/10: UNPRICED DUE TO SCARCITY
*ORANGE/5: UNPRICED DUE TO SCARCITY
*GOLD/1: UNPRICED DUE TO SCARCITY

1 British Bulldog
2 Drew McIntyre
3 Paige
4 Bret "Hit Man" Hart vs. British Bulldog
5 Macho Man Randy Savage vs. Ultimate Warrior
6 Papa Shango vs. Tito Santana
7 Grizzled Young Veterans
8 William Regal
9 Wade Barrett
10 Tyler Bate
11 Pete Dunne
12 Flash Morgan Webster
13 Piper Niven
14 Zack Gibson
15 Joe Coffey
16 Mark Coffey
17 Wolfgang
18 Danny Burch
19 Trent Seven
20 Mark Andrews
21 Gallus
22 Nikki Cross
23 Kay Lee Ray
24 James Drake
25 AJ Styles vs. Jinder Mahal
26 Becky Lynch
27 Finn Balor
28 Sheamus
29 Jordan Devlin
30 Killian Dain

2021 Topps On-Demand WWE Best of British Autographs

*RED/10: UNPRICED DUE TO SCARCITY
*ORANGE/5: UNPRICED DUE TO SCARCITY
*GOLD/1: UNPRICED DUE TO SCARCITY

NNO AJ Styles
NNO Becky Lynch
NNO Bret Hart
NNO Drew McIntyre
NNO Finn Balor
NNO James Drake
NNO Kay Lee Ray
NNO Killian Dain
NNO Mark Andrews
NNO Mark Coffey
NNO Nikki Cross
NNO Pete Dunne
NNO Sheamus
NNO Trent Seven
NNO Tyler Bate
NNO Wade Barrett
NNO William Regal
NNO Wolfgang

2019 Topps On-Demand WWE Mother's Day

COMPLETE SET (9)		12.00	30.00
STATED PRINT RUN 107 ANNCD SETS			
1	Beth Phoenix	2.00	5.00
2	Eve Torres	1.50	4.00
3	Lacey Evans	2.50	6.00
4	Maryse	1.50	4.00
5	Mickie James	3.00	8.00
6	Naomi	2.00	5.00
7	Tamina	1.25	3.00
8	Trish Stratus	6.00	15.00
9	Stephanie McMahon	3.00	8.00

2021 Topps On-Demand WWE Summer of Cena

COMPLETE SET (15)		20.00	50.00
*PURPLE/25: 2X TO 5X BASIC CARDS			
*RED/10: UNPRICED DUE TO SCARCITY			
*ORANGE/5: UNPRICED DUE TO SCARCITY			
*GOLD/1: UNPRICED DUE TO SCARCITY			
STATED PRINT RUN ANNCD SETS			
NNO	Contract Is Signed	2.50	6.00
NNO	Crushing Corbin	2.50	6.00
NNO	John Cena	2.50	6.00
NNO	John Cena By the Numbers	2.50	6.00
NNO	John Cena vs. Batista	2.50	6.00
NNO	John Cena vs. Booker T	2.50	6.00
NNO	John Cena vs. Randy Orton	2.50	6.00
NNO	Masters of the Mic	2.50	6.00
NNO	Meeting the Bro	2.50	6.00
NNO	Opening RAW	2.50	6.00
NNO	Shocking Return	2.50	6.00
NNO	SummerSlam 2021 Poster Image	2.50	6.00
NNO	The Ultimate Face-Off	2.50	6.00
NNO	Vegas Can See Him!	2.50	6.00
NNO	Vegas Classic	2.50	6.00

2020 Topps On-Demand WWE 30 Years of the Deadman

COMPLETE SET (40)		12.00	30.00
STATED PRINT RUN 278 SER.#'d SETS			

2020 Topps On-Demand WWE 30 Years of the Deadman Rest in Peace Relic

*NAVY BLUE/50: .75X TO 2X BASIC MEM
*PURPLE/30: 1X TO 2.5X BASIC MEM
*GRAY/15: UNPRICED DUE TO SCARCITY
*BLACK/5: UNPRICED DUE TO SCARCITY
*GOLD/1: UNPRICED DUE TO SCARCITY
STATED PRINT RUN 99 SER.#'d SETS

C1	Undertaker	12.00	30.00

2019 Topps On-Demand WWE WrestleMania 35 Roster

COMPLETE SET (10)		25.00	60.00
STATED PRINT RUN 75 SER.#'d SETS			
1	Kurt Angle	3.00	8.00
2	Kofi Kingston	2.50	6.00
3	The New Daniel Bryan	6.00	15.00
4	Becky Lynch	6.00	15.00
5	Charlotte Flair	6.00	15.00
6	Ronda Rousey	8.00	20.00
7	Seth Rollins	4.00	10.00
8	Brock Lesnar	6.00	15.00
9	Triple H	4.00	10.00
10	Dave Batista	4.00	10.00

2010 Topps Platinum WWE

COMPLETE SET (125)		12.00	30.00
UNOPENED BOX (24 PACKS)			
UNOPENED PACK (7 CARDS)			
*RAINBOW: .8X TO 2X BASIC CARDS			
*X-FRACTOR: 1X TO 2.5X BASIC CARDS			
*GREEN/499: 1.25X TO 3X BASIC CARDS			
*BLUE/199: 2X TO 5X BASIC CARDS			
*GOLD/50: 3X TO 8X BASIC CARDS			
*RED/1: UNPRICED DUE TO SCARCITY			
*P.P.BLACK/1: UNPRICED DUE TO SCARCITY			
*P.P.CYAN/1: UNPRICED DUE TO SCARCITY			
*P.P.MAGENTA/1: UNPRICED DUE TO SCARCITY			
*P.P.YELLOW/1: UNPRICED DUE TO SCARCITY			
1	John Cena	1.00	2.50
2	Finlay	.30	.75
3	Shad	.20	.50
4	Dean Malenko	.30	.75
5	Christian	.30	.75
6	Kane	.50	1.25
7	Luke Gallows	.20	.50
8	The Miz	.30	.75
9	Gail Kim	.50	1.25
10	Iron Sheik	.50	1.25
11	Eli Cottonwood	.20	.50
12	High Chief Peter Maivia	.20	.50
13	Earthquake	.30	.75
14	Melina	.75	2.00
15	Paul Bearer	.30	.75
16	Rosa Mendes	.30	.75
17	Ricky The Dragon Steamboat	.30	.75
18	Darren Young	.30	.75
19	Animal UER/Hawk on Front	.20	.50
20	JTG	.20	.50
21	Evan Bourne	.20	.50
22	Jake The Snake Roberts	.50	1.25
23	Edge	.75	2.00
24	Beth Phoenix	.75	2.00
25	Jey Uso	.20	.50
26	The Great Khali	.20	.50
27	Jimmy Superfly Snuka	.50	1.25
28	Layla	.50	1.25
29	Mark Henry	.30	.75
30	Arn Anderson	.30	.75
31	Jimmy Uso	.20	.50
32	Bushwhacker Luke	.20	.50
33	Jerry The King Lawler	.30	.75
34	Chris Masters	.20	.50
35	Bushwhacker Butch	.20	.50
36	Hawk UER/Animal on Front	.20	.50
37	Big Show	.50	1.25
38	Tamina	.20	.50
39	Hacksaw Jim Duggan	.30	.75
40	Cowboy Bob Orton	.30	.75
41	Percy Watson	.20	.50
42	Ted DiBiase	.30	.75
43	Curt Hawkins	.20	.50
44	Husky Harris	.40	1.00
45	Tyler Reks	.20	.50
46	Mr. Perfect Curt Hennig	.30	.75
47	Jillian	.75	2.00
48	CM Punk	.75	2.00
49	Vance Archer	.20	.50
50	Tiffany	.30	.75
51	Hillbilly Jim	.30	.75
52	David Otunga	.30	.75
53	Jack Swagger	.20	.50
54	Maryse	.75	2.00
55	Triple H	1.00	2.50
56	Michelle McCool	.75	2.00
57	Alex Riley	.20	.50
58	One Man Gang	.30	.75
59	Kofi Kingston	.30	.75
60	Zack Ryder	.20	.50
61	Doink	.20	.50
62	Sergeant Slaughter	.50	1.25
63	Dusty Rhodes	.50	1.25
64	Kelly Kelly	.75	2.00
65	Theodore Long	.20	.50
66	Chris Jericho	.50	1.25
67	Heath Slater	.30	.75
68	Natalya	.75	2.00
69	Rocky Johnson	.20	.50
70	Kaval	.20	.50
71	Eve	.75	2.00
72	Bobby The Brain Heenan	.30	.75
73	Undertaker	.75	2.00
74	Bam Bam Bigelow	.30	.75
75	Classy Freddie Blassie	.50	1.25
76	MVP	.30	.75
77	Goldust	.30	.75
78	Chavo Guerrero	.30	.75
79	Brian Pillman	.50	1.25
80	Lucky Cannon	.20	.50
81	Drew McIntyre	.30	.75
82	Ranjin Singh	.20	.50
83	Papa Shango	.20	.50
84	William Regal	.50	1.25
85	Titus O'Neil	.20	.50
86	Trent Barreta	.20	.50
87	Nikki Bella	.75	2.00
88	R-Truth	.20	.50
89	Vader	.30	.75
90	Skip Sheffield	.30	.75
91	Tyson Kidd	.20	.50
92	Michael Tarver	.30	.75
93	John Morrison	.30	.75
94	Michael McGillicutty	.20	.50
95	Koko B. Ware	.30	.75
96	Don Muraco	.30	.75
97	Randy Orton	.75	2.00
98	Harley Race	.30	.75
99	British Bulldog	.30	.75
100	Sheamus	.30	.75
101	Justin Gabriel	.30	.75
102	Yoshi Tatsu	.20	.50
103	Ezekiel Jackson	.20	.50
104	Terry Funk	.50	1.25
105	Mr. Wonderful Paul Orndorff	.50	1.25
106	David Hart Smith	.20	.50
107	Ravishing Rick Rude	.30	.75
108	Nikolai Volkoff	.30	.75
109	Cody Rhodes	.20	.50
110	Hornswoggle	.30	.75
111	Primo	.20	.50
112	Santino Marella	.20	.50
113	Rey Mysterio	.50	1.25
114	Wade Barrett	.30	.75
115	Dolph Ziggler	.30	.75
116	Million Dollar Man Ted DiBiase	.30	.75
117	Chief Jay Strongbow	.20	.50
118	Vladimir Kozlov	.30	.75
119	Junkyard Dog	.50	1.25
120	Vickie Guerrero	.20	.50

121	Rowdy Roddy Piper	.75	2.00
122	Kamala	.30	.75
123	Brie Bella	.75	2.00
124	Caylen Croft	.20	.50
125	Alicia Fox	.30	.75
CL	Checklist	.20	.50

2010 Topps Platinum WWE Autographed Relics

*BLUE/99: .75X TO 1.5X BASIC AUTOS
*GOLD/25: 1X TO 2X BASIC AUTOS
STATED PRINT RUN 275 SER. #'d SETS

1	John Cena	20.00	50.00
5	Christian	10.00	25.00
8	The Miz	10.00	25.00
21	Evan Bourne	12.00	30.00
23	Edge	15.00	40.00
37	Big Show	15.00	40.00
48	CM Punk	35.00	70.00
59	Kofi Kingston	12.00	30.00
76	MVP	10.00	25.00
97	Randy Orton	15.00	40.00

2010 Topps Platinum WWE Autographs

*BLUE/99: .75X TO 1.5X BASIC AUTOS
*GOLD/25: 1X TO 2X BASIC AUTOS
*RED/1: UNPRICED DUE TO SCARCITY
*P.P.BLACK/1: UNPRICED DUE TO SCARCITY
*P.P.CYAN/1: UNPRICED DUE TO SCARCITY
*P.P.MAGENTA/1: UNPRICED DUE TO SCARCITY
*P.P.YELLOW/1: UNPRICED DUE TO SCARCITY
STATED PRINT RUN 271 SER.#'d SETS

6	Kane	15.00	40.00
42	Ted DiBiase	12.00	30.00
43	Curt Hawkins	6.00	15.00
45	Tyler Reks	6.00	15.00
52	David Otunga	8.00	20.00
54	Maryse	20.00	50.00
56	Michelle McCool	20.00	50.00
60	Zack Ryder	8.00	20.00
64	Kelly Kelly	20.00	50.00
65	Theodore Long	8.00	20.00
66	Chris Jericho	25.00	60.00
81	Drew McIntyre	12.00	30.00
86	Trent Barreta	8.00	20.00
114	Wade Barrett	12.00	30.00
115	Dolph Ziggler	12.00	30.00
124	Caylen Croft UER/Misspelled Caylan	8.00	20.00
125	Alicia Fox	12.00	30.00

2010 Topps Platinum WWE Legendary Superstars

COMPLETE SET (25) 5.00 12.00
*GREEN/499: .5X TO 1.25X BASIC CARDS
*BLUE/199: .6X TO 1.5X BASIC CARDS
*GOLD/50: 1.2X TO 3X BASIC CARDS
*RED/1: UNPRICED DUE TO SCARCITY
STATED ODDS 1:4

LS1	Evan Bourne/Jimmy Snuka	.60	1.50
LS2	Dolph Ziggler/Paul Orndorff	.60	1.50
LS3	Randy Orton/Jake Roberts	1.00	2.50
LS4	Goldust/Papa Shango	.40	1.00
LS5	R-Truth/Koko B. Ware	.40	1.00
LS6	The Miz/Michael Hayes	.40	1.00
LS7	Mark Henry/One Man Gang	.40	1.00
LS8	Big Show/Vader	.60	1.50
LS9	William Regal/Arn Anderson	.60	1.50
LS10	John Cena/Dusty Rhodes	1.25	3.00
LS11	Drew McIntyre/Rick Rude	.40	1.00
LS12	Edge/Brian Pillman	1.00	2.50
LS13	Chris Jericho/Roddy Piper	1.00	2.50
LS14	The Usos/Wild Samoans	.40	1.00
LS15	Kane/Bam Bam Bigelow	.60	1.50
LS16	Daniel Bryan/Dean Malenko	.40	1.00
LS17	Sheamus/Iron Sheik	.60	1.50
LS18	Triple H/Harley Race	1.25	3.00
LS19	Curt Hawkins/Curt Hennig	.40	1.00
LS20	Ted DiBiase/Tully Blanchard	.40	1.00
LS21	MVP/Ted DiBiase	.40	1.00
LS22	Rey Mysterio/Ricky Steamboat	.60	1.50
LS23	CM Punk/Terry Funk	1.00	2.50
LS24	Brothers of Destruction	1.00	2.50
	Legion of Doom		
LS25	Wade Barrett/British Bulldog	.40	1.00

2010 Topps Platinum WWE Platinum Performance

COMPLETE SET (25) 6.00 15.00
*GREEN/499: .5X TO 1.25X BASIC CARDS
*BLUE/199: .6X TO 1.5X BASIC CARDS
*GOLD/50: 1.2X TO 3X BASIC CARDS
*RED/1: UNPRICED DUE TO SCARCITY
STATED ODDS 1:4

PP1	Pat Patterson	.40	1.00
PP2	Bobby The Brain Heenan	.40	1.00
PP3	Chris Jericho	.60	1.50
PP4	Randy Orton	1.00	2.50
PP5	Hacksaw Jim Duggan	.40	1.00
PP6	Triple H	1.25	3.00
PP7	CM Punk	1.00	2.50
PP8	The British Bulldog	.40	1.00
PP9	Beth Phoenix	1.00	2.50
PP10	John Cena	1.25	3.00
PP11	Jimmy Superfly Snuka	.60	1.50
PP12	Sheamus	.40	1.00
PP13	Chris Jericho	.60	1.50
PP14	Big Show	.60	1.50
PP15	Rey Mysterio	.60	1.50
PP16	The Hart Dynasty	.40	1.00
PP17	Undertaker	1.00	2.50
PP18	Million Dollar Man Ted DiBiase	.40	1.00
PP19	Vladimir Kozlov	.40	1.00
PP20	Edge	1.00	2.50
PP21	John Morrison	.40	1.00
PP22	Harley Race	.40	1.00
PP23	MVP	.40	1.00
PP24	Eve	1.00	2.50
PP25	Ricky The Dragon Steamboat	.40	1.00

2010 Topps Platinum WWE Relics

*GREEN/399: .5X TO 1.25X BASIC MEM
*BLUE/99: .6X TO 1.5X BASIC MEM
*GOLD/50: 1.2X TO 3X BASIC MEM
*RED/10: UNPRICED DUE TO SCARCITY
STATED ODDS ONE PER HOBBY BOX

1	John Cena	8.00	20.00
5	Christian	5.00	12.00
8	The Miz	5.00	12.00
23	Edge	6.00	15.00
37	Big Show	6.00	15.00
48	CM Punk	8.00	20.00
55	Triple H	8.00	20.00
59	Kofi Kingston	5.00	12.00
76	MVP	5.00	12.00
88	R-Truth	5.00	12.00
91	Tyson Kidd	6.00	15.00
93	John Morrison	8.00	20.00
97	Randy Orton	10.00	25.00
100	Sheamus	6.00	15.00
106	David Hart Smith	5.00	12.00

2010 Topps Platinum WWE Triple Relics

STATED PRINT RUN 99 SER.#'d SETS

PTR1	HHH/Cena/Edge	25.00	50.00
PTR2	Morrison/Kingston/Miz	20.00	40.00
PTR3	Bourne/Truth/Christian	20.00	40.00
PTR4	Rhodes/Bourne/MVP	20.00	40.00
PTR5	Christian/Edge/Kidd	20.00	40.00
PTR6	Sheamus/Mysterio/Orton/75	25.00	50.00
PTR7	Cena/Sheamus/Morrison	25.00	50.00
PTR8	Orton/Smith/Marella	25.00	50.00
PTR9	Show/Edge/Punk	20.00	40.00
PTR10	Punk/Miz/Mysterio/75	20.00	40.00

1999 Topps WCW Embossed

COMPLETE SET (72) 10.00 25.00
UNOPENED BOX (36 PACKS)
UNOPENED PACK (8 CARDS)

1	Title Card	.12	.30
2	Buff Bagwell	.12	.30
3	Lash LeRoux	.12	.30
4	Chris Benoit	.20	.50
5	Rick Steiner	.20	.50
6	Diamond Dallas Page	.25	.60
7	Disco Inferno	.12	.30
8	Bobby Duncum, Jr.	.12	.30
9	Vampiro	.12	.30
10	Rowdy Roddy Piper	.40	1.00
11	Arn Anderson	.25	.60
12	Sid Vicious	.12	.30
13	Macho Man Randy Savage	.40	1.00
14	Ric Flair	1.00	2.50
15	Saturn	.12	.30
16	Goldberg	.30	1.00
17	Steven Regal	.12	.30
18	Juventud Guerrera	.20	.50
19	Chavo Guerrero, Jr.	.12	.30
20	Eddy Guerrero	.20	.50
21	Shane Douglas	.12	.30
22	Sting	.60	1.50
23	Rey Mysterio, Jr.	.30	.75
24	Booker T.	.20	.50
25	Stevie Ray	.12	.30
26	Bret Hart	.20	.50
27	Barry Windham	.12	.30
28	Scott Norton	.12	.30
29	Curt Hennig	.25	.60
30	Kaos	.12	.30
31	Scotty Riggs	.12	.30
32	Hugh Morrus	.12	.30
33	Ernest The Cat Miller	.12	.30
34	Kanyon	.12	.30
35	Kaz Hayashi	.12	.30
36	Billy Kidman	.12	.30
37	Konnan	.12	.30
38	Psychosis	.12	.30
39	Lenny Lane	.12	.30
40	Lodi	.12	.30
41	Meng	.12	.30
42	Dean Malenko	.12	.30
43	Prince Iaukea	.12	.30
44	Berlyn	.12	.30
45	David Flair	.12	.30
46	Evan Karagias	.12	.30
47	Jimmy Hart P	.20	.50
48	JJ Dillon P	.12	.30
49	Charles Robinson P	.12	.30
50	Hardcore Hak DHD	.12	.30
51	Brian Knobs DHD	.12	.30
52	Bam Bam Bigelow DHD	.20	.50
53	Jerry Flynn DHD	.12	.30
54	Fit Finlay DHD	.12	.30
55	Hulk Hogan	2.00	5.00
56	Kevin Nash	.30	.75
57	Scott Steiner	.30	.75
58	Lex Luger	.25	.60
59	Scott Hall	.12	.30
60	Horace Hogan	.12	.30
61	Vincent	.12	.30
62	Kimberly WOW	.20	.50
63	Chae WOW	.20	.50
64	Spice WOW	.20	.50
65	Tygress WOW	.20	.50
66	Fyre WOW	.20	.50
67	A.C. Jazz WOW	.20	.50
68	Storm WOW	.20	.50
69	Asya WOW	.20	.50
70	Madusa WOW	.20	.50
71	Gorgeous George WOW	.20	.50
72	Miss Elizabeth WOW	.30	.75
NNO	Hulk Hogan RR	25.00	50.00

1999 Topps WCW Embossed Authentic Signatures

STATED ODDS 1:49

NNO	Asya	20.00	50.00
NNO	Barbarian	50.00	100.00
NNO	Blitzkrieg	15.00	40.00
NNO	Brad Armstrong	25.00	60.00
NNO	Buff Bagwell	75.00	150.00
NNO	Chastity	30.00	75.00
NNO	Chris Adams	50.00	100.00
NNO	Dave Taylor	20.00	50.00
NNO	Doug Dillinger	15.00	40.00
NNO	Eric Watts	30.00	75.00
NNO	Gorgeous George	100.00	200.00
NNO	Hacksaw Jim Duggan	30.00	75.00
NNO	Horace Hogan	25.00	60.00
NNO	Jerry Flynn	25.00	60.00
NNO	Kendall Windham	75.00	150.00
NNO	Lash Laroux	20.00	50.00
NNO	Lex Luger	60.00	120.00
NNO	Lizmark, Jr.	20.00	50.00
NNO	Madusa	50.00	100.00
NNO	Outrageous Evan Karagias	20.00	50.00
NNO	Sarge Buddy Lee Parker	20.00	50.00
NNO	Scott Hudson	30.00	75.00
NNO	Scotty Putsky	25.00	60.00
NNO	Steve Regal	50.00	100.00
NNO	Tank Abbott	50.00	100.00
NNO	Tough Tom	20.00	50.00
NNO	Van Hammer	30.00	75.00

1999 Topps WCW Embossed Chrome

COMPLETE SET (5) 12.00
STATED ODDS 1:6

1	Buff Bagwell/Lex Luger	1.50	4.00
2	Goldberg/Kevin Nash	2.50	6.00
3	Randy Savage/Gorgeous George	2.50	6.00
4	Ric Flair/David Flair	2.00	5.00
5	Scott Steiner/Rick Steiner	1.25	3.00

1999 Topps WCW Embossed Promos

P1	Buff Bagwell	1.00	2.50
P2	Gorgeous George	1.50	4.00

1998 Topps WCW/nWo

COMPLETE SET (72) 30.00 75.00
UNOPENED BOX (36 PACKS)
UNOPENED PACK (4 CARDS)

1	Hollywood Hogan	4.00	10.00
2	Sting	1.25	3.00
3	Kevin Nash	.40	1.00
4	Macho Man Randy Savage	1.25	3.00
5	Bret Hart	1.25	3.00
6	Lex Luger	.30	.75
7	Giant	3.00	8.00
8	Diamond Dallas Page	.40	1.00
9	Goldberg	10.00	25.00
10	Scott Hall	.75	2.00
11	Rick Steiner	.20	.50
12	Scott Steiner	.30	.75
13	Buff Bagwell	.60	1.50
14	Scott Norton	.12	.30
15	Booker T	.20	.50
16	Rowdy Roddy Piper	1.50	4.00
17	Chris Benoit	1.50	4.00
18	Raven	.12	.30
19	Chris Jericho	4.00	10.00
20	Ravishing Rick Rude	.30	.75
21	Konnan	.12	.30
22	Saturn	.12	.30
23	Sick Boy	.12	.30
24	British Bulldog	.20	.50
25	Juventud Guerrera	.12	.30
26	Dean Malenko	.12	.30
27	Eddy Guerrero	4.00	10.00
28	Chavo Guerrero Jr.	.12	.30
29	Ultimo Dragon	.12	.30
30	Disco Inferno	.12	.30
31	Wrath	.12	.30
32	Rey Mysterio Jr.	8.00	20.00
33	Psychosis	.12	.30
34	Stevie Ray	.12	.30
35	Jimmy Hart	.20	.50
36	Steve McMichael	.20	.50
37	Curt Hennig	.30	.75
38	Meng	.12	.30
39	Vincent	.12	.30
40	Fit Finley	.12	.30
41	Jay Leno	3.00	8.00
42	Alex Wright	.12	.30
43	Tenay/Schiavone/Heenan	.12	.30
44	Hugh Morrus	.12	.30
45	Kaz Hayashi	.12	.30
46	Kanyon	.12	.30
47	The Disciple	.20	.50
48	Jim Neidhart	.12	.30
49	Arn Anderson	.20	.50
50	Eric Bischoff	1.25	3.00
51	Ernest Miller	.12	.30
52	Miss Elizabeth	2.00	5.00
53	Gene Okerlund	.20	.50
54	Ric Flair	.75	2.00
55	Brian Adams	.20	.50
56	Lodi	.12	.30
57	Riggs	.12	.30
58	Fyre NG	1.25	3.00
59	Chae NG	1.25	3.00
60	Kimberly NG	1.25	3.00
61	Spice NG	1.25	3.00
62	A.C. Jazz NG	1.25	3.00
63	Tygress NG	1.25	3.00
64	Whisper NG	1.25	3.00
65	Hollywood Hogan ICON	5.00	12.00
66	Macho Man Randy Savage ICON	1.25	3.00
67	Rowdy Roddy Piper ICON	1.25	3.00
68	Goldberg CH	2.00	5.00
69	Chris Jericho CH	3.00	8.00
70	Bret Hart CH	.30	.75
71	Kidman CH	.12	.30
72	Hogan/Goldberg CL	.12	2.00

1998 Topps WCW/nWo Authentic Signatures

STATED ODDS 1:40 HOBBY

NNO	Alex Wright	25.00	60.00
NNO	Arn Anderson	75.00	150.00
NNO	Bobby Heenan	125.00	250.00
NNO	Chris Benoit	500.00	1000.00
NNO	Chris Jericho	300.00	600.00
NNO	Dean Malenko	100.00	200.00
NNO	Diamond Dallas Page	125.00	250.00
NNO	The Disciple	25.00	60.00
NNO	Disco Inferno	25.00	60.00
NNO	Eddy Guerrero	750.00	1500.00
NNO	Ernest Miller	100.00	200.00
NNO	Fit Finley	30.00	75.00
NNO	Fyre	30.00	75.00
NNO	Gene Okerlund	100.00	200.00
NNO	Giant	125.00	250.00
NNO	Hollywood Hogan	300.00	500.00
NNO	Jimmy Hart	30.00	75.00
NNO	Juventud Guerrera	30.00	75.00
NNO	Kanyon	25.00	60.00
NNO	Kaz Hayashi	30.00	75.00
NNO	Kevin Nash	50.00	100.00
NNO	Kidman	60.00	120.00
NNO	Konnan	30.00	75.00
NNO	Lodi	20.00	50.00
NNO	Meng	30.00	75.00
NNO	Mike Tenay	15.00	40.00
NNO	Psychosis	75.00	150.00
NNO	Raven	50.00	100.00
NNO	Riggs	50.00	100.00
NNO	Saturn	30.00	75.00
NNO	Sick Boy	50.00	100.00
NNO	Spice	30.00	75.00
NNO	Tony Schiavone	60.00	120.00
NNO	Tygress	25.00	60.00
NNO	Vincent	15.00	40.00
NNO	Whisper	25.00	60.00
NNO	Wrath	30.00	75.00

1998 Topps WCW/nWo Chrome

COMPLETE SET (10) 20.00 40.00
STATED ODDS 1:12 HOBBY EXCLUSIVE

C1	Goldberg	8.00	20.00
C2	Diamond Dallas Page	2.50	6.00
C3	Macho Man Randy Savage	6.00	15.00
C4	Sting	6.00	15.00
C5	Hollywood Hogan	12.00	30.00
C6	Kevin Nash	2.50	6.00
C7	Konnan	1.25	3.00
C8	Bret Hart	3.00	8.00
C9	Giant	2.00	5.00
C10	Lex Luger	2.00	5.00

1998 Topps WCW/nWo Retail Stickers

COMPLETE SET (10) 5.00 12.00
STATED ODDS 1:1 RETAIL EXCLUSIVE

S1	Goldberg	2.00	5.00
S2	Diamond Dallas Page	.60	1.50
S3	Macho Man Randy Savage	1.50	4.00
S4	Sting	2.50	6.00
S5	Hollywood Hogan	2.00	5.00
S6	Kevin Nash	.50	1.25
S7	Konnan	.40	1.00
S8	Bret Hart	1.25	3.00
S9	Giant	.60	1.50
S10	Lex Luger	.40	1.00

1998 Topps WCW/nWo Promos

P1	Hollywood Hogan	1.00	2.50
P2	Sting	1.25	3.00
P3	Macho Man	.75	2.00
P4	Diamond Dallas Page	.60	1.50
P5	Goldberg	1.00	2.50

1999 Topps WCW/nWo Nitro

COMPLETE SET (72) 6.00 15.00
UNOPENED BOX (36 PACKS)
UNOPENED PACK (8 CARDS)

1	Checklist	.12	.30
2	Bret Hart	.25	.60
3	Diamond Dallas Page	.25	.60
4	Goldberg	.30	.75
5	Rick Steiner	.20	.50
6	Booker T	.20	.50
7	Chris Jericho	.20	.50
8	Saturn	.12	.30
9	Bam Bam Bigelow	.20	.50
10	Chavo Guerrero, Jr.	.12	.30
11	Disco Inferno	.12	.30
12	Wrath	.12	.30
13	Rey Misterio, Jr.	.25	.60
14	Meng	.12	.30
15	Super Calo	.12	.30
16	Glacier	.12	.30
17	Silver King	.12	.30
18	Kaos	.12	.30
19	Lenny Lane	.12	.30
20	Norman Smiley	.12	.30
21	Kidman	.12	.30
22	Alex Wright	.12	.30
23	Kanyon	.12	.30
24	Raven	.12	.30
25	Lodi	.12	.30
26	Ernest Miller	.20	.50
27	The Disciple	.20	.50
28	Bobby Duncum, Jr.	.12	.30
29	Barry Windham	.12	.30
30	Konnan	.12	.30
31	Buff Bagwell	.12	.30
32	Eric Bischoff	.12	.30
33	Hollywood Hogan	1.50	4.00
34	Scott Hall	.12	.30
35	Horace Hogan	.12	.30
36	Scott Steiner	.25	.60
37	Stevie Ray	.12	.30
38	Brian Adams	.12	.30
39	Vincent	.12	.30
40	Curt Hennig	.25	.60
41	Macho Man Randy Savage	.40	1.00
42	Sting	.60	1.50
43	Kevin Nash	.30	.75
44	Lex Luger	.25	.60
45	Ric Flair	1.00	2.50
46	Arn Anderson	.20	.50
47	Dean Malenko	.12	.30
48	Chris Benoit	.25	.60
49	Steve McMichael	.20	.50
50	Juventud Guerrera	.12	.30
51	Eddie Guerrero	.20	.50
52	Psychosis	.12	.30
53	La Parka	.12	.30
54	Damian	.12	.30
55	Hector Garza	.12	.30
56	Miss Elizabeth	.30	.75
57	Kimberly	.20	.50
58	Spice	.20	.50
59	A.C. Jazz	.20	.50
60	Tygress	.20	.50
61	Whisper	.20	.50
62	Chae	.20	.50
63	Fyre	.20	.50
64	Storm	.20	.50
65	Goldberg Triumphant	.30	.75
66	The Venomous Bite of Sting	.40	1.00
67	Hogan for President	.60	1.50
68	Kevin Nash Is God	.30	.75
69	DDP Is Back Again	.25	.60
70	Larry Zbyszko/Bobby Heenan	.20	.50
71	Doug Dellinger	.12	.30
72	Sonny Onoo	.12	.30

1999 Topps WCW/nWo Nitro Authentic Signatures

COMPLETE SET (37)
STATED ODDS 1:40 HOBBY

NNO	A.C. Jazz	25.00	60.00
NNO	Bam Bam Bigelow	150.00	300.00
NNO	Billy Silverman	30.00	75.00
NNO	Bret Hart	100.00	200.00
NNO	Brian Adams	100.00	200.00
NNO	Chae	20.00	50.00
NNO	Charles Robinson	25.00	60.00
NNO	Chavo Guerrero, Jr.	15.00	40.00
NNO	Curt Hennig	250.00	400.00
NNO	Cyclope	12.00	30.00
NNO	Damian	50.00	100.00
NNO	David Penzer	15.00	40.00
NNO	El Dandy	10.00	25.00
NNO	Glacier	75.00	150.00
NNO	Goldberg	200.00	400.00
NNO	Hector Garza	12.00	30.00
NNO	Hugh Morrus	25.00	60.00
NNO	Jim Neidhart	50.00	100.00
NNO	Kenny Kaos	15.00	40.00
NNO	Kimberly	125.00	250.00
NNO	La Parka	50.00	100.00
NNO	Larry Zbyszko	25.00	60.00
NNO	Lenny Lane	25.00	60.00
NNO	Macho Man Randy Savage	500.00	1000.00
NNO	Ms. Elizabeth	400.00	800.00

NNO	Nick Patrick	10.00	25.00
NNO	Norman Smiley	12.00	30.00
NNO	Prince Iaukea	10.00	25.00
NNO	Rick Steiner	100.00	200.00
NNO	Scott Hall	125.00	250.00
NNO	Scott Norton	20.00	50.00
NNO	Silver King	10.00	25.00
NNO	Sonny Onoo	30.00	75.00
NNO	Sting	150.00	300.00
NNO	Storm	50.00	100.00
NNO	Super Calo	10.00	25.00
NNO	Ultimo Dragon	30.00	75.00

1999 Topps WCW/nWo Nitro Chrome

COMPLETE SET (12)		30.00	60.00
STATED ODDS 1:12 HOBBY			
C1	Sting/Luger v. Hogan/Nash	3.00	8.00
C2	Hogan v. Sting	4.00	10.00
C3	Hogan v. Savage	3.00	8.00
C4	Savage v. Sting	2.50	6.00
C5	Nash v. Giant	3.00	8.00
C6	Hogan/Hart v. Savage/Piper	4.00	10.00
C7	DDP v. Hogan	3.00	8.00
C8	DDP v. Hogan	3.00	8.00
C9	WCW v. The Pac v. Hollywood	3.00	8.00
C10	Goldberg v. DDP	2.50	6.00
C11	60 Man 3 Ring Battle Royal	1.50	4.00
C12	Nash v. Goldberg	3.00	8.00

1999 Topps WCW/nWo Nitro Stickers

COMPLETE SET (12)		3.00	6.00
STATED ODDS 1:1 RETAIL			
S1	Sting/Luger v. Hogan/Nash	.40	1.00
S2	Hogan v. Sting	.40	1.00
S3	Hogan v. Savage	.30	.75
S4	Savage v. Sting	.20	.50
S5	Nash v. Giant	.20	.50
S6	Hogan/Hart v. Savage/Piper	.40	1.00
S7	DDP v. Hogan	.40	1.00
S8	DDP v. Hogan	.40	1.00
S9	WCW v. The Pac v. Hollywood	.40	1.00
S10	Goldberg v. DDP	.30	.75
S11	60 Man 3 Ring Battle Royal	.20	.50
S12	Nash v. Goldberg	.30	.75

1999 Topps WCW/nWo Nitro Promos

D1 IS DEALER EXCLUSIVE			
B1	Nash and Nitro Girls DE	3.00	8.00
H1	Goldberg	2.00	5.00
H2	Kevin Nash	.75	2.00
H3	Goldberg	1.25	3.00
R1	Goldberg		

2009 Topps WWE

COMPLETE SET (90)		15.00	30.00
UNOPENED BOX (24 PACKS)			
UNOPENED PACK (7 CARDS)			
*GOLD/500: 1.2X TO 3X BASIC CARDS			
*BLACK/40: 5X TO 12X BASIC CARDS			
*PLATINUM/1: UNPRICED DUE TO SCARCITY			
1	Hurricane Helms	.15	.40
2	Carlito	.40	1.00
3	CM Punk	.25	.60
4	Maria	.60	1.50
5	Kofi Kingston	.15	.40
6	Primo	.15	.40
7	Rey Mysterio	.40	1.00

8	Natalya	.60	1.50
9	Tommy Dreamer	.15	.40
10	Michelle McCool	.60	1.50
11	Undertaker	.75	2.00
12	Big Show	.40	1.00
13	Charlie Haas	.15	.40
14	Chris Jericho	.40	1.00
15	Evan Bourne	.15	.40
16	Layla	.40	1.00
17	Christian	.40	1.00
18	Cody Rhodes	.15	.40
19	Dolph Ziggler	.25	.60
20	Randy Orton	.40	1.00
21	Edge	.60	1.50
22	Mickie James	.75	2.00
23	Festus	.15	.40
24	Finlay	.25	.60
25	Ted DiBiase	.25	.60
26	Goldust	.25	.60
27	Melina	.60	1.50
28	Hornswoggle	.25	.60
29	Jack Swagger	.15	.40
30	Jim Ross	.15	.40
31	Mark Henry	.25	.60
32	Katie Lea Burchill	.40	1.00
33	Mike Knox	.15	.40
34	Kelly Kelly	.60	1.50
35	Matt Hardy	.60	1.50
36	Montel Vontavious Porter	.25	.60
37	R-Truth	.15	.40
38	John Cena	1.00	2.50
39	William Regal	.40	1.00
40	Santino Marella	.15	.40
41	Tyson Kidd	.15	.40
42	Maryse	.40	1.00
43	Shelton Benjamin	.15	.40
44	The Brian Kendrick	.25	.60
45	The Great Khali	.15	.40
46	Eve	.60	1.50
47	The Miz	.25	.60
48	Triple H	1.00	2.50
49	Vladimir Kozlov	.25	.60
50	Alicia Fox	.25	.60
51	Beth Phoenix	.75	2.00
52	Gail Kim	.40	1.00
53	Jerry The King Lawler	.25	.60
54	Theodore Long	.15	.40
55	Batista	.60	1.50
56	Tiffany	.25	.60
57	Ranjin Singh	.15	.40
58	Tony Atlas	.15	.40
59	Kane	.60	1.50
60	Shawn Michaels	1.00	2.50
61	Chavo Guerrero	.25	.60
62	John Morrison	.25	.60
63	Jamie Noble	.15	.40
64	Jimmy Wang Yang	.15	.40
65	Kung Fu Naki	.15	.40
66	Paul Burchill	.15	.40
67	Jillian Hall	.60	1.50
68	David Hart Smith	.15	.40
69	Curt Hawkins	.15	.40
70	DJ Gabriel	.15	.40
71	Ezekiel Jackson	.15	.40
72	Jesse	.15	.40
73	Zack Ryder	.15	.40
74	JTG	.15	.40
75	Shad Gaspard	.15	.40

76	Ricky Ortiz	.15	.40
77	Brie Bella	5.00	12.00
78	Nikki Bella	6.00	15.00
79	CM Punk	.25	.60
80	Santina Marella	.15	.40
81	Chris Jericho	.40	1.00
82	Matt Hardy	.60	1.50
83	Rey Mysterio	.40	1.00
84	Undertaker/Shawn Michaels	1.00	2.50
85	Edge	.60	1.50
86	John Cena	1.00	2.50
87	Randy Orton	.40	1.00
88	Triple H	1.00	2.50
89	Stone Cold Steve Austin	1.00	2.50
90	John Cena CL	1.00	2.50

2009 Topps WWE Autographs

STATED ODDS 1:54 HOBBY; 1:172 RETAIL			
NNO	Arn Anderson	20.00	50.00
NNO	Beth Phoenix	12.00	30.00
NNO	Evan Bourne	6.00	15.00
NNO	Gail Kim	12.00	30.00
NNO	Jim Ross	10.00	25.00
NNO	John Cena	30.00	75.00
NNO	John Morrison	15.00	40.00
NNO	Maryse	30.00	75.00
NNO	Michelle McCool	12.00	30.00
NNO	Mickie James	15.00	40.00
NNO	Ricky Steamboat	12.00	30.00
NNO	Santino Marella	6.00	15.00
NNO	Tiffany	12.00	30.00

2009 Topps WWE Dual Autographs

STATED ODDS 1:55 HOBBY EXCLUSIVE			
NNO	Bob & Randy Orton	60.00	120.00
NNO	Carlito/Primo	12.00	30.00
NNO	Dusty & Cody Rhodes	150.00	300.00
NNO	Ted DiBiase Sr. & Jr.	12.00	30.00

2009 Topps WWE Event-Worn Ringside Relics

STATED ODDS 1:24 HOBBY; 1:84 RETAIL			
NNO	Christian	6.00	15.00
NNO	Cody Rhodes	6.00	15.00
NNO	Miz (looking left)	5.00	12.00
NNO	Miz (looking right)	5.00	12.00
NNO	Santino Marella (hands apart)	6.00	15.00
NNO	Santino Marella (hands clasped)	6.00	15.00
NNO	Shawn Michaels (no hat)	8.00	20.00
NNO	Shawn Michaels (w/hat)	8.00	20.00
NNO	Ted DiBiase	6.00	15.00
NNO	Triple H	8.00	20.00

2009 Topps WWE Historical Commemorative Patches

COMPLETE SET (4)		12.00	30.00
STATED ODDS 1:RETAIL BLASTER BOX			
P1	John Cena WrestleMania	6.00	15.00
P2	John Cena The Bash	6.00	15.00
P3	John Cena SummerSlam	6.00	15.00
P4	John Cena Royal Rumble	6.00	15.00

2009 Topps WWE Judgment Day Mat Relic Autographs

STATED ODDS 1:215 HOBBY EXCLUSIVE			
NNO	Christian	25.00	60.00
NNO	Edge	30.00	75.00
NNO	Randy Orton	30.00	75.00
NNO	Rey Mysterio	20.00	50.00

2009 Topps WWE Legends of the Ring

COMPLETE SET (20)		8.00	20.00
*GOLD/2250: .75X TO 2X BASIC CARDS			
*PLATINUM/1: UNPRICE DUE TO SCARCITY			
STATED ODDS 1:1 HOBBY AND RETAIL			
1	Bam Bam Bigelow	1.00	2.50
2	British Bulldog	1.00	2.50
3	Chief Jay Strongbow	.60	1.50
4	Dean Malenko	1.00	2.50
5	Don Muraco	.40	1.00
6	Dusty Rhodes	1.00	2.50
7	Iron Sheik	1.00	2.50
8	Jake The Snake Roberts	1.00	2.50
9	Jimmy Superfly Snuka	1.00	2.50
10	Junkyard Dog	1.00	2.50
11	Mr. Perfect	1.00	2.50
12	Nikolai Volkoff	.60	1.50
13	Ravishing Rick Rude	1.00	2.50
14	Sgt. Slaughter	1.00	2.50
15	Superstar Billy Graham	1.00	2.50
16	Terry Funk	.60	1.50
17	Vader	.60	1.50
18	The Wild Samoans	.60	1.50
19	Gorilla Monsoon	1.00	2.50
20	Mr. Wonderful Paul Orndorff	.60	1.50

2009 Topps WWE Reign of Honor

COMPLETE SET (10)		6.00	15.00
STATED ODDS 1:6 HOBBY AND RETAIL			
1	John Cena	1.50	4.00
2	Triple H	1.50	4.00
3	Jack Swagger	.25	.60
4	Rey Mysterio	.60	1.50
5	MVP	.40	1.00
6	Melina	1.00	2.50
7	Maryse	.60	1.50
8	Primo & Carlito	.60	1.50
9	Shawn Michaels	1.50	4.00
10	Undertaker	1.25	3.00

2009 Topps WWE Sketches

STATED ODDS 1:2,857 HOBBY EXCLUSIVE
UNPRICED DUE TO SCARCITY

NNO Eve/Beauty...
NNO Eve/Musical Notes
NNO Eve/Passion
NNO Eve/Speak What You Feel
NNO J.Lawler/Batista
NNO J.Lawler/Big Show
NNO J.Lawler/Edge
NNO J.Lawler/Jack Swagger
NNO J.Lawler/Rey Mysterio
NNO J.Lawler/Triple H
NNO J.Lawler/Undertaker
NNO Natalya/Balance
NNO Natalya/Calm
NNO Natalya/Energy
NNO Natalya/Glory

NNO Natalya/Happy
NNO Natalya/Honour
NNO Natalya/Peace
NNO Natalya/Pride
NNO Natalya/Sparkle
NNO Natalya/Spirit
NNO Santino/Island
NNO Santino/Landscape
NNO Santino/Map of Italy
NNO Santino/Muscle
NNO Santino/Santina
NNO Santino/Santino
NNO Santino/Self Portrait 1
NNO Santino/Self Portrait 2
NNO Santino/Self Portrait 3
NNO Santino/Self Portrait w/belt

2009 Topps WWE Tin Inserts

COMPLETE SET (4)

1 Jack Swagger
2 Triple H
3 Chris Jericho
4 Rey Mysterio

2009 Topps WWE Topps Town

COMPLETE SET (30)		6.00	15.00
STATED ODDS 1:1 HOBBY AND RETAIL			
1	Batista	.50	1.25
2	Beth Phoenix	.60	1.50
3	Chris Jericho	.30	.75
4	Christian	.30	.75
5	CM Punk	.20	.50
6	Cody Rhodes	.12	.30
7	Dolph Ziggler	.20	.50
8	Edge	.50	1.25
9	Evan Bourne	.12	.30
10	Gail Kim	.30	.75
11	Jack Swagger	.12	.30
12	John Cena	.75	2.00
13	John Morrison	.20	.50
14	Kofi Kingston	.12	.30
15	Maria	.50	1.25
16	Maryse	.30	.75
17	Matt Hardy	.50	1.25
18	Melina	.50	1.25
19	Michelle McCool	.50	1.25
20	Mickie James	.60	1.50
21	Montel Vontavious Porter	.20	.50
22	Randy Orton	.30	.75
23	Rey Mysterio	.30	.75
24	R-Truth	.12	.30
25	Santino Marella	.12	.30
26	Shawn Michaels	.75	2.00
27	Ted DiBiase	.20	.50
28	The Miz	.20	.50
29	Triple H	.75	2.00
30	Undertaker	.60	1.50

2010 Topps WWE

COMPLETE SET (110)		10.00	25.00
UNOPENED BOX (24 PACKS)			
UNOPENED PACK (7 CARDS)			
*BLUE/2010: 1X TO 2.5X BASIC CARDS			
*SILVER/999: 1.2X TO 3X BASIC CARDS			
*GOLD/50: 4X TO 10X BASIC CARDS			
*RED/1: UNPRICED DUE TO SCARCITY			
*P.P.BLACK/1: UNPRICED DUE TO SCARCITY			
*P.P.CYAN/1: UNPRICED DUE TO SCARCITY			
*P.P.MAGENTA/1: UNPRICED DUE TO SCARCITY			
*P.P.YELLOW/1: UNPRICED DUE TO SCARCITY			
1	John Cena	.75	2.00
2	Layla	.40	1.00
3	William Regal	.40	1.00
4	John Morrison	.25	.60
5	Matt Hardy	.40	1.00
6	Alicia Fox	.25	.60
7	Yoshi Tatsu	.15	.40
8	Nikki Bella	.60	1.50
9	Randy Orton	.60	1.50
10	Luke Gallows	.15	.40
11	MVP	.25	.60
12	Michelle McCool	.60	1.50
13	JTG	.15	.40
14	Rosa Mendes	.25	.60
15	Beth Phoenix	.60	1.50
16	Chris Jericho	.40	1.00
17	Kane	.40	1.00
18	Mark Henry	.25	.60
19	Tyson Kidd	.15	.40
20	Santino Marella	.15	.40
21	Theodore Long	.15	.40
22	Big Show	.40	1.00
23	Kofi Kingston	.25	.60
24	Vladimir Kozlov	.25	.60
25	Vance Archer	.15	.40
26	Brie Bella	.60	1.50
27	Ezekiel Jackson	.15	.40
28	David Hart Smith	.15	.40
29	Trent Baretta	.15	.40
30	Kelly Kelly	.60	1.50
31	Goldust	.25	.60
32	Maryse	.60	1.50
33	Tyler Reks	.15	.40
34	Serena	.25	.60
35	Melina	.60	1.50
36	CM Punk	.60	1.50
37	Drew McIntyre	.25	.60
38	Jillian	.60	1.50
39	Cody Rhodes	.15	.40
40	Ted DiBiase	.25	.60
41	Finlay	.25	.60
42	Dolph Ziggler	.25	.60
43	Triple H	.75	2.00
44	Hornswoggle	.25	.60
45	R-Truth	.15	.40
46	The Miz	.25	.60
47	Primo	.15	.40
48	Jack Swagger	.15	.40
49	Caylen Croft	.15	.40
50	Rey Mysterio	.40	1.00
51	Chris Masters	.15	.40
52	Chavo Guerrero	.25	.60
53	Shad	.15	.40
54	Ranjin Singh	.15	.40
55	Sheamus	.25	.60
56	Vickie Guerrero	.15	.40
57	Evan Bourne	.15	.40
58	Edge	.60	1.50
59	The Undertaker	.60	1.50
60	Zack Ryder	.15	.40
61	Natalya	.60	1.50
62	The Great Khali	.15	.40
63	Eve	.60	1.50
64	Christian	.25	.60
65	Michael Tarver	.25	.60
66	Skip Sheffield	.25	.60
67	Wade Barrett	.25	.60
68	Daniel Bryan	8.00	20.00
69	Darren Young	.25	.60
70	David Otunga	.25	.60
71	Heath Slater	.25	.60
72	Justin Gabriel	.25	.60
73	Undertaker 18-0	.60	1.50
74	ShowMiz	.40	1.00
75	The Dude Busters	.15	.40
76	The Straight Edge Society	.60	1.50
77	Hart Dynasty	.60	1.50
78	Mr. Perfect Curt Hennig	.25	.60
79	Dean Malenko	.25	.60
80	Don Muraco	.25	.60
81	Akeem	.25	.60
82	Doink the Clown	.15	.40
83	Earthquake	.25	.60
84	Hillbilly Jim	.25	.60
85	Mr. Wonderful Paul Orndorff	.40	1.00
86	Nikolai Volkoff	.25	.60
87	Papa Shango	.15	.40
88	Vader	.25	.60
89	Sgt. Slaughter	.40	1.00
90	Junkyard Dog	.40	1.00
91	Bobby The Brain Heenan	.25	.60
92	Harley Race	.25	.60
93	The American Dream Dusty Rhodes	.40	1.00
94	Jake The Snake Roberts	.40	1.00
95	The Iron Sheik	.40	1.00
96	Koko B. Ware	.25	.60
97	Brian Pillman	.40	1.00
98	Jimmy Superfly Snuka	.40	1.00
99	Mean Gene Okerland UER	.25	.60
100	Million Dollar Man Ted DiBiase	.25	.60
101	The Bushwackers	.15	.40
102	Paul Bearer	.25	.60
103	Rowdy Roddy Piper	.60	1.50
104	Terry Funk	.40	1.00
105	Kamala	.25	.60
106	Cowboy Bob Orton	.25	.60
107	The Road Warriors	.40	1.00
108	Ravishing Rick Rude	.25	.60
109	Bam Bam Bigelow	.25	.60
110	Classy Freddie Blassie	.40	1.00
CH1	Checklist 1/2	.15	.40
CH3	Checklist 3/4	.15	.40

2010 Topps WWE Autographs

*GOLD/25: .6X TO 1.5X BASIC AUTOS			
*RED/1: UNPRICED DUE TO SCARCITY			
*P.P.BLACK/1: UNPRICED DUE TO SCARCITY			
*P.P.CYAN/1: UNPRICED DUE TO SCARCITY			
*P.P.MAGENTA/1: UNPRICED DUE TO SCARCITY			
*P.P.YELLOW/1: UNPRICED DUE TO SCARCITY			
OVERALL AUTO ODDS 1:BOX			
ABP	Beth Phoenix		
ABS	Big Show	12.00	30.00
ACC	Caylen Croft	6.00	15.00
ACH	Christian		
ACM	CM Punk	20.00	50.00
ACR	Cody Rhodes	8.00	20.00
ADM	Drew McIntyre	10.00	25.00
ADS	David Hart Smith	8.00	20.00
AEB	Evan Bourne	6.00	15.00
AED	Edge	12.00	30.00
AEJ	Ezekiel Jackson	6.00	15.00
AGK	Gail Kim	12.00	30.00
AJC	John Cena	30.00	75.00
AJM	John Morrison	10.00	25.00
AJT	JTG	6.00	15.00
AKK	Kofi Kingston	8.00	20.00
ALG	Luke Gallows	6.00	15.00
AMM	Michelle McCool	12.00	30.00
ARM	Rosa Mendes	10.00	25.00
ARO	Randy Orton	20.00	50.00
ART	R-Truth	8.00	20.00
ASE	Serena	10.00	25.00
ASH	Shad	6.00	15.00
ATB	Trent Baretta	6.00	15.00
ATD	Ted DiBiase	10.00	25.00
ATH	Triple H		
ATK	Tyson Kidd	8.00	20.00
ATM	Miz	12.00	30.00
AVA	Vance Archer	6.00	15.00
AZR	Zack Ryder	8.00	20.00
ASAN	Santino Marella	10.00	25.00
ASHE	Sheamus	12.00	30.00
JCA1	John Cena	50.00	100.00

2010 Topps WWE Championship Material

COMPLETE SET (50)		20.00	50.00
*PUZZLE BACK: .5X TO 1.2X BASIC CARDS			
*IC PUZZLE: .5X TO 1.2X BASIC CARDS			
STATED ODDS 1:6 HOBBY AND RETAIL			
C1	Christian	.50	1.25
C2	John Morrison	.50	1.25
C3	John Morrison	.50	1.25
C4	The Miz & John Morrison	.50	1.25
C5	CM Punk	1.25	3.00
C6	CM Punk	1.25	3.00
C7	Kofi Kingston & CM Punk	1.25	3.00
C8	The Miz	.50	1.25
C9	The Hart Dynasty	1.25	3.00
C10	Goldust	.50	1.25
C11	Triple H	1.50	4.00
C12	Edge & Chris Jericho	1.25	3.00
C13	Christian	.50	1.25
C14	Chris Jericho & Big Show	.75	2.00
C15	Chris Jericho	.75	2.00
C16	Randy Orton	1.25	3.00
C17	Big Show & The Miz	.75	2.00
C18	Edge & Christian	1.25	3.00
C19	Edge	1.25	3.00
C20	Mark Henry	.50	1.25
C21	Chavo Guerrero	.50	1.25
C22	Matt Hardy	.75	2.00
C23	Undertaker & Kane	1.25	3.00
C24	Kane	.75	2.00
C25	Kane	.75	2.00
C26	R-Truth	.30	.75
C27	John Cena	1.50	4.00
C28	Big Show	.75	2.00
C29	Ted DiBiase & Cody Rhodes	.50	1.25
C30	Drew McIntyre	.50	1.25
C31	Rey Mysterio	.75	2.00
C32	Jack Swagger	.30	.75
C33	William Regal	.75	2.00
C34	Kofi Kingston	.50	1.25
C35	Santino Marella	.30	.75
C36	Ted DiBiase	.75	2.00
C37	Michelle McCool	1.25	3.00
C38	Maryse	1.25	3.00
C39	Edge & Randy Orton	1.25	3.00
C40	Jillian	1.25	3.00

C41 Melina	1.25	3.00
C42 MVP	.50	1.25
C43 Kofi Kingston	.50	1.25
C44 Matt Hardy	.75	2.00
C45 Finlay	.50	1.25
C46 Mr. Perfect	.50	1.25
C47 Don Muraco	.50	1.25
C48 Ravishing Rick Rude	.50	1.25
C49 Rowdy Roddy Piper	1.25	3.00
C50 British Bulldog	.50	1.25

2010 Topps WWE Dual Autographs

*GOLD/25: .5X TO 1.2X BASIC AUTOS
*RED/1: UNPRICED DUE TO SCARCITY
*P.P.BLACK/1: UNPRICED DUE TO SCARCITY
*P.P.CYAN/1: UNPRICED DUE TO SCARCITY
*P.P.MAGENTA/1: UNPRICED DUE TO SCARCITY
*P.P.YELLOW/1: UNPRICED DUE TO SCARCITY
STATED PRINT RUN 99 SER.#'d SETS

DABM E.Bourne/D.McIntyre	10.00	25.00
DACB C.Croft/T.Baretta	8.00	20.00
DACO J.Cena/R.Orton	50.00	100.00
DADR T.DiBiase/C.Rhodes	12.00	30.00
DAES Edge/Big Show	15.00	40.00
DAJC E.Jackson/Christian		
DAJS JTG/Shad	8.00	20.00
DAJT E.Jackson/R-Truth	8.00	20.00
DAKM K.Kingston/Miz	12.00	30.00
DAMP J.Morrison/CM Punk	20.00	50.00
DAPG CM Punk/L.Gallows	20.00	50.00
DAPS CM Punk/Serena	15.00	40.00
DARM Z.Ryder/R.Mendes	12.00	30.00
DASK D.Smith/T.Kidd	8.00	20.00
DASP S.Marella/B.Phoenix		
DASS S.Marella/Sheamus	12.00	30.00
DAKMC G.Kim/M.McCool	15.00	40.00

2010 Topps WWE Elimination Chamber Canvas

COMPLETE SET (19) 60.00 120.00
*GOLD/50: .75X TO 2X BASIC CARDS
*RED/1: UNPRICED DUE TO SCARCITY
OVERALL RELIC ODDS 1:2 RETAIL EXCLUSIVE

EC1 John Cena	8.00	20.00
EC2 Sheamus	2.50	6.00
EC3 Triple H	8.00	20.00
EC4 Randy Orton	6.00	15.00
EC5 Ted DiBiase Jr.	2.50	6.00
EC6 Kofi Kingston	2.50	6.00
EC7 Drew McIntyre	2.50	6.00
EC8 Kane	4.00	10.00
EC9 Michelle McCool	6.00	15.00
EC10 Layla	4.00	10.00
EC11 Maryse	6.00	15.00
EC12 The Miz	2.50	6.00
EC13 MVP	2.50	6.00
EC14 Chris Jericho	4.00	10.00
EC15 The Undertaker	6.00	15.00
EC16 John Morrison	2.50	6.00
EC17 CM Punk	6.00	15.00
EC18 Rey Mysterio	4.00	10.00
EC19 R-Truth	2.50	6.00

2010 Topps WWE Favorite Finishers

COMPLETE SET (25) 8.00 20.00
STATED ODDS 1:4 HOBBY AND RETAIL

FF1 Dolph Ziggler	.40	1.00
FF2 Jack Swagger	.25	.60
FF3 Edge	1.00	2.50
FF4 CM Punk	1.00	2.50
FF5 Sheamus	.40	1.00
FF6 Evan Bourne	.25	.60
FF7 Undertaker	1.00	2.50
FF8 John Cena	1.25	3.00
FF9 The Hart Dynasty	1.00	2.50
FF10 Yoshi Tatsu	.25	.60
FF11 Drew McIntyre	.40	1.00
FF12 MVP	.40	1.00
FF13 John Morrison	.40	1.00
FF14 Randy Orton	1.00	2.50
FF15 Big Show	.60	1.50
FF16 Kofi Kingston	.40	1.00
FF17 Matt Hardy	.60	1.50
FF18 Kane	.60	1.50
FF19 Christian	.40	1.00
FF20 Mark Henry	.40	1.00
FF21 Triple H	1.25	3.00
FF22 Beth Phoenix	1.00	2.50
FF23 Rey Mysterio	.60	1.50
FF24 Chris Jericho	.60	1.50
FF25 The Miz	.40	1.00

2010 Topps WWE History Of

COMPLETE SET (25) 10.00 25.00
STATED ODDS 1:8 HOBBY AND RETAIL

HO1 Chris Jericho	.75	2.00
HO2 Triple H	1.50	4.00
HO3 Edge	1.25	3.00
HO4 Jack Swagger	.30	.75
HO5 John Morrison	.50	1.25
HO6 The Undertaker	1.25	3.00
HO7 Kane	.75	2.00
HO8 The Miz	.50	1.25
HO9 Finlay	.50	1.25
HO10 Michelle McCool	1.25	3.00
HO11 Rey Mysterio	.75	2.00
HO12 Natalya	1.25	3.00
HO13 John Cena	1.50	4.00
HO14 Kelly Kelly	1.25	3.00
HO15 Ted DiBiase	.50	1.25
HO16 Randy Orton	1.25	3.00
HO17 Kofi Kingston	.50	1.25
HO18 Big Show	.75	2.00
HO19 Santino Marella	.30	.75
HO20 Goldust	.50	1.25
HO21 Christian	.50	1.25
HO22 William Regal	.75	2.00
HO23 British Bulldog	.50	1.25
HO24 Junkyard Dog	.75	2.00
HO25 Mr. Perfect	.50	1.25

2010 Topps WWE National Heroes

COMPLETE SET (25) 10.00 25.00
STATED ODDS 1:8 HOBBY AND RETAIL

NH1 John Cena	1.50	4.00
NH2 Maryse	1.25	3.00
NH3 Jack Swagger	.30	.75
NH4 Edge	1.25	3.00
NH5 Chris Jericho	.75	2.00
NH6 William Regal	.75	2.00
NH7 Finlay	.50	1.25
NH8 Yoshi Tatsu	.30	.75
NH9 Sheamus	.50	1.25
NH10 Sgt. Slaughter	.75	2.00
NH11 Vladimir Kozlov	.50	1.25
NH12 The Great Khali	.30	.75
NH13 Kamala	.50	1.25
NH14 Nikolai Volkoff	.50	1.25
NH15 Iron Shiek	.75	2.00
NH16 Wild Samoans	.30	.75
NH17 Kofi Kingston	.50	1.25
NH18 Drew McIntyre	.50	1.25
NH19 Santino Marella	.30	.75
NH20 Rey Mysterio	.75	2.00
NH21 Mark Henry	.50	1.25
NH22 Christian	.50	1.25
NH23 Tyson Kidd	.30	.75
NH24 Chavo Guerrero	.50	1.25
NH25 The British Bulldog	.50	1.25

2010 Topps WWE Signature Swatches

STATED PRINT RUN 25 SER. #'d SETS

SSSBS Big Show	60.00	120.00
SSSCG Chavo Guerrero	25.00	60.00
SSSCH Christian	30.00	80.00
SSSCJ Chris Jericho	50.00	100.00
SSSCM CM Punk	60.00	120.00
SSSCR Cody Rhodes	25.00	60.00
SSSDS David Hart Smith	25.00	60.00
SSSEB Evan Bourne	25.00	60.00
SSSED Edge	50.00	100.00
SSSJC John Cena	100.00	200.00
SSSJM John Morrison	50.00	100.00
SSSKK Kofi Kingston	30.00	80.00
SSSMH Matt Hardy	30.00	80.00
SSSRM Rey Mysterio	50.00	100.00
SSSRO Randy Orton	100.00	200.00
SSSSA Santino Marella EXCH	50.00	100.00
SSSSH Shad	25.00	60.00
SSSTD Ted DiBiase Jr.	25.00	60.00
SSSTK Tyson Kidd	30.00	80.00
SSSTM The Miz	30.00	80.00
SSSJTG JTG	25.00	60.00
SSSMVP MVP	30.00	80.00

2010 Topps WWE Superstar Jumbo Swatches

STATED PRINT RUN 30 SER.#'d SETS

SSSBS Big Show	50.00	100.00
SSSCG Chavo Guerrero		
SSSCH Christian	40.00	80.00
SSSCJ Chris Jericho		
SSSCM CM Punk	50.00	100.00
SSSCR Cody Rhodes	20.00	50.00
SSSDS David Hart Smith	25.00	60.00
SSSEB Evan Bourne	25.00	60.00
SSSED Edge	50.00	100.00
SSSJC John Cena	60.00	120.00
SSSJM John Morrison	40.00	80.00
SSSKK Kofi Kingston	40.00	80.00
SSSMH Matt Hardy EXCH	50.00	100.00
SSSRM Rey Mysterio	40.00	80.00
SSSRO Randy Orton	40.00	80.00
SSSSA Santino Marella EXCH	25.00	60.00
SSSSH Shad		
SSSTD Ted DiBiase Jr.		
SSSTH Triple H		
SSSTK Tyson Kidd	25.00	60.00
SSSTM The Miz	40.00	80.00
SSSTU The Undertaker		
SSSJTG JTG		
SSSMVP MVP	25.00	60.00

2010 Topps WWE Superstar Swatches

*GOLD/99: .5X TO 2X BASIC CARDS
*RED/1: UNPRICED DUE TO SCARCITY
OVERALL RELIC ODDS 1:BOX

JCR1 John Cena	15.00	30.00
SBS Big Show	5.00	12.00
SCG Chavo Guerrero		
SCH Christian	5.00	12.00
SCJ Chris Jericho		
SCM CM Punk	5.00	12.00
SCR Cody Rhodes	4.00	10.00
SDS David Hart Smith	4.00	10.00
SEB Evan Bourne	5.00	12.00
SED Edge	6.00	15.00
SJC John Cena	10.00	25.00
SJM John Morrison	6.00	15.00
SKK Kofi Kingston	5.00	12.00
SMH Matt Hardy EXCH	8.00	20.00
SRM Rey Mysterio	8.00	20.00
SRO Randy Orton	10.00	25.00
SSA Santino Marella EXCH	5.00	12.00
SSH Shad		
STD Ted DiBiase EXCH	6.00	15.00
STH Triple H EXCH	20.00	50.00
STK Tyson Kidd	4.00	10.00
STM The Miz	4.00	10.00
STU The Undertaker		
SJTG JTG		
SMVP MVP	4.00	10.00

2010 Topps WWE Topps Town

COMPLETE SET (25) 10.00 25.00
STATED ODDS 1:6 HOBBY AND RETAIL

TT1 John Cena	1.25	3.00
TT2 Jack Swagger	.25	.60
TT3 Rey Mysterio	.60	1.50
TT4 The Miz	.40	1.00
TT5 Kane	.60	1.50
TT6 Triple H	1.25	3.00
TT7 MVP	.40	1.00
TT8 The Undertaker	1.00	2.50
TT9 John Morisson	.40	1.00
TT10 Randy Orton	1.00	2.50
TT11 Kofi Kingston	.40	1.00
TT12 Michelle McCool	1.00	2.50
TT13 Cody Rhodes	.25	.60
TT14 Edge	1.00	2.50
TT15 Kelly Kelly	1.00	2.50
TT16 Ted DiBiase	.40	1.00
TT17 Chris Jericho	.60	1.50
TT18 CM Punk	1.00	2.50
TT19 Big Show	.60	1.50
TT20 Beth Phoenix	1.00	2.50
TT21 Sheamus	.40	1.00
TT22 Christian	.40	1.00
TT23 R-Truth	.25	.60
TT24 Ezekiel Jackson	.25	.60
TT25 Maryse	1.00	2.50

2010 Topps WWE When They Were Young

RANDOMLY INSERTED INTO PACKS

WTWY1 John Cena
WTWY2 William Regal
WTWY3 Jack Swagger
WTWY4 Chris Jericho

WTWY5	Big Show
WTWY6	Natalya
WTWY7	The Miz
WTWY8	Sheamus
WTWY9	Chavo Guerrero
WTWY10	Shad
WTWY11	Hornswoggle
WTWY12	Jerry Lawler
WTWY13	Santino Marella
WTWY14	Melina
WTWY15	Ted DiBiase Jr.
WTWY16	Cody Rhodes
WTWY17	Christian
WTWY18	Kelly Kelly
WTWY19	Rosa Mendes
WTWY20	CM Punk
WTWY21	Shelton Benjamin
WTWY22	Evan Bourne
WTWY23	R-Truth
WTWY24	Zack Ryder
WTWY25	Triple H

2010 Topps WWE World Championship Material

COMPLETE SET (25)		12.00	30.00

*PUZZLE: .5X TO 1.2X BASIC CARDS
STATED ODDS 1:6 HOBBY AND RETAIL

W1	John Cena	1.50	4.00
W2	John Cena	1.50	4.00
W3	Triple H	1.50	4.00
W4	Triple H	1.50	4.00
W5	Chris Jericho	.75	2.00
W6	Superstar Billy Graham	.75	2.00
W7	Chris Jericho	.75	2.00
W8	Sheamus	.50	1.25
W9	Randy Orton	1.25	3.00
W10	Randy Orton	1.25	3.00
W11	Kane	.75	2.00
W12	Undertaker	1.25	3.00
W13	Undertaker	1.25	3.00
W14	Rey Mysterio	.75	2.00
W15	Jack Swagger	.30	.75
W16	Melina	1.25	3.00
W17	Edge	1.25	3.00
W18	Beth Phoenix	1.25	3.00
W19	Edge	1.25	3.00
W20	Michelle McCool	1.25	3.00
W21	Big Show	.75	2.00
W22	CM Punk	1.25	3.00
W23	Sgt. Slaughter	.75	2.00
W24	The Iron Sheik	.75	2.00
W25	John Cena	1.50	4.00

2011 Topps WWE

COMPLETE SET (113)		10.00	25.00
UNOPENED BOX (24 PACKS)			
UNOPENED PACK (7 CARDS)			

*BLUE/2011: .8X TO 2X BASIC CARDS
*BLACK/999: 1.5X TO 4X BASIC CARDS
*GOLD/50: 4X TO 10X BASIC CARDS
*RED/1: UNPRICED DUE TO SCARCITY
*P.P.BLACK/1: UNPRICED DUE TO SCARCITY
*P.P.CYAN/1: UNPRICED DUE TO SCARCITY
*P.P.MAGENTA/1: UNPRICED DUE TO SCARCITY
*P.P.YELLOW/1: UNPRICED DUE TO SCARCITY

1	John Cena	.75	2.00
2	Randy Orton	.60	1.50
3	Rey Mysterio	.40	1.00
4	Wade Barrett	.15	.40
5	John Morrison	.25	.60
6	Natalya	.60	1.50
7	Primo	.15	.40
8	Justin Gabriel	.15	.40
9	Johnny Curtis	.15	.40
10	Josh Mathews	.15	.40
11	Michael McGillicutty	.15	.40
12	Jey Uso	.15	.40
13	Dolph Ziggler	.25	.60
14	Alex Riley	.15	.40
15	Kharma	.25	.60
16	Ranjin Singh	.15	.40
17	Chris Masters	.15	.40
18	Ted DiBiase	.25	.60
19	Percy Watson	.15	.40
20	Hornswoggle	.25	.60
21	David Otunga	.15	.40
22	Booker T	.25	.60
23	Mason Ryan	.15	.40
24	Tamina	.15	.40
25	CM Punk	.40	1.00
26	Jack Korpela	.15	.40
27	Kelly Kelly	.60	1.50
28	William Regal	.25	.60
29	Beth Phoenix	.40	1.00
30	The Great Khali	.15	.40
31	Michael Cole	.15	.40
32	Brodus Clay	.15	.40
33	Goldust	.15	.40
34	Jimmy Uso	.15	.40
35	Kofi Kingston	.15	.40
36	Matt Striker	.15	.40
37	Nikki Bella	.60	1.50
38	Yoshi Tatsu	.15	.40
39	Ricardo Rodriguez	.15	.40
40	Cody Rhodes	.15	.40
41	Brie Bella	.60	1.50
42	Ezekiel Jackson	.25	.60
43	Vladimir Kozlov	.25	.60
44	Sheamus	.25	.60
45	Vickie Guerrero	.25	.60
46	Alicia Fox	.25	.60
47	Drew McIntyre	.15	.40
48	Todd Grisham	.15	.40
49	Jack Swagger	.25	.60
50	Tyson Kidd	.15	.40
51	Alberto Del Rio	.40	1.00
52	Heath Slater	.15	.40
53	Evan Bourne	.15	.40
54	JTG	.15	.40
55	Kaitlyn	.40	1.00
56	Big Show	.40	1.00
57	Tyler Reks	.15	.40
58	Layla	.40	1.00
59	Justin Roberts	.15	.40
60	R-Truth	.15	.40
61	Daniel Bryan	.15	.40
62	Gail Kim	.40	1.00
63	The Miz	.25	.60
64	Chavo Guerrero	.15	.40
65	Curt Hawkins	.15	.40
66	Maryse	.60	1.50
67	Kane	.40	1.00
68	Santino Marella	.25	.60
69	Mark Henry	.25	.60
70	David Hart Smith	.15	.40
71	Rosa Mendes	.25	.60
72	Jerry The King Lawler	.40	1.00
73	Undertaker	.60	1.50
74	Melina	.60	1.50
75	Sin Cara	.40	1.00
76	Eve	.60	1.50
77	Theodore Long	.15	.40
78	Zack Ryder	.15	.40
79	Christian	.15	.40
80	Triple H	.75	2.00
81	Edge	.60	1.50
82	The Rock	.75	2.00
83	Darren Young	.15	.40
84	Lucky Cannon	.15	.40
85	Titus O'Neil	.15	.40
86	Byron Saxton	.15	.40
87	Conor O'Brian	.15	.40
88	Jacob Novak	.15	.40
89	The American Dream Dusty Rhodes	.25	.60
90	The British Bulldog	.25	.60
91	Million Dollar Man Ted DiBiase	.25	.60
92	Rowdy Roddy Piper	.60	1.50
93	Mr. Perfect	.40	1.00
94	The Iron Sheik	.40	1.00
95	Cowboy Bob Orton	.25	.60
96	Jake The Snake Roberts	.40	1.00
97	Ravishing Rick Rude	.25	.60
98	Doink the Clown	.25	.60
99	Big Boss Man	.25	.60
100	Bushwhacker Luke	.25	.60
101	Bushwhacker Butch	.25	.60
102	Yokozuna	.25	.60
103	Sgt. Slaughter	.40	1.00
104	Papa Shango	.15	.40
105	Hawk	.40	1.00
106	Animal	.40	1.00
107	Kamala	.25	.60
108	Terry Funk	.25	.60
109	Junkyard Dog	.40	1.00
110	Hacksaw Jim Duggan	.40	1.00
CL1	Checklist 1	.15	.40
CL2	Checklist 2	.15	.40
CL3	Checklist 3	.15	.40

2011 Topps WWE Autographs

NNO	Alberto Del Rio	15.00	40.00
NNO	Alex Riley	10.00	25.00
NNO	Big Show	12.00	30.00
NNO	Brie Bella	20.00	50.00
NNO	Christian	10.00	25.00
NNO	David Otunga	6.00	15.00
NNO	Drew McIntyre	8.00	20.00
NNO	Evan Bourne	6.00	15.00
NNO	Eve	12.00	30.00
NNO	Ezekiel Jackson	10.00	25.00
NNO	John Cena	25.00	60.00
NNO	Kane	12.00	30.00
NNO	Kofi Kingston	10.00	25.00
NNO	Mark Henry	10.00	25.00
NNO	Michael McGillicutty	6.00	15.00
NNO	Nikki Bella	20.00	50.00
NNO	Randy Orton	20.00	50.00
NNO	R-Truth	8.00	20.00
NNO	Sin Cara	10.00	25.00
NNO	The Miz	10.00	25.00

2011 Topps WWE Catchy Phrases

COMPLETE SET (10)		5.00	10.00

*P.P.BLACK/1: UNPRICED DUE TO SCARCITY
*P.P.CYAN/1: UNPRICED DUE TO SCARCITY
*P.P.MAGENTA/1: UNPRICED DUE TO SCARCITY
*P.P.YELLOW/1: UNPRICED DUE TO SCARCITY
STATED ODDS 1:8 HOBBY AND RETAIL

CP1	John Cena	1.50	4.00
CP2	The Miz	.50	1.25
CP3	The Rock	1.50	4.00
CP4	Undertaker	1.25	3.00
CP5	Triple H	1.50	4.00
CP6	Rey Mysterio	.75	2.00
CP7	Christian	.30	.75
CP8	Zack Ryder	.30	.75
CP9	Goldust	.30	.75
CP10	Vickie Guerrero	.50	1.25

2011 Topps WWE Dual Autographs

STATED PRINT RUN 70 SER.#'d SETS

NNO	A.Del Rio/Christian	25.00	60.00
NNO	Big Show/M.Henry	20.00	50.00
NNO	Brie & Nikki Bella	60.00	120.00
NNO	D.Otunga/M.McGillicutty	12.00	30.00
NNO	Eve/K.Kingston	25.00	60.00
NNO	J.Cena/R-Truth	30.00	75.00
NNO	Kane/E.Jackson	15.00	40.00
NNO	R.Orton/E.Bourne	25.00	60.00
NNO	S.Cara/D.McIntyre	15.00	40.00
NNO	Miz/A.Riley	20.00	50.00

2011 Topps WWE Electrifying Entrances

COMPLETE SET (25)		10.00	25.00

*P.P.BLACK/1: UNPRICED DUE TO SCARCITY
*P.P.CYAN/1: UNPRICED DUE TO SCARCITY
*P.P.MAGENTA/1: UNPRICED DUE TO SCARCITY
*P.P.YELLOW/1: UNPRICED DUE TO SCARCITY
STATED ODDS 1:8 HOBBY AND RETAIL

EE1	Undertaker	1.25	3.00
EE2	John Cena	1.50	4.00
EE3	Triple H	1.50	4.00
EE4	Rey Mysterio	.75	2.00
EE5	R-Truth	.30	.75
EE6	Randy Orton	1.25	3.00
EE7	The Miz	.50	1.25
EE8	Big Show	.75	2.00
EE9	Kofi Kingston	.30	.75
EE10	Sheamus	.50	1.25
EE11	Alberto Del Rio	.75	2.00
EE12	Kane	.75	2.00
EE13	Christian	.30	.75
EE14	Jack Swagger	.50	1.25
EE15	Sin Cara	.75	2.00
EE16	Wade Barrett	.30	.75
EE17	John Morrison	.50	1.25
EE18	Drew McIntyre	.30	.75
EE19	Daniel Bryan	.30	.75
EE20	Cody Rhodes	.30	.75
EE21	Ted DiBiase	.50	1.25
EE22	Dolph Ziggler	.50	1.25
EE23	Santino Marella	.50	1.25
EE24	The Great Khali	.30	.75
EE25	Kharma	.50	1.25

2011 Topps WWE Heritage

COMPLETE SET (50)		12.00	30.00

P.P.BLACK/1: UNPRICED DUE TO SCARCITY
P.P.CYAN/1: UNPRICED DUE TO SCARCITY
P.P.MAGENTA/1: UNPRICED DUE TO SCARCITY
P.P.YELLOW/1: UNPRICED DUE TO SCARCITY

STATED ODDS 1:4 HOBBY AND RETAIL

H1	Stone Cold Steve Austin	1.00	2.50
H2	Shawn Michaels	1.00	2.50
H3	Trish Stratus	1.25	3.00
H4	Booker T	.40	1.00
H5	Jerry The King Lawler	.60	1.50
H6	Michael PS Hayes	.25	.60
H7	The American Dream Dusty Rhodes	.40	1.00
H8	The British Bulldog	.40	1.00
H9	Million Dollar Man Ted DiBiase	.40	1.00
H10	Rowdy Roddy Piper	1.00	2.50
H11	Mr. Perfect	.60	1.50
H12	Mean Gene Okerlund	.40	1.00
H13	Jimmy Superfly Snuka	.60	1.50
H14	Paul Bearer	.40	1.00
H15	Irwin R. Schyster	.25	.60
H16	Vader	.40	1.00
H17	Akeem	.25	.60
H18	Bobby The Brain Heenan	.40	1.00
H19	Kama Mustafa	.25	.60
H20	Howard Finkel	.25	.60
H21	Don Muraco	.40	1.00
H22	Harley Race	.40	1.00
H23	Brian Pillman	.40	1.00
H24	The Iron Sheik	.60	1.50
H25	Koko B. Ware	.40	1.00
H26	Gorilla Monsoon	.40	1.00
H27	Jake The Snake Roberts	.60	1.50
H28	Ravishing Rick Rude	.40	1.00
H29	Doink the Clown	.25	.60
H30	Big Boss Man	.40	1.00
H31	Jim Ross	.25	.60
H32	Rocky Johnson	.40	1.00
H33	Terry Funk	.40	1.00
H34	Big John Studd	.25	.60
H35	The Godfather	.25	.60
H36	Hillbilly Jim	.40	1.00
H37	Barry Windham	.25	.60
H38	Tito Santana	.25	.60
H39	Nikolai Volkoff	.40	1.00
H40	Arn Anderson	.40	1.00
H41	Tully Blanchard	.40	1.00
H42	One Man Gang	.25	.60
H43	Dean Malenko	.25	.60
H44	Classy Freddie Blassie	.40	1.00
H45	Tom Prichard	.25	.60
H46	Yokozuna	.40	1.00
H47	Mr. Wonderful Paul Orndorff	.40	1.00
H48	Sgt. Slaughter	.60	1.50
H49	Diesel	.40	1.00
H50	Batista	.40	1.00

2011 Topps WWE Masters of the Mat Relics

*GOLD/50: 1X TO 2.5X BASIC MEM
*RED/1: UNPRICED DUE TO SCARCITY
STATED ODDS 1:69

NNO	Alberto Del Rio	2.50	6.00
NNO	Big Show	2.50	6.00
NNO	Christian	2.50	6.00
NNO	Cody Rhodes	2.50	6.00
NNO	Daniel Bryan	2.50	6.00
NNO	Dolph Ziggler	2.50	6.00
NNO	Drew McIntyre	2.50	6.00
NNO	Jack Swagger	2.50	6.00
NNO	John Cena	5.00	12.00
NNO	John Morrison	2.50	6.00
NNO	Kane	2.50	6.00
NNO	Kofi Kingston	2.50	6.00

NNO	Mark Henry	2.50	6.00
NNO	Randy Orton	4.00	10.00
NNO	Rey Mysterio	3.00	8.00
NNO	R-Truth	2.50	6.00
NNO	Santino Marella	2.50	6.00
NNO	Sheamus	2.50	6.00
NNO	Sin Cara	2.50	6.00
NNO	Ted DiBiase	2.50	6.00
NNO	The Great Khali	2.50	6.00
NNO	The Miz	2.50	6.00
NNO	Triple H	4.00	10.00
NNO	Undertaker	4.00	10.00
NNO	Wade Barrett	2.50	6.00

2011 Topps WWE Prestigious Pairings

COMPLETE SET (15)		6.00	15.00

*P.P.BLACK/1: UNPRICED DUE TO SCARCITY
*P.P.CYAN/1: UNPRICED DUE TO SCARCITY
*P.P.MAGENTA/1: UNPRICED DUE TO SCARCITY
*P.P.YELLOW/1: UNPRICED DUE TO SCARCITY
STATED ODDS 1:8 HOBBY AND RETAIL

PP1	Big Show/Kane	.75	2.00
PP2	Marella/Kozlov	.50	1.25
PP3	Phoenix/Kelly	1.25	3.00
PP4	Lawler/Ross	.75	2.00
PP5	Swagger/Cole	.50	1.25
PP6	Orton/Mysterio	1.25	3.00
PP7	Cena/Cara	1.50	4.00
PP8	Jimmy Uso/Jay Uso	.30	.75
PP9	Ziggler/Guerrero	.50	1.25
PP10	Edge/Christian	1.25	3.00
PP11	Del Rio/Clay	.75	2.00
PP12	Ziggler/Sheamus	.50	1.25
PP13	Morrison/Bryan	.50	1.25
PP14	Torres/Kim	1.25	3.00
PP15	R-Truth/Morrison	.50	1.25

2011 Topps WWE Ringside Relics Ring Skirts

*GOLD/50: .6X TO 1.5X BASIC MEM
*RED/1: UNPRICED DUE TO SCARCITY
STATED ODDS 1:180

NNO	Alberto Del Rio	3.00	8.00
NNO	Big Show	3.00	8.00
NNO	Christian	3.00	8.00
NNO	Daniel Bryan	3.00	8.00
NNO	Dolph Ziggler	3.00	8.00
NNO	Jack Swagger	3.00	8.00
NNO	John Cena	6.00	15.00
NNO	John Morrison	3.00	8.00
NNO	Kane	3.00	8.00
NNO	Kofi Kingston	3.00	8.00
NNO	Randy Orton	5.00	12.00
NNO	Rey Mysterio	4.00	10.00
NNO	R-Truth	3.00	8.00
NNO	Santino Marella	3.00	8.00
NNO	Sheamus	3.00	8.00
NNO	Sin Cara	3.00	8.00
NNO	The Miz	3.00	8.00
NNO	Triple H	5.00	12.00
NNO	Undertaker	6.00	15.00
NNO	Wade Barrett	3.00	8.00

2011 Topps WWE Superstar Swatches

*GOLD/50: .6X TO 1.5X BASIC CARDS
*RED/1: UNPRICED DUE TO SCARCITY

STATED ODDS 1:126

NNO	Christian	4.00	10.00
NNO	Cody Rhodes	4.00	10.00
NNO	Daniel Bryan	5.00	12.00
NNO	Drew McIntyre	4.00	10.00
NNO	Heath Slater	4.00	10.00
NNO	Jack Swagger	4.00	10.00
NNO	Kofi Kingston	4.00	10.00
NNO	Randy Orton	5.00	12.00
NNO	R-Truth	4.00	10.00
NNO	Santino Marella	4.00	10.00
NNO	Sheamus	4.00	10.00
NNO	Stone Cold Steve Austin	6.00	15.00
NNO	Ted DiBiase	4.00	10.00
NNO	The Miz	4.00	10.00
NNO	Wade Barrett	4.00	10.00

2012 Topps WWE

COMPLETE SET (93)		15.00	40.00
COMPLETE SET W/O SP (90)		10.00	25.00
UNOPENED BOX (24 PACKS)			
UNOPENED PACK (7 CARDS)			

*BLUE: 1X TO 2.5X BASIC CARDS
*GOLD: 2.5X TO 6X BASIC CARDS
*PURPLE: 2.5X TO 6X BASIC CARDS
*RED: 2.5X TO 6X BASIC CARDS
*SILVER: 2.5X TO 6X BASIC CARDS
*BLACK: 8X TO 20X BASIC CARDS
*PLATINUM/1: UNPRICED DUE TO SCARCITY
*P.P.BLACK/1: UNPRICED DUE TO SCARCITY
*P.P.CYAN/1: UNPRICED DUE TO SCARCITY
*P.P.MAGENTA/1: UNPRICED DUE TO SCARCITY
*P.P.YELLOW/1: UNPRICED DUE TO SCARCITY

1	John Cena	.75	2.00
2	Randy Orton	.60	1.50
3	Beth Phoenix	.40	1.00
4	Sheamus	.40	1.00
5	Brock Lesnar	.60	1.50
6	Daniel Bryan	.15	.40
7A	Mick Foley	.60	1.50
7B	Cactus Jack SP	4.00	10.00
7C	Dude Love SP	4.00	10.00
7D	Mankind SP	4.00	10.00
8	Cody Rhodes	.15	.40
9	Cameron	.25	.60
10	Christian	.15	.40
11	Kelly Kelly	.60	1.50
12	Hornswoggle	.25	.60
13	Brodus Clay	.15	.40
14	Aksana	.40	1.00
15	Epico	.15	.40
16	Mark Henry	.25	.60
17	Maxine	.40	1.00
18	Jey Uso	.15	.40
19	Zack Ryder	.15	.40
20	Ricardo Rodriguez	.15	.40
21	JTG	.15	.40
22	Hunico	.15	.40
23	Kofi Kingston	.15	.40
24	Matt Striker	.15	.40
25	Kane	.40	1.00
26	Jimmy Uso	.15	.40
27	Naomi	.25	.60
28	The Great Khali	.15	.40
29	Tyler Reks	.15	.40
30	Josh Matthews	.15	.40
31	Derrick Bateman	.15	.40
32	Camacho	.15	.40

33	Kharma	.25	.60
34	Heath Slater	.15	.40
35	Evan Bourne	.15	.40
36	Yoshi Tatsu	.15	.40
37	Big Show	.40	1.00
38	Ryback	.15	.40
39	Percy Watson	.15	.40
40	Kaitlyn	.40	1.00
41	The Miz	.25	.60
42	William Regal	.25	.60
43	Michael Cole	.15	.40
44	Wade Barrett	.15	.40
45	Rey Mysterio	.40	1.00
46	Alicia Fox	.25	.60
47	Triple H	.60	1.50
48	Layla	.40	1.00
49	Chris Jericho	.60	1.50
50	Jinder Mahal	.15	.40
51	Eve	.60	1.50
52	Johnny Curtis	.15	.40
53	Tensai	.15	.40
54	Titus O'Neil	.15	.40
55	Vickie Guerrero	.25	.60
56	Justin Gabriel	.15	.40
57	Primo	.15	.40
58	Booker T	.25	.60
59	Goldust	.15	.40
60	Natalya	.60	1.50
61	Jack Swagger	.25	.60
62	Ezekiel Jackson	.25	.60
63	John Laurinaitis	.15	.40
64	Ted DiBiase	.25	.60
65	R-Truth	.15	.40
66	Trent Barreta	.15	.40
67	Jerry The King Lawler	.40	1.00
68	Tyson Kidd	.15	.40
69	David Otunga	.15	.40
70	Rosa Mendes	.25	.60
71	Michael McGillicutty	.15	.40
72	Drew McIntyre	.15	.40
73	Alex Riley	.15	.40
74	Theodore Long	.15	.40
75	Dolph Ziggler	.25	.60
76	Sin Cara	.40	1.00
77	Justin Roberts	.15	.40
78	Alberto Del Rio	.40	1.00
79	Curt Hawkins	.15	.40
80	Tamina Snuka	.25	.60
81	Mason Ryan	.15	.40
82	Darren Young	.15	.40
83	Scott Stanford	.15	.40
84	Lilian Garcia	.40	1.00
85	Santino Marella	.25	.60
86	Antonio Cesaro	.15	.40
87	The Rock	.75	2.00
88	AJ	.75	2.00
89	CM Punk	.60	1.50
90	Undertaker	.60	1.50

2012 Topps WWE Autographs

STATED ODDS 1:470 HOBBY AND RETAIL

NNO	Booker T	15.00	40.00
NNO	Cactus Jack	50.00	100.00
NNO	Chris Jericho	30.00	75.00
NNO	Dude Love	50.00	100.00
NNO	Epico	8.00	20.00
NNO	Hunico	8.00	20.00
NNO	John Laurinaitis	12.00	30.00

NNO Mankind	50.00	100.00
NNO Mick Foley	30.00	75.00
NNO Primo	8.00	20.00
NNO Triple H		

2012 Topps WWE Classic Hall of Famers

COMPLETE SET (35)	10.00	25.00

*P.P.BLACK/1: UNPRICED DUE TO SCARCITY
*P.P.CYAN/1: UNPRICED DUE TO SCARCITY
*P.P.MAGENTA/1: UNPRICED DUE TO SCARCITY
*P.P.YELLOW/1: UNPRICED DUE TO SCARCITY
STATED ODDS 1:4 HOBBY AND RETAIL

1 Chief Jay Strongbow	.40	1.00
2 Classy Freddie Blassie	.40	1.00
3 Gorilla Monsoon	.40	1.00
4 Jimmy Superfly Snuka	.40	1.00
5 Big John Studd	.40	1.00
6 Bobby The Brain Heenan	.40	1.00
7 Don Muraco	.40	1.00
8 Greg The Hammer Valentine	.40	1.00
9 Harley Race	.40	1.00
10 Junkyard Dog	.40	1.00
11 Sgt. Slaughter	.40	1.00
12 Tito Santana	.40	1.00
13 Cowboy Bob Orton	.40	1.00
14 The Iron Sheik	.40	1.00
15 Mr. Wonderful Paul Orndorff	.40	1.00
16 Nikolai Volkoff	.40	1.00
17 Rowdy Roddy Piper	.60	1.50
18 Mean Gene Okerlund	.40	1.00
19 The American Dream Dusty Rhodes	.40	1.00
20 Mr. Perfect Curt Hennig	.40	1.00
21 Rocky Johnson	.40	1.00
22 Terry Funk	.40	1.00
23 Howard Finkel	.40	1.00
24 Koko B. Ware	.40	1.00
25 Ricky The Dragon Steamboat	.40	1.00
26 Stone Cold Steve Austin	1.25	3.00
27 Million Dollar Man Ted DiBiase	.40	1.00
28 Hacksaw Jim Duggan	.40	1.00
29 Road Warrior Hawk	.40	1.00
30 Road Warrior Animal	.40	1.00
31 Shawn Michaels	1.00	2.50
32 Edge	.60	1.50
33 Arn Anderson	.40	1.00
34 Barry Windham	.40	1.00
35 Tully Blanchard	.40	1.00

2012 Topps WWE Classic Hall of Famers Autographs

STATED ODDS 1:269 HOBBY AND RETAIL

NNO Animal	25.00	60.00
NNO Barry Windham	12.00	30.00
NNO Don Muraco	20.00	50.00
NNO Greg The Hammer Valentine	25.00	60.00
NNO Harley Race	50.00	100.00
NNO Jimmy Superfly Snuka	100.00	200.00
NNO Koko B. Ware	15.00	40.00
NNO Mr. Wonderful Paul Orndorff	100.00	200.00
NNO Nikolai Volkoff	15.00	30.00
NNO Terry Funk	75.00	150.00
NNO Tito Santana	20.00	50.00
NNO Tully Blanchard	15.00	40.00

2012 Topps WWE Diva Kiss

STATED ODDS 1:1,125

NNO AJ	100.00	175.00

NNO Aksana	30.00	80.00
NNO Alicia Fox	30.00	80.00
NNO Beth Phoenix	30.00	80.00
NNO Kaitlyn	20.00	50.00
NNO Kelly Kelly	25.00	60.00
NNO Layla	50.00	100.00
NNO Maxine	20.00	50.00
NNO Natalya	30.00	80.00
NNO Rosa Mendes	30.00	80.00
NNO Cameron	20.00	50.00
NNO Naomi	30.00	80.00
NNO Tamina Snuka	30.00	80.00

2012 Topps WWE Divas Class of 2012

COMPLETE SET (15)	8.00	20.00

*P.P.BLACK/1: UNPRICED DUE TO SCARCITY
*P.P.CYAN/1: UNPRICED DUE TO SCARCITY
*P.P.MAGENTA/1: UNPRICED DUE TO SCARCITY
*P.P.YELLOW/1: UNPRICED DUE TO SCARCITY
STATED ODDS 1:4 HOBBY AND RETAIL

1 AJ	2.50	6.00
2 Aksana	1.25	3.00
3 Alicia Fox	.75	2.00
4 Beth Phoenix	1.25	3.00
5 Cameron	.75	2.00
6 Eve	2.00	5.00
7 Kaitlyn	1.25	3.00
8 Kelly Kelly	2.00	5.00
9 Layla	1.25	3.00
10 Lilian Garcia	1.25	3.00
11 Maxine	1.25	3.00
12 Naomi	.75	2.00
13 Natalya	2.00	5.00
14 Rosa Mendes	.75	2.00
15 Tamina Snuka	.75	2.00

2012 Topps WWE Divas Class of 2012 Autographs

STATED ODDS 1:364

NNO Aksana	20.00	50.00
NNO Alicia Fox	15.00	40.00
NNO Beth Phoenix	15.00	40.00
NNO Kaitlyn	30.00	75.00
NNO Kelly Kelly	30.00	75.00
NNO Lilian Garcia	20.00	50.00
NNO Maxine	15.00	40.00
NNO Rosa Mendes	15.00	40.00
NNO Tamina Snuka	20.00	50.00

2012 Topps WWE Dual Autographs

STATED ODDS 1:2,245 HOBBY EXCLUSIVE

NNO Jimmy & Tamina Snuka	100.00	200.00
NNO Maxine/Kaitlyn	30.00	75.00
NNO Primo/Epico	20.00	50.00
NNO T.Blanchard/B.Windham	25.00	60.00

2012 Topps WWE First Class Champions

COMPLETE SET (20)	10.00	25.00

*P.P.BLACK/1: UNPRICED DUE TO SCARCITY
*P.P.CYAN/1: UNPRICED DUE TO SCARCITY
*P.P.MAGENTA/1: UNPRICED DUE TO SCARCITY
*P.P.YELLOW/1: UNPRICED DUE TO SCARCITY
STATED ODDS 1:6 HOBBY AND RETAIL

1 The Iron Shiek	.50	1.25
2 Sgt. Slaughter	.50	1.25
3 Undertaker	1.25	3.00
4 Yokozuna	.50	1.25
5 Diesel	.50	1.25
6 Shawn Michaels	1.25	3.00
7 Stone Cold Steve Austin	1.50	4.00
8 The Rock	1.50	4.00
9 Mankind	1.25	3.00
10 Triple H	1.25	3.00
11 Big Show	.75	2.00
12 Chris Jericho	1.25	3.00
13 Brock Lesnar	1.25	3.00
14 John Cena	1.50	4.00
15 Edge	.75	2.00
16 Randy Orton	1.25	3.00
17 Batista	.50	1.25
18 Sheamus	.75	2.00
19 The Miz	.50	1.25
20 CM Punk	1.25	3.00

2012 Topps WWE Shirt Relics

*BLACK/50: .8X TO 2X BASIC MEM
*PLATINUM/1: UNPRICED DUE TO SCARCITY
STATED ODDS 1:112

NNO Alberto Del Rio	5.00	12.00
NNO Big Show	6.00	15.00
NNO Brodus Clay	5.00	12.00
NNO Camacho	5.00	12.00
NNO CM Punk	6.00	15.00
NNO Cody Rhodes	5.00	12.00
NNO Daniel Bryan	5.00	12.00
NNO Dolph Ziggler	6.00	15.00
NNO Hornswoggle	5.00	12.00
NNO Hunico	4.00	10.00
NNO Jerry Lawler	6.00	15.00
NNO John Cena	10.00	25.00
NNO Kofi Kingston	5.00	12.00
NNO Mark Henry	4.00	10.00
NNO Randy Orton	6.00	15.00
NNO R-Truth	4.00	10.00
NNO Santino Marella	4.00	10.00
NNO Sheamus	5.00	12.00
NNO The Miz	5.00	12.00
NNO Zack Ryder	5.00	12.00
NNO Natalya	5.00	12.00
NNO Christian	5.00	12.00
NNO Chris Jericho	6.00	15.00
NNO Evan Bourne	3.00	8.00
NNO Heath Slater	4.00	10.00
NNO Jack Swagger	4.00	10.00
NNO Justin Gabriel	3.00	8.00
NNO Michael McGillicutty	3.00	8.00
NNO Ted DiBiase	3.00	8.00
NNO Wade Barrett	4.00	10.00

2012 Topps WWE Top Class Matches Punk's Picks

COMPLETE SET (10)	5.00	12.00

*P.P.BLACK/1: UNPRICED DUE TO SCARCITY
*P.P.CYAN/1: UNPRICED DUE TO SCARCITY
*P.P.MAGENTA/1: UNPRICED DUE TO SCARCITY
*P.P.YELLOW/1: UNPRICED DUE TO SCARCITY
STATED ODDS 1:6

1 Wins ECW Championship	1.00	2.50
2 Wins Money in the Bank	1.00	2.50
3 Wins Intercontinental Title	1.00	2.50
4 Wins World Heavyweight Championship	1.00	2.50
5 Loses His Hair	1.00	2.50
6 Wins the WWE Championship	1.00	2.50
7 Unifies the WWE Championship	1.00	2.50
8 Reclaims the WWE Championship	1.00	2.50
9 Victorious at WrestleMania XXVIII	1.00	2.50
10 Turns Back Jericho Again	1.00	2.50

2012 Topps WWE World Class Events

COMPLETE SET (10)	5.00	12.00

*P.P.BLACK/1: UNPRICED DUE TO SCARCITY
*P.P.CYAN/1: UNPRICED DUE TO SCARCITY
*P.P.MAGENTA/1: UNPRICED DUE TO SCARCITY
*P.P.YELLOW/1: UNPRICED DUE TO SCARCITY
STATED ODDS 1:6

1 WrestleMania XXVII	1.00	2.50
2 Money in the Bank 2011	1.00	2.50
3 SummerSlam 2011	1.00	2.50
4 Hell in a Cell 2011	1.00	2.50
5 Vengeance 2011	1.00	2.50
6 Survivor Series 2011	1.00	2.50
7 Tables, Ladders and Chairs 2011	1.00	2.50
8 Royal Rumble 2012	1.00	2.50
9 Elimination Chamber 2012	1.00	2.50
10 WrestleMania XXVIII	1.00	2.50

2012 Topps WWE WrestleMania XXVIII Mat Relics

*BLACK/50: .8X TO 2X BASIC MEM
*PLATINUM/1: UNPRICED DUE TO SCARCITY
STATED ODDS 1:109

NNO Beth Phoenix	6.00	15.00
NNO Big Show	6.00	15.00
NNO Booker T	5.00	12.00
NNO Chris Jericho	6.00	15.00
NNO CM Punk	10.00	25.00
NNO Cody Rhodes	5.00	12.00
NNO Daniel Bryan	5.00	12.00
NNO David Otunga	5.00	12.00
NNO Dolph Ziggler	5.00	12.00
NNO Eve	6.00	15.00
NNO Jack Swagger	6.00	15.00
NNO John Cena	10.00	25.00
NNO Kane	6.00	15.00
NNO Kelly Kelly	8.00	20.00
NNO Kofi Kingston	5.00	12.00
NNO Mark Henry	5.00	12.00
NNO Randy Orton	6.00	15.00
NNO R-Truth	5.00	12.00
NNO Santino Marella	5.00	12.00
NNO Sheamus	6.00	15.00
NNO The Miz	5.00	12.00
NNO The Rock	10.00	25.00
NNO Triple H	8.00	20.00
NNO Undertaker	10.00	25.00
NNO Zack Ryder	6.00	15.00

2013 Topps WWE

COMPLETE SET (110)	8.00	20.00
UNOPENED BOX (24 PACKS)		
UNOPENED PACK (7 CARDS)		

*BLACK: 2.5X TO 6X BASIC CARDS
*SILVER: 4X TO 10X BASIC CARDS
*GOLD/10: 15X TO 40X BASIC CARDS
*P.P.BLACK/1: UNPRICED DUE TO SCARCITY
*P.P.CYAN/1: UNPRICED DUE TO SCARCITY
*P.P.MAGENTA/1: UNPRICED DUE TO SCARCITY
*P.P.YELLOW/1: UNPRICED DUE TO SCARCITY

1 AJ Lee	.75	2.00

2	Alex Riley	.15	.40
3	Big E Langston	.15	.40
4	Big Show	.30	.75
5	Brock Lesnar	.60	1.50
6	Brodus Clay	.15	.40
7	Cameron	.25	.60
8	CM Punk	.60	1.50
9	Daniel Bryan	.40	1.00
10	David Otunga	.15	.40
11	Dean Ambrose	.25	.60
12	Dolph Ziggler	.25	.60
13	Epico	.15	.40
14	Evan Bourne	.15	.40
15	Eve	.60	1.50
16	Jack Swagger	.25	.60
17	Jerry The King Lawler	.30	.75
18	John Cena	.75	2.00
19	JTG	.15	.40
20	Justin Roberts	.15	.40
21	Kane	.30	.75
22	Kofi Kingston	.15	.40
23	Mason Ryan	.15	.40
24	Michael Cole	.15	.40
25	Michael McGillicutty	.15	.40
26	The Miz	.25	.60
27	Naomi	.40	1.00
28	Paul Heyman	.15	.40
29	Primo	.15	.40
30	R-Truth	.15	.40
31	Rey Mysterio	.40	1.00
32	The Rock	.75	2.00
33	Roman Reigns	.25	.60
34	Rosa Mendes	.25	.60
35	Ryback	.15	.40
36	Santino Marella	.15	.40
37	Scott Stanford	.15	.40
38	Seth Rollins	.15	.40
39	Tamina Snuka	.20	.50
40	Tensai	.15	.40
41	Triple H	.60	1.50
42	Vickie Guerrero	.25	.60
43	Zack Ryder	.15	.40
44	Aksana	.25	.60
45	Alberto Del Rio	.30	.75
46	Alicia Fox	.25	.60
47	Antonio Cesaro	.15	.40
48	Booker T	.25	.60
49	Camacho	.15	.40
50	Christian	.15	.40
51	Cody Rhodes	.15	.40
52	Damien Sandow	.15	.40
53	Darren Young	.15	.40
54	Drew McIntyre	.15	.40
55	Ezekiel Jackson	.15	.40
56	The Great Khali	.15	.40
57	Heath Slater	.15	.40
58	Hornswoggle	.15	.40
59	Hunico	.15	.40
60	Jey Uso	.15	.40
61	Jimmy Uso	.15	.40
62	Jinder Mahal	.15	.40
63	Fandango	.15	.40
64	Josh Mathews	.15	.40
65	Justin Gabriel	.15	.40
66	Kaitlyn	.30	.75
67	Layla	.30	.75
68	Lilian Garcia	.40	1.00
69	Mark Henry	.20	.50
70	Matt Striker	.15	.40
71	Natalya	.30	.75
72	Percy Watson	.15	.40
73	Randy Orton	.50	1.25
74	Ricardo Rodriguez	.15	.40
75	Sheamus	.30	.75
76	Sin Cara	.25	.60
77	Ted DiBiase	.20	.50
78	Theodore Long	.15	.40
79	Titus O'Neil	.15	.40
80	Tyson Kidd	.15	.40
81	Undertaker	.60	1.50
82	Wade Barrett	.15	.40
83	William Regal	.20	.50
84	Yoshi Tatsu	.15	.40
85	The American Dream Dusty Rhodes	.25	.60
86	Big John Studd	.25	.60
87	The British Bulldog	.25	.60
88	The Bushwhackers	.15	.40
89	Cowboy Bob Orton	.25	.60
90	Dean Malenko	.15	.40
91	Hacksaw Jim Duggan	.25	.60
92	Greg The Hammer Valentine	.15	.40
93	Harley Race	.25	.60
94	The Iron Sheik	.25	.60
95	Jake The Snake Roberts	.25	.60
96	Jimmy Superfly Snuka	.25	.60
97	Junkyard Dog	.25	.60
98	Million Dollar Man Ted DiBiase	.25	.60
99	Mr. Perfect	.25	.60
100	Mr. Wonderful Paul Orndorff	.25	.60
101	Nikolai Volkoff	.25	.60
102	Ravishing Rick Rude	.25	.60
103	Ricky The Dragon Steamboat	.25	.60
104	Rowdy Roddy Piper	.40	1.00
105	Sgt. Slaughter	.25	.60
106	Terry Funk	.25	.60
107	Tito Santana	.25	.60
108	Tom Prichard	.15	.40
109	Vader	.15	.40
110	Yokozuna	.15	.40

2013 Topps WWE Autographed Relics

STATED ODDS 1:9,550
UNPRICED DUE TO SCARCITY

NNO Alicia Fox
NNO Daniel Bryan
NNO Dolph Ziggler
NNO Kofi Kingston
NNO Ryback
NNO Sin Cara

2013 Topps WWE Autographs

STATED ODDS 1:79 HOBBY AND RETAIL

NNO	AJ Lee	75.00	150.00
NNO	Alicia Fox	8.00	20.00
NNO	Antonio Cesaro	10.00	25.00
NNO	Bushwhacker Butch	12.00	30.00
NNO	Bushwhacker Luke	8.00	20.00
NNO	Cowboy Bob Orton	10.00	25.00
NNO	Daniel Bryan	15.00	40.00
NNO	Dean Malenko	12.00	30.00
NNO	Dolph Ziggler	12.00	30.00
NNO	Eve	12.00	30.00
NNO	Jack Swagger	10.00	25.00
NNO	Kaitlyn	15.00	40.00
NNO	Kofi Kingston	8.00	20.00
NNO	Michael Cole	8.00	20.00
NNO	Million Dollar Man Ted DiBiase	15.00	40.00
NNO	Randy Orton	20.00	50.00
NNO	Rosa Mendes	10.00	25.00
NNO	Ryback	10.00	25.00
NNO	Sin Cara	10.00	25.00
NNO	Tom Prichard	8.00	20.00

2013 Topps WWE Diva Kiss

STATED ODDS 1:568 HOBBY AND RETAIL

NNO	AJ Lee	100.00	175.00
NNO	Aksana	25.00	50.00
NNO	Alicia Fox	15.00	40.00
NNO	Cameron	25.00	50.00
NNO	Eve	40.00	80.00
NNO	Kaitlyn	40.00	80.00
NNO	Layla	30.00	60.00
NNO	Naomi	15.00	40.00
NNO	Natalya	30.00	60.00
NNO	Rosa Mendes	25.00	50.00

2013 Topps WWE Diva Snapshots

COMPLETE SET (10)		20.00	40.00

STATED ODDS 1:24 HOBBY AND RETAIL

NNO	AJ Lee	6.00	15.00
NNO	Aksana	2.00	5.00
NNO	Alicia Fox	2.00	5.00
NNO	Cameron	2.00	5.00
NNO	Eve	5.00	12.00
NNO	Kaitlyn	2.50	6.00
NNO	Layla	2.50	6.00
NNO	Naomi	3.00	8.00
NNO	Natalya	2.50	6.00
NNO	Rosa Mendes	2.00	5.00

2013 Topps WWE Shirt Relics

STATED ODDS 1:24 HOBBY; 1:96 RETAIL

NNO	Alicia Fox Skirt	6.00	15.00
NNO	Big Show/Hat	6.00	15.00
NNO	Brodus Clay/Pants	4.00	10.00
NNO	CM Punk/Shirt	9.00	20.00
NNO	Damien Sandow/Shirt	5.00	12.00
NNO	Daniel Bryan/Shirt	5.00	12.00
NNO	Dolph Ziggler/Shirt	5.00	12.00
NNO	Kofi Kingston/Shirt	5.00	12.00
NNO	Paul Heyman/Suit	6.00	15.00
NNO	R-Truth/Shirt	5.00	12.00
NNO	Rey Mysterio/Shirt	5.00	12.00
NNO	Ryback/Shirt	8.00	20.00
NNO	Santino Marella/Puppet	6.00	15.00
NNO	Sheamus/Shirt	6.00	15.00
NNO	Sin Cara Shirt	5.00	12.00
NNO	The Miz/Shirt	4.00	10.00
NNO	Titus O'Neil/Shirt	4.00	10.00
NNO	Wade Barrett/Shirt	5.00	12.00
NNO	CM Punk/Sock SP	30.00	60.00

2013 Topps WWE SummerSlam Mat Relics

STATED ODDS 1:102

NNO	AJ Lee	8.00	20.00
NNO	Aksana	4.00	10.00
NNO	Alberto Del Rio	5.00	12.00
NNO	Antonio Cesaro	4.00	10.00
NNO	Big Show	4.00	10.00
NNO	Brock Lesnar	6.00	15.00
NNO	CM Punk	6.00	15.00
NNO	Daniel Bryan	4.00	10.00
NNO	Darren Young	4.00	10.00
NNO	Dolph Ziggler	5.00	12.00
NNO	Jerry The King Lawler	5.00	12.00
NNO	John Cena	8.00	20.00
NNO	Kane	5.00	12.00
NNO	Kofi Kingston	4.00	10.00
NNO	Paul Heyman	5.00	12.00
NNO	R-Truth	4.00	10.00
NNO	Santino Marella	4.00	10.00
NNO	Sheamus	4.00	10.00
NNO	The Miz	4.00	10.00
NNO	Titus O'Neil	4.00	10.00
NNO	Triple H	6.00	15.00
NNO	Vickie Guerrero	4.00	10.00

2013 Topps WWE Triple Autographs

STATED ODDS 1:12,637 HOBBY AND RETAIL
UNPRICED DUE TO SCARCITY

NNO Luke/Butch/DiBiase
NNO Bryan/Cesaro/Kaitlyn
NNO Eve/Fox/Mendes
NNO Swagger/SinCara/Ryback
NNO R.Orton/B.Orton/Cole

2013 Topps WWE Triple Threat Tier Three

COMPLETE SET (30)		5.00	12.00

*TIER TWO: .5X TO 1.2X TIER THREE
*TIER ONE: .8X TO 2X TIER THREE
*T3 P.P.BLACK/1: UNPRICED DUE TO SCARCITY
*T3 P.P.CYAN/1: UNPRICED DUE TO SCARCITY
*T3 P.P.MAGENTA/1: UNPRICED DUE TO SCARCITY
*T3 P.P.YELLOW/1: UNPRICED DUE TO SCARCITY
*T2 P.P.BLACK/1: UNPRICED DUE TO SCARCITY
*T2 P.P.CYAN/1: UNPRICED DUE TO SCARCITY
*T2 P.P.MAGENTA/1: UNPRICED DUE TO SCARCITY
*T2 P.P.YELLOW/1: UNPRICED DUE TO SCARCITY
*T1 P.P.BLACK/1: UNPRICED DUE TO SCARCITY
*T1 P.P.CYAN/1: UNPRICED DUE TO SCARCITY
*T1 P.P.MAGENTA/1: UNPRICED DUE TO SCARCITY
*T1 P.P.YELLOW/1: UNPRICED DUE TO SCARCITY
STATED ODDS 1:2 HOBBY AND RETAIL

TT1	Dolph Ziggler	.30	.75
TT2	John Cena	1.00	2.50
TT3	Jack Swagger	.30	.75
TT4	The Miz	.30	.75
TT5	Prime Time Players	.20	.50
TT6	Wade Barrett	.20	.50
TT7	Santino Marella	.20	.50
TT8	Brock Lesnar	.75	2.00
TT9	Sin Cara	.30	.75
TT10	Rey Mysterio	.50	1.25
TT11	Damien Sandow	.20	.50
TT12	Randy Orton	.60	1.50
TT13	Cody Rhodes	.20	.50
TT14	Eve	.75	2.00
TT15	Kane	.40	1.00
TT16	Big Show	.40	1.00
TT17	AJ Lee	1.00	2.50
TT18	Mark Henry	.25	.60
TT19	Triple H	.75	2.00
TT20	Ryback	.20	.50
TT21	Zack Ryder	.20	.50
TT22	Daniel Bryan	.50	1.25
TT23	Alberto Del Rio	.40	1.00

TT24 Christian	.20	.50
TT25 Tyson Kidd	.20	.50
TT26 CM Punk	.75	2.00
TT27 The Rock	1.00	2.50
TT28 Undertaker	.75	2.00
TT29 Kofi Kingston	.20	.50
TT30 Sheamus	.40	1.00

2013 Topps WWE 2K14 Phenom Edition Promo

NNO Undertaker

2014 Topps WWE

COMPLETE SET (110)	10.00	25.00
UNOPENED BOX (24 PACKS)		
UNOPENED PACK (7 CARDS)		
*BLACK: .75X TO 2X BASIC CARDS		
*SILVER: 1.5X TO 4X BASIC CARDS		
*GOLD/10: 6X TO 15X BASIC CARDS		
*RED/1: UNPRICED DUE TO SCARCITY		
*P.P.BLACK/1: UNPRICED DUE TO SCARCITY		
*P.P.CYAN/1: UNPRICED DUE TO SCARCITY		
*P.P.MAGENTA/1: UNPRICED DUE TO SCARCITY		
*P.P.YELLOW/1: UNPRICED DUE TO SCARCITY		
1 AJ Lee	.75	2.00
2 Alex Riley	.15	.40
3 Big E Langston	.15	.40
4 Bo Dallas	.15	.40
5 Brad Maddox	.15	.40
6 Bray Wyatt	.40	1.00
7 Brie Bella	.50	1.25
8 Brock Lesnar	.60	1.50
9 Brodus Clay	.15	.40
10 Cameron	.25	.60
11 Chris Jericho	.40	1.00
12 CM Punk	.60	1.50
13 Curtis Axel	.15	.40
14 Daniel Bryan	.25	.60
15 David Otunga	.15	.40
16 Dean Ambrose	.40	1.00
17 Diego	.15	.40
18 Dolph Ziggler	.25	.60
19 Erick Rowan	.25	.60
20 Eva Marie	.60	1.50
21 Fandango	.25	.60
22 Fernando	.15	.40
23 Jack Swagger	.25	.60
24 Jerry The King Lawler	.40	1.00
25 John Cena	.75	2.00
26 Jojo	.25	.60
27 Justin Roberts	.15	.40
28 Kane	.40	1.00
29 Kofi Kingston	.15	.40
30 Luke Harper	.25	.60
31 El Torito	.15	.40
32 Michael Cole	.15	.40
33 The Miz	.25	.60
34 Naomi	.25	.60
35 Nikki Bella	.50	1.25
36 Paul Heyman	.15	.40
37 R-Truth	.15	.40
38 Randy Orton	.60	1.50
39 Rey Mysterio	.40	1.00
40 The Rock	.75	2.00
41 Rob Van Dam	.40	1.00
42 Roman Reigns	.40	1.00
43 Ryback	.15	.40
44 Santino Marella	.25	.60

45 Scott Stanford	.15	.40
46 Seth Rollins	.15	.40
47 Stephanie McMahon	.25	.60
48 Summer Rae	.60	1.50
49 Tamina Snuka	.25	.60
50 Tensai	.15	.40
51 Triple H	.60	1.50
52 Zack Ryder	.15	.40
53 Zeb Colter	.25	.60
54 Aksana	.40	1.00
55 Alberto Del Rio	.40	1.00
56 Alicia Fox	.25	.60
57 Antonio Cesaro	.15	.40
58 Big Show	.40	1.00
59 Booker T	.25	.60
60 Camacho	.15	.40
61 Christian	.15	.40
62 Cody Rhodes	.15	.40
63 Curt Hawkins	.15	.40
64 Damien Sandow	.15	.40
65 Darren Young	.15	.40
66 Drew McIntyre	.15	.40
67 Ezekiel Jackson	.25	.60
68 The Great Khali	.15	.40
69 Heath Slater	.15	.40
70 Hornswoggle	.25	.60
71 Hunico	.15	.40
72 JBL	.25	.60
73 Jey Uso	.15	.40
74 Jimmy Uso	.15	.40
75 Jinder Mahal	.15	.40
76 Josh Mathews	.15	.40
77 Justin Gabriel	.15	.40
78 Kaitlyn	.40	1.00
79 Layla	.40	1.00
80 Lilian Garcia	.40	1.00
81 Mark Henry	.25	.60
82 Natalya	.50	1.25
83 Renee Young	.60	1.50
84 Ricardo Rodriguez	.15	.40
85 Rosa Mendes	.25	.60
86 Sheamus	.40	1.00
87 Sin Cara	.40	1.00
88 Theodore Long	.15	.40
89 Titus O'Neil	.15	.40
90 Tony Chimel	.15	.40
91 Tyson Kidd	.15	.40
92 Undertaker	.60	1.50
93 Vickie Guerrero	.25	.60
94 Wade Barrett	.15	.40
95 William Regal	.25	.60
96 Andre The Giant L	.60	1.50
97 Billy Gunn L	.25	.60
98 Bob Backlund L	.25	.60
99 Diamond Dallas Page L	.25	.60
100 Eddie Guerrero L	.25	.60
101 Honky Tonk Man L	.25	.60
102 Jim Ross L	.25	.60
103 Junkyard Dog L	.25	.60
104 Kevin Nash L	.40	1.00
105 Larry Zbyszko L	.25	.60
106 Mick Foley L	.40	1.00
107 Paul Bearer L	.25	.60
108 Road Dogg L	.25	.60
109 Shawn Michaels L	.60	1.50
110 X-Pac L	.15	.40

2014 Topps WWE Autographs

*BLACK/50: .5X TO 1.2X BASIC AUTOS		
*SILVER/25: .6X TO 1.5X BASIC AUTOS		
*GOLD/10: UNPRICED DUE TO SCARCITY		
*RED/1: UNPRICED DUE TO SCARCITY		
*P.P.BLACK/1: UNPRICED DUE TO SCARCITY		
*P.P.CYAN/1: UNPRICED DUE TO SCARCITY		
*P.P.MAGENTA/1: UNPRICED DUE TO SCARCITY		
*P.P.YELLOW/1: UNPRICED DUE TO SCARCITY		
NNO AJ Lee	60.00	120.00
NNO Billy Gunn	8.00	20.00
NNO Bray Wyatt	30.00	75.00
NNO Daniel Bryan	15.00	40.00
NNO Erick Rowan	6.00	15.00
NNO Eva Marie	12.00	30.00
NNO Jack Swagger	8.00	20.00
NNO John Cena	75.00	150.00
NNO Jojo	6.00	15.00
NNO Luke Harper	8.00	20.00
NNO Randy Orton	30.00	75.00
NNO Renee Young	15.00	40.00
NNO Road Dogg	12.00	30.00
NNO Shawn Michaels	30.00	75.00
NNO Summer Rae	15.00	40.00
NNO X-Pac	8.00	20.00

2014 Topps WWE Champions

COMPLETE SET (30)	10.00	25.00
*P.P.BLACK/1: UNPRICED DUE TO SCARCITY		
*P.P.CYAN/1: UNPRICED DUE TO SCARCITY		
*P.P.MAGENTA/1: UNPRICED DUE TO SCARCITY		
*P.P.YELLOW/1: UNPRICED DUE TO SCARCITY		
STATED ODDS 1:4 HOBBY AND RETAIL		
1 Bruno Sammartino	.40	1.00
2 Bob Backlund	.40	1.00
3 The Iron Sheik	.40	1.00
4 Andre The Giant	1.00	2.50
5 Sgt. Slaughter	.60	1.50
6 Undertaker	1.00	2.50
7 Yokozuna	.40	1.00
8 Diesel	.60	1.50
9 Shawn Michaels	1.00	2.50
10 Stone Cold Steve Austin	1.25	3.00
11 Kane	.60	1.50
12 The Rock	1.25	3.00
13 Mankind	.60	1.50
14 Triple H	1.00	2.50
15 Big Show	.60	1.50
16 Chris Jericho	.60	1.50
17 Brock Lesnar	1.00	2.50
18 Eddie Guerrero	.40	1.00
19 JBL	.40	1.00
20 John Cena	1.25	3.00
21 Edge	.60	1.50
22 Rob Van Dam	.60	1.50
23 Randy Orton	1.00	2.50
24 Batista	.75	2.00
25 Sheamus	.60	1.50
26 The Miz	.40	1.00
27 CM Punk	1.00	2.50
28 Rey Mysterio	.60	1.50
29 Alberto Del Rio	.60	1.50
30 Daniel Bryan	.40	1.00

2014 Topps WWE Championship Belts

STATED PRINT RUN 400 SETS		
NNO AJ Lee	10.00	25.00

NNO Andre The Giant	8.00	20.00
NNO Brie Bella	6.00	15.00
NNO British Bulldog	4.00	10.00
NNO Chris Jericho	5.00	12.00
NNO Christian	2.00	5.00
NNO CM Punk	12.00	30.00
NNO Daniel Bryan	3.00	8.00
NNO D-Generation X	8.00	20.00
NNO Edge	5.00	12.00
NNO Jeri-Show	5.00	12.00
NNO Jimmy Superfly Snuka	3.00	8.00
NNO John Cena	10.00	25.00
NNO Kaitlyn	5.00	12.00
NNO Kofi Kingston	2.00	5.00
NNO Kofi Kingston/R-Truth	2.00	5.00
NNO Layla	5.00	12.00
NNO The Miz	3.00	8.00
NNO Mr. Perfect Curt Hennig	2.50	6.00
NNO Nikki Bella	6.00	15.00
NNO Randy Orton	8.00	20.00
NNO Ravishing Rick Rude	2.00	5.00
NNO Rey Mysterio/Eddie Guerrero	5.00	12.00
NNO Ricky The Dragon Steamboat	2.00	5.00
NNO The Rock	10.00	25.00
NNO Rowdy Roddy Piper	5.00	12.00
NNO Stone Cold Steve Austin	10.00	25.00
NNO Team Hell No	5.00	12.00
NNO Triple H	8.00	20.00
NNO Undertaker	8.00	20.00

2014 Topps WWE Diva Kiss

STATED PRINT RUN 100 SETS		
NNO AJ Lee	150.00	225.00
NNO Brie Bella	50.00	100.00
NNO Eva Marie	30.00	75.00
NNO Jojo	25.00	60.00
NNO Kaitlyn	25.00	60.00
NNO Lilian Garcia	25.00	60.00
NNO Natalya	25.00	60.00
NNO Nikki Bella	50.00	100.00
NNO Renee Young	35.00	75.00
NNO Summer Rae	60.00	120.00

2014 Topps WWE Diva Kiss Autographs

COMMON AUTO	60.00	120.00
STATED PRINT RUN 20 SETS		
NNO AJ Lee	200.00	400.00
NNO Eva Marie	125.00	250.00
NNO Jojo	60.00	120.00
NNO Renee Young	75.00	150.00
NNO Summer Rae	125.00	250.00

2014 Topps WWE Greatest Championship Contenders

COMPLETE SET (10)	5.00	12.00
*P.P.BLACK/1: UNPRICED DUE TO SCARCITY		
*P.P.CYAN/1: UNPRICED DUE TO SCARCITY		
*P.P.MAGENTA/1: UNPRICED DUE TO SCARCITY		
*P.P.YELLOW/1: UNPRICED DUE TO SCARCITY		
STATED ODDS 1:12		
1 Ricky The Dragon Steamboat	.50	1.25
2 Mr. Perfect	.60	1.50
3 Ravishing Rick Rude	.50	1.25
4 Million Dollar Man Ted DiBiase	.60	1.50
5 Rowdy Roddy Piper	1.25	3.00
6 Mr. Wonderful Paul Orndorff	.50	1.25

7	Jake The Snake Roberts	.75	2.00
8	Jimmy Superfly Snuka	.75	2.00
9	The British Bulldog	1.00	2.50
10	The American Dream Dusty Rhodes	1.00	2.50

2014 Topps WWE Greatest Championship Matches

COMPLETE SET (20)		8.00	20.00

*P.P.BLACK/1: UNPRICED DUE TO SCARCITY
*P.P.CYAN/1: UNPRICED DUE TO SCARCITY
*P.P.MAGENTA/1: UNPRICED DUE TO SCARCITY
*P.P.YELLOW/1: UNPRICED DUE TO SCARCITY
STATED ODDS 1:8 HOBBY AND RETAIL

1	The Rock/Steve Austin	.75	2.00
2	John Cena/CM Punk	.75	2.00
3	John Cena/HBK	.75	2.00
4	The Rock/Mankind	.75	2.00
5	Triple H/Cactus Jack	.60	1.50
6	HBK/Mankind	.60	1.50
7	John Cena/RVD	.75	2.00
8	Brock Lesnar/Undertaker	.60	1.50
9	Rey Mysterio/John Cena	.75	2.00
10	HHH/Chris Jericho	.60	1.50
11	Steve Austin/The Rock	.75	2.00
12	Randy Orton/John Cena	.75	2.00
13	CM Punk/John Cena	.75	2.00
14	The Rock/HHH	.75	2.00
15	Brock Lesnar/Eddie Guerrero	.60	1.50
16	John Cena/JBL	.75	2.00
17	The Rock/Brock Lesnar	.75	2.00
18	Steve Austin/Chris Jericho	.75	2.00
19	CM Punk/Chris Jericho	.60	1.50
20	Mankind/The Rock	.75	2.00

2014 Topps WWE NXT Prospects

COMPLETE SET (20)		15.00	40.00

*P.P.BLACK/1: UNPRICED DUE TO SCARCITY
*P.P.CYAN/1: UNPRICED DUE TO SCARCITY
*P.P.MAGENTA/1: UNPRICED DUE TO SCARCITY
*P.P.YELLOW/1: UNPRICED DUE TO SCARCITY
STATED ODDS 1:2 HOBBY AND RETAIL

1	Adrian Neville	.60	1.50
2	Alexander Rusev	.75	2.00
3	Baron Corbin	.30	.75
4	Bayley	3.00	8.00
5	Charlotte	6.00	15.00
6	CJ Parker	.30	.75
7	Konnor O'Brian	.30	.75
8	Corey Graves	.30	.75
9	Emma	1.50	4.00
10	Enzo Amore	.60	1.50
11	Jason Jordan	.30	.75
12	Leo Kruger	.30	.75
13	Mojo Rawley	.30	.75
14	Paige	5.00	12.00
15	Rick Viktor	.30	.75
16	Sami Zayn	.60	1.50
17	Sasha Banks	8.00	20.00
18	Sylvester Lefort	.30	.75
19	Tyler Breeze	.30	.75
20	Xavier Woods	.30	.75

2014 Topps WWE Quad Autograph

NNO	HBK/X-Pac/Dogg/Gunn		

2014 Topps WWE Stone Cold Steve Austin Tribute

COMPLETE SET (10)		5.00	12.00

*P.P.BLACK/1: UNPRICED DUE TO SCARCITY
*P.P.CYAN/1: UNPRICED DUE TO SCARCITY
*P.P.MAGENTA/1: UNPRICED DUE TO SCARCITY
*P.P.YELLOW/1: UNPRICED DUE TO SCARCITY
STATED ODDS 1:12 HOBBY AND RETAIL

1	Stone Cold Steve Austin	1.00	2.50
2	Stone Cold Steve Austin	1.00	2.50
3	Stone Cold Steve Austin	1.00	2.50
4	Stone Cold Steve Austin	1.00	2.50
5	Stone Cold Steve Austin	1.00	2.50
6	Stone Cold Steve Austin	1.00	2.50
7	Stone Cold Steve Austin	1.00	2.50
8	Stone Cold Steve Austin	1.00	2.50
9	Stone Cold Steve Austin	1.00	2.50
10	Stone Cold Steve Austin	1.00	2.50

2014 Topps WWE SummerSlam Mat Relics

NNO	AJ Lee	12.00	30.00
NNO	Alberto Del Rio	6.00	15.00
NNO	Big E Langston	2.50	6.00
NNO	Bray Wyatt	6.00	15.00
NNO	Brie Bella	8.00	20.00
NNO	Brock Lesnar	10.00	25.00
NNO	Christian	2.50	6.00
NNO	CM Punk	10.00	25.00
NNO	Cody Rhodes	2.50	6.00
NNO	Damien Sandow	2.50	6.00
NNO	Daniel Bryan	4.00	10.00
NNO	Dean Ambrose	10.00	25.00
NNO	Dolph Ziggler	4.00	10.00
NNO	John Cena	12.00	30.00
NNO	Kaitlyn	6.00	15.00
NNO	Kane	6.00	15.00
NNO	Natalya	8.00	20.00
NNO	Randy Orton	10.00	25.00
NNO	Rob Van Dam	6.00	15.00
NNO	Triple H	10.00	25.00

2014 Topps WWE Swatch Relics

NNO	Brodus Clay/Shirt	3.00	8.00
NNO	Christian/Shirt	3.00	8.00
NNO	CM Punk/Shirt	6.00	15.00
NNO	Damien Sandow/Shirt	3.00	8.00
NNO	Daniel Bryan/Shirt	4.00	10.00
NNO	Darren Young/Shirt	3.00	8.00
NNO	Dean Ambrose/Shirt	8.00	20.00
NNO	Dolph Ziggler/Shirt	5.00	12.00
NNO	Hornswoggle/Shirt	3.00	8.00
NNO	John Cena/Shirt	8.00	20.00
NNO	Mark Henry/Shirt	4.00	10.00
NNO	The Miz/Shirt	3.00	8.00
NNO	Randy Orton/Shirt	6.00	15.00
NNO	Roman Reigns/Shirt	12.00	30.00
NNO	Ryback/Shirt	3.00	8.00
NNO	Seth Rollins	6.00	15.00
	Shirt		
NNO	Undertaker/Pants	12.00	30.00
NNO	Wade Barrett/Shirt	3.00	8.00

2014 Topps WWE Triple Autographs

OVERALL TRIPLE AUTO PRINT RUN 25
UNPRICED DUE TO SCARCITY

NNO	Lee/Rae/Young		

NNO	Wyatt/Harper/Rowan		
NNO	Marie/Jojo/Swagger		
NNO	Cena/Bryan/Orton		

2014 Topps WWE Promo

P1 Shawn Michaels
(WWE 50 Book Exclusive)

2015 Topps WWE

COMPLETE SET (100)		8.00	20.00
UNOPENED BOX (24 PACKS)			
UNOPENED PACK (7 CARDS)			

*BLACK: 2X TO 5X BASIC CARDS
*SILVER: 3X TO 8X BASIC CARDS
*GOLD/10: 6X TO 15X BASIC CARDS
*RED/1: UNPRICED DUE TO SCARCITY
*P.P.BLACK/1: UNPRICED DUE TO SCARCITY
*P.P.CYAN/1: UNPRICED DUE TO SCARCITY
*P.P.MAGENTA/1: UNPRICED DUE TO SCARCITY
*P.P.YELLOW/1: UNPRICED DUE TO SCARCITY

1	Adam Rose	.20	.50
2	AJ Lee	.75	2.00
3	Alex Riley	.15	.40
4	Alicia Fox	.30	.75
5	Bad News Barrett	.15	.40
6	Batista	.40	1.00
7	Big E	.25	.60
8	Big Show	.40	1.00
9	Bo Dallas	.15	.40
10	Booker T	.25	.60
11	Bray Wyatt	.60	1.50
12	Brie Bella	.50	1.25
13	Brock Lesnar	.60	1.50
14	Byron Saxton	.15	.40
15	Cameron	.25	.60
16	Cesaro	.15	.40
17	Chris Jericho	.40	1.00
18	Christian	.15	.40
19	Curtis Axel	.15	.40
20	Damien Mizdow	.15	.40
21	Daniel Bryan	.60	1.50
22	Darren Young	.15	.40
23	David Otunga	.15	.40
24	Dean Ambrose	.40	1.00
25	Diego	.15	.40
26	Dolph Ziggler	.25	.60
27	Eden	.25	.60
28	Emma	.25	.60
29	Erick Rowan	.25	.60
30	Eva Marie	.60	1.50
31	Fandango	.15	.40
32	Fernando	.15	.40
33	Goldust	.15	.40
34	Heath Slater	.15	.40
35	Hornswoggle	.25	.60
36	Jack Swagger	.25	.60
37	Jason Albert	.15	.40
38	JBL	.15	.40
39	Jerry The King Lawler	.25	.60
40	Jey Uso	.15	.40
41	Jimmy Uso	.15	.40
42	John Cena	.75	2.00
43	Justin Gabriel	.15	.40
44	Kane	.40	1.00
45	Kofi Kingston	.15	.40
46	Lana	.60	1.50
47	Layla	.40	1.00
48	Lilian Garcia	.40	1.00
49	Luke Harper	.25	.60
50	Mark Henry	.25	.60
51	Michael Cole	.15	.40
52	The Miz	.25	.60
53	Naomi	.25	.60
54	Natalya	.50	1.25
55	Nikki Bella	.50	1.25
56	Paige	.75	2.00
57	Paul Heyman	.15	.40
58	R-Truth	.15	.40
59	Randy Orton	.60	1.50
60	Renee Young	.60	1.50
61	Rey Mysterio	.40	1.00
62	The Rock	.75	2.00
63	Rob Van Dam	.40	1.00
64	Roman Reigns	.40	1.00
65	Rosa Mendes	.25	.60
66	Rusev	.40	1.00
67	Ryback	.15	.40
68	Santino Marella	.15	.40
69	Scott Stanford	.15	.40
70	Seth Rollins	.25	.60
71	Sheamus	.40	1.00
72	Sin Cara	.25	.60
73	Stardust	.15	.40
74	Stephanie McMahon	.25	.60
75	Summer Rae	.60	1.50
76	Tamina Snuka	.25	.60
77	Titus O'Neil	.15	.40
78	Tom Phillips	.15	.40
79	Tony Chimel	.15	.40
80	El Torito	.15	.40
81	Triple H	.60	1.50
82	Tyson Kidd	.15	.40
83	Undertaker	.60	1.50
84	William Regal	.25	.60
85	Xavier Woods	.25	.60
86	Zack Ryder	.15	.40
87	Zeb Colter	.25	.60
88	Bret The Hit Man Hart	.50	1.25
89	Bruno Sammartino	.40	1.00
90	George The Animal Steele	.20	.50
91	Gerald Brisco	.25	.60
92	Hulk Hogan	.75	2.00
93	Larry Zbyszko	.25	.60
94	Mouth of the South Jimmy Hart	.20	.50
95	Pat Patterson	.15	.40
96	Ric Flair	.75	2.00
97	Rowdy Roddy Piper	.50	1.25
98	Sting	.40	1.00
99	Ultimate Warrior	.50	1.25
100	Virgil	.15	.40

2015 Topps WWE Athletic Tape Relics

*RED/1: UNPRICED DUE TO SCARCITY
STATED PRINT RUN 20 SER.#'d SETS

NNO	Cesaro	30.00	80.00
NNO	Curtis Axel	25.00	60.00
NNO	Daniel Bryan	120.00	200.00
NNO	Darren Young	15.00	40.00
NNO	Jack Swagger	15.00	40.00
NNO	Rey Mysterio	30.00	80.00
NNO	Ryback	25.00	60.00
NNO	Zack Ryder	50.00	100.00

2015 Topps WWE Autographs

*BLACK/50: .6X TO 1.5X BASIC AUTOS
*SILVER/25: .75X TO 2X BASIC AUTOS

*GOLD/10: 1X TO 2.5X BASIC AUTOS
*RED/1: UNPRICED DUE TO SCARCITY
*P.P.BLACK/1: UNPRICED DUE TO SCARCITY
*P.P.CYAN/1: UNPRICED DUE TO SCARCITY
*P.P.MAGENTA/1: UNPRICED DUE TO SCARCITY
*P.P.YELLOW/1: UNPRICED DUE TO SCARCITY
RANDOMLY INSERTED INTO PACKS

NNO	AJ Lee	75.00	150.00
NNO	Bray Wyatt	15.00	40.00
NNO	Bret Hit Man Hart	25.00	60.00
NNO	Eden	20.00	50.00
NNO	Emma	15.00	40.00
NNO	George The Animal Steele	15.00	40.00
NNO	Hulk Hogan	125.00	250.00
NNO	Jack Swagger	6.00	15.00
NNO	John Cena	25.00	60.00
NNO	Larry Zbyszko	6.00	15.00
NNO	Mouth of the South Jimmy Hart	6.00	15.00
NNO	Paige	75.00	150.00
NNO	Ric Flair	15.00	40.00
NNO	Rowdy Roddy Piper	25.00	60.00
NNO	Rusev	20.00	50.00
NNO	Seth Rollins	15.00	40.00

2015 Topps WWE Championship Plates

*GOLD/10: UNPRICED DUE TO SCARCITY
*RED/1: UNPRICED DUE TO SCARCITY
RANDOMLY INSERTED INTO PACKS

NNO	AJ Lee	15.00	40.00
NNO	Batista and Rey Mysterio	6.00	15.00
NNO	Big Show	6.00	15.00
NNO	Booker T	6.00	15.00
NNO	Brie Bella	8.00	20.00
NNO	Brock Lesnar	8.00	20.00
NNO	Bruno Sammartino	6.00	15.00
NNO	Cesaro	6.00	15.00
NNO	Dean Ambrose	8.00	20.00
NNO	Dolph Ziggler	8.00	20.00
NNO	Edge and Chris Jericho	6.00	15.00
NNO	Eve	10.00	25.00
NNO	Hulk Hogan	12.00	30.00
NNO	John Cena	10.00	25.00
NNO	Kane	6.00	15.00
NNO	Kane and Big Show	6.00	15.00
NNO	Lex Luger	6.00	15.00
NNO	New Age Outlaws	8.00	20.00
NNO	Nikki Bella	12.00	30.00
NNO	Paige	15.00	40.00
NNO	Randy Orton	6.00	15.00
NNO	Razor Ramon	8.00	20.00
NNO	Rey Mysterio	6.00	15.00
NNO	Ric Flair/US Title	10.00	25.00
NNO	Ric Flair/WWE Title	12.00	30.00
NNO	Rock	8.00	20.00
NNO	Triple H	6.00	15.00
NNO	Ultimate Warrior/IC Title	6.00	15.00
NNO	Ultimate Warrior/WWE Title	10.00	25.00
NNO	Usos	8.00	20.00

2015 Topps WWE Crowd Chants Oh No

COMPLETE SET (10)   4.00   10.00
*P.P.BLACK/1: UNPRICED DUE TO SCARCITY
*P.P.CYAN/1: UNPRICED DUE TO SCARCITY
*P.P.MAGENTA/1: UNPRICED DUE TO SCARCITY
*P.P.YELLOW/1: UNPRICED DUE TO SCARCITY

RANDOMLY INSERTED INTO PACKS

1	The Montreal Incident	.40	1.00
2	Mr. McMahon/The Rock	.40	1.00
3	Eve/Zack Ryder	1.00	2.50
4	Brad Maddox/Ryback	.40	1.00
5	Damien Sandow/Cody Rhodes	.40	1.00
6	Big Show/John Cena	.40	1.00
7	Randy Orton/Daniel Bryan	1.25	3.00
8	Triple H/Daniel Bryan	.75	2.00
9	Wyatt Family/John Cena	.50	1.25
10	Streak Ends	1.00	2.50

2015 Topps WWE Crowd Chants One More Match

COMPLETE SET (10)   4.00   10.00
*P.P.BLACK/1: UNPRICED DUE TO SCARCITY
*P.P.CYAN/1: UNPRICED DUE TO SCARCITY
*P.P.MAGENTA/1: UNPRICED DUE TO SCARCITY
*P.P.YELLOW/1: UNPRICED DUE TO SCARCITY
RANDOMLY INSERTED INTO PACKS

1	Cowboy Bob Orton	.40	1.00
2	Edge	.50	1.25
3	Shawn Michaels	.50	1.25
4	Million Dollar Man Ted DiBiase	.40	1.00
5	Bruno Sammartino	.40	1.00
6	Ric Flair	.75	2.00
7	Rowdy Roddy Piper	.50	1.25
8	Hulk Hogan	1.25	3.00
9	Jake The Snake Roberts	.40	1.00
10	Stone Cold Steve Austin	1.25	3.00

2015 Topps WWE Crowd Chants This Is Awesome

COMPLETE SET (10)   4.00   10.00
*P.P.BLACK/1: UNPRICED DUE TO SCARCITY
*P.P.CYAN/1: UNPRICED DUE TO SCARCITY
*P.P.MAGENTA/1: UNPRICED DUE TO SCARCITY
*P.P.YELLOW/1: UNPRICED DUE TO SCARCITY
RANDOMLY INSERTED INTO PACKS

1	Rock beats Cena	.75	2.00
2	DX Reunites	.75	2.00
3	Bob Backlund HOF	.40	1.00
4	Dolph Ziggler/Alberto Del Rio	.40	1.00
5	Big Show/Triple H	.40	1.00
6	Kofi Kingston	.40	1.00
7	Wyatt Family/The Shield	.40	1.00
8	Hogan/Austin/Rock	1.25	3.00
9	Daniel Bryan	.40	1.00
10	Paige/AJ Lee	2.50	6.00

2015 Topps WWE Crowd Chants USA

COMPLETE SET (10)   5.00   12.00
*P.P.BLACK/1: UNPRICED DUE TO SCARCITY
*P.P.CYAN/1: UNPRICED DUE TO SCARCITY
*P.P.MAGENTA/1: UNPRICED DUE TO SCARCITY
*P.P.YELLOW/1: UNPRICED DUE TO SCARCITY
RANDOMLY INSERTED INTO PACKS

1	Hulk Hogan	1.50	4.00
2	Sgt. Slaughter	.75	2.00
3	Hacksaw Jim Duggan	.40	1.00
4	Lex Luger	.40	1.00
5	The US Express	.40	1.00
6	Jack Swagger	.40	1.00
7	The American Dream Dusty Rhodes	.40	1.00
8	John Cena	1.25	3.00
9	The Rock	1.50	4.00
10	Undertaker	1.25	3.00

2015 Topps WWE Crowd Chants WOOOOOO

COMPLETE SET (10)   4.00   10.00
*P.P.BLACK/1: UNPRICED DUE TO SCARCITY
*P.P.CYAN/1: UNPRICED DUE TO SCARCITY
*P.P.MAGENTA/1: UNPRICED DUE TO SCARCITY
*P.P.YELLOW/1: UNPRICED DUE TO SCARCITY
RANDOMLY INSERTED INTO PACKS

1	Ric Flair/Royal Rumble	.75	2.00
2	Ric Flair/Randy Savage	.60	1.50
3	Ric Flair/Eric Bischoff	.60	1.50
4	Ric Flair/Jeff Jarrett	.60	1.50
5	Evolution	.60	1.50
6	Ric Flair/Carlito	.60	1.50
7	Ric Flair/Roddy Piper	.60	1.50
8	Ric Flair HOF	1.25	3.00
9	Shawn Michaels/Ric Flair	.60	1.50
10	Four Horsemen HOF	1.25	3.00

2015 Topps WWE Crowd Chants YES! YES! YES!

COMPLETE SET (10)   5.00   12.00
*P.P.BLACK/1: UNPRICED DUE TO SCARCITY
*P.P.CYAN/1: UNPRICED DUE TO SCARCITY
*P.P.MAGENTA/1: UNPRICED DUE TO SCARCITY
*P.P.YELLOW/1: UNPRICED DUE TO SCARCITY
RANDOMLY INSERTED INTO PACKS

1	Daniel Bryan/Kane	.75	2.00
2	Team Hell No/Tag Champs	1.25	3.00
3	Team Hell No/Ziggler & Big E	.75	2.00
4	Daniel Bryan/WWE Title	.75	2.00
5	Locker Room/Daniel Bryan	.75	2.00
6	Daniel Bryan/Second Title	.75	2.00
7	Daniel Bryan/Wyatt Family	.75	2.00
8	Yes Movement	.75	2.00
9	Daniel Bryan/Triple H	.75	2.00
10	Daniel Bryan	1.25	3.00
	WWE World Title		

2015 Topps WWE Crowd Chants You Still Got It

COMPLETE SET (10)   2.50   6.00
*P.P.BLACK/1: UNPRICED DUE TO SCARCITY
*P.P.CYAN/1: UNPRICED DUE TO SCARCITY
*P.P.MAGENTA/1: UNPRICED DUE TO SCARCITY
*P.P.YELLOW/1: UNPRICED DUE TO SCARCITY
RANDOMLY INSERTED INTO PACKS

1	Ricky The Dragon Steamboat	.40	1.00
2	Booker T	.40	1.00
3	Chris Jericho	.40	1.00
4	Vader	.40	1.00
5	Road Warrior Animal	.40	1.00
6	Jerry The King Lawler	.40	1.00
7	Rob Van Dam	.40	1.00
8	Goldust	.40	1.00
9	Billy Gunn	.40	1.00
10	Road Dogg	.40	1.00

2015 Topps WWE Diva Kiss

*GOLD/10: .5X TO 1.2X BASIC KISS
*RED/1: UNPRICED DUE TO SCARCITY
RANDOMLY INSERTED INTO PACKS

NNO	Alicia Fox	20.00	50.00
NNO	Eva Marie	25.00	60.00
NNO	Eve Torres	25.00	60.00
NNO	Lana	30.00	80.00
NNO	Layla	15.00	40.00

NNO	Lilian Garcia	15.00	40.00
NNO	Paige	150.00	300.00
NNO	Rosa Mendes	15.00	40.00
NNO	Trish Stratus	30.00	80.00
NNO	Lita	25.00	60.00

2015 Topps WWE Diva Kiss Autographs

*GOLD/10: UNPRICED DUE TO SCARCITY
*RED/1: UNPRICED DUE TO SCARCITY
STATED PRINT RUN 15 SER.#'d SETS

NNO	Alicia Fox	40.00	100.00
NNO	Eva Marie	80.00	200.00
NNO	Eve Torres	40.00	100.00
NNO	Lana	80.00	200.00
NNO	Layla	50.00	125.00
NNO	Lilian Garcia	50.00	125.00
NNO	Paige	100.00	250.00
NNO	Rosa Mendes	30.00	80.00
NNO	Trish Stratus	100.00	250.00
NNO	Lita	80.00	200.00

2015 Topps WWE King of the Ring Relics

*RED/1: UNPRICED DUE TO SCARCITY
RANDOMLY INSERTED INTO PACKS

NNO	Billy Gunn	12.00	30.00
NNO	Bret Hit Man Hart	25.00	60.00
NNO	Brock Lesnar	15.00	40.00
NNO	Don Muraco	12.00	30.00
NNO	Edge	20.00	50.00
NNO	Harley Race	20.00	50.00
NNO	King Booker	15.00	40.00
NNO	Million Dollar Man Ted DiBiase	20.00	50.00
NNO	Sheamus	15.00	40.00
NNO	Stone Cold Steve Austin	25.00	60.00
NNO	Tito Santana	15.00	40.00
NNO	Triple H	25.00	60.00
NNO	William Regal	12.00	30.00

2015 Topps WWE NXT Prospects

COMPLETE SET (10)   6.00   15.00
STATED ODDS 1:3

1	Aiden English	1.00	2.50
2	Alexa Bliss	12.00	30.00
3	Angelo Dawkins	1.00	2.50
4	Bull Dempsey	1.50	4.00
5	Colin Cassady	1.25	3.00
6	Hideo Itami	2.00	5.00
7	Kalisto	1.25	3.00
8	Marcus Louis	1.00	2.50
9	Sawyer Fulton	1.00	2.50
10	Tye Dillinger	1.00	2.50

2015 Topps WWE SummerSlam Mat Relics

*GOLD/10: UNPRICED DUE TO SCARCITY
*RED/1: UNPRICED DUE TO SCARCITY
RANDOMLY INSERTED INTO PACKS

NNO	AJ Lee	12.00	30.00
NNO	Bray Wyatt	6.00	15.00
NNO	Brie Bella	6.00	15.00
NNO	Brock Lesnar	8.00	20.00
NNO	Cesaro	5.00	12.00
NNO	Chris Jericho	8.00	20.00
NNO	Dean Ambrose	6.00	15.00
NNO	Dolph Ziggler	8.00	20.00

NNO	Jack Swagger	5.00	12.00
NNO	John Cena	6.00	15.00
NNO	Miz	5.00	12.00
NNO	Nikki Bella	6.00	15.00
NNO	Paige	15.00	40.00
NNO	Randy Orton	5.00	12.00
NNO	Rob Van Dam	5.00	12.00
NNO	Roman Reigns	8.00	20.00
NNO	Rusev	6.00	15.00
NNO	Seth Rollins	5.00	12.00
NNO	Stephanie McMahon	8.00	20.00
NNO	Triple H	8.00	20.00

2015 Topps WWE Swatch Relics

*GOLD/10: UNPRICED DUE TO SCARCITY
*RED/1: UNPRICED DUE TO SCARCITY
RANDOMLY INSERTED INTO PACKS

NNO	AJ Lee	15.00	40.00
NNO	Big E	5.00	12.00
NNO	Big Show	5.00	12.00
NNO	Bo Dallas	6.00	15.00
NNO	Bray Wyatt	10.00	25.00
NNO	Brie Bella	6.00	15.00
NNO	Dolph Ziggler	6.00	15.00
NNO	Fandango	5.00	12.00
NNO	Goldust	5.00	12.00
NNO	Jey Uso	5.00	12.00
NNO	John Cena	6.00	15.00
NNO	The Miz	5.00	12.00
NNO	Natalya	6.00	15.00
NNO	Nikki Bella	6.00	15.00
NNO	Paige	15.00	40.00
NNO	Randy Orton	6.00	15.00
NNO	Seth Rollins	6.00	15.00
NNO	Stardust	5.00	12.00

2015 Topps WWE Triple Autographs

STATED PRINT RUN 5 SER.#'d SETS
UNPRICED DUE TO SCARCITY

NNO	AJ/Paige/Emma
NNO	Wyatt/Rusev/Hart
NNO	Hogan/Flair/Piper
NNO	Cena/Ambrose/Rollins
NNO	Paige/Emma/Eden

2016 Topps WWE

COMPLETE SET (100)		10.00	25.00
UNOPENED BOX (24 PACKS)			
UNOPENED PACK (8 CARDS)			

*BRONZE: 1.2X TO 3X BASIC CARDS
*SILVER: 2X TO 5X BASIC CARDS
*GOLD/10: UNPRICED DUE TO SCARCITY
*RED/1: UNPRICED DUE TO SCARCITY
*P.P.BLACK/1: UNPRICED DUE TO SCARCITY
*P.P.CYAN/1: UNPRICED DUE TO SCARCITY
*P.P.MAGENTA/1: UNPRICED DUE TO SCARCITY
*P.P.YELLOW/1: UNPRICED DUE TO SCARCITY

1	Adam Rose	.20	.50
2	Alberto Del Rio	.30	.75
3	Alicia Fox	.30	.75
4	The Ascension	.20	.50
5	Becky Lynch	.60	1.50
6	Big Show	.40	1.00
7	Bo Dallas	.20	.50
8	Booker T	.40	1.00
9	Brie Bella	.40	1.00
10	Bubba Ray Dudley	.40	1.00
11	The Bunny	.20	.50
12	Byron Saxton	.20	.50
13	Cesaro	.40	1.00
14	Charlotte	.60	1.50
15	Corey Graves	.12	.30
16	Curtis Axel	.20	.50
17	D-Von Dudley	.30	.75
18	Damien Sandow	.20	.50
19	Dolph Ziggler	.25	.60
20	Fandango	.20	.50
21	Goldust	.30	.75
22	Jason Albert	.20	.50
23	JBL	.25	.60
24	Jerry The King Lawler	.40	1.00
25	Kalisto	.50	1.25
26	Kevin Owens	.50	1.25
27	Lana	.75	2.00
28	Mandy Rose	2.00	5.00
29	Mark Henry	.25	.60
30	The Miz	.30	.75
31	Naomi	.30	.75
32	Natalya	.30	.75
33	Neville	.50	1.25
34	Nikki Bella	.60	1.50
35	Paige	.60	1.50
36	Titus O'Neil	.20	.50
37	R-Truth	.20	.50
38	Rusev	.50	1.25
39	Ryback	.25	.60
40	Sasha Banks	.60	1.50
41	Sin Cara	.25	.60
42	Stardust	.20	.50
43	Summer Rae	.50	1.25
44	Tamina	.25	.60
45	Tyler Breeze	.20	.50
46	Tyson Kidd	.20	.50
47	The Usos	.20	.50
48	William Regal	.20	.50
49	Zeb Colter	.20	.50
50	Alundra Blayze L	.25	.60
51	American Dream Dusty Rhodes L	.20	.50
52	Andre the Giant L	.60	1.50
53	Bam Bam Bigelow L	.25	.60
54	Barry Windham L	.20	.50
55	Batista L	.40	1.00
56	The Brain Busters L	.20	.50
57	The British Bulldog L	.25	.60
58	The Bushwackers L	.20	.50
59	Christian L	.30	.75
60	Dangerous Danny Davis L	.20	.50
61	Doink the Clown L	.20	.50
62	Edge L	.50	1.25
63	Eve Torres L	.40	1.00
64	George The Animal Steele L	.25	.60
65	The Godfather L	.25	.60
66	Irwin R. Schyster L	.20	.50
67	Jake The Snake Roberts L	.40	1.00
68	Jim Ross L	.30	.75
69	J.J. Dillon L	.20	.50
70	Kamala L	.20	.50
71	Kerry Von Erich L	.30	.75
72	Kevin Nash L	.50	1.25
73	Kevin Von Erich L	.30	.75
74	Lita L	.60	1.50
75	Macho King Randy Savage L	.50	1.25
76	Mike Rotunda L	.20	.50
77	Million Dollar Man Ted DiBiase L	.25	.60
78	Miss Elizabeth L	.20	.50
79	Mr. X L	.20	.50
80	The Nasty Boys L	.20	.50
81	The Natural Disasters L	.20	.50
82	Bret Hit Man Hart L	.50	1.25
83	Papa Shango L	.25	.60
84	Ric Flair L	.75	2.00
85	Rikishi L	.25	.60
86	Road Dogg L	.30	.75
87	Rob Van Dam L	.40	1.00
88	Faarooq L	.50	1.25
89	Rowdy Roddy Piper L	.60	1.50
90	Santino Marella L	.25	.60
91	Scott Hall L	.50	1.25
92	Sensational Sherri L	.30	.75
93	Shawn Michaels L	.75	2.00
94	Stevie Ray L	.20	.50
95	Superstar Billy Graham L	.20	.50
96	Tatsumi Fujinami L	.20	.50
97	Trish Stratus L	1.00	2.50
98	Ultimate Warrior L	.50	1.25
99	Virgil L	.20	.50
100	X-Pac L	.30	.75

2016 Topps WWE 2K17 NXT TakeOver London Mat Relics

*PURPLE/299: SAME VALUE AS BASIC
*GREEN/199: .5X TO 1.2X BASIC MEM
*BRONZE/99: .6X TO 1.5X BASIC MEM
*SILVER/50: .75X TO 2X BASIC MEM
*BLUE/25: UNPRICED DUE TO SCARCITY
*GOLD/10: UNPRICED DUE TO SCARCITY
RANDOMLY INSERTED INTO PACKS

NNO	Asuka	5.00	12.00
NNO	Emma	6.00	15.00
NNO	Dana Brooke	3.00	8.00
NNO	Dash Wilder	2.50	6.00
NNO	Scott Dawson	2.50	6.00
NNO	Enzo Amore	3.00	8.00
NNO	Colin Cassady	3.00	8.00
NNO	Carmella	6.00	15.00
NNO	Baron Corbin	4.00	10.00
NNO	Apollo Crews	3.00	8.00
NNO	Bayley	5.00	12.00
NNO	Nia Jax	3.00	8.00
NNO	Finn Balor	5.00	12.00
NNO	Samoa Joe	3.00	8.00

2016 Topps WWE Authority Perspectives

COMPLETE SET (18)		12.00	30.00

*P.P.BLACK/1: UNPRICED DUE TO SCARCITY
*P.P.CYAN/1: UNPRICED DUE TO SCARCITY
*P.P.MAGENTA/1: UNPRICED DUE TO SCARCITY
*P.P.YELLOW/1: UNPRICED DUE TO SCARCITY
RANDOMLY INSERTED INTO PACKS
*ANTI-AUTHORITY: SAME VALUE

1A	Triple H	2.50	6.00
2A	Stephanie McMahon	1.00	2.50
3A	Seth Rollins	1.00	2.50
4A	Kane	1.00	2.50
5A	J&J Security	.60	1.50
6A	The New Day	1.50	4.00
7A	The Wyatt Family	1.25	3.00
8A	King Barrett	.60	1.50
9A	Sheamus	1.50	4.00
10A	John Cena	3.00	8.00
11A	Sting	1.50	4.00
12A	The Rock	3.00	8.00
13A	Reigns/Ambrose	2.00	5.00
14A	Randy Orton	1.50	4.00
15A	Brock Lesnar	3.00	8.00
16A	Undertaker	2.50	6.00
17A	Chris Jericho	1.50	4.00
18A	Daniel Bryan	2.50	6.00

2016 Topps WWE Autographs

*BRONZE/50: .5X TO 1.2X BASIC AUTOS
*SILVER/25: .75X TO 2X BASIC AUTOS
*GOLD/10: UNPRICED DUE TO SCARCITY
*RED/1: UNPRICED DUE TO SCARCITY
*P.P.BLACK/1: UNPRICED DUE TO SCARCITY
*P.P.CYAN/1: UNPRICED DUE TO SCARCITY
*P.P.MAGENTA/1: UNPRICED DUE TO SCARCITY
*P.P.YELLOW/1: UNPRICED DUE TO SCARCITY
RANDOMLY INSERTED INTO PACKS

NNO	Apollo Crews	10.00	25.00
NNO	Alberto Del Rio	10.00	25.00
NNO	Asuka	30.00	80.00
NNO	Bayley	25.00	60.00
NNO	Becky Lynch	15.00	40.00
NNO	Braun Strowman	10.00	25.00
NNO	Bray Wyatt	10.00	25.00
NNO	Bubba Ray Dudley	8.00	20.00
NNO	Charlotte	12.00	30.00
NNO	D-Von Dudley	6.00	15.00
NNO	Dean Ambrose	10.00	25.00
NNO	Finn Balor	15.00	40.00
NNO	JJ Dillion	6.00	15.00
NNO	John Cena	15.00	40.00
NNO	Luke Harper	25.00	60.00
NNO	Natalya	8.00	20.00
NNO	Nia Jax	12.00	30.00
NNO	Ric Flair	30.00	75.00
NNO	Rikishi	6.00	15.00
NNO	Roman Reigns	10.00	25.00
NNO	Samoa Joe	8.00	20.00
NNO	Seth Rollins	8.00	20.00
NNO	Sting	25.00	60.00
NNO	Superstar Billy Graham	15.00	40.00

2016 Topps WWE Diva Kiss

*GOLD/10: UNPRICED DUE TO SCARCITY
*RED/1: UNPRICED DUE TO SCARCITY
STATED PRINT RUN 99 SER.#'d SETS

NNO	Alicia Fox	30.00	75.00
NNO	Alundra Blayze	60.00	120.00
NNO	Bayley	75.00	150.00
NNO	Becky Lynch	150.00	300.00
NNO	Brie Bella	30.00	75.00
NNO	Charlotte	125.00	250.00
NNO	Lana	50.00	100.00
NNO	Lita	25.00	60.00
NNO	Nikki Bella	60.00	120.00
NNO	Sasha Banks	150.00	300.00
NNO	Trish Stratus	200.00	400.00

2016 Topps WWE Diva Kiss Autographs

*GOLD/10: UNPRICED DUE TO SCARCITY
*RED/1: UNPRICED DUE TO SCARCITY
*P.P.BLACK/1: UNPRICED DUE TO SCARCITY
*P.P.CYAN/1: UNPRICED DUE TO SCARCITY
*P.P.MAGENTA/1: UNPRICED DUE TO SCARCITY
*P.P.YELLOW/1: UNPRICED DUE TO SCARCITY

NNO	Alicia Fox	30.00	80.00
NNO	Alundra Blayze	30.00	80.00
NNO	Bayley	100.00	200.00
NNO	Becky Lynch	400.00	800.00
NNO	Brie Bella	150.00	300.00
NNO	Charlotte	150.00	300.00
NNO	Lana	60.00	120.00
NNO	Lita	50.00	100.00
NNO	Nikki Bella	50.00	100.00
NNO	Sasha Banks	250.00	500.00
NNO	Trish Stratus	250.00	500.00

2016 Topps WWE Medallions

*BRONZE/50: .5X TO 1.2X BASIC MEM
*SILVER/25: .6X TO 1.5X BASIC MEM
*GOLD/10: UNPRICED DUE TO SCARCITY
*RED/1: UNPRICED DUE TO SCARCITY
STATED PRINT RUN 299 SER.#'d SETS

NNO	Big E	2.00	5.00
NNO	Braun Strowman	2.50	6.00
NNO	Bray Wyatt	8.00	20.00
NNO	Brock Lesnar	10.00	25.00
NNO	Chris Jericho	5.00	12.00
NNO	Daniel Bryan	8.00	20.00
NNO	Dean Ambrose	6.00	15.00
NNO	Jamie Noble	2.00	5.00
NNO	Joey Mercury	2.00	5.00
NNO	John Cena	10.00	25.00
NNO	Kane	3.00	8.00
NNO	King Barrett	2.00	5.00
NNO	Kofi Kingston	2.00	5.00
NNO	Luke Harper	2.00	5.00
NNO	Randy Orton	5.00	12.00
NNO	The Rock	10.00	25.00
NNO	Roman Reigns	6.00	15.00
NNO	Seth Rollins	3.00	8.00
NNO	Sheamus	5.00	12.00
NNO	Stephanie McMahon	3.00	8.00
NNO	Sting	5.00	12.00
NNO	Triple H	8.00	20.00
NNO	Undertaker	8.00	20.00
NNO	Xavier Woods	2.00	5.00

2016 Topps WWE NXT Inserts

COMPLETE SET (28) 8.00 20.00
*P.P.BLACK/1: UNPRICED DUE TO SCARCITY
*P.P.CYAN/1: UNPRICED DUE TO SCARCITY
*P.P.MAGENTA/1: UNPRICED DUE TO SCARCITY
*P.P.YELLOW/1: UNPRICED DUE TO SCARCITY
STATED ODDS 1:1

1	Aiden English	.30	.75
2	Alexa Bliss	4.00	10.00
3	Angelo Dawkins	.30	.75
4	Apollo Crews	.30	.75
5	Asuka	4.00	10.00
6	Baron Corbin	.40	1.00
7	Bayley	.75	2.00
8	Billie Kay	.75	2.00
9	Blake	.30	.75
10	Carmella	.75	2.00
11	Chad Gable	.40	1.00
12	Colin Cassady	.60	1.50
13	Dana Brooke	.75	2.00
14	Dash Wilder	.40	1.00
15	Scott Dawson	.30	.75
16	Enzo Amore	.60	1.50
17	Finn Balor	2.00	5.00
18	Hideo Itami	.40	1.00
19	Jason Jordan	.40	1.00
20	Mojo Rawley	.30	.75
21	Murphy	.30	.75
22	Nia Jax	.50	1.25
23	Peyton Royce	.75	2.00
24	Sami Zayn	.50	1.25
25	Samoa Joe	.75	2.00
26	Sawyer Fulton	.40	1.00
27	Simon Gotch	.50	1.25
28	Tye Dillinger	.40	1.00

2016 Topps WWE NXT TakeOver Brooklyn Mat Relics

*BRONZE/50: .5X TO 1.2X BASIC MEM
*SILVER/25: .6X TO 1.5X BASIC MEM
*GOLD/10: UNPRICED DUE TO SCARCITY
*RED/1: UNPRICED DUE TO SCARCITY
*P.P.BLACK/1: UNPRICED DUE TO SCARCITY
*P.P.CYAN/1: UNPRICED DUE TO SCARCITY
*P.P.MAGENTA/1: UNPRICED DUE TO SCARCITY
*P.P.YELLOW/1: UNPRICED DUE TO SCARCITY
STATED PRINT RUN 199 SER.#'d SETS

NNO	Aiden English	2.50	6.00
NNO	Alexa Bliss	12.00	30.00
NNO	Apollo Crews	2.50	6.00
NNO	Baron Corbin	3.00	8.00
NNO	Bayley	6.00	15.00
NNO	Blake	2.50	6.00
NNO	Finn Balor	8.00	20.00
NNO	Kevin Owens	6.00	15.00
NNO	Murphy	2.50	6.00
NNO	Samoa Joe	6.00	15.00
NNO	Sasha Banks	8.00	20.00
NNO	Simon Gotch	4.00	10.00
NNO	Tye Dillinger	3.00	8.00
NNO	Tyler Breeze	2.50	6.00

2016 Topps WWE Shirt Relics

*BRONZE/50: .5X TO 1.2X BASIC MEM
*SILVER/25: .6X TO 1.5X BASIC MEM
*GOLD/10: UNPRICED DUE TO SCARCITY
*RED/1: UNPRICED DUE TO SCARCITY
*P.P.BLACK/1: UNPRICED DUE TO SCARCITY
*P.P.CYAN/1: UNPRICED DUE TO SCARCITY
*P.P.MAGENTA/1: UNPRICED DUE TO SCARCITY
*P.P.YELLOW/1: UNPRICED DUE TO SCARCITY
RANDOMLY INSERTED INTO PACKS

NNO	Aiden English	3.00	8.00
NNO	Alberto Del Rio	5.00	12.00
NNO	Alicia Fox	5.00	12.00
NNO	Apollo Crews	3.00	8.00
NNO	Bayley	8.00	20.00
NNO	Becky Lynch	10.00	25.00
NNO	Braun Strowman	4.00	10.00
NNO	Bray Wyatt	12.00	30.00
NNO	Brie Bella	6.00	15.00
NNO	Bubba Ray Dudley	6.00	15.00
NNO	Cesaro	6.00	15.00
NNO	Charlotte	10.00	25.00
NNO	Dean Ambrose	10.00	25.00
NNO	D-Von Dudley	5.00	12.00
NNO	Finn Balor	10.00	25.00
NNO	John Cena	15.00	40.00
NNO	Kevin Owens	8.00	20.00
NNO	Luke Harper	3.00	8.00
NNO	Naomi	5.00	12.00
NNO	Natalya	5.00	12.00
NNO	Neville	8.00	20.00
NNO	Paige	10.00	25.00
NNO	Roman Reigns	10.00	25.00
NNO	Samoa Joe	8.00	20.00
NNO	Sasha Banks	10.00	25.00
NNO	Seth Rollins	5.00	12.00
NNO	Simon Gotch	5.00	12.00
NNO	Tamina	4.00	10.00
NNO	Tyler Breeze	3.00	8.00
NNO	Zack Ryder	3.00	8.00

2016 Topps WWE SummerSlam Mat Relics

*BRONZE/50: .5X TO 1.2X BASIC MEM
*SILVER/25: .6X TO 1.5X BASIC MEM
*GOLD/10: UNPRICED DUE TO SCARCITY
*RED/1: UNPRICED DUE TO SCARCITY
*P.P.BLACK/1: UNPRICED DUE TO SCARCITY
*P.P.CYAN/1: UNPRICED DUE TO SCARCITY
*P.P.MAGENTA/1: UNPRICED DUE TO SCARCITY
*P.P.YELLOW/1: UNPRICED DUE TO SCARCITY
STATED PRINT RUN 199 SER.#'d SETS

NNO	Big Show	4.00	10.00
NNO	Bray Wyatt	8.00	20.00
NNO	Brock Lesnar	10.00	25.00
NNO	Cesaro	4.00	10.00
NNO	Dean Ambrose	6.00	15.00
NNO	Dolph Ziggler	2.50	6.00
NNO	John Cena	10.00	25.00
NNO	Kevin Owens	5.00	12.00
NNO	King Barrett	2.00	5.00
NNO	Luke Harper	2.00	5.00
NNO	The Miz	3.00	8.00
NNO	Neville	5.00	12.00
NNO	Randy Orton	5.00	12.00
NNO	Roman Reigns	6.00	15.00
NNO	Rusev	5.00	12.00
NNO	Ryback	2.50	6.00
NNO	Seth Rollins	3.00	8.00
NNO	Sheamus	5.00	12.00
NNO	Stardust	2.00	5.00
NNO	Undertaker	8.00	20.00

2016 Topps WWE Superstars of Canada Autographs

STATED PRINT RUN 25 SER.#'d SETS

NNO	Chris Jericho	15.00	40.00
NNO	Christian	12.00	30.00
NNO	Edge	25.00	60.00
NNO	Kevin Owens	12.00	30.00
NNO	Natalya	12.00	30.00
NNO	Renee Young	15.00	40.00
NNO	Sami Zayn	10.00	25.00
NNO	Trish Stratus	50.00	100.00
NNO	Tyson Kidd	6.00	15.00
NNO	Viktor	6.00	15.00

2016 Topps WWE Triple Autographs

STATED PRINT RUN 11 SER.#'d SETS

NNO	Del Rio/Graham/Rikishi	50.00	100.00
NNO	Bayley/Asuka/Nia Jax	75.00	150.00
NNO	Wyatt/Harper/Strowman	100.00	200.00
NNO	Charlotte/Lynch/Natalya	100.00	200.00
NNO	Balor/Samoa Joe/Crews	100.00	200.00
NNO	Cena/Dudley Boyz	75.00	150.00
NNO	Rollins/Ambrose/Reigns	125.00	250.00
NNO	Sting/Flair/Dillon	150.00	300.00

2017 Topps WWE

COMPLETE SET W/O SP (100) 8.00 20.00
COMPLETE SET W/SP (120)
UNOPENED BOX (24 PACKS)
UNOPENED PACK (7 CARDS)
*BRONZE: .5X TO 1.2X BASIC CARDS
*BLUE/99: 1X TO 2.5X BASIC CARDS
*SILVER/25: 2X TO 5X BASIC CARDS
*GOLD/10: 4X TO 10X BASIC CARDS
*RED/1: UNPRICED DUE TO SCARCITY
*P.P.BLACK/1: UNPRICED DUE TO SCARCITY
*P.P.CYAN/1: UNPRICED DUE TO SCARCITY
*P.P.MAGENTA/1: UNPRICED DUE TO SCARCITY
*P.P.YELLOW/1: UNPRICED DUE TO SCARCITY

1A	The Rock	1.25	3.00
1B	The Rock SP Just Bring It	10.00	25.00
2	Tyson Kidd	.25	.60
3	Booker T	.30	.75
4	Byron Saxton	.25	.60
5A	Bayley	.75	2.00
5B	Bayley SP Leaping	5.00	12.00
6	Big Cass	.30	.75
7A	Big E	.30	.75
7B	Big E SP Big Splash	3.00	8.00
8	Bob Backlund	.25	.60
9A	Brian Kendrick	.25	.60
9B	Brian Kendrick SP Jacket	3.00	8.00
10A	Brock Lesnar	1.25	3.00
10B	Brock Lesnar SP Outside Ring	8.00	20.00
11	Chad Patton	.25	.60
12	Charly Caruso	.25	.60
13A	Chris Jericho	.60	1.50
13B	Chris Jericho SP Walls of Jericho	6.00	15.00
14	Corey Graves	.25	.60
15	Darrick Moore	.25	.60
16	Enzo Amore	.75	2.00
17A	Finn Balor	1.00	2.50
17B	Finn Balor SP Entrance/No Logo	10.00	25.00
18A	Goldberg	1.00	2.50
18B	Goldberg SP Jacket	12.00	30.00
19	JoJo	.40	1.00
20	John Cone	.25	.60
21	Karl Anderson	.25	.60
22A	Kofi Kingston	.30	.75
22B	Kofi Kingston SP Leaping	6.00	15.00
23	Luke Gallows	.40	1.00
24	Michael Cole	.25	.60
25	Mick Foley	.60	1.50
26A	Nia Jax	.40	1.00
26B	Nia Jax SP Pink Gear	5.00	12.00
27	Paige	.60	1.50
28	Paul Heyman	.25	.60
29	Rod Zapata	.25	.60
30	Shawn Bennett	.25	.60
31	TJ Perkins	.25	.60
32	Titus O'Neil	.25	.60
33A	Triple H	.60	1.50
33B	Triple H SP No Mic	10.00	25.00
34A	Xavier Woods	.30	.75
34B	Xavier Woods	2.50	6.00
35A	AJ Styles	1.25	3.00
35B	AJ Styles	12.00	30.00
36A	Alexa Bliss	1.25	3.00
36B	Alexa Bliss SP Flip	15.00	40.00
37	Andrea D'Marco	.25	.60

#	Card		
38A	Carmella	.60	1.50
38B	Carmella SP Microphone	6.00	15.00
39	Chad Gable	.30	.75
40	Charles Robinson	.25	.60
41	Dan Engler	.25	.60
42	David Otunga	.25	.60
43	Greg Hamilton	.25	.60
44	Jason Ayers	.25	.60
45	Jason Jordan	.30	.75
46	JBL	.30	.75
47A	John Cena	1.25	3.00
47B	John Cena SP		
48A	Kane	.30	.75
48B	Kane SP Facing Forward	8.00	20.00
49	Luke Harper	.25	.60
50	Maryse	.50	1.25
51	Mauro Ranallo	.25	.60
52	Mike Chioda	.25	.60
53A	The Miz	.50	1.25
53B	Miz SP In the Ring	8.00	20.00
54	Mojo Rawley	.30	.75
55A	Randy Orton	.60	1.50
55B	Randy Orton SP RKO	6.00	15.00
56	Renee Young	.40	1.00
57	Ryan Tran	.25	.60
58A	Undertaker	1.00	2.50
58B	Undertaker SP Silhouette	20.00	50.00
59	Zack Ryder	.25	.60
60	Alexander Wolfe	.30	.75
61	Aliyah	.30	.75
62A	Asuka	.75	2.00
62B	Asuka SP/(mask)	8.00	20.00
63A	Austin Aries	.50	1.25
63B	Austin Aries SP Cape	6.00	15.00
64	Billie Kay	.30	.75
65A	Bobby Roode	.60	1.50
65B	Bobby Roode SP	8.00	20.00
66	Cathy Kelley	.25	.60
67	Dash Wilder	.25	.60
68	Dasha Fuentes	.30	.75
69	Danilo Anfibio	.25	.60
70	Drake Wuertz	.25	.60
71	Eddie Orengo	.25	.60
72	Ember Moon	.60	1.50
73	Eric Young	.50	1.25
74	Hideo Itami	.40	1.00
75	Johnny Gargano	.25	.60
76	Liv Morgan	.40	1.00
77	Nick Miller	.25	.60
78	Nikki Cross	.50	1.25
79	Oney Lorcan	.25	.60
80	Paul Ellering	.25	.60
81	Peyton Royce	.40	1.00
82	Roderick Strong	.30	.75
83A	Samoa Joe	.75	2.00
83B	Samoa Joe SP		
84	Scott Dawson	.25	.60
85	Shane Thorne	.25	.60
86A	Shinsuke Nakamura	.60	1.50
86B	Shinsuke Nakamura SP Jacket	6.00	15.00
87	Tommaso Ciampa	.25	.60
88	Tye Dillinger	.25	.60
89	William Regal	.30	.75
90	Norman Smiley	.30	.75
91	Ric Flair	.60	1.50
92	Terri Runnels	.25	.60
93	Beth Phoenix	.25	.60
94	Eric Bischoff	.25	.60

#	Card		
95	Ivory	.25	.60
96	Judy Martin	.25	.60
97	Kelly Kelly	.50	1.25
98	Leilani Kai	.25	.60
99	Princess Victoria	.25	.60
100	Torrie Wilson	.60	1.50

2017 Topps WWE Autographed Shirt Relics

STATED ODDS 1:3,524

NNO	Bayley	30.00	75.00
NNO	Big E	15.00	40.00
NNO	Bray Wyatt	30.00	75.00
NNO	Carmella	25.00	60.00
NNO	Cesaro	15.00	40.00
NNO	Dolph Ziggler	15.00	40.00
NNO	John Cena	50.00	100.00
NNO	Karl Anderson	15.00	40.00
NNO	Kevin Owens	15.00	40.00
NNO	Kofi Kingston	15.00	40.00
NNO	The Miz	30.00	75.00
NNO	Randy Orton	30.00	80.00
NNO	Roman Reigns		
NNO	Seth Rollins	25.00	60.00
NNO	Shinsuke Nakamura		
NNO	Xavier Woods		

2017 Topps WWE Autographs

*BLUE/50: .6X TO 1.5X BASIC AUTOS
*SILVER/25: .75X TO 2X BASIC AUTOS
*GOLD/10: UNPRICED DUE TO SCARCITY
*RED/1: UNPRICED DUE TO SCARCITY
STATED ODDS 1:50

5	Bayley	15.00	40.00
6	Big Cass	8.00	20.00
7	Big E	6.00	15.00
10	Brock Lesnar	50.00	100.00
13	Chris Jericho	12.00	30.00
16	Enzo Amore	10.00	25.00
18	Goldberg	50.00	100.00
21	Karl Anderson	6.00	15.00
22	Kofi Kingston	6.00	15.00
23	Luke Gallows	5.00	12.00
34	Xavier Woods	6.00	15.00
38	Carmella	10.00	25.00
53	The Miz	5.00	12.00
62	Asuka	15.00	40.00
64	Billie Kay	8.00	20.00
81	Peyton Royce	10.00	25.00
83	Samoa Joe	6.00	15.00
91	Ric Flair	15.00	40.00
92	Terri Runnels	10.00	25.00
93	Beth Phoenix	6.00	15.00
94	Eric Bischoff	8.00	20.00
96	Judy Martin	6.00	15.00
97	Kelly Kelly	15.00	40.00
98	Leilani Kai	6.00	15.00
100	Torrie Wilson	10.00	25.00

2017 Topps WWE Autographs Blue

STATED ODDS 1:99
STATED PRINT RUN 50 SER.#'d SETS

58	Undertaker	150.00	300.00

2017 Topps WWE Autographs Silver

STATED ODDS 1:116
STATED PRINT RUN 25 SER.#'d SETS

25	Mick Foley	15.00	40.00

2017 Topps WWE Breaking Ground

COMPLETE SET (10) 5.00 12.00
STATED ODDS 1:2

1	Baron Corbin	1.00	2.50
2	Dana Brooke	1.25	3.00
3	Tyler Breeze	.60	1.50
4	Jason Jordan	.75	2.00
5	Tyler Breeze	.60	1.50
6	The Superstars	1.00	2.50
7	Bayley	2.00	5.00
8	Scott Hall	.75	2.00
9	Sami Zayn	.75	2.00
10	Tyler Breeze	.60	1.50

2017 Topps WWE Championship Relics

*BLUE/50: .5X TO 1.2X BASIC MEM
*SILVER/25: .6X TO 1.5X BASIC MEM
*GOLD/10: 1X TO 2.5X BASIC MEM
*RED/1: UNPRICED DUE TO SCARCITY
STATED ODDS 1:277

NNO	AJ Styles	10.00	25.00
NNO	Becky Lynch	6.00	15.00
NNO	Charlotte Flair	8.00	20.00
NNO	Dean Ambrose	6.00	15.00
NNO	Dean Ambrose	6.00	15.00
NNO	Dolph Ziggler	3.00	8.00
NNO	Finn Balor	8.00	20.00
NNO	Kalisto	3.00	8.00
NNO	Kevin Owens/NXT Title	5.00	12.00
NNO	Kevin Owens/Universal Title	5.00	12.00
NNO	The Miz	4.00	10.00
NNO	The New Day	4.00	10.00
NNO	Rhyno & Heath Slater	2.00	5.00
NNO	Roman Reigns/US Title	6.00	15.00
NNO	Roman Reigns/WWE Title	6.00	15.00
NNO	Rusev	4.00	10.00
NNO	Sasha Banks	6.00	15.00
NNO	Seth Rollins	6.00	15.00
NNO	Triple H	5.00	12.00
NNO	Zack Ryder	2.00	5.00

2017 Topps WWE Kiss

*GOLD/10: .6X TO 1.5X BASIC KISS
*RED/1: UNPRICED DUE TO SCARCITY
STATED ODDS 1:125

NNO	Asuka	25.00	60.00
NNO	Becky Lynch	15.00	40.00
NNO	Charlotte Flair	25.00	60.00
NNO	Maryse	20.00	50.00
NNO	Naomi	15.00	40.00
NNO	Summer Rae	12.00	30.00

2017 Topps WWE NXT Autographed TakeOver Brooklyn II Mat Relics

STATED PRINT RUN 10 SER.#'d SETS

NNO	Asuka
NNO	Austin Aries
NNO	Bayley
NNO	Samoa Joe
NNO	Shinsuke Nakamura

2017 Topps WWE NXT TakeOver Brooklyn II Mat Relics

*BRONZE/199: SAME VALUE AS BASIC MEM
*BLUE/50: .5X TO 1.2X BASIC MEM
*SILVER/25: .6X TO 1.5X BASIC MEM
*GOLD/10: 1X TO 2.5X BASIC MEM
*RED/1: UNPRICED DUE TO SCARCITY
STATED ODDS 1:369

NNO	Andrade Cien Almas	2.00	5.00
NNO	Asuka	6.00	15.00
NNO	Austin Aries	4.00	10.00
NNO	Bayley	6.00	15.00
NNO	Bobby Roode	5.00	12.00
NNO	Johnny Gargano	2.00	5.00
NNO	No Way Jose	2.00	5.00
NNO	Samoa Joe	6.00	15.00
NNO	Shinsuke Nakamura	5.00	12.00
NNO	Tommaso Ciampa	2.00	5.00

2017 Topps WWE Roster Updates

COMPLETE SET (20) 8.00 20.00
RANDOMLY INSERTED INTO PACKS

R1	Tamina	1.25	3.00
R2	Cedric Alexander	1.50	4.00
R3	Gran Metalik	2.00	5.00
R4	Jack Gallagher	2.00	5.00
R5	Lince Dorado	1.25	3.00
R6	Noam Dar	1.00	2.50
R7	Rich Swann	1.00	2.50
R8	Stephanie McMahon	1.25	3.00
R9	Shane McMahon	1.50	4.00
R10	Tom Phillips	1.00	2.50
R11	Andrade Cien Almas	1.00	2.50
R12	Mandy Rose	1.25	3.00
R13	Mike Rome	1.00	2.50
R14	No Way Jose	1.00	2.50
R15	Otis Dozovic	1.25	3.00
R16	Riddick Moss	1.25	3.00
R17	Tian Bing	1.00	2.50
R18	Tino Sabbatelli	1.25	3.00
R19	Tye Dillinger	1.00	2.50
R20	Tucker Knight	2.50	6.00

2017 Topps WWE Shirt Relics

*BLUE/50: .5X TO 1.2X BASIC MEM
*SILVER/25: .6X TO 1.5X BASIC MEM
*GOLD/10: 1X TO 2.5X BASIC MEM
*RED/1: UNPRICED DUE TO SCARCITY
STATED ODDS 1:185
STATED PRINT RUN 199 SER.#'d SETS

NNO	Andrade Cien Almas	2.00	5.00
NNO	Baron Corbin	3.00	8.00
NNO	Bayley	6.00	15.00
NNO	Big E	2.50	6.00
NNO	Bobby Roode	5.00	12.00
NNO	Bray Wyatt	5.00	12.00
NNO	Carmella	5.00	12.00
NNO	Cesaro	4.00	10.00
NNO	Chad Gable	2.50	6.00
NNO	Dolph Ziggler	3.00	8.00
NNO	Heath Slater	2.00	5.00
NNO	Jason Jordan	2.50	6.00
NNO	John Cena	10.00	25.00
NNO	Johnny Gargano	2.00	5.00
NNO	Karl Anderson	2.00	5.00
NNO	Kevin Owens	5.00	12.00
NNO	Kofi Kingston	2.50	6.00
NNO	The Miz	4.00	10.00
NNO	No Way Jose	2.00	5.00
NNO	Randy Orton	5.00	12.00
NNO	Roman Reigns	6.00	15.00
NNO	Seth Rollins	6.00	15.00

NNO Shinsuke Nakamura	5.00	12.00
NNO Tommaso Ciampa	2.00	5.00
NNO Xavier Woods	2.50	6.00

2017 Topps WWE Stone Cold Podcast

COMPLETE SET (8)	8.00	20.00
STATED ODDS 1:4		
1 Triple H	2.00	5.00
2 Paul Heyman	.75	2.00
3 Edge & Christian	2.00	5.00
4 Brock Lesnar	4.00	10.00
5 Big Show	1.00	2.50
6 Mick Foley	2.00	5.00
7 AJ Styles	4.00	10.00
8 Dean Ambrose	2.50	6.00

2017 Topps WWE Autographed SummerSlam 2016 Mat Relics

STATED PRINT RUN 10 SER.#'d SETS
UNPRICED DUE TO SCARCITY

NNO AJ Styles
NNO Big Cass
NNO Brock Lesnar
NNO Charlotte Flair
NNO Chris Jericho
NNO Dean Ambrose
NNO Dolph Ziggler
NNO Enzo Amore
NNO Finn Balor
NNO John Cena
NNO Karl Anderson
NNO Kevin Owens
NNO Kofi Kingston
NNO Luke Gallows
NNO Randy Orton
NNO Roman Reigns
NNO Rusev
NNO Sasha Banks
NNO Seth Rollins
NNO Xavier Woods

2017 Topps WWE SummerSlam 2016 Mat Relics

*BRONZE/199: SAME VALUE AS BASIC MEM
*BLUE/50: .5X TO 1.2X BASIC MEM
*SILVER/25: .6X TO 1.5X BASIC MEM
*GOLD/10: 1X TO 2.5X BASIC MEM
*RED/1: UNPRICED DUE TO SCARCITY
STATED ODDS 1:184
STATED PRINT RUN 299 SER.#'d SETS

NNO AJ Styles	10.00	25.00
NNO Big Cass	2.50	6.00
NNO Brock Lesnar	10.00	25.00
NNO Charlotte Flair	8.00	20.00
NNO Chris Jericho	5.00	12.00
NNO Dean Ambrose	6.00	15.00
NNO Dolph Ziggler	3.00	8.00
NNO Enzo Amore	6.00	15.00
NNO Finn Balor	8.00	20.00
NNO John Cena	10.00	25.00
NNO Karl Anderson	2.00	5.00
NNO Kevin Owens	5.00	12.00
NNO Kofi Kingston	2.50	6.00
NNO Luke Gallows	3.00	8.00
NNO Randy Orton	5.00	12.00
NNO Roman Reigns	6.00	15.00
NNO Rusev	4.00	10.00
NNO Sasha Banks	6.00	15.00
NNO Seth Rollins	6.00	15.00
NNO Xavier Woods	2.50	6.00

2017 Topps WWE Total Divas

COMPLETE SET (20)	12.00	30.00
STATED ODDS 1:2		
1 Nikki Bella	1.25	3.00
2 Brie Bella	1.25	3.00
3 Natalya	1.00	2.50
4 The Bellas	1.25	3.00
5 Mandy Rose	.60	1.50
6 Natalya	1.00	2.50
7 Nikki Bella	1.25	3.00
8 Nikki Bella	1.25	3.00
9 Alicia Fox	.75	2.00
10 Natalya	1.00	2.50
11 Brie Bella	1.25	3.00
12 Brie Bella	1.25	3.00
13 John Cena	2.50	6.00
14 Daniel Bryan	2.00	5.00
15 Natalya	1.00	2.50
16 The Bella Twins	1.25	3.00
17 Nikki Bella	1.25	3.00
18 Mandy Rose	.60	1.50
19 Alicia Fox	.75	2.00
20 Nikki Bella	1.25	3.00

2017 Topps WWE Triple Autographs

STATED ODDS 1:1,762		
NNO Bayley/Jax/Morgan		
NNO Big E/Kingston/Woods	60.00	120.00
NNO Kay/Royce/Aliyah		
NNO Lesnar/Goldberg/Bischoff	250.00	400.00
NNO C.Kelly/Fuentes/Young	75.00	150.00
NNO Martin/Kai/Victoria		
NNO K.Kelly/Wilson/Phoenix	75.00	150.00

2017 Topps WWE Undertaker Tribute

COMPLETE SET (40)	15.00	40.00
1 Undertaker	2.00	5.00
2 Undertaker	2.00	5.00
3 Undertaker	2.00	3.00
4 Undertaker	2.00	5.00
5 Undertaker	2.00	5.00
6 Undertaker	2.00	5.00
7 Undertaker	2.00	5.00
8 Undertaker	2.00	5.00
9 Undertaker	2.00	5.00
10 Undertaker	2.00	5.00
11 Undertaker	2.00	5.00
12 Undertaker	2.00	5.00
13 Undertaker	2.00	5.00
14 Undertaker	2.00	5.00
15 Undertaker	2.00	5.00
16 Undertaker	2.00	5.00
17 Undertaker	2.00	5.00
18 Undertaker	2.00	5.00
19 Undertaker	2.00	5.00
20 Undertaker	2.00	5.00
21 Undertaker	2.00	5.00
22 Undertaker	2.00	5.00
23 Undertaker	2.00	5.00
24 Undertaker	2.00	5.00
25 Undertaker	2.00	5.00
26 Undertaker	2.00	5.00
27 Undertaker	2.00	5.00
28 Undertaker	2.00	5.00
29 Undertaker	2.00	5.00
30 Undertaker	2.00	5.00
31 Undertaker	2.00	5.00
32 Undertaker	2.00	5.00
33 Undertaker	2.00	5.00
34 Undertaker	2.00	5.00
35 Undertaker	2.00	5.00
36 Undertaker	2.00	5.00
37 Undertaker	2.00	5.00
38 Undertaker	2.00	5.00
39 Undertaker	2.00	5.00
40 Undertaker	2.00	5.00

2018 Topps WWE

COMPLETE SET W/O SP (100)	8.00	20.00
UNOPENED BOX (24 PACKS)		
UNOPENED PACK (7 CARDS)		
*BRONZE: .5X TO 1.2X BASIC CARDS		
*BLUE/99: .75X TO 2X BASIC CARDS		
*SILVER/25: 2X TO 5X BASIC CARDS		
*GOLD/10: UNPRICED DUE TO SCARCITY		
*RED/1: UNPRICED DUE TO SCARCITY		
*P.P.BLACK/1: UNPRICED DUE TO SCARCITY		
*P.P.CYAN/1: UNPRICED DUE TO SCARCITY		
*P.P.MAGENTA/1: UNPRICED DUE TO SCARCITY		
*P.P.YELLOW/1: UNPRICED DUE TO SCARCITY		
1A Adam Cole	.30	.75
1B Adam Cole SP Shirtless	12.00	30.00
2A AJ Styles	1.00	2.50
2B AJ Styles SP Shirtless	20.00	50.00
3 Akam	.25	.60
4 Akira Tozawa	.40	1.00
5A Aleister Black	.30	.75
5B Aleister Black SP Mid-Air	6.00	15.00
6 Alicia Fox	.40	1.00
7 Andrade Cien Almas	.40	1.00
8 Apollo Crews	.25	.60
9 Ariya Daivari	.25	.60
10 Asuka	.75	2.00
11A Big E	.30	.75
11B Big E SP Microphone	2.50	6.00
12 Billie Kay	.50	1.25
13 Bo Dallas	.25	.60
14A Bobby Roode	.40	1.00
14B Bobby Roode SP In Action	10.00	25.00
15 Bobby Fish	.25	.60
16 Booker T	.40	1.00
17 The Brian Kendrick	.40	1.00
18 Brie Bella	.50	1.25
19 Byron Saxton	.25	.60
20A Carmella	.50	1.25
20B Carmella SP In Ring	12.00	30.00
21 Cathy Kelley	.50	1.25
22 Cedric Alexander	.25	.60
23 Chad Gable	.25	.60
24A Charlotte Flair	.75	2.00
24B Charlotte Flair SP Close-Up	12.00	30.00
25 Christy St. Cloud	.30	.75
26 Curt Hawkins	.25	.60
27 Curtis Axel	.25	.60
28 Daniel Bryan	.60	1.50
29 Drew Gulak	.25	.60
30A Drew McIntyre	.40	1.00
30B Drew McIntyre SP Close-Up	2.50	6.00
31 Elias	.60	1.50
32A Ember Moon	.50	1.25
32B Ember Moon SP In Between Ropes	6.00	15.00
33 Gentleman Jack Gallagher	.30	.75
34 Gran Metalik	.25	.60
35 Greg Hamilton	.40	1.00
36 Heath Slater	.25	.60
37 Hideo Itami	.25	.60
38 Jerry The King Lawler	.50	1.25
39 Jey Uso	.25	.60
40 Jim Ross	.40	1.00
41 Jimmy Uso	.25	.60
42A Jinder Mahal	.30	.75
42B Jinder Mahal SP Shirtless		
43 John Cena	1.00	2.50
44 Johnny Gargano	.25	.60
45A Kairi Sane	.60	1.50
45B Kairi Sane SP Mid-Air		
46 Kayla Braxton	.25	.60
47A Kevin Owens	.60	1.50
47B Kevin Owens SP Red Background	8.00	20.00
48A Kofi Kingston	.30	.75
48B Kofi Kingston SP Cross Body	2.50	6.00
49 Kurt Angle	.60	1.50
50A Kyle O'Reilly	.30	.75
50B Kyle O'Reilly SP Straightfaced	2.50	6.00
51 Lana	.60	1.50
52 Lita	.60	1.50
53 Maria Kanellis	.60	1.50
54 Maryse	.50	1.25
55 Mauro Ranallo	.25	.60
56 Mean Gene Okerlund	.30	.75
57 Michael Cole	.25	.60
58 Mickie James	.50	1.25
59 Mike Kanellis	.60	1.50
60 Mike Rome	.25	.60
61 The Miz	.50	1.25
62 Montez Ford	.25	.60
63 Mr. McMahon	.50	1.25
64 Mustafa Ali	.25	.60
65 Naomi	.30	.75
66A Natalya	.30	.75
66B Natalya SP Pointing Up	12.00	30.00
67 Neville	.40	1.00
68 Nia Jax	.40	1.00
69 Nigel McGuinness	.25	.60
70 Noam Dar	.25	.60
71 Paige	.60	1.50
72 Paul Ellering	.30	.75
73 Percy Watson	.25	.60
74 Pete Dunne	.25	.60
75 Peyton Royce	.60	1.50
76 Rezar	.25	.60
77 Rhyno	.25	.60
78 Big Cass	.30	.75
79 The Rock	1.25	3.00
80 Roderick Strong	.25	.60
81 Samir Singh	.25	.60
82 Shane McMahon	.50	1.25
83 Shelton Benjamin	.30	.75
84 Sin Cara	.30	.75
85 Sonya Deville	.50	1.25
86 Stephanie McMahon	.50	1.25
87 Sunil Singh	.25	.60
88 Tamina	.25	.60
89 Titus O'Neil	.25	.60
90 TJP	.30	.75
91 Tommaso Ciampa	.25	.60
92 Tony Nese	.25	.60
93 Tony Chimel	.25	.60
94 Triple H	.60	1.50

95	Tyler Bate	.25	.60
96A	Undertaker	1.00	2.50
96B	Undertaker SP Kneeling	10.00	25.00
97	William Regal	.40	1.00
98A	Xavier Woods	.30	.75
98B	Xavier Woods SP Cross Body	5.00	12.00
99	Zack Ryder	.25	.60
100	Zelina Vega	.25	.60

2018 Topps WWE Autographed Commemorative Championship Medallions

STATED PRINT RUN 10 SER.#'d SETS
UNPRICED DUE TO SCARCITY

CCAJ AJ Styles
CCAT Akira Tozawa
CCBW Bray Wyatt
CCCJ Chris Jericho
CCJM Jinder Mahal
CCKO Kevin Owens
CCNA Natalya
CCNO Naomi
CCRO Randy Orton
CCTM The Miz

2018 Topps WWE Autographed Dual Mat Relics

STATED PRINT RUN 10 SER.#'d SETS
UNPRICED DUE TO SCARCITY

DMRDB Daniel Bryan
DMRSM Stephanie McMahon
DMRTH Triple H
DMRUT Undertaker
DNRDA Dean Ambrose

2018 Topps WWE Autographed NXT TakeOver Brooklyn III Mat Relics

STATED PRINT RUN 10 SER.#'d SETS
UNPRICED DUE TO SCARCITY

TBRAB Aleister Black
TBRAC Adam Cole
TBRAS Asuka
TBRBR Bobby Roode
TBRDM Drew McIntyre
TBREM Ember Moon
TBREY Eric Young
TBRHI Hideo Itami
TBRJG Johnny Gargano

2018 Topps WWE Autographed Shirt Relics

STATED PRINT RUN 10 SER.#'d SETS
UNPRICED DUE TO SCARCITY

SRAE Aiden English
SRAF Alicia Fox
SREY Eric Young
SRGD Goldust
SRJJ Jojo
SRNA Natalya
SRRY Renee Young
SRSJ Samoa Joe

2018 Topps WWE Autographed SummerSlam 2017 Mat Relics

STATED PRINT RUN 10 SER.#'d SETS
UNPRICED DUE TO SCARCITY

SMRAJ AJ Styles
SMRBC Baron Corbin
SMRBS Braun Strowman
SMRBW Bray Wyatt
SMRCO Cesaro
SMRDA Dean Ambrose
SMRJM Jinder Mahal
SMRKO Kevin Owens
SMRNA Natalya
SMRNO Naomi
SMRSB Sasha Banks
SMRSH Sheamus
SMRSJ Samoa Joe
SMRSN Shinsuke Nakamura

2018 Topps WWE Autographs

*BLUE/50: .5X TO 1.2X BASIC AUTOS
*SILVER/25: .6X TO 1.5X BASIC AUTOS
*GOLD/10: UNPRICED DUE TO SCARCITY
*RED/1: UNPRICED DUE TO SCARCITY

1	Adam Cole	20.00	50.00
2	AJ Styles	15.00	40.00
4	Akira Tozawa	5.00	12.00
5	Aleister Black	10.00	25.00
8	Apollo Crews	4.00	10.00
10	Asuka	15.00	40.00
11	Big E	8.00	20.00
14	Bobby Roode	6.00	15.00
15	Bobby Fish	12.00	30.00
18	Brie Bella	10.00	25.00
20	Carmella	12.00	30.00
24	Charlotte Flair	15.00	40.00
30	Drew McIntyre	8.00	20.00
32	Ember Moon	10.00	25.00
42	Jinder Mahal	5.00	12.00
45	Kairi Sane	30.00	75.00
47	Kevin Owens	6.00	15.00
48	Kofi Kingston	6.00	15.00
49	Kurt Angle	12.00	30.00
50	Kyle O'Reilly	12.00	30.00
61	The Miz	5.00	12.00
65	Naomi	4.00	10.00
66	Natalya	6.00	15.00
68	Nia Jax	10.00	25.00
80	Roderick Strong	5.00	12.00
83	Shelton Benjamin	5.00	12.00
88	Tamina	4.00	10.00
89	Titus O'Neil	5.00	12.00
98	Xavier Woods	6.00	15.00

2018 Topps WWE Commemorative Championship Medallions

*BRONZE/99: .5X TO 1.2X BASIC MEM
*BLUE/50: .6X TO 1.5X BASIC MEM
*SILVER/25: .75X TO 2X BASIC MEM
*GOLD/10: UNPRICED DUE TO SCARCITY
*RED/1: UNPRICED DUE TO SCARCITY

CCAA	American Alpha	3.00	8.00
CCAB	Alexa Bliss	10.00	25.00
CCAJ	AJ Styles	6.00	15.00
CCAS	Dean Ambrose & Seth Rollins	8.00	20.00
CCAT	Akira Tozawa	3.00	8.00
CCAX	Alexa Bliss	8.00	20.00
CCBA	Bayley	8.00	20.00
CCBL	Brock Lesnar	10.00	25.00
CCBW	Bray Wyatt	3.00	8.00
CCCJ	Chris Jericho	4.00	10.00
CCCS	Cesaro & Sheamus	2.50	6.00
CCGA	Luke Gallows & Karl Anderson	2.50	6.00
CCHB	The Hardy Boyz	6.00	15.00
CCJC	John Cena	5.00	12.00
CCJM	Jinder Mahal	2.50	6.00
CCKA	Kalisto	2.50	6.00
CCKO	Kevin Owens	4.00	10.00
CCNA	Natalya	2.50	6.00
CCND	The New Day	2.50	6.00
CCNO	Naomi	2.50	6.00
CCRO	Randy Orton	4.00	10.00
CCTM	The Miz	2.50	6.00
CCTU	The Usos	3.00	8.00
CCWF	The Wyatt Family	5.00	12.00

2018 Topps WWE Dual Mat Relics

*SILVER/25: .6X TO 1.5X BASIC MEM
*GOLD/10: UNPRICED DUE TO SCARCITY
*RED/1: UNPRICED DUE TO SCARCITY

DMRBL	Brock Lesnar	10.00	25.00
DMRBY	Bayley	10.00	25.00
DMRDA	Dean Ambrose	6.00	15.00
DMRDB	Daniel Bryan	8.00	20.00
DMRRR	Roman Reigns	6.00	15.00
DMRSM	Stephanie McMahon	15.00	40.00
DMRSR	Seth Rollins	5.00	12.00
DMRTH	Triple H	6.00	15.00
DMRTR	The Rock	8.00	20.00
DMRUT	Undertaker	12.00	30.00

2018 Topps WWE Evolution

COMPLETE SET (50)		15.00	40.00
E1	The Giant	.40	1.00
E2	Big Show	.40	1.00
E3	Big Show	.40	1.00
E4	Booker T	.60	1.50
E5	G.I. Bro	.60	1.50
E6	King Booker	.60	1.50
E7	Booker T	.60	1.50
E8	Brock Lesnar	1.50	4.00
E9	Brock Lesnar	1.50	4.00
E10	Chris Jericho	1.00	2.50
E11	Chris Jericho	1.00	2.50
E12	Daniel Bryan	1.00	2.50
E13	Daniel Bryan	1.00	2.50
E14	Daniel Bryan	1.00	2.50
E15	The Rock	2.00	5.00
E16	The Rock	2.00	5.00
E17	Goldust	.75	2.00
E18	Seven	.75	2.00
E19	American Nightmare Dustin Rhodes	.75	2.00
E20	Goldust	.75	2.00
E21	Jerry The King Lawler	.75	2.00
E22	Jerry The King Lawler	.75	2.00
E23	John Cena	1.50	4.00
E24	Doctor of Thuganomics John Cena	1.50	4.00
E25	John Cena	1.50	4.00
E26	Kane	.60	1.50
E27	Kane	.60	1.50
E28	Corporate Kane	.60	1.50
E29	Kane	.60	1.50
E30	Kurt Angle	1.00	2.50
E31	Kurt Angle	1.00	2.50
E32	Mark Henry	.50	1.25
E33	Mark Henry	.50	1.25
E34	Mark Henry	.50	1.25
E35	Cactus Jack	.75	2.00
E36	Mankind	.75	2.00
E37	Dude Love	.75	2.00
E38	Mick Foley	.75	2.00
E39	Randy Orton	1.00	2.50
E40	Randy Orton	1.00	2.50
E41	Hunter Hearst Helmsley	1.00	2.50
E42	Triple H	1.00	2.50
E43	The Game Triple H	1.00	2.50
E44	COO Triple H	1.00	2.50
E45	Undertaker	1.50	4.00
E46	Undertaker	1.50	4.00
E47	Undertaker	1.50	4.00
E48	The American Bad-Ass Undertaker	1.50	4.00
E49	Big Evil Undertaker	1.50	4.00
E50	Undertaker	1.50	4.00

2018 Topps WWE Kiss

*GOLD/10: UNPRICED DUE TO SCARCITY
*RED/1: UNPRICED DUE TO SCARCITY

KBX	Billie Kay	20.00	50.00
KDB	Dana Brooke	15.00	40.00
KEM	Ember Moon	20.00	50.00
KKS	Kairi Saine	30.00	75.00
KLM	Liv Morgan	25.00	60.00
KMA	Maryse	15.00	40.00
KNA	Natalya	15.00	40.00
KPR	Peyton Royce	25.00	60.00
KSD	Sonya Deville	50.00	100.00

2018 Topps WWE Kiss Autographs

*GOLD/10: UNPRICED DUE TO SCARCITY
*RED/1: UNPRICED DUE TO SCARCITY
STATED PRINT RUN 25 SER.#'d SETS

NNO	Billie Kay	30.00	75.00
NNO	Dana Brooke	30.00	75.00
NNO	Ember Moon	60.00	120.00
NNO	Kairi Saine	50.00	100.00
NNO	Liv Morgan	50.00	100.00
NNO	Maryse	50.00	100.00
NNO	Mickie James	75.00	150.00
NNO	Natalya	30.00	75.00
NNO	Peyton Royce	30.00	75.00
NNO	Sonya Deville	60.00	120.00

2018 Topps WWE NXT TakeOver Brooklyn III Mat Relics

*BRONZE/199: .5X TO 1.2X BASIC MEM
*BLUE/50: .6X TO 1.5X BASIC MEM
*SILVER/25: .75X TO 2X BASIC MEM
*GOLD/10: UNPRICED DUE TO SCARCITY
*RED/1: UNPRICED DUE TO SCARCITY

TBRAA	Andrade Cien Almas	3.00	8.00
TBRAB	Aleister Black	3.00	8.00
TBRAC	Adam Cole	6.00	15.00
TBRAS	Asuka	6.00	15.00
TBRBR	Bobby Roode	3.00	8.00
TBRDM	Drew McIntyre	3.00	8.00
TBREM	Ember Moon	4.00	10.00
TBREY	Eric Young	3.00	8.00
TBRHI	Hideo Itami	3.00	8.00
TBRJG	Johnny Gargano	3.00	8.00

2018 Topps WWE Roster Updates

COMPLETE SET (20)		15.00	40.00
R1	Aiden English	1.00	2.50
R2	Aliyah	1.50	4.00
R3	Angelo Dawkins	1.00	2.50
R4	Buddy Murphy	1.25	3.00

R5 Charly Caruso	1.50	4.00
R6 Corey Graves	1.25	3.00
R7 Dana Brooke	2.00	5.00
R8 Dasha Fuentes	1.50	4.00
R9 Epico Colon	1.00	2.50
R10 JoJo	1.00	2.50
R11 Konnor	1.00	2.50
R12 Lars Sullivan	1.00	2.50
R13 Lio Rush	1.00	2.50
R14 Primo Colon	1.00	2.50
R15 R-Truth	1.25	3.00
R16 Renee Young	1.50	4.00
R17 Sarah Logan	1.00	2.50
R18 Tom Phillips	1.00	2.50
R19 Viktor	1.00	2.50
R20 Wesley Blake	1.25	3.00

2018 Topps WWE Shirt Relics

*BLUE/50: .6X TO 1.5X BASIC MEM
*SILVER/25: .75X TO 2X BASIC MEM
*GOLD/10: UNPRICED DUE TO SCARCITY
*RED/1: UNPRICED DUE TO SCARCITY

SRAE Aiden English	3.00	8.00
SRAF Alicia Fox	3.00	8.00
SRAW Alexander Wolfe	2.50	6.00
SRBL Brock Lesnar	6.00	15.00
SRDW Dash Wilder	2.50	6.00
SREY Eric Young	3.00	8.00
SRGD Goldust	3.00	8.00
SRJC John Cena	8.00	20.00
SRJJ JoJo	5.00	12.00
SRNA Natalya	3.00	8.00
SRNC Nikki Cross	6.00	15.00
SRRR Roman Reigns	4.00	10.00
SRRY Renee Young	6.00	15.00
SRSD Scott Dawson	3.00	8.00
SRSJ Samoa Joe	4.00	10.00

2018 Topps WWE SummerSlam 2017 Mat Relics

*BRONZE/199: .5X TO 1.2X BASIC MEM
*BLUE/50: .6X TO 1.5X BASIC MEM
*SILVER/25: .75X TO 2X BASIC MEM
*GOLD/10: UNPRICED DUE TO SCARCITY
*RED/1: UNPRICED DUE TO SCARCITY

SMRAB Alexa Bliss	8.00	20.00
SMRAJ AJ Styles	5.00	12.00
SMRBC Baron Corbin	2.50	6.00
SMRBL Brock Lesnar	4.00	10.00
SMRBS Braun Strowman	5.00	12.00
SMRBW Bray Wyatt	2.50	6.00
SMRCO Cesaro	2.50	6.00
SMRDA Dean Ambrose	2.50	6.00
SMRFB Finn Balor	4.00	10.00
SMRJC John Cena	5.00	12.00
SMRJM Jinder Mahal	2.50	6.00
SMRKO Kevin Owens	2.50	6.00
SMRNA Natalya	3.00	8.00
SMRNO Naomi	2.50	6.00
SMRRR Roman Reigns	3.00	8.00
SMRSB Sasha Banks	8.00	20.00
SMRSH Sheamus	2.50	6.00
SMRSJ Samoa Joe	2.50	6.00
SMRSN Shinsuke Nakamura	4.00	10.00
SMRSR Seth Rollins	2.50	6.00

2018 Topps WWE Triple Autographs

STATED PRINT RUN 10 SER.#'d SETS
UNPRICED DUE TO SCARCITY

TADAY Big E/Kingston/Woods
TAERA Cole/Fish/O'Reilly
TAHOJ Ambrose/Rollins/Reigns
TAMIZ Miz/Axel/Dallas
TARAW HHH/S.McMahon/Angle
TATWF Wyatt/Harper/Rowan

2021 Topps WWE

COMPLETE SET (200) 15.00 40.00
*AQUA/299: .75X TO 2X BASIC CARDS
*LT GREEN/199: 1.2X TO 3X BASIC CARDS
*DK GREEN/99: 1.5X TO 4X BASIC CARDS
*CITRINE/75: 2X TO 5X BASIC CARDS
*ORANGE/50: 2.5X TO 6X BASIC CARDS
*PURPLE/25: UNPRICED DUE TO SCARCITY
*BLUE/10: UNPRICED DUE TO SCARCITY
*BLACK/5: UNPRICED DUE TO SCARCITY
*RED/1: UNPRICED DUE TO SCARCITY
*P.P.BLACK/1: UNPRICED DUE TO SCARCITY
*P.P.CYAN/1: UNPRICED DUE TO SCARCITY
*P.P.MAGENTA/1: UNPRICED DUE TO SCARCITY
*P.P.YELLOW/1: UNPRICED DUE TO SCARCITY

1 Kofi Kingston	.60	1.50
2 Otis	.30	.75
3 Usos	.50	1.25
4 Miz	.40	1.00
5 King Corbin's Court	.50	1.25
6 Drew McIntyre	.60	1.50
7 John Morrison	.50	1.25
8 John Morrison	.50	1.25
9 Roman Reigns	1.25	3.00
10 Edge	1.00	2.50
11 Drew McIntyre	.60	1.50
12 Miz & John Morrison	.50	1.25
13 King Corbin	.25	.60
14 Randy Orton	.75	2.00
15 Angel Garza	.30	.75
16 Drew McIntyre	.60	1.50
17 Angel Garza	.30	.75
18 King Corbin	.25	.60
19 Drew McIntyre	.60	1.50
20 Street Profits	.50	1.25
21 Usos	.60	1.50
22 Seth Rollins	.60	1.50
23 Randy Orton	.75	2.00
24 Roman Reigns	1.25	3.00
25 Undertaker	1.25	3.00
26 Miz & John Morrison	.50	1.25
27 Angel Garza	.30	.75
28 Goldberg	1.00	2.50
29 Usos	.40	1.00
30 Angel Garza	.30	.75
31 Randy Orton	.75	2.00
32 Dolph Ziggler	.50	1.25
33 Miz & John Morrison	.50	1.25
34 Sami Zayn	.60	1.50
35 AJ Styles	.75	2.00
36 Edge	1.00	2.50
37 Elias	.25	.60
38 Edge	1.00	2.50
39 Elias	.25	.60
40 Dolph Ziggler	.50	1.25
41 Street Profits	.30	.75
42 Miz & John Morrison	.50	1.25
43 King Corbin	.25	.60
44 Kevin Owens & Street Profits	.25	.60
45 Cesaro	.25	.60
46 John Morrison	.50	1.25
47 Kevin Owens	.50	1.25
48 Undertaker	1.25	3.00
49 Elias	.25	.60
50 Otis	.30	.75
51 Edge	1.00	2.50
52 Street Profits	.50	1.25
53 Drew McIntyre	.60	1.50
54 Drew McIntyre	.60	1.50
55 Sheamus	.40	1.00
56 Seth Rollins	.60	1.50
57 Big E	.60	1.50
58 Apollo Crews	.30	.75
59 Rey Mysterio	.60	1.50
60 Drew McIntyre	.60	1.50
61 King Corbin	.25	.60
62 Lucha House Party	.40	1.00
63 Drew McIntyre	.60	1.50
64 Otis	.30	.75
65 AJ Styles	.75	2.00
66 Viking Raiders	.25	.60
67 New Day	.50	1.25
68 Drew McIntyre	.60	1.50
69 Otis	.30	.75
70 Bobby Lashley	.60	1.50
71 Rey Mysterio	.60	1.50
72 Randy Orton	1.00	2.50
73 Elias	.25	.60
74 Bobby Lashley	.25	.60
75 Drew McIntyre	.60	1.50
76 AJ Styles	.75	2.00
77 Jeff Hardy	.60	1.50
78 Apollo Crews	.30	.75
79 Drew McIntyre	.60	1.50
80 Drew McIntyre	.60	1.50
81 Sheamus	.40	1.00
82 Jeff Hardy	.60	1.50
83 Bobby Lashley	.60	1.50
84 Bobby Lashley & MVP	.60	1.50
85 AJ Styles	.75	2.00
86 Cesaro & Nakamura	.60	1.50
87 Sheamus	.40	1.00
88 Drew McIntyre	.60	1.50
89 Randy Orton	.75	2.00
90 Cesaro & Nakamura	.60	1.50
91 Seth Rollins	.60	1.50
92 Drew McIntyre	.60	1.50
93 Street Profits	.30	.75
94 Seth Rollins	.60	1.50
95 Drew McIntyre	.60	1.50
96 AJ Styles	.75	2.00
97 Alexa Bliss	1.50	4.00
98 Aliyah	.50	1.25
99 Asuka	1.00	2.50
100 Becky Lynch	1.00	2.50
101 Bobby Lashley	.60	1.50
102 Cedric Alexander	.25	.60
103 Charlotte Flair	1.25	3.00
104 Damian Priest	.40	1.00
105 Dana Brooke	.25	.60
106 Drew Gulak	.30	.75
107 Drew McIntyre	.60	1.50
108 Doudrop	.40	1.00
109 Elias	.25	.60
110 Eva Marie	.60	1.50
111 Jeff Hardy	.60	1.50
112 Jaxson Ryker	.25	.60
113 John Morrison	.50	1.25
114 Keith Lee	.50	1.25
115 Kofi Kingston	.60	1.50
116 Lacey Evans	1.00	2.50
117 Mace	.25	.60
118 Mansoor	.25	.60
119 MVP	.25	.60
120 Mustafa Ali	.30	.75
121 Naomi	.30	.75
122 Nia Jax	.50	1.25
123 Nikki A.S.H.	.50	1.25
124 Omos	.25	.60
125 Randy Orton	.75	2.00
126 Reggie	.25	.60
127 Rhea Ripley	1.00	2.50
128 Ricochet	.40	1.00
129 Riddle	.60	1.50
130 Shayna Baszler	.60	1.50
131 Sheamus	.40	1.00
132 Shelton Benjamin	.40	1.00
133 T-Bar	.30	.75
134 The Miz	.40	1.00
135 Xavier Woods	.25	.60
136 Angelo Dawkins	.30	.75
137 Apollo Crews	.30	.75
138 Baron Corbin	.25	.60
139 Bayley	.60	1.50
140 Bianca Belair	.60	1.50
141 Big E	.60	1.50
142 Carmella	.60	1.50
143 Cesaro	.25	.60
144 Chad Gable	.25	.60
145 Commander Azeez	.30	.75
146 Dolph Ziggler	.50	1.25
147 Dominik Mysterio	.30	.75
148 Finn Balor	.60	1.50
149 Jey Uso	.25	.60
150 Jimmy Uso	.25	.60
151 Kevin Owens	.50	1.25
152 King Nakamura	.60	1.50
153 Liv Morgan	1.00	2.50
154 Montez Ford	.25	.60
155 Natalya	.40	1.00
156 Nox	.60	1.50
157 Otis	.30	.75
158 Rey Mysterio	.60	1.50
159 Rick Boogs	.25	.60
160 Robert Roode	.30	.75
161 Roman Reigns	1.25	3.00
162 Sami Zayn	.40	1.00
163 Sasha Banks	1.25	3.00
164 Seth Rollins	.60	1.50
165 Shotzi	1.25	3.00
166 Sonya Deville	.60	1.50
167 Tamina	.25	.60
168 Toni Storm	1.00	2.50
169 Zelina Vega	.50	1.25
170 Austin Theory	.50	1.25
171 Candice LeRae	1.00	2.50
172 Dakota Kai	.50	1.25
173 Dexter Lumis	.25	.60
174 Ember Moon	.30	.75
175 Io Shirai	.50	1.25
176 Indi Hartwell	.75	2.00
177 Isaiah "Swerve" Scott	.40	1.00
178 Johnny Gargano	.50	1.25

179	Karrion Kross	1.00	2.50
180	Kyle O'Reilly	.40	1.00
181	Mandy Rose	1.25	3.00
182	Pete Dunne	.60	1.50
183	Raquel Gonzalez	1.00	2.50
184	Roderick Strong	.50	1.25
185	Samoa Joe	.50	1.25
186	Santos Escobar	.50	1.25
187	Sarray	.30	.75
188	Scarlett	1.25	3.00
189	Timothy Thatcher	.25	.60
190	Tommaso Ciampa	.60	1.50
191	Walter	.75	2.00
192	Batista	.50	1.25
193	British Bulldog	.40	1.00
194	Edge	1.00	2.50
195	Goldberg	1.00	2.50
196	JBL	.25	.60
197	Kane	.40	1.00
198	Molly Holly	.30	.75
199	Rob Van Dam	.50	1.25
200	John Cena	1.25	3.00

2021 Topps WWE Autographed Mat Relics

*RED/1: UNPRICED DUE TO SCARCITY
STATED ODDS 1:4,986
STATED PRINT RUN 10 SER.#'d SETS

MRAB	Big E
MRAR	Riddle
MRMY	Mia Yim
MRAAG	Angel Garza
MRAFA	Fabian Aichner
MRAFB	Finn Balor
MRAJD	Jordan Devlin
MRAJG	Johnny Gargano
MRAKL	Keith Lee
MRAMB	Marcel Barthel
MRARM	Rey Mysterio
MRARR	Rhea Ripley
MRARS	Roderick Strong
MRATC	Tommaso Ciampa
MRAWT	WALTER
MRABOB	Bobby Lashley
MRADOM	Dominik Mysterio
MRANIA	Nia Jax
MRAROM	Roman Reigns
MRASHA	Shayna Baszler

2021 Topps WWE Autographs

*GREEN/99: .6X TO 1.5X BASIC AUTOS
*ORANGE/50: .75X TO 2X BASIC AUTOS
*PURPLE/25: UNPRICED DUE TO SCARCITY
*BLUE/10: UNPRICED DUE TO SCARCITY
*BLACK/5: UNPRICED DUE TO SCARCITY
*RED/1: UNPRICED DUE TO SCARCITY
*P.P.BLACK/1: UNPRICED DUE TO SCARCITY
*P.P.CYAN/1: UNPRICED DUE TO SCARCITY
*P.P.MAGENTA/1: UNPRICED DUE TO SCARCITY
*P.P.YELLOW/1: UNPRICED DUE TO SCARCITY

AC	Carmella	12.00	30.00
AE	Big E	6.00	15.00
AAS	AJ Styles	10.00	25.00
AAT	Austin Theory		
ABB	Bianca Belair	12.00	30.00
ABE	Becky Lynch	50.00	100.00
ABL	Bobby Lashley	10.00	25.00

ACF	Charlotte Flair	30.00	75.00
ADM	Drew McIntyre	15.00	40.00
ADP	Damian Priest	6.00	15.00
AED	Edge	25.00	60.00
AFB	Finn Balor	10.00	25.00
AJH	Jeff Hardy	15.00	40.00
AJU	Jey Uso	6.00	15.00
AKC	King Corbin	5.00	12.00
AKF	Kofi Kingston	6.00	15.00
AKK	Karrion Kross		
AKL	Keith Lee		
AKN	Asuka	25.00	60.00
AKO	Kevin Owens	8.00	20.00
ALM	Liv Morgan	30.00	75.00
AMR	Riddle	10.00	25.00
AOT	Otis	6.00	15.00
AQS	Shayna Baszler	6.00	15.00
ARH	Rhea Ripley	12.00	30.00
ARM	Rey Mysterio	15.00	40.00
ARR	Roman Reigns	30.00	75.00
ARU	Robert Roode	5.00	12.00
ASB	Sasha Banks	50.00	100.00
ASD	Sonya Deville	8.00	20.00
ASN	Shinsuke Nakamura	10.00	25.00
ASR	Seth Rollins	10.00	25.00
ASZ	Sami Zayn	6.00	15.00
AUN	Apollo Crews	5.00	12.00
AXW	Xavier Woods	5.00	12.00
AMVP	MVP	5.00	12.00

2021 Topps WWE Coolest Mixed Tag Teams

COMPLETE SET (11)		6.00	15.00
STATED ODDS 1:10			
MT1	Charlotte Flair & AJ Styles	1.50	4.00
MT2	Finn Balor & Bayley	.75	2.00
MT3	John Cena & Trish Stratus	1.50	4.00
MT4	Sasha Banks & Roman Reigns	1.50	4.00
MT5	R-Truth & Carmella	.75	2.00
MT6	The Miz & Asuka	1.25	3.00
MT7	Stephanie McMahon & Triple H	1.00	2.50
MT8	Jimmy Uso & Naomi	.40	1.00
MT9	Seth Rollins & Becky Lynch	1.25	3.00
MT10	Johnny Gargano & Candice LeRae	1.25	3.00
MT11	Natalya & Shinsuke Nakamura	.75	2.00

2021 Topps WWE Hall of Fame Tribute

COMPLETE SET (18)		8.00	20.00
STATED ODDS 1:12			
HOF1	Razor	.50	1.25
HOF2	Diesel	.50	1.25
HOF3	...The New World Order	.50	1.25
HOF4	Hollywood Hulk Hogan	1.50	4.00
HOF5	The Outsiders	.50	1.25
HOF6	The nWo PPV	1.50	4.00
HOF7	Syxx	.40	1.00
HOF8	Kevin Nash		
HOF9	Fingerpoke of Doom	.50	1.25
HOF10	Scott Hall	.75	2.00
HOF11	Hollywood Hulk Hogan	1.50	4.00
HOF12	Kevin Nash	.50	1.25
HOF13	Scott Hall	.50	1.25
HOF14	Scott Hall	.50	1.25
HOF15	The nWo	1.50	4.00
HOF16	The nWo	.50	1.25
HOF17	Scott Hall	.50	1.25
HOF18	Icon vs. Icon	2.00	5.00

2021 Topps WWE Hall of Fame Tribute Autographs

STATED PRINT RUN 25 SER.#'d SETS

NWOKN	Kevin Nash	15.00	40.00
NWOSW	Syxx	12.00	30.00

2021 Topps WWE Locker Room Veterans Booklet Autograph

ABC The Miz/R-Truth/Rey Mysterio/Randy Orton/Jeff Hardy/Shelton Benjamin Sheamus/Natalya/Edge/Bobby Lashley/MVP/Kofi Kingston

2021 Topps WWE Manufactured Match Film Strip Relics

*AQUA/299: .5X TO 1.2X BASIC MEM
*LT GREEN/199: .6X TO 1.5X BASIC MEM
*DK GREEN/99: .75X TO 2X BASIC MEM
*CITRINE/75: 1X TO 2.5X BASIC MEM
*ORANGE/50: 1.2X TO 3X BASIC MEM
*PURPLE/25: UNPRICED DUE TO SCARCITY
*BLUE/10: UNPRICED DUE TO SCARCITY
*BLACK/5: UNPRICED DUE TO SCARCITY
*RED/1: UNPRICED DUE TO SCARCITY
STATED ODDS 1:74

FSAJ	AJ Styles vs. John Cena	6.00	15.00
FSBB	Bret Hart vs. British Bulldog	5.00	12.00
FSBC	Becky Lynch vs. Charlotte Flair	8.00	20.00
FSBP	Bret Hart vs. Mr. Perfect	5.00	12.00
FSHA	Bret Hart vs. Steve Austin	6.00	15.00
FSHG	Hulk Hogan vs. Andre the Giant	10.00	25.00
FSHM	Bret Hart vs. Shawn Michaels	5.00	12.00
FSHU	Hulk Hogan vs. Ultimate Warrior	15.00	40.00
FSJE	John Cena vs. Edge		
FSKU	Undertaker vs. Kane	5.00	12.00
FSLU	Bobby Lashley vs. Umaga	5.00	12.00
FSMF	Shawn Michaels vs. Ric Flair	5.00	12.00
FSMR	Randy Savage vs. Ric Flair	6.00	15.00
FSNC	Natalya vs. Charlotte Flair		
FSPR	Mr. Perfect vs. Ric Flair	4.00	12.00
FSRC	The Rock vs. John Cena	6.00	15.00
FSRH	The Rock vs. Hulk Hogan	10.00	25.00
FSRS	Razor Ramon vs. Shawn Michaels	10.00	25.00
FSSB	Sasha Banks vs. Bayley	6.00	15.00
FSSC	Sami Zayn vs. Cesaro	4.00	12.00
FSSM	Shawn Michaels vs. Mankind	5.00	12.00
FSSS	Randy Savage vs. Ricky Steamboat	12.00	30.00
FSST	Shawn Michaels vs. Triple H	5.00	12.00
FSSW	Randy Savage vs. Ultimate Warrior	8.00	20.00
FSTJ	The Miz vs. John Cena		
FSBCA	Becky Lynch vs. Charlotte Flair vs. Asuka	6.00	15.00
FSFBL	Charlotte Flair vs. Sasha Banks vs. Becky Lynch	5.00	12.00
FSRA2	The Rock vs. Steve Austin	8.00	20.00
FSRA3	The Rock vs. Steve Austin	8.00	20.00
FSRC2	The Rock vs. John Cena	6.00	15.00
FSUH2	Undertaker vs. Triple H	6.00	15.00
FSUH3	Undertaker vs. Triple H	6.00	15.00
FSUM1	Undertaker vs. Shawn Michaels	6.00	15.00
FSUM2	Undertaker vs. Shawn Michaels	6.00	15.00
FSUM3	Undertaker vs. Shawn Michaels	6.00	15.00
FSUMK	Undertaker vs. Mankind	5.00	12.00
FSACJG	Adam Cole vs. Johnny Gargano	5.00	12.00
FSKOSZ	Kevin Owens vs. Sami Zayn	5.00	12.00
FSTCJG	Tommaso Ciampa vs. Johnny Gargano	5.00	12.00

2021 Topps WWE Mat Relics

*AQUA/299: .5X TO 1.2X BASIC MEM
*LT GREEN/199: .6X TO 1.5X BASIC MEM
*DK GREEN/99: .75X TO 2X BASIC MEM
*CITRINE/75: 1X TO 2.5X BASIC MEM
*ORANGE/50: 1.2X TO 3X BASIC MEM
*PURPLE/25: UNPRICED DUE TO SCARCITY
*BLUE/10: UNPRICED DUE TO SCARCITY
*BLACK/5: UNPRICED DUE TO SCARCITY
*RED/1: UNPRICED DUE TO SCARCITY
STATED ODDS 1:49

MRB	Big E	1.50	4.00
MRR	Riddle	1.50	4.00
MRAC	Adam Cole	2.00	5.00
MRAG	Angel Garza	.75	2.00
MRAS	Asuka	2.50	6.00
MRBA	Bayley	1.50	4.00
MRBB	Bianca Belair	1.50	4.00
MRBF	Bobby Fish	.75	2.00
MRBL	Becky Lynch	8.00	20.00
MRBR	Robert Roode	2.50	6.00
MRCS	Cesaro	2.00	5.00
MRDA	Dana Brooke	2.00	5.00
MRDK	Dakota Kai	4.00	10.00
MRDM	Finn Balor	5.00	12.00
MRFA	Fabian Aichner	2.50	6.00
MRFB	Finn Balor	5.00	12.00
MRGM	Gran Metalik	2.00	5.00
MRID	Ilja Dragunov	2.00	5.00
MRIS	Isaiah "Swerve" Scott	3.00	8.00
MRJD	Jordan Devlin	2.00	5.00
MRJG	Johnny Gargano	4.00	10.00
MRJH	Jeff Hardy	5.00	12.00
MRJM	Jinder Mahal	2.50	6.00
MRKL	Keith Lee	4.00	10.00
MRKO	Kevin Owens	4.00	10.00
MRKR	Kyle O'Reilly	3.00	8.00
MRLA	Bobby Lashley	5.00	12.00
MRLM	Liv Morgan	8.00	20.00
MRMA	Mustafa Ali	2.50	6.00
MRMB	Marcel Barthel	2.50	6.00
MRMY	Mia Yim	2.50	6.00
MRNJ	Nia Jax	4.00	10.00
MROT	Otis	2.50	6.00
MRRM	Rey Mysterio	5.00	12.00
MRRR	Rhea Ripley	8.00	20.00
MRRS	Roderick Strong	4.00	10.00
MRSB	Sasha Banks	10.00	25.00
MRSD	Sonya Deville	5.00	12.00
MRSG	Chad Gable	2.00	5.00
MRSN	Shinsuke Nakamura	5.00	12.00
MRSR	Seth Rollins	5.00	12.00
MRT7	Trent Seven	2.50	6.00
MRTC	Tommaso Ciampa	5.00	12.00
MRTO	Titus O'Neil	2.00	5.00
MRTS	Toni Storm	8.00	20.00
MRTY	Tyler Bate	2.50	6.00
MRWT	WALTER	6.00	15.00
MRBOB	Bobby Lashley	5.00	12.00
MRDOM	Dominik Mysterio	2.50	6.00
MRKLR	Kay Lee Ray	5.00	12.00
MRMIZ	The Miz	3.00	8.00
MRNIA	Nia Jax	4.00	10.00
MRROM	Roman Reigns	10.00	25.00
MRSHA	Shayna Baszler	5.00	12.00

2021 Topps WWE Memorable Entrances

COMPLETE SET (9)	6.00	15.00
STATED ODDS 1:10		
ME1 Rhythm & Blues	.40	1.00
ME2 Bobby "The Brain" Heenan	.50	1.25
ME3 Macho King Randy Savage	2.00	5.00
ME4 Shawn Michaels	1.25	3.00
ME5 John Cena	1.50	4.00
ME6 Undertaker	1.50	4.00
ME7 Triple H	1.00	2.50
ME8 Sasha Banks	1.50	4.00
ME9 Roman Reigns	1.50	4.00

2021 Topps WWE RKO Outta Nowhere

COMPLETE SET (10)	6.00	15.00
STATED ODDS 1:10		
RKO1 Undertaker	1.50	4.00
RKO2 Hulk Hogan	1.50	4.00
RKO3 Jeff Hardy	.75	2.00
RKO4 Triple H	1.00	2.50
RKO5 Dolph Ziggler	.60	1.50
RKO6 Seth Rollins	.75	2.00
RKO7 Rey Mysterio	.75	2.00
RKO8 Ricochet	.50	1.25
RKO9 AJ Styles	1.00	2.50
RKO10 Alexa Bliss	2.00	5.00

2021 Topps WWE Tag Team Autographs

*BLUE/10: UNPRICED DUE TO SCARCITY
*RED/1: UNPRICED DUE TO SCARCITY
RANDOMLY INSERTED INTO PACKS
STATED PRINT RUN 25 SER.#'d SETS

DADD Robert Roode/Dolph Ziggler	15.00	40.00
DASN Shayna Baszler/Nia Jax	15.00	40.00
DALHP Lince Dorado/Gran Metalik	12.00	30.00

2007 Topps WWE Action

COMPLETE SET (90)	8.00	20.00
UNOPENED BOX (24 PACKS)		
UNOPENED PACK (7 CARDS)		
1 John Cena	.60	1.50
2 Carlito	.40	1.00
3 Charlie Haas	.10	.25
4 Chris Masters	.40	1.00
5 Edge	.40	1.00
6 Eugene	.10	.25
7 Jim Duggan	.40	1.00
8 John Morrison	.10	.25
9 JTG	.10	.25
10 Kenny Dykstra	.15	.40
11 Lance Cade	.15	.40
12 Randy Orton	.40	1.00
13 Robbie McAllister	.10	.25
14 Rory McAllister	.10	.25
15 Shad	.10	.25
16 Shawn Michaels	.60	1.50
17 Shelton Benjamin	.10	.25
18 Super Crazy	.15	.40
19 Trevor Murdoch	.10	.25
20 Triple H	.60	1.50
21 Umaga	.15	.40
22 Val Venis	.25	.60
23 Viscera	.25	.60
24 Ric Flair	.40	1.00
25 The Great Khali	.15	.40
26 Jeff Hardy	.25	.60
27 Matt Hardy	.25	.60
28 Batista	.40	1.00
29 Boogeyman	.15	.40
30 Brian Kendrick	.15	.40
31 Chavo Guerrero	.15	.40
32 Santino Marella	.25	.60
33 Dave Taylor	.10	.25
34 Deuce	.10	.25
35 Domino	.10	.25
36 Finlay	.25	.60
37 Funaki	.15	.40
38 Gregory Helms	.10	.25
39 Hornswoggle	.15	.40
40 Jamie Noble	.10	.25
41 Jimmy Wang Yang	.10	.25
42 Kane	.40	1.00
43 King Booker	.40	1.00
44 Mark Henry	.15	.40
45 Montel Vontavious Porter	.15	.40
46 Mr. Kennedy	.25	.60
47 Paul London	.25	.60
48 Rey Mysterio	.25	.60
49 Scotty 2 Hotty	.15	.40
50 The Miz	.40	1.00
51 Balls Mahoney	.10	.25
52 Bobby Lashley	.40	1.00
53 CM Punk	.15	.40
54 Elijah Burke	.10	.25
55 Hardcore Holly	.25	.60
56 Kevin Thorn	.10	.25
57 Nunzio	.15	.40
58 Marcus CorVan	.10	.25
59 Matt Striker	.10	.25
60 Tazz	.15	.40
61 Joey Styles	.10	.25
62 Sabu	.10	.25
63 Sandman	.15	.40
64 Snitsky	.15	.40
65 Steve Richards	.15	.40
66 Tommy Dreamer	.15	.40
67 Undertaker/Batista	.50	1.25
68 Undertaker/Batista	.50	1.25
69 Undertaker/Batista	.50	1.25
70 J. Cena/S. Michaels	.60	1.50
71 J. Cena/S. Michaels	.60	1.50
72 J. Cena/S. Michaels	.60	1.50
73 Bobby Lashley/Umaga	.40	1.00
74 Bobby Lashley/Umaga	.40	1.00
75 Bobby Lashley/Umaga	.40	1.00
76 Mr. Kennedy	.25	.60
77 Mr. Kennedy	.25	.60
78 Mr. Kennedy	.25	.60
79 ECW Originals/New Breed	.10	.25
80 ECW Originals/New Breed	.10	.25
81 ECW Originals/New Breed	.10	.25
82 The Great Khali/Kane	.40	1.00
83 The Great Khali/Kane	.40	1.00
84 The Great Khali/Kane	.40	1.00
85 The Great Khali/Kane	.40	1.00
86 Mr. McMahon	.40	1.00
87 Mr. McMahon	.40	1.00
88 Mr. McMahon	.40	1.00
89 Mr. McMahon	.40	1.00
90 Checklist Card	.10	.25

2007 Topps WWE Action Autographs

STATED ODDS 1:48 HOBBY EXCLUSIVE
WILLIAM PERRY ODDS 1:1,392

NNO Bobby Lashley	10.00	25.00
NNO Carlito	5.00	12.00
NNO CM Punk	30.00	60.00
NNO Edge	10.00	25.00
NNO Jeff Hardy	20.00	40.00
NNO John Cena	25.00	50.00
NNO Matt Hardy	10.00	25.00
NNO Mr. Kennedy	10.00	25.00
NNO William Refrigerator Perry	40.00	80.00

2007 Topps WWE Action Lenticular Motion

COMPLETE SET (10)	5.00	12.00
STATED ODDS 1:8 RETAIL EXCLUSIVE		
1 John Cena	1.25	3.00
2 Carlito	.60	1.50
3 Shawn Michaels	1.00	2.50
4 Batista	1.00	2.50
5 Mr. Kennedy	.40	1.00
6 Bobby Lashley	.40	1.00
7 Ric Flair	1.50	4.00
8 Edge	.75	2.00
9 Rey Mysterio	.75	2.00
10 Rob Van Dam	.40	1.00

2007 Topps WWE Action Ringside Relics

COMPLETE SET (4)	10.00	25.00
STATED ODDS 1:48 HOBBY EXCLUSIVE		
NNO Carlito	3.00	8.00
NNO Edge	4.00	10.00
NNO Mr. Kennedy	3.00	8.00
NNO Shawn Michaels	5.00	12.00

2007 Topps WWE Action Tattoos

COMPLETE SET (10)	4.00	10.00
STATED ODDS 1:4 RETAIL EXCLUSIVE		
1 Batista	.50	1.25
2 Booker T	.50	1.25
3 John Cena	.75	2.00
4 Edge	.50	1.25
5 Triple H	.75	2.00
6 Undertaker	.60	1.50
7 Carlito	.50	1.25
8 Ric Flair	.50	1.25
9 Rob Van Dam	.50	1.25
10 Rey Mysterio	.30	.75

2015-16 Topps WWE Bret Hart Tribute

COMPLETE SET (20)	15.00	40.00
CANADIAN EXCLUSIVES		
1 Bret Hit Man Hart	2.50	6.00
2 Bret Hit Man Hart	2.50	6.00
3 Bret Hit Man Hart	2.50	6.00
4 Bret Hit Man Hart	2.50	6.00
5 Bret Hit Man Hart	2.50	6.00
6 Bret Hit Man Hart	2.50	6.00
7 Bret Hit Man Hart	2.50	6.00
8 Bret Hit Man Hart	2.50	6.00
9 Bret Hit Man Hart	2.50	6.00
10 Bret Hit Man Hart	2.50	6.00
11 Bret Hit Man Hart	2.50	6.00
12 Bret Hit Man Hart	2.50	6.00
13 Bret Hit Man Hart	2.50	6.00
14 Bret Hit Man Hart	2.50	6.00
15 Bret Hit Man Hart	2.50	6.00
16 Bret Hit Man Hart	2.50	6.00
17 Bret Hit Man Hart	2.50	6.00
18 Bret Hit Man Hart	2.50	6.00
19 Bret Hit Man Hart	2.50	6.00
20 Bret Hit Man Hart	2.50	6.00

2015-16 Topps WWE Bret Hart Tribute Autographs and Relics

NNO Bret Hart AU/100	50.00	100.00
NNO Bret Hart MEM/100	30.00	80.00
NNO Bret Hart AU MEM/10	150.00	300.00

2016 Topps WWE Brock Lesnar Tribute

COMPLETE SET (10)	15.00	40.00
WALMART EXCLUSIVE		
1 Brock Lesnar	1.00	2.50
2 Brock Lesnar	1.00	2.50
3 Brock Lesnar	1.00	2.50
4 Brock Lesnar	1.00	2.50
5 Brock Lesnar	1.00	2.50
6 Brock Lesnar	1.00	2.50
7 Brock Lesnar	1.00	2.50
8 Brock Lesnar	1.00	2.50
9 Brock Lesnar	1.00	2.50
10 Brock Lesnar	1.00	2.50
11 Brock Lesnar	1.00	2.50
12 Brock Lesnar	1.00	2.50
13 Brock Lesnar	1.00	2.50
14 Brock Lesnar	1.00	2.50
15 Brock Lesnar	1.00	2.50
16 Brock Lesnar	1.00	2.50
17 Brock Lesnar	1.00	2.50
18 Brock Lesnar	1.00	2.50
19 Brock Lesnar	1.00	2.50
20 Brock Lesnar	1.00	2.50
21 Brock Lesnar	1.00	2.50
22 Brock Lesnar	1.00	2.50
23 Brock Lesnar	1.00	2.50
24 Brock Lesnar	1.00	2.50
25 Brock Lesnar	1.00	2.50
26 Brock Lesnar	1.00	2.50
27 Brock Lesnar	1.00	2.50
28 Brock Lesnar	1.00	2.50
29 Brock Lesnar	1.00	2.50
30 Brock Lesnar	1.00	2.50
31 Brock Lesnar	1.00	2.50
32 Brock Lesnar	1.00	2.50
33 Brock Lesnar	1.00	2.50
34 Brock Lesnar	1.00	2.50
35 Brock Lesnar	1.00	2.50
36 Brock Lesnar	1.00	2.50
37 Brock Lesnar	1.00	2.50
38 Brock Lesnar	1.00	2.50
39 Brock Lesnar	1.00	2.50
40 Brock Lesnar	1.00	2.50

2016 Topps WWE Brock Lesnar Tribute Autographs and Relics

NNO Brock Lesnar AU	
NNO Brock Lesnar MEM	
NNO Brock Lesnar AU MEM	

2011 Topps WWE Champions

COMPLETE SET (90)	10.00	25.00
UNOPENED BOX (24 PACKS)		
UNOPENED PACK (7 CARDS)		
1 Undertaker/Shawn Michaels	.60	1.50
2 ShowMiz/Morrison & R-Truth	.40	1.00
3 Randy Orton/Rhodes & DiBiase	.60	1.50
4 Jack Swagger MITB	.25	.60
5 Triple H/Sheamus	.75	2.00
6 Rey Mysterio/CM Punk	.40	1.00
7 10-Diva Tag Match	.60	1.50
8 John Cena/Batista	.75	2.00
9 Sheamus	.25	.60
10 Randy Orton	.60	1.50
11 The Miz	.60	1.50
12 Rey Mysterio	.40	1.00
13 Kane	.40	1.00
14 Edge	.60	1.50
15 Dolph Ziggler	.25	.60
16 Edge	.60	1.50
17 Kofi Kingston	.15	.40
18 Dolph Ziggler	.25	.60
19 Kofi Kingston	.15	.40
20 Wade Barrett	.15	.40
21 R-Truth	.15	.40
22 The Miz	.25	.60
23 Daniel Bryan	.15	.40
24 Sheamus	.25	.60
25 David Hart Smith/Tyson Kidd	.15	.40
26 Cody Rhodes/Drew McIntyre	.15	.40
27 David Otunga/John Cena	.75	2.00
28 Heath Slater/Justin Gabriel	.15	.40
29 Santino Marella/Vladimir Kozlov	.25	.60
30 Heath Slater/Justin Gabriel	.15	.40
31 John Cena/The Miz	.75	2.00
32 Heath Slater/Justin Gabriel	.15	.40
33 Eve	.60	1.50
34 Alicia Fox	.25	.60
35 Melina	.60	1.50
36 Michelle McCool	.60	1.50
37 Natalya	.60	1.50
38 Eve	.60	1.50
39 Beth Phoenix	.40	1.00
40 Layla	.40	1.00
41 Nexus	.15	.40
42 Alberto Del Rio	.40	1.00
43 Alex Riley	.15	.40
44 Mason Ryan	.15	.40
45 Sin Cara	.40	1.00
46 Ted DiBiase	.25	.60
47 Big Show/Miz	.40	1.00
48 Randy Orton/Evan Bourne	.60	1.50
49 Big Show/CM Punk	.40	1.00
50 Kane MITB	.40	1.00
51 The Miz MITB	.25	.60
52 Kane/Undertaker	.60	1.50
53 Team SmackDown	.60	1.50
54 Sheamus KOTR	.25	.60
55 Team Mysterio	.40	1.00
56 CM Punk	.40	1.00
57 Wade Barrett	.15	.40
58 John Morrison	.25	.60
59 Booker T	.25	.60
60 Diesel	.25	.60
61 Alberto Del Rio	.40	1.00
62 Edge	.60	1.50
63 John Cena	.75	2.00
64 The Rock Returns	.75	2.00
65 Stone Cold Steve Austin	.60	1.50
66 Trish Stratus/Vickie Guerrero	.75	2.00
67 Mean Gene Okerlund	.25	.60
68 Cowboy Bob Orton	.25	.60
69 Nikolai Volkoff	.25	.60
70 Jimmy Superfly Snuka	.40	1.00
71 Tito Santana	.15	.40
72 Sgt. Slaughter	.40	1.00
73 Jim Ross	.15	.40
74 Rowdy Roddy Piper	.60	1.50
75 Daniel Bryan	.15	.40
76 The Miz	.25	.60
77 CM Punk/John Cena	.75	2.00
78 Wade Barrett	.15	.40
79 John Morrison	.25	.60
80 Drew McIntyre	.15	.40
81 Daniel Bryan	.15	.40
82 Cody Rhodes	.15	.40
83 Edge/Alberto Del Rio	.60	1.50
84 Big Show/Kane/Santino/Kofi	.40	1.00
85 Randy Orton/CM Punk	.60	1.50
86 Michael Cole/Jerry Lawler	.40	1.00
87 Undertaker/Triple H	.75	2.00
88 Trish & Morrison/LayCool & Ziggler	.75	2.00
89 The Miz/John Cena	.75	2.00
90 Checklist	.15	.40

2011 Topps WWE Champions Autographs

STATED ODDS 1:150

NNO Dolph Ziggler	8.00	20.00
NNO Edge	15.00	40.00
NNO John Cena	25.00	60.00
NNO Kofi Kingston	12.00	30.00
NNO Layla	10.00	25.00
NNO Michelle McCool	12.00	30.00
NNO The Miz	12.00	30.00
NNO Natalya	12.00	30.00
NNO Randy Orton	20.00	50.00
NNO Santino Marella	8.00	20.00
NNO Sheamus	12.00	30.00
NNO Vladimir Kozlov	8.00	20.00

2011 Topps WWE Champions Foil

COMPLETE SET (10)	4.00	10.00
STATED ODDS 1:3		
F1 Stone Cold Steve Austin	1.00	2.50
F2 Triple H	1.25	3.00
F3 Ravishing Rick Rude	.40	1.00
F4 John Morrison	.40	1.00
F5 Edge & Christian	1.00	2.50
F6 Michelle McCool	1.00	2.50
F7 Melina	1.00	2.50
F8 The British Bulldog	.40	1.00
F9 Terry Funk	.40	1.00
F10 Booker T	.40	1.00

2009 Topps WWE Chipz

COMPLETE SET (63)	15.00	30.00
UNOPENED BOX (24 PACKS)		
UNOPENED PACK (3 CHIPS)		
1 John Cena	1.00	2.50
2 Randy Orton	.40	1.00
3 Charlie Haas	.15	.40
4 JTG	.15	.40
5 Snitsky	.25	.60
6 Shad	.15	.40
7 Shawn Michaels	1.00	2.50
8 Santino Marella	.15	.40
9 D-Lo Brown	.25	.60
10 William Regal	.40	1.00
11 Jerry Lawler	.25	.60
12 Chris Jericho	.40	1.00
13 Ted DiBiase	.40	1.00
14 Cody Rhodes	.15	.40
15 Hardcore Holly	.25	.60
16 JBL	.25	.60
17 Michael Cole	.15	.40
18 Rey Mysterio	.40	1.00
19 Batista	.60	1.50
20 Chuck Palumbo	.25	.60
21 Jamie Noble	.15	.40
22 CM Punk	.25	.60
23 Kofi Kingston	.15	.40
24 Kane	.60	1.50
25 Triple H	1.00	2.50
26 Brian Kendrick	.25	.60
27 Undertaker	.75	2.00
28 Jeff Hardy	.60	1.50
29 Umaga	.25	.60
30 Jim Ross	.15	.40
31 Edge	.60	1.50
32 Big Show	.40	1.00
33 Kenny Dykstra	.25	.60
34 Jimmy Wang Yang	.15	.40
35 Zack Ryder	.15	.40
36 Curt Hawkins	.15	.40
37 Deuce	.15	.40
38 Kung Fu Naki	.15	.40
39 R-Truth	.15	.40
40 MVP	.25	.60
41 Vladimir Kozlov	.25	.60
42 Primo	.15	.40
43 Jesse	.15	.40
44 Festus	.15	.40
45 Tazz	.15	.40
46 Shelton Benjamin	.15	.40
47 Elijah Burke	.15	.40
48 Hornswoggle	.25	.60
49 Tommy Dreamer	.15	.40
50 Mike Knox	.15	.40
51 Evan Bourne	.15	.40
52 Matt Striker	.15	.40
53 Matt Hardy	.60	1.50
54 John Morrison	.25	.60
55 Chavo Guerrero	.25	.60
56 Candice	.75	2.00
57 Jillian	.60	1.50
58 Maria	.60	1.50
59 Melina	.60	1.50
60 Michelle McCool	.60	1.50
61 Eve	.60	1.50
62 Kelly Kelly	.60	1.50
63 Victoria	.60	1.50

2009 Topps WWE Chipz Foil

COMPLETE SET (17)	10.00	20.00
STATED ODDS 1:2		
1 Randy Orton	.50	1.25
2 Shawn Michaels	1.25	3.00
3 Mr. Kennedy	.50	1.25
4 Carlito	.50	1.25
5 Shad	.20	.50
6 Chris Jericho	.50	1.25
7 The Great Khali	.20	.50
8 Matt Hardy	.75	2.00
9 MVP	.30	.75
10 Hurricane Helms	.20	.50
11 Mark Henry	.30	.75
12 Finlay	.30	.75
13 John Morrison	.30	.75
14 Boogeyman	.30	.75
15 The Miz	.30	.75
16 Beth Phoenix	1.00	2.50
17 Mickie James	1.00	2.50

2009 Topps WWE Chipz Silver

SILVER STATED ODDS 1:24		
GOLD STATED ODDS 1:72		
1 Shawn Michaels	12.00	30.00
2 Rey Mysterio	10.00	25.00
3 CM Punk	8.00	20.00
4 Kane	10.00	25.00
5 Triple H	10.00	25.00
6 Batista	10.00	25.00
7 Jeff Hardy	10.00	25.00
8 Edge	8.00	20.00
9 Randy Orton	10.00	25.00
10 John Cena GOLD	10.00	25.00

2011 Topps WWE Classic

COMPLETE SET (90)	8.00	20.00
UNOPENED BOX (24 PACKS)		
UNOPENED PACK (8 CARDS)		
*GOLD: 4X TO 10X BASIC CARDS		
1 AJ	.75	2.00
2 Alberto Del Rio	.40	1.00
3 Alex Riley	.15	.40
4 Alicia Fox	.25	.60
5 Batista	.25	.60
6 Beth Phoenix	.40	1.00
7 Big Show	.40	1.00
8 Booker T	.25	.60
9 Brie Bella	.60	1.50
10 Brodus Clay	.15	.40
11 Christian	.15	.40
12 CM Punk	.40	1.00
13 Cody Rhodes	.15	.40
14 Curt Hawkins	.15	.40
15 Daniel Bryan	.15	.40
16 David Otunga	.15	.40
17 Dolph Ziggler	.25	.60
18 Drew McIntyre	.15	.40
19 Eden Stiles	.60	1.50
20 Edge	.60	1.50
21 Evan Bourne	.15	.40
22 Eve	.60	1.50
23 Ezekiel Jackson	.25	.60
24 Goldust	.15	.40
25 Heath Slater	.15	.40
26 Hornswoggle	.25	.60
27 Jack Swagger	.25	.60
28 Jerry The King Lawler	.40	1.00
29 Jey Uso	.15	.40
30 Jim Ross	.15	.40
31 Jimmy Uso	.15	.40
32 Jinder Mahal	.25	.60
33 John Cena	.75	2.00
34 John Morrison	.25	.60
35 Johnny Curtis	.15	.40
36 JTG	.15	.40
37 Justin Gabriel	.15	.40
38 Kaitlyn	.40	1.00

117

39	Kane	.40	1.00
40	Kelly Kelly	.60	1.50
41	Kofi Kingston	.15	.40
42	Layla	.40	1.00
43	Mark Henry	.25	.60
44	Mason Ryan	.15	.40
45	Matt Striker	.15	.40
46	Michael Cole	.15	.40
47	Michael McGillicutty	.15	.40
48	The Miz	.25	.60
49	Natalya	.60	1.50
50	Nikki Bella	.60	1.50
51	Percy Watson	.15	.40
52	Primo	.15	.40
53	R-Truth	.15	.40
54	Randy Orton	.60	1.50
55	Rey Mysterio	.40	1.00
56	Ricardo Rodriguez	.15	.40
57	The Rock	.75	2.00
58	Rosa Mendes	.25	.60
59	Santino Marella	.25	.60
60	Shawn Michaels	.60	1.50
61	Sheamus	.25	.60
62	Sin Cara	.40	1.00
63	Stone Cold Steve Austin	.60	1.50
64	Tamina	.15	.40
65	Ted DiBiase	.25	.60
66	Theodore Long	.15	.40
67	Trent Barreta	.15	.40
68	Triple H	.75	2.00
69	Trish Stratus	.75	2.00
70	Tyler Reks	.15	.40
71	Tyson Kidd	.15	.40
72	Undertaker	.60	1.50
73	Vickie Guerrero	.25	.60
74	Wade Barrett	.15	.40
75	William Regal	.25	.60
76	Yoshi Tatsu	.15	.40
77	Zack Ryder	.15	.40
78	The American Dream Dusty Rhodes	.25	.60
79	Arn Anderson	.25	.60
80	Big Boss Man	.25	.60
81	Bobby The Brain Heenan	.25	.60
82	Diesel	.25	.60
83	Jimmy Superfly Snuka	.40	1.00
84	Junkyard Dog	.40	1.00
85	Michael PS Hayes	.15	.40
86	Ricky The Dragon Steamboat	.40	1.00
87	The Road Warriors	.40	1.00
88	Rowdy Roddy Piper	.60	1.50
89	Sgt. Slaughter	.40	1.00
90	Yokozuna	.25	.60

2011 Topps WWE Classic Autographs

STATED ODDS 1:24 HOBBY; 1:153 RETAIL

NNO	AJ	75.00	150.00
NNO	CM Punk	15.00	40.00
NNO	Daniel Bryan	15.00	40.00
NNO	Dolph Ziggler	8.00	20.00
NNO	Hornswoggle	8.00	20.00
NNO	Jack Swagger	8.00	20.00
NNO	Jinder Mahal	15.00	40.00
NNO	Johnny Curtis	8.00	20.00
NNO	Justin Gabriel	8.00	20.00
NNO	Mason Ryan	8.00	20.00
NNO	Rey Mysterio	20.00	50.00
NNO	R-Truth	10.00	25.00
NNO	Santino Marella	8.00	20.00
NNO	Sheamus	12.00	30.00
NNO	Wade Barrett	8.00	20.00
NNO	Zack Ryder	8.00	20.00

2011 Topps WWE Classic Relics

STATED ODDS 1:24 HOBBY; 1:48 RETAIL

NNO	Alberto Del Rio	5.00	12.00
NNO	Christian	5.00	12.00
NNO	CM Punk	8.00	20.00
NNO	Daniel Bryan	5.00	12.00
NNO	Dolph Ziggler	6.00	15.00
NNO	Drew McIntyre	5.00	12.00
NNO	Hornswoggle	5.00	12.00
NNO	Jack Swagger	5.00	12.00
NNO	Kofi Kingston	5.00	12.00
NNO	The Miz	5.00	12.00
NNO	Santino Marella	8.00	20.00
NNO	Sheamus	5.00	12.00
NNO	Zack Ryder	6.00	15.00

2011 Topps WWE Classic Promo

P1 The Rock vs. John Cena
(WWE '12 People's Edition Exclusive)

2020 Topps WWE Countdown to WrestleMania

COMPLETE SET (20)

1	Hulk Hogan/Andre the Giant/207*	6.00	15.00
2	Hulk Hogan/Randy Savage/207*	5.00	12.00
3	Ultimate Warrior/Hulk Hogan/208*	6.00	15.00
4	Razor Ramon/170*	4.00	10.00
5	Shawn Michaels/Bret Hart/147*	5.00	12.00
6	Bret Hart/Steve Austin/149*	5.00	12.00
7	Stone Cold Steve Austin/164*	5.00	12.00
8	The Rock/172*	4.00	10.00
9	Brock Lesnar/132*		
10	Eddie Guerrero/134*		
11	Undertaker/123*	5.00	12.00
12	Undertaker/129*	4.00	10.00
13	John Cena/113*	4.00	10.00
14	Daniel Bryan/116*	4.00	10.00
15	Brock Lesnar/106*	8.00	20.00
16	Seth Rollins/116*	4.00	10.00
17	Charlotte Flair/183*	5.00	12.00
18	Kurt Angle & Ronda Rousey/194*	10.00	25.00
19	Becky Lynch/206*	8.00	20.00
20	Kofi Kingston/113*	4.00	10.00

2017 Topps WWE Daniel Bryan Tribute

COMPLETE SET (20) 8.00 20.00

1	Daniel Bryan	1.25	3.00
2	Daniel Bryan	1.25	3.00
3	Daniel Bryan	1.25	3.00
4	Daniel Bryan	1.25	3.00
5	Daniel Bryan	1.25	3.00
6	Daniel Bryan	1.25	3.00
7	Daniel Bryan	1.25	3.00
8	Daniel Bryan	1.25	3.00
9	Daniel Bryan	1.25	3.00
10	Daniel Bryan	1.25	3.00
11	Daniel Bryan	1.25	3.00
12	Daniel Bryan	1.25	3.00
13	Daniel Bryan	1.25	3.00
14	Daniel Bryan	1.25	3.00
15	Daniel Bryan	1.25	3.00
16	Daniel Bryan	1.25	3.00
17	Daniel Bryan	1.25	3.00
18	Daniel Bryan	1.25	3.00
19	Daniel Bryan	1.25	3.00
20	Daniel Bryan	1.25	3.00
21	Daniel Bryan	1.25	3.00
22	Daniel Bryan	1.25	3.00
23	Daniel Bryan	1.25	3.00
24	Daniel Bryan	1.25	3.00
25	Daniel Bryan	1.25	3.00
26	Daniel Bryan	1.25	3.00
27	Daniel Bryan	1.25	3.00
28	Daniel Bryan	1.25	3.00
29	Daniel Bryan	1.25	3.00
30	Daniel Bryan	1.25	3.00
31	Daniel Bryan	1.25	3.00
32	Daniel Bryan	1.25	3.00
33	Daniel Bryan	1.25	3.00
34	Daniel Bryan	1.25	3.00
35	Daniel Bryan	1.25	3.00
36	Daniel Bryan	1.25	3.00
37	Daniel Bryan	1.25	3.00
38	Daniel Bryan	1.25	3.00
39	Daniel Bryan	1.25	3.00
40	Daniel Bryan	1.25	3.00

2017 Topps WWE Daniel Bryan Tribute Autographs and Relics

NNO Daniel Bryan AU
NNO Daniel Bryan MEM
NNO Daniel Bryan AU MEM

2017 Topps WWE Daniel Bryan Tribute Topps Heritage WWE Autographs and Relics

RANDOMLY INSERTED INTO PACKS

1	Daniel Bryan AU	15.00	40.00
2	Daniel Bryan MEM		
3	Daniel Bryan AU MEM		

2017 Topps WWE Daniel Bryan Tribute Topps WWE Road to WrestleMania Autographs and Relics

NNO	Daniel Bryan AU	12.00	30.00
NNO	Daniel Bryan MEM		
NNO	Daniel Bryan AU MEM		

2017 Topps WWE Daniel Bryan Tribute Topps WWE Then Now Forever Autographs and Relics

NNO	Daniel Bryan AU	12.00	30.00
NNO	Daniel Bryan MEM	8.00	20.00
NNO	Daniel Bryan AU MEM		

2008 Topps WWE Decade of Decadence Ultimate Fan Edition DVD Memorabilia Promo

NNO Edge
Shirt

2016 Topps WWE Divas Revolution

COMPLETE SET (43) 15.00 40.00
*SILVER/50: 1X TO 2.5X BASIC CARDS
*PINK/25: 2.5X TO 6X BASIC CARDS
*GOLD/10: 4X TO 10X BASIC CARDS
*RED/1: UNPRICED DUE TO SCARCITY

1	Wendi Richter	.25	.60
2	Miss Elizabeth	.25	.60
3	Sensational Sherri	.40	1.00
4	Alundra Blayze	.30	.75
5	Ivory	.25	.60
6	Lita	.75	2.00
7	Trish Stratus	1.25	3.00
8	Torrie Wilson	.60	1.50
9	Leilani Kai	.25	.60
10	Kelly Kelly	.40	1.00
11	Beth Phoenix	.40	1.00
12	Eve Torres	.50	1.25
13	Alexa Bliss	6.00	15.00
14	Alicia Fox	.40	1.00
15	Cathy Kelley	.25	.60
16	Becky Lynch	4.00	10.00
17	Brie Bella	.50	1.25
18	Carmella	.60	1.50
19	Charlotte	3.00	8.00
20	Dana Brooke	.60	1.50
21	Dasha Fuentes	.25	.60
22	Emma	.50	1.25
23	Eva Marie	.50	1.25
24	JoJo	.25	.60
25	Lana	1.00	2.50
26	Maryse	.50	1.25
27	Naomi	.40	1.00
28	Natalya	.40	1.00
29	Nia Jax	.40	1.00
30	Nikki Bella	.75	2.00
31	Renee Young	.60	1.50
32	Rosa Mendes	.25	.60
33	Sasha Banks	3.00	8.00
34	Stephanie McMahon	.40	1.00
35	Summer Rae	.60	1.50
36	Tamina	.30	.75
37	Aliyah	.30	.75
38	Asuka	2.50	6.00
39	Bayley	.60	1.50
40	Billie Kay	.60	1.50
41	Liv Morgan	.30	.75
42	Peyton Royce	.60	1.50
43	Mandy Rose	3.00	8.00

2016 Topps WWE Divas Revolution Autographs

*SILVER/50: .6X TO 1.5X BASIC AUTOS
*PINK/25: .75X TO 2X BASIC AUTOS
*GOLD/10: 1.2X TO 3X BASIC AUTOS
*RED/1: UNPRICED DUE TO SCARCITY
STATED ODDS 1:9

1	Wendi Richter	12.00	30.00
4	Alundra Blayze	10.00	25.00
6	Lita	15.00	40.00
7	Trish Stratus	20.00	50.00
8	Torrie Wilson	20.00	50.00
9	Leilani Kai	6.00	15.00
10	Kelly Kelly	15.00	40.00
11	Beth Phoenix	10.00	25.00
12	Eve Torres	20.00	50.00
13	Alexa Bliss	60.00	120.00
14	Alicia Fox	12.00	30.00
16	Becky Lynch	25.00	60.00
17	Brie Bella	12.00	30.00
18	Carmella	15.00	40.00
19	Charlotte	20.00	50.00
22	Emma	15.00	40.00
26	Maryse	12.00	30.00
27	Naomi	10.00	25.00
28	Natalya	12.00	30.00

30	Nikki Bella	15.00	40.00
32	Rosa Mendes	6.00	15.00
33	Sasha Banks	20.00	50.00
35	Summer Rae	10.00	25.00
36	Tamina	10.00	25.00
38	Asuka	15.00	40.00
43	Mandy Rose	50.00	100.00

2016 Topps WWE Divas Revolution Best Matches

COMPLETE SET (9)   6.00   15.00
*SILVER/50: .5X TO 1.5X BASIC CARDS
*PINK/25: X TO 2X BASIC CARDS
*GOLD/10: 1.2X TO 3X BASIC CARDS
*RED/1: UNPRICED DUE TO SCARCITY

1	Alundra Blayze/Bull Nakano	.60	1.50
2	Trish Stratus/Lita	2.50	6.00
3	Charlotte/Natalya	1.50	4.00
4	Stephanie McMahon/Brie Bella	.75	2.00
5	Charlotte/Sasha Banks	1.50	4.00
6	Sasha Banks/Becky Lynch	1.50	4.00
7	Bayley	1.25	3.00
8	Bayley/Sasha Banks	1.25	3.00
9	Asuka/Bayley	2.00	5.00

2016 Topps WWE Divas Revolution Diva Kiss

*GOLD/10: .75X TO 2X BASIC KISS
*RED/1: UNPRICED DUE TO SCARCITY
STATED ODDS 1:15

NNO	Alexa Bliss	60.00	120.00
NNO	Alicia Fox	12.00	30.00
NNO	Asuka	25.00	60.00
NNO	Becky Lynch	20.00	50.00
NNO	Billie Kay	25.00	60.00
NNO	Carmella	25.00	60.00
NNO	Charlotte	20.00	50.00
NNO	Dana Brooke	25.00	60.00
NNO	Emma	25.00	60.00
NNO	Mandy Rose	20.00	40.00
NNO	Maryse	20.00	50.00
NNO	Natalya	20.00	50.00
NNO	Nia Jax	12.00	30.00
NNO	Peyton Royce	12.00	30.00
NNO	Renee Young	20.00	50.00

2016 Topps WWE Divas Revolution Diva Kiss Autographs

*GOLD/10: .75X TO 2X BASIC AUTOS
*RED/1: UNPRICED DUE TO SCARCITY
STATED ODDS 1:56

NNO	Alexa Bliss	120.00	200.00
NNO	Alicia Fox	15.00	40.00
NNO	Asuka	40.00	100.00
NNO	Becky Lynch	60.00	120.00
NNO	Billie Kay	25.00	60.00
NNO	Carmella	60.00	120.00
NNO	Charlotte	60.00	120.00
NNO	Dana Brooke	25.00	60.00
NNO	Emma	25.00	60.00
NNO	Mandy Rose	25.00	60.00
NNO	Maryse	25.00	60.00
NNO	Natalya	15.00	40.00
NNO	Nia Jax	15.00	40.00
NNO	Peyton Royce	15.00	40.00
NNO	Renee Young	20.00	50.00

2016 Topps WWE Divas Revolution Historic Women's Champions

COMPLETE SET (10)   6.00   15.00
*SILVER/50: .75X TO 2X BASIC CARDS
*PINK/25: 2X TO 5X BASIC CARDS
*GOLD/10: 3X TO 8X BASIC CARDS
*RED/1: UNPRICED DUE TO SCARCITY

1	Alundra Blayze	.50	1.25
2	Lita	1.25	3.00
3	Trish Stratus	2.00	5.00
4	Maryse	.75	2.00
5	Eve Torres	.75	2.00
6	Nikki Bella	1.25	3.00
7	Charlotte	1.25	3.00
8	Charlotte	1.25	3.00
9	Bayley	1.00	2.50
10	Charlotte	1.25	3.00

2016 Topps WWE Divas Revolution Mat Relics

*SILVER/50: .5X TO 1.2X BASIC MEM
*PINK/25: .6X TO 1.5X BASIC MEM
*GOLD/10: .75X TO 2X BASIC MEM
*RED/1: UNPRICED DUE TO SCARCITY
STATED ODDS 1:8

NNO	Alexa Bliss Belfast	10.00	25.00
NNO	Alexa Bliss DMF	10.00	25.00
NNO	Alicia Fox Summerslam	3.00	8.00
NNO	Alicia Fox WrestleMania	3.00	8.00
NNO	Asuka Belfast	8.00	20.00
NNO	Asuka DMF	8.00	20.00
NNO	Bayley Takeover	5.00	12.00
NNO	Bayley DMF	5.00	12.00
NNO	Bayley Belfast	5.00	12.00
NNO	Becky Lynch SummerSlam	6.00	15.00
NNO	Becky Lynch NXT	6.00	15.00
NNO	Brie Bella SummerSlam	4.00	10.00
NNO	Brie Bella WrestleMania	4.00	10.00
NNO	Carmella Belfast	5.00	12.00
NNO	Carmella DMF	5.00	12.00
NNO	Charlotte SummerSlam	6.00	15.00
NNO	Charlotte NXT	6.00	15.00
NNO	Dana Brooke NXT	5.00	12.00
NNO	Emma WrestleMania	4.00	10.00
NNO	Emma NXT	4.00	10.00
NNO	Eve Torres WrestleMania	4.00	10.00
NNO	Naomi SummerSlam	3.00	8.00
NNO	Naomi WrestleMania	3.00	8.00
NNO	Naomi WrestleMania	3.00	8.00
NNO	Nia Jax Belfast	3.00	8.00
NNO	Nia Jax DMF	3.00	8.00
NNO	Nikki Bella MITB	6.00	15.00
NNO	Nikki Bella SummerSlam	6.00	15.00
NNO	Nikki Bella WrestleMania	6.00	15.00
NNO	Peyton Royce Belfast	5.00	12.00
NNO	Peyton Royce DMF	5.00	12.00
NNO	Rosa Mendes WrestleMania	2.00	5.00
NNO	Sasha Banks Takeover	6.00	15.00
NNO	Sasha Banks SummerSlam	6.00	15.00
NNO	Tamina SummerSlam	2.50	6.00

2016 Topps WWE Divas Revolution Power Couples

COMPLETE SET (10)   6.00   15.00
*RED/50: .75X TO 2X BASIC CARDS
*PINK/25: 1.2X TO 3X BASIC CARDS
*GOLD/10: 2X TO 5X BASIC CARDS

RANDOMLY INSERTED INTO PACKS

1	Miss Elizabeth/Randy Savage	1.00	2.50
2	Stephanie McMahon/HHH	1.50	4.00
3	Lita/Edge	1.25	3.00
4	Sensational Sherri/HBK	1.50	4.00
5	Trish Stratus/Christian	2.00	5.00
6	Brie Bella/Daniel Bryan	1.50	4.00
7	Queen Sherri/Randy Savage	1.00	2.50
8	Naomi/Jimmy Uso	.60	1.50
9	Rusev/Lana	1.50	4.00
10	Lita/Kane	1.25	3.00

2016 Topps WWE Divas Revolution The Revolution

COMPLETE SET (4)   4.00   10.00
*SILVER/50: .75X TO 2X BASIC CARDS
*PINK/25: 1.2X TO 3X BASIC CARDS
*GOLD/10: 1.5X TO 4X BASIC CARDS
*RED/1: UNPRICED DUE TO SCARCITY

1	Charlotte	1.50	4.00
2	Team PCB	1.25	3.00
3	Charlotte	1.50	4.00
4	Charlotte	1.50	4.00

2016 Topps WWE Divas Revolution Rivalries

COMPLETE SET (8)   5.00   12.00
*SILVER/50: 1X TO 2.5X BASIC CARDS
*PINK/25: 1.2X TO 3X BASIC CARDS
*GOLD/10: 1.5X TO 4X BASIC CARDS
*RED//1: UNPRICED DUE TO SCARCITY
RANDOMLY INSERTED INTO PACKS

1	Trish Stratus/Lita	2.00	5.00
2	Trish Stratus/Stephanie McMahon	2.00	5.00
3	Bayley/Sasha Banks	1.25	3.00
4	Charlotte/Sasha Banks	1.25	3.00
5	Charlotte/Nikki Bella	1.25	3.00
6	Becky Lynch/Charlotte	1.25	3.00
7	Brie Bella/Nikki Bella	1.25	3.00
8	Miss Elizabeth	.60	1.50
	Sensational Sherri		

2016 Topps WWE Divas Revolution Shirt Relics

*SILVER/50: .5X TO 1.2X BASIC MEM
*PINK/25: .6X TO 1.5X BASIC MEM
*GOLD/10: UNPRICED DUE TO SCARCITY
*RED/1: UNPRICED DUE TO SCARCITY

NNO	Alexa Bliss	12.00	30.00
NNO	Alicia Fox	4.00	10.00
NNO	Asuka	10.00	25.00
NNO	Becky Lynch	8.00	20.00
NNO	Brie Bella	5.00	12.00
NNO	Carmella	6.00	15.00
NNO	Charlotte	8.00	20.00
NNO	JoJo	2.50	6.00
NNO	Lana	10.00	25.00
NNO	Naomi	4.00	10.00
NNO	Natalya	4.00	10.00
NNO	Renee Young	6.00	15.00
NNO	Sasha Banks	8.00	20.00
NNO	Summer Rae	6.00	15.00
NNO	Tamina	3.00	8.00

2007 Topps WWE Dog Tags

COMPLETE SET (24)   40.00   80.00
UNOPENED BOX (24 PACKS)

UNOPENED PACK (1 TAG+1 CARD)
*GOLD: 1X TO 2.5X BASIC TAGS

1	John Cena	4.00	10.00
2	Batista	2.50	6.00
3	Johnny Nitro	1.00	2.50
4	Carlito	2.50	6.00
5	Ric Flair	2.50	6.00
6	Undertaker	3.00	8.00
7	Chris Benoit	1.50	4.00
8	CM Punk	1.00	2.50
9	Booker T	2.50	6.00
10	Rob Van Dam	2.50	6.00
11	Ken Kennedy	1.50	4.00
12	Shawn Michaels	4.00	10.00
13	The Rock	5.00	12.00
14	Jeff Hardy	1.50	4.00
15	Stone Cold Steve Austin	4.00	10.00
16	Edge	2.50	6.00
17	Rey Mysterio	1.50	4.00
18	Kane	2.50	6.00
19	Randy Orton	2.50	6.00
20	Triple H	4.00	10.00
21	Sabu	.60	1.50
22	Umaga	1.00	2.50
23	Sandman	1.00	2.50
24	Bobby Lashley	2.50	6.00

2007 Topps WWE Dog Tags Trading Cards

COMPLETE SET (25)   15.00   40.00

1	John Cena	2.00	5.00
2	Batista	1.25	3.00
3	Johnny Nitro	.50	1.25
4	Carlito	1.25	3.00
5	Ric Flair	1.25	3.00
6	Undertaker	1.50	4.00
7	Chris Benoit	.75	2.00
8	CM Punk	.50	1.25
9	Booker T	1.25	3.00
10	Rob Van Dam	1.25	3.00
11	Ken Kennedy	.75	2.00
12	Shawn Michaels	2.00	5.00
13	The Rock	2.50	6.00
14	Jeff Hardy	.75	2.00
15	Stone Cold Steve Austin	2.00	5.00
16	Edge	1.25	3.00
17	Rey Mysterio	.75	2.00
18	Kane	1.25	3.00
19	Randy Orton	1.25	3.00
20	Triple H	2.00	5.00
21	Sabu	.30	.75
22	Umaga	.50	1.25
23	Sandman	.50	1.25
24	Bobby Lashley	1.25	3.00
NNO	Checklist	.30	.75

2015 Topps WWE Dog Tags

COMPLETE SET (30)   15.00   40.00

1	AJ Lee	1.50	4.00
2	Bad News Barrett	.30	.75
3	Batista	.75	2.00
4	Big Show	.75	2.00
5	Bray Wyatt	1.25	3.00
6	Brock Lesnar	1.25	3.00
7	Cesaro	.30	.75
8	Chris Jericho	.75	2.00
9	Daniel Bryan	1.25	3.00

10	Dean Ambrose	.75	2.00
11	Dolph Ziggler	.50	1.25
12	Edge	.75	2.00
13	Hulk Hogan	1.50	4.00
14	Jake The Snake Roberts	.50	1.25
15	John Cena	1.50	4.00
16	Kane	.75	2.00
17	Kofi Kingston	.30	.75
18	Randy Orton	1.25	3.00
19	Rey Mysterio	.75	2.00
20	Ric Flair	1.50	4.00
21	Rob Van Dam	.75	2.00
22	The Rock	1.50	4.00
23	Roman Reigns	.75	2.00
24	Seth Rollins	.50	1.25
25	Shawn Michaels	1.25	3.00
26	Sheamus	.75	2.00
27	Stone Cold Steve Austin	1.50	4.00
28	Triple H	1.25	3.00
29	Ultimate Warrior	1.00	2.50
30	Undertaker	1.25	3.00

2015 Topps WWE Dog Tags Trading Cards

COMPLETE SET (30)		8.00	20.00
STATED ODDS 1:1			
1	AJ Lee	.75	2.00
2	Bad News Barrett	.15	.40
3	Batista	.40	1.00
4	Big Show	.40	1.00
5	Bray Wyatt	.60	1.50
6	Brock Lesnar	.60	1.50
7	Cesaro	.15	.40
8	Chris Jericho	.40	1.00
9	Daniel Bryan	.60	1.50
10	Dean Ambrose	.40	1.00
11	Dolph Ziggler	.25	.60
12	Edge	.40	1.00
13	Hulk Hogan	.75	2.00
14	Jake The Snake Roberts	.25	.60
15	John Cena	.75	2.00
16	Kane	.40	1.00
17	Kofi Kingston	.15	.40
18	Randy Orton	.60	1.50
19	Rey Mysterio	.40	1.00
20	Ric Flair	.75	2.00
21	Rob Van Dam	.40	1.00
22	The Rock	.75	2.00
23	Roman Reigns	.40	1.00
24	Seth Rollins	.25	.60
25	Shawn Michaels	.60	1.50
26	Sheamus	.40	1.00
27	Stone Cold Steve Austin	.75	2.00
28	Triple H	.60	1.50
29	Ultimate Warrior	.50	1.25
30	Undertaker	.60	1.50

2015 Topps WWE Dog Tags Relic Tags

1	Bad News Barrett
2	Big Show
3	Bray Wyatt
4	Cesaro
5	Chris Jericho
6	Daniel Bryan
7	Dolph Ziggler
8	Edge
9	Hulk Hogan

10	Kofi Kingston		
11	John Cena		
12	Randy Orton		
13	Rey Mysterio		
14	Rob Van Dam		
15	Roman Reigns		
16	Seth Rollins		

2010 Topps WWE Dog Tags Pyrotechno Edition

COMPLETE SET (24)		12.00	30.00
UNOPENED BOX (24 PACKS)			
UNOPENED PACK (1 TAG+1 CARD)			
*GOLD: .75X TO 2X BASIC TAGS			
1	John Cena	2.50	6.00
2	Kofi Kingston	.75	2.00
3	Big Show	1.25	3.00
4	Cody Rhodes	.50	1.25
5	Ted DiBiase	.75	2.00
6	Santino Marella	.50	1.25
7	The Miz	.75	2.00
8	Triple H	2.50	6.00
9	Shawn Michaels	3.00	8.00
10	CM Punk	2.00	5.00
11	John Morrison	.75	2.00
12	Chris Jericho	1.25	3.00
13	Matt Hardy	1.25	3.00
14	Christian	.75	2.00
15	Tommy Dreamer	.50	1.25
16	Undertaker	2.00	5.00
17	Yoshi Tatsu	.50	1.25
18	Sheamus	.75	2.00
19	Finlay	.75	2.00
20	Hornswoggle	.75	2.00
21	Edge	2.00	5.00
22	Batista	2.00	5.00
23	Evan Bourne	.50	1.25
24	Randy Orton	2.00	5.00

2010 Topps WWE Dog Tags Pyrotechno Edition Trading Cards

COMPLETE SET (24)		10.00	25.00
1	John Cena	2.00	5.00
2	Kofi Kingston	.60	1.50
3	Big Show	1.00	2.50
4	Cody Rhodes	.40	1.00
5	Ted DiBiase	.60	1.50
6	Santino Marella	.40	1.00
7	The Miz	.60	1.50
8	Triple H	2.00	5.00
9	Shawn Michaels	2.50	6.00
10	CM Punk	1.50	4.00
11	John Morrison	.60	1.50
12	Chris Jericho	1.00	2.50
13	Matt Hardy	1.00	2.50
14	Christian	.60	1.50
15	Tommy Dreamer	.40	1.00
16	Undertaker	1.50	4.00
17	Yoshi Tatsu	.40	1.00
18	Sheamus	.60	1.50
19	Finlay	.60	1.50
20	Hornswoggle	.60	1.50
21	Edge	1.50	4.00
22	Batista	1.50	4.00
23	Evan Bourne	.40	1.00
24	Randy Orton	1.50	4.00

2011 Topps WWE Dog Tags Ringside Relic Edition

COMPLETE SET (24)		10.00	20.00
UNOPENED BOX (24 PACKS)			
UNOPENED PACK (1 TAG+1 CARD)			
1	CM Punk	1.00	2.50
2	Daniel Bryan	.40	1.00
3	David Otunga	.40	1.00
4	John Cena	2.00	5.00
5	John Morrison	.60	1.50
6	Justin Gabriel	.40	1.00
7	Ezekiel Jackson	.60	1.50
8	Randy Orton	1.50	4.00
9	Sheamus	.60	1.50
10	The Miz	.60	1.50
11	Wade Barrett	.40	1.00
12	Heath Slater	.40	1.00
13	Dolph Ziggler	.60	1.50
14	Edge	1.50	4.00
15	Kane	1.00	2.50
16	Undertaker	1.50	4.00
17	Alberto Del Rio	1.00	2.50
18	Jack Swagger	.60	1.50
19	Tyler Reks	.40	1.00
20	Drew McIntyre	.40	1.00
21	Rey Mysterio	1.00	2.50
22	Kaval	1.00	2.50
23	Kofi Kingston	.40	1.00
24	Big Show	1.00	2.50

2011 Topps WWE Dog Tags Ringside Relic Edition Memorabilia Tags

STATED ODDS 1:24			
1	Hornswoggle	2.50	6.00
2	Sheamus	2.50	6.00
3	Kofi Kingston	2.50	6.00
4	Edge	6.00	15.00
5	Jack Swagger	2.50	6.00
6	Justin Gabriel	2.50	6.00
7	David Hart Smith	2.50	6.00
8	The Miz	2.50	6.00
9	John Cena	8.00	20.00
10	Randy Orton	6.00	15.00
11	Alex Riley	2.50	6.00
12	Heath Slater	2.50	6.00
13	Wade Barrett	2.50	6.00
14	John Morrison	2.50	6.00
15	David Otunga	2.50	6.00
16	Tyson Kidd	2.50	6.00
17	Rey Mysterio	4.00	10.00
18	Big Show	4.00	10.00

2011 Topps WWE Dog Tags Ringside Relic Edition Trading Cards

COMPLETE SET (24)		4.00	10.00
1	CM Punk	.40	1.00
2	Daniel Bryan	.15	.40
3	David Otunga	.15	.40
4	John Cena	.75	2.00
5	John Morrison	.25	.60
6	Justin Gabriel	.15	.40
7	Ezekiel Jackson	.25	.60
8	Randy Orton	.60	1.50
9	Sheamus	.25	.60
10	The Miz	.25	.60
11	Wade Barrett	.15	.40
12	Heath Slater	.15	.40

13	Dolph Ziggler	.25	.60
14	Edge	.60	1.50
15	Kane	.40	1.00
16	Undertaker	.60	1.50
17	Alberto Del Rio	.40	1.00
18	Jack Swagger	.25	.60
19	Tyler Reks	.15	.40
20	Drew McIntyre	.15	.40
21	Rey Mysterio	.40	1.00
22	Kaval	.40	1.00
23	Kofi Kingston	.15	.40
24	Big Show	.40	1.00

2011 Topps WWE Dog Tags Ringside Relic Edition Silver Insert Cards

COMPLETE SET (18)		4.00	10.00
STATED ODDS 1:24			
1	Hornswoggle	.40	1.00
2	Sheamus	.40	1.00
3	Kofi Kingston	.25	.60
4	Edge	1.00	2.50
5	Jack Swagger	.40	1.00
6	Justin Gabriel	.25	.60
7	David Hart Smith	.25	.60
8	The Miz	.40	1.00
9	John Cena	1.25	3.00
10	Randy Orton	1.00	2.50
11	Alex Riley	.25	.60
12	Heath Slater	.25	.60
13	Wade Barrett	.25	.60
14	John Morrison	.40	1.00
15	David Otunga	.25	.60
16	Tyson Kidd	.25	.60
17	Rey Mysterio	.60	1.50
18	Big Show	.60	1.50

2012 Topps WWE Dog Tags Ringside Relic Edition

COMPLETE SET (24)		15.00	40.00
UNOPENED BOX (24 PACKS)			
UNOPENED PACK (1 TAG+1 CARD)			
STATED ODDS 1:1			
1	CM Punk	2.50	6.00
2	Ted Dibiase	1.00	2.50
3	Sheamus	1.50	4.00
4	David Otunga	.60	1.50
5	The Miz	1.00	2.50
6	Jack Swagger	1.00	2.50
7	R-Truth	.60	1.50
8	Heath Slater	.60	1.50
9	Christian	.60	1.50
10	John Cena	3.00	8.00
11	Zack Ryder	.60	1.50
12	Daniel Bryan	.60	1.50
13	Hornswoggle	1.00	2.50
14	Rey Mysterio	1.50	4.00
15	Dolph Ziggler	1.00	2.50
16	Kofi Kingston	.60	1.50
17	Evan Bourne	.60	1.50
18	Santino Marella	1.00	2.50
19	Triple H	2.50	6.00
20	Sin Cara	1.50	4.00
21	The Miz	1.00	2.50
22	Stone Cold Steve Austin	3.00	8.00
23	Undertaker	2.50	6.00
24	Randy Orton	2.50	6.00

2012 Topps WWE Dog Tags Ringside Relic Edition Memorabilia Tags

STATED ODDS 1:24

1 CM Punk	6.00	15.00
2 Ted Dibiase	2.50	6.00
3 Sheamus	4.00	10.00
4 David Otunga	1.50	4.00
5 The Miz	2.50	6.00
6 Jack Swagger	2.50	6.00
7 R-Truth	1.50	4.00
8 Heath Slater	1.50	4.00
9 Christian	1.50	4.00
10 John Cena	8.00	20.00
11 Zack Ryder	1.50	4.00
12 Daniel Bryan	1.50	4.00
13 Hornswoggle	2.50	6.00
14 Rey Mysterio	4.00	10.00
15 Dolph Ziggler	2.50	6.00
16 Kofi Kingston	1.50	4.00
17 Evan Bourne	1.50	4.00

2012 Topps WWE Dog Tags Ringside Relic Edition Trading Cards

COMPLETE SET (24)	5.00	12.00
1 CM Punk	1.00	2.50
2 Ted Dibiase	.40	1.00
3 Sheamus	.60	1.50
4 David Otunga	.25	.60
5 The Miz	.40	1.00
6 Jack Swagger	.40	1.00
7 R-Truth	.25	.60
8 Heath Slater	.25	.60
9 Christian	.25	.60
10 John Cena	1.25	3.00
11 Zack Ryder	.25	.60
12 Daniel Bryan	.25	.60
13 Hornswoggle	.40	1.00
14 Rey Mysterio	.60	1.50
15 Dolph Ziggler	.40	1.00
16 Kofi Kingston	.25	.60
17 Evan Bourne	.25	.60
18 Santino Marella	.40	1.00
19 Triple H	1.00	2.50
20 Sin Cara	.60	1.50
21 The Miz	.40	1.00
22 Stone Cold Steve Austin	1.25	3.00
23 Undertaker	1.00	2.50
24 Randy Orton	1.00	2.50

2013 Topps WWE Dog Tags Signature Series

UNOPENED BOX (24 PACKS)		
UNOPENED PACK (1 TAG+1 CARD)		
STATED ODDS 1:1		
1 John Cena	3.00	8.00
2 CM Punk	2.50	6.00
3 Ryback	.60	1.50
4 Sheamus	1.25	3.00
5 Big Show	1.25	3.00
6 Randy Orton	2.00	5.00
7 Alberto Del Rio	1.25	3.00
8 Christian	.60	1.50
9 Cody Rhodes	.60	1.50
10 Rey Mysterio	1.50	4.00
11 Sin Cara	1.00	2.50
12 Dolph Ziggler	1.00	2.50
13 Zack Ryder	.60	1.50

14 Santino	.60	1.50
15 Triple H	2.50	6.00
16 Undertaker	2.50	6.00
17 Kane	1.25	3.00
18 Daniel Bryan	1.50	4.00
19 The Miz	1.00	2.50
20 Kofi Kingston	.60	1.50
21 R-Truth	.60	1.50
22 Brodus Clay	.60	1.50
23 Wade Barrett	.60	1.50
24 The Rock	3.00	8.00
25 Cactus Jack	2.50	6.00
26 Jerry King Lawler	1.25	3.00
27 Shawn Michaels	2.50	6.00
28 Kevin Nash	.75	2.00
29 Booker T	1.00	2.50
30 Stone Cold Steve Austin	2.50	6.00

2013 Topps WWE Dog Tags Signature Series Autographed Tags

STATED ODDS 1:107

NNO AJ Lee	75.00	150.00
NNO Aksana	6.00	15.00
NNO Booker T	12.00	30.00
NNO Brodus Clay	6.00	15.00
NNO Daniel Bryan	15.00	40.00
NNO Kane	12.00	30.00
NNO Layla	6.00	15.00
NNO Natalya	10.00	25.00
NNO Tamina	6.00	15.00
NNO Zack Ryder	6.00	15.00

2013 Topps WWE Dog Tags Signature Series Divas Trading Cards

COMPLETE SET (5)		
STATED ODDS 1:107		
1 AJ Lee	15.00	40.00
2 Aksana	5.00	12.00
3 Layla	6.00	15.00
4 Natalya	6.00	15.00
5 Tamina	4.00	10.00

2013 Topps WWE Dog Tags Signature Series Memorabilia Tags

STATED ODDS 1:24

NNO Alberto Del Rio	3.00	8.00
NNO Brodus Clay	1.50	4.00
NNO CM Punk	6.00	15.00
NNO Cody Rhodes	1.50	4.00
NNO Daniel Bryan	4.00	10.00
NNO Dolph Ziggler	2.50	6.00
NNO John Cena	8.00	20.00
NNO Kofi Kingston	1.50	4.00
NNO The Miz	2.50	6.00
NNO Rey Mysterio	4.00	10.00
NNO R-Truth	1.50	4.00
NNO Ryback	1.50	4.00
NNO Santino	1.50	4.00
NNO Shawn Michaels	6.00	15.00
NNO Sheamus	3.00	8.00
NNO Sin Cara	2.50	6.00
NNO Wade Barrett	1.50	4.00
NNO Zack Ryder	1.50	4.00

2013 Topps WWE Dog Tags Signature Series Trading Cards

COMPLETE SET (30)	6.00	15.00
1 John Cena	1.25	3.00
2 CM Punk	1.00	2.50
3 Ryback	.25	.60
4 Sheamus	.50	1.25
5 Big Show	.50	1.25
6 Randy Orton	.75	2.00
7 Alberto Del Rio	.50	1.25
8 Christian	.25	.60
9 Cody Rhodes	.25	.60
10 Rey Mysterio	.60	1.50
11 Sin Cara	.40	1.00
12 Dolph Ziggler	.40	1.00
13 Zack Ryder	.25	.60
14 Santino	.25	.60
15 Triple H	1.00	2.50
16 Undertaker	1.00	2.50
17 Kane	.50	1.25
18 Daniel Bryan	.60	1.50
19 The Miz	.40	1.00
20 Kofi Kingston	.25	.60
21 R-Truth	.25	.60
22 Brodus Clay	.25	.60
23 Wade Barrett	.25	.60
24 The Rock	1.25	3.00
25 Cactus Jack	1.00	2.50
26 Jerry King Lawler	.50	1.25
27 Shawn Michaels	1.00	2.50
28 Kevin Nash	.30	.75
29 Booker T	.40	1.00
30 Stone Cold Steve Austin	1.00	2.50

2007 Topps WWE Dog Tags UK

COMPLETE SET (21)	25.00	60.00
UNOPENED BOX (24 PACKS)		
UNOPENED PACK (1 TAG+1 CARD)		
*GOLD: 1X TO 2.5X BASIC TAGS		
1 John Cena	4.00	10.00
2 Batista	2.50	6.00
3 Johnny Nitro	1.00	2.50
4 Carlito	2.50	6.00
5 Ric Flair	2.50	6.00
6 Undertaker	3.00	8.00
7 CM Punk	1.00	2.50
8 Booker T	2.50	6.00
9 Ken Kennedy	1.50	4.00
10 Shawn Michaels	4.00	10.00
11 The Rock	5.00	12.00
12 Jeff Hardy	1.50	4.00
13 Stone Cold Steve Austin	4.00	10.00
14 Edge	2.50	6.00
15 Rey Mysterio	1.50	4.00
16 Kane	2.50	6.00
17 Randy Orton	2.50	6.00
18 Triple H	4.00	10.00
19 Umaga	1.00	2.50
20 Sandman	1.00	2.50
21 Bobby Lashley	2.50	6.00

2007 Topps WWE Dog Tags UK Trading Cards

COMPLETE SET (21)	12.00	30.00
1 John Cena	2.00	5.00
2 Batista	1.25	3.00
3 Johnny Nitro	.50	1.25

4 Carlito	1.25	3.00
5 Ric Flair	1.25	3.00
6 Undertaker	1.50	4.00
7 CM Punk	.50	1.25
8 Booker T	1.25	3.00
9 Ken Kennedy	.75	2.00
10 Shawn Michaels	2.00	5.00
11 The Rock	2.50	6.00
12 Jeff Hardy	.75	2.00
13 Stone Cold Steve Austin	2.00	5.00
14 Edge	1.25	3.00
15 Rey Mysterio	.75	2.00
16 Kane	1.25	3.00
17 Randy Orton	1.25	3.00
18 Triple H	2.00	5.00
19 Umaga	.50	1.25
20 Sandman	.50	1.25
21 Bobby Lashley	1.25	3.00
CL Checklist	.30	.75

2007 Topps WWE Face-Off

COMPLETE SET (132)	20.00	50.00
1 Bobby Lashley	1.25	3.00
2 Armando Estrada	.30	.75
3 Brian Kendrick	.50	1.25
4 Carlito	1.25	3.00
5 Charlie Haas	.30	.75
6 Daivari	.30	.75
7 Jim Duggan	.50	1.25
8 Jeff Hardy	.75	2.00
9 Jerry Lawler	.75	2.00
10 Jim Ross	.40	1.00
11 John Cena	2.00	5.00
12 Jonathan Coachman	.30	.75
13 JTG	.30	.75
14 King Booker	1.25	3.00
15 Lance Cade	.30	.75
16 Mr. Kennedy	.75	2.00
17 Paul London	.75	2.00
18 Randy Orton	1.25	3.00
19 Robbie McAllister	.30	.75
20 Rory McAllister	.30	.75
21 Roddy Piper	1.25	3.00
22 Sandman	.50	1.25
23 Santino Marella	.40	1.00
24 Shad	.30	.75
25 Shane McMahon	.75	2.00
26 Shawn Michaels	2.00	5.00
27 Shelton Benjamin	.30	.75
28 Snitsky	.50	1.25
29 Stone Cold	2.00	5.00
30 Super Crazy	.50	1.25
31 Todd Grisham	.30	.75
32 Trevor Murdoch	.30	.75
33 Triple H	2.00	5.00
34 Umaga	.50	1.25
35 Val Venis	.75	2.00
36 William Regal	.75	2.00
37 Batista	1.25	3.00
38 Brett Major	.50	1.25
39 Brian Major	.30	.75
40 Chavo Guerrero	.50	1.25
41 Chris Masters	1.25	3.00
42 Dave Taylor	.30	.75
43 Deuce	.30	.75
44 Domino	.30	.75
45 Edge	1.25	3.00
46 Eugene	.30	.75

47	Finlay	.75	2.00
48	Funaki	.50	1.25
49	Gregory Helms	.30	.75
50	Hardcore Holly	.75	2.00
51	Hornswoggle	.40	1.00
52	Jamie Noble	.30	.75
53	JBL	.75	2.00
54	Jimmy Wang Yang	.30	.75
55	Kane	1.25	3.00
56	Kenny Dykstra	.50	1.25
57	Mark Henry	.50	1.25
58	Matt Hardy	.75	2.00
59	Michael Cole	.30	.75
60	MVP	.50	1.25
61	Rey Mysterio	.75	2.00
62	Ric Flair	1.25	3.00
63	Shannon Moore	.30	.75
64	The Great Khali	.50	1.25
65	Theodore Long	.40	1.00
66	Undertaker	1.50	4.00
67	Ashley	1.25	3.00
68	Candice	1.50	4.00
69	Cherry	.30	.75
70	Jillian	1.50	4.00
71	Kelly Kelly	.75	2.00
72	Maria	1.25	3.00
73	Melina	1.25	3.00
74	Michelle McCool	1.50	4.00
75	Mickie James	1.50	4.00
76	Queen Sharmell	.75	2.00
77	Torrie Wilson	2.50	6.00
78	Victoria	1.50	4.00
79	Balls Mahoney	.30	.75
80	Boogeyman	.50	1.25
81	CM Punk	.50	1.25
82	Elijah Burke	.30	.75
83	Joey Styles	.30	.75
84	John Morrison	.50	1.25
85	Kevin Thorn	.30	.75
86	Nunzio	.50	1.25
87	Marcus Cor Von	.30	.75
88	Matt Striker	.30	.75
89	Mike Knox	.30	.75
90	Stevie Richards	.50	1.25
91	Tazz	.50	1.25
92	The Miz	.60	1.50
93	Tommy Dreamer	.40	1.00
94	Big Daddy V	.30	.75
95	Kendrick / London	.75	2.00
96	Hass / Benjamin	.30	.75
97	Carlito / Masters	1.25	3.00
98	Cryme Tyme	.30	.75
99	Taylor / Regal	.75	2.00
100	Deuce / Domino	.30	.75
101	D-Generation X	1.00	2.50
102	Burke / Cor Von	.30	.75
103	Undertaker / Kane	1.50	4.00
104	Finlay / Hornswoggle	.75	2.00
105	Michaels / Cena	2.00	5.00
106	Cade / Murdoch	.30	.75
107	Kane / Boogeyman	1.25	3.00
108	Flair / Piper	1.25	3.00
109	Hardy Boys	.75	2.00
110	Highlanders	.50	1.25
111	Major Brothers	.50	1.25
112	Dusty / Cody Rhodes	.75	2.00
113	Candice / Victoria	1.50	4.00
114	Vince / Shane McMahon	1.25	3.00
115	Junkyard Dog	.60	1.50
116	British Bulldog	1.25	3.00
117	Bushwhacker Butch	.50	1.25
118	Bushwhacker Luke	.50	1.25
119	Curt Hennig	.50	1.25
120	Doink the Clown	.30	.75
121	Dusty Rhodes	.75	2.00
122	Jake Roberts	.75	2.00
123	Jimmy Snuka	.50	1.25
124	Ted Dibiase	.60	1.50
125	Nikolai Volkoff	.60	1.50
126	Paul Bearer	.50	1.25
127	Sgt. Slaughter	.75	2.00
128	Billy Graham	.50	1.25
129	Terry Funk	.30	.75
130	Bobby Heenan	.60	1.50
131	Checklist 1 CL		
132	Checklist 2 CL		.75

2007 Topps WWE Face-Off Royal Rumble Champions

COMPLETE SET (10)		12.00	30.00

RANDOMLY INSERTED INTO PACKS

R1	Batista	2.00	5.00
R2	Triple H	3.00	8.00
R3	The Rock	4.00	10.00
R4	Jim Duggan	.75	2.00
R5	Rey Mysterio	1.25	3.00
R6	Ric Flair	2.00	5.00
R7	Shawn Michaels	3.00	8.00
R8	Stone Cold Steve Austin	3.00	8.00
R9	Undertaker	2.50	6.00
R10	Mr. McMahon	2.00	5.00

2007 Topps WWE Face-Off Superstar Foil

COMPLETE SET (22)		12.00	30.00

RANDOMLY INSERTED INTO PACKS

S1	Bobby Lashley	1.50	4.00
S2	Boogeyman	.60	1.50
S3	Carlito	1.50	4.00
S4	Chavo Guerrero	.60	1.50
S5	Chris Masters	1.50	4.00
S6	CM Punk	.60	1.50
S7	Edge	1.50	4.00
S8	Fit Finlay	1.00	2.50
S9	Jeff Hardy	1.00	2.50
S10	John Cena	2.50	6.00
S11	John Morrison	.60	1.50
S12	Kane	1.50	4.00
S13	King Booker	1.50	4.00
S14	Mark Henry	.60	1.50
S15	Matt Hardy	1.00	2.50
S16	Mr. Kennedy	1.00	2.50
S17	MVP	.60	1.50
S18	Randy Orton	1.50	4.00
S19	Shelton Benjamin	.40	1.00
S20	The Great Khali	.60	1.50
S21	Tommy Dreamer	.50	1.25
S22	Umaga	.60	1.50

2020 Topps WWE Fully Loaded Autographed Gear Relics

*GREEN/50: .5X TO 1.2X BASIC AUTOS
*PURPLE/25: UNPRICED DUE TO SCARCITY
*BLUE/10: UNPRICED DUE TO SCARCITY
*RED/5: UNPRICED DUE TO SCARCITY
*GOLD/1: UNPRICED DUE TO SCARCITY
STATED ODDS 1:23
STATED PRINT RUN 199 SER.#'d SETS

SGAJ	AJ Styles	20.00	50.00
SGBL	Becky Lynch	75.00	150.00
SGFB	Finn Balor	20.00	50.00
SGSN	Shinsuke Nakamura	20.00	50.00

2020 Topps WWE Fully Loaded Autographed Chair Relics

*GREEN/50: .5X TO 1.2X BASIC AUTOS
*PURPLE/25: UNPRICED DUE TO SCARCITY
*BLUE/10: UNPRICED DUE TO SCARCITY
*RED/5: UNPRICED DUE TO SCARCITY
*GOLD/1: UNPRICED DUE TO SCARCITY
STATED ODDS 1:20
STATED PRINT RUN 99 SER.#'d SETS

CAS	Asuka	50.00	100.00
CCL	Candice LeRae	30.00	75.00
CDK	Dakota Kai	30.00	75.00
CKC	King Corbin	12.00	30.00
CRR	Rhea Ripley	60.00	120.00
CSB	Shayna Baszler	15.00	40.00
CTN	Tegan Nox	30.00	75.00

2020 Topps WWE Fully Loaded Autographed Kiss

*PURPLE/25: .5X TO 1.2X BASIC AUTOS
*BLUE/10: UNPRICED DUE TO SCARCITY
*RED/5: UNPRICED DUE TO SCARCITY
*GOLD/1: UNPRICED DUE TO SCARCITY
STATED ODDS 1:118
STATED PRINT RUN 50 SER.#'d SETS

KBK	Billie Kay		
KBL	Becky Lynch		
KCC	Charly Caruso		
KCF	Charlotte Flair		
KCM	Carmella		
KEM	Ember Moon		
KLM	Liv Morgan		
KMJ	Mickie James	75.00	150.00
KMM	Maryse		
KMR	Mandy Rose		
KNC	Nikki Cross	125.00	250.00
KNJ	Nia Jax		
KNT	Natalya	50.00	100.00
KPR	Peyton Royce		
KRR	Ruby Riott		
KRY	Renee Young		
KSD	Sonya Deville		
KVB	Vanessa Borne		

2020 Topps WWE Fully Loaded Autographed Ladder Relics

*GREEN/50: .5X TO 1.2X BASIC AUTOS
*PURPLE/25: UNPRICED DUE TO SCARCITY
*BLUE/10: UNPRICED DUE TO SCARCITY
*RED/5: UNPRICED DUE TO SCARCITY
*GOLD/1: UNPRICED DUE TO SCARCITY
STATED ODDS 1:15
STATED PRINT RUN 99 SER.#'d SETS

LAJ	AJ Styles	25.00	60.00
LAS	Asuka	30.00	75.00
LBE	Big E	15.00	40.00
LCS	Cesaro	15.00	40.00
LKC	King Corbin	12.00	30.00
LKK	Kofi Kingston	15.00	40.00
LKO	Kevin Owens	25.00	60.00
LLE	Lacey Evans	30.00	75.00
LNJ	Nia Jax	20.00	50.00
LOT	Otis	12.00	30.00
LSZ	Sami Zayn	12.00	30.00

2020 Topps WWE Fully Loaded Autographed Microphone Box Relics

*GOLD/1: UNPRICED DUE TO SCARCITY
STATED PRINT RUN 5 SER.#'d SETS
UNPRICED DUE TO SCARCITY

MCBE Big E
MCRT R-Truth
MCTM The Miz

2020 Topps WWE Fully Loaded Autographed Oversized Mat Relics

*GREEN/50: .5X TO 1.2X BASIC AUTOS
*PURPLE/25: UNPRICED DUE TO SCARCITY
*BLUE/10: UNPRICED DUE TO SCARCITY
*RED/5: UNPRICED DUE TO SCARCITY
*GOLD/1: UNPRICED DUE TO SCARCITY
STATED ODDS 1:6
STATED PRINT RUN 199 SER.#'d SETS

MAB	Alexa Bliss	75.00	150.00
MAJ	AJ Styles	20.00	50.00
MBA	Bayley	30.00	75.00
MBL	The Fiend Bray Wyatt	60.00	120.00
MBS	Braun Strowman	15.00	40.00
MCF	Becky Lynch	60.00	120.00
MCM	Carmella	30.00	75.00
MJG	Johnny Gargano	12.00	30.00
MKK	Kofi Kingston	12.00	30.00
MSB	Sasha Banks	75.00	150.00
MSH	Sheamus	15.00	40.00
MSN	Shinsuke Nakamura	15.00	40.00
MSR	Seth Rollins	20.00	50.00
MTM	The Miz	15.00	40.00

2020 Topps WWE Fully Loaded Autographed Table Relics

*GREEN/50: .5X TO 1.2X BASIC AUTOS
*PURPLE/25: UNPRICED DUE TO SCARCITY
*BLUE/10: UNPRICED DUE TO SCARCITY
*RED/5: UNPRICED DUE TO SCARCITY
*GOLD/1: UNPRICED DUE TO SCARCITY
STATED ODDS 1:11
STATED PRINT RUN 99 SER.#'d SETS

TAB	Aleister Black	20.00	50.00
TAC	Adam Cole	20.00	50.00
TAJ	AJ Styles	20.00	50.00
TAS	Asuka	50.00	100.00
TBF	Bobby Fish	15.00	40.00
TBS	Braun Strowman	15.00	40.00
TCM	Carmella	30.00	75.00
TCS	Cesaro	15.00	40.00
TDD	Dominik Dijakovic	12.00	30.00
TKL	Keith Lee	15.00	40.00
TKO	Kevin Owens	15.00	40.00
TKR	Kyle O'Reilly	12.00	30.00
TLA	Bobby Lashley	12.00	30.00
TRS	Roderick Strong	15.00	40.00
TSN	Shinsuke Nakamura	15.00	40.00
TTC	Tommaso Ciampa	15.00	40.00

2020 Topps WWE Fully Loaded Autographed Turnbuckle Relics

*GREEN/50: .5X TO 1.2X BASIC AUTOS
*PURPLE/25: UNPRICED DUE TO SCARCITY
*BLUE/10: UNPRICED DUE TO SCARCITY
*RED/5: UNPRICED DUE TO SCARCITY
*GOLD/1: UNPRICED DUE TO SCARCITY
STATED ODDS 1:11
STATED PRINT RUN 99 SER.#'d SETS

AAC	Apollo Crews	12.00	30.00
AAG	Angel Garza	12.00	30.00
AAN	Andrade	15.00	40.00
AAT	Austin Theory	20.00	50.00
ADM	Drew McIntyre	20.00	50.00
ADZ	Dolph Ziggler	12.00	30.00
AJH	Jeff Hardy	25.00	60.00
ALE	Lacey Evans	25.00	60.00
AMA	Mustafa Ali	12.00	30.00
AMR	Mandy Rose	75.00	150.00
AOT	Otis	15.00	40.00
ARC	Ricochet	12.00	30.00
ART	R-Truth	15.00	40.00
ASB	Shayna Baszler		
ASJ	Samoa Joe	15.00	40.00
ATM	The Miz	12.00	30.00

2020 Topps WWE Fully Loaded Autographs

STATED ODDS 1:430

AVM	Mr. McMahon	300.00	600.00

2021 Topps WWE Fully Loaded Future Stars Autographs

*GOLD/99: .5X TO 1.2X BASIC AUTOS
*CITRINE/75: .6X TO 1.5X BASIC AUTOS
*ONYX/50: .75X TO 2X BASIC AUTOS
*SAPPHIRE/25: UNPRICED DUE TO SCARCITY
*RUBY/1: UNPRICED DUE TO SCARCITY
*P.P.BLACK/1: UNPRICED DUE TO SCARCITY
*P.P.CYAN/1: UNPRICED DUE TO SCARCITY
*P.P.MAGENTA/1: UNPRICED DUE TO SCARCITY
*P.P.YELLOW/1: UNPRICED DUE TO SCARCITY
STATED ODDS 1:12

SS	Sarray	25.00	60.00
SW	WALTER	15.00	40.00
SAT	Austin Theory	12.00	30.00
SDM	Dominik Mysterio		
SIH	Indi Hartwell	20.00	50.00
SKK	Karrion Kross		
SLK	LA Knight	15.00	40.00
SNC	Nash Carter	8.00	20.00
SSB	Shotzi Blackheart	30.00	75.00
SSC	Scarlett	50.00	100.00
STB	Tyler Bate	8.00	20.00
STS	Toni Storm		
STV	Franky Monet	20.00	50.00
SWL	Wes Lee	8.00	20.00
SZS	Zoey Stark	15.00	40.00

2021 Topps WWE Fully Loaded Autographed Ladder Relics

*SAPPHIRE/25: UNPRICED DUE TO SCARCITY
*RUBY/1: UNPRICED DUE TO SCARCITY
*DIE-CUT/1: UNPRICED DUE TO SCARCITY
STATED ODDS 1:26
STATED PRINT RUN 99 SER.#'d SETS

LCG	Cameron Grimes	15.00	40.00
LCL	Candice LeRae	25.00	60.00
LDP	Damian Priest	12.00	30.00
LIS	Io Shirai	50.00	100.00
LJG	Johnny Gargano		
LJU	Jimmy Uso	12.00	30.00
LSZ	Sami Zayn	15.00	40.00

2021 Topps WWE Fully Loaded Autographed Metal Chair Relics

*SAPPHIRE/25: UNPRICED DUE TO SCARCITY
*RUBY/1: UNPRICED DUE TO SCARCITY
*DIE-CUT/1: UNPRICED DUE TO SCARCITY
STATED ODDS 1:23
STATED PRINT RUN 99 SER.#'d SETS

CO	Omos	25.00	60.00
CBB	Bianca Belair	30.00	75.00
CDR	Drew McIntyre	20.00	50.00
CIS	Io Shirai	30.00	75.00
CJM	John Morrison	12.00	30.00
CKO	Kevin Owens	15.00	40.00
CRG	Raquel Gonzalez	30.00	75.00
CSB	Sasha Banks	60.00	120.00
CROM	Roman Reigns	75.00	150.00

2021 Topps WWE Fully Loaded Autographed Oversized Mat Relics

*SAPPHIRE/25: UNPRICED DUE TO SCARCITY
*RUBY/1: UNPRICED DUE TO SCARCITY
STATED ODDS 1:26

MA	Asuka	30.00	75.00
ME	Edge	25.00	60.00
MBC	Baron Corbin	12.00	30.00
MCF	Charlotte Flair	50.00	100.00
MFB	The Demon King Finn Balor	25.00	60.00

2021 Topps WWE Fully Loaded Autographed Trash Can Relics

*SAPPHIRE/25: UNPRICED DUE TO SCARCITY
*RUBY/1: UNPRICED DUE TO SCARCITY
STATED ODDS 1:34

TIS	Io Shirai	50.00	100.00
TRM	Raul Mendoza	10.00	25.00
TSE	Santos Escobar	10.00	25.00

2021 Topps WWE Fully Loaded Autographed Superstar Gear Relics

*SAPPHIRE/25: UNPRICED DUE TO SCARCITY
*RUBY/1: UNPRICED DUE TO SCARCITY
*DIE-CUT/1: UNPRICED DUE TO SCARCITY
STATED ODDS 1:34
STATED PRINT RUN 99 SER.#'d SETS

GC	Carmella	30.00	75.00
GR	Ricochet	12.00	30.00
GBE	Big E	15.00	40.00
GSB	Shayna Baszler	12.00	30.00
GXW	Xavier Woods	12.00	30.00
GKOR	Kyle O'Reilly	12.00	30.00

2021 Topps WWE Fully Loaded Autographed Table Relics

*SAPPHIRE/25: UNPRICED DUE TO SCARCITY
*RUBY/1: UNPRICED DUE TO SCARCITY
*DIE-CUT/1: UNPRICED DUE TO SCARCITY
STATED ODDS 1:19
STATED PRINT RUN 99 SER.#'d SETS

TE	Elias	10.00	25.00
TAS	AJ Styles	15.00	40.00
TJH	Jeff Hardy	20.00	50.00
TJU	Jey Uso	10.00	25.00
TKK	Kofi Kingston	15.00	40.00
TPD	Pete Dunne	10.00	25.00
TRM	Rey Mysterio	20.00	50.00
TRR	Rhea Ripley	30.00	75.00
TSR	Seth Rollins	15.00	40.00
TTM	The Miz	15.00	40.00

2021 Topps WWE Fully Loaded Autographed Turnbuckle Pad Relics

*RUBY/1: UNPRICED DUE TO SCARCITY
STATED ODDS 1:23

PN	Natalya	15.00	40.00
PAD	Angelo Dawkins	10.00	25.00
PKL	Keith Lee	12.00	30.00
PMF	Montez Ford	10.00	25.00
PSR	Seth Rollins		

2021 Topps WWE Fully Loaded Legends Autographs

STATED ODDS 1:23

LG	Goldberg		
LK	Kane		
LU	Undertaker		
LBH	Bret "Hit Man" Hart		
LDL	Dude Love	50.00	100.00
LPS	Papa Shango	20.00	50.00
LSA	Stone Cold Steve Austin		
LSK	Stacy Keibler	50.00	100.00
LSM	Shawn Michaels		
LTS	Trish Stratus	30.00	75.00
L123	1-2-3 Kid		
LDDP	Diamond Dallas Page	25.00	60.00
LHHH	Triple H		
LJBL	John "Bradshaw" Layfield	10.00	25.00

2019 Topps WWE Garbage Pail Kids

COMPLETE SET (13)		25.00	60.00

STATED PRINT RUN 1028 SETS PRODUCED

1	Gigantic Andre	2.50	6.00
2	Breakin' Becky	8.00	20.00
3	C-Thru Cena	4.00	10.00
4	Savage Randy	2.50	6.00
5	Mixed-Up Mick	3.00	8.00
6	Mouthy Miz & Maryse	2.50	6.00
7	Slick Ric	4.00	10.00
8	Rowdy Ronda	6.00	15.00
9	Brawlin' Rollins	3.00	8.00
10	Seething Steve	3.00	8.00
11	Chipped Rock	4.00	10.00
12	Unravelled Warrior	3.00	8.00
13	Undead Taker	5.00	10.00

2018 Topps WWE Hall of Fame Tribute

1	Andre the Giant	.60	1.50
2	Andre the Giant	.60	1.50
3	Andre the Giant	.60	1.50
4	Andre the Giant	.60	1.50
5	Andre the Giant	.60	1.50
6	Andre the Giant	.60	1.50
7	Andre the Giant	.60	1.50
8	Andre the Giant	.60	1.50
9	Andre the Giant	.60	1.50
10	Andre the Giant	.60	1.50
11	Ultimate Warrior	.60	1.50
12	Ultimate Warrior	.60	1.50
13	Ultimate Warrior	.60	1.50
14	Ultimate Warrior	.60	1.50
15	Ultimate Warrior	.60	1.50
16	Ultimate Warrior	.60	1.50
17	Ultimate Warrior	.60	1.50
18	Ultimate Warrior	.60	1.50
19	Ultimate Warrior	.60	1.50
20	Ultimate Warrior	.60	1.50
21	Ric Flair	.60	1.50
22	Ric Flair	.60	1.50
23	Ric Flair	.60	1.50
24	Ric Flair	.60	1.50
25	Ric Flair	.60	1.50
26	Ric Flair	.60	1.50
27	Ric Flair	.60	1.50
28	Ric Flair	.60	1.50
29	Ric Flair	.60	1.50
30	Ric Flair	.60	1.50
31	Rowdy Roddy Piper	.60	1.50
32	Rowdy Roddy Piper	.60	1.50
33	Rowdy Roddy Piper	.60	1.50
34	Rowdy Roddy Piper	.60	1.50
35	Rowdy Roddy Piper	.60	1.50
36	Rowdy Roddy Piper	.60	1.50
37	Rowdy Roddy Piper	.60	1.50
38	Rowdy Roddy Piper	.60	1.50
39	Rowdy Roddy Piper	.60	1.50
40	Rowdy Roddy Piper	.60	1.50

2015 Topps WWE Hulk Hogan Tribute

COMPLETE SET (30)		12.00	30.00

*GOLD/10: 4X TO 10X BASIC CARDS
*RED/1: UNPRICED DUE TO SCARCITY

1	Hulk Hogan	.75	2.00
2	Hulk Hogan	.75	2.00
3	Hulk Hogan	.75	2.00
4	Hulk Hogan	.75	2.00
5	Hulk Hogan	.75	2.00
6	Hulk Hogan	.75	2.00
7	Hulk Hogan	.75	2.00
8	Hulk Hogan	.75	2.00
9	Hulk Hogan	.75	2.00
10	Hulk Hogan	.75	2.00
11	Hulk Hogan	.75	2.00
12	Hulk Hogan	.75	2.00
13	Hulk Hogan	.75	2.00
14	Hulk Hogan	.75	2.00
15	Hulk Hogan	.75	2.00
16	Hulk Hogan	.75	2.00
17	Hulk Hogan	.75	2.00
18	Hulk Hogan	.75	2.00
19	Hulk Hogan	.75	2.00
20	Hulk Hogan	.75	2.00
21	Hulk Hogan	.75	2.00
22	Hulk Hogan	.75	2.00
23	Hulk Hogan	.75	2.00
24	Hulk Hogan	.75	2.00
25	Hulk Hogan	.75	2.00
26	Hulk Hogan	.75	2.00
27	Hulk Hogan	.75	2.00
28	Hulk Hogan	.75	2.00
29	Hulk Hogan	.75	2.00
30	Hulk Hogan	.75	2.00

2006 Topps WWE Insider

COMPLETE SET (72)		8.00	20.00
UNOPENED BOX (24 PACKS)			
UNOPENED PACK (7 CARDS)			
1	Lashley	.30	.75
2	Big Show	.50	1.25
3	Carlito	.50	1.25
4	Chris Masters	.20	.50
5	Edge	.50	1.25
6	Gene Snitsky	.20	.50
7	Hulk Hogan	.75	2.00
8	Jerry The King Lawler	.40	1.00
9	John Cena	.75	2.00
10	Jonathan Coachman	.12	.30
11	Kane	.50	1.25
12	Chavo Guerrero	.20	.50
13	Kurt Angle	.50	1.25
14	Lance Cade	.12	.30
15	Lilian Garcia	.60	1.50
16	Lita	.75	2.00
17	Maria	.50	1.25
18	Matt Hardy	.30	.75
19	Rene Dupree	.20	.50
20	Ric Flair	.60	1.50
21	Rob Conway	.20	.50
22	Rob Van Dam	.30	.75
23	Paul Burchill	.12	.30
24	Kid Kash	.12	.30
25	Shawn Michaels	.75	2.00
26	Shelton Benjamin	.12	.30
27	Mickie James	.75	2.00
28	Stone Cold	.75	2.00
29	Gregory Helms	.12	.30
30	Trevor Murdoch	.12	.30
31	Triple H	.75	2.00
32	Trish Stratus	1.25	3.00
33	Mark Henry	.20	.50
34	Val Venis	.20	.50
35	Victoria	.75	2.00
36	Viscera	.20	.50
37	Batista	.50	1.25
38	Booker T	.30	.75
39	Candice Michelle	.75	2.00
40	Chris Benoit	.50	1.25
41	Boogeyman	.20	.50
42	Funaki	.20	.50
43	Hardcore Holly	.20	.50
44	Joey Styles	.12	.30
45	JBL	.30	.75
46	Joey Mercury	.12	.30
47	Johnny Nitro	.20	.50
48	Ashley	.50	1.25
49	Finlay	.30	.75
50	Ken Kennedy	.30	.75
51	Melina	.50	1.25
52	Michael Cole	.12	.30
53	Nunzio	.12	.30
54	Orlando Jordan	.12	.30
55	Paul London	.12	.30
56	Psicosis	.12	.30
57	Randy Orton	.30	.75
58	Rey Mysterio	.50	1.25
59	Road Warrior Animal	.25	.60
60	Kristal	.30	.75
61	Sharmell	.50	1.25
62	Simon Dean	.12	.30
63	Steven Richards	.20	.50
64	Super Crazy	.20	.50
65	Goldust	.20	.50
66	Tazz	.20	.50
67	Theodore Long	.12	.30
68	Torrie Wilson	1.25	3.00
69	Undertaker	.60	1.50
70	Vito	.12	.30
71	William Regal	.30	.75
72	Checklist	.10	.25

2006 Topps WWE Insider Autographs

STATED ODDS 1:24 HOBBY EXCLUSIVE

NNO	Ashley	6.00	15.00
NNO	Candice Michelle	12.00	30.00
NNO	Carlito	30.00	80.00
NNO	Chris Masters	6.00	15.00
NNO	Edge	15.00	40.00
NNO	Eugene	12.00	30.00
NNO	Goldust	8.00	20.00
NNO	Gregory Helms	8.00	20.00
NNO	John Cena	75.00	150.00
NNO	Kristal	8.00	20.00
NNO	Lita	12.00	30.00
NNO	Maria	20.00	50.00
NNO	Matt Hardy	12.00	30.00
NNO	Melina	8.00	20.00
NNO	Mickie James	20.00	50.00
NNO	Randy Orton	25.00	60.00
NNO	Road Warrior (Animal)	15.00	50.00
NNO	Shelton Benjamin	12.00	30.00
NNO	Torrie Wilson	30.00	75.00
NNO	Trish Stratus	50.00	100.00
NNO	Victoria	12.00	30.00
NNO	Viscera	15.00	40.00

2006 Topps WWE Insider Champions

COMPLETE SET (12)		5.00	12.00

STATED ODDS 1:6 RETAIL EXCLUSIVE

C1	John Cena	.75	2.00
C2	Ric Flair	.60	1.50
C3	Trish Stratus	1.25	3.00
C4	Rey Mysterio	.50	1.25
C5	Eddie Guerrero	.50	1.25
C6	Booker T	.30	.75
C7	Chris Benoit	.50	1.25
C8	Kurt Angle	.50	1.25
C9	Undertaker	.60	1.50
C10	Triple H	.75	2.00
C11	Stone Cold	.75	2.00
C12	Hulk Hogan	.75	2.00

2006 Topps WWE Insider Coins

COMPLETE SET (24)		12.00	30.00

STATED ODDS 1:1 RETAIL EXCLUSIVE

1	John Cena	1.50	4.00
2	Edge	1.00	2.50
3	Carlito	1.00	2.50
4	Kurt Angle	1.00	2.50
5	Randy Orton	.60	1.50
6	Shawn Michaels	1.50	4.00
7	Undertaker	1.25	3.00
8	Batista	1.00	2.50
9	Ric Flair	1.25	3.00
10	Chris Masters	.40	1.00
11	Triple H	1.50	4.00
12	Kane	1.00	2.50
13	Boogeyman	.40	1.00
14	Steve Austin	1.50	4.00
15	Trish Stratus	2.50	6.00
16	Rob Van Dam	.60	1.50
17	Chris Benoit	1.00	2.50
18	Hulk Hogan	1.50	4.00
19	JBL	.60	1.50
20	Rey Mysterio	1.00	2.50
21	Big Show	1.00	2.50
22	Booker T	.60	1.50
23	Torrie Wilson	2.50	6.00
24	Candice Michelle	1.50	4.00

2006 Topps WWE Insider Divas

COMPLETE SET (12)		10.00	25.00

STATED ODDS 1:3 RETAIL EXCLUSIVE

D1	Candice Michelle	.60	1.50
D2	Ashley	4.00	10.00
D3	Mickie James	.60	1.50
D4	Sharmell	.40	1.00
D5	Torrie Wilson	6.00	15.00
D6	Trish Stratus	5.00	12.00
D7	Jillian Hall	.40	1.00
D8	Lilian Garcia	.50	1.25
D9	Lita	.60	1.50
D10	Maria	.40	1.00
D11	Kristal	.25	.60
D12	Victoria	.60	1.50

2006 Topps WWE Insider Memorabilia

STATED ODDS 1:24 HOBBY EXCLUSIVE

NNO	John Cena	6.00	15.00
NNO	Kurt Angle	3.00	8.00
NNO	Matt Hardy	2.00	5.00
NNO	Rey Mysterio	2.00	5.00
NNO	Shawn Michaels	8.00	20.00

2006 Topps WWE Insider Promos

COMPLETE SET (2)			
P1	Undertaker		
P2	Batista		

2019 Topps WWE Intercontinental Championship 40th Anniversary

COMPLETE SET (40)		15.00	40.00

RANDOMLY INSERTED INTO PACKS

IC1	Don Muraco	.50	1.25
IC2	Macho Man Randy Savage	1.25	3.00
IC3	Ricky The Dragon Steamboat	.60	1.50
IC4	The Honky Tonk Man	.50	1.25
IC5	Ultimate Warrior	1.25	3.00
IC6	Ravishing Rick Rude	.60	1.50
IC7	Mr. Perfect	.75	2.00
IC8	Texas Tornado	.75	2.00
IC9	Bret Hit Man Hart	1.25	3.00
IC10	Rowdy Roddy Piper	1.25	3.00
IC11	Shawn Michaels	1.25	3.00
IC12	Razor Ramon	.75	2.00
IC13	Diesel	.75	2.00
IC14	Triple H	1.25	3.00
IC15	The Rock	2.50	6.00
IC16	Stone Cold Steve Austin	2.50	6.00
IC17	Ken Shamrock	.75	2.00
IC18	Road Dogg	.50	1.25
IC19	The Godfather	.50	1.25
IC20	Edge	1.25	3.00
IC21	D'Lo Brown	.50	1.25
IC22	Kurt Angle	1.00	2.50
IC23	Eddie Guerrero	1.25	3.00
IC24	Billy Gunn	.60	1.50
IC25	Jeff Hardy	1.25	3.00
IC26	Kane	.75	2.00
IC27	Albert	.50	1.25
IC28	William Regal	.75	2.00
IC29	Booker T	1.25	3.00
IC30	Randy Orton	1.25	3.00
IC31	Shelton Benjamin	.60	1.50
IC32	Ric Flair	1.50	4.00
IC33	Umaga	.50	1.25
IC34	Kofi Kingston	.75	2.00
IC35	Rey Mysterio	1.25	3.00
IC36	Drew McIntyre	.60	1.50
IC37	Dolph Ziggler	1.00	2.50
IC38	Big Show	.75	2.00
IC39	The Miz	1.00	2.50
IC40	Curtis Axel	.60	1.50

2017 Topps WWE John Cena Tribute

COMPLETE SET (40)		6.00	15.00

STATED ODDS 1:6

1	John Cena	1.00	2.50
2	John Cena	1.00	2.50
3	John Cena	1.00	2.50
4	John Cena	1.00	2.50
5	John Cena	1.00	2.50
6	John Cena	1.00	2.50
7	John Cena	1.00	2.50
8	John Cena	1.00	2.50
9	John Cena	1.00	2.50
10	John Cena	1.00	2.50
11	John Cena	1.00	2.50
12	John Cena	1.00	2.50
13	John Cena	1.00	2.50
14	John Cena	1.00	2.50
15	John Cena	1.00	2.50
16	John Cena	1.00	2.50
17	John Cena	1.00	2.50
18	John Cena	1.00	2.50
19	John Cena	1.00	2.50
20	John Cena	1.00	2.50
21	John Cena	1.00	2.50
22	John Cena	1.00	2.50
23	John Cena	1.00	2.50
24	John Cena	1.00	2.50
25	John Cena	1.00	2.50
26	John Cena	1.00	2.50
27	John Cena	1.00	2.50
28	John Cena	1.00	2.50
29	John Cena	1.00	2.50
30	John Cena	1.00	2.50
31	John Cena	1.00	2.50
32	John Cena	1.00	2.50
33	John Cena	1.00	2.50
34	John Cena	1.00	2.50
35	John Cena	1.00	2.50
36	John Cena	1.00	2.50
37	John Cena	1.00	2.50
38	John Cena	1.00	2.50
39	John Cena	1.00	2.50
40	John Cena	1.00	2.50

2018 Topps WWE Macho Man Randy Savage Tribute

1	Macho Man Randy Savage	1.25	3.00
2	Macho Man Randy Savage	1.25	3.00
3	Macho Man Randy Savage	1.25	3.00

4	Macho Man Randy Savage	1.25	3.00
5	Macho Man Randy Savage	1.25	3.00
6	Macho Man Randy Savage	1.25	3.00
7	Macho Man Randy Savage	1.25	3.00
8	Macho Man Randy Savage	1.25	3.00
9	Macho Man Randy Savage	1.25	3.00
10	Macho Man Randy Savage	1.25	3.00
11	Macho Man Randy Savage	1.25	3.00
12	Macho Man Randy Savage	1.25	3.00
13	Macho Man Randy Savage	1.25	3.00
14	Macho Man Randy Savage	1.25	3.00
15	Macho Man Randy Savage	1.25	3.00
16	Macho Man Randy Savage	1.25	3.00
17	Macho Man Randy Savage	1.25	3.00
18	Macho Man Randy Savage	1.25	3.00
19	Macho Man Randy Savage	1.25	3.00
20	Macho Man Randy Savage	1.25	3.00
21	Macho Man Randy Savage	1.25	3.00
22	Macho Man Randy Savage	1.25	3.00
23	Macho Man Randy Savage	1.25	3.00
24	Macho Man Randy Savage	1.25	3.00
25	Macho Man Randy Savage	1.25	3.00
26	Macho Man Randy Savage	1.25	3.00
27	Macho Man Randy Savage	1.25	3.00
28	Macho Man Randy Savage	1.25	3.00
29	Macho Man Randy Savage	1.25	3.00
30	Macho Man Randy Savage	1.25	3.00
31	Macho Man Randy Savage	1.25	3.00
32	Macho Man Randy Savage	1.25	3.00
33	Macho Man Randy Savage	1.25	3.00
34	Macho Man Randy Savage	1.25	3.00
35	Macho Man Randy Savage	1.25	3.00
36	Macho Man Randy Savage	1.25	3.00
37	Macho Man Randy Savage	1.25	3.00
38	Macho Man Randy Savage	1.25	3.00
39	Macho Man Randy Savage	1.25	3.00
40	Macho Man Randy Savage	1.25	3.00

2019 Topps WWE Money in the Bank

COMPLETE SET (90)		10.00	25.00

*BRONZE: .5X TO 1.2X BASIC CARDS
*GREEN/99: .75X TO 2X BASIC CARDS
*BLUE/50: 1.2X TO 3X BASIC CARDS
*PURPLE/25: 2X TO 5X BASIC CARDS
*GOLD/10: UNPRICED DUE TO SCARCITY
*BLACK/5: UNPRICED DUE TO SCARCITY
*RED/1: UNPRICED DUE TO SCARCITY

1	Aiden English	.25	.60
2	AJ Styles	1.25	3.00
3	Alexa Bliss	1.25	3.00
4	Alicia Fox	.50	1.25
5	Andrade	.30	.75
6	Ariya Daivari	.25	.60
7	Apollo Crews	.30	.75
8	Asuka	.75	2.00
9	Baron Corbin	.40	1.00
10	Bayley	.50	1.25
11	Becky Lynch	1.00	2.50
12	Beth Phoenix	.40	1.00
13	Big Show	.40	1.00
14	Big E	.25	.60
15	Bobby Lashley	.50	1.25
16	Robert Roode	.50	1.25
17	Booker T	.60	1.50
18	Braun Strowman	.60	1.50
19	Bray Wyatt	.60	1.50
20	Brock Lesnar	1.00	2.50
21	Carmella	.60	1.50
22	Cesaro	.30	.75
23	Charlotte Flair	1.00	2.50
24	Christian	.40	1.00
25	Curt Hawkins	.25	.60
26	Curtis Axel	.30	.75
27	Dana Brooke	.50	1.25
28	Daniel Bryan	1.00	2.50
29	Drew McIntyre	.30	.75
30	Elias	.50	1.25
31	Ember Moon	.60	1.50
32	Eve Torres	.30	.75
33	Fandango	.25	.60
34	Finlay	.25	.60
35	Finn Balor	.60	1.50
36	Gran Metalik	.25	.60
37	Heath Slater	.25	.60
38	Jeff Hardy	.60	1.50
39	Jey Uso	.30	.75
40	Jimmy Uso	.30	.75
41	Jinder Mahal	.50	1.25
42	John Cena	1.00	2.50
43	Kalisto	.25	.60
44	Kane	.40	1.00
45	Karl Anderson	.40	1.00
46	Kevin Owens	.60	1.50
47	Kofi Kingston	.40	1.00
48	Lacey Evans	.50	1.25
49	Lince Dorado	.25	.60
50	Luke Gallows	.40	1.00
51	Mark Henry	.30	.75
52	Maria Kanellis	.60	1.50
53	Mandy Rose	.60	1.50
54	Matt Hardy	.50	1.25
55	Mike Kanellis	.25	.60
56	Mojo Rawley	.30	.75
57	Ali	.25	.60
58	Naomi	.40	1.00
59	Natalya	.50	1.25
60	Nikki Cross	.40	1.00
61	Nia Jax	.50	1.25
62	Paige	1.00	2.50
63	Paul Heyman	.30	.75
64	Randy Orton	.60	1.50
65	Rey Mysterio	.60	1.50
66	Ric Flair	.75	2.00
67	Ricochet	.60	1.50
68	Roman Reigns	.60	1.50
69	Ronda Rousey	1.25	3.00
70	Rowan	.25	.60
71	R-Truth	.30	.75
72	Sami Zayn	.50	1.25
73	Samir Singh	.25	.60
74	Samoa Joe	.50	1.25
75	Sonya Deville	.50	1.25
76	Seth Rollins	.60	1.50
77	Sheamus	.40	1.00
78	Shelton Benjamin	.30	.75
79	Shinsuke Nakamura	.60	1.50
80	Sunil Singh	.25	.60
81	Tamina	.25	.60
82	Lord Tensai	.25	.60
83	The Miz	.50	1.25
84	Titus O'Neil	.30	.75
85	Tony Nese	.25	.60
86	Tyler Breeze	.30	.75
87	Xavier Woods	.30	.75
88	William Regal	.40	1.00
89	Zack Ryder	.30	.75
90	Zelina Vega	.40	1.00

2019 Topps WWE Money in the Bank
Autographed Mat Relics

COMMON AUTO		5.00	12.00

*BLUE/50: .5X TO 1.2X BASIC AUTOS
*PURPLE/25: UNPRICED DUE TO SCARCITY
*GOLD/10: UNPRICED DUE TO SCARCITY
*BLACK/5: UNPRICED DUE TO SCARCITY
*RED/1: UNPRICED DUE TO SCARCITY
STATED ODDS 1:227
STATED PRINT RUN 99 SER.#'d SETS

MRACM	Carmella	12.00	30.00
MRAFB	Finn Balor	10.00	25.00
MRAKA	Karl Anderson	8.00	20.00
MRAKK	Kofi Kingston	6.00	15.00
MRAKO	Kevin Owens	8.00	20.00
MRALG	Luke Gallows	6.00	15.00
MRANT	Natalya	6.00	15.00
MRART	R-Truth	6.00	15.00
MRASA	Samir Singh	5.00	12.00
MRASJ	Samoa Joe	6.00	15.00
MRASM	Sheamus	8.00	20.00
MRASN	Shinsuke Nakamura	6.00	15.00
MRASR	Seth Rollins	8.00	20.00
MRASU	Sunil Singh	5.00	12.00
MRATO	Titus O'Neil	5.00	12.00
MRATS	Tamina	5.00	12.00
MRAXW	Xavier Woods	5.00	12.00
MRAZR	Zack Ryder	6.00	15.00

2019 Topps WWE Money in the Bank
Autographed Shirt Relics

*BLUE/50: .5X TO 1.2X BASIC AUTOS
*PURPLE/25: .6X TO 1.5X BASIC AUTOS
*GOLD/10: UNPRICED DUE TO SCARCITY
*BLACK/5: UNPRICED DUE TO SCARCITY
*RED/1: UNPRICED DUE TO SCARCITY
STATED ODDS 1:453
STATED PRINT RUN 99 SER.#'d SETS

SRAAC	Apollo Crews	5.00	12.00
SRAAJ	AJ Styles	10.00	25.00
SRABS	Braun Strowman	12.00	30.00
SRACS	Cesaro	5.00	12.00
SRAHS	Heath Slater	5.00	12.00
SRAKK	Kofi Kingston	6.00	15.00
SRARI	Ricochet	10.00	25.00
SRARR	Roman Reigns		
SRASR	Seth Rollins	12.00	30.00
SRASZ	Sami Zayn		

2019 Topps WWE Money in the Bank
Autographs

*GREEN/99: .5X TO 1.2X BASIC AUTOS
*BLUE/50: .6X TO 1.5X BASIC AUTOS
*PURPLE/25: UNPRICED DUE TO SCARCITY
*GOLD/10: UNPRICED DUE TO SCARCITY
*BLACK/5: UNPRICED DUE TO SCARCITY
*RED/1: UNPRICED DUE TO SCARCITY
STATED ODDS 1:41
STATED PRINT RUN 99 SER.#'d SETS

AAB	Alexa Bliss	20.00	50.00
AAD	Andrade	4.00	10.00
AAE	Aiden English	4.00	10.00
AAJ	AJ Styles	8.00	20.00
AAK	Asuka	10.00	25.00
AAL	Ali	4.00	10.00
ABC	Baron Corbin	4.00	10.00
ABE	Big E	4.00	10.00
ABJ	Shelton Benjamin	4.00	10.00
ABK	Dana Brooke	10.00	25.00
ABL	Becky Lynch	12.00	30.00
ABM	Matt Hardy	5.00	12.00
ABR	Robert Roode	4.00	10.00
ABS	Braun Strowman	5.00	12.00
ABW	Bray Wyatt	6.00	15.00
ACF	Charlotte Flair EXCH	12.00	30.00
ACM	Carmella	6.00	15.00
ACS	Cesaro	4.00	10.00
ADB	Daniel Bryan	6.00	15.00
ADM	Drew McIntyre	4.00	10.00
ADZ	Dolph Ziggler	4.00	10.00
AEL	Elias	5.00	12.00
AEM	Ember Moon	6.00	15.00
AFB	Finn Balor	5.00	12.00
AKK	Kofi Kingston	4.00	10.00
AKL	Kalisto	4.00	10.00
AKO	Kevin Owens	5.00	12.00
AMA	Maria Kanellis	8.00	20.00
AMG	Karl Anderson	4.00	10.00
AMI	Mike Kanellis	4.00	10.00
ANT	Natalya	5.00	12.00
ARM	Rey Mysterio	10.00	25.00
ARS	Rusev	4.00	10.00
ARW	Rowan	4.00	10.00
ASA	Samir Singh	4.00	10.00
ASB	Sasha Banks	10.00	25.00
ASJ	Samoa Joe	4.00	10.00
ASM	Sheamus	4.00	10.00
ASN	Shinsuke Nakamura	5.00	12.00
ASR	Seth Rollins	.60	15.00
ASU	Sunil Singh	4.00	10.00
ASZ	Sami Zayn	4.00	10.00
ATM	The Miz	5.00	12.00
ATO	Titus O'Neil	4.00	10.00
AXW	Xavier Woods	4.00	10.00
AZR	Zack Ryder	5.00	12.00
AZV	Zelina Vega	8.00	20.00

2019 Topps WWE Money in the Bank
Cash-In Moments

COMPLETE SET (13)		8.00	20.00
STATED ODDS 1:6			

CM1	Kane	.60	1.50
CM2	The Miz	.75	2.00
CM3	Daniel Bryan	1.50	4.00
CM4	John Cena	1.50	4.00
CM5	Randy Orton	1.00	2.50
CM6	Seth Rollins	1.00	2.50
CM7	Sheamus	.60	1.50
CM8	Baron Corbin	.60	1.50
CM9	Braun Strowman	1.00	2.50
CM10	Carmella	1.00	2.50
CM11	Alexa Bliss	2.00	5.00
CM12	Bayley	.75	2.00
CM13	Brock Lesnar	1.50	4.00

2019 Topps WWE Money in the Bank
Dual Autographs

*GOLD/10: UNPRICED DUE TO SCARCITY
*BLACK/5: UNPRICED DUE TO SCARCITY
*RED/1: UNPRICED DUE TO SCARCITY
STATED ODDS 1:3,663
STATED PRINT RUN 25 SER.#'d SETS

DANEW	X.Woods/Big E	25.00	60.00
DABROS	The Singhs	25.00	60.00

DAGOOD K.Anderson/L.Gallows 20.00 50.00
DAHRDY The Hardys 30.00 75.00

2019 Topps WWE Money in the Bank Greatest Matches and Moments

COMPLETE SET (22)		6.00	15.00
STATED ODDS 1:3			
GMM1	Shelton Benjamin	.40	1.00
GMM2	Matt Hardy	.60	1.50
GMM3	Kofi Kingston	.50	1.25
GMM4	Kofi Kingston	.50	1.25
GMM5	Kofi Kingston	.50	1.25
GMM6	The Miz	.60	1.50
GMM7	Daniel Bryan	1.25	3.00
GMM8	Christian	.50	1.25
GMM9	Big Show	.50	1.25
GMM10	The Shield	.75	2.00
GMM11	John Cena	1.25	3.00
GMM12	Seth Rollins	.75	2.00
GMM13	John Cena	1.25	3.00
GMM14	Bray Wyatt	.75	2.00
GMM15	AJ Styles	1.50	4.00
GMM16	Seth Rollins	.75	2.00
GMM17	Mike & Maria Kanellis	.75	2.00
GMM18	Carmella	.75	2.00
GMM19	AJ Styles and Nakamura	1.50	4.00
GMM20	Carmella	.75	2.00
GMM21	Ember Moon	.75	2.00
GMM22	Brock Lesnar	1.25	3.00

2019 Topps WWE Money in the Bank Mat Relics

*GREEN/99: .5X TO 1.2X BASIC MEM
*BLUE/50: .6X TO 1.5X BASIC MEM
*PURPLE/25: UNPRICED DUE TO SCARCITY
*GOLD/10: UNPRICED DUE TO SCARCITY
*BLACK/5: UNPRICED DUE TO SCARCITY
*RED/1: UNPRICED DUE TO SCARCITY
STATED ODDS 1:20

MRBC	Baron Corbin	2.50	6.00
MRBE	Big E.	2.50	6.00
MRBL	Bobby Lashley	2.50	6.00
MRBR	Robert Roode	2.50	6.00
MRCM	Carmella	4.00	10.00
MRFB	Finn Balor	5.00	12.00
MRJE	Jey Uso	2.50	6.00
MRJI	Jimmy Uso	2.50	6.00
MRKK	Kofi Kingston	3.00	8.00
MRKO	Kevin Owens	4.00	10.00
MRLK	Becky Lynch	5.00	12.00
MRNM	Naomi	2.50	6.00
MRNT	Natalya	2.50	6.00
MRRO	Randy Orton	3.00	8.00
MRRT	R-Truth	3.00	8.00
MRSJ	Samoa Joe	2.50	6.00
MRSM	Sheamus	2.50	6.00
MRSR	Seth Rollins	4.00	10.00
MRTO	Titus O'Neil	2.50	6.00
MRTS	Tamina	2.50	6.00
MRXW	Xavier Woods	2.50	6.00
MRZR	Zack Ryder	2.50	6.00

2019 Topps WWE Money in the Bank Money Cards

COMPLETE SET (13)		8.00	20.00
STATED ODDS 1:6			
MC1	Kane	.60	1.50

MC2	The Miz	.75	2.00
MC3	Daniel Bryan	1.50	4.00
MC4	John Cena	1.50	4.00
MC5	Randy Orton	1.00	2.50
MC6	Seth Rollins	1.00	2.50
MC7	Sheamus	.60	1.50
MC8	Baron Corbin	.60	1.50
MC9	Braun Strowman	1.00	2.50
MC10	Carmella	1.00	2.50
MC11	Alexa Bliss	2.00	5.00
MC12	Bayley	.75	2.00
MC13	Brock Lesnar	1.50	4.00

2019 Topps WWE Money in the Bank Quad Autograph

STATED ODDS 1:47,616
STATED PRINT RUN 5 SER.#'d SETS
UNPRICED DUE TO SCARCITY
QABC Owens/Styles/Nakamura/Corbin

2019 Topps WWE Money in the Bank Shirt Relics

*GREEN/99: .5X TO 1.2X BASIC MEM
*BLUE/50: .6X TO 1.5X BASIC MEM
*PURPLE/25: UNPRICED DUE TO SCARCITY
*GOLD/10: UNPRICED DUE TO SCARCITY
*BLACK/5: UNPRICED DUE TO SCARCITY
*RED/1: UNPRICED DUE TO SCARCITY
STATED ODDS 1:23
STATED PRINT RUN 199 SER.#'d SETS

SRAC	Apollo Crews	1.50	4.00
SRAJ	AJ Styles		
SRBL	Brock Lesnar	5.00	12.00
SRBS	Braun Strowman	2.50	6.00
SRCS	Cesaro	4.00	10.00
SRFB	Finn Balor		
SRHS	Heath Slater		
SRJE	Jey Uso		
SRJI	Jimmy Uso		
SRKB	Booker T	3.00	8.00
SRKK	Kofi Kingston	3.00	8.00
SRKO	Kevin Owens	3.00	8.00
SRLA	Bobby Lashley	2.50	6.00
SRMZ	The Miz	3.00	8.00
SRRI	Ricochet	5.00	12.00
SRRM	Rey Mysterio	5.00	12.00
SRRR	Roman Reigns		
SRSR	Seth Rollins	5.00	12.00
SRSZ	Sami Zayn	2.50	6.00

2019 Topps WWE Money in the Bank Triple Autographs

*GOLD/10: UNPRICED DUE TO SCARCITY
*BLACK/5: UNPRICED DUE TO SCARCITY
*RED/1: UNPRICED DUE TO SCARCITY
STATED ODDS 1:6,802
STATED PRINT RUN SER.#'d SETS

TABC	Anderson/Gallows/Styles	60.00	120.00
TANEW	Woods/Big E/Kingston	50.00	100.00

2019 Topps WWE Money in the Bank Promo

NYCC19 John Cena NYCC 5.00 12.00

2016 Topps WWE NXT

*BRONZE/50: .6X TO 1.5X BASIC CARDS
*SILVER/25: .75X TO 2X BASIC CARDS

*GOLD/10: 1.5X TO 4X BASIC CARDS
*RED/1: UNPRICED DUE TO SCARCITY

1	Aliyah	.75	2.00
2	Akam	.60	1.50
3	Andrade "Cien" Almas	.60	1.50
4	Angelo Dawkins	.60	1.50
5	Asuka	2.50	6.00
6	Austin Aries	.75	2.00
7	Billie Kay	1.50	4.00
8	Blake	.60	1.50
9	Dash Wilder	.75	2.00
10	Elias Samson	.60	1.50
11	Hideo Itami	.75	2.00
12	Johnny Gargano	.60	1.50
13	Liv Morgan	.75	2.00
14	Buddy Murphy	.60	1.50
15	No Way Jose	.60	1.50
16	Peyton Royce	1.50	4.00
17	Rezar	.60	1.50
18	Samoa Joe	1.50	4.00
19	Sawyer Fulton	.75	2.00
20	Scott Dawson	.60	1.50
21	Shinsuke Nakamura	2.50	6.00
22	Tommaso Ciampa	.75	2.00
23	Tye Dillinger	.75	2.00
24	Roman Reigns	2.00	5.00
25	Seth Rollins	1.00	2.50
26	Big E	.60	1.50
27	Bray Wyatt	2.50	6.00
28	Xavier Woods	.60	1.50
29	Rusev	1.50	4.00
30	Kalisto	1.50	4.00
31	Neville	1.50	4.00
32	Kevin Owens	1.50	4.00
33	Charlotte	2.00	5.00
34	Sasha Banks	2.00	5.00
35	Becky Lynch	2.00	5.00
36	Sami Zayn	1.00	2.50
37	Baron Corbin	.75	2.00
38	Big Cass	1.25	3.00
39	Enzo Amore	1.25	3.00
40	Aiden English	.60	1.50
41	Simon Gotch	1.00	2.50
42	Dana Brooke	1.50	4.00
43	Alexa Bliss	3.00	8.00
44	Carmella	1.50	4.00
45	Chad Gable	.75	2.00
46	Finn Balor	2.00	5.00
47	Jason Jordan	.75	2.00
48	Mojo Rawley	.60	1.50
49	Nia Jax	1.00	2.50
50	Bayley	1.50	4.00

2016 Topps WWE NXT Autographs

*BRONZE/50: .5X TO 1.2X BASIC AUTOS
*SILVER/25: .6X TO 1.5X BASIC AUTOS
*GOLD/10: UNPRICED DUE TO SCARCITY
*RED/1: UNPRICED DUE TO SCARCITY
STATED OVERALL ODDS 1:MINIBOX

NNO	Alexa Bliss	50.00	100.00
NNO	Aliyah	8.00	15.00
NNO	Andrade Cien Almas	6.00	15.00
NNO	Angelo Dawkins	6.00	15.00
NNO	Asuka	20.00	50.00
NNO	Austin Aries	10.00	25.00
NNO	Bayley	15.00	40.00
NNO	Billie Kay	20.00	50.00
NNO	Blake	6.00	15.00

NNO	Buddy Murphy	6.00	15.00
NNO	Dash Wilder	12.00	30.00
NNO	Elias Samson	15.00	40.00
NNO	Finn Balor	15.00	40.00
NNO	Hideo Itami	6.00	15.00
NNO	Johnny Gargano	6.00	15.00
NNO	Liv Morgan	12.00	30.00
NNO	Nia Jax	8.00	20.00
NNO	No Way Jose	10.00	25.00
NNO	Peyton Royce	15.00	40.00
NNO	Samoa Joe	10.00	25.00
NNO	Sawyer Fulton	10.00	25.00
NNO	Scott Dawson	6.00	15.00
NNO	Shinsuke Nakamura	10.00	25.00
NNO	Tommaso Ciampa	6.00	15.00
NNO	Tye Dillinger	10.00	25.00

2017 Topps WWE NXT

UNOPENED BOX (10 PACKS)
UNOPENED PACK (7 CARDS)
*BRONZE: .6X TO 1.5X BASIC CARDS
*BLUE/50: .75X TO 2X BASIC CARDS
*SILVER/25: 1.2X TO 3X BASIC CARDS
*GOLD/10: UNPRICED DUE TO SCARCITY
*RED/1: UNPRICED DUE TO SCARCITY
*P.P.BLACK/1: UNPRICED DUE TO SCARCITY
*P.P.CYAN/1: UNPRICED DUE TO SCARCITY
*P.P.MAGENTA/1: UNPRICED DUE TO SCARCITY
*P.P.YELLOW/1: UNPRICED DUE TO SCARCITY

1	Asuka	1.25	3.00
2	Akam	.40	1.00
3	Alexander Wolfe	.50	1.25
4	Aliyah	.50	1.25
5	Andrade Cien Almas	.40	1.00
6	Angelo Dawkins	.40	1.00
7	Killian Dain	.40	1.00
8	Billie Kay	.50	1.25
9	Bobby Roode	1.00	2.50
10	Buddy Murphy	.40	1.00
11	Elias Samson	.60	1.50
12	Ember Moon	1.00	2.50
13	Eric Young	.75	2.00
14	Hideo Itami	.60	1.50
15	Johnny Gargano	.40	1.00
16	Liv Morgan	.60	1.50
17	Mandy Rose	.50	1.25
18	Nick Miller	.40	1.00
19	Nikki Cross	.75	2.00
20	No Way Jose	.40	1.00
21	Oney Lorcan	.40	1.00
22	Otis Dozovic	.50	1.25
23	Peyton Royce	.60	1.50
24	Rezar	.40	1.00
25	Riddick Moss	.50	1.25
26	Roderick Strong	.50	1.25
27	Ruby Riot	.50	1.25
28	Sawyer Fulton	.40	1.00
29	Shane Thorne	.40	1.00
30	Tian Bing	.40	1.00
31	Tino Sabbatelli	.50	1.25
32	Tommaso Ciampa	.40	1.00
33	Tucker Knight	1.00	2.50
34	Wesley Blake	.40	1.00
35	Cathy Kelley	.40	1.00
36	Charly Caruso	.40	1.00
37	Mike Rome	.40	1.00
38	Paul Ellering	.40	1.00
39	Tom Phillips	.40	1.00

40	William Regal	.50	1.25
41	Corey Graves	.40	1.00
42	Dasha Fuentes	.50	1.25
43	Baron Corbin	.60	1.50
44	Bayley	1.25	3.00
45	Dash Wilder	.40	1.00
46	Finn Balor	1.50	4.00
47	Samoa Joe	1.25	3.00
48	Scott Dawson	.40	1.00
49	Shinsuke Nakamura	1.00	2.50
50	Tye Dillinger	.40	1.00

2017 Topps WWE NXT Autographs

*BRONZE/99: .5X TO 1.2X BASIC AUTOS
*BLUE/50: .6X TO 1.5X BASIC AUTOS
*SILVER/25: .75X TO 2X BASIC AUTOS
*GOLD/10: UNPRICED DUE TO SCARCITY
*RED/1: UNPRICED DUE TO SCARCITY
*P.P.BLACK/1: UNPRICED DUE TO SCARCITY
*P.P.CYAN/1: UNPRICED DUE TO SCARCITY
*P.P.MAGENTA/1: UNPRICED DUE TO SCARCITY
*P.P.YELLOW/1: UNPRICED DUE TO SCARCITY
RANDOMLY INSERTED INTO PACKS

RAAC	Andrade Cien Almas	5.00	12.00
RAAD	Angelo Dawkins	5.00	12.00
RAAK	Akam	8.00	20.00
RAAL	Aliyah	6.00	15.00
RAAS	Asuka	20.00	50.00
RAAW	Alexander Wolfe	8.00	20.00
RABD	Killian Dain	5.00	12.00
RABK	Billie Kay	10.00	25.00
RABM	Buddy Murphy	5.00	12.00
RABR	Bobby Roode	10.00	25.00
RACC	Charly Caruso	8.00	20.00
RACK	Cathy Kelley	8.00	20.00
RADF	Dasha Fuentes	8.00	20.00
RADW	Dash Wilder	5.00	12.00
RAEM	Ember Moon	10.00	25.00
RAEY	Eric Young	6.00	15.00
RAHI	Hideo Itami	5.00	12.00
RAJG	Johnny Gargano	5.00	12.00
RALM	Liv Morgan	15.00	40.00
RAMR	Mandy Rose	20.00	50.00
RANC	Nikki Cross	10.00	25.00
RANM	Nick Miller	5.00	12.00
RANW	No Way Jose	5.00	12.00
RAOD	Otis Dozovic	5.00	12.00
RAOL	Oney Lorcan	6.00	15.00
RAPR	Peyton Royce	8.00	20.00
RARE	Rezar	5.00	12.00
RARM	Riddick Moss	5.00	12.00
RARS	Roderick Strong	5.00	12.00
RASD	Scott Dawson	5.00	12.00
RASF	Sawyer Fulton	5.00	12.00
RASN	Shinsuke Nakamura	12.00	30.00
RAST	Shane Thorne	5.00	12.00
RATB	Tian Bing	5.00	12.00
RATC	Tommaso Ciampa	5.00	12.00
RATK	Tucker Knight	5.00	12.00
RATP	Tom Phillips	5.00	12.00
RATS	Tino Sabbatelli	5.00	12.00
RAWB	Wesley Blake	5.00	12.00

2017 Topps WWE NXT Dual Relics

RANDOMLY INSERTED INTO PACKS
STATED PRINT RUN 25 SER.#'d SETS
UNPRICED DUE TO SCARCITY

DRAA	Andrade Cien Almas	

DRAS	Asuka	
DRBR	Bobby Roode	
DRBY	Bayley	
DREM	Ember Moon	
DRFB	Finn Balor	
DRJG	Johnny Gargano	
DRNJ	No Way Jose	
DRSD	Scott Dawson	
DRSJ	Samoa Joe	
DRSN	Shinsuke Nakamura	
DRTC	Tommaso Ciampa	

2017 Topps WWE NXT Mat Relics

*BRONZE/99: .5X TO 1.2X BASIC MEM
*BLUE/50: .6X TO 1.5X BASIC MEM
*SILVER/25: .75X TO 2X BASIC MEM
*GOLD/10: UNPRICED DUE TO SCARCITY
*RED/1: UNPRICED DUE TO SCARCITY
RANDOMLY INSERTED INTO PACKS

MRAA	Andrade Cien Almas	2.00	5.00
MRAC	Apollo Crews	2.50	6.00
MRAE	Aiden English	2.00	5.00
MRAK	Asuka	6.00	15.00
MRAS	Asuka	6.00	15.00
MRAU	Austin Aries	4.00	10.00
MRBC	Big Cass	2.50	6.00
MRBR	Bobby Roode	5.00	12.00
MRBY	Bayley	6.00	15.00
MRCG	Chad Gable	2.50	6.00
MRDW	Dash Wilder	2.00	5.00
MREA	Enzo Amore	6.00	15.00
MREM	Ember Moon	5.00	12.00
MRFB	Finn Balor	8.00	20.00
MRJG	Johnny Gargano	2.00	5.00
MRJJ	Jason Jordan	2.50	6.00
MRKO	Kevin Owens	5.00	12.00
MRMR	Mojo Rawley	2.50	6.00
MRSB	Sasha Banks	6.00	15.00
MRSD	Scott Dawson	2.00	5.00
MRSH	Shinsuke Nakamura	5.00	12.00
MRSJ	Samoa Joe	6.00	15.00
MRSK	Asuka	6.00	15.00
MRSN	Shinsuke Nakamura	5.00	12.00
MRSZ	Sami Zayn	2.50	6.00
MRTB	Tyler Breeze	2.00	5.00
MRTC	Tommaso Ciampa	2.00	5.00
MRTD	Tye Dillinger	2.00	5.00
MRZR	Zack Ryder	2.00	5.00
MRBCB	Baron Corbin	3.00	8.00
MRBEY	Bayley	6.00	15.00
MRBLY	Bayley	6.00	15.00
MRBRD	Bobby Roode	5.00	12.00
MRBRH	Bobby Roode	5.00	12.00
MRBYY	Bayley	6.00	15.00
MRFBL	Finn Balor	8.00	20.00
MRFBR	Finn Balor	8.00	20.00
MRNWJ	No Way Jose	2.00	5.00
MRNYJ	No Way Jose	2.00	5.00
MRSJE	Samoa Joe	6.00	15.00
MRSJO	Samoa Joe	6.00	15.00
MRSNK	Shinsuke Nakamura	5.00	12.00
MRSZN	Sami Zayn	2.50	6.00
MRTDL	Tye Dillinger	2.00	5.00

2017 Topps WWE NXT Matches and Moments

*BRONZE: .5X TO 1.5X BASIC CARDS
*BLUE/50: .75X TO 2X BASIC CARDS

*SILVER/25: 1.2X TO 3X BASIC CARDS
*GOLD/10: UNPRICED DUE TO SCARCITY
*RED/1: UNPRICED DUE TO SCARCITY
*P.P.BLACK/1: UNPRICED DUE TO SCARCITY
*P.P.CYAN/1: UNPRICED DUE TO SCARCITY
*P.P.MAGENTA/1: UNPRICED DUE TO SCARCITY
*P.P.YELLOW/1: UNPRICED DUE TO SCARCITY

#			
1	Jason Jordan & Chad Gable	.50	1.25
2	Finn Balor/Samoa Joe	1.50	4.00
3	Apollo Crews	.50	1.25
4	Finn Balor/Samoa Joe	1.50	4.00
5	Finn Balor/Samoa Joe	1.50	4.00
6	Bayley	1.25	3.00
7	Apollo Crews	.50	1.25
8	Baron Corbin	.60	1.50
9	Samoa Joe	1.25	3.00
10	Samoa Joe	1.25	3.00
11	Dash/Dawson	.40	1.00
12	Dash/Dawson	.40	1.00
13	Jason Jordan/Chad Gable	.50	1.25
14	Samoa Joe/Baron Corbin	1.25	3.00
15	Dash/Dawson	.40	1.00
16	Finn Balor	1.50	4.00
17	Elias Samson	.60	1.50
18	Sami Zayn	.50	1.25
19	Finn Balor	1.50	4.00
20	Sami Zayn vs. Samoa Joe	1.25	3.00
21	Baron Corbin	.60	1.50
22	Finn Balor	1.50	4.00
23	Samoa Joe	1.25	3.00
24	The Revival	.40	1.00
25	American Alpha	.50	1.25
26	Finn Balor	1.50	4.00
27	American Alpha	.50	1.25
28	Shinsuke Nakamura	1.00	2.50
29	Asuka	1.25	3.00
30	Finn Balor	1.50	4.00
31	Apollo Crews	.50	1.25
32	Shinsuke Nakamura	1.00	2.50
33	No Way Jose	.40	1.00
34	Samoa Joe	1.25	3.00
35	Samoa Joe	1.50	4.00
36	Shinsuke Nakamura	1.00	2.50
37	Finn Balor	1.50	4.00
38	Blake/Murphy	.40	1.00
39	Johnny Gargano/Tommaso Ciampa	.40	1.00
40	Andrade Cien Almas	.40	1.00
41	The Revival	.50	1.25
42	The Authors of Pain	.40	1.00
43	Samoa Joe	1.50	4.00
44	TM-61	.40	1.00
45	Oney Lorcan	.40	1.00
46	Johnny Gargano/Tommaso Ciampa	.40	1.00
47	The Revival	.50	1.25
48	Shinsuke Nakamura	1.50	4.00
49	Shinsuke Nakamura	1.00	2.50
50	Bobby Roode	1.00	2.50

2017 Topps WWE NXT Shirt Relics

*BRONZE/99: .5X TO 1.2X BASIC MEM
*BLUE/50: .6X TO 1.5X BASIC MEM
*SILVER/25: .75X TO 2X BASIC MEM
*GOLD/10: UNPRICED DUE TO SCARCITY
*RED/1: UNPRICED DUE TO SCARCITY
RANDOMLY INSERTED INTO PACKS

SRAK	Akam	2.00	5.00
SRAW	Alexander Wolfe	2.50	6.00
SRBR	Bobby Roode	5.00	12.00

SREM	Ember Moon	5.00	12.00
SREY	Eric Young	4.00	10.00
SRHI	Hideo Itami	3.00	8.00
SRNC	Nikki Cross	4.00	10.00
SRRZ	Rezar	2.00	5.00
SRSD	Scott Dawson	2.00	5.00
SRSN	Shinsuke Nakamura	5.00	12.00
SRACA	Andrade Cien Almas	2.00	5.00
SRAKA	Asuka	6.00	15.00
SRBLY	Bayley	6.00	15.00
SRNWJ	No Way Jose	2.00	5.00

2018 Topps WWE NXT

UNOPENED BOX (10 PACKS)
UNOPENED PACK (7 CARDS)
*BRONZE: .6X TO 1.5X BASIC CARDS
*BLUE/50: .75X TO 2X BASIC CARDS
*SILVER/25: 1.2X TO 3X BASIC CARDS
*GOLD/10: UNPRICED DUE TO SCARCITY
*RED/1: UNPRICED DUE TO SCARCITY
*P.P.BLACK/1: UNPRICED DUE TO SCARCITY
*P.P.CYAN/1: UNPRICED DUE TO SCARCITY
*P.P.MAGENTA/1: UNPRICED DUE TO SCARCITY
*P.P.YELLOW/1: UNPRICED DUE TO SCARCITY

#			
R1	Adam Cole	.50	1.25
R2	Akam	.40	1.00
R3	Aleister Black	.50	1.25
R4	Alexander Wolfe	.40	1.00
R5	Andrade Cien Almas	.60	1.50
R6	Angelo Dawkins	.40	1.00
R7	Bobby Fish	.40	1.00
R8	Buddy Murphy	.50	1.25
R9	Cezar Bononi	.40	1.00
R10	Drew McIntyre	.60	1.50
R11	Eric Young	.50	1.25
R12	Fabian Aichner	.40	1.00
R13	Gabriel Ealy	.40	1.00
R14	Kassius Ohno	.40	1.00
R15	Killian Dain	.50	1.25
R16	Kyle O'Reilly	.50	1.25
R17	Lars Sullivan	.40	1.00
R18	Lio Rush	.40	1.00
R19	Montez Ford	.40	1.00
R20	Nick Miller	.40	1.00
R21	No Way Jose	.50	1.25
R22	Oney Lorcan	.50	1.25
R23	Otis Dozovic	.40	1.00
R24	Paul Ellering	.50	1.25
R25	Pete Dunne	.40	1.00
R26	Rezar	.40	1.00
R27	Riddick Moss	.40	1.00
R28	Roderick Strong	.40	1.00
R29	Shane Thorne	.40	1.00
R30	Tino Sabbatelli	.50	1.25
R31	Tommaso Ciampa	.40	1.00
R32	Tucker Knight	.40	1.00
R33	Tyler Bate	.40	1.00
R34	Trent Seven	.40	1.00
R35	Velveteen Dream	.40	1.00
R36	Wesley Blake	.50	1.25
R37	Aliyah	.60	1.50
R38	Bianca Belair	.50	1.25
R39	Billie Kay	.75	2.00
R40	Ember Moon	.75	2.00
R41	Kairi Sane	1.00	2.50
R42	Lacey Evans	.50	1.25
R43	Nikki Cross	.60	1.50
R44	Peyton Royce	1.00	2.50

R45	Shayna Baszler	1.00	2.50
R46	Taynara Conti	.40	1.00
R47	Vanessa Borne	.40	1.00
R48	Zelina Vega	.40	1.00
R49	William Regal	.50	1.25
R50	Triple H	1.00	2.50

2018 Topps WWE NXT Autographed Shirt Relics

*BLUE/50: .5X TO 1.2X BASIC AUTOS
*SILVER/25: .6X TO 1.5X BASIC AUTOS
*GOLD/10: UNPRICED DUE TO SCARCITY
*RED/1: UNPRICED DUE TO SCARCITY
STATED PRINT RUN 99 SER.#'d SETS

ARAA	Andrade Cien Almas	8.00	20.00
ARAK	Akam	6.00	15.00
ARAW	Alexander Wolfe	5.00	12.00
AREM	Ember Moon	12.00	30.00
AREY	Eric Young	8.00	20.00
ARNC	Nikki Cross	10.00	25.00
ARNW	No Way Jose	8.00	20.00
ARRZ	Rezar	6.00	15.00

2018 Topps WWE NXT Autographs

*BRONZE/99: SAME VALUE AS BASIC
*BLUE/50: .5X TO 1.2X BASIC AUTOS
*SILVER/25: .6X TO 1.5X BASIC AUTOS
*GOLD/10: UNPRICED DUE TO SCARCITY
*RED/1: UNPRICED DUE TO SCARCITY
*P.P.BLACK/1: UNPRICED DUE TO SCARCITY
*P.P.CYAN/1: UNPRICED DUE TO SCARCITY
*P.P.MAGENTA/1: UNPRICED DUE TO SCARCITY
*P.P.YELLOW/1: UNPRICED DUE TO SCARCITY
RANDOMLY INSERTED INTO PACKS

AAA	Andrade Cien Almas	4.00	10.00
AAB	Aleister Black	6.00	15.00
AAC	Adam Cole	8.00	20.00
AAD	Angelo Dawkins	4.00	10.00
AAK	Akam	4.00	10.00
AAW	Alexander Wolfe	4.00	10.00
AAY	Aliyah	6.00	15.00
ABB	Bianca Belair	50.00	100.00
ABF	Bobby Fish	10.00	25.00
ABK	Billie Kay	10.00	25.00
ABM	Buddy Murphy	5.00	12.00
ABY	Bayley	8.00	20.00
ACB	Cezar Bononi	5.00	12.00
ADA	Dean Ambrose	20.00	50.00
ADM	Drew McIntyre	8.00	20.00
AEM	Ember Moon	8.00	20.00
AEY	Eric Young	5.00	12.00
AFA	Fabian Aichner	6.00	15.00
AJG	Johnny Gargano	6.00	15.00
AKD	Killian Dain	5.00	12.00
AKS	Kairi Sane	20.00	50.00
ALE	Lacey Evans	10.00	25.00
ALR	Lio Rush	10.00	25.00
ALS	Lars Sullivan	10.00	25.00
AMF	Montez Ford	10.00	25.00
ANC	Nikki Cross	6.00	15.00
ANM	Nick Miller	5.00	12.00
ANW	No Way Jose	4.00	10.00
AOD	Otis Dozovic	5.00	12.00
AOL	Oney Lorcan	5.00	12.00
AON	Kassius Ohno	4.00	10.00
APD	Pete Dunne	15.00	40.00
APR	Peyton Royce	6.00	15.00

ARE	Rezar	4.00	10.00
ARM	Riddick Moss	4.00	10.00
ARS	Roderick Strong	4.00	10.00
ASH	Shayna Baszler	12.00	30.00
AST	Shane Thorne	5.00	12.00
ATB	Tyler Bate	10.00	25.00
ATC	Tommaso Ciampa	5.00	12.00
ATK	Tucker Knight	4.00	10.00
ATS	Tino Sabbatelli	4.00	10.00
ATY	Taynara Conti	20.00	50.00
AUA	Kyle O'Reilly	6.00	15.00
AVB	Vanessa Borne	12.00	30.00
AVD	Velveteen Dream	6.00	15.00
AWB	Wesley Blake	4.00	10.00
AZV	Zelina Vega	20.00	50.00

2018 Topps WWE NXT Dual Autographs

*GOLD/10: UNPRICED DUE TO SCARCITY
*RED/1: UNPRICED DUE TO SCARCITY
STATED PRINT RUN 25 SER.#'d SETS

DADY	Triple H/William Regal	75.00	150.00
DAID	Peyton Royce/Billie Kay	75.00	150.00

2018 Topps WWE NXT Matches and Moments

*BRONZE: .6X TO 1.5X BASIC CARDS
*BLUE/50: .75X TO 2X BASIC CARDS
*SILVER/25: 1.2X TO 3X BASIC CARDS
*GOLD/10: UNPRICED DUE TO SCARCITY
*RED/1: UNPRICED DUE TO SCARCITY
*P.P.BLACK/1: UNPRICED DUE TO SCARCITY
*P.P.CYAN/1: UNPRICED DUE TO SCARCITY
*P.P.MAGENTA/1: UNPRICED DUE TO SCARCITY
*P.P.YELLOW/1: UNPRICED DUE TO SCARCITY

1	Samoa Joe	.75	2.00
2	Bobby Roode	.60	1.50
3	The Revival	.50	1.25
4	Shinsuke Nakamura	1.00	2.50
5	The Authors of Pain	.50	1.25
6	Tye Dillinger	.40	1.00
7	Bobby Roode	.60	1.50
8	Andrade "Cien" Almas	.60	1.50
9	SAnitY Debut	.60	1.50
10	#DIY Advance	.40	1.00
11	Shane Thorne	.40	1.00
12	The Authors of Pain	.50	1.25
13	Andrade "Cien" Almas	.60	1.50
14	Bobby Roode	.60	1.50
15	The Authors of Pain	.50	1.25
16	#DIY	.40	1.00
17	Samoa Joe	.75	2.00
18	SAnitY	.60	1.50
19	Samoa Joe	.75	2.00
20	Shinsuke Nakamura	1.00	2.50
21	Shinsuke Nakamura	1.00	2.50
22	Bobby Roode	.60	1.50
23	#DIY	.40	1.00
24	#DIY	.50	1.25
25	TM61	.50	1.25
26	Eric Young	.50	1.25
27	The Authors of Pain	.50	1.25
28	Seth Rollins	1.00	2.50
29	Bobby Roode	1.00	2.50
30	SAnitY	.50	1.25
31	Kassius Ohno	.40	1.00
32	The Authors of Pain	.50	1.25

33	Shinsuke Nakamura	1.00	2.50
34	Bobby Roode	.60	1.50
35	Kassius Ohno	1.00	2.50
36	SAnitY	.50	1.25
37	Aleister Black	.50	1.25
38	The Authors of Pain	.50	1.25
39	Bobby Roode	1.00	2.50
40	Oney Lorcan	.50	1.25
41	Drew McIntyre	.60	1.50
42	Tye Dillinger	.40	1.00
43	Tyler Bate	.50	1.25
44	Hideo Itami	.40	1.00
45	Hideo Itami	.40	1.00
46	Roderick Strong	.50	1.25
47	Pete Dunne	.40	1.00
48	Bobby Roode	.60	1.50
49	The Authors of Pain	.40	1.00
50	Tommaso Ciampa	.40	1.00

2018 Topps WWE NXT Triple Autographs

*GOLD/10: UNPRICED DUE TO SCARCITY
*RED/1: UNPRICED DUE TO SCARCITY

TAERA	Cole/Fish/O'Reilly	50.00	100.00
TAMAG	McIntyre/Almas/Gargano	30.00	75.00
TAMCA	Moon/Cross/Aliyah	50.00	100.00
TASAY	Young/Wolfe/Dain	25.00	60.00

2019 Topps WWE NXT

COMPLETE SET (100)		12.00	30.00

*BRONZE: .6X TO 1.5X BASIC CARDS
*BLUE/50: .75X TO 2X BASIC CARDS
*SILVER/25: 2X TO 5X BASIC CARDS
*GOLD/10: UNPRICED DUE TO SCARCITY
*RED/1: UNPRICED DUE TO SCARCITY

1	Velveteen Dream	.50	1.25
2	The Undisputed Era	.40	1.00
3	Aleister Black	.30	.75
4	Andrade	.30	.75
5	Roderick Strong	.50	1.25
6	Pete Dunne	.50	1.25
7	Johnny Gargano	.25	.60
8	Pete Dunne & Roderick Strong	.50	1.25
9	Adam Cole	.30	.75
10	Johnny Gargano	.25	.60
11	Pete Dunne & Roderick Strong	.50	1.25
12	EC3	.25	.60
13	Ricochet	.60	1.50
14	Adam Cole	.30	.75
15	Roderick Strong	.50	1.25
16	Aleister Black	.30	.75
17	Johnny Gargano	.50	1.25
18	The Viking Raiders	.30	.75
19	Ricochet	.60	1.50
20	Lars Sullivan	.25	.60
21	Kona Reeves	.30	.75
22	Pete Dunne	.50	1.25
23	The Viking Raiders	.30	.75
24	Tommaso Ciampa	.40	1.00
25	Kona Reeves	.30	.75
26	Dunne/Danny Burch/Oney Lorcan	.50	1.25
27	Lars Sullivan	.25	.60
28	EC3	.40	1.00
29	Pete Dunne	.50	1.25
30	The Undisputed Era	.50	1.25
31	Ricochet	.60	1.50
32	Aleister Black	.30	.75

33	Tommaso Ciampa	.25	.60
34	British Strong Style	.50	1.25
35	Aleister Black & Ricochet	.60	1.50
36	Moustache Mountain	.40	1.00
37	The Undisputed Era	.50	1.25
38	Johnny Gargano	.25	.60
39	The Undisputed Era	.50	1.25
40	Tommaso Ciampa	.30	.75
41	EC3	.25	.60
42	Aleister Black	.30	.75
43	Keith Lee	.25	.60
44	The Undisputed Era	.50	1.25
45	Velveteen Dream	.50	1.25
46	Ricochet	.60	1.50
47	Tommaso Ciampa	.25	.60
48	Lars Sullivan	.25	.60
49	The Undisputed Era	.50	1.25
50	The Forgotten Sons	.40	1.00
51	Jaxson Ryker	.25	.60
52	Pete Dunne	.60	1.50
53	Lars Sullivan	.25	.60
54	Keith Lee	.25	.60
55	Ricochet	.60	1.50
56	Bobby Fish	.40	1.00
57	Pete Dunne	.50	1.25
58	EC3	.25	.60
59	Johnny Gargano	.30	.75
60	Matt Riddle	.40	1.00
61	Heavy Machinery	.25	.60
62	Pete Dunne	.50	1.25
63	Aleister Black	.30	.75
64	Tommaso Ciampa	.25	.60
65	Dunne/Ricochet/Viking Raiders	.60	1.50
66	The Forgotten Sons	.40	1.00
67	EC3	.25	.60
68	Ricochet	.60	1.50
69	Dominik Dijakovic	.25	.60
70	Walter	.50	1.25
71	Tommaso Ciampa	.25	.60
72	The Viking Raiders	.30	.75
73	Johnny Gargano	.25	.60
74	Matt Riddle	.40	1.00
75	Black/Ricochet/Velveteen Dream	.25	.60
76	Rik Bugez	.40	1.00
77	Ricochet	.60	1.50
78	Velveteen Dream	.50	1.25
79	Keith Lee	.25	.60
80	DIY	.25	.60
81	Aleister Black/Ricochet	.60	1.50
82	Aleister Black/Ricochet	.60	1.50
83	Johnny Gargano	.25	.60
84	Adam Cole	.30	.75
85	Aleister Black & Ricochet	.60	1.50
86	The Viking Raiders	.30	.75
87	Velveteen Dream	.50	1.25
88	Walter	.50	1.25
89	Johnny Gargano	.50	1.25
90	Velveteen Dream	.50	1.25
91	Kushida	.25	.60
92	Matt Riddle	.40	1.00
93	The Viking Raiders	.30	.75
94	Tyler Breeze	.30	.75
95	Walter	.50	1.25
96	Imperium	.50	1.25
97	Matt Riddle	.50	1.25
98	The Street Profits	.30	.75
99	Velveteen Dream	.50	1.25
100	Adam Cole	.30	.75

2019 Topps WWE NXT Autographed Shirt Relics

*BLUE/50: .5X TO 1.2X BASIC AUTOS
*SILVER/25: UNPRICED DUE TO SCARCITY
*GOLD/10: UNPRICED DUE TO SCARCITY
*RED/1: UNPRICED DUE TO SCARCITY
STATED ODDS 1:364
STATED PRINT RUN 99 SER.#'d SETS

ASAC Adam Cole	8.00	20.00
ASRS Roderick Strong	.6.00	15.00
ASSB Shayna Baszler	10.00	25.00
ASVD Velveteen Dream	6.00	15.00

2019 Topps WWE NXT Autographs

*BRONZE/99: SAME VALUE AS BASIC
*BLUE/50: .5X TO 1.2X BASIC AUTOS
*SILVER/25: UNPRICE DUE TO SCARCITY
*GOLD/10: UNPRICED DUE TO SCARCITY
*RED/1: UNPRICED DUE TO SCARCITY
*P.P.BLACK/1: UNPRICED DUE TO SCARCITY
*P.P.CYAN/1: UNPRICED DUE TO SCARCITY
*P.P.MAGENTA/1: UNPRICED DUE TO SCARCITY
*P.P.YELLOW/1: UNPRICED DUE TO SCARCITY
STATED ODDS 1:20

AE Erik	5.00	12.00
AI Ivar	5.00	12.00
AAC Adam Cole	8.00	20.00
ABB Bianca Belair	12.00	30.00
ABF Bobby Fish	5.00	12.00
ABM Buddy Murphy	5.00	12.00
ACG Chelsea Green	15.00	40.00
ACL Candice LeRae	6.00	15.00
ADD Dominik Dijakovic	6.00	15.00
ADP Deonna Purrazzo	6.00	15.00
AIS Io Shirai	25.00	60.00
AJD Jessamyn Duke	8.00	20.00
AJG Johnny Gargano	5.00	12.00
AKL Keith Lee	12.00	30.00
AKY Kyle O'Reilly	5.00	12.00
ALE Lacey Evans	15.00	40.00
AMS Marina Shafir	5.00	12.00
AMY Mia Yim	10.00	25.00
ANC Nikki Cross	8.00	20.00
AOD Otis	6.00	15.00
AOH Kassius Ohno	5.00	12.00
APD Pete Dunne	8.00	20.00
APM Damian Priest	5.00	12.00
ARC Ricochet	12.00	30.00
ARS Roderick Strong	5.00	12.00
ASB Shayna Baszler	6.00	15.00
ATK Tucker	5.00	12.00
ATM Tommaso Ciampa	8.00	20.00
ATS Toni Storm	75.00	150.00
AVD Velveteen Dream	5.00	12.00
AWT Walter	15.00	40.00
ABRO Matt Riddle	15.00	40.00

2019 Topps WWE NXT Dual Autographs

*GOLD/10: UNPRICED DUE TO SCARCITY
*RED/1: UNPRICED DUE TO SCARCITY
STATED ODDS 1:1,149
STATED PRINT RUN 25 SER.#'d SETS

DAAB M.Barthel/F.Aichner	25.00	60.00
DAGL C.LeRae/J.Gargano	60.00	120.00
DAMG V.Borne/Aliyah	50.00	100.00
DASO K.O'Reilly/R.Strong	20.00	50.00

2019 Topps WWE NXT Kiss Autographs

*GOLD/10: UNPRICED DUE TO SCARCITY
*RED/1: UNPRICED DUE TO SCARCITY
STATED ODDS 1:1,910
STATED PRINT RUN 25 SER.#'d SETS

AKAL Aliyah	50.00	100.00
AKBB Bianca Belair	125.00	250.00
AKCG Chelsea Green	100.00	200.00
AKIS Io Shirai	200.00	350.00

2019 Topps WWE NXT Roster

COMPLETE SET (50)	15.00	40.00

STATED ODDS 2:1

1 Adam Cole	.60	1.50
2 Jordan Myles	.30	.75
3 Aliyah	.50	1.25
4 Angelo Dawkins	.50	1.25
5 Bianca Belair	.30	.75
6 Bobby Fish	.75	2.00
7 Candice LeRae	1.00	2.50
8 Cathy Kelly	1.25	3.00
9 Chelsea Green	.50	1.25
10 Dakota Kai	1.00	2.50
11 Damian Priest	.50	1.25
12 Danny Burch	.50	1.25
13 Deonna Purrazzo	.50	1.25
14 Dominik Dijakovic	.50	1.25
15 Fabian Aichner	1.00	2.50
16 Humberto Carrillo	1.00	2.50
17 Io Shirai	.50	1.25
18 Jaxson Ryker	.50	1.25
19 Jessamyn Duke	.60	1.50
20 Jessi Kamea	.50	1.25
21 Johnny Gargano	.50	1.25
22 Kacy Catanzaro	1.25	3.00
23 Kassius Ohno	.75	2.00
24 Keith Lee	.50	1.25
25 Kona Reeves	.60	1.50
26 Kushida	.50	1.25
27 Kyle O'Reilly	.75	2.00
28 Marcel Barthel	1.00	2.50
29 Marina Shafir	.50	1.25
30 Matt Riddle	.75	2.00
31 Mauro Ranallo	.50	1.25
32 Mia Yim	.50	1.25
33 Montez Ford	.50	1.25
34 Oney Lorcan	.60	1.50
35 Pete Dunne	1.00	2.50
36 Raul Mendoza	.50	1.25
37 Rik Bugez	.50	1.25
38 Riddick Moss	.50	1.25
39 Roderick Strong	1.00	2.50
40 Shayna Baszler	1.00	2.50
41 Steve Cutler	.75	2.00
42 Toni Storm	2.00	5.00
43 Trent Seven	.75	2.00
44 Tyler Bate	.60	1.50
45 Vanessa Borne	.60	1.50
46 Velveteen Dream	1.00	2.50
47 Walter	1.00	2.50
48 Wesley Blake	.75	2.00
49 William Regal	.75	2.00
50 Xia Li	.50	1.25

2019 Topps WWE NXT Triple Autographs

*GOLD/10: UNPRICED DUE TO SCARCITY
*RED/1: UNPRICED DUE TO SCARCITY
STATED ODDS 1:1,442
STATED PRINT RUN 25 SER.#'d SETS

TA4H Shafir/Baszler/Duke	60.00	120.00
TAFS Ryker/Blake/Cutler	30.00	75.00
TAMYC Purrazzo/Shirai/Yim	100.00	200.00

2020 Topps WWE NXT

COMPLETE SET (100)	8.00	20.00

*BRONZE: .5X TO 1.2X BASIC CARDS
*BLUE/50: .75X TO 2X BASIC CARDS
*SILVER/25: UNPRICED DUE TO SCARCITY
*GOLD/10: UNPRICED DUE TO SCARCITY
*RED/1: UNPRICED DUE TO SCARCITY

1 Imperium	.60	1.50
2 Alexander Wolfe	.60	1.50
3 Angel Garza	.40	1.00
4 Adam Cole	.75	2.00
5 Imperium	.50	1.25
6 Isaiah Swerve Scott	.40	1.00
7 Trent Seven	.30	.75
8 Killian Dain	.40	1.00
9 Johnny Gargano	.75	2.00
10 WALTER	.60	1.50
11 Pete Dunne	.30	.75
12 Tyler Bate	.50	1.25
13 Pete Dunne	.60	1.50
14 Dave Mastiff	.40	1.00
15 Street Profits	.30	.75
16 Velveteen Dream	.40	1.00
17 Adam Cole	.75	2.00
18 Flash Morgan Webster	.40	1.00
19 Mark Andrews	.30	.75
20 Moustache Mountain	.60	1.50
21 Killian Dain	.40	1.00
22 Dominik Dijakovic	.30	.75
23 Undisputed ERA	.75	2.00
24 Joe Coffey	.40	1.00
25 Mark Andrews	.40	1.00
26 WALTER	.60	1.50
27 Roderick Strong	.60	1.50
28 Mark Andrews & Flash Webster	.40	1.00
29 Roderick Strong	.60	1.50
30 Matt Riddle	.60	1.50
31 Keith Lee	.30	.75
32 Matt Riddle	.60	1.50
33 Adam Cole	.75	2.00
34 Undisputed ERA	.60	1.50
35 Finn Balor	.75	2.00
36 Tommaso Ciampa	.75	2.00
37 Gallus	.40	1.00
38 Roderick Strong	.60	1.50
39 Tommaso Ciampa	.60	1.50
40 Pete Dunne	.30	.75
41 Damian Priest	.30	.75
42 Gallus	.40	1.00
43 Angel Garza	.40	1.00
44 Roderick Strong	.60	1.50
45 Finn Balor	.75	2.00
46 Undisputed ERA	.75	2.00
47 NXT Invades SmackDown	1.00	2.50
48 Adam Cole	.75	2.00
49 Pete Dunne	.30	.75
50 Angel Garza	.40	1.00
51 Ilja Dragunov	.60	1.50
52 Imperium	.50	1.25
53 WALTER	.60	1.50
54 Finn Balor	.75	2.00
55 Keith Lee	.60	1.50
56 Damian Priest	.30	.75
57 Adam Cole	.75	2.00
58 Alexander Wolfe	.30	.75
59 NXT Invades SD DX-Style	.75	2.00
60 Pete Dunne	.30	.75
61 Finn Balor	.75	2.00
62 Team Ciampa	.60	1.50
63 Roderick Strong	.60	1.50
64 Adam Cole	.75	2.00
65 Keith Lee	.75	2.00
66 Undisputed ERA	.75	2.00
67 Finn Balor	.75	2.00
68 Gallus & Ilja Dragunov	.60	1.50
69 Tommaso Ciampa	.30	.75
70 Imperium	.60	1.50
71 Angel Garza	.40	1.00
72 Finn Balor	.75	2.00
73 Brawl Leads to Ladder Match	.30	.75
74 Johnny Gargano	.60	1.50
75 Isaiah Swerve Scott	.40	1.00
76 Austin Theory	.50	1.25
77 Ilja Dragunov	.50	1.25
78 Austin Theory	.50	1.25
79 Imperium	.30	.75
80 Undisputed ERA	.75	2.00
81 Keith Lee	.30	.75
82 Tyler Bate	.50	1.25
83 Gallus	.40	1.00
84 WALTER	.60	1.50
85 Undisputed ERA	.75	2.00
86 BroserWeights	.60	1.50
87 Johnny Gargano	.60	1.50
88 Grizzled Young Veterans	.40	1.00
89 Isaiah Swerve Scott	.40	1.00
90 Imperium	.75	2.00
91 Grizzled Young Veterans	.40	1.00
92 BroserWeights	.60	1.50
93 Keith Lee	.60	1.50
94 Jordan Devlin	.30	.75
95 Travis Banks	.30	.75
96 Finn Balor	.75	2.00
97 Jordan Devlin	.40	1.00
98 Imperium	.60	1.50
99 #DIY	.60	1.50
100 BroserWeights	.60	1.50

2020 Topps WWE NXT Autographed Mat Relics

*BLUE/50: .5X TO 1.2X BASIC AUTOS
*SILVER/25: UNPRICED DUE TO SCARCITY
*GOLD/10: UNPRICED DUE TO SCARCITY
*RED/1: UNPRICED DUE TO SCARCITY
STATED ODDS 1:12
STATED PRINT RUN 99 SER.#'d SETS

MRAAC Adam Cole	20.00	50.00
MRABB Bianca Belair	15.00	40.00
MRABF Bobby Fish	12.00	30.00
MRACL Candice LeRae	25.00	60.00
MRADK Dakota Kai	30.00	75.00
MRAIS Io Shirai	30.00	75.00
MRAJG Johnny Gargano	10.00	25.00
MRAKL Keith Lee	12.00	30.00
MRAKO Kyle O'Reilly	10.00	25.00

MRAMR Matt Riddle	15.00	40.00
MRARR Rhea Ripley	50.00	100.00
MRATC Tommaso Ciampa	12.00	30.00
MRATN Tegan Nox	25.00	60.00
MRAVT Velveteen Dream	12.00	30.00

2020 Topps WWE NXT Autographed Shirt Relics

*SILVER/25: UNPRICED DUE TO SCARCITY
*GOLD/10: UNPRICED DUE TO SCARCITY
*RED/1: UNPRICED DUE TO SCARCITY
STATED ODDS 1:33
STATED PRINT RUN 50 SER.#'d SETS

SRAAC Adam Cole	20.00	50.00
SRABF Bobby Fish	12.00	30.00
SRAFB Finn Balor	15.00	40.00
SRAJG Johnny Gargano	12.00	30.00
SRAKO Kyle O'Reilly	10.00	25.00
SRAKU Kushida	10.00	25.00
SRAMY Mia Yim	12.00	30.00
SRAT7 Trent Seven	20.00	50.00
SRATC Tommaso Ciampa	10.00	25.00
SRAVD Velveteen Dream		

2020 Topps WWE NXT Called Up

COMPLETE SET (9) 6.00 15.00
RANDOMLY INSERTED INTO PACKS

CU1 Aleister Black	1.50	4.00
CU2 Angelo Dawkins	.75	2.00
CU3 Lacey Evans	2.00	5.00
CU4 Lars Sullivan	.75	2.00
CU5 Montez Ford	.75	2.00
CU6 Nikki Cross	1.50	4.00
CU7 Otis	1.25	3.00
CU8 Ricochet	1.25	3.00
CU9 Tucker	.75	2.00

2020 Topps WWE NXT Called Up Autographs

STATED PRINT RUN 25 SER.#'d SETS

CUAAB Aleister Black		
CUAAD Angelo Dawkins		
CUALE Lacey Evans		
CUAMF Montez Ford	15.00	40.00
CUANC Nikki Cross		
CUAOT Otis		
CUARC Ricochet		

2020 Topps WWE NXT Dual Autographs

STATED PRINT RUN 25 SER.#'d SETS

DABB V.Borne/Aliyah	100.00	200.00
DATK T.Nox/D.Kai	125.00	250.00
DAUE B.Fish/K.O'Reilly	25.00	60.00

2020 Topps WWE NXT Johnny Gargano Tribute

COMPLETE SET (20) 12.00 30.00
RANDOMLY INSERTED INTO PACKS

JG1 Johnny Gargano	1.50	4.00
JG2 Johnny Gargano	1.50	4.00
JG3 Johnny Gargano	1.50	4.00
JG4 Johnny Gargano	1.50	4.00
JG5 Johnny Gargano	1.50	4.00
JG6 Johnny Gargano	1.50	4.00
JG7 Johnny Gargano	1.50	4.00
JG8 Johnny Gargano	1.50	4.00
JG9 Johnny Gargano	1.50	4.00
JG10 Johnny Gargano	1.50	4.00
JG11 Johnny Gargano	1.50	4.00
JG12 Johnny Gargano	1.50	4.00
JG13 Johnny Gargano	1.50	4.00
JG14 Johnny Gargano	1.50	4.00
JG15 Johnny Gargano	1.50	4.00
JG16 Johnny Gargano	1.50	4.00
JG17 Johnny Gargano	1.50	4.00
JG18 Johnny Gargano	1.50	4.00
JG19 Johnny Gargano	1.50	4.00
JG20 Johnny Gargano	1.50	4.00

2020 Topps WWE NXT Johnny Gargano Tribute Autographs

*GOLD/10: UNPRICED DUE TO SCARCITY
*RED/1: UNPRICED DUE TO SCARCITY
STATED PRINT RUN 25 SER.#'d SETS

JG15 Johnny Gargano	10.00	25.00
JG16 Johnny Gargano	10.00	25.00
JG17 Johnny Gargano	10.00	25.00
JG18 Johnny Gargano	10.00	25.00
JG19 Johnny Gargano	10.00	25.00

2020 Topps WWE NXT Roster

COMPLETE SET (66) 15.00 40.00
RANDOMLY INSERTED INTO PACKS

NXT1 Adam Cole	.75	2.00
NXT2 Aliyah	.60	1.50
NXT3 Angel Garza	.40	1.00
NXT4 Austin Theory	.50	1.25
NXT5 Bianca Belair	.75	2.00
NXT6 Boa	.30	.75
NXT7 Bobby Fish	.30	.75
NXT8 Bronson Reed	.30	.75
NXT9 Cameron Grimes	.30	.75
NXT10 Candice LeRae	1.00	2.50
NXT11 Chelsea Green	1.50	4.00
NXT12 Dakota Kai	.60	1.50
NXT13 Damian Priest	.30	.75
NXT14 Danny Burch	.40	1.00
NXT15 Dexter Lumis	.30	.75
NXT16 Dominik Dijakovic	.30	.75
NXT17 Fandango	.30	.75
NXT18 Finn Balor	.75	2.00
NXT19 Io Shirai	.50	1.25
NXT20 Isaiah "Swerve" Scott	.40	1.00
NXT21 Jaxson Ryker	.40	1.00
NXT22 Jessamyn Duke	.50	1.25
NXT23 Joaquin Wilde	.30	.75
NXT24 Johnny Gargano	.60	1.50
NXT25 Keith Lee	.30	.75
NXT26 Killian Dain	.40	1.00
NXT27 Kona Reeves	.30	.75
NXT28 Kyle O'Reilly	.40	1.00
NXT29 Kushida	.30	.75
NXT30 Mansoor	.30	.75
NXT31 Marina Shafir	.50	1.25
NXT32 Matt Riddle	.60	1.50
NXT33 Mia Yim	.60	1.50
NXT34 Oney Lorcan	.40	1.00
NXT35 Pete Dunne	.30	.75
NXT36 Raul Mendoza	.30	.75
NXT37 Rhea Ripley	1.25	3.00
NXT38 Roderick Strong	.60	1.50
NXT39 Santana Garrett	.30	.75
NXT40 Shane Thorne	.30	.75
NXT41 Shayna Baszler	1.00	2.50
NXT42 Shotzi Blackheart	1.00	2.50
NXT43 Steve Cutler	.30	.75
NXT44 Tegan Nox	.75	2.00
NXT45 Tommaso Ciampa	.60	1.50
NXT46 Tyler Breeze	.40	1.00
NXT47 Vanessa Borne	.60	1.50
NXT48 Velveteen Dream	.40	1.00
NXT49 Wesley Blake	.40	1.00
NXT50 Xia Li	.60	1.50
NXT51 Alexander Wolfe	.30	.75
NXT52 Fabian Aichner	.30	.75
NXT53 Flash Morgan Webster	.40	1.00
NXT54 Joe Coffey	.30	.75
NXT55 Jordan Devlin	.30	.75
NXT56 Kay Lee Ray	.50	1.25
NXT57 Marcel Barthel	.30	.75
NXT58 Mark Andrews	.30	.75
NXT59 Mark Coffey	.40	1.00
NXT60 Toni Storm	.75	2.00
NXT61 Trent Seven	.30	.75
NXT62 Tyler Bate	.50	1.25
NXT63 WALTER	.60	1.50
NXT64 Wolfgang	.30	.75
NXT65 James Drake	.40	1.00
NXT66 Zack Gibson	.30	.75

2020 Topps WWE NXT Roster Autographs

*BRONZE/99: .5X TO 1.2X BASIC AUTOS
*BLUE/50: .6X TO 1.5X BASIC AUTOS
*SILVER/25: UNPRICED DUE TO SCARCITY
*GOLD/10: UNPRICED DUE TO SCARCITY
*RED/1: UNPRICED DUE TO SCARCITY

AAC Adam Cole	10.00	25.00
AAG Angel Garza	6.00	15.00
AAL Aliyah	10.00	25.00
AAR Arturo Ruas	6.00	15.00
AAT Austin Theory	12.00	30.00
ABB Bianca Belair	20.00	50.00
ABF Bobby Fish	5.00	12.00
ABL Shotzi Blackheart	60.00	120.00
ABR Bronson Reed	10.00	25.00
ACG Cameron Grimes	6.00	15.00
ACL Candice LeRae	20.00	50.00
ADD Dominik Dijakovic	5.00	12.00
ADK Dakota Kai	15.00	40.00
ADL Dexter Lumis	20.00	50.00
ADP Damian Priest	6.00	15.00
AFA Fabian Aichner	5.00	12.00
AFB Finn Balor	10.00	25.00
AIO Io Shirai	20.00	50.00
AIS Isaiah Swerve Scott	5.00	12.00
AJG Johnny Gargano	8.00	20.00
AJW Joaquin Wilde	8.00	20.00
AKC Kayden Carter	10.00	25.00
AKL Keith Lee	6.00	15.00
AKU Kushida	10.00	25.00
AMB Marcel Barthel	5.00	12.00
AMR Matt Riddle	15.00	40.00
AMY Mia Yim	8.00	20.00
AOL Oney Lorcan	5.00	12.00
ARM Raul Mendoza	6.00	15.00
ARR Rhea Ripley	50.00	100.00
ARS Roderick Strong	5.00	12.00
ATN Tegan Nox	30.00	75.00
ATO Tommaso Ciampa	6.00	15.00
AVD Velveteen Dream	5.00	12.00

2021 Topps WWE NXT

COMPLETE SET (100) 10.00 25.00
*PURPLE: .75X TO 2X BASIC CARDS
*BLUE: 1.5X TO 4X BASIC CARDS
*RED/25: 2X TO 5X BASIC CARDS
*GOLD/10: UNPRICED DUE TO SCARCITY
*PLATINUM/1: UNPRICED DUE TO SCARCITY

1 Roderick Strong	.60	1.50
2 Keith Lee	.60	1.50
3 The BroserWeights	.75	2.00
4 Adam Cole	1.00	2.50
5 Johnny Gargano	.60	1.50
6 The BroserWeights	.75	2.00
7 Tommaso Ciampa	.75	2.00
8 Keith Lee	.60	1.50
9 Johnny Gargano	.60	1.50
10 Timothy Thatcher	.30	.75
11 Karrion Kross	1.50	4.00
12 Akira Tozawa	.50	1.25
13 El Hijo	.60	1.50
14 Jake Atlas	.30	.75
15 Kushida	.50	1.25
16 Isaiah "Swerve" Scott	.60	1.50
17 Imperium	.40	1.00
18 Drake Maverick	.30	.75
19 Keith Lee	.60	1.50
20 Johnny Gargano	.60	1.50
21 Karrion Kross	1.50	4.00
22 Adam Cole	1.00	2.50
23 Akira Tozawa	.40	1.00
24 Kushida	.50	1.25
25 Jake Atlas	.30	.75
26 Imperium	.40	1.00
27 Damian Priest	.75	2.00
28 Riddle	.75	2.00
29 El Hijo	.60	1.50
30 Roderick Strong	.60	1.50
31 Drake Maverick	.50	1.25
32 Tommaso Ciampa	.75	2.00
33 Timothy Thatcher	.30	.75
34 El Hijo	.60	1.50
35 Finn B-lor	.75	2.00
36 Keith Lee	.60	1.50
37 Karrion Kross	1.25	3.00
38 El Hijo	.60	1.50
39 Adam Cole	1.00	2.50
40 Imperium	.40	1.00
41 Karrion Kross	1.25	3.00
42 Dexter Lumis	.30	.75
43 Keith Lee	.60	1.50
44 Dexter Lumis	.30	.75
45 Legado del Fantasma	.60	1.50
46 Keith Lee	.60	1.50
47 Keith Lee	.60	1.50
48 Breezango	.50	1.25
49 Bronson Reed	.40	1.00
50 Karrion Kross	1.25	3.00
51 Imperium	.40	1.00
52 Dexter Lumis	.30	.75
53 Damian Priest	.50	1.25
54 Keith Lee	.60	1.50
55 Imperium	.40	1.00
56 Karrion Kross	1.25	3.00
57 Bronson Reed	.40	1.00
58 Cameron Grimes	.60	1.50
59 Breezango	.50	1.25
60 Finn B-lor	.75	2.00
61 Damian Priest	.50	1.25

62	Karrion Kross	1.25	3.00
63	Karrion Kross	1.50	4.00
64	Breezango	.50	1.25
65	Adam Cole	1.00	2.50
66	Finn B-lor	.75	2.00
67	Breezango	.50	1.25
68	Damian Priest	.50	1.25
69	Damian Priest	.50	1.25
70	Roderick Strong & Danny Burch	.60	1.50
71	Kyle O'Reilly	.50	1.25
72	Damian Priest	.50	1.25
73	Santos Escobar	.60	1.50
74	Finn B-lor	.75	2.00
75	Cameron Grimes	.60	1.50
76	Johnny Gargano	.60	1.50
77	Undisputed ERA	.60	1.50
78	Damian Priest	.50	1.25
79	Legado del Fantasma	.60	1.50
80	Oney Lorcan & Danny Burch	.40	1.00
81	Pete Dunne	.75	2.00
82	Johnny Gargano	.60	1.50
83	Dexter Lumis	.60	1.50
84	Kushida	.50	1.25
85	Leon Ruff	.30	.75
86	Santos Escobar	.60	1.50
87	Oney Lorcan & Danny Burch	.30	.75
88	Damian Priest	.60	1.50
89	Dexter Lumis and Cameron Grimes	.60	1.50
90	Kushida	.50	1.25
91	Tommaso Ciampa	.75	2.00
92	Dexter Lumis	.60	1.50
93	Johnny Gargano	.60	1.50
94	Finn B-lor	1.50	4.00
95	Karrion Kross	1.25	3.00
96	The Way	.60	1.50
97	Kyle O'Reilly	.50	1.25
98	Leon Ruff	.30	.75
99	Damian Priest	1.25	3.00
100	Johnny Gargano	1.25	3.00

2021 Topps WWE NXT Finn Balor Tribute

COMPLETE SET (10)	5.00	12.00

RANDOMLY INSERTED INTO PACKS

FB1	Finn Balor	1.00	2.50
FB2	Finn Balor	1.00	2.50
FB3	Finn Balor	1.00	2.50
FB4	Finn Balor	1.00	2.50
FB5	Finn Balor	1.00	2.50
FB6	Finn Balor	1.00	2.50
FB7	Finn Balor	1.00	2.50
FB8	Finn Balor	1.00	2.50
FB9	Finn Balor	1.00	2.50
FB10	Finn Balor	1.00	2.50

2021 Topps WWE NXT Finn Balor Tribute Autographs

*GOLD/10: UNPRICED DUE TO SCARCITY
*PLATINUM/1: UNPRICED DUE TO SCARCITY
STATED PRINT RUN 25 SER.#'d SETS

FB14	Finn Balor	25.00	60.00
FB15	Finn Balor	25.00	60.00
FB16	Finn Balor	25.00	60.00
FB19	Finn Balor	25.00	60.00
FB20	Finn Balor	25.00	60.00

2021 Topps WWE NXT Migs Media Illustrations

COMPLETE SET (10)	6.00	15.00

RANDOMLY INSERTED INTO PACKS

MM1	Cameron Grimes	1.25	3.00
MM2	Dakota Kai	1.25	3.00
MM3	Damian Priest	1.00	2.50
MM4	Io Shirai	1.25	3.00
MM5	Kushida	1.00	2.50
MM6	Rhea Ripley	2.50	6.00
MM7	Santos Escobar	1.25	3.00
MM8	Bronson Reed	.75	2.00
MM9	Tegan Nox	1.50	4.00
MM10	Timothy Thatcher	.60	1.50

2021 Topps WWE NXT NXT Alumni

COMPLETE SET (9)	5.00	12.00

RANDOMLY INSERTED INTO PACKS

NA1	Angel Garza	.75	2.00
NA2	Bianca Belair	1.50	4.00
NA3	Jaxson Ryker	.60	1.50
NA4	Keith Lee	1.25	3.00
NA5	Riddle	1.50	4.00
NA6	Riddick Moss	.75	2.00
NA7	Shayna Baszler	1.50	4.00
NA8	Damian Priest	1.00	2.50
NA9	Rhea Ripley	2.50	6.00

2021 Topps WWE NXT NXT Alumni Autographs

*GOLD/10: UNPRICED DUE TO SCARCITY
*PLATINUM/1: UNPRICED DUE TO SCARCITY
RANDOMLY INSERTED INTO PACKS

NAAG	Angel Garza	8.00	20.00
NAJR	Jaxson Ryker	8.00	20.00
NAKL	Keith Lee	10.00	25.00
NAMR	Riddle	15.00	40.00
NARM	Riddick Moss	20.00	50.00
NASB	Shayna Baszler	15.00	40.00

2021 Topps WWE NXT Tag Team Autographs

*GOLD/10: UNPRICED DUE TO SCARCITY
*PLATINUM/1: UNPRICED DUE TO SCARCITY
STATED PRINT RUN 25 SER.#'d SETS

DABZ	Tyler Breeze/Fandango	15.00	40.00
DAER	Chase Parker/Matt Martel	50.00	100.00
DAIP	Marcel Barthel/Fabian Aichner	30.00	75.00
DAJC	Candice LeRae/Johnny Gargano	100.00	200.00
DAKS	Scarlett/Karrion Kross	250.00	500.00
DALF	Joaquin Wilde/Raul Mendoza		
DAOD	Danny Burch/Oney Lorcan	30.00	75.00
DATN	Kacy Catanzaro/Kayden Carter	100.00	200.00
DAUE	Bobby Fish/Kyle O'Reilly	20.00	50.00
DAGYV	James Drake/Zack Gibson	15.00	40.00

2021 Topps WWE NXT We Are NXT

RANDOMLY INSERTED INTO PACKS

NXT1	Adam Cole	1.25	3.00
NXT2	Aliyah	.75	2.00
NXT3	Austin Theory	.75	2.00
NXT4	Arturo Ruas	.40	1.00
NXT5	Bobby Fish	.50	1.25
NXT6	Bronson Reed	.50	1.25
NXT7	Cameron Grimes	.75	2.00
NXT8	Candice LeRae	1.50	4.00
NXT9	Chase Parker	.40	1.00
NXT10	Dakota Kai	.75	2.00
NXT11	Danny Burch	.50	1.25
NXT12	Dave Mastiff	.40	1.00
NXT13	Dexter Lumis	.40	1.00
NXT14	Drake Maverick	.40	1.00
NXT15	Fabian Aichner	.50	1.25
NXT16	Fandango	.60	1.50
NXT17	Finn Balor	1.00	2.50
NXT18	Flash Morgan Webster	.50	1.25
NXT19	Ilja Dragunov	.40	1.00
NXT20	Indi Hartwell	1.25	3.00
NXT21	Io Shirai	.75	2.00
NXT22	Isaiah Swerve Scott	.60	1.50
NXT23	Jake Atlas	.40	1.00
NXT24	James Drake	.40	1.00
NXT25	Jessi Kamea	.75	2.00
NXT26	Joaquin Wilde	.60	1.50
NXT27	Johnny Gargano	.75	2.00
NXT28	Kacy Catanzaro	.75	2.00
NXT29	Karrion Kross	1.50	4.00
NXT30	Kay Lee Ray	1.00	2.50
NXT31	Kayden Carter	.75	2.00
NXT32	Killian Dain	.40	1.00
NXT33	Kushida	.60	1.50
NXT34	Kyle O'Reilly	.60	1.50
NXT35	Malcolm Bivens	.40	1.00
NXT36	Marcel Barthel	.50	1.25
NXT37	Marina Shafir	.75	2.00
NXT38	Matt Martel	.50	1.25
NXT39	Noam Dar	.50	1.25
NXT40	Oney Lorcan	.40	1.00
NXT41	Pete Dunne	1.00	2.50
NXT42	Piper Niven	.60	1.50
NXT43	Raquel Gonzalez	1.50	4.00
NXT44	Raul Mendoza	.60	1.50
NXT45	Ridge Holland	.40	1.00
NXT46	Robert Stone	.40	1.00
NXT47	Roderick Strong	.75	2.00
NXT48	Santos Escobar	.75	2.00
NXT49	Saurav	.40	1.00
NXT50	Scarlett	2.00	5.00
NXT51	Shotzi Blackheart	2.00	5.00
NXT52	Tegan Nox	1.00	2.50
NXT53	Ashante Thee Adonis	.50	1.25
NXT54	Timothy Thatcher	.40	1.00
NXT55	Tommaso Ciampa	1.00	2.50
NXT56	Toni Storm	1.50	4.00
NXT57	Trent Seven	.50	1.25
NXT58	Tyler Bate	.50	1.25
NXT59	Tyler Breeze	.50	1.25
NXT60	WALTER	1.25	3.00
NXT61	Xia Li	.75	2.00
NXT62	Zack Gibson	.40	1.00

2021 Topps WWE NXT We Are NXT Autographs

*GREEN/99: .5X TO 1.2X BASIC AUTOS
*PURPLE/75: .6X TO 1.5X BASIC AUTOS
*BLUE/50: .75X TO 2X BASIC AUTOS
*RED/25: 1.2X TO 3X BASIC AUTOS
*GOLD/10: UNPRICED DUE TO SCARCITY
*PLATINUM/1: UNPRICED DUE TO SCARCITY
*P.P.BLACK/1: UNPRICED DUE TO SCARCITY
*P.P.CYAN/1: UNPRICED DUE TO SCARCITY
*P.P.MAGENTA/1: UNPRICED DUE TO SCARCITY
*P.P.YELLOW/1: UNPRICED DUE TO SCARCITY
RANDOMLY INSERTED INTO PACKS

AAC	Adam Cole		
AAL	Aliyah		
AAT	Austin Theory	10.00	25.00
ABA	Marcel Barthel	6.00	15.00
ABF	Bobby Fish	5.00	12.00
ABR	Bronson Reed	10.00	25.00
ACG	Cameron Grimes	6.00	15.00
ACL	Candice LeRae		
ACP	Chase Parker	8.00	20.00
ADB	Danny Burch		
ADK	Dakota Kai	15.00	40.00
ADL	Dexter Lumis	10.00	25.00
ADM	Dave Mastiff	6.00	15.00
ADR	Drake Maverick	5.00	12.00
AFA	Fabian Aichner	6.00	15.00
AFD	Fandango	5.00	12.00
AFS	Kayden Carter	8.00	20.00
AID	Ilja Dragunov	15.00	40.00
AIH	Indi Hartwell	20.00	50.00
AIS	Io Shirai	15.00	40.00
AJA	Jake Atlas	5.00	12.00
AJD	James Drake	5.00	12.00
AJG	Johnny Gargano		
AJK	Jessi Kamea	10.00	25.00
AJW	Joaquin Wilde	5.00	12.00
AKC	Kacy Catanzaro	15.00	40.00
AKD	Killian Dain		
AKK	Karrion Kross	25.00	60.00
AKS	Kushida	8.00	20.00
AMM	Matt Martel	6.00	15.00
AOL	Oney Lorcan		
APD	Pete Dunne	6.00	15.00
APN	Piper Niven		
ARE	Robert Stone	4.00	12.00
ARG	Raquel Gonzalez	30.00	75.00
ARH	Ridge Holland	6.00	15.00
ARM	Raul Mendoza	5.00	12.00
ARS	Roderick Strong	8.00	20.00
ASB	Shotzi Blackheart	20.00	50.00
ASC	Scarlett		
ASE	Santos Escobar	5.00	12.00
ASW	Isaiah Swerve Scott	5.00	12.00
AT7	Trent Seven	6.00	15.00
ATB	Tyler Breeze	5.00	10.00
ATC	Tommaso Ciampa		
ATM	Ashante Thee Adonis	5.00	12.00
ATN	Tegan Nox	10.00	25.00
ATO	Toni Storm	25.00	60.00
ATT	Timothy Thatcher	6.00	15.00
ATY	Tyler Bate		
AWT	WALTER	10.00	25.00
AXL	Xia Li	10.00	25.00
AZG	Zack Gibson	6.00	15.00
AKLR	Kay Lee Ray		
AKOR	Kyle O'Reilly	6.00	15.00

2012 Topps WWE Power Plates

NNO	Alberto Del Rio
	Destiny
NNO	The American Dream Dusty Rhodes
	Dream SP
NNO	Big Show
	Giant
NNO	The British Bulldog
	Bulldog SP
NNO	Christian
	Charisma
NNO	CM Punk

GTS		
NNO Cody Rhodes		
Xrhodes /		
NNO Daniel Bryan		
Skills		
NNO Evan Bourne		
Air		
NNO John Cena		
Champ		
NNO Kane		
Big Red		
NNO Kevin Nash		
Diesel		
NNO Kofi Kingston		
SOS		
NNO Mark Henry		
Strongman		
NNO Million Dollar Man Ted DiBiase		
$$$ SP		
NNO The Miz		
Awesome		
NNO Randy Orton		
RKO		
NNO Rey Mysterio		
619		
NNO Rowdy Roddy Piper		
Hotrod SP		
NNO R-Truth		
Truth		
NNO Santino Marella		
Cobra		
NNO Sgt. Slaughter		
USA SP		
NNO Sheamus		
Celtic		
NNO Zack Ryder		
WWWYKI		

2019 Topps WWE RAW

COMPLETE SET (90) 10.00 25.00
*BRONZE: .6X TO 1.5X BASIC CARDS
*BLUE/99: .75X TO 2X BASIC CARDS
*SILVER/25: 2X TO 5X BASIC CARDS
*GOLD/10: UNPRICED DUE TO SCARCITY
*BLACK/1: UNPRICED DUE TO SCARCITY
*P.P.BLACK/1: UNPRICED DUE TO SCARCITY
*P.P.CYAN/1: UNPRICED DUE TO SCARCITY
*P.P.MAGENTA/1: UNPRICED DUE TO SCARCITY
*P.P.YELLOW/1: UNPRICED DUE TO SCARCITY

1 Akam	.25	.60
2 Alexa Bliss	1.25	3.00
3 Alicia Fox	.50	1.25
4 Apollo Crews	.30	.75
5 Baron Corbin	.40	1.00
6 Batista	.60	1.50
7 Bayley	.50	1.25
8 Bo Dallas	.30	.75
9 Bobby Lashley	.50	1.25
10 Bobby Roode	.50	1.25
11 Booker T	.60	1.50
12 Braun Strowman	.60	1.50
13 Bray Wyatt	.60	1.50
14 Brie Bella	.60	1.50
15 Brock Lesnar	1.00	2.50
16 Chad Gable	.25	.60
17 Charly Caruso	.40	1.00
18 Corey Graves	.30	.75
19 Curt Hawkins	.25	.60
20 Curtis Axel	.30	.75
21 Dana Brooke	.50	1.25
22 Dash Wilder	.25	.60
23 David Otunga	.25	.60
24 Dean Ambrose	.60	1.50
25 Dolph Ziggler	.50	1.25
26 Drake Maverick	.25	.60
27 Drew McIntyre	.30	.75
28 Elias	.50	1.25
29 Ember Moon	.60	1.50
30 Fandango	.25	.60
31 Finn Balor	.60	1.50
32 Gran Metalik	.25	.60
33 Heath Slater	.25	.60
34 Jason Jordan	.30	.75
35 Jinder Mahal	.50	1.25
36 Jonathan Coachman	.25	.60
37 John Cena	1.00	2.50
38 JoJo	.40	1.00
39 Kalisto	.25	.60
40 Kane	.40	1.00
41 Kayla Braxton	.40	1.00
42 Kevin Owens	.60	1.50
43 Konnor	.25	.60
44 Kurt Angle	.50	1.25
45 Lince Dorado	.25	.60
46 Lio Rush	.30	.75
47 Liv Morgan	.75	2.00
48 Michael Cole	.25	.60
49 Mickie James	.60	1.50
50 Mike Rome	.30	.75
51 Mojo Rawley	.30	.75
52 Natalya	.50	1.25
53 Nia Jax	.50	1.25
54 Nikki Bella	.60	1.50
55 No Way Jose	.30	.75
56 Paul Heyman	.30	.75
57 Renee Young	.40	1.00
58 Rezar	.25	.60
59 Rhyno	.25	.60
60 Roman Reigns	.60	1.50
61 Ronda Rousey	1.25	3.00
62 Ruby Riott	.50	1.25
63 Sami Zayn	.50	1.25
64 Samir Singh	.25	.60
65 Sarah Logan	.30	.75
66 Sasha Banks	1.00	2.50
67 Scott Dawson	.25	.60
68 Seth Rollins	.60	1.50
69 Stephanie McMahon	.60	1.50
70 Sunil Singh	.25	.60
71 Titus O'Neil	.30	.75
72 Tyler Breeze	.30	.75
73 Viktor	.25	.60
74 Zack Ryder	.30	.75
75 Akira Tozawa	.25	.60
76 Ariya Daivari	.25	.60
77 Buddy Murphy	.30	.75
78 Cedric Alexander	.25	.60
79 Drew Gulak	.25	.60
80 Gentleman Jack Gallagher	.30	.75
81 Hideo Itami	.25	.60
82 Maria Kanellis	.60	1.50
83 Mark Andrews	.25	.60
84 Mike Kanellis	.25	.60
85 Nigel McGuinness	.25	.60
86 Noam Dar	.25	.60
87 The Brian Kendrick	.40	1.00
88 TJP	.40	1.00
89 Tony Nese	.25	.60
90 Vic Joseph	.25	.60

2019 Topps WWE RAW Autographed Commemorative Intercontinental Championship Relics

STATED PRINT RUN 10 SER.#'d SETS

ICRAHH Triple H
ICRASM Shawn Michaels

2019 Topps WWE RAW Autographed Commemorative RAW Championship Relics

STATED PRINT RUN 10 SER.#'d SETS
UNPRICED DUE TO SCARCITY

RACAB Alexa Bliss
RACBL Bayley
RACBS Braun Strowman
RACCF Charlotte Flair
RACDA Dean Ambrose
RACFB Finn Balor
RACKO Kevin Owens
RACRRR Ronda Rousey
RACSB Sasha Banks
RACSR Seth Rollins
RACTM The Miz

2019 Topps WWE RAW Autographed Mat Relics

STATED PRINT RUN 10 SER.#'d SETS
UNPRICED DUE TO SCARCITY

DMARAB Aleister Black
DMARAJ AJ Styles
DMARAK Asuka
DMARAS Shayna Baszler
DMARBL Bobby Lashley
DMARBR Bobby Roode
DMARBS Braun Strowman
DMARCF Charlotte Flair
DMAREM Ember Moon
DMARFB Finn Balor
DMARJG Johnny Gargano
DMARJN Natalya
DMARKK Kofi Kingston
DMARKO Kevin Owens
DMARKR Kyle O'Reilly
DMARLK Becky Lynch
DMARMB Alexa Bliss
DMARNC Nikki Cross
DMARNM Naomi
DMARRC Ricochet
DMARRD Rusev
DMARRS Roderick Strong
DMARSB Sasha Banks
DMARSJ Samoa Joe
DMARSN Shinsuke Nakamura
DMARSR Seth Rollins
DMARSZ Sami Zayn
DMARTC Tomasso Ciampa
DMARTM The Miz
DMARVD Velveteen Dream
DMARRRR Ronda Rousey

2019 Topps WWE RAW Autographed Shirt Relics

STATED PRINT RUN 10 SER.#'d SETS
UNPRICED DUE TO SCARCITY

SARAB Alexa Bliss
SARDA Dean Ambrose
SARFB Finn Balor
SARKO Kevin Owens
SARRY Renee Young
SARSR Seth Rollins
SARWJ No Way Jose

2019 Topps WWE RAW Autographed Women's Revolution Relics

STATED PRINT RUN 10 SER.#'d SETS
UNPRICED DUE TO SCARCITY

DRACAB Alexa Bliss
DRACSB Sasha Banks
DRACRRR Ronda Rousey

2019 Topps WWE RAW Autographs

*BLUE/50: .5X TO 1.2X BASIC AUTOS
*SILVER/25: .6X TO 1.5X BASIC AUTOS
*GOLD/10: UNPRICED DUE TO SCARCITY
*BLACK/1: UNPRICED DUE TO SCARCITY
STATED PRINT RUN 99 SER.#'d SETS

AAB Alexa Bliss	25.00	60.00
AAC Apollo Crews		
ABC Baron Corbin	5.00	12.00
ABL Bobby Lashley	5.00	12.00
ABR Bobby Roode	4.00	10.00
ABS Braun Strowman/94	5.00	12.00
ABT Booker T	5.00	12.00
ACA Cedric Alexander	4.00	10.00
ACC Charly Caruso	6.00	15.00
ACG Chad Gable	3.00	8.00
ADA Dean Ambrose	6.00	15.00
ADB Dana Brooke	6.00	15.00
ADM Drew McIntyre	5.00	12.00
AEM Ember Moon/63	8.00	20.00
AFB Finn Balor/88	12.00	30.00
AGR Corey Graves	6.00	15.00
AHO Hideo Itami	3.00	8.00
AJG Gentleman Jack Gallagher	12.00	30.00
AJJ Jason Jordan/77	5.00	12.00
AJN Natalya		
AKA Kurt Angle	8.00	20.00
AKT Kalisto	4.00	10.00
ALD Lince Dorado/98	10.00	25.00
ALR Lio Rush	6.00	15.00
ARY Renee Young	6.00	12.00
ASL Sarah Logan	6.00	15.00
ASR Seth Rollins	8.00	20.00
ATB Tyler Breeze	4.00	10.00
ATN Titus O'Neil	4.00	10.00

2019 Topps WWE RAW Commemorative Intercontinental Championship Relics

RANDOMLY INSERTED INTO PACKS

ICRED Edge
ICRHH Triple H
ICRRM The Rock
ICRRR Razor Ramon
ICRSM Shawn Michaels

2019 Topps WWE RAW Commemorative RAW Championship Relics

*BRONZE/99: SAME VALUE AS BASIC
*BLUE/50: .5X TO 1.2X BASIC MEM

RCAB	Alexa Bliss	10.00	25.00
RCBC	Karl Anderson/Luke Gallows	2.00	5.00
RCBD	Roman Reigns	5.00	12.00
RCBL	Bayley	5.00	12.00
RCBS	Braun Strowman	2.50	6.00
RCBT	Curtis Axel/Bo Dallas	2.50	6.00
RCCF	Charlotte Flair	4.00	10.00
RCDA	Dean Ambrose	5.00	12.00
RCDZ	Dolph Ziggler	2.50	6.00
RCFB	Finn Balor	3.00	8.00
RCGB	Goldberg	6.00	15.00
RCKO	Kevin Owens	2.00	5.00
RCNJ	Nia Jax	2.00	5.00
RCRR	Roman Reigns	5.00	12.00
RCSB	Sasha Banks	6.00	15.00
RCSD	Seth Rollins/Dean Ambrose	3.00	8.00
RCSR	Seth Rollins	4.00	10.00
RCTB	Cesaro/Sheamus	2.00	5.00
RCTM	The Miz	2.00	5.00
RCZM	Drew McIntyre/Dolph Ziggler	2.50	6.00
RCRRR	Ronda Rousey	12.00	30.00

2019 Topps WWE RAW Hometown Heroes

COMPLETE SET (48)		12.00	30.00
RANDOMLY INSERTED INTO PACKS			
HH1	Alexa Bliss	2.00	5.00
HH2	Apollo Crews	.50	1.25
HH3	Baron Corbin	.60	1.50
HH4	Bayley	.75	2.00
HH5	Big Show	.60	1.50
HH6	Bo Dallas	.50	1.25
HH7	Bobby Lashley	.75	2.00
HH8	Bobby Roode	.75	2.00
HH9	Booker T	1.00	2.50
HH10	Curtis Axel	.50	1.25
HH11	Dana Brooke	.75	2.00
HH12	Dean Ambrose	1.00	2.50
HH13	Dolph Ziggler	.75	2.00
HH14	Drew McIntyre	.50	1.25
HH15	Elias	.75	2.00
HH16	Ember Moon	1.00	2.50
HH17	Finn Balor	1.00	2.50
HH18	Heath Slater	.40	1.00
HH19	Jason Jordan	.50	1.25
HH20	Jinder Mahal	.75	2.00
HH21	John Cena	1.50	4.00
HH22	Kevin Owens	1.00	2.50
HH23	Liv Morgan	1.25	3.00
HH24	Mickie James	1.00	2.50
HH25	Mojo Rawley	.50	1.25
HH26	Natalya	.75	2.00
HH27	Nia Jax	.75	2.00
HH28	No Way Jose	.50	1.25
HH29	Lince Dorado	.40	1.00
HH30	Lio Rush	.50	1.25
HH31	Rhyno	.40	1.00
HH32	Roman Reigns	1.00	2.50
HH33	Ronda Rousey	2.00	5.00
HH34	Ruby Riott	.75	2.00
HH35	Sarah Logan	.50	1.25
HH36	Sasha Banks	1.50	4.00
HH37	Seth Rollins	1.00	2.50
HH38	Titus O'Neil	.50	1.25
HH39	Zack Ryder	.50	1.25
HH40	Buddy Murphy	.50	1.25
HH41	Cedric Alexander	.40	1.00
HH42	Drew Gulak	.40	1.00
HH43	Gentleman Jack Gallagher	.50	1.25
HH44	Gran Metalik	.40	1.00
HH45	Hideo Itami	.40	1.00
HH46	Kalisto	.40	1.00
HH47	Mark Andrews	.40	1.00
HH48	TJP	.60	1.50

2019 Topps WWE RAW Image Variations

IVAB	Alexa Bliss	30.00	75.00
IVAC	Apollo Crews	2.50	6.00
IVBL	Bobby Lashley	12.00	30.00
IVBR	Bobby Roode		
IVBY	Bayley	8.00	20.00
IVDG	Drew Gulak		
IVDM	Drew McIntyre	3.00	8.00
IVDZ	Dolph Ziggler		
IVEM	Ember Moon	4.00	10.00
IVFB	The Demon Finn Balor	15.00	40.00
IVJN	Natalya	5.00	12.00
IVKO	Kevin Owens	4.00	10.00
IVLL	Kalisto	2.50	6.00
IVLR	Lio Rush	3.00	8.00
IVMK	Mike Kanellis	4.00	10.00
IVMR	Mojo Rawley	4.00	10.00
IVNJ	Nia Jax	4.00	10.00
IVRR	Roman Reigns	6.00	15.00
IVRS	Drake Maverick	6.00	15.00
IVSB	Sasha Banks	12.00	30.00
IVSR	Seth Rollins	5.00	12.00
IVSZ	Sami Zayn	3.00	8.00
IVTJ	TJP	5.00	12.00
IVZR	Zack Ryder	8.00	20.00

2019 Topps WWE RAW Intercontinental Champions Autographs

ICAHH	Triple H	100.00	200.00
ICASM	Shawn Michaels	50.00	100.00

2019 Topps WWE RAW Kiss

KCAF	Alicia Fox	15.00	40.00
KCEM	Ember Moon	15.00	40.00
KCNJ	Nia Jax	12.00	30.00

2019 Topps WWE RAW Kiss Autographs

KARAF	Alicia Fox	30.00	75.00
KARMJ	Mickie James	60.00	120.00
KARNJ	Nia Jax	20.00	50.00

2019 Topps WWE RAW Legends of RAW

COMPLETE SET (20)		6.00	15.00
RANDOMLY INSERTED INTO PACKS			
LR1	Batista	.60	1.50
LR2	Bret Hitman Hart	.60	1.50
LR3	Edge	.60	1.50
LR4	Faarooq	.40	1.00
LR5	Goldberg	.75	2.00
LR6	Jerry The King Lawler	.50	1.25
LR7	Ken Shamrock	.40	1.00
LR8	Lita	.60	1.50
LR9	Mr. Perfect	.40	1.00
LR10	Mark Henry	.30	.75
LR11	Mankind	.50	1.25
LR12	Sycho Sid	.25	.60
LR13	Rikishi	.25	.60
LR14	Ric Flair	.75	2.00
LR15	Road Dogg	.25	.60
LR16	Shawn Michaels	.60	1.50
LR17	Stone Cold Steve Austin	1.25	3.00
LR18	Trish Stratus	1.25	3.00
LR19	Vader	.30	.75
LR20	X-Pac	.25	.60

2019 Topps WWE RAW Mat Relics

SEMISTARS		2.00	5.00
UNLISTED STARS		2.50	6.00

DMRAB	Aleister Black	1.50	4.00
DMRAJ	AJ Styles	3.00	8.00
DMRAK	Asuka	6.00	15.00
DMRAS	Shayna Baszler	4.00	10.00
DMRBL	Bobby Lashley	1.50	4.00
DMRBR	Bobby Roode	2.50	6.00
DMRBS	Braun Strowman	2.00	5.00
DMRCF	Charlotte Flair	4.00	10.00
DMRCM	Carmella	5.00	12.00
DMRDB	Daniel Bryan	2.50	6.00
DMRDN	Danny Burch	2.50	6.00
DMREM	Ember Moon	3.00	8.00
DMRFB	Finn Balor	4.00	10.00
DMRJG	Johnny Gargano	2.00	5.00
DMRJN	Natalya	3.00	8.00
DMRKK	Kofi Kingston	3.00	8.00
DMRKO	Kevin Owens	2.50	6.00
DMRKR	Kyle O'Reilly	3.00	8.00
DMRLD	Lana	2.50	6.00
DMRLK	Becky Lynch	6.00	15.00
DMRLS	Lars Sullivan	1.50	4.00
DMRMB	Alexa Bliss	12.00	30.00
DMRNC	Nikki Cross	1.50	4.00
DMRNJ	Nia Jax	2.00	5.00
DMRNM	Naomi	2.50	6.00
DMROL	Oney Lorcan	2.00	5.00
DMRRC	Ricochet	3.00	8.00
DMRRD	Rusev	2.50	6.00
DMRRR	Roman Reigns	4.00	10.00
DMRRS	Roderick Strong	2.00	5.00
DMRSB	Sasha Banks	8.00	20.00
DMRSJ	Samoa Joe	2.00	5.00
DMRSN	Shinsuke Nakamura	3.00	8.00
DMRSR	Seth Rollins	4.00	10.00
DMRSZ	Sami Zayn	2.00	5.00
DMRTC	Tommaso Ciampa	2.00	5.00
DMRTM	The Miz	2.50	6.00
DMRVD	Velveteen Dream	2.00	5.00
DMRWE	Elias	2.00	5.00
DMRRRR	Ronda Rousey	10.00	25.00

2019 Topps WWE RAW Shirt Relics

SRAB	Alexa Bliss	15.00	40.00
SRDA	Dean Ambrose	6.00	15.00
SREL	Elias	4.00	10.00
SRFB	Finn Balor	8.00	20.00
SRKO	Kevin Owens	3.00	8.00
SRRR	Roman Reigns	5.00	15.00
SRSR	Seth Rollins	6.00	15.00
SRWJ	No Way Jose	3.00	6.00

2019 Topps WWE RAW Triple Autographs

TAAB Bliss/Fox/James
TARS Morgan/Riott/Logan

2019 Topps WWE RAW Women's Revolution Autographs

WABL	Bayley	20.00	50.00
WARR	Ronda Rousey		
WASB	Sasha Banks	30.00	75.00

2019 Topps WWE RAW Women's Revolution Relics

DRCAB Alexa Bliss
DRCNJ Nia Jax
DRCSB Sasha Banks

2009 Topps WWE Rivals Stickers

1	Emblem WWE	.12	.30
2	WWE 1	.12	.30
3	WWE 2		.30
4	John Cena	.75	2.00
5	John Cena	.75	2.00
6	John Cena	.75	2.00
7	John Cena	.75	2.00
8	John Cena	.75	2.00
9	John Cena	.75	2.00
10	John Cena	.75	2.00
11	John Cena	.75	2.00
12	John Cena	.75	2.00
13	John Cena	.75	2.00
14	Edge	.50	1.25
15	Edge	.50	1.25
16	Edge	.50	1.25
17	Edge	.50	1.25
18	Edge	.50	1.25
19	Edge	.50	1.25
20	Edge	.50	1.25

#	Name			#	Name			#	Name			#	Name		
21	Edge	.50	1.25	89	Jeff Hardy	.50	1.25	157	Cody Rhodes & Ted Dibiase	.20	.50	225	Mark Henry	.20	.50
22	Edge	.50	1.25	90	Jeff Hardy	.50	1.25	158	Cody Rhodes & Ted Dibiase	.20	.50	226	Mark Henry	.20	.50
23	Edge	.50	1.25	91	Jeff Hardy	.50	1.25	159	Cryme Tyme	.12	.30	227	Mark Henry	.20	.50
24	Kane	.50	1.25	92	Jeff Hardy	.50	1.25	160	Cryme Tyme	.12	.30	228	Mark Henry	.20	.50
25	Kane	.50	1.25	93	Jeff Hardy	.50	1.25	161	Cryme Tyme	.12	.30	229	Batista	.50	1.25
26	Kane	.50	1.25	94	John Morrison	.20	.50	162	Cryme Tyme	.12	.30	230	Batista	.50	1.25
27	Kane	.50	1.25	95	John Morrison	.20	.50	163	Cryme Tyme	.12	.30	231	Batista	.50	1.25
28	Kane	.50	1.25	96	John Morrison	.20	.50	164	Triple H	.75	2.00	232	Batista	.50	1.25
29	The Miz	.20	.50	97	John Morrison	.20	.50	165	Triple H	.75	2.00	233	Batista	.50	1.25
30	The Miz	.20	.50	98	John Morrison	.20	.50	166	Triple H	.75	2.00	234	Jack Swagger	.12	.30
31	The Miz	.20	.50	99	John Morrison	.20	.50	167	Triple H	.75	2.00	235	Jack Swagger	.12	.30
32	The Miz	.20	.50	100	John Morrison	.20	.50	168	Triple H	.75	2.00	236	Jack Swagger	.12	.30
33	The Miz	.20	.50	101	John Morrison	.20	.50	169	Triple H	.75	2.00	P1	RAW	.12	.30
34	Mr. Kennedy	.30	.75	102	John Morrison	.20	.50	170	Triple H	.75	2.00	P2	John Cena	.75	2.00
35	Mr. Kennedy	.30	.75	103	John Morrison	.20	.50	171	Triple H	.75	2.00	P3	Randy Orton	.30	.75
36	Mr. Kennedy	.30	.75	104	Shawn Michaels	.75	2.00	172	Triple H	.75	2.00	P4	JBL	.20	.50
37	Mr. Kennedy	.30	.75	105	Shawn Michaels	.75	2.00	173	Triple H	.75	2.00	P5	Rey Mysterio	.30	.75
38	Mr. Kennedy	.30	.75	106	Shawn Michaels	.75	2.00	174	Rey Mysterio	.30	.75	P6	ECW	.12	.30
39	William Regal	.30	.75	107	Shawn Michaels	.75	2.00	175	Rey Mysterio	.30	.75	P7	John Morrison	.20	.50
40	William Regal	.30	.75	108	Shawn Michaels	.75	2.00	176	Rey Mysterio	.30	.75	P8	Mark Henry	.20	.50
41	William Regal	.30	.75	109	Vladimir Kozlov	.20	.50	177	Rey Mysterio	.30	.75	P9	Chavo Guerrero	.20	.50
42	William Regal	.30	.75	110	Vladimir Kozlov	.20	.50	178	Rey Mysterio	.30	.75	P10	SMACK DOWN	.12	.30
43	William Regal	.30	.75	111	Vladimir Kozlov	.20	.50	179	Rey Mysterio	.30	.75	P11	Edge	.50	1.25
44	Chavo Guerrero	.20	.50	112	Vladimir Kozlov	.20	.50	180	Rey Mysterio	.30	.75	P12	Triple H	.75	2.00
45	Chavo Guerrero	.20	.50	113	Vladimir Kozlov	.20	.50	181	Rey Mysterio	.30	.75	P13	Jeff Hardy	.50	1.25
46	Chavo Guerrero	.20	.50	114	Big Show	.30	.75	182	Rey Mysterio	.30	.75	P14	Vladimir Kozlov	.20	.50
47	Chavo Guerrero	.20	.50	115	Big Show	.30	.75	183	Rey Mysterio	.30	.75				
48	Chavo Guerrero	.20	.50	116	Big Show	.30	.75	184	Shelton Benjamin	.12	.30				
49	Chavo Guerrero	.20	.50	117	Big Show	.30	.75	185	Shelton Benjamin	.12	.30				
50	Chavo Guerrero	.20	.50	118	Big Show	.30	.75	186	Shelton Benjamin	.12	.30				
51	Chavo Guerrero	.20	.50	119	JBL	.20	.50	187	Shelton Benjamin	.12	.30				
52	Chavo Guerrero	.20	.50	120	JBL	.20	.50	188	Shelton Benjamin	.12	.30				
53	Chavo Guerrero	.20	.50	121	JBL	.20	.50	189	Tommy Dreamer	.12	.30				
54	CM Punk	.20	.50	122	JBL	.20	.50	190	Tommy Dreamer	.12	.30				
55	CM Punk	.20	.50	123	JBL	.20	.50	191	Tommy Dreamer	.12	.30				
56	CM Punk	.20	.50	124	Beth Phoenix	.60	1.50	192	Tommy Dreamer	.12	.30				
57	CM Punk	.20	.50	125	Beth Phoenix	.60	1.50	193	Tommy Dreamer	.12	.30				
58	CM Punk	.20	.50	126	Maria	.50	1.25	194	Santino Marella	.12	.30				
59	CM Punk	.20	.50	127	Maria	.50	1.25	195	Santino Marella	.12	.30				
60	CM Punk	.20	.50	128	Candice	.60	1.50	196	Santino Marella	.12	.30				
61	CM Punk	.20	.50	129	Melina	.50	1.25	197	Santino Marella	.12	.30				
62	CM Punk	.20	.50	130	Mickie James	.60	1.50	198	Santino Marella	.12	.30				
63	CM Punk	.20	.50	131	Candice	.60	1.50	199	Umaga	.20	.50				
64	The Great Khali	.12	.30	132	Melina	.50	1.25	200	Umaga	.20	.50				
65	The Great Khali	.12	.30	133	Mickie James	.60	1.50	201	Umaga	.20	.50				
66	The Great Khali	.12	.30	134	Matt Hardy	.50	1.25	202	Umaga	.20	.50				
67	The Great Khali	.12	.30	135	Matt Hardy	.50	1.25	203	Umaga	.20	.50				
68	The Great Khali	.12	.30	136	Matt Hardy	.50	1.25	204	Randy Orton	.30	.75				
69	Finlay & Hornswoggle	.20	.50	137	Matt Hardy	.50	1.25	205	Randy Orton	.30	.75				
70	Finlay & Hornswoggle	.20	.50	138	Matt Hardy	.50	1.25	206	Randy Orton	.30	.75				
71	Finlay & Hornswoggle	.20	.50	139	Matt Hardy	.50	1.25	207	Randy Orton	.30	.75				
72	Finlay & Hornswoggle	.20	.50	140	Matt Hardy	.50	1.25	208	Randy Orton	.30	.75				
73	Finlay & Hornswoggle	.20	.50	141	Matt Hardy	.50	1.25	209	Randy Orton	.30	.75				
74	Kofi Kingston	.12	.30	142	Matt Hardy	.50	1.25	210	Randy Orton	.30	.75				
75	Kofi Kingston	.12	.30	143	Matt Hardy	.50	1.25	211	Randy Orton	.30	.75				
76	Kofi Kingston	.12	.30	144	MVP	.20	.50	212	Randy Orton	.30	.75				
77	Kofi Kingston	.12	.30	145	MVP	.20	.50	213	Randy Orton	.30	.75				
78	Kofi Kingston	.12	.30	146	MVP	.20	.50	214	Undertaker	.60	1.50				
79	Carlito	.30	.75	147	MVP	.20	.50	215	Undertaker	.60	1.50				
80	Carlito	.30	.75	148	MVP	.20	.50	216	Undertaker	.60	1.50				
81	Carlito	.30	.75	149	Chris Jericho	.30	.75	217	Undertaker	.60	1.50				
82	Carlito	.30	.75	150	Chris Jericho	.30	.75	218	Undertaker	.60	1.50				
83	Carlito	.30	.75	151	Chris Jericho	.30	.75	219	Undertaker	.60	1.50				
84	Jeff Hardy	.50	1.25	152	Chris Jericho	.30	.75	220	Undertaker	.60	1.50				
85	Jeff Hardy	.50	1.25	153	Chris Jericho	.30	.75	221	Undertaker	.60	1.50				
86	Jeff Hardy	.50	1.25	154	Cody Rhodes & Ted Dibiase	.20	.50	222	Undertaker	.60	1.50				
87	Jeff Hardy	.50	1.25	155	Cody Rhodes & Ted Dibiase	.20	.50	223	Undertaker	.60	1.50				
88	Jeff Hardy	.50	1.25	156	Cody Rhodes & Ted Dibiase	.20	.50	224	Mark Henry	.20	.50				

2014 Topps WWE Road to WrestleMania

COMPLETE SET (110)		12.00	30.00
UNOPENED BOX (24 PACKS)			
UNOPENED PACK (7 CARDS)			
*BRONZE: .6X TO 1.5X BASIC CARDS			
*BLUE: .75X TO 2X BASIC CARDS			
*PURPLE: .75X TO 2X BASIC CARDS			
*BLACK: 2.5X TO 6X BASIC CARDS			
*GOLD/10: UNPRICED DUE TO SCARCITY			
*P.P.BLACK/1: UNPRICED DUE TO SCARCITY			
*P.P.CYAN/1: UNPRICED DUE TO SCARCITY			
*P.P.MAGENTA/1: UNPRICED DUE TO SCARCITY			
*P.P.YELLOW/1: UNPRICED DUE TO SCARCITY			
1	Wade Barrett	.15	.40
2	Dolph Ziggler	.25	.60
3	Ryback	.15	.40
4	Kofi Kingston	.15	.40
5	Undertaker	.60	1.50
6	AJ Lee	.75	2.00
7	Brock Lesnar	.60	1.50
8	Mark Henry	.15	.40
9	Dean Ambrose	.60	1.50
10	The Shield	.75	2.00
11	Brock Lesnar	.60	1.50
12	Curtis Axel	.15	.40
13	Team Hell No	.50	1.25
14	Curtis Axel	.15	.40
15	AJ Lee	.75	2.00
16	Alberto Del Rio	.40	1.00
17	John Cena	.75	2.00
18	Mark Henry	.15	.40
19	Brad Maddox	.15	.40
20	Wyatt Family	.60	1.50
21	Damien Sandow	.25	.60
22	John Cena	.75	2.00
23	Randy Orton	.60	1.50
24	AJ Lee	.75	2.00
25	Rob Van Dam	.40	1.00
26	Vickie Guerrero	.15	.40
27	Eva Marie and Jojo	.15	.40

28	Cody Rhodes	.15	.40
29	Daniel Bryan	.75	2.00
30	Alberto Del Rio	.40	1.00
31	Bray Wyatt	.75	2.00
32	Cody Rhodes	.15	.40
33	Daniel Bryan	.75	2.00
34	Randy Orton	.60	1.50
35	Daniel Bryan	.75	2.00
36	Randy Orton	.60	1.50
37	Randy Orton	.60	1.50
38	Edge	.60	1.50
39	Randy Orton	.60	1.50
40	The Miz	.25	.60
41	Natalya & Tyson Kidd	.75	2.00
42	Daniel Bryan	.75	2.00
43	Triple H	.60	1.50
44	Daniel Bryan	.75	2.00
45	The Rhodes Brothers	.25	.60
46	Los Matadores	.15	.40
47	The Rhodes Brothers	.25	.60
48	Big Show	.40	1.00
49	The Rhodes Brothers	.25	.60
50	The Rhodes Brothers	.25	.60
51	John Cena	.75	2.00
52	Randy Orton	.60	1.50
53	John Cena	.75	2.00
54	The Authority	.25	.60
55	Big E	.15	.40
56	Xavier Woods	.15	.40
57	Rey Mysterio	.40	1.00
58	The Shield	.75	2.00
59	Team Total Divas	1.25	3.00
60	Titus O'Neil	.15	.40
61	Sin Cara	.15	.40
62	Triple H	.60	1.50
63	Daniel Bryan	.75	2.00
64	Randy Orton	.60	1.50
65	Brodus Clay	.15	.40
66	The Total Divas	1.25	3.00
67	Brock Lesnar	.60	1.50
68	Jake The Snake Roberts	.40	1.00
69	Daniel Bryan	.75	2.00
70	Batista	.60	1.50
71	New Age Outlaws	.25	.60
72	Rusev	.40	1.00
73	Kevin Nash	.40	1.00
74	Sheamus	.40	1.00
75	Batista	.40	1.00
76	Titus O'Neil	.15	.40
77	Christian	.25	.60
78	Emma	.40	1.00
79	The Wyatt Family	.60	1.50
80	Randy Orton	.60	1.50
81	Hulk Hogan	.75	2.00
82	Undertaker	.60	1.50
83	Lana	.60	1.50
84	The Usos	.25	.60
85	Big Show	.40	1.00
86	Hulk Hogan	.75	2.00
87	Daniel Bryan	.75	2.00
88	The Shield	.75	2.00
89	Kane	.40	1.00
90	The Wyatt Family	.60	1.50
91	Undertaker	.60	1.50
92	Brock Lesnar	.60	1.50
93	The Wyatt Family	.60	1.50
94	Rowdy Roddy Piper	.40	1.00
95	Jake The Snake Roberts	.40	1.00
96	Kane	.40	1.00
97	Razor Ramon	.40	1.00
98	Ultimate Warrior	.40	1.00
99	The Usos	.25	.60
100	The Real Americans	.25	.60
101	Triple H	.60	1.50
102	Daniel Bryan	.75	2.00
103	The Shield	.75	2.00
104	Kofi Kingston	.15	.40
105	Cesaro	.25	.60
106	John Cena	.75	2.00
107	Brock Lesnar	.60	1.50
108	AJ Lee	.75	2.00
109	Daniel Bryan	.75	2.00
110	Daniel Bryan	.75	2.00

2014 Topps WWE Road to WrestleMania 30 Years of WrestleMania

COMPLETE SET (60) 12.00 30.00
*P.P.BLACK/1: UNPRICED DUE TO SCARCITY
*P.P.CYAN/1: UNPRICED DUE TO SCARCITY
*P.P.MAGENTA/1: UNPRICED DUE TO SCARCITY
*P.P.YELLOW/1: UNPRICED DUE TO SCARCITY
STATED ODDS 2:1

1	The Foreign Legion	.20	.50
2	Hulk Hogan & Mr. T	1.25	3.00
3	The British Bulldogs	.20	.50
4	Hulk Hogan/King Kong Bundy	1.25	3.00
5	Ricky "The Dragon" Steamboat	.20	.50
6	Hulk Hogan vs. Andre	1.25	3.00
7	Hulk Hogan vs. Andre	1.25	3.00
8	Macho Man Randy Savage	.20	.50
9	Rick Rude	.20	.50
10	Hulk Hogan	1.25	3.00
11	Million Dollar Man Ted DiBiase	.20	.50
12	Ultimate Warrior	1.50	4.00
13	Ultimate Warrior	.60	1.50
14	Hulk Hogan	1.25	3.00
15	Macho Man Randy Savage	.75	2.00
16	Hulk Hogan	1.25	3.00
17	Yokozuna	.20	.50
18	Hulk Hogan	1.25	3.00
19	Yokozuna	.20	.50
20	Bret "Hit Man" Hart	.20	.50
21	Yokozuna & Owen Hart	.20	.50
22	Diesel	.20	.50
23	Ultimate Warrior	.60	1.50
24	Shawn Michaels	.60	1.50
25	British Bulldog & Owen Hart	.40	1.00
26	Bret "Hit Man" Hart	1.00	2.50
27	Triple H	.75	2.00
28	Stone Cold Steve Austin	1.25	3.00
29	Road Dogg	.20	.50
30	Stone Cold Steve Austin	2.00	5.00
31	Edge & Christian	.60	1.50
32	Triple H	.75	2.00
33	Edge & Christian	.60	1.50
34	Stone Cold Steve Austin	1.00	2.50
35	The Rock	2.00	5.00
36	Triple H	.75	2.00
37	Triple H	.75	2.00
38	Brock Lesnar	.75	2.00
39	Eddie Guerrero	.20	.50
40	Triple Threat Match	1.25	3.00
41	John Cena	1.00	2.50
42	Batista	.20	.50
43	Rey Mysterio	.20	.50
44	John Cena	1.25	3.00
45	Vince McMahon	.20	.50
46	John Cena	1.25	3.00
47	Shawn Michaels Retires Ric Flair	.60	1.50
48	Randy Orton	1.25	3.00
49	John Cena	1.25	3.00
50	Triple H	.75	2.00
51	Chris Jericho	.60	1.50
52	John Cena	1.25	3.00
53	Edge	.60	1.50
54	The Miz	1.25	3.00
55	CM Punk	.50	1.25
56	The Rock	1.50	4.00
57	Triple H	1.00	2.50
58	John Cena	1.50	4.00
59	Daniel Bryan	1.25	3.00
60	Daniel Bryan	1.25	3.00

2014 Topps WWE Road to WrestleMania Autographed WrestleMania 30 Mat Relics

RANDOMLY INSERTED INTO PACKS

NNO	Bray Wyatt	40.00	100.00
NNO	Cameron	12.00	30.00
NNO	Cesaro	15.00	40.00
NNO	Eve	20.00	50.00
NNO	Hulk Hogan	150.00	300.00
NNO	Jimmy Hart	20.00	30.00
NNO	Kane	25.00	60.00
NNO	Kevin Nash	30.00	80.00
NNO	Layla	12.00	30.00
NNO	Lex Luger	30.00	80.00
NNO	Naomi	20.00	50.00
NNO	Nikki Bella	30.00	80.00
NNO	Roman Reigns	40.00	100.00
NNO	Ron Simmons	30.00	80.00
NNO	Summer Rae	40.00	100.00
NNO	Trish Stratus	60.00	120.00

2014 Topps WWE Road to WrestleMania Dual Autographs

RANDOMLY INSERTED INTO PACKS

NNO	B.Wyatt/R.Reigns	120.00	250.00
NNO	H.Hogan/J.Hart	125.00	250.00
NNO	Kane/Layla	20.00	50.00
NNO	K.Nash/R.Simmons	30.00	80.00
NNO	L.Luger/Cesaro	50.00	100.00
NNO	Naomi/N.Bella	25.00	60.00
NNO	T.Stratus/Eve	50.00	100.00

2014 Topps WWE Road to WrestleMania Queen of WrestleMania

COMPLETE SET (8) 10.00 25.00
*P.P.BLACK/1: UNPRICED DUE TO SCARCITY
*P.P.CYAN/1: UNPRICED DUE TO SCARCITY
*P.P.MAGENTA/1: UNPRICED DUE TO SCARCITY
*P.P.YELLOW/1: UNPRICED DUE TO SCARCITY
STATED ODDS 1:12

#			
1	Leads T&A to Victory	2.00	5.00
2	Triple Threat Match/Women's Title	2.00	5.00
3	Defeats Victoria and Jazz	2.00	5.00
4	Turns on Chris Jericho	2.00	5.00
5	Defeats Christy Hemme	2.00	5.00
6	Battles Mickie James	2.00	5.00
7	With John Morrison and Snooki	2.00	5.00
8	Hall of Fame Induction	2.00	5.00

2014 Topps WWE Road to WrestleMania The Streak

COMPLETE SET (22) 8.00 20.00
*P.P.BLACK/1: UNPRICED DUE TO SCARCITY
*P.P.CYAN/1: UNPRICED DUE TO SCARCITY
*P.P.MAGENTA/1: UNPRICED DUE TO SCARCITY
*P.P.YELLOW/1: UNPRICED DUE TO SCARCITY
STATED ODDS 1:1

1	Jimmy Superfly Snuka	.60	1.50
2	Jake The Snake Roberts	.60	1.50
3	Giant Gonzales	.60	1.50
4	King Kong Bundy	.60	1.50
5	Diesel	.60	1.50
6	Sycho Sid	.60	1.50
7	Kane	.60	1.50
8	Big Boss Man	.60	1.50
9	Triple H	.60	1.50
10	Ric Flair	.60	1.50
11	Big Show/A-Train	.60	1.50
12	Kane	.60	1.50
13	Randy Orton	.60	1.50
14	Mark Henry	.60	1.50
15	Batista	.60	1.50
16	Edge	.60	1.50
17	Shawn Michaels	.60	1.50
18	Shawn Michaels	.60	1.50
19	Triple H	.60	1.50
20	Triple H	.60	1.50
21	CM Punk	.60	1.50
22	Brock Lesnar	2.00	5.00

2014 Topps WWE Road to WrestleMania Swatch Relics

*P.P.BLACK/1: UNPRICED DUE TO SCARCITY
*P.P.CYAN/1: UNPRICED DUE TO SCARCITY
*P.P.MAGENTA/1: UNPRICED DUE TO SCARCITY
*P.P.YELLOW/1: UNPRICED DUE TO SCARCITY
RANDOMLY INSERTED INTO PACKS

NNO	Alberto Del Rio/Shirt	3.00	8.00
NNO	Big Show/Shirt	3.00	8.00
NNO	Billy Gunn/Shirt	3.00	8.00
NNO	Bray Wyatt/Shirt	4.00	10.00
NNO	Curtis Axel/Shirt	3.00	8.00
NNO	Damien Sandow/Shirt	3.00	8.00
NNO	Daniel Bryan/Shirt	10.00	25.00
NNO	Darren Young/Shirt	4.00	10.00
NNO	Dolph Ziggler/Shirt	5.00	12.00
NNO	Goldust/Shirt	3.00	8.00
NNO	Jack Swagger/Shirt	3.00	8.00
NNO	Jey Uso/Shirt	8.00	20.00
NNO	John Cena/Shirt	120.00	200.00
NNO	John Cena/Shoe	8.00	20.00
NNO	Mark Henry/Shirt	4.00	10.00
NNO	The Miz/Shirt	3.00	8.00
NNO	Natalya/Shirt	4.00	10.00
NNO	Ryback/Shirt	3.00	8.00
NNO	Tamina Snuka/Shirt	3.00	8.00
NNO	T.Stratus/Green Pants	30.00	60.00
NNO	T.Stratus/Purple Pants	30.00	60.00
NNO	Undertaker/Pants & Hat	150.00	300.00

2014 Topps WWE Road to WrestleMania Ultimate Warrior Tribute

COMPLETE SET (10) 5.00 12.00
*P.P.BLACK/1: UNPRICED DUE TO SCARCITY
*P.P.CYAN/1: UNPRICED DUE TO SCARCITY

*P.P.MAGENTA/1: UNPRICED DUE TO SCARCITY
*P.P.YELLOW/1: UNPRICED DUE TO SCARCITY
STATED ODDS 1:4

1	Defeats Honky Tonk Man	.75	2.00
2	Defeats Ravishing Rick Rude	.75	2.00
3	Defeats The Heenan Family	.75	2.00
4	Defeats Hulk Hogan for WWE Title	.75	2.00
5	Defeats Ravishing Rick Rude	.75	2.00
6	Wins Match at Survivor Series	.75	2.00
7	Defeats Macho King Randy Savage	.75	2.00
8	Returns to WWE, Defeats Triple H	.75	2.00
9	Joins WCW	.75	2.00
10	Addresses WWE Universe	.75	2.00

2014 Topps WWE Road to WrestleMania WrestleMania 30 Mat Relics

RANDOMLY INSERTED INTO PACKS

NNO	AJ Lee	12.00	30.00
NNO	Batista	4.00	10.00
NNO	Big Show	5.00	12.00
NNO	Bray Wyatt	6.00	15.00
NNO	Brock Lesnar	4.00	10.00
NNO	Cesaro	3.00	8.00
NNO	Daniel Bryan	8.00	20.00
NNO	Dean Ambrose	5.00	12.00
NNO	Hulk Hogan	10.00	25.00
NNO	Jey Uso	3.00	8.00
NNO	Jimmy Uso	3.00	8.00
NNO	John Cena	8.00	20.00
NNO	Randy Orton	6.00	15.00
NNO	The Rock	6.00	15.00
NNO	Roman Reigns	8.00	20.00
NNO	Seth Rollins	6.00	15.00
NNO	Sheamus	3.00	8.00
NNO	Stone Cold Steve Austin	6.00	15.00
NNO	Triple H	5.00	12.00
NNO	Undertaker	6.00	15.00

2014 Topps WWE Road to WrestleMania WrestleMania Autographs

*BRONZE/25: .5X TO 1.2X BASIC AUTOS
RANDOMLY INSERTED INTO PACKS

NNO	Bray Wyatt	15.00	40.00
NNO	Cameron	8.00	20.00
NNO	Cesaro	12.00	30.00
NNO	Eve	12.00	20.00
NNO	Hulk Hogan	100.00	200.00
NNO	Jimmy Hart	12.00	25.00
NNO	Kane	15.00	40.00
NNO	Kevin Nash	15.00	40.00
NNO	Layla	12.00	25.00
NNO	Lex Luger	12.00	30.00
NNO	Naomi	12.00	30.00
NNO	Nikki Bella	15.00	40.00
NNO	Roman Reigns	20.00	50.00
NNO	Ron Simmons	12.00	30.00
NNO	Summer Rae	15.00	40.00
NNO	Trish Stratus	30.00	75.00

2014 Topps WWE Road to WrestleMania WWE 2K15

STATED ODDS 1:613

1	AJ Lee	50.00	100.00
2	Bray Wyatt	15.00	40.00
3	Brock Lesnar	10.00	25.00

4	Cesaro	8.00	20.00
5	Daniel Bryan	15.00	40.00
6	Dolph Ziggler	8.00	20.00
7	Hulk Hogan	30.00	80.00
8	John Cena	30.00	80.00
9	Roman Reigns	20.00	50.00
10	Seth Rollins	20.00	50.00

2015 Topps WWE Road to WrestleMania

COMPLETE SET (110) 10.00 25.00
UNOPENED BOX (24 PACKS)
UNOPENED PACK (7 CARDS)
*BRONZE: .6X TO 1.5X BASIC CARDS
*BLUE: .75X TO 2X BASIC CARDS
*PURPLE: .75X TO 2X BASIC CARDS
*SILVER: 2.5X TO 6X BASIC CARDS
*GOLD/10: UNPRICED DUE TO SCARCITY
*RED/1: UNPRICED DUE TO SCARCITY
*P.P. BLACK/1: UNPRICED DUE TO SCARCITY
*P.P. CYAN/1: UNPRICED DUE TO SCARCITY
*P.P. MAGENTA/1: UNPRICED DUE TO SCARCITY
*P.P. YELLOW/1: UNPRICED DUE TO SCARCITY

1	Paige	.60	1.50
2	The Shield/Daniel Bryan	.30	.75
3	Daniel Bryan/Hulk Hogan	.50	1.25
4	Fandango/Summer Rae/Layla	.12	.30
5	Ultimate Warrior Tribute	.12	.30
6	Cesaro/Mark Henry	.12	.30
7	Evolution/The Shield	.50	1.25
8	Jimmy Uso/Naomi	.12	.30
9	Kane/Daniel Bryan	.30	.75
10	Bray Wyatt/John Cena	.50	1.25
11	Kane/Brie Bella	.30	.75
12	Bad News Barrett/Big E	.12	.30
13	The Shield/Evolution	.30	.75
14	Bray Wyatt/John Cena	.50	1.25
15	Daniel Bryan/Kane	.50	1.25
16	Sheamus/Dean Ambrose	.30	.75
17	Adam Rose	.15	.40
18	Bo Dallas	.12	.30
19	The Authority/Brad Maddox	.50	1.25
20	Daniel Bryan/Brie Bella	.50	1.25
21	Brie Bella	.40	1.00
22	John Cena/Bray Wyatt	.60	1.50
23	The Shield/Evolution	.30	.75
24	Batista	.30	.75
25	Seth Rollins/The Shield	.20	.50
26	The Authority/Daniel Bryan	.50	1.25
27	John Cena/Shield/Wyatts	.60	1.50
28	Stardust	.12	.30
29	John Cena/Kane	.60	1.50
30	Seth Rollins MITB	.20	.50
31	John Cena	.60	1.50
32	Bret Hit Man Hart/Damien Sandow	.40	1.00
33	Funkadactyls	.20	.50
34	Summer Rae/Layla/Fandango	.50	1.25
35	The Miz	.20	.50
36	John Cena	.60	1.50
37	Brock Lesnar/John Cena	.50	1.25
38	Stephanie McMahon/Brie Bella	.20	.50
39	Brock Lesnar/Hulk Hogan	.50	1.25
40	Dolph Ziggler/The Miz	.20	.50
41	Paige/AJ Lee	.60	1.50
42	Seth Rollins/Dean Ambrose	.20	.50
43	Roman Reigns/Randy Orton	.30	.75
44	Brock Lesnar/John Cena	.50	1.25
45	Gold & Stardust/Usos	.12	.30
46	The Miz/Dolph Ziggler	.20	.50

47	Dean Ambrose/Seth Rollins	.30	.75
48	John Cena/Brock Lesnar	.60	1.50
49	Dolph Ziggler/The Miz	.20	.50
50	The Bunny	.12	.30
51	Seth Rollins/Dean Ambrose	.20	.50
52	The Rock/Rusev	.60	1.50
53	Dean Ambrose/The Authority	.30	.75
54	Dean Ambrose/John Cena	.30	.75
55	Nikki Bella/Brie Bella	.40	1.00
56	John Cena/Randy Orton	.60	1.50
57	Bray Wyatt/Dean Ambrose	.50	1.25
58	The Authority/Randy Orton	.50	1.25
59	Rusev/Sheamus	.30	.75
60	Luke Harper/Dolph Ziggler	.20	.50
61	Miz & Mizdow/Goldust & Stardust	.20	.50
62	Divas Survivor Series Match	.12	.30
63	Nikki Bella/AJ Lee	.40	1.00
64	Sting WWE Debut	.30	.75
65	Team Cena/Team Authority	.60	1.50
66	Dolph Ziggler/Luke Harper	.20	.50
67	John Cena/Seth Rollins	.60	1.50
68	Roman Reigns	.30	.75
69	Bray Wyatt/Dean Ambrose	.50	1.25
70	Brock Lesnar/Chris Jericho	.50	1.25
71	Seth Rollins/John Cena	.20	.50
72	Dean Ambrose/Bray Wyatt	.30	.75
73	Edge & Christian	.30	.75
74	Usos/The Miz & Mizdow	.12	.30
75	The Ascension/Miz & Mizdow	.12	.30
76	Seth Rollins/John Cena	.20	.50
77	Bad New Barrett/Dolph Ziggler	.12	.30
78	Authority/Ziggler/Ryback/Rowan	.50	1.25
79	Rollins/Cena/Lesnar	.20	.50
80	Daniel Bryan	.50	1.25
81	The Ascension/nWo	.12	.30
82	Sting/Team Cena	.30	.75
83	Lesnar/Rollins/Cena	.50	1.25
84	Kane	.30	.75
85	Roman Reigns	.30	.75
86	Daniel Bryan/Kane	.50	1.25
87	Daniel Bryan/Seth Rollins	.50	1.25
88	Stardust/Goldust	.12	.30
89	Ric Flair/Triple H	.60	1.50
90	Prime Time Players	.12	.30
91	Randy Orton/The Authority	.50	1.25
92	Tyson Kidd & Cesaro/Usos	.12	.30
93	Sting/Triple H	.30	.75
94	Rusev/John Cena	.30	.75
95	Roman Reigns/Daniel Bryan	.30	.75
96	Sting/Randy Orton	.30	.75
97	Larry Zbyszko HOF	.20	.50
98	Bushwhackers HOF	.12	.30
99	Hulk Hogan/Macho Man HOF	.60	1.50
100	Kevin Nash HOF	.30	.75
101	Tyson Kidd & Cesaro	.12	.30
102	Big Show	.30	.75
103	Daniel Bryan	.50	1.25
104	Randy Orton/Seth Rollins	.50	1.25
105	Triple H/Sting	.50	1.25
106	AJ Lee & Paige/Bella Twins	.60	1.50
107	John Cena/Rusev	.60	1.50
108	The Rock/The Authority	.60	1.50
109	Undertaker/Bray Wyatt	.50	1.25
110	Rollins/Lesnar/Reigns	.20	.50

2015 Topps WWE Road to WrestleMania Autographs

*BRONZE/50: .5X TO 1.2X BASIC AUTOS
*SILVER/25: .6X TO 1.5X BASIC AUTOS

*GOLD/10: .75X TO 2X BASIC AUTOS
*RED/1: UNPRICED DUE TO SCARCITY
*P.P.BLACK/1: UNPRICED DUE TO SCARCITY
*P.P.CYAN/1: UNPRICED DUE TO SCARCITY
*P.P.MAGENTA/1: UNPRICED DUE TO SCARCITY
*P.P.YELLOW/1: UNPRICED DUE TO SCARCITY
RANDOMLY INSERTED INTO PACKS

NNO	Afa	8.00	20.00
NNO	Alicia Fox	6.00	15.00
NNO	Bray Wyatt	12.00	30.00
NNO	Brie Bella	12.00	30.00
NNO	Brock Lesnar	60.00	120.00
NNO	Damien Mizdow	6.00	15.00
NNO	Daniel Bryan	12.00	30.00
NNO	Dean Ambrose	12.00	30.00
NNO	Dolph Ziggler	8.00	20.00
NNO	Emma	10.00	25.00
NNO	Hulk Hogan	125.00	250.00
NNO	Jack Swagger	6.00	15.00
NNO	Jimmy Hart	10.00	25.00
NNO	Nikki Bella	15.00	40.00
NNO	Razor Ramon	20.00	50.00
NNO	Roman Reigns	15.00	40.00
NNO	R-Truth	8.00	20.00
NNO	Ryback	8.00	20.00
NNO	Sika	8.00	20.00

2015 Topps WWE Road to WrestleMania Bizarre WrestleMania Matches

COMPLETE SET (10) 5.00 12.00
*P.P.BLACK/1: UNPRICED DUE TO SCARCITY
*P.P.CYAN/1: UNPRICED DUE TO SCARCITY
*P.P.MAGENTA/1: UNPRICED DUE TO SCARCITY
*P.P.YELLOW/1: UNPRICED DUE TO SCARCITY
STATED ODDS 1:4

1	Andre the Giant/Big John Studd	1.00	2.50
2	Mr.T/Rowdy Roddy Piper	1.00	2.50
3	Corporal Kirchner/Nikolai Volkoff	1.00	2.50
4	Battle Royal	1.00	2.50
5	Rowdy Roddy Piper/Adrian Adonis	1.00	2.50
6	Jake Roberts/Rick Martel	1.00	2.50
7	Rowdy Roddy Piper/Goldust	1.00	2.50
8	C.Jack & C.Charlie/New Age Outlaws	1.00	2.50
9	Gimmick Battle Royal	1.00	2.50
10	Akebono/Big Show	1.00	2.50

2015 Topps WWE Road to WrestleMania Classic WrestleMania Matches

COMPLETE SET (30) 6.00 15.00
*P.P.BLACK/1: UNPRICED DUE TO SCARCITY
*P.P.CYAN/1: UNPRICED DUE TO SCARCITY
*P.P.MAGENTA/1: UNPRICED DUE TO SCARCITY
*P.P.YELLOW/1: UNPRICED DUE TO SCARCITY
RANDOMLY INSERTED INTO PACKS

1	Harley Race/JYD	.50	1.25
2	Honky Tonk Man	.50	1.25
	Jake The Snake Roberts		
3	Twin Towers/Rockers	.50	1.25
4	Nasty Boys/Hart Foundation	.50	1.25
5	Bret Hit Man Hart	.50	1.25
	Rowdy Roddy Piper		
6	Money Inc/Mega-Maniacs	.50	1.25
7	Lex Luger/Mr. Perfect	.50	1.25
8	Bret Hit Man Hart	.50	1.25
9	Razor Ramon/Shawn Michaels	.50	1.25

10	Stone Cold Steve Austin Savio Vega	.50	1.25
11	Chris Jericho/Kurt Angle	.50	1.25
12	Chris Jericho/William Regal	.50	1.25
13	Eddie Guerrero/Test	.50	1.25
14	Stone Cold Steve Austin Chris Jericho	.50	1.25
15	Shawn Michaels/Chris Jericho	.50	1.25
16	John Cena/Big Show	.50	1.25
17	Christian/Chris Jericho	.50	1.25
18	Goldberg/Brock Lesnar	.50	1.25
19	Rey Mysterio/Eddie Guerrero	.50	1.25
20	Edge MITB	.50	1.25
21	Kurt Angle/Shawn Michaels	.50	1.25
22	Rob Van Dam MITB	.50	1.25
23	Edge/Mick Foley	.50	1.25
24	Shawn Michaels/Mr. McMahon	.50	1.25
25	Jack Swagger MITB	.50	1.25
26	Bret Hit Man Hart Mr. McMahon	.50	1.25
27	Randy Orton/CM Punk	.50	1.25
28	Sheamus/Daniel Bryan	.50	1.25
29	Shield/Orton Sheamus Big Show	.50	1.25
30	Team Hell No/Ziggler & Big E	.50	1.25

2015 Topps WWE Road to WrestleMania Dual Autographs

STATED PRINT RUN 10 SER.#'d SETS
UNPRICED DUE TO SCARCITY

NNO	Afa/Sika	
NNO	Brie & Nikki Bella	
NNO	D.Mizdow/J.Hart	
NNO	D.Bryan/B.Wyatt	
NNO	D.Ambrose/R.Reigns	
NNO	D.Ziggler/Ryback	
NNO	Emma/A.Fox	
NNO	H.Hogan/R.Ramon	

2015 Topps WWE Road to WrestleMania Hall of Fame

COMPLETE SET (30) 4.00 10.00
*P.P.BLACK/1: UNPRICED DUE TO SCARCITY
*P.P.CYAN/1: UNPRICED DUE TO SCARCITY
*P.P.MAGENTA/1: UNPRICED DUE TO SCARCITY
*P.P.YELLOW/1: UNPRICED DUE TO SCARCITY
STATED ODDS 1:1

1	Chief Jay Strongbow	.40	1.00
2	Classy Freddie Blassie	.25	.60
3	Gorilla Monsoon	.30	.75
4	George The Animal Steele	.30	.75
5	Jimmy Superfly Snuka	.40	1.00
6	Pat Patterson	.25	.60
7	The Magnificent Don Muraco	.40	1.00
8	Greg The Hammer Valentine	.30	.75
9	The King Harley Race	.40	1.00
10	Sgt. Slaughter	.40	1.00
11	Tito Santana	.40	1.00
12	Hulk Hogan	1.25	3.00
13	Rowdy Roddy Piper	.75	2.00
14	Cowboy Bob Orton	.25	.60
15	Mr. Wonderful Paul Orndorff	.40	1.00
16	Nikolai Volkoff	.25	.60
17	The Iron Sheik	.40	1.00
18	Bret Hit Man Hart	.75	2.00
19	The American Dream Dusty Rhodes	.40	1.00
20	Jerry The King Lawler	.40	1.00
21	Nature Boy Ric Flair	1.25	3.00

22	Rocky Johnson	.40	1.00
23	Stone Cold Steve Austin	1.25	3.00
24	Ricky The Dragon Steamboat	.40	1.00
25	Koko B. Ware	.30	.75
26	Million Dollar Man Ted DiBiase	.40	1.00
27	Heartbreak Kid Shawn Michaels	1.00	2.50
28	Hacksaw Jim Duggan	.40	1.00
29	Edge	.60	1.50
30	Ron Simmons	.40	1.00

2015 Topps WWE Road to WrestleMania HHH at WrestleMania

COMPLETE SET (10) 4.00 10.00
*P.P.BLACK/1: UNPRICED DUE TO SCARCITY
*P.P.CYAN/1: UNPRICED DUE TO SCARCITY
*P.P.MAGENTA/1: UNPRICED DUE TO SCARCITY
*P.P.YELLOW/1: UNPRICED DUE TO SCARCITY
STATED ODDS 1:2

1	Defeats Goldust	.75	2.00
2	Battles Kane	.75	2.00
3	Wins 4-Way Elimination Match	.75	2.00
4	Defeats Y2J for WWE Title	.75	2.00
5	Defeats Booker T	.75	2.00
6	Defeats Randy Orton	.75	2.00
7	Defeats Sheamus	.75	2.00
8	Faces Undertaker No Holds Barred	.75	2.00
9	Faces Undertaker Hell in a Cell	.75	2.00
10	Defeats Brock Lesnar	.75	2.00

2015 Topps WWE Road to WrestleMania Mat Relics

*SILVER/25: .6X TO 1.5X BASIC MEM
*GOLD/10: UNPRICED DUE TO SCARCITY
*RED/1: UNPRICED DUE TO SCARCITY
*P.P.BLACK/1: UNPRICED DUE TO SCARCITY
*P.P.CYAN/1: UNPRICED DUE TO SCARCITY
*P.P.MAGENTA/1: UNPRICED DUE TO SCARCITY
*P.P.YELLOW/1: UNPRICED DUE TO SCARCITY
RANDOMLY INSERTED INTO PACKS

NNO	Bad News Barrett	2.00	5.00
NNO	Big Show	2.50	6.00
NNO	Bray Wyatt	3.00	8.00
NNO	Brie Bella	4.00	10.00
NNO	Brock Lesnar	3.00	8.00
NNO	Damien Mizdow	2.50	6.00
NNO	Daniel Bryan	5.00	12.00
NNO	Dean Ambrose	3.00	8.00
NNO	Dolph Ziggler	2.00	5.00
NNO	John Cena	4.00	10.00
NNO	Nikki Bella	4.00	10.00
NNO	Paige	6.00	15.00
NNO	Randy Orton	3.00	8.00
NNO	Roman Reigns	4.00	10.00
NNO	Rusev	2.50	6.00
NNO	Ryback	2.00	5.00
NNO	Seth Rollins	3.00	8.00
NNO	Sting	6.00	15.00
NNO	Triple H	3.00	8.00
NNO	Undertaker	5.00	12.00

2015 Topps WWE Road to WrestleMania Rocking WrestleMania

COMPLETE SET (8) 5.00 12.00
*P.P.BLACK/1: UNPRICED DUE TO SCARCITY
*P.P.CYAN/1: UNPRICED DUE TO SCARCITY
*P.P.MAGENTA/1: UNPRICED DUE TO SCARCITY
*P.P.YELLOW/1: UNPRICED DUE TO SCARCITY

RANDOMLY INSERTED INTO PACKS

1	Faces Stone Cold Steve Austin	1.25	3.00
2	Takes on Stone Cold Steve Austin	1.25	3.00
3	Defeats Hollywood Hulk Hogan	1.25	3.00
4	Defeats Stone Cold Steve Austin	1.25	3.00
5	Rock 'n' Sock Reunite	1.25	3.00
6	Rock Bottoms John Cena	1.25	3.00
7	Defeats John Cena	1.25	3.00
8	Battles John Cena	1.25	3.00

2015 Topps WWE Road to WrestleMania Superstars of Canada

COMPLETE SET (10) 25.00 60.00
RANDOMLY INSERTED INTO PACKS

1	Chris Jericho	5.00	12.00
2	Christian	2.00	5.00
3	Edge	5.00	12.00
4	Kevin Owens	6.00	15.00
5	Natalya	6.00	15.00
6	Renee Young	8.00	20.00
7	Sami Zayn	3.00	8.00
8	Trish Stratus	10.00	25.00
9	Tyson Kidd	2.00	5.00
10	Viktor	2.00	5.00

2015 Topps WWE Road to WrestleMania Superstars of Canada Autographs

RANDOMLY INSERTED INTO PACKS
STATED PRINT RUN 25 SER.#'d SETS
CANADIAN EXCLUSIVES

NNO	Chris Jericho	50.00	100.00
NNO	Christian	25.00	60.00
NNO	Edge	50.00	100.00
NNO	Kevin Owens	15.00	40.00
NNO	Natalya	20.00	50.00
NNO	Renee Young	20.00	50.00
NNO	Sami Zayn	10.00	25.00
NNO	Trish Stratus	100.00	200.00
NNO	Tyson Kidd	6.00	15.00
NNO	Viktor	6.00	15.00

2015 Topps WWE Road to WrestleMania Swatch Relics

*P.P.BLACK/1: UNPRICED DUE TO SCARCITY
*P.P.CYAN/1: UNPRICED DUE TO SCARCITY
*P.P.MAGENTA/1: UNPRICED DUE TO SCARCITY
*P.P.YELLOW/1: UNPRICED DUE TO SCARCITY
RANDOMLY INSERTED INTO PACKS

NNO	Adam Rose	4.00	10.00
NNO	Brie Bella	6.00	15.00
NNO	Cesaro	4.00	10.00
NNO	Charlotte	10.00	25.00
NNO	Dean Ambrose	8.00	20.00
NNO	Damien Mizdow	4.00	10.00
NNO	Dolph Ziggler	4.00	10.00
NNO	Goldust	6.00	15.00
NNO	Hulk Hogan	10.00	25.00
NNO	John Cena	6.00	15.00
NNO	Jack Swagger	5.00	12.00
NNO	Nikki Bella	10.00	25.00
NNO	Paige	12.00	30.00
NNO	Roman Reigns	8.00	20.00
NNO	Rusev	5.00	12.00
NNO	Ryback	5.00	12.00
NNO	Stardust	5.00	12.00
NNO	Sami Zayn	6.00	15.00

2015 Topps WWE Road to WrestleMania Turnbuckle Pad Relics

RANDOMLY INSERTED INTO PACKS
STATED PRINT RUN 25 SER.#'d SETS

NNO	Bad News Barrett	6.00	15.00
NNO	Big Show	15.00	40.00
NNO	Bray Wyatt	25.00	60.00
NNO	Brie Bella	20.00	50.00
NNO	Brock Lesnar	25.00	60.00
NNO	Damien Mizdow	6.00	15.00
NNO	Daniel Bryan	25.00	60.00
NNO	Dean Ambrose	15.00	40.00
NNO	Dolph Ziggler	10.00	25.00
NNO	John Cena	30.00	80.00
NNO	Nikki Bella	20.00	50.00
NNO	Paige	30.00	80.00
NNO	Randy Orton	25.00	60.00
NNO	Roman Reigns	15.00	40.00
NNO	Rusev	15.00	40.00
NNO	Ryback	6.00	15.00
NNO	Seth Rollins	10.00	25.00
NNO	Sting	15.00	40.00
NNO	Triple H	25.00	60.00
NNO	Undertaker	25.00	60.00

2016 Topps WWE Road to WrestleMania

COMPLETE SET (110) 12.00 30.00
UNOPENED BOX (24 PACKS)
UNOPENED PACK (7 CARDS)
*BRONZE: .5X TO 1.2X BASIC CARDS
*SILVER: 2X TO 5X BASIC CARDS
*GOLD/10: UNPRICED DUE TO SCARCITY
*RED/1: UNPRICED DUE TO SCARCITY
*PP BLACK/1: UNPRICED DUE TO SCARCITY
*PP CYAN/1: UNPRICED DUE TO SCARCITY
*PP MAGENTA/1: UNPRICED DUE TO SCARCITY
*PP YELLOW/1: UNPRICED DUE TO SCARCITY
NUMBERS 111-113 ARE WWE DVD EXCLUSIVES

1	Daniel Bryan	.75	2.00
2	The Usos	.20	.50
3	Alundra Blayze	.25	.60
4	Ric Flair	.75	2.00
5	Triple H	.75	2.00
6	Hideo Itami	.25	.60
7	Damien Mizdow	.30	.75
8	Sting	.50	1.25
9	Triple H	.75	2.00
10	D-Generation X	.60	1.50
11	Rusev	.50	1.25
12	Bray Wyatt	.75	2.00
13	Roman Reigns	1.00	2.50
14	Sheamus	.50	1.25
15	Kalisto	.50	1.25
16	Brock Lesnar	1.00	2.50
17	Neville	.50	1.25
18	Big Show	.60	1.50
19	Fandango	.20	.50
20	Daniel Bryan/John Cena	1.00	2.50
21	The Miz	.30	.75
22	The New Day	.50	1.25
23	Roman Reigns	.60	1.50
24	Seth Rollins	.30	.75
25	Bad New Barrett	.20	.50
26	Sami Zayn	1.00	2.50
27	Erick Rowan	.20	.50
28	Neville	1.00	2.50

#	Player		
29	Daniel Bryan	.75	2.00
30	John Cena	1.00	2.50
31	Seth Rollins	.30	.75
32	Rusev	.75	2.00
33	Kevin Owens	1.00	2.50
34	Lana	.75	2.00
35	The New Day	.50	1.25
36	Kalisto	.50	1.25
37	The New Day	.50	1.25
38	Nikki Bella	.60	1.50
39	Kevin Owens	.50	1.25
40	Ryback	.25	.60
41	Dean Ambrose	.60	1.50
42	Dusty Rhodes Tribute	.20	.50
43	Bray Wyatt	.75	2.00
44	Sheamus	.50	1.25
45	Nikki Bella	.60	1.50
46	John Cena	1.00	2.50
47	The Prime Time Players	.20	.50
48	Seth Rollins	.60	1.50
49	Brock Lesnar	1.00	2.50
50	Brock Lesnar	1.00	2.50
51	Cesaro	1.00	2.50
52	Chris Jericho	.50	1.25
53	Nikki Bella	.60	1.50
54	Brock Lesnar	1.00	2.50
55	Rusev/Summer Rae	.75	2.00
56	Brock Lesnar	1.00	2.50
57	John Cena	1.00	2.50
58	Rusev	.50	1.25
59	Stardust	.20	.50
60	Brock Lesnar	1.00	2.50
61	Cesaro	.50	1.25
62	Bray Wyatt	.75	2.00
63	Charlotte	.60	1.50
64	John Cena	1.00	2.50
65	Undertaker	1.00	2.50
66	Brock Lesnar	1.00	2.50
67	John Cena/Cesaro/Randy Orton	1.00	2.50
68	Seth Rollins	.30	.75
69	John Cena	1.00	2.50
70	Dean Ambrose/Cesaro	.60	1.50
71	Rowdy Roddy Piper Tribute	.60	1.50
72	Ambrose/Reigns/Orton	.50	1.25
73	The New Day	.50	1.25
74	Undertaker	1.00	2.50
75	Ryback	.30	.75
76	Roman Reigns/Dean Ambrose	.75	2.00
77	Seth Rollins	.30	.75
78	Team PCB	.60	1.50
79	Undertaker	1.00	2.50
80	Brock Lesnar	1.00	2.50
81	The Dudley Boyz	.40	1.00
82	Braun Strowman	.25	.60
83	Sting	.50	1.25
84	Charlotte	.60	1.50
85	Sting/John Cena	1.00	2.50
86	Hideo Itami	.25	.60
87	Sami Zayn	.30	.75
88	Becky Lynch	.60	1.50
89	Kevin Owens	.50	1.25
90	Tyler Breeze/Adam Rose	.20	.50
91	Finn Balor	.60	1.50
92	Charlotte/Bayley	.60	1.50
93	Sasha Banks	.60	1.50
94	Kevin Owens	.50	1.25
95	Samoa Joe	.50	1.25
96	Kevin Owens	.50	1.25

#	Player		
97	Samoa Joe	.50	1.25
98	Samoa Joe	.50	1.25
99	Finn Balor/Samoa Joe	.60	1.50
100	Finn Balor	.60	1.50
101	The Vaudevillains	.20	.50
102	Sasha Banks	.60	1.50
103	Blake/Murphy	.20	.50
104	Bayley	.60	1.50
105	Bayley	.50	1.25
106	The Vaudevillains	.20	.50
107	Apollo Crews	.20	.50
108	Samoa Joe	.50	1.25
109	Bayley	.50	1.25
110	Finn Balor	.60	1.50
111	The Dudley Boyz SP		
112	Stone Cold Steve Austin SP		
113	Daniel Bryan SP		

2016 Topps WWE Road to WrestleMania Autographs

*BRONZE/50: .5X TO 1.2X BASIC AUTOS
*SILVER/25: .60X TO 1.5X BASIC AUTOS
*GOLD/10: UNPRICED DUE TO SCARCITY
*RED/1: UNPRICED DUE TO SCARCITY
*PP BLACK/1: UNPRICED DUE TO SCARCITY
*PP CYAN/1: UNPRICED DUE TO SCARCITY
*PP MAGENTA/1: UNPRICED DUE TO SCARCITY
*PP YELLOW/1: UNPRICED DUE TO SCARCITY
STATED PRINT RUN 99 SER.#'d SETS

NNO	Baron Corbin	10.00	25.00
NNO	Bayley	15.00	40.00
NNO	Becky Lynch	25.00	60.00
NNO	Brie Bella	10.00	25.00
NNO	Brock Lesnar	100.00	200.00
NNO	Charlotte	25.00	60.00
NNO	Daniel Bryan	10.00	25.00
NNO	Dean Ambrose	10.00	25.00
NNO	Dory Funk Jr.	12.00	30.00
NNO	Dusty Rhodes	50.00	100.00
NNO	Eva Marie	15.00	40.00
NNO	Gerald Brisco	6.00	15.00
NNO	John Cena	20.00	50.00
NNO	Kalisto	12.00	30.00
NNO	Kevin Von Erich	25.00	60.00
NNO	Lana	20.00	50.00
NNO	Michael P.S. Hayes	10.00	25.00
NNO	Neville	6.00	15.00
NNO	Nikki Bella	15.00	40.00
NNO	Pat Patterson	6.00	15.00
NNO	Ric Flair	15.00	40.00
NNO	Roman Reigns	12.00	30.00
NNO	Samoa Joe	8.00	20.00
NNO	Sasha Banks	25.00	60.00
NNO	Seth Rollins	10.00	25.00
NNO	Sting	30.00	80.00
NNO	Terry Funk	50.00	100.00

2016 Topps WWE Road to WrestleMania Battleground Mat Relics

*BRONZE/50: .5X TO 1.2X BASIC MEM
*SILVER/25: .6X TO 1.5X BASIC MEM
*GOLD/10: UNPRICED DUE TO SCARCITY
*RED/1: UNPRICED DUE TO SCARCITY
*PP BLACK/1: UNPRICED DUE TO SCARCITY
*PP CYAN/1: UNPRICED DUE TO SCARCITY
*PP MAGENTA/1: UNPRICED DUE TO SCARCITY
*PP YELLOW/1: UNPRICED DUE TO SCARCITY

STATED PRINT RUN 199 SER.#'d SETS

NNO	Big E	2.00	5.00
NNO	Bray Wyatt	8.00	20.00
NNO	Brie Bella	4.00	10.00
NNO	Brock Lesnar	10.00	25.00
NNO	Charlotte	6.00	15.00
NNO	Darren Young	2.00	5.00
NNO	John Cena	10.00	25.00
NNO	Kevin Owens	5.00	12.00
NNO	Kofi Kingston	2.00	5.00
NNO	Luke Harper	2.00	5.00
NNO	Randy Orton	5.00	12.00
NNO	Roman Reigns	6.00	15.00
NNO	R-Truth	2.00	5.00
NNO	Sasha Banks	6.00	15.00
NNO	Seth Rollins	3.00	8.00
NNO	Sheamus	5.00	12.00
NNO	Titus O'Neil	2.00	5.00
NNO	Undertaker	8.00	20.00
NNO	Wade Barrett	2.00	5.00
NNO	Xavier Woods	2.00	5.00

2016 Topps WWE Road to WrestleMania Battleground Turnbuckle Pad Relics

STATED PRINT RUN 25 SER.#'d SETS

NNO	Big E	5.00	12.00
NNO	Bray Wyatt	20.00	50.00
NNO	Brie Bella	10.00	25.00
NNO	Brock Lesnar	25.00	60.00
NNO	Charlotte	15.00	40.00
NNO	Darren Young	5.00	12.00
NNO	John Cena	25.00	60.00
NNO	Kevin Owens	12.00	30.00
NNO	Kofi Kingston	5.00	12.00
NNO	Luke Harper	5.00	12.00
NNO	Randy Orton	12.00	30.00
NNO	Roman Reigns	15.00	40.00
NNO	R-Truth	5.00	12.00
NNO	Sasha Banks	15.00	40.00
NNO	Seth Rollins	8.00	20.00
NNO	Sheamus	12.00	30.00
NNO	Titus O'Neil	5.00	12.00
NNO	Undertaker	20.00	50.00
NNO	Wade Barrett	5.00	12.00
NNO	Xavier Woods	5.00	12.00

2016 Topps WWE Road to WrestleMania Dual Autographs

STATED PRINT RUN 11 SER.#'d SETS

NNO	Charlotte/Bayley	100.00	200.00
NNO	Lana/E.Marie	100.00	200.00
NNO	Neville/Kalisto	30.00	75.00
NNO	P.Patterson/G.Brisco	25.00	60.00
NNO	Samoa Joe/B.Corbin	50.00	100.00
NNO	S.Banks/B.Lynch	200.00	300.00
NNO	Sting/R.Flair	225.00	350.00
NNO	T.Funk/D.Funk Jr.	50.00	100.00

2016 Topps WWE Road to WrestleMania Dusty Rhodes Tribute

COMPLETE SET (10) 3.00 8.00
STATED ODDS 1:6

1	Dusty Rhodes	.60	1.50
2	Dusty Rhodes	.60	1.50
3	Dusty Rhodes	.60	1.50
4	Dusty Rhodes	1.00	2.50
5	Dusty Rhodes	.60	1.50
6	Dusty Rhodes	1.00	2.50
7	Dusty Rhodes	.60	1.50
8	Dusty Rhodes	.60	1.50
9	Dusty Rhodes	.60	1.50
10	Dusty Rhodes	1.50	4.00

2016 Topps WWE Road to WrestleMania Immortals

COMPLETE SET (10) 6.00 15.00
STATED ODDS 1:6

1	Roman Reigns	1.00	2.50
2	Daniel Bryan	1.25	3.00
3	Randy Orton	.75	2.00
4	The Bellas	1.00	2.50
5	Paige	1.00	2.50
6	Triple H	1.25	3.00
7	Undertaker	1.25	3.00
8	The Rock	1.50	4.00
9	Brock Lesnar	1.50	4.00
10	John Cena	1.50	4.00

2016 Topps WWE Road to WrestleMania NXT Diva Kiss

STATED PRINT RUN 99 SER.#'d SETS

NNO	Alexa Bliss	50.00	100.00
NNO	Bayley	80.00	150.00
NNO	Becky Lynch	50.00	100.00
NNO	Carmella	25.00	60.00
NNO	Charlotte	50.00	100.00
NNO	Dana Brooke	20.00	50.00
NNO	Eva Marie	30.00	80.00
NNO	Jojo	20.00	50.00
NNO	Sasha Banks	100.00	200.00

2016 Topps WWE Road to WrestleMania NXT Diva Kiss Autographs

*GOLD/10: UNPRICED DUE TO SCARCITY
*RED/1: UNPRICED DUE TO SCARCITY
*PP BLACK/1: UNPRICED DUE TO SCARCITY
*PP CYAN/1: UNPRICED DUE TO SCARCITY
*PP MAGENTA/1: UNPRICED DUE TO SCARCITY
*PP YELLOW/1: UNPRICED DUE TO SCARCITY
STATED PRINT RUN 25 SER.#'d SETS

NNO	Alexa Bliss	250.00	500.00
NNO	Bayley	75.00	150.00
NNO	Becky Lynch	120.00	200.00
NNO	Carmella	60.00	120.00
NNO	Charlotte	150.00	250.00
NNO	Dana Brooke	50.00	100.00
NNO	Eva Marie	50.00	100.00
NNO	Jojo	50.00	100.00
NNO	Sasha Banks	150.00	250.00

2016 Topps WWE Road to WrestleMania Roster

COMPLETE SET (30) 10.00 25.00
*P.P.BLACK/1: UNPRICED DUE TO SCARCITY
*P.P.CYAN/1: UNPRICED DUE TO SCARCITY
*P.P.MAGENTA/1: UNPRICED DUE TO SCARCITY
*P.P.YELLOW/1: UNPRICED DUE TO SCARCITY
STATED ODDS 1:1

1	The Rock	1.50	4.00
2	Triple H	1.25	3.00
3	Undertaker	1.25	3.00
4	Sting	.75	2.00

5	Brock Lesnar	1.50	4.00
6	Seth Rollins	.50	1.25
7	Roman Reigns	1.00	2.50
8	Randy Orton	.75	2.00
9	Dean Ambrose	1.00	2.50
10	John Cena	1.50	4.00
11	Rusev	.75	2.00
12	Daniel Bryan	1.25	3.00
13	Dolph Ziggler	.40	1.00
14	King Barrett	.30	.75
15	Luke Harper	.30	.75
16	Bray Wyatt	1.25	3.00
17	The Miz	.50	1.25
18	Ryback	.40	1.00
19	Big Show	.60	1.50
20	Cesaro	.60	1.50
21	Tyson Kidd	.30	.75
22	Kofi Kingston	.30	.75
23	Big E	.30	.75
24	Xavier Woods	.30	.75
25	Brie Bella	.60	1.50
26	Nikki Bella	1.00	2.50
27	Paige	1.00	2.50
28	Naomi	.50	1.25
29	Natalya	.50	1.25
30	Lana	1.25	3.00

2016 Topps WWE Road to WrestleMania Rowdy Roddy Piper Tribute

COMPLETE SET (10) 4.00 10.00
STATED ODDS 1:6

1	Rowdy Roddy Piper	.75	2.00
2	Rowdy Roddy Piper	1.25	3.00
3	Rowdy Roddy Piper	.75	2.00
4	Rowdy Roddy Piper	.75	2.00
5	Rowdy Roddy Piper	.75	2.00
6	Rowdy Roddy Piper	.75	2.00
7	Rowdy Roddy Piper	.75	2.00
8	Rowdy Roddy Piper	.75	2.00
9	Rowdy Roddy Piper	.75	2.00
10	Rowdy Roddy Piper	.75	2.00

2016 Topps WWE Road to WrestleMania Shirt Relics

*BRONZE/50: .5X TO 1.2X BASIC MEM
*SILVER/25: .6X TO 1.5X BASIC MEM
*GOLD/10: UNPRICED DUE TO SCARCITY
*RED/1: UNPRICED DUE TO SCARCITY
*PP BLACK/1: UNPRICED DUE TO SCARCITY
*PP CYAN/1: UNPRICED DUE TO SCARCITY
*PP MAGENTA/1: UNPRICED DUE TO SCARCITY
*PP YELLOW/1: UNPRICED DUE TO SCARCITY
STATED PRINT RUN 350 SER.#'d SETS

NNO	Alicia Fox	3.00	8.00
NNO	Baron Corbin	2.50	6.00
NNO	Bayley	10.00	25.00
NNO	Becky Lynch	10.00	25.00
NNO	Big Show	4.00	10.00
NNO	Bray Wyatt	8.00	20.00
NNO	Colin Cassady	4.00	10.00
NNO	Darren Young	2.00	5.00
NNO	Dean Ambrose	6.00	15.00
NNO	John Cena	10.00	25.00
NNO	Kalisto	5.00	12.00
NNO	Kevin Owens	5.00	12.00
NNO	Kofi Kingston	2.00	5.00

NNO	Miz	3.00	8.00
NNO	Mojo Rawley	2.00	5.00
NNO	Neville	5.00	12.00
NNO	Paige	8.00	20.00
NNO	Randy Orton	5.00	12.00
NNO	Rob Van Dam	4.00	10.00
NNO	Roman Reigns	6.00	15.00
NNO	Ryback	2.50	6.00
NNO	Sami Zayn	3.00	8.00
NNO	Samoa Joe	5.00	12.00
NNO	Sasha Banks	8.00	20.00
NNO	Seth Rollins	3.00	8.00
NNO	Sheamus	5.00	12.00
NNO	Sin Cara	2.50	6.00
NNO	Summer Rae	5.00	12.00
NNO	Tyler Breeze	2.00	5.00
NNO	Xavier Woods	2.00	5.00

2016 Topps WWE Road to WrestleMania SP Inserts

STATED ODDS 1:24 HOBBY EXCLUSIVE

1	Kevin Owens	4.00	10.00
2	Charlotte	5.00	12.00
3	John Cena	8.00	20.00
4	Seth Rollins	4.00	10.00
5	Brock Lesnar	8.00	20.00
6	Tyler Breeze	1.50	4.00
7	Alberto Del Rio	8.00	20.00
8	Roman Reigns	6.00	15.00
9	Seth Rollins	2.50	6.00
10	Brock Lesnar	8.00	20.00
11	Paige	5.00	12.00
12	Goldust	2.50	6.00
13	Ryback	2.00	5.00
14	Undertaker/Kane	6.00	15.00
15	Roman Reigns	5.00	12.00
16	Sheamus	5.00	12.00
17	The New Day	1.50	4.00
18	Alberto Del Rio	2.50	6.00
19	Dean Ambrose	5.00	12.00
20	Sheamus	5.00	12.00

2016 Topps WWE Road to WrestleMania Triple Threat Autographed Dual Relics

STATED PRINT RUN 11 SER.#'d SETS

NNO	Bray Wyatt	50.00	100.00
NNO	Daniel Bryan	100.00	150.00
NNO	Dean Ambrose	25.00	60.00
NNO	John Cena	50.00	100.00
NNO	Nikki Bella	60.00	120.00
NNO	Roman Reigns	60.00	120.00
NNO	Seth Rollins	30.00	80.00

2016 Topps WWE Road to WrestleMania WWE Hall of Fame Commemorative Ring Relics

*BRONZE/50: .5X TO 1.2X BASIC MEM
*SILVER/25: .6X TO 1.5X BASIC MEM
*GOLD/10: UNPRICED DUE TO SCARCITY
RED/1: UNPRICED DUE TO SCARCITY
*P.P. BLACK/1: UNPRICED DUE TO SCARCITY
*P.P. CYAN/1: UNPRICED DUE TO SCARCITY
*P.P. MAGENTA/1: UNPRICED DUE TO SCARCITY
*P.P. YELLOW/1: UNPRICED DUE TO SCARCITY
STATED PRINT RUN 299 SER.#'d SETS

NNO	Alundra Blayze	2.00	5.00

NNO	American Dream Dusty Rhodes	1.50	4.00
NNO	Bob Backlund	1.50	4.00
NNO	Booker T	3.00	8.00
NNO	Bret Hit Man Hart	4.00	10.00
NNO	Bruno Sammartino	2.00	5.00
NNO	Don Muraco	1.50	4.00
NNO	Edge	4.00	10.00
NNO	George The Animal Steele	2.00	5.00
NNO	Hacksaw Jim Duggan	1.50	4.00
NNO	Harley Race	1.50	4.00
NNO	Iron Sheik	1.50	4.00
NNO	Jake The Snake Roberts	3.00	8.00
NNO	Jerry The King Lawler	3.00	8.00
NNO	Kevin Nash	4.00	10.00
NNO	Koko B. Ware	1.50	4.00
NNO	Larry Zbyszko	1.50	4.00
NNO	Lita	5.00	12.00
NNO	Million Dollar Man Ted DiBiase	2.00	5.00
NNO	Mr. Wonderful Paul Orndorff	1.50	4.00
NNO	Razor Ramon	4.00	10.00
NNO	Ric Flair	6.00	15.00
NNO	Ricky The Dragon Steamboat	2.00	5.00
NNO	Ron Simmons	4.00	10.00
NNO	Rowdy Roddy Piper	5.00	12.00
NNO	Sgt. Slaughter	2.00	5.00
NNO	Shawn Michaels	6.00	15.00
NNO	Stone Cold Steve Austin	8.00	20.00
NNO	Trish Stratus	8.00	20.00
NNO	Ultimate Warrior	4.00	10.00

2017 Topps WWE Road to WrestleMania

COMPLETE SET (100) 10.00 25.00
UNOPENED BOX (24 PACKS)
UNOPENED PACK (7 CARDS)
*BRONZE: .5X TO 1.2X BASIC CARDS
*BLUE/99: 1X TO 2.5X BASIC CARDS
*SILVER/25: 1.5X TO 4X BASIC CARDS
*GOLD/10: 3X TO 8X BASIC CARDS
*RED/1: UNPRICED DUE TO SCARCITY
*P.P.BLACK/1: UNPRICED DUE TO SCARCITY
*P.P.CYAN/1: UNPRICED DUE TO SCARCITY
*P.P.MAGENTA/1: UNPRICED DUE TO SCARCITY
*P.P.YELLOW/1: UNPRICED DUE TO SCARCITY

1	Roman Reigns	.60	1.50
2	Dean Ambrose	.60	1.50
3	Dean Ambrose	.60	1.50
4	John Cena	1.00	2.50
5	Charlotte	.75	2.00
6	Kalisto	.30	.75
7	Brock Lesnar	1.00	2.50
8	The Wyatt Family	.50	1.25
9	Dean Ambrose	.60	1.50
10	Kalisto	.30	.75
11	Sasha Banks	.60	1.50
12	AJ Styles	1.00	2.50
13	The Wyatt Family	.50	1.25
14	Triple H	.50	1.25
15	Triple H	.50	1.25
16	AJ Styles	1.00	2.50
17	The Rock	1.00	2.50
18	Roman Reigns/Dean Ambrose	.60	1.50
19	Brock Lesnar	1.00	2.50
20	Brock Lesnar	1.00	2.50
21	Daniel Bryan Retires	.75	2.00
22	Chris Jericho	.50	1.25
23	Kevin Owens	.50	1.25
24	Brock Lesnar	1.00	2.50

25	Kalisto	.30	.75
26	Charlotte	.75	2.00
27	AJ Styles	1.00	2.50
28	Roman Reigns/Dean Ambrose	.60	1.50
29	Brock Lesnar	1.00	2.50
30	Roman Reigns	.60	1.50
31	Shane McMahon	.30	.75
32	Dean Ambrose	.60	1.50
33	Triple H	.50	1.25
34	Undertaker	.75	2.00
35	Triple H	.50	1.25
36	Shane McMahon	.30	.75
37	Sami Zayn	.25	.60
38	The New Day	.40	1.00
39	Dean Ambrose	.60	1.50
40	Brock Lesnar	1.00	2.50
41	Triple H	.50	1.25
42	Triple H	.50	1.25
43	Roman Reigns	.60	1.50
44	Undertaker	.75	2.00
45	Brock Lesnar	1.00	2.50
46	Shane McMahon	.30	.75
47	The Godfather	.20	.50
48	Vader	.20	.50
49	The Fabulous Freebirds	.20	.50
50	John Cena	1.00	2.50
51	Sting Retires	.60	1.50
52	Kalisto	.30	.75
53	Team Total Divas	.20	.50
54	Lita	.40	1.00
55	The Usos	.25	.60
56	Zack Ryder	.20	.50
57	Chris Jericho	.50	1.25
58	Brock Lesnar	1.00	2.50
59	Charlotte	.75	2.00
60	Shane McMahon	.30	.75
61	Undertaker	.75	2.00
62	Diamond Dallas Page	.25	.60
63	Tatanka	.20	.50
64	Baron Corbin	.30	.75
65	The Rock	1.00	2.50
66	HHH/Stephanie	.50	1.25
67	Roman Reigns	.60	1.50
68	Apollo Crews	.25	.60
69	The Miz	.40	1.00
70	Maryse	.40	1.00
71	Enzo Amore/Big Cass	.60	1.50
72	Cesaro	.40	1.00
73	AJ Styles	1.00	2.50
74	Vaudevillains	.20	.50
75	Cesaro	.40	1.00
76	Gallows & Anderson	.30	.75
77	Roman Reigns	.60	1.50
	Bray Wyatt		
78	Sami Zayn	.25	.60
79	League of Nations	.20	.50
80	Dean Ambrose	.60	1.50
81	Charlotte	.75	2.00
82	Shane & Stephanie McMahon	.30	.75
83	Roman Reigns	.60	1.50
84	Dana Brooke	.40	1.00
85	Rusev	.40	1.00
86	Dean Ambrose	.60	1.50
87	Charlotte	.75	2.00
88	Roman Reigns	.60	1.50
89	Seth Rollins	.60	1.50
90	The Club	.20	.50
91	AJ Styles	1.00	2.50
92	Dean Ambrose	.60	1.50
93	Seth Rollins	.60	1.50

94	Dean Ambrose	.60	1.50
95	Team USA	.20	.50
96	Daniel Bryan	.75	2.00
	Mick Foley		
97	WWE Draft	.20	.50
98	Sasha Banks/Bayley	.60	1.50
99	John Cena/Enzo & Cass	1.00	2.50
100	Dean Ambrose	.60	1.50

2017 Topps WWE Road to WrestleMania Autographed Andre the Giant Battle Royal Trophy Relics

STATED ODDS 1:33,024
UNPRICED DUE TO SCARCITY

NNO Big Show
NNO Cesaro
NNO Curtis Axel
NNO Darren Young
NNO Goldust
NNO Heath Slater
NNO Hideo Itami
NNO Jack Swagger
NNO Kane
NNO Konnor
NNO Mark Henry
NNO The Miz
NNO Viktor

2017 Topps WWE Road to WrestleMania Andre the Giant Battle Royal Trophy Relics

*BLUE/50: .5X TO 1.2X BASIC MEM
*SILVER/25: .6X TO 1.5X BASIC MEM
*GOLD/10: .75X TO 2X BASIC MEM
*RED/1: UNPRICED DUE TO SCARCITY
*P.P.BLACK/1: UNPRICED DUE TO SCARCITY
*P.P.CYAN/1: UNPRICED DUE TO SCARCITY
*P.P.MAGENTA/1: UNPRICED DUE TO SCARCITY
*P.P.YELLOW/1: UNPRICED DUE TO SCARCITY
STATED ODDS 1:1,296

NNO	Baron Corbin	3.00	8.00
NNO	Big Show	2.50	6.00
NNO	Bo Dallas	2.00	5.00
NNO	Cesaro	4.00	10.00
NNO	Curtis Axel	2.00	5.00
NNO	Darren Young	2.00	5.00
NNO	Diamond Dallas Page	2.50	6.00
NNO	Fandango	2.00	5.00
NNO	Goldust	2.50	6.00
NNO	Heath Slater	2.00	5.00
NNO	Hideo Itami	3.00	8.00
NNO	Jack Swagger	2.00	5.00
NNO	Kane	2.50	6.00
NNO	Konnor	2.00	5.00
NNO	Mark Henry	2.00	5.00
NNO	R-Truth	2.00	5.00
NNO	Tatanka	2.00	5.00
NNO	The Miz	4.00	10.00
NNO	Tyler Breeze	2.00	5.00
NNO	Viktor	2.00	5.00

2017 Topps WWE Road to WrestleMania Autographed Shirt Relics

STATED ODDS 1:22,016
UNPRICED DUE TO SCARCITY

NNO Asuka
NNO Austin Aries
NNO Bayley
NNO Becky Lynch
NNO Big Cass
NNO Big E
NNO Bray Wyatt
NNO Cesaro
NNO Darren Young
NNO Dolph Ziggler
NNO Enzo Amore
NNO Hideo Itami
NNO John Cena
NNO Kevin Owens
NNO Kofi Kingston
NNO Natalya
NNO Randy Orton
NNO Roman Reigns
NNO Sami Zayn
NNO Sasah Banks
NNO Seth Rollins
NNO Shinsuke Nakamura
NNO Simon Gotch
NNO Xavier Woods
NNO Zack Ryder

2017 Topps WWE Road to WrestleMania Autographs

*BLUE/50: .6X TO 1.5X BASIC AUTOS
*SILVER/25: .75X TO 2X BASIC AUTOS
*GOLD/10: 1X TO 2.5X BASIC AUTOS
*RED/1: UNPRICED DUE TO SCARCITY
*P.P.BLACK/1: UNPRICED DUE TO SCARCITY
*P.P.CYAN/1: UNPRICED DUE TO SCARCITY
*P.P.MAGENTA/1: UNPRICED DUE TO SCARCITY
*P.P.YELLOW/1: UNPRICED DUE TO SCARCITY
STATED ODDS 1:36

NNO	Asuka	15.00	40.00
NNO	Austin Aries	8.00	20.00
NNO	Bayley	20.00	50.00
NNO	Becky Lynch	15.00	40.00
NNO	Big E	8.00	20.00
NNO	Bray Wyatt	12.00	30.00
NNO	Cesaro	10.00	25.00
NNO	Charlotte	12.00	30.00
NNO	Dean Ambrose	12.00	30.00
NNO	Finn Balor	12.00	30.00
NNO	Hideo Itami	6.00	15.00
NNO	John Cena		
NNO	Kevin Owens	15.00	40.00
NNO	Kofi Kingston	6.00	15.00
NNO	Lana	8.00	20.00
NNO	Lex Luger	10.00	25.00
NNO	Maryse	12.00	30.00
NNO	The Miz	6.00	15.00
NNO	Nikki Bella	15.00	40.00
NNO	Roman Reigns	30.00	75.00
NNO	Rusev	6.00	15.00
NNO	Sasha Banks	30.00	75.00
NNO	Seth Rollins	12.00	30.00
NNO	Shinsuke Nakamura	20.00	50.00
NNO	Sting	25.00	60.00

2017 Topps WWE Road to WrestleMania Kiss

*GOLD/10: .6X TO 1.5X BASIC KISS
*RED/1: UNPRICED DUE TO SCARCITY
STATED ODDS 1:91

NNO	Alexa Bliss	60.00	120.00
NNO	Becky Lynch	20.00	50.00
NNO	Carmella	20.00	50.00
NNO	Charlotte	15.00	40.00
NNO	Liv Morgan	20.00	50.00
NNO	Natalya	12.00	30.00
NNO	Nia Jax	12.00	30.00
NNO	Renee Young	12.00	30.00

2017 Topps WWE Road to WrestleMania Kiss Autographs

*GOLD/10: UNPRICED DUE TO SCARCITY
*RED/1: UNPRICED DUE TO SCARCITY
STATED ODDS 1:354

NNO	Alexa Bliss	250.00	500.00
NNO	Becky Lynch	150.00	300.00
NNO	Carmella	30.00	80.00
NNO	Charlotte	125.00	250.00
NNO	Liv Morgan	60.00	120.00
NNO	Natalya	25.00	60.00
NNO	Nia Jax	20.00	50.00
NNO	Nikki Bella	60.00	120.00
NNO	Renee Young	25.00	60.00

2017 Topps WWE Road to WrestleMania Dual Autographs

STATED ODDS 1:726
STATED PRINT RUN 10 SER.#'d SETS

NNO	Asuka/Bayley	100.00	200.00
NNO	Charlotte/R.Flair	100.00	200.00
NNO	F.Balor/H.Itami	60.00	120.00
NNO	J.Cena/N.Bella	125.00	250.00
NNO	K.Kingston/Big E	30.00	75.00
NNO	Miz/Maryse	60.00	120.00
NNO	R.Reigns/D.Ambrose		
NNO	Rusev/Lana	75.00	150.00
NNO	S.Banks/B.Lynch	100.00	200.00
NNO	S.Rollins/Cesaro	60.00	120.00
NNO	S.Nakamura/A.Aries		
NNO	Sting/L.Luger	75.00	150.00

2017 Topps WWE Road to WrestleMania Autographed NXT TakeOver Dallas Mat Relics

STATED PRINT RUN 10 SER.#'d SETS
UNPRICED DUE TO SCARCITY

NNO Asuka
NNO Austin Aries
NNO Bayley
NNO Sami Zayn
NNO Samoa Joe
NNO Shinsuke Nakamura

2017 Topps WWE Road to WrestleMania NXT TakeOver Dallas Mat Relics

*BLUE/50: .5X TO 1.2X BASIC MEM
*SILVER/25: .6X TO 1.5X BASIC MEM
*GOLD/10: .75X TO 2X BASIC MEM
*RED/1: UNPRICED DUE TO SCARCITY
*P.P.BLACK/1: UNPRICED DUE TO SCARCITY
*P.P.CYAN/1: UNPRICED DUE TO SCARCITY
*P.P.MAGENTA/1: UNPRICED DUE TO SCARCITY
*P.P.YELLOW/1: UNPRICED DUE TO SCARCITY
STATED ODDS 1:2,642

NNO	Asuka	5.00	12.00
NNO	Austin Aries	3.00	8.00
NNO	Baron Corbin	2.50	6.00
NNO	Bayley	5.00	12.00
NNO	Chad Gable	2.00	5.00
NNO	Finn Balor	6.00	15.00
NNO	Jason Jordan	2.00	5.00
NNO	Sami Zayn	2.00	5.00
NNO	Samoa Joe	5.00	12.00
NNO	Shinsuke Nakamura	4.00	10.00

2017 Topps WWE Road to WrestleMania Shirt Relics

*BLUE/50: .5X TO 1.2X BASIC MEM
*SILVER/25: .6X TO 1.5X BASIC MEM
*GOLD/10: UNPRICED DUE TO SCARCITY
*RED/1: UNPRICED DUE TO SCARCITY
*P.P.BLACK/1: UNPRICED DUE TO SCARCITY
*P.P.CYAN/1: UNPRICED DUE TO SCARCITY
*P.P.MAGENTA/1: UNPRICED DUE TO SCARCITY
*P.P.YELLOW/1: UNPRICED DUE TO SCARCITY
STATED ODDS 1:870

NNO	Asuka	4.00	10.00
NNO	Austin Aries	2.50	6.00
NNO	Becky Lynch	4.00	10.00
NNO	Big Cass	1.50	4.00
NNO	Bray Wyatt	3.00	8.00
NNO	Cesaro	2.50	6.00
NNO	Charlotte	5.00	12.00
NNO	Darren Young	1.25	3.00
NNO	Dolph Ziggler	2.00	5.00
NNO	Finn Balor	5.00	12.00
NNO	Hideo Itami	2.00	5.00
NNO	John Cena	6.00	15.00
NNO	Kofi Kingston	1.50	4.00
NNO	Natalya	2.50	6.00
NNO	No Way Jose	1.25	3.00
NNO	Randy Orton	3.00	8.00
NNO	Roman Reigns	4.00	10.00
NNO	Sasha Banks	4.00	10.00
NNO	Seth Rollins	4.00	10.00
NNO	Shinsuke Nakamura	3.00	8.00
NNO	Simon Gotch	1.25	3.00
NNO	Zack Ryder	1.25	3.00

2017 Topps WWE Road to WrestleMania Autographed Triple Threat Dual Relics

STATED ODDS 1:66,048
STATED PRINT RUN 10 SER.#'d SETS

NNO	Brock Lesnar	125.00	250.00
NNO	John Cena	125.00	200.00
NNO	Roman Reigns	60.00	120.00
NNO	Sasha Banks	120.00	200.00

2017 Topps WWE Road to WrestleMania Autographed WrestleMania 32 Mat Relics

STATED ODDS 1:33,024
UNPRICED DUE TO SCARCITY

NNO AJ Styles
NNO Becky Lynch
NNO Bray Wyatt
NNO Brie Bella
NNO Brock Lesnar
NNO Chris Jericho
NNO Dean Ambrose
NNO John Cena
NNO Kevin Owens

NNO	Natalya
NNO	Roman Reigns
NNO	Sasha Banks
NNO	Zack Ryder

2017 Topps WWE Road to WrestleMania WrestleMania 32 Mat Relics

*BLUE/50: .5X TO 1.2X BASIC MEM
*SILVER/25: .6X TO 1.5X BASIC MEM
*GOLD/10: .75X TO 2X BASIC MEM
*RED/1: UNPRICED DUE TO SCARCITY
*P.P.BLACK/1: UNPRICED DUE TO SCARCITY
*P.P.CYAN/1: UNPRICED DUE TO SCARCITY
*P.P.MAGENTA/1: UNPRICED DUE TO SCARCITY
*P.P.YELLOW/1: UNPRICED DUE TO SCARCITY
STATED ODDS 1:1,296

NNO	AJ Styles	10.00	25.00
NNO	Baron Corbin	3.00	8.00
NNO	Becky Lynch	6.00	15.00
NNO	Bray Wyatt	5.00	12.00
NNO	Brie Bella	5.00	12.00
NNO	Brock Lesnar	10.00	25.00
NNO	Charlotte	8.00	20.00
NNO	Chris Jericho	5.00	12.00
NNO	Dean Ambrose	6.00	15.00
NNO	John Cena	10.00	25.00
NNO	Kevin Owens	5.00	12.00
NNO	Lana	6.00	15.00
NNO	Natalya	4.00	10.00
NNO	The Rock	10.00	25.00
NNO	Roman Reigns	6.00	15.00
NNO	Sasha Banks	6.00	15.00
NNO	Shane McMahon	3.00	8.00
NNO	Triple H	5.00	12.00
NNO	Undertaker	8.00	20.00
NNO	Zack Ryder	2.00	5.00

2017 Topps WWE Road to WrestleMania WrestleMania 33 Roster

COMPLETE SET (50)		10.00	25.00
STATED ODDS 2:1			
WMR1	Triple H	.75	2.00
WMR2	Stephanie McMahon	.40	1.00
WMR3	Roman Reigns	1.00	2.50
WMR4	The Rock	1.50	4.00
WMR5	John Cena	1.50	4.00
WMR6	Bray Wyatt	.75	2.00
WMR7	Erick Rowan	.30	.75
WMR8	Braun Strowman	.40	1.00
WMR9	Luke Harper	.30	.75
WMR10	Undertaker	1.25	3.00
WMR11	Shane McMahon	.50	1.25
WMR12	Brock Lesnar	1.50	4.00
WMR13	Dean Ambrose	1.00	2.50
WMR14	Charlotte	1.25	3.00
WMR15	Ric Flair	.75	2.00
WMR16	Sasha Banks	1.00	2.50
WMR17	Becky Lynch	1.00	2.50
WMR18	Chris Jericho	.75	2.00
WMR19	AJ Styles	1.50	4.00
WMR20	Baron Corbin	.50	1.25
WMR21	Kane	.40	1.00
WMR22	Big Show	.40	1.00
WMR23	Mark Henry	.30	.75
WMR24	Zack Ryder	.30	.75
WMR25	Kevin Owens	.75	2.00
WMR26	Sami Zayn	.40	1.00
WMR27	The Miz	.60	1.50
WMR28	Dolph Ziggler	.50	1.25
WMR29	Sin Cara	.40	1.00
WMR30	Kalisto	.50	1.25
WMR31	Kofi Kingston	.40	1.00
WMR32	Big E	.40	1.00
WMR33	Xavier Woods	.40	1.00
WMR34	Sheamus	.60	1.50
WMR35	Rusev	.60	1.50
WMR36	Jey Uso	.40	1.00
WMR37	Jimmy Uso	.40	1.00
WMR38	Darren Young	.30	.75
WMR39	R-Truth	.30	.75
WMR40	Goldust	.40	1.00
WMR41	Heath Slater	.30	.75
WMR42	Brie Bella	.75	2.00
WMR43	Natalya	.60	1.50
WMR44	Alicia Fox	.50	1.25
WMR45	Eva Marie	.75	2.00
WMR46	Lana	1.00	2.50
WMR47	Naomi	.60	1.50
WMR48	Tamina	.40	1.00
WMR49	Emma	.75	2.00
WMR50	Summer Rae	.75	2.00

2018 Topps WWE Road to WrestleMania

COMPLETE SET (100)		8.00	20.00
UNOPENED BOX (24 PACKS)			
UNOPENED PACK (7 CARDS)			
*BRONZE: .5X TO 1.2X BASIC CARDS			
*BLUE/99: .75X TO 2X BASIC CARDS			
*SILVER/25: 2X TO 5X BASIC CARDS			
*GOLD/10: UNPRICED DUE TO SCARCITY			
*RED/1: UNPRICED DUE TO SCARCITY			
*P.P.BLACK/1: UNPRICED DUE TO SCARCITY			
*P.P.CYAN/1: UNPRICED DUE TO SCARCITY			
*P.P.MAGENTA/1: UNPRICED DUE TO SCARCITY			
*P.P.YELLOW/1: UNPRICED DUE TO SCARCITY			
1	Roman Reigns	.60	1.50
2	Cesaro & Sheamus	.50	1.25
3	Roman Reigns	.60	1.50
4	Universal Champion Kevin Owens	.60	1.50
5	Roman Reigns	.60	1.50
6	Kevin Owens	.60	1.50
7	Team Raw defeats Team SmackDown	.50	1.25
8	Cesaro & Sheamus	.50	1.25
9	Undertaker Returns	1.00	2.50
10	Chris Jericho	.60	1.50
11	Luke Gallows & Karl Anderson	.30	.75
12	Kevin Owens	.60	1.50
13	Samoa Joe Debuts	.50	1.25
14	Kevin Owens	.60	1.50
15	Roman Reigns	.60	1.50
16	Kevin Owens	1.00	2.50
17	Roman Reigns	1.00	2.50
18	Mick Foley	.60	1.50
19	Undertaker	1.00	2.50
20	Undertaker	1.00	2.50
21	Ricky The Dragon Steamboat	.40	1.00
22	Diamond Dallas Page	.40	1.00
23	Kurt Angle Returns	.60	1.50
24	Kevin Owens	.60	1.50
25	The Hardy Boyz Return	.60	1.50
26	Seth Rollins	.60	1.50
27	Brock Lesnar	1.00	2.50
28	Roman Reigns	.60	1.50
29	Kurt Angle	.60	1.50
30	The Revival	.30	.75
31	Finn Balor	.60	1.50
32	Alexa Bliss	1.25	3.00
33	Elias	.60	1.50
34	Chris Jericho	.60	1.50
35	Bray Wyatt	.60	1.50
36	Braun Strowman	.60	1.50
37	Goldust	.50	1.25
38	The Miz	.50	1.25
39	Cesaro & Sheamus	.50	1.25
40	Samoa Joe	.50	1.25
41	Big Cass Turns	.30	.75
42	Cesaro & Sheamus	.50	1.25
43	Universal Champion Brock Lesnar	1.00	2.50
44	Kurt Angle	.60	1.50
45	Braun Strowman	.60	1.50
46	Dean Ambrose	.60	1.50
47	TJP	.30	.75
48	The Brian Kendrick	.40	1.00
49	The Brian Kendrick	.40	1.00
50	Rich Swann	.30	.75
51	Neville Returns	.40	1.00
52	Neville	.40	1.00
53	Neville	.40	1.00
54	Noam Dar	.40	1.00
55	Akira Tozawa	.40	1.00
56	WWE Champion AJ Styles	1.00	2.50
57	Dolph Ziggler	.50	1.25
58	Bray Wyatt	.60	1.50
59	Randy Orton	.60	1.50
60	The Miz	.50	1.25
61	Edge and Undertaker Return	1.00	2.50
62	Team SmackDown defeats Team Raw	1.00	2.50
63	James Ellsworth	.25	.60
64	The New Wyatt Family	.60	1.50
65	The Miz	.50	1.25
66	Baron Corbin	.40	1.00
67	AJ Styles	1.00	2.50
68	American Alpha	.25	.60
69	Dean Ambrose	.50	1.25
70	John Cena	1.00	2.50
71	Randy Orton	.60	1.50
72	Randy Orton	.60	1.50
73	Bray Wyatt	.60	1.50
74	Randy Orton	.60	1.50
75	The Usos	.40	1.00
76	Shane McMahon	1.00	2.50
77	Mojo Rawley	.25	.60
78	Dean Ambrose	.50	1.25
79	AJ Styles	1.00	2.50
80	John Cena Proposes to Nikki Bella	1.00	2.50
81	Randy Orton	.60	1.50
82	Tye Dillinger	.25	.60
83	Shinsuke Nakamura	.60	1.50
84	The Superstar Shake-Up	.75	2.00
85	Jinder Mahal	.30	.75
86	Kevin Owens	.60	1.50
87	Shinsuke Nakamura	.60	1.50
88	The Usos	.40	1.00
89	Jinder Mahal	.30	.75
90	Maria Kanellis	.60	1.50
91	WWE Champion Jinder Mahal	.30	.75
92	Baron Corbin	.40	1.00
93	AJ Styles	1.00	2.50
94	The New Day	.40	1.00
95	Kevin Owens	.60	1.50
96	John Cena	1.00	2.50
97	WWE Champion Jinder Mahal	.30	.75
98	AJ Styles	1.00	2.50
99	Shinsuke Nakamura	1.00	2.50
100	Jinder Mahal	.30	.75

2018 Topps WWE Road to WrestleMania Commemorative Andre the Giant Battle Royal Trophy Relics

*BRONZE/99: .5X TO 1.2X BASIC MEM
*BLUE/50: .6X TO 1.5X BASIC MEM
*SILVER/25: .75X TO 2X BASIC MEM
*GOLD/10: UNPRICED DUE TO SCARCITY
*RED/1: UNPRICED DUE TO SCARCITY
STATED ODDS 1:936

ACBR	Braun Strowman	6.00	15.00
ACBS	Big Show	2.50	6.00
ACCG	Chad Gable	2.50	6.00
ACDZ	Dolph Ziggler	2.50	6.00
ACFA	Fandango	5.00	12.00
ACGO	Goldust	2.50	6.00
ACHS	Heath Slater	2.50	6.00
ACJI	Jimmy Uso	5.00	12.00
ACJJ	Jason Jordan	2.50	6.00
ACJM	Jinder Mahal	2.50	6.00
ACJU	Jey Uso	2.50	6.00
ACKD	Killian Dain	3.00	8.00
ACLH	Luke Harper	3.00	8.00
ACMH	Mark Henry	2.50	6.00
ACMR	Mojo Rawley	3.00	8.00
ACRH	Rhyno	3.00	8.00
ACRT	R-Truth	2.50	6.00
ACSZ	Sami Zayn	4.00	10.00
ACTB	Tian Bing	2.50	6.00
ACTBR	Tyler Breeze	2.50	6.00

2018 Topps WWE Road to WrestleMania Autographed Commemorative Andre the Giant Battle Royal Trophy Relics

STATED ODDS 1:24,096
STATED PRINT RUN 10 SER.#'d SETS
UNPRICED DUE TO SCARCITY

NNO	Big Show
NNO	Braun Strowman
NNO	Dolph Ziggler
NNO	Fandango
NNO	Goldust
NNO	Heath Slater
NNO	Jey Uso
NNO	Jimmy Uso
NNO	Jinder Mahal
NNO	Killian Dain
NNO	Luke Harper
NNO	Mark Henry
NNO	Mojo Rawley
NNO	Sami Zayn
NNO	Tyler Breeze

2018 Topps WWE Road to WrestleMania Autographed Dual Relics

STATED ODDS 1:96,384
STATED PRINT RUN 10 SER.#'d SETS
UNPRICED DUE TO SCARCITY

| NNO | Alexa Bliss |
| NNO | John Cena |

NNO Kevin Owens
NNO Naomi
NNO Roman Reigns
NNO Shinsuke Nakamura

2018 Topps WWE Road to WrestleMania Autographed NXT TakeOver Orlando Mat Relics

STATED ODDS 1:32,128
STATED PRINT RUN 10 SER.#'d SETS
UNPRICED DUE TO SCARCITY

NNO Aleister Black
NNO Asuka
NNO Bobby Roode
NNO Eric Young
NNO Johnny Gargano
NNO Kassius Ohno
NNO Nikki Cross
NNO Roderick Strong
NNO Ruby Riot
NNO Shinsuke Nakamura
NNO Tommaso Ciampa

2018 Topps WWE Road to WrestleMania Autographed Shirt Relics

STATED ODDS 1:32,128
STATED PRINT RUN 10 SER.#'d SETS
UNPRICED DUE TO SCARCITY

NNO Becky Lynch
NNO Carmella
NNO Cesaro
NNO Goldust
NNO Karl Anderson
NNO Kevin Owens
NNO Luke Gallows
NNO Luke Harper
NNO Naomi
NNO Roman Reigns
NNO Sting
NNO Xavier Woods

2018 Topps WWE Road to WrestleMania Autographed Wrestlemania 33 Mat Relics

STATED ODDS 1:24,096
STATED PRINT RUN 10 SER.#'d SETS
UNPRICED DUE TO SCARCITY

NNO AJ Styles
NNO Charlotte Flair
NNO Chris Jericho
NNO Jeff Hardy
NNO Kevin Owens
NNO Maryse
NNO Naomi
NNO Randy Orton
NNO Roman Reigns
NNO Sasha Banks
NNO Stephanie McMahon
NNO The Miz
NNO Triple H
NNO Undertaker

2018 Topps WWE Road to WrestleMania Autographs

*BLUE/50: .5X TO 1.2X BASIC AUTOS
*SILVER/25: .6X TO 1.5X BASIC AUTOS

---

*GOLD/10: UNPRICED DUE TO SCARCITY
*RED/1: UNPRICED DUE TO SCARCITY
*P.P.BLACK/1: UNPRICED DUE TO SCARCITY
*P.P.CYAN/1: UNPRICED DUE TO SCARCITY
*P.P.MAGENTA/1: UNPRICED DUE TO SCARCITY
*P.P.YELLOW/1: UNPRICED DUE TO SCARCITY
STATED ODDS 1:32

AAB	Aleister Black	12.00	30.00
AAL	Alexa Bliss	30.00	75.00
AAS	AJ Styles	15.00	40.00
ABA	Bayley	12.00	30.00
ABL	Becky Lynch	15.00	40.00
ABW	Bray Wyatt	8.00	20.00
ACA	Carmella	10.00	25.00
ACF	Charlotte Flair	15.00	40.00
ADA	Dean Ambrose	12.00	30.00
ADW	Dash Wilder	6.00	15.00
AEM	Ember Moon	12.00	30.00
AEY	Eric Young	5.00	12.00
AFB	Finn Balor	15.00	40.00
AJG	Johnny Gargano	10.00	25.00
AJH	Jeff Hardy	15.00	40.00
AJM	Jinder Mahal	10.00	25.00
AKA	Kassius Ohno	6.00	15.00
AKO	Kevin Owens	8.00	20.00
AMH	Matt Hardy	15.00	40.00
ANA	Naomi	6.00	15.00
ANC	Nikki Cross	10.00	25.00
ARS	Roderick Strong	5.00	12.00
ASB	Sasha Banks	20.00	50.00
ASD	Scott Dawson	5.00	12.00
ASJ	Samoa Joe	8.00	20.00
ASN	Shinsuke Nakamura	12.00	30.00
ASR	Seth Rollins	12.00	30.00
ATC	Tommaso Ciampa	5.00	12.00
ATD	Tye Dillinger	6.00	15.00
ATM	The Miz	8.00	20.00
AASU	Asuka	15.00	40.00
ABOR	Bobby Roode	10.00	25.00
AKUA	Kurt Angle	15.00	40.00
ARRI	Ruby Riot	12.00	30.00

2018 Topps WWE Road to WrestleMania Autographs Silver

STATED ODDS 1:105
STATED PRINT RUN 25 SER.#'d SETS

ASM	Stephanie McMahon	125.00	250.00
ATH	Triple H	150.00	300.00
AUN	Undertaker	150.00	300.00
ANAT	Natalya	10.00	25.00

2018 Topps WWE Road to WrestleMania Dual Autographs

STATED ODDS 1:1,928
STATED PRINT RUN 10 SER.#'d SETS

DABR	A.Black/B.Roode/10	60.00	120.00
DAFS	F.Balor/Samoa Joe/4		
DAJT	T.Ciampa/J.Gargano/10	30.00	75.00
DAMJ	Matt & Jeff Hardy/10	30.00	75.00
DARK	K.Ohno/R.Strong/10		
DARN	N.Cross/R.Riot/10	20.00	50.00
DAUK	K.Angle/Undertaker/10	250.00	400.00

2018 Topps WWE Road to WrestleMania Dual Relics

*SILVER/25: .5X TO 1.2X BASIC MEM
*GOLD/10: UNPRICED DUE TO SCARCITY
*RED/1: UNPRICED DUE TO SCARCITY

STATED PRINT RUN 50 SER.#'d SETS

DRAB	Alexa Bliss	30.00	75.00
DRBL	Brock Lesnar	10.00	25.00
DRJC	John Cena	15.00	40.00
DRKO	Kevin Owens	10.00	25.00
DRNA	Naomi	12.00	30.00
DRRR	Roman Reigns	10.00	25.00
DRSN	Shinsuke Nakamura		
DRSR	Seth Rollins	12.00	30.00

2018 Topps WWE Road to WrestleMania Kiss

*GOLD/10: UNPRICED DUE TO SCARCITY
*RED/1: UNPRICED DUE TO SCARCITY
STATED ODDS 1:112

KAB	Alexa Bliss	60.00	120.00
KAS	Asuka	30.00	75.00
KCA	Carmella	25.00	60.00
KCF	Charlotte Flair/99	25.00	60.00
KMA	Maryse	20.00	50.00
KNA	Naomi	12.00	30.00
KRR	Ruby Riot	20.00	50.00

2018 Topps WWE Road to WrestleMania Kiss Autographs

*GOLD/10: UNPRICED DUE TO SCARCITY
*RED/1: UNPRICED DUE TO SCARCITY
STATED ODDS 1:445

NNO	Alexa Bliss	120.00	250.00
NNO	Asuka	50.00	100.00
NNO	Becky Lynch	60.00	120.00
NNO	Carmella	50.00	100.00
NNO	Charlotte Flair	75.00	150.00
NNO	Goldust	75.00	150.00
NNO	Maryse	50.00	100.00
NNO	Nikki Cross	50.00	100.00
NNO	Ruby Riot	50.00	100.00

2018 Topps WWE Road to WrestleMania NXT TakeOver Orlando Mat Relics

*BRONZE/99: SAME VALUE AS BASIC MEM
*BLUE/50: .5X TO 1.2X BASIC MEM
*SILVER/25: .6X TO 1.5X BASIC MEM
*GOLD/10: UNPRICED DUE TO SCARCITY
*RED/1: UNPRICED DUE TO SCARCITY
STATED ODDS 1:1,236

MRAB	Aleister Black	6.00	15.00
MRAS	Asuka	6.00	15.00
MRBR	Bobby Roode	6.00	15.00
MRDW	Dash Wilder	2.50	6.00
MREM	Ember Moon	3.00	8.00
MREY	Eric Young	2.50	6.00
MRJG	Johnny Gargano	3.00	8.00
MRKO	Kassius Ohno	6.00	15.00
MRNC	Nikki Cross	4.00	10.00
MRRR	Ruby Riot	5.00	12.00
MRRS	Roderick Strong	2.50	6.00
MRSD	Scott Dawson	3.00	8.00
MRSN	Shinsuke Nakamura	4.00	10.00
MRTC	Tommaso Ciampa	3.00	8.00
MRTD	Tye Dillinger	3.00	8.00

2018 Topps WWE Road to WrestleMania Road to WrestleMania 34

RTW1	The Miz & Miztourage	1.25	3.00
RTW2	Big Cass	.75	2.00
RTW3	Finn Balor	1.50	4.00
RTW4	Dean Ambrose & Seth Rollins	1.50	4.00
RTW5	Brock Lesnar	2.50	6.00
RTW6	Braun Strowman	1.50	4.00
RTW7	John Cena	2.50	6.00
RTW8	Jeff Hardy	1.25	3.00
RTW9	John Cena and Roman Reigns	2.50	6.00
RTW10	Neville	1.00	2.50
RTW11	Enzo Amore	.60	1.50
RTW12	The Brian Kendrick	1.00	2.50
RTW13	The Usos	.60	1.50
RTW14	John Cena	2.50	6.00
RTW15	Randy Orton	1.50	4.00
RTW16	AJ Styles	2.50	6.00
RTW17	Jinder Mahal	.75	2.00
RTW18	Bobby Roode	1.00	2.50
RTW19	Shelton Benjamin	.75	2.00
RTW20	Shinsuke Nakamura	1.50	4.00

2018 Topps WWE Road to WrestleMania Shirt Relics

*BLUE/50: .5X TO 1.2X BASIC MEM
*SILVER/25: .6X TO 1.5X BASIC MEM
*GOLD/10: UNPRICED DUE TO SCARCITY
*RED/1: UNPRICED DUE TO SCARCITY
STATED ODDS 1:1,890
STATED PRINT RUN 99 SER.#'d SETS

SRAB	Alexa Bliss	12.00	30.00
SRBL	Becky Lynch	10.00	25.00
SRBR	Brock Lesnar	5.00	12.00
SRCA	Carmella	6.00	15.00
SRCE	Cesaro	3.00	8.00
SRCG	Chad Gable	2.50	6.00
SRGO	Goldust	3.00	8.00
SRJC	John Cena	6.00	15.00
SRJI	Jimmy Uso	2.50	6.00
SRJJ	Jason Jordan	3.00	8.00
SRKA	Karl Anderson	2.50	6.00
SRKO	Kevin Owens	2.50	6.00
SRLG	Luke Gallows	2.50	6.00
SRLH	Luke Harper	3.00	8.00
SRNA	Naomi	4.00	10.00
SRNW	No Way Jose	2.50	6.00
SRRR	Roman Reigns	4.00	10.00
SRSR	Seth Rollins	4.00	10.00
SRST	Sting	10.00	25.00
SRXW	Xavier Woods	2.50	6.00

2018 Topps WWE Road to WrestleMania WrestleMania 33 Mat Relics

*BRONZE/99: SAME VALUE AS BASIC MEM
*BLUE/50: .5X TO 1.2X BASIC MEM
*SILVER/25: .6X TO 1.5X BASIC MEM
*GOLD/10: UNPRICED DUE TO SCARCITY
*RED/1: UNPRICED DUE TO SCARCITY
STATED ODDS 1:748
STATED PRINT RUN 199 SER.#'d SETS

WMAB	Alexa Bliss	10.00	25.00
WMAS	AJ Styles	8.00	20.00
WMBA	Bayley	6.00	15.00
WMBR	Brock Lesnar	6.00	15.00
WMBY	Bray Wyatt	10.00	25.00
WMCA	Carmella	5.00	12.00
WMCF	Charlotte Flair	6.00	15.00
WMCJ	Chris Jericho	4.00	10.00
WMDA	Dean Ambrose	5.00	12.00

WMJC	John Cena	6.00	15.00
WMJH	Jeff Hardy	6.00	15.00
WMKO	Kevin Owens	4.00	10.00
WMMA	Maryse	6.00	15.00
WMMH	Matt Hardy	4.00	10.00
WMNA	Naomi	4.00	10.00
WMNB	Nikki Bella	5.00	12.00
WMRO	Randy Orton	3.00	8.00
WMRR	Roman Reigns	10.00	25.00
WMSB	Sasha Banks	6.00	15.00
WMSM	Stephanie McMahon	6.00	15.00
WMSR	Seth Rollins	5.00	12.00
WMTH	Triple H	8.00	20.00
WMTM	The Miz	3.00	8.00
WMUN	Undertaker	15.00	40.00
WMNAT	Natalya	3.00	8.00

2018 Topps WWE Road to WrestleMania WrestleMania 34 Roster

	COMPLETE SET (50)	12.00	30.00
R1	Roman Reigns	.75	2.00
R2	Brock Lesnar	1.25	3.00
R3	Randy Orton	.75	2.00
R4	Bray Wyatt	.75	2.00
R5	Seth Rollins	.75	2.00
R6	Triple H	.75	2.00
R7	John Cena	1.25	3.00
R8	The Miz	.60	1.50
R9	Kevin Owens	.75	2.00
R10	Chris Jericho	.75	2.00
R11	AJ Styles	1.25	3.00
R12	Dean Ambrose	.60	1.50
R13	Baron Corbin	.50	1.25
R14	Mojo Rawley	.30	.75
R15	Jinder Mahal	.40	1.00
R16	Asuka	1.00	2.50
R17	Matt Hardy	.75	2.00
R18	Jeff Hardy	.60	1.50
R19	Luke Gallows	.40	1.00
R20	Karl Anderson	.30	.75
R21	Cesaro	.60	1.50
R22	Sheamus	.60	1.50
R23	Enzo Amore	.30	.75
R24	Big Cass	.40	1.00
R25	Bayley	.50	1.25
R26	Charlotte Flair	1.00	2.50
R27	Sasha Banks	1.00	2.50
R28	Nia Jax	.50	1.25
R29	Naomi	.40	1.00
R30	Alexa Bliss	1.50	4.00
R31	Becky Lynch	.75	2.00
R32	Mickie James	.60	1.50
R33	Natalya	.40	1.00
R34	Carmella	.60	1.50
R35	Braun Strowman	.75	2.00
R36	Big Show	.30	.75
R37	Sami Zayn	.30	.75
R38	Luke Harper	.50	1.25
R39	Dolph Ziggler	.40	1.00
R40	Fandango	.30	.75
R41	Tyler Breeze	.30	.75
R42	Jason Jordan	.30	.75
R43	Chad Gable	.30	.75
R44	Jey Uso	.30	.75
R45	Jimmy Uso	.30	.75
R46	Heath Slater	.30	.75
R47	Rhyno	.30	.75

R48	Goldust	.60	1.50
R49	R-Truth	.40	1.00
R50	Titus O'Neil	.30	.75

2019 Topps WWE Road to WrestleMania

COMPLETE SET (100)		10.00	25.00
UNOPENED BOX (24 PACKS)			
UNOPENED PACK (7 CARDS)			
*BRONZE: .5X TO 1.2X BASIC CARDS			
*BLUE/99: .75X TO 2X BASIC CARDS			
*SILVER/25: 2X TO 5X BASIC CARDS			
*GOLD/10: UNPRICED DUE TO SCARCITY			
*RED/1: UNPRICED DUE TO SCARCITY			
*P.P.BLACK/1: UNPRICED DUE TO SCARCITY			
*P.P.CYAN/1: UNPRICED DUE TO SCARCITY			
*P.P.MAGENTA/1: UNPRICED DUE TO SCARCITY			
*P.P.YELLOW/1: UNPRICED DUE TO SCARCITY			

1	Braun Strowman	.60	1.50
2	Braun Strowman	1.00	2.50
3	Roman Reigns	1.00	2.50
4	The Shield	.60	1.50
5	Kane	.40	1.00
6	Demon Finn Balor	.60	1.50
7	Kurt Angle	.50	1.25
8	SmackDown Live Siege	.50	1.25
9	Cesaro & Sheamus	.40	1.00
10	The Shield	.60	1.50
11	Triple H	.60	1.50
12	Braun Strowman	.60	1.50
13	The Shield	.60	1.50
14	Team Raw Defeat Team SmackDown	.60	1.50
15	Roman Reigns	.60	1.50
16	Matt Hardy Snaps	.50	1.25
17	Braun Strowman	.60	1.50
18	Seth Rollins & Jason Jordan	.60	1.50
19	Roman Reigns	.60	1.50
20	The Balor Club	.60	1.50
21	Stone Cold Steve Austin Returns	1.25	3.00
22	The Miz	.50	1.25
23	Cesaro & Sheamus	.40	1.00
24	John Cena	1.00	2.50
25	Elias	.50	1.25
26	Finn Balor and Seth Rollins	.60	1.50
27	Braun Strowman	.60	1.50
28	Roman Reigns	.60	1.50
29	Kurt Angle	.50	1.25
30	Braun Strowman	.60	1.50
31	John Cena	1.00	2.50
32	Braun Strowman	.60	1.50
33	John Cena	1.00	2.50
34	Woken Matt Hardy	.60	1.50
35	Seth Rollins	.60	1.50
36	Kurt Angle & Ronda Rousey	1.25	3.00
37	Undertaker	1.25	3.00
38	Braun Strowman	.60	1.50
39	Breezango	.30	.75
40	Gentleman Jack Gallagher	.40	1.00
41	Kalisto	.25	.60
42	Kalisto	.25	.60
43	Drew Gulak	.25	.60
44	Akira Tozawa	.25	.60
45	Hideo Itami	.25	.60
46	Cedric Alexander & Goldust	.25	.60
47	Drake Maverick	.25	.60
48	Mark Andrews	.25	.60
49	Buddy Murphy	.30	.75
50	Cedric Alexander	.25	.60

51	Mustafa Ali	.25	.60
52	Cedric Alexander	.25	.60
53	Buddy Murphy	.30	.75
54	Cedric Alexander	.25	.60
55	Shinsuke Nakamura	.60	1.50
56	The New Day	.40	1.00
57	Rusev	.50	1.25
58	Kevin Owens	.60	1.50
59	The Usos	.30	.75
60	Baron Corbin	.40	1.00
61	Jinder Mahal	.60	1.50
62	Kevin Owens	.60	1.50
63	Kevin Owens and Sami Zayn	.60	1.50
64	Baron Corbin	.40	1.00
65	Kevin Owens & Sami Zayn	.60	1.50
66	Shinsuka Nakamura	.60	1.50
67	AJ Styles	1.25	3.00
68	Raw Launches Counter-Siege	.60	1.50
69	Baron Corbin	.40	1.00
70	The Usos	.30	.75
71	Kevin Owens & Sami Zayn	.60	1.50
72	Mojo Rawley	.30	.75
73	Kevin Owens	.60	1.50
74	Rusev & Aiden English	.50	1.25
75	Kevin Owens & Sami Zayn	1.00	2.50
76	Kevin Owens	.60	1.50
77	Dolph Ziggler	.50	1.25
78	Kevin Owens & Sami Zayn	1.00	2.50
79	AJ Styles	1.25	3.00
80	Dolph Ziggler	.50	1.25
81	Kevin Owens	.60	1.50
82	Sami Zayn	1.25	3.00
83	Bobby Roode	.50	1.25
84	AJ Styles	1.25	3.00
85	Shinsuke Nakamura	.60	1.50
86	AJ Styles & Nakamura	1.25	3.00
87	John Cena	1.00	2.50
88	Sami Zayn	.50	1.25
89	Randy Orton	.60	1.50
90	AJ Styles	1.25	3.00
91	Daniel Bryan	1.00	2.50
92	Daniel Bryan	1.00	2.50
93	Jinder Mahal	.60	1.50
94	Bludgeon Brothers	.30	.75
95	Daniel Bryan & Shane McMahon	1.00	2.50
96	AJ Styles	1.25	3.00
97	Braun Strowman	.60	1.50
98	Shinsuka Nakamura	.60	1.50
99	The Usos	.30	.75
100	Woken Matt Hardy	.50	1.25

2019 Topps WWE Road to WrestleMania Autographed Commemorative Andre the Giant Battle Royal Trophy Re

STATED PRINT RUN 10 SER.#'d SETS
UNPRICED DUE TO SCARCITY

BRABC	Baron Corbin
BRACG	Chad Gable
BRADZ	Dolph Ziggler
BRAFN	Fandango
BRAGD	Goldust
BRAKA	Karl Anderson
BRALG	Luke Gallows
BRAMH	Woken Matt Hardy
BRAMR	Mojo Rawley
BRASB	Shelton Benjamin
BRASC	Sin Cara

BRATB	Tyler Breeze
BRATO	Titus O'Neil

2019 Topps WWE Road to WrestleMania Autographed Commemorative Intercontinental Championship Relics

STATED PRINT RUN 10 SER.#'d SETS
UNPRICED DUE TO SCARCITY

ICRBH	Bret Hit Man Hart
ICRRS	Ricky The Dragon Steamboat

2019 Topps WWE Road to WrestleMania Autographed Divas Revolution Relic

UNPRICED DUE TO SCARCITY

DRRABB	Brie Bella

2019 Topps WWE Road to WrestleMania Autographed Mat Relics

STATED PRINT RUN 10 SER.#'d SETS
UNPRICED DUE TO SCARCITY

MRAAB	Alexa Bliss
MRAAC	Adam Cole
MRAAS	Asuka
MRACF	Charlotte Flair
MRAEM	Ember Moon
MRAJG	Johnny Gargano
MRAKA	Kurt Angle
MRAKD	Killian Dain
MRAKO	Kevin Owens
MRAMH	Woken Matt Hardy
MRANA	Naomi
MRARC	Ricochet
MRASB	Shayna Baszler
MRASN	Shinsuke Nakamura
MRASR	Seth Rollins
MRASZ	Sami Zayn
MRATC	Tommaso Ciampa
MRAUN	Undertaker
MRAALB	Aleister Black
MRAERA	Kyle O'Reilly
MRAHHH	Triple H
MRARRR	Ronda Rousey
MRASMC	Stephanie McMahon

2019 Topps WWE Road to WrestleMania Autographed Shirt Relics

STATED PRINT RUN 10 SER.#'d SETS
UNPRICED DUE TO SCARCITY

SRAAB	Alexa Bliss
SRAAF	Alicia Fox
SRACM	Carmella
SRAFB	Finn Balor
SRAMH	Woken Matt Hardy
SRARD	Rusev
SRARY	Renee Young
SRASR	Seth Rollins

2019 Topps WWE Road to WrestleMania Autographs

*BLUE/50: .5X TO 1.2X BASIC AUTOS
*SILVER/25: .6X TO 1.5X BASIC AUTOS
*GOLD/10: UNPRICED DUE TO SCARCITY

*RED/1: UNPRICED DUE TO SCARCITY
*P.P.BLACK/1: UNPRICED DUE TO SCARCITY
*P.P.CYAN/1: UNPRICED DUE TO SCARCITY
*P.P.MAGENTA/1: UNPRICED DUE TO SCARCITY
*P.P.YELLOW/1: UNPRICED DUE TO SCARCITY
RANDOMLY INSERTED INTO PACKS

AAB	Alexa Bliss	30.00	75.00
AAE	Aiden English	5.00	12.00
AAJ	AJ Styles	15.00	40.00
AAS	Asuka	15.00	40.00
ABE	Big E	6.00	15.00
ABR	Bobby Roode	6.00	15.00
ABS	Braun Strowman	15.00	40.00
ACE	Cesaro	5.00	12.00
ACF	Charlotte Flair	20.00	50.00
ACM	Carmella	12.00	30.00
ADB	Daniel Bryan	10.00	25.00
AEM	Ember Moon	10.00	25.00
AFB	Finn Balor	15.00	40.00
AJH	Jeff Hardy	15.00	40.00
AKA	Kurt Angle	10.00	25.00
AKK	Kofi Kingston	6.00	15.00
AKO	Kevin Owens	10.00	25.00
ALM	Liv Morgan EXCH	15.00	40.00
AMH	Woken Matt Hardy	8.00	20.00
ANA	Naomi	8.00	20.00
ANJ	Nia Jax	6.00	15.00
ARD	Rusev	8.00	20.00
ARW	Rowan	5.00	12.00
ASB	Sasha Banks	20.00	50.00
ASH	Sheamus	6.00	15.00
ASJ	Samoa Joe	8.00	20.00
ASN	Shinsuke Nakamura	10.00	25.00
ASR	Seth Rollins	10.00	25.00
ASZ	Sami Zayn	5.00	12.00
ATM	The Miz	6.00	15.00
AXW	Xavier Woods	6.00	15.00
ARRR	Ronda Rousey	125.00	250.00
ARTT	Ruby Riott	12.00	30.00
AWWE	Elias	12.00	30.00

2019 Topps WWE Road to WrestleMania Autographs Blue

AJM	Jinder Mahal	8.00	20.00
AJEY	Jey Uso	6.00	15.00
AJIM	Jimmy Uso	6.00	15.00

2019 Topps WWE Road to WrestleMania Autographs Silver

AUN	Undertaker	125.00	250.00
AHHH	Triple H	100.00	200.00
ASMC	Stephanie McMahon	75.00	150.00

2019 Topps WWE Road to WrestleMania Commemorative Andre the Giant Battle Royal Trophy Relics

*BRONZE/99: .5X TO 1.2X BASIC MEM
*BLUE/50: .6X TO 1.5X BASIC MEM
*SILVER/25: .75X TO 2X BASIC MEM
*GOLD/10: UNPRICED DUE TO SCARCITY
*RED/1: UNPRICED DUE TO SCARCITY
RANDOMLY INSERTED INTO PACKS

BRAE	Aiden English	2.00	5.00
BRBC	Baron Corbin	2.50	6.00
BRCG	Chad Gable	3.00	8.00
BRDZ	Dolph Ziggler	2.50	6.00
BRFN	Fandango	2.00	5.00
BRGD	Goldust	2.50	6.00
BRHS	Heath Slater	2.00	5.00
BRKA	Karl Anderson	2.50	6.00
BRKN	Kane	3.00	8.00
BRLG	Luke Gallows	2.50	6.00
BRMH	Woken Matt Hardy	3.00	8.00
BRMR	Mojo Rawley	2.00	5.00
BRRT	R-Truth	2.00	5.00
BRRY	Rhyno	2.50	6.00
BRSB	Shelton Benjamin	3.00	8.00
BRSC	Sin Cara	4.00	10.00
BRTB	Tyler Breeze	2.50	6.00
BRTD	Tye Dillinger	2.50	6.00
BRTO	Titus O'Neil	2.50	6.00
BRZR	Zack Ryder	3.00	8.00

2019 Topps WWE Road to WrestleMania Divas Revolution Autographs

RANDOMLY INSERTED INTO PACKS

DRABB	Brie Bella	
DRABL	Becky Lynch	
DRACF	Charlotte Flair	

2019 Topps WWE Road to WrestleMania Divas Revolution Relics

RANDOMLY INSERTED INTO PACKS

DRRBB	Brie Bella	
DRRNB	Nikki Bella	

2019 Topps WWE Road to WrestleMania Dual Autographs

STATED PRINT RUN 10 SER.#'d SETS
UNPRICED DUE TO SCARCITY

DAAP	Akam/Rezar
DABB	Rowan/Harper
DABR	T.Breeze/Fandango
DABT	B.Dallas/C.Axel
DADW	B.Wyatt/M.Hardy
DAUSO	The Usos
DAYEP	S.Zayn/K.Owens

2019 Topps WWE Road to WrestleMania Intercontinental Champions Autographs

*GOLD/10: UNPRICED DUE TO SCARCITY
*RED/1: UNPRICED DUE TO SCARCITY
*P.P.BLACK/1: UNPRICED DUE TO SCARCITY
*P.P.CYAN/1: UNPRICED DUE TO SCARCITY
*P.P.MAGENTA/1: UNPRICED DUE TO SCARCITY
*P.P.YELLOW/1: UNPRICED DUE TO SCARCITY
RANDOMLY INSERTED INTO PACKS

ICABH	Bret Hit Man Hart
ICARS	Ricky The Dragon Steamboat

2019 Topps WWE Road to WrestleMania Kiss

*SILVER/25: .6X TO 1.2X BASIC KISS
*GOLD/10: UNPRICED DUE TO SCARCITY
*RED/1: UNPRICED DUE TO SCARCITY
STATED PRINT RUN 50 SER.#'d SETS

KCEM	Ember Moon	20.00	50.00
KCKS	Kairi Sane	25.00	60.00
KCLE	Lacey Evans	30.00	75.00
KCNA	Naomi	15.00	40.00
KCTC	Taynara Conti	30.00	75.00
KCVB	Vanessa Borne	15.00	40.00

2019 Topps WWE Road to WrestleMania Mat Relics

*BRONZE/99: .5X TO 1.2X BASIC MEM
*BLUE/50: .6X TO 1.5X BASIC MEM
*SILVER/25: .75X TO 2X BASIC MEM
*GOLD/10: UNPRICED DUE TO SCARCITY
*RED/1: UNPRICED DUE TO SCARCITY
RANDOMLY INSERTED INTO PACKS

MRAA	Andrade Cien Almas	2.50	6.00
MRAB	Alexa Bliss	10.00	25.00
MRAC	Adam Cole	3.00	8.00
MRAJ	AJ Styles	3.00	8.00
MRAS	Asuka	5.00	12.00
MRBA	Batista		
MRBS	Braun Strowman	2.50	6.00
MRCA	Cedric Alexander	2.00	5.00
MRCF	Charlotte Flair	5.00	12.00
MRDB	Daniel Bryan	3.00	8.00
MREM	Ember Moon	3.00	8.00
MRFB	Finn Balor	3.00	8.00
MRJC	John Cena	4.00	10.00
MRJG	Johnny Gargano	2.50	6.00
MRKA	Kurt Angle	3.00	8.00
MRKD	Killian Dain	2.00	5.00
MRKO	Kevin Owens	2.00	5.00
MRLS	Lars Sullivan	1.50	4.00
MRMH	Woken Matt Hardy	2.50	6.00
MRNA	Naomi	4.00	10.00
MRNJ	Nia Jax	2.00	5.00
MRPD	Pete Dunne	3.00	8.00
MRRC	Ricochet	3.00	8.00
MRRR	Roman Reigns	4.00	10.00
MRRS	Roderick Strong		
MRSB	Shayna Baszler	3.00	8.00
MRSN	Shinsuke Nakamura	2.50	6.00
MRSR	Seth Rollins	3.00	8.00
MRSZ	Sami Zayn	1.50	4.00
MRTC	Tommaso Ciampa	2.50	6.00
MRTM	The Miz	2.00	5.00
MRUN	Undertaker	5.00	12.00
MRVD	Velveteen Dream	3.00	8.00
MRALB	Aleister Black	3.00	8.00
MREC3	EC3	1.50	4.00
MRERA	Kyle O'Reilly	2.50	6.00
MRHHH	Triple H	3.00	8.00
MRRRR	Ronda Rousey	6.00	15.00
MRSMC	Stephanie McMahon	3.00	8.00
MRWWE	Elias	2.00	5.00

2019 Topps WWE Road to WrestleMania Shirt Relics

*BRONZE/99: .5X TO 1.2X BASIC MEM
*BLUE/50: .6X TO 1.5X BASIC MEM
*SILVER/25: .75X TO 2X BASIC MEM
*GOLD/10: UNPRICED DUE TO SCARCITY
*RED/1: UNPRICED DUE TO SCARCITY
RANDOMLY INSERTED INTO PACKS

SRAB	Alexa Bliss	15.00	30.00
SRAE	Aiden English	2.50	6.00
SRAF	Alicia Fox	5.00	12.00
SRBS	Braun Strowman	2.50	6.00
SRCM	Carmella	4.00	10.00
SRDB	Daniel Bryan	3.00	8.00
SRFB	Finn Balor	3.00	8.00
SRJC	John Cena	4.00	10.00
SRJH	Jeff Hardy	2.50	6.00
SRMH	Woken Matt Hardy	4.00	10.00
SRRD	Rusev		
SRRR	Roman Reigns	5.00	12.00
SRRY	Renee Young	2.50	6.00
SRSR	Seth Rollins	4.00	10.00
SRTM	The Miz	2.50	6.00
SRWWE	Elias	5.00	12.00

2019 Topps WWE Road to WrestleMania Update

COMPLETE SET (20)		8.00	20.00

RANDOMLY INSERTED INTO PACKS

U1	No Way Jose	.50	1.25
U2	Jeff Hardy	1.00	2.50
U3	Bobby Lashley	.75	2.00
U4	Samoa Joe	.75	2.00
U5	Jeff Hardy	1.00	2.50
U6	AOP	.60	1.50
U7	Kevin Owens and Sami Zayn	1.00	2.50
U8	Dolph Ziggler and Drew McIntyre	.75	2.00
U9	Kalisto	.40	1.00
U10	Drew Gulak	.40	1.00
U11	Buddy Murphy	.50	1.25
U12	Lince Dorado	.40	1.00
U13	Paige	1.50	4.00
U14	Usos	.50	1.25
U15	Randy Orton	1.00	2.50
U16	Shinsuke Nakamura	1.00	2.50
U17	Jeff Hardy	1.00	2.50
U18	Harper	.50	1.25
U19	Samoa Joe	.75	2.00
U20	AJ Styles & Daniel Bryan	2.00	5.00

2019 Topps WWE Road to WrestleMania WrestleMania 35 Roster

COMPLETE SET (50)		6.00	15.00

RANDOMLY INSERTED INTO PACKS

WM1	Paul Heyman	.40	1.00
WM2	AJ Styles	1.50	4.00
WM3	Shinsuke Nakamura	.75	2.00
WM4	Undertaker	1.50	4.00
WM5	John Cena	1.25	3.00
WM6	Elias	.60	1.50
WM7	Kurt Angle	.60	1.50
WM8	Ronda Rousey	1.50	4.00
WM9	Triple H	.75	2.00
WM10	Stephanie McMahon	.75	2.00
WM11	Charlotte Flair	1.25	3.00
WM12	Asuka	1.00	2.50
WM13	Nia Jax	.60	1.50
WM14	Alexa Bliss	1.50	4.00
WM15	Daniel Bryan	1.25	3.00
WM16	Shane McMahon	.75	2.00
WM17	Kevin Owens	.75	2.00
WM18	Sami Zayn	.60	1.50
WM19	Seth Rollins	.75	2.00
WM20	The Miz	.60	1.50
WM21	Finn Balor	.75	2.00
WM22	Jinder Mahal	.60	1.50
WM23	Randy Orton	.75	2.00
WM24	Bobby Roode	.60	1.50
WM25	Rusev	.60	1.50
WM26	Aiden English	.30	.75
WM27	Braun Strowman	.75	2.00

WM28	Cesaro	.40	1.00
WM29	Sheamus	.50	1.25
WM30	Harper	.40	1.00
WM31	Rowan	.30	.75
WM32	Jey Uso	.40	1.00
WM33	Jimmy Uso	.40	1.00
WM34	Big E	.30	.75
WM35	Kofi Kingston	.50	1.25
WM36	Xavier Woods	.40	1.00
WM37	Cedric Alexander	.30	.75
WM38	Mustafa Ali	.30	.75
WM39	Woken Matt Hardy	.60	1.50
WM40	Bray Wyatt	.75	2.00
WM41	Naomi	.50	1.25
WM42	Bayley	.60	1.50
WM43	Sasha Banks	1.25	3.00
WM44	Samoa Joe	.60	1.50
WM45	Jeff Hardy	.75	2.00
WM46	Bobby Lashley	.60	1.50
WM47	Ember Moon	.75	2.00
WM48	Carmella	.75	2.00
WM49	Ruby Riott	.60	1.50
WM50	Liv Morgan	1.00	2.50

2020 Topps WWE Road to WrestleMania

COMPLETE SET (100)		12.00	30.00

*FOILBOARD: .5X TO 1.2X BASIC CARDS
*BLUE/99: 1.2X TO 3X BASIC CARDS
*SILVER/25: UNPRICED DUE TO SCARCITY
*GOLD/10: UNPRICED DUE TO SCARCITY
*RED/1: UNPRICED DUE TO SCARCITY
*P.P.BLACK/1: UNPRICED DUE TO SCARCITY
*P.P.CYAN/1: UNPRICED DUE TO SCARCITY
*P.P.MAGENTA/1: UNPRICED DUE TO SCARCITY
*P.P.YELLOW/1: UNPRICED DUE TO SCARCITY

1	Lince Dorado & Gran Metalik	.25	.60
2	Buddy Murphy	.30	.75
3	Buddy Murphy	.30	.75
4	Buddy Murphy	.30	.75
5	Buddy Murphy	.30	.75
6	Noam Dar	.25	.60
7	Buddy Murphy	.40	1.00
8	Buddy Murphy	.30	.75
9	Tony Nese	.25	.60
10	Buddy Murphy	.30	.75
11	Tony Nese	.25	.60
12	Tony Nese	.25	.60
13	Tony Nese	.25	.60
14	Tony Nese	.25	.60
15	Roman Reigns	.60	1.50
16	Seth Rollins	.50	1.25
17	Dolph Ziggler & Drew McIntyre	.50	1.25
18	Brock Lesnar	1.00	2.50
19	Dolph Ziggler & Drew McIntyre	.50	1.25
20	Seattle Hates The Elias & KO Show	.30	.75
21	Triple H	1.00	2.50
22	Roman Reigns	.60	1.50
23	Dolph Ziggler	.25	.60
24	Brock Lesnar	1.00	2.50
25	D-Generation X	1.00	2.50
26	Drew McIntyre	.50	1.25
27	AOP	.30	.75
28	Seth Rollins	.50	1.25
29	Brock Lesnar	1.00	2.50
30	Team RAW Def. Team SmackDown	.60	1.50
31	AOP	.30	.75
32	Robert Roode & Chad Gable	.25	.60

33	Finn Balor	.60	1.50
34	Cena/Balor/Rollins	.60	1.50
35	Bobby Lashley	.50	1.25
36	Seth Rollins	.50	1.25
37	Brock Lesnar	1.00	2.50
38	The Revival	.25	.60
39	Baron Corbin	.30	.75
40	Seth Rollins	1.00	2.50
41	The Revival	.25	.60
42	Finn Balor	.60	1.50
43	Baron Corbin	.30	.75
44	Batista Returns	.40	1.00
45	Roman Reigns Returns	.60	1.50
46	Seth Rollins	.50	1.25
47	Bobby Lashley	.50	1.25
48	Kurt Angle	.60	1.50
49	Kurt Angle	.60	1.50
50	Drew McIntyre	.50	1.25
51	Baron Corbin	.30	.75
52	Curt Hawkins & Zack Ryder	.25	.60
53	Braun Strowman	.60	1.50
54	Seth Rollins	.50	1.25
55	Roman Reigns	.60	1.50
56	Triple H	.60	1.50
57	Baron Corbin	.30	.75
58	The Demon Finn Balor	.60	1.50
59	The New Day	.40	1.00
60	Daniel Bryan	.75	2.00
61	Randy Orton	.60	1.50
62	AJ Styles	.75	2.00
63	Shinsuke Nakamura	.50	1.25
64	The New Day	.40	1.00
65	AJ Styles	.75	2.00
66	Randy Orton	.60	1.50
67	Big Show Helps The Bar	.30	.75
68	The Miz	.40	1.00
69	The Miz	.50	1.25
70	Rey Mysterio	.50	1.25
71	Daniel Bryan	.75	2.00
72	The New Daniel Bryan	.75	2.00
73	The New Daniel Bryan	.75	2.00
74	The Bar	.30	.75
75	AJ Styles & Mustafa Ali	.75	2.00
76	Mustafa Ali	.40	1.00
77	Rusev	.30	.75
78	AJ Styles	.75	2.00
79	Samoa Joe & Andrade	.40	1.00
80	Andrade	.50	1.25
81	Rey Mysterio and Andrade	.50	1.25
82	Shinsuke Nakamura	.50	1.25
83	The Miz & Shane McMahon	.40	1.00
84	Erick Rowan	.25	.60
85	R-Truth	.25	.60
86	R-Truth	.25	.60
87	The Usos	.25	.60
88	The New Daniel Bryan	.75	2.00
89	Samoa Joe	.40	1.00
90	The Usos	.25	.60
91	The Bar	.30	.75
92	Samoa Joe	.40	1.00
93	The New Daniel Bryan	.75	2.00
94	Kofi Kingston	.40	1.00
95	The New Day	.25	.60
96	AJ Styles	.75	2.00
97	The Usos	.25	.60
98	Shane McMahon	.40	1.00
99	Samoa Joe	.40	1.00
100	Kofi Kingston	.75	2.00

2020 Topps WWE Road to WrestleMania Andre the Giant Battle Royal Commemorative Trophy Relics

*BRONZE/99: .5X TO 1.2X BASIC MEM
*BLUE/50: .6X TO 1.5X BASIC MEM
*SILVER/25: UNPRICED DUE TO SCARCITY
*GOLD/10: UNPRICED DUE TO SCARCITY
*RED/1: UNPRICED DUE TO SCARCITY
STATED PRINT RUN 199 SER.#'d SETS

AGAC	Apollo Crews	2.00	5.00
AGAD	Andrade	2.50	6.00
AGAL	Ali	2.50	6.00
AGBS	Braun Strowman	4.00	10.00
AGCA	Curtis Axel	2.00	5.00
AGGM	Gran Metalik	4.00	10.00
AGJH	Jeff Hardy	5.00	12.00
AGJM	Jinder Mahal	2.00	5.00
AGKA	Karl Anderson	2.50	6.00
AGKL	Kalisto	2.50	6.00
AGLD	Lince Dorado	2.00	5.00
AGMH	Matt Hardy	4.00	10.00
AGOT	Otis	6.00	15.00
AGRR	Robert Roode	3.00	8.00
AGSB	Shelton Benjamin	2.50	6.00
AGTB	Tyler Breeze	2.50	6.00
AGTK	Tucker	2.00	5.00

2020 Topps WWE Road to WrestleMania Autographed Andre the Giant Battle Royal Commemorative Trophy Relics

*RED/1: UNPRICED DUE TO SCARCITY
STATED PRINT RUN 10 SER.#'d SETS
UNPRICED DUE TO SCARCITY

AGAAC	Apollo Crews
AGAAD	Andrade
AGAAL	Ali
AGABS	Braun Strowman
AGAGM	Gran Metalik
AGAJH	Jeff Hardy
AGAJM	Jinder Mahal
AGAMH	Matt Hardy
AGAOT	Otis
AGATK	Tucker

2020 Topps WWE Road to WrestleMania Autographed Hall of Fame Headliner Tribute Relic

HOFHTM	Honky Tonk Man

2020 Topps WWE Road to WrestleMania Autographed Mat Relics

*RED/1: UNPRICED DUE TO SCARCITY
STATED PRINT RUN 10 SER.#'d SETS
UNPRICED DUE TO SCARCITY

MRAAC	Adam Cole
MRAAJ	AJ Styles
MRABC	Becky Lynch
MRABK	Billie Kay
MRABP	Beth Phoenix
MRACM	Carmella
MRAKA	Kurt Angle
MRAKK	Kofi Kingston
MRAPR	Peyton Royce
MRARR	Roman Reigns

MRASB	Shayna Baszler
MRASJ	Samoa Joe
MRAVD	Velveteen Dream
MRAZR	Zack Ryder

2020 Topps WWE Road to WrestleMania Autographed Shirt Relics

*RED/1: UNPRICED DUE TO SCARCITY
STATED PRINT RUN 10 SER.#'d SETS
UNPRICED DUE TO SCARCITY

SRAAB	Aleister Black
SRAAD	Andrade
SRAAJ	AJ Styles
SRABB	Bobby Lashley
SRABD	Bo Dallas
SRABS	Braun Strowman
SRACA	Curtis Axel
SRAEL	Elias
SRAFB	Finn Balor
SRANJ	No Way Jose
SRARC	Ricochet
SRARR	Ronda Rousey
SRAZR	Zack Ryder

2020 Topps WWE Road to WrestleMania Autographed Women's WrestleMania Battle Royal Commemorative Trop

*RED/1: UNPRICED DUE TO SCARCITY
STATED PRINT RUN 10 SER.#'d SETS
UNPRICED DUE TO SCARCITY

WRAAS	Asuka
WRACM	Carmella
WRADB	Dana Brooke
WRAEM	Ember Moon
WRAKS	Kairi Sane
WRAMJ	Mickie James
WRAMK	Maria Kanellis
WRAMR	Mandy Rose
WRANC	Nikki Cross
WRANM	Naomi
WRASD	Sonya Deville
WRASL	Sarah Logan
WRAZV	Zelina Vega

2020 Topps WWE Road to WrestleMania Autographs

*BLUE/50: .5X TO 1.2X BASIC AUTOS
*SILVER/25: UNPRICED DUE TO SCARCITY
*GOLD/10: UNPRICED DUE TO SCARCITY
*RED/1: UNPRICED DUE TO SCARCITY
*P.P.BLACK/1: UNPRICED DUE TO SCARCITY
*P.P.CYAN/1: UNPRICED DUE TO SCARCITY
*P.P.MAGENTA/1: UNPRICED DUE TO SCARCITY
*P.P.YELLOW/1: UNPRICED DUE TO SCARCITY
STATED PRINT RUN 99 SER.#'d SETS

AAB	Alexa Bliss	60.00	120.00
AAJ	AJ Styles	10.00	25.00
AAL	Aleister Black	12.00	30.00
AAS	Asuka	25.00	60.00
ABK	Becky Lynch	30.00	75.00
ABS	Braun Strowman	15.00	40.00
ABW	Bray Wyatt	12.00	30.00
ACM	Carmella	15.00	40.00
ADB	Daniel Bryan	10.00	25.00
AKK	Kofi Kingston	6.00	15.00

AKO	Kevin Owens	8.00	20.00
AKS	Kairi Sane	15.00	40.00
ALE	Lacey Evans	12.00	30.00
AMA	Ali	6.00	15.00
ARC	Ricochet	10.00	25.00
ARR	Roman Reigns	10.00	25.00
ASB	Sasha Banks	25.00	60.00
ASJ	Samoa Joe	6.00	15.00
ASN	Shinsuke Nakamura	8.00	20.00
ASR	Seth Rollins	12.00	30.00
ATM	The Miz	6.00	15.00

2020 Topps WWE Road to WrestleMania Dual Autographs

*GOLD/10: UNPRICED DUE TO SCARCITY
*RED/1: UNPRICED DUE TO SCARCITY
STATED PRINT RUN 25 SER.#'d SETS

DAGB	K.Anderson/L.Gallows	25.00	60.00
DAHB	The Hardy Boyz	100.00	200.00
DAHM	Tucker/Otis	60.00	120.00
DAIG	Andrade/Z.Vega	30.00	75.00
DAII	B.Kay/P.Royce	100.00	200.00
DARV	S.Dawson/D.Wilder		

2020 Topps WWE Road to WrestleMania Hall of Fame Headliner Tribute

COMPLETE SET (16) 10.00 25.00
RANDOMLY INSERTED INTO PACKS

HF1	Honky Tonk Man	1.00	2.50
HF2	Honky Tonk Man	1.00	2.50
HF3	Honky Tonk Man	1.00	2.50
HF4	Honky Tonk Man	1.50	4.00
HF5	Honky Tonk Man	1.00	2.50
HF6	Honky Tonk Man	1.00	2.50
HF7	Honky Tonk Man	1.00	2.50
HF8	Honky Tonk Man	1.00	2.50
HF9	Honky Tonk Man	1.00	2.50
HF10	Honky Tonk Man	1.00	2.50
HF11	Honky Tonk Man	1.00	2.50
HF12	Honky Tonk Man	1.00	2.50
HF13	Honky Tonk Man	1.00	2.50
HF14	Honky Tonk Man	1.00	2.50
HF15	Honky Tonk Man	1.00	2.50
HF16	Honky Tonk Man	1.00	2.50

2020 Topps WWE Road to WrestleMania Hall of Fame Headliner Tribute Autographs

STATED PRINT RUN 10 SER.#'d SETS
UNPRICED DUE TO SCARCITY

HFA1 Honky Tonk Man
HFA2 Honky Tonk Man
HFA3 Honky Tonk Man
HFA4 Honky Tonk Man
HFA5 Honky Tonk Man
HFA6 Honky Tonk Man
HFA7 Honky Tonk Man
HFA8 Honky Tonk Man
HFA9 Honky Tonk Man
HFA10 Honky Tonk Man
HFA11 Honky Tonk Man
HFA12 Honky Tonk Man
HFA13 Honky Tonk Man
HFA14 Honky Tonk Man
HFA15 Honky Tonk Man
HFA16 Honky Tonk Man

2020 Topps WWE Road to WrestleMania Mat Relics

*BRONZE/99: .5X TO 1.2X BASIC MEM
*BLUE/50: .6X TO 1.5X BASIC MEM
*SILVER/25: UNPRICED DUE TO SCARCITY
*GOLD/10: UNPRICED DUE TO SCARCITY
*RED/1: UNPRICED DUE TO SCARCITY
STATED PRINT RUN 199 SER.#'d SETS

MRAB	Aleister Black	2.00	5.00
MRAC	Adam Cole	5.00	12.00
MRAJ	AJ Styles	5.00	12.00
MRBB	Bianca Belair	4.00	10.00
MRBC	Becky Lynch	10.00	25.00
MRBK	Billie Kay	8.00	20.00
MRBM	Buddy Murphy	2.00	5.00
MRBP	Beth Phoenix	2.50	6.00
MRBS	Braun Strowman	4.00	10.00
MRBT	Batista	6.00	15.00
MRCF	Charlotte Flair	6.00	15.00
MRCH	Curt Hawkins	2.00	5.00
MRCM	Carmella	5.00	12.00
MRDB	Daniel Bryan	3.00	8.00
MRDM	Drew McIntyre	4.00	10.00
MRER	Erik	2.00	5.00
MRIS	Io Shirai	2.00	5.00
MRIV	Ivar	2.00	5.00
MRJG	Johnny Gargano	2.50	6.00
MRKA	Kurt Angle	3.00	8.00
MRKK	Kofi Kingston	4.00	10.00
MRKS	Kairi Sane	2.50	6.00
MRMR	Matt Riddle	2.00	5.00
MRNT	Natalya	3.00	8.00
MRPD	Pete Dunne	2.00	5.00
MRPR	Peyton Royce	6.00	15.00
MRRC	Ricochet	2.50	6.00
MRRM	Rey Mysterio	2.50	6.00
MRRR	Roman Reigns	4.00	10.00
MRRS	Ronda Rousey	8.00	20.00
MRSB	Shayna Baszler	5.00	12.00
MRSJ	Samoa Joe	3.00	8.00
MRTH	Triple H	3.00	8.00
MRTM	The Miz	2.50	6.00
MRTN	Tony Nese	2.00	5.00
MRVD	Velveteen Dream	2.00	5.00
MRWT	Walter	2.50	6.00
MRZR	Zack Ryder	10.00	25.00
MRJEY	Jey Uso	2.50	6.00
MRJIM	Jimmy Uso	2.50	6.00

2020 Topps WWE Road to WrestleMania Shirt Relics

*BRONZE/99: .5X TO 1.2X BASIC MEM
*BLUE/50: .6X TO 1.5X BASIC MEM
*SILVER/25: UNPRICED DUE TO SCARCITY
*GOLD/10: UNPRICED DUE TO SCARCITY
*RED/1: UNPRICED DUE TO SCARCITY
STATED PRINT RUN 199 SER.#'d SETS

SRAB	Aleister Black	4.00	10.00
SRAD	Andrade	2.50	6.00
SRAJ	AJ Styles	5.00	12.00
SRBB	Bobby Lashley	3.00	8.00
SRBD	Bo Dallas	2.00	5.00
SRBH	Bret Hit Man Hart	8.00	20.00
SRBL	Brock Lesnar	4.00	10.00
SRBS	Braun Strowman	3.00	8.00
SRBT	Booker T	3.00	8.00
SRCA	Curtis Axel	2.50	6.00

SREL	Elias	2.50	6.00
SRFB	Finn Balor	5.00	12.00
SRNJ	No Way Jose	2.00	5.00
SRRR	Ronda Rousey	20.00	50.00
SRSM	Shawn Michaels	5.00	12.00
SRSR	Stevie Ray	2.00	5.00
SRZR	Zack Ryder	2.50	6.00

2020 Topps WWE Road to WrestleMania Six-Person Autograph Booklet

STATED PRINT RUN 10 SER.#'d SETS
UNPRICED DUE TO SCARCITY

ABCMITB Rousey/Flair/Rollins/Reigns/Kingston/Lynch

2020 Topps WWE Road to WrestleMania Triple Autographs

*GOLD/10: UNPRICED DUE TO SCARCITY
*RED/1: UNPRICED DUE TO SCARCITY
STATED PRINT RUN 25 SER.#'d SETS

TALP	Dorado/Metalik/Kalisto	60.00	120.00
TAND	Woods/Big E/Kingston	75.00	150.00

2020 Topps WWE Road to WrestleMania Winningest Superstars in WrestleMania History

COMPLETE SET (10) 6.00 15.00
RANDOMLY INSERTED INTO PACKS

WS1	Randy Orton	1.00	2.50
WS2	Shawn Michaels	1.00	2.50
WS3	Seth Rollins	.75	2.00
WS4	Macho Man Randy Savage	1.25	3.00
WS5	Rey Mysterio	.75	2.00
WS6	Kane	.50	1.25
WS7	Bret Hit Man Hart	1.00	2.50
WS8	Triple H	1.00	2.50
WS9	John Cena	1.50	4.00
WS10	Undertaker	1.50	4.00

2020 Topps WWE Road to WrestleMania Winningest Superstars in WrestleMania History Autographs

*RED/1: UNPRICED DUE TO SCARCITY
STATED PRINT RUN 10 SER.#'d SETS
UNPRICED DUE TO SCARCITY

WSA1 Randy Orton
WSA2 Shawn Michaels
WSA3 Seth Rollins
WSA4 Rey Mysterio
WSA5 Bret Hit Man Hart

2020 Topps WWE Road to WrestleMania Women's WrestleMania Battle Royal Commemorative Trophy Relics

*BRONZE/99: .5X TO 1.2X BASIC MEM
*BLUE/50: .6X TO 1.5X BASIC MEM
*SILVER/25: UNPRICED DUE TO SCARCITY
*GOLD/10: UNPRICED DUE SCARCITY
*RED/1: UNPRICED DUE TO SCARCITY
STATED PRINT RUN 199 SER.#'d SETS

WRAS	Asuka	6.00	15.00
WRCM	Carmella	5.00	12.00
WRDB	Dana Brooke	2.50	6.00
WREM	Ember Moon	3.00	8.00
WRKS	Kairi Sane	2.50	6.00

WRMJ	Mickie James	4.00	10.00
WRMK	Maria Kanellis	5.00	12.00
WRMR	Mandy Rose	8.00	20.00
WRNC	Nikki Cross	4.00	10.00
WRNM	Naomi	2.50	6.00
WRSD	Sonya Deville	3.00	8.00
WRSL	Sarah Logan	2.50	6.00
WRZV	Zelina Vega	3.00	8.00

2020 Topps WWE Road to WrestleMania WrestleMania Roster

COMPLETE SET (50) 12.00 30.00
RANDOMLY INSERTED INTO PACKS

WM1	AJ Styles	1.00	2.50
WM2	Aleister Black	.60	1.50
WM3	Alexa Bliss	2.00	5.00
WM4	Mustafa Ali	.50	1.25
WM5	Andrade	.50	1.25
WM6	Asuka	1.25	3.00
WM7	King Corbin	.40	1.00
WM8	Bayley	.60	1.50
WM9	Becky Lynch	1.25	3.00
WM10	Big E	.30	.75
WM11	Billie Kay	.60	1.50
WM12	Bobby Lashley	.60	1.50
WM13	Braun Strowman	.75	2.00
WM14	The Fiend Bray Wyatt	1.00	2.50
WM15	Brock Lesnar	1.25	3.00
WM16	Buddy Murphy	.40	1.00
WM17	Carmella	.75	2.00
WM18	Cesaro	.30	.75
WM19	Charlotte Flair	1.25	3.00
WM20	Daniel Bryan	1.00	2.50
WM21	Drew McIntyre	.60	1.50
WM22	Elias	.30	.75
WM23	Ember Moon	.60	1.50
WM24	Erik	.30	.75
WM25	Finn Balor	.75	2.00
WM26	Ivar	.30	.75
WM27	Jeff Hardy	.75	2.00
WM28	John Cena	1.25	3.00
WM29	Kairi Sane	.60	1.50
WM30	Kevin Owens	.40	1.00
WM31	Kofi Kingston	.50	1.25
WM32	Lacey Evans	.75	2.00
WM33	Lars Sullivan	.30	.75
WM34	Mandy Rose	1.50	4.00
WM35	Matt Hardy	.60	1.50
WM36	Nikki Cross	.60	1.50
WM37	Peyton Royce	.60	1.50
WM38	Randy Orton	.75	2.00
WM39	Rey Mysterio	.60	1.50
WM40	Ricochet	.50	1.25
WM41	Roman Reigns	.75	2.00
WM42	R-Truth	.30	.75
WM43	Sami Zayn	.40	1.00
WM44	Samoa Joe	.50	1.25
WM45	Seth Rollins	.60	1.50
WM46	Shinsuke Nakamura	.60	1.50
WM47	Sonya Deville	.75	2.00
WM48	The Miz	.50	1.25
WM49	Xavier Woods	.30	.75
WM50	Zelina Vega	.60	1.50

2020 Topps WWE Road to WrestleMania Yearly Records

COMPLETE SET (10) 8.00 20.00
BLASTER EXCLUSIVE

YR1	Asuka	2.50	6.00
YR2	Braun Strowman	1.50	4.00
YR3	Brock Lesnar	2.50	6.00
YR4	Carmella	1.50	4.00
YR5	Charlotte Flair	2.50	6.00
YR6	Daniel Bryan	2.00	5.00
YR7	Kofi Kingston	1.00	2.50
YR8	Mickie James	1.00	2.50
YR9	Pete Dunne	.60	1.50
YR10	Seth Rollins	1.25	3.00

2020 Topps WWE Road to WrestleMania Yearly Records Autographs

*RED/1: UNPRICED DUE TO SCARCITY
STATED PRINT RUN 10 SER.#'d SETS
UNPRICED DUE TO SCARCITY

YRA1	Asuka
YRA2	Braun Strowman
YRA3	Carmella
YRA4	Kofi Kingston
YRA5	Seth Rollins

2021 Topps WWE Road to WrestleMania Stickers

1	Intro	.15	.40
2	Intro	.15	.40
3	Intro	.15	.40
4	Intro	.15	.40
5	Drew McIntyre	.60	1.50
6	Drew McIntyre	.60	1.50
7	Drew McIntyre	.60	1.50
8	Drew McIntyre	.60	1.50
9	Drew McIntyre	.60	1.50
10	Drew McIntyre	.60	1.50
11	Drew McIntyre	.60	1.50
12	Drew McIntyre	.60	1.50
13	Drew McIntyre	.60	1.50
14	Drew McIntyre	.60	1.50
15	Becky Lynch	1.00	2.50
16	Becky Lynch	1.00	2.50
17	Becky Lynch	1.00	2.50
18	Becky Lynch	1.00	2.50
19	Becky Lynch	1.00	2.50
20	Becky Lynch	1.00	2.50
21	Becky Lynch	1.00	2.50
22	Becky Lynch	1.00	2.50
23	Becky Lynch	1.00	2.50
24	Becky Lynch	1.00	2.50
25	The Fiend Bray Wyatt	1.00	2.50
26	The Fiend Bray Wyatt	1.00	2.50
27	The Fiend Bray Wyatt	1.00	2.50
28	The Fiend Bray Wyatt	1.00	2.50
29	The Fiend Bray Wyatt	1.00	2.50
30	The Fiend Bray Wyatt	1.00	2.50
31	The Fiend Bray Wyatt	1.00	2.50
32	The Fiend Bray Wyatt	1.00	2.50
33	The Fiend Bray Wyatt	1.00	2.50
34	The Fiend Bray Wyatt	1.00	2.50
35	Charlotte Flair	1.25	3.00
36	Charlotte Flair	1.25	3.00
37	Charlotte Flair	1.25	3.00
38	Charlotte Flair	1.25	3.00
39	Angel Garza	.30	.75
40	Drew Gulak	.30	.75
41	Big Show	.50	1.25
42	Shayna Baszler	.60	1.50
43	Lacey Evans	1.00	2.50
44	AJ Styles	.75	2.00
45	AJ Styles	.75	2.00
46	AJ Styles	.75	2.00
47	AJ Styles	.75	2.00
48	Mandy Rose	1.25	3.00
49	Dana Brooke	.25	.60
50	Elias	.25	.60
51	Nia Jax	.50	1.25
52	Braun Strowman	.60	1.50
53	Braun Strowman	.60	1.50
54	Bobby Lashley	.60	1.50
55	Bobby Lashley	.60	1.50
56	Cedric Alexander	.25	.60
57	MVP	.25	.60
58	Shelton Benjamin	.40	1.00
59	Akira Tozawa	.30	.75
60	Randy Orton	.75	2.00
61	Viking Raiders	.25	.60
62	R-Truth	.30	.75
63	Naomi	.30	.75
64	Andrade	.40	1.00
65	Nikki Cross	.50	1.25
66	The New Day	.50	1.25
67	The New Day	.50	1.25
68	The Miz	.40	1.00
69	Ricochet	.40	1.00
70	Keith Lee	.50	1.25
71	Keith Lee	.50	1.25
72	Keith Lee	.50	1.25
73	Keith Lee	.50	1.25
74	Ali	.30	.75
75	Retribution	.25	.60
76	Retribution	.25	.60
77	Lana	.30	.75
78	Sheamus	.40	1.00
79	Alexa Bliss	1.50	4.00
80	Alexa Bliss	1.50	4.00
81	Alexa Bliss	1.50	4.00
82	Gran Metalik	.25	.60
83	John Morrison	.50	1.25
84	Humberto Carrillo	.25	.60
85	Humberto Carrillo	.25	.60
86	Humberto Carrillo	.25	.60
87	Jeff Hardy	.60	1.50
88	Tucker	.25	.60
89	Asuka	1.00	2.50
90	Asuka	1.00	2.50
91	Asuka	1.00	2.50
92	Edge	1.00	2.50
93	Edge	1.00	2.50
94	Charlotte Flair	1.25	3.00
95	Number One	.15	.40
96	Surprise	.15	.40
97	Most Eliminations	.15	.40
98	Most Wins	.15	.40
99	Champion	.15	.40
100	History Maker	.15	.40
101	1988	.15	.40
102	The People's Rumble	.15	.40
103	Undertaker The Streak	1.25	3.00
104	Undertaker The Streak #1	1.25	3.00
105	Undertaker The Streak #6	1.25	3.00
106	Undertaker The Streak #7	1.25	3.00
107	Undertaker The Streak #9	1.25	3.00
108	Undertaker The Streak #12	1.25	3.00
109	Undertaker The Streak #14	1.25	3.00
110	Undertaker The Streak #17	1.25	3.00
111	Undertaker The Streak #21	1.25	3.00
112	WrestleMania	.15	.40
113	WrestleMania X	.15	.40
114	WrestleMania 13	.15	.40
115	WrestleMania XV	.15	.40
116	WrestleMania X-Seven	.15	.40
117	WrestleMania XX	.15	.40
118	WrestleMania 25	.15	.40
119	WrestleMania XXX	.15	.40
120	WrestleMania 36	.15	.40
121	Adam Cole	.75	2.00
122	Adam Cole	.75	2.00
123	Adam Cole	.75	2.00
124	The Undisputed Era	.40	1.00
125	Shotzi Blackheart	1.25	3.00
126	Dexter Lumis	.25	.60
127	Johnny Gargano	.50	1.25
128	Candice LeRae	1.00	2.50
129	Rhea Ripley	1.00	2.50
130	Damian Priest	.40	1.00
131	Finn Balor	.60	1.50
132	Karrion Kross	1.00	2.50
133	Dakota Kai	.50	1.25
134	Pete Dunne	.60	1.50
135	Kushida	.40	1.00
136	Kushida	.40	1.00
137	Kushida	.40	1.00
138	Ember Moon	.30	.75
139	Tommaso Ciampa	.60	1.50
140	NXT UK	.15	.40
141	Moustache Mountain	.25	.60
142	Moustache Mountain	.25	.60
143	Trent Seven	.30	.75
144	Tyler Bate	.30	.75
145	Ilja Dragunov	.25	.60
146	Jordan Devlin	.25	.60
147	Piper Niven	.40	1.00
148	Gallus	.30	.75
149	Kay Lee Ray	.60	1.50
150	Andre the Giant	3.00	8.00
151	Macho Man Randy Savage	1.50	4.00
152	Ultimate Warrior	1.50	4.00
153	Rowdy Roddy Piper	.60	1.50
154	Bret "Hit Man" Hart	.60	1.50
155	Shawn Michaels	1.00	2.50
156	Undertaker	1.25	3.00
157	Stone Cold Steve Austin	1.25	3.00
158	The Rock	1.50	4.00
159	Triple H	.75	2.00
160	Trish Stratus	1.25	3.00
161	Eddie Guerrero	1.25	3.00
162	Edge	1.00	2.50
163	John Cena	1.25	3.00
164	Randy Orton	.75	2.00
165	Batista	.50	1.25
166	Charlotte Flair	1.25	3.00
167	Becky Lynch	1.00	2.50
168	Roman Reigns	1.25	3.00
169	Roman Reigns	1.25	3.00
170	Roman Reigns	1.25	3.00
171	Roman Reigns	1.25	3.00
172	Roman Reigns	1.25	3.00
173	Roman Reigns	1.25	3.00
174	Roman Reigns	1.25	3.00
175	Roman Reigns	1.25	3.00
176	Roman Reigns	1.25	3.00
177	Roman Reigns	1.25	3.00
178	Roman Reigns	1.25	3.00
179	Sasha Banks	1.25	3.00
180	Sasha Banks	1.25	3.00
181	Sasha Banks	1.25	3.00
182	Sasha Banks	1.25	3.00
183	Sasha Banks	1.25	3.00
184	Sasha Banks	1.25	3.00
185	Sasha Banks	1.25	3.00
186	Sasha Banks	1.25	3.00
187	Sasha Banks	1.25	3.00
188	Sasha Banks	1.25	3.00
189	Seth Rollins	.60	1.50
190	Seth Rollins	.60	1.50
191	Seth Rollins	.60	1.50
192	Seth Rollins	.60	1.50
193	Seth Rollins	.60	1.50
194	Seth Rollins	.60	1.50
195	Seth Rollins	.60	1.50
196	Seth Rollins	.60	1.50
197	Seth Rollins	.60	1.50
198	Seth Rollins	.60	1.50
199	Bayley	.60	1.50
200	Bayley	.60	1.50
201	Bayley	.60	1.50
202	Bayley	.60	1.50
203	Rey Mysterio	.60	1.50
204	Rey Mysterio	.60	1.50
205	Rey Mysterio	.60	1.50
206	Baron Corbin	.25	.60
207	Baron Corbin	.25	.60
208	SmackDown Fact	.15	.40
209	Usos	.25	.60
210	Usos	.25	.60
211	Kevin Owens	.50	1.25
212	Bo Dallas	.25	.60
213	Big E	.60	1.50
214	Big E	.60	1.50
215	Big E	.60	1.50
216	Mojo Rawley	.25	.60
217	Tamina	.25	.60
218	Cesaro	.25	.60
219	Cesaro	.25	.60
220	Cesaro	.25	.60
221	Billie Kay	.50	1.25
222	Dolph Ziggler	.50	1.25
223	Dolph Ziggler	.50	1.25
224	Dolph Ziggler	.50	1.25
225	Street Profits	.25	.60
226	Street Profits	.25	.60
227	Street Profits	.25	.60
228	Chad Gable	.25	.60
229	Apollo Crews	.30	.75
230	Murphy	.30	.75
231	The Riott Squad	.40	1.00
232	The Riott Squad	.40	1.00
233	Aleister Black	.60	1.50
234	Bianca Belair	.60	1.50
235	Bianca Belair	.60	1.50
236	Bianca Belair	.60	1.50
237	Sami Zayn	.40	1.00
238	Kalisto	.30	.75
239	SmackDown Fact	.15	.40
240	Daniel Bryan	1.00	2.50
241	Daniel Bryan	1.00	2.50
242	Daniel Bryan	1.00	2.50
243	Natalya	.40	1.00
244	Lars Sullivan	.25	.60
245	Otis	.30	.75
246	Otis	.30	.75
247	Kane	.40	1.00

248	Shinsuke Nakamura	.60	1.50
249	Shinsuke Nakamura	.60	1.50
250	Wesley Blake	.25	.60
251	Jaxson Ryker	.25	.60
252	Steve Cutler	.25	.60
253	Carmella	.60	1.50
254	Carmella	.60	1.50
255	Carmella	.60	1.50
256	Robert Roode	.30	.75
257	Mickie James	.50	1.25
258	Main Event Shocker	.15	.40
259	Fantastic Flair	.15	.40
260	Super Cena	1.25	3.00
261	Hardcore Hell	.15	.40
262	Air Shane	.50	1.25
263	Macho Marathon	1.50	4.00
264	Asuka's Run Ended	1.00	2.50
265	Magic Mysterio	.60	1.50
266	Money, Money, Money	.15	.40
267	Mega Match	.15	.40
268	Bret Wins Big	.60	1.50
269	His Time Is Now	1.25	3.00
270	KO to Big Show	.15	.40
271	The Last Ride	.15	.40
272	I'm Sorry, I Love You	.15	.40
273	You Never Saw It Coming	.15	.40
274	Warrior to the Rescue	1.50	4.00
275	Greatest Rivals	.15	.40
276	Wyatt's World	1.00	2.50
277	Legends of the Ladder	.15	.40
278	Super Spear	.15	.40
279	The Boyz Are Back	.60	1.50
280	Dream Match	.15	.40
281	Austin Era Begins	1.25	3.00
282	Match Made in Heaven	.15	.40
283	Kofi-Mania	.60	1.50
284	The Ultimate Challenge	.15	.40
285	Best of British	.15	.40
286	The Boyhood Dream	1.00	2.50
287	Becky Two Belts	1.00	2.50
288	Stone Cold Classic	1.25	3.00
289	Icon vs. Icon	1.50	4.00
290	Drama in the Cell	.15	.40
291	Yes	.15	.40
292	End of the Streak	1.25	3.00
293	Heist of the Century	.15	.40
294	The Greatest of Them All	.15	.40
295	Sami Zayn	.40	1.00
296	Bianca Belair	.60	1.50
297	Seth Rollins	.60	1.50
298	Alexa Bliss	1.50	4.00
299	Kofi Kingston	.60	1.50
300	Big Show	.50	1.25
301	Becky Lynch	1.00	2.50
302	Charlotte Flair	1.25	3.00
303	Cesaro	.25	.60
304	Mandy Rose	1.25	3.00

2021 Topps WWE Road to WrestleMania Stickers Autographs

STATED PRINT RUN 100 ANNCD SETS

AA1	Big E	20.00	50.00
AA2	Becky Lynch	60.00	120.00
AA3	Walter	30.00	75.00
AA4	Trent Seven	30.00	75.00
AA5	Naomi	50.00	100.00

2021 Topps WWE Road to WrestleMania Stickers Firefly Funhouse Pop-Up Card

NNO Bray Wyatt

2021 Topps WWE Road to WrestleMania Stickers Gold XL

T1 Icons
T2 Superstars
T3 Future Legends

2021 Topps WWE Road to WrestleMania Stickers Limiited Edition

LE1	The Rock	2.00	5.00
LE2	The Fiend Bray Wyatt	2.50	6.00
LE3	Roman Reigns	1.50	4.00
LE4	Sasha Banks	1.50	4.00

2021 Topps WWE Road to WrestleMania Stickers Tins

NNO McIntyre/Bliss/Orton/Lashley/Strowman
NNO Rose/Banks/Bayley/Rollins/Styles
NNO Ripley/Fiend/Shirai/Reigns/Big E

2016 Topps WWE The Rock Tribute

COMPLETE SET (40)		6.00	15.00
STATED ODDS 1:6			
1	The Rock	1.00	2.50
2	The Rock	1.00	2.50
3	The Rock	1.00	2.50
4	The Rock	1.00	2.50
5	The Rock	1.00	2.50
6	The Rock	1.00	2.50
7	The Rock	1.00	2.50
8	The Rock	1.00	2.50
9	The Rock	1.00	2.50
10	The Rock	1.00	2.50
11	The Rock	1.00	2.50
12	The Rock	1.00	2.50
13	The Rock	1.00	2.50
14	The Rock	1.00	2.50
15	The Rock	1.00	2.50
16	The Rock	1.00	2.50
17	The Rock	1.00	2.50
18	The Rock	1.00	2.50
19	The Rock	1.00	2.50
20	The Rock	1.00	2.50
21	The Rock	1.00	2.50
22	The Rock	1.00	2.50
23	The Rock	1.00	2.50
24	The Rock	1.00	2.50
25	The Rock	1.00	2.50
26	The Rock	1.00	2.50
27	The Rock	1.00	2.50
28	The Rock	1.00	2.50
29	The Rock	1.00	2.50
30	The Rock	1.00	2.50
31	The Rock	1.00	2.50
32	The Rock	1.00	2.50
33	The Rock	1.00	2.50
34	The Rock	1.00	2.50
35	The Rock	1.00	2.50
36	The Rock	1.00	2.50
37	The Rock	1.00	2.50
38	The Rock	1.00	2.50
39	The Rock	1.00	2.50
40	The Rock	1.00	2.50

2019 Topps WWE Roman Reigns Leukemia and Lymphoma Society Set

COMPLETE SET (11)		8.00	20.00
STATED PRINT RUN 101 ANNCD SETS			
1	Survivor Series 2013	1.25	3.00
2	Royal Rumble 2014	1.25	3.00
3	Fastlane 2015	1.25	3.00
4	Extreme Rules 2015	1.25	3.00
5	WrestleMania 32	1.25	3.00
6	Extreme Rules 2016	1.25	3.00
7	WrestleMania 33	1.25	3.00
8	No Mercy 2017	1.25	3.00
9	SummerSlam 2018	1.25	3.00
10	RAW Return 2019	1.25	3.00
11	LLS	1.25	3.00

2019 Topps WWE Ronda Rousey Spotlight Complete Series

COMPLETE SET (40)		25.00	60.00
1	Helps The Rock Fend Off Triple H and Stephanie McMahon	1.25	3.00
2	Crashes Women's Royal Rumble	1.25	3.00
3	WWE Contract	1.25	3.00
4	Confronts HHH & Stephanie	1.25	3.00
5	Takes Down Stephanie	1.25	3.00
6	Rebuffs Absolution	1.25	3.00
7	Teams w/Kurt Angle	1.25	3.00
8	Armbars Stephanie Twice	1.25	3.00
9	Helps Natalya	1.25	3.00
10	Armbars Mickie James	1.25	3.00
11	Chases off Alexa Bliss	1.25	3.00
12	Confronts Nia Jax	1.25	3.00
13	Signs Contract for Title Match	1.25	3.00
14	Armbars Nia Jax	1.25	3.00
15	Defeats Nia Jax by DQ	1.25	3.00
16	Is Suspended	1.25	3.00
17	Violates Her Suspension	1.25	3.00
18	Wins Her RAW Debut	1.25	3.00
19	Defeats Alexa Bliss for Women's Title	1.25	3.00
20	Attacks Stephanie McMahon	1.25	3.00
21	Works with Trish Stratus	1.25	3.00
22	Stops Alexa Bliss & Alicia Fox	1.25	3.00
23	Teams with Natalya	1.25	3.00
24	Successfully Defends Title Against Bliss	1.25	3.00
25	Defeats Rudy Riott	1.25	3.00
26	Crashes Negotiations	1.25	3.00
27	Goes Toe-to-Toe with Charlotte Flair	1.25	3.00
28	Defeats Mickie James	1.25	3.00
29	Teams with Ember Moon	1.25	3.00
30	Watches Ember Moon's Back	1.25	3.00
31	Defends Women's Title Against Nia	1.25	3.00
32	Tries to Issue Open Challenge	1.25	3.00
33	Defeats Natalya to Retain Title	1.25	3.00
34	Teams with Natalya	1.25	3.00
35	Appears A Moment of Bliss	1.25	3.00
36	Tags with Sasha Banks	1.25	3.00
37	Defeats Bayley in Open Challenge	1.25	3.00
38	Defeats Liv Morgan & Sarah Logan	1.25	3.00
39	Attacks Becky Lynch	1.25	3.00
40	Defeats Dana Brooke	1.25	3.00

2010 Topps WWE Rumble Pack

COMPLETE SET (50)		5.00	12.00
UNOPENED BOX (24 PACKS)			
UNOPENED PACK (6 CARDS)			
1	Big Show	.30	.75
2	Big Show	.30	.75
3	Carlito	.30	.75
4	Chris Jericho	.30	.75
5	Christian	.20	.50
6	Christian	.20	.50
7	CM Punk	.50	1.25
8	Cody Rhodes	.12	.30
9	Cody Rhodes	.12	.30
10	Evan Bourne	.12	.30
11	Evan Bourne	.12	.30
12	Hornswoggle	.20	.50
13	Hornswoggle	.20	.50
14	Yoshi Tatsu	.12	.30
15	Yoshi Tatsu	.12	.30
16	Jack Swagger	.12	.30
17	Jack Swagger	.12	.30
18	John Cena	.60	1.50
19	John Cena	.60	1.50
20	John Morrison	.15	.40
21	John Morrison	.15	.40
22	Kane	.30	.75
23	Kane	.30	.75
24	Kofi Kingston	.20	.50
25	Kofi Kingston	.20	.50
26	Kung Fu Naki	.12	.30
27	Matt Hardy	.30	.75
28	MVP	.20	.50
29	MVP	.20	.50
30	Primo	.12	.30
31	R-Truth	.12	.30
32	R-Truth	.12	.30
33	Randy Orton	.50	1.25
34	Randy Orton	.50	1.25
35	Rey Mysterio	.30	.75
36	Rey Mysterio	.30	.75
37	Santino Marella	.12	.30
38	Shawn Michaels	.75	2.00
39	Shawn Michaels	.75	2.00
40	Sheamus	.20	.50
41	Ted DiBiase	.20	.50
42	The Miz	.20	.50
43	Undertaker	.50	1.25
44	Triple H	.60	1.50
45	Triple H	.60	1.50
46	Edge	.50	1.25
47	Edge	.50	1.25
48	Batista	.50	1.25
49	Batista	.50	1.25
50	Checklist	.12	.30

2010 Topps WWE Rumble Pack Finger Puppets

COMPLETE SET (10)		3.00	8.00
STATED ODDS 1:4			
1	Shawn Michaels	1.25	3.00
2	Rey Mysterio	.50	1.25
3	CM Punk	.75	2.00
4	Hornswoggle	.30	.75
5	Mark Henry	.30	.75
6	Hurricane Helms	.20	.50
7	Triple H	1.00	2.50
8	R-Truth	.20	.50
9	Dolph Ziggler	.30	.75
10	MVP	.30	.75

2010 Topps WWE Rumble Pack Glow-in-the-Dark

COMPLETE SET (10)		4.00	10.00
STATED ODDS 1:6			

1	John Cena	1.25	3.00
2	Undertaker	1.00	2.50
3	Rey Mysterio	.60	1.50
4	Yoshi Tatsu	.25	.60
5	The Miz	.40	1.00
6	Big Show	.60	1.50
7	Shawn Michaels	1.50	4.00
8	Triple H	1.25	3.00
9	Carlito	.60	1.50
10	Jack Swagger	.25	.60

2010 Topps WWE Rumble Pack Hidden Images

COMPLETE SET (10)		4.00	10.00
STATED ODDS 1:6			
1	John Cena	1.25	3.00
2	MVP	.40	1.00
3	Undertaker	1.00	2.50
4	Evan Bourne	.25	.60
5	CM Punk	1.00	2.50
6	Triple H	1.25	3.00
7	Christian	.40	1.00
8	Kane	.60	1.50
9	Chris Jericho	.60	1.50
10	Rey Mysterio	.60	1.50

2010 Topps WWE Rumble Pack Pop-Ups

COMPLETE SET (9)		3.00	8.00
STATED ODDS 1:4			
1	John Cena	1.00	2.50
2	Sheamus	.30	.75
3	Undertaker	.75	2.00
4	Triple H	1.00	2.50
5	Evan Bourne	.20	.50
6	Randy Orton	.75	2.00
7	John Morrison	.25	.60
8	The Miz	.30	.75
9	Edge	.75	2.00

2010 Topps WWE Rumble Pack Stickers

COMPLETE SET (30)		6.00	15.00
STATED ODDS 2:1			
1	John Cena	.75	2.00
2	John Cena	.75	2.00
3	John Cena	.75	2.00
4	Triple H	.75	2.00
5	Triple H	.75	2.00
6	Triple H	.75	2.00
7	Undertaker	.60	1.50
8	Undertaker	.60	1.50
9	Undertaker	.60	1.50
10	Rey Mysterio	.40	1.00
11	Rey Mysterio	.40	1.00
12	Rey Mysterio	.40	1.00
13	Edge	.60	1.50
14	Edge	.60	1.50
15	Edge	.60	1.50
16	Batista	.60	1.50
17	Batista	.60	1.50
18	Batista	.60	1.50
19	Shawn Michaels	1.00	2.50
20	Shawn Michaels	1.00	2.50
21	Shawn Michaels	1.00	2.50
22	CM Punk	.60	1.50
23	CM Punk	.60	1.50
24	CM Punk	.60	1.50
25	Randy Orton	.60	1.50
26	Randy Orton	.60	1.50
27	Randy Orton	.60	1.50
28	Kane	.40	1.00
29	Kofi Kingston	.25	.60
30	DX CL	1.00	2.50

2010 Topps WWE Rumble Pack Tattoos

COMPLETE SET (10)		5.00	12.00
STATED ODDS 1:6			
1	Kofi Kingston/Randy Orton	1.00	2.50
2	Christian/William Regal	.60	1.50
3	Triple H/Edge	1.25	3.00
4	Kane/Big Show	.60	1.50
5	Batista/The Undertaker	1.00	2.50
6	MVP/Jack Swagger	.40	1.00
7	Shawn Michaels/Chris Jericho	1.50	4.00
8	Rey Mysterio/CM Punk	1.00	2.50
9	John Morrison/The Miz	.40	1.00
10	John Cena/Sheamus	1.25	3.00

2018 Topps WWE Shawn Michaels Tribute

1	Shawn Michaels	1.25	3.00
2	Shawn Michaels	1.25	3.00
3	Shawn Michaels	1.25	3.00
4	Shawn Michaels	1.25	3.00
5	Shawn Michaels	1.25	3.00
6	Shawn Michaels	1.25	3.00
7	Shawn Michaels	1.25	3.00
8	Shawn Michaels	1.25	3.00
9	Shawn Michaels	1.25	3.00
10	Shawn Michaels	1.25	3.00
11	Shawn Michaels	1.25	3.00
12	Shawn Michaels	1.25	3.00
13	Shawn Michaels	1.25	3.00
14	Shawn Michaels	1.25	3.00
15	Shawn Michaels	1.25	3.00
16	Shawn Michaels	1.25	3.00
17	Shawn Michaels	1.25	3.00
18	Shawn Michaels	1.25	3.00
19	Shawn Michaels	1.25	3.00
20	Shawn Michaels	1.25	3.00
21	Shawn Michaels	1.25	3.00
22	Shawn Michaels	1.25	3.00
23	Shawn Michaels	1.25	3.00
24	Shawn Michaels	1.25	3.00
25	Shawn Michaels	1.25	3.00
26	Shawn Michaels	1.25	3.00
27	Shawn Michaels	1.25	3.00
28	Shawn Michaels	1.25	3.00
29	Shawn Michaels	1.25	3.00
30	Shawn Michaels	1.25	3.00
31	Shawn Michaels	1.25	3.00
32	Shawn Michaels	1.25	3.00
33	Shawn Michaels	1.25	3.00
34	Shawn Michaels	1.25	3.00
35	Shawn Michaels	1.25	3.00
36	Shawn Michaels	1.25	3.00
37	Shawn Michaels	1.25	3.00
38	Shawn Michaels	1.25	3.00
39	Shawn Michaels	1.25	3.00
40	Shawn Michaels	1.25	3.00

2018 Topps WWE Shawn Michaels Tribute Topps Heritage WWE Autographs and Relics

SMA1	Shawn Michaels AU	30.00	75.00
SMR1	Shawn Michaels RELIC	8.00	20.00
SMAR1	Shawn Michaels AU RELIC	60.00	120.00

2018 Topps WWE Shawn Michaels Tribute Topps WWE Road to WrestleMania Autographs and Relics

SM	Shawn Michaels AU	30.00	75.00
SMR	Shawn Michaels RELIC	10.00	25.00
SMAR	Shawn Michaels AU RELIC	50.00	100.00

2020 Topps WWE Signature Performance Autographs

*BLUE/25: UNPRICED DUE TO SCARCITY
*RED/10: UNPRICED DUE TO SCARCITY
*ORANGE/5: UNPRICED DUE TO SCARCITY
*GOLD/1: UNPRICED DUE TO SCARCITY
STATED PRINT RUN 50 SER.#'d SETS

NNO	Drew McIntyre	50.00	100.00

2008 Topps WWE Slam Attax

COMPLETE SET (172)		15.00	40.00
1	John Cena CH	1.25	3.00
2	Edge CH	.75	2.00
3	Chavo Guerrero CH	.30	.75
4	Matt Hardy CH	.75	2.00
5	Chris Jericho CH	.50	1.25
6	Triple H CH	1.25	3.00
7	Jeff Hardy CH	.75	2.00
8	Rey Mysterio CH	.50	1.25
9	Randy Orton CH	.50	1.25
10	CM Punk CH	.20	.50
11	William Regal CH	.50	1.25
12	Batista CH	.75	2.00
13	Shawn Michaels CH	1.25	3.00
14	Beth Phoenix CH	1.00	2.50
15	Kofi Kingston CH	.50	1.25
16	Undertaker CH	1.00	2.50
17	Montel Vontavious Porter FM	.30	.75
18	Kane FM	.75	2.00
19	Mr. Kennedy FM	.50	1.25
20	Big Show FM	.50	1.25
21	Carlito FM	.50	1.25
22	D-Generation X FM	.60	1.50
23	The Hardys FM	.75	2.00
24	Cryme Tyme FM	.25	.60
25	Umaga FM	.30	.75
26	JBL FM	.20	.50
27	Mark Henry FM	.30	.75
28	John Morrison FM	.20	.50
29	The Great Khali FM	.20	.50
30	Snitsky FM	.30	.75
31	Shelton Benjamin FM	.20	.50
32	Stone Cold Steve Austin FM	1.25	3.00
33	Mickie James FM	1.25	3.00
34	Finlay FM	.30	.75
35	Vladimir Kozlov FM	.20	.50
36	WWE Championship TC	.20	.50
37	Intercontinental Championship TC	.20	.50
38	Women's Championship TC	.20	.50
39	World Tag Team Championship TC	.20	.50
40	World Heavyweight Championship TC	.20	.50
41	United States Championship TC	.20	.50
42	WWE Tag Team Championship TC	.20	.50
43	WWE Diva Championship TC	.20	.50
44	ECW Championship TC	.20	.50
45	WWE Money in the Bank Briefcase TC	.20	.50
46	Deuce	.20	.50
47	Kofi Kingston	.50	1.25
48	JBL	.20	.50
49	Charlie Haas	.20	.50
50	Ron Simmons	.20	.50
51	CM Punk	.20	.50
52	Chuck Palumbo	.30	.75
53	William Regal	.50	1.25
54	Paul Burchill	.20	.50
55	Rey Mysterio	.50	1.25
56	Snitsky	.30	.75
57	Paul London	.20	.50
58	Chris Jericho	.50	1.25
59	Val Venis	.25	.60
60	Jerry Lawler	.40	1.00
61	Ted DiBiase Jr.	.50	1.25
62	Stone Cold Steve Austin	1.25	3.00
63	Hacksaw Jim Duggan	.50	1.25
64	Todd Grisham	.20	.50
65	Jamie Noble	.20	.50
66	Batista	.75	2.00
67	D'Lo Brown	.30	.75
68	Santino Marella	.20	.50
69	Shawn Michaels	1.25	3.00
70	Michael Cole	.20	.50
71	John Cena	1.25	3.00
72	JTG	.20	.50
73	Shad	.20	.50
74	Randy Orton	.50	1.25
75	Lance Cade	.20	.50
76	Hardcore Holly	.30	.75
77	Cody Rhodes	.20	.50
78	Kane	.75	2.00
79	Mike Adamle	.20	.50
80	Ezekiel Jackson	.20	.50
81	Montel Vontavious Porter	.30	.75
82	Funaki	.20	.50
83	Undertaker	1.00	2.50
84	DH Smith	.20	.50
85	Gregory Helms	.25	.60
86	Jeff Hardy	.75	2.00
87	Vladimir Kozlov	.20	.50
88	The Great Khali	.20	.50
89	Jesse	.20	.50
90	Festus	.20	.50
91	Edge	.75	2.00
92	Carlito	.50	1.25
93	Vickie Guerrero	.25	.60
94	Kenny Dykstra	.30	.75
95	Mr. Kennedy	.50	1.25
96	Shelton Benjamin	.20	.50
97	Triple H	1.25	3.00
98	Justin Roberts	.20	.50
99	Jimmy Wang Yang	.20	.50
100	Curt Hawkins	.20	.50
101	Zack Ryder	.20	.50
102	Brian Kendrick	.30	.75
103	Big Show	.50	1.25
104	Jim Ross	.40	1.00
105	Umaga	.30	.75
106	Tazz	.30	.75
107	John Morrison	.20	.50
108	Tommy Dreamer	.20	.50
109	Mike Knox	.20	.50
110	Super Crazy	.30	.75

#	Name	Lo	Hi
111	Boogeyman	.30	.75
112	Mark Henry	.30	.75
113	Chavo Guerrero	.30	.75
114	Tony Chimel	.20	.50
115	Finlay	.30	.75
116	Bam Neely	.20	.50
117	Matt Hardy	.75	2.00
118	Armando Estrada	.20	.50
119	Elijah Burke	.20	.50
120	Hornswoggle	.30	.75
121	The Miz	.30	.75
122	Ricky Ortiz	.20	.50
123	Evan Bourne	.20	.50
124	Theodore Long	.25	.60
125	Matt Striker	.20	.50
126	Natalya DV	.40	1.00
127	Eve DV	.40	1.00
128	Maria DV	.75	2.00
129	Tiffany DV	.30	.75
130	Katie Lea Burchill DV	.25	.60
131	Kelly Kelly DV	.75	2.00
132	Layla DV	.50	1.25
133	Beth Phoenix DV	1.00	2.50
134	Candice DV	1.00	2.50
135	Lilian Garcia DV	.50	1.25
136	Lena Yada DV	.25	.60
137	Victoria DV	1.00	2.50
138	Melina DV	.75	2.00
139	Maryse DV	.75	2.00
140	Michelle McCool DV	1.00	2.50
141	Jillian DV	.75	2.00
142	Mickie James DV	1.25	3.00
143	Kane & Undertaker	1.00	2.50
144	The Bushwhackers	.25	.60
145	Curt Hawkins & Zack Ryder	.20	.50
146	Finlay & Hornswoggle	.30	.75
147	Chris Jericho & Lance Cade	.50	1.25
148	Cody Rhodes & Ted Dibiase	.50	1.25
149	John Morrison & The Miz	.30	.75
150	The Hardys TT	.75	2.00
151	Jesse & Festus TT	.20	.50
152	Cryme Tyme TT	.25	.60
153	D-Generation X TT	.60	1.50
154	Chavo Guerrero / Bam Neely TT	.30	.75
155	Sgt. Slaughter HOF	.50	1.25
156	The Mouth of the South Jimmy Hart HOF	.30	.75
157	Cowboy Bob Orton HOF	.50	1.25
158	The Iron Sheik HOF	.75	2.00
159	Rowdy Roddy Piper HOF	.75	2.00
160	Pat Patterson HOF	.20	.50
161	Gerald Brisco HOF	.20	.50
162	Junkyard Dog HOF	.30	.75
163	Dusty Rhodes HOF	.50	1.25
164	Jimmy Superfly Snuka	.50	1.25
165	Tony Atlas HOF	.20	.50
166	Bobby The Brain Heenan	.50	1.25
167	Superstar Billy Graham	.25	.60
168	Gorilla Monsoon L	.50	1.25
169	Nikolai Volkoff L	.30	.75
170	Curt Hennig L	.50	1.25
171	Vader L	.30	.75
172	Stone Cold Steve Austin L	1.25	3.00

2010 Topps WWE Slam Attax

		Lo	Hi
COMPLETE SET (130)		12.00	30.00
UNOPENED BOX (24 PACKS)			
UNOPENED PACK (8 CARDS)			

#	Name	Lo	Hi
1	Kofi Kingston	.20	.50
2	Carlito	.30	.75
3	Primo	.12	.30
4	Jerry Lawler	.20	.50
5	Ted DiBiase	.20	.50
6	Jim Duggan	.20	.50
7	Festus	.12	.30
8	Chris Masters	.12	.30
9	Hornswoggle	.20	.50
10	Jamie Noble	.12	.30
11	Mark Henry	.20	.50
12	Justin Roberts	.12	.30
13	Santino Marella	.12	.30
14	Shawn Michaels	.75	2.00
15	Jack Swagger	.12	.30
16	Michael Cole	.12	.30
17	The Miz	.20	.50
18	Triple H	.60	1.50
19	Chavo Guerrero	.20	.50
20	Evan Bourne	.12	.30
21	Big Show	.30	.75
22	Montel Vontavious Porter	.20	.50
23	John Cena	.60	1.50
24	Randy Orton	.50	1.25
25	Cody Rhodes	.12	.30
26	Eve	.50	1.25
27	Melina	.50	1.25
28	Alicia Fox	.20	.50
29	Kelly Kelly	.50	1.25
30	Gail Kim	.30	.75
31	Jillian	.50	1.25
32	Maryse	.50	1.25
33	Sheamus	.20	.50
34	Brie Bella	.50	1.25
35	Nikki Bella	.50	1.25
36	Kung Fu Naki	.12	.30
37	Undertaker	.50	1.25
38	Charlie Haas	.12	.30
39	Kane	.30	.75
40	CM Punk	.50	1.25
41	Dolph Ziggler	.20	.50
42	Rey Mysterio	.30	.75
43	Chris Jericho	.30	.75
44	The Great Khali	.12	.30
45	Slam Master J	.12	.30
46	Matt Hardy	.30	.75
47	Edge	.50	1.25
48	JTG	.12	.30
49	Shad	.12	.30
50	David Hart Smith	.12	.30
51	Tyson Kidd	.12	.30
52	Mike Knox	.12	.30
53	R-Truth	.12	.30
54	John Morrison	.20	.50
55	Finlay	.20	.50
56	Beth Phoenix	.50	1.25
57	Batista	.50	1.25
58	Theodore Long	.12	.30
59	Todd Grisham	.12	.30
60	Ranjin Singh	.12	.30
61	Jimmy Wang Yang	.12	.30
62	Curt Hawkins	.12	.30
63	Jim Ross	.12	.30
64	Natalya	.50	1.25
65	Michelle McCool	.50	1.25
66	Mickie James	.60	1.50
67	Layla	.30	.75
68	Maria	.50	1.25
69	Tommy Dreamer	.12	.30
70	The Hurricane	.12	.30
71	Vladimir Kozlov	.20	.50
72	Tony Chimel	.12	.30
73	Ezekiel Jackson	.12	.30
74	Shelton Benjamin	.12	.30
75	Josh Mathews	.12	.30
76	William Regal	.30	.75
77	Paul Burchill	.12	.30
78	Gabriel	.12	.30
79	Goldust	.20	.50
80	Zack Ryder	.12	.30
81	Yoshi Tatsu	.12	.30
82	Abraham Washington	.12	.30
83	Tyler Reks	.12	.30
84	Savannah	.20	.50
85	Matt Striker	.12	.30
86	Christian	.20	.50
87	Rosa Mendes	.20	.50
88	Katie Lea Burchill	.30	.75
89	Tiffany	.20	.50
90	C.Rhodes/T.DiBiase	.20	.50
91	Cryme Tyme	.12	.30
92	D.Smith/T.Kidd	.12	.30
93	S.Benjamin/C.Haas	.12	.30
94	C.Jericho/Big Show	.30	.75
95	M.Henry/Hornswoggle	.20	.50
96	Iron Sheik	.30	.75
97	Ted DiBiase	.20	.50
98	Jake Roberts	.30	.75
99	Koko B. Ware	.20	.50
100	British Bulldog	.20	.50
101	Sgt. Slaughter	.30	.75
102	Rick Rude	.20	.50
103	Bam Bam Bigelow	.20	.50
104	Junkyard Dog	.30	.75
105	Roddy Piper	.50	1.25
106	Paul Orndorff	.30	.75
107	Jimmy Snuka	.30	.75
108	Nikolai Volkoff	.20	.50
109	Dusty Rhodes	.30	.75
110	Bobby Heenan	.20	.50
111	Hillbilly Jim	.20	.50
112	Curt Hennig	.20	.50
113	Bob Orton	.20	.50
114	Jerry Lawler	.20	.50
115	Earthquake	.20	.50
116	TLC Match	.12	.30
117	Steel Cage Match	.12	.30
118	Hell in a Cell Match	.12	.30
119	Stretcher Match	.12	.30
120	Casket Match	.12	.30
121	Royal Rumble	.12	.30
122	No Way Out	.12	.30
123	WrestleMania	.12	.30
124	Backlash	.12	.30
125	Judgement Day	.12	.30
126	Extreme Rules	.12	.30
127	The Bash	.12	.30
128	Night Of Champions	.12	.30
129	Summerslam	.12	.30
130	Survivor Series	.12	.30

2010 Topps WWE Slam Attax Champions

		Lo	Hi
COMPLETE SET (16)		8.00	20.00
STATED ODDS 1:5			
1	John Cena	2.00	5.00
2	Edge	1.50	4.00
3	Matt Hardy	1.00	2.50
4	Chris Jericho	1.00	2.50
5	Triple H	2.00	5.00
6	Rey Mysterio	1.00	2.50
7	Randy Orton	1.50	4.00
8	CM Punk	1.50	4.00
9	Batista	1.50	4.00
10	C.Jericho/Big Show	1.00	2.50
11	Michelle McCool	1.50	4.00
12	Kofi Kingston	.60	1.50
13	Christian	.60	1.50
14	Montel Vontavious Porter	.60	1.50
15	Maryse	1.50	4.00
16	Undertaker	1.50	4.00

2010 Topps WWE Slam Attax Finishing Moves

		Lo	Hi
COMPLETE SET (19)		6.00	15.00
STATED ODDS 1:6			
1	Kane	.75	2.00
2	Cody Rhodes	.30	.75
3	Ted DiBiase	.50	1.25
4	Shawn Michaels	2.00	5.00
5	John Morrison	.50	1.25
6	Carlito	.75	2.00
7	Beth Phoenix	1.25	3.00
8	Jack Swagger	.30	.75
9	Mark Henry	.50	1.25
10	Tommy Dreamer	.30	.75
11	Evan Bourne	.30	.75
12	The Great Khali	.30	.75
13	Chavo Guerrero	.50	1.25
14	Melina	1.25	3.00
15	Finlay	.50	1.25
16	Big Show	.75	2.00
17	Shelton Benjamin	.30	.75
18	R-Truth	.30	.75
19	Maria	1.25	3.00

2010 Topps WWE Slam Attax Props

		Lo	Hi
COMPLETE SET (10)		5.00	12.00
STATED ODDS 1:5			
1	Steel Chair	.75	2.00
2	Sledgehammer	.75	2.00
3	Table	.75	2.00
4	Trash Can	.75	2.00
5	Ladder	.75	2.00
6	Steel Steps	.75	2.00
7	Ring Bell	.75	2.00
8	Brass Knuckles	.75	2.00
9	Shillelagh	.75	2.00
10	Kendo Stick	.75	2.00

2010 Topps WWE Slam Attax Starter Box Exclusives

		Lo	Hi
COMPLETE SET (5)		6.00	15.00
STATED ODDS ONE PER STARTER BOX			
1	Chris Jericho	1.25	3.00
2	Undertaker	2.00	5.00
3	Randy Orton	2.00	5.00
4	Triple H	2.50	6.00
5	John Cena	2.50	6.00

2010 Topps WWE Slam Attax Titles

		Lo	Hi
COMPLETE SET (11)		5.00	12.00
STATED ODDS 1:6			

#	Card	Lo	Hi
1	WWE Championship	.75	2.00
2	Intercontinental Championship	.75	2.00
3	Women's Championship	.75	2.00
4	Word Tag Team Championship	.75	2.00
5	World Heavyweight Championship	.75	2.00
6	United States Championship	.75	2.00
7	WWE Tag Team Championship	.75	2.00
8	WWE Divas Championship	.75	2.00
9	ECW Championship	.75	2.00
10	WWE Money in the Bank Briefcase	.75	2.00
11	WWE Slammy Award	.75	2.00

2010 Topps WWE Slam Attax WrestleMania XXVI

COMPLETE SET (5) — 6.00 — 15.00
ONE SET PER WRESTLEMANIA XXVI TIN

#	Card	Lo	Hi
1	Chris Jericho	1.00	2.50
2	John Cena	2.00	5.00
3	Randy Orton	1.50	4.00
4	Triple H	2.00	5.00
5	Undertaker	1.50	4.00

2021 Topps WWE Slam Attax

COMPLETE SET (368) — 100.00 — 200.00

#	Card	Lo	Hi
1	Adam Cole	.60	1.50
2	AJ Styles	.60	1.50
3	Akira Tozawa	.25	.60
4	Aleister Black	.50	1.25
5	Alexa Bliss	1.25	3.00
6	Alexander Wolfe	.20	.50
7	Aliyah	.40	1.00
8	August Grey	.20	.50
9	Angel Garza	.25	.60
10	Angelo Dawkins	.25	.60
11	Apollo Crews	.25	.60
12	Ariya Daivari	.25	.60
13	Arturo Ruas	.20	.50
14	Asuka	.75	2.00
15	Austin Theory	.40	1.00
16	Bayley	.50	1.25
17	Becky Lynch	.75	2.00
18	Bianca Belair	.50	1.25
19	Big E	.50	1.25
20	Billie Kay	.40	1.00
21	Bo Dallas	.20	.50
22	Boa	.20	.50
23	Bobby Fish	.25	.60
24	Bobby Lashley	.50	1.25
25	Braun Strowman	.50	1.25
26	Bronson Reed	.25	.60
27	Cameron Grimes	.40	1.00
28	Candice LeRae	.75	2.00
29	Carmella	.50	1.25
30	Cedric Alexander	.20	.50
31	Cesaro	.20	.50
32	Chad Gable	.20	.50
33	Charlotte Flair	1.00	2.50
34	Chelsea Green	.50	1.25
35	Dabba Kato	.25	.60
36	Dakota Kai	.40	1.00
37	Damian Priest	.30	.75
38	Dana Brooke	.20	.50
39	Daniel Bryan	.75	2.00
40	Danny Burch	.25	.60
41	Dave Mastiff	.20	.50
42	Dexter Lumis	.20	.50
43	Dolph Ziggler	.40	1.00
44	Dominik Mysterio	.25	.60
45	Drew Gulak	.25	.60
46	Drew McIntyre	.50	1.25
47	Edge	.75	2.00
48	Elias	.20	.50
49	Ember Moon	.25	.60
50	Erik	.20	.50
51	Fabian Aichner	.25	.60
52	Fandango	.30	.75
53	Finn Balor	.50	1.25
54	Flash Morgan	.25	.60
55	Gran Metalik	.20	.50
56	Humberto Carrillo	.20	.50
57	Ilja Dragunov	.20	.50
58	Indi Hartwell	.60	1.50
59	Io Shirai	.40	1.00
60	Isaiah "Swerve" Scott	.30	.75
61	Ivar	.20	.50
62	Jake Atlas	.20	.50
63	James Drake	.20	.50
64	Jaxson Ryker	.20	.50
65	Jeff Hardy	.50	1.25
66	Jessamyn Duke	.20	.50
67	Jey Uso	.20	.50
68	Jimmy Uso	.20	.50
69	Jinder Mahal	.25	.60
70	Joaquin Wilde	.30	.75
71	Joe Coffey	.20	.50
72	John Morrison	.40	1.00
73	Johnny Gargano	.40	1.00
74	Jordan Devlin	.20	.50
75	Kacy Catanzaro	.40	1.00
76	Kalisto	.25	.60
77	Kane	.30	.75
78	Karrion Kross	.75	2.00
79	Kay Lee Ray	.50	1.25
80	Kayden Carter	.40	1.00
81	Keith Lee	.40	1.00
82	Kevin Owens	.40	1.00
83	Killian Dain	.20	.50
84	King Corbin	.20	.50
85	Kofi Kingston	.50	1.25
86	Kona Reeves	.20	.50
87	Kushida	.30	.75
88	Kyle O'Reilly	.30	.75
89	Lacey Evans	.75	2.00
90	Lana	.25	.60
91	Leon Ruff	.20	.50
92	Lince Dorado	.20	.50
93	Liv Morgan	.75	2.00
94	Mace	.20	.50
95	Mandy Rose	1.00	2.50
96	Mansoor	.20	.50
97	Marcel Barthel	.25	.60
98	Marina Shafir	.40	1.00
99	Mark Andrews	.20	.50
100	Mark Coffey	.20	.50
101	Mercedes Martinez	.30	.75
102	Montez Ford	.20	.50
103	Murphy	.25	.60
104	Mustafa Ali	.25	.60
105	MVP	.20	.50
106	Naomi	.25	.60
107	Nash Carter	.20	.50
108	Natalya	.30	.75
109	Nia Jax	.40	1.00
110	Nikki Cross	.40	1.00
111	Noam Dar	.25	.60
112	Oney Lorcan	.20	.50
113	Otis	.25	.60
114	Pete Dunne	.50	1.25
115	Peyton Royce	.40	1.00
116	Piper Niven	.30	.75
117	R-Truth	.25	.60
118	Randy Orton	.60	1.50
119	Raquel Gonzalez	.75	2.00
120	Raul Mendoza	.30	.75
121	Reckoning	.25	.60
122	Rey Mysterio	.50	1.25
123	Rhea Ripley	.75	2.00
124	Ricochet	.30	.75
125	Riddick Moss	.25	.60
126	Riddle	.50	1.25
127	Rinku	.20	.50
128	Robert Roode	.25	.60
129	Roderick Strong	.40	1.00
130	Roman Reigns	1.00	2.50
131	Ruby Riott	.40	1.00
132	Sami Zayn	.20	.50
133	Samir Singh	.20	.50
134	Santos Escobar	.40	1.00
135	Sasha Banks	1.00	2.50
136	Saurav	.20	.50
137	Scarlett	1.00	2.50
138	Seth Rollins	.50	1.25
139	Shayna Baszler	.50	1.25
140	Sheamus	.30	.75
141	Shelton Benjamin	.30	.75
142	Shinsuke Nakamura	.50	1.25
143	Shotzi Blackheart	1.00	2.50
144	Slapjack	.20	.50
145	Sunil Singh	.20	.50
146	T-Bar	.25	.60
147	Tamina	.20	.50
148	Tegan Nox	.50	1.25
149	The Brian Kendrick	.20	.50
150	The Fiend Bray Wyatt	.75	2.00
151	The Miz	.30	.75
152	Timothy Thatcher	.20	.50
153	Tomasso Ciampa	.50	1.25
154	Toni Storm	.75	2.00
155	Tony Nese	.20	.50
156	Trent Seven	.25	.60
157	Tucker	.20	.50
158	Tyler Bate	.25	.60
159	Tyler Breeze	.25	.60
160	Tyler Rust	.20	.50
161	Vanessa Borne	.25	.60
162	Velveteen Dream	.25	.60
163	Walter	.60	1.50
164	Wes Lee	.20	.50
165	Wesley Blake	.20	.50
166	Wolfgang	.20	.50
167	Xavier Woods	.20	.50
168	Xia Lee	.40	1.00
169	Zack Gibson	.20	.50
170	Ariya Daivari & Tony Nese TT	.25	.60
171	Asuka & Charlotte TT	1.00	2.50
172	Breezango TT	.30	.75
173	Cesaro & Daniel Bryan TT	.75	2.00
174	Dakota Kai & Raquel TT	.40	1.00
175	Danny Burch & Oney Lorcan TT	.25	.60
176	Elias & Jaxson TT	.20	.50
177	Ever Rise TT	.25	.60
178	Flash Morgan Webster & Mark Andrews TT	.25	.60
179	Alpha Academy TT	.25	.60
180	Gallus TT	.25	.60
181	Grizzled Young Veterans TT	.20	.50
182	The Hurt Business TT	.30	.75
183	Imperium TT	.25	.60
184	Indus Sher TT	.20	.50
185	Kacy Catanzaro & Kayden Carter TT	.40	1.00
186	Kushida & Leon Ruff TT	.30	.75
187	Legado Del Fantasma TT	.25	.60
188	Mandy Rose & Dana Brooke TT	1.00	2.50
189	Moustache Mountain TT	.25	.60
190	MSK TT	.20	.50
191	Retribution TT	.25	.60
192	Shayna Baszler & Nia Jax TT	.50	1.25
193	Shotzi Blackheart & Ember Moon TT	1.00	2.50
194	The Bollywood Boys TT	.20	.50
195	The Dirty Dawgs TT	.40	1.00
196	The Lucha House Party TT	.20	.50
197	The Miz & John Morrison TT	.40	1.00
198	The New Day TT	.40	1.00
199	The Riott Squad TT	.30	.75
200	The Robert Stone Brand TT	.20	.50
201	The Street Profits TT	.25	.60
202	The Viking Raiders TT	.20	.50
203	The Way TT	.20	.50
204	Tomasso Ciampa & Timothy Thatcher TT	.50	1.25
205	The Way FAC	.20	.50
206	The Hurt Business FAC	.30	.75
207	Imperium FAC	.25	.60
208	Retribution FAC	.25	.60
209	Styles Clash	.60	1.50
210	Twisted Bliss	1.25	3.00
211	Bayley-to-Belly	.50	1.25
212	Big Ending	.50	1.25
213	The Hurt Lock	.50	1.25
214	Powerslam	.50	1.25
215	Figure-Eight Leg-Lock	1.00	2.50
216	Claymore	.50	1.25
217	Moonsault	.40	1.00
218	Uso Splash	.20	.50
219	RKO	.60	1.50
220	Riptide	.75	2.00
221	Spear	1.00	2.50
222	Brogue Kick	.30	.75
223	Sister Abigail	.75	2.00
224	Skull-Crushing Finale	.30	.75
225	Sasha Banks	1.00	2.50
226	Sasha Banks	1.00	2.50
227	Sasha Banks	1.00	2.50
228	Riddle	.50	1.25
229	Riddle	.50	1.25
230	Riddle	.50	1.25
231	Mankind	.30	.75
232	Stone Cold Steve Austin	1.00	2.50
233	Hulk Hogan	1.00	2.50
234	The Rock	1.25	3.00
235	Universal Championship	.15	.40
236	WWE Championship	.15	.40
237	RAW Women's Championship	.15	.40
238	SmackDown Women's Championship	.15	.40
239	Intercontinental Championship	.15	.40
240	United States Championship	.15	.40
241	24/7 Championship	.15	.40
242	RAW Tag Team Championship	.15	.40
243	SmackDown Championship	.15	.40
244	WWE Women's Tag Team Championship	.15	.40

#	Card	Low	High
245	NXT Championship	.15	.40
246	NXT Women's Championship	.15	.40
247	NXT North American Championship	.15	.40
248	NXT Cruiserweight Championship	.15	.40
249	NXT Tag Team Championship	.15	.40
250	NXT UK Championship	.15	.40
251	NXT UK Women's Championship	.15	.40
252	NXT UK Tag Team Championship	.15	.40
253	AJ Styles	.60	1.50
254	Alexa Bliss	1.25	3.00
255	Charlotte Flair	1.00	2.50
256	Drew McIntyre	.50	1.25
257	Randy Orton	.60	1.50
258	The Fiend Bray Wyatt	.75	2.00
259	Bayley	.50	1.25
260	Bianca Belair	.50	1.25
261	Daniel Bryan	.75	2.00
262	Kevin Owens	.40	1.00
263	Roman Reigns	1.00	2.50
264	Sasha Banks	1.00	2.50
265	Adam Cole	.60	1.50
266	Finn Balor	.50	1.25
267	Io Shirai	.40	1.00
268	Karrion Kross	.75	2.00
269	Pete Dunne	.50	1.25
270	Toni Storm	.75	2.00
271	Flash Morgan Webster	.25	.60
272	Ilja Dragunov	.20	.50
273	Kay Lee Ray	.50	1.25
274	Trent Seven	.25	.60
275	Walter	.60	1.50
276	Wolfgang	.20	.50
277	Thank You Taker	1.00	2.50
278	Thank You Taker	1.00	2.50
279	Thank You Taker	1.00	2.50
280	Thank You Taker	1.00	2.50
281	Thank You Taker	1.00	2.50
282	Daniel Bryan	.75	2.00
283	Ricochet	.30	.75
284	Shotzi Blackheart	1.00	2.50
285	WWE Logo	.15	.40
286	RAW Logo	.15	.40
287	SmackDown Logo	.15	.40
288	NXT Logo	.15	.40
289	NXT UK Logo	.15	.40
290	Andre the Giant L	2.50	6.00
291	Batista L	.40	1.00
292	Bret "Hit Man" Hart L	.50	1.25
293	Hulk Hogan L	1.00	2.50
294	Macho Man Randy Savage L	1.25	3.00
295	Mankind L	.30	.75
296	Ric Flair L	.75	2.00
297	Stone Cold Steve Austin L	1.00	2.50
298	Trish Stratus L	1.00	2.50
299	Ultimate Warrior L	1.25	3.00
300	Apollo Crews	.25	.60
301	Bianca Belair	.50	1.25
302	Big E	.50	1.25
303	Billie Kay	.40	1.00
304	Cesaro	.20	.50
305	Damien Priest	.30	.75
306	Jey Uso	.20	.50
307	Liv Morgan	.75	2.00
308	Rhea Ripley	.75	2.00
309	Riddle	.50	1.25
310	Firefly Funhouse Logo	.15	.40
311	Mercy the Buzzard	.15	.40
312	Huskus the Pig Boy	.15	.40
313	Abby the Witch	.15	.40

#	Card	Low	High
314	Ramblin' Rabbit	.15	.40
315	The Boss	1.00	2.50
316	Friendship Frog	.15	.40
317	Apollo Crews	.25	.60
318	Bayley	.50	1.25
319	Braun Strowman	.50	1.25
320	Sheamus	.30	.75
321	Asuka	.75	2.00
322	Cesaro	.20	.50
323	Kevin Owens	.40	1.00
324	Seth Rollins	.50	1.25
325	Drew McIntyre	.50	1.25
326	Mandy Rose	1.00	2.50
327	Montez Ford	.20	.50
328	Roman Reigns	1.00	2.50
329	Dominik Mysterio	.25	.60
330	Keith Lee	.40	1.00
331	Riddle	.50	1.25
332	Shayna Baszler	.50	1.25
333	Angelo Dawkins	.25	.60
334	Bobby Lashley	.50	1.25
335	Sami Zayn	.30	.75
336	Shinsuke Nakamura	.50	1.25
337	AJ Styles	.60	1.50
338	Lacey Evans	.75	2.00
339	Lana	.25	.60
340	The Miz	.30	.75
341	Big E	.50	1.25
342	Cedric Alexander	.20	.50
343	Daniel Bryan	.75	2.00
344	Randy Orton	.60	1.50
345	Bianca Belair	.50	1.25
346	Billie Kay	.40	1.00
347	Edge	.75	2.00
348	Rhea Ripley	.75	2.00
349	Asuka ICON	.75	2.00
350	Bayley ICON	.50	1.25
351	Becky Lynch ICON	.75	2.00
352	Charlotte Flair ICON	1.00	2.50
353	Daniel Bryan ICON	.75	2.00
354	Kofi Kingston ICON	.50	1.25
355	Randy Orton ICON	.60	1.50
356	Seth Rollins ICON	.50	1.25
357	Hollywood Hulk Hogan SR	1.00	2.50
358	Alexa Bliss 100C	1.25	3.00
359	Bianca Belair 100C	.50	1.25
360	Drew McIntyre 100C	.50	1.25
361	Bobby Lashley 100C	.50	1.25
362	Sasha Banks 100C	1.00	2.50
363	The Fiend Bray Wyatt 100C	.75	2.00
364	Edge 100C	.75	2.00
365	Roman Reigns 100C	1.00	2.50
366	Alexa Bliss/Firefly Funhouse	1.25	3.00
367	Bray Wyatt/Firefly Funhouse	.75	2.00
368	John Cena nWo UR	1.00	2.50

2021 Topps WWE Slam Attax Autographs

RANDOMLY INSERTED INTO PACKS

#	Card	Low	High
AT1	Adam Cole		
AT2	Alexa Bliss		
AT3	Becky Lynch		
AT4	Bianca Belair		
AT5	Billie Kay		
AT6	The Fiend Bray Wyatt		
AT7	Candice LeRae		
AT8	Carmella	30.00	75.00
AT9	Cesaro		
AT10	Elias		
AT11	Ember Moon		
AT12	Finn Balor		
AT13	Flash Morgan Webster		
AT14	Io Shirai		
AT15	Kevin Owens		
AT17	Mark Coffey		
AT18	Mustafa Ali		
AT19	Finn Balor		
AT20	Riddle	60.00	120.00
AT21	Ruby Riott		
AT22	Pete Dunne		
AT23	Rhea Ripley		
AT24	Sasha Banks		
AT25	Shinsuke Nakamura		
AT26	Shotzi Blackheart		
AT27	The Miz	15.00	40.00
AT28	Tommaso Ciampa	25.00	60.00
AT29	Wolfgang		
AT30	Xavier Woods	15.00	40.00
AT34	Keith Lee	15.00	40.00
AT35	Lacey Evans	25.00	60.00
AT37	Asuka	50.00	100.00
AT38	Bayley		
AT39	Charlotte Flair		
AT40	Naomi	12.00	30.00
AT41	Natalya	20.00	50.00
AT42	Nikki Cross	20.00	50.00
AT43	Peyton Royce	30.00	75.00
AT44	Trish Stratus	50.00	100.00
FINDDREW	Drew McIntyre/99		

2021 Topps WWE Slam Attax Boneyard Match Relics

STATED PRINT RUN 200 SER.#'d SETS

#	Card	Low	High
BY1	Undertaker vs. AJ Styles	50.00	100.00

2021 Topps WWE Slam Attax Champion Edition

STATED PRINT RUN 100 SER.#'d SETS

#	Card	Low	High
NNO	Nikki A.S.H.	15.00	40.00
NNO	Reggie	4.00	10.00
NNO	Roman Reigns	12.00	30.00

2021 Topps WWE Slam Attax The Impossible Autographs

AT31	The Fiend/Alexa Bliss
AT32	John Cena
AT33	Roman Reigns

2021 Topps WWE Slam Attax Limited Edition Bronze

RANDOMLY INSERTED INTO PACKS

#	Card	Low	High
LE3B	The Fiend Bray Wyatt	2.00	5.00
LE4B	Alexa Bliss	2.50	6.00
LE5B	Roman Reigns	2.00	5.00

2021 Topps WWE Slam Attax Limited Edition Gold

#	Card	Low	High
COMPLETE SET (24)		75.00	150.00

RANDOMLY INSERTED INTO PACKS

#	Card	Low	High
LE1G	Drew McIntyre	1.50	4.00
LE2G	Sasha Banks	3.00	8.00
LE3G	The Fiend Bray Wyatt	4.00	10.00
LE4G	Alexa Bliss	6.00	15.00
LE5G	Roman Reigns	4.00	10.00
LE6G	Bianca Belair	2.00	5.00
LE7G	AJ Styles	2.50	6.00
LE8G	Billie Kay	2.00	5.00
LE9G	Big E	1.50	4.00
LE10G	Daniel Bryan	2.50	6.00
LE11G	Keith Lee	1.50	4.00
LE12G	Liv Morgan	2.00	5.00
LE13G	Riddle	3.00	8.00
LE14G	Charlotte Flair	3.00	8.00
LE15G	Bobby Lashley	2.00	5.00
LE16G	Seth Rollins	1.50	4.00
LE17G	Rhea Ripley	2.50	6.00
LE18G	Becky Lynch	4.00	10.00
LE19G	The Rock	6.00	15.00
LE20G	John Cena	4.00	10.00
LE21G	Randy Orton	3.00	8.00
LE22G	Mandy Rose	4.00	10.00
LE23G	Sami Zayn	1.50	4.00
LE24G	Bayley	15.00	40.00

2021 Topps WWE Slam Attax Limited Edition Platinum Blue

RANDOMLY INSERTED INTO PACKS

#	Card	Low	High
LE3R	The Fiend Bray Wyatt	10.00	25.00
LE4R	Alexa Bliss	20.00	50.00
LE5R	Roman Reigns	10.00	25.00

2021 Topps WWE Slam Attax Limited Edition Silver

RANDOMLY INSERTED INTO PACKS

#	Card	Low	High
LE3S	The Fiend Bray Wyatt	3.00	8.00
LE4S	Alexa Bliss	5.00	12.00
LE5S	Roman Reigns	3.00	8.00

2021 Topps WWE Slam Attax Oversized

#	Card	Low	High
COMPLETE SET (20)		30.00	75.00
OV1	Roman Reigns	4.00	10.00
OV2	Hulk Hogan	4.00	10.00
OV3	Batista	1.50	4.00
OV4	Bret "Hit Man" Hart	2.00	5.00
OV5	Stone Cold Steve Austin	4.00	10.00
OV6	Becky Lynch	3.00	8.00
OV7	Drew McIntyre	2.00	5.00
OV8	Trish Stratus	4.00	10.00
OV9	Ultimate Warrior	5.00	12.00
OV10	Ric Flair	3.00	8.00
OV11	Karrion Kross	3.00	8.00
OV12	The Fiend Bray Wyatt	3.00	8.00
OV13	Alexa Bliss	5.00	12.00
OV14	Apollo Crews	1.00	2.50
OV15	Kevin Owens	1.50	4.00
OV16	Bianca Belair	2.00	5.00
OV17	Asuka	3.00	8.00
OV18	Cesaro	.75	2.00
OV19	Sasha Banks	4.00	10.00
OV20	Big E	2.00	5.00

2021 Topps WWE Slam Attax SP

STATED PRINT RUN 100 SER.#'d SETS

#	Card	Low	High
NNO	The Fiend Bray Wyatt	12.00	30.00
NNO	Lilly	8.00	20.00
NNO	Omos	6.00	15.00

2021 Topps WWE Slam Attax Tactic Cards

#	Card	Low	High
COMPLETE SET (4)		3.00	8.00

RANDOMLY INSERTED INTO PACKS

T1 Ladder	1.00	2.50
T2 Table	1.00	2.50
T3 Steel Chair	1.00	2.50
T4 Special Counsel Paul Heyman	1.00	2.50

2021 Topps WWE Slam Attax Women of WWE

COMPLETE SET (32)	10.00	25.00
RANDOMLY INSERTED INTO PACKS		
W1 Alexa Bliss	1.50	4.00
W2 Asuka	1.00	2.50
W3 Bayley	.60	1.50
W4 Becky Lynch	1.00	2.50
W5 Bianca Belair	.60	1.50
W6 Billie Kay	.50	1.25
W7 Candice LeRae	1.00	2.50
W8 Carmella	.60	1.50
W9 Charlotte Flair	1.25	3.00
W10 Dakota Kai	.50	1.25
W11 Dana Brooke	.25	.60
W12 Ember Moon	.30	.75
W13 Io Shirai	.50	1.25
W14 Kacy Catanzaro	.50	1.25
W15 Kay Lee Ray	.60	1.50
W16 Lacey Evans	1.00	2.50
W17 Lana	.30	.75
W18 Liv Morgan	1.00	2.50
W19 Mandy Rose	1.25	3.00
W20 Naomi	.30	.75
W21 Natalya	.40	1.00
W22 Nia Jax	.50	1.25
W23 Nikki Cross	.50	1.25
W24 Peyton Royce	.50	1.25
W25 Piper Niven	.40	1.00
W26 Rhea Ripley	1.00	2.50
W27 Ruby Riott	.50	1.25
W28 Sasha Banks	1.25	3.00
W29 Scarlett	1.25	3.00
W30 Shayna Baszler	.60	1.50
W31 Tamina	.25	.60
W32 Toni Storm	1.00	2.50

2018 Topps WWE Slam Attax Live!

COMPLETE SET (392)	25.00	60.00
1 Alexa Bliss FOIL	1.00	2.50
2 Baron Corbin FOIL	.30	.75
3 Bobby Roode FOIL	.30	.75
4 Braun Strowman FOIL	.50	1.25
5 Elias FOIL	.50	1.25
6 Finn Balor FOIL	.50	1.25
7 John Cena FOIL	.75	2.00
8 Kevin Owens FOIL	.50	1.25
9 Nia Jax FOIL	.30	.75
10 Roman Reigns FOIL	.50	1.25
11 Sami Zayn FOIL	.20	.50
12 Seth Rollins FOIL	.50	1.25
13 AJ Styles FOIL	.75	2.00
14 Rusev FOIL	.30	.75
15 Asuka FOIL	.60	1.50
16 Bludgeon Brothers FOIL	.30	.75
17 Carmella FOIL	.40	1.00
18 Charlotte Flair FOIL	.60	1.50
19 Jeff Hardy FOIL	.40	1.00
20 The Miz FOIL	.40	1.00
21 Rusev FOIL	.30	.75
22 Samoa Joe FOIL	.40	1.00
23 Shinsuke Nakamura FOIL	.50	1.25

24 The Usos FOIL	.30	.75
25 Adam Cole FOIL	.25	.60
26 Aleister Black FOIL	.25	.60
27 Kairi Sane FOIL	.50	1.25
28 Pete Dunne FOIL	.20	.50
29 Roderick Strong FOIL	.20	.50
30 Shayna Baszler FOIL	.50	1.25
31 Undisputed Era FOIL	.25	.60
32 Cedric Alexander FOIL	.20	.50
33 Alexa Bliss/Nia Jax FOIL	1.00	2.50
34 Bray Wyatt/Woken Matt Hardy FOIL	.50	1.25
35 Roman Reigns/Jinder Mahal FOIL	.50	1.25
36 Seth Rollins/Finn Balor FOIL	.50	1.25
37 AJ Styles/Nakamura FOIL	.75	2.00
38 Asuka/Charlotte Flair FOIL	.60	1.50
39 Bobby Roode/Randy Orton FOIL	.50	1.25
40 Daniel Bryan/The Miz FOIL	.50	1.25
41 Adam Cole/Velveteen Dream FOIL	.25	.60
42 Andrade/Aleister Black FOIL	.30	.75
43 Ember Moon/Shayna Baszler FOIL	.50	1.25
44 Bret Hart/Shawn Michaels FOIL	.60	1.50
45 Ric Flair/Chris Jericho FOIL	.60	1.50
46 Trish Stratus/Lita FOIL	.75	2.00
47 Undertaker/Kane FOIL	.75	2.00
48 X-Pac/Shane McMahon FOIL	.40	1.00
49 1-2-3 Kid	.25	.60
50 Braun Strowman	.50	1.25
51 Bret Hit Man Hart	.50	1.25
52 Chris Jericho	.50	1.25
53 Chris Jericho	.50	1.25
54 D-Generation X	.60	1.50
55 Daniel Bryan	.50	1.25
56 Daniel Bryan	.50	1.25
57 Finn Balor	.50	1.25
58 Jeff Hardy	.40	1.00
59 John Cena	.75	2.00
60 John Cena & Shawn Michaels	.75	2.00
61 Kane	.30	.75
62 Mark Henry	.25	.60
63 The Miz	.40	1.00
64 Paige	.50	1.25
65 Randy Orton	.50	1.25
66 Ric Flair	.60	1.50
67 Roman Reigns	.50	1.25
68 Sasha Banks	.60	1.50
69 Seth Rollins	.50	1.25
70 Shane McMahon	.40	1.00
71 Stephanie McMahon	.40	1.00
72 Sting	.50	1.25
73 Stone Cold Steve Austin	1.00	2.50
74 Stone Cold Steve Austin	1.00	2.50
75 Stone Cold Steve Austin	1.00	2.50
76 The Rock	1.00	2.50
77 Trish Stratus & Lita	.75	2.00
78 Ultimate Warrior	.75	2.00
79 Undertaker & Triple H	.75	2.00
80 Yokozuna	.25	.60
81 Akam	.20	.50
82 Alexa Bliss	1.00	2.50
83 Alicia Fox	.30	.75
84 Apollo Crews	.20	.50
85 Baron Corbin	.30	.75
86 Bayley	.30	.75
87 Big Show	.20	.50
88 Bo Dallas	.20	.50
89 Bobby Roode	.30	.75
90 Braun Strowman	.50	1.25
91 Bray Wyatt	.50	1.25

92 Chad Gable	.20	.50
93 Charly Caruso	.30	.75
94 Corey Graves	.25	.60
95 Curt Hawkins	.20	.50
96 Curtis Axel	.20	.50
97 Dana Brooke	.40	1.00
98 Dash Wilder	.25	.60
99 David Otunga	.25	.60
100 Dean Ambrose	.40	1.00
101 Drew McIntyre	.30	.75
102 Elias	.50	1.25
103 Ember Moon	.40	1.00
104 Fandango	.20	.50
105 Finn Balor	.50	1.25
106 Goldust	.40	1.00
107 Heath Slater	.20	.50
108 Jason Jordan	.20	.50
109 Jinder Mahal	.25	.60
110 John Cena	.75	2.00
111 Jojo	.20	.50
112 Jonathan Coachman	.20	.50
113 Kane	.30	.75
114 Kevin Owens	.50	1.25
115 Konnor	.20	.50
116 Kurt Angle	.50	1.25
117 Bobby Lashley	.40	1.00
118 Liv Morgan	.40	1.00
119 Maryse	.40	1.00
120 Woken Matt Hardy	.50	1.25
121 Michael Cole	.20	.50
122 Mickie James	.40	1.00
123 Mike Kanellis	.20	.50
124 Mike Rome	.20	.50
125 Mojo Rawley	.20	.50
126 Natalya	.25	.60
127 Nia Jax	.30	.75
128 No Way Jose	.25	.60
129 Renee Young	.30	.75
130 Rezar	.20	.50
131 Rhyno	.20	.50
132 Roman Reigns	.50	1.25
133 Ronda Rousey	1.00	2.50
134 Ruby Riott	.30	.75
135 Sami Zayn	.20	.50
136 Sarah Logan	.20	.50
137 Sasha Banks	.60	1.50
138 Scott Dawson	.25	.60
139 Seth Rollins	.50	1.25
140 Stephanie McMahon	.40	1.00
141 Titus O'Neil	.20	.50
142 Triple H	.50	1.25
143 Tyler Breeze	.20	.50
144 Viktor	.20	.50
145 Zack Ryder	.20	.50
146 Aiden English	.20	.50
147 AJ Styles	.75	2.00
148 Alexander Wolfe	.20	.50
149 Andrade Cien Almas	.30	.75
150 Asuka	.60	1.50
151 Becky Lynch	.50	1.25
152 Big Cass	.25	.60
153 Big E	.25	.60
154 Billie Kay	.40	1.00
155 Byron Saxton	.20	.50
156 Carmella	.40	1.00
157 Cesaro	.40	1.00
158 Charlotte Flair	.60	1.50
159 Chris Jericho	.50	1.25

160 Daniel Bryan	.50	1.25
161 Dasha Fuentes	.30	.75
162 Eric Young	.25	.60
163 Greg Hamilton	.30	.75
164 Harper	.30	.75
165 Jeff Hardy	.40	1.00
166 Jey Uso	.20	.50
167 Jimmy Uso	.20	.50
168 Karl Anderson	.20	.50
169 Killian Dain	.25	.60
170 Kofi Kingston	.25	.60
171 Lana	.50	1.25
172 Luke Gallows	.25	.60
173 Mandy Rose	.50	1.25
174 Maria Kanellis	.50	1.25
175 The Miz	.40	1.00
176 Naomi	.25	.60
177 Nikki Bella	.40	1.00
178 Paige	.50	1.25
179 Peyton Royce	.50	1.25
180 R-Truth	.25	.60
181 Randy Orton	.50	1.25
182 Rowan	.30	.75
183 Rusev	.30	.75
184 Samir Singh	.20	.50
185 Samoa Joe	.40	1.00
186 Shane McMahon	.40	1.00
187 Sheamus	.40	1.00
188 Shelton Benjamin	.25	.60
189 Shinsuke Nakamura	.50	1.25
190 Sin Cara	.25	.60
191 Sonya Deville	.40	1.00
192 Sunil Singh	.20	.50
193 Tamina	.20	.50
194 Tom Phillips	.20	.50
195 Tye Dillinger	.20	.50
196 Xavier Woods	.25	.60
197 Zelina Vega	.20	.50
198 Adam Cole	.25	.60
199 Aleister Black	.25	.60
200 Aliyah	.30	.75
201 Angelo Dawkins	.20	.50
202 Bianca Belair	.25	.60
203 Bobby Fish	.20	.50
204 Buddy Murphy	.25	.60
205 Cezar Bononi	.20	.50
206 Danny Burch	.20	.50
207 EC3	.20	.50
208 Fabian Aichner	.20	.50
209 Johnny Gargano	.20	.50
210 Kairi Sane	.50	1.25
211 Kassius Ohno	.20	.50
212 Kyle O'Reilly	.25	.60
213 Lacey Evans	.25	.60
214 Lars Sullivan	.20	.50
215 Lio Rush	.20	.50
216 Mauro Ranallo	.20	.50
217 Montez Ford	.20	.50
218 Nick Miller	.20	.50
219 Nigel McGuinness	.20	.50
220 Nikki Cross	.30	.75
221 Oney Lorcan	.25	.60
222 Otis Dozovic	.20	.50
223 Percy Watson	.20	.50
224 Pete Dunne	.20	.50
225 Ricochet	.40	1.00
226 Riddick Moss	.20	.50
227 Roderick Strong	.20	.50

228	Shane Thorne	.20	.50
229	Shayna Baszler	.50	1.25
230	Taynara Conti	.20	.50
231	Tino Sabatelli	.25	.60
232	Tommaso Ciampa	.20	.50
233	Trent Seven	.20	.50
234	Tucker Knight	.20	.50
235	Tyler Bate	.20	.50
236	Vanessa Borne	.20	.50
237	Velveteen Dream	.20	.50
238	Wesley Blake	.25	.60
239	William Regal	.30	.75
240	Akira Tozawa	.30	.75
241	Ariya Daivari	.20	.50
242	The Brian Kendrick	.30	.75
243	Cedric Alexander	.20	.50
244	Drake Maverick	.25	.60
245	Drew Gulak	.20	.50
246	Gentleman Jack Gallagher	.25	.60
247	Gran Metalik	.20	.50
248	Hideo Itami	.20	.50
249	Kalisto	.20	.50
250	Lince Dorado	.20	.50
251	Mustafa Ali	.20	.50
252	Neville	.30	.75
253	Noam Dar	.20	.50
254	TJP	.25	.60
255	Tony Nese	.20	.50
256	Alundra Blayze	.20	.50
257	Andre the Giant	.40	1.00
258	Bam Bam Bigelow	.30	.75
259	Batista	.30	.75
260	Beth Phoenix	.40	1.00
261	Big Boss Man	.20	.50
262	Billy Gunn	.25	.60
263	Bob Backlund	.20	.50
264	Bobby The Brain Heenan	.30	.75
265	Booker T	.30	.75
266	Bret Hit Man Hart	.50	1.25
267	British Bulldog	.30	.75
268	Bruno Sammartino	.30	.75
269	Chief Jay Strongbow	.30	.75
270	Classy Freddie Blassie	.20	.50
271	Cowboy Bob Orton	.20	.50
272	D'Lo Brown	.20	.50
273	Dean Malenko	.20	.50
274	Diamond Dallas Page	.30	.75
275	Dusty Rhodes	.40	1.00
276	Eddie Guerrero	.50	1.25
277	Edge	.50	1.25
278	Eve	.40	1.00
279	The Godfather	.20	.50
280	Hacksaw Jim Duggan	.20	.50
281	Harley Race	.20	.50
282	Honky Tonk Man	.20	.50
283	Howard Finkel	.20	.50
284	Iron Sheik	.20	.50
285	Irwin R. Schyster	.20	.50
286	Jake The Snake Roberts	.25	.60
287	Jerry The King Lawler	.40	1.00
288	Jim The Anvil Neidhart	.30	.75
289	Jimmy Hart	.30	.75
290	Junkyard Dog	.20	.50
291	Ken Shamrock	.25	.60
292	Kevin Nash	.40	1.00
293	Lex Luger	.25	.60
294	Lita	.50	1.25
295	Macho Man Randy Savage	.60	1.50

296	Magnificent Don Muraco	.20	.50
297	Mark Henry	.25	.60
298	Mean Gene Okerlund	.25	.60
299	Million Dollar Man Ted DiBiase	.25	.60
300	Mr. Perfect Curt Hennig	.25	.60
301	Mr. Wonderful Paul Orndorff	.20	.50
302	Norman Smiley	.20	.50
303	Papa Shango	.20	.50
304	Paul Bearer	.30	.75
305	Prince Albert	.20	.50
306	Psycho Sid	.20	.50
307	Ravishing Rick Rude	.25	.60
308	Razor Ramon	.40	1.00
309	Ric Flair	.60	1.50
310	Ricky The Dragon Steamboat	.30	.75
311	Rikishi	.20	.50
312	Road Dogg	.20	.50
313	The Rock	1.00	2.50
314	Rowdy Roddy Piper	.50	1.25
315	Sgt. Slaughter	.25	.60
316	Shawn Michaels	.60	1.50
317	Sting	.50	1.25
318	Stone Cold Steve Austin	1.00	2.50
319	Tatanka	.20	.50
320	Trish Stratus	.75	2.00
321	Ultimate Warrior	.75	2.00
322	Umaga	.20	.50
323	Undertaker	.75	2.00
324	Viscera	.20	.50
325	X-Pac	.25	.60
326	Yokozuna	.25	.60
327	The Ascension	.20	.50
328	Authors of Pain	.20	.50
329	Bray Wyatt & Woken Matt Hardy	.50	1.25
330	Breezango	.20	.50
331	Heath Slater & Rhyno	.20	.50
332	The Miztourage	.40	1.00
333	The Revival	.25	.60
334	The Riott Squad	.40	1.00
335	The Shield	.50	1.25
336	Titus Worldwide	.40	1.00
337	Absolution	.50	1.25
338	The Bar	.40	1.00
339	Bludgeon Brothers	.30	.75
340	Gallows & Anderson	.25	.60
341	The New Day	.30	.75
342	Rusev Day	.30	.75
343	The Iiconics	.50	1.25
344	SanitY	.30	.75
345	The Singh Brothers	.25	.60
346	The Usos	.30	.75
347	Danny Burch & Oney Lorcan	.25	.60
348	Heavy Machinery	.20	.50
349	Moustache Mountain	.20	.50
350	Riddick Moss & Tino Sabbatelli	.25	.60
351	The Street Profits	.20	.50
352	TM-61	.20	.50
353	Undisputed Era	.25	.60
354	Bushwhackers		.50
355	D-Generation X	.60	1.50
356	Nasty Boys	.20	.50
357	nWo	.40	1.00
358	WWE Title	.20	.50
359	Intercontinental Title	.20	.50
360	RAW Women's Title	.20	.50
361	WWE UK Title	.20	.50
362	SmackDown Women's Title	.20	.50
363	NXT Title	.20	.50

364	WWE Universal Title	.20	.50
365	NXT Women's Title	.20	.50
366	RAW Tag Team Title	.20	.50
367	SmackDown Tag Team Title	.20	.50
368	United States Title	.20	.50
369	WWE Cruiserweight Title	.20	.50
370	NXT Tag Team Title	.20	.50
371	Puzzle	.50	1.25
372	Puzzle	.75	2.00
373	Puzzle	.30	.75
374	Puzzle	.50	1.25
375	Puzzle	1.00	2.50
376	Puzzle	.50	1.25
377	Puzzle	.40	1.00
378	Puzzle	.75	2.00
379	Puzzle	.50	1.25
380	Puzzle	.50	1.25
381	Puzzle	.75	2.00
382	Puzzle	.60	1.50
383	Puzzle	1.00	2.50
384	Puzzle	1.00	2.50
385	Puzzle	.75	2.00
386	Puzzle	.20	.50
387	Puzzle	.20	.50
388	Puzzle	.20	.50
389	Steel Chair	.20	.50
390	Table	.20	.50
391	Ladder	.20	.50
392	Trash Can	.20	.50

2018 Topps WWE Slam Attax Live! Authentic Ring Mat Memorabilia

RMAA	John Cena & Nikki Bella		
RMAB	Triple H & Stephanie McMahon		
RMAC	Seth Rollins		
RMBA	The Usos		
RMBB	Carmella		
RMBC	Baron Corbin		
RMCA	Sasha Banks		
RMCB	Braun Strowman		
RMCC	AJ Styles		
RMDA	Kurt Angle		
RMDB	The Miz		
RMDC	Dean Ambrose/Seth Rollins		
RMEA	Charlotte Flair		
RMEB	Alexa Bliss		
RMEC	Finn Balor		
RMFA	Shinsuke Nakamura		
RMFB	Kevin Owens		
RMFC	Asuka		
RMGA	Drew McIntyre		
RMGB	Braun Strowman		
RMGC	Andrade Cien Almas		
RMHA	Undisputed Era		
RMHB	Velveteen Dream		
RMHC	Kairi Sane		
RMIA	Aleister Black		
RMIB	Adam Cole		
RMIC	Ember Moon		
RMJA	Finn Balor		
RMJB	Elias		
RMJC	Jason Jordan		

2018 Topps WWE Slam Attax Live! Authentic T-Shirt Memorabilia

TS1	AJ Styles
TS3	Bayley
TS5	John Cena

TS7	Karl Anderson
TS9	Roman Reigns
TS10	Sami Zayn
TS11	Tye Dillinger

2018 Topps WWE Slam Attax Live! Collector Cards

CC1	Bret Hit Man Hart
CC2	Eddie Guerrero
CC3	Shawn Michaels
CC4	Sting
CC5	Stone Cold Steve Austin
CC6	Ultimate Warrior

2018 Topps WWE Slam Attax Live! Gold Limited Edition

LEPA	Roman Reigns
LEPB	Daniel Bryan
LEPC	Andrade Cien Almas
LEPD	Sasha Banks
LEPE	Asuka
LEPF	Seth Rollins
LEPG	John Cena
LEPH	Kevin Owens

2018 Topps WWE Slam Attax Live! Silver Limited Edition

LEMB	Braun Strowman
LEMC	Adam Cole
LEMD	Charlotte Flair
LEMF	Randy Orton
LESA	Ronda Rousey

2010 Topps WWE Slam Attax Mayhem

COMPLETE SET (161)	12.00	30.00
UNOPENED BOX (24 PACKS)		
UNOPENED PACK (8 CARDS)		

1	Chris Jericho	.30	.75
2	David Hart Smith	.12	.30
3	Edge	.50	1.25
4	Evan Bourne	.12	.30
5	Ezekiel Jackson	.12	.30
6	Goldust	.20	.50
7	Jerry Lawler	.20	.50
8	Jay Uso	.12	.30
9	Jimmy Uso	.12	.30
10	John Cena	.60	1.50
11	John Morrison	.20	.50
12	Justin Roberts	.12	.30
13	Mark Henry	.20	.50
14	Michael Cole	.12	.30
15	Primo	.12	.30
16	R-Truth	.12	.30
17	Randy Orton	.50	1.25
18	Ranjin Singh	.12	.30
19	Santino Marella	.12	.30
20	Sheamus	.20	.50
21	Ted DiBiase	.20	.50
22	The Great Khali	.12	.30
23	The Miz	.20	.50
24	Triple H	.60	1.50
25	Tyson Kidd	.12	.30
26	Vladimir Kozlov	.20	.50
27	William Regal	.30	.75
28	Yoshi Tatsu	.12	.30
29	Zack Ryder	.12	.30

30 Alicia Fox	.20	.50
31 Brie Bella	.50	1.25
32 Eve	.50	1.25
33 Gail Kim	.30	.75
34 Jillian	.50	1.25
35 Maryse	.50	1.25
36 Melina	.50	1.25
37 Natalya	.50	1.25
38 Nikki Bella	.50	1.25
39 Tamina	.12	.30
40 Big Show	.30	.75
41 Caylen Croft	.12	.30
42 Chavo Guerrero	.20	.50
43 Chris Masters	.12	.30
44 Christian	.20	.50
45 CM Punk	.50	1.25
46 Cody Rhodes	.12	.30
47 Curt Hawkins	.12	.30
48 Dolph Ziggler	.20	.50
49 Drew McIntyre	.20	.50
50 Finlay	.20	.50
51 Hornswoggle	.20	.50
52 Jack Swagger	.12	.30
53 JTG	.12	.30
54 Kane	.30	.75
55 Kofi Kingston	.20	.50
56 Luke Gallows	.12	.30
57 Matt Hardy	.30	.75
58 Matt Striker	.12	.30
59 Montel Vontavious Porter	.20	.50
60 Rey Mysterio	.30	.75
61 Shad	.12	.30
62 Theodore Long	.12	.30
63 Todd Grisham	.12	.30
64 Tony Chimel	.12	.30
65 Trent Barreta	.12	.30
66 Tyler Reks	.12	.30
67 Undertaker	.50	1.25
68 Vance Archer	.12	.30
69 Beth Phoenix	.50	1.25
70 Kelly Kelly	.50	1.25
71 Layla	.30	.75
72 Michelle McCool	.50	1.25
73 Rosa Mendes	.20	.50
74 Serena	.20	.50
75 Darren Young	.20	.50
76 David Otunga	.20	.50
77 Heath Slater	.20	.50
78 Justin Gabriel	.20	.50
79 Michael Tarver	.20	.50
80 Skip Sheffield	.20	.50
81 Wade Barrett	.20	.50
82 Alex Riley	.12	.30
83 Husky Harris	.25	.60
84 Kaval	.12	.30
85 Lucky Cannon	.12	.30
86 Eli Cottonwood	.12	.30
87 Michael McGillicutty	.12	.30
88 Percy Watson	.12	.30
89 Titus O'Neil	.12	.30
90 Jamie Keyes	.12	.30
91 David Hart Smith/Tyson Kidd	.12	.30
92 Trent Barreta/Caylen Croft	.12	.30
93 Chris Jericho/The Miz	.30	.75
94 Montel Vontavious Porter/JTG	.20	.50
95 Curt Hawkins/Vance Archer	.12	.30
96 William Regal/Vladimir Kozlov	.30	.75
97 THE USO Brothers	.12	.30
98 Iron Sheik	.30	.75

99 Jake The Snake Roberts	.30	.75
100 Koko B. Ware	.20	.50
101 British Bulldog	.20	.50
102 Sgt. Slaughter	.30	.75
103 Ravishing Rick Rude	.20	.50
104 Bam Bam Bigelow	.20	.50
105 Junkyard Dog	.30	.75
106 Ted DiBiase	.20	.50
107 Rowdy Roddy Piper	.50	1.25
108 Mr. Wonderful Paul Orndorff	.30	.75
109 Jimmy Superfly Snuka	.30	.75
110 Nikolai Volkoff	.20	.50
111 Dusty Rhodes	.30	.75
112 Bobby The Brain Heenan	.20	.50
113 Hillbilly Jim	.20	.50
114 Mr. Perfect Curt Hennig	.20	.50
115 Barry Windham	.20	.50
116 Cowboy Bob Orton	.20	.50
117 Jerry The King Lawler	.20	.50
118 Earthquake	.20	.50
119 Ricky Dragon Steamboat	.20	.50
120 Vader	.20	.50
121 Gorilla Monsoon	.12	.30
122 Terry Funk	.30	.75
123 IRS	.12	.30
124 Yokozuna	.12	.30
125 Steel Chair	.12	.30
126 Sledgehammer	.12	.30
127 Table	.12	.30
128 Trash Can	.12	.30
129 Ladder	.12	.30
130 Steel Steps	.12	.30
131 Ring Bell	.12	.30
132 Brass Knuckles	.12	.30
133 Baseball Bat	.12	.30
134 Handcuffs	.12	.30
135 Fire Extinguisher	.12	.30
136 Announcers Table	.12	.30
137 Steel Pipe	.12	.30
138 Microphone	.12	.30
139 Steel Cage Match	.12	.30
140 Hell in a Cell Match	.12	.30
141 Stretcher Match	.12	.30
142 Casket Match	.12	.30
143 Elimination Chamber Match	.12	.30
144 Ambulance Match	.12	.30
145 Backstage Brawl	.12	.30
146 Royal Rumble	.12	.30
147 Elimination Chamber	.12	.30
148 WrestleMania XXVI	.12	.30
149 Extreme Rules	.12	.30
150 WWE Over The Limit	.12	.30
151 Fatal 4 Way	.12	.30
152 Money In The Bank	.12	.30
153 SummerSlam	.12	.30
154 Night Of Champions	.12	.30
155 Hell In A Cell	.12	.30
156 WWE Bragging Rights	.12	.30
157 TLC:Tables, Ladders and Chairs	.12	.30
158 John Cena	.60	1.50
159 The Miz	.20	.50
160 Undertaker	.50	1.25
161 Rey Mysterio	.30	.75

2010 Topps WWE Slam Attax Mayhem Champions

COMPLETE SET (16) 8.00 20.00
STATED ODDS 1:6

1 Jack Swagger	.40	1.00
2 Drew McIntyre	.60	1.50
3 John Cena	2.00	5.00
4 The Miz	.60	1.50
5 David Hart Smith/Tyson Kidd	.40	1.00
6 Eve	1.50	4.00
7 Layla	1.00	2.50
8 Triple H	2.00	5.00
9 Randy Orton	1.50	4.00
10 Chris Jericho	1.00	2.50
11 Undertaker	1.50	4.00
12 Big Show	1.00	2.50
13 Edge	1.50	4.00
14 Sheamus	.60	1.50
15 Melina	1.50	4.00
16 Kofi Kingston	.60	1.50

2010 Topps WWE Slam Attax Mayhem Finishing Moves

COMPLETE SET (26) 10.00 25.00
STATED ODDS

1 Chavo Guerrero	.50	1.25
2 Chris Masters	.30	.75
3 Christian	.50	1.25
4 Dolph Ziggler	.50	1.25
5 Kane	.75	2.00
6 Luke Gallows	.30	.75
7 Matt Hardy	.75	2.00
8 Montel Vontavious Porter	.50	1.25
9 Undertaker	1.25	3.00
10 Evan Bourne	.30	.75
11 Mark Henry	.50	1.25
12 Rey Mysterio	.75	2.00
13 R-Truth	.30	.75
14 Ted DiBiase	.50	1.25
15 The Great Khali	.30	.75
16 The Miz	.50	1.25
17 Zack Ryder	.30	.75
18 Edge	1.25	3.00
19 Randy Orton	1.25	3.00
20 John Cena	1.50	4.00
21 John Morrison	.50	1.25
22 Jack Swagger	.30	.75
23 Beth Phoenix	1.25	3.00
24 Michelle McCool	1.25	3.00
25 Maryse	1.25	3.00
26 Gail Kim	.75	2.00

2010 Topps WWE Slam Attax Mayhem General Managers

COMPLETE SET (6) 2.50 6.00
STATED ODDS 1:6

1 T.Long/You're Kicked Out	.75	2.00
2 T.Long/You're Kicked Out	.75	2.00
3 T.Long/You're Kicked Out	.75	2.00
4 T.Long/Return to the Ring	.75	2.00
5 T.Long/Return to the Ring	.75	2.00
6 T.Long/Return to the Ring	.75	2.00

2010 Topps WWE Slam Attax Mayhem Starter Box Exclusives

COMPLETE SET (3) 2.50 6.00
STATED ODDS ONE PER STARTER BOX

1 Montel Vontavious Porter	.75	2.00
2 Triple H	2.50	6.00
3 Drew McIntyre	.75	2.00

2010 Topps WWE Slam Attax Mayhem Titles

COMPLETE SET (10) 5.00 12.00
STATED ODDS

1 WWE Championship	.75	2.00
2 Intercontinental Championship	.75	2.00
3 Women's Championship	.75	2.00
4 World Tag Team Championship	.75	2.00
5 World Heavyweight Championship	.75	2.00
6 United States Championship	.75	2.00
7 WWE Tag Team Championship	.75	2.00
8 WWE Divas Championship	.75	2.00
9 WWE Money in the Bank Briefcase	.75	2.00
10 WWE Slammy Award	.75	2.00

2020 Topps WWE Slam Attax Reloaded

COMPLETE SET (352) 20.00 50.00

1 Akam	.40	1.00
2 Akira Tozawa	.30	.75
3 Aleister Black	.60	1.50
4 Andrade	.50	1.25
5 Angel Garza	.40	1.00
6 Angelo Dawkins	.30	.75
7 Apollo Crews	.40	1.00
8 Asuka	1.25	3.00
9 Becky Lynch	1.25	3.00
10 Bianca Belair	.75	2.00
11 Big Show	.40	1.00
12 Billie Kay	.60	1.50
13 Bobby Lashley	.60	1.50
14 Cedric Alexander	.30	.75
15 Charlotte Flair	1.25	3.00
16 Drew McIntyre	.60	1.50
17 Edge	.60	1.50
18 Erik	.30	.75
19 Humberto Carrillo	.50	1.25
20 Ivar	.30	.75
21 Jason Jordan	.30	.75
22 Jinder Mahal	.30	.75
23 Kairi Sane	.60	1.50
24 Kevin Owens	.40	1.00
25 Liv Morgan	.75	2.00
26 Montez Ford	.30	.75
27 Murphy	.40	1.00
28 Natalya	.50	1.25
29 Nia Jax	.50	1.25
30 Peyton Royce	.60	1.50
31 R-Truth	.30	.75
32 Randy Orton	.75	2.00
33 Rey Mysterio	.60	1.50
34 Rezar	.30	.75
35 Ricochet	.50	1.25
36 Shayna Baszler	1.00	2.50
37 Ruby Riott	.50	1.25
38 Samoa Joe	.50	1.25
39 Seth Rollins	.60	1.50
40 Shelton Benjamin	.40	1.00
41 Titus O'Neil	.30	.75
42 Undertaker	1.25	3.00
43 Zelina Vega	.60	1.50
44 AJ Styles	1.00	2.50
45 Alexa Bliss	2.00	5.00
46 Bayley	.60	1.50
47 Big E	.30	.75
48 Bo Dallas	.30	.75
49 Braun Strowman	.75	2.00

50	Carmella	.75	2.00
51	Cesaro	.30	.75
52	Dana Brooke	.50	1.25
53	Daniel Bryan	1.00	2.50
54	Dolph Ziggler	.30	.75
55	Elias	.30	.75
56	Ember Moon	.60	1.50
57	Goldberg	1.25	3.00
58	Gran Metalik	.30	.75
59	Jaxson Ryker	.40	1.00
60	Jeff Hardy	.75	2.00
61	Jey Uso	.30	.75
62	Jimmy Uso	.30	.75
63	John Morrison	.30	.75
64	Kalisto	.30	.75
65	Kane	.40	1.00
66	King Corbin	.40	1.00
67	Kofi Kingston	.50	1.25
68	Lacey Evans	.75	2.00
69	Lars Sullivan	.30	.75
70	Lince Dorado	.30	.75
71	Mandy Rose	1.50	4.00
72	Maryse	.60	1.50
73	Mickie James	.50	1.25
74	Mojo Rawley	.30	.75
75	Mustafa Ali	.50	1.25
76	Naomi	.60	1.50
77	Nikki Cross	.60	1.50
78	Otis	.50	1.25
79	Robert Roode	.30	.75
80	Roman Reigns	.75	2.00
81	Sami Zayn	.40	1.00
82	Sasha Banks	1.50	4.00
83	Sheamus	.40	1.00
84	Shinsuke Nakamura	.60	1.50
85	Shorty G	.30	.75
86	Sonya Deville	.75	2.00
87	Steve Cutler	.30	.75
88	Tamina	.40	1.00
89	The Fiend Bray Wyatt	1.00	2.50
90	The Miz	.50	1.25
91	Tucker	.30	.75
92	Wesley Blake	.40	1.00
93	Xavier Woods	.30	.75
94	Adam Cole	.75	2.00
95	Aliyah	.60	1.50
96	Arturo Ruas	.30	.75
97	Mercedes Martinez	.50	1.25
98	Boa	.30	.75
99	Bobby Fish	.30	.75
100	Bronson Reed	.30	.75
101	Cameron Grimes	.30	.75
102	Candice LeRae	1.00	2.50
103	Chelsea Green	1.50	4.00
104	Dakota Kai	.60	1.50
105	Damian Priest	.30	.75
106	Danny Burch	.40	1.00
107	Dexter Lumis	.30	.75
108	Dominik Dijakovic	.30	.75
109	Fandango	.30	.75
110	Finn Balor	.75	2.00
111	Io Shirai	.50	1.25
112	Isaiah Swerve Scott	.40	1.00
113	Jessamyn Duke	.50	1.25
114	Joaquin Wilde	.30	.75
115	Johnny Gargano	.60	1.50
116	Kacy Catanzaro	.60	1.50
117	Karrion Kross	.60	1.50
118	Keith Lee	.30	.75
119	Killian Dain	.40	1.00
120	Kona Reeves	.30	.75
121	Kushida	.40	1.00
122	Kyle O'Reilly	.40	1.00
123	Mansoor	.30	.75
124	Marina Shafir	.50	1.25
125	Matt Riddle	.60	1.50
126	Mia Yim	.60	1.50
127	Pete Dunne	.30	.75
128	Racquel Gonzalez	.50	1.25
129	Rhea Ripley	1.25	3.00
130	Roderick Strong	.60	1.50
131	Scarlett	1.25	3.00
132	Shane Thorne	.30	.75
133	Santana Garett	.30	.75
134	Shotzi Blackheart	1.00	2.50
135	Tegan Nox	.75	2.00
136	Tommaso Ciampa	.60	1.50
137	Tyler Breeze	.40	1.00
138	Vanessa Borne	.60	1.50
139	Velveteen Dream	.40	1.00
140	Xia Li	.60	1.50
141	Alexander Wolfe	.30	.75
142	Dave Mastiff	.40	1.00
143	Fabian Aichner	.12	.30
144	Flash Morgan Webster	.40	1.00
145	Ilja Dragunov	.50	1.25
146	James Drake	.40	1.00
147	Joe Coffey	.30	.75
148	Jordan Devlin	.30	.75
149	Kay Lee Ray	.50	1.25
150	Ligero	.30	.75
151	Marcel Barthel	.30	.75
152	Mark Andrews	.30	.75
153	Mark Coffey	.40	1.00
154	Noam Dar	.30	.75
155	Piper Niven	.40	1.00
156	Toni Storm	.75	2.00
157	Travis Banks	.30	.75
158	Trent Seven	.30	.75
159	Tyler Bate	.50	1.25
160	Walter	.60	1.50
161	Wolfgang	.30	.75
162	Zack Gibson	.30	.75
163	Ariya Daivari	.30	.75
164	Gentleman Jack Gallagher	.40	1.00
165	Oney Lorcan	.40	1.00
166	Raul Mendoza	.30	.75
167	Samir Singh	.30	.75
168	Sunil Singh	.30	.75
169	The Brian Kendrick	.30	.75
170	Tony Nese	.30	.75
171	AOP TT	.40	1.00
172	Murphy/Austin Theory TT	.50	1.25
173	Miz/John Morrison TT	.50	1.25
174	Seth Rollins/Murphy TT	.60	1.50
175	Usos TT	.30	.75
176	Heavy Machinery TT	.50	1.25
177	Robert Roode/Dolph Ziggler TT	.30	.75
178	Street Profits TT	.30	.75
179	Viking Raiders TT	.30	.75
180	Broserweights TT	.60	1.50
181	Ever Rise TT	.30	.75
182	Danny Burch/Oney Lorcan TT	.40	1.00
183	Ricochet/Cedric Alexander TT	.50	1.25
184	Grizzled Young Veterans TT	.40	1.00
185	Alexa Bliss/Nikki Cross TT	2.00	5.00
186	Kabuki Warriors TT	1.25	3.00
187	Nakamura/Cesaro TT	.60	1.50
188	Lucha House Party TT	.30	.75
189	New Day TT	.50	1.25
190	Forgotten Sons TT	.40	1.00
191	British Strong Style TT	.50	1.25
192	Gallus TT	.40	1.00
193	The Undisputed Era TT	.75	2.00
194	Imperium TT	.60	1.50
195	Adam Cole FL	.75	2.00
196	Aleister Black FL	.60	1.50
197	Bianca Belair FL	.75	2.00
198	Dominik Dijakovic FL	.30	.75
199	Io Shirai FL	.50	1.25
200	Keith Lee FL	.30	.75
201	King Corbin FL	.40	1.00
202	Liv Morgan FL	.75	2.00
203	Matt Riddle FL	.60	1.50
204	Pete Dunne FL	.30	.75
205	Rhea Ripley FL	1.25	3.00
206	Ricochet FL	.50	1.25
207	Shayna Baszler FL	1.00	2.50
208	Tommaso Ciampa FL	.60	1.50
209	Velveteen Dream FL	.40	1.00
210	Walter FL	.60	1.50
211	Angel Garza FL	.40	1.00
212	Austin Theory FL	.50	1.25
213	Cameron Grimes FL	.30	.75
214	Candice LeRae FL	1.00	2.50
215	Dakota Kai FL	.60	1.50
216	Johnny Gargano FL	.60	1.50
217	Montez Ford FL	.30	.75
218	Toni Storm FL	.75	2.00
219	Lacey Evans FL	.75	2.00
220	Otis FL	.50	1.25
221	AJ Styles R	1.00	2.50
222	Asuka R	1.25	3.00
223	Rey Mysterio R	.60	1.50
224	Ruby Riott R	.50	1.25
225	Table	.20	.50
226	Ladder	.20	.50
227	Steel Chair	.20	.50
228	Trash Can	.20	.50
229	The Fiend Bray Wyatt FFH	1.00	2.50
230	Bray Wyatt FFH	1.00	2.50
231	Mercy the Buzzard FFH		1.00
232	Huskus the Pig Boy FFH	.40	
233	Ramblin' Rabbit FFH		1.00
234	Abby the Witch FFH	1.00	2.50
235	Beth Phoenix HOF	.50	1.25
236	Brutus Beefcake HOF	.30	.75
237	Dusty Rhodes HOF	.60	1.50
238	Jerry Lawler HOF	.75	2.00
239	Mark Henry HOF	.50	1.25
240	Road Dogg HOF	.40	1.00
241	Faarooq HOF	.50	1.25
242	X-Pac HOF	.30	.75
243	Big Boss Man HOF	.50	1.25
244	British Bulldog HOF	.50	1.25
245	Diamond Dallas Page HOF	.60	1.50
246	Hacksaw Jim Duggan HOF	.60	1.50
247	Kevin Nash HOF	.50	1.25
248	Mr. Perfect HOF	.50	1.25
249	Rick Rude HOF	.40	1.00
250	Razor Ramon HOF	.50	1.25
251	Ricky Steamboat HOF	.50	1.25
252	Rikishi HOF	.30	.75
253	Rowdy Roddy Piper HOF	.75	2.00
254	Sgt. Slaughter HOF	.60	1.50
255	The Honky Tonk Man HOF	.50	1.25
256	The Million Dollar Man HOF	.60	1.50
257	Andre the Giant HOF	.75	2.00
258	Batista HOF	.50	1.25
259	Booker T HOF	.60	1.50
260	Bret Hit Man Hart HOF	.75	2.00
261	Chyna HOF	.75	2.00
262	Eddie Guerrero HOF	.75	2.00
263	Lita HOF	.75	2.00
264	Randy Savage HOF	1.00	2.50
265	Mick Foley HOF	.60	1.50
266	Ric Flair HOF	1.25	3.00
267	Shawn Michaels HOF	.75	2.00
268	Diesel HOF	.50	1.25
269	Sting HOF	1.00	2.50
270	Trish Stratus HOF	1.50	4.00
271	Ultimate Warrior HOF	.75	2.00
272	Yokozuna HOF	.50	1.25
273	Andrade B	.50	1.25
274	Charlotte Flair B	1.25	3.00
275	Drew McIntyre B	.60	1.50
276	Edge B	.60	1.50
277	Sheamus B	.40	1.00
278	AJ Styles B	1.00	2.50
279	Alexa Bliss B	2.00	5.00
280	Murphy B	.40	1.00
281	The Fiend Bray Wyatt B	1.00	2.50
282	Nikki Cross B	.60	1.50
283	Adam Cole B	.75	2.00
284	Dolph Ziggler B	.30	.75
285	Rhea Ripley B	1.25	3.00
286	Io Shirai B	.50	1.25
287	Shayna Baszler B	1.00	2.50
288	Seth Rollins B	.60	1.50
289	Angel Garza B	.40	1.00
290	Goldberg B	1.25	3.00
291	Roman Reigns B	.75	2.00
292	The Miz B	.50	1.25
293	Bayley B	.60	1.50
294	Natalya B	.50	1.25
295	Randy Orton B	.75	2.00
296	Daniel Bryan B	1.00	2.50
297	Kairi Sane B	.60	1.50
298	Shorty G B	.30	.75
299	Aleister Black B	.60	1.50
300	Kevin Owens B	.40	1.00
301	Kofi Kingston B	.50	1.25
302	Shinsuke Nakamura B	.60	1.50
303	Asuka MITB	1.25	3.00
304	Otis MITB	.50	1.25
305	Universal Title	.20	.50
306	WWE Title	.20	.50
307	RAW Women's Title	.20	.50
308	SmackDown Women's Title	.20	.50
309	Intercontinental Title	.20	.50
310	United States Title	.20	.50
311	24/7 Title	.20	.50
312	RAW Tag Team Title	.20	.50
313	SmackDown Tag Team Title	.20	.50
314	WWE Women's Tag Team Title	.20	.50
315	NXT Title	.20	.50
316	NXT Women's Title	.20	.50
317	NXT North American Title	.20	.50
318	NXT Cruiserweight Title	.20	.50
319	NXT Tag Team Title	.20	.50
320	NXT UK Title	.20	.50
321	NXT UK Women's Title	.20	.50
322	NXT UK Tag Team Title	.20	.50

323	Orton/RKO	.75	2.00
324	Balor/Coup de Grace	.75	2.00
325	Goldberg/Jackhammer	1.25	3.00
326	Black/Black Mass	.60	1.50
327	Edge/Spear	.60	1.50
328	Styles/Phenomenal Forearm	1.00	2.50
329	Hardy/Swanton Bomb	.75	2.00
330	McIntyre/Claymore Kick	.60	1.50
331	Hart/Sharpshooter	.75	2.00
332	Austin/Stone Cold Stunner	1.50	4.00
333	Undertaker/Tombstone	1.25	3.00
334	Triple H/Pedigree	.75	2.00
335	Kane/Chokeslam	.40	1.00
336	Cena/Attitude Adjustment	1.25	3.00
337	Braun Strowman B	.75	2.00
338	Otis B	.50	1.25
339	Sasha Banks ICONS	1.50	4.00
340	Charlotte Flair ICONS	1.25	3.00
341	Daniel Bryan ICONS	1.00	2.50
342	Seth Rollins ICONS	.60	1.50
343	Triple H ICONS	.75	2.00
344	The Rock ICONS	1.50	4.00
345	Bret Hart ICONS	.75	2.00
346	Steve Austin ICONS	1.50	4.00
347	Roman Reigns 100 CLUB	.75	2.00
348	Asuka 100 CLUB	1.25	3.00
349	Drew McIntyre 100 CLUB	.60	1.50
350	Bray Wyatt 100 CLUB	1.00	2.50
351	Undertaker SR	1.25	3.00
352	John Cena SR	1.25	3.00

2020 Topps WWE Slam Attax Reloaded Autographs

AAB	Alexa Bliss
AAC	Adam Cole
AAD	Angelo Dawkins
AAJ	AJ Styles
AAN	Andrade
AAS	Asuka
ABA	Bayley
ABB	Bianca Belair
ABE	Big E
ABL	Becky Lynch
ABM	Murphy
ACS	Cesaro
ADB	Daniel Bryan
ADM	Drew McIntyre
AED	Edge
AEL	Elias
AEM	Ember Moon
AFB	Finn Balor
AJG	Johnny Gargano
AKO	Kevin Owens
AKS	Kairi Sane
ALA	Bobby Lashley
ALE	Lacey Evans
AMA	Mustafa Ali
AMR	Mandy Rose
ANJ	Nia Jax
ANM	Naomi
ANT	Natalya
AOO	Otis
APD	Pete Dunne
ARB	Ruby Riott
ARC	Ricochet
ARR	Robert Roode
ARS	Roderick Strong
ART	R-Truth
ASB	Shayna Baszler
ASD	Sonya Deville
ASG	Shorty G
ASH	Shinsuke Nakamura
ATB	Tyler Bate
ATC	Tommaso Ciampa
ATE	Aleister Black
ATM	The Miz
ATS	Trent Seven
AVD	Velveteen Dream/50
	(Topps.com Exclusive)
AXW	Xavier Woods

2020 Topps WWE Slam Attax Reloaded Collector Tins

NNO	Edge
NNO	John Cena
NNO	Sasha Banks

2020 Topps WWE Slam Attax Reloaded Exclusives

T1	Bret Hit Man Hart
T2	British Bulldog
T3	Eddie Guerrero
T4	Yokozuna
T5	Batista
T6	Diesel
T7	Lita
T8	Bayley
T9	The Fiend Bray Wyatt
T10	Kofi Kingston
T11	Velveteen Dream
T12	Kevin Owens
T13	Rhea Ripley
T14	Sasha Banks
T15	Macho Man Randy Savage
T16	Ric Flair
T17	Shawn Michaels
T18	Stone Cold Steve Austin
T19	Papa Shango
T20	Vader
T21	Booker T
T22	Daniel Bryan
T23	Drew McIntyre
T24	Randy Orton
T25	Roman Reigns
T26	King Corbin
T27	Alexa Bliss
T28	Becky Lynch
T29	Andre the Giant
T30	Bam Bam Bigelow
T31	Ultimate Warrior
T32	Rowdy Roddy Piper
T33	Razor Ramon
T34	Chyna
T35	Trish Stratus
T36	AJ Styles
T37	Braun Strowman
T38	The Miz
T39	Seth Rollins
T40	Adam Cole
T41	Charlotte Flair
T42	Asuka

2020 Topps WWE Slam Attax Reloaded Limited Edition Bronze

LEBB	Becky Lynch
LECB	Drew McIntyre
LERB	Roman Reigns

2020 Topps WWE Slam Attax Reloaded Limited Edition Gold

LEDA	The Rock
	(Mega Tins Exclusive)
LEDB	Undertaker
	(Mega Tins Exclusive)
LEDC	Stone Cold Steve Austin
	(Mega Tins Exclusive)
LESA	The Fiend Bray Wyatt
LETA	John Cena
	(Collector Tins Exclusive)
LETB	Sasha Banks
	(Collector Tins Exclusive)
LETC	Edge
	(Collector Tins Exclusive)
LEXA	Daniel Bryan
	(Web Wednesday Exclusive)
LEXB	Charlotte Flair
	(WWE Kids Magazine Exclusive)
LEXC	Seth Rollins
	(Web Wednesday Exclusive)
LEXD	Nikki Cross
	(Web Wednesday Exclusive)

2020 Topps WWE Slam Attax Reloaded Relics

M1	Drew McIntyre/T-Shirt
M2	Humberto Carrllo/T-Shirt
M3	Samoa Joe/T-Shirt
M4	Shayna Baszler/T-Shirt
M5	Sonya Deville/T-Shirt
M6	Roman Reigns vs. King Corbin/Table
M7	Triple H vs. Batista/Mat

2020 Topps WWE Slam Attax Reloaded XL

XL1	John Cena
XL2	Charlotte Flair
XL3	Braun Strowman
XL4	Bayley
XL5	Becky Lynch
XL6	Roman Reigns
XL7	Undertaker
XL8	The Fiend Bray Wyatt
XL9	Drew McIntyre
XL10	Rhea Ripley
XL11	Kofi Kingston

2016 Topps WWE Slam Attax TakeOver

COMPLETE SET (299)		25.00	60.00
1	AJ Styles	.50	1.25
2	Asuka	.50	1.25
3	Alberto Del Rio	.20	.50
4	Brock Lesnar	.60	1.50
5	Charlotte	.40	1.00
6	Dean Ambrose	.40	1.00
7	Finn Balor	.40	1.00
8	John Cena	.60	1.50
9	Kalisto	.30	.75
10	Kevin Owens	.30	.75
11	Roman Reigns	.40	1.00
12	Samoa Joe	.30	.75
13	Sasha Banks	.40	1.00
14	Seth Rollins	.20	.50
15	The New Day	.30	.75
16	Triple H	.50	1.25
17	AJ Styles	.50	1.25
18	Asuka	.50	1.25
19	Alberto Del Rio	.20	.50
20	Brock Lesnar	.60	1.50
21	Charlotte	.40	1.00
22	Dean Ambrose	.40	1.00
23	Finn Balor	.40	1.00
24	John Cena	.60	1.50
25	Kalisto	.30	.75
26	Kevin Owens	.30	.75
27	Roman Reigns	.40	1.00
28	Samoa Joe	.30	.75
29	Sasha Banks	.40	1.00
30	Seth Rollins	.20	.50
31	The New Day	.30	.75
32	Triple H	.50	1.25
33	Becky Lynch	.40	1.00
34	Big E	.12	.30
35	Bo Dallas	.12	.30
36	Bray Wyatt	.50	1.25
37	Charlotte	.40	1.00
38	Kalisto	.30	.75
39	Kevin Owens	.30	.75
40	Luke Harper	.12	.30
41	Neville	.25	.60
42	Paige	.40	1.00
43	Roman Reigns	.40	1.00
44	Rusev	.30	.75
45	Sasha Banks	.40	1.00
46	Seth Rollins	.20	.50
47	Tyler Breeze	.12	.30
48	Xavier Woods	.12	.30
49	MITB Briefcase	.12	.30
50	NXT Women's Title	.12	.30
51	NXT Title	.12	.30
52	NXT Tag Team Title	.12	.30
53	WWE Tag Team Title	.12	.30
54	WWE Women's Title	.12	.30
55	WWE United States Title	.12	.30
56	WWE Title	.12	.30
57	AJ Styles	.50	1.25
58	Alberto Del Rio	.20	.50
59	Apollo Crews	.12	.30
60	Asuka	.50	1.25
61	Baron Corbin	.15	.40
62	Bayley	.30	.75
63	Becky Lynch	.40	1.00
64	Big Cass	.25	.60
65	Braun Strowman	.15	.40
66	Bray Wyatt	.50	1.25
67	Brock Lesnar	.60	1.50
68	Charlotte	.40	1.00
69	Chris Jericho	.30	.75
70	Dean Ambrose	.40	1.00
71	Dolph Ziggler	.15	.40
72	Elias Samson	.12	.30
73	Erick Rowan	.12	.30
74	Heath Slater	.12	.30
75	Hideo Itami	.15	.40
76	Jason Jordan	.15	.40
77	John Cena	.60	1.50
78	Kalisto	.30	.75
79	Kevin Owens	.30	.75
80	Mojo Rawley	.12	.30
81	Neville	.25	.60
82	Paige	.40	1.00
83	Roman Reigns	.40	1.00
84	Rusev	.30	.75

85	Samoa Joe	.30	.75
86	Sasha Banks	.40	1.00
87	Sheamus	.30	.75
88	Triple H	.50	1.25
89	Aiden English	.12	.30
90	AJ Styles	.50	1.25
91	Alberto Del Rio	.20	.50
92	Alicia Fox	.20	.50
93	Apollo Crews	.12	.30
94	Baron Corbin	.15	.40
95	Becky Lynch	.40	1.00
96	Big Cass	.25	.60
97	Big E	.12	.30
98	Big Show	.25	.60
99	Bo Dallas	.12	.30
100	Booker T	.25	.60
101	Braun Strowman	.15	.40
102	Bray Wyatt	.50	1.25
103	Brie Bella	.25	.60
104	Brock Lesnar	.60	1.50
105	Bubba Ray Dudley	.25	.60
106	Byron Saxton	.12	.30
107	Cesaro	.25	.60
108	Charlotte	.40	1.00
109	Chris Jericho	.30	.75
110	Curtis Axel	.12	.30
111	Dana Brooke	.30	.75
112	Daniel Bryan	.50	1.25
113	Darren Young	.12	.30
114	David Otunga	.12	.30
115	Dean Ambrose	.40	1.00
116	Dolph Ziggler	.15	.40
117	D-Von Dudley	.20	.50
118	Emma	.25	.60
119	Enzo Amore	.25	.60
120	Epico	.12	.30
121	Erick Rowan	.12	.30
122	Eva Marie	.25	.60
123	Fandango	.12	.30
124	Goldust	.20	.50
125	Heath Slater	.12	.30
126	Jack Swagger	.12	.30
127	JBL	.15	.40
128	Jerry Lawler	.25	.60
129	Jey Uso	.12	.30
130	Jimmy Uso	.12	.30
131	John Cena	.60	1.50
132	Jojo	.12	.30
133	Kalisto	.30	.75
134	Kane	.20	.50
135	Karl Anderson	.12	.30
136	Kevin Owens	.30	.75
137	Kofi Kingston	.12	.30
138	Konnor	.12	.30
139	Lana	.50	1.25
140	Luke Gallows	.15	.40
141	Luke Harper	.12	.30
142	Mark Henry	.15	.40
143	Maryse	.25	.60
144	Mauro Ranallo	.12	.30
145	Michael Cole	.12	.30
146	Naomi	.20	.50
147	Natalya	.20	.50
148	Neville	.25	.60
149	Nikki Bella	.40	1.00
150	Paige	.40	1.00
151	Primo	.12	.30
152	Randy Orton	.30	.75

153	Renee Young	.30	.75
154	Roman Reigns	.40	1.00
155	Rosa Mendes	.12	.30
156	R-Truth	.12	.30
157	Rusev	.30	.75
158	Ryback	.15	.40
159	Sami Zayn	.20	.50
160	Sasha Banks	.40	1.00
161	Seth Rollins	.20	.50
162	Sheamus	.30	.75
163	Simon Gotch	.20	.50
164	Sin Cara	.15	.40
165	Summer Rae	.30	.75
166	Tamina	.15	.40
167	The Miz	.20	.50
168	The Rock	.60	1.50
169	Titus O'Neil	.12	.30
170	Tony Chimel	.12	.30
171	Triple H	.50	1.25
172	Tyler Breeze	.12	.30
173	Tyson Kidd	.12	.30
174	Undertaker	.50	1.25
175	Viktor	.12	.30
176	Xavier Woods	.12	.30
177	Zack Ryder	.12	.30
178	Alexa Bliss	.60	1.50
179	Angelo Dawkins	.12	.30
180	Asuka	.50	1.25
181	Austin Aries	.15	.40
182	Bayley	.30	.75
183	Billie Kay	.30	.75
184	Blake	.12	.30
185	Carmella	.30	.75
186	Cathy Kelley	.12	.30
187	Chad Gable	.15	.40
188	Corey Graves	.12	.30
189	Dash Wilder	.15	.40
190	Dasha Fuentes	.12	.30
191	Elias Samson	.12	.30
192	Finn Balor	.40	1.00
193	Greg Hamilton	.12	.30
194	Hideo Itami	.15	.40
195	Jason Jordan	.15	.40
196	Mandy Rose	.30	.75
197	Mojo Rawley	.12	.30
198	Murphy	.12	.30
199	Nia Jax	.20	.50
200	No Way Jose	.12	.30
201	Peyton Royce	.30	.75
202	Samoa Joe	.30	.75
203	Sawyer Fulton	.15	.40
204	Scott Dawson	.12	.30
205	Shinsuke Nakamura	.50	1.25
206	Tom Phillips	.12	.30
207	Tye Dillinger	.15	.40
208	William Regal	.12	.30
209	Adrienne Reese	.30	.75
210	Bronson Matthews	.12	.30
211	Oney Lorcan	.12	.30
212	Hugo Knox	.12	.30
213	King Constantine	.12	.30
214	Manny Andrade	.20	.50
215	Noah Kekoa	.12	.30
216	Tino Sabbatelli	.12	.30
217	Bam Bam Bigelow	.15	.40
218	Big Boss Man	.20	.50
219	Bob Backlund	.12	.30
220	Bobby Heenan	.20	.50

221	Booker T	.25	.60
222	Bret Hart	.30	.75
223	Brian Pillman	.15	.40
224	British Bulldog	.15	.40
225	Bruno Sammartino	.15	.40
226	Chief Jay Strongbow	.20	.50
227	Freddie Blassie	.15	.40
228	Bob Orton	.20	.50
229	Dean Malenko	.12	.30
230	Diamond Dallas Page	.20	.50
231	Diesel	.30	.75
232	Doink The Clown	.12	.30
233	Dusty Rhodes	.12	.30
234	Eddie Guerrero	.30	.75
235	Edge	.30	.75
236	Greg Valentine	.15	.40
237	Jim Duggan	.12	.30
238	Harley Race	.12	.30
239	Honky Tonk Man	.12	.30
240	Iron Shiek	.12	.30
241	Irwin R. Schyster	.12	.30
242	Jake Roberts	.25	.60
243	Jim Neidhart	.12	.30
244	Jimmy Hart	.15	.40
245	Junkyard Dog	.20	.50
246	Kevin Nash	.30	.75
247	Lex Luger	.20	.50
248	Lita	.40	1.00
249	Randy Savage	.30	.75
250	Don Muraco	.12	.30
251	Gene Okerlund	.15	.40
252	Ted Dibiase	.15	.40
253	Curt Hennig	.30	.75
254	Paul Orndorf	.12	.30
255	Paul Bearer	.20	.50
256	Rick Rude	.20	.50
257	Razor Ramon	.30	.75
258	Ric Flair	.50	1.25
259	Ricky Steamboat	.15	.40
260	Rikishi	.15	.40
261	Rhyno	.12	.30
262	Road Dogg	.20	.50
263	Ron Simmons	.30	.75
264	Rowdy Roddy Piper	.40	1.00
265	Sgt. Slaughter	.15	.40
266	Shawn Michaels	.50	1.25
267	Sting	.30	.75
268	Stone Cold Steve Austin	.60	1.50
269	Terry Funk	.12	.30
270	The Godfather	.15	.40
271	Trish Stratus	.60	1.50
272	Ultimate Warrior	.30	.75
273	Vader	.25	.60
274	X-Pac	.20	.50
275	Yokozuna	.25	.60
276	American Alpha	.15	.40
277	Blake/Murphy	.12	.30
278	Enzo/Cass	.25	.60
279	Gargano/Ciampa	.15	.40
280	Gallows/Anderson	.15	.40
281	The Shining Stars	.12	.30
282	Team B.A.D.	.40	1.00
283	The Ascension	.12	.30
284	The Bella Twins	.40	1.00
285	The Bushwhackers	.12	.30
286	The Dudley Boyz	.25	.60
287	The Hype Bros	.12	.30
288	The Lucha Dragons	.30	.75

289	The New Day	.30	.75
290	The Prime Time Players	.12	.30
291	The Revival	.15	.40
292	The Social Outcasts	.12	.30
293	The Usos	.12	.30
294	The Vaudevillains	.20	.50
295	The Wyatt Family	.50	1.25
296	Ladder	.12	.30
297	Steel Chair	.12	.30
298	Table	.12	.30
299	Trash Can	.12	.30

2019 Topps WWE SmackDown Live

COMPLETE SET (90)		10.00	25.00
*GREEN: .5X TO 1.5X BASIC CARDS			
*PURPLE/99: .75X TO 3X BASIC CARDS			
*20TH ANN./20: UNPRICED DUE TO SCARCITY			
*GOLD/10: UNPRICED DUE TO SCARCITY			
*RED/1: UNPRICED DUE TO SCARCITY			
*P.P.BLACK/1: UNPRICED DUE TO SCARCITY			
*P.P.CYAN/1: UNPRICED DUE TO SCARCITY			
*P.P.MAGENTA/1: UNPRICED DUE TO SCARCITY			
*P.P.YELLOW/1: UNPRICED DUE TO SCARCITY			

1	Aiden English	.25	.60
2	Aleister Black	.30	.75
3	Ali	.25	.60
4	Andrade	.30	.75
5	Apollo Crews	.30	.75
6	Asuka	.75	2.00
7	Bayley	.50	1.25
8	Becky Lynch	1.00	2.50
9	Big E	.25	.60
10	Billie Kay	.50	1.25
11	Bo Dallas	.30	.75
12	Buddy Murphy	.30	.75
13	Byron Saxton	.25	.60
14	Carmella	.60	1.50
15	Cesaro	.30	.75
16	Chad Gable	.25	.60
17	Charlotte Flair	1.00	2.50
18	Corey Graves	.30	.75
19	Curtis Axel	.30	.75
20	Daniel Bryan	1.00	2.50
21	Elias	.50	1.25
22	Ember Moon	.60	1.50
23	Finn Balor	.60	1.50
24	Greg Hamilton	.25	.60
25	Jeff Hardy	.60	1.50
26	Jinder Mahal	.50	1.25
27	Kairi Sane	.50	1.25
28	Kevin Owens	.60	1.50
29	Kofi Kingston	.40	1.00
30	Lana	.50	1.25
31	Lars Sullivan	.25	.60
32	Liv Morgan	.75	2.00
33	Mandy Rose	.60	1.50
34	Maryse	.30	.75
35	Matt Hardy	.50	1.25
36	Mickie James	.60	1.50
37	Otis	.25	.60
38	Paige	1.00	2.50
39	Peyton Royce	.60	1.50
40	R-Truth	.30	.75
41	Randy Orton	.60	1.50
42	Roman Reigns	.60	1.50
43	Rowan	.25	.60
44	Rusev	.50	1.25
45	Samir Singh	.25	.60

46	Sarah Schreiber	.25	.60
47	Sheamus	.40	1.00
48	Shelton Benjamin	.30	.75
49	Shinsuke Nakamura	.60	1.50
50	Sin Cara	.25	.60
51	Sonya Deville	.50	1.25
52	Sunil Singh	.25	.60
53	Tom Phillips	.25	.60
54	Tucker	.25	.60
55	Xavier Woods	.30	.75
56	Zelina Vega	.40	1.00
57	Big Show	.40	1.00
58	The Rock	1.25	3.00
59	Triple H	.60	1.50
60	Undertaker	1.25	3.00
61	Albert	.25	.60
62	Beth Phoenix	.40	1.00
63	Big Boss Man	.30	.75
64	The British Bulldog	.60	1.50
65	Boogeyman	.25	.60
66	King Booker	.60	1.50
67	Cactus Jack	.50	1.25
68	Christian	.40	1.00
69	Chyna	.50	1.25
70	Cowboy Bob Orton	.25	.60
71	D-Lo Brown	.25	.60
72	Diamond Dallas Page	.50	1.25
73	Eddie Guerrero	.60	1.50
74	Faarooq	.40	1.00
75	Finlay	.25	.60
76	The Godfather	.25	.60
77	Goldberg	.75	2.00
78	Jerry The King Lawler	.50	1.25
79	Kevin Nash	.40	1.00
80	Lita	.60	1.50
81	Mankind	.50	1.25
82	Paul Bearer	.30	.75
83	Rikishi	.25	.60
84	Road Dogg Jesse James	.25	.60
85	Rowdy Roddy Piper	.60	1.50
86	Scott Hall	.40	1.00
87	Stone Cold Steve Austin	1.25	3.00
88	Tatanka	.25	.60
89	Trish Stratus	1.25	3.00
90	X-Pac	.25	.60

2019 Topps WWE SmackDown Live 20 Years of SmackDown

COMPLETE SET (46)   12.00   30.00
RANDOMLY INSERTED INTO PACKS

SD1	Undertaker & Big Show	1.50	4.00
SD2	The Rock & Mankind	1.50	4.00
SD3	Stone Cold Steve Austin	1.50	4.00
SD4	Jeff Hardy	.75	2.00
SD5	Kurt Angle	.60	1.50
SD6	Batista	.75	2.00
SD7	Rey Mysterio	.75	2.00
SD8	John Cena	1.25	3.00
SD9	Kurt Angle	.60	1.50
SD10	Kurt Angle	.60	1.50
SD11	Rey Mysterio	.75	2.00
SD12	Brock Lesnar	1.25	3.00
SD13	Brock Lesnar	1.25	3.00
SD14	Eddie Guerrero	.75	2.00
SD15	Stone Cold Steve Austin	1.50	4.00
SD16	Eddie Guerrero	.75	2.00
SD17	Undertaker	1.50	4.00
SD18	Kurt Angle	.60	1.50

SD19	Eddie Guerrero	.75	2.00
SD20	Undertaker	1.50	4.00
SD21	Kurt Angle	.60	1.50
SD22	Booker T	.75	2.00
SD23	Shawn Michaels	.75	2.00
SD24	Jeff Hardy	.75	2.00
SD25	Jeff Hardy	.75	2.00
SD26	Shawn Michaels	.75	2.00
SD27	Randy Orton	.75	2.00
SD28	Daniel Bryan	1.25	3.00
SD29	Beth Phoenix	.50	1.25
SD30	Daniel Bryan	1.25	3.00
SD31	John Cena	1.25	3.00
SD32	Cesaro	.40	1.00
SD33	Batista	.75	2.00
SD34	Wyatt Family	.40	1.00
SD35	Kevin Owens	.75	2.00
SD36	The Miz	.60	1.50
SD37	Alexa Bliss	1.50	4.00
SD38	Bray Wyatt	.75	2.00
SD39	The Usos	.40	1.00
SD40	Carmella	.75	2.00
SD41	Shinsuke Nakamura	.75	2.00
SD42	The New Day	.60	1.50
SD43	AJ Styles	1.50	4.00
SD44	John Cena	1.25	3.00
SD45	Rusev	.60	1.50
SD46	The New Day	.60	1.50

2019 Topps WWE SmackDown Live Autographed Intercontinental Championship 40th Anniversary Relics

RANDOMLY INSERTED INTO PACKS

ICRKK	Kofi Kingston	
ICRSB	Shelton Benjamin	
ICRTM	The Miz	

2019 Topps WWE SmackDown Live Autographed Mat Relics

STATED PRINT RUN 10 SER.#'d SETS
UNPRICED DUE TO SCARCITY

MRAAJ	AJ Styles
MRABD	Daniel Bryan
MRABE	Big E
MRABM	Buddy Murphy
MRACM	Carmella
MRAJE	Jey Uso
MRAJH	Jeff Hardy
MRAJI	Jimmy Uso
MRAKA	Karl Anderson
MRAKK	Kofi Kingston
MRAKS	Shinsuke Nakamura
MRALG	Luke Gallows
MRAMA	Ali
MRAMR	Mandy Rose
MRARJ	Rey Mysterio
MRARM	Rey Mysterio
MRART	R-Truth
MRASD	Sonya Deville
MRASN	Shinsuke Nakamura
MRAXW	Xavier Woods

2019 Topps WWE SmackDown Live Autographed Shirt Relics

STATED PRINT RUN 10 SER.#'d SETS
UNPRICED DUE TO SCARCITY

SRAC	Apollo Crews
SREM	Ember Moon
SRMH	Matt Hardy
SRXW	Xavier Woods
SRAAA	Andrade
SRAAB	Aleister Black
SRAEL	Elias
SRAKK	Kofi Kingston

2019 Topps WWE SmackDown Live Autographed SmackDown Championship Commemorative Relics

STATED PRINT RUN 10 SER.#'d SETS
UNPRICED DUE TO SCARCITY

ASCAB	Alexa Bliss
ASCAJ	AJ Styles
ASCBC	Baron Corbin
ASCBL	Becky Lynch
ASCBR	Robert Roode
ASCCM	Carmella
ASCKK	Kofi Kingston
ASCKO	Kevin Owens
ASCNM	Naomi
ASCNT	Natalya
ASCRO	Randy Orton
ASCRT	R-Truth
ASCSJ	Samoa Joe
ASCSN	Shinsuke Nakamura

2019 Topps WWE SmackDown Live Autographed Women's Evolution Relics

DRACCM	Carmella

2019 Topps WWE SmackDown Live Autographs

*ORANGE/50: .5X TO 1.2X BASIC AUTOS
*20TH ANN./20: UNPRICED DUE TO SCARCITY
*GOLD/10: UNPRICED DUE TO SCARCITY
*RED/1: UNPRICED DUE TO SCARCITY
STATED PRINT RUN 99 SER.#'d SETS

AAA	Andrade	4.00	10.00
AAL	Aleister Black	12.00	30.00
ABA	Bayley	10.00	25.00
ABE	Becky Lynch		
ABK	Billie Kay	8.00	20.00
ABL	Big E	4.00	10.00
ABU	Buddy Murphy	8.00	20.00
ACH	Chad Gable	4.00	10.00
ACM	Carmella	10.00	25.00
AEL	Elias	4.00	10.00
AEM	Ember Moon	8.00	20.00
AFI	Finn Balor	12.00	30.00
AGH	Greg Hamilton	4.00	10.00
AKE	Kevin Owens	6.00	15.00
AKK	Kofi Kingston	6.00	15.00
ALI	Liv Morgan	15.00	40.00
AMA	Ali	4.00	10.00
AMH	Matt Hardy	6.00	15.00
AMR	Mandy Rose	15.00	40.00
AOT	Otis	10.00	25.00
APR	Peyton Royce	10.00	25.00
ARR	Roman Reigns	10.00	25.00
ART	R-Truth	5.00	12.00
ARW	Rowan	4.00	10.00
ASD	Sonya Deville	6.00	15.00
ASN	Shinsuke Nakamura	5.00	12.00
ATU	Tucker	4.00	10.00

AXW	Xavier Woods	5.00	12.00
AZV	Zelina Vega	12.00	30.00

2019 Topps WWE SmackDown Live Corey Says

COMPLETE SET (19)   6.00   15.00
RANDOMLY INSERTED INTO PACKS

CG1	AJ Styles	1.50	4.00
CG2	Asuka	1.00	2.50
CG3	Becky Lynch	1.25	3.00
CG4	Carmella	.75	2.00
CG5	Cesaro	.40	1.00
CG6	Charlotte Flair	1.25	3.00
CG7	Daniel Bryan	1.25	3.00
CG8	Jeff Hardy	.75	2.00
CG9	Randy Orton	.75	2.00
CG10	Rey Mysterio	.75	2.00
CG11	Rusev	.60	1.50
CG12	Samoa Joe	.60	1.50
CG13	Shane McMahon	.75	2.00
CG14	Sheamus	.50	1.25
CG15	Shinsuke Nakamura	.75	2.00
CG16	The Miz	.60	1.50
CG17	The New Day	.60	1.50
CG18	The Usos	.40	1.00
CG19	Undertaker	1.50	4.00

2019 Topps WWE SmackDown Live Dual Autographs

*GOLD/10: UNPRICED DUE TO SCARCITY
*RED/1: UNPRICED DUE TO SCARCITY
STATED PRINT RUN 25 SER.#'d SETS

DADB	R-Truth/Carmella	20.00	50.00
DAGB	K.Anderson/L.Gallows	30.00	75.00
DAII	B.Kay/P.Royce	75.00	150.00
DATQ	Z.Vega/Andrade	20.00	50.00
DAABS	S.Deville/M.Rose	75.00	150.00

2019 Topps WWE SmackDown Live Image Variations

IV1	Aleister Black		
IV2	Andrade	6.00	15.00
IV3	Big E		
IV4	Billie Kay	6.00	15.00
IV5	Charlotte Flair	15.00	40.00
IV6	Daniel Bryan	12.00	30.00
IV7	Jeff Hardy	4.00	10.00
IV8	Killian Dain		
IV9	Kofi Kingston	6.00	15.00
IV10	Mandy Rose	12.00	30.00
IV11	Peyton Royce		
IV12	R-Truth		
IV13	Shinsuke Nakamura		
IV14	Sheamus		
IV15	Shelton Benjamin	8.00	20.00
IV16	Sonya Deville	10.00	25.00
IV17	Xavier Woods	4.00	10.00
IV18	Zelina Vega		
IV19	Ali		
IV20	Matt Hardy	8.00	20.00

2019 Topps WWE SmackDown Live Intercontinental Championship 40th Anniversary Autographs

ICAKK	Kofi Kingston	8.00	20.00
ICASB	Shelton Benjamin	12.00	30.00
ICATM	The Miz	10.00	25.00

2019 Topps WWE SmackDown Live Intercontinental Championship 40th Anniversary Relics

RANDOMLY INSERTED INTO PACKS

ICRDM Drew McIntyre
ICRKK Kofi Kingston
ICRRM Rey Mysterio
ICRSB Shelton Benjamin
ICRTM The Miz

2019 Topps WWE SmackDown Live Mat Relics

*PURPLE/99: .6X TO 1.5X BASIC MEM
*ORANGE/50: .75X TO 2X BASIC MEM
*20TH ANN./20: UNPRICED DUE TO SCARCITY
*GOLD/10: UNPRICED DUE TO SCARCITY
*RED/1: UNPRICED DUE TO SCARCITY
STATED PRINT RUN 199 SER.#'d SETS

MR4H	Charlotte Flair	8.00	20.00
MRAJ	AJ Styles	4.00	10.00
MRAS	Asuka	6.00	15.00
MRAW	Alexander Wolfe	3.00	8.00
MRBD	Daniel Bryan	4.00	10.00
MRBE	Big E	2.50	6.00
MRBL	Becky Lynch	6.00	15.00
MRBM	Buddy Murphy	2.50	6.00
MRBS	Big Show	2.50	6.00
MRBT	Batista	3.00	8.00
MRCF	Charlotte Flair	6.00	15.00
MRCM	Carmella	4.00	10.00
MRCS	Cesaro	2.50	6.00
MRDB	Daniel Bryan	4.00	10.00
MREY	Eric Young	2.50	6.00
MRJE	Jey Uso	2.50	6.00
MRJH	Jeff Hardy	4.00	10.00
MRJI	Jimmy Uso	2.50	6.00
MRKA	Karl Anderson	2.50	6.00
MRKD	Killian Dain	2.50	6.00
MRKK	Kofi Kingston	3.00	8.00
MRKS	Shinsuke Nakamura	3.00	8.00
MRLG	Luke Gallows	2.50	6.00
MRLN	Lana	3.00	8.00
MRMA	Ali	2.50	6.00
MRMH	Stephanie McMahon	4.00	10.00
MRMR	Mandy Rose	6.00	15.00
MRRF	Ric Flair	5.00	12.00
MRRJ	Rey Mysterio	4.00	10.00
MRRM	Rey Mysterio	4.00	10.00
MRRO	Randy Orton	4.00	10.00
MRRS	Rusev	2.50	6.00
MRRT	R-Truth	2.50	6.00
MRSD	Sonya Deville	3.00	8.00
MRSH	Sheamus	2.50	6.00
MRSJ	Samoa Joe	2.50	6.00
MRSN	Shinsuke Nakamura	3.00	8.00
MRTH	Triple H	3.00	8.00
MRTM	The Miz	2.50	6.00
MRUT	Undertaker	6.00	15.00
MRXW	Xavier Woods	2.50	6.00

2019 Topps WWE SmackDown Live Shirt Relics

*PURPLE/99: .6X TO 1.5X BASIC MEM
*ORANGE/50: .75X TO 2X BASIC MEM
20TH ANN./20: UNPRICED DUE TO SCARCITY
*GOLD/10: UNPRICED DUE TO SCARCITY
*RED/1: UNPRICED DUE TO SCARCITY

STATED PRINT RUN 199 SER.#'d SETS

SRAA	Andrade/199	5.00	12.00
SRAB	Aleister Black/199	5.00	12.00
SRAC	Apollo Crews/199	4.00	10.00
SREL	Elias/199	5.00	12.00
SREM	Ember Moon/199	6.00	15.00
SRJH	Jeff Hardy/199	5.00	12.00
SRKA	Karl Anderson/199	4.00	10.00
SRKK	Kofi Kingston/199	4.00	10.00
SRKS	Kairi Sane/199	5.00	12.00
SRLG	Luke Gallows/199	4.00	10.00
SRLM	Liv Morgan/160	12.00	30.00
SRMH	Matt Hardy/199	4.00	10.00
SRSM	Sheamus/199	4.00	10.00
SRXW	Xavier Woods/199	6.00	15.00

2019 Topps WWE SmackDown Live SmackDown Championship Commemorative Relics

*PURPLE/99: .6X TO 1.5X BASIC MEM
*ORANGE/50: .75X TO 2X BASIC MEM
20TH ANN./20: UNPRICED DUE TO SCARCITY
*GOLD/10: UNPRICED DUE TO SCARCITY
*RED/1: UNPRICED DUE TO SCARCITY
STATED PRINT RUN 199 SER.#'d SETS

SCAB	Alexa Bliss	8.00	20.00
SCAJ	AJ Styles	5.00	12.00
SCAS	Asuka	6.00	15.00
SCBC	Baron Corbin	2.50	6.00
SCBL	Becky Lynch	10.00	25.00
SCBR	Robert Roode	2.50	6.00
SCBW	Bray Wyatt	6.00	15.00
SCCF	Charlotte Flair	4.00	10.00
SCCM	Carmella	8.00	20.00
SCDB	Daniel Bryan	5.00	12.00
SCJC	John Cena	6.00	15.00
SCJH	Jeff Hardy	5.00	12.00
SCKK	Kofi Kingston	5.00	12.00
SCKO	Kevin Owens	2.50	6.00
SCMH	Jinder Mahal	2.50	6.00
SCNM	Naomi	2.50	6.00
SCNT	Natalya	2.50	6.00
SCRO	Randy Orton	5.00	12.00
SCRT	R-Truth	3.00	8.00
SCRV	Rusev	2.50	6.00
SCSJ	Samoa Joe	2.50	6.00
SCSN	Shinsuke Nakamura	4.00	10.00
SCVP	Randy Orton	5.00	12.00

2019 Topps WWE SmackDown Live SmackDown Tag Team Championship Commemorative Relics

*PURPLE/99: .6X TO 1.5X BASIC MEM
*ORANGE/50: .75X TO 2X BASIC MEM
20TH ANN./20: UNPRICED DUE TO SCARCITY
*GOLD/10: UNPRICED DUE TO SCARCITY
*RED/1: UNPRICED DUE TO SCARCITY
STATED PRINT RUN 199 SER.#'d SETS

SCAA	Jason Jordan/Chad Gable	4.00	10.00
SCBB	Matt Hardy/Jeff Hardy	6.00	15.00
SCND	Xavier Woods/Kofi Kingston	5.00	12.00
SCPE	Rowan/Daniel Bryan	4.00	10.00
SCTB	Cesaro/Sheamus	4.00	10.00
SCUS	Jey Uso/Jimmy Uso	6.00	15.00
SCWF	Randy Orton/Bray Wyatt	5.00	12.00

2019 Topps WWE SmackDown Live Triple Autographs

*GOLD/10: UNPRICED DUE TO SCARCITY
*RED/1: UNPRICED DUE TO SCARCITY
STATED PRINT RUN 25 SER.#'d SETS

TAND	Woods/Big E/Kingston	100.00	200.00

2019 Topps WWE SmackDown Live Women's Evolution Autographs

RANDOMLY INSERTED INTO PACKS

WACM Carmella
WAMR Mandy Rose
WASD Sonya Deville

2019 Topps WWE SmackDown Live Women's Evolution Relics

RANDOMLY INSERTED INTO PACKS

DRCAK Asuka
DRCCM Carmella
DRCKS Kairi Sane

2015 Topps WWE Sting Tribute

COMPLETE SET (40)   15.00   40.00
*GOLD/10: 2X TO 5X BASIC CARDS
*RED/1: UNPRICED DUE TO SCARCITY

1	Sting	1.25	3.00
2	Sting	1.25	3.00
3	Sting	1.25	3.00
4	Sting	1.25	3.00
5	Sting	1.25	3.00
6	Sting	1.25	3.00
7	Sting	1.25	3.00
8	Sting	1.25	3.00
9	Sting	1.25	3.00
10	Sting	1.25	3.00
11	Sting	1.25	3.00
12	Sting	1.25	3.00
13	Sting	1.25	3.00
14	Sting	1.25	3.00
15	Sting	1.25	3.00
16	Sting	1.25	3.00
17	Sting	1.25	3.00
18	Sting	1.25	3.00
19	Sting	1.25	3.00
20	Sting	1.25	3.00
21	Sting	1.25	3.00
22	Sting	1.25	3.00
23	Sting	1.25	3.00
24	Sting	1.25	3.00
25	Sting	1.25	3.00
26	Sting	1.25	3.00
27	Sting	1.25	3.00
28	Sting	1.25	3.00
29	Sting	1.25	3.00
30	Sting	1.25	3.00
31	Sting	1.25	3.00
32	Sting	1.25	3.00
33	Sting	1.25	3.00
34	Sting	1.25	3.00
35	Sting	1.25	3.00
36	Sting	1.25	3.00
37	Sting	1.25	3.00
38	Sting	1.25	3.00
39	Sting	1.25	3.00
40	Sting	1.25	3.00

2015 Topps WWE Sting Tribute Autographs and Relics

*GOLD/10: UNPRICED DUE TO SCARCITY
*RED/1: UNPRICED DUE TO SCARCITY

NNO	Sting AU/Red White Blue	25.00	60.00
NNO	Sting MEM/Shirt	10.00	25.00
NNO	Sting AU MEM/Shirt	50.00	100.00

2015 Topps WWE Sting Tribute Topps Chrome WWE Autographs and Relics

*GOLD/10: UNPRICED DUE TO SCARCITY

NNO	Sting AU/WCW Belt	50.00	100.00
NNO	Sting MEM/Tights	15.00	40.00
NNO	Sting AU MEM/Tights	75.00	150.00

2015 Topps WWE Sting Tribute Topps Heritage WWE Autographs and Relics

*GOLD/10: UNPRICED DUE TO SCARCITY
*RED/1: UNPRICED DUE TO SCARCITY

NNO	Sting AU	50.00	100.00
NNO	Sting AU MEM/Glove		

2015 Topps WWE Sting Tribute Topps WWE Road to WrestleMania Autographs and Relics

*GOLD/10: UNPRICED DUE TO SCARCITY
*RED/1: UNPRICED DUE TO SCARCITY

NNO	Sting AU	50.00	100.00
NNO	Sting MEM/Boots	30.00	75.00
NNO	Sting AU MEM/Boots	75.00	150.00

2019 Topps WWE SummerSlam

COMPLETE SET (100)   10.00   25.00
*BRONZE: .6X TO 1.5X BASIC CARDS
*BLUE/99: .75X TO 2X BASIC CARDS
*SILVER/25: 2X TO 5X BASIC CARDS
*GOLD/10: UNPRICED DUE TO SCARCITY
*RED/1: UNPRICED DUE TO SCARCITY
*P.P.BLACK/1: UNPRICED DUE TO SCARCITY
*P.P.CYAN/1: UNPRICED DUE TO SCARCITY
*P.P.MAGENTA/1: UNPRICED DUE TO SCARCITY
*P.P.YELLOW/1: UNPRICED DUE TO SCARCITY

1	Akam	.25	.60
2	Baron Corbin	.40	1.00
3	Bobby Lashley	.50	1.25
4	Braun Strowman	.60	1.50
5	Bray Wyatt	.60	1.50
6	Brock Lesnar	1.00	2.50
7	Dolph Ziggler	.50	1.25
8	Drew McIntyre	.30	.75
9	Elias	.50	1.25
10	Finn Balor	.60	1.50
11	Kevin Owens	.60	1.50
12	Kurt Angle	.50	1.25
13	Rezar	.25	.60
14	Roman Reigns	.60	1.50
15	Sami Zayn	.50	1.25
16	Seth Rollins	.60	1.50
17	Titus O'Neil	.30	.75
18	Alexa Bliss	1.25	3.00
19	Bayley	.50	1.25
20	Ember Moon	.60	1.50
21	Liv Morgan	.75	2.00
22	Natalya	.50	1.25
23	Nia Jax	.50	1.25

#	Player		
24	Ronda Rousey	1.25	3.00
25	Ruby Riott	.50	1.25
26	Sarah Logan	.30	.75
27	Sasha Banks	1.00	2.50
28	Ali	.25	.60
29	AJ Styles	1.25	3.00
30	Andrade	.30	.75
31	Big E	.25	.60
32	Cesaro	.30	.75
33	Daniel Bryan	1.00	2.50
34	Jeff Hardy	.60	1.50
35	Kofi Kingston	.40	1.00
36	The Miz	.50	1.25
37	Randy Orton	.60	1.50
38	Rey Mysterio	.60	1.50
39	Samoa Joe	.50	1.25
40	Sheamus	.40	1.00
41	Shinsuke Nakamura	.60	1.50
42	Xavier Woods	.30	.75
43	Asuka	.75	2.00
44	Becky Lynch	1.00	2.50
45	Carmella	.60	1.50
46	Charlotte Flair	1.00	2.50
47	Mandy Rose	.60	1.50
48	Naomi	.40	1.00
49	Peyton Royce	.60	1.50
50	Zelina Vega	.40	1.00
51	Matt Hardy & Bray Wyatt	.60	1.50
52	Shelton Benjamin	.60	1.50
53	Nakamura, Rusev & English	1.25	3.00
54	The Deleters of Worlds	.60	1.50
55	Cedric Alexander	.25	.60
56	Jeff Hardy	.60	1.50
57	The Bludgeon Brothers	.30	.75
58	Seth Rollins	.60	1.50
59	AJ Styles	1.25	3.00
60	Brock Lesnar	1.00	2.50
61	Seth Rollins	.60	1.50
62	Jeff Hardy	.60	1.50
63	AJ Styles and Nakamura	.60	1.50
64	Braun Strowman	.60	1.50
65	The Deleters of Worlds	.60	1.50
66	Finn Balor	.60	1.50
67	Rusev	1.00	2.50
68	Andrade	.40	1.00
69	Cedric Alexander	.30	.75
70	The B-Team	.30	.75
71	Braun Strowman	.60	1.50
72	Shinsuke Nakamura	.60	1.50
73	Seth Rollins	.60	1.50
74	AJ Styles	1.25	3.00
75	Braun Strowman	.60	1.50
76	Dolph Ziggler	.50	1.25
77	Rusev	1.25	3.00
78	Drew McIntyre	.30	.75
79	AJ Styles & Jeff Hardy	1.25	3.00
80	The B-Team	.30	.75
81	Bobby Lashley	.50	1.25
82	AJ Styles	1.25	3.00
83	Dolph Ziggler	.60	1.50
84	Roman Reigns	.60	1.50
85	Bobby Lashley	.50	1.25
86	Randy Orton	.60	1.50
87	Drew Gulak	.25	.60
88	Baron Corbin	.60	1.50
89	Nakamura & Randy Orton	.60	1.50
90	The New Day	.40	1.00
91	Brock Lesnar	1.00	2.50
92	Cedric Alexander	.25	.60
93	Seth Rollins	.60	1.50
94	The New Day	.25	.60
95	Braun Strowman	.60	1.50
96	Samoa Joe	.50	1.25
97	The Miz	1.00	2.50
98	Finn Balor	.60	1.50
99	Shinsuke Nakamura	.60	1.50
100	Roman Reigns	.60	1.50

2019 Topps WWE SummerSlam Autographed Intercontinental Championship Manufactured Relics

UNPRICED DUE TO SCARCITY

ICRAJH Jeff Hardy
ICRAKA Kurt Angle
ICRAWR William Regal

2019 Topps WWE SummerSlam Autographed Manufactured Logo Relics

STATED PRINT RUN 10 SER.#'d SETS
UNPRICED DUE TO SCARCITY

LRABS Braun Strowman
LRAKA Kurt Angle
LRALL Lex Luger
LRAMK Mankind
LRARO Randy Orton
LRATD Ted DiBiase

2019 Topps WWE SummerSlam Autographed Mat Relics

STATED PRINT RUN 10 SER.#'d SETS
UNPRICED DUE TO SCARCITY

MRAAB Alexa Bliss
MRAAC Adam Cole
MRAAJ AJ Styles
MRABC Baron Corbin
MRABE Big E
MRABL Becky Lynch
MRABM Drew McIntyre
MRABS Braun Strowman
MRACM Carmella
MRADB Daniel Bryan
MRAEC Velveteen Dream
MRAFB Finn Balor
MRAJG Johnny Gargano
MRAJH Jeff Hardy
MRAKK Kofi Kingston
MRAKO Kevin Owens
MRAKR Kyle O'Reilly
MRAKS Kairi Sane
MRANT Natalya
MRARC Ricochet
MRARS Roderick Strong
MRARW Rowan
MRASB Shayna Baszler
MRASJ Samoa Joe
MRASN Shinsuke Nakamura
MRASR Seth Rollins
MRATB Tyler Bate
MRATM The Miz
MRATS Trent Seven
MRAVD EC3
MRAXW Xavier Woods

2019 Topps WWE SummerSlam Autographed Superstar Relics

STATED PRINT RUN 10 SER.#'d SETS
UNPRICED DUE TO SCARCITY

SRAAE Aiden English
SRAAW Alexander Wolfe
SRABS Braun Strowman
SRACS Cesaro
SRADW Dash Wilder
SRAEY Eric Young
SRAKD Killian Dain
SRASD Scott Dawson
SRASM Shawn Michaels
SRASZ Sami Zayn

2019 Topps WWE SummerSlam Autographed Women's Evolution Relics

UNPRICED DUE TO SCARCITY

ERARR Ruby Riott
ERATS Tamina

2019 Topps WWE SummerSlam Autographs

*BLUE/50: .5X TO 1.2X BASIC AUTOS
*SILVER/25: .6X TO 1.5X BASIC AUTOS
*GOLD/10: UNPRICED DUE TO SCARCITY
*RED/1: UNPRICED DUE TO SCARCITY
*P.P.BLACK/1: UNPRICED DUE TO SCARCITY
*P.P.CYAN/1: UNPRICED DUE TO SCARCITY
*P.P.MAGENTA/1: UNPRICED DUE TO SCARCITY
*P.P.YELLOW/1: UNPRICED DUE TO SCARCITY
STATED ODDS 1:24

Code	Name		
OCAA	Andrade	4.00	10.00
OCAB	Alexa Bliss	30.00	75.00
OCAJ	AJ Styles	12.00	30.00
OCBE	Big E	4.00	10.00
OCBL	Bayley	10.00	25.00
OCBR	Bobby Roode	5.00	12.00
OCBS	Braun Strowman	6.00	15.00
OCCF	Charlotte Flair	15.00	40.00
OCCM	Carmella	8.00	20.00
OCDM	Drew McIntyre	6.00	15.00
OCEL	Elias	8.00	20.00
OCFB	Finn Balor	12.00	30.00
OCJH	Jeff Hardy	12.00	30.00
OCKK	Kofi Kingston	8.00	20.00
OCKO	Kevin Owens	5.00	12.00
OCMM	Bobby Lashley	5.00	12.00
OCMR	Mandy Rose	20.00	50.00
OCRM	Rey Mysterio	12.00	30.00
OCRR	Ruby Riott	15.00	40.00
OCRT	R-Truth	4.00	10.00
OCSD	Sonya Deville	10.00	25.00
OCSJ	Samoa Joe	6.00	15.00
OCSN	Shinsuke Nakamura	8.00	20.00
OCTM	The Miz	6.00	15.00
OCXW	Xavier Woods	4.00	10.00
OCZV	Zelina Vega	12.00	30.00

2019 Topps WWE SummerSlam Dual Autographs

STATED PRINT RUN 10 SER.#'d SETS
UNPRICED DUE TO SCARCITY

DAAB S.Deville/M.Rose
DABT B.Dallas/C.Axel
DAII B.Kay/P.Royce
DAMK Maria & Mike Kanellis
DAND X.Woods/K.Kingston

2019 Topps WWE SummerSlam Greatest Matches and Moments

COMPLETE SET (40)		6.00	15.00
RANDOMLY INSERTED INTO PACKS			
GM1	Ultimate Warrior Def. Honky Tonk Man	.50	1.25
GM2	Warrior/Rick Rude	.60	1.50
GM3	Dusty Rhodes/Honky Tonk Man	.50	1.25
GM4	The Texas Tornado Def. Mr. Perfect	.30	.75
GM5	Macho Man Marries Elizabeth	.60	1.50
GM6	Virgil/Ted DiBiase	.25	.60
GM7	British Bulldog/Bret Hart	.50	1.25
GM8	Warrior/Randy Savage	.60	1.50
GM9	Lex Luger/Yokozuna	.30	.75
GM10	Alundra Blayze/Bull Nakano	.25	.60
GM11	Shawn Michaels/Razor Ramon	.50	1.25
GM12	Mankind/Undertaker	.40	1.00
GM13	Shawn Michaels/Vader	.60	1.50
GM14	Mankind/Triple H	.50	1.25
GM15	Steve Austin wins IC Title	1.00	2.50
GM16	Ken Shamrock/Owen Hart	.40	1.00
GM17	Steve Austin/Undertaker	1.25	3.00
GM18	Mankind/Steve Austin/HHH	.50	1.25
GM19	Rock/HHH/Kurt Angle	1.00	2.50
GM20	Kurt Angle/Steve Austin	1.25	3.00
GM21	Shawn Michaels/HHH	.60	1.50
GM22	Kurt Angle/Rey Mysterio	.40	1.00
GM23	Kurt Angle/Brock Lesnar	.50	1.25
GM24	Kurt Angle/Eddie Guerrero	.40	1.00
GM25	Rey Mysterio/Eddie Guerrero	.60	1.50
GM26	Ric Flair/Mick Foley	.75	2.00
GM27	John Cena/Randy Orton	1.00	2.50
GM28	Batista/John Cena	.50	1.25
GM29	Rey Mysterio/Dolph Ziggler	.60	1.50
GM30	Randy Orton/Sheamus	.50	1.25
GM31	Randy Orton/Christian	.60	1.50
GM32	Kane/Rey Mysterio/Undertaker	.30	.75
GM33	Miz/Rey Mysterio	.50	1.25
GM34	Daniel Bryan/John Cena	.75	2.00
GM35	Roman Reigns/Randy Orton	.60	1.50
GM36	Seth Rollins/John Cena	.50	1.25
GM37	Charlotte Flair/Sasha Banks	1.00	2.50
GM38	Finn Balor/Seth Rollins	.60	1.50
GM39	AJ Styles/John Cena	1.25	3.00
GM40	Usos/New Day	.30	.75

2019 Topps WWE SummerSlam Intercontinental Champion Autographs

STATED PRINT RUN 25 SER.#'d SETS

Code	Name		
ICRJH	Jeff Hardy	15.00	40.00
ICRWR	William Regal	10.00	25.00

2019 Topps WWE SummerSlam Intercontinental Championship Manufactured Relics

RANDOMLY INSERTED INTO PACKS

ICRBT Booker T
ICRDL D'Lo Brown
ICRJH Jeff Hardy
ICRKA Kurt Angle
ICRWR William Regal

2019 Topps WWE SummerSlam Manufactured Logo Relics

*BRONZE/99: .5X TO 1.2X BASIC MEM
*BLUE/50: .6X TO 1.5X BASIC MEM
*SILVER/25: .75X TO 2X BASIC MEM
*GOLD/10: UNPRICED DUE TO SCARCITY
*RED/1: UNPRICED DUE TO SCARCITY
STATED ODDS 1:152

LRBH	Bret Hit Man Hart	3.00	8.00
LRBL	Brock Lesnar	6.00	15.00
LRBS	Braun Strowman	3.00	8.00
LRBT	Booker T	3.00	8.00
LRED	Edge	3.00	8.00
LRJC	John Cena	4.00	10.00
LRKA	Kurt Angle	3.00	8.00
LRLL	Lex Luger	2.50	6.00
LRMK	Mankind	2.50	6.00
LRRO	Randy Orton	4.00	10.00
LRSA	Stone Cold Steve Austin	6.00	15.00
LRSM	Shawn Michaels	4.00	10.00
LRTD	Ted DiBiase	2.50	6.00
LRUT	Undertaker	4.00	10.00
LRBDC	Diesel	3.00	8.00

2019 Topps WWE SummerSlam Mat Relics

*BRONZE/99: .5X TO 1.2X BASIC MEM
*BLUE/50: .6X TO 1.5X BASIC MEM
*SILVER/25: .75X TO 2X BASIC MEM
*GOLD/10: UNPRICED DUE TO SCARCITY
*RED/1: UNPRICED DUE TO SCARCITY
RANDOMLY INSERTED INTO PACKS

MRAB	Alexa Bliss	12.00	30.00
MRAC	Adam Cole	3.00	8.00
MRAJ	AJ Styles	3.00	8.00
MRBC	Baron Corbin	1.50	4.00
MRBD	Roman Reigns	3.00	8.00
MRBE	Big E	1.50	4.00
MRBI	Brock Lesnar	3.00	8.00
MRBL	Becky Lynch	6.00	15.00
MRBM	Drew McIntyre	2.50	6.00
MRBS	Braun Strowman	2.50	6.00
MRCF	Charlotte Flair	5.00	12.00
MRCM	Carmella	4.00	10.00
MRDB	Daniel Bryan		
MRDZ	Dolph Ziggler	2.50	6.00
MREC	Velveteen Dream	2.50	6.00
MRFB	Finn Balor	4.00	10.00
MRHP	Harper	2.50	6.00
MRJG	Johnny Gargano	2.50	6.00
MRJH	Jeff Hardy	4.00	10.00
MRKK	Kofi Kingston	3.00	8.00
MRKO	Kevin Owens	2.00	5.00
MRKR	Kyle O'Reilly	2.00	5.00
MRKS	Kairi Sane	3.00	8.00
MRNT	Natalya	3.00	8.00
MRPH	Paul Heyman	2.50	6.00
MRRC	Ricochet	3.00	8.00
MRRR	Ronda Rousey	10.00	25.00
MRRS	Roderick Strong	2.50	6.00
MRRW	Rowan	1.50	4.00
MRSB	Shayna Baszler		
MRSJ	Samoa Joe	2.00	5.00
MRSN	Shinsuke Nakamura	2.00	5.00
MRSR	Seth Rollins	3.00	8.00
MRTB	Tyler Bate	2.50	6.00
MRTC	Tommaso Ciampa	2.50	6.00

MRTM	The Miz	2.00	5.00
MRTS	Trent Seven	1.50	4.00
MRVD	EC3	1.50	4.00
MRXW	Xavier Woods	1.50	4.00

2019 Topps WWE SummerSlam Mr. SummerSlam

RANDOMLY INSERTED INTO PACKS

MSS1	Lesnar/Rock	1.25	3.00
MSS2	Lesnar/HHH	1.00	2.50
MSS3	Lesnar/Cena	1.00	2.50
MSS4	Lesnar/Orton	1.00	2.50
MSS5	Lesnar/Samoa Joe/Strowman/Reigns	1.00	2.50
MSS6	Undertaker Returns	1.25	3.00
MSS7	Undertaker/Kama	1.25	3.00
MSS8	Unholy Alliance/Kane/X-Pac	.40	1.00
MSS9	Undertaker/Edge	1.25	3.00
MSS10	Undertaker/Brock Lesnar	1.25	3.00
MSS11	Edge & Christian	.60	1.50
MSS12	Edge/Eddie Guerrero	.60	1.50
MSS13	Edge IC Title	.60	1.50
MSS14	Edge/Matt Hardy	.60	1.50
MSS15	Edge/John Cena	.60	1.50
MSS16	HHH PPV Debut	.60	1.50
MSS17	Triple H/Rock	1.25	3.00
MSS18	DX/Mr. McMahon & Shane	.60	1.50
MSS19	HHH/King Booker	.60	1.50
MSS20	HHH/A Giant	.60	1.50
MSS21	Hart Foundation	.60	1.50
MSS22	Bret Hart/Mr. Perfect	.60	1.50
MSS23	Bret Hart/Lawler	.60	1.50
MSS24	Bret Hart/Undertaker	.60	1.50
MSS25	Bret Hart Returns	.60	1.50

2019 Topps WWE SummerSlam Posters Spotlight

COMPLETE SET (4)		3.00	8.00
STATED ODDS 1:6			
SS14	'14 Cena/Lesnar	1.25	3.00
SS15	'15 Lesnar/Undertaker	1.00	2.50
SS16	'17 Collage	1.00	2.50
SS17	'18 Lesnar/Bliss/Rousey/Reigns	1.50	4.00

2019 Topps WWE SummerSlam Superstar Relics

*BRONZE/99: SAME VALUE AS BASIC
*BLUE/50: .5X TO 1.2X BASIC MEM
*SILVER/25: .6X TO 1.5X BASIC MEM
*GOLD/10: UNPRICED DUE TO SCARCITY
*RED/1: UNPRICED DUE TO SCARCITY
RANDOMLY INSERTED INTO PACKS

SRAC	Apollo Crews	2.50	6.00
SRAW	Alexander Wolfe	2.50	6.00
SRBS	Braun Strowman	5.00	12.00
SRCS	Cesaro	3.00	8.00
SRDW	Dash Wilder	2.50	6.00
SRED	Edge	4.00	10.00
SREY	Eric Young	2.50	6.00
SRHS	Heath Slater	2.50	6.00
SRJC	John Cena	5.00	12.00
SRKD	Killian Dain	2.50	6.00
SRRR	Roman Reigns	4.00	10.00
SRSD	Scott Dawson	2.50	6.00
SRSM	Shawn Michaels	4.00	10.00
SRSR	Seth Rollins	3.00	8.00
SRSZ	Sami Zayn	2.50	6.00

2019 Topps WWE SummerSlam Women's Evolution Autographs

*GOLD/10: UNPRICED DUE TO SCARCITY
*P.P.BLACK/1: UNPRICED DUE TO SCARCITY
*P.P.CYAN/1: UNPRICED DUE TO SCARCITY
*P.P.MAGENTA/1: UNPRICED DUE TO SCARCITY
*P.P.YELLOW/1: UNPRICED DUE TO SCARCITY
STATED PRINT RUN 25 SER.#'d SETS
UNPRICED DUE TO SCARCITY

WAAF	Alicia Fox
WAEM	Ember Moon
WAMJ	Mickie James
WANL	Natalya
WARR	Ruby Riott
WATS	Tamina

2019 Topps WWE SummerSlam Women's Evolution Relics

STATED PRINT RUN 25 SER.#'d SETS
UNPRICED DUE TO SCARCITY

ERAF	Alicia Fox
EREM	Ember Moon
ERRR	Ruby Riott
ERTS	Tamina

2021 Topps WWE Superstars

COMPLETE SET (225)		30.00	80.00
1	Adam Cole	.60	1.50
2	AJ Styles	.60	1.50
3	Akira Tozawa	.25	.60
4	Alexa Bliss	1.25	3.00
5	Aliyah	.40	1.00
6	Angel Garza	.25	.60
7	Angelo Dawkins	.25	.60
8	Apollo Crews	.25	.60
9	Asuka	.75	2.00
10	Austin Theory	.40	1.00
11	Bayley	.40	1.00
12	Becky Lynch	.75	2.00
13	Bianca Belair	.50	1.25
14	Big E	.50	1.25
15	Bobby Lashley	.50	1.25
16	Cameron Grimes	.40	1.00
17	Candice LeRae	.75	2.00
18	Carmella	.50	1.25
19	Cedric Alexander	.20	.50
20	Cesaro	.20	.50
21	Chad Gable	.20	.50
22	Charlotte Flair	1.00	2.50
23	Commander Azeez	.25	.60
24	Dakota Kai	.40	1.00
25	Damian Priest	.30	.75
26	Dana Brooke	.20	.50
27	Danny Burch	.25	.60
28	Dave Mastiff	.20	.50
29	Dexter Lumis	.20	.50
30	Dolph Ziggler	.40	1.00
31	Dominik Mysterio	.25	.60
32	Drake Maverick	.20	.50
33	Drew Gulak	.25	.60
34	Drew McIntyre	.50	1.25
35	Edge	.75	2.00
36	Elias	.20	.50
37	Ember Moon	.25	.60
38	Erik	.20	.50
39	Eva Marie	.50	1.25
40	Fabian Aichner	.25	.60
41	Finn Balor	.50	1.25
42	Flash Morgan Webster	.25	.60
43	Franky Monet	.40	1.00
44	Gigi Dolin	.20	.50
45	Gran Metalik	.20	.50
46	Humberto Carrillo	.20	.50
47	Ilja Dragunov	.20	.50
48	Indi Hartwell	.60	1.50
49	Io Shirai	.40	1.00
50	Isaiah "Swerve" Scott	.30	.75
51	Ivar	.20	.50
52	James Drake	.20	.50
53	Jaxson Ryker	.20	.50
54	Jeff Hardy	.50	1.25
55	Jey Uso	.20	.50
56	Jimmy Uso	.20	.50
57	Jinder Mahal	.25	.60
58	Joaquin Wilde	.30	.75
59	Joe Coffey	.20	.50
60	John Morrison	.40	1.00
61	Johnny Gargano	.40	1.00
62	Jordan Devlin	.40	1.00
63	Kacy Catanzaro	.40	1.00
64	Karrion Kross	.75	2.00
65	Kay Lee Ray	.50	1.25
66	Kayden Carter	.40	1.00
67	Keith Lee	.40	1.00
68	Kevin Owens	.40	1.00
69	Baron Corbin	.20	.50
70	Kofi Kingston	.50	1.25
71	Kushida	.30	.75
72	Kyle O'Reilly	.30	.75
73	LA Knight	.20	.50
74	Lacey Evans	.75	2.00
75	Liv Morgan	.75	2.00
76	Mace	.20	.50
77	Mandy Rose	1.00	2.50
78	Mansoor	.20	.50
79	Marcel Barthel	.25	.60
80	Mark Andrews	.20	.50
81	Mark Coffey	.20	.50
82	Montez Ford	.20	.50
83	Mustafa Ali	.25	.60
84	MVP	.25	.60
85	Naomi	.25	.60
86	Nash Carter	.20	.50
87	Natalya	.30	.75
88	Nia Jax	.40	1.00
89	Nikki A.S.H.	.40	1.00
90	Noam Dar	.25	.60
91	Oney Lorcan	.20	.50
92	Omos	.20	.50
93	Otis	.25	.60
94	Pete Dunne	.50	1.25
95	Doudrop	.30	.75
96	R-Truth	.25	.60
97	Randy Orton	.60	1.50
98	Raquel Gonzalez	.75	2.00
99	Mia Yim	.25	.60
100	Reggie	.20	.50
101	Rey Mysterio	.50	1.25
102	Rhea Ripley	.75	2.00
103	Ricochet	.30	.75
104	Riddick Moss	.25	.60
105	Riddle	.50	1.25
106	Robert Roode	.25	.60
107	Roderick Strong	.40	1.00
108	Roman Reigns	1.00	2.50

#	Player		
109	Sami Zayn	.30	.75
110	Santos Escobar	.40	1.00
111	Sarray	.25	.60
112	Sasha Banks	1.00	2.50
113	Scarlett	1.00	2.50
114	Seth Rollins	.50	1.25
115	Shayna Baszler	.50	1.25
116	Sheamus	.30	.75
117	Shelton Benjamin	.30	.75
118	Shinsuke Nakamura	.50	1.25
119	Shotzi	1.00	2.50
120	Shane Thorne	.20	.50
121	T-Bar	.25	.60
122	Tamina	.20	.50
123	Tegan Nox	.50	1.25
124	Samoa Joe	.40	1.00
125	The Miz	.30	.75
126	Timothy Thatcher	.20	.50
127	Tommaso Ciampa	.50	1.25
128	Toni Storm	.75	2.00
129	Trent Seven	.25	.60
130	Tyler Bate	.25	.60
131	Walter	.60	1.50
132	Wes Lee	.20	.50
133	Wolfgang	.20	.50
134	Xavier Woods	.20	.50
135	Xia Li	.40	1.00
136	Zack Gibson	.20	.50
137	Zoey Stark	.25	.60
138	Andre the Giant L	2.50	6.00
139	Bam Bam Bigelow L	.40	1.00
140	Batista L	.40	1.00
141	Big Boss Man L	.30	.75
142	Booker T L	.40	1.00
143	Bret "Hit Man" Hart L	.50	1.25
144	British Bulldog L	.30	.75
145	Chyna L	.40	1.00
146	Doink the Clown L	.20	.50
147	Eddie Guerrero L	1.00	2.50
148	Goldberg L	.75	2.00
149	Honky Tonk Man L	.20	.50
150	Hulk Hogan L	1.00	2.50
151	Jake "The Snake" Roberts L	.30	.75
152	Kevin Nash L	.30	.75
153	Lex Luger L	.25	.60
154	Macho Man Randy Savage L	1.25	3.00
155	Mick Foley L	.30	.75
156	Mr. Perfect L	.60	1.50
157	Papa Shango L	.25	.60
158	Razor Ramon L	.30	.75
159	Ricky "The Dragon" Steamboat L	.30	.75
160	Rikishi L	.25	.60
161	Rowdy Roddy Piper L	.50	1.25
162	RVD L	.40	1.00
163	Sgt. Slaughter L	.30	.75
164	Shawn Michaels L	.75	2.00
165	Stacy Keibler L	.60	1.50
166	Stone Cold Steve Austin L	1.00	2.50
167	Trish Stratus L	1.00	2.50
168	Ultimate Warrior L	1.25	3.00
169	Undertaker L	1.00	2.50
170	Vader L	.30	.75
171	Yokozuna L	.30	.75
172	Bianca Belair UF	.50	1.25
173	Bobby Lashley UF	.50	1.25
174	Drew McIntyre UF	.50	1.25
175	Io Shirai UF	.40	1.00
176	Kevin Owens UF	.40	1.00
177	Randy Orton UF	.60	1.50
178	Rhea Ripley UF	.75	2.00
179	Roman Reigns UF	1.00	2.50
180	John Cena UF	1.00	2.50
181	The Austin Era Begins	1.00	2.50
182	Five-Star Classic	1.00	2.50
183	Ticket to the Title	1.00	2.50
184	First WWE Championship	1.00	2.50
185	Dominating the Dude	1.00	2.50
186	The People's Stunner	1.00	2.50
187	Third Royal Rumble Win	1.00	2.50
188	Main Event Shocker	1.00	2.50
189	Last-Ever Match	1.00	2.50
190	The Winning Business WMFB	.50	1.25
191	A Swiss Masterclass WMFB	.20	.50
192	Omos Makes His Mark WMFB	.20	.50
193	Triumphant Turmoil WMFB	.30	.75
194	Bianca Becomes the Great-est WMFB	.40	1.00
195	RKO Stuns the Fiend WMFB	.60	1.50
196	Owens KO's His Rival WMFB	.40	1.00
197	Sheamus Solves the Riddle WMFB	.30	.75
198	Crews Control WMFB	.25	.60
199	Rhea Wins the Big One WMFB	.75	2.00
200	Smash 'Em, Stack 'Em, Pin 'Em WMFB	1.00	2.50
201	Alexa Bliss RTWM	1.25	3.00
202	Becky Lynch RTWM	.75	2.00
203	Bianca Belair RTWM	.50	1.25
204	Charlotte Flair RTWM	1.00	2.50
205	Drew McIntyre RTWM	.50	1.25
206	Kofi Kingston RTWM	.50	1.25
207	Randy Orton RTWM	.60	1.50
208	Roman Reigns RTWM	1.00	2.50
209	Seth Rollins RTWM	.50	1.25
210	The Rock	1.25	3.00
211	The Rock	1.25	3.00
212	The Rock	1.25	3.00
213	The Rock	1.25	3.00
214	The Rock	1.25	3.00
215	The Rock	1.25	3.00
216	The Rock	1.25	3.00
217	The Rock	1.25	3.00
218	SummerSlam 2020 SUW	1.00	2.50
219	Payback 2020 SUW	1.00	2.50
220	Clash of Champions 2020 SUW	1.00	2.50
221	Hell in a Cell 2020 SUW	1.00	2.50
222	Survivor Series 2020 SUW	1.00	2.50
223	Royal Rumble 2021 SUW	1.00	2.50
224	WrestleMania 37 SUW	1.00	2.50
225	WrestleMania Backlash SUW	1.00	2.50

2021 Topps WWE Superstars 25 Years of The Rock

COMPLETE SET (3) 8.00 20.00
*GREEN/50: .5X TO 1.2X BASIC CARDS
*PURPLE/25: .6X TO 1.5X BASIC CARDS
*TURQUOISE/10: UNPRICED DUE TO SCARCITY
*RED/5: UNPRICED DUE TO SCARCITY
*GOLD/1: UNPRICED DUE TO SCARCITY

TR1	Survivor Series Shocker	4.00	10.00
TR2	Icon vs. Icon	4.00	10.00
TR3	Magic in Miami	4.00	10.00

2021 Topps WWE Superstars Autographs Orange

*TURQUOISE/10: UNPRICED DUE TO SCARCITY
*RED/5: UNPRICED DUE TO SCARCITY
*GOLD/1: UNPRICED DUE TO SCARCITY
STATED PRINT RUN 99 SER.#'d SETS

NNO	Kofi Kingston
	(2021 Black Friday Exclusive)
NNO	Kofi Kingston (Kofi-Mania)
	(2021 Black Friday Exclusive)
NNO	Big E
NNO	Erik
NNO	King Nakamura
NNO	Naomi
NNO	Roderick Strong
NNO	Samoa Joe
NNO	Tyler Bate
NNO	Zelina Vega

2021 Topps WWE Superstars Crystal

COMPLETE SET (6) 15.00 40.00
RANDOMLY INSERTED INTO PACKS

CR1	Alexa Bliss	6.00	15.00
CR2	Bianca Belair	3.00	8.00
CR3	Drew McIntyre	6.00	15.00
CR4	Roman Reigns	5.00	12.00
CR5	Sasha Banks	6.00	15.00
CR6	John Cena	4.00	10.00

2021 Topps WWE Superstars Iconic Matches

*TURQUOISE/10: UNPRICED DUE TO SCARCITY
*RED/5: UNPRICED DUE TO SCARCITY
*GOLD/1: UNPRICED DUE TO SCARCITY
RANDOMLY INSERTED INTO PACKS

MA1	WrestleMania III
MA2	WrestleMania VI
MA3	SummerSlam 1992
MA4	SummerSlam 1995
MA5	WrestleMania XII
MA6	Royal Rumble 2000
MA7	WrestleMania X-Seven
MA8	WrestleMania 25
MA9	WrestleMania 28
MA10	NXT TakeOver: Brooklyn
MA11	SummerSlam 2016

2021 Topps WWE Superstars John Cena's Greatest Moments

COMPLETE SET (6) 12.00 30.00
*GREEN/50: .5X TO 1.2X BASIC CARDS
*PURPLE/25: .6X TO 1.5X BASIC CARDS
*TURQUOISE/10: UNPRICED DUE TO SCARCITY
*RED/5: UNPRICED DUE TO SCARCITY
*GOLD/1: UNPRICED DUE TO SCARCITY
RANDOMLY INSERTED INTO PACKS

JC1	First WWE Title	3.00	8.00
JC2	Legend of the Ladder	3.00	8.00
JC3	Rumble Shocker	3.00	8.00
JC4	Iconic Entrance	3.00	8.00
JC5	Revenge on the Rock	3.00	8.00
JC6	Thuganomics 4 Life	3.00	8.00

2021 Topps WWE Superstars Legends Autographs Orange

*TURQUOISE/10: UNPRICED DUE TO SCARCITY
*RED/5: UNPRICED DUE TO SCARCITY
*GOLD/1: UNPRICED DUE TO SCARCITY
STATED PRINT RUN 99 SER.#'d SETS

NNO	Booker T
NNO	Million Dollar Man Ted DiBiase

2021 Topps WWE Superstars Return of the Fans

COMPLETE SET (5) 6.00 15.00
*GREEN/50: .5X TO 1.2X BASIC CARDS
*PURPLE/25: .6X TO 1.5X BASIC CARDS
*TURQUOISE/10: UNPRICED DUE TO SCARCITY
*RED/5: UNPRICED DUE TO SCARCITY
*GOLD/1: UNPRICED DUE TO SCARCITY
RANDOMLY INSERTED INTO PACKS

RF1	Big E Wins the Big One	2.00	5.00
RF2	Roman Reigns Supreme	2.50	6.00
RF3	Return Heard Around the World	2.50	6.00
RF4	The Bro-Off	4.00	10.00
RF5	Superhero Cash-In	1.50	4.00

2021 Topps WWE Superstars Super Elite

COMPLETE SET (16) 15.00 40.00
*YELLOW: .5X TO 1.2X BASIC CARDS
*BLUE/299: .6X TO 1.5X BASIC CARDS
*ORANGE/99: .75X TO 2X BASIC CARDS
*GREEN/50: 1X TO 2.5X BASIC CARDS
*PURPLE/25: UNPRICED DUE TO SCARCITY
*TURQUOISE/10: UNPRICED DUE TO SCARCITY
*RED/5: UNPRICED DUE TO SCARCITY
*GOLD/1: UNPRICED DUE TO SCARCITY
RANDOMLY INSERTED INTO PACKS

SE1	AJ Styles	1.50	4.00
SE2	Alexa Bliss	3.00	8.00
SE3	Asuka	2.00	5.00
SE4	Bayley	1.00	2.50
SE5	Becky Lynch	2.00	5.00
SE6	Bianca Belair	1.25	3.00
SE7	Bobby Lashley	1.25	3.00
SE8	Charlotte Flair	2.50	6.00
SE9	Drew McIntyre	1.25	3.00
SE10	Riddle	1.25	3.00
SE11	Randy Orton	1.50	4.00
SE12	Roman Reigns	2.50	6.00
SE13	Sasha Banks	2.50	6.00
SE14	Seth Rollins	1.25	3.00
SE15	Shinsuke Nakamura	1.25	3.00
SE16	Big E	1.25	3.00

2021 Topps WWE Superstars Super Elite Icons

COMPLETE SET (9) 12.00 30.00
*YELLOW: .5X TO 1.2X BASIC CARDS
*BLUE/299: .6X TO 1.5X BASIC CARDS
*ORANGE/99: .75X TO 2X BASIC CARDS
*GREEN/50: 1X TO 2.5X BASIC CARDS
*PURPLE/25: UNPRICED DUE TO SCARCITY
*TURQUOISE/10: UNPRICED DUE TO SCARCITY
*RED/5: UNPRICED DUE TO SCARCITY
*GOLD/1: UNPRICED DUE TO SCARCITY
RANDOMLY INSERTED INTO PACKS

IC1	Andre the Giant	6.00	15.00
IC2	Bret Hit Man Hart	1.25	3.00
IC3	Hulk Hogan	2.50	6.00
IC4	John Cena	2.50	6.00
IC5	Shawn Michaels	2.00	5.00
IC6	Stone Cold Steve Austin	2.50	6.00
IC7	The Rock	3.00	8.00
IC8	Triple H	1.50	4.00
IC9	Undertaker	2.50	6.00

2016 Topps WWE Then Now Forever

COMPLETE SET (100)	10.00	25.00
UNOPENED BOX (24 PACKS)		
UNOPENED PACK (7 CARDS)		

*BRONZE: 1.2X TO 3X BASIC CARDS
*SILVER: 2X TO 5X BASIC CARDS
*GOLD/10: 4X TO 10X BASIC CARDS
*RED/1: UNPRICED DUE TO SCARCITY
*P.P.BLACK/1: UNPRICED DUE TO SCARCITY
*P.P.CYAN/1: UNPRICED DUE TO SCARCITY
*P.P.MAGENTA/1: UNPRICED DUE TO SCARCITY
*P.P.YELLOW/1: UNPRICED DUE TO SCARCITY

101	Aiden English	.20	.50
102	AJ Styles	.75	2.00
103	Apollo Crews	.20	.50
104	Baron Corbin	.25	.60
105	Big Cass	.40	1.00
106	Big E	.20	.50
107	Braun Strowman	.25	.60
108	Bray Wyatt	.75	2.00
109	Brock Lesnar	1.00	2.50
110	Cathy Kelley	.20	.50
111	Chris Jericho	.50	1.25
112	Dana Brooke	.50	1.25
113	Darren Young	.20	.50
114	Dasha Fuentes	.20	.50
115	David Otunga	.20	.50
116	Dean Ambrose	.60	1.50
117	Emma	.40	1.00
118	Enzo Amore	.40	1.00
119	Epico	.20	.50
120	Erick Rowan	.20	.50
121	Eva Marie	.40	1.00
122	Greg Hamilton	.20	.50
123	Heath Slater	.20	.50
124	Jack Swagger	.20	.50
125	John Cena	1.00	2.50
126	JoJo	.20	.50
127	Kane	.30	.75
128	Karl Anderson	.20	.50
129	Kofi Kingston	.20	.50
130	Luke Gallows	.25	.60
131	Luke Harper	.20	.50
132	Maryse	.40	1.00
133	Mauro Ranallo	.20	.50
134	Primo	.20	.50
135	Randy Orton	.50	1.25
136	Renee Young	.50	1.25
137	The Rock	1.00	2.50
138	Roman Reigns	.60	1.50
139	Rosa Mendes	.20	.50
140	Sami Zayn	.30	.75
141	Scott Stanford	.20	.50
142	Seth Rollins	.30	.75
143	Shane McMahon	.30	.75
144	Sheamus	.50	1.25
145	Simon Gotch	.30	.75
146	Stephanie McMahon	.30	.75
147	Tom Phillips	.20	.50
148	Tony Chimel	.20	.50
149	Triple H	.75	2.00
150	Undertaker	.75	2.00
151	Xavier Woods	.20	.50
152	Zack Ryder	.20	.50
153	Big Boss Man L	.30	.75
154	Big John Studd L	.30	.75
155	Bob Backlund L	.20	.50
156	Bobby The Brain Heenan L	.30	.75
157	Brian Pillman L	.25	.60
158	Bruno Sammartino L	.25	.60
159	Chief Jay Strongbow L	.30	.75
160	Cowboy Bob Orton L	.30	.75
161	Daniel Bryan L	.75	2.00
162	Dean Malenko L	.20	.50
163	Diamond Dallas Page L	.30	.75
164	Eddie Guerrero L	.50	1.25
165	The Funks L	.20	.50
166	Gerald Brisco L	.20	.50
167	Gorilla Monsoon L	.30	.75
168	General Adnan L	.20	.50
169	Greg The Hammer Valentine L	.25	.60
170	Hacksaw Jim Duggan L	.20	.50
171	High Chief Peter Maivia L	.20	.50
172	The Honky Tonk Man L	.20	.50
173	Howard Finkel L	.20	.50
174	Jamie Noble L	.20	.50
175	Jim The Anvil Neidhart L	.20	.50
176	Joey Mercury L	.20	.50
177	Junkyard Dog L	.30	.75
178	The King Harley Race L	.20	.50
179	Larry Zbyszko L	.20	.50
180	Lex Luger L	.30	.75
181	Mean Gene Okerlund L	.25	.60
182	Michael P.S. Hayes L	.20	.50
183	Mouth of the South Jimmy Hart L	.25	.60
184	Mr. Perfect Curt Henning L	.50	1.25
185	Mr. Wonderful Paul Orndorff L	.20	.50
186	Nikolai Volkoff L	.25	.60
187	Norman Smiley L	.20	.50
188	Pat Patterson L	.20	.50
189	Paul Bearer L	.30	.75
190	Ravishing Rick Rude L	.30	.75
191	Ricky The Dragon Steamboat L	.25	.60
192	Rocky Johnson L	.25	.60
193	Sgt. Slaughter L	.25	.60
194	Sting L	.50	1.25
195	Stone Cold Steve Austin L	1.00	2.50
196	Tatanka L	.20	.50
197	Tom Prichard L	.20	.50
198	Vader L	.40	1.00
199	Viscera L	.20	.50
200	Yokozuna L	.40	1.00

2016 Topps WWE Then Now Forever Autographs

*BRONZE/50: .5X TO 1.2X BASIC AUTOS
*SILVER/25: .75X TO 2X BASIC AUTOS
*GOLD/10: 1.2X TO 3X BASIC AUTOS
*RED/1: UNPRICED DUE TO SCARCITY
*P.P.BLACK/1: UNPRICED DUE TO SCARCITY
*P.P.CYAN/1: UNPRICED DUE TO SCARCITY
*P.P.MAGENTA/1: UNPRICED DUE TO SCARCITY
*P.P.YELLOW/1: UNPRICED DUE TO SCARCITY
STATED ODDS 1:51

NNO	Aiden English	6.00	15.00
NNO	AJ Styles	20.00	50.00
NNO	Becky Lynch	15.00	60.00
NNO	Charlotte	20.00	50.00
NNO	Chris Jericho	15.00	40.00
NNO	Dean Ambrose	10.00	25.00
NNO	Enzo Amore	12.00	30.00
NNO	Hideo Itami	6.00	15.00
NNO	Karl Anderson	8.00	20.00
NNO	Luke Gallows	8.00	20.00
NNO	Maryse	12.00	30.00
NNO	Naomi	6.00	15.00
NNO	Natalya	8.00	20.00
NNO	Norman Smiley	6.00	15.00
NNO	Ric Flair	60.00	120.00
NNO	Roman Reigns	20.00	50.00
NNO	R-Truth	6.00	15.00
NNO	Sami Zayn	10.00	25.00
NNO	Samoa Joe	6.00	15.00
NNO	Sasha Banks	50.00	100.00
NNO	Seth Rollins	8.00	20.00
NNO	Shinsuke Nakamura	30.00	80.00
NNO	Simon Gotch	6.00	15.00
NNO	Sting	20.00	50.00

2016 Topps WWE Then Now Forever Diva Kiss

*GOLD/10: UNPRICED DUE TO SCARCITY
*RED/1: UNPRICED DUE TO SCARCITY
STATED ODDS 1:125
STATED PRINT RUN 99 SER.#'d SETS

NNO	Alicia Fox	15.00	40.00
NNO	Asuka	30.00	80.00
NNO	Bayley	30.00	80.00
NNO	Becky Lynch	25.00	60.00
NNO	Brie Bella	20.00	50.00
NNO	Carmella	25.00	60.00
NNO	Charlotte	20.00	50.00
NNO	Lana	20.00	50.00
NNO	Nikki Bella	20.00	50.00
NNO	Sasha Banks	30.00	80.00

2016 Topps WWE Then Now Forever Diva Kiss Autographs

*GOLD/10: UNPRICED DUE TO SCARCITY
*RED/1: UNPRICED DUE TO SCARCITY
STATED ODDS 1:482
STATED PRINT RUN 25 SER.#'d SETS

NNO	Alicia Fox	25.00	60.00
NNO	Asuka	80.00	150.00
NNO	Bayley	150.00	300.00
NNO	Becky Lynch	60.00	120.00
NNO	Brie Bella	80.00	150.00
NNO	Carmella	50.00	100.00
NNO	Charlotte	60.00	120.00
NNO	Lana	50.00	100.00
NNO	Nikki Bella	60.00	120.00
NNO	Sasha Banks	150.00	300.00

2016 Topps WWE Then Now Forever Mask and Face Paint Medallions

*BRONZE: .5X TO 1.2X BASIC MEM
*SILVER: .6X TO 1.5X BASIC MEM
*GOLD/10: UNPRICED DUE TO SCARCITY
*RED/1: UNPRICED DUE TO SCARCITY
*P.P.BLACK/1: UNPRICED DUE TO SCARCITY
*P.P.CYAN/1: UNPRICED DUE TO SCARCITY
*P.P.MAGENTA/1: UNPRICED DUE TO SCARCITY
*P.P.YELLOW/1: UNPRICED DUE TO SCARCITY
STATED ODDS 1:338

NNO	Asuka	8.00	20.00
NNO	Braun Strowman	5.00	12.00
NNO	Goldust	10.00	25.00
NNO	Kalisto	6.00	15.00
NNO	Kane	5.00	12.00
NNO	Papa Shango	5.00	12.00
NNO	Sin Cara	5.00	12.00
NNO	Sting	8.00	20.00
NNO	Undertaker	10.00	25.00

2016 Topps WWE Then Now Forever NXT Prospects

COMPLETE SET (15)	12.00	30.00
STATED ODDS 1:1		

1	Angelo Dawkins	1.00	2.50
2	Austin Aries	1.25	3.00
3	Asuka	4.00	10.00
4	Billie Kay	2.50	6.00
5	Blake	1.00	2.50
6	Dash Wilder	1.25	3.00
7	Elias Samson	1.00	2.50
8	Hideo Itami	1.25	3.00
9	No Way Jose	1.00	2.50
10	Peyton Royce	2.50	6.00
11	Samoa Joe	2.50	6.00
12	Sawyer Fulton	1.25	3.00
13	Scott Dawson	1.00	2.50
14	Shinsuke Nakamura	2.50	6.00
15	Tye Dillinger	1.25	3.00

2016 Topps WWE Then Now Forever NXT Rivalries

COMPLETE SET (20)	10.00	25.00
STATED ODDS 1:2		

1	Shinsuke Nakamura vs. Samoa Joe	2.00	5.00
2	Finn Balor vs. Samoa Joe	1.25	3.00
3	Kevin Owens vs. Finn Balor	1.25	3.00
4	Asuka vs. Bayley	.75	2.00
5	Nia Jax vs. Asuka	1.25	3.00
6	Nia Jax vs. Bayley	1.50	4.00
7	Emma vs. Asuka	.75	2.50
8	No Way Jose vs. Austin Aries	.75	2.00
9	Baron Corbin vs. Austin Aries	.75	2.00
10	Elias Samson vs. Apollo Crews	.75	2.00
11	Baron Corbin vs. Samoa Joe	1.25	3.00
12	Emma vs. Bayley	1.25	3.00
13	Sami Zayn vs. Cesaro	.75	2.00
14	Tyler Breeze vs. Hideo Itami	.75	2.00
15	Tyler Breeze vs. Neville	.75	2.00
16	Summer Rae vs. Paige	2.00	5.00
17	Bo Dallas vs. Neville	.75	2.00
18	Bray Wyatt vs. Neville	.75	2.00
19	Big E vs. Bo Dallas	.75	2.00
20	Big E vs. Seth Rollins	.75	2.00

2016 Topps WWE Then Now Forever Royal Rumble 2016 Mat Relics

*BRONZE/50: .5X TO 1.2X BASIC MEM
*SILVER/25: .6X TO 1.5X BASIC MEM
*GOLD/10: UNPRICED DUE TO SCARCITY
*RED/1: UNPRICED DUE TO SCARCITY
*P.P.BLACK/1: UNPRICED DUE TO SCARCITY
*P.P.CYAN/1: UNPRICED DUE TO SCARCITY
*P.P.MAGENTA/1: UNPRICED DUE TO SCARCITY
*P.P.YELLOW/1: UNPRICED DUE TO SCARCITY
STATED ODDS 1:92

NNO	AJ Styles	8.00	20.00
NNO	Alberto Del Rio	3.00	8.00
NNO	Becky Lynch	6.00	15.00
NNO	Big E	2.00	5.00
NNO	Big Show	4.00	10.00
NNO	Braun Strowman	2.50	6.00
NNO	Bray Wyatt	8.00	20.00
NNO	Brock Lesnar	10.00	25.00
NNO	Charlotte	6.00	15.00
NNO	Chris Jericho	5.00	12.00
NNO	Dean Ambrose	6.00	15.00

NNO Dolph Ziggler	2.50	6.00
NNO Erick Rowan	2.00	5.00
NNO Kalisto	5.00	12.00
NNO Kane	3.00	8.00
NNO Kevin Owens	5.00	12.00
NNO Kofi Kingston	2.00	5.00
NNO Luke Harper	2.00	5.00
NNO The Miz	3.00	8.00
NNO Ric Flair	8.00	20.00
NNO Roman Reigns	6.00	15.00
NNO Sami Zayn	3.00	8.00
NNO Sheamus	5.00	12.00
NNO Triple H	8.00	20.00
NNO Xavier Woods	2.00	5.00

2016 Topps WWE Then Now Forever Shirt Relics

*BRONZE/50: .5X TO 1.2X BASIC MEM
*SILVER/25: .6X TO 1.5X BASIC MEM
*GOLD/10: UNPRICED DUE TO SCARCITY
*RED/1: UNPRICED DUE TO SCARCITY
*P.P.BLACK/1: UNPRICED DUE TO SCARCITY
*P.P.CYAN/1: UNPRICED DUE TO SCARCITY
*P.P.MAGENTA/1: UNPRICED DUE TO SCARCITY
*P.P.YELLOW/1: UNPRICED DUE TO SCARCITY
STATED ODDS 1:102

1 Aiden English	2.00	5.00
2 Alberto Del Rio	3.00	8.00
3 Apollo Crews	2.00	5.00
4 Asuka	8.00	20.00
5 Austin Aries	2.50	6.00
6 Baron Corbin	2.50	6.00
7 Bayley	5.00	12.00
8 Big Cass	4.00	10.00
9 Big Show	4.00	10.00
10 Bo Dallas	2.00	5.00
11 Braun Strowman	2.50	6.00
12 Bray Wyatt	8.00	20.00
13 Bubba Ray Dudley	4.00	10.00
14 Cesaro	4.00	10.00
15 Curtis Axel	2.00	5.00
16 Darren Young	2.00	5.00
17 Finn Balor	6.00	15.00
18 Heath Slater	2.00	5.00
19 Jey Uso	2.00	5.00
20 Jimmy Uso	2.00	5.00
21 John Cena	10.00	25.00
22 Kalisto	5.00	12.00
23 Kevin Owens	5.00	12.00
24 Luke Harper	2.00	5.00
25 Randy Orton	5.00	12.00
26 Roman Reigns	6.00	15.00
27 Sheamus	5.00	12.00
28 Simon Gotch	3.00	8.00
29 Xavier Woods	2.00	5.00
30 Zack Ryder	2.00	5.00

2016 Topps WWE Then Now Forever Triple Autographs

STATED ODDS 1:1,362
STATED PRINT RUN 11 SER.#'d SETS

NNO English/Gotch/Amore	50.00	100.00
NNO Styles/Anderson/Gallows	125.00	250.00
NNO Cena/Jericho/R-Truth	75.00	150.00
NNO Naomi/Banks/Bailey	125.00	250.00
NNO Natalya/Charlotte/Lynch	125.00	250.00
NNO Samoa Joe/Balor/Itami	100.00	200.00
NNO Rollins/Ambrose/Reigns	120.00	250.00
NNO Nakamura/Zayn/Asuka	100.00	200.00

2016 Topps WWE Then Now Forever WWE Rivalries

COMPLETE SET (20)	10.00	25.00

STATED ODDS 1:2

1 AJ Styles vs. John Cena	1.00	2.50
2 Seth Rollins vs. Roman Reigns	1.00	2.50
3 Seth Rollins vs. Dean Ambrose	1.25	3.00
4 Dean Ambrose vs. Chris Jericho	1.25	3.00
5 Roman Reigns vs. AJ Styles	1.50	4.00
6 Chris Jericho vs. AJ Styles	.75	2.00
7 Sami Zayn vs. Kevin Owens	1.25	3.00
8 Kevin Owens vs. Cesaro	1.50	4.00
9 Kevin Owens vs. Dolph Ziggler	1.25	3.00
10 Undertaker vs. Brock Lesnar	2.00	5.00
11 Roman Reigns vs. Triple H	1.25	3.00
12 Dean Ambrose vs. Triple H	1.25	3.00
13 Natalya vs. Charlotte	1.00	2.50
14 Natalya vs. Becky Lynch	1.25	3.00
15 Dolph Ziggler vs. Baron Corbin	.75	2.00
16 Enzo Amore vs. Chris Jericho	1.00	2.50
17 Kalisto vs. Rusev	.75	2.00
18 Rusev vs. Jack Swagger	.75	2.00
19 Lana vs. Brie Bella	1.50	4.00
20 Dolph Ziggler vs. The Miz	.75	2.00

2017 Topps WWE Then Now Forever

COMPLETE SET (100)	10.00	25.00

UNOPENED BOX (24 PACKS)
UNOPENED PACK (7 CARDS)
*BRONZE: .5X TO 1.2X BASIC CARDS
*BLUE/99: 1X TO 2.5X BASIC CARDS
*SILVER/25: 2X TO 5X BASIC CARDS
*GOLD/10: 4X TO 10X BASIC CARDS
*RED/1: UNPRICED DUE TO SCARCITY
*P.P.BLACK/1: UNPRICED DUE TO SCARCITY
*P.P.CYAN/1: UNPRICED DUE TO SCARCITY
*P.P.MAGENTA/1: UNPRICED DUE TO SCARCITY
*P.P.YELLOW/1: UNPRICED DUE TO SCARCITY

101 Tyler Bate		
102 Brie Bella	.60	1.50
103 Jerry The King Lawler	.30	.75
104A Akira Tozawa	.25	.60
104B Akira Tozawa SP Arms Up	8.00	20.00
105 Alicia Fox	.40	1.00
106 Apollo Crews	.30	.75
107 Ariya Daivari	.25	.60
108 Harley Race	.30	.75
109A Big Show	.30	.75
109B Big Show SP Red/White/Blue	4.00	10.00
110 Bo Dallas	.25	.60
111A Braun Strowman	.30	.75
111B Braun Strowman SP Stomping	5.00	12.00
112A Bray Wyatt	.60	1.50
112B Bray Wyatt SP White Ropes	5.00	12.00
113A Cesaro	.50	1.25
113B Cesaro SP Mid-Air	5.00	12.00
114 Charly Caruso	.25	.60
115 Curt Hawkins	.25	.60
116 Curtis Axel	.25	.60
117 Dana Brooke	.50	1.25
118 Darren Young	.25	.60
119 Dean Ambrose	.75	2.00
120 Emma	.60	1.50
121 Jeff Hardy	.50	1.25
122 Goldust	.30	.75
123 Heath Slater	.25	.60
124 JoJo	.40	1.00
125 Kalisto	.40	1.00
126 Kurt Angle	.50	1.25
127 Mark Henry	.25	.60
128 Matt Hardy	.60	1.50
129 Mickie James	.40	1.00
130 Neville	.40	1.00
131 R-Truth	.25	.60
132 Rhyno	.25	.60
133 Roman Reigns	.75	2.00
134 Sasha Banks	.75	2.00
135 Seth Rollins	.75	2.00
136A Sheamus	.50	1.25
136B Sheamus SP Mid-Air	4.00	10.00
137 Summer Rae	.60	1.50
138 Aiden English	.25	.60
139 Baron Corbin	.40	1.00
140 Becky Lynch	.75	2.00
141 Charlotte Flair	1.00	2.50
142A Daniel Bryan	1.00	2.50
142B Daniel Bryan SP YES!	5.00	12.00
143A Dolph Ziggler	.40	1.00
143B Dolph Ziggler SP Drops Elbow	5.00	12.00
144 Epico	.25	.60
145 Erick Rowan	.25	.60
146 Fandango	.25	.60
147 James Ellsworth	.25	.60
148 Jey Uso	.30	.75
149 Jimmy Uso	.30	.75
150 Jinder Mahal	.40	1.00
151A Kevin Owens	.60	1.50
151B Kevin Owens SP Red/White/Blue	5.00	12.00
152 Konnor	.25	.60
153 Lana	.75	2.00
154 Naomi	.50	1.25
155A Natalya	.50	1.25
155B Natalya SP Arms Raised	6.00	15.00
156 Nikki Bella	.60	1.50
157 Primo	.25	.60
158A Rusev	.50	1.25
158B Rusev SP Man Bun	5.00	12.00
159 Sami Zayn	.30	.75
160 Shinsuke Nakamura	.60	1.50
161 Sin Cara	.30	.75
162 Tyler Breeze	.25	.60
163 Viktor	.25	.60
164 Akam	.25	.60
165 Aleister Black	.25	.60
166 Andrade Cien Almas	.25	.60
167 Angelo Dawkins	.25	.60
168 Buddy Murphy	.25	.60
169 Drew McIntyre	.25	.60
170 Elias	.40	1.00
171 Kassius Ohno	.25	.60
172 Killian Dain	.25	.60
173 Abbey Laith	.25	.60
174 Lacey Evans	.40	1.00
175 Mandy Rose	.30	.75
176 No Way Jose	.25	.60
177 Rezar	.25	.60
178 Ruby Riot	.30	.75
179 Sawyer Fulton	.25	.60
180 Wesley Blake	.25	.60
181 Alundra Blayze	.30	.75
182 Andre the Giant	.50	1.25
183 Bret Hit Man Hart	.50	1.25
184 British Bulldog	.25	.60
185 Bruno Sammartino	.40	1.00
186 Dusty Rhodes	.30	.75
187 Edge	.60	1.50
188 Jake The Snake Roberts	.30	.75
189 Lex Luger	.30	.75
190 Macho Man Randy Savage	.50	1.25
191 Million Dollar Man Ted DiBiase	.30	.75
192 Mr. Perfect	.50	1.25
193 Ravishing Rick Rude	.40	1.00
194 Rowdy Roddy Piper	.50	1.25
195 Shawn Michaels	.60	1.50
196 Sting	.75	2.00
197 Stone Cold Steve Austin	1.00	2.50
198 Trish Stratus	1.00	2.50
199 Ultimate Warrior	.50	1.25
200 Wendi Richter	.30	.75

2017 Topps WWE Then Now Forever Autographed Dual Relics

STATED PRINT RUN 10 SER.#'d SETS
UNPRICED DUE TO SCARCITY

NNO Asuka
NNO Bayley
NNO Bobby Roode
NNO Bray Wyatt
NNO Charlotte Flair
NNO John Cena
NNO Nikki Bella
NNO Randy Orton
NNO Shinsuke Nakamura

2017 Topps WWE Then Now Forever Autographed NXT TakeOver San Antonio 2017 Mat Relics

STATED PRINT RUN 10 SER.#'d SETS
UNPRICED DUE TO SCARCITY

NNO Asuka
NNO Billie Kay
NNO Bobby Roode
NNO Eric Young
NNO Peyton Royce
NNO Roderick Strong
NNO Shinsuke Nakamura

2017 Topps WWE Then Now Forever Autographed Royal Rumble 2017 Mat Relics

STATED PRINT RUN 10 SER.#'d SETS
UNPRICED DUE TO SCARCITY

NNO AJ Styles
NNO Braun Strowman
NNO Bray Wyatt
NNO Charlotte Flair
NNO Chris Jericho
NNO Goldberg
NNO Karl Anderson
NNO Kevin Owens
NNO Luke Gallows
NNO Naomi
NNO Neville
NNO Nia Jax
NNO Nikki Bella
NNO Randy Orton
NNO Roman Reigns
NNO Undertaker

2017 Topps WWE Then Now Forever
Autographed Shirt Relics

STATED PRINT RUN 10 SER.#'d SETS
UNPRICED DUE TO SCARCITY

- NNO Aiden English
- NNO Becky Lynch
- NNO Big Show
- NNO Charlotte Flair
- NNO Curtis Axel
- NNO JoJo
- NNO Kevin Owens
- NNO Naomi
- NNO Natalya
- NNO Sasha Banks
- NNO Seth Rollins
- NNO Sheamus
- NNO Sting
- NNO Summer Rae

2017 Topps WWE Then Now Forever
Autographs

*BLUE/50: .6X TO 1.5X BASIC AUTOS
*SILVER/25: .75X TO 2X BASIC AUTOS
*GOLD/10: UNPRICED DUE TO SCARCITY
*RED/1: UNPRICED DUE TO SCARCITY

102	Brie Bella	10.00	25.00
104	Akira Tozawa	8.00	20.00
105	Alicia Fox	8.00	20.00
106	Apollo Crews	6.00	15.00
111	Braun Strowman	12.00	30.00
112	Bray Wyatt	8.00	20.00
113	Cesaro	6.00	15.00
119	Dean Ambrose	10.00	25.00
121	Jeff Hardy	15.00	40.00
123	Heath Slater	5.00	12.00
126	Kurt Angle	15.00	40.00
128	Matt Hardy	15.00	40.00
134	Sasha Banks	25.00	60.00
136	Sheamus	5.00	12.00
139	Baron Corbin	5.00	12.00
140	Becky Lynch	15.00	40.00
154	Naomi	10.00	25.00
159	Sami Zayn	5.00	12.00
160	Shinsuke Nakamura	15.00	40.00
165	Aleister Black	8.00	20.00
169	Drew McIntyre	8.00	20.00
171	Kassius Ohno	6.00	15.00
172	Killian Dain	6.00	15.00
174	Lacey Evans	12.00	30.00
178	Ruby Riot	15.00	40.00
189	Lex Luger	8.00	20.00

2017 Topps WWE Then Now Forever
Championship Medallion Relics

*BRONZE/99: .5X TO 1.2X BASIC MEM
*BLUE/50: .6X TO 1.5X BASIC MEM
*SILVER/25: .75X TO 2X BASIC MEM
*GOLD/10: UNPRICED DUE TO SCARCITY
*RED/1: UNPRICED DUE TO SCARCITY
RANDOMLY INSERTED INTO PACKS

NNO	Aiden English	1.50	4.00
NNO	American Alpha	2.00	5.00
NNO	Asuka	5.00	12.00
NNO	The Authors of Pain	1.50	4.00
NNO	Bayley	5.00	12.00
NNO	Blake & Murphy	1.50	4.00
NNO	Bobby Roode	4.00	10.00

NNO	The Brian Kendrick	1.50	4.00
NNO	DIY	1.50	4.00
NNO	Finn Balor	6.00	15.00
NNO	Kevin Owens	4.00	10.00
NNO	Neville	2.50	6.00
NNO	The Revival	1.50	4.00
NNO	Rich Swann	1.50	4.00
NNO	Sami Zayn	2.00	5.00
NNO	Samoa Joe	5.00	12.00
NNO	Sasha Banks	5.00	12.00
NNO	Shinsuke Nakamura	4.00	10.00
NNO	TJ Perkins	1.50	4.00

2017 Topps WWE Then Now Forever
Dual Relics

*SILVER/25: .6X TO 1.5X BASIC MEM
*GOLD/10: UNPRICED DUE TO SCARCITY
*RED/1: UNPRICED DUE TO SCARCITY
STATED PRINT RUN 50 SER.#'d SETS

NNO	Asuka		
NNO	Bayley		
NNO	Bobby Roode	10.00	25.00
NNO	Bray Wyatt		
NNO	Brock Lesnar		
NNO	Charlotte Flair		
NNO	John Cena	12.00	30.00
NNO	Nikki Bella	10.00	25.00
NNO	Randy Orton		
NNO	Shinsuke Nakamura	20.00	50.00

2017 Topps WWE Then Now Forever
Finishers and Signature Moves

COMPLETE SET (50)		10.00	25.00
STATED ODDS 2:1			
F1	John Cena	1.50	4.00
F2	John Cena	1.50	4.00
F3	Brock Lesnar	1.50	4.00
F4	Brock Lesnar	1.50	4.00
F5	Goldberg	1.25	3.00
F6	Goldberg	1.25	3.00
F7	The Rock	1.50	4.00
F8	The Rock	1.50	4.00
F9	Triple H	.75	2.00
F10	Randy Orton	.75	2.00
F11	Undertaker	1.25	3.00
F12	Undertaker	1.25	3.00
F13	Undertaker	1.25	3.00
F14	Kane	.40	1.00
F15	Big Show	.40	1.00
F16	Big Show	.40	1.00
F17	Chris Jericho	.75	2.00
F18	Chris Jericho	.75	2.00
F19	Chris Jericho	.75	2.00
F20	Daniel Bryan	1.25	3.00
F21	Mick Foley	.75	2.00
F22	Mick Foley	.75	2.00
F23	Booker T	.40	1.00
F24	AJ Styles	1.50	4.00
F25	AJ Styles	1.50	4.00
F26	AJ Styles	1.50	4.00
F27	Finn Balor	1.25	3.00
F28	Finn Balor	1.25	3.00
F29	The Miz	.60	1.50
F30	The Miz	.60	1.50
F31	Bobby Roode	.75	2.00
F32	Shinsuke Nakamura	.75	2.00
F33	Drew McIntyre	.30	.75

F34	Aliyah	.40	1.00
F35	Andrade Cien Almas	.30	.75
F36	Dean Ambrose	1.00	2.50
F37	No Way Jose	.30	.75
F38	Ember Moon	.75	2.00
F39	Eric Young	.60	1.50
F40	Hideo Itami	.50	1.25
F41	Nikki Cross	.60	1.50
F42	Billie Kay	.40	1.00
F43	Tye Dillinger	.30	.75
F44	Buddy Murphy	.30	.75
F45	Peyton Royce	.50	1.25
F46	The Authors of Pain	.30	.75
F47	The Revival	.30	.75
F48	TM-61	.30	.75
F49	The Hype Bros.	.40	1.00
F50	#DIY	.30	.75

2017 Topps WWE Then Now Forever
Kiss

*GOLD/10: UNPRICED DUE TO SCARCITY
*RED/1: UNPRICED DUE TO SCARCITY
STATED PRINT RUN 99 SER.#'d SETS

NNO	Alexa Bliss	200.00	400.00
NNO	Asuka	50.00	100.00
NNO	Becky Lynch	125.00	250.00
NNO	Billie Kay	15.00	40.00
NNO	Charlotte Flair	125.00	250.00
NNO	Ember Moon	30.00	75.00
NNO	Liv Morgan	100.00	200.00
NNO	Peyton Royce	15.00	40.00

2017 Topps WWE Then Now Forever
Kiss Autographs

*GOLD/10: UNPRICED DUE TO SCARCITY
*RED/1: UNPRICED DUE TO SCARCITY
STATED PRINT RUN 25 SER.#'d SETS

NNO	Alexa Bliss		
NNO	Asuka	50.00	100.00
NNO	Becky Lynch	50.00	100.00
NNO	Billie Kay	30.00	75.00
NNO	Charlotte Flair	60.00	120.00
NNO	Ember Moon	25.00	60.00
NNO	Liv Morgan	50.00	100.00
NNO	Mickie James	60.00	120.00
NNO	Nikki Bella	50.00	100.00
NNO	Peyton Royce	30.00	75.00

2017 Topps WWE Then Now Forever
NXT TakeOver San Antonio 2017 Mat Relics

*BRONZE/99: .5X TO 1.2X BASIC MEM
*BLUE/50: .6X TO 1.5X BASIC MEM
*SILVER/25: .75X TO 2X BASIC MEM
*GOLD/10: UNPRICED DUE TO SCARCITY
*RED/1: UNPRICED DUE TO SCARCITY
STATED PRINT RUN 350 SER.#'d SETS

NNO	Akam	1.50	4.00
NNO	Asuka	5.00	12.00
NNO	Billie Kay	2.00	5.00
NNO	Bobby Roode	4.00	10.00
NNO	Eric Young	3.00	8.00
NNO	Peyton Royce	2.50	6.00
NNO	Rezar	1.50	4.00
NNO	Roderick Strong	2.00	5.00
NNO	Shinsuke Nakamura	4.00	10.00
NNO	Tye Dillinger	1.50	4.00

2017 Topps WWE Then Now Forever
Roster Updates

COMPLETE SET (20)		12.00	30.00
R21	Alexa Bliss	5.00	12.00
R22	Dash Wilder	1.00	2.50
R23	Jason Jordan	1.25	3.00
R24	Maryse	2.00	5.00
R25	The Miz	2.00	5.00
R26	Mustafa Ali	1.00	2.50
R27	Scott Dawson	1.00	2.50
R28	Tony Nese	1.00	2.50
R29	The New Day	2.00	5.00
R30	Samir Singh	1.00	2.50
R31	Sunil Singh	1.00	2.50
R32	Tamina	1.25	3.00
R33	Tye Dillinger	1.00	2.50
R34	Dan Matha	1.00	2.50
R35	Vanessa Borne	1.25	3.00
R36	Gabriel Ealy	1.00	2.50
R37	Kona Reeves	1.00	2.50
R38	The Velveteen Dream	1.25	3.00
R39	Steve Cutler	1.00	2.50
R40	Uriel Ealy	1.00	2.50

2017 Topps WWE Then Now Forever
Royal Rumble 2017 Mat Relics

*BRONZE/99: .5X TO 1.2X BASIC MEM
*BLUE/50: .6X TO 1.5X BASIC MEM
*SILVER/25: .75X TO 2X BASIC MEM
*GOLD/10: UNPRICED DUE TO SCARCITY
*RED/1: UNPRICED DUE TO SCARCITY
RANDOMLY INSERTED INTO PACKS

NNO	AJ Styles	6.00	15.00
NNO	Bayley	4.00	10.00
NNO	Braun Strowman	1.50	4.00
NNO	Bray Wyatt	3.00	8.00
NNO	Brock Lesnar	6.00	15.00
NNO	Charlotte Flair	5.00	12.00
NNO	Chris Jericho	3.00	8.00
NNO	Goldberg	5.00	12.00
NNO	John Cena	6.00	15.00
NNO	Karl Anderson	1.25	3.00
NNO	Kevin Owens	3.00	8.00
NNO	Luke Gallows	2.00	5.00
NNO	Naomi	2.50	6.00
NNO	Neville	2.00	5.00
NNO	Nia Jax	2.00	5.00
NNO	Nikki Bella	3.00	8.00
NNO	Randy Orton	3.00	8.00
NNO	Rich Swann	1.25	3.00
NNO	Roman Reigns	4.00	10.00
NNO	Undertaker	5.00	12.00

2017 Topps WWE Then Now Forever
Shirt Relics

*BLUE/50: .5X TO 1.2X BASIC MEM
*SILVER/25: .6X TO 1.5X BASIC MEM
*GOLD/10: UNPRICED DUE TO SCARCITY
*RED/1: UNPRICED DUE TO SCARCITY
RANDOMLY INSERTED INTO PACKS

NNO	Aiden English	1.25	3.00
NNO	Andrade Cien Almas	1.25	3.00
NNO	Becky Lynch	4.00	10.00
NNO	Big Show	1.50	4.00
NNO	Brock Lesnar	6.00	15.00
NNO	Charlotte Flair	5.00	12.00
NNO	Curtis Axel	1.25	3.00

NNO	Darren Young	1.25	3.00
NNO	John Cena	6.00	15.00
NNO	JoJo	2.00	5.00
NNO	Kevin Owens	3.00	8.00
NNO	Naomi	2.50	6.00
NNO	Natalya	2.50	6.00
NNO	No Way Jose	1.25	3.00
NNO	Sasha Banks	4.00	10.00
NNO	Seth Rollins	4.00	10.00
NNO	Sheamus	2.50	6.00
NNO	Sting	4.00	10.00
NNO	Summer Rae	3.00	8.00

2017 Topps WWE Then Now Forever Triple Autographs

STATED PRINT RUN 10 SER.#'d SETS
RANDOMLY INSERTED INTO PACKS

NNO	Bayley/Banks/Flair	125.00	250.00
NNO	Wyatt/Orton/Harper	75.00	150.00
NNO	Rollins/Reigns/Ambrose	150.00	300.00
NNO	Undertaker/Lesnar/Goldberg	400.00	600.00
NNO	Undertaker/Kane/Bryan	250.00	400.00

2018 Topps WWE Then Now Forever

COMPLETE SET W/O SP (100) 8.00 20.00
UNOPENED BOX (24 PACKS)
UNOPENED PACK (7 CARDS)
*BRONZE: .5X TO 1.2X BASIC CARDS
*BLUE/99: .75X TO 2X BASIC CARDS
*SILVER/25: 2X TO 5X BASIC CARDS
*GOLD/10: UNPRICED DUE TO SCARCITY
*RED/1: UNPRICED DUE TO SCARCITY
*P.P.BLACK/1: UNPRICED DUE TO SCARCITY
*P.P.CYAN/1: UNPRICED DUE TO SCARCITY
*P.P.MAGENTA/1: UNPRICED DUE TO SCARCITY
*P.P.YELLOW/1: UNPRICED DUE TO SCARCITY

101	Ronda Rousey	2.50	6.00
102	Alexa Bliss	1.25	3.00
102A	Alexa Bliss SP		
103	Akam	.25	.60
104	Alexander Wolfe	.25	.60
105	Andrade	.40	1.00
105A	Andrade SP		
106	Constable Baron Corbin	.40	1.00
107	Bayley	.40	1.00
107A	Bayley SP		
108	Becky Lynch	.60	1.50
108A	Becky Lynch SP		
109	Bianca Belair	.30	.75
110	Big Show	.25	.60
111	Billie Kay	.50	1.25
112	Bobby Lashley	.50	1.25
112A	Bobby Lashley SP		
113	Braun Strowman	.60	1.50
113A	Braun Strowman SP		
114	Bray Wyatt	.60	1.50
114A	Bray Wyatt SP		
115	Candice LeRae	.30	.75
116	Cesaro	.50	1.25
116A	Cesaro SP		
117	Cezar Bononi	.25	.60
118	Dakota Kai	.30	.75
119	Danny Burch	.25	.60
120	Dash Wilder	.30	.75
121	David Otunga	.30	.75
122	Dean Ambrose	.50	1.25
122A	Dean Ambrose SP		

123	Dolph Ziggler	.30	.75
124	Drake Maverick	.30	.75
125	Drew McIntyre	.40	1.00
125A	Drew McIntyre SP		
126	EC3	.30	.75
127	Ember Moon	.50	1.25
127A	Ember Moon SP		
128	Eric Young	.30	.75
128A	Eric Young SP		
129	Fabian Aichner	.25	.60
130	Fandango	.25	.60
131	Finn Balor	.60	1.50
131A	Finn Balor SP		
132	Goldust	.50	1.25
133	Hanson	.30	.75
134	Harper	.40	1.00
135	Hideo Itami	.25	.60
136	Jason Jordan	.25	.60
137	Jeff Hardy	.50	1.25
137A	Jeff Hardy SP		
138	Jonathan Coachman	.25	.60
139	Kalisto	.25	.60
140	Kane	.40	1.00
141	Karl Anderson	.25	.60
142	Kassius Ohno	.25	.60
143	Killian Dain	.30	.75
144	Kona Reeves	.25	.60
145	Lacey Evans	.30	.75
146	Lince Dorado	.25	.60
147	Liv Morgan	.50	1.25
148	Luke Gallows	.30	.75
149	Mandy Rose	.60	1.50
150	Mark Andrews	.25	.60
151	Woken Matt Hardy	.60	1.50
152	Mojo Rawley	.25	.60
153	Nick Miller	.25	.60
154	Nikki Bella	.50	1.25
155	Nikki Cross	.40	1.00
156	No Way Jose	.30	.75
157	Otis Dozovic	.25	.60
158	Peyton Royce	.60	1.50
159	Randy Orton	.60	1.50
159A	Randy Orton SP		
160	Raul Mendoza	.25	.60
161	Rezar	.25	.60
162	Ricochet	.50	1.25
163	Riddick Moss	.25	.60
164	Roman Reigns	.60	1.50
164A	Roman Reigns SP		
165	Rowan	.40	1.00
166	Rowe	.25	.60
167	Ruby Riott	.40	1.00
167A	Ruby Riott SP		
168	Rusev	.40	1.00
168A	Rusev SP		
169	Sami Zayn	.25	.60
169A	Sami Zayn SP		
170	Samoa Joe	.50	1.25
170A	Samoa Joe SP		
171	Sasha Banks	.75	2.00
171A	Sasha Banks SP		
172	Scott Dawson	.30	.75
173	Scott Stanford	.25	.60
174	Seth Rollins	.60	1.50
174A	Seth Rollins SP		
175	Shane Thorne	.25	.60
176	Shayna Baszler	.60	1.50
177	Sheamus	.50	1.25

177A	Sheamus SP		
178	Shinsuke Nakamura	.60	1.50
178A	Shinsuke Nakamura SP		
179	Taynara Conti	.25	.60
180	Tino Sabbatelli	.30	.75
181	Trent Seven	.25	.60
182	Tucker Knight	.25	.60
183	Tye Dillinger	.25	.60
184	Tyler Breeze	.25	.60
185	Vanessa Borne	.25	.60
186	Velveteen Dream	.25	.60
187	Zelina Vega	.25	.60
188	Andre the Giant	.50	1.25
189	Beth Phoenix	.50	1.25
190	Bret Hit Man Hart	.60	1.50
191	Eddie Guerrero	.60	1.50
192	Edge	.60	1.50
193	Jake The Snake Roberts	.30	.75
194	Lita	.60	1.50
195	Macho Man Randy Savage	.75	2.00
196	Million Dollar Man Ted DiBiase	.30	.75
197	Mr. Perfect	.30	.75
198	Shawn Michaels	.75	2.00
199	Sting	.60	1.50
200	Stone Cold Steve Austin	1.25	3.00

2018 Topps WWE Then Now Forever 25 Years of RAW

COMPLETE SET (50) 12.00 30.00
RANDOMLY INSERTED INTO PACKS

RAW1	Monday Night RAW Premieres	.40	1.00
RAW2	Mr. Perfect Def. Ric Flair	.40	1.00
RAW3	123 Kid vs. Bret Hart	.40	1.00
RAW4	Ringmaster Debuts	1.50	4.00
RAW5	Bret Hart Snaps	.75	2.00
RAW6	Austin injures Bret Hart	1.50	4.00
RAW7	NA Outlaws/Chainsaw Charlie	.40	1.00
RAW8	HHH Leads DX	.75	2.00
RAW9	DX Invades WCW	.75	2.00
RAW10	Stone Cold/Zamboni	1.50	4.00
RAW11	Undertaker Captures Austin	1.25	3.00
RAW12	Stone Cold/Beer Truck	1.50	4.00
RAW13	The Higher Power	.40	1.00
RAW14	Rock/This Is Your Life	.40	1.00
RAW15	HHH and Stephanie Elope	.75	2.00
RAW16	Angle/Milk Truck	.75	2.00
RAW17	HHH Returns	.75	2.00
RAW18	WWE Draft	.40	1.00
RAW19	Hardy/Undertaker	.60	1.50
RAW20	HHH Turns on HBK	.75	2.00
RAW21	HHH/Evolution	.75	2.00
RAW22	Goldberg Debuts	1.25	3.00
RAW23	HHH Def. Ric Flair	.75	2.00
RAW24	Lita Def. Trish	.75	2.00
RAW25	Batista Thumbs Down	.50	1.25
RAW26	Cena Joins RAW	1.25	3.00
RAW27	HBK/Montreal	1.00	2.50
RAW28	Mr. McMahon's Limo	.60	1.50
RAW29	Hardy Swantons Orton	.60	1.50
RAW30	Ric Flair Retires	1.00	2.50
RAW31	Bret Hart Returns	.75	2.00
RAW32	HBK Farewell	1.00	2.50
RAW33	Nexus Invades	.40	1.00
RAW34	Miz Cashes In	.60	1.50
RAW35	HHH/Taker WrestleMania	.75	2.00
RAW36	Edge Retires	.75	2.00
RAW37	Daniel Bryan Kane Hug	.75	2.00
RAW38	Dolph Ziggler Cashes In	.40	1.00

RAW39	Mark Henry Fake Retires	.40	1.00
RAW40	Yes! Movement	.75	2.00
RAW41	Seth Rollins Turns	.75	2.00
RAW42	Kevin Owens Debuts	.75	2.00
RAW43	Shane McMahon Returns	.60	1.50
RAW44	Styles Confronts Cena	1.25	3.00
RAW45	Goldberg Returns	1.25	3.00
RAW46	Angle New GM	.75	2.00
RAW47	Roman Reigns/My Yard	.75	2.00
RAW48	The Shield Reunite	.40	1.00
RAW49	Miz Wins 8th IC Title	.60	1.50
RAW50	Scott Hall Returns	.60	1.50

2018 Topps WWE Then Now Forever Autographed Royal Rumble 2018 Mat Relics

STATED PRINT RUN 10 SER.#'d SETS
UNPRICED DUE TO SCARCITY

MRARRAC Adam Cole
MRARRAJ AJ Styles
MRARRAS Asuka
MRARRBS Braun Strowman
MRARRFB Finn Balor
MRARRKK Kofi Kingston
MRARRKO Kevin Owens
MRARRMH Woken Matt Hardy
MRARRRS Rusev
MRARRSN Shinsuke Nakamura
MRARRSR Seth Rollins
MRARRSZ Sami Zayn

2018 Topps WWE Then Now Forever Autographed Shirt Relics

STATED PRINT RUN 10 SER.#'d SETS
UNPRICED DUE TO SCARCITY

SRAB Alexa Bliss
SRAK Akam
SRCG Chad Gable
SRCR Carmella
SRDZ Dolph Ziggler
SRJC John Cena
SRJJ Jason Jordan
SRKA Karl Anderson
SRLG Luke Gallows
SRNA Naomi
SRRZ Rezar
SRSR Seth Rollins

2018 Topps WWE Then Now Forever Autographs

*BLUE/99: .5X TO 1.2X BASIC AUTOS
*SILVER/25: .6X TO 1.5X BASIC AUTOS
*GOLD/10: UNPRICED DUE TO SCARCITY
*RED/1: UNPRICED DUE TO SCARCITY
RANDOMLY INSERTED INTO PACKS

102	Alexa Bliss	30.00	75.00
106	Baron Corbin	4.00	10.00
108	Becky Lynch	15.00	40.00
111	Billie Kay	10.00	25.00
113	Braun Strowman	10.00	25.00
114	Bray Wyatt	8.00	20.00
115	Candice LeRae	12.00	30.00
125	Drew McIntyre	6.00	15.00
126	EC3	10.00	25.00
127	Ember Moon	8.00	20.00
128	Eric Young	5.00	12.00
131	Finn Balor	8.00	20.00

133	Hanson	12.00	30.00
137	Jeff Hardy	8.00	20.00
142	Kassius Ohno	4.00	10.00
147	Liv Morgan	15.00	40.00
151	Woken Matt Hardy	8.00	20.00
152	Mojo Rawley	5.00	12.00
158	Peyton Royce	12.00	30.00
162	Ricochet	25.00	60.00
166	Rowe	8.00	20.00
167	Ruby Riott	12.00	30.00
168	Rusev	6.00	15.00
169	Sami Zayn	6.00	15.00
170	Samoa Joe	5.00	12.00
178	Shinsuke Nakamura	10.00	25.00
189	Beth Phoenix	10.00	25.00

2018 Topps WWE Then Now Forever Four Corner Mat Relics

*SILVER/25: .5X TO 1.2X BASIC MEM
*GOLD/10: UNPRICED DUE TO SCARCITY
STATED PRINT RUN 50 SER.#'d SETS

FCAJ	AJ Styles	12.00	30.00
FCAS	Asuka	10.00	25.00
FCDA	Dean Ambrose	4.00	10.00
FCJC	John Cena	12.00	30.00
FCRO	Randy Orton	6.00	15.00
FCRR	Roman Reigns	6.00	15.00
FCSN	Shinsuke Nakamura	10.00	25.00
FCSR	Seth Rollins	12.00	30.00
FCTH	Triple H	10.00	25.00
FCUN	Undertaker	15.00	40.00

2018 Topps WWE Then Now Forever Kiss

*GOLD/10: UNPRICED DUE TO SCARCITY
*RED/1: UNPRICED DUE TO SCARCITY

KCAB	Alexa Bliss		
KCAS	Asuka		
KCMR	Mandy Rose	30.00	75.00

2018 Topps WWE Then Now Forever Kiss Autographs

*GOLD/10: UNPRICED DUE TO SCARCITY
*RED/1: UNPRICED DUE TO SCARCITY
STATED PRINT RUN 25 SER.#'d SETS

KCMJ	Mickie James	60.00	120.00
KCMR	Mandy Rose	50.00	100.00
KCRR	Ruby Riott		

2018 Topps WWE Then Now Forever Money in the Bank 2017 Mat Relics

*BRONZE/99: .5X TO 1.2X BASIC MEM
*BLUE/50: .6X TO 1.5X BASIC MEM
*SILVER/25: .75X TO 2X BASIC MEM
*GOLD/10: UNPRICED DUE TO SCARCITY
*RED/1: UNPRICED DUE TO SCARCITY

MRMBAJ	AJ Styles	8.00	20.00
MRMBBC	Baron Corbin	2.50	6.00
MRMBBL	Becky Lynch	6.00	15.00
MRMBCF	Charlotte Flair	10.00	25.00
MRMBCR	Carmella	5.00	12.00
MRMBDZ	Dolph Ziggler	3.00	8.00
MRMBKO	Kevin Owens	2.50	6.00
MRMBNT	Natalya	3.00	8.00
MRMBSN	Shinsuke Nakamura	4.00	10.00
MRMBSZ	Sami Zayn	2.50	6.00
MRMBTA	Tamina	2.50	6.00

2018 Topps WWE Then Now Forever NXT TakeOver Philadelphia 2018 Mat Relics

*BRONZE/99: .5X TO 1.2X BASIC MEM
*BLUE/50: .6X TO 1.5X BASIC MEM
*SILVER/25: .75X TO 2X BASIC MEM
*GOLD/10: UNPRICED DUE TO SCARCITY
*RED/1: UNPRICED DUE TO SCARCITY

MRPHAA	Andrade Cien Almas	4.00	10.00
MRPHAB	Aleister Black	2.50	6.00
MRPHAC	Adam Cole	3.00	8.00
MRPHBF	Bobby Fish	2.00	5.00
MRPHEM	Ember Moon	3.00	8.00
MRPHJG	Johnny Gargano	2.00	5.00
MRPHKO	Kassius Ohno	3.00	8.00
MRPHOR	Kyle O'Reilly	4.00	10.00
MRPHSB	Shayna Baszler	3.00	8.00
MRPHVD	Velveteen Dream	5.00	12.00

2018 Topps WWE Then Now Forever RAW 25 Mat Relics

*BRONZE/99: .5X TO 1.2X BASIC MEM
*BLUE/50: .6X TO 1.5X BASIC MEM
*SILVER/25: .75X TO 2X BASIC MEM
*GOLD/10: UNPRICED DUE TO SCARCITY
*RED/1: UNPRICED DUE TO SCARCITY

MR25AS	Asuka	5.00	12.00
MR25EL	Elias	2.50	6.00
MR25JC	John Cena	6.00	15.00
MR25RR	Roman Reigns	4.00	10.00
MR25SA	Stone Cold Steve Austin	12.00	30.00
MR25TM	The Miz	3.00	8.00

2018 Topps WWE Then Now Forever Roster Updates

COMPLETE SET (20)		15.00	40.00
RANDOMLY INSERTED INTO PACKS			
R21	Asuka	2.50	6.00
R22	Bobby Roode	1.25	3.00
R23	Chad Gable	.75	2.00
R24	Jinder Mahal	1.00	2.50
R25	Kevin Owens	2.00	5.00
R26	Konnor	.75	2.00
R27	Maria Kanellis	2.00	5.00
R28	Mike Kanellis	2.00	5.00
R29	Natalya	1.00	2.50
R30	Paige	2.00	5.00
R31	R-Truth	1.00	2.50
R32	Samir Singh	.75	2.00
R33	Sarah Logan	.75	2.00
R34	Sonya Deville	1.50	4.00
R35	Sunil Singh	.75	2.00
R36	The Miz	1.50	4.00
R37	Vic Joseph	.75	2.00
R38	Viktor	.75	2.00
R39	Zack Ryder	.75	2.00
R40	Maryse	1.50	4.00

2018 Topps WWE Then Now Forever Royal Rumble 2018 Mat Relics

*BRONZE/199: .5X TO 1.2X BASIC MEM
*BLUE/99: .6X TO 1.5X BASIC MEM
*SILVER/25: .75X TO 2X BASIC MEM
*GOLD/10: UNPRICED DUE TO SCARCITY
*RED/1: UNPRICED DUE TO SCARCITY

MRRRAA	Andrade Cien Almas	2.00	5.00
MRRRAC	Adam Cole	4.00	10.00
MRRRAJ	AJ Styles	6.00	15.00
MRRRAS	Asuka	4.00	10.00
MRRRBE	Big E	2.00	5.00
MRRRBS	Braun Strowman	3.00	8.00
MRRRCE	Cesaro	2.50	6.00
MRRRDZ	Dolph Ziggler	2.50	6.00
MRRREL	Elias	3.00	8.00
MRRRFB	Finn Balor	5.00	12.00
MRRRJC	John Cena	6.00	15.00
MRRRJJ	Jason Jordan	2.50	6.00
MRRRJM	Jinder Mahal	2.00	5.00
MRRRKK	Kofi Kingston	2.50	6.00
MRRRKN	Kane	2.50	6.00
MRRRKO	Kevin Owens	2.00	5.00
MRRRMH	Woken Matt Hardy	2.50	6.00
MRRRNB	Nikki Bella	5.00	12.00
MRRRRO	Randy Orton	4.00	10.00
MRRRRR	Roman Reigns	4.00	10.00
MRRRRS	Rusev	2.50	6.00
MRRRSH	Sheamus	3.00	8.00
MRRRSN	Shinsuke Nakamura	3.00	8.00
MRRRSR	Seth Rollins	4.00	10.00
MRRRSZ	Sami Zayn	2.50	6.00
MRRRTM	The Miz	2.50	6.00
MRRRXW	Xavier Woods	2.50	6.00

2018 Topps WWE Then Now Forever Shirt Relics

*BLUE/99: .5X TO 1.2X BASIC MEM
*SILVER/25: .75X TO 2X BASIC MEM
*GOLD/10: UNPRICED DUE TO SCARCITY
*RED/1: UNPRICED DUE TO SCARCITY

SRAB	Alexa Bliss	8.00	20.00
SRAK	Akam		
SRCG	Chad Gable	1.50	4.00
SRCR	Carmella	3.00	8.00
SRDZ	Dolph Ziggler	1.50	4.00
SRJC	John Cena	4.00	10.00
SRJJ	Jason Jordan	2.00	5.00
SRKA	Karl Anderson		
SRLG	Luke Gallows		
SRNA	Naomi		
SRRZ	Rezar		
SRSR	Seth Rollins		

2018 Topps WWE Then Now Forever Triple Autographs

STATED PRINT RUN 10 SER.#'d SETS
UNPRICED DUE TO SCARCITY

TAABS Paige/Rose/Deville
TACLB Styles/Gallows/Anderson
TATRS Riott/Morgan/Logan
TATWW O'Neil/Crews/Brooke

2018 Topps WWE Then Now Forever Promo

NYCC2	Alexa Bliss NYCC	4.00	10.00

2016 Topps WWE Then Now Forever Stickers

1	WWE Logo FOIL	.20	.50
2	Raw Logo	.20	.50
3	Smackdown Logo	.20	.50
4	NXT Logo	.20	.50
5	WWE Legends Logo	.20	.50
6	Brock Lesnar FOIL	.60	1.50
7	Brock Lesnar	.60	1.50
8	Brock Lesnar	.60	1.50
9	Brock Lesnar	.60	1.50
10	Brock Lesnar	.60	1.50
11	Neville	.30	.75
12	Neville	.30	.75
13	Neville	.30	.75
14	Neville	.30	.75
15	Neville	.30	.75
16	The New Day FOIL	.30	.75
17	The New Day	.30	.75
18	The New Day	.30	.75
19	The New Day	.30	.75
20	The New Day	.30	.75
21	Dudley Boyz	.12	.30
22	Dudley Boyz	.12	.30
23	D-Von Dudley	.20	.50
24	Bubba Ray Dudley	.25	.60
25	Dudley Boyz	.12	.30
26	Finn Balor FOIL	.40	1.00
27	Finn Balor	.40	1.00
28	Finn Balor	.40	1.00
29	Finn Balor	.40	1.00
30	Finn Balor	.40	1.00
31	Samoa Joe	.30	.75
32	Samoa Joe	.30	.75
33	Samoa Joe	.30	.75
34	Samoa Joe	.30	.75
35	Samoa Joe	.30	.75
36	Apollo Crews	.12	.30
37	Apollo Crews	.12	.30
38	Apollo Crews	.12	.30
39	Apollo Crews	.12	.30
40	Apollo Crews	.12	.30
41	Baron Corbin	.15	.40
42	Baron Corbin	.15	.40
43	Baron Corbin	.15	.40
44	Baron Corbin	.15	.40
45	Baron Corbin	.15	.40
46	John Cena FOIL	.60	1.50
47	John Cena	.60	1.50
48	John Cena	.60	1.50
49	John Cena	.60	1.50
50	John Cena	.60	1.50
51	Seth Rollins	.20	.50
52	Seth Rollins	.20	.50
53	Seth Rollins	.20	.50
54	Seth Rollins	.20	.50
55	Seth Rollins	.20	.50
56	Roman Reigns FOIL	.40	1.00
57	Roman Reigns	.40	1.00
58	Roman Reigns	.40	1.00
59	Roman Reigns	.40	1.00
60	Roman Reigns	.40	1.00
61	Dean Ambrose FOIL	.40	1.00
62	Dean Ambrose	.40	1.00
63	Dean Ambrose	.40	1.00
64	Dean Ambrose	.40	1.00
65	Dean Ambrose	.40	1.00
66	The Wyatt Family FOIL	.50	1.25
67	Bray Wyatt	.50	1.25
68	Braun Strowman	.15	.40
69	Luke Harper	.12	.30
70	Erick Rowan	.12	.30
71	Kalisto FOIL	.30	.75
72	Kalisto	.30	.75
73	Kalisto	.30	.75
74	Kalisto	.30	.75

#			
75 Kalisto	.30	.75
76 Bret Hart FOIL	.30	.75
77 Bret Hart	.30	.75
78 Bret Hart	.30	.75
79 Bret Hart	.30	.75
80 Bret Hart	.30	.75
81 Edge FOIL	.30	.75
82 Edge	.30	.75
83 Edge	.30	.75
84 Edge	.30	.75
85 Edge	.30	.75
86 Sting	.30	.75
87 Sting	.30	.75
88 Sting	.30	.75
89 Sting	.30	.75
90 Sting	.30	.75
91 Shawn Michaels FOIL	.50	1.25
92 Shawn Michaels	.50	1.25
93 Shawn Michaels	.50	1.25
94 Shawn Michaels	.50	1.25
95 Shawn Michaels	.50	1.25
96 Charlotte FOIL	.40	1.00
97 Alicia Fox	.20	.50
98 Becky Lynch	.40	1.00
99 Brie Bella	.25	.60
100 Lana	.50	1.25
101 Nikki Bella FOIL	.40	1.00
102 Natalya	.20	.50
103 Paige	.40	1.00
104 Sasha Banks	.40	1.00
105 Summer Rae	.30	.75
106 Naomi	.20	.50
107 Bayley FOIL	.30	.75
108 Alexa Bliss	.60	1.50
109 Asuka	.50	1.25
110 Billie Kay	.30	.75
111 Carmella	.30	.75
112 Eva Marie FOIL	.25	.60
113 Dana Brooke	.30	.75
114 Emma	.25	.60
115 Nia Jax	.20	.50
116 Peyton Royce	.30	.75
117 Dasha Fuentes	.12	.30
118 Randy Orton FOIL	.30	.75
119 Randy Orton	.30	.75
120 Randy Orton	.30	.75
121 Randy Orton	.30	.75
122 Randy Orton	.30	.75
123 Daniel Bryan FOIL	.50	1.25
124 Daniel Bryan	.50	1.25
125 Daniel Bryan	.50	1.25
126 Daniel Bryan	.50	1.25
127 Daniel Bryan	.50	1.25
128 Ryback FOIL	.15	.40
129 Ryback	.15	.40
130 Ryback	.15	.40
131 Ryback	.15	.40
132 Ryback	.15	.40
133 Dolph Ziggler FOIL	.15	.40
134 Dolph Ziggler	.15	.40
135 Dolph Ziggler	.15	.40
136 Dolph Ziggler	.15	.40
137 Dolph Ziggler	.15	.40
138 Chris Jericho	.30	.75
139 Shawn Michaels	.50	1.25
140 Steve Austin/Beer Truck	.60	1.50
141 Samoa Joe	.30	.75
142 no info		
143 Randy Orton	.30	.75
144 Bayley/Sasha Banks	.40	1.00
145 Bray Wyatt	.50	1.25
146 no info		
147 The Rock	.60	1.50
148 Ric Flair	.50	1.25
149 Daniel Bryan	.50	1.25
150 Brock Lesnar	.60	1.50
151 Kevin Owens	.30	.75
152 Finn Balor	.40	1.00
153 Bret Hart	.30	.75
154 The Rock/John Cena	.60	1.50
155 The Bellas	.40	1.00
156 Seth Rollins		
157 no info		
158 Ultimate Warrior	.30	.75
159 Roman Reigns	.40	1.00
160 League of Nations FOIL	.30	.75
161 Alberto Del Rio	.20	.50
162 Sheamus	.30	.75
163 Wade Barrett	.20	
164 Rusev	.30	.75
165 Kane FOIL	.20	.50
166 Kane	.20	.50
167 Kane	.20	.50
168 Kane	.20	.50
169 Kane	.20	.50
170 Kevin Owens FOIL	.30	.75
171 Kevin Owens	.30	.75
172 Kevin Owens	.30	.75
173 Kevin Owens	.30	.75
174 Kevin Owens	.30	.75
175 Chris Jericho FOIL	.30	.75
176 Chris Jericho	.30	.75
177 Chris Jericho	.30	.75
178 Chris Jericho	.30	.75
179 Chris Jericho	.30	.75
180 Dash/Dawson	.15	.40
181 Dash/Dawson	.15	.40
182 Dash/Dawson	.15	.40
183 Dash/Dawson	.15	.40
184 Dash/Dawson	.15	.40
185 Blake/Murphy FOIL	.12	.30
186 Murphy	.12	.30
187 Blake	.12	.30
188 Alexa Bliss/Murphy/Blake	.60	1.50
189 Blake	.12	.30
190 Enzo Amore	.25	.60
191 Enzo Amore	.25	.60
192 Enzo Amore	.25	.60
193 Enzo Amore	.25	.60
194 Enzo Amore	.25	.60
195 Colin Cassady FOIL	.25	.60
196 Colin Cassady	.25	.60
197 Colin Cassady	.25	.60
198 Colin Cassady	.25	.60
199 Colin Cassady	.25	.60
200 Eddie Guerrero FOIL	.30	.75
201 Eddie Guerrero	.30	.75
202 Eddie Guerrero	.30	.75
203 Eddie Guerrero	.30	.75
204 Eddie Guerrero	.30	.75
205 Stone Cold Steve Austin FOIL	.60	1.50
206 Stone Cold Steve Austin	.60	1.50
207 Stone Cold Steve Austin	.60	1.50
208 Stone Cold Steve Austin	.60	1.50
209 Stone Cold Steve Austin	.60	1.50
210 Razor Ramon	.30	.75
211 Razor Ramon	.30	.75
212 Razor Ramon	.30	.75
213 Razor Ramon	.30	.75
214 Razor Ramon	.30	.75
215 Ultimate Warrior FOIL	.30	.75
216 Ultimate Warrior	.30	.75
217 Ultimate Warrior	.30	.75
218 Ultimate Warrior	.30	.75
219 Ultimate Warrior	.30	.75
220 The Usos FOIL	.12	.30
221 The Usos	.12	.30
222 The Usos	.12	.30
223 The Usos	.12	.30
224 The Usos	.12	.30
225 Cesaro	.25	.60
226 Cesaro	.25	.60
227 Cesaro	.25	.60
228 Cesaro	.25	.60
229 Cesaro	.25	.60
230 The Rock FOIL	.60	1.50
231 The Rock	.60	1.50
232 The Rock	.60	1.50
233 The Rock/John Cena	.60	1.50
234 The Rock	.60	1.50
235 Undertaker FOIL	.50	1.25
236 Undertaker	.50	1.25
237 Undertaker	.50	1.25
238 Undertaker	.50	1.25
239 Undertaker	.50	1.25
240 Brock Lesnar	.60	1.50
241 Kalisto	.30	.75
242 Brock Lesnar/Undertaker	.60	1.50
243 Sting	.30	.75
244 Seth Rollins	.20	.50

2020-21 Topps WWE This Month in History

COMPLETE SET
DEC.'20 PRINT RUN SETS
JAN.'21 PRINT RUN SETS

1 Jeff Hardy/95*
2 Evolution/85*
3 Boogeyman/85*
4 Trish Stratus/188*
5 Wade Barrett/78*
6 Sgt. Slaughter/89*
7 Eddie Guerrero/122*
8 Daniel Bryan/102*
9 Andre the Giant/282*
10 Mr. T/269*
11 Bret Hit Man Hart/187*
12 Road Dogg/130*
13 Mankind/147*
14 Shelton Benjamin/70*
15 Asuka/110*
16 Rob Van Dam/103*
17 Hulk Hogan/175*
18 Scott Hall/96*
19 Honky Tonk Man/
20 Yokozuna/
21 Diamond Dallas Page/
22 Sherri Martel/
23 Goldberg/
24 Undertaker/
25 Ultimate Warrior/
26 Macho Man & Elizabeth/
27 British Bulldog/
28 Stone Cold Steve Austin/
29 Shawn Michaels/
30 Trish Stratus/
31 Bayley/
32 Batista/
33 Alundra Blayze/

2020 Topps WWE 3:16 Day

COMPLETE SET (6)	15.00	40.00
STATED PRINT RUN 137 SETS		
1 Stone Cold Steve Austin	4.00	10.00
2 Stone Cold Steve Austin	4.00	10.00
3 Stone Cold Steve Austin	4.00	10.00
4 Stone Cold Steve Austin	4.00	10.00
5 Stone Cold Steve Austin	4.00	10.00
6 Stone Cold Steve Austin	6.00	15.00

2019 Topps WWE Transcendent

*BLUE/15: UNPRICED DUE TO SCARCITY
*PURPLE/10: UNPRICED DUE TO SCARCITY
*BLACK/5: UNPRICED DUE TO SCARCITY
*GOLD/1: UNPRICED DUE TO SCARCITY
*RED/1: UNPRICED DUE TO SCARCITY
STATED PRINT RUN 25 SER.#'d SETS

AAB Alexa Bliss	150.00	300.00
AAC Adam Cole	50.00	100.00
AAJ AJ Styles	75.00	150.00
AAL Aleister Black	50.00	100.00
AAS Asuka	100.00	200.00
ABB Brie Bella	30.00	75.00
ABE Becky Lynch	75.00	150.00
ABH Bret Hit Man Hart	60.00	120.00
ABK Billie Kay	30.00	75.00
ABL Brock Lesnar	50.00	100.00
ABO Bobby Lashley	25.00	60.00
ABR Bobby Roode	20.00	50.00
ABS Braun Strowman	30.00	75.00
ABY Bayley	50.00	100.00
ACA Carmella	30.00	75.00
ACF Charlotte Flair	100.00	200.00
ACJ Chris Jericho	60.00	120.00
ADA Dean Ambrose	30.00	75.00
ADB Daniel Bryan	50.00	100.00
AEL Elias	15.00	40.00
AFB Finn Balor	20.00	50.00
AJC John Cena	100.00	200.00
AJG Johnny Gargano	30.00	75.00
AKO Kevin Owens	15.00	40.00
ALL Lex Luger	25.00	60.00
ALV Liv Morgan	75.00	150.00
AMA Maryse	20.00	50.00
AMJ Mickie James	30.00	75.00
AMM Mr. McMahon	500.00	1000.00
AMR Mandy Rose	60.00	120.00
ANA Naomi	15.00	40.00
ANB Nikki Bella	50.00	100.00
ANT Natalya	25.00	60.00
APG Paige	100.00	200.00
APR Peyton Royce	75.00	150.00
ARD Ricky The Dragon Steamboat	20.00	50.00
ARO Randy Orton	30.00	75.00
ASA Stone Cold Steve Austin	225.00	450.00
ASB Sasha Banks	75.00	150.00
ASH Shane McMahon	200.00	400.00
ASJ Samoa Joe	15.00	40.00
ASM Stephanie McMahon	100.00	200.00
ASN Shinsuke Nakamura	25.00	60.00
ASR Seth Rollins	20.00	50.00
AST Sting	60.00	120.00

ASW Shawn Michaels	100.00	200.00
ATH Triple H	150.00	300.00
ATS Trish Stratus	75.00	150.00
AUN Undertaker	175.00	350.00
ARRR Ronda Rousey	200.00	400.00

2019 Topps WWE Transcendent Autographed Championship Titles

NNO Dean Ambrose
NNO Jeff Hardy
NNO Randy Orton
NNO Rey Mysterio
NNO Seth Rollins

2019 Topps WWE Transcendent Autographed Kiss

*BLACK/5: UNPRICED DUE TO SCARCITY
*GOLD/1: UNPRICED DUE TO SCARCITY
*RED/1: UNPRICED DUE TO SCARCITY
STATED PRINT RUN 10 SER.#'d SETS
UNPRICED DUE TO SCARCITY

KAS Asuka
KBB Brie Bella
KNB Nikki Bella
KPR Peyton Royce

2019 Topps WWE Transcendent Autographed Sketches

STATED PRINT RUN 1 SER.#'d SET
UNPRICED DUE TO SCARCITY

1 Adam Cole
2 AJ Styles
3 Aleister Black
4 Alexa Bliss
5 Asuka
6 Bayley
7 Becky Lynch
8 Billie Kay
9 Bobby Lashley
10 Bobby Roode
11 Braun Strowman
12 Bray Wyatt
13 Bret Hart
14 Brie Bella
15 Charlotte Flair
16 Daniel Bryan
17 Dean Ambrose
18 Dolph Ziggler
19 Drew McIntyre
20 Elias
21 Ember Moon
22 Finn Balor
23 Jeff Hardy
24 John Cena
25 Johnny Gargano
26 Kairi Sane
27 Kane
28 Kevin Owens
29 Kofi Kingston
30 Matt Hardy
31 Naomi
32 Nikki Bella
33 Randy Orton
34 Ric Flair
35 Ricochet
36 Roman Reigns
37 Ronda Rousey

38 Samoa Joe
39 Sasha Banks
40 Seth Rollins
41 Shawn Michaels
42 Shinsuke Nakamura
43 Sting
44 Stone Cold Steve Austin
45 The Miz
46 The Rock
47 Tommaso Ciampa
48 Triple H
49 Trish Stratus
50 Undertaker

2019 Topps WWE Transcendent Oversized Tribute Cut Signatures

STATED PRINT RUN 1 SER.#'d SET
UNPRICED DUE TO SCARCITY

CAG Andre The Giant
CBH Bobby Heenan
CBS Bruno Sammartino
CCH Mr. Perfect
CDR Dusty Rhodes
CEG Eddie Guerrero
CFB Freddie Blassie
CGM Gorilla Monsoon
CGS George Steele
CJN Jim The Anvil Neidhart
CJS Chief Jay Strongbow
CKV Kerry Von Erich
CME Miss Elizabeth
CMY Mae Young
CPB Paul Bearer
CRR Ravishing Rick Rude
CRS Macho Man Randy Savage
CSM Sherri Martel
CUG Umaga
CUM Ultimate Warrior
CYK Yokozuna
CBBB Bam Bam Bigelow
CBJS Big John Studd
CBVV Vader
CJYD Junkyard Dog
CRRR Rowdy Roddy Piper

2019 Topps WWE Transcendent Oversized Tribute Dual Cut Signatures

STATED PRINT RUN 1 SER.#'d SET
UNPRICED DUE TO SCARCITY

DCAB Andre the Giant/B.Heenan
DCBC P. Bearer/Vader
DCDS G.Steele/Junkyard Dog
DCEM Elizabeth/S.Martel
DCES G.Steele/Elizabeth
DCHH Mr. Perfect/B.Heenan
DCPE K.Von Erich/R.Piper
DCPG E.Guerrero/R.Piper
DCPW Warrior/R.Piper
DCRE D.Rhodes/Elizabeth
DCRS R.Savage/S.Martel
DCSB G.Steele/F.Blassie
DCSE R.Savage/Elizabeth
DCSH B.Heenan/J.Studd
DCSN J.Neidhart/R.Savage
DCSR B.Sammartino/R.Piper
DCSS B.Sammartino/J.Strongbow

DCSW Warrior/R.Savage
DCVB B.Bigelow/Vader
DCVM Vader/R.Savage
DCYU Umaga/Yokozuna
DCYV Vader/Yokozuna
DCNWO1 C.Hennig/D.Rhodes
DCNWO2 R.Savage/C.Hennig

2019 Topps WWE Transcendent VIP Party Autographs

B1 Big Show	15.00	40.00
B2 Big Show	15.00	40.00
F1 Ric Flair	75.00	150.00
F2 Ric Flair	75.00	150.00
S1 Sting	50.00	100.00
S2 Sting	50.00	100.00

2019 Topps WWE Transcendent VIP Party Dual Autograph

NNO Stephanie McMahon/Triple H	225.00	450.00

2020 Topps WWE Transcendent

COMPLETE SET (50)	500.00	750.00

STATED PRINT RUN 50 SER.#'d SETS

1 Adam Cole	15.00	40.00
2 Andre the Giant	30.00	75.00
3 Angelo Dawkins	6.00	15.00
4 Bianca Belair	15.00	40.00
5 Big Show	8.00	20.00
6 Bruno Sammartino	15.00	40.00
7 Cain Velasquez	6.00	15.00
8 Cameron Grimes	6.00	15.00
9 Candice LeRae	20.00	50.00
10 Chyna	15.00	40.00
11 Damian Priest	6.00	15.00
12 Dusty Rhodes	12.00	30.00
13 Eddie Guerrero	15.00	40.00
14 Harley Race	10.00	25.00
15 Hulk Hogan	20.00	50.00
16 Io Shirai	10.00	25.00
17 Jim The Anvil Neidhart	8.00	20.00
18 John Cena	25.00	60.00
19 John Morrison	6.00	15.00
20 Johnny Gargano	12.00	30.00
21 Keith Lee	6.00	15.00
22 Kevin Nash	10.00	25.00
23 Lana	15.00	40.00
24 Lio Rush	6.00	15.00
25 Macho Man Randy Savage	20.00	50.00
26 Mandy Rose	30.00	80.00
27 Mr. Perfect Curt Hennig	10.00	25.00
28 Montez Ford	6.00	15.00
29 Mustafa Ali	10.00	25.00
30 Naomi	12.00	30.00
31 Natalya	10.00	25.00
32 Nikki Cross	12.00	30.00
33 Paul Heyman	6.00	15.00
34 Ravishing Rick Rude	8.00	20.00
35 Renee Young	8.00	20.00
36 Rhea Ripley	25.00	60.00
37 Robert Roode	6.00	15.00
38 Roderick Strong	12.00	30.00
39 Rowdy Roddy Piper	15.00	40.00
40 Rusev	8.00	20.00
41 Scott Hall	10.00	25.00
42 Shorty G	6.00	15.00
43 Sting	20.00	50.00
44 Sonya Deville	15.00	40.00
45 The British Bulldog	10.00	25.00
46 The Rock	30.00	80.00
47 Ultimate Warrior	30.00	75.00
48 Undertaker	25.00	60.00
49 Vader	10.00	25.00
50 Yokozuna	10.00	25.00

2020 Topps WWE Transcendent Autographed Replica Championship Side Plates

UNPRICED DUE TO SCARCITY

NNO AJ Styles
NNO Becky Lynch
NNO Charlotte Flair
NNO Daniel Bryan
NNO Kofi Kingston
NNO Randy Orton
NNO Roman Reigns
NNO Seth Rollins
NNO Triple H

2020 Topps WWE Transcendent Autographs

*GREEN/15: UNPRICED DUE TO SCARCITY
*PURPLE/10: UNPRICED DUE TO SCARCITY
*BLUE/5: UNPRICED DUE TO SCARCITY
*RED/1: UNPRICED DUE TO SCARCITY

AAA Andrade	25.00	60.00
AAB Aleister Black	30.00	75.00
AAJ AJ Styles	60.00	120.00
AAK Asuka	100.00	200.00
AAX Alexa Bliss	150.00	300.00
ABC King Corbin	25.00	60.00
ABD Diesel	30.00	75.00
ABH Bret Hit Man Hart	75.00	150.00
ABI Brock Lesnar	125.00	250.00
ABL Becky Lynch	75.00	150.00
ABR Braun Strowman	50.00	100.00
ABT Booker T	30.00	75.00
ABW The Fiend Bray Wyatt	100.00	200.00
ABY Bayley	50.00	100.00
ACF Charlotte Flair	100.00	200.00
ACW Sheamus	25.00	60.00
ADB Daniel Bryan	50.00	100.00
ADR Drew McIntyre	60.00	120.00
AFB Finn Balor	50.00	100.00
AGB Goldberg	75.00	150.00
AHH Hulk Hogan	250.00	500.00
AJH Jeff Hardy	60.00	120.00
AKA Kurt Angle	50.00	100.00
AKK Kofi Kingston	60.00	120.00
AKN Kane	50.00	100.00
AKO Kevin Owens	50.00	100.00
AKS Kairi Sane	75.00	150.00
ALE Lacey Evans	60.00	120.00
ALT Lita	75.00	150.00
AMF Mick Foley	30.00	75.00
AMR Matt Riddle	60.00	120.00
AQS Shayna Baszler	50.00	100.00
ARC Ricochet	25.00	60.00
ARO Randy Orton	60.00	120.00
ARR Roman Reigns	75.00	150.00
ASB Sasha Banks	125.00	250.00
ASC Stone Cold Steve Austin	350.00	700.00
ASM Shane McMahon	125.00	250.00
ASN Shinsuke Nakamura	30.00	75.00
ASR Seth Rollins	50.00	100.00

AST Stephanie McMahon	250.00	400.00
ATC Tommaso Ciampa	50.00	100.00
ATM The Miz	30.00	75.00
AUT Undertaker	300.00	500.00
AZV Zelina Vega	60.00	120.00
AHBK Shawn Michaels	125.00	250.00
AHHH Triple H	250.00	400.00
AVKM Mr. McMahon	600.00	1000.00

2020 Topps WWE Transcendent Bat Relic Autographs

RCST Sting	250.00	400.00

2020 Topps WWE Transcendent Dual Autographs

*GREEN/15: UNPRICED DUE TO SCARCITY
*PURPLE/10: UNPRICED DUE TO SCARCITY
*BLUE/5: UNPRICED DUE TO SCARCITY
*RED/1: UNPRICED DUE TO SCARCITY
STATED PRINT RUN 25 SER.#'d SETS

DAVR Erik/Ivar	75.00	150.00
DAUSO Jimmy Uso/Jey Uso	75.00	150.00

2020 Topps WWE Transcendent Image Variation Autographs

STATED PRINT RUN 1 SER.#'d SET
UNPRICED DUE TO SCARCITY

AIVAA Andrade
AIVAB Aleister Black
AIVAJ AJ Styles
AIVAK Asuka
AIVAX Alexa Bliss
AIVBC King Corbin
AIVBD Diesel
AIVBH Bret Hit Man Hart
AIVBI Brock Lesnar
AIVBL Becky Lynch
AIVBR Braun Strowman
AIVBT Booker T
AIVBW Bray Wyatt
AIVBY Bayley
AIVCF Charlotte Flair
AIVCW Sheamus
AIVDB Daniel Bryan
AIVDR Drew McIntyre
AIVFB Finn Balor
AIVGB Goldberg
AIVHH Hulk Hogan
AIVJH Jeff Hardy
AIVKA Kurt Angle
AIVKK Kofi Kingston
AIVKN Kane
AIVKO Kevin Owens
AIVKS Kairi Sane
AIVLE Lacey Evans
AIVLT Lita
AIVMF Mick Foley
AIVMR Matt Riddle
AIVQS Shayna Baszler
AIVRC Ricochet
AIVRO Randy Orton
AIVRR Roman Reigns
AIVSB Sasha Banks
AIVSC Stone Cold Steve Austin
AIVSJ Samoa Joe
AIVSM Shane McMahon
AIVSN Shinsuke Nakamura

AIVSR Seth Rollins
AIVST Stephanie McMahon
AIVTC Tommaso Ciampa
AIVTM The Miz
AIVUT Undertaker
AIVZV Zelina Vega
AIVHBK Shawn Michaels
AIVHHH Triple H
AIVVKM Mr. McMahon

2020 Topps WWE Transcendent Image Variation Dual Autographs

STATED PRINT RUN 1 SER.#'d SET
UNPRICED DUE TO SCARCITY

DAIVVR Erik/Ivar
DAIVUSO Jimmy Uso/Jey Uso

2020 Topps WWE Transcendent John Cena Superstar Tribute

COMPLETE SET (50)	250.00	500.00
JCRP1 John Cena	10.00	25.00
JCRP2 John Cena	10.00	25.00
JCRP3 John Cena	10.00	25.00
JCRP4 John Cena	10.00	25.00
JCRP5 John Cena	10.00	25.00
JCRP6 John Cena	10.00	25.00
JCRP7 John Cena	10.00	25.00
JCRP8 John Cena	10.00	25.00
JCRP9 John Cena	10.00	25.00
JCRP10 John Cena	10.00	25.00
JCRP11 John Cena	10.00	25.00
JCRP12 John Cena	10.00	25.00
JCRP13 John Cena	10.00	25.00
JCRP14 John Cena	10.00	25.00
JCRP15 John Cena	10.00	25.00
JCRP16 John Cena	10.00	25.00
JCRP17 John Cena	10.00	25.00
JCRP18 John Cena	10.00	25.00
JCRP19 John Cena	10.00	25.00
JCRP20 John Cena	10.00	25.00
JCRP21 John Cena	10.00	25.00
JCRP22 John Cena	10.00	25.00
JCRP23 John Cena	10.00	25.00
JCRP24 John Cena	10.00	25.00
JCRP25 John Cena	10.00	25.00
JCRP26 John Cena	10.00	25.00
JCRP27 John Cena	10.00	25.00
JCRP28 John Cena	10.00	25.00
JCRP29 John Cena	10.00	25.00
JCRP30 John Cena	10.00	25.00
JCRP31 John Cena	10.00	25.00
JCRP32 John Cena	10.00	25.00
JCRP33 John Cena	10.00	25.00
JCRP34 John Cena	10.00	25.00
JCRP35 John Cena	10.00	25.00
JCRP36 John Cena	10.00	25.00
JCRP37 John Cena	10.00	25.00
JCRP38 John Cena	10.00	25.00
JCRP39 John Cena	10.00	25.00
JCRP40 John Cena	10.00	25.00
JCRP41 John Cena	10.00	25.00
JCRP42 John Cena	10.00	25.00
JCRP43 John Cena	10.00	25.00
JCRP44 John Cena	10.00	25.00
JCRP45 John Cena	10.00	25.00
JCRP46 John Cena	10.00	25.00
JCRP47 John Cena	10.00	25.00
JCRP48 John Cena	10.00	25.00
JCRP49 John Cena	10.00	25.00
JCRP50 John Cena	10.00	25.00

2020 Topps WWE Transcendent John Cena Superstar Tribute Autographs

STATED PRINT RUN 1 SER.#'d SET
UNPRICED DUE TO SCARCITY

2020 Topps WWE Transcendent Sketches

STATED PRINT RUN 1 SER.#'d SET
UNPRICED DUE TO SCARCITY
ART BY DAN BERGREN

NNO AJ Styles
NNO Alexa Bliss
NNO Andrade
NNO Angel Garza
NNO Asuka
NNO Batista
NNO Bayley
NNO Becky Lynch
NNO Braun Strowman
NNO The Fiend Bray Wyatt
NNO Bret Hit Man Hart
NNO Brock Lesnar
NNO Charlotte Flair
NNO Eddie Guerrero
NNO Ember Moon
NNO Finn Balor
NNO Goldberg
NNO Hulk Hogan
NNO Jeff Hardy
NNO John Cena
NNO Kairi Sane
NNO Kane
NNO Keith Lee
NNO Kevin Owens
NNO Kofi Kingston
NNO Lacey Evans
NNO Lita
NNO Matt Riddle
NNO Mustafa Ali
NNO Pete Dunne
NNO Randy Orton
NNO Macho Man Randy Savage
NNO Ricochet
NNO Rowdy Roddy Piper
NNO Roman Reigns
NNO Ronda Rousey
NNO Sami Zayn
NNO Samoa Joe
NNO Sasha Banks
NNO Seth Rollins
NNO Shawn Michaels
NNO Shayna Baszler
NNO Shinsuke Nakamura
NNO Sting
NNO Stone Cold Steve Austin
NNO The Miz
NNO The Rock
NNO Triple H
NNO Ultimate Warrior
NNO Undertaker

2020 Topps WWE Transcendent VIP Party Black and White Pattern 1

*BLACK/WHITE 2: UNPRICED DUE TO SCARCITY
*BLACK/WHITE 3: UNPRICED DUE TO SCARCITY
*BLACK/WHITE 4: UNPRICED DUE TO SCARCITY
*BLACK/WHITE 5: UNPRICED DUE TO SCARCITY
*AQUA/PURPLE 1: UNPRICED DUE TO SCARCITY
*AQUA/PURPLE 2: UNPRICED DUE TO SCARCITY
*AQUA/PURPLE 3: UNPRICED DUE TO SCARCITY
*AQUA/PURPLE 4: UNPRICED DUE TO SCARCITY
*AQUA/PURPLE 5: UNPRICED DUE TO SCARCITY
*GREEN/YELLOW 1: UNPRICED DUE TO SCARCITY
*GREEN/YELLOW 2: UNPRICED DUE TO SCARCITY
*GREEN/YELLOW 3: UNPRICED DUE TO SCARCITY
*GREEN/YELLOW 4: UNPRICED DUE TO SCARCITY
*GREEN/YELLOW 5: UNPRICED DUE TO SCARCITY
*PURPLE/RED 1: UNPRICED DUE TO SCARCITY
*PURPLE/RED 2: UNPRICED DUE TO SCARCITY
*PURPLE/RED 3: UNPRICED DUE TO SCARCITY
*PURPLE/RED 4: UNPRICED DUE TO SCARCITY
*PURPLE/RED 5: UNPRICED DUE TO SCARCITY
*RED/YELLOW 1: UNPRICED DUE TO SCARCITY
*RED/YELLOW 2: UNPRICED DUE TO SCARCITY
*RED/YELLOW 3: UNPRICED DUE TO SCARCITY
*RED/YELLOW 4: UNPRICED DUE TO SCARCITY
*RED/YELLOW 5: UNPRICED DUE TO SCARCITY
STATED PRINT RUN 1 SER.#'d SET
UNPRICED DUE TO SCARCITY
SUMMERSLAM VIP EXCLUSIVE
ALL CARDS ARE 1/1

1 AJ Styles
2 Akira Tozawa
3 Alexa Bliss
4 Apollo Crews
5 Asuka
6 Batista
7 Bayley
8 Bianca Belair
9 Bobby Lashley
10 The Fiend Bray Wyatt
11 Carmella
12 Cesaro
13 Dakota Kai
14 Dolph Ziggler
15 Dominik Mysterio
16 Drew McIntyre
17 Edge
18 Finn Balor
19 Hulk Hogan
20 Jey Uso
21 Jinder Mahal
22 TBD
23 Kevin Owens
24 Kofi Kingston
25 Kushida
26 MVP
27 Nia Jax
28 Omos
29 Pete Dunne
30 Randy Orton
31 Raquel Gonzalez
32 Razor Ramon
33 TBD
34 Rhea Ripley
35 Ric Flair
36 Riddle
37 Roman Reigns

38 Sami Zayn
39 Santos Escobar
40 Sasha Banks
41 Scarlett
42 Seth Rollins
43 Sgt. Slaughter
44 Shayna Baszler
45 Sheamus
46 Shotzi Blackheart
47 The Miz
48 Walter
49 Xavier Woods
50 X-Pac

2020 Topps WWE Transcendent VIP Party Autographs

*AQUA/PURPLE 1: UNPRICED DUE TO SCARCITY
*AQUA/PURPLE 2: UNPRICED DUE TO SCARCITY
*BLACK/WHITE 1: UNPRICED DUE TO SCARCITY
*BLACK/WHITE 2: UNPRICED DUE TO SCARCITY
*GREEN/YELLOW 1: UNPRICED DUE TO SCARCITY
*GREEN/YELLOW 2: UNPRICED DUE TO SCARCITY
*PURPLE/RED 1: UNPRICED DUE TO SCARCITY
*PURPLE/RED 2: UNPRICED DUE TO SCARCITY
*RED/YELLOW 1: UNPRICED DUE TO SCARCITY
*RED/YELLOW 2: UNPRICED DUE TO SCARCITY
STATED PRINT RUN 1 SER.#'d SET
UNPRICED DUE TO SCARCITY
SUMMERSLAM VIP EXCLUSIVE
ALL CARDS 1/1

ABE Big E
ABP Beth Phoenix
AEM Ember Moon
AJC John Cena
AJL Jerry ïThe Kingî Lawler
AJN Jim ïThe Anvilî Neidhart
AJR Jaxson Ryker
AMK Mankind
ANN Natalya
ATA Tamina
ATR Trish Stratus
ATS Toni Storm
AJBL JBL
AKOR Kyle OíReilly

2020 Topps WWE Transcendent VIP Party On-Card Autographs

STATED PRINT RUN 25 SER.#'d SETS
SUMMERSLAM VIP EXCLUSIVE

VIPDM1	Drew McIntyre	30.00	75.00
VIPDM2	Drew McIntyre	30.00	75.00
VIPJH1	Jeff Hardy		
VIPJH2	Jeff Hardy		
VIPNC1	Nikki Ash	50.00	100.00
VIPNC2	Nikki Ash	50.00	100.00
VIPRR1	Rhea Ripley		
VIPRR2	Rhea Ripley		

2021 Topps WWE Transcendent

COMPLETE SET (50)		200.00	500.00
1	Aleister Black	8.00	20.00
2	Andre the Giant	40.00	100.00
3	Apollo Crews	4.00	10.00
4	Bam Bam Bigelow	6.00	15.00
5	Beth Phoenix	6.00	15.00
6	Big Boss Man	5.00	12.00
7	Braun Strowman	8.00	20.00

8	Candice LeRae	12.00	30.00
9	Cedric Alexander	3.00	8.00
10	Diamond Dallas Page	5.00	12.00
11	Dusty Rhodes	10.00	25.00
12	Earthquake	8.00	20.00
13	Eddie Guerrero	15.00	40.00
14	Faarooq	5.00	12.00
15	Finlay	3.00	8.00
16	Finn Balor	8.00	20.00
17	George The Animal Steele	6.00	15.00
18	Gorilla Monsoon	6.00	15.00
19	Indi Hartwell	10.00	25.00
20	Jerry The King Lawler	5.00	12.00
21	Jimmy Hart	4.00	10.00
22	Junkyard Dog	3.00	8.00
23	Kay Lee Ray	8.00	20.00
24	Kevin Owens	6.00	15.00
25	King Corbin	3.00	8.00
26	Lacey Evans	12.00	30.00
27	Mae Young	5.00	12.00
28	Macho King Randy Savage	20.00	50.00
29	Marlena	5.00	12.00
30	Michael Cole	3.00	8.00
31	Mr. Perfect	10.00	25.00
32	Naomi	4.00	10.00
33	Natalya	5.00	12.00
34	Nikolai Volkoff	3.00	8.00
35	Nikki Cross	6.00	15.00
36	Paul Bearer	6.00	15.00
37	Ricky The Dragon Steamboat	5.00	12.00
38	Raquel Gonzalez	12.00	30.00
39	Rob Van Dam	6.00	15.00
40	Roderick Strong	6.00	15.00
41	Rowdy Roddy Piper	8.00	20.00
42	Shayna Baszler	8.00	20.00
43	Sheamus	5.00	12.00
44	Sensational Sherri Martel	8.00	20.00
45	Shinsuke Nakamura	8.00	20.00
46	The Brian Kendrick	3.00	8.00
47	The Honky Tonk Man	3.00	8.00
48	Trent Seven	4.00	10.00
49	Tyler Bate	4.00	10.00
50	Ultimate Warrior	20.00	50.00

2021 Topps WWE Transcendent Autographed Championships

NNO AJ Styles
WWE Championship
NNO Bobby Lashley
WWE Championship
NNO Braun Strowman
SmackDown Universal Championship
NNO Drew McIntyre
WWE Championship
NNO Finn Balor
RAW Universal Championship
NNO Goldberg
RAW Universal Championship
NNO Kevin Owens
RAW Universal Championship
NNO Kofi Kingston
WWE Championship
NNO Roman Reigns
SmackDown Universal Championship
NNO Seth Rollins
RAW Universal Championship

2021 Topps WWE Transcendent Autographs

*GREEN/15: UNPRICED DUE TO SCARCITY
*PURPLE/10: UNPRICED DUE TO SCARCITY
*BLUE/5: UNPRICED DUE TO SCARCITY
*RED/1: UNPRICED DUE TO SCARCITY
*SUPERFR/1: UNPRICED DUE TO SCARCITY
STATED PRINT RUN 25 SER.#'d SETS

AAB	Alexa Bliss	200.00	400.00
AAC	Adam Cole	50.00	100.00
AAJ	AJ Styles	25.00	60.00
AAS	Asuka	100.00	200.00
ABA	Bayley	30.00	75.00
ABB	Bianca Belair	50.00	100.00
ABE	Big E	20.00	50.00
ABH	Bret "Hit Man" Hart	150.00	300.00
ABL	Becky Lynch EXCH	100.00	200.00
ACF	Charlotte Flair	75.00	150.00
ACS	Cesaro	15.00	40.00
ADK	Dakota Kai	50.00	100.00
ADP	Damian Priest	15.00	40.00
ADR	Drew McIntyre	25.00	60.00
AED	Edge	60.00	120.00
AGB	Goldberg	75.00	150.00
AIR	Iron Sheik	50.00	100.00
AIS	Io Shirai	75.00	150.00
AJC	John Cena	150.00	300.00
AJR	Jake "The Snake" Roberts	75.00	150.00
AJU	Jey Uso	15.00	40.00
AKK	Karrion Kross	20.00	50.00
AKL	Keith Lee	15.00	40.00
AKN	Kane	50.00	100.00
ALA	Bobby Lashley	20.00	50.00
AMK	Mankind	100.00	200.00
ANJ	Nia Jax	25.00	60.00
ARM	Rey Mysterio	100.00	200.00
ARO	Randy Orton	50.00	100.00
ARP	Rhea Ripley	60.00	120.00
ARR	Roman Reigns	125.00	250.00
ASA	Stone Cold Steve Austin	500.00	800.00
ASC	Scarlett	60.00	120.00
ASD	Sonya Deville	20.00	50.00
ASR	Seth Rollins	30.00	75.00
ASS	Sgt. Slaughter	50.00	100.00
AST	Stephanie McMahon	150.00	300.00
ATD	Million Dollar Man Ted DiBiase	30.00	75.00
ATS	Toni Storm	75.00	150.00
AUT	Undertaker	300.00	500.00
AVM	Mr. McMahon	750.00	1500.00
AWT	WALTER	15.00	40.00
AXP	X-Pac	30.00	75.00
ABRO	Riddle	15.00	40.00
AHBK	Shawn Michaels	150.00	300.00
AHHH	Triple H	200.00	400.00
AMVP	MVP	15.00	40.00

2021 Topps WWE Transcendent Dual Autographs

*GREEN/15: UNPRICED DUE TO SCARCITY
*PURPLE/10: UNPRICED DUE TO SCARCITY
*BLUE/5: UNPRICED DUE TO SCARCITY
*RED/1: UNPRICED DUE TO SCARCITY
*SUPERFR/1: UNPRICED DUE TO SCARCITY
STATED PRINT RUN 25 SER.#'d SETS

TAKW	The New Day	30.00	75.00
TAMM	The Miz & John Morrison	25.00	60.00
TASP	The Street Profits	25.00	60.00

2021 Topps WWE Transcendent Quad Autograph

*GREEN/15: UNPRICED DUE TO SCARCITY
*PURPLE/10: UNPRICED DUE TO SCARCITY
*BLUE/5: UNPRICED DUE TO SCARCITY
*RED/1: UNPRICED DUE TO SCARCITY
STATED PRINT RUN 25 SER.#'d SETS

QA4HW	Becky/Sasha/Charlotte/Bayley	600.00	1000.00

2021 Topps WWE Transcendent Ric Flair Legends Tribute

COMPLETE SET (25)		125.00	300.00

STATED ODDS 1:SET PER BOX
STATED PRINT RUN 50 SER.#'d SETS

RF1	Ric Flair	8.00	20.00
RF2	Ric Flair	8.00	20.00
RF3	Ric Flair	8.00	20.00
RF4	Ric Flair	8.00	20.00
RF5	Ric Flair	8.00	20.00
RF6	Ric Flair	8.00	20.00
RF7	Ric Flair	8.00	20.00
RF8	Ric Flair	8.00	20.00
RF9	Ric Flair	8.00	20.00
RF10	Ric Flair	8.00	20.00
RF11	Ric Flair	8.00	20.00
RF12	Ric Flair	8.00	20.00
RF13	Ric Flair	8.00	20.00
RF14	Ric Flair	8.00	20.00
RF15	Ric Flair	8.00	20.00
RF16	Ric Flair	8.00	20.00
RF17	Ric Flair	8.00	20.00
RF18	Ric Flair	8.00	20.00
RF19	Ric Flair	8.00	20.00
RF20	Ric Flair	8.00	20.00
RF21	Ric Flair	8.00	20.00
RF22	Ric Flair	8.00	20.00
RF23	Ric Flair	8.00	20.00
RF24	Ric Flair	8.00	20.00
RF25	Ric Flair	8.00	20.00

2021 Topps WWE Transcendent The Rock Legends Tribute

COMPLETE SET (25)		200.00	500.00

STATED ODDS 1:SET PER BOX
STATED PRINT RUN 50 SER.#'d SETS

DJ1	The Rock	15.00	40.00
DJ2	The Rock	15.00	40.00
DJ3	The Rock	15.00	40.00
DJ4	The Rock	15.00	40.00
DJ5	The Rock	15.00	40.00
DJ6	The Rock	15.00	40.00
DJ7	The Rock	15.00	40.00
DJ8	The Rock	15.00	40.00
DJ9	The Rock	15.00	40.00
DJ10	The Rock	15.00	40.00
DJ11	The Rock	15.00	40.00
DJ12	The Rock	15.00	40.00
DJ13	The Rock	15.00	40.00
DJ14	The Rock	15.00	40.00
DJ15	The Rock	15.00	40.00
DJ16	The Rock	15.00	40.00
DJ17	The Rock	15.00	40.00
DJ18	The Rock	15.00	40.00
DJ19	The Rock	15.00	40.00
DJ20	The Rock	15.00	40.00
DJ21	The Rock	15.00	40.00
DJ22	The Rock	15.00	40.00

DJ23	The Rock	15.00	40.00
DJ24	The Rock	15.00	40.00
DJ25	The Rock	15.00	40.00

2021 Topps WWE Transcendent Sketches

UNPRICED DUE TO SCARCITY

NNO	Alexa Bliss	
NNO	Asuka	
NNO	Batista	
NNO	Bayley	
NNO	Becky Lynch	
NNO	Booker T	
NNO	Braun Strowman	
NNO	Bray Wyatt	
NNO	Bret "Hit Man" Hart	
NNO	Charlotte Flair	
NNO	Daniel Bryan	
NNO	Drew McIntyre	
NNO	Eddie Guerrero	
NNO	Edge	
NNO	Finn Balor	
NNO	Goldberg	
NNO	Hulk Hogan	
NNO	Jeff Hardy	
NNO	John Cena	
NNO	Kane	
NNO	Keith Lee	
NNO	Kevin Owens	
NNO	King Corbin	
NNO	Macho Man Randy Savage	
NNO	Mick Foley	
NNO	Million Dollar Man Ted DiBiase	
NNO	Mr. Perfect	
NNO	Nia Jax	
NNO	Otis	
NNO	Randy Orton	
NNO	Razor Ramon	
NNO	Rey Mysterio	
NNO	Ric Flair	
NNO	Riddle	
NNO	Rikishi	
NNO	Roman Reigns	
NNO	Rowdy Roddy Piper	
NNO	Sasha Banks	
NNO	Sami Zayn	
NNO	Seth Rollins	
NNO	Shawn Michaels	
NNO	Sheamus	
NNO	Sgt. Slaughter	
NNO	Shinsuke Nakamura	
NNO	Stone Cold Steve Austin	
NNO	The New Day	
NNO	The Rock	
NNO	Ultimate Warrior	
NNO	Undertaker	

2016 Topps WWE Triple H Tribute

COMPLETE SET (10)		12.00	30.00
TARGET EXCLUSIVES			
1	Triple H	.50	1.25
2	Triple H	.50	1.25
3	Triple H	.50	1.25
4	Triple H	.50	1.25
5	Triple H	.50	1.25
6	Triple H	1.25	3.00
7	Triple H	1.50	4.00
8	Triple H	1.25	3.00
9	Triple H	1.25	3.00

10	Triple H	1.25	3.00
11	Triple H	.50	1.25
12	Triple H	.50	1.25
13	Triple H	.50	1.25
14	Triple H	.50	1.25
15	Triple H	.50	1.25
16	Triple H	1.25	3.00
17	Triple H	1.25	3.00
18	Triple H	1.25	3.00
19	Triple H	1.25	3.00
20	Triple H	1.25	3.00
21	Triple H	.50	1.25
22	Triple H	.50	1.25
23	Triple H	.50	1.25
24	Triple H	.50	1.25
25	Triple H	.50	1.25
26	Triple H	1.25	3.00
27	Triple H	1.25	3.00
28	Triple H	1.25	3.00
29	Triple H	1.25	3.00
30	Triple H	1.25	3.00
31	Triple H	.50	1.25
32	Triple H	.50	1.25
33	Triple H	.50	1.25
34	Triple H	.50	1.25
35	Triple H	.50	1.25
36	Triple H	1.25	3.00
37	Triple H	1.25	3.00
38	Triple H	1.25	3.00
39	Triple H	1.25	3.00
40	Triple H	1.25	3.00

2020 Topps WWE Triple H 25th Anniversary

COMPLETE SET (25)		8.00	20.00
STATED PRINT RUN 260 SETS			
1	Hunter Hearst Helmsley Makes His WWE Debut	.75	2.00
2	Hunter Hearst Helmsley Is Victorious in an Arkansas Hog Pen Match	.75	2.00
3	Hunter Hearst Helmsley Wins the Intercontinental Championship for the First Time	.75	2.00
4	Triple H Wins the 1997 King of the Ring Tournament	.75	2.00
5	Triple H Becomes the Leader of D-Generation X	.75	2.00
6	D-Generation X Invade WCW Monday Nitro	.75	2.00
7	Triple H Def. The Rock in a Ladder Match for the Intercontinental Title	.75	2.00
8	WWE Champion Triple H Def. Stone Cold Steve Austin in a No Holds Barred Match	.75	2.00
9	WWE Champion Triple H Def. Cactus Jack in a Street Fight	.75	2.00
10	Triple H Def. Kurt Angle in a No Disqualification Match	.75	2.00
11	Triple H Def. Stone Cold Steve Austin in a Three Stages of Hell Match	.75	2.00
12	The Two Man Power Trip Def. The Brothers Of Destruction in a Winners-Take-All Match	.75	2.00
13	Triple H Returns from a Career-Threatening Injury	.75	2.00
14	Triple H Wins the 2002 Royal Rumble	.75	2.00
15	Triple H Goes to War with Shawn Michaels	.75	2.00
16	Triple H Advances in the Road to WrestleMania Tournament	.75	2.00
17	Triple H Reunites with Shawn Michaels	.75	2.00
18	Triple H Def. King Booker	.75	2.00

19	D-Generation X Wins the Unified WWE Tag Team Championship	.75	2.00
20	Triple H The End of an Era	.75	2.00
21	Triple H Def. Brock Lesnar in a No Holds Barred Match	.75	2.00
22	The King of Kings Makes an Unforgettable Entrance	.75	2.00
23	Triple H Def. Sting	.75	2.00
24	Triple H Introduces Brooklyn to NXT	.75	2.00
25	D-Generation X Is Inducted into the WWE Hall of Fame	.75	2.00

2020 Topps WWE Triple H 25th Anniversary Autographs

COMPLETE SET (5)
*GREEN/15: UNPRICED DUE TO SCARCITY
*GOLD/1: UNPRICED DUE TO SCARCITY
STATED OVERALL ODDS 1:2 W/RELICS
STATED PRINT RUN 99 SER.#'d SETS

1A	Triple H	100.00	200.00
2A	Triple H	100.00	200.00
3A	Triple H	100.00	200.00
4A	Triple H	100.00	200.00
5A	Triple H	100.00	200.00

2020 Topps WWE Triple H 25th Anniversary Cerebral Moments

COMPLETE SET (11)		5.00	12.00
STATED PRINT RUN 260 SETS			
C1	Triple H Turns His Back on D-Generation X	.75	2.00
C2	Triple H Attacks The Rock While Trapped in a Casket	.75	2.00
C3	D-Generation X Reforms?	.75	2.00
C4	Triple H Kicks Randy Orton Out of Evolution	.75	2.00
C5	Triple H Tames íThe Animalí	.75	2.00
C6	Triple H Betrays His Mentor	.75	2.00
C7	Triple H Breaks Big Showís Hand with a Sledgehammer	.75	2.00
C8	Triple H Deals a Merciless Steel Chair Attack to Undertaker	.75	2.00
C9	Triple H Does Whatís Best for Business.	.75	2.00
C10	Triple H Brutalizes Daniel Bryan & the Yes! Movement	.75	2.00
C11	Triple H Sends a Harsh Message to Roman Reigns	.75	2.00
C12	Triple H Costs Seth Rollins His Universal Championship Opportunity	.75	2.00

2020 Topps WWE Triple H 25th Anniversary Relics

*GREEN/9: UNPRICED DUE TO SCARCITY
*GOLD/1: UNPRICED DUE TO SCARCITY
STATED OVERALL ODDS 1:2 W/AUTOGRAPHS
STATED PRINT RUN 15 SER.#'d SETS

1R	Triple H	30.00	75.00
2R	Triple H	30.00	75.00
3R	Triple H	30.00	75.00
4R	Triple H	30.00	75.00
5R	Triple H	30.00	75.00

2020 Topps WWE Triple H 25th Anniversary World Title Victories

COMPLETE SET (14)		6.00	15.00
STATED PRINT RUN 260 SETS			
T1	Triple H Def. Mankind for His First WWE Championship	.75	2.00
T2	Triple H Wins a Six Pack Challenge	.75	2.00

T3	Triple H Def. Big Show	.75	2.00
T4	Triple H Def. The Rock in a 60-Minute Iron Man Match	.75	2.00
T5	Triple H Wins His Fifth WWE Championship	.75	2.00
T6	Triple H Is Awarded the World Heavyweight Championship	.75	2.00
T7	Triple H Def. Shawn Michaels in a Three Stages of Hell Match	.75	2.00
T8	Triple H Def. Goldberg And Kane in a Triple Threat Match	.75	2.00
T9	Triple H Def. Randy Orton	.75	2.00
T10	Triple H Def. Newly-Crowned WWE Champion Randy Orton	.75	2.00
T11	Triple H Wins A Fatal 4-Way Elimination Match	.75	2.00
T12	Triple H Wins the Elimination Chamber Match	.75	2.00
T13	Triple H Wins His 14th World Championship	.75	2.00

2008 Topps WWE Ultimate Rivals

COMPLETE SET (90)		8.00	20.00
UNOPENED BOX (24 PACKS)			
UNOPENED PACK (7 CARDS)			
1	Kane vs. Chavo Guerrero	.40	1.00
2	Batista vs. Mark Henry	.40	1.00
3	Batisita vs. The Great Khali	.40	1.00
4	Batista vs. Undertaker	.50	1.25
5	Big Daddy V vs. Boogeyman	.15	.40
6	Kendrick/London vs. Regal/Taylor	.25	.60
7	Chris Jericho vs. JBL	.25	.60
8	CM Punk vs. John Morrison	.10	.25
9	CM Punk vs. Mike Knox	.10	.25
10	CM Punk vs. Shannon Moore	.10	.25
11	C.Rhodes vs. Hardcore Holly	.15	.40
12	D-Generation X vs. Rated RKO	.25	.60
13	Elijah Burke vs. CM Punk	.10	.25
14	Finlay vs. Rey Mysterio	.25	.60
15	Finlay vs. JBL	.15	.40
16	Jamie Noble vs. The Hurricane	.12	.30
17	Jamie Noble vs. Hornswoggle	.15	.40
18	Jeff Hardy vs. John Morrison	.40	1.00
19	Jeff Hardy vs. Umaga	.40	1.00
20	John Cena vs. Carlito	.60	1.50
21	John Cena vs. Edge	.60	1.50
22	John Cena vs. Randy Orton	.60	1.50
23	Kane vs. MVP	.40	1.00
24	Kane vs. Snitsky	.40	1.00
25	Umaga vs. Kane	.40	1.00
26	Kane vs. Undertaker	.50	1.25
27	K.Dykstra vs. Chuck Palumbo	.15	.40
28	K.Dykstra vs. Shawn Michaels	.60	1.50
29	Cade/Murdoch vs. Rhodes/Holly	.15	.40
30	Deuce/Domino vs. London/Kendrick	.15	.40
31	Matt Hardy vs. Edge	.40	1.00
32	Matt Hardy vs. MVP	.40	1.00
33	T.Dreamer vs. Matt Striker	.10	.25
34	Mr. Kennedy vs. Undertaker	.50	1.25
35	Big Show vs. John Cena	.60	1.50
36	R.Mysterio vs. Chavo Guerrero	.25	.60
37	Rey Mysterio vs. MVP	.25	.60
38	Ric Flair vs. Carlito	.40	1.00
39	S.Marella vs. Steve Austin	.60	1.50
40	Shawn Michaels vs. Undertaker	.60	1.50
41	Funaki vs. Val Venis	.10	.25
42	Steve Austin vs. Mr. McMahon	.60	1.50
43	Kevin Thorn vs. Stevie Richards	.15	.40
44	Tommy Dreamer vs. Mick Foley	.50	1.25
45	Triple H vs. Batista	.60	1.50

46	Triple H vs. Mick Foley	.60	1.50
47	Randy Orton vs. Triple H	.60	1.50
48	Triple H vs. Umaga	.60	1.50
49	Shane McMahon vs. Mr. McMahon	.25	.60
50	Randy Orton vs. Jeff Hardy	.40	1.00
51	Steve Austin vs. Brian Pillman	.60	1.50
52	S.Michaels vs. British Bulldog	.60	1.50
53	Chris Jericho vs. Dean Malenko	.25	.60
54	Big Show vs. Undertaker	.50	1.25
55	Randy Orton vs. Dusty Rhodes	.25	.60
56	Shane McMahon vs. Chris Jericho	.25	.60
57	Jerry Lawler vs. Tazz	.25	.60
58	Ric Flair vs. Terry Funk	.40	1.00
59	Paul Bearer vs. Undertaker	.50	1.25
60	Rey Mysterio vs. JBL	.25	.60
61	Arn Anderson vs. Ric Flair	.40	1.00
62	Ric Flair vs. Mr.Perfect	.40	1.00
63	Ric Flair vs. Dusty Rhodes	.40	1.00
64	Kama Mustafa vs. Undertaker	.50	1.25
65	Santino Marella vs. Maria	.40	1.00
66	Mickie James vs. Melina	.60	1.50
67	Candice Michelle vs. Beth Phoenix	.50	1.25
68	Melina vs. Candice Michelle	.50	1.25
69	Kelly Kelly vs. Layla	.40	1.00
70	Victoria vs. Michelle McCool	.50	1.25
71	Mickie James vs. Beth Phoenix	.60	1.50
72	Maria vs. Melina	.40	1.00
73	Doink vs. Bam Bam Bigelow	.25	.60
74	Iron Shiek vs. Sgt. Slaughter	.40	1.00
75	Paul Orndorff vs. Bobby Heenan	.25	.60
76	J.Strongbow vs. Peter Maivia	.25	.60
77	Mick Foley vs. Terry Funk	.25	.60
78	Dusty Rhodes vs. Billy Graham	.25	.60
79	Ron Simmons vs. Vader	.15	.40
80	Jake Roberts vs. Kamala	.25	.60
81	Jake Roberts vs. Rick Rude	.25	.60
82	Jake Roberts vs. Ted DiBiase	.25	.60
83	Jake Roberts vs. Jerry Lawler	.25	.60
84	Bam Bam vs. One Man Gang	.25	.60
85	Ric Flair vs. Roddy Piper	.40	1.00
86	Rocky Johnson vs. Wild Samoans	.15	.40
87	Ted DiBiase vs. Dusty Rhodes	.25	.60
88	Sgt. Slaughter vs. Pat Patterson	.25	.60
89	Gorilla Monsoon vs. Vader	.25	.60
90	Checklist	.10	.25

2008 Topps WWE Ultimate Rivals Autographs

STATED ODDS 1:48 HOBBY EXCLUSIVE

NNO	CM Punk	100.00	200.00
NNO	Edge	20.00	50.00
NNO	Elijah Burke	6.00	15.00
NNO	John Morrison	8.00	20.00
NNO	Matt Hardy	8.00	20.00
NNO	Michelle McCool	12.00	30.00
NNO	The Miz	8.00	20.00
NNO	Stevie Richards	6.00	15.00
NNO	Super Crazy	6.00	15.00
NNO	Victoria	8.00	20.00

2008 Topps WWE Ultimate Rivals Motion Cards

COMPLETE SET (10)		4.00	10.00

STATED ODDS 1:8 HOBBY AND RETAIL

1	Batista vs. Edge	.60	1.50
2	Lance Cade vs. Hardcore Holly	.20	.50
3	Carlito vs. Brian Kendrick	.30	.75
4	Chavo Guerrero vs. CM Punk	.30	.75
5	Hornswoggle/Finley vs. Edge	.60	1.50

6	Lance Cade	.20	.50
7	Jeff Hardy vs. Randy Orton	.60	1.50
8	Rey Mysterio vs. Edge	.60	1.50
9	Triple H vs. Umaga	1.00	2.50
10	Undertaker vs. MVP	1.00	2.50

2008 Topps WWE Ultimate Rivals Ringside Relics

STATED ODDS 1:48 HOBBY EXCLUSIVE

NNO	Carlito	3.00	8.00
NNO	Charlie Haas	3.00	8.00
NNO	CM Punk	3.00	8.00
NNO	Edge	4.00	10.00
NNO	John Cena	6.00	15.00
NNO	Matt Hardy	5.00	12.00
NNO	Mr. Kennedy	3.00	8.00

2008 Topps WWE Ultimate Rivals Tattoos

COMPLETE SET (10)		4.00	10.00

STATED ODDS 1:4 RETAIL EXCLUSIVE

1	John Cena	1.00	3.00
2	Batista	.60	1.50
3	Shawn Michaels	1.00	2.50
4	Edge	.60	1.50
5	Mr. Kennedy	.30	.75
6	The Undertaker	.60	1.50
7	Ric Flair	.60	1.50
8	Triple H	1.00	2.50
9	Rey Mysterio	.30	.75
10	John Morrison	.30	.75

2008 Topps WWE Ultimate Rivals Promos

P1	John Cena vs. Edge	1.00	2.50

2015 Topps WWE Undisputed

COMPLETE SET (100)		30.00	80.00
UNOPENED BOX (10 PACKS)			
UNOPENED PACKS (5 CARDS)			

*RED: .5X TO 1.2X BASIC CARDS
*BLACK/99: .6X TO 1.5X BASIC CARDS
*PURPLE/50: .75X TO 2X BASIC CARDS
*SILVER/25: 1.2X TO 3X BASIC CARDS
*GOLD/1: UNPRICED DUE TO SCARCITY
*PP BLACK/1: UNPRICED DUE TO SCARCITY
*PP CYAN/1: UNPRICED DUE TO SCARCITY
*PP MAGENTA/1: UNPRICED DUE TO SCARCITY
*PP YELLOW/1: UNPRICED DUE TO SCARCITY

1	Undertaker	2.50	6.00
2	Rosa Mendes	1.00	2.50
3	Lita	2.50	6.00
4	Kofi Kingston	.60	1.50
5	George The Animal Steele	.75	2.00
6	Titus O'Neil	.60	1.50
7	Stardust	.60	1.50
8	The American Dream Dusty Rhodes	1.00	2.50
9	Alicia Fox	1.25	3.00
10	Brock Lesnar	2.50	6.00
11	Zack Ryder	.60	1.50
12	Summer Rae	2.50	6.00
13	The Miz	1.00	2.50
14	Roman Reigns	1.50	4.00
15	Natalya	2.00	5.00
16	Rob Van Dam	1.50	4.00
17	Lana	2.50	6.00
18	Shawn Michaels	2.50	6.00
19	R-Truth	.60	1.50
20	Nature Boy Ric Flair	3.00	8.00
21	Jey Uso	.60	1.50
22	Hacksaw Jim Duggan	1.00	2.50
23	Booker T	1.00	2.50
24	Randy Orton	2.50	6.00
25	John Cena	3.00	8.00
26	Big Show	1.50	4.00
27	Cesaro	.60	1.50
28	Kevin Nash	1.50	4.00
29	Honky Tonk Man	1.00	2.50
30	Bret Hit Man Hart	2.00	5.00
31	Paige	3.00	8.00
32	Dolph Ziggler	1.00	2.50
33	Christian	.60	1.50
34	Ricky The Dragon Steamboat	1.00	2.50
35	Chris Jericho	1.50	4.00
36	Jerry The King Lawler	1.00	2.50
37	Kane	1.50	4.00
38	Bo Dallas	.60	1.50
39	Darren Young	.60	1.50
40	Daniel Bryan	2.50	6.00
41	Paul Heyman	.60	1.50
42	Big E	1.00	2.50
43	Sin Cara	1.00	2.50
44	Doink The Clown	.60	1.50
45	Naomi	1.00	2.50
46	Paul Bearer	1.00	2.50
47	Rusev	1.50	4.00
48	Mark Henry	1.00	2.50
49	Erick Rowan	1.00	2.50
50	Triple H	2.50	6.00
51	Diamond Dallas Page	1.25	3.00
52	Tyson Kidd	.60	1.50
53	The British Bulldog	1.00	2.50
54	Razor Ramon	1.50	4.00
55	Million Dollar Man Ted DiBiase	1.00	2.50
56	King Barrett	.60	1.50
57	Seth Rollins	1.00	2.50
58	Rowdy Roddy Piper	2.00	5.00
59	Ultimate Warrior	2.00	5.00
60	Trish Stratus	3.00	8.00
61	Eve Torres	1.25	3.00
62	Adam Rose	.75	2.00
63	Bruno Sammartino	1.50	4.00
64	JBL	.60	1.50
65	The Iron Sheik	1.00	2.50
66	Emma	1.00	2.50
67	Jack Swagger	1.00	2.50
68	Luke Harper	1.00	2.50
69	Konnor	.75	2.00
70	Sting	1.50	4.00
71	Bray Wyatt	2.50	6.00
72	Bob Backlund	.60	1.50
73	Eva Marie	2.50	6.00
74	Jake The Snake Roberts	1.00	2.50
75	Yokozuna	1.00	2.50
76	Nikki Bella	2.00	5.00
77	Sheamus	1.50	4.00
78	Jimmy Uso	.60	1.50
79	Fandango	.60	1.50
80	Neville	1.25	3.00
81	Viktor	.60	1.50
82	Cowboy Bob Orton	.60	1.50
83	Arn Anderson	.75	2.00
84	Damien Sandow	.60	1.50
85	Edge	1.50	4.00
86	Classy Freddie Blassie	.60	1.50
87	Dean Ambrose	1.50	4.00
88	Stephanie McMahon	1.00	2.50
89	Sgt. Slaughter	1.00	2.50
90	Mr. Perfect Curt Hennig	1.00	2.50
91	Ryback	.60	1.50
92	Big Boss Man	.60	1.50
93	Bam Bam Bigelow	.75	2.00
94	Pat Patterson	.60	1.50
95	Brie Bella	2.00	5.00
96	Cameron	1.00	2.50
97	Kalisto	1.00	2.50
98	The Rock	3.00	8.00
99	Goldust	.60	1.50
100	Ravishing Rick Rude	1.00	2.50

2015 Topps WWE Undisputed Autographed Relics

*BLACK/50: .6X TO 1.5X BASIC AUTOS
*PURPLE/25: 1X TO 2.5X BASIC AUTOS
*GOLD/1: UNPRICED DUE TO SCARCITY

UARAF	Alicia Fox	6.00	15.00
UARAR	Adam Rose	5.00	12.00
UARBB	Brie Bella	12.00	30.00
UARBD	Bo Dallas	5.00	12.00
UARBS	Big Show	8.00	20.00
UARBW	Bray Wyatt	12.00	30.00
UARCA	Curtis Axel	5.00	12.00
UARCE	Cesaro	10.00	25.00
UARDA	Dean Ambrose	12.00	30.00
UARDB	Daniel Bryan	15.00	40.00
UARDM	Damien Sandow	5.00	12.00
UARDY	Darren Young	5.00	12.00
UARDZ	Dolph Ziggler	6.00	15.00
UARFA	Fandango	5.00	12.00
UARGO	Goldust	8.00	20.00
UARHS	Heath Slater	5.00	12.00
UARJC	John Cena	25.00	60.00
UARJS	Jack Swagger	5.00	12.00
UARJU	Jimmy Uso	8.00	20.00
UARKO	Konnor	5.00	12.00
UARMH	Mark Henry	6.00	15.00
UARNA	Natalya	8.00	20.00
UARNB	Nikki Bella	50.00	100.00
UARRO	Randy Orton	12.00	30.00
UARRR	Roman Reigns	25.00	60.00
UARSH	Sheamus	10.00	25.00
UARSR	Seth Rollins	15.00	40.00
UARTK	Tyson Kidd	5.00	12.00
UARTM	The Miz	8.00	20.00
UARTO	Titus O'Neil	5.00	12.00
UARVI	Viktor	5.00	12.00
UARZR	Zack Ryder	5.00	12.00
UARBNB	King Barrett	6.00	15.00
UARJKL	Jerry The King Lawler	15.00	40.00
UARSRA	Summer Rae	10.00	25.00

2015 Topps WWE Undisputed Autographs

*BLACK/50: .6X TO 1.5X BASIC AUTOS
*PURPLE/25: .75X TO 2X BASIC AUTOS
*GOLD/1: UNPRICED DUE TO SCARCITY

UAAB	Alundra Blayze	8.00	20.00
UABB	Brie Bella	12.00	30.00
UABL	Brock Lesnar	120.00	200.00
UABS	Bruno Sammartino	10.00	25.00
UABW	Bray Wyatt	8.00	20.00
UACJ	Chris Jericho	15.00	40.00
UADA	Dean Ambrose	8.00	20.00
UADB	Daniel Bryan	10.00	25.00
UADZ	Dolph Ziggler	6.00	15.00
UAED	Edge	10.00	25.00
UAEV	Eve Torres	6.00	15.00
UAIS	The Iron Sheik	20.00	50.00

UAJC	John Cena	75.00	150.00
UAJL	Jerry The King Lawler	8.00	20.00
UALI	Lita	10.00	25.00
UALT	Lawrence Taylor	75.00	150.00
UAMM	Million Dollar Man Ted DiBiase	12.00	30.00
UANA	Natalya	6.00	15.00
UANB	Nikki Bella	12.00	30.00
UANE	Neville	6.00	15.00
UAPH	Paul Heyman	8.00	20.00
UAPR	Pete Rose	20.00	50.00
UARF	Nature Boy Ric Flair	15.00	40.00
UARO	Randy Orton	25.00	60.00
UARR	Razor Ramon	60.00	120.00
UARU	Rusev	6.00	15.00
UARY	Ryback	6.00	15.00
UASM	Shawn Michaels	50.00	100.00
UASR	Seth Rollins	15.00	40.00
UATM	The Miz	8.00	20.00
UATS	Trish Stratus	50.00	100.00
UABHH	Bret Hit Man Hart	50.00	100.00
UABSH	Big Show	6.00	15.00
UARRE	Roman Reigns	50.00	100.00
UASRA	Summer Rae	12.00	30.00

2015 Topps WWE Undisputed Cage Evolution Moments

COMPLETE SET (20)   10.00   25.00
*RED: .5X TO 1.2X BASIC CARDS
*BLACK/99: .6X TO 1.5X BASIC CARDS
*PURPLE/50: .75X TO 2X BASIC CARDS
*SILVER/25: 1.2X TO 3X BASIC CARDS
*GOLD/1: UNPRICED DUE TO SCARCITY
*PP BLACK/1: UNPRICED DUE TO SCARCITY
*PP CYAN/1: UNPRICED DUE TO SCARCITY
*PP MAGENTA/1: UNPRICED DUE TO SCARCITY
*PP YELLOW/1: UNPRICED DUE TO SCARCITY

CEM1	Ultimate Warrior/Rick Rude	1.25	3.00
CEM2	Undertaker/Shawn Michaels	1.50	4.00
CEM3	Edge/Christian	1.00	2.50
CEM4	John Cena/Big Show	2.00	5.00
CEM5	Sheamus/Ryback/R-Truth	1.00	2.50
	Barrett/Ziggler/Henry		
CEM6	Triple H/Randy Orton	1.50	4.00
CEM7	JBL/Big Show	1.00	2.50
CEM8	John Cena/Edge	2.00	5.00
CEM9	Undertaker/Edge	1.50	4.00
CEM10	Mark Henry/Big Show	1.00	2.50
CEM11	Big Show/Bryan/Henry	1.50	4.00
CEM12	Undertaker/Triple H	1.50	4.00
CEM13	Triple H/Brock Lesnar	1.50	4.00
CEM14	Cesaro/Orton/Bryan	2.00	5.00
	Cena/Christian/Sheamus		
CEM15	John Cena/Bray Wyatt	2.00	5.00
CEM16	RVD/Jericho/HHH	1.50	4.00
	Booker T/Kane/HBK		
CEM17	Shawn Michaels/Triple H	1.50	4.00
CEM18	Dean Ambrose/Seth Rollins	1.00	2.50
CEM19	Randy Orton/Seth Rollins	1.50	4.00
CEM20	John Cena/Seth Rollins	2.00	5.00

2015 Topps WWE Undisputed Cut Signatures

STATED PRINT RUN 1 SER.#'d SET
UNPRICED DUE TO SCARCITY

CUTBB	British Bulldog
CUTJD	Junkyard Dog
CUTMP	Mr. Perfect Curt Hennig
CUTBBM	Big Boss Man
CUTCJS	Chief Jay Strongbow

2015 Topps WWE Undisputed Famous Finishers

COMPLETE SET (30)   12.00   30.00
*RED: .5X TO 1.2X BASIC CARDS
*BLACK/99: .6X TO 1.5X BASIC CARDS
*PURPLE/50: .75X TO 2X BASIC CARDS
*SILVER/25: 1.2X TO 3X BASIC CARDS
*GOLD/1: UNPRICED DUE TO SCARCITY
*PP BLACK/1: UNPRICED DUE TO SCARCITY
*PP CYAN/1: UNPRICED DUE TO SCARCITY
*PP MAGENTA/1: UNPRICED DUE TO SCARCITY
*PP YELLOW/1: UNPRICED DUE TO SCARCITY

FF1	Sweet Chin Music	2.00	5.00
FF2	Pedigree	2.00	5.00
FF3	Stratusfaction	2.50	6.00
FF4	Zig Zag	.75	2.00
FF5	Tombstone	2.00	5.00
FF6	Figure-4 Leglock	2.50	6.00
FF7	RKO	2.00	5.00
FF8	Rude Awakening	.75	2.00
FF9	Codebreaker	1.25	3.00
FF10	Brogue Kick	1.25	3.00
FF11	Sharpshooter	1.50	4.00
FF12	Attitude Adjustment	2.50	6.00
FF13	Million Dollar Dream	.75	2.00
FF14	KO Punch	1.25	3.00
FF15	Sister Abigail	2.00	5.00
FF16	F-5	2.00	5.00
FF17	Running Knee Smash	2.00	5.00
FF18	Camel Clutch	.75	2.00
FF19	Texas Cloverleaf	.75	2.00
FF20	World's Strongest Slam	.75	2.00
FF21	Razor's Edge	1.25	3.00
FF22	Banzai Drop	.75	2.00
FF23	Patriot Lock	.75	2.00
FF24	Spear	1.25	3.00
FF25	Perfectplex	.75	2.00
FF26	DDT	.75	2.00
FF27	Coup de Grace	1.50	4.00
FF28	Figure Eight	1.50	4.00
FF29	Skull-Crushing Finale	.75	2.00
FF30	Red Arrow	1.00	2.50

2015 Topps WWE Undisputed Famous Rivalries Dual Autographed Jumbo Relics

STATED PRINT RUN 5 SER.#'d SETS
UNPRICED DUE TO SCARCITY

FRARAR	D.Ambrose/S.Rollins
FRARBB	Nikki & Brie Bella
FRARCO	J.Cena/R.Orton
FRARSH	Big Show/M.Henry
FRARZM	D.Ziggler/Miz

2015 Topps WWE Undisputed Famous Rivalries Dual Autographs

STATED PRINT RUN 25 SER.#'d SETS

FRACO	J.Cena/R.Orton	150.00	300.00
FRAHL	B.Hart/J.Lawler	75.00	150.00
FRAMR	S.Michaels/R.Ramon	100.00	200.00

2015 Topps WWE Undisputed Fistographs

STATED PRINT RUN 10 SER.#'d SETS

NNO	Big Show	100.00	200.00
NNO	Bray Wyatt	100.00	200.00
NNO	Bret Hit Man Hart	125.00	250.00
NNO	Bruno Sammartino	125.00	250.00

NNO	Daniel Bryan		
NNO	Dean Ambrose	150.00	300.00
NNO	Edge	125.00	250.00
NNO	Jack Swagger		
NNO	John Cena		
NNO	Kane	100.00	200.00
NNO	King Barrett		
NNO	Lita	150.00	300.00
NNO	Mark Henry	75.00	150.00
NNO	Randy Orton	125.00	250.00
NNO	Ric Flair		
NNO	Roman Reigns	250.00	500.00
NNO	Rowdy Roddy Piper		
NNO	Rusev	75.00	150.00
NNO	Shawn Michaels	300.00	450.00
NNO	Sheamus		
NNO	Trish Stratus	250.00	400.00

2015 Topps WWE Undisputed Four Corners Quadragraphs

STATED PRINT RUN 10 SER.#'d SETS

FCQBBSL	Lita/Trish/Bellas	300.00	600.00
FCQBBYS	Bryan/Young/Barrett/Slater	125.00	250.00
FCQDNZO	Dallas/Neville/Zayn/Owens	125.00	250.00
FCQHHLD	J.Hart/B.Hart/Lawler/DiBiase	150.00	300.00

2015 Topps WWE Undisputed NXT In Line Autographs

*BLACK/50: .6X TO 1.5X BASIC AUTOS
*PURPLE/25: .75X TO 2X BASIC AUTOS
*GOLD/1: UNPRICED DUE TO SCARCITY

NABD	Bull Dempsey	5.00	12.00
NABL	Becky Lynch	150.00	300.00
NABM	Murphy	5.00	12.00
NACC	Colin Cassady	6.00	15.00
NACH	Charlotte	125.00	250.00
NAEA	Enzo Amore	10.00	25.00
NAFB	Finn Balor	50.00	100.00
NAHI	Hideo Itami	8.00	20.00
NAKO	Kevin Owens	25.00	60.00
NASB	Sasha Banks	150.00	300.00
NASJ	Samoa Joe	10.00	25.00
NASZ	Sami Zayn	10.00	25.00
NATB	Tyler Breeze	8.00	20.00
NAWB	Blake	5.00	12.00
NABCO	Baron Corbin	6.00	15.00

2015 Topps WWE Undisputed NXT Prospects

COMPLETE SET (25)   100.00   200.00
*RED: .5X TO 1.2X BASIC CARDS
*BLACK/99: .6X TO 1.5X BASIC CARDS
*PURPLE/50: .75X TO 2X BASIC CARDS
*SILVER/25: 1.2X TO 3X BASIC CARDS
*GOLD/1: UNPRICED DUE TO SCARCITY
*PP BLACK/1: UNPRICED DUE TO SCARCITY
*PP CYAN/1: UNPRICED DUE TO SCARCITY
*PP MAGENTA/1: UNPRICED DUE TO SCARCITY
*PP YELLOW/1: UNPRICED DUE TO SCARCITY

NXT1	Angelo Dawkins	1.50	4.00
NXT2	Sasha Banks	12.00	30.00
NXT3	Finn Balor	4.00	10.00
NXT4	Sami Zayn	2.00	5.00
NXT5	Charlotte	10.00	25.00
NXT6	Blake	1.25	3.00
NXT7	Murphy	1.25	3.00
NXT8	Carmella	5.00	12.00
NXT9	Enzo Amore	1.25	3.00
NXT10	Baron Corbin	2.00	5.00
NXT11	Hideo Itami	1.25	3.00
NXT12	Tyler Breeze	1.25	3.00
NXT13	Solomon Crowe	1.25	3.00
NXT14	Becky Lynch	15.00	40.00
NXT15	Bayley	5.00	12.00
NXT16	Bull Dempsey	2.00	5.00
NXT17	Alexa Bliss	50.00	100.00
NXT18	Tye Dillinger	2.00	5.00
NXT19	Jason Jordan	1.25	3.00
NXT20	Colin Cassady	2.00	5.00
NXT21	Aiden English	1.50	4.00
NXT22	Simon Gotch	1.25	3.00
NXT23	Mojo Rawley	1.25	3.00
NXT24	Marcus Louis	2.00	5.00
NXT25	Samoa Joe	3.00	8.00

2016 Topps WWE Undisputed

COMPLETE SET (100)   25.00   60.00
UNOPENED BOX (10 PACKS)
UNOPENED PACK (5 CARDS)
*BRONZE/99: .5X TO 1.2X BASIC CARDS
*SILVER/50: .75X TO 2X BASIC CARDS
*BLUE/25: 1.2X TO 3X BASIC CARDS
*GOLD/10: 2X TO 5X BASIC CARDS
*RED/1: UNPRICED DUE TO SCARCITY
*P.P.BLACK/1: UNPRICED DUE TO SCARCITY
*P.P.CYAN/1: UNPRICED DUE TO SCARCITY
*P.P.MAGENTA/1: UNPRICED DUE TO SCARCITY
*P.P.YELLOW/1: UNPRICED DUE TO SCARCITY

1	Alberto Del Rio	1.00	2.50
2	Big E	.60	1.50
3	Big Show	1.25	3.00
4	Braun Strowman	.75	2.00
5	Bray Wyatt	2.50	6.00
6	Brock Lesnar	3.00	8.00
7	Bubba Ray Dudley	1.25	3.00
8	Cesaro	1.25	3.00
9	Chris Jericho	1.50	4.00
10	D-Von Dudley	1.00	2.50
11	Dean Ambrose	2.00	5.00
12	Dolph Ziggler	.75	2.00
13	Erick Rowan	.60	1.50
14	Goldust	1.00	2.50
15	Jerry The King Lawler	1.25	3.00
16	John Cena	3.00	8.00
17	Kane	1.00	2.50
18	Kevin Owens	1.50	4.00
19	King Barrett	.60	1.50
20	Kofi Kingston	.60	1.50
21	Luke Harper	.60	1.50
22	Mark Henry	.75	2.00
23	The Miz	1.00	2.50
24	Neville	1.50	4.00
25	Paul Heyman	.75	2.00
26	R-Truth	.60	1.50
27	Randy Orton	1.50	4.00
28	The Rock	3.00	8.00
29	Roman Reigns	2.00	5.00
30	Rusev	1.50	4.00
31	Ryback	.75	2.00
32	Seth Rollins	1.00	2.50
33	Sheamus	1.50	4.00
34	Sting	1.50	4.00
35	Triple H	2.50	6.00
36	Tyler Breeze	.60	1.50
37	Tyson Kidd	.60	1.50
38	Undertaker	2.50	6.00
39	Xavier Woods	.60	1.50
40	Zack Ryder	.60	1.50
41	The American Dream Dusty Rhodes	.60	1.50

42	Andre the Giant	2.00	5.00
43	Bam Bam Bigelow	.75	2.00
44	Batista	1.25	3.00
45	Big Boss Man	1.00	2.50
46	Big John Studd	1.00	2.50
47	Bob Backlund	.60	1.50
48	Bobby The Brain Heenan	1.00	2.50
49	Bret Hit Man Hart	1.50	4.00
50	Brian Pillman	.75	2.00
51	The British Bulldog	.75	2.00
52	Cowboy Bob Orton	1.00	2.50
53	Diamond Dallas Page	1.00	2.50
54	Doink the Clown	.60	1.50
55	Eddie Guerrero	1.50	4.00
56	Edge	1.50	4.00
57	General Adnan	.60	1.50
58	George The Animal Steele	.75	2.00
59	Hacksaw Jim Duggan	.60	1.50
60	High Chief Peter Maivia	.60	1.50
61	Honky Tonk Man	.60	1.50
62	Jake The Snake Roberts	1.25	3.00
63	Jim The Anvil Neidhart	.60	1.50
64	Jim Ross	1.00	2.50
65	J.J. Dillon	.60	1.50
66	Junkyard Dog	1.00	2.50
67	Kamala	.60	1.50
68	The King Harley Race	.60	1.50
69	Kevin Nash	1.50	4.00
70	Lex Luger	1.00	2.50
71	Macho Man Randy Savage	1.50	4.00
72	Mean Gene Okerlund	.75	2.00
73	Michael P.S. Hayes	.60	1.50
74	Million Dollar Man Ted DiBiase	.75	2.00
75	The Mouth of the South Jimmy Hart	.75	2.00
76	Mr. Perfect Curt Hennig	1.50	4.00
77	Mr. Wonderful Paul Orndorff	.60	1.50
78	Papa Shango	.75	2.00
79	Paul Bearer	1.00	2.50
80	Ravishing Rick Rude	1.00	2.50
81	Ric Flair	2.50	6.00
82	Ricky The Dragon Steamboat	.75	2.00
83	Rikishi	.75	2.00
84	Road Dogg	1.00	2.50
85	Rob Van Dam	1.25	3.00
86	Rocky Johnson	.75	2.00
87	Rowdy Roddy Piper	2.00	5.00
88	Scott Hall	1.50	4.00
89	Sgt. Slaughter	.75	2.00
90	Shawn Michaels	2.50	6.00
91	Superstar Billy Graham	.60	1.50
92	Stone Cold Steve Austin	3.00	8.00
93	Tatanka	.60	1.50
94	Tatsumi Fujinami	.60	1.50
95	Tito Santana	.75	2.00
96	Ultimate Warrior	1.50	4.00
97	Vader	1.25	3.00
98	Virgil	.60	1.50
99	X-Pac	1.00	2.50
100	Yokozuna	1.25	3.00

2016 Topps WWE Undisputed Autographed Diva Kiss and Relic Booklets

STATED PRINT RUN 5 SER. #'d SETS
UNPRICED DUE TO SCARCITY

ADRAF Alicia Fox
ADRBA Bayley
ADRBB Brie Bella
ADRLA Lana
ADRNB Nikki Bella

2016 Topps WWE Undisputed Autographed Relics

*SILVER/50: .6X TO 1.5X BASIC AUTOS
*BLUE/25: 1X TO 2.5X BASIC MEM
*GOLD/10: 1.2X TO 3X BASIC AUTOS
*RED/1: UNPRICED DUE TO SCARCITY
*P.P.BLACK/1: UNPRICED DUE TO SCARCITY
*P.P.CYAN/1: UNPRICED DUE TO SCARCITY
*P.P.MAGENTA/1: UNPRICED DUE TO SCARCITY
*P.P.YELLOW/1: UNPRICED DUE TO SCARCITY
STATED PRINT RUN 99 SER.#'d SETS

Code	Name		
UARAC	Alicia Fox	6.00	15.00
UARAE	Aiden English	6.00	15.00
UARBB	Brie Bella	12.00	30.00
UARBC	Baron Corbin	6.00	15.00
UARBE	Big E	6.00	15.00
UARBL	Becky Lynch	20.00	50.00
UARBW	Bray Wyatt	10.00	25.00
UARCC	Colin Cassady	8.00	20.00
UARCH	Charlotte	15.00	40.00
UARDA	Dean Ambrose	12.00	30.00
UARDD	D-Von Dudley	6.00	15.00
UARDZ	Dolph Ziggler	6.00	15.00
UAREA	Enzo Amore	12.00	30.00
UARFB	Finn Balor	15.00	40.00
UARJU	Jey Uso	6.00	15.00
UARKA	Kalisto	6.00	15.00
UARKK	Kofi Kingston	6.00	15.00
UARKO	Kevin Owens	12.00	30.00
UARMR	Mojo Rawley	6.00	15.00
UARNE	Neville	8.00	20.00
UARRR	Roman Reigns	10.00	25.00
UARRY	Ryback	6.00	15.00
UARSB	Sasha Banks	25.00	60.00
UARSC	Sin Cara	8.00	20.00
UARSG	Simon Gotch	6.00	15.00
UARSH	Sheamus	6.00	15.00
UARSJ	Samoa Joe	6.00	15.00
UARSR	Seth Rollins	10.00	25.00
UARTB	Tyler Breeze	6.00	15.00
UARTM	The Miz	6.00	15.00
UARXW	Xavier Woods	6.00	15.00
UARZR	Zack Ryder	6.00	15.00
UARADR	Alberto Del Rio	6.00	15.00
UARAPC	Apollo Crews	6.00	15.00
UARBAY	Bayley	20.00	50.00
UARBRD	Bubba Ray Dudley	6.00	15.00
UARJIU	Jimmy Uso	8.00	20.00

2016 Topps WWE Undisputed Autographs

*BRONZE/99: .5X TO 1.2X BASIC AUTOS
*SILVER/50: .75X TO 2X BASIC AUTOS
*BLUE/25: 1.2X TO 3X BASIC AUTOS
*GOLD/10: 1.5X TO 4X BASIC AUTOS
*RED/1: UNPRICED DUE TO SCARCITY
*P.P.BLACK/1: UNPRICED DUE TO SCARCITY
*P.P.CYAN/1: UNPRICED DUE TO SCARCITY
*P.P.MAGENTA/1: UNPRICED DUE TO SCARCITY
*P.P.YELLOW/1: UNPRICED DUE TO SCARCITY
RANDOMLY INSERTED INTO PACKS

Code	Name		
UAAF	Alicia Fox	5.00	12.00
UAAS	Asuka	25.00	60.00
UABA	Bayley	15.00	40.00
UABB	Brie Bella	8.00	20.00
UABE	Big E	6.00	15.00
UABH	Bret Hit Man Hart	12.00	30.00
UABL	Becky Lynch	30.00	75.00
UABS	Braun Strowman	6.00	15.00
UABT	Booker T	6.00	15.00
UACA	Carmella	10.00	25.00
UACC	Colin Cassady	6.00	15.00
UACE	Cesaro	6.00	15.00
UACH	Charlotte	25.00	60.00
UADA	Dean Ambrose	10.00	25.00
UADB	Daniel Bryan	10.00	25.00
UADD	D-Von Dudley	6.00	15.00
UAEA	Enzo Amore	10.00	25.00
UAER	Erick Rowan	5.00	12.00
UAFB	Finn Balor	10.00	25.00
UAGO	Goldust	10.00	25.00
UAHI	Hideo Itami	5.00	12.00
UAJC	John Cena	75.00	150.00
UAJN	Jim The Anvil Neidhart	6.00	15.00
UAKA	Kalisto	5.00	12.00
UAKK	Kofi Kingston	10.00	25.00
UALA	Lana	10.00	25.00
UALH	Luke Harper	6.00	15.00
UALI	Lita	25.00	60.00
UANA	Natalya	10.00	25.00
UANB	Nikki Bella	10.00	25.00
UANJ	Nia Jax	5.00	12.00
UARR	Roman Reigns	20.00	50.00
UASB	Sasha Banks	30.00	75.00
UASC	Sin Cara	6.00	15.00
UASJ	Samoa Joe	5.00	12.00
UASR	Seth Rollins	8.00	20.00
UAST	Sting	25.00	60.00
UATS	Trish Stratus	30.00	75.00
UAXW	Xavier Woods	5.00	12.00
UAAJS	AJ Styles	10.00	25.00
UABAC	Baron Corbin	6.00	15.00
UABRD	Bubba Ray Dudley	6.00	15.00
UABRW	Bray Wyatt	6.00	15.00
UANAO	Naomi	5.00	12.00
UASTR	Stevie Ray	5.00	12.00

2016 Topps WWE Undisputed Cut Signatures

STATED PRINT RUN 1 SER.#'d SET
UNPRICED DUE TO SCARCITY

UCSRS Macho Man Randy Savage
UCSCFB Classy Freddie Blassie
UCSMIE Miss Elizabeth

2016 Topps WWE Undisputed Divas Revolution

	COMPLETE SET (30)	60.00	120.00

*BRONZE/99: .5X TO 1.2X BASIC CARDS
*SILVER/50: .75X TO 2X BASIC CARDS
*BLUE/25: 1.2X TO 3X BASIC CARDS
*GOLD/10: UNPRICED DUE TO SCARCITY
*RED/1: UNPRICED DUE TO SCARCITY
*P.P.BLACK/1 UNPRICED DUE TO SCARCITY
*P.P.CYAN/1 UNPRICED DUE TO SCARCITY
*P.P.MAGENTA/1 UNPRICED DUE TO SCARCITY
*P.P.YELLOW/1 UNPRICED DUE TO SCARCITY
RANDOMLY INSERTED INTO PACKS

Code	Name		
DR1	Alundra Blayze	1.50	4.00
DR2	Eve	2.50	6.00
DR3	Lita	4.00	10.00
DR4	Miss Elizabeth	1.25	3.00
DR5	Sensational Sherri	2.00	5.00
DR6	Trish Stratus	6.00	15.00
DR7	Alicia Fox	2.00	5.00
DR8	Asuka	5.00	12.00
DR9	Bayley	3.00	8.00
DR10	Becky Lynch	4.00	10.00
DR11	Brie Bella	2.50	6.00
DR12	Cameron	1.25	3.00
DR13	Charlotte	4.00	10.00
DR14	Dasha Fuentes	1.25	3.00
DR15	Eden	1.50	4.00
DR16	Emma	2.50	6.00
DR17	Eva Marie	2.50	6.00
DR18	JoJo	1.25	3.00
DR19	Lana	5.00	12.00
DR20	Mandy Rose	3.00	8.00
DR21	Naomi	2.00	5.00
DR22	Natalya	2.00	5.00
DR23	Nikki Bella	4.00	10.00
DR24	Paige	4.00	10.00
DR25	Renee Young	3.00	8.00
DR26	Rosa Mendes	1.25	3.00
DR27	Sasha Banks	4.00	10.00
DR28	Maryse	2.50	6.00
DR29	Summer Rae	3.00	8.00
DR30	Tamina	1.50	4.00

2016 Topps WWE Undisputed Faction Triple Autograph Booklets

STATED PRINT RUN 10 SER. #'d SETS

Code	Name		
FTAARR	Ambrose/Rollins/Reigns	125.00	250.00
FTABBF	The Bellas/Fox	100.00	200.00
FTAKBW	Kingston/Big E/Woods	75.00	150.00
FTANBT	Naomi/Banks/Tamina	125.00	250.00
FTASKV	Stardust/Konnor/Viktor	60.00	120.00

2016 Topps WWE Undisputed Family Ties Dual Autographs

STATED PRINT RUN 25 SER.#'d SETS

Code	Name		
FTABB	Nikki & Brie Bella	120.00	200.00
FTAFC	Ric & Charlotte Flair	120.00	200.00
FTAGS	Goldust/Stardust	60.00	120.00
FTANN	J.Neidhart/Natalya	60.00	120.00
FTATR	Booker T/S. Ray	30.00	75.00

2016 Topps WWE Undisputed NXT Prospects

	COMPLETE SET (30)	30.00	80.00

*BRONZE/99: .5X TO 1.2X BASIC CARDS
*SILVER/50: .75X TO 2X BASIC CARDS
*BLUE/25: 1.2X TO 3X BASIC CARDS
*GOLD/10: UNPRICED DUE TO SCARCITY
*RED/1: UNPRICED DUE TO SCARCITY
*P.P.BLACK/1: UNPRICED DUE TO SCARCITY
*P.P.CYAN/1: UNPRICED DUE TO SCARCITY
*P.P.MAGENTA/1: UNPRICED DUE TO SCARCITY
*P.P.YELLOW/1: UNPRICED DUE TO SCARCITY
RANDOMLY INSERTED INTO PACKS

Code	Name		
NXT1	Aiden English	1.25	3.00
NXT2	Alexa Bliss	6.00	15.00
NXT3	Angelo Dawkins	1.25	3.00
NXT4	Apollo Crews	1.25	3.00
NXT5	Asuka	5.00	12.00
NXT6	Austin Aries	1.50	4.00
NXT7	Baron Corbin	1.50	4.00
NXT8	Bayley	3.00	8.00
NXT9	Billie Kay	3.00	8.00
NXT10	Blake	1.25	3.00
NXT11	Carmella	3.00	8.00
NXT12	Chad Gable	1.50	4.00
NXT13	Colin Cassady	2.50	6.00
NXT14	Dana Brooke	3.00	8.00
NXT15	Dash Wilder	1.50	4.00
NXT16	Elias Samson	1.25	3.00

NXT17 Enzo Amore	2.50	6.00
NXT18 Finn Balor	4.00	10.00
NXT19 Hideo Itami	1.50	4.00
NXT20 Jason Jordan	1.50	4.00
NXT21 Mojo Rawley	1.25	3.00
NXT22 Murphy	1.25	3.00
NXT23 Nia Jax	2.00	5.00
NXT24 Peyton Royce	3.00	8.00
NXT25 Sami Zayn	2.00	5.00
NXT26 Samoa Joe	3.00	8.00
NXT27 Sawyer Fulton	1.50	4.00
NXT28 Scott Dawson	1.25	3.00
NXT29 Simon Gotch	2.00	5.00
NXT30 Tye Dillinger	1.50	4.00

2016 Topps WWE Undisputed Relics

STATED PRINT RUN 175 SER.#'d SETS

UARAC Alicia Fox	3.00	8.00
UARAE Aiden English	2.00	5.00
UARBB Brie Bella	4.00	10.00
UARBC Baron Corbin	2.50	6.00
UARBE Big E	2.00	5.00
UARBL Becky Lynch	6.00	15.00
UARBW Bray Wyatt	8.00	20.00
UARCC Colin Cassady	4.00	10.00
UARCH Charlotte	6.00	15.00
UARDA Dean Ambrose	6.00	15.00
UARDD D-Von Dudley	3.00	8.00
UARDZ Dolph Ziggler	2.50	6.00
UAREA Enzo Amore	4.00	10.00
UARFB Finn Balor	6.00	15.00
UARJU Jey Uso	2.00	5.00
UARKA Kalisto	5.00	12.00
UARKB King Barrett	2.00	5.00
UARKK Kofi Kingston	2.00	5.00
UARKO Kevin Owens	5.00	12.00
UARMR Mojo Rawley	2.00	5.00
UARNE Neville	5.00	12.00
UARRR Roman Reigns	6.00	15.00
UARRY Ryback	2.50	6.00
UARSB Sasha Banks	6.00	15.00
UARSC Sin Cara	2.50	6.00
UARSG Simon Gotch	3.00	8.00
UARSH Sheamus	5.00	12.00
UARSJ Samoa Joe	5.00	12.00
UARSR Seth Rollins	3.00	8.00
UARTB Tyler Breeze	2.00	5.00
UARTM The Miz	3.00	8.00
UARXW Xavier Woods	2.00	5.00
UARZR Zack Ryder	2.00	5.00
UARADR Alberto Del Rio	3.00	8.00
UARAPC Apollo Crews	2.00	5.00
UARBAY Bayley	5.00	12.00
UARBRD Bubba Ray Dudley	4.00	10.00
UARJIU Jimmy Uso	2.00	5.00

2016 Topps WWE Undisputed Tag Teams

COMPLETE SET (40)	50.00	100.00
*BRONZE/99: .5X TO 1.2X BASIC CARDS		
*SILVER/50: .75X TO 2X BASIC CARDS		
*BLUE/25: 1.2X TO 3X BASIC CARDS		
*GOLD/10: UNPRICED DUE TO SCARCITY		
*RED/1: UNPRICED DUE TO SCARCITY		
*P.P.BLACK/1: UNPRICED DUE TO SCARCITY		
*P.P.CYAN/1: UNPRICED DUE TO SCARCITY		
*P.P.MAGENTA/1: UNPRICED DUE TO SCARCITY		
*P.P.YELLOW/1: UNPRICED DUE TO SCARCITY		
RANDOMLY INSERTED INTO PACKS		

UTT1 The Allied Powers	1.50	4.00
UTT2 The APA	2.50	6.00
UTT3 The Ascension	1.00	2.50
UTT4 Blake and Murphy	1.00	2.50
UTT5 The Brain Busters	1.00	2.50
UTT6 Brothers of Destruction	4.00	10.00
UTT7 The Bushwhackers	1.00	2.50
UTT8 D-Generation X	3.00	8.00
UTT9 The Dudley Boyz	2.00	5.00
UTT10 Edge and Christian	2.50	6.00
UTT11 The Enforcers	1.00	2.50
UTT12 The Foreign Legion	1.25	3.00
UTT13 The Funks	1.00	2.50
UTT14 Gold and Stardust	1.50	4.00
UTT15 Harlem Heat	2.00	5.00
UTT16 The Hart Foundation	2.50	6.00
UTT17 The Hollywood Blonds	5.00	12.00
UTT18 The Hype Bros.	1.00	2.50
UTT19 J and J Security	1.00	2.50
UTT20 Jeri-Show	2.50	6.00
UTT21 The Insiders	2.50	6.00
UTT22 The Lucha Dragons	2.50	6.00
UTT23 The Mega Bucks	3.00	8.00
UTT24 Money Inc.	1.25	3.00
UTT25 The Nasty Boys	1.25	3.00
UTT26 The Natural Disasters	1.00	2.50
UTT27 The Outsiders	2.50	6.00
UTT28 The Prime Time Players	1.00	2.50
UTT29 Rated-RKO	2.50	6.00
UTT30 Rhythm and Blues	1.25	3.00
UTT31 ShoMiz	2.00	5.00
UTT32 Team Hell No	4.00	10.00
UTT33 Team Rhodes Scholars	1.00	2.50
UTT34 Dudes with Attitude	4.00	10.00
UTT35 Two Man Power Trip	5.00	12.00
UTT36 Unholy Alliance	4.00	10.00
UTT37 Miz/Mizdow	1.50	4.00
UTT38 The Usos	1.00	2.50
UTT39 The Vaudevillains	1.50	4.00
UTT40 The Revival	1.25	3.00

2017 Topps WWE Undisputed

COMPLETE SET (70)	20.00	50.00
UNOPENED BOX (10 PACKS)		
UNOPENED PACK (5 CARDS)		
*BRONZE/99: .5X TO 1.2X BASIC CARDS		
*SILVER/50: .75X TO 2X BASIC CARDS		
*GREEN/25: 1.2X TO 3X BASIC CARDS		
*GOLD/10: 2X TO 5X BASIC CARDS		
*RED/1: UNPRICED DUE TO SCARCITY		
*P.P.BLACK/1: UNPRICED DUE TO SCARCITY		
*P.P.CYAN/1: UNPRICED DUE TO SCARCITY		
*P.P.MAGENTA/1: UNPRICED DUE TO SCARCITY		
*P.P.YELLOW/1: UNPRICED DUE TO SCARCITY		

1 John Cena	3.00	8.00
2 AJ Styles	3.00	8.00
3 Big Cass	.75	2.00
4 Big E	.75	2.00
5 The Brian Kendrick	.60	1.50
6 Bray Wyatt	1.50	4.00
7 Brock Lesnar	3.00	8.00
8 Cesaro	1.25	3.00
9 Chad Gable	.75	2.00
10 Chris Jericho	1.50	4.00
11 Daniel Bryan	2.50	6.00
12 Dean Ambrose	2.00	5.00
13 Dolph Ziggler	1.00	2.50
14 Finn Balor	2.50	6.00
15 Goldberg	2.50	6.00
16 James Ellsworth	.60	1.50
17 Jason Jordan	.75	2.00
18 Kane	.75	2.00
19 Karl Anderson	.60	1.50
20 Kevin Owens	1.50	4.00
21 Kofi Kingston	.75	2.00
22 Luke Gallows	1.00	2.50
23 Luke Harper	.60	1.50
24 Mick Foley	1.50	4.00
25 The Miz	1.25	3.00
26 Neville	1.00	2.50
27 Randy Orton	1.50	4.00
28 Rich Swann	.60	1.50
29 The Rock	3.00	8.00
30 Roman Reigns	2.00	5.00
31 Rusev	1.25	3.00
32 Sami Zayn	.75	2.00
33 Seth Rollins	2.00	5.00
34 Shane McMahon	1.00	2.50
35 Sheamus	1.25	3.00
36 TJ Perkins	.60	1.50
37 Triple H	1.50	4.00
38 Undertaker	2.50	6.00
39 Xavier Woods	.75	2.00
40 Zack Ryder	.60	1.50
41 Alexander Wolfe	.75	2.00
42 Andrade Cien Almas	.60	1.50
43 Austin Aries	1.25	3.00
44 Bobby Roode	1.50	4.00
45 Dash Wilder	.60	1.50
46 Eric Young	1.25	3.00
47 Hideo Itami	1.00	2.50
48 Johnny Gargano	.60	1.50
49 Nick Miller	.60	1.50
50 No Way Jose	.60	1.50
51 Oney Lorcan	.60	1.50
52 Roderick Strong	.75	2.00
53 Samoa Joe	2.00	5.00
54 Sawyer Fulton	.60	1.50
55 Scott Dawson	.60	1.50
56 Shane Thorne	.60	1.50
57 Shinsuke Nakamura	1.50	4.00
58 Tommaso Ciampa	.60	1.50
59 Tye Dillinger	.60	1.50
60 William Regal	.75	2.00
61 Andre the Giant	1.25	3.00
62 Bret Hit Man Hart	1.25	3.00
63 Macho Man Randy Savage	1.25	3.00
64 Million Dollar Man Ted DiBiase	.75	2.00
65 Ric Flair	1.50	4.00
66 Rowdy Roddy Piper	1.25	3.00
67 Shawn Michaels	1.50	4.00
68 Sting	2.00	5.00
69 Stone Cold Steve Austin	2.50	6.00
70 Ultimate Warrior	1.25	3.00

2017 Topps WWE Undisputed Autographed Relics

*SILVER/50: .5X TO 1.2X BASIC AUTOS		
*GREEN/25: .6X TO 1.5X BASIC AUTOS		
*GOLD/10: UNPRICED DUE TO SCARCITY		
*RED/1: UNPRICED DUE TO SCARCITY		
RANDOMLY INSERTED INTO PACKS		

UARAE Aiden English	5.00	12.00
UARAB Alexa Bliss	60.00	120.00
UARAF Alicia Fox	6.00	15.00
UARAS Asuka	25.00	60.00
UARAA Austin Aries	5.00	12.00
UARBC Baron Corbin	6.00	15.00
UARBE Becky Lynch	25.00	60.00

UARBCA Big Cass	5.00	12.00
UARBIG Big E	6.00	15.00
UARBS Big Show	6.00	15.00
UARBD Bo Dallas	6.00	15.00
UARBR Bobby Roode	6.00	15.00
UARBRS Braun Strowman	15.00	40.00
UARBW Bray Wyatt	10.00	25.00
UARBB Brie Bella	12.00	30.00
UARCA Carmella	12.00	30.00
UARCU Curtis Axel	5.00	12.00
UARDY Darren Young	6.00	15.00
UARDZ Dolph Ziggler	6.00	15.00
UARFA Fandango	5.00	12.00
UARFB Finn Balor	12.00	30.00
UARGO Goldust	6.00	15.00
UARHS Heath Slater	5.00	12.00
UARJG Johnny Gargano	5.00	12.00
UARJO Jojo	6.00	15.00
UARKA Kalisto	8.00	20.00
UARLH Luke Harper	50.00	100.00
UARMR Mojo Rawley	5.00	12.00
UARNA Natalya	6.00	15.00
UARNE Neville	8.00	20.00
UARRO Randy Orton	15.00	40.00
UARRY Renee Young	8.00	20.00
UARRR Roman Reigns	15.00	40.00
UARSJ Samoa Joe	6.00	15.00
UARSB Sasha Banks	60.00	120.00
UARSR Seth Rollins	12.00	30.00
UARSH Sheamus	6.00	15.00
UARSG Simon Gotch	5.00	12.00
UARSU Summer Rae	8.00	20.00
UARTA Tamina	6.00	15.00
UARTC Tommaso Ciampa	8.00	20.00
UARVI Viktor	5.00	12.00
UARZR Zack Ryder	6.00	15.00

2017 Topps WWE Undisputed Autographs

*BRONZE/99: SAME VALUE AS BASIC AUTOS		
*SILVER/50: .5X TO 1.2X BASIC AUTOS		
*GREEN/25: .6X TO 1.5X BASIC AUTOS		
*GOLD/10: UNPRICED DUE TO SCARCITY		
*BLACK/5: UNPRICED DUE TO SCARCITY		
*RED/1: UNPRICED DUE TO SCARCITY		
*P.P.BLACK/1: UNPRICED DUE TO SCARCITY		
*P.P.CYAN/1: UNPRICED DUE TO SCARCITY		
*P.P.MAGENTA/1: UNPRICED DUE TO SCARCITY		
*P.P.YELLOW/1: UNPRICED DUE TO SCARCITY		
RANDOMLY INSERTED INTO PACKS		

UAA Asuka	15.00	40.00
UAC Cesaro	6.00	15.00
UAE Edge	10.00	25.00
UAM Maryse	12.00	30.00
UAN Natalya	8.00	20.00
UAR Rhyno	6.00	15.00
UAS Sting	25.00	60.00
UAAA Austin Aries	6.00	15.00
UAAB Alexa Bliss	60.00	120.00
UAAF Alicia Fox	8.00	20.00
UAAS AJ Styles	20.00	50.00
UABA Bayley	15.00	40.00
UABC Big Cass	6.00	15.00
UABE Big E	5.00	12.00
UABH Bret Hit Man Hart	15.00	40.00
UABL Becky Lynch	25.00	60.00
UABR Bobby Roode	10.00	25.00
UABW Bray Wyatt	8.00	20.00

177

UACA	Carmella	12.00	30.00
UACF	Charlotte Flair	15.00	40.00
UACJ	Chris Jericho	10.00	25.00
UADA	Dean Ambrose	10.00	25.00
UADB	Dana Brooke	10.00	25.00
UADD	Diamond Dallas Page	12.00	30.00
UAEA	Enzo Amore	8.00	20.00
UAEM	Ember Moon	8.00	20.00
UAEY	Eric Young	6.00	15.00
UAFB	Finn Balor	15.00	40.00
UAHS	Heath Slater	5.00	12.00
UAJG	Johnny Gargano	6.00	15.00
UAKA	Karl Anderson	6.00	15.00
UAKO	Kevin Owens	8.00	20.00
UALG	Luke Gallows	5.00	12.00
UALM	Liv Morgan	12.00	30.00
UANA	Naomi	8.00	20.00
UANB	Nikki Bella	10.00	25.00
UARR	Roman Reigns	25.00	60.00
UARS	Roderick Strong	6.00	15.00
UARY	Renee Young	8.00	20.00
UASB	Sasha Banks	15.00	40.00
UASH	Sheamus	5.00	12.00
UASN	Shinsuke Nakamura	20.00	50.00
UASR	Seth Rollins	10.00	25.00
UASZ	Sami Zayn	6.00	15.00
UATC	Tommaso Ciampa	6.00	15.00
UATM	The Miz	5.00	12.00
UATP	TJ Perkins	5.00	12.00
UATS	Trish Stratus	25.00	60.00
UAXW	Xavier Woods	5.00	12.00
UABAC	Baron Corbin	8.00	20.00
UAEMM	Emma	10.00	25.00
UAKOK	Kofi Kingston	5.00	12.00

2017 Topps WWE Undisputed Autographs Bronze

UAG	Goldberg	50.00	100.00
UAU	Undertaker	150.00	300.00
UARO	Randy Orton	15.00	40.00
UABRL	Brock Lesnar	50.00	100.00

2017 Topps WWE Undisputed Dream Matches

COMPLETE SET (10) 10.00 25.00
*BRONZE/99: .5X TO 1.2X BASIC CARDS
*SILVER/50: .6X TO 1.5X BASIC CARDS
*GREEN/25: .75X TO 2X BASIC CARDS
*GOLD/10: UNPRICED DUE TO SCARCITY
*RED/1: UNPRICED DUE TO SCARCITY
*P.P.BLACK/1: UNPRICED DUE TO SCARCITY
*P.P.CYAN/1: UNPRICED DUE TO SCARCITY
*P.P.MAGENTA/1: UNPRICED DUE TO SCARCITY
*P.P.YELLOW/1: UNPRICED DUE TO SCARCITY
STATED ODDS 1:

D1	Sting/Undertaker	2.00	5.00
D2	Goldberg/Steve Austin	1.50	4.00
D3	Steve Austin/Brock Lesnar	1.50	4.00
D4	Shawn Michaels/The Rock	2.00	5.00
D5	Shawn Michaels/Eddie Guerrero	1.25	3.00
D6	John Cena/Steve Austin	1.50	4.00
D7	Edge/Bret Hit Man Hart	1.00	2.50
D8	Undertaker/Goldberg	1.50	4.00
D9	Batista/Brock Lesnar	1.25	3.00
D10	Nakamura/Daniel Bryan	1.00	2.50

2017 Topps WWE Undisputed Dual Autographs

STATED PRINT RUN 25 SER.#'d SETS

UDAAE	Asuka/E.Moon	60.00	120.00
UDABA	B.Roode/A.Aries	30.00	75.00
UDABG	B.Lesnar/Goldberg	120.00	250.00
UDACR	Charlotte & Ric Flair	75.00	150.00
UDAJT	J.Gargano/T.Ciampa	50.00	100.00
UDAKC	K.Owens/C.Jericho	60.00	120.00
UDASB	S.Banks/Bayley	75.00	150.00
UDASR	S.Rollins/R.Reigns	100.00	200.00

2017 Topps WWE Undisputed Quad Autographed Booklets

STATED PRINT RUN 5 SER.#'d SETS
UNPRICED DUE TO SCARCITY

UQACSBB Charlotte/Banks/Lynch/Bayley
UQAFAKL Balor/Styles/Anderson/Gallows
UQAGBJR Goldberg/Lesnar/Cena/Orton
UQASBER Nakamura/Roode/Young/Strong

2017 Topps WWE Undisputed Relics

*SILVER/50: .5X TO 1.2X BASIC MEM
*GREEN/25: .6X TO 1.5X BASIC MEM
*GOLD/10: UNPRICED DUE TO SCARCITY
*RED/1: UNPRICED DUE TO SCARCITY
RANDOMLY INSERTED INTO PACKS

URAA	Austin Aries	3.00	8.00
URAB	Alexa Bliss	8.00	20.00
URAE	Aiden English	1.50	4.00
URAF	Alicia Fox	2.50	6.00
URAS	Asuka	5.00	12.00
URBB	Brie Bella	4.00	10.00
URBD	Bo Dallas	1.50	4.00
URBE	Becky Lynch	5.00	12.00
URBL	Brock Lesnar	8.00	20.00
URBR	Bobby Roode	4.00	10.00
URBS	Big Show	2.00	5.00
URBW	Bray Wyatt	4.00	10.00
URCA	Carmella	4.00	10.00
URCU	Curtis Axel	1.50	4.00
URDY	Darren Young	1.50	4.00
URFB	Finn Balor	6.00	15.00
URGO	Goldust	2.00	5.00
URJC	John Cena	8.00	20.00
URJO	Jojo	2.50	6.00
URLH	Luke Harper	1.50	4.00
URMR	Mojo Rawley	2.00	5.00
URNA	Natalya	3.00	8.00
URNE	Neville	2.50	6.00
URRO	Randy Orton	4.00	10.00
URRY	Renee Young	2.50	6.00
URSB	Sasha Banks	5.00	12.00
URSG	Simon Gotch	1.50	4.00
URSH	Sheamus	3.00	8.00
URSJ	Samoa Joe	5.00	12.00
URSR	Seth Rollins	5.00	12.00
URSR	Summer Rae	4.00	10.00
URTA	Tamina	2.00	5.00
URVI	Viktor	1.50	4.00
URXW	Xavier Woods	2.00	5.00
URZR	Zack Ryder	1.50	4.00
URBCA	Big Cass	2.00	5.00
URBIG	Big E	2.00	5.00

2017 Topps WWE Undisputed Cut Signature

STATED PRINT RUN 1 SER.#'d SET
UNPRICED DUE TO SCARCITY

UTCYO Yokozuna

2017 Topps WWE Undisputed Triple Autographs

STATED PRINT RUN 10 SER.#'d SETS

UTAAKL	Styles/Anderson/Gallows	100.00	200.00
UTABAE	Bayley/Asuka/Moon	150.00	300.00
UTACSB	Flair/Banks/Lynch	250.00	400.00
UTADSR	Ambrose/Rollins/Reigns	125.00	250.00
UTANCA	N.Bella/Carmella/Bliss	200.00	350.00

2017 Topps WWE Undisputed Women's Division

*BRONZE/99: .75X TO 2X BASIC CARDS
*SILVER/50: 1X TO 2.5X BASIC CARDS
*GREEN/25: 1.5X TO 4X BASIC CARDS
*GOLD/10: UNPRICED DUE TO SCARCITY
*RED/1: UNPRICED DUE TO SCARCITY
*P.P.BLACK/1: UNPRICED DUE TO SCARCITY
*P.P.CYAN/1: UNPRICED DUE TO SCARCITY
*P.P.MAGENTA/1: UNPRICED DUE TO SCARCITY
*P.P.YELLOW/1: UNPRICED DUE TO SCARCITY
RANDOMLY INSERTED INTO PACKS

W1	Alexa Bliss	4.00	10.00
W2	Alicia Fox	1.25	3.00
W3	Bayley	2.50	6.00
W4	Becky Lynch	2.50	6.00
W5	Carmella	2.00	5.00
W6	Charlotte Flair	3.00	8.00
W7	Dana Brooke	1.50	4.00
W8	Eva Marie	2.00	5.00
W9	Lana	2.50	6.00
W10	Maryse	1.50	4.00
W11	Mickie James	1.25	3.00
W12	Naomi	1.50	4.00
W13	Natalya	1.50	4.00
W14	Nia Jax	1.25	3.00
W15	Nikki Bella	2.00	5.00
W16	Sasha Banks	2.50	6.00
W17	Asuka	2.50	6.00
W18	Ember Moon	2.00	5.00
W19	Liv Morgan	1.25	3.00

2018 Topps WWE Undisputed

COMPLETE SET (50) 20.00 50.00
UNOPENED BOX (10 PACKS) 200.00 250.00
UNOPENED PACK (5 CARDS) 20.00 25.00
*ORANGE/99: .6X TO 1.5X BASIC CARDS
*GREEN/50: .75X TO 2X BASIC CARDS
*BLUE/25: 1X TO 2.5X BASIC CARDS
*GOLD/10: 2X TO 5X BASIC CARDS
*PURPLE/5: UNPRICED DUE TO SCARCITY
*RED/1: UNPRICED DUE TO SCARCITY
*P.P.BLACK/1: UNPRICED DUE TO SCARCITY
*P.P.CYAN/1: UNPRICED DUE TO SCARCITY
*P.P.MAGENTA/1: UNPRICED DUE TO SCARCITY
*P.P.YELLOW/1: UNPRICED DUE TO SCARCITY

1	AJ Styles	2.50	6.00
2	Alexa Bliss	3.00	8.00
3	Asuka	2.00	5.00
4	Bayley	1.00	2.50
5	Becky Lynch	1.50	4.00
6	Big E	.75	2.00
7	Bobby Roode	1.00	2.50
8	Brie Bella	1.25	3.00
9	Braun Strowman	1.50	4.00
10	Bray Wyatt	1.50	4.00
11	Brock Lesnar	2.50	6.00
12	Carmella	1.25	3.00
13	Cesaro	1.25	3.00
14	Charlotte Flair	2.00	5.00
15	Chris Jericho	1.50	4.00
16	Daniel Bryan	1.50	4.00
17	Dean Ambrose	1.25	3.00
18	Finn Balor	1.50	4.00
19	Jason Jordan	.60	1.50
20	Jeff Hardy	1.25	3.00
21	John Cena	2.50	6.00
22	Kane	1.00	2.50
23	Kevin Owens	1.50	4.00
24	Kofi Kingston	.75	2.00
25	Kurt Angle	1.50	4.00
26	Woken Matt Hardy	1.50	4.00
27	Mickie James	1.25	3.00
28	Naomi	.75	2.00
29	Natalya	.75	2.00
30	Nia Jax	1.00	2.50
31	Nikki Bella	1.25	3.00
32	Paige	1.50	4.00
33	Randy Orton	1.50	4.00
34	Roman Reigns	1.50	4.00
35	Ruby Riott	1.00	2.50
36	Sami Zayn	.60	1.50
37	Samoa Joe	1.25	3.00
38	Sasha Banks	2.00	5.00
39	Seth Rollins	1.50	4.00
40	Sheamus	1.25	3.00
41	Shinsuke Nakamura	1.50	4.00
42	The Miz	1.25	3.00
43	Triple H	1.50	4.00
44	Undertaker	2.50	6.00
45	Xavier Woods	.75	2.00
46	Adam Cole	.75	2.00
47	Aleister Black	.75	2.00
48	Drew McIntyre	1.00	2.50
49	Ember Moon	1.25	3.00
50	Kairi Sane	1.50	4.00

2018 Topps WWE Undisputed 30 Years of Royal Rumble

COMPLETE SET (25) 12.00 30.00
*ORANGE/99: .5X TO 1.2X BASIC CARDS
*GREEN/50: .6X TO 1.5X BASIC CARDS
*BLUE/25: .75X TO 2X BASIC CARDS
*GOLD/10: 1.2X TO 3X BASIC CARDS
*PURPLE/5: UNPRICED DUE TO SCARCITY
*RED/1: UNPRICED DUE TO SCARCITY
*P.P.BLACK/1: UNPRICED DUE TO SCARCITY
*P.P.CYAN/1: UNPRICED DUE TO SCARCITY
*P.P.MAGENTA/1: UNPRICED DUE TO SCARCITY
*P.P.YELLOW/1: UNPRICED DUE TO SCARCITY
RANDOMLY INSERTED INTO PACKS

RR1	Hacksaw Jim Duggan	.60	1.50
RR2	Big John Studd	.60	1.50
RR3	Ric Flair	2.00	5.00
RR4	Yokozuna	.75	2.00
RR5	Bret Hit Man Hart	1.50	4.00
RR6	Lex Luger	.75	2.00
RR7	Shawn Michaels	2.00	5.00
RR8	Shawn Michaels	2.00	5.00
RR9	Stone Cold Steve Austin	3.00	8.00

RR10	Stone Cold Steve Austin	3.00	8.00
RR11	The Rock	3.00	8.00
RR12	Stone Cold Steve Austin	3.00	8.00
RR13	Triple H	1.50	4.00
RR14	Brock Lesnar	2.50	6.00
RR15	Batista	1.00	2.50
RR16	Undertaker	2.50	6.00
RR17	John Cena	2.50	6.00
RR18	Randy Orton	1.50	4.00
RR19	Edge	1.50	4.00
RR20	Sheamus	1.25	3.00
RR21	John Cena	2.50	6.00
RR22	Batista	1.00	2.50
RR23	Roman Reigns	1.50	4.00
RR24	Triple H	1.50	4.00
RR25	Randy Orton	1.50	4.00

2018 Topps WWE Undisputed 30 Years of Survivor Series

COMPLETE SET (25) 12.00 30.00
*ORANGE/99: .5X TO 1.2X BASIC CARDS
*GREEN/50: .6X TO 1.5X BASIC CARDS
*BLUE/25: .75X TO 2X BASIC CARDS
*GOLD/10: 1.2X TO 3X BASIC CARDS
*PURPLE/5: UNPRICED DUE TO SCARCITY
*RED/1: UNPRICED DUE TO SCARCITY
*P.P.BLACK/1: UNPRICED DUE TO SCARCITY
*P.P.CYAN/1: UNPRICED DUE TO SCARCITY
*P.P.MAGENTA/1: UNPRICED DUE TO SCARCITY
*P.P.YELLOW/1: UNPRICED DUE TO SCARCITY
RANDOMLY INSERTED INTO PACKS

SS1	Andre The Giant	1.25	3.00
SS2	Macho Man Randy Savage	2.00	5.00
SS3	Ultimate Warrior	2.50	6.00
SS4	Ultimate Warrior	2.50	6.00
SS5	Big Boss Man	.60	1.50
SS6	The Nasty Boys	.60	1.50
SS7	Lex Luger	.75	2.00
SS8	Million Dollar Man Ted DiBiase	.75	2.00
SS9	Shawn Michaels	2.00	5.00
SS10	Ken Shamrock	.75	2.00
SS11	The Rock	3.00	8.00
SS12	Chris Jericho	1.50	4.00
SS13	Randy Orton	1.50	4.00
SS14	Batista	1.00	2.50
SS15	John Cena	2.50	6.00
SS16	Randy Orton	1.50	4.00
SS17	Mickie James	1.25	3.00
SS18	Kofi Kingston	.75	2.00
SS19	Dolph Ziggler	.75	2.00
SS20	Dolph Ziggler	.75	2.00
SS21	Natalya	.75	2.00
SS22	John Cena	2.50	6.00
SS23	The Usos	1.00	2.50
SS24	AJ Styles	2.50	6.00
SS25	Kurt Angle	1.50	4.00

2018 Topps WWE Undisputed Autographed Kiss and Shirt Relic Booklets

STATED ODDS 1:1,500
STATED PRINT RUN 5 SER.#'d SETS
UNPRICED DUE TO SCARCITY

KSAF Alicia Fox
KSEM Ember Moon
KSNA Natalya
KSNB Nikki Bella
KSRY Renee Young

2018 Topps WWE Undisputed Autographed Relics

*SILVER/50: .5X TO 1.2X BASIC AUTOS
*BLUE/25: UNPRICED DUE TO SCARCITY
*GOLD/10: UNPRICED DUE TO SCARCITY
*PURPLE/5: UNPRICED DUE TO SCARCITY
*RED/1: UNPRICED DUE TO SCARCITY
*P.P.BLACK/1: UNPRICED DUE TO SCARCITY
*P.P.CYAN/1: UNPRICED DUE TO SCARCITY
*P.P.MAGENTA/1: UNPRICED DUE TO SCARCITY
*P.P.YELLOW/1: UNPRICED DUE TO SCARCITY
STATED ODDS 1:10
STATED PRINT RUN 99 SER.#'d SETS

URAA	Andrade Cien Almas	8.00	20.00
URAB	Alexa Bliss	60.00	120.00
URAE	Aiden English	5.00	12.00
URAF	Alicia Fox	15.00	40.00
URAK	Akam	6.00	15.00
URAP	Apollo Crews	5.00	12.00
URAW	Alexander Wolfe	6.00	15.00
URAX	Curtis Axel	5.00	12.00
URBK	Becky Lynch	30.00	75.00
URCA	Carmella	20.00	50.00
URCF	Charlotte Flair	20.00	50.00
URCG	Chad Gable	6.00	15.00
URDW	Dash Wilder	6.00	15.00
UREY	Eric Young	8.00	20.00
URFN	Fandango	5.00	12.00
URGD	Goldust	10.00	25.00
URHA	Harper	6.00	15.00
URJJ	JoJo	15.00	40.00
URJO	Jason Jordan	5.00	12.00
URJU	Jimmy Uso	6.00	15.00
URKA	Karl Anderson	5.00	12.00
URLG	Luke Gallows	6.00	15.00
URNA	Naomi	10.00	25.00
URNC	Nikki Cross	10.00	25.00
URNT	Natalya	12.00	30.00
URNW	No Way Jose	8.00	20.00
URRE	Rezar	6.00	15.00
URRY	Renee Young	15.00	40.00
URSB	Sasha Banks	25.00	60.00
URSD	Scott Dawson	6.00	15.00
URSR	Seth Rollins	15.00	40.00
URTC	Tommaso Ciampa	8.00	20.00
URZR	Zack Ryder	6.00	15.00

2018 Topps WWE Undisputed Autographs

*ORANGE/99: .5X TO 1.2X BASIC AUTOS
*GREEN/50: .6X TO 1.5X BASIC AUTOS
*BLUE/25: UNPRICED DUE TO SCARCITY
*GOLD/10: UNPRICED DUE TO SCARCITY
*PURPLE/5: UNPRICED DUE TO SCARCITY
*RED/1: UNPRICED DUE TO SCARCITY
*P.P.BLACK/1: UNPRICED DUE TO SCARCITY
*P.P.CYAN/1: UNPRICED DUE TO SCARCITY
*P.P.MAGENTA/1: UNPRICED DUE TO SCARCITY
*P.P.YELLOW/1: UNPRICED DUE TO SCARCITY
RANDOMLY INSERTED INTO PACKS

UAAB	Alexa Bliss	30.00	75.00
UAAC	Adam Cole	12.00	30.00
UAAJ	AJ Styles	20.00	50.00
UAAS	Asuka	15.00	40.00
UABA	Bayley	15.00	40.00
UABC	Baron Corbin	6.00	15.00
UABE	Big E	6.00	15.00

UABF	Bobby Fish	8.00	20.00
UABL	Becky Lynch	25.00	60.00
UABR	Bobby Roode	10.00	25.00
UABW	Bray Wyatt	10.00	25.00
UACA	Carmella	12.00	30.00
UACE	Cesaro	6.00	15.00
UACF	Charlotte Flair	15.00	40.00
UACG	Chad Gable	4.00	10.00
UADA	Dean Ambrose	8.00	20.00
UADB	Daniel Bryan	15.00	40.00
UADM	Drew McIntyre	10.00	25.00
UADW	Dash Wilder	5.00	12.00
UAEL	Elias	15.00	40.00
UAEY	Eric Young	5.00	12.00
UAFA	Fandango	8.00	20.00
UAFB	Finn Balor	15.00	40.00
UAHI	Hideo Itami	6.00	15.00
UAJH	Jeff Hardy	12.00	30.00
UAJJ	Jason Jordan	6.00	15.00
UAJM	Jinder Mahal	6.00	15.00
UAKA	Karl Anderson	4.00	10.00
UAKK	Kofi Kingston	4.00	10.00
UAKO	Kevin Owens	12.00	30.00
UAKS	Kairi Sane	25.00	60.00
UALA	Lana	8.00	20.00
UAMH	Matt Hardy	10.00	25.00
UAMK	Maria Kanellis	8.00	20.00
UAMR	Mojo Rawley	4.00	10.00
UANA	Naomi	5.00	12.00
UANJ	Nia Jax	10.00	25.00
UARS	Roderick Strong	6.00	15.00
UARU	Rusev	5.00	12.00
UASB	Sasha Banks	20.00	50.00
UASD	Scott Dawson	4.00	10.00
UASH	Sheamus	6.00	15.00
UASJ	Samoa Joe	10.00	25.00
UASN	Shinsuke Nakamura	10.00	25.00
UASR	Seth Rollins	12.00	30.00
UAST	Sting	15.00	40.00
UASZ	Sami Zayn	5.00	12.00
UATB	Tyler Breeze	6.00	15.00
UATD	Tye Dillinger	5.00	12.00
UATM	The Miz	8.00	20.00
UAVD	Velveteen Dream	15.00	40.00
UAXW	Xavier Woods	5.00	12.00
UAZR	Zack Ryder	4.00	10.00
UAABL	Aleister Black	10.00	20.00
UABCA	Big Cass	5.00	12.00
UABRS	Braun Strowman	12.00	30.00
UAEMB	Ember Moon	12.00	30.00
UAKOH	Kassius Ohno	6.00	15.00
UAKUA	Kurt Angle	12.00	30.00
UAKYO	Kyle O'Reilly	6.00	15.00
UAMAR	Maryse	10.00	25.00
UANAT	Natalya	8.00	20.00
UARRI	Ruby Riott	8.00	20.00
UASBE	Shelton Benjamin	6.00	15.00

2018 Topps WWE Undisputed Classic Matches Dual Autographed Relics

*PURPLE/5: UNPRICED DUE TO SCARCITY
*RED/1: UNPRICED DUE TO SCARCITY
STATED ODDS 1:766
STATED PRINT RUN 10 SER.#'d SETS
UNPRICED DUE TO SCARCITY

ARBH HHH/D.Bryan
ARDS Sheamus/D.Bryan
ARRH HHH/S.Rollins
ARRU Undertaker/R.Reigns

2018 Topps WWE Undisputed Cut Signatures

STATED ODDS 1:19,120
STATED PRINT RUN 1 SER.#'d SET
UNPRICED DUE TO SCARCITY

CSCH Mr. Perfect Curt Hennig
CSEG Eddie Guerrero

2018 Topps WWE Undisputed Dual Autographs

*GOLD/10: UNPRICED DUE TO SCARCITY
*PURPLE/5: UNPRICED DUE TO SCARCITY
*RED/1: UNPRICED DUE TO SCARCITY
STATED ODDS 1:154
STATED PRINT RUN 25 SER.#'d SETS

DAAJ	K.Angle/J.Jordan	25.00	60.00
DAAR	D.Ambrose/S.Rollins	30.00	75.00
DABG	S.Benjamin/C.Gable	15.00	40.00
DACS	Sheamus/Cesaro	15.00	40.00
DAFB	T.Breeze/Fandango	30.00	75.00
DAGA	K.Anderson/L.Gallows	25.00	60.00
DAHH	J.Hardy/M.Hardy	60.00	120.00
DARR	M.Rawley/Z.Ryder	30.00	75.00
DATM	HHH/S.McMahon	150.00	300.00
DAWD	S.Dawson/D.Wilder	15.00	40.00

2018 Topps WWE Undisputed Quad Autographed Booklets

QAAUTH HHH/McMahon/Rollins/Orton
QATEAMA Benjamin/Jordan/Gable/Angle
QAWYATT Wyatt/Strowman/Harper/Rowan
QASANITY Cross/Wolfe/Dain/Young
QATHEMIZ Axel/Maryse/Miz/Dallas

2018 Topps WWE Undisputed Relics

*GREEN/50: .6X TO 1.2X BASIC MEM
*BLUE/25: .75X TO 2X BASIC MEM
*GOLD/10: 1.5X TO 4X BASIC MEM
*PURPLE/5: UNPRICED DUE TO SCARCITY
*RED/1: UNPRICED DUE TO SCARCITY
*P.P.BLACK/1: UNPRICED DUE TO SCARCITY
*P.P.CYAN/1: UNPRICED DUE TO SCARCITY
*P.P.MAGENTA/1: UNPRICED DUE TO SCARCITY
*P.P.YELLOW/1: UNPRICED DUE TO SCARCITY
STATED ODDS 1:10
STATED PRINT RUN 99 SER.#'d SETS

URAA	Andrade Cien Almas	5.00	12.00
URAB	Alexa Bliss	12.00	30.00
URAE	Aiden English	2.00	5.00
URAF	Alicia Fox	5.00	12.00
URAK	Akam	2.00	5.00
URAW	Alexander Wolfe	2.50	6.00
URAX	Curtis Axel	3.00	8.00
URBC	Baron Corbin	2.50	6.00
URBE	Big E	2.50	6.00
URBK	Becky Lynch	10.00	25.00
URBL	Brock Lesnar	6.00	15.00
URBR	Bobby Roode	2.50	6.00
URCA	Carmella	8.00	20.00
URCF	Charlotte Flair	6.00	15.00
URCG	Chad Gable	2.50	6.00
URDB	Daniel Bryan	5.00	12.00
URDW	Dash Wilder	3.00	8.00
UREM	Ember Moon	5.00	12.00
UREY	Eric Young	2.50	6.00
URGD	Goldust	3.00	8.00
URHA	Harper	2.00	5.00

URHI	Hideo Itami	2.00	5.00
URJC	John Cena	10.00	25.00
URJJ	JoJo	6.00	15.00
URJO	Jason Jordan	2.00	5.00
URJU	Jimmy Uso	3.00	8.00
URKA	Karl Anderson	3.00	8.00
URKK	Kofi Kingston	2.50	6.00
URKO	Kevin Owens	2.50	6.00
URLG	Luke Gallows	2.00	5.00
URNA	Naomi	2.50	6.00
URNC	Nikki Cross	6.00	15.00
URNT	Natalya	3.00	8.00
URNW	No Way Jose	2.00	5.00
URRE	Rezar	2.00	5.00
URRR	Roman Reigns	6.00	15.00
URRY	Renee Young	5.00	12.00
URSB	Sasha Banks	12.00	30.00
URSD	Scott Dawson	2.00	5.00
URSR	Seth Rollins	2.50	6.00
URTC	Tommaso Ciampa	6.00	15.00
URXW	Xavier Woods	2.50	6.00

2018 Topps WWE Undisputed Rivals Dual Autograph and Championship Booklets

STATED ODDS 1:1,500
STATED PRINT RUN 5 SER.#'d SETS
UNPRICED DUE TO SCARCITY

ACAC	B.Corbin/D.Ambrose
ACBF	Bayley/C.Flair
ACNB	A.Bliss/Naomi
ACOJ	C.Jericho/K.Owens
ACOW	B.Wyatt/R.Orton

2018 Topps WWE Undisputed Triple Autographs

*PURPLE/5: UNPRICED DUE TO SCARCITY
*RED/1: UNPRICED DUE TO SCARCITY
STATED ODDS 1:475
STATED PRINT RUN 10 SER.#'d SETS

TACFO	O'Reilly/Cole/Fish
TAKBW	Kingston/Woods/Big E
TAMAD	Miz/Axel/Dallas
TAOTC	O'Neil/Crews/Tozawa
TASGA	Anderson/Gallows/Styles
TAUUN	J.Uso/J.Uso/Naomi
TAYWD	Dain/Young/Wolfe

2018 Topps WWE Undisputed Triple Shirt Relics

*GOLD/10: UNPRICED DUE TO SCARCITY
*PURPLE/5: UNPRICED DUE TO SCARCITY
*RED/1: UNPRICED DUE TO SCARCITY
STATED ODDS 1:310
STATED PRINT RUN 25 SER.#'d SETS

TSBGA	Gallows/Balor/Anderson	20.00	50.00
TSDAY	Woods/Kingston/Big E	12.00	30.00
TSNUU	The Usos/Naomi	15.00	40.00
TSOZB	Zayn/Bryan/Owens	12.00	30.00
TSRRJ	Rollins/Reigns/Jordan	15.00	40.00

2019 Topps WWE Undisputed

COMPLETE SET (100)	25.00	60.00
UNOPENED BOX (10 PACKS)		
UNOPENED PACK (5 CARDS)		
*ORANGE/99: .6X TO 1.5X BASIC CARDS		
*GREEN/50: .75X TO 2X BASIC CARDS		

*BLUE/25: 1X TO 2.5X BASIC CARDS
*GOLD/10: UNPRICED DUE TO SCARCITY
*PURPLE/5: UNPRICED DUE TO SCARCITY
*RED/1: UNPRICED DUE TO SCARCITY
*P.P.BLACK/1: UNPRICED DUE TO SCARCITY
*P.P.CYAN/1: UNPRICED DUE TO SCARCITY
*P.P.MAGENTA/1: UNPRICED DUE TO SCARCITY
*P.P.YELLOW/1: UNPRICED DUE TO SCARCITY

1	Aiden English	.50	1.25
2	AJ Styles	2.50	6.00
3	Alexa Bliss	2.50	6.00
4	Alexander Wolfe	.50	1.25
5	Andrade	.60	1.50
6	Asuka	1.50	4.00
7	Baron Corbin	.75	2.00
8	Bayley	1.00	2.50
9	Becky Lynch	2.00	5.00
10	Big E	.50	1.25
11	Billie Kay	1.00	2.50
12	Bo Dallas	.60	1.50
13	Bobby Lashley	1.00	2.50
14	Bobby Roode	1.00	2.50
15	Braun Strowman	1.25	3.00
16	Bray Wyatt	1.25	3.00
17	Carmella	1.25	3.00
18	Cedric Alexander	.50	1.25
19	Cesaro	.60	1.50
20	Charlotte Flair	2.00	5.00
21	Curtis Axel	.60	1.50
22	Daniel Bryan	2.00	5.00
23	Dash Wilder	.50	1.25
24	Dolph Ziggler	1.00	2.50
25	Drake Maverick	.50	1.25
26	Drew Gulak	.50	1.25
27	Drew McIntyre	.60	1.50
28	Elias	1.00	2.50
29	Ember Moon	1.25	3.00
30	Eric Young	.60	1.50
31	Finn Balor	1.25	3.00
32	Harper	.60	1.50
33	Jeff Hardy	1.25	3.00
34	Jey Uso	.60	1.50
35	Jimmy Uso	.60	1.50
36	Jinder Mahal	1.00	2.50
37	John Cena	2.00	5.00
38	Karl Anderson	.75	2.00
39	Kevin Owens	1.25	3.00
40	Killian Dain	.50	1.25
41	Kofi Kingston	.75	2.00
42	Kurt Angle	1.00	2.50
43	Lacey Evans	1.00	2.50
44	Lio Rush	.60	1.50
45	Liv Morgan	1.50	4.00
46	Luke Gallows	.75	2.00
47	Mustafa Ali	.50	1.25
48	Naomi	.75	2.00
49	Natalya	1.00	2.50
50	Nia Jax	1.00	2.50
51	Paige	2.00	5.00
52	Peyton Royce	1.25	3.00
53	Randy Orton	1.25	3.00
54	Rey Mysterio	1.25	3.00
55	Roman Reigns	1.25	3.00
56	Ronda Rousey	2.50	6.00
57	Rowan	.50	1.25
58	Ruby Riott	1.00	2.50
59	Rusev	1.00	2.50
60	Sami Zayn	1.00	2.50

61	Samoa Joe	1.00	2.50
62	Sarah Logan	.60	1.50
63	Sasha Banks	2.00	5.00
64	Scott Dawson	.50	1.25
65	Seth Rollins	1.25	3.00
66	Sheamus	.75	2.00
67	Shelton Benjamin	.60	1.50
68	Shinsuke Nakamura	1.25	3.00
69	The Miz	1.00	2.50
70	The Rock	2.50	6.00
71	Titus O'Neil	.60	1.50
72	Triple H	1.25	3.00
73	Undertaker	2.50	6.00
74	Xavier Woods	.60	1.50
75	Zelina Vega	.75	2.00
76	Adam Cole	.60	1.50
77	Aleister Black	.60	1.50
78	Deonna Purrazzo	.50	1.25
79	EC3	.50	1.25
80	Johnny Gargano	.50	1.25
81	Kairi Sane	1.00	2.50
82	Keith Lee	.50	1.25
83	Nikki Cross	.75	2.00
84	Ricochet	1.25	3.00
85	Shayna Baszler	1.00	2.50
86	Tommaso Ciampa	.50	1.25
87	Goldberg	1.50	4.00
88	Shawn Michaels	1.25	3.00
89	Sting	1.25	3.00
90	Trish Stratus	2.50	6.00
RS1	Finn Balor	1.25	3.00
RS2	Jeff Hardy	1.25	3.00
RS3	Sasha Banks	2.00	5.00
RS4	Bayley	1.00	2.50
RS5	Seth Rollins	1.25	3.00
RS6	Shinsuke Nakamura	1.25	3.00
RS7	Aleister Black	.60	1.50
RS8	Ricochet	1.25	3.00
RS9	Sting	1.25	3.00
RS10	Ric Flair	1.50	4.00

2019 Topps WWE Undisputed Autographed Kiss and Shirt Relic Booklet

STATED PRINT RUN 5 SER.#'d SETS
UNPRICED DUE TO SCARCITY

| AKSAF | Alicia Fox |

2019 Topps WWE Undisputed Autographed Relics

*GREEN/50: .5X TO 1.2X BASIC AUTOS
*BLUE/25: .6X TO 1.5X BASIC AUTOS
*GOLD/10: UNPRICED DUE TO SCARCITY
*PURPLE/5: UNPRICED DUE TO SCARCITY
*RED/1: UNPRICED DUE TO SCARCITY
STATED PRINT RUN 120 SER.#'d SETS

UAR4H	Shayna Baszler	10.00	25.00
UARAA	Andrade	12.00	30.00
UARAB	Alexa Bliss	60.00	120.00
UARAC	Adam Cole	10.00	25.00
UARAE	Aiden English	6.00	15.00
UARAK	Asuka	20.00	50.00
UARBD	Bo Dallas	6.00	15.00
UARBS	Braun Strowman	12.00	30.00
UARCA	Curtis Axel	6.00	15.00
UARCM	Carmella	15.00	40.00
UARCS	Cesaro	6.00	15.00

UARDW	Dash Wilder	6.00	15.00
UAREL	Elias	10.00	25.00
UARFB	Finn Balor	12.00	30.00
UARJH	Jeff Hardy	12.00	30.00
UARKD	Killian Dain	6.00	15.00
UARKK	Kofi Kingston	12.00	30.00
UARLG	Luke Gallows	6.00	15.00
UARLM	Liv Morgan	25.00	60.00
UARMG	Karl Anderson	6.00	15.00
UARNJ	Nia Jax	8.00	20.00
UARNM	Naomi	8.00	20.00
UARNN	Natalya	10.00	25.00
UARNW	No Way Jose	6.00	15.00
UARRB	Ruby Riott	12.00	30.00
UARRC	Ricochet	20.00	50.00
UARSB	Sasha Banks	20.00	50.00
UARSD	Scott Dawson	6.00	15.00
UARSM	Sheamus	6.00	15.00
UARSR	Seth Rollins	8.00	20.00
UARSZ	Sami Zayn	6.00	15.00
UARTC	Tommaso Ciampa	10.00	25.00
UARTM	The Miz	10.00	25.00
UARVD	Velveteen Dream	10.00	25.00
UARXW	Xavier Woods	6.00	15.00
UARZR	Zack Ryder	6.00	15.00

2019 Topps WWE Undisputed Autographed Relics Blue

| UARCH | Curt Hawkins | 10.00 | 25.00 |

2019 Topps WWE Undisputed Autographed Relics Green

| UARAF | Alicia Fox | 8.00 | 20.00 |

2019 Topps WWE Undisputed Autographed Tag Team Championship Medallion Booklets

STATED PRINT RUN 5 SER.#'d SETS
UNPRICED DUE TO SCARCITY

DACBT	C.Axel/B.Dallas
DACND	X.Woods/K.Kingston
DACTB	Cesaro/Sheamus
DACUSO	Jey and Jimmy Uso

2019 Topps WWE Undisputed Autographs

*GOLD/10: UNPRICED DUE TO SCARCITY
*PURPLE/5: UNPRICED DUE TO SCARCITY
*RED/1: UNPRICED DUE TO SCARCITY
*P.P.BLACK/1: UNPRICED DUE TO SCARCITY
*P.P.CYAN/1: UNPRICED DUE TO SCARCITY
*P.P.MAGENTA/1: UNPRICED DUE TO SCARCITY
*P.P.YELLOW/1: UNPRICED DUE TO SCARCITY
STATED PRINT RUN 199 SER.#'d SETS

AAA	Andrade Almas	5.00	12.00
AAB	Alexa Bliss	50.00	100.00
AAC	Adam Cole	10.00	25.00
AAL	Aleister Black	8.00	20.00
AAS	AJ Styles	15.00	40.00
AAW	Alexander Wolfe	5.00	12.00
ABC	Baron Corbin	5.00	12.00
ABD	Bo Dallas	5.00	12.00
ABE	Big E	6.00	15.00
ABL	Becky Lynch	25.00	60.00
ABR	Bobby Roode	8.00	20.00
ABS	Braun Strowman	10.00	25.00
ACA	Cedric Alexander	5.00	12.00

ACE	Cesaro	5.00	12.00
ACF	Charlotte Flair	20.00	50.00
ACJ	Cactus Jack	15.00	40.00
ACU	Curtis Axel	5.00	12.00
ADK	Dakota Kai	12.00	30.00
ADM	Drew McIntyre	6.00	15.00
ADP	Deonna Purrazzo	20.00	50.00
AEC	EC3	5.00	12.00
AEY	Eric Young	5.00	12.00
AFB	Finn Balor	12.00	30.00
AJF	Jeff Hardy	12.00	30.00
AJG	Johnny Gargano	6.00	15.00
AJM	Jinder Mahal	5.00	12.00
AKA	Kurt Angle	10.00	25.00
AKD	Killian Dain	5.00	12.00
AKK	Kofi Kingston	10.00	25.00
AKL	Keith Lee	6.00	15.00
AKR	Kyle O'Reilly	5.00	12.00
AKS	Kairi Sane	15.00	40.00
ALR	Lio Rush	5.00	12.00
AMA	Maryse	10.00	25.00
AME	Carmella	10.00	25.00
AMR	Mandy Rose	15.00	40.00
ANA	Naomi	6.00	15.00
ANJ	Nia Jax	8.00	20.00
ANN	Natalya	5.00	12.00
APD	Pete Dunne	6.00	15.00
ARI	Ricochet	20.00	50.00
ARM	Rey Mysterio	12.00	30.00
ARS	Roderick Strong	5.00	12.00
ARU	Rusev	5.00	12.00
ARY	Renee Young	6.00	15.00
ASD	Sonya Deville	12.00	30.00
ASH	Sheamus	5.00	12.00
ASN	Shinsuke Nakamura	10.00	25.00
AST	Sting	15.00	40.00
ASU	Asuka	15.00	40.00
ASZ	Sami Zayn	5.00	12.00
ATC	Tommaso Ciampa	8.00	20.00
ATM	The Miz	10.00	25.00
ATN	Titus O'Neil	5.00	12.00
AVD	Velveteen Dream	10.00	25.00
AXW	Xavier Woods	5.00	12.00
AZV	Zelina Vega	12.00	30.00
ABAS	Shayna Baszler	10.00	25.00
AE	Elias	8.00	20.00

2019 Topps WWE Undisputed Cut Signatures

STATED PRINT RUN 1 SER.#'d SET

UNPRICED DUE TO SCARCITY

CSDR	Dusty Rhodes		
CSEG	Eddie Guerrero		
CSJN	Jim "The Anvil" Neidhart		

2019 Topps WWE Undisputed Dual Autographs

*GOLD/10: UNPRICED DUE TO SCARCITY

*PURPLE/5: UNPRICED DUE TO SCARCITY

*RED/1: UNPRICED DUE TO SCARCITY

STATED PRINT RUN 25 SER.#'d SETS

DTI	B.Kay/P.Royce	125.00	250.00
DTR	D.Wilder/S.Dawson	50.00	100.00
DUE	R.Strong/K.O'Reilly	25.00	60.00
DWR	Hanson/Rowe	100.00	200.00

2019 Topps WWE Undisputed Quad Autographs Booklets

STATED PRINT RUN 5 SER.#'d SETS

UNPRICED DUE TO SCARCITY

QHW Flair/Lynch/Banks/Bayley

QUE Strong/O'Reilly/Fish/Cole

2019 Topps WWE Undisputed Relics

*GREEN/50: .5X TO 1.2X BASIC MEM

*BLUE/25: .6X TO 1.5X BASIC MEM

*GOLD/10: UNPRICED DUE TO SCARCITY

*PURPLE/5: UNPRICED DUE TO SCARCITY

*RED/1: UNPRICED DUE TO SCARCITY

STATED PRINT RUN 99 SER.#'d SETS

UR4H	Shayna Baszler	4.00	10.00
URAA	Andrade	4.00	10.00
URAB	Alexa Bliss	12.00	30.00
URAC	Adam Cole	6.00	15.00
URAF	Alicia Fox	4.00	10.00
URAK	Asuka	5.00	12.00
URBD	Bo Dallas	4.00	10.00
URBS	Braun Strowman	5.00	12.00
URCA	Curtis Axel	5.00	12.00
URCF	Charlotte Flair	10.00	25.00
URCM	Carmella	6.00	15.00
URCS	Cesaro	3.00	8.00
URDW	Dash Wilder	3.00	8.00
URDZ	Dolph Ziggler	4.00	10.00
UREL	Elias	3.00	8.00
UREM	Ember Moon	5.00	12.00
URFB	Finn Balor	5.00	12.00
URJC	John Cena	6.00	15.00
URJH	Jeff Hardy	5.00	12.00
URKD	Killian Dain	5.00	12.00
URKK	Kofi Kingston	4.00	10.00
URKO	Kevin Owens	5.00	12.00
URLG	Luke Gallows	4.00	10.00
URLM	Liv Morgan	10.00	25.00
URMG	Karl Anderson	4.00	10.00
URNJ	Nia Jax	5.00	12.00
URNM	Naomi	3.00	8.00
URNN	Natalya	4.00	10.00
URNW	No Way Jose	4.00	10.00
URRB	Ruby Riott	4.00	10.00
URRC	Ricochet	5.00	12.00
URRR	Roman Reigns	6.00	15.00
URSB	Sasha Banks	8.00	20.00
URSD	Scott Dawson	3.00	8.00
URSM	Sheamus	3.00	8.00
URSR	Seth Rollins	5.00	12.00
URSZ	Sami Zayn	3.00	8.00
URTC	Tommaso Ciampa	5.00	12.00
URTM	The Miz	3.00	8.00
URVD	Velveteen Dream	4.00	10.00
URXW	Xavier Woods	4.00	10.00
URZR	Zack Ryder	5.00	12.00
URUCE	Jey Uso	3.00	8.00
URUSO	Jimmy Uso	3.00	8.00

2019 Topps WWE Undisputed Triple Autographs

*PURPLE/5: UNPRICED DUE TO SCARCITY

*RED/1: UNPRICED DUE TO SCARCITY

STATED PRINT RUN 10 SER.#'d SETS

UNPRICED DUE TO SCARCITY

TLP Kalisto/Metalik/Dorado

TND Big E/Woods/Kingston

TRD Rusev/Lana/English

TRS Logan/Riott/Morgan

2020 Topps WWE Undisputed

COMPLETE SET (90)		25.00	60.00

*ORANGE/99: .75X TO 2X BASIC CARDS

*GREEN/50: 1.2X TO 3X BASIC CARDS

*BLUE/25: UNPRICED DUE TO SCARCITY

*GOLD/10: UNPRICED DUE TO SCARCITY

*PURPLE/5: UNPRICED DUE TO SCARCITY

*RED/1: UNPRICED DUE TO SCARCITY

*P.P.BLACK/1: UNPRICED DUE TO SCARCITY

*P.P.CYAN/1: UNPRICED DUE TO SCARCITY

*P.P.MAGENTA/1: UNPRICED DUE TO SCARCITY

*P.P.YELLOW/1: UNPRICED DUE TO SCARCITY

1	Aleister Black	1.00	2.50
2	Andrade	.75	2.00
3	Asuka	2.00	5.00
4	Becky Lynch	2.00	5.00
5	Bianca Belair	1.25	3.00
6	Bobby Lashley	1.00	2.50
7	Buddy Murphy	.60	1.50
8	Charlotte Flair	2.00	5.00
9	Drew McIntyre	1.00	2.50
10	Edge	1.00	2.50
11	Erik	.50	1.25
12	Humberto Carrillo	.75	2.00
13	Ivar	.50	1.25
14	Kairi Sane	1.00	2.50
15	Kevin Owens	.60	1.50
16	Lana	1.25	3.00
17	Nia Jax	.75	2.00
18	Randy Orton	1.25	3.00
19	Ricochet	.75	2.00
20	Ruby Riott	.75	2.00
21	R-Truth	.50	1.25
22	Samoa Joe	.75	2.00
23	Seth Rollins	1.00	2.50
24	Zelina Vega	1.00	2.50
25	AJ Styles	1.50	4.00
26	Alexa Bliss	3.00	8.00
27	Bayley	1.00	2.50
28	Big E	.50	1.25
29	Braun Strowman	1.25	3.00
30	The Fiend Bray Wyatt	1.50	4.00
31	Carmella	1.25	3.00
32	Cesaro	.50	1.25
33	Dana Brooke	.75	2.00
34	Daniel Bryan	1.50	4.00
35	Dolph Ziggler	.50	1.25
36	Elias	.50	1.25
37	King Corbin	.60	1.50
38	Kofi Kingston	.75	2.00
39	Lacey Evans	1.25	3.00
40	Matt Riddle	1.00	2.50
41	Mustafa Ali	.75	2.00
42	Naomi	1.00	2.50
43	Nikki Cross	1.00	2.50
44	Robert Roode	.50	1.25
45	Roman Reigns	1.25	3.00
46	Sami Zayn	.60	1.50
47	Sasha Banks	2.50	6.00
48	Sheamus	.60	1.50
49	Shinsuke Nakamura	1.00	2.50
50	The Miz	.75	2.00
51	Xavier Woods	.50	1.25
52	Adam Cole	1.25	3.00
53	Bobby Fish	.50	1.25
54	Candice LeRae	1.50	4.00
55	Dakota Kai	1.00	2.50
56	Damian Priest	.50	1.25
57	Dominik Dijakovic	.50	1.25
58	Finn Balor	1.25	3.00
59	Io Shirai	.75	2.00
60	Johnny Gargano	1.00	2.50
61	Kay Lee Ray	.75	2.00
62	Karrion Kross	1.00	2.50
63	Keith Lee	.50	1.25
64	Kushida	.60	1.50
65	Kyle OíReilly	.60	1.50
66	Mia Yim	1.00	2.50
67	Pete Dunne	.50	1.25
68	Rhea Ripley	2.00	5.00
69	Roderick Strong	1.00	2.50
70	Scarlett	2.00	5.00
71	Shayna Baszler	1.50	4.00
72	Tommaso Ciampa	1.00	2.50
73	Toni Storm	1.25	3.00
74	Velveteen Dream	.60	1.50
75	Walter	1.00	2.50
76	John Cena	2.00	5.00
77	Ronda Rousey	2.50	6.00
78	Undertaker	2.00	5.00
79	Batista	.75	2.00
80	Booker T	1.00	2.50
81	Bret Hit Man Hart	1.25	3.00
82	Diesel	.75	2.00
83	Howard Finkel	.50	1.25
84	Hulk Hogan	1.50	4.00
85	Lita	1.25	3.00
86	Mr. T	1.00	2.50
87	Razor Ramon	.75	2.00
88	Rowdy Roddy Piper	1.25	3.00
89	Trish Stratus	2.50	6.00
90	Stone Cold Steve Austin	2.50	6.00

2020 Topps WWE Undisputed Autographed Dual Relics

*GREEN/50: .75X TO 2X BASIC AUTOS

*BLUE/25: UNPRICED DUE TO SCARCITY

*GOLD/10: UNPRICED DUE TO SCARCITY

*PURPLE/5: UNPRICED DUE TO SCARCITY

*RED/1: UNPRICED DUE TO SCARCITY

*P.P.BLACK/1: UNPRICED DUE TO SCARCITY

*P.P.CYAN/1: UNPRICED DUE TO SCARCITY

*P.P.MAGENTA/1: UNPRICED DUE TO SCARCITY

*P.P.YELLOW/1: UNPRICED DUE TO SCARCITY

STATED PRINT RUN 99 SER.#'d SETS

DRAAB	Aleister Black	12.00	30.00
DRAAC	Adam Cole	8.00	20.00
DRAAD	Angelo Dawkins	8.00	20.00
DRAAJ	AJ Styles	15.00	40.00
DRAAN	Andrade/62	8.00	20.00
DRABB	Bianca Belair	15.00	40.00
DRABF	Bobby Fish	8.00	20.00
DRABO	Bobby Lashley	8.00	20.00
DRABS	Braun Strowman	10.00	25.00
DRACC	Cesaro	6.00	15.00
DRACF	Charlotte Flair	25.00	60.00
DRACS	Cesaro	6.00	15.00
DRADZ	Dolph Ziggler	6.00	15.00
DRAEK	Erik	6.00	15.00
DRAFB	Finn Balor	10.00	25.00
DRAJD	Mia Yim	12.00	30.00
DRAJG	Johnny Gargano	10.00	25.00
DRAKD	Killian Dain	6.00	15.00
DRAKE	Kevin Owens	8.00	20.00
DRAKK	Kofi Kingston	8.00	20.00

Code	Name		
DRAKO	Kevin Owens	8.00	20.00
DRAKR	Kyle OiReilly	6.00	15.00
DRALE	Lacey Evans	15.00	40.00
DRALS	Bobby Lashley	8.00	20.00
DRAMR	Matt Riddle	12.00	30.00
DRAMZ	The Miz	8.00	20.00
DRANJ	Nia Jax	6.00	15.00
DRANT	Natalya	10.00	25.00
DRAOT	Otis	12.00	30.00
DRAPD	The Demon Finn Balor	15.00	40.00
DRAPP	Ricochet	10.00	25.00
DRARB	Ruby Riott	15.00	40.00
DRARC	Ricochet	10.00	25.00
DRARH	Rhea Ripley	50.00	100.00
DRARS	Roderick Strong	6.00	15.00
DRASH	Shayna Baszler	15.00	40.00
DRASR	Seth Rollins	8.00	20.00
DRATC	Tommaso Ciampa	6.00	15.00
DRAVD	Velveteen Dream/46		
DRAXW	Xavier Woods	6.00	15.00

2020 Topps WWE Undisputed Autographed Match Books

STATED PRINT RUN 5 SER.#'d SETS
UNPRICED DUE TO SCARCITY

MBCAS AJ Styles/Samoa Joe
MBCDT D.Bryan/Miz
MBCJT J.Gargano/T.Ciampa

2020 Topps WWE Undisputed Autographed Oversized Boxloaders

STATED PRINT RUN 5 SER.#'d SETS
UNPRICED DUE TO SCARCITY

BLAC Adam Cole
BLAJ AJ Styles
BLBA Bayley
BLBW The Fiend Bray Wyatt
BLKK Kofi Kingston
BLMR Matt Riddle
BLSB Sasha Banks
BLSN Shinsuke Nakamura
BLTM The Miz
BL4HW Shayna Baszler

2020 Topps WWE Undisputed Autographs

*ORANGE/99: .5X TO 1.2X BASIC AUTOS
*GREEN/50: .6X TO 1.5X BASIC AUTOS
*BLUE/25: UNPRICED DUE TO SCARCITY
*GOLD/10: UNPRICED DUE TO SCARCITY
*PURPLE/5: UNPRICED DUE TO SCARCITY
*RED/1: UNPRICED DUE TO SCARCITY
*P.P.BLACK/1: UNPRICED DUE TO SCARCITY
*P.P.CYAN/1: UNPRICED DUE TO SCARCITY
*P.P.MAGENTA/1: UNPRICED DUE TO SCARCITY
*P.P.YELLOW/1: UNPRICED DUE TO SCARCITY
STATED PRINT RUN 199 SER.#'d SETS

Code	Name		
AAB	Alexa Bliss	50.00	100.00
AAC	Adam Cole	10.00	25.00
AAJ	AJ Styles	12.00	30.00
AAN	Andrade	6.00	15.00
AAS	Asuka	30.00	75.00
AAT	Aleister Black	8.00	20.00
AAZ	Zelina Vega	15.00	40.00
ABA	Bayley EXCH	15.00	40.00
ABB	Bianca Belair	12.00	30.00
ABD	Daniel Bryan	10.00	25.00

Code	Name		
ABE	Big E	6.00	15.00
ABF	Bobby Fish	8.00	20.00
ABM	Buddy Murphy	6.00	15.00
ABS	Braun Strowman EXCH	10.00	25.00
ABT	Booker T	10.00	25.00
ABW	The Fiend Bray Wyatt	50.00	100.00
ACF	Charlotte Flair	20.00	50.00
ACL	Candice LeRae	15.00	40.00
ACM	Carmella EXCH	15.00	40.00
ACS	Cesaro	5.00	15.00
ADB	Dana Brooke	10.00	25.00
ADD	Dominik Dijakovic	8.00	20.00
ADK	Dakota Kai	20.00	50.00
ADM	Drew McIntyre	12.00	30.00
ADP	Damian Priest	8.00	20.00
ADZ	Dolph Ziggler	8.00	20.00
AHC	Humberto Carrillo	6.00	15.00
AIO	Io Shirai	30.00	75.00
AIV	Ivar	6.00	15.00
AJG	Johnny Gargano	6.00	15.00
AKC	King Corbin	8.00	20.00
AKK	Kofi Kingston	6.00	15.00
AKO	Kevin Owens	6.00	15.00
AKS	Kairi Sane	20.00	50.00
AKU	Kushida	8.00	20.00
ALE	Lacey Evans	15.00	40.00
ALN	Lana EXCH	10.00	25.00
ALT	Lita	20.00	50.00
AMA	Mustafa Ali	8.00	20.00
AMR	Matt Riddle	12.00	30.00
AMY	Mia Yim	10.00	25.00
ANC	Nikki Cross	10.00	25.00
ARB	Ruby Riott	12.00	30.00
ARC	Ricochet	8.00	20.00
ARD	Kyle OiReilly	6.00	15.00
ARR	Roman Reigns EXCH	15.00	40.00
ART	R-Truth	12.00	30.00
ASB	Sasha Banks	30.00	75.00
ASG	Shorty G EXCH	8.00	20.00
ASJ	Samoa Joe	6.00	15.00
ASM	Sheamus	8.00	20.00
ASN	Shinsuke Nakamura	6.00	15.00
ASR	Seth Rollins	10.00	25.00
ASZ	Sami Zayn	6.00	15.00
ATC	Tommaso Ciampa	8.00	20.00
ATM	The Miz	8.00	20.00
AVD	Velveteen Dream EXCH	6.00	15.00
AVR	Erik	8.00	20.00
A4HW	Shayna Baszler	12.00	30.00
ABOB	Bobby Lashley	8.00	20.00
ALEE	Keith Lee	10.00	25.00
ARIP	Rhea Ripley	60.00	120.00
AROD	Roderick Strong EXCH	8.00	20.00

2020 Topps WWE Undisputed Cut Signatures

CSBB Bam Bam Bigelow
CSBH Bobby The Brain Heenan
CSBM Big Boss Man
CSBS Bruno Sammartino
CSDR Dusty Rhodes
CSEG Eddie Guerrero
CSGO Mean Gene Okerlund
CSJN Jim The Anvil Neidhart
CSJS Big John Studd
CSJT Earthquake
CSMP Mr. Perfect
CSNV Nikolai Volkoff

CSPB Paul Bearer
CSRP Rowdy Roddy Piper
CSRR Ravishing Rick Rude
CSRS Macho Man Randy Savage
CSUM Umaga
CSUW Ultimate Warrior
CSVD Big Van Vader
CSYO Yokozuna
CSDBS Davey Boy Smith

2020 Topps WWE Undisputed Dual Relics

*GREEN/50: .75X TO 2X BASIC MEM
*BLUE/25: UNPRICED DUE TO SCARCITY
*GOLD/10: UNPRICED DUE TO SCARCITY
*PURPLE/5: UNPRICED DUE TO SCARCITY
*RED/1: UNPRICED DUE TO SCARCITY
*P.P.BLACK/1: UNPRICED DUE TO SCARCITY
*P.P.CYAN/1: UNPRICED DUE TO SCARCITY
*P.P.MAGENTA/1: UNPRICED DUE TO SCARCITY
*P.P.YELLOW/1: UNPRICED DUE TO SCARCITY
STATED PRINT RUN 99 SER.#'d SETS

Code	Name		
DRAB	Aleister Black	3.00	8.00
DRAC	Adam Cole	2.50	6.00
DRAD	Angelo Dawkins	2.50	6.00
DRAJ	AJ Styles	4.00	10.00
DRAN	Andrade	2.00	5.00
DRBB	Bianca Belair	3.00	8.00
DRBF	Bobby Fish	2.00	5.00
DRBO	Bobby Lashley	2.50	6.00
DRBS	Braun Strowman	3.00	8.00
DRCF	Charlotte Flair	5.00	12.00
DRCM	Carmella	8.00	20.00
DRCS	Cesaro	2.50	6.00
DRDZ	Dolph Ziggler	2.50	6.00
DREK	Erik	2.00	5.00
DREL	Elias	2.50	6.00
DRFB	Finn Balor	6.00	15.00
DRJD	Mia Yim	5.00	12.00
DRJG	Johnny Gargano	4.00	10.00
DRKD	Killian Dain	2.00	5.00
DRKE	Kevin Owens	3.00	8.00
DRKK	Kofi Kingston	3.00	8.00
DRKO	Kevin Owens	3.00	8.00
DRKR	Kyle OiReilly	2.50	6.00
DRKS	Kairi Sane	12.00	30.00
DRLE	Lacey Evans	6.00	15.00
DRMR	Matt Riddle	4.00	10.00
DRMZ	The Miz	2.50	6.00
DRNJ	Nia Jax	2.50	6.00
DRNT	Natalya	3.00	8.00
DROT	Otis	2.00	5.00
DRPD	The Demon Finn Balor	6.00	15.00
DRRB	Ruby Riott	5.00	12.00
DRRC	Ricochet	3.00	8.00
DRRO	Randy Orton	3.00	8.00
DRRR	Roman Reigns	4.00	10.00
DRRS	Roderick Strong	2.00	5.00
DRSM	Shawn Michaels	4.00	10.00
DRSR	Seth Rollins	3.00	8.00
DRTC	Tommaso Ciampa	2.50	6.00
DRVD	Velveteen Dream	2.00	5.00
DRXW	Xavier Woods	2.50	6.00
DRHHH	Triple H	4.00	10.00

2020 Topps WWE Undisputed Framed Autograph

STATED PRINT RUN 150 SER.#'d SETS

Code	Name		
AFF	Bray Wyatt	50.00	100.00

2020 Topps WWE Undisputed Quad Autographs

STATED PRINT RUN 5 SER.#'d SETS
UNPRICED DUE TO SCARCITY

QHW Banks/Flair/Lynch/Bayley
QIP Walter/Barthel/Aichner/Wolfe
QUE Cole/Fish/O'Reilly/Strong

2020 Topps WWE Undisputed Schamberger Art

COMPLETE SET (10) 20.00 50.00
RANDOMLY INSERTED INTO PACKS

Code	Name		
RS1	Mustafa Ali	3.00	8.00
RS2	Asuka	5.00	12.00
RS3	Becky Lynch	5.00	12.00
RS4	Bianca Belair	3.00	8.00
RS5	Eddie Guerrero	4.00	10.00
RS6	Macho Man Randy Savage	6.00	15.00
RS7	The Miz	2.50	6.00
RS8	Toni Storm	6.00	15.00
RS9	Undertaker	4.00	10.00
RS10	Walter	2.00	5.00

2020 Topps WWE Undisputed Schamberger Art Autographs

STATED PRINT RUN 10 SER.#'d SETS
UNPRICED DUE TO SCARCITY

RSRSAS Schamberger/Ali
RSRSBB Schamberger/Asuka
RSRSBL Schamberger/Lynch
RSRSMA Schamberger/Belair
RSRSRG Schamberger/Guerrero
RSRSRS Schamberger/Savage
RSRSTM Schamberger/Miz
RSRSTS Schamberger/Storm
RSRSUT Schamberger/Undertaker
RSRSWT Schamberger/WALTER

2020 Topps WWE Undisputed Schamberger Art Superstar Autographs

STATED PRINT RUN 10 SER.#'d SETS
UNPRICED DUE TO SCARCITY

ARSAS Asuka
ARSBB Bianca Belair
ARSMA Mustafa Ali
ARSTM The Miz

2020 Topps WWE Undisputed Tag Team Autographs

*GOLD/10: UNPRICED DUE TO SCARCITY
*PURPLE/5: UNPRICED DUE TO SCARCITY
*RED/1: UNPRICED DUE TO SCARCITY
STATED PRINT RUN 25 SER.#'d SETS

Code	Name		
DAKW	K.Sane/Asuka	125.00	250.00
DASP	A.Dawkins/M.Ford	30.00	75.00
DAVR	Erik/Ivar	20.00	50.00

2020 Topps WWE Undisputed Triple Autographs

*PURPLE/5: UNPRICED DUE TO SCARCITY
*RED/1: UNPRICED DUE TO SCARCITY
STATED PRINT RUN 10 SER.#'d SETS
UNPRICED DUE TO SCARCITY

TALP Dorado/Metalik/Kalisto
TAND Woods/Big E/Kingston

2021 Topps WWE Undisputed

COMPLETE SET (74)   20.00   50.00
*PURPLE/99: .75X TO 2X BASIC CARDS
*GREEN/50: 1.2X TO 3X BASIC CARDS
*BLACK/25: UNPRICED DUE TO SCARCITY
*BLUE/10: UNPRICED DUE TO SCARCITY
*RED/5: UNPRICED DUE TO SCARCITY
*GOLD/1: UNPRICED DUE TO SCARCITY
*P.P.BLACK/1: UNPRICED DUE TO SCARCITY
*P.P.CYAN/1: UNPRICED DUE TO SCARCITY
*P.P.MAGENTA/1: UNPRICED DUE TO SCARCITY
*P.P.YELLOW/1: UNPRICED DUE TO SCARCITY

1	AJ Styles	1.50	4.00
2	Alexa Bliss	3.00	8.00
3	Angel Garza	.60	1.50
4	Becky Lynch	2.00	5.00
5	Bobby Lashley	1.25	3.00
6	The Fiend Bray Wyatt	2.00	5.00
7	Charlotte Flair	2.50	6.00
8	Damian Priest	.75	2.00
9	Dana Brooke	.50	1.25
10	Drew McIntyre	1.25	3.00
11	Elias	.50	1.25
12	Eva Marie	1.25	3.00
13	John Morrison	1.00	2.50
14	Keith Lee	1.00	2.50
15	MACE	.50	1.25
16	Mandy Rose	2.50	6.00
17	Mustafa Ali	.60	1.50
18	MVP	.50	1.25
19	Nia Jax	1.00	2.50
20	Omos	.50	1.25
21	Rhea Ripley	2.00	5.00
22	Riddle	1.25	3.00
23	R-Truth	.60	1.50
24	Shayna Baszler	1.25	3.00
25	Sheamus	.75	2.00
26	T-BAR	.60	1.50
27	Xavier Woods	.50	1.25
28	Angelo Dawkins	.60	1.50
29	Apollo Crews	.60	1.50
30	Bianca Belair	1.25	3.00
31	Big E	1.25	3.00
32	Carmella	1.25	3.00
33	Cesaro	.50	1.25
34	Chad Gable	.50	1.25
35	Commander Azeez	.60	1.50
36	Dominik Mysterio	.60	1.50
37	Jey Uso	.50	1.25
38	Jimmy Uso	.50	1.25
39	Kevin Owens	1.00	2.50
40	Baron Corbin	.50	1.25
41	Liv Morgan	2.00	5.00
42	Mia Yim	.60	1.50
43	Montez Ford	.50	1.25
44	Natalya	.75	2.00
45	Otis	.60	1.50
46	Sami Zayn	.75	2.00
47	Shinsuke Nakamura	1.25	3.00
48	Tamina	.50	1.25
49	Adam Cole	1.50	4.00
50	Candice LeRae	2.00	5.00
51	Dakota Kai	1.00	2.50
52	Danny Burch	.60	1.50
53	Ember Moon	.60	1.50
54	Finn Balor	1.25	3.00
55	Indi Hartwell	1.50	4.00
56	Io Shirai	1.00	2.50
57	Johnny Gargano	1.00	2.50
58	Karrion Kross	2.00	5.00
59	Kushida	.75	2.00
60	LA Knight	.50	1.25
61	Nash Carter	.50	1.25
62	Oney Lorcan	.50	1.25
63	Pete Dunne	1.25	3.00
64	Santos Escobar	1.00	2.50
65	Tommaso Ciampa	1.25	3.00
66	Toni Storm	2.00	5.00
67	Wes Lee	.50	1.25
68	Lex Luger	.60	1.50
69	Ric Flair	2.00	5.00
70	The Godfather	.60	1.50
71	Undertaker	2.50	6.00
72	William Regal	.75	2.00
73	Yokozuna	.75	2.00
74	John Cena	2.50	6.00

2021 Topps WWE Undisputed Autographed Framed Boxloaders

*BLUE/25: UNPRICED DUE TO SCARCITY
*GOLD/10: UNPRICED DUE TO SCARCITY
*BLACK/5: UNPRICED DUE TO SCARCITY
*ORANGE/3: UNPRICED DUE TO SCARCITY
STATED PRINT RUN 150 SER.#'d SETS

FRA	Asuka	30.00	75.00
FRK	Kane	25.00	60.00
FRM	MVP	8.00	20.00
FRR	Riddle	15.00	40.00
FRAB	Alexa Bliss	100.00	200.00
FRCA	Cedric Alexander	10.00	25.00
FRIS	Io Shirai	20.00	50.00
FRJH	Jeff Hardy	30.00	75.00
FRJM	John Morrison	12.00	30.00
FRKU	Kushida		
FRLL	Lex Luger	15.00	40.00
FRMA	Mustafa Ali	8.00	20.00
FRRM	Rey Mysterio	25.00	60.00
FRRR	Robert Roode	8.00	20.00
FRSB	Shelton Benjamin	10.00	25.00
FRTC	Tommaso Ciampa	12.00	30.00
FRWR	William Regal	15.00	40.00

2021 Topps WWE Undisputed Autographed Mat Relics

*GREEN/50: .5X TO 1.2X BASIC AUTOS
*BLUE/25: UNPRICED DUE TO SCARCITY
*GOLD/10: UNPRICED DUE TO SCARCITY
*BLACK/5: UNPRICED DUE TO SCARCITY
STATED PRINT RUN 99 SER.#'d SETS

MB	Bayley	15.00	40.00
MC	Cesaro	8.00	20.00
ME	Edge	20.00	50.00
MG	Goldberg		
MM	MVP	6.00	15.00
MO	Otis	6.00	15.00
M$$	Sasha Banks	30.00	75.00
MAC	Adam Cole	15.00	40.00
MAD	Angelo Dawkins	5.00	12.00
MAG	Angel Garza	5.00	12.00
MAN	Angelo Dawkins	5.00	12.00
MAP	Apollo Crews	5.00	12.00
MAS	Asuka	15.00	40.00
MAT	Austin Theory	6.00	15.00
MBF	Bobby Fish	5.00	12.00
MBL	Becky Lynch	30.00	75.00
MBO	Bobby Lashley	10.00	25.00
MBW	The Fiend Bray Wyatt		
MCF	Charlotte Flair		
MDD	Dominik Dijakovic		
MDG	Drew Gulak	5.00	12.00
MDM	Drew McIntyre	10.00	25.00
MDO	Dominik Mysterio	12.00	30.00
MDR	Drew McIntyre	10.00	25.00
MES	Elias	6.00	15.00
MFB	Finn Balor	10.00	25.00
MGA	Angel Garza	5.00	12.00
MJC	John Cena	100.00	200.00
MJG	Johnny Gargano	5.00	12.00
MJM	John Morrison		
MJU	Jimmy Uso	5.00	12.00
MKC	King Corbin	5.00	12.00
MKK	Kofi Kingston	6.00	15.00
MKL	Keith Lee	10.00	25.00
MKO	Kevin Owens	8.00	20.00
MKR	Kyle O'Reilly	8.00	20.00
MMF	Montez Ford	5.00	12.00
MMO	Montez Ford	5.00	12.00
MMR	Matt Riddle	12.00	30.00
MPD	Pete Dunne	6.00	15.00
MRR	Rhea Ripley	25.00	60.00
MSB	Shayna Baszler	6.00	15.00
MSE	Seth Rollins	12.00	30.00
MSR	Seth Rollins	12.00	30.00
MTC	Tommaso Ciampa	8.00	20.00

2021 Topps WWE Undisputed Autographed Match-Up Dual Relics

*GOLD/10: UNPRICED DUE TO SCARCITY
*BLACK/5: UNPRICED DUE TO SCARCITY
STATED PRINT RUN 25 SER.#'d SETS

AMABN	Natalia/Becky Lynch
AMABS	Shayna Baszler/Becky Lynch
AMACD	Drew Gulak/Cesaro
AMACT	Charlotte Flair/Trish Stratus
AMADG	Goldberg/Drew McIntyre
AMADO	Drew Gulak/Oney Lorcan
AMADT	Tegan Nox/Dakota Kai
AMAEK	Elias/King Corbin
AMAFJ	Johnny Gargano/Finn Balor
AMAFR	Charlotte Flair/Rhea Ripley
AMAIC	Io Shirai/Candice LeRae
AMAKD	Keith Lee/Dominik Dijakovic
AMAKS	Seth Rollins/Kevin Owens
AMALK	Asuka/Bayley
AMALN	Natalia/Liv Morgan
AMAMS	Mandy Rose/Sonya Deville
AMARJ	Ricochet/Johnny Gargano
AMARO	Kevin Owens/Roman Reigns
AMART	Rhea Ripley/Toni Storm
AMASA	Sasha Banks/Asuka
AMASC	Sasha Banks/Carmella
AMASM	Mia Yim/Shayna Baszler

2021 Topps WWE Undisputed Autographed Oversized Boxloaders

STATED ODDS 1:93 BOXES
STATED PRINT RUN 5 SER.#'d SETS
UNPRICED DUE TO SCARCITY

OAC	Carmella
OAR	Ricochet
OAAG	Angel Garza
OACF	Charlotte Flair
OADZ	Dolph Ziggler
OAJG	Johnny Gargano
OAJU	Jey Uso
OAKO	Kevin Owens
OANJ	Nia Jax
OAPD	Pete Dunne
OASZ	Sami Zayn

2021 Topps WWE Undisputed Autographs

*PURPLE/99: .5X TO 1.2X BASIC AUTOS
*GREEN/50: .6X TO 1.5X BASIC AUTOS
*BLUE/25: UNPRICED DUE TO SCARCITY
*GOLD/10: UNPRICED DUE TO SCARCITY
*BLACK/5: UNPRICED DUE TO SCARCITY
*RED/1: UNPRICED DUE TO SCARCITY
*P.P.BLACK/1: UNPRICED DUE TO SCARCITY
*P.P.CYAN/1: UNPRICED DUE TO SCARCITY
*P.P.MAGENTA/1: UNPRICED DUE TO SCARCITY
*P.P.YELLOW/1: UNPRICED DUE TO SCARCITY
STATED PRINT RUN 199 SER.#'d SETS

AC	Carmella	12.00	30.00
AE	Elias	6.00	15.00
AK	Kushida	4.00	10.00
AM	MACE	4.00	10.00
AO	Omos	12.00	30.00
AR	Riddle	10.00	25.00
AU	Undertaker		
AAB	Alexa Bliss	30.00	75.00
AAC	Adam Cole	10.00	25.00
AAD	Angelo Dawkins	6.00	15.00
AAG	Angel Garza	3.00	8.00
AAS	AJ Styles	10.00	25.00
ABB	Bianca Belair EXCH	15.00	40.00
ABE	Big E	4.00	10.00
ABL	Becky Lynch	25.00	60.00
ABO	Bobby Lashley EXCH	8.00	20.00
ACF	Charlotte Flair EXCH	20.00	50.00
ACG	Chad Gable	6.00	15.00
ACL	Candice LeRae	10.00	25.00
ACS	Cesaro	5.00	12.00
ADB	Danny Burch	3.00	8.00
ADK	Dakota Kai	10.00	25.00
ADM	Drew McIntyre		
ADO	Dominik Mysterio	6.00	15.00
ADZ	Dolph Ziggler	5.00	12.00
AEM	Ember Moon	6.00	15.00
AFB	Finn Balor	8.00	20.00
AIH	Indi Hartwell	10.00	25.00
AIS	Io Shirai	12.00	30.00
AJC	John Cena		
AJG	Johnny Gargano	5.00	12.00
AJU	Jey Uso	4.00	10.00
AKC	King Corbin	5.00	12.00
AKK	Karrion Kross	8.00	20.00
AKL	Keith Lee	6.00	15.00
AKO	Kevin Owens	8.00	20.00
ALL	Lex Luger	12.00	30.00
AMA	Mustafa Ali	4.00	10.00
AMF	Montez Ford	4.00	10.00
AMR	Mandy Rose	20.00	50.00
AMVP	MVP	5.00	12.00
ANJ	Nia Jax	4.00	10.00
AOD	Otis	6.00	15.00
ARP	Rhea Ripley	15.00	40.00
ARR	Robert Roode	5.00	12.00
ART	R-Truth	4.00	10.00
ASB	Shayna Baszler	5.00	12.00

ASE	Santos Escobar	5.00	12.00
ASH	Sheamus	6.00	15.00
ASN	Shinsuke Nakamura	8.00	20.00
ASZ	Sami Zayn	6.00	15.00
ATB	T-BAR	5.00	12.00
ATC	Tommaso Ciampa	6.00	15.00
ATG	The Godfather	8.00	20.00
ATS	Toni Storm	12.00	30.00
AWR	William Regal	10.00	25.00
AXW	Xavier Woods	4.00	10.00

2021 Topps WWE Undisputed Cut Signatures

CSBB	Bam Bam Bigelow
CSBH	Bobby "The Brain" Heenan
CSCJS	Chief Jay Strongbow

2021 Topps WWE Undisputed Dual Autographs

*BLUE/25: UNPRICED DUE TO SCARCITY
*GOLD/10: UNPRICED DUE TO SCARCITY
*BLACK/5: UNPRICED DUE TO SCARCITY
*RED/1: UNPRICED DUE TO SCARCITY
STATED PRINT RUN 50 SER.#'d SETS

DACS	Cesaro/Shinsuka Nakamura	25.00	60.00
DADM	Dana Brooke/Mandy Rose		
DADR	Raquel Gonzalez/Dakota Kai	20.00	50.00
DAHB	Shelton Benjamin/Cedric Alexander		
DAIM	Marcel Barthel/Fabian Aichner	10.00	25.00
DAKS	Scarlett/Karrion Kross	50.00	100.00
DALF	Joaquin Wilde/Raul Mendoza	12.00	30.00
DALH	Gran Metalik/Lince Dorado	12.00	30.00
DAMF	Dominik and Rey Mysterio	30.00	75.00
DAND	Kofi Kingston/Xavier Woods	10.00	25.00
DANS	Nia Jax/Shayna Baszler	10.00	25.00
DAOD	Oney Lorcan/Danny Burch	10.00	25.00
DAPC	Candice LeRae/Johnny Gargano	50.00	100.00
DARB	Mace/T-Bar	10.00	25.00
DAVR	Ivar/Erik	10.00	25.00
DAZR	Dolph Ziggler/Robert Roode	10.00	25.00
DAGYZ	Zack Gibson/James Drake	10.00	25.00

2021 Topps WWE Undisputed Fistographs

STATED ODDS 1:19 BOXES
STATED PRINT RUN 25 SER.#'d SETS

FIO	Omos	125.00	250.00
FIAS	AJ Styles	200.00	400.00
FIBB	Bianca Belair	200.00	400.00
FIBE	Big E	100.00	200.00
FIDM	Drew McIntyre	200.00	400.00
FIOD	Otis	100.00	200.00
FIRR	Rhea Ripley	250.00	500.00
FISB	Sasha Banks	400.00	800.00
FISN	Shinsuke Nakamura	200.00	400.00
FISR	Seth Rollins	250.00	500.00

2021 Topps WWE Undisputed Grand Slam Champions Autographs

*PURPLE/99: .5X TO 1.2X BASIC AUTOS
*GREEN/50: .6X TO 1.5X BASIC AUTOS
*BLUE/25: UNPRICED DUE TO SCARCITY
*GOLD/10: UNPRICED DUE TO SCARCITY
*BLACK/5: UNPRICED DUE TO SCARCITY
*RED/1: UNPRICED DUE TO SCARCITY
*P.P.BLACK/1: UNPRICED DUE TO SCARCITY
*P.P.CYAN/1: UNPRICED DUE TO SCARCITY
*P.P.MAGENTA/1: UNPRICED DUE TO SCARCITY
*P.P.YELLOW/1: UNPRICED DUE TO SCARCITY
STATED PRINT RUN 199 SER.#'d SETS

GAA	Asuka	15.00	40.00
GAE	Edge	15.00	40.00
GAK	Kane	20.00	50.00
GABT	Booker T	12.00	30.00
GAJH	Jeff Hardy	12.00	30.00
GAKK	Kofi Kingston	6.00	15.00
GARM	Rey Mysterio	15.00	40.00
GATM	The Miz	10.00	25.00

2021 Topps WWE Undisputed Grand Slam Champions Autographs Purple

STATED PRINT RUN 99 SER.#'d SETS

GASB	Sasha Banks	50.00	100.00
GASR	Seth Rollins	12.00	30.00

2021 Topps WWE Undisputed Grand Slam Champions

COMPLETE SET (16)		20.00	50.00
RANDOMLY INSERTED INTO PACKS			
GS1	Asuka	3.00	8.00
GS2	Bayley	2.00	5.00
GS3	Booker T	1.50	4.00
GS4	Eddie Guerrero	4.00	10.00
GS5	Edge	3.00	8.00
GS6	Jeff Hardy	2.00	5.00
GS7	Kane	1.25	3.00
GS8	Kofi Kingston	2.00	5.00
GS9	Randy Orton	2.50	6.00
GS10	Rey Mysterio	2.00	5.00
GS11	Roman Reigns	4.00	10.00
GS12	Sasha Banks	4.00	10.00
GS13	Seth Rollins	2.00	5.00
GS14	Shawn Michaels	3.00	8.00
GS15	The Miz	1.25	3.00
GS16	Triple H	2.50	6.00

2021 Topps WWE Undisputed Mat Relics

*GREEN/50: .5X TO 1.2X BASIC MEM
*BLUE/25: UNPRICED DUE TO SCARCITY
*GOLD/10: UNPRICED DUE TO SCARCITY
*BLACK/5: UNPRICED DUE TO SCARCITY
*RED/1: UNPRICED DUE TO SCARCITY
*P.P.BLACK/1: UNPRICED DUE TO SCARCITY
*P.P.CYAN/1: UNPRICED DUE TO SCARCITY
*P.P.MAGENTA/1: UNPRICED DUE TO SCARCITY
*P.P.YELLOW/1: UNPRICED DUE TO SCARCITY
STATED PRINT RUN 99 SER.#'d SETS

MB	Bayley	4.00	10.00
MC	Cesaro	1.50	4.00
MG	Goldberg	6.00	15.00
MM	MVP	1.50	4.00
M$$	Sasha Banks	8.00	20.00
MAC	Adam Cole	5.00	12.00
MAD	Angelo Dawkins	2.00	5.00
MAG	Angel Garza	2.00	5.00
MAP	Apollo Crews	2.00	5.00
MBF	Bobby Fish	2.00	5.00
MBL	Becky Lynch	6.00	15.00
MCF	Charlotte Flair	8.00	20.00
MDD	Dominik Dijakovic	2.00	5.00
MDG	Drew Gulak	2.00	5.00
MES	Elias	1.50	4.00
MFB	Finn Balor	4.00	10.00

MJG	Johnny Gargano	3.00	8.00
MKC	King Corbin	1.50	4.00
MKL	Keith Lee	3.00	8.00
MKR	Kyle O'Reilly	2.50	6.00
MMF	Montez Ford	1.50	4.00
MMR	Matt Riddle	4.00	10.00
MPD	Pete Dunne	4.00	10.00
MRA	Randy Orton	5.00	12.00
MRR	Rhea Ripley	6.00	15.00
MSB	Shayna Baszler	4.00	10.00
MSE	Seth Rollins	4.00	10.00
MTC	Tommaso Ciampa	4.00	10.00

2021 Topps WWE Undisputed Match-Up Dual Autographed Books

*GOLD/5: UNPRICED DUE TO SCARCITY
*RED/1: UNPRICED DUE TO SCARCITY
STATED PRINT RUN 10 SER.#'d SETS
UNPRICED DUE TO SCARCITY

MAC	Charlotte Flair/Asuka
MAS	AJ Styles/Shinsuke Nakamura
MBS	Sasha Banks/Bayley
MCS	Cesaro/Sheamus
MEJ	Edge/Jeff Hardy
MJR	Roman Reigns/John Cena
MSR	Seth Rollins/Finn Balor
MTM	Triple H/Mankind
MUK	Kane/Undertaker

2021 Topps WWE Undisputed Match-Up Dual Relics

*GREEN/50: .5X TO 1.2X BASIC MEM
*BLUE/25: UNPRICED DUE TO SCARCITY
*RED/1: UNPRICED DUE TO SCARCITY
*GOLD/10: UNPRICED DUE TO SCARCITY
*P.P.BLACK/1: UNPRICED DUE TO SCARCITY
*P.P.CYAN/1: UNPRICED DUE TO SCARCITY
*P.P.MAGENTA/1: UNPRICED DUE TO SCARCITY
*P.P.YELLOW/1: UNPRICED DUE TO SCARCITY
STATED PRINT RUN 99 SER.#'d SETS

MABA	Asuka/B.Lynch	6.00	15.00
MABJ	B.Wyatt/J.Cena	8.00	20.00
MABL	L.Evans/Bayley	6.00	15.00
MABS	B.Lynch/S.Baszler	6.00	15.00
MACP	A.Crews/MVP	2.00	5.00
MACS	S.Baszler/C.Flair	8.00	20.00
MADG	D.McIntyre/Goldberg	6.00	15.00
MADR	R.Reigns/D.McIntyre	8.00	20.00
MAEK	King Corbin/Elias	1.50	4.00
MAER	R.Orton/Edge	6.00	15.00
MAFR	C.Flair/R.Ripley	8.00	20.00
MAKS	K.Owens/S.Rollins	4.00	10.00
MALK	Bayley/Asuka	6.00	15.00
MAMO	R.Orton/D.McIntyre	5.00	12.00
MAMS	S.Deville/M.Rose	8.00	20.00
MARB	B.Belair/R.Ripley	6.00	15.00
MARM	D.Mysterio/S.Rollins	4.00	10.00
MARO	K.Owens/R.Reigns	8.00	20.00
MASA	S.Banks/Asuka	8.00	20.00
MASC	S.Bannks/Carmella	8.00	20.00

2021 Topps WWE Undisputed Rob Schamberger Illustrations

COMPLETE SET (10)		12.00	30.00
RANDOMLY INSERTED INTO PACKS			
RS1	AJ Styles	2.00	5.00
RS2	Big E	1.50	4.00

RS3	Charlotte Flair	3.00	8.00
RS4	Johnny Gargano	1.25	3.00
RS5	Natalya	1.00	2.50
RS6	Rey Mysterio	1.50	4.00
RS7	Roman Reigns	3.00	8.00
RS8	Shotzi Blackheart	3.00	8.00
RS9	Stone Cold Steve Austin	3.00	8.00
RS10	The Fiend Bray Wyatt	2.50	6.00

2021 Topps WWE Undisputed Rob Schamberger Illustrations Artist Autographs

STATED PRINT RUN 10 SER.#'d SETS
UNPRICED DUE TO SCARCITY

AAAS	Rob Schamberger
AABE	Rob Schamberger
AABW	Rob Schamberger
AACF	Rob Schamberger
AAJG	Rob Schamberger
AANT	Rob Schamberger
AARM	Rob Schamberger
AARR	Rob Schamberger
AASA	Rob Schamberger
AASB	Rob Schamberger

2021 Topps WWE Undisputed Rob Schamberger Illustrations Superstar Autographs

STATED PRINT RUN 10 SER.#'d SETS
UNPRICED DUE TO SCARCITY

SAAS	AJ Styles
SABE	Big E
SABW	The Fiend Bray Wyatt
SAJG	Johnny Gargano
SANT	Natalya
SARM	Rey Mysterio
SASB	Shotzi Blackheart

2017 Topps WWE Women's Division

UNOPENED BLASTER BOX (81 CARDS)
UNOPENED HANGER BOX (40 CARDS)
UNOPENED FAT PACK (18 CARDS)
*SILVER/50: 1.2X TO 3X BASIC CARDS
*BLUE/25: 2X TO 5X BASIC CARDS
*GOLD/10: UNPRICED DUE TO SCARCITY
*RED/1: UNPRICED DUE TO SCARCITY

R1	Aliyah	.40	1.00
R2	Asuka	1.00	2.50
R3	Billie Kay	.40	1.00
R4	Cathy Kelley	.30	.75
R5	Ember Moon	.75	2.00
R6	Kimberly Frankele	.30	.75
R7	Liv Morgan	.50	1.25
R8	Mandy Rose	.40	1.00
R9	Nikki Cross	.60	1.50
R10	Peyton Royce	.50	1.25
R11	Ruby Riot	.40	1.00
R12	Brie Bella	.75	2.00
R13	Alexa Bliss	1.50	4.00
R14	Alicia Fox	.50	1.25
R15	Bayley	1.00	2.50
R16	Charly Caruso	.30	.75
R17	Dana Brooke	.60	1.50
R18	Emma	.75	2.00
R19	JoJo	.50	1.25
R20	Maryse	.60	1.50
R21	Mickie James	.50	1.25

R22 Nia Jax	.50	1.25
R23 Sasha Banks	1.00	2.50
R24 Stephanie McMahon	.40	1.00
R25 Summer Rae	.75	2.00
R26 Lita	.60	1.50
R27 Becky Lynch	1.00	2.50
R28 Carmella	.75	2.00
R29 Charlotte Flair	1.25	3.00
R30 Dasha Fuentes	.40	1.00
R31 Lana	1.00	2.50
R32 Naomi	.60	1.50
R33 Natalya	.60	1.50
R34 Nikki Bella	.75	2.00
R35 Renee Young	.50	1.25
R36 Tamina	.40	1.00
R37 Alundra Blayze	.40	1.00
R38 Eve Torres	.50	1.25
R39 Miss Elizabeth	.50	1.25
R40 Sherri Martel	.40	1.00
R41 Terri Runnels	.30	.75
R42 Trish Stratus	1.25	3.00
R43 Wendi Richter	.40	1.00
R44 Beth Phoenix	.30	.75
R45 Ivory	.30	.75
R46 Judy Martin	.30	.75
R47 Kelly Kelly	.60	1.50
R48 Leilani Kai	.30	.75
R49 Princess Victoria	.30	.75
R50 Torrie Wilson	.75	2.00

2017 Topps WWE Women's Division Autographed Kiss and Mat Relics

STATED ODDS 1:1,054 BLASTER BOX EXCLUSIVE
STATED PRINT RUN 5 SER.#'d SETS
UNPRICED DUE TO SCARCITY

WARCA Carmella
WARNA Natalya

2017 Topps WWE Women's Division Autographed Mat Relics

STATED ODDS 1:68 BLASTER BOX
STATED ODDS 1:6,012 HANGER BOX
STATED ODDS 1:11,988 HANGER PACK
STATED PRINT RUN 10 SER.#'d SETS
UNPRICED DUE TO SCARCITY

MRAB Alexa Bliss
MRAF Alicia Fox
MRAS Asuka
MRBA Bayley
MRBL Becky Lynch
MRCA Carmella
MRCF Charlotte Flair
MRNJ Nia Jax
MRSR Summer Rae
MRSU Summer Rae
MRTA Tamina
MRASA Asuka
MRASU Asuka
MRBAY Bayley
MRBEC Becky Lynch
MRBLY Bayley
MRCAR Carmella
MRCHA Charlotte Flair
MRCHF Charlotte Flair
MRCRM Carmella
MREMM Emma
MRNAO Naomi

MRNAT Natalya
MRNIA Nia Jax
MRSUM Summer Rae
MRTAM Tamina
MRCHAR Charlotte Flair
MREMMA Emma

2017 Topps WWE Women's Division Autographs

*SILVER/50: .5X TO 1.2X BASIC AUTOS
*BLUE/25: .6X TO 1.5X BASIC AUTOS
*GOLD/10: UNPRICED DUE TO SCARCITY
*RED/1: UNPRICED DUE TO SCARCITY
STATED ODDS 1:13 BLASTER BOX
STATED ODDS 1:802 HANGER BOX
STATED ODDS 1:1,599 HANGER PACK
STATED PRINT RUN 99 OR FEWER SER.#'d SETS

R1 Aliyah/99	6.00	15.00
R2 Asuka/99	20.00	50.00
R3 Billie Kay/99	10.00	25.00
R4 Cathy Kelley/99	8.00	20.00
R5 Ember Moon/94	8.00	20.00
R7 Liv Morgan/99	25.00	60.00
R8 Mandy Rose/99	20.00	50.00
R10 Peyton Royce/99	10.00	25.00
R11 Ruby Riot/99	20.00	50.00
R12 Brie Bella/56	10.00	25.00
R13 Alexa Bliss/99	50.00	100.00
R14 Alicia Fox/61	10.00	25.00
R18 Emma/99	12.00	30.00
R19 JoJo/99	6.00	15.00
R22 Nia Jax/99	10.00	25.00
R23 Sasha Banks/68	25.00	60.00
R27 Becky Lynch/99	15.00	40.00
R28 Carmella/99	20.00	50.00
R29 Charlotte Flair/57	20.00	50.00
R30 Dasha Fuentes/99	6.00	15.00
R32 Naomi/99	8.00	20.00
R33 Natalya/78	8.00	20.00
R34 Nikki Bella/99	10.00	25.00
R36 Tamina/99	6.00	15.00
R37 Alundra Blayze/99	8.00	20.00
R41 Terri Runnels/99	10.00	25.00
R43 Wendi Richter/99	6.00	15.00
R44 Beth Phoenix/99	8.00	20.00
R45 Ivory/99	6.00	15.00
R46 Judy Martin/99	6.00	15.00
R47 Kelly Kelly/99	10.00	25.00
R48 Leilani Kai/99	6.00	15.00
R49 Princess Victoria/99	10.00	25.00
R50 Torrie Wilson/99	12.00	30.00

2017 Topps WWE Women's Division Autographs Blue

STATED ODDS 1:39 BLASTER BOX
STATED ODDS 1:3,280 HANGER BOX
STATED ODDS 1:6,539 HANGER PACK
STATED PRINT RUN 25 SER.#'d SETS

R25 Summer Rae	15.00	40.00

2017 Topps WWE Women's Division Autographs Silver

STATED ODDS 1:20 BLASTER BOX
STATED ODDS 1:1,569 HANGER BOX
STATED ODDS 1:3,128 HANGER PACK
STATED PRINT RUN 50 SER.#'d SETS

R15 Bayley	15.00	40.00

R20 Maryse	8.00	20.00
R38 Eve Torres	20.00	50.00
R42 Trish Stratus	25.00	60.00

2017 Topps WWE Women's Division Diva's Championship Medallions

*SILVER/50: .5X TO 1.2X BASIC MEM
*BLUE/25: .6X TO 1.5X BASIC MEM
*GOLD/10: UNPRICED DUE TO SCARCITY
*RED/1: UNPRICED DUE TO SCARCITY
STATED ODDS 1:15 BLASTER BOX
STATED ODDS 1:1,203 HANGER BOX
STATED ODDS 1:2,398 HANGER PACK
STATED PRINT RUN 99 SER.#'d SETS

DCM Maryse	5.00	12.00
DCN Natalya	5.00	12.00
DCAF Alicia Fox	4.00	10.00
DCBB Brie Bella	6.00	15.00
DCBP Beth Phoenix	2.50	6.00
DCCF Charlotte Flair	10.00	25.00
DCET Eve Torres	4.00	10.00
DCKK Kelly Kelly	5.00	12.00
DCMJ Mickie James	4.00	10.00
DCNB Nikki Bella	6.00	15.00

2017 Topps WWE Women's Division Finishers and Signature Moves

*SILVER/50: 1X TO 2.5X BASIC CARDS
*BLUE/25: 1.2X TO 3X BASIC CARDS
*GOLD/10: 2X TO 5X BASIC CARDS
*RED/1: UNPRICED DUE TO SCARCITY
STATED ODDS 5:1 HANGER BOX EXCLUSIVE

F1 Alexa Bliss	3.00	8.00
F2 Nikki Bella	1.50	4.00
F3 Bayley	2.00	5.00
F4 Natalya	1.25	3.00
F5 Brie Bella	1.50	4.00
F6 Sasha Banks	2.00	5.00
F7 Becky Lynch	2.00	5.00
F8 Beth Phoenix	.60	1.50
F9 Sasha Banks	2.00	5.00
F10 Charlotte Flair	2.50	6.00
F11 Eve Torres	1.00	2.50
F12 Mickie James	1.00	2.50
F13 Trish Stratus	2.50	6.00
F14 Naomi	1.25	3.00
F15 Alicia Fox	1.00	2.50
F16 Tamina	.75	2.00
F17 Dana Brooke	1.25	3.00
F18 Emma	1.50	4.00
F19 Carmella	1.50	4.00
F20 Summer Rae	1.50	4.00
F21 Nia Jax	1.00	2.50
F22 Stephanie McMahon	.75	2.00
F23 Kelly Kelly	1.25	3.00
F24 Charlotte Flair	2.50	6.00

2017 Topps WWE Women's Division Kiss

*GOLD/10: UNPRICED DUE TO SCARCITY
*RED/1: UNPRICED DUE TO SCARCITY
STATED ODDS 1:67 BLASTER BOX
STATED ODDS 1:1,503 HANGER BOX
STATED ODDS 1:2,997 HANGER PACK
STATED PRINT RUN 99 SER.#'d SETS

KAF Alicia Fox/99	15.00	40.00
KBK Billie Kay/99	25.00	60.00

KCA Carmella/99	25.00	60.00
KDB Dana Brooke/69	15.00	40.00
KNA Naomi/54	15.00	40.00
KPR Peyton Royce/99	20.00	50.00
KRY Renee Young/68	25.00	60.00

2017 Topps WWE Women's Division Kiss Autographs

*GOLD/10: UNPRICED DUE TO SCARCITY
*RED/1: UNPRICED DUE TO SCARCITY
STATED ODDS 1:211 BLASTER BOX
STATED ODDS 1:6,012 HANGER BOX
STATED ODDS 1:11,988 HANGER PACK
STATED PRINT RUN 25 SER.#'d SETS

KAF Alicia Fox		
KAS Asuka		
KBK Billie Kay	50.00	100.00
KCA Carmella	50.00	100.00
KDB Dana Brooke	30.00	75.00
KMR Mandy Rose	125.00	250.00
KPR Peyton Royce	125.00	250.00
KRY Renee Young	30.00	75.00

2017 Topps WWE Women's Division Mat Relics

*SILVER/50: .5X TO 1.2X BASIC MEM
*BLUE/25: .6X TO 1.5X BASIC MEM
*GOLD/10: UNPRICED DUE TO SCARCITY
*RED/1: UNPRICED DUE TO SCARCITY
STATED ODDS 1:10 BLASTER BOX
STATED ODDS 1:262 HANGER BOX
STATED ODDS 1:522 HANGER PACK
STATED PRINT RUN 199 SER.#'d SETS

MRAB Alexa Bliss	8.00	20.00
MRAF Alicia Fox	2.50	6.00
MRAL Alexa Bliss	8.00	20.00
MRAS Asuka	5.00	12.00
MRBA Bayley	5.00	12.00
MRBB Brie Bella	4.00	10.00
MRBL Becky Lynch	5.00	12.00
MRBR Brie Bella	4.00	10.00
MRCA Carmella	4.00	10.00
MRCF Charlotte Flair	6.00	15.00
MRDB Dana Brooke	3.00	8.00
MRLA Lana	5.00	12.00
MRNB Nikki Bella	4.00	10.00
MRNC Nikki Cross	3.00	8.00
MRNI Nikki Bella	4.00	10.00
MRNJ Nia Jax	2.50	6.00
MRSB Sasha Banks	5.00	12.00
MRSM Stephanie McMahon	2.00	5.00
MRSR Summer Rae	4.00	10.00
MRSU Summer Rae	4.00	10.00
MRTA Tamina	2.00	5.00
MRASA Asuka	5.00	12.00
MRASU Asuka	5.00	12.00
MRBAY Bayley	5.00	12.00
MRBEC Becky Lynch	5.00	12.00
MRBLY Bayley	5.00	12.00
MRBRI Brie Bella	4.00	10.00
MRCAR Carmella	4.00	10.00
MRCHA Charlotte Flair	6.00	15.00
MRCHF Charlotte Flair	6.00	15.00
MRCRM Carmella	4.00	10.00
MREMM Emma	4.00	10.00
MRLAA Lana	5.00	12.00
MRLAN Lana	5.00	12.00

MRNAO	Naomi	3.00	8.00
MRNAT	Natalya	3.00	8.00
MRNIA	Nia Jax	2.50	6.00
MRNIK	Nikki Cross	3.00	8.00
MRSAS	Sasha Banks	5.00	12.00
MRSTE	Stephanie McMahon	2.00	5.00
MRSUM	Summer Rae	4.00	10.00
MRTAM	Tamina	2.00	5.00
MRCHAR	Charlotte Flair	6.00	15.00
MREMMA	Emma	4.00	10.00

2017 Topps WWE Women's Division NXT Matches and Moments

*SILVER/50: 1.2X TO 3X BASIC CARDS
*BLUE/25: 2X TO 5X BASIC CARDS
*GOLD/10: UNPRICED DUE TO SCARCITY
*RED/1: UNPRICED DUE TO SCARCITY

NXT1	Emma	.75	2.00
NXT2	Billie Kay	.40	1.00
NXT3	Peyton Royce	.50	1.25
NXT4	Asuka	1.00	2.50
NXT5	Asuka	1.00	2.50
NXT6	Bayley	1.00	2.50
NXT7	Nia Jax	.50	1.25
NXT8	Bayley	1.50	4.00
NXT9	Bayley	1.00	2.50
NXT10	Carmella	1.00	2.50
NXT11	Bayley	1.00	2.50
NXT12	Bayley	1.00	2.50
NXT13	Asuka	1.00	2.50
NXT14	Asuka	1.00	2.50
NXT15	Nia Jax	.50	1.25
NXT16	Nia Jax	.50	1.25
NXT17	Asuka	1.00	2.50
NXT18	Bayley	1.00	2.50
NXT19	Mandy Rose	.40	1.00
NXT20	Ember Moon	.75	2.00
NXT21	Asuka	1.00	2.50
NXT22	Asuka	1.00	2.50
NXT23	Nikki Cross	.60	1.50
NXT24	Asuka	1.00	2.50
NXT25	Asuka	1.00	2.50
NXT26	Ember Moon	.75	2.00

2017 Topps WWE Women's Division Rivalries

*SILVER/50: 1.2X TO 3X BASIC CARDS
*BLUE/25: 2X TO 5X BASIC CARDS
*GOLD/10: UNPRICED DUE TO SCARCITY
*RED/1: UNPRICED DUE TO SCARCITY
STATED ODDS 3:1 HANGER PACK EXCLUSIVE

RV1	Charlotte Flair/Bayley	1.25	3.00
RV2	Charlotte Flair/Dana Brooke	1.25	3.00
RV3	Sasha Banks/Dana Brooke	1.00	2.50
RV4	Sasha Banks/Nia Jax	1.00	2.50
RV5	Bayley/Dana Brooke	1.00	2.50
RV6	Nikki Bella/Maryse	.75	2.00
RV7	Nikki Bella/Natalya	.75	2.00
RV8	Nikki Bella/Carmella	.75	2.00
RV9	Becky Lynch/Alexa Bliss	1.50	4.00
RV10	Becky Lynch/Mickie James	1.00	2.50
RV11	Alexa Bliss/Mickie James	1.50	4.00
RV12	Alexa Bliss/Naomi	1.50	4.00
RV13	Alexa Bliss/Bayley	1.50	4.00
RV14	Naomi/Charlotte Flair	1.25	3.00
RV15	Asuka/Ember Moon	1.00	2.50
RV16	Asuka/Peyton Royce	1.00	2.50
RV17	Asuka/Billie Kay	1.00	2.50
RV18	Asuka/Nikki Cross	1.00	2.50
RV19	Ruby Riot/Nikki Cross	.60	1.50
RV20	Wendi Richter/Leilani Kai	.40	1.00
RV21	Trish Stratus/Mickie James	1.25	3.00
RV22	Mickie James/Beth Phoenix	.50	1.25
RV23	Mickie James/Maryse	.60	1.50
RV24	Eve Torres/Maryse	.60	1.50
RV25	Eve Torres/Natalya	.60	1.50

2017 Topps WWE Women's Division Shirt Relics

*SILVER/50: .5X TO 1.2X BASIC MEM
*BLUE/25: .6X TO 1.5X BASIC MEM
*GOLD/10: UNPRICED DUE TO SCARCITY
*RED/1: UNPRICED DUE TO SCARCITY
STATED ODDS 1:12 BLASTER BOX
STATED ODDS 1:950 HANGER BOX
STATED ODDS 1:1,893 HANGER PACK
STATED PRINT RUN 199 SER.#'d SETS

SRAB	Alexa Bliss	15.00	40.00
SRAF	Alicia Fox	5.00	12.00
SRBA	Bayley	10.00	25.00
SRBL	Becky Lynch	10.00	25.00
SRCA	Carmella	8.00	20.00
SRCF	Charlotte Flair	12.00	30.00
SRJO	JoJo	5.00	12.00
SRNA	Naomi	6.00	15.00
SRNT	Natalya	6.00	15.00
SRRY	Renee Young	5.00	12.00
SRSB	Sasha Banks	10.00	25.00
SRSR	Summer Rae	8.00	20.00

2017 Topps WWE Women's Division Women's Championship Medallions

*SILVER/50: .5X TO 1.2X BASIC MEM
*BLUE/25: .6X TO 1.5X BASIC MEM
*GOLD/10: UNPRICED DUE TO SCARCITY
*RED/1: UNPRICED DUE TO SCARCITY
STATED ODDS 1:15 BLASTER BOX
STATED ODDS 1:1,203 HANGER BOX
STATED ODDS 1:2,398 HANGER PACK
STATED PRINT RUN 99 SER.#'d SETS

WCI	Ivory	2.50	6.00
WCAB	Alundra Blayze	3.00	8.00
WCBP	Beth Phoenix	2.50	6.00
WCLK	Leilani Kai	2.50	6.00
WCMJ	Mickie James	4.00	10.00
WCSM	Stephanie McMahon	3.00	8.00
WCSS	Sensational Sherri	3.00	8.00
WCTS	Trish Stratus	10.00	25.00
WCWR	Wendi Richter	3.00	8.00

2017 Topps WWE Women's Division WWE Matches and Moments

*SILVER/50: 1.2X TO 3X BASIC CARDS
*BLUE/25: 2X TO 5X BASIC CARDS
*GOLD/10: UNPRICED DUE TO SCARCITY
*RED/1: UNPRICED DUE TO SCARCITY

WWE1	Sasha Banks	1.00	2.50
WWE2	Charlotte	1.25	3.00
WWE3	Nikki Bella	.75	2.00
WWE4	Bayley	1.00	2.50
WWE5	Becky Lynch	1.00	2.50
WWE6	Alexa Bliss	1.50	4.00
WWE7	Charlott Flair	1.25	3.00
WWE8	Alexa Bliss	1.50	4.00
WWE9	Charlotte Flair	1.25	3.00
WWE10	Sasha Banks	1.00	2.50
WWE11	Nikki Bella	.75	2.00
WWE12	Charlotte Flair	1.25	3.00
WWE13	Team Raw	1.25	3.00
WWE14	Sasha Banks	1.00	2.50
WWE15	Nikki Bella	.75	2.00
WWE16	Alexa Bliss	1.50	4.00
WWE17	Charlotte Flair	1.25	3.00
WWE18	Charlotte Flair	1.25	3.00
WWE19	Bayley	1.00	2.50
WWE20	Natalya	.75	2.00
WWE21	La Luchadora	.50	1.25
WWE22	Bayley	1.00	2.50
WWE23	Alexa Bliss	1.50	4.00
WWE24	Mickie James	1.50	4.00

2018 Topps WWE Women's Division

UNOPENED BOX (24 PACKS)
UNOPENED PACK (7 CARDS)
*SILVER/50: .6X TO 1.5X BASIC CARDS
*BLUE/25: 1.2X TO 3X BASIC CARDS
*GOLD/10: UNPRICED DUE TO SCARCITY
*RED/1: UNPRICED DUE TO SCARCITY

1	Alexa Bliss	2.00	5.00
2	Alicia Fox	.60	1.50
3	Asuka	1.25	3.00
4	Bayley	.60	1.50
5	Becky Lynch	1.00	2.50
6	Brie Bella	.75	2.00
7	Carmella	.75	2.00
8	Cathy Kelley	.75	2.00
9	Charlotte Flair	1.25	3.00
10	Charly Caruso	.60	1.50
11	Dana Brooke	.75	2.00
12	Dasha Fuentes	.60	1.50
13	JoJo	.40	1.00
14	Lana	1.00	2.50
15	Liv Morgan	.75	2.00
16	Mandy Rose	1.00	2.50
17	Maria Kanellis	1.00	2.50
18	Maryse	.75	2.00
19	Mickie James	.75	2.00
20	Naomi	.50	1.25
21	Natalya	.50	1.25
22	Nia Jax	.60	1.50
23	Nikki Bella	.75	2.00
24	Renee Young	.60	1.50
25	Ronda Rousey	2.00	5.00
26	Ruby Riott	.60	1.50
27	Sarah Logan	.40	1.00
28	Sasha Banks	1.25	3.00
29	Sonya Deville	.75	2.00
30	Stephanie McMahon	.75	2.00
31	Tamina	.40	1.00
32	Aliyah	.60	1.50
33	Bianca Belair	.50	1.25
34	Billie Kay	.75	2.00
35	Candice LeRae	.50	1.25
36	Dakota Kai	.50	1.25
37	Ember Moon	.75	2.00
38	Kairi Sane	1.00	2.50
39	Kayla Braxton	.40	1.00
40	Lacey Evans	.50	1.25
41	Nikki Cross	.60	1.50
42	Peyton Royce	1.00	2.50
43	Shayna Baszler	1.00	2.50
44	Taynara Conti	.40	1.00
45	Vanessa Borne	.40	1.00
46	Zelina Vega	.40	1.00
47	Alundra Blayze	.40	1.00
48	Lita	1.00	2.50
49	Trish Stratus	1.50	4.00
50	Wendi Richter	.40	1.00

2018 Topps WWE Women's Division Autographed Kiss and Shirt Relic Booklets

STATED PRINT RUN 5 SER.#'d SETS
UNPRICED DUE TO SCARCITY

ASKAB	Alexa Bliss
ASKCF	Charlotte Flair
ASKCR	Carmella
ASKEM	Ember Moon

2018 Topps WWE Women's Division Autographed Mat Relics

STATED ODDS 1:1,866
STATED PRINT RUN 10 SER.#'d SETS
UNPRICED DUE TO SCARCITY

AMRAK	Asuka
AMRAS	Asuka
AMRBB	Brie Bella
AMRBL	Becky Lynch
AMRBP	Beth Phoenix
AMRBY	Bayley
AMRCR	Carmella
AMRDB	Dana Brooke
AMREB	Ember Moon
AMREM	Ember Moon
AMRKR	Kairi Sane
AMRKS	Kairi Sane
AMRLA	Lana
AMRLM	Liv Morgan
AMRLT	Lita
AMRMJ	Mickie James
AMRMR	Mandy Rose
AMRNA	Naomi
AMRNB	Nikki Bella
AMRNC	Nikki Cross
AMRNJ	Nia Jax
AMRNT	Natalya
AMRNY	Natalya
AMRPR	Peyton Royce
AMRRR	Ruby Riott
AMRSB	Sasha Banks
AMRSD	Sonya Deville
AMRSL	Sarah Logan
AMRTM	Tamina
AMRTS	Trish Stratus

2018 Topps WWE Women's Division Autographed Shirt Relics

STATED ODDS 1:4,547
STATED PRINT RUN 10 SER.#'d SETS
UNPRICED DUE TO SCARCITY

ASRAB	Alexa Bliss
ASRAF	Alicia Fox
ASRBL	Becky Lynch
ASRCF	Charlotte Flair
ASRCM	Carmella
ASREM	Ember Moon
ASRJO	JoJo
ASRNA	Naomi
ASRNC	Nikki Cross

ASRNT Natalya
ASRRY Renee Young
ASRSB Sasha Banks

2018 Topps WWE Women's Division Autographs

*GREEN/150: SAME VALUE AS BASIC AUTOS
*PURPLE/99: .5X TO 1.2X BASIC AUTOS
*BRONZE/75: .6X TO 1.5X BASIC AUTOS
*SILVER/50: .75X TO 2X BASIC AUTOS
*BLUE/25: 1X TO 2.5X BASIC AUTOS
*GOLD/10: UNPRICED DUE TO SCARCITY
*BLACK/5: UNPRICED DUE TO SCARCITY
*RED/1: UNPRICED DUE TO SCARCITY
*P.P.BLACK/1: UNPRICED DUE TO SCARCITY
*P.P.CYAN/1: UNPRICED DUE TO SCARCITY
*P.P.MAGENTA/1: UNPRICED DUE TO SCARCITY
*P.P.YELLOW/1: UNPRICED DUE TO SCARCITY
STATED ODDS 1:86
STATED PRINT RUN 199 SER.#'d SETS

1	Alexa Bliss	30.00	75.00
2	Alicia Fox	5.00	12.00
3	Asuka	12.00	30.00
4	Bayley	10.00	25.00
5	Becky Lynch	12.00	30.00
6	Brie Bella	10.00	25.00
7	Carmella	8.00	20.00
9	Charlotte Flair	15.00	40.00
11	Dana Brooke	6.00	15.00
12	Dasha Fuentes	5.00	12.00
14	Lana	6.00	15.00
15	Liv Morgan	15.00	40.00
16	Mandy Rose	12.00	30.00
19	Mickie James	10.00	25.00
20	Naomi	6.00	15.00
21	Natalya	8.00	20.00
22	Nia Jax	12.00	30.00
23	Nikki Bella	10.00	25.00
26	Ruby Riott	15.00	40.00
27	Sarah Logan	10.00	25.00
28	Sasha Banks	15.00	40.00
29	Sonya Deville	8.00	20.00
31	Tamina	5.00	12.00
32	Aliyah	6.00	15.00
33	Bianca Belair	15.00	40.00
34	Billie Kay	10.00	25.00
35	Candice LeRae	15.00	40.00
36	Dakota Kai	25.00	60.00
37	Ember Moon	10.00	25.00
38	Kairi Sane	15.00	40.00
40	Lacey Evans	12.00	30.00
42	Peyton Royce	15.00	40.00
43	Shayna Baszler	8.00	20.00
44	Taynara Conti	12.00	30.00
45	Vanessa Borne	8.00	20.00

2018 Topps WWE Women's Division Autographs Green

24	Renee Young	6.00	15.00

2018 Topps WWE Women's Division Commemorative Championship Relics

*PURPLE/99: SAME VALUE AS BASIC
*SILVER/50: .5X TO 1.2X BASIC MEM
*BLUE/25: .6X TO 1.5X BASIC MEM
*GOLD/10: UNPRICED DUE TO SCARCITY

*BLACK/5: UNPRICED DUE TO SCARCITY
*RED/1: UNPRICED DUE TO SCARCITY
STATED ODDS 1:183
STATED PRINT RUN 199 SER.#'d SETS

CCAB	Alundra Blayze	2.00	5.00
CCAL	Alexa Bliss	10.00	25.00
CCAS	Asuka	5.00	12.00
CCBL	Becky Lynch	8.00	20.00
CCBP	Beth Phoenix	2.50	6.00
CCBY	Bayley	2.50	6.00
CCCF	Charlotte Flair	6.00	15.00
CCCH	Charlotte Flair	6.00	15.00
CCET	Eve Torres	2.00	5.00
CCLT	Lita	4.00	10.00
CCMJ	Mickie James	5.00	12.00
CCMR	Maryse	2.00	5.00
CCNA	Naomi	2.50	6.00
CCNB	Nikki Bella	3.00	8.00
CCNT	Natalya	3.00	8.00
CCPG	Paige	10.00	25.00
CCSB	Sasha Banks	6.00	15.00
CCSS	Sensational Sherri	2.00	5.00
CCTS	Trish Stratus	4.00	10.00
CCWR	Wendi Richter	2.00	5.00

2018 Topps WWE Women's Division Kiss

*GOLD/10: UNPRICED DUE TO SCARCITY
*RED/1: UNPRICED DUE TO SCARCITY
STATED ODDS 1:1,797
STATED PRINT RUN 99 SER.#'d SETS

KCCF	Charlotte Flair	30.00	75.00
KCCR	Carmella	25.00	60.00
KCEM	Ember Moon	25.00	60.00
KCLM	Liv Morgan	20.00	50.00

2018 Topps WWE Women's Division Kiss Autographs

*GOLD/10: UNPRICED DUE TO SCARCITY
*RED/1: UNPRICED DUE TO SCARCITY
STATED ODDS 1:7,658
STATED PRINT RUN 25 SER.#'d SETS

AKCAB	Alexa Bliss	150.00	300.00
AKCCF	Charlotte Flair	200.00	400.00
AKCLM	Liv Morgan	60.00	120.00

2018 Topps WWE Women's Division Mat Relics

*GREEN/150: SAME AS BASIC MEM
*PURPLE/99: .5X TO 1.2X BASIC MEM
*BRONZE/75: .6X TO 1.5X BASIC MEM
*SILVER/50: .75X TO 2X BASIC MEM
*BLUE/25: 1X TO 2.5X BASIC MEM
*GOLD/10: UNPRICED DUE TO SCARCITY
*BLACK/5: UNPRICED DUE TO SCARCITY
*RED/1: UNPRICED DUE TO SCARCITY
STATED ODDS 1:123

AMRAK	Asuka	4.00	10.00
AMRAS	Asuka	4.00	10.00
AMRBB	Brie Bella	3.00	8.00
AMRBL	Becky Lynch	5.00	12.00
AMRBP	Beth Phoenix	3.00	8.00
AMRBY	Bayley	2.50	6.00
AMRCR	Carmella	4.00	10.00
AMRDB	Dana Brooke	2.50	6.00
AMREB	Ember Moon	5.00	12.00
AMREM	Ember Moon	5.00	12.00
AMRKR	Kairi Sane	5.00	12.00
AMRKS	Kairi Sane	5.00	12.00
AMRLA	Lana	5.00	12.00
AMRLM	Liv Morgan	4.00	10.00
AMRLT	Lita	3.00	8.00
AMRMJ	Mickie James	4.00	10.00
AMRMR	Mandy Rose	3.00	8.00
AMRNA	Naomi	2.00	5.00
AMRNB	Nikki Bella	5.00	12.00
AMRNC	Nikki Cross	2.00	5.00
AMRNJ	Nia Jax	2.00	5.00
AMRNT	Natalya	5.00	12.00
AMRNY	Natalya	5.00	12.00
AMRPR	Peyton Royce	3.00	8.00
AMRRR	Ruby Riott	4.00	10.00
AMRSB	Sasha Banks	6.00	15.00
AMRSD	Sonya Deville	3.00	8.00
AMRSL	Sarah Logan	3.00	8.00
AMRTM	Tamina	2.00	5.00
AMRTS	Trish Stratus	8.00	20.00

2018 Topps WWE Women's Division Matches and Moments

*SILVER/50: .6X TO 1.5X BASIC CARDS
*BLUE/25: 1.2X TO 3X BASIC CARDS
*GOLD/10: UNPRICED DUE TO SCARCITY
*RED/1: UNPRICED DUE TO SCARCITY

NXT1	Ember Moon	.75	2.00
NXT2	Asuka	1.25	3.00
NXT3	Asuka	1.25	3.00
NXT4	Ruby Riott	.60	1.50
NXT5	Asuka	1.25	3.00
NXT6	Asuka	1.25	3.00
NXT7	Asuka	1.25	3.00
NXT8	Sarah Logan	.40	1.00
NXT9	NXT Women's Triple Threat	1.25	3.00
NXT10	Asuka	1.25	3.00
NXT11	Bianca Belair	.50	1.25
NXT12	Vanessa Borne	.40	1.00
NXT13	Ember Moon	.75	2.00
NXT14	Asuka	1.25	3.00
NXT15	Shayna Baszler	1.00	2.50
NXT16	Dakota Kai	.50	1.25
NXT17	Bianca Belair	.50	1.25
NXT18	Candice LeRae	.50	1.25
NXT19	Lacey Evans	.50	1.25
NXT20	Kairi Sane	1.00	2.50
NXT21	Kairi Sane	1.00	2.50
NXT22	Shayna Baszler	1.00	2.50
NXT23	Dakota Kai	.50	1.25
NXT24	Candice LeRae	.50	1.25
NXT25	Shayna Baszler	1.00	2.50
NXT26	Kairi Sane	1.00	2.50
NXT27	Shayna Baszler	1.00	2.50
NXT28	Kairi Sane	1.00	2.50
NXT29	Asuka	1.25	3.00
NXT30	Kairi Sane	1.00	2.50
RAW1	Charlotte Flair	1.25	3.00
RAW2	Bayley	.60	1.50
RAW3	Sasha Banks	1.25	3.00
RAW4	Sasha Banks	1.25	3.00
RAW5	Bayley	.60	1.50
RAW6	Sasha Banks	1.25	3.00
RAW7	Nia Jax	.60	1.50
RAW8	Bayley & Sasha Banks	1.25	3.00
RAW9	Bayley	.60	1.50
RAW10	Alexa Bliss/Mickie James	2.00	5.00
SDL1	Becky Lynch	1.00	2.50
SDL2	Naomi	.50	1.25
SDL3	Naomi	.50	1.25
SDL4	Alexa Bliss	2.00	5.00
SDL5	Natalya	.50	1.25
SDL6	Mickie James	.75	2.00
SDL7	John Cena & Nikki Bella	1.50	4.00
SDL8	Naomi	.50	1.25
SDL9	Charlotte Flair	1.25	3.00
SDL10	Charlotte Flair	1.25	3.00

2018 Topps WWE Women's Division Mixed Match Challenge

COMPLETE SET (24)		8.00	20.00

*SILVER/50: .6X TO 1.5X BASIC CARDS
*BLUE/25: .75X TO 2X BASIC CARDS
*GOLD/10: UNPRICED DUE TO SCARCITY
*RED/1: UNPRICED DUE TO SCARCITY
RANDOMLY INSERTED INTO PACKS

MM1	Bliss/Strowman	1.50	4.00
MM2	Banks/Balor	1.00	2.50
MM3	Jax/Crews	.50	1.25
MM4	Miz/Asuka	1.00	2.50
MM5	Rose/Goldust	.75	2.00
MM6	Bayley/Elias	.75	2.00
MM7	Roode/Flair	1.00	2.50
MM8	Lana/Rusev	.75	2.00
MM9	Natalya/Nakamura	.75	2.00
MM10	Jimmy Uso/Naomi	.40	1.00
MM11	Zayn/Lynch	.75	2.00
MM12	Big E/Carmella	.60	1.50
MM13	The Boss Club	1.00	2.50
MM14	Team Awe-ska	1.00	2.50
MM15	Team Little Big	1.50	4.00
MM16	Glowish	.30	.75
MM17	Ravishing Rusev Day!	.50	1.25
MM18	The Robe Warriors	.50	1.25
MM19	Team Awe-ska	1.00	2.50
MM20	Team Little Big	.75	2.00
MM21	The Robe Warriors	1.00	2.50
MM22	Team Awe-ska	1.00	2.50
MM23	Roode & Lynch	.75	2.00
MM24	Team Awe-ska	1.00	2.50

2018 Topps WWE Women's Division Power Couples

*SILVER/50: .5X TO 1.2X BASIC CARDS
*BLUE/25: .6X TO 1.5X BASIC CARDS
*GOLD/10: UNPRICED DUE TO SCARCITY
*RED/1: UNPRICED DUE TO SCARCITY
RANDOMLY INSERTED INTO PACKS

PC1	Brie Bella/Daniel Bryan	1.50	4.00
PC2	Stephanie McMahon/Triple H	1.50	4.00
PC3	Maryse/The Miz	1.25	3.00
PC4	Renee Young/Dean Ambrose	1.25	3.00
PC5	Naomi/Jimmy Uso	.75	2.00
PC6	Lana/Rusev	1.50	4.00
PC7	Maria Kanellis/Mike Kanellis	1.50	4.00
PC8	Candice LeRae/Johnny Gargano	.75	2.00
PC9	Beth Phoenix/Edge	1.50	4.00
PC10	Alicia Fox/Noam Dar	1.00	2.50
PC11	Alicia Fox/Cedric Alexander	1.00	2.50
PC12	Lana/Dolph Ziggler	1.50	4.00
PC13	Eve Torres/Zack Ryder	1.25	3.00
PC14	Maria Kanellis/Dolph Ziggler	1.50	4.00
PC15	Stephanie McMahon/Kurt Angle	1.50	4.00
PC16	Trish Stratus/Chris Jericho	2.50	6.00
PC17	Trish Stratus/Jeff Hardy	2.50	6.00

2018 Topps WWE Women's Division

PC18	Marlena/Goldust	1.25	3.00
PC19	Miss Elizabeth/Randy Savage	2.00	5.00
PC20	Queen Sherri/Randy Savage	2.00	5.00
PC21	Sherri/Shawn Michaels	2.00	5.00
PC22	Lita/Kane	1.50	4.00

2018 Topps WWE Women's Division Shirt Relics

*PURPLE/99: .5X TO 1.2X BASIC MEM
*SILVER/50: .6X TO 1.5X BASIC MEM
*BLUE/25: .75X TO 2X BASIC MEM
*GOLD/10: UNPRICED DUE TO SCARCITY
*BLACK/5: UNPRICED DUE TO SCARCITY
*RED/1: UNPRICED DUE TO SCARCITY
STATED ODDS 1:516

ASRAB	Alexa Bliss	15.00	40.00
ASRAF	Alicia Fox	5.00	12.00
ASRBL	Becky Lynch	8.00	20.00
ASRCF	Charlotte Flair	10.00	25.00
ASRCM	Carmella	6.00	15.00
ASREM	Ember Moon	6.00	15.00
ASRJO	JoJo	5.00	10.00
ASRNA	Naomi	5.00	12.00
ASRNC	Nikki Cross	4.00	10.00
ASRNT	Natalya	6.00	15.00
ASRRY	Renee Young	5.00	12.00
ASRSB	Sasha Banks	8.00	20.00

2018 Topps WWE Women's Division Women's Champion

COMPLETE SET (25) 10.00 25.00
RANDOMLY INSERTED INTO PACKS

WC1	Maryse	.75	2.00
WC2	Mickie James	.75	2.00
WC3	Eve Torres	.75	2.00
WC4	Alicia Fox	.60	1.50
WC5	Natalya	.50	1.25
WC6	Brie Bella	.75	2.00
WC7	Beth Phoenix	.75	2.00
WC8	Nikki Bella	.75	2.00
WC9	Paige	1.00	2.50
WC10	Charlotte Flair	1.25	3.00
WC11	Paige	1.00	2.50
WC12	Charlotte Flair	1.25	3.00
WC13	Sasha Banks	1.25	3.00
WC14	Bayley	.60	1.50
WC15	Asuka	1.25	3.00
WC16	Ember Moon	.75	2.00
WC17	Charlotte Flair	1.25	3.00
WC18	Sasha Banks	1.25	3.00
WC19	Bayley	.60	1.50
WC20	Alexa Bliss	2.00	5.00
WC21	Becky Lynch	1.00	2.50
WC22	Alexa Bliss	2.00	5.00
WC23	Naomi	.50	1.25
WC24	Natalya	.50	1.25
WC25	Charlotte Flair	1.25	3.00

2018 Topps WWE Women's Division Women's Royal Rumble

COMPLETE SET (24) 12.00 30.00
*SILVER/50: .5X TO 1.5X BASIC CARDS
*BLUE/25: 1.2X TO 3X BASIC CARDS
*GOLD/10: UNPRICED DUE TO SCARCITY
*RED/1: UNPRICED DUE TO SCARCITY
STATED ODDS 1:2

RR1	Sasha Banks	2.00	5.00
RR2	Becky Lynch	1.50	4.00
RR3	Sarah Logan	.60	1.50
RR4	Mandy Rose	1.50	4.00
RR5	Lita	1.50	4.00
RR6	Kairi Sane	1.50	4.00
RR7	Tamina	.60	1.50
RR8	Dana Brooke	1.25	3.00
RR9	Sonya Deville	1.25	3.00
RR10	Liv Morgan	1.25	3.00
RR11	Lana	1.50	4.00
RR12	Ruby Riott	1.00	2.50
RR13	Carmella	1.25	3.00
RR14	Natalya	.75	2.00
RR15	Naomi	.75	2.00
RR16	Nia Jax	1.00	2.50
RR17	Ember Moon	1.25	3.00
RR18	Beth Phoenix	1.25	3.00
RR19	Asuka	2.00	5.00
RR20	Mickie James	1.25	3.00
RR21	Nikki Bella	1.25	3.00
RR22	Brie Bella	1.25	3.00
RR23	Bayley	1.00	2.50
RR24	Trish Stratus	2.50	6.00

2019 Topps WWE Women's Division

COMPLETE SET (100) 8.00 20.00
*PURPLE/99: .6X TO 1.5X BASIC CARDS
*BRONZE/75: .75X TO 2X BASIC CARDS
*ORANGE/50: 1X TO 2.5X BASIC CARDS
*BLUE/25: 1.5X TO 4X BASIC CARDS
*GOLD/10: UNPRICED DUE TO SCARCITY
*RED/1: UNPRICED DUE TO SCARCITY
*P.P.BLACK/1: UNPRICED DUE TO SCARCITY
*P.P.CYAN/1: UNPRICED DUE TO SCARCITY
*P.P.MAGENTA/1: UNPRICED DUE TO SCARCITY
*P.P.YELLOW/1: UNPRICED DUE TO SCARCITY

1	Alexa Bliss	1.25	3.00
2	Alicia Fox	.50	1.25
3	Bayley	.50	1.25
4	Dana Brooke	.50	1.25
5	Ember Moon	.60	1.50
6	Lacey Evans	.50	1.25
7	Liv Morgan	.75	2.00
8	Mickie James	.60	1.50
9	Natalya	.50	1.25
10	Nia Jax	.50	1.25
11	Ronda Rousey	1.25	3.00
12	Ruby Riott	.50	1.25
13	Sarah Logan	.30	.75
14	Sasha Banks	1.00	2.50
15	Tamina	.25	.60
16	Renee Young	.40	1.00
17	Stephanie McMahon	.60	1.50
18	Maria Kanellis	.60	1.50
19	Asuka	.75	2.00
20	Becky Lynch	1.00	2.50
21	Billie Kay	.50	1.25
22	Carmella	.60	1.50
23	Mandy Rose	.60	1.50
24	Maryse	.30	.75
25	Naomi	.40	1.00
26	Nikki Cross	.40	1.00
27	Peyton Royce	.60	1.50
28	Sonya Deville	.50	1.25
29	Zelina Vega	.40	1.00
30	Paige	1.00	2.50
31	Aliyah	.25	.60
32	Bianca Belair	.25	.60
33	Candice LeRae	.50	1.25
34	Chelsea Green	.25	.60
35	Dakota Kai	.50	1.25
36	Deonna Purrazzo	.25	.60
37	Io Shirai	.25	.60
38	Jessamyn Duke	.30	.75
39	Jessi Kamea	.25	.60
40	Kacy Catanzaro	.60	1.50
41	Kairi Sane	.50	1.25
42	Lacey Lane	.25	.60
43	Marina Shafir	.25	.60
44	Mia Yim	.25	.60
45	MJ Jenkins	.25	.60
46	Shayna Baszler	.50	1.25
47	Taynara Conti	.30	.75
48	Vanessa Borne	.30	.75
49	Xia Li	.25	.60
50	Toni Storm	1.00	2.50
51	Nina Samuels	.30	.75
52	Alundra Blayze	.30	.75
53	Beth Phoenix	.40	1.00
54	Eve Torres	.30	.75
55	Marlena	.25	.60
56	Lita	.60	1.50
57	Sherri Martel	.40	1.00
58	Miss Elizabeth	.50	1.25
59	Trish Stratus	1.25	3.00
60	Wendi Richter	.25	.60
61	Asuka	.75	2.00
62	Ember Moon	.60	1.50
63	Asuka	.75	2.00
64	Asuka	.75	2.00
65	Alexa Bliss	1.25	3.00
66	Shayna Baszler	.50	1.25
67	Naomi	.40	1.00
68	Nia Jax	1.25	3.00
69	Ronda Rousey	1.25	3.00
70	Candice LeRae	.50	1.25
71	Carmella	.60	1.50
72	Asuka	.75	2.00
73	Shayna Baszler	.50	1.25
74	Kairi Sane	.50	1.25
75	Shayna Baszler	.50	1.25
76	Bayley	.50	1.25
77	Alexa Bliss	1.25	3.00
78	Carmella	.75	2.00
79	Alexa Bliss	1.25	3.00
80	Sasha Banks & Bayley	1.00	2.50
81	Kairi Sane	.50	1.25
82	Ronda Rousey	1.25	3.00
83	Asuka	.75	2.00
84	Ronda Rousey	1.25	3.00
85	Iiconics	.60	1.50
86	Io Shirai	.25	.60
87	Becky Lynch	1.00	2.50
88	Bianca Belair	.25	.60
89	Shayna Baszler	.50	1.25
90	Team RAW/Team SmackDown	.75	2.00
91	Nikki Cross	.40	1.00
92	Mia Yim	.25	.60
93	Io Shirai	.50	1.25
94	Natalya	.50	1.25
95	Ronda Rousey	1.25	3.00
96	Asuka	.75	2.00
97	Natalya	.50	1.25
98	Asuka	.75	2.00
99	Bayley/Sasha Banks/Ember Moon	.60	1.50
100	Bianca Belair	.25	.60

2019 Topps WWE Women's Division Autographed Mat Relics

*RED/1: UNPRICED DUE TO SCARCITY
STATED PRINT RUN 10 SER.#'d SETS
UNPRICED DUE TO SCARCITY

MRAAS	Asuka
MRABL	Becky Lynch
MRABY	Bayley
MRACA	Carmella
MRAIS	Io Shirai
MRAKS	Kairi Sane
MRANA	Natalya
MRANM	Naomi
MRAQA	Shayna Baszler
MRASD	Sonya Deville
MRATA	Tamina

2019 Topps WWE Women's Division Autographed Shirt Relics

*RED/1: UNPRICED DUE TO SCARCITY
STATED PRINT RUN 10 SER.#'d SETS
UNPRICED DUE TO SCARCITY

SRAAB	Alexa Bliss
SRACM	Carmella
SRALE	Lacey Evans
SRANM	Naomi
SRANT	Natalya
SRAQA	Shayna Baszler
SRARY	Renee Young
SRATM	Tamina

2019 Topps WWE Women's Division Autographs

*GREEN/150: SAME VALUE AS BASIC
*PURPLE/99: .5X TO 1.2X BASIC AUTOS
*BRONZE/75: .5X TO 1.2X BASIC AUTOS
*ORANGE/50: .6X TO 1.5X BASIC AUTOS
*BLUE/25: UNPRICED DUE TO SCARCITY
*GOLD/10: UNPRICED DUE TO SCARCITY
*BLACK/5: UNPRICED DUE TO SCARCITY
*RED/1: UNPRICED DUE TO SCARCITY
*P.P.BLACK/1: UNPRICED DUE TO SCARCITY
*P.P.CYAN/1: UNPRICED DUE TO SCARCITY
*P.P.MAGENTA/1: UNPRICED DUE TO SCARCITY
*P.P.YELLOW/1: UNPRICED DUE TO SCARCITY
RANDOMLY INSERTED INTO PACKS

AAB	Alexa Bliss	30.00	75.00
ABE	Bayley	12.00	30.00
ABK	Billie Kay	10.00	25.00
ABZ	Shayna Baszler	8.00	20.00
ACG	Chelsea Green	20.00	50.00
ACL	Candice LeRae	10.00	25.00
ACM	Carmella	12.00	30.00
ADB	Dana Brooke	6.00	15.00
ADK	Dakota Kai	10.00	25.00
ADP	Deonna Purrazzo	6.00	15.00
AEM	Ember Moon	8.00	20.00
AIS	Io Shirai	30.00	75.00
AJD	Jessamyn Duke	10.00	25.00
AJE	Jessi Kamea	8.00	20.00
AKC	Kacy Catanzaro	15.00	40.00
ALE	Lacey Evans	10.00	25.00
AMR	Mandy Rose	15.00	40.00
AMS	Marina Shafir	8.00	20.00
AMY	Mia Yim	12.00	30.00
ANC	Nikki Cross	8.00	20.00
ANT	Natalya	6.00	15.00

APR	Peyton Royce	10.00	25.00
ARY	Renee Young	6.00	15.00
ASD	Sonya Deville	10.00	25.00
ATC	Taynara Conti	6.00	15.00
ATM	Tamina	6.00	15.00
AVB	Vanessa Borne	6.00	15.00
AEST	Bianca Belair	10.00	25.00

2019 Topps WWE Women's Division
Championship Side Plate
Commemorative Patches

*PURPLE/99: .5X TO 1.2X BASIC MEM
*ORANGE/50: .6X TO 1.5X BASIC MEM
*BLUE/25: .75X TO 2X BASIC MEM
*GOLD/10: UNPRICED DUE TO SCARCITY
*RED/1: UNPRICED DUE TO SCARCITY
STATED PRINT RUN 199 SER.#'d SETS

PCAB	Alexa Bliss	15.00	40.00
PCAK	Asuka	8.00	20.00
PCBL	Becky Lynch	10.00	25.00
PCBY	Bayley	8.00	20.00
PCCM	Carmella	6.00	15.00
PCEM	Ember Moon	5.00	12.00
PCKS	Kairi Sane	12.00	30.00
PCNJ	Nia Jax	5.00	12.00
PCNM	Naomi	4.00	10.00
PCNT	Natalya	4.00	10.00
PCQA	Shayna Baszler	5.00	12.00
PCRR	Ronda Rousey	12.00	30.00
PCSB	Sasha Banks	8.00	20.00

2019 Topps WWE Women's Division
Dual Autographs

*GOLD/10: UNPRICED DUE TO SCARCITY
*BLACK/5: UNPRICED DUE TO SCARCITY
*RED/1: UNPRICED DUE TO SCARCITY
RANDOMLY INSERTED INTO PACKS
STATED PRINT RUN 25 SER.#'d SETS

DABC	A.Bliss/N.Cross	200.00	300.00
DADD	B.Phoenix/Natalya	60.00	120.00
DAII	B.Kay/P/Royce	125.00	250.00

2019 Topps WWE Women's Division
Mat Relics

*GREEN/150: SAME VALUE AS BASIC
*PURPLE/99: .5X TO 1.2X BASIC MEM
*BRONZE/75: .6X TO 1.5X BASIC MEM
*ORANGE/50: .75X TO 2X BASIC MEM
*BLUE/25: 1.2X TO 3X BASIC MEM
*GOLD/10: UNPRICED DUE TO SCARCITY
*BLACK/5: UNPRICED DUE TO SCARCITY
*RED/1: UNPRICED DUE TO SCARCITY
RANDOMLY INSERTED INTO PACKS
STATED PRINT RUN 199 SER.#'d SETS

MRAB	Alexa Bliss	10.00	25.00
MRAF	Alicia Fox	3.00	8.00
MRAK	Asuka	5.00	12.00
MRAS	Asuka	4.00	10.00
MRBE	Becky Lynch	10.00	25.00
MRBK	Billie Kay	4.00	10.00
MRBL	Becky Lynch	10.00	25.00
MRBP	Beth Phoenix	3.00	8.00
MRBY	Bayley	2.50	6.00
MRCA	Carmella	3.00	8.00
MRCH	Charlotte Flair	4.00	10.00
MRCM	Carmella	3.00	8.00
MREM	Ember Moon	4.00	10.00

MRIS	Io Shirai	6.00	15.00
MRJJ	JoJo	2.50	6.00
MRKS	Kairi Sane	5.00	12.00
MRLI	Liv Morgan	6.00	15.00
MRLM	Liv Morgan	5.00	12.00
MRLT	Lita	3.00	8.00
MRMD	Alundra Blayze	2.50	6.00
MRMJ	Mickie James	2.50	6.00
MRNA	Natalya	2.50	6.00
MRNI	Nia Jax	3.00	8.00
MRNJ	Nia Jax	3.00	8.00
MRNM	Naomi	2.50	6.00
MRNT	Natalya	2.50	6.00
MRQA	Shayna Baszler	2.50	6.00
MRRB	Ruby Riott	3.00	8.00
MRRO	Ronda Rousey	10.00	25.00
MRRR	Ronda Rousey	10.00	25.00
MRRU	Ruby Riott	3.00	8.00
MRRY	Renee Young	3.00	8.00
MRSA	Sarah Logan	2.50	6.00
MRSB	Sasha Banks	6.00	15.00
MRSD	Sonya Deville	5.00	12.00
MRSF	Trish Stratus	4.00	10.00
MRSL	Sarah Logan	2.50	6.00
MRTA	Tamina	2.50	6.00
MRTM	Tamina	2.50	6.00
MRTS	Toni Storm	8.00	20.00

2019 Topps WWE Women's Division
Mixed Match Challenge Season 2

COMPLETE SET (25) 8.00 20.00
*ORANGE/50: 1.2X TO 3X BASIC CARDS
*BLUE/25: 2X TO 5X BASIC CARDS
*GOLD/10: UNPRICED DUE TO SCARCITY
*RED/1: UNPRICED DUE TO SCARCITY
RANDOMLY INSERTED INTO PACKS

MMC1	Monster Eclipse	.60	1.50
MMC2	Country Dominance	.60	1.50
MMC3	B'N'B	.60	1.50
MMC4	Mahalicia	.50	1.25
MMC5	Team Pawz	.50	1.25
MMC6	Awe-ska	.75	2.00
MMC7	Day One Glow	.40	1.00
MMC8	Ravishing Rusev Day	.50	1.25
MMC9	Fabulous Truth	.60	1.50
MMC10	Monster Eclipse	.60	1.50
MMC11	Country Dominance	.60	1.50
MMC12	Awe-ska	.75	2.00
MMC13	B'N'B	.60	1.50
MMC14	Robert Roode/Team Pawz	.50	1.25
MMC15	Awe-ska	.75	2.00
MMC16	Monster Eclipse	.60	1.50
MMC17	Fabulous Truth	.60	1.50
MMC18	Curt Hawkins/Monster Eclipse	.60	1.50
MMC19	Mahalicia	.50	1.25
MMC20	B'N'B	.60	1.50
MMC21	Awe-ska	.75	2.00
MMC22	Apollo Crews/B'N'B	.50	1.25
MMC23	Mahalicia	.50	1.25
MMC24	Fabulous Truth	.60	1.50
MMC25	Fabulous Truth Win	.60	1.50

2019 Topps WWE Women's Division
Shirt Relics

*PURPLE/99: .5X TO 1.2X BASIC CARDS
*ORANGE/50: .6X TO 1.5X BASIC CARDS
*BLUE/25: .75X TO 2X BASIC CARDS
*GOLD/10: UNPRICED DUE TO SCARCITY

	*RED/1: UNPRICED DUE TO SCARCITY		
	STATED PRINT RUN 199 SER.#'d SETS		
SRAB	Alexa Bliss	12.00	30.00
SRAF	Alicia Fox	5.00	12.00
SRAS	Asuka	6.00	15.00
SRCM	Carmella	5.00	12.00
SRJJ	JoJo	4.00	10.00
SRLE	Lacey Evans	5.00	12.00
SRNM	Naomi	4.00	10.00
SRNT	Natalya	4.00	10.00
SRQA	Shayna Baszler	4.00	10.00
SRSB	Sasha Banks		

2019 Topps WWE Women's Division
Team Bestie

COMPLETE SET (20) 8.00 20.00
*ORANGE/50: 1.5X TO 4X BASIC CARDS
*BLUE/25: 2.5X TO 6X BASIC CARDS
*GOLD/10: UNPRICED DUE TO SCARCITY
*RED/1: UNPRICED DUE TO SCARCITY
RANDOMLY INSERTED INTO PACKS

TB1	Trish Stratus	.75	2.00
TB2	Trish Stratus	.75	2.00
TB3	Trish Stratus	.75	2.00
TB4	Trish Stratus	.75	2.00
TB5	Team Bestie	1.00	2.50
TB6	Trish Stratus	.75	2.00
TB7	Trish Stratus	.75	2.00
TB8	Trish Stratus	.75	2.00
TB9	Trish Stratus	1.25	3.00
TB10	Trish Stratus	.75	2.00
TB11	Lita	.60	1.50
TB12	Lita/The Rock	1.00	2.50
TB13	Lita	.60	1.50
TB14	Team Bestie	.75	2.00
TB15	Lita	.60	1.50
TB16	Lita	.60	1.50
TB17	Lita	.60	1.50
TB18	Lita	.60	1.50
TB19	Lita	.60	1.50
TB20	Lita	.60	1.50

2019 Topps WWE Women's Division
Triple Autographs

STATED PRINT RUN 10 SER.#'d SETS
UNPRICED DUE TO SCARCITY

TA4H	Shafir/Duke/Baszler	

2019 Topps WWE Women's Division
Women's Evolution

COMPLETE SET (10) 8.00 20.00
*ORANGE/50: 1.2X TO 1.5X BASIC CARDS
*BLUE/25: 2X TO 3X BASIC CARDS
*GOLD/10: UNPRICED DUE TO SCARCITY
*RED/1: UNPRICED DUE TO SCARCITY

WE1	Lita	1.50	4.00
WE2	Alundra Blayze	.75	2.00
WE3	Nia Jax/Tamina	.60	1.50
WE4	Carmella	1.50	4.00
WE5	Mandy Rose	1.50	4.00
WE6	Toni Storm	2.50	6.00
WE7	Sasha/Bayley/Natalya	2.50	6.00
WE8	Jessamyn Duke/Marina Shafir	.75	2.00
WE9	Becky Lynch	2.50	6.00
WE10	Women's Division	3.00	8.00

2019 Topps WWE Women's Division
Women's Royal Rumble

COMPLETE SET (25) 12.00 30.00
*ORANGE/50: 2X TO 5X BASIC CARDS
*BLUE/25: 3X TO 8X BASIC CARDS
*GOLD/10: UNPRICED DUE TO SCARCITY
*RED/1: UNPRICED DUE TO SCARCITY
RANDOMLY INSERTED INTO PACKS

RR1	Lacey Evans	1.00	2.50
RR2	Natalya	1.00	2.50
RR3	Mandy Rose	1.25	3.00
RR4	Mickie James	1.25	3.00
RR5	Ember Moon	1.25	3.00
RR6	Billie Kay	1.00	2.50
RR7	Nikki Cross	.75	2.00
RR8	Peyton Royce	1.25	3.00
RR9	Tamina	.50	1.25
RR10	Kairi Sane	1.00	2.50
RR11	Naomi	.75	2.00
RR12	Candice LeRae	1.00	2.50
RR13	Alicia Fox	1.00	2.50
RR14	Kacy Catanzaro	1.25	3.00
RR15	Zelina Vega	.75	2.00
RR16	Ruby Riott	1.00	2.50
RR17	Io Shirai	.50	1.25
RR18	Sonya Deville	1.00	2.50
RR19	Alexa Bliss	2.50	6.00
RR20	Bayley	1.00	2.50
RR21	Becky Lynch	2.00	5.00
RR22	Nia Jax	1.00	2.50
RR23	Carmella	1.25	3.00
RR24	Maria Kanellis	1.25	3.00
RR25	Xia Li	.50	1.25

2020 Topps WWE Women's Division

COMPLETE SET (100) 15.00 40.00
*PURPLE/99: .6X TO 1.5X BASIC CARDS
*GREEN/75: .75X TO 2X BASIC CARDS
*ORANGE/50: 1X TO 2.5X BASIC CARDS
*BLUE/25: UNPRICED DUE TO SCARCITY
*GOLD/10: UNPRICED DUE TO SCARCITY
*BLACK/5: UNPRICED DUE TO SCARCITY
*RED/1: UNPRICED DUE TO SCARCITY
*P.P.BLACK/1: UNPRICED DUE TO SCARCITY
*P.P.CYAN/1: UNPRICED DUE TO SCARCITY
*P.P.MAGENTA/1: UNPRICED DUE TO SCARCITY
*P.P.YELLOW/1: UNPRICED DUE TO SCARCITY

1	Becky Lynch	1.00	2.50
2	Toni Storm	.60	1.50
3	Nikki Cross	.50	1.25
4	Becky Lynch	1.00	2.50
5	Asuka	1.00	2.50
6	Shayna Baszler	.75	2.00
7	Ronda Rousey	1.25	3.00
8	Asuka	1.00	2.50
9	Lacey Evans	.60	1.50
10	Becky Lynch	1.00	2.50
11	Boss 'n' Hug Connection	1.25	3.00
12	Ronda Rousey	1.25	3.00
13	Mandy Rose	1.25	3.00
14	Shayna Baszler	.75	2.00
15	Asuka	1.00	2.50
16	Becky Lynch	1.00	2.50
17	Boss 'n' Hug Connection	1.25	3.00
18	Iiconics	.50	1.25
19	Charlotte Flair	1.00	2.50
20	Shayna Baszler	.75	2.00

#	Card		
21	Iiconics	.50	1.25
22	Becky Lynch	1.25	3.00
23	Lacey Evans	.60	1.50
24	Kairi Sane	.50	1.25
25	Shayna Baszler	.75	2.00
26	Charlotte Flair	1.00	2.50
27	Toni Storm	.60	1.50
28	Kabuki Warriors	.50	1.25
29	Bayley	.50	1.25
30	Becky Lynch	1.00	2.50
31	Charlotte Flair	1.00	2.50
32	Bayley	.50	1.25
33	Shayna Baszler	.75	2.00
34	Alexa Bliss	1.50	4.00
35	Kay Lee Ray	.40	1.00
36	Bayley	.50	1.25
37	Becky Lynch	1.00	2.50
38	Baron Corbin & Lacey Evans	.60	1.50
39	Nikki Cross	.50	1.25
40	Shayna Baszler	.75	2.00
41	Io Shirai	.75	2.00
42	Nikki Cross	1.50	4.00
43	Mia Yim	.50	1.25
44	Nikki Cross	.50	1.25
45	Seth Rollins & Becky Lynch	1.00	2.50
46	Io Shirai	.40	1.00
47	Bayley	.50	1.25
48	Seth Rollins & Becky Lynch	1.00	2.50
49	Natalya	.40	1.00
50	Bayley & Ember Moon	.50	1.25
51	Iiconics	.50	1.25
52	Ember Moon	.50	1.25
53	Candice LeRae	.75	2.00
54	Natalya	1.00	2.50
55	Alexa Bliss & Nikki Cross	1.50	4.00
56	Charlotte Flair	1.25	3.00
57	Shayna Baszler	.75	2.00
58	Becky Lynch & Charlotte Flair	1.00	2.50
59	Alexa Bliss & Nikki Cross	1.50	4.00
60	Io Shirai	.40	1.00
61	Shayna Baszler	.75	2.00
62	Alexa Bliss & Nikki Cross	1.50	4.00
63	Becky Lynch	1.00	2.50
64	Bayley	.50	1.25
65	Charlotte Flair	1.25	3.00
66	Alexa Bliss & Nikki Cross	1.50	4.00
67	Sasha Banks	1.25	3.00
68	Charlotte Flair	1.00	2.50
69	Alexa Bliss & Nikki Cross	1.50	4.00
70	Charlotte Flair	1.50	4.00
71	Mia Yim	.50	1.25
72	Sasha Banks	1.25	3.00
73	Rhea Ripley	1.00	2.50
74	Kay Lee Ray	.40	1.00
75	Sasha Banks	1.25	3.00
76	Bayley	.50	1.25
77	Bayley & Sasha Banks	1.25	3.00
78	Fire & Desire	1.25	3.00
79	Becky Lynch & Charlotte Flair	1.00	2.50
80	Nikki Cross	1.50	4.00
81	Shayna Baszler	1.00	2.50
82	Alexa Bliss & Nikki Cross	1.50	4.00
83	Bayley	.50	1.25
84	Sasha Banks	1.25	3.00
85	Becky Lynch & Charlotte Flair	1.00	2.50
86	Candice LeRae	.75	2.00
87	Kabuki Warriors	1.00	2.50
88	Dakota Kai	.50	1.25
89	Shayna Baszler	.75	2.00
90	Charlotte Flair	1.00	2.50
91	Kabuki Warriors	1.00	2.50
92	Becky Lynch	1.00	2.50
93	Kabuki Warriors	1.00	2.50
94	Bayley	1.00	2.50
95	Tegan Nox	.60	1.50
96	Nikki Cross	.50	1.25
97	Rhea Ripley	1.00	2.50
98	Dakota Kai & Tegan Nox	.60	1.50
99	Kabuki Warriors	.60	1.50
100	Kabuki Warriors	1.00	2.50

2020 Topps WWE Women's Division Autographed Championship Plate Patches

*RED/1: UNPRICED DUE TO SCARCITY
STATED PRINT RUN 10 SER.#'d SETS
UNPRICED DUE TO SCARCITY

CPAB	Alexa Bliss		
CPAS	Asuka		
CPCM	Carmella		
CPKS	Kairi Sane		
CPNJ	Nia Jax		
CPNM	Naomi		
CPNT	Natalya		
CPQU	Charlotte Flair		
CPSB	Sasha Banks		
CPSP	Shayna Baszler		
CPALX	Alexa Bliss		
CPBAY	Bayley		
CPRIP	Rhea Ripley		

2020 Topps WWE Women's Division Autographed Mat Relics

*RED/1: UNPRICED DUE TO SCARCITY
STATED PRINT RUN 10 SER.#'d SETS
UNPRICED DUE TO SCARCITY

MRABA	Bayley		
MRABB	Bianca Belair		
MRABP	Beth Phoenix		
MRACG	Chelsea Green		
MRACL	Candice LeRae		
MRADB	Dana Brooke		
MRADK	Dakota Kai		
MRAKS	Kairi Sane		
MRALE	Lacey Evans		
MRALM	Liv Morgan		
MRAMM	Mercedes Martinez		
MRAMR	Mandy Rose		
MRAMY	Mia Yim		
MRANM	Naomi		
MRAZI	Shotzi Blackheart		
MRAZV	Zelina Vega		

2020 Topps WWE Women's Division Autographs

*PINK/150: SAME PRICE AS BASIC
*PURPLE/99: .5X TO 1.2X BASIC AUTO
*GREEN/75: .6X TO 1.5X BASIC AUTO
*ORANGE/50: .75X TO 2X BASIC AUTO
*BLUE/25: UNPRICED DUE TO SCARCITY
*GOLD/10: UNPRICED DUE TO SCARCITY
*BLACK/5: UNPRICED DUE TO SCARCITY
*RED/1: UNPRICED DUE TO SCARCITY
*P.P.BLACK/1: UNPRICED DUE TO SCARCITY
*P.P.CYAN/1: UNPRICED DUE TO SCARCITY
*P.P.MAGENTA/1: UNPRICED DUE TO SCARCITY
*P.P.YELLOW/1: UNPRICED DUE TO SCARCITY

AAB	Alexa Bliss	60.00	120.00
AAL	Aliyah	12.00	30.00
AAS	Asuka	20.00	50.00
ABB	Bianca Belair	25.00	60.00
ABI	Billie Kay	10.00	25.00
ABL	Bayley	15.00	40.00
ACC	Charly Caruso	10.00	25.00
ACG	Chelsea Green	15.00	40.00
ACL	Candice LeRae	12.00	30.00
ACM	Carmella	15.00	40.00
ADK	Dakota Kai	20.00	50.00
AEM	Ember Moon	8.00	20.00
AIS	Io Shirai	30.00	75.00
AJD	Jessamyn Duke	8.00	20.00
AKB	Kayla Braxton	20.00	50.00
AKC	Kayden Carter	10.00	25.00
ALE	Lacey Evans	15.00	40.00
ALM	Liv Morgan	20.00	50.00
ALN	Lana	12.00	30.00
AMJ	Mickie James	12.00	30.00
AMR	Mandy Rose	15.00	40.00
AMS	Marina Shafir	6.00	15.00
AMY	Mia Yim	6.00	15.00
ANC	Nikki Cross	10.00	25.00
ANJ	Nia Jax	6.00	15.00
ANM	Naomi	8.00	20.00
ANT	Natalya	6.00	15.00
APR	Peyton Royce	15.00	40.00
ARB	Ruby Riott	12.00	30.00
ARR	Rhea Ripley	50.00	100.00
ASB	Sasha Banks	30.00	75.00
ASG	Santana Garrett	15.00	40.00
ASH	Shotzi Blackheart	75.00	150.00
ASP	Shayna Baszler	10.00	25.00
ATN	Tegan Nox	25.00	60.00
ATS	Toni Storm	50.00	100.00
AXL	Xia Li	20.00	50.00
AKLR	Kay Lee Ray	20.00	50.00

2020 Topps WWE Women's Division Breaking Barriers

COMPLETE SET (10)		8.00	20.00

*BLUE/25: UNPRICED DUE TO SCARCITY
*GOLD/10: UNPRICED DUE TO SCARCITY
*BLACK/5: UNPRICED DUE TO SCARCITY
*RED/1: UNPRICED DUE TO SCARCITY

BB1	Chyna	1.25	3.00
BB2	Chyna	1.25	3.00
BB3	Chyna	1.25	3.00
BB4	Chyna	1.25	3.00
BB5	Alundra Blayze	.75	2.00
BB6	Chyna	1.25	3.00
BB7	Ronda Rousey	2.50	6.00
BB8	WWE Evolution	2.00	5.00
BB9	Nia Jax	.75	2.00
BB10	Main Event WrestleMania	2.00	5.00

2020 Topps WWE Women's Division Championship Plate Patches

*PURPLE/99: .5X TO 1.2X BASIC MEM
*ORANGE/50: .6X TO 1.5X BASIC MEM
*BLUE/25: UNPRICED DUE TO SCARCITY
*GOLD/10: UNPRICED DUE TO SCARCITY
*RED/1: UNPRICED DUE TO SCARCITY
STATED PRINT RUN 150 SER.#'d SETS

CPA	Asuka	12.00	30.00
CPC	Charlotte Flair	6.00	15.00
CPAB	Alexa Bliss	15.00	40.00
CPAS	Asuka	12.00	30.00
CPBL	Becky Lynch	10.00	25.00
CPBS	Sasha Banks	10.00	25.00
CPCF	Charlotte Flair	6.00	15.00
CPCM	Carmella	5.00	12.00
CPEM	Ember Moon	4.00	10.00
CPHG	Bayley	6.00	15.00
CPKS	Kairi Sane	5.00	12.00
CPNJ	Nia Jax	4.00	10.00
CPNM	Naomi	3.00	8.00
CPNT	Natalya	3.00	8.00
CPPG	Paige		
CPQU	Charlotte Flair	6.00	15.00
CPRH	Rhea Ripley	15.00	40.00
CPRM	Bayley	6.00	15.00
CPRR	Ronda Rousey	12.00	30.00
CPSB	Sasha Banks	10.00	25.00
CPSP	Shayna Baszler	10.00	25.00
CPTS	Toni Storm	15.00	40.00
CPALX	Alexa Bliss	15.00	40.00
CPBAY	Bayley	6.00	15.00
CPKLR	Kay Lee Ray	8.00	20.00
CPMAN	Becky Lynch	10.00	25.00
CPRIP	Rhea Ripley	15.00	40.00

2020 Topps WWE Women's Division Cut Signatures

CSCY	Chyna	
CSMA	Mae Young	
CSME	Miss Elizabeth	

2020 Topps WWE Women's Division Dual Autographs

*GOLD/10: UNPRICED DUE TO SCARCITY
*BLACK/5: UNPRICED DUE TO SCARCITY
*RED/1: UNPRICED DUE TO SCARCITY

DAAN	A.Bliss/N.Cross	100.00	200.00
DAHI	V.Borne/Aliyah	50.00	100.00
DAKW	K.Sane/Asuka	125.00	250.00

2020 Topps WWE Women's Division Four Horsewomen of MMA Autographed Book

QMMA	Shafir/Rousey/Baszler/Duke	500.00	1000.00

2020 Topps WWE Women's Division Four Horsewomen of WWE Autographed Book

QWWE	Bayley/Lynch/Flair/Banks	1000.00	1500.00

2020 Topps WWE Women's Division Mat Relics

*PURPLE/99: .5X TO 1.2X BASIC MEM
*ORANGE/50: .6X TO 1.5X BASIC MEM
*BLUE/25: UNPRICED DUE TO SCARCITY
*GOLD/10: UNPRICED DUE TO SCARCITY
*RED/1: UNPRICED DUE TO SCARCITY
STATED PRINT RUN 150 SER.#'d SETS

MRAB	Alexa Bliss	12.00	30.00
MRAS	Asuka	10.00	25.00
MRBA	Bayley	5.00	12.00
MRBB	Bianca Belair	3.00	8.00
MRBL	Becky Lynch	8.00	20.00
MRBP	Beth Phoenix	2.00	5.00

MRCF	Charlotte Flair	6.00	15.00
MRCG	Chelsea Green	4.00	10.00
MRCL	Candice LeRae	6.00	15.00
MRDB	Dana Brooke	2.50	6.00
MRDK	Dakota Kai	8.00	20.00
MRET	Asuka	10.00	25.00
MRIS	Io Shirai	5.00	12.00
MRKS	Kairi Sane	6.00	15.00
MRLE	Lacey Evans	4.00	10.00
MRLM	Liv Morgan	8.00	20.00
MRMH	Mighty Molly	3.00	8.00
MRMM	Mercedes Martinez	3.00	8.00
MRMR	Mandy Rose	6.00	15.00
MRMY	Mia Yim	3.00	8.00
MRNC	Nikki Cross	4.00	10.00
MRNM	Naomi	3.00	8.00
MRNT	Natalya	2.50	6.00
MRQU	Charlotte Flair	6.00	15.00
MRRR	Rhea Ripley	6.00	15.00
MRSB	Shayna Baszler	6.00	15.00
MRSD	Sonya Deville	2.00	5.00
MRTM	Becky Lynch	8.00	20.00
MRTN	Tegan Nox	5.00	12.00
MRTO	Toni Storm	10.00	25.00
MRTS	Tamina	2.00	5.00
MRXL	Xia Li	4.00	10.00
MRZI	Shotzi Blackheart	12.00	30.00
MRZV	Zelina Vega	3.00	8.00
MREST	Bianca Belair	3.00	8.00

2020 Topps WWE Women's Division Roster

COMPLETE SET (60)		20.00	50.00

*BLUE/25: UNPRICED DUE TO SCARCITY
*GOLD/10: UNPRICED DUE TO SCARCITY
*BLACK/5: UNPRICED DUE TO SCARCITY
*RED/1: UNPRICED DUE TO SCARCITY

RC1	Alexa Bliss	2.50	6.00
RC2	Alicia Taylor	.40	1.00
RC3	Aliyah	.75	2.00
RC4	Asuka	1.50	4.00
RC5	Bayley	.75	2.00
RC6	Becky Lynch	1.50	4.00
RC7	Beth Phoenix	.60	1.50
RC8	Bianca Belair	1.00	2.50
RC9	Billie Kay	.75	2.00
RC10	Candice LeRae	1.25	3.00
RC11	Carmella	1.00	2.50
RC12	Charlotte Flair	1.50	4.00
RC13	Charly Caruso	.40	1.00
RC14	Chelsea Green	2.00	5.00
RC15	Chyna	1.00	2.50
RC16	Dakota Kai	.75	2.00
RC17	Dana Brooke	.60	1.50
RC18	Ember Moon	.75	2.00
RC19	Io Shirai	.60	1.50
RC20	Jessamyn Duke	.60	1.50
RC21	Jessi Kamea	.40	1.00
RC22	Kairi Sane	.75	2.00
RC23	Kay Lee Ray	.60	1.50
RC24	Kayden Carter	.40	1.00
RC25	Kayla Braxton	.50	1.25
RC26	Lacey Evans	1.00	2.50
RC27	Lana	1.00	2.50
RC28	Liv Morgan	1.00	2.50
RC29	Lita	1.00	2.50
RC30	Mandy Rose	2.00	5.00
RC31	Marina Shafir	.60	1.50

RC32	Maryse	.75	2.00
RC33	Mia Yim	.75	2.00
RC34	Mickie James	.60	1.50
RC35	Naomi	.75	2.00
RC36	Natalya	.60	1.50
RC37	Nia Jax	.60	1.50
RC38	Nikki Cross	.75	2.00
RC39	Paige	1.00	2.50
RC40	Peyton Royce	.75	2.00
RC41	Piper Niven	.50	1.25
RC42	Renee Young	.50	1.25
RC43	Rhea Ripley	1.50	4.00
RC44	Ronda Rousey	2.00	5.00
RC45	Ruby Riott	.60	1.50
RC46	Santana Garrett	.40	1.00
RC47	Sarah Schreiber	.40	1.00
RC48	Sasha Banks	2.00	5.00
RC49	Shayna Baszler	1.25	3.00
RC50	Shotzi Blackheart	1.25	3.00
RC51	Sonya Deville	1.00	2.50
RC52	Stephanie McMahon	1.00	2.50
RC53	Tamina	.50	1.25
RC54	Tegan Nox	1.00	2.50
RC55	Toni Storm	1.00	2.50
RC56	Trish Stratus	2.00	5.00
RC57	Vanessa Borne	.75	2.00
RC58	Xia Li	.75	2.00
RC59	Zelina Vega	.75	2.00
RC60	Raquel Gonzalez	.60	1.50

2020 Topps WWE Women's Division Superstar Transformations

COMPLETE SET (15)		20.00	50.00

*BLUE/25: UNPRICED DUE TO SCARCITY
*GOLD/10: UNPRICED DUE TO SCARCITY
*BLACK/5: UNPRICED DUE TO SCARCITY
*RED/1: UNPRICED DUE TO SCARCITY

ST1	Alexa Bliss	6.00	15.00
ST2	Asuka	3.00	8.00
ST3	Bayley	2.50	6.00
ST4	Becky Lynch	4.00	10.00
ST5	Carmella	2.00	5.00
ST6	Charlotte Flair	4.00	10.00
ST7	Io Shirai	2.50	6.00
ST8	Kairi Sane	3.00	8.00
ST9	Liv Morgan	2.50	6.00
ST10	Naomi	1.50	4.00
ST11	Paige	1.50	4.00
ST12	Peyton Royce	2.50	6.00
ST13	Ruby Riott	2.50	6.00
ST14	Sasha Banks	5.00	12.00
ST15	Sonya Deville	1.50	4.00

2020 Topps WWE Women's Division Triple Autographs

*GOLD/10: UNPRICED DUE TO SCARCITY
*BLACK/5: UNPRICED DUE TO SCARCITY
*RED/1: UNPRICED DUE TO SCARCITY
STATED PRINT RUN 25 SER.#'d SETS

TAUK	Ray/Storm/Ripley	150.00	300.00
TABAD	Naomi/Tamina/Banks	100.00	200.00

2019 Topps WWE Women's Revolution

COMPLETE SET (40)		25.00	60.00
SEMISTARS		1.00	2.50
UNLISTED STARS		1.25	3.00

RANDOMLY INSERTED INTO PACKS

DR1	Paige	2.00	5.00
DR2	Charlotte/Becky/Sasha	2.00	5.00
DR3	Charlotte Flair	2.00	5.00
DR4	Team PCB	2.00	5.00
DR5	Charlotte Flair	2.00	5.00
DR6	Nikki Bella	2.00	5.00
DR7	Charlotte Flair	2.00	5.00
DR8	Paige	2.00	5.00
DR9	Natalya	2.00	5.00
DR10	Charlotte Flair	2.00	5.00
DR11	Paige	2.00	5.00
DR12	Charlotte Flair	2.00	5.00
DR13	Paige	2.00	5.00
DR14	Charlotte Flair	2.00	5.00
DR15	Charlotte Flair	2.00	5.00
DR16	Nikki Bella	1.25	3.00
DR17	Charlotte Flair	2.00	5.00
DR18	Sasha Banks	2.00	5.00
DR19	Brie Bella	1.25	3.00
DR20	Team B.A.D./Sasha Banks	2.00	5.00
DR21	Lita	1.25	3.00
DR22	Charlotte Flair	2.00	5.00
DR23	Charlotte Flair	2.00	5.00
DR24	SD Women's Championship	2.50	6.00
DR25	Becky Lynch	2.00	5.00
DR26	Charlotte Flair	2.00	5.00
DR27	Sasha Banks & Charlotte Flair	2.00	5.00
DR28	Mickie James & Asuka	1.25	3.00
DR29	Alexa Bliss	2.50	6.00
DR30	Mickie James & Alexa Bliss	2.50	6.00
DR31	Bayley	1.00	2.50
DR32	Naomi	.75	2.00
DR33	Naomi & Charlotte	.75	2.00
DR34	Alexa Bliss	2.50	6.00
DR35	Carmella	1.25	3.00
DR36	Asuka	1.50	4.00
DR37	Charlotte Flair	2.00	5.00
DR38	Absolution	2.00	5.00
DR39	Riott Squad	1.50	4.00
DR40	Asuka	1.50	4.00

1985 Topps WWF

COMPLETE SET W/HOGAN (66)	200.00	400.00
COMPLETE SET W/O HOGAN (60)	100.00	200.00
UNOPENED BOX (36 PACKS)	1000.00	1500.00
UNOPENED PACK (9 CARDS+1 STICKER)	30.00	40.00
RACK PACK (26 CARDS+3 STICKERS)	150.00	200.00
RINGSIDE ACTION (22-56)		
SUPERSTARS SPEAK (57-66)		

*OPC: SAME VALUE AS TOPPS

1	Hulk Hogan	150.00	300.00
2	The Iron Sheik	1.00	2.50
3	Captain Lou Albano	.75	2.00
4	Junk Yard Dog	1.00	2.50
5	Paul Mr. Wonderful Orndorff	.60	1.50
6	Jimmy Superfly Snuka	.60	1.50
7	Rowdy Roddy Piper	8.00	20.00
8	Wendi Richter	.75	2.00
9	Greg The Hammer Valentine	1.00	2.50
10	Brutus Beefcake	1.00	2.50
11	Jesse The Body Ventura	3.00	8.00
12	Big John Studd	.60	1.50
13	Fabulous Moolah	1.25	3.00
14	Tito Santana	1.25	3.00
15	Hillbilly Jim	1.00	2.50
16	Hulk Hogan	75.00	150.00
17	Mr. Fuji	.75	2.00

18	Rotundo & Windham	.75	2.00
19	Moondog Spot	.50	1.25
20	Chief Jay Strongbow	.50	1.25
21	George The Animal Steele	1.25	3.00
22	Let Go of My Toe! RA	.50	1.25
23	Lock 'Em Up! RA	.50	1.25
24	Scalp 'Em! RA	.50	1.25
25	Going for the Midsection! RA	.75	2.00
26	Up in the Air! RA	.60	1.50
27	All Tied Up! RA	1.50	4.00
28	Here She Comes! RA	.50	1.25
29	Stretched to the Limit! RA	3.00	8.00
30	Over He Goes! RA	1.00	2.50
31	An Appetite for Mayhem! RA	.60	1.50
32	Putting on Pressure! RA	.50	1.25
33	Smashed on a Knee! RA	.75	2.00
34	A Fist Comes Flying! RA	.50	1.25
35	Lemme' Out of This! RA	.50	1.25
36	No Fair Chokin'! RA	.50	1.25
37	Attacked by an Animal! RA	.50	1.25
38	One Angry Man! RA	1.25	3.00
39	Someone's Going Down! RA	1.25	3.00
40	Strangle Hold! RA	2.00	5.00
41	Bending an Arm! RA	.50	1.25
42	Ready for a Pile Driver! RA	.75	2.00
43	Face to the Canvas! RA	.50	1.25
44	Paul Wants It All! RA	.75	2.00
45	Kick to the Face! RA	3.00	8.00
46	Ready for Action! RA	.50	1.25
47	Putting on the Squeeze! RA	.60	1.50
48	Giants in Action! RA	1.50	4.00
49	Camel Clutch! RA	.60	1.50
50	Pile Up! RA	2.00	5.00
51	Can't Get Away! RA	.60	1.50
52	Going for the Pin! RA	.50	1.25
53	Ready to Fly! RA	2.00	5.00
54	Crusher in a Crusher! RA	.50	1.25
55	Fury of the Animal! RA	.75	2.00
56	Wrong Kind of Music! RA	6.00	15.00
57	Who's your next challenger? SS	2.50	6.00
58	This dog has got a mean bite! SS	.75	2.00
59	I don't think I'll ask that... SS	1.25	3.00
60	You Hulkster fans lift... SS	8.00	20.00
61	This ain't my idea... SS	1.00	2.50
62	You mean Freddie Blassie is... SS	1.25	3.00
63	Mppgh Ecch Oong. SS	1.00	2.50
64	It's the rock n' wrestling... SS	.75	2.00
65	Arrrgggghhhh! SS	.60	1.50
66	They took my reindeer! SS	.60	1.50

1985 Topps WWF Stickers

COMPLETE SET W/HOGAN (22)	50.00	100.00
COMPLETE SET W/O HOGAN (17)	12.00	30.00
1	Hulk Hogan	15.00	40.00
2	Captain Lou Albano	.75	2.00
3	Brutus Beefcake	1.25	3.00
4	Jesse Ventura	2.00	5.00
5	The Iron Sheik	1.50	4.00
6	Wendi Richter	1.25	3.00
7	Jimmy Snuka	.75	2.00
8	Ivan Putski	1.00	2.50
9	Hulk Hogan	4.00	10.00
10	Junk Yard Dog	1.25	3.00
11	Hulk Hogan	6.00	15.00
12	Captain Lou Albano	.75	2.00
13	Captain Lou Albano	.75	2.00
14	Freddie Blassie & The Iron Sheik	.75	2.00
15	Jimmy Snuka	.75	2.00

16	Hulk Hogan	10.00	25.00
17	Iron Sheik	1.50	4.00
18	Rene Goulet & S.D. Jones	1.25	3.00
19	Junk Yard Dog	.75	2.00
20	Wendi Richter	1.25	3.00
21	Andre the Giant	3.00	8.00
22	Hulk Hogan	8.00	20.00

1987 Topps WWF

COMPLETE SET (75)		60.00	120.00
UNOPENED BOX (36 PACKS)			
UNOPENED PACK (9 CARDS+1 STICKER)			
1	Bret "Hit Man" Hart	25.00	60.00
2	Andre the Giant	6.00	15.00
3	Hulk Hogan	5.00	12.00
4	Frankie	.75	2.00
5	Koko B. Ware	.75	2.00
6	Tito Santana	.60	1.50
7	Randy Savage & Elizabeth	10.00	25.00
8	Billy Jack Haynes	.40	1.00
9	Hercules & Bobby Heenan	.40	1.00
10	King Harley Race	.60	1.50
11	Kimchee & Kamala	.40	1.00
12	Bravo/Johnny V/Valentine	.50	1.25
13	Honky Tonk Man	1.00	2.50
14	Outback Jack	.40	1.00
15	King Kong Bundy	1.25	3.00
16	The Magnificent Muraco	.40	1.00
17	Mr. Fuji and Killer Khan	.75	2.00
18	The Natural Butch Reed	.60	1.50
19	Davey Boy Smith	.75	2.00
20	The Dynamite Kid	.40	1.00
21	Ricky The Dragon Steamboat	1.50	4.00
22	Two-Man Clothesline RA	.40	1.00
23	Ref Turned Wrestler RA	.75	2.00
24	Ready to Strike RA	.60	1.50
25	In the Outback RA	.40	1.00
26	The Hulkster Explodes RA	2.00	5.00
27	Double Whammy RA	.40	1.00
28	Spoiling for a Fight RA	.40	1.00
29	Flip Flop RA	.40	1.00
30	Islanders Attack RA	.40	1.00
31	King Harley Parades RA	.40	1.00
32	Backbreaker RA	.40	1.00
33	Double Dropkick RA	.40	1.00
34	The Loser Must Bow RA	.40	1.00
35	American-Made RA	2.50	6.00
36	A Challenge Answered RA	2.00	5.00
37	Champ in the Ring RA	4.00	10.00
38	Listening to Hulkamania RA	2.00	5.00
39	Heading for the Ring RA	.40	1.00
40	Out to Destroy RA	.40	1.00
41	Tama Takes a Beating RA	.40	1.00
42	Bundy in Mid-Air RA	.40	1.00
43	Karate Stance RA	.40	1.00
44	Her Eyes on Randy RA	2.50	6.00
45	The Olympian Returns RA	.40	1.00
46	Reed Is Riled RA	.40	1.00
47	Flying Bodypress RA	.40	1.00
48	Hooking the Leg RA	.40	1.00
49	A Belly Buster WMIII	.40	1.00
50	Revenge on Randy WMIII	.75	2.00
51	Fighting the Full Nelson WMIII	.40	1.00
52	Honky Tonk Goes Down WMIII	.40	1.00
53	Over the Top WMIII	.40	1.00
54	The Giant Is Slammed WMIII	1.25	3.00
55	Out of the Ring WMIII	.75	2.00
56	And Still Champion WMIII	1.50	4.00

57	Harts Hit Concrete WMIII	.40	1.00
58	The Challenge RA	1.25	3.00
59	Bearhug RA	.40	1.00
60	Fantastic Bodypress RA	.40	1.00
61	Aerial Maneuvers RA	.40	1.00
62	Ready to Sting! RA	.40	1.00
63	Showing Off RA	.40	1.00
64	Scare Tactics RA	.40	1.00
65	Taking a Bow RA	.60	1.50
66	Out to Eat a Turnbuckle RA	.40	1.00
67	Nice guys finish last! SS	.40	1.00
68	Here's how we keep... SS	.40	1.00
69	Urrggh. Nice! SS	.40	1.00
70	No Kamala...him not dinner! SS	.40	1.00
71	We are the original destroyers. SS	.40	1.00
72	I think the fans are mad at me. SS	.40	1.00
73	You ain't nothin'... SS	.40	1.00
74	I'm gonna take a big bit... SS	.40	1.00
75	Good! SS	.40	1.00

1987 Topps WWF Stickers

COMPLETE SET (22)		20.00	50.00
1	Bret Hit Man Hart	5.00	12.00
2	Hulk Hogan	8.00	20.00
3	Koko B. Ware	.40	1.00
4	Randy Savage & Elizabeth	10.00	25.00
5	Billy Jack Haynes	.40	1.00
6	Hercules & Bobby Heenan	.60	1.50
7	King Harley Race	.60	1.50
8	Kimchee & Kamala	.40	1.00
9	Bravo/Johnny V/Valentine	.60	1.50
10	Honky Tonk Man	.60	1.50
11	Outback Jack	.40	1.00
12	King Kong Bundy	.60	1.50
13	Magnificent Muraco	.40	1.00
14	Mr. Fuji & Killer Khan	.40	1.00
15	Ricky The Dragon Steamboat	.60	1.50
16	Danny Davis	.40	1.00
17	Andre the Giant	6.00	15.00
18	Ken Patera	.40	1.00
19	Smash Demolition	.40	1.00
20	Jim The Anvil Neidhart	.40	1.00
21	George The Animal Steele	.60	1.50
22	WWF Logo	.40	1.00

1985 Topps WWF 3-D Pro Wrestling Stars

COMPLETE SET (12)		500.00	1000.00
UNOPENED BOX			
UNOPENED PACK (1 CARD)			
1	Hulk Hogan	250.00	500.00
2	Wendi Richter	50.00	100.00
3	Jimmy Superfly Snuka	50.00	100.00
4	The Iron Sheik	60.00	120.00
5	Hillbilly Jim	30.00	75.00
6	Captain Lou Albano	50.00	100.00
7	Paul Orndorff	75.00	150.00
8	Jesse The Body Ventura	60.00	120.00
9	Brutus Beefcake	30.00	75.00
10	Andre the Giant	200.00	350.00
11	Rocky Johnson	30.00	75.00
12	Junk Yard Dog	60.00	120.00

2009 TRISTAR Hulk Hogan Joins TNA Commemoratives

COMPLETE SET (2)			
H1	Hulk Hogan		
H2	Hulk Hogan		

2008 TRISTAR TNA Cross The Line

COMPLETE SET (100)		8.00	20.00
UNOPENED BOX (20 PACKS)			
UNOPENED PACK (6 CARDS)			
*GOLD/50: 2X TO 5X BASIC CARDS			
*RED/10: UNPRICED DUE TO SCARCITY			
*PURPLE/1: UNPRICED DUE TO SCARCITY			
1	A.J. Styles	.40	1.00
2	Motor City Machineguns	.15	.40
3	Brother Ray	.20	.50
4	LAX	.15	.40
5	Consequences Creed	.15	.40
6	Taylor Wilde	.60	1.50
7	Sheik Abdul Bashir	.20	.50
8	Main Event Mafia	.20	.50
9	Hector Guerrero & Willie Urbina	.12	.30
10	Lauren	.40	1.00
11	Kyra Angle	.40	1.00
12	Suicide	.12	.30
13	Rhaka Khan	.20	.50
14	Mick Foley	.60	1.50
15	Shane Sewell	.12	.30
16	Dutch Mantel	.12	.30
17	Beer Money Inc.	.15	.40
18	Prince Justice Brotherhood	.12	.30
19	Jeff Jarrett	.75	2.00
20	A.J. Styles	.40	1.00
21	Cowboy James Storm	.15	.40
22	Mike Tenay	.15	.40
23	Don West	.12	.30
24	Rudy Charles	.12	.30
25	Andrew Thomas	.12	.30
26	Jeremy Borash	.12	.30
27	Hermie Sadler	.12	.30
28	Kevin Nash	.60	1.50
29	Brother Devon	.20	.50
30	Beautiful People	.60	1.50
31	Roxxi	.40	1.00
32	Abyss	.40	1.00
33	Dixie Carter	.30	.75
34	Christian Cage	.30	.75
35	Booker T	.75	2.00
36	Shark Boy	.12	.30
37	Johnny Devine	.15	.40
38	Petey Williams	.12	.30
39	Homicide	.15	.40
40	Angelina Love	.60	1.50
41	Scott Steiner	.60	1.50
42	Alex Shelley	.15	.40
43	Jacqueline	.40	1.00
44	Curry Man	.12	.30
45	Kip James	.15	.40
46	Earl Hebner	.15	.40
47	Velvet Sky	.50	1.25
48	Kurt Angle	.75	2.00
49	Jim Cornette	.15	.40
50	Sting	.60	1.50
51	Traci Brooks	.50	1.25
52	Jay Lethal	.12	.30
53	Robert Roode	.12	.30
54	Petey Williams	.12	.30
55	Sonjay Dutt	.12	.30
56	Sharmell	.40	1.00
57	Chris Sabin	.12	.30
58	Matt Morgan	.15	.40
59	ODB	.40	1.00
60	Tomko	.12	.30
61	Kurt Angle	.75	2.00

62	Christian Cage	.30	.75
63	ODB	.40	1.00
64	Team 3D	.20	.50
65	A.J. Styles	.40	1.00
66	James Storm	.15	.40
67	Raisha Saeed	.30	.75
68	Sonjay Dutt	.12	.30
69	Kevin Nash	.60	1.50
70	Matt Morgan	.15	.40
71	BG James	.12	.30
72	Hernandez	.15	.40
73	A.J. Styles	.40	1.00
74	Kurt Angle	.75	2.00
75	Christian Cage	.30	.75
76	Jeff Jarrett	.75	2.00
77	Sting	.60	1.50
78	Christian Cage	.30	.75
79	Jeff Jarrett	.75	2.00
80	Kurt Angle Meets Samoa Joe	.75	2.00
81	Sharmell	.40	1.00
82	Sting	.60	1.50
83	Most Important Moment in TNA History	.12	.30
84	Christian†Cage vs. Abyss	.40	1.00
85	Samoa Joe vs. Daniels vs. Styles	.40	1.00
86	Kurt Angle	.75	2.00
87	Styles vs. Angle	.75	2.00
88	Eric Young	.12	.30
89	Rhino	.30	.75
90	Samoa Joe	.20	.50
91	SoCal Val	.60	1.50
92	Curry Man	.12	.30
93	Lance Rock	.15	.40
94	Jimmy Rave	.15	.40
95	Sting vs. Samoa Joe	.60	1.50
96	Kurt Angle vs. Jeff Jarrett	.75	2.00
97	Awesome Kong/TNA Knockouts	.30	.75
98	Beer Money vs. LAX	.15	.40
99	Steve McMichael	.30	.75
100	Checklist	.12	.30

2008 TRISTAR TNA Cross the Line Autographed Memorabilia Silver

*GOLD/50: .6X TO 1.2X BASIC AU MEM
*RED/25: .75X TO 1.5 BASIC AU MEM
*GREEN/5: UNPRICED DUE TO SCARCITY
*PURPLE/1: UNPRICED DUE TO SCARCITY
STATED PRINT RUN 99 SER.#'d SETS

MAA	Abyss	15.00	30.00
MOA	ODB	15.00	30.00
MSA	Sting	25.00	50.00
MABA	Sheik Abdul Bashir	10.00	20.00
MALA	Angelina Love	20.00	40.00
MASA	A.J. Styles	20.00	40.00
MCCA	Christian Cage	15.00	30.00
MCHA	Christy Hemme	20.00	40.00
MCMA	Curry Man	10.00	20.00
MDCA	Dixie Carter	15.00	30.00
MJBA	Jeremy Borash	10.00	20.00
MKAA	Kurt Angle	15.00	30.00
MKNA	Kevin Nash	20.00	40.00
MRCA	Rudy Charles	10.00	20.00
MRSA	Raisha Saeed	10.00	20.00
MSEA	Super Eric	10.00	20.00
MSJA	Samoa Joe	20.00	40.00
MSVA	SoCal Val	15.00	30.00
MTWA	Taylor Wilde	15.00	30.00
MVSA	Velvet Sky	20.00	40.00

2008 TRISTAR TNA Cross the Line Autographs Silver

*GOLD/50: .5X TO 1.2X BASIC AUTOS
*RED/25: .6X TO 1.5X BASIC AUTOS
*PURPLE/1: UNPRICED DUE TO SCARCITY
*P.P.BLACK/1: UNPRICED DUE TO SCARCITY
*P.P.CYAN/1: UNPRICED DUE TO SCARCITY
*P.P.MAGENTA/1: UNPRICED DUE TO SCARCITY
*P.P.YELLOW/1: UNPRICED DUE TO SCARCITY

CA	Abyss	8.00	20.00
CJ	Jacqueline	6.00	15.00
CL	Lauren	6.00	15.00
CO	ODB	6.00	15.00
CS	Sting	20.00	50.00
CAB	Sheik Abdul Bashir	6.00	15.00
CAJ	A.J. Styles	10.00	25.00
CAK	Awesome Kong	6.00	15.00
CAL	Angelina Love	10.00	25.00
CAS	Alex Shelley	6.00	15.00
CAT	Andrew Thomas	6.00	15.00
CBD	Brother Devon	8.00	20.00
CBR	Brother Ray	8.00	20.00
CBT	Booker T	8.00	20.00
CCC	Christian Cage	8.00	20.00
CCH	Christy Hemme	10.00	25.00
CCM	Curry Man	8.00	20.00
CCS	Chris Sabin	6.00	15.00
CDC	Dixie Carter	8.00	20.00
CDW	Don West	8.00	20.00
CEH	Earl Hebner	6.00	15.00
CEY	Eric Young	6.00	15.00
CH1	Hernandez	6.00	15.00
CH2	Homicide	6.00	15.00
CHG	Hector Guerrero	6.00	15.00
CHS	Hermie Sadler	6.00	15.00
CJB	Jeremy Borash	6.00	15.00
CJC	Jim Cornette	6.00	15.00
CJD	Johnny Devine	6.00	15.00
CJJ	Jeff Jarrett	8.00	20.00
CJL	Jay Lethal	6.00	15.00
CJR	Jimmy Rave	6.00	15.00
CJS	James Storm	6.00	15.00
CKA	Kurt Angle	12.00	30.00
CKJ	Kip James	6.00	15.00
CKN	Kevin Nash	12.00	30.00
CLR	Lance Rock	6.00	15.00
CMF	Mick Foley	12.00	30.00
CMM	Matt Morgan	8.00	20.00
CMT	Mike Tenay	6.00	15.00
CPW	Petey Williams	6.00	15.00
CR2	Roxxi	8.00	20.00
CRC	Rudy Charles		
CRR	Robert Roode	6.00	15.00
CRS	Raisha Saeed	8.00	20.00
CRS	Rhino	6.00	15.00
CS2	Sharmell	6.00	15.00
CS3	Suicide	8.00	20.00
CSB	Shark Boy	6.00	15.00
CSD	Sonjay Dutt	6.00	15.00
CSE	Super Eric	6.00	15.00
CSJ	Slick Johnson	6.00	15.00
CSJ	Samoa Joe	12.00	30.00
CSM	Steve McMichael	8.00	20.00
CSS	Scott Steiner	12.00	30.00
CSV	SoCal Val	8.00	20.00
CTB	Traci Brooks	8.00	20.00
CTW	Taylor Wilde	8.00	20.00

CVS	Velvet Sky	10.00	25.00
CWU	Willie Urbina	8.00	20.00
CCC2	Consequences Creed	6.00	15.00
CKA2	Karen Angle	8.00	20.00
CSS2	Shane Sewell	6.00	15.00

2008 TRISTAR TNA Cross the Line Dual Autographs Silver

*GOLD/50: .5X TO 1.2X BASIC AUTOS
*RED/25: .6X TO 1.5X BASIC AUTOS
*BLUE/5: UNPRICED DUE TO SCARCITY
*PURPLE/1: UNPRICED DUE TO SCARCITY
*P.P.BLACK/1: UNPRICED DUE TO SCARCITY
*P.P.CYAN/1: UNPRICED DUE TO SCARCITY
*P.P.MAGENTA/1: UNPRICED DUE TO SCARCITY
*P.P.YELLOW/1: UNPRICED DUE TO SCARCITY
RANDOMLY INSERTED INTO PACKS

C2BS	Booker T/Sharmell	15.00	30.00
C2CB	J.Cornette/T.Brooks	12.50	25.00
C2CR	C.Cage/Rhino	12.50	25.00
C2HH	Hernandez/Homicide	7.50	15.00
C2JK	S.Joe/K.Nash	15.00	30.00
C2KS	A.Kong/R.Saeed	12.50	25.00
C2KW	A.Kong/T.Wilde	20.00	40.00
C2LS	A.Love/V.Sky	20.00	40.00
C2RD	BroRay/BroDevon	15.00	30.00
C2SA	A.J. Styles/K.Angle	15.00	30.00
C2SA	Sting/K.Angle	20.00	40.00
C2SR	J.Storm/R.Roode	15.00	30.00
C2SS	A.Shelley/C.Sabin	15.00	30.00
C2SW	S.Steiner/P.Williams	12.50	25.00
C2WC	P.Williams/C.Creed	7.50	15.00

2008 TRISTAR TNA Cross the Line Dual Memorabilia Silver

*GOLD/50: .5X TO 1.2X BASIC MEM
*RED/25: .6X TO 1.5X BASIC MEM
*GREEN/5: UNPRICED DUE TO SCARCITY
*PURPLE/1: UNPRICED DUE TO SCARCITY
STATED PRINT RUN 99 SER.#'d SETS

MS2	Sting	20.00	50.00
MAS2	Kurt Angle/A.J. Styles	8.00	20.00
MDL2	Sonjay Dutt/Jay Lethal	6.00	15.00
MLV2	Jay Lethal	5.00	12.00
	SoCal Val		

2008 TRISTAR TNA Cross the Line High Impact Championship Inserts

STATED ODDS 1:CASE
NO PRICING DUE TO SCARCITY

NNO Velvet Sky Auto Baseball EXCH
NNO Booker T Auto Baseball EXCH
NNO A.J. Styles Auto Baseball EXCH
NNO TNA Wrestler Auto Photo EXCH

2008 TRISTAR TNA Cross the Line Memorabilia Silver

*GOLD/50: .5X TO 1.2X BASIC MEM
*RED/25: .6X TO 1.5X BASIC MEM
*GREEN/5: UNPRICED DUE TO SCARCITY
*PURPLE/1: UNPRICED DUE TO SCARCITY
STATED PRINT RUN 99 SER.#'d SETS

MA	Abyss	8.00	20.00
MS	Sting	10.00	25.00
MAB	Sheik Abdul Bashir	6.00	15.00
MAS	A.J. Styles	8.00	20.00
MBP	The Beautiful People	10.00	25.00

MCC	Christian Cage	8.00	20.00
MCM	Curry Man	6.00	15.00
MDC	Dixie Carter	8.00	20.00
MKA	Kurt Angle	10.00	25.00
MKN	Kevin Nash	8.00	20.00
MSE	Super Eric	6.00	15.00
MTW	Taylor Wilde	8.00	20.00

2008 TRISTAR TNA Cross the Line Quad Autographs Silver

*GOLD/50: .6X TO 1.2X BASIC AUTOS
*RED/25: .75X TO 1.5X BASIC AUTOS
*BLUE/5: UNPRICED DUE TO SCARCITY
*PURPLE/1: UNPRICED DUE TO SCARCITY
*P.P.BLACK/1: UNPRICED DUE TO SCARCITY
*P.P.CYAN/1: UNPRICED DUE TO SCARCITY
*P.P.MAGENTA/1: UNPRICED DUE TO SCARCITY
*P.P.YELLOW/1: UNPRICED DUE TO SCARCITY
RANDOMLY INSERTED INTO PACKS

1	Love/Sky/Brooks/Hemme	60.00	120.00
2	Sting/Nash/Jarrett/Steiner	125.00	200.00
3	Hebner/Johnson/Thomas/Charles	25.00	50.00
4	Tenay/West/Guerrero/Urbina	25.00	50.00
5	Storm/Roode/Homic/Hrndz	25.00	50.00
6	Love/Sky/Kong/Jacqueline	30.00	60.00
7	Bashir/Dutt/Curry/Guer	25.00	50.00

2008 TRISTAR TNA Cross the Line Triple Autographs Silver

*GOLD/50: .6X TO 1.2X BASIC AUTOS
*RED/25: .75X TO 1.5X BASIC AUTOS
*BLUE/5: UNPRICED DUE TO SCARCITY
*PURPLE/1: UNPRICED DUE TO SCARCITY
*P.P.BLACK/1: UNPRICED DUE TO SCARCITY
*P.P.CYAN/1: UNPRICED DUE TO SCARCITY
*P.P.MAGENTA/1: UNPRICED DUE TO SCARCITY
*P.P.YELLOW/1: UNPRICED DUE TO SCARCITY
RANDOMLY INSERTED INTO PACKS

C3B	Tenay/West/Borash	20.00	40.00
C3BP	Love/Sky/James	40.00	80.00
C3RR	Hemme/Rock/Rave	25.00	50.00
C3BSS	Booker/Sting/Samoa	40.00	80.00
C3LVD	Lethal/SoCal/Dutt	25.00	50.00
C3PJB	Shark/Curry/SuperEric	20.00	40.00

2010 TRISTAR TNA Icons

COMPLETE SET (100)	10.00	25.00
UNOPENED BOX (20 PACKS)		
UNOPENED PACK (6 CARDS)		

*GOLD/25: 2.5X TO 6X BASIC CARDS
*RED/5: UNPRICED DUE TO SCARCITY
*PURPLE/1: UNPRICED DUE TO SCARCITY

1	Hulk Hogan	1.00	2.50
2	Ric Flair	.75	2.00
3	Sting	.60	1.50
4	Jeff Hardy	.60	1.50
5	Mick Foley	.75	2.00
6	Kevin Nash	.60	1.50
7	Rob Van Dam	.40	1.00
8	Jeff Jarrett	.40	1.00
9	Kurt Angle	.60	1.50
10	Eric Bischoff	.15	.40
11	Earl Hebner	.15	.40
12	Mr. Anderson	.25	.60
13	Team 3D	.25	.60
14	AJ Styles	.40	1.00
15	Tara	.60	1.50

16	Tommy Dreamer	.15	.40
17	Ric Flair	.75	2.00
18	Sting	.60	1.50
19	Jeff Hardy	.60	1.50
20	Jeff Jarrett	.40	1.00
21	Kevin Nash	.60	1.50
22	Kurt Angle	.60	1.50
23	Mick Foley	.75	2.00
24	Rob Van Dam	.40	1.00
25	Ric Flair	.75	2.00
26	Sting	.60	1.50
27	Jeff Hardy	.60	1.50
28	Mick Foley	.75	2.00
29	Kevin Nash	.60	1.50
30	Rob Van Dam	.40	1.00
31	Team 3D	.25	.60
32	Kurt Angle	.60	1.50
33	Eric Bischoff	.15	.40
34	Dixie Carter	.40	1.00
35	Desmond Wolfe	.15	.40
36	Jay Lethal	.15	.40
37	Matt Morgan	.15	.40
38	Abyss	.25	.60
39	AJ Styles	.40	1.00
40	Hulk Hogan	1.00	2.50
41	Velvet Sky	.75	2.00
42	Angelina Love	.60	1.50
43	Taylor Wilde	.40	1.00
44	Sarita	.40	1.00
45	Daffney	.60	1.50
46	Madison Rayne	.60	1.50
47	Lacey Von Erich	.75	2.00
48	Christy Hemme	.60	1.50
49	SoCal Val	.60	1.50
50	Chelsea	.60	1.50
51	Miss Tessmacher	.75	2.00
52	Rosie Lottalove	.40	1.00
53	Motor City Machineguns	.20	.50
54	Rob Terry	.15	.40
55	Kazarian	.15	.40
56	D'Angelo Dinero	.15	.40
57	Douglas Williams	.15	.40
58	Desmond Wolfe	.15	.40
59	Eric Young	.15	.40
60	Generation Me	.15	.40
61	Beer Money Inc.	.25	.60
62	Abyss	.25	.60
63	Matt Morgan	.15	.40
64	Samoa Joe	.25	.60
65	Hernandez	.15	.40
66	Ink Inc.	.15	.40
67	Jay Lethal	.15	.40
68	Magnus	.15	.40
69	Lacey Von Erich	.75	2.00
70	Hulk Hogan	.75	2.00
71	Ric Flair	.60	1.50
72	Sting	.50	1.25
73	Jeff Hardy	.50	1.25
74	Mick Foley	.60	1.50
75	Kevin Nash	.50	1.25
76	Rob Van Dam	.30	.75
77	Jeff Jarrett	.30	.75
78	Kurt Angle	.50	1.25
79	Mr. Anderson	.20	.50
80	Tommy Dreamer	.15	.40
81	Hulk Hogan	.75	2.00
82	Ric Flair	.60	1.50
83	Sting	.50	1.25

#	Player		
84	Jeff Hardy	.50	1.25
85	Mick Foley	.60	1.50
86	Kevin Nash	.50	1.25
87	Rob Van Dam	.30	.75
88	Jeff Jarrett	.30	.75
89	Kurt Angle	.50	1.25
90	Mick Foley	.60	1.50
91	Mick Foley	.60	1.50
92	Mick Foley	.60	1.50
93	Mick Foley	.60	1.50
94	Mick Foley	.60	1.50
95	Sting	.50	1.25
96	Kevin Nash	.50	1.25
97	Rob Van Dam	.30	.75
98	Mr. Anderson	.20	.50
99	Jeff Jarrett	.30	.75
100	Kurt Angle	.50	1.25

2010 TRISTAR TNA Icons Dual Memorabilia Silver

STATED PRINT RUN 199 SER.#'d SETS

M8 Rob Van Dam
Jeff Hardy
M9 Ric Flair
AJ Styles

2010 TRISTAR TNA Icons Hogangraphs Green

OVERALL AUTO ODDS TWO PER BOX

H1	Hulk Hogan	75.00	150.00
H2	Hulk Hogan	75.00	150.00
H3	Hulk Hogan	75.00	150.00
H4	Hulk Hogan	75.00	150.00
H5	Hulk Hogan	75.00	150.00

2010 TRISTAR TNA Icons Hulk Hogan Die-Cut Letter Memorabilia Silver

*GOLD/50: .5X TO 1.2X BASIC MEM
*RED/25: .6X TO 1.5 BASIC MEM
*PURPLE/1: UNPRICED DUE TO SCARCITY
STATED ODDS OVERALL MEM 1:BOX
STATED PRINT RUN 199 SER.#'d SETS

HH1	Hulk Hogan Bandana H	12.00	30.00
HH2	Hulk Hogan Bandana O	12.00	30.00
HH3	Hulk Hogan Bandana G	12.00	30.00
HH4	Hulk Hogan Bandana A	12.00	30.00
HH5	Hulk Hogan Bandana N	12.00	30.00

2010 TRISTAR TNA Icons Hulk Hogan Dual Autographs Gold

*GREEN/50: UNPRICED DUE TO SCARCITY
*RED/5: UNPRICED DUE TO SCARCITY
*PURPLE/1: UNPRICED DUE TO SCARCITY
STATED PRINT RUN 99 SER.#'d SETS

H21 Hulk Hogan/Abyss
H22 Hulk Hogan/AJ Styles
H23 Hulk Hogan/Jeff Hardy
H24 Hulk Hogan/Jeff Jarrett
H25 Hulk Hogan/Kevin Nash
H26 Hulk Hogan/Kurt Angle
H27 Hulk Hogan/Lacey Von Erich
H28 Hulk Hogan/Mick Foley
H29 Hulk Hogan/Ric Flair
H210 Hulk Hogan/Rob Van Dam
H211 Hulk Hogan/Sting
H212 Hulk Hogan/Tara
H213 Hulk Hogan/Velvet Sky

2010 TRISTAR TNA Icons Hulk Hogan Quad Autographs Gold

*GREEN/50: UNPRICED DUE TO SCARCITY
*RED/5: UNPRICED DUE TO SCARCITY
*PURPLE/1: UNPRICED DUE TO SCARCITY
STATED PRINT RUN 99 SER. #'d SETS

H41 Hogan/Sky/Rayne/Von Erich
H42 Hogan/Magnus/Williams/Terry
H43 Hogan/Flair/Abyss/Styles
H44 Hogan/Flair/Sting/Foley

2010 TRISTAR TNA Icons Iconigraphs Gold

*GREEN/25: .5X TO 1.2X BASIC AUTOS
*RED/5: UNPRICED DUE TO SCARCITY
*PURPLE/1: UNPRICED DUE TO SCARCITY
STATED ODDS OVERALL 2:BOX
STATED PRINT RUN 50 SER.#'d SETS

I1	Ric Flair		
I2	Sting		
I3	Jeff Hardy	25.00	50.00
I4	Mick Foley	12.00	30.00
I5	Kevin Nash	10.00	20.00
I6	Rob Van Dam	20.00	40.00
I7	Jeff Jarrett	10.00	20.00
I8	Kurt Angle	12.00	25.00
I9	Earl Hebner	12.00	25.00
I10	Mr. Anderson	12.00	25.00
I11	AJ Styles	10.00	20.00
I12	Syxx-Pac	12.00	25.00
I13	Tara	12.00	25.00
I14	Tommy Dreamer	10.00	20.00
I15	Sting/Icon		
I16	Jeff Hardy/Twist of Fate		
I17	Mick Foley/Bang Bang		
I18	Kevin Nash (inscribed)		
I19	Rob Van Dam/Mr. Monday Night		
I20	Rob Van Dam/Whole F'n Show		
I21	Rob Van Dam/420		
I22	Jeff Jarrett/TNA Founder		
I23	Jeff Jarrett/Guitar Show		
I24	Jeff Jarrett/Slapnutz		
I25	Jeff Jarrett/The Chosen One		
I26	Jeff Jarrett/Music City USA		
I27	Kurt Angle/Olympic Champ		
I28	Kurt Angle/It's Real		
I29	Earl Hebner/Montreal Screw Job		
I30	Mr. Anderson/Mic Check		
I31	Mr. Anderson/Go Pack Go		
I32	AJ Styles/Grand Slam Winner		
I33	AJ Styles/Phenomenal		
I34	AJ Styles/TNA Original		
I35	Tommy Dreamer/Extreme Original		

2010 TRISTAR TNA Icons Memorabilia Silver

*GOLD: .5X TO 1.2X BASIC MEM
*RED: .6X TO 1.5X BASIC MEM
*PURPLE/1: UNPRICED DUE TO SCARCITY
STATED ODDS OVERALL 1:BOX
STATED PRINT RUN 199 SER.#'d SETS

M1	Ric Flair		
M2	Rob Van Dam	4.00	10.00
M3	Jeff Hardy	6.00	15.00
M4	Sting		
M5	Mick Foley	8.00	20.00
M6	Kevin Nash	6.00	15.00
M7	Tommy Dreamer	4.00	10.00

2010 TRISTAR TNA Icons Memorabilia Gold

*GOLD: .5X TO 1.2X BASIC MEM
STATED PRINT RUN 50 SER.#'d SETS

M1	Ric Flair		
M2	Rob Van Dam	5.00	12.00
M3	Jeff Hardy	8.00	20.00
M4	Sting	10.00	25.00
M5	Mick Foley	10.00	25.00
M6	Kevin Nash	8.00	20.00
M7	Tommy Dreamer	5.00	12.00

2010 TRISTAR TNA Icons The Next Generation Autographs Gold

*GREEN/25: .5X TO 1.2X BASIC AUTOS
*RED/5: UNPRICED DUE TO SCARCITY
*PURPLE/1: UNPRICED DUE TO SCARCITY
STATED ODDS OVERALL 2:BOX
STATED PRINT RUN 50 SER.#'d SETS

NEXT1	Alex Shelley	6.00	15.00
NEXT2	Chris Sabin	4.00	10.00
NEXT3	Rob Terry	4.00	10.00
NEXT4	Kazarian	4.00	10.00
NEXT5	D'Angelo Dinero	4.00	10.00
NEXT6	Douglas Williams	4.00	10.00
NEXT7	Desmond Wolfe	4.00	10.00
NEXT8	Eric Young	4.00	10.00
NEXT9	Abyss	6.00	15.00
NEXT10	Matt Morgan	4.00	10.00
NEXT11	Samoa Joe	6.00	15.00
NEXT12	Hernandez	4.00	10.00
NEXT13	Jay Lethal	4.00	10.00
NEXT14	Magnus	4.00	10.00

2010 TRISTAR TNA Icons Quad Memorabilia Silver

COMPLETE SET (1)

HH8 Hogan/Flair/Sting/Foley

2010 TRISTAR TNA Icons Six Autographs Gold

*GREEN/50: UNPRICED DUE TO SCARCITY
*RED/5: UNPRICED DUE TO SCARCITY
*PURPLE/1: UNPRICED DUE TO SCARCITY
STATED PRINT RUN 99 SER.#'d SETS

A61 Hogan/Foley/Sting/Nash/Flair/Jarr
A62 RVD/Moore/Hardy/Foley/Anderson/Angle
A63 Devon/Young/Ray/Storm/Nash/Roode
A64 Sky/Love/Rayne/Wilde/Von Erich/Sarita

2010 TRISTAR TNA Icons Sugar and Spice Autographs Gold

*GREEN/25: .5X TO 1.2X BASIC AUTOS
*RED/5: UNPRICED DUE TO SCARCITY
*PURPLE/1: UNPRICED DUE TO SCARCITY
STATED ODDS OVERALL 2:BOX
STATED PRINT RUN 50 SER.#'d SETS

SS1	Velvet Sky	10.00	25.00
SS2	Angelina Love	8.00	20.00
SS3	Taylor Wilde	8.00	20.00
SS4	Sarita	8.00	20.00
SS5	Daffney	10.00	25.00
SS6	Madison Rayne	8.00	20.00
SS7	Lacey Von Erich	12.00	30.00
SS8	Christy Hemme	8.00	20.00
SS9	SoCal Val	8.00	20.00
SS10	Chelsea	10.00	25.00
SS11	Miss Tessmacher	12.00	30.00
SS12	Rosie Lottalove	10.00	25.00

2010 TRISTAR TNA Icons Triple Memorabilia Silver

STATED PRINT RUN 199 SER.#'d SETS

HH6 Hulk Hogan/Bandana
HH7 Hulk Hogan/Bandana/Shirt/Mat
M10 Sky/Rayne/Von Erich

2008 TRISTAR TNA Impact

COMPLETE SET (69) 8.00 20.00
UNOPENED BOX (18 PACKS) 30.00 50.00
UNOPENED PACK (8 CARDS)
*GOLD/50: 2X TO 5X BASIC CARDS
*RUBY/10: UNPRICED DUE TO SCARCITY
*P.P.BLACK/1: UNPRICED DUE TO SCARCITY
*P.P.CYAN/1: UNPRICED DUE TO SCARCITY
*P.P.MAGENTA/1: UNPRICED DUE TO SCARCITY
*P.P.YELLOW/1: UNPRICED DUE TO SCARCITY

1	Kurt Angle	.75	2.00
2	Christian Cage	.30	.75
3	Samoa Joe	.20	.50
4	A.J. Styles	.40	1.00
5	Tomko	.12	.30
6	Booker T	.75	2.00
7	Jay Lethal	.12	.30
8	Jeff Jarrett	.75	2.00
9	Rhino	.30	.75
10	Curry Man	.12	.30
11	Sting	.60	1.50
12	Scott Steiner	.60	1.50
13	Robert Roode	.12	.30
14	Eric Young	.12	.30
15	Homicide	.15	.40
16	Hernandez	.15	.40
17	Petey Williams	.12	.30
18	Shark Boy	.12	.30
19	Consequences Creed	.15	.40
20	Alex Shelley	.15	.40
21	Jimmy Rave	.15	.40
22	Rellik	.15	.40
23	Brother Devon	.20	.50
24	Brother Ray	.20	.50
25	Kip James	.15	.40
26	Abyss	.40	1.00
27	Lance Hoyt	.15	.40
28	BG James	.12	.30
29	Chris Sabin	.12	.30
30	Kaz	.12	.30
31	Johnny Devine	.15	.40
32	Super Eric	.12	.30
33	Black Reign	.15	.40
34	James Storm	.15	.40
35	Sonjay Dutt	.12	.30
36	A.Styles/Tomko	.40	1.00
37	Team 3D	.20	.50
38	LAX	.40	1.00
39	Rock n' Rave Infection	.75	2.00
40	Motor Sity Machineguns	.15	.40
41	Karen Angle	.50	1.25
42	ODB	.40	1.00
43	Awesome Kong	.30	.75

#	Name	Lo	Hi
44	Traci Brooks	.50	1.25
45	Christy Hemme	.75	2.00
46	Sharmell	.40	1.00
47	Gail Kim	.40	1.00
48	Angelina Love	.60	1.50
49	Raisha Saeed	.30	.75
50	SoCal Val	.60	1.50
51	Velvet Sky	.50	1.25
52	Hermie Sadler	.40	1.00
53	Jacqueline	.40	1.00
54	Roxxi Laveaux	.40	1.00
55	Salinas	.40	1.00
56	Vince Russo	.12	.30
57	James Mitchell	.15	.40
58	Matt Morgan	.15	.40
59	Jim Cornette	.15	.40
60	Earl Hebner	.15	.40
61	Andrew Thomas	.12	.30
62	Rudy Charles	.12	.30
63	Mark Johnson	.12	.30
64	Mike Tenay	.15	.40
65	Don West	.12	.30
66	Jeremy Borash	.12	.30
67	Terry Taylor	.12	.30
68	Dixie Carter	.30	.75
69	Kevin Nash	.60	1.50

2008 TRISTAR TNA Impact Autographs Silver

*GOLD/50: .5X TO 1.2X BASIC AUTOS
*RED/25: .6X TO 1.5X BASIC AUTOS
*BLUE/5: UNPRICED DUE TO SCARCITY
*PURPLE/1: UNPRICED DUE TO SCARCITY

Code	Name	Lo	Hi
AA	Abyss	6.00	15.00
AJ	Jacqueline	4.00	10.00
AK	Kaz	4.00	10.00
AO	ODB	4.00	10.00
AR	Rellik	4.00	10.00
AS	Sting SP	40.00	80.00
AT	Tomko	6.00	15.00
AAJ	A.J. Styles	15.00	40.00
AAK	Awesome Kong	5.00	12.00
AAL	Angelina Love	6.00	15.00
AAS	Alex Shelley	5.00	12.00
ABD	Brother Devon	6.00	15.00
ABG	BG James	5.00	12.00
ABR	Black Reign	4.00	10.00
ABR	Brother Ray	6.00	15.00
ABT	Booker T SP	15.00	40.00
ACC	Christian Cage SP	6.00	15.00
ACH	Christy Hemme	10.00	25.00
ACM	Curry Man	4.00	10.00
ACS	Chris Sabin	5.00	12.00
ADC	Dixie Carter SP	15.00	40.00
ADW	Don West	4.00	10.00
AEY	Eric Young	4.00	10.00
AGK	Gail Kim	20.00	40.00
AH1	Hernandez	4.00	10.00
AH2	Homicide	4.00	10.00
AJB	Jeremy Borash	4.00	10.00
AJC	Jim Cornette	5.00	12.00
AJD	Johnny Devine	4.00	10.00
AJJ	Jeff Jarrett	6.00	15.00
AJL	Jay Lethal	4.00	10.00
AJM	James Mitchell	4.00	10.00
AJR	Jimmy Rave	5.00	12.00
AJS	James Storm	4.00	10.00
AKA	Kurt Angle SP	30.00	60.00
AKJ	Kip James	5.00	12.00
AKN	Kevin Nash	12.00	30.00
ALH	Lance Hoyt	4.00	10.00
AMM	Matt Morgan	5.00	12.00
AMT	Mike Tenay	4.00	10.00
APB	Payton Banks	5.00	12.00
APW	Petey Williams	4.00	10.00
AR2	Rhino	5.00	12.00
ARL	Roxxi Laveaux	5.00	12.00
ARR	Robert Roode	5.00	12.00
ARS	Raisha Saeed	4.00	10.00
AS2	Sharmell	4.00	10.00
AS3	Salinas	5.00	12.00
ASB	Shark Boy	4.00	10.00
ASD	Sonjay Dutt	4.00	10.00
ASE	Super Eric	4.00	10.00
ASJ	Samoa Joe SP	15.00	40.00
ASS	Scott Steiner	12.00	30.00
ASV	SoCal Val	5.00	12.00
ATB	Traci Brooks	5.00	12.00
AVS	Velvet Sky	10.00	25.00
ACC2	Consequences Creed	4.00	10.00
AKA2	Karen Angle SP	20.00	40.00

2008 TRISTAR TNA Impact Dual Autographs Gold

COMPLETE SET (10)
*RED/25: .5X TO 1.2X BASIC AUTOS
*BLUE/5: UNPRICED DUE TO SCARCITY
*PURPLE/1: UNPRICED DUE TO SCARCITY
STATED PRINT RUN 50 SER.#'d SETS

Code	Name	Lo	Hi
A2AA	Ku.Angle/Ka.Angle	50.00	100.00
A2BS	Booker T/Sharmell	25.00	50.00
A2DR	Brothers Devon & Ray	25.00	50.00
A2HH	Homicide/Hernandez	20.00	40.00
A2LS	A.Love/V.Sky	40.00	80.00
A2LV	J.Lethal/S.Val	20.00	40.00
A2RB	R.Roode/P.Banks	25.00	50.00
A2SJ	J.Storm/Jacqueline	20.00	40.00
A2SS	A.Shelley/C.Sabin	30.00	60.00
A2TW	M.Tenay/D.West	15.00	30.00

2008 TRISTAR TNA Impact Memorabilia Black

*RAINBOW FOIL/10-50
*GOLD/25: .5X TO 1.2X BASIC MEM
*RED/1: UNPRICED DUE TO SCARCITY
STATED PRINT RUN 250 SER.#'d SETS

Code	Name	Lo	Hi
AAO	ODB	6.00	15.00
AAS	Sting	10.00	25.00
AAT	Tomko	5.00	12.00
AAAL	Angelina Love	10.00	25.00
AAAS	A.J. Styles	6.00	15.00
AACC	Christian Cage	5.00	12.00
AACH	Christy Hemme	8.00	20.00
AAGK	Gail Kim	8.00	20.00
AAJL	Jay Lethal	6.00	15.00
AAKA	Kurt Angle	8.00	20.00
AAKN	Kevin Nash	8.00	20.00
AASD	Sonjay Dutt	5.00	12.00
AASJ	Samoa Joe	5.00	12.00
AASS	Scott Steiner	8.00	20.00
AASV	SoCal Val	8.00	20.00
AATB	Traci Brooks	8.00	20.00
AAVS	Velvet Sky	10.00	25.00
AAKA2	Karen Angle	10.00	25.00

2008 TRISTAR TNA Impact Mike's Magical Moments

	Lo	Hi
COMPLETE SET (5)	1.00	2.50

*GOLD/50: 2X TO 5X BASIC CARDS
*RED/10: UNPRICED DUE TO SCARCITY
*PURPLE/1: UNPRICED DUE TO SCARCITY
*P.P.BLACK/1: UNPRICED DUE TO SCARCITY
*P.P.CYAN/1: UNPRICED DUE TO SCARCITY
*P.P.MAGENTA/1: UNPRICED DUE TO SCARCITY
*P.P.YELLOW/1: UNPRICED DUE TO SCARCITY

Code	Name	Lo	Hi
M1	First Night	.12	.30
M2	Kurt Angle/Samoa Joe	.75	2.00
M3	Big Name Newcomers/Arrivals	.12	.30
M4	X Division	.12	.30
M5	Sporting Superstars	.12	.30

2008 TRISTAR TNA Impact Muscles Ink

	Lo	Hi
COMPLETE SET (10)	3.00	8.00

*GOLD/50: 2X TO 5X BASIC CARDS
*RED/10: UNPRICED DUE TO SCARCITY
*PURPLE/1: UNPRICED DUE TO SCARCITY
*P.P.BLACK/1: UNPRICED DUE TO SCARCITY
*P.P.CYAN/1: UNPRICED DUE TO SCARCITY
*P.P.MAGENTA/1: UNPRICED DUE TO SCARCITY
*P.P.YELLOW/1: UNPRICED DUE TO SCARCITY

Code	Name	Lo	Hi
MI1	Scott Steiner	.60	1.50
MI2	Robert Roode	.12	.30
MI3	Petey Williams	.12	.30
MI4	Traci Brooks	.50	1.25
MI5	Brother Devon	.20	.50
MI6	Booker T	.75	2.00
MI7	Christy Hemme	.75	2.00
MI8	Kevin Nash	.60	1.50
MI9	Tomko	.12	.30
MI10	Kurt Angle	.75	2.00

2008 TRISTAR TNA Impact Then and Now

	Lo	Hi
COMPLETE SET (4)	1.50	4.00

*GOLD/50: 2X TO 5X BASIC CARDS
*RED/10: UNPRICED DUE TO SCARCITY
*PURPLE/1: UNPRICED DUE TO SCARCITY
*P.P.BLACK/1: UNPRICED DUE TO SCARCITY
*P.P.CYAN/1: UNPRICED DUE TO SCARCITY
*P.P.MAGENTA/1: UNPRICED DUE TO SCARCITY
*P.P.YELLOW/1: UNPRICED DUE TO SCARCITY

Code	Name	Lo	Hi
TN1	Jeff Jarrett	.75	2.00
TN2	Robert Roode	.12	.30
TN3	Kevin Nash	.60	1.50
TN4	Scott Steiner	.60	1.50

2008 TRISTAR TNA Impact Thoughts by Big Sexy Kevin Nash

	Lo	Hi
COMPLETE SET (5)	2.00	5.00

*GOLD/50: 2X TO 5X BASIC CARDS
*RED/10: UNPRICED DUE TO SCARCITY
*PURPLE/1: UNPRICED DUE TO SCARCITY
*P.P.BLACK/1: UNPRICED DUE TO SCARCITY
*P.P.CYAN/1: UNPRICED DUE TO SCARCITY
*P.P.MAGENTA/1: UNPRICED DUE TO SCARCITY
*P.P.YELLOW/1: UNPRICED DUE TO SCARCITY

Code	Name	Lo	Hi
BS1	TNA's X-Division	.60	1.50
BS2	Samoa Joe	.60	1.50
BS3	Sting	.60	1.50
BS4	Scott Steiner	.60	1.50
BS5	Trading Cards	.60	1.50

2008 TRISTAR TNA Impact Triple Autographs Red

STATED PRINT RUN 25 SER.#'d SETS

Code	Name	Lo	Hi
A3AAS	Angle/Angle/Styles	75.00	150.00
A3RHH	Rave/Hoyt/Hemme	25.00	50.00

2008 TRISTAR TNA Impact We Are TNA

	Lo	Hi
COMPLETE SET (7)	2.50	6.00

*GOLD/50: 2X TO 5X BASIC CARDS
*RED/10: UNPRICED DUE TO SCARCITY
*PURPLE/1: UNPRICED DUE TO SCARCITY
*P.P.BLACK/1: UNPRICED DUE TO SCARCITY
*P.P.CYAN/1: UNPRICED DUE TO SCARCITY
*P.P.MAGENTA/1: UNPRICED DUE TO SCARCITY
*P.P.YELLOW/1: UNPRICED DUE TO SCARCITY

Code	Name	Lo	Hi
T1	6-Sided Ring	.40	1.00
T2	X-Division	.20	.50
T3	History	.75	2.00
T4	TNA World Championship	.75	2.00
T5	TNA X-Division Championship	.40	1.00
T6	TNA World Tag Team Champ.	.40	1.00
T7	TNA Womens Championship	.40	1.00

2009 TRISTAR TNA Impact

	Lo	Hi
COMPLETE SET (100)	12.50	25.00
UNOPENED BOX (20 PACKS)		
UNOPENED PACK (6 CARDS)		

*WHITE: SAME VALUE
*SILVER/20: 4X TO 10X BASIC CARDS
*GOLD/5: UNPRICED DUE TO SCARCITY
*PURPLE/1: UNPRICED DUE TO SCARCITY

#	Name	Lo	Hi
1	Sting	.60	1.50
2	Mick Foley	.60	1.50
3	Daniels	.12	.30
4	Angelina Love	.60	1.50
5	Bobby Lashley	.30	.75
6	James Storm	.15	.40
7	Jeff Jarrett	.60	1.50
8	Taz	.12	.30
9	Brother Ray	.20	.50
10	Tara	.50	1.25
11	Samoa Joe	.20	.50
12	Kevin Nash	.75	2.00
13	Suicide	.12	.30
14	Velvet Sky	.60	1.50
15	Scott Steiner	.60	1.50
16	Daffney	.30	.75
17	Amazing Red	.12	.30
18	Matt Morgan	.15	.40
19	Hernandez	.15	.40
20	ODB	.20	.50
21	AJ Styles	.30	.75
22	Jay Lethal	.12	.30
23	Awesome Kong	.20	.50
24	Robert Roode	.15	.40
25	Kurt Angle	.75	2.00
26	Brutus Magnus	.12	.30
27	SoCal Val	.50	1.25
28	Mike Tenay	.12	.30
29	Jenna Morasca	.50	1.25
30	Booker T	.12	.30
31	Alex Shelley	.15	.40
32	Kiyoshi	.12	.30
33	Sojournor Bolt	.20	.50
34	Abyss	.30	.75
35	Christy Hemme	.75	2.00

#	Player		
36	Doug Williams	.12	.30
37	Consequences Creed	.12	.30
38	Taylor Wilde	.50	1.25
39	Jesse Neal	.12	.30
40	Brother Devon	.20	.50
41	Lauren Brooke	.30	.75
42	Shark Boy	.12	.30
43	Homicide	.15	.40
44	Sharmell	.20	.50
45	Jim Cornette	.12	.30
46	Cody Deaner	.12	.30
47	Eric Young	.12	.30
48	Raisha Saeed	.20	.50
49	Rhino	.20	.50
50	Sarita	.30	.75
51	Don West	.12	.30
52	Traci Brooks	.50	1.25
53	Sheik Abdul Bashir	.12	.30
54	Dr. Stevie	.15	.40
55	Madison Rayne	.50	1.25
56	Chris Sabin	.12	.30
57	Kip James	.15	.40
58	Dixie Carter	.30	.75
59	Jeremy Borash	.12	.30
60	Rob Terry	.12	.30
61	Hermie Sadler	.12	.30
62	Rocco & Sally Boy	.12	.30
63	Ayako Hamada	.30	.75
64	The Beautiful People	.60	1.50
65	Beer Money, Inc.	.15	.40
66	Danny Bonaduce	.30	.75
67	Curtis Granderson	.20	.50
68	THE ICON: STING	.60	1.50
69	THE ICON: STING	.60	1.50
70	THE ICON: STING	.60	1.50
71	THE ICON: STING	.60	1.50
72	THE ICON: STING	.60	1.50
73	Mick Foley	.60	1.50
74	Kurt Angle	.75	2.00
75	Booker T	.12	.30
76	AJ Styles	.30	.75
77	Suicide	.12	.30
78	Daniels	.12	.30
79	Team 3D	.20	.50
80	Sting/Kurt Angle	.75	2.00
81	Angelina Love	.60	1.50
82	Awesome Kong	.20	.50
83	Kurt Angle	.75	2.00
84	Jenna Morasca	.50	1.25
85	Daniels	.12	.30
86	Madison Rayne	.50	1.25
87	Mike Tenay	.12	.30
88	Alex Shelley	.15	.40
89	Sheik Abdul Bashir	.12	.30
90	Jeff Jarrett	.60	1.50
91	Consequences Creed	.12	.30
92	Lauren Brooke	.30	.75
93	Mick Foley	.60	1.50
94	James Storm	.15	.40
95	Jenna Morasca	.50	1.25
96	Kip James	.15	.40
97	Mike Tenay	.12	.30
98	Daniels	.12	.30
99	Tweet n' Tweak Connection	.20	.50
NNO	Checklist	.12	.30

2009 TRISTAR TNA Impact Autographs Silver

SEMISTARS (IA1-IA84)
UNLISTED STARS (IA1-IA84)
*GOLD/60: .5X TO 1.2X BASIC AUTOS
*BLUE/25: .6X TO 1.5X BASIC AUTOS
*GREEN/10: UNPRICED DUE TO SCARCITY
*PURPLE/1: UNPRICED DUE TO SCARCITY

Card	Player		
IA1	Abyss	5.00	12.00
IA2	AJ Styles	6.00	15.00
IA3	Alex Shelley	4.00	10.00
IA4	Amazing Red	4.00	10.00
IA5	Angelina Love	8.00	20.00
IA6	Awesome Kong	5.00	12.00
IA7	Bobby Lashley		
IA8	Booker T		
IA9	Brother Devon	4.00	10.00
IA10	Brother Ray	4.00	10.00
IA11	Brutus Magnus	4.00	10.00
IA12	Chris Sabin	5.00	12.00
IA13	Christy Hemme		
IA14	Cody Deaner	4.00	10.00
IA15	Consequences Creed	4.00	10.00
IA16	Curtis Granderson		
IA17	Daffney	8.00	20.00
IA18	Daniels	5.00	12.00
IA19	Danny Bonaduce	6.00	15.00
IA20	Dixie Carter	5.00	12.00
IA21	Doug Williams	4.00	10.00
IA22	Dr. Stevie	5.00	12.00
IA23	Eric Young	4.00	10.00
IA24	Hernandez		
IA25	Homicide	4.00	10.00
IA26	Hermie Sadler	4.00	10.00
IA27	James Storm	5.00	12.00
IA28	Jay Lethal	4.00	10.00
IA29	Jeff Jarrett	6.00	15.00
IA30	Jenna Morasca	6.00	15.00
IA31	Jesse Neal	4.00	10.00
IA32	Jeremy Borash	4.00	10.00
IA33	Jim Cornette		
IA34	Kevin Nash		
IA35	Kip James	4.00	10.00
IA36	Kiyoshi	4.00	10.00
IA37	Kurt Angle		
IA38	Lauren Brooke	5.00	12.00
IA39	Madison Rayne	6.00	15.00
IA40	Matt Morgan		
IA41	Mick Foley		
IA42	ODB	4.00	10.00
IA43	Raisha Saeed	5.00	12.00
IA44	Rhino		
IA45	Rob Terry	5.00	12.00
IA46	Robert Roode	5.00	12.00
IA47	Samoa Joe	5.00	12.00
IA48	Sarita	6.00	15.00
IA49	Scott Steiner		
IA50	Shark Boy	5.00	12.00
IA51	Sharmell		
IA52	Sheik Abdul Bashir		10.00
IA53	SoCal Val	6.00	15.00
IA54	Sojournor Bolt		
IA55	Sting		
IA56	Suicide	4.00	10.00
IA57	Tara	8.00	20.00
IA58	Taylor Wilde	8.00	20.00
IA59	Traci Brooks	6.00	15.00
IA60	Velvet Sky	8.00	20.00
IA61	Jeff Jarrett		
	Mick Foley		
IA62	Angelina Love	12.00	30.00
	Velvet Sky		
IA63	Chris Sabin		
	Alex Shelley		
IA64	Daffney	12.00	30.00
	The Governor		
IA65	Bobby Lashley		
	Kurt Angle		
IA66	Kevin Nash		
	Jenna Morasca		
IA67	Abyss		
	Lauren		
IA68	Mick Foley		
	Sting		
IA69	Consequences Creed		
	Jay Lethal		
IA70	Jesse Neal		
	Rhino		
IA71	Mike Tenay		
	Don West		
IA72	ODB		
	Cody Deaner		
IA73	Brother Devon		
	Brother Ray		
IA74	Sting		
	Kurt Angle		
IA75	Kevin Nash		
	Samoa Joe		
IA76	Scott Steiner		
	Booker T		
IA77	Angelina Love		
	Velvet Sky/Madison Rayne		
IA78	Sting		
	Kurt Angle/Mick Foley		
IA79	Tara		
	Christy Hemme/Traci Brooks		
IA80	Brutus Magnus		
	Rob Terry/Doug Williams		
IA81	Brother Devon		
	Brother Ray/James Storm/Robert Roode		
IA82	Kurt Angle		
	Kevin Nash/Booker T/Scott Steiner		
IA83	Angelina Love		
	Velvet Sky/Tara/Christy Hemme		
IA84	Chris Sabin		
	Alex Shelley/Jay Lethal/Consequences Creed		

2009 TRISTAR TNA Impact High Impact Championship Inserts

NNO Phone Call EXCH
NNO 2 Tickets and Backstage Pass EXCH
NNO 2 Tickets EXCH
NNO Autographed Baseball EXCH
NNO Autographed Photo EXCH

2009 TRISTAR TNA Impact Knockout Autographed Dual Kiss Gold

*BLUE/10: UNPRICED DUE TO SCARCITY
*PURPLE/1: UNPRICED DUE TO SCARCITY
STATED PRINT RUN 25 SER.#'d SETS

Card	Players		
2K1	A.Love/V.Sky		
2K2	C.Hemme/T.Brooks		
2K3	J.Morasca/Sharmell	15.00	30.00
2K4	SoCal Val/L.Brooke	25.00	50.00

2009 TRISTAR TNA Impact Knockout Kiss Gold

*BLUE/25: .6X TO 1.5X BASIC KISS
*GREEN/10: UNPRICED DUE TO SCARCITY
*PURPLE/1: UNPRICED DUE TO SCARCITY
STATED PRINT RUN 99 SER.#'d SETS

Card	Player		
K1	Angelina Love	15.00	40.00
K2	Awesome Kong	8.00	20.00
K3	Christy Hemme	15.00	40.00
K4	Jenna Morasca	10.00	25.00
K5	ODB	8.00	20.00
K6	Sharmell	8.00	20.00
K7	Tara	15.00	40.00
K8	Taylor Wilde	12.00	30.00
K9	Traci Brooks	12.00	30.00
K10	Velvet Sky	15.00	40.00

2009 TRISTAR TNA Impact Sting Autographed Face Paint Silver

STATED PRINT RUN 10 SER. #'d SETS
NOT PRICED DUE TO SCARCITY

S1 Sting Black
S2 Sting White

2009 TRISTAR TNA Impact Sting Event-Worn Face Paint Silver

*PURPLE/1: UNPRICED DUE TO SCARCITY
STATED PRINT RUN 5 SER. #'d SETS
UNPRICED DUE TO SCARCITY

S1 Sting Black
S2 Sting White

2009 TRISTAR TNA Impact Sting Face Paint Gold

*GREEN/10: UNPRICED DUE TO SCARCITY
*PURPLE/1: UNPRICED DUE TO SCARCITY
STATED PRINT RUN 60 SER.#'d SETS

S1	Sting Black	25.00	60.00
S2	Sting White	25.00	60.00

2013 TRISTAR TNA Impact Glory

COMPLETE SET (109) 20.00 50.00
COMPLETE SET W/O SP (100) 8.00 20.00
UNOPENED BOX (20 PACKS)
UNOPENED PACK (6 CARDS)
*RED/40: 2X TO 5X BASIC CARDS
*RED SP/40: .5X TO 1.2X BASIC CARDS
*BLUE/10: UNPRICED DUE TO SCARCITY
*BLUE SP/10: UNPRICED DUE TO SCARCITY
*RAINBOW/1: UNPRICED DUE TO SCARCITY
*RAINBOW SP/1: UNPRICED DUE TO SCARCITY
STATED ODDS SP 1:1 HOBBY BOX

#	Player		
1	Jeff Hardy	.60	1.50
2	Hulk Hogan	.75	2.00
3	Kurt Angle	.25	.60
4	Sting	.60	1.50
5	Rampage Jackson	.25	.60
6	Tito Ortiz	.25	.60
7	Mickie James	.75	2.00
8	Chris Sabin	.15	.40
9	Bully Ray	.15	.40
10	Bobby Roode	.15	.40
11	AJ Styles	.25	.60
12	Gail Kim	.40	1.00
13	Velvet Sky	.60	1.50
14	Chavo Guerrero Jr.	.15	.40

15	James Storm	.15	.40
16	ODB	.15	.40
17	Christopher Daniels	.15	.40
18	Sting	.60	1.50
19	Joseph Park	.25	.60
20	Jessie Godderz	.15	.40
21	Mr. Anderson	.25	.60
22	Garett Bischoff	.25	.60
23	Samoa Joe	.15	.40
24	Austin Aries	.25	.60
25	Hernandez	.15	.40
26	Jeremy Borash	.15	.40
27	Manik	.15	.40
28	Velvet Sky	.60	1.50
29	Jeff Hardy	.60	1.50
30	Christy Hemme	.50	1.25
31	Robbie E	.15	.40
32	Dixie Carter	.25	.60
33	Christopher Daniels	.15	.40
34	Taryn Terrell	.40	1.00
35	Eric Young	.15	.40
36	Miss Tessmacher	.40	1.00
37	Magnus	.15	.40
38	AJ Styles	.25	.60
39	Hulk Hogan	.75	2.00
40	Sting	.60	1.50
41	Gail Kim	.40	1.00
42	Wes Brisco	.15	.40
43	Rob Terry	.15	.40
44	Chavo Guerrero Jr.	.15	.40
45	Gunner	.15	.40
46	Velvet Sky	.60	1.50
47	Knux	.15	.40
48	Jeff Hardy	.60	1.50
49	Chris Sabin	.15	.40
50	Kazarian	.15	.40
51	King Mo	.15	.40
52	Austin Aries	.25	.60
53	Jay Bradley	.15	.40
54	Kenny King	.15	.40
55	Taz	.15	.40
56	Hernandez	.15	.40
57	Eric Young	.15	.40
58	Hulk Hogan	.75	2.00
59	Velvet Sky	.60	1.50
60	Sting	.60	1.50
61	AJ Styles	.25	.60
62	Rockstar Spud	.15	.40
63	Bully Ray	.15	.40
64	Dixie Carter	.25	.60
65	Velvet Sky	.60	1.50
66	Rampage Jackson	.25	.60
67	Jeff Hardy	.60	1.50
68	Christopher Daniels	.15	.40
69	Abyss	.25	.60
70	Chris Sabin	.15	.40
71	Mike Tenay	.15	.40
72	Mickie James	.75	2.00
73	AJ Styles	.25	.60
74	ODB	.15	.40
75	Magnus	.15	.40
76	Hector Guerrero	.15	.40
77	Hulk Hogan	.75	2.00
78	Brooke Hogan	.40	1.00
79	Austin Aries	.25	.60
80	Jessie Godderz	.15	.40
81	Jessie Godderz	.15	.40
82	Jessie Godderz	.15	.40
83	Garett Bischoff	.25	.60
84	Chavo Guerrero Jr.	.15	.40
85	Sam Shaw	.15	.40
86	Bobby Roode	.15	.40
87	Dixie Carter	.25	.60
88	Jeff Hardy	.60	1.50
89	Hulk Hogan	.75	2.00
90	Jeff Hardy Original Art	.50	1.25
91	Jeff Hardy Original Art	.50	1.25
92	Jeff Hardy Original Art	.50	1.25
93	Jeff Hardy Original Art	.50	1.25
94	Jeff Hardy Original Art	.50	1.25
95	Jeff Hardy Original Art	.50	1.25
96	Jeff Hardy Original Art	.50	1.25
97	Jeff Hardy Original Art	.50	1.25
98	Jeff Hardy Original Art	.50	1.25
99	Jeff Hardy Original Art	.50	1.25
100	Aces and Eights SP	3.00	8.00
101	Jeff Hardy SP	3.00	8.00
102	Rampage Jackson SP	1.25	3.00
103	Velvet Sky SP	3.00	8.00
104	AJ Styles SP	1.25	3.00
105	Gail Kim SP	2.00	5.00
106	Sting SP	3.00	8.00
107	Jeff Hardy SP	3.00	8.00
108	Dixie Carter SP	1.25	3.00
109	Hulk Hogan SP	4.00	10.00

2013 TRISTAR TNA Impact Glory Autographed Mat Relics Gold

*BLUE/10: UNPRICED DUE TO SCARCITY
*RED/5: UNPRICED DUE TO SCARCITY
*RAINBOW/1: UNPRICED DUE TO SCARCITY
STATED PRINT RUN 50 SER.#'d SETS

MAS	AJ Styles	12.00	30.00
MBH	Brooke Hogan	20.00	50.00
MBR	Bully Ray	8.00	20.00
MBR	Bobby Roode	8.00	20.00
MCG	Chavo Guerrero Jr.	8.00	20.00
MCH	Christy Hemme	12.00	30.00
MCS	Chris Sabin	8.00	20.00
MD	Devon	8.00	20.00
MHH	Hulk Hogan	50.00	100.00
MJG	Jessie Godderz	8.00	20.00
MJH	Jeff Hardy	20.00	50.00
MKA	Kurt Angle	15.00	40.00
MMA	Mr. Anderson	8.00	20.00
MMJ	Mickie James	20.00	50.00
MRJ	Rampage Jackson	12.00	30.00
MS	Sting	30.00	60.00
MT	Tara	8.00	20.00
MTT	Taryn Terrell	12.00	30.00

2013 TRISTAR TNA Impact Glory Autographed Memorabilia Red

M1	Hulk Hogan		
M2	Jeff Hardy		
M3	Sting	40.00	80.00
M4	Austin Aries		
M5	Rampage Jackson	15.00	40.00
M6	Tito Ortiz		

2013 TRISTAR TNA Impact Glory Dual Autographs Gold

*RED/50: .5X TO 1.2X BASIC AUTOS
*BLUE/10: UNPRICED DUE TO SCARCITY
*GREEN/5: UNPRICED DUE TO SCARCITY
*RAINBOW/1: UNPRICED DUE TO SCARCITY
*P.P.BLACK/1: UNPRICED DUE TO SCARCITY
*P.P.CYAN/1: UNPRICED DUE TO SCARCITY
*P.P.MAGENTA/1: UNPRICED DUE TO SCARCITY
*P.P.YELLOW/1: UNPRICED DUE TO SCARCITY
STATED PRINT RUN 99 SER.#'d SETS

4	J.Park/Abyss	8.00	20.00
7	M.James/G.Kim	10.00	25.00
8	C.Daniels/Kazarian	4.00	10.00
10	E.Young/ODB	4.00	10.00
12	G.Kim/V.Sky	8.00	20.00
14	B.Roode/J.Storm	5.00	12.00
16	J.Storm/Gunner	5.00	12.00
20	A.Styles/S.Joe	8.00	20.00
21	C.Hemme/S.Val	8.00	20.00

2013 TRISTAR TNA Impact Glory Dual Memorabilia Gold

*RED/50: .5X TO 1.2X BASIC MEM
*BLUE/10: UNPRICED DUE TO SCARCITY
*GREEN/5: UNPRICED DUE TO SCARCITY
*RAINBOW/1: UNPRICED DUE TO SCARCITY
STATED PRINT RUN 99 SER.#'d SETS

M8	B.Ray/M.Tessmacher	5.00	12.00
M9	T.Ortiz/R.Jackson	5.00	12.00

2013 TRISTAR TNA Impact Glory Dual Memorabilia Red

*RED/50: .5X TO 1.2X BASIC MEM

M8	B.Ray/M.Tessmacher	6.00	15.00
M9	T.Ortiz/R.Jackson	6.00	15.00

2013 TRISTAR TNA Impact Glory Jeff Hardy Autographed Face Paint Green

H1	Jeff Hardy		
H2	Jeff Hardy		

2013 TRISTAR TNA Impact Glory Memorabilia Red

STATED PRINT RUN 50 SER.#'d SETS

M10	Tito Ortiz	5.00	12.00
M11	Rampage Jackson	5.00	12.00
M12	Bully Ray	5.00	12.00
M13	Mickie James	15.00	40.00
M14	Sting	12.00	30.00

2013 TRISTAR TNA Impact Glory On-Card Autographs Gold

*RED/50: .5X TO 1.2X BASIC AUTOS
*BLUE/10: UNPRICED DUE TO SCARCITY
*GREEN/5: UNPRICED DUE TO SCARCITY
*RAINBOW/1: UNPRICED DUE TO SCARCITY
STATED PRINT RUN 199 SER.#'d SETS

GAS	AJ Styles	8.00	20.00
GBR	Bobby Roode	6.00	15.00
GCH	Christy Hemme	6.00	15.00
GGK	Gail Kim	8.00	20.00
GJG	Jessie Godderz	5.00	12.00
GJS	James Storm	5.00	12.00
GKA	Kurt Angle	12.00	30.00
GMJ	Mickie James	8.00	20.00
GT	Tara	6.00	15.00
GVS	Velvet Sky	10.00	25.00

2013 TRISTAR TNA Impact Glory Quad Memorabilia Gold

*RED/50: X TO X BASIC MEM
*BLUE/10: UNPRICED DUE TO SCARCITY
*GREEN/5: UNPRICED DUE TO SCARCITY
*RAINBOW/1: UNPRICED DUE TO SCARCITY
STATED PRINT RUN 99 SER.#'d SETS

M7 Kim/James/Tessmacher/Sky

2013 TRISTAR TNA Impact Glory Sticker Autographs Gold

*RED/50: .5X TO 1.2X BASIC AUTOS
*BLUE/10: UNPRICED DUE TO SCARCITY
*GREEN/5: UNPRICED DUE TO SCARCITY
*RAINBOW/1: UNPRICED DUE TO SCARCITY
*P.P.BLACK/1: UNPRICED DUE TO SCARCITY
*P.P.CYAN/1: UNPRICED DUE TO SCARCITY
*P.P.MAGENTA/1: UNPRICED DUE TO SCARCITY
*P.P.YELLOW/1: UNPRICED DUE TO SCARCITY
STATED PRINT RUN 99 SER.#'d SETS

G5	Chris Sabin	4.00	10.00
G11	Manik	4.00	10.00
G15	Knux	4.00	10.00
G26	Wes Brisco	4.00	10.00
G27	Jay Bradley	4.00	10.00
G31	Brooke Hogan	15.00	40.00
G32	Garett Bischoff	4.00	10.00
G33	Magnus	4.00	10.00
G37	Devon	4.00	10.00

2013 TRISTAR TNA Impact Glory Triple Autographs Red

*BLUE/10: UNPRICED DUE TO SCARCITY
*GREEN/5: UNPRICED DUE TO SCARCITY
*RAINBOW/1: UNPRICED DUE TO SCARCITY
STATED PRINT RUN 50 SER.#'d SETS

1	Bobby Roode Christopher Daniels/ Kazarian	8.00	20.00
3	Brisco/G.Bischoff/Knux	8.00	20.00
5	James/ODB/Tessmacher	12.00	30.00

2013 TRISTAR TNA Impact Live

COMPLETE SET (109)		25.00	50.00
COMPLETE SET W/O SP (99)		8.00	20.00
UNOPENED BOX (20 PACKS)			
UNOPENED PACK (6 CARDS)			

*GOLD/50: 2X TO 5X BASIC CARDS
*GOLD SP/50: .6X TO 1.5X BASIC CARDS
*RED/10: UNPRICED DUE TO SCARCITY
*RED SP/10: UNPRICED DUE TO SCARCITY
*RAINBOW/1: UNPRICED DUE TO SCARCITY
*RAINBOW/1: UNPRICED DUE TO SCARCITY
STATED SP ODDS 1:BOX

1	Hulk Hogan	.75	2.00
2	Brooke Hogan	.40	1.00
3	Hulk Hogan/Brooke Hogan	.75	2.00
4	Sting	.60	1.50
5	Jeff Hardy	.60	1.50
6	Austin Aries	.25	.60
7	Gail Kim	.40	1.00
8	AJ Styles	.25	.60
9	Bobby Roode	.15	.40
10	Bully Ray	.15	.40
11	Kurt Angle	.25	.60
12	Garett Bischoff	.25	.60
13	Hernandez	.15	.40
14	King Mo	.15	.40

15	Jessie Godderz	.15	.40
16	Tara	.50	1.25
17	James Storm	.15	.40
18	Kazarian	.15	.40
19	Christopher Daniels	.15	.40
20	Matt Morgan	.15	.40
21	Rob Van Dam	.25	.60
22	Douglas Williams	.15	.40
23	SoCal Val	.40	1.00
24	Sting	.60	1.50
25	Christy Hemme	.50	1.25
26	Jesse Sorensen	.15	.40
27	Taz	.15	.40
28	Earl Hebner	.15	.40
29	Magnus	.15	.40
30	AJ Styles	.25	.60
31	Kenny King	.15	.40
32	Taryn Terrell	.40	1.00
33	Devon	.15	.40
34	Velvet Sky	.60	1.50
35	Jeff Hardy	.60	1.50
36	Joseph Park	.25	.60
37	Eric Young	.15	.40
38	Tara	.50	1.25
39	Chris Sabin	.15	.40
40	Sting	.60	1.50
41	Bully Ray	.15	.40
42	Robbie E	.15	.40
43	Rob Terry	.15	.40
44	James Storm	.15	.40
45	Crimson	.15	.40
46	DOC	.15	.40
47	Jessie Godderz	.15	.40
48	Samoa Joe	.15	.40
49	Rob Van Dam	.25	.60
50	Hulk Hogan	.75	2.00
51	Jeff Hardy	.60	1.50
52	Christy Hemme	.50	1.25
53	Jessie Godderz	.15	.40
54	Madison Rayne	.40	1.00
55	TNA Referees	.15	.40
56	Zema Ion	.15	.40
57	Christopher Daniels	.15	.40
58	Mr. Anderson	.25	.60
59	Garett Bischoff	.25	.60
60	AJ Styles	.25	.60
61	Mike Tenay	.15	.40
62	Aces and Eights	.15	.40
63	Matt Morgan	.15	.40
64	James Storm	.15	.40
65	Hernandez	.15	.40
66	Kurt Angle	.25	.60
67	Douglas Williams	.15	.40
68	Jeff Hardy	.60	1.50
69	ODB	.15	.40
70	Abyss	.25	.60
71	Bully Ray	.15	.40
72	Jeremy Borash	.15	.40
73	Gunner	.15	.40
74	Christopher Daniels	.15	.40
75	AJ Styles	.25	.60
76	Gut Check	.15	.40
77	Alex Silva	.15	.40
78	Christian York	.15	.40
79	Sam Shaw	.15	.40
80	Joey Ryan	.15	.40
81	Taeler Hendrix	.25	.60
82	Wes Brisco	.15	.40
83	Al Snow	.25	.60

84	D'Lo Brown	.15	.40
85	Chavo Guerrero Jr.	.15	.40
86	Hector Guerrero	.15	.40
87	World Tag Team Champions: Hernandez and Chavo Guerrero Jr.	.15	.40
88	The Guerrero Legacy	.15	.40
89	Gail Kim	.40	1.00
90	Mr. Anderson	.25	.60
91	Miss Tessmacher	.40	1.00
92	Robbie E	.15	.40
93	Tara	.50	1.25
94	Mickie James	.75	2.00
95	Chavo Guerrero Jr.	.15	.40
96	Destination X	.15	.40
97	Slammiversary	.15	.40
98	Bound For Glory	.15	.40
99	Sting's Hall of Fame Induction	.60	1.50
100	Hulk Hogan SP	4.00	10.00
101	Sting SP	3.00	8.00
102	Bully Ray SP	.75	2.00
103	Samoa Joe SP	.75	2.00
104	Kurt Angle SP	1.25	3.00
105	Hulk Hogan SP	4.00	10.00
106	Sting SP	3.00	8.00
107	Kurt Angle SP	1.25	3.00
108	Miss Tessmacher SP	2.00	5.00
109	Jeff Hardy SP	3.00	8.00
CL	Checklist	.15	.40

2013 TRISTAR TNA Impact Live Autographed Memorabilia Gold

M17 Gail Kim

2013 TRISTAR TNA Impact Live Autographed Memorabilia Rainbow

STATED PRINT RUN 1 SER.#'d SET
UNPRICED DUE TO SCARCITY

M15 Hulk Hogan
M16 Jeff Hardy
M17 Gail Kim
M18 Sting

2013 TRISTAR TNA Impact Live Autographs Gold

*GREEN/50: .5X TO 1.2X BASIC AUTOS
*BLUE/25: .6X TO 1.5X BASIC AUTOS
*RED/5: UNPRICED DUE TO SCARCITY
*RAINBOW/1: UNPRICED DUE TO SCARCITY
STATED PRINT RUN 99 SER. #'d SETS

L16	Gail Kim	8.00	20.00
L17	James Storm	5.00	12.00
L20	Mr. Anderson	6.00	15.00
L23	Taryn Terrell	12.00	30.00
L24	Doug Williams	3.00	8.00
L25	Matt Morgan	5.00	12.00
L26	Christy Hemme	10.00	25.00
L27	Abyss	3.00	8.00
L29	Samoa Joe	3.00	8.00
L32	Bully Ray	5.00	12.00
L33	Robbie E	3.00	8.00
L34	Winter	4.00	10.00
L35	Jesse Sorensen	3.00	8.00
L36	Kazarian	4.00	10.00
L37	Garett Bischoff	3.00	8.00
L38	Kenny King	6.00	15.00
L39	Christian York	8.00	20.00
L40	Hector Guerrero	3.00	8.00
L41	ODB	5.00	12.00
L42	Bobby Roode	3.00	8.00
L43	Chris Sabin	4.00	10.00
L44	SoCal Val	5.00	12.00
L45	Rosita	5.00	12.00
L46	Hernandez	3.00	8.00
L47	Kid Kash	3.00	8.00
L48	Austin Aries	8.00	20.00

2013 TRISTAR TNA Impact Live Dual Autographs Gold

*GREEN/50: .5X TO 1.2X BASIC AUTOS
*BLUE/25: .6X TO 1.5X BASIC AUTOS
*RED/5: UNPRICED DUE TO SCARCITY
*RAINBOW/1: UNPRICED DUE TO SCARCITY
STATED PRINT RUN 99 SER.#'d SETS

2	Chavo & Hector Guerrero		
3	K.Angle/W.Brisco		
4	E.Young/ODB		
5	C.Daniels/Kazarian	4.00	10.00
6	Tara/J.Godderz	6.00	15.00
7	C.Hemme/J.Borash	6.00	15.00
8	M.Morgan/J.Ryan	6.00	15.00
9	Sarita/Rosita	5.00	12.00
10	C.Guerrero/Hernandez		
11	G.Kim/M.James	12.00	30.00
12	J.Storm/B.Roode		
13	B.Roode/J.Hardy		
14	B.Hogan/B.Ray		
15	A.Aries/M.Morgan		
16	M.Tessmacher/Tara	8.00	20.00
17	W.Brisco/G.Bischoff	5.00	12.00
18	S.Shaw/C.York		
19	M.James/Tara		
20	C.Daniels/C.Sabin	4.00	10.00
21	C.Sabin/J.Sorensen	4.00	10.00
22	K.Angle/M.Anderson		
23	B.Roode/A.Aries		
24	M.Anderson/Devon		
25	Sting/J.Hardy		

2013 TRISTAR TNA Impact Live Dual Memorabilia Silver

*GOLD/50: .5X TO 1.2X BASIC MEM
*BLUE/25: .6X TO 1.5X BASIC MEM
*RED/5: UNPRICED DUE TO SCARCITY
*RAINBOW/1: UNPRICED DUE TO SCARCITY
.STATED ODDS OVERALL 1:BOX

M11	Tara	4.00	10.00
	Jessie Godderz		
M12	C.Guerrero Jr./Hernandez	4.00	10.00

2013 TRISTAR TNA Impact Live Eight Autographs Gold

*GREEN/50: X TO X BASIC AUTOS
*BLUE/25: UNPRICED DUE TO SCARCITY
*RED/5: UNPRICED DUE TO SCARCITY
*RAINBOW/1: UNPRICED DUE TO SCARCTIY
STATED PRINT RUN 99 SER.#'d SETS

3 Brooke Hogan
Tara/ Velvet Sky/ Madison Rayne/ Gail Kim/ Mickie James/ Christy Hemme/ Ms. Tessmacher

2013 TRISTAR TNA Impact Live Jeff Hardy Die-Cut Letter Memorabilia Gold

*BLUE/25: .5X TO 1.2X BASIC MEM
*RED/5: .75X TO 2X BASIC MEM

*RAINBOW/1: UNPRICED DUE TO SCARCITY
STATED PRINT RUN 50 SER.#'d SETS

M1	Jeff Hardy H	15.00	40.00
M2	Jeff Hardy A	15.00	40.00
M3	Jeff Hardy R	15.00	40.00
M4	Jeff Hardy D	15.00	40.00
M5	Jeff Hardy Y	15.00	40.00

2013 TRISTAR TNA Impact Live Memorabilia Silver

*GOLD/50: .5X TO 1.2X BASIC MEM
*BLUE/25: .6X TO 1.5X BASIC MEM
*RED/5: UNPRICED DUE TO SCARCITY
*RAINBOW/1: UNPRICED DUE TO SCARCITY
STATED ODDS OVERALL 1:BOX

M6	Hulk Hogan	10.00	25.00
M7	Sting	8.00	20.00
M8	Kurt Angle	6.00	15.00
M9	Austin Aries	4.00	10.00
M10	Chavo Guerrero Jr.	4.00	10.00

2013 TRISTAR TNA Impact Live Quad Autographs Gold

*GREEN/50: X TO X BASIC AUTOS
*BLUE/25: UNPRICED DUE TO SCARCITY
*RED/5: UNPRICED DUE TO SCARCITY
*RAINBOW/1: UNPRICED DUE TO SCARCITY
STATED PRINT RUN 99 SER.#'d SETS

1 Gail Kim
Mickie James/ Tara/ Velvet Sky
2 Angle/Brisco/G.Bischoff/Samoa Joe

2013 TRISTAR TNA Impact Live Quad Memorabilia Silver

*GOLD/50: .5X TO 1.2X BASIC MEM
*BLUE/25: .6X TO 1.5X BASIC MEM
*RED/5: UNPRICED DUE TO SCARCITY
*RAINBOW/1: UNPRICED DUE TO SCARCITY
STATED ODDS OVERALL 1:BOX

M13	Hulk Hogan		
	Sting/ Jeff Hardy/ Kurt Angle		
M14	Kim/James/Tessmacher/Sky	12.00	30.00

2013 TRISTAR TNA Impact Live Six Autographs Gold

2 Kim/Tara/James
Sky/Tessmacher/Rayne

2013 TRISTAR TNA Impact Live Ten Autographs Gold

2 Styles/Morgan/Sabin/Daniels/Roode
Young/Hernandez/Kazarian/Storm/Robbie

2013 TRISTAR TNA Impact Live Triple Autographs Gold

2 Jeff Hardy
Austin Aries/ Bobby Roode
4 Angle/Anderson/Hardy

2013 TRISTAR TNA Impact Live Twelve Autographs Gold

2 Brooke/Tara/Hemme/Sarita
Kim/Sky/Tessmacher/Terrell/James/Rayne/ODB/Val

2012 TRISTAR TNA Impact Reflexxions

COMPLETE SET (100)	10.00	25.00
UNOPENED BOX (20 PACKS)		
UNOPENED PACK (6 CARDS)		

*SILVER/40: 2.5X TO 6X BASIC CARDS
*GOLD/10: UNPRICED DUE TO SCARCITY
*PURPLE/1: UNPRICED DUE TO SCARCITY
SUBSET CARDS SAME PRICE AS BASE CARDS
EXCHANGE DEADLINE 6/1/2013

1	Hulk Hogan	1.00	2.50
2	Ric Flair	.75	2.00
3	Sting	.60	1.50
4	Bobby Roode	.15	.40
5	James Storm	.15	.40
6	Jeff Hardy	.60	1.50
7	AJ Styles	.25	.60
8	Dixie Carter	.40	1.00
9	Jeff Jarrett	.25	.60
10	Rob Van Dam	.25	.60
11	Velvet Sky	.75	2.00
12	Bully Ray	.15	.40
13	Angelina Love	.60	1.50
14	Kurt Angle	.25	.60
15	Crimson	.15	.40
16	Christy Hemme	.60	1.50
17	Gail Kim	.40	1.00
18	Austin Aries	.25	.60
19	Mickie James	1.00	2.50
20	Samoa Joe	.15	.40
21	Eric Bischoff	.15	.40
22	Garrett Bischoff	.25	.60
23	Mr. Anderson	.25	.60
24	Alex Shelley	.15	.40
25	Mark Haskins	.15	.40
26	Rob Terry	.15	.40
27	Karen Jarrett	.25	.60
28	Douglas Williams	.15	.40
29	Rosita	.25	.60
30	Kazarian	.15	.40
31	Scott Steiner	.25	.60
32	Zema Ion	.15	.40
33	Anarquia	.15	.40
34	Gunner	.15	.40
35	Kid Kash	.25	.60
36	D'Angelo Dinero	.15	.40
37	Magnus	.15	.40
38	Tara	.60	1.50
39	Abyss	.25	.60
40	Matt Morgan	.15	.40
41	ODB	.15	.40
42	Chris Sabin	.15	.40
43	Jesse Sorensen	.15	.40
44	Mike Tenay	.15	.40
45	Madison Rayne	.40	1.00
46	Devon	.15	.40
47	Sarita	.25	.60
48	Eric Young	.15	.40
49	Traci Brooks	.40	1.00
50	Anthony Nese	.15	.40
51	Taz	.15	.40
52	Hernandez	.15	.40
53	Brooke Tessmacher	.40	1.00
54	Christopher Daniels	.15	.40
55	Jesse Neal	.15	.40
56	Robbie E	.15	.40
57	SoCal Val	.40	1.00
58	Brian Kendrick	.15	.40
59	Jeremy Borash	.15	.40
60	Shannon Moore	.15	.40
61	Winter	.60	1.50
62	Ric Flair US	.75	2.00
63	Sting US	.60	1.50
64	Christy Hemme US	.60	1.50
65	Jeff Jarrett US	.25	.60
66	Velvet Sky US	.75	2.00
67	Mr. Anderson US	.25	.60
68	Gail Kim US	.40	1.00
69	Scott Steiner US	.25	.60
70	Traci Brooks US	.40	1.00
71	Jeff Hardy US	.60	1.50
72	Dixie Carter US	.40	1.00
73	Sting FT	.60	1.50
74	Ric Flair FT	.75	2.00
75	Velvet Sky FT	.75	2.00
76	Jeff Jarrett FT	.25	.60
77	Scott Steiner FT	.25	.60
78	Jeff Hardy FT	.60	1.50
79	Mr. Anderson FT	.25	.60
80	Velvet Sky BMV	.75	2.00
81	Christy Hemme BMV	.60	1.50
82	Gail Kim BMV	.40	1.00
83	Karen Jarrett BMV	.25	.60
84	Traci Brooks BMV	.40	1.00
85	Madison Rayne BMV	.40	1.00
86	Brooke Tessmacher BMV	.40	1.00
87	Hulk Hogan SW	1.00	2.50
88	Sting SW	.60	1.50
89	Kurt Angle SW	.25	.60
90	Crimson SW	.15	.40
91	Jeff Hardy LH	.60	1.50
92	Sting LH	.60	1.50
93	Christy Hemme LH	.60	1.50
94	Ric Flair LH	.75	2.00
95	Mr. Anderson LH	.25	.60
96	Velvet Sky LH	.75	2.00
97	Scott Steiner LH	.25	.60
98	Gail Kim LH	.40	1.00
99	Jeff Jarrett LH	.25	.60
CL	Checklist	.15	.40
NNO	Jeff Hardy Art Redemption EXCH		

2012 TRISTAR TNA Impact Reflexxions Autographed Mat Relics Gold

*BLUE/25: X TO X BASIC AU RELICS
*RED/5: UNPRICED DUE TO SCARCITY
*PURPLE/1: UNPRICED DUE TO SCARCITY
STATED PRINT RUN 50 SER.#'d SETS

M3	Kurt Angle		
M4	Velvet Sky	25.00	50.00
M5	AJ Styles		
M6	Bobby Roode		
M7	Tara		
M8	Mr. Anderson		
M9	James Storm	15.00	30.00
M10	Angelina Love	20.00	40.00
M11	Jeff Jarrett		
M12	Gail Kim	20.00	40.00
M13	Rob Van Dam		

2012 TRISTAR TNA Impact Reflexxions Autographed Memorabilia Blue

*RED/5: UNPRICED DUE TO SCARCITY
*PURPLE/1: UNPRICED DUE TO SCARCITY

STATED PRINT RUN 25 SER.#'d SETS

M14	Hulk Hogan		
M15	Ric Flair	75.00	125.00
M16	Sting	50.00	100.00
M17	Rob Van Dam	20.00	40.00
M18	Kurt Angle	25.00	50.00
M19	Mickie James	75.00	125.00
M20	Jeff Hardy	40.00	80.00
M21	Mr. Anderson	15.00	30.00
M22	Garett Bischoff	15.00	30.00
M23	Velvet Sky	40.00	80.00

2012 TRISTAR TNA Impact Reflexxions Autographs Silver

*GOLD/50: .5X TO 1.2X BASIC AUTOS
*RED/25: X TO X BASIC AUTOS
*GREEN/5: UNPRICED DUE TO SCARCITY
*PURPLE/1: UNPRICED DUE TO SCARCITY
STATED PRINT RUN 99 SER.#'d SETS

16	Christy Hemme	10.00	25.00
20	Samoa Joe	4.00	10.00
22	Garrett Bischoff	4.00	10.00
26	Rob Terry	4.00	10.00
29	Rosita	6.00	15.00
30	Kazarian	4.00	10.00
33	Anarquia	4.00	10.00
34	Gunner	4.00	10.00
35	Kid Kash	6.00	15.00
36	D'Angelo Dinero	4.00	10.00
37	Magnus	4.00	10.00
39	Abyss	5.00	12.00
41	ODB	4.00	10.00
43	Jesse Sorensen	5.00	12.00
45	Madison Rayne	6.00	15.00
47	Sarita	5.00	12.00
48	Eric Young	4.00	10.00
49	Traci Brooks	5.00	12.00
52	Hernandez	4.00	10.00
53	Brooke Tessmacher	8.00	20.00
55	Jesse Neal	4.00	10.00
56	Robbie E	4.00	10.00
57	SoCal Val	5.00	12.00
61	Winter	8.00	20.00

2012 TRISTAR TNA Impact Reflexxions Blue Foil Inserts

COMPLETE SET (50)		60.00	120.00

*RED/10: UNPRICED DUE TO SCARCITY
*PURPLE/1: UNPRICED DUE TO SCARCITY
STATED PRINT RUN 40 SER.#'d SETS

R1	Hulk Hogan	4.00	10.00
R2	Hulk Hogan	4.00	10.00
R3	Hulk Hogan	4.00	10.00
R4	Hulk Hogan	4.00	10.00
R5	Hulk Hogan	4.00	10.00
R6	Ric Flair	3.00	8.00
R7	Ric Flair	3.00	8.00
R8	Sting	2.50	6.00
R9	Sting	2.50	6.00
R10	Kurt Angle	1.00	2.50
R11	Kurt Angle	1.00	2.50
R12	Jeff Jarrett	1.00	2.50
R13	Rob Van Dam	1.00	2.50
R14	Velvet Sky	3.00	8.00
R15	AJ Styles	1.00	2.50
R16	Eric Bischoff	.60	1.50
R17	Scott Steiner	1.00	2.50
R18	Angelina Love	2.50	6.00
R19	Mr. Anderson	1.00	2.50
R20	Bobby Roode	.60	1.50
R21	James Storm	.60	1.50
R22	Abyss	1.00	2.50
R23	Gail Kim	1.50	4.00
R24	Samoa Joe	.60	1.50
R25	Crimson	.60	1.50
R26	Dixie Carter	1.50	4.00
R27	Tara	2.50	6.00
R28	Hernandez	.60	1.50
R29	Christopher Daniels	.60	1.50
R30	Devon	.60	1.50
R31	Mickie James	4.00	10.00
R32	Matt Morgan	.60	1.50
R33	Bully Ray	.60	1.50
R34	Garett Bischoff	1.00	2.50
R35	Brooke Tessmacher	1.50	4.00
R36	Karen Jarrett	1.00	2.50
R37	The Immortal Battles	4.00	10.00
R38	The Immortal Battles	4.00	10.00
R39	The Immortal Battles	4.00	10.00
R40	Jeff Hardy	2.50	6.00
R41	Jeff Hardy Original Art	5.00	12.00
R42	Jeff Hardy Original Art	5.00	12.00
R43	Jeff Hardy Original Art	5.00	12.00
R44	Jeff Hardy Original Art	5.00	12.00
R45	Jeff Hardy Original Art	5.00	12.00
R46	Jeff Hardy Original Art	5.00	12.00
R47	Jeff Hardy Original Art	5.00	12.00
R48	Jeff Hardy Original Art	5.00	12.00
R49	Jeff Hardy Original Art	5.00	12.00
R50	Jeff Hardy Original Art	5.00	12.00

2012 TRISTAR TNA Impact Reflexxions Dual Autographs Silver

*GOLD/50: .5X TO 1.25X BASIC AUTOS
*RED/25: .6X TO 1.5X BASIC AUTOS
*GREEN/5: UNPRICED DUE TO SCARCITY
*PURPLE/1: UNPRICED DUE TO SCARCITY
STATED PRINT RUN 99 SER.#'d SETS

7	Tara/Tessmacher	8.00	20.00
8	Crimson/Morgan	6.00	15.00
9	Kim/Sky	15.00	30.00
10	K.Jarrett/Brooks	10.00	25.00
12	Hernandez/Anarquia	5.00	12.00
14	Robbie E/Robbie T	5.00	12.00
15	Sarita/Rosita	8.00	20.00
17	Aries/Kash	8.00	20.00
19	Hemme/SoCal Val	8.00	20.00
20	Tenay/Borash	5.00	12.00
29	Aries/Kendrick	6.00	15.00
30	Sky/Love	8.00	20.00

2012 TRISTAR TNA Impact Reflexxions Dual Memorabilia Silver

*GOLD/50: .5X TO 1.2X BASIC MEM
*BLUE/25: .6X TO 1.5X BASIC MEM
*RED/5: UNPRICED DUE TO SCARCITY
*PURPLE/1: UNPRICED DUE TO SCARCITY
STATED PRINT RUN 199 SER.#'d SETS

M26	J.Jarrett/K.Jarrett	4.00	10.00
M27	Roode/Storm	4.00	10.00
M29	Jarrett/Brooks	5.00	12.00

2012 TRISTAR TNA Impact Reflexxions Quad Memorabilia Silver

*GOLD/50: X TO X BASIC MEM
*BLUE/25: X TO X BASIC MEM
*RED/5: UNPRICED DUE TO SCARCITY
*PURPLE/1: UNPRICED DUE TO SCARCITY
STATED PRINT RUN 199 SER.#'d SETS

M36	Styles/Abyss/Mrgn/Dnls	8.00	20.00

2012 TRISTAR TNA Impact Reflexxions Quad Memorabilia Gold

*GOLD: .5X TO 1.2X BASIC MEM
STATED PRINT RUN 50 SER.#'d SETS

M34	James/Tara/Sky/Love	15.00	40.00
M36	Styles/Abyss/Mrgn/Dnls	10.00	25.00

2012 TRISTAR TNA Impact Reflexxions Quad Memorabilia Red

STATED PRINT RUN 5 SER.#'d SETS
UNPRICED DUE TO SCARCITY

M34 James/Tara/Sky/Love
M35 Hulk/Flair/Sting/Angle
M36 Styles/Abyss/Mrgn/Dnls

2012 TRISTAR TNA Impact Reflexxions Six Autographs Red

*GREEN/5: UNPRICED DUE TO SCARCITY
*PURPLE/1: UNPRICED DUE TO SCARCITY
STATED PRINT RUN 25 SER.#'d SETS

1 Sky/Tara/Tess/Love/Wint/Rayn
3 Rood/Strm/Styl/VDam/Hard/Angle

2012 TRISTAR TNA Impact Reflexxions Triple Autographs Red

*GREEN/5: UNPRICED DUE TO SCARCITY
*PURPLE/1: UNPRICED DUE TO SCARCITY
STATED PRINT RUN 25 SER.#'d SETS

2	Angle/Jarrett/Jarrett	20.00	40.00
3	Roode/Styles/Hardy	40.00	80.00
4	Kim/James/Sky	40.00	80.00
5	Hemme/Kim/Brooks	30.00	60.00

2012 TRISTAR TNA Impact Reflexxions Triple Memorabilia Silver

*GOLD/50: .5X TO 1.2X BASIC MEM
*BLUE/25: X TO X BASIC MEM
*RED/5: UNPRICED DUE TO SCARCITY
*PURPLE/1: UNPRICED DUE TO SCARCITY
STATED PRINT RUN 199 SER.#'d SETS

M32	Sting/Steiner/Jarrett	8.00	20.00
M33	RVD/Anderson/Styles	6.00	15.00

2012 TRISTAR TNA Impact Reflexxions Triple Memorabilia Blue

*BLUE: .6X TO 1.5X BASIC MEM
STATED PRINT RUN 25 SER.#'d SETS

M31	Hogan/Flair/Sting		
M32	Sting/Steiner/Jarrett	12.00	30.00
M33	RVD/Anderson/Styles	10.00	25.00

2012 TRISTAR TNA Impact Reflexxions Triple Memorabilia Purple

STATED PRINT RUN 1 SER.#'d SET
UNPRICED DUE TO SCARCITY

M31 Hogan/Flair/Sting
M32 Sting/Steiner/Jarrett
M33 RVD/Anderson/Styles

2012 TRISTAR TNA Impact TENacious

COMPLETE SET (120)

COMPLETE SET W/O SP (100)		8.00	20.00
UNOPENED BOX (20 PACKS)			
UNOPENED PACK (6 CARDS)			

*SILVER/30: 2.5X TO 6X BASIC CARDS
*GOLD/RED/10: UNPRICED DUE TO SCARCITY
*PURPLE/1: UNPRICED DUE TO SCARCITY

1	Jeff Jarrett	.25	.60
2	AJ Styles	.25	.60
3	James Storm	.15	.40
4	Jeremy Borash	.15	.40
5	Mike Tenay	.15	.40
6	Hulk Hogan	1.00	2.50
7	Brooke Hogan	.60	1.50
8	Sting	.60	1.50
9	Gail Kim	.40	1.00
10	Jeff Jarrett	.25	.60
11	Jeff Hardy	.60	1.50
12	Kurt Angle	.25	.60
13	Chris Sabin	.15	.40
14	Austin Aries	.25	.60
15	Bully Ray	.15	.40
16	Hector Guerrero	.15	.40
17	Kazarian	.15	.40
18	Eric Bischoff	.15	.40
19	Hernandez	.15	.40
20	Jeff Jarrett	.25	.60
21	Mickie James	1.00	2.50
22	Christopher Daniels	.15	.40
23	Mr. Anderson	.25	.60
24	ODB	.15	.40
25	Devon	.15	.40
26	Matt Morgan	.15	.40
27	Ric Flair	.75	2.00
28	AJ Styles	.25	.60
29	Rob Terry	.15	.40
30	Jeff Jarrett	.25	.60
31	Rob Van Dam	.25	.60
32	Jeff Hardy	.60	1.50
33	Kid Kash	.25	.60
34	Robbie E	.15	.40
35	Madison Rayne	.40	1.00
36	Bobby Roode	.15	.40
37	Bobby Roode	.15	.40
38	Bobby Roode	.15	.40
39	Bobby Roode	.15	.40
40	Jeff Jarrett	.25	.60
41	Jeremy Borash	.15	.40
42	Jeremy Borash	.15	.40
43	Jeremy Borash	.15	.40
44	Joseph Park	.25	.60
45	Alex Silva	.15	.40
46	Gunner	.15	.40
47	Mr. Anderson	.25	.60
48	Rosita	.25	.60
49	Samoa Joe	.15	.40
50	Jeff Jarrett	.25	.60
51	Sarita	.25	.60
52	Eric Young	.15	.40
53	Kurt Angle	.25	.60
54	Miss Tessmacher	.40	1.00
55	Sting	.60	1.50
56	Tara	.60	1.50
57	Garett Bischoff	.25	.60
58	Taz	.15	.40
59	SoCal Val	.40	1.00
60	Jeff Jarrett	.25	.60
61	Velvet Sky	.75	2.00
62	Angelina Love	.60	1.50
63	Jeff Hardy	.60	1.50
64	Zema Ion	.15	.40
65	Winter	.60	1.50
66	James Storm	.15	.40
67	Jessie Godderz	.15	.40
68	Matt Morgan	.15	.40
69	ODB	.15	.40
70	Jeff Jarrett	.25	.60
71	Christopher Daniels	.15	.40
72	Gail Kim	.40	1.00
73	Velvet Sky	.75	2.00
74	Doug Williams	.15	.40
75	Abyss	.25	.60
76	Crimson	.15	.40
77	Karen Jarrett	.25	.60
78	Eric Young	.15	.40
79	Magnus	.15	.40
80	Jeff Jarrett	.25	.60
81	D'Angelo Dinero	.15	.40
82	Jesse Sorensen	.15	.40
83	Jeff Hardy	.60	1.50
84	Christy Hemme	.60	1.50
85	Christopher Daniels	.15	.40
86	Hulk Hogan	1.00	2.50
87	Tara	.60	1.50
88	ODB	.15	.40
89	Magnus	.15	.40
90	AJ Styles	.25	.60
91	Miss Tessmacher	.40	1.00
92	Joe vs. Daniels vs. Styles	.15	.40
93	MSG Hulk Hogan Press Conference	1.00	2.50
94	IMPACT Wrestling Live on 1/4/2010	1.00	2.50
95	Beer Money vs. MCMG Best of 5	.15	.40
96	RVD Defeats Hardy and Styles	.25	.60
97	Sting Defeats Jarrett	.60	1.50
98	Samoa Joe vs. Kurt Angle	.25	.60
99	Gail Kim Wins 1st Knockouts Title	.40	1.00
100	Jeff Hardy/100	8.00	20.00
101	Team 3D/100	2.50	6.00
102	Kurt Angle/100	3.00	8.00
103	Hulk Hogan/100	4.00	10.00
104	Ric Flair/100	4.00	10.00
105	Jeff Hardy ART/100	8.00	20.00
106	Jeff Hardy ART/100	8.00	20.00
107	Jeff Hardy ART/100	8.00	20.00
108	Jeff Hardy ART/100	8.00	20.00
109	Jeff Hardy ART/100	8.00	20.00
110	Hulk Hogan/100	4.00	10.00
111	Hulk Hogan/100	4.00	10.00
112	Hulk Hogan/100	4.00	10.00
113	Hulk Hogan/100	4.00	10.00
114	Hulk Hogan/100	4.00	10.00
115	Sting/100	3.00	8.00
116	Sting/100	3.00	8.00
117	Sting/100	3.00	8.00
118	Sting/100	3.00	8.00
119	Sting/100	3.00	8.00
CL	Checklist	.15	.40

2012 TRISTAR TNA Impact TENacious Autographed Memorabilia Silver

COMPLETE SET (5)
*GOLD/80: .5X TO 1.2X BASIC AU MEM
*BLUE/50: .6X TO 1.5X BASIC AU MEM
*RED/10: UNPRICED DUE TO SCARCITY
*PURPLE/1: UNPRICED DUE TO SCARCITY
STATED PRINT RUN 100 SER.#'d SETS

T2	Jeff Hardy	12.00	30.00
T3	Bobby Roode	5.00	12.00
T4	Sting	25.00	60.00
T5	Mickie James	15.00	40.00
T6	Rob Van Dam	10.00	25.00

2012 TRISTAR TNA Impact TENacious Autographed Memorabilia Blue

T2	Jeff Hardy	20.00	50.00
T3	Bobby Roode	8.00	20.00
T4	Sting	50.00	100.00
T5	Mickie James	30.00	60.00
T6	Rob Van Dam	15.00	40.00

2012 TRISTAR TNA Impact TENacious Autographs Gold

*RED/10: UNPRICED DUE TO SCARCITY
*PURPLE/1: UNPRICED DUE TO SCARCITY
STATED PRINT RUN 100 SER.#'d SETS

TEN1	Jeff Jarrett	6.00	15.00
TEN2	AJ Styles	5.00	12.00
TEN3	James Storm	4.00	10.00
TEN4	Gail Kim		
TEN8	Sting		
TEN9	Bobby Roode	4.00	10.00
TEN10	Jeff Hardy	25.00	50.00
TEN11	Kurt Angle	10.00	25.00
TEN12	Eric Bischoff		
TEN13	Mickie James	12.00	30.00
TEN14	Mr. Anderson	5.00	12.00
TEN15	Ric Flair		
TEN16	Rob Van Dam	10.00	25.00
TEN17	Austin Aries	10.00	25.00
TEN18	Brooke Tessmacher	10.00	25.00
TEN19	Samoa Joe	4.00	10.00
TEN20	Tara	8.00	20.00
TEN21	Bully Ray	5.00	12.00
TEN22	Devon	4.00	10.00
TEN23	Velvet Sky	8.00	20.00
TEN24	Garett Bischoff	4.00	10.00
TEN25	Abyss	4.00	10.00
TEN26	Christy Hemme	10.00	25.00
TEN27	Jeremy Borash	4.00	10.00
TEN28	ODB	4.00	10.00
TEN29	Magnus	4.00	10.00
TEN30	Crimson	4.00	10.00
TEN31	Doug Williams	4.00	10.00
TEN32	Robbie E	4.00	10.00
TEN33	Alex Shelley	4.00	10.00
TEN34	Rosita	5.00	12.00
TEN35	Gunner	5.00	12.00
TEN36	Kazarian	4.00	10.00
TEN37	Angelina Love	8.00	20.00
TEN38	Matt Morgan	4.00	10.00
TEN39	Chris Sabin	4.00	10.00
TEN40	Gail Kim	10.00	25.00
TEN41	Hernandez	5.00	12.00
TEN42	Madison Rayne	8.00	20.00
TEN43	Anarquia	4.00	10.00
TEN44	Winter	6.00	15.00
TEN45	Eric Young	4.00	10.00
TEN46	Sarita	5.00	12.00
TEN47	Shannon Moore	4.00	10.00
TEN48	Christopher Daniels	4.00	10.00

TEN49 Mike Tenay	4.00	10.00
TEN50 SoCal Val	5.00	12.00

2012 TRISTAR TNA Impact TENacious
Celebrity Cut Signatures Gold

STATED PRINT RUN 5 SER.#'d SETS
UNPRICED DUE TO SCARCITY

1 Ace Young
2 Adam Pac-Man Jones
3 AJ Pierzynski
4 Brandon Jacobs
5 Brian Urlacher
6 Brooke Hogan
7 Chris Rock
8 Curtis Granderson
9 David Eckstein
10 Dennis Rodman
11 Johnny Damon
12 Juan Pablo Montoya
13 Ken Shamrock
14 Rowdy Roddy Piper
15 Steve McMichael
16 Tito Ortiz
17 Toby Keith
18 Tom Arnold

2012 TRISTAR TNA Impact TENacious
Dual Autographs Gold

*RED/10: UNPRICED DUE TO SCARCITY
*PURPLE/1: UNPRICED DUE TO SCARCITY
STATED PRINT RUN 100 SER.#'d SETS

TEN21 B.Roode/J.Storm	8.00	20.00
TEN22 Eric & Garett Bischoff		
TEN23 J.Hardy/K.Angle		
TEN24 V.Sky/G.Kim	12.00	30.00
TEN25 K.Angle/AJ Styles		
TEN26 Sting/J.Hardy		
TEN28 ODB/E.Young	5.00	12.00
TEN210 B.Roode/E.Young	5.00	12.00
TEN211 A.Shelley/C.Sabin	5.00	12.00
TEN212 K.Angle/Samoa Joe	10.00	25.00
TEN213 Sting/B.Roode		
TEN214 Sting/J.Jarrett		
TEN215 B.Ray/Devon		
TEN216 Jeff & Karen Jarrett		
TEN217 Kazarian/T.Brooks	8.00	20.00
TEN218 K.Angle/Sting		
TEN219 Hernandez/Anarquia	5.00	12.00
TEN220 Kazarian/C.Daniels	5.00	12.00

2012 TRISTAR TNA Impact TENacious
Dual Memorabilia Silver

*GOLD/80: .5X TO 1.2X BASIC MEM
*BLUE/50: .6X TO 1.5X BASIC MEM
*RED/10: UNPRICED DUE TO SCARCITY
*PURPLE/1: UNPRICED DUE TO SCARCITY
STATED PRINT RUN 100 SER.#'d SETS

T10 Eric & Garett Bischoff	3.00	8.00
T11 Devon/B.Ray	3.00	8.00
T12 B.Roode/J.Storm	3.00	8.00
T13 J.Hardy/Mr.Anderson	6.00	15.00
T14 K.Angle/AJ Styles	3.00	8.00

2012 TRISTAR TNA Impact TENacious
Quad Autographs Gold

*RED/10: UNPRICED DUE TO SCARCITY
*PURPLE/1: UNPRICED DUE TO SCARCITY

TEN41 Jarrett/Styles/Storm/Borash		
TEN43 Storm/Roode/Sabin/Shelley	10.00	25.00

2012 TRISTAR TNA Impact TENacious
Six Autographs Gold

*RED/10: UNPRICED DUE TO SCARCITY
*PURPLE/1: UNPRICED DUE TO SCARCITY
STATED ODDS

TEN61 Styles/Samoa Joe/Daniels
 Aries/Sabin/Kash
TEN62 Young/Styles/Terry
 Abyss/Williams/Devon
TEN63 Angle/Sting/Styles
 Roode/RVD/Hardy
TEN64 Kim/Love/Tara
 Rayne/James/Sky

2012 TRISTAR TNA Impact TENacious
Triple Autographs Gold

*RED/10: UNPRICED DUE TO SCARCITY
*PURPLE/1: UNPRICED DUE TO SCARCITY
STATED ODDS

TEN31 Styles/Samoa Joe/Daniels
TEN32 Kurt & Karen Angle/Jarrett

2012 TRISTAR TNA Impact TENacious
Triple Memorabilia Blue

T15 Jarrett/Storm/Styles	6.00	15.00
T17 Kim/Sky/James	10.00	25.00

2009 TRISTAR TNA Knockouts

COMPLETE SET W/SP (108)	20.00	50.00
COMPLETE SET W/O SP (90)	12.00	30.00
UNOPENED BOX (18 PACKS)		
UNOPENED PACK (4 CARDS)		

*SILVER: 4X TO 10X BASIC CARDS
*GOLD/10: UNPRICED DUE TO SCARCITY
*PURPLE/1: UNPRICED DUE TO SCARCITY
*P.P.BLACK/1: UNPRICED DUE TO SCARCITY
*P.P.CYAN/1: UNPRICED DUE TO SCARCITY
*P.P.MAGENTA/1: UNPRICED DUE TO SCARCITY
*P.P.YELLOW/1: UNPRICED DUE TO SCARCITY
INSTANT WIN CARD RANDOMLY INSERTED
90-107 ARE REVEALED PACKS EXCLUSIVE

1 Angelina Love	.50	1.25
2 Awesome Kong	.15	.40
3 Christy Hemme	.60	1.50
4 The Governor	.25	.60
5 Jacqueline	.20	.50
6 Jenna Morasca	.40	1.00
7 Lauren	.25	.60
8 Madison Rayne	.40	1.00
9 ODB	.15	.40
10 Raisha Saeed	.15	.40
11 Rhaka Khan	.20	.50
12 Roxxi	.20	.50
13 Sharmell	.15	.40
14 SoCal Val	.40	1.00
15 Sojournor Bolt	.15	.40
16 Taylor Wilde	.40	1.00
17 Traci Brooks	.40	1.00
18 Velvet Sky	.50	1.25
19 Cute Kip	.12	.30
20 The Beautiful People	.50	1.25
21 Angelina Love	.50	1.25
22 Christy Hemme	.60	1.50
23 Lauren	.25	.60
24 ODB	.15	.40
25 Roxxi	.20	.50
26 Sharmell	.15	.40
27 SoCal Val	.40	1.00
28 Taylor Wilde	.40	1.00
29 Traci Brooks	.40	1.00
30 Velvet Sky	.50	1.25
31 Angelina Love	.50	1.25
32 Awesome Kong	.15	.40
33 Dixie Carter	.25	.60
34 Jacqueline	.20	.50
35 Lauren	.25	.60
36 ODB	.15	.40
37 Raisha Saeed	.15	.40
38 Traci Brooks	.40	1.00
39 Christy Hemme	.60	1.50
40 Rhaka Khan	.20	.50
41 Roxxi	.20	.50
42 Sharmell	.15	.40
43 SoCal Val	.40	1.00
44 Sojournor Bolt	.15	.40
45 Taylor Wilde	.40	1.00
46 Velvet Sky	.50	1.25
47 Jacqueline	.20	.50
48 Sojournor Bolt	.15	.40
49 ODB	.15	.40
50 Traci Brooks	.40	1.00
51 Angelina Love	.50	1.25
52 Awesome Kong	.15	.40
53 Christy Hemme	.60	1.50
54 Jacqueline	.20	.50
55 Lauren	.25	.60
56 ODB	.15	.40
57 Sharmell	.15	.40
58 SoCal Val	.40	1.00
59 Sojournor Bolt	.15	.40
60 Taylor Wilde	.40	1.00
61 Traci Brooks	.40	1.00
62 Velvet Sky	.50	1.25
63 Angelina Love	.50	1.25
64 Awesome Kong	.15	.40
65 Christy Hemme	.60	1.50
66 Dixie Carter	.25	.60
67 Roxxi	.20	.50
68 Sharmell	.15	.40
69 ODB	.15	.40
70 Taylor Wilde	.40	1.00
71 Traci Brooks	.40	1.00
72 Velvet Sky	.50	1.25
73 Angelina Love / AJ Styles	.50	1.25
74 Awesome Kong / Samoa Joe	.15	.40
75 Christy Hemme / Robert Roode	.60	1.50
76 Dixie Carter / Mick Foley	.50	1.25
77 Jacqueline / James Storm	.20	.50
78 Jenna Morasca / Brother Ray	.40	1.00
79 Lauren / Chris Sabin	.25	.60
80 ODB / Rhino	.15	.40
81 Raisha Saeed / Alex Shelley	.15	.40
82 Rhaka Khan / Kurt Angle	.60	1.50
83 Roxxi / Jim Cornette	.20	.50
84 Sharmell / Mike Tenay	.15	.40
85 SoCal Val / Consequences Creed	.40	1.00
86 Sojournor Bolt / Don West	.15	.40
87 Taylor Wilde / Jay Lethal	.40	1.00
88 Traci Brooks / Sting	.50	1.25
89 Velvet Sky / Brother Devon	.50	1.25
90 Traci Brooks	1.25	3.00
91 Angelina Love	1.50	4.00
92 SoCal Val	1.25	3.00
93 Christy Hemme	2.00	5.00
94 Velvet Sky	1.50	4.00
95 Lauren	.75	2.00
96 ODB	.50	1.25
97 Traci Brooks	1.25	3.00
98 SoCal Val	1.25	3.00
99 Christy Hemme	2.00	5.00
100 Angelina Love	1.50	4.00
101 Roxxi	.60	1.50
102 Jenna Morasca	1.25	3.00
103 Velvet Sky	1.50	4.00
104 SoCal Val	1.25	3.00
105 Christy Hemme	2.00	5.00
106 Angelina Love/Velvet Sky	1.50	4.00
107 Traci Brooks/SoCal Val	1.25	3.00
CL Checklist	.20	.50
NNO Instant Winner		

2009 TRISTAR TNA Knockouts
Autographed Dual Kiss Gold

*TURQUOISE/10: UNPRICED DUE TO SCARCITY
*PURPLE/1: UNPRICED DUE TO SCARCITY
STATED PRINT RUN 25 SER.#'d SETS

2K1 A.Love/V.Sky
2K2 C.Hemme/T.Brooks
2K3 Jenna/Sharmell
2K4 S.Val/Lauren

2009 TRISTAR TNA Knockouts
Autographed Kiss

STATED PRINT RUN 10 SER.#'d SETS

K1 Angelina Love
K2 Awesome Kong
K3 Jacqueline
K4 Jenna
K5 Lauren
K6 Madison Rayne
K7 ODB
K8 Roxxi
K9 Sharmell
K10 Sojournor Bolt
K11 Taylor Wilde
K12 Velvet Sky
K13 Christy Hemme
K14 SoCal Val
K15 Traci Brooks

2009 TRISTAR TNA Knockouts
Knockout Kiss

*TURQUOISE/25: .5X TO 1.25X BASIC KISS
*GREEN/5: UNPRICED DUE TO SCARCITY
*PURPLE/1: UNPRICED DUE TO SCARCITY
*P.P.BLACK/1: UNPRICED DUE TO SCARCITY
*P.P.CYAN/1: UNPRICED DUE TO SCARCITY
*P.P.MAGENTA/1: UNPRICED DUE TO SCARCITY
*P.P.YELLOW/1: UNPRICED DUE TO SCARCITY
STATED PRINT RUN 75 SER.#'d SETS
K12-K15 ARE REVEALED PACKS EXCLUSIVE

K1 Angelina Love	30.00	60.00
K2 Awesome Kong	12.00	30.00
K3 Jacqueline	8.00	20.00
K4 Jenna	25.00	50.00
K5 Lauren	15.00	40.00
K6 Madison Rayne	25.00	50.00
K7 ODB	12.00	30.00
K8 Roxxi	10.00	25.00

K9 Sharmell	10.00	25.00
K10 Sojournor Bolt	8.00	20.00
K11 Taylor Wilde	25.00	50.00
K12 Velvet Sky	30.00	60.00
K13 Christy Hemme	25.00	50.00
K14 SoCal Val	15.00	40.00
K15 Traci Brooks	12.00	30.00

2009 TRISTAR TNA Knockouts Signature Curves

*GOLD/75: .5X TO 1.2X BASIC AUTOS
*TURQUOISE/25: UNPRICED DUE TO SCARCITY
*PINK/10: UNPRICED DUE TO SCARCITY
*GREEN/5: UNPRICED DUE TO SCARCITY
*PURPLE/1: UNPRICED DUE TO SCARCITY
*P.P.BLACK/1: UNPRICED DUE TO SCARCITY
*P.P.CYAN/1: UNPRICED DUE TO SCARCITY
*P.P.MAGENTA/1: UNPRICED DUE TO SCARCITY
*P.P.YELLOW/1: UNPRICED DUE TO SCARCITY
STATED ODDS 1:9

KA1 Angelina Love	10.00	25.00
KA2 Awesome Kong	6.00	15.00
KA3 Christy Hemme	10.00	25.00
KA4 Dixie Carter	6.00	15.00
KA5 Jacqueline	6.00	15.00
KA6 Jenna	8.00	20.00
KA7 Madison Rayne	10.00	25.00
KA8 Raisha Saeed	6.00	15.00
KA9 Roxxi	6.00	15.00
KA10 Sharmell	6.00	15.00
KA11 SoCal Val	8.00	20.00
KA12 Sojournor Bolt	8.00	20.00
KA13 Taylor Wilde	8.00	20.00
KA14 Traci Brooks	8.00	20.00
KA15 Velvet Sky	10.00	25.00
KA24 Lauren	10.00	25.00
KA25 ODB	8.00	20.00

2009 TRISTAR TNA Knockouts Six-Person Signature Curves Gold

*TURQUOISE/25: X TO X BASIC AUTOS
*GREEN/5: UNPRICED DUE TO SCARCITY
*PURPLE/1: UNPRICED DUE TO SCARCITY
*P.P.BLACK/1: UNPRICED DUE TO SCARCITY
*P.P.CYAN/1: UNPRICED DUE TO SCARCITY
*P.P.MAGENTA/1: UNPRICED DUE TO SCARCITY
*P.P.YELLOW/1: UNPRICED DUE TO SCARCITY
STATED ODDS

KA27 Sharmell/Booker T/Nash
Angle/Sting/Steiner

2009 TRISTAR TNA Knockouts Top Drawer Memorabilia Gold

*TURQUOISE/75: .5X TO 1.2X BASIC MEM
*PINK/10: UNPRICED DUE TO SCARCITY
*PURPLE/1: UNPRICED DUE TO SCARCITY
STATED PRINT RUN 175 SER.#'d SETS

TD1 Angelina Love	10.00	25.00
TD2 Christy Hemme	10.00	25.00
TD3 Jenna Morasca	6.00	15.00
TD4 Lauren	10.00	25.00
TD5 Madison Rayne	10.00	25.00
TD6 Roxxi	6.00	15.00
TD7 SoCal Val	8.00	20.00
TD8 Sojournor Bolt	6.00	15.00
TD9 Taylor Wilde	10.00	25.00
TD10 Traci Brooks	6.00	15.00
TD11 Velvet Sky	10.00	25.00

2010 TRISTAR TNA New Era

COMPLETE SET (101)	30.00	75.00
UNOPENED BOX (20 PACKS)		
UNOPENED PACK (6 CARDS)		
COMPLETE SET W/O SP (90)	10.00	25.00

*SILVER: 2.5X TO 6X BASIC CARDS
*GOLD/10: UNPRICED DUE TO SCARCITY
*PURPLE/1: UNPRICED DUE TO SCARCITY
OBAK STATED ODDS 2:HOBBY BOX
OBAK ANNOUNCED PRINT RUN 600

1 Hulk Hogan	1.00	2.50
2 Hulk Hogan	1.00	2.50
3 Hulk Hogan	1.00	2.50
4 Hulk Hogan	1.00	2.50
5 Hulk Hogan	1.00	2.50
6 Hulk Hogan	1.00	2.50
7 Hulk Hogan	1.00	2.50
8 Ric Flair	.75	2.00
9 Jeff Hardy	.60	1.50
10 Scott Hall	.15	.40
11 Syxx-Pac	.25	.60
12 Eric Bischoff	.15	.40
13 Shannon Moore	.15	.40
14 Orlando Jordan	.15	.40
15 Bubba The Love Sponge	.25	.60
16 Mr. Anderson	.25	.60
17 The Nasty Boys	.15	.40
18 Generation Me	.15	.40
19 The Pope D'Angelo Dinero	.15	.40
20 Desmond Wolfe	.15	.40
21 Brian Kendrick	.25	.60
22 Jimmy Hart	.25	.60
23 Sting	.60	1.50
24 Kurt Angle	.60	1.50
25 Mick Foley	.75	2.00
26 Kevin Nash	.60	1.50
27 Jeff Jarrett	.40	1.00
28 James Storm	.25	.60
29 Alex Shelley	.25	.60
30 AJ Styles	.40	1.00
31 Team 3D	.25	.60
32 British Invasion	.15	.40
33 Taz & Mike Tenay	.15	.40
34 Motor City Machineguns	.25	.60
35 Matt Morgan	.15	.40
36 Amazing Red	.15	.40
37 Robert Roode	.15	.40
38 Suicide	.15	.40
39 Abyss	.25	.60
40 Lethal Consequences	.15	.40
41 Eric Young	.15	.40
42 Beer Money, Inc.	.25	.60
43 Samoa Joe	.25	.60
44 Daniels	.15	.40
45 Taylor Wilde	.40	1.00
46 Homicide	.20	.50
47 Daffney	.60	1.50
48 Hernandez	.15	.40
49 The Beautiful People	.75	2.00
50 Rob Terry	.15	.40
51 Lacey Von Erich	.75	2.00
52 Tara	.60	1.50
53 Hamada	.40	1.00
54 Sarita	.40	1.00
55 ODB	.25	.60
56 Jesse Neal	.15	.40
57 Velvet Sky	.75	2.00
58 Magnus	.15	.40
59 Angelina Love	.60	1.50
60 Doug Williams	.15	.40
61 Madison Rayne	.60	1.50
62 Rhino	.25	.60
63 Kazarian	.15	.40
64 Chris Sabin	.15	.40
65 Dr. Stevie	.15	.40
66 Christy Hemme	.60	1.50
67 Jeremy Borash	.15	.40
68 Dixie Carter	.40	1.00
69 Bob Carter	.15	.40
70 Rob Van Dam	.40	1.00
71 Destination X	.15	.40
72 Lockdown	.15	.40
73 Hulk Hogan/Eric Bischoff	.75	2.00
74 Ric Flair/AJ Styles	.60	1.50
75 Scott Hall/Syxx-Pac	.20	.50
76 Hulk Hogan/Abyss	.75	2.00
77 Matt Morgan/Hernandez	.15	.40
78 Ric Flair	.60	1.50
79 Ric Flair	.60	1.50
80 Ric Flair	.60	1.50
81 TNA iMPACT! Moves	.75	2.00
82 Hogan's Wrestling Return	.75	2.00
83 H.Hogan/R.Flair	.75	2.00
84 The Main Event	.75	2.00
85 Why, Sting, Why?	.50	1.25
86 Van Dam Arrives in TNA	.30	.75
87 The Band: Off Key	.20	.50
88 Kurt Angle	.50	1.25
89 Jeff Hardy Returns	.50	1.25
90 What A Night!	.75	2.00
91 Hulk Hogan OBAK SP	4.00	10.00
92 Ric Flair OBAK SP	3.00	8.00
93 Sting OBAK SP	2.50	6.00
94 Kevin Nash OBAK SP	2.50	6.00
95 Jeff Jarrett OBAK SP	1.50	4.00
96 Kurt Angle OBAK SP	2.50	6.00
97 Mick Foley OBAK SP	3.00	8.00
98 AJ Styles OBAK SP	1.50	4.00
99 Beautiful People OBAK SP	3.00	8.00
100 Hogan/Flair OBAK SP	4.00	10.00
CL Checklist	.15	.40

2010 TRISTAR TNA New Era Autographed Hulk Hogan Bonus Red

*PURPLE/1: UNPRICED DUE TO SCARCITY
STATED PRINT RUN 9 SER.#'d SETS
UNPRICED DUE TO SCARCITY

H1 Hulk Hogan holding rope
H2 Hulk Hogan black shirt in ring
H3 Hulk Hogan ripping shirt
H4 Hulk Hogan no shirt white bkgrnd
H5 Hulk Hogan w/boa
H6 Hulk Hogan black shirt white bkgrnd

2010 TRISTAR TNA New Era Autographed Memorabilia Silver

STATED PRINT RUN 199 SER.#'d SETS

M13 Hulk Hogan		
M14 Ric Flair		
M15 Mick Foley		
M16 Sting		
M17 AJ Styles		
M18 Velvet Sky	15.00	40.00

2010 TRISTAR TNA New Era Autographs Silver

*GOLD/50: .5X TO 1.2X BASIC AUTOS
*GREEN/15-25: X TO X BASIC AUTOS
*RED/5: UNPRICED DUE TO SCARCITY
*PURPLE/1: UNPRICED DUE TO SCARCITY

A1 Hulk Hogan		
A2 Sting		
A3 Mick Foley	10.00	25.00
A4 Kurt Angle	8.00	20.00
A5 Sean Morley	6.00	15.00
A6 Mr. Anderson	8.00	20.00
A7 Orlando Jordan	8.00	20.00
A8 D'Angelo Dinero	8.00	20.00
A9 Tara	6.00	15.00
A10 Desmond Wolfe	4.00	10.00
A11 Taz	4.00	10.00
A12 Kevin Nash	8.00	20.00
A13 Brian Kendrick	6.00	15.00
A14 AJ Styles	8.00	20.00
A15 Jeff Jarrett	5.00	12.00
A16 Sarita	6.00	15.00
A17 Amazing Red	4.00	10.00
A18 Lacey Von Erich	12.00	30.00
A19 Abyss	4.00	10.00
A20 Rob Van Dam	12.00	30.00
A21 Hernandez	4.00	10.00
A22 Taylor Wilde	6.00	15.00
A23 Samoa Joe	8.00	20.00
A24 Awesome Kong	5.00	12.00
A25 Dr. Stevie	5.00	12.00
A26 Brutus Magnus	4.00	10.00
A27 Velvet Sky	10.00	25.00
A28 Jeremy Borash	4.00	10.00
A29 Madison Rayne	8.00	20.00
A30 Doug Williams	4.00	10.00
A31 Christy Hemme	10.00	25.00
A32 Suicide	4.00	10.00
A33 Hamada	8.00	20.00
A34 Robert Roode	4.00	10.00
A35 Brian Knobs	4.00	10.00
A36 Dixie Carter	5.00	12.00
A37 Daniels	4.00	10.00
A38 Bubba The Love Sponge	10.00	25.00
A39 ODB	5.00	12.00
A40 Homicide	4.00	10.00
A41 Matt Morgan	4.00	10.00
A42 Daffney	10.00	25.00
A43 Jesse Neal	4.00	10.00
A44 James Storm	4.00	10.00
A45 SoCal Val	6.00	15.00
A46 Jeff Hardy	20.00	40.00
A47 Traci Brooks	6.00	15.00
A48 Jerry Sags	4.00	10.00
A49 Angelina Love	8.00	20.00
A50 Alex Shelley	4.00	10.00
A51 Syxx-Pac	6.00	15.00
A52 Shannon Moore	6.00	15.00
A53 Jay Lethal	4.00	10.00
A54 Rob Terry	4.00	10.00
A55 Ric Flair		

2010 TRISTAR TNA New Era Dual Autographs Silver

*GOLD/50: X TO X BASIC AUTOS
*GREEN/25: X TO X BASIC AUTOS
*RED/5: UNPRICED DUE TO SCARCITY

1 H.Hogan/Sting
2 M.Foley/Abyss
3 H.Hogan/D.Carter
4 K.Angle/J.Jarrett
5 K.Nash/E.Young
6 H.Hogan/M.Foley
7 K.Angle/Mr.Anderson
8 Taz/M.Tenay
9 H.Hogan/K.Nash
10 A.Love/Lacey Von Erich
11 D.Dinero/O.Jordan
12 B.Knobs/J.Sags
13 A.Kong/Hamada
14 K.Angle/D.Wolfe
15 M.Morgan/Hernandez
16 V.Sky/M.Rayne
17 H.Hogan/K.Angle
18 A.Shelley/C.Sabin
19 J.Storm/R.Roode
20 R.Flair/AJ Styles
21 Sting/R.Flair
22 H.Hogan/R.Flair

2010 TRISTAR TNA New Era Dual Autographs Gold

STATED PRINT RUN 50 SER.#'d SETS

1 H.Hogan/Sting
2 M.Foley/Abyss
3 H.Hogan/D.Carter
4 K.Angle/J.Jarrett
5 K.Nash/E.Young
6 H.Hogan/M.Foley
7 K.Angle/Mr.Anderson
8 Taz/M.Tenay
9 H.Hogan/K.Nash
10 Angelina Love/L.Von Erich
11 D.Dinero/O.Jordan
12 B.Knobs/J.Sags
13 A.Kong/Hamada
14 K.Angle/D.Wolfe
15 M.Morgan/Hernandez
16 V.Sky/M.Rayne
17 H.Hogan/K.Angle
18 A.Shelley/C.Sabin
19 J.Storm/R.Roode
20 R.Flair/AJ Styles
21 Sting/R.Flair
22 H.Hogan/R.Flair

2010 TRISTAR TNA New Era Dual Autographs Green

*GREEN: X TO X BASIC AUTOS
STATED PRINT RUN 25 SER.#'d SETS

1 H.Hogan/Sting		
2 M.Foley/Abyss	20.00	40.00
3 H.Hogan/D.Carter		
4 K.Angle/J.Jarrett	25.00	50.00
5 K.Nash/E.Young	15.00	30.00
6 H.Hogan/M.Foley		
7 K.Angle/Mr.Anderson	20.00	40.00
8 Taz/M.Tenay	10.00	20.00
9 H.Hogan/K.Nash		
10 Angelina Love/L.Von Erich	20.00	40.00
11 D.Dinero/O.Jordan	20.00	40.00
12 B.Knobs/J.Sags	15.00	30.00

13 A.Kong/Hamada	15.00	30.00
14 K.Angle/D.Wolfe	20.00	40.00
15 M.Morgan/Hernandez	15.00	30.00
16 V.Sky/M.Rayne	20.00	40.00
17 H.Hogan/K.Angle		
18 A.Shelley/C.Sabin	10.00	20.00
19 J.Storm/R.Roode	15.00	30.00
20 R.Flair/AJ Styles		
21 Sting/R.Flair		
22 H.Hogan/R.Flair		

2010 TRISTAR TNA New Era Dual Memorabilia Silver

STATED ODDS

M10 J.Storm/R.Roode	4.00	10.00

2010 TRISTAR TNA New Era Memorabilia Silver

*GOLD/50: .5X TO 1.2X BASIC MEM
*RED/25: .6X TO 1.5X BASIC MEM
*PURPLE/1: UNPRICED DUE TO SCARCITY
OVERALL MEM ODDS ONE PER HOBBY BOX
STATED PRINT RUN 99-199

M1 Hulk Hogan		
M2 Ric Flair		
M3 Mick Foley	5.00	12.00
M4 Sting	6.00	15.00
M5 Kurt Angle	5.00	12.00
M6 Rob Van Dam	4.00	10.00
M7 Mr. Anderson	4.00	10.00
M8 Syxx-Pac	4.00	10.00

2010 TRISTAR TNA New Era Quad Autographs Silver

*GOLD/50: X TO X BASIC AUTOS
*GREEN/25: X TO X BASIC AUTOS
*RED/5: UNPRICED DUE TO SCARCITY
*PURPLE/1: UNPRICED DUE TO SCARCITY
RANDOMLY INSERTED INTO RETAIL PACKS

1 Hogan/Jarrett/Angle/Foley
2 Sky/Rayne/Von Erich/Love
3 Hogan/Flair/Sting/Nash
4 Wilde/Sarita/Hamada/A.Kong
5 Hogan/Abyss/Flair/Styles

2010 TRISTAR TNA New Era Triple Autographs Silver

*GOLD/50: X TO X BASIC AUTOS
*GREEN/25: X TO X BASIC AUTOS
*RED/5: UNPRICED DUE TO SCARCITY
*PURPLE/1: UNPRICED DUE TO SCARCITY
RANDOMLY INSERTED INTO RETAIL PACKS

1 Hogan/Nash/6-Pac
2 Sky/Rayne/Von Erich
3 Terry/Magnus/Williams
4 Tara/Hemme/Brooks

2010 TRISTAR TNA New Era Triple Autographs Green

*GREEN: X TO X BASIC AUTOS
STATED PRINT RUN 25 SER.#'d SETS

1 Hogan/Nash/6-Pac		
2 Sky/Rayne/Von Erich	30.00	60.00
3 Terry/Magnus/Williams	15.00	30.00
4 Tara/Hemme/Brooks	20.00	40.00

2010 TRISTAR TNA New Era Triple Autographs Red

STATED PRINT RUN 5 SER.#'d SETS
UNPRICED DUE TO SCARCITY

1 Hogan/Nash/6-Pac
2 Sky/Rayne/Von Erich
3 Terry/Magnus/Williams
4 Tara/Hemme/Brooks

2010 TRISTAR TNA Obak National Convention

COMPLETE SET (3)	4.00	10.00
TNA1 Rob Van Dam	2.00	5.00
TNA2 Mick Foley	2.50	6.00
TNA3 Kurt Angle	2.00	5.00

2011 TRISTAR TNA Signature Impact

COMPLETE SET (100)	20.00	40.00
COMPLETE SET W/O SP (90)	10.00	25.00
UNOPENED BOX (20 PACKS)		
UNOPENED PACK (6 CARDS)		
*SILVER/50: 2.5X TO 6X BASIC CARDS		
*SILVER SP/50: .75X TO 2X BASIC CARDS		
*GOLD/5: UNPRICED DUE TO SCARCITY		
*PURPLE/1: UNPRICED DUE TO SCARCITY		

1 Hulk Hogan	1.00	2.50
2 Ric Flair	.75	2.00
3 Sting	.60	1.50
4 Jeff Jarrett	.25	.60
5 Scott Steiner	.25	.60
6 Jeff Hardy	.60	1.50
7 Matt Hardy	.40	1.00
8 Velvet Sky	.75	2.00
9 Abyss	.25	.60
10 Kurt Angle	.25	.60
11 Sting	.60	1.50
12 Ric Flair	.75	2.00
13 Matt Hardy/Jeff Hardy	.60	1.50
14 AJ Styles	.25	.60
15 Velvet Sky	.75	2.00
16 Scott Steiner	.25	.60
17 Mr. Anderson	.25	.60
18 Anarquia	.15	.40
19 Devon	.15	.40
20 Dixie Carter	.40	1.00
21 Crimson	.15	.40
22 Angelina Love	.60	1.50
23 Eric Bischoff	.15	.40
24 AJ Styles	.25	.60
25 Daniels	.15	.40
26 Gunner	.15	.40
27 Murphy	.15	.40
28 Tara	.60	1.50
29 Ric Flair	.75	2.00
30 Hulk Hogan	1.00	2.50
31 Mickie James	1.00	2.50
32 Sting	.60	1.50
33 Abyss	.25	.60
34 Mr. Anderson	.25	.60
35 James Storm	.15	.40
36 Karen Jarrett	.25	.60
37 Bully Ray	.15	.40
38 Douglas Williams	.15	.40
39 Mickie James	1.00	2.50
40 Mr. Anderson	.25	.60
41 Alex Shelley	.15	.40
42 Chris Sabin	.15	.40

43 Matt Morgan	.15	.40
44 Rob Van Dam	.25	.60
45 Hulk Hogan	1.00	2.50
46 Samoa Joe	.15	.40
47 Taz	.15	.40
48 RVD	.25	.60
49 Madison Rayne	.40	1.00
50 Orlando Jordan	.15	.40
51 Mike Tenay	.15	.40
52 Taz	.15	.40
53 Jeremy Borash	.15	.40
54 Christy Hemme	.60	1.50
55 Eric Young	.15	.40
56 Ms. Tessmacher	.40	1.00
57 Rob Terry	.15	.40
58 Amazing Red	.15	.40
59 Hernandez	.15	.40
60 Magnus	.15	.40
61 K.Angle/J.Jarrett	.25	.60
62 Lockdown 2011	.15	.40
63 Karen Jarrett's TNA Return	.25	.60
64 Karen on Angle & Jarrett	.25	.60
65 The Jarrett/Angle Bunch	.15	.40
66 Robbie E	.15	.40
67 Robert Roode	.15	.40
68 Shannon Moore	.15	.40
69 Jesse Neal	.15	.40
70 Cookie	.15	.40
71 D'Angelo Dinero	.15	.40
72 Rosita	.25	.60
73 Generation Me	.15	.40
74 Samoa Joe	.15	.40
75 Mexican America	.15	.40
76 Sarita	.25	.60
77 Suicide	.15	.40
78 Brian Kendrick	.15	.40
79 Winter	.60	1.50
80 Kazarian	.15	.40
81 Immortal	.15	.40
82 Fortune	.15	.40
83 Bully Ray	.15	.40
84 Christy Hemme	.60	1.50
85 Kurt Angle	.25	.60
86 Beer Money	.15	.40
87 Eric Bischoff	.15	.40
88 Scott Steiner	.25	.60
89 Samoa Joe	.15	.40
90 Hogan/Flair/Sting	3.00	8.00
91 Hulk Hogan SP	3.00	8.00
92 Hulk Hogan SP	3.00	8.00
93 Hulk Hogan SP	3.00	8.00
94 Ric Flair SP	3.00	8.00
95 Ric Flair SP	3.00	8.00
96 Ric Flair SP	3.00	8.00
97 Sting SP	3.00	8.00
98 Sting SP	3.00	8.00
99 Sting SP	3.00	8.00
CL Checklist	.15	.40

2011 TRISTAR TNA Signature Impact Autographs Silver

*GOLD/25: .6X TO 1.25X BASIC AUTOS
*RED/5: UNPRICED DUE TO SCARCITY
*PURPLE/1: UNPRICED DUE TO SCARCITY
STATED PRINT RUN 99 SER.#'d SETS

S8 Jeff Hardy	25.00	50.00
S9 Matt Hardy	15.00	30.00
S10 Rob Van Dam	15.00	30.00

S11	Mickie James	30.00	60.00
S12	Scott Steiner		
S13	Anarquia	15.00	30.00
S14	Jeff Jarrett	12.00	25.00
S15	Kazarian	6.00	15.00
S16	Winter	12.00	25.00
S17	Kurt Angle	20.00	40.00
S18	Karen Jarrett	6.00	15.00
S19	Abyss	6.00	15.00
S20	Matt Morgan	6.00	15.00
S21	Kendrick	6.00	15.00
S22	Mr. Anderson	10.00	20.00
S23	Velvet Sky	20.00	40.00
S24	Robert Roode	10.00	20.00
S25	Ms. Tessmacher	12.00	25.00
S26	Sarita	6.00	15.00
S27	Jesse Neal	6.00	15.00
S28	Amazing Red	6.00	15.00
S29	D'Angelo Dinero	6.00	15.00
S30	Magnus	6.00	15.00
S31	Angelina Love	10.00	20.00
S32	Orlando Jordan	6.00	15.00
S33	Mick Foley	10.00	20.00
S34	Crimson	6.00	15.00
S35	Daniels	6.00	15.00
S36	Madison Rayne	10.00	20.00
S37	Murphy		
S38	Tara	10.00	20.00
S39	James Storm	6.00	15.00
S40	Jeremy Buck	6.00	15.00
S41	Rosita	12.00	25.00
S42	Rob Terry	6.00	15.00
S43	SoCal Val	10.00	20.00
S44	Jay Lethal	6.00	15.00
S45	Mike Tenay	6.00	15.00
S46	Jeremy Borash	6.00	15.00
S47	Samoa Joe	6.00	15.00
S48	Eric Young	6.00	15.00
S49	AJ Styles	10.00	20.00
S50	Christy Hemme	10.00	20.00
S51	Shannon Moore	6.00	15.00
S52	Max Buck	6.00	15.00
S53	Chyna	10.00	25.00
S54	Eric Bischoff		

2011 TRISTAR TNA Signature Impact Dual Autographs Silver

*GOLD/25: .6X TO 1.25X BASIC AUTOS
*RED/5: UNPRICED DUE TO SCARCITY
*PURPLE/1: UNPRICED DUE TO SCARCITY
STATED PRINT RUN 99 SER.#'d SETS

1	H.Hogan/R.Flair		
2	Jeff & Matt Hardy		
3	Jeff & Karen Jarrett		
4	Sting/RVD		
5	H.Hogan/Sting		
6	M.Hardy/RVD		
7	H.Hogan/M.Hardy		
8	Sarita/Rosita	10.00	20.00
9	Hernandez/Anarquia		
10	AJ Styles/Daniels	10.00	20.00
11	RVD/H.Hogan		
12	M.James/Tara	20.00	40.00
13	Tara/M.Rayne	10.00	20.00
14	Gunner/Murphy	6.00	15.00
15	Magnus/D.Williams	6.00	15.00
16	Max & Jeremy Buck	6.00	15.00
17	S.Steiner/H.Hogan		
18	Crimson/Abyss	6.00	15.00
19	K.Angle/J.Jarrett		
20	S.Moore/J.Neal		
21	M.Foley/RVD		
22	C.Hemme/S.Val	10.00	20.00
23	Hernandez/M.Morgan	6.00	15.00
24	Robbie E/Cookie	6.00	15.00
25	Winter/A.Love	10.00	20.00
26	A.Love/V.Sky	15.00	30.00
27	Chyna/K.Angle		

2011 TRISTAR TNA Signature Impact Dual Memorabilia Silver

STATED PRINT RUN 199 SER.#'d SETS

M11 Jeff & Matt Hardy

2011 TRISTAR TNA Signature Impact Eight Autographs Silver

*GOLD/25: UNPRICED DUE TO SCARCITY
*RED/5: UNPRICED DUE TO SCARCITY
*PURPLE/1: UNPRICED DUE TO SCARCITY
STATED PRINT RUN 99 SER.#'d SETS

1 Hogan/Flair/Sting/Steiner
Angle/J.Hardy/RVD/M.Hardy
2 Hogan/Tara/Flair/James
Sting/Sky/J.Hardy/Love
3 James/Tara/Love/Sky
Rayne/Winter/Rosita/Sarita

2011 TRISTAR TNA Signature Impact Five Autographs Silver

*GOLD/25: X TO X BASIC AUTOS
*RED/5: UNPRICED DUE TO SCARCITY
*PURPLE/1: UNPRICED DUE TO SCARCITY
STATED PRINT RUN 99 SER.#'d SETS

1	Hogan/Steiner/Sting/Jarrett/Flair		
2	Love/Sky/Tara/James/Rayne	30.00	60.00
3	Jeff & Matt Hardy/RVD/Foley/Angle		

2011 TRISTAR TNA Signature Impact Memorabilia Silver

*GOLD/50: .6X TO 1.25X BASIC MEM
*BLUE/25: .75X TO 1.5X BASIC MEM
*RED/5: UNPRICED DUE TO SCARCITY
*PURPLE/1: UNPRICED DUE TO SCARCITY
STATED PRINT RUN 199 SER.#'d SETS

M6	Hulk Hogan		
M7	Sting	12.00	25.00
M8	Chyna	12.00	25.00
M9	Jeff Hardy		
M10	Rob Van Dam	10.00	20.00

2011 TRISTAR TNA Signature Impact Quad Autographs Silver

*GOLD/25: .6X TO 1.25X BASIC AUTOS
*RED/5: UNPRICED DUE TO SCARCITY
*PURPLE/1: UNPRICED DUE TO SCARCITY
STATED PRINT RUN 99 SER.#'d SETS

1	Flair/Hardy/Abyss/Styles		
2	Hogan/Flair/The Hardys		
3	Hernandez/Anarquia/Sarita/Rosita	15.00	30.00
4	Angle/Chyna/Karen & Jeff Jarrett		

2011 TRISTAR TNA Signature Impact Quad Memorabilia Silver

M14	Sky/Love/Winter/James	15.00	40.00
M15	Hernandez/Anarquia	8.00	20.00
	Sarita/Rosita		

2011 TRISTAR TNA Signature Impact Ric Flair Die-Cut Letter Memorabilia Silver

COMPLETE SET (5)

M1 Ric Flair F
M2 Ric Flair L
M3 Ric Flair A
M4 Ric Flair I
M5 Ric Flair R

2011 TRISTAR TNA Signature Impact Seven Autographs Silver

*GOLD/25: UNPRICED DUE TO SCARCITY
*RED/5: UNPRICED DUE TO SCARCITY
*PURPLE/1: UNPRICED DUE TO SCARCITY
STATED PRINT RUN 99 SER.#'d SETS
UNPRICED DUE TO SCARCITY

1 Sting/RVD/Anderson/Hogan
Flair/Jeff & Matt Hardy
2 Hogan/James/Flair
Love/RVD/Sky/J.Hardy

2011 TRISTAR TNA Signature Impact Six Autographs Silver

*GOLD/25: UNPRICED DUE TO SCARCITY
*RED/5: UNPRICED DUE TO SCARCITY
*PURPLE/1: UNPRICED DUE TO SCARCITY
STATED PRINT RUN 99 SER.#'d SETS
UNPRICED DUE TO SCARCITY

1 Hogan/Flair/Sting
Angle/Jarrett/Steiner
2 Tara/James/Sky
Love/Rayne/Hemme

2011 TRISTAR TNA Signature Impact Triple Autographs Silver

*GOLD/25: UNPRICED DUE TO SCARCITY
*RED/5: UNPRICED DUE TO SCARCITY
*PURPLE/1: UNPRICED DUE TO SCARCITY
STATED PRINT RUN 99 SER.#'d SETS
UNPRICED DUE TO SCARCITY

1 Jeff & Karen Jarrett/Angle
2 Sky/Winter/Love
3 Sting/RVD/Anderson
4 Hogan/Flair/Sting
5 Jeff & Matt Hardy/RVD

2011 TRISTAR TNA Signature Impact Triple Memorabilia Silver

M12	Hogan/Flair/Sting		
M13	Jeff & Karen Jarrett/Angle	8.00	20.00

2010 TRISTAR TNA Xtreme

COMPLETE SET W/SP (111)	60.00	120.00
COMPLETE SET W/O SP (101)	10.00	25.00
UNOPENED BOX (20 PACKS)		
UNOPENED PACK (6 CARDS)		

*SILVER/40: 3X TO 8X BASIC CARDS

*GOLD/10: UNPRICED DUE TO SCARCITY
*PURPLE/1: UNPRICED DUE TO SCARCITY
SP STATED ODDS 1:BOX

1	Hulk Hogan	1.00	2.50
2	Eric Bischoff	.15	.40
3	Jeff Jarrett	.40	1.00
4	Samoa Joe	.25	.60
5	Robbie E	.15	.40
6	Sting	.60	1.50
7	Ric Flair	.75	2.00
8	AJ Styles	.40	1.00
9	Matt Morgan	.15	.40
10	Cowboy James Storm	.25	.60
11	Robert Roode	.15	.40
12	Kazarian	.15	.40
13	Tommy Dreamer	.15	.40
14	Mick Foley	.75	2.00
15	Brother Devon	.25	.60
16	Stevie Richards	.15	.40
17	Rhino	.25	.60
18	Brian Kendrick	.25	.60
19	Raven	.25	.60
20	Taz	.15	.40
21	Sabu	.15	.40
22	Al Snow	.40	1.00
23	Hardcore Justice	.15	.40
24	RVD/Sabu	.40	1.00
25	Raven/Tommy Dreamer	.25	.60
26	So.Philly Street Fight	.15	.40
27	Rhino/Al Snow/Brother Runt	.40	1.00
28	Stevie Richards/PJ Polaco	.15	.40
29	Too Cold Scorpio/CW Anderson	.15	.40
30	The FBI/Kash/Diamond/Swinger	.15	.40
31	Jason Hervey	.15	.40
32	Rob Van Dam	.40	1.00
33	Jeff Hardy	.60	1.50
34	Kurt Angle	.60	1.50
35	D'Angelo Dinero	.15	.40
36	Brother Ray	.25	.60
37	Mr. Anderson	.25	.60
38	TNA Tag Team Champ	.15	.40
39	Falls Count Anywhere	.25	.60
40	Jarrett/Joe/Sting/Nash	.60	1.50
41	Tommy Dreamer/AJ Styles	.40	1.00
42	Jeff Hardy/Kurt Angle	.60	1.50
43	London Brawling	.15	.40
44	Generation Me	.15	.40
45	Rob Terry	.15	.40
46	Douglas Williams	.15	.40
47	Motorcity Machine Guns	.25	.60
48	Amazing Red	.15	.40
49	Magnus	.15	.40
50	Hernandez	.15	.40
51	Jeremy Borash	.15	.40
52	Orlando Jordan	.15	.40
53	TNA Tag Team Champ	.15	.40
54	Classic Knockouts	.25	.60
55	RVD Overcomes the Odds	.40	1.00
56	Lethal Lockdown	.15	.40
57	Cookie	.25	.60
58	Mickie James	.75	2.00
59	Angelina Love	.60	1.50
60	Velvet Sky	.75	2.00
61	Lacey Von Erich	.75	2.00
62	Madison Rayne	.60	1.50
63	Taylor Wilde	.40	1.00
64	Hamada	.40	1.00
65	Daffney	.60	1.50

No.	Card		
66	Sarita	.40	1.00
67	SoCal Val	.60	1.50
68	Tara	.60	1.50
69	Miss Tessmacher	.75	2.00
70	Ink Inc.	.15	.40
71	Abyss SS	.25	.60
72	AJ Styles SS	.40	1.00
73	Hulk Hogan SS	1.00	2.50
74	Kurt Angle SS	.60	1.50
75	Jeff Jarrett SS	.40	1.00
76	Jeff Hardy SS	.60	1.50
77	Dixie Carter SS	.40	1.00
78	Rob Van Dam SS	.40	1.00
79	Lacey Von Erich SS	.75	2.00
80	Jay Lethal SS	.15	.40
81	Tommy Dreamer SS	.15	.40
82	Mick Foley SS	.75	2.00
83	Sting PC	.60	1.50
84	Madison Rayne PC	.60	1.50
85	D'Angelo Dinero PC	.15	.40
86	Christy Hemme PC	.60	1.50
87	Jeff Hardy PC	.60	1.50
88	Angelina Love PC	.60	1.50
89	Mickie James PC	.75	2.00
90	Dixie Carter PC	.40	1.00
91	Kurt Angle PC	.60	1.50
92	Mike Tenay PC	.15	.40
93	Mickie James	.75	2.00
94	Rob Van Dam UX	.40	1.00
95	Sting UX	.60	1.50
96	Jeff Hardy UX	.60	1.50
97	Abyss UX	.25	.60
98	Tommy Dreamer UX	.15	.40
99	AJ Styles UX	.40	1.00
100	Hulk Hogan UX	1.00	2.50
101	Jeff Hardy Original Art SP	6.00	15.00
102	Jeff Hardy Original Art SP	6.00	15.00
103	Jeff Hardy Original Art SP	6.00	15.00
104	Jeff Hardy Original Art SP	6.00	15.00
105	Jeff Hardy Original Art SP	6.00	15.00
106	Jeff Hardy Original Art SP	6.00	15.00
107	Jeff Hardy Original Art SP	6.00	15.00
108	Jeff Hardy Original Art SP	6.00	15.00
109	Jeff Hardy Original Art SP	6.00	15.00
110	Jeff Hardy Original Art SP	6.00	15.00
CL	Checklist	.15	.40

2010 TRISTAR TNA Xtreme Autographed Memorabilia Gold

*GREEN/25: UNPRICED DUE TO SCARCITY
*RED/5: UNPRICED DUE TO SCARCITY
*PURPLE/1: UNPRICED DUE TO SCARCITY
STATED PRINT RUN 99 SER.#'d SETS
UNPRICED DUE TO SCARCITY

XA1 Hulk Hogan
XA2 Mickie James
XA3 Rob Van Dam
XA4 Jeff Hardy
XA5 Sting
XA6 AJ Styles

2010 TRISTAR TNA Xtreme Autographs Gold

COMMON AUTO		5.00	12.00

*GREEN/25: .6X TO 1.5X BASIC AUTOS
*RED/5: UNPRICED DUE TO SCARCITY

---

*PURPLE/1: UNPRICED DUE TO SCARCITY
STATED PRINT RUN 99 SER.#'d SETS

X1	Rob Van Dam		
X2	Rhino	6.00	15.00
X3	Mick Foley		
X4	Tommy Dreamer	6.00	15.00
X5	Sabu	6.00	15.00
X6	Raven		
X7	Stevie Richards	6.00	15.00
X8	Al Snow	8.00	20.00
X9	Kid Kash	5.00	12.00
X10	New Jack	5.00	12.00
X11	P.J. Polaco	5.00	12.00
X12	Tracy Smothers	5.00	12.00
X13	Axl Rotten	5.00	12.00
X14	Too Cold Scorpio	5.00	12.00
X15	Bill Alfonso	5.00	12.00
X16	Tony Luke	5.00	12.00
X17	Blue Tillie	5.00	12.00
X18	Swinger	5.00	12.00
X19	Brother Runt	5.00	12.00
X20	Stephen DeAngelis	5.00	12.00
X21	Simon Diamond	5.00	12.00
X22	Nova	5.00	12.00
X23	Guido Maritato	5.00	12.00
X24	Big Sal	5.00	12.00
X25	Mustafa	5.00	12.00
X26	C.W. Anderson	5.00	12.00
X27	Joel Gertner		
X28	John Rechner		
X29	Taz	5.00	12.00
X30	Brian Kendrick	6.00	15.00
X31	Tara	8.00	20.00
X32	Jason Hervey	6.00	15.00
X33	Mickie James	15.00	30.00
X34	Jeremy Borash	5.00	12.00
X35	Samoa Joe	8.00	20.00
X36	Alex Shelley	5.00	12.00
X37	Shannon Moore	8.00	20.00
X38	Jay Lethal	5.00	12.00
X39	Jeff Hardy		
X40	Chris Sabin	5.00	12.00
X41	Kazarian	5.00	12.00
X42	Mr. Anderson	6.00	15.00
X43	Sting		
X44	Abyss	6.00	15.00
X45	AJ Styles	8.00	20.00
X46	Angelina Love	10.00	25.00
X47	Madison Rayne	10.00	25.00
X48	Velvet Sky	10.00	25.00
X49	Lacey Von Erich	10.00	25.00
X50	Christy Hemme	10.00	25.00
X51	Kevin Nash	10.00	25.00
X52	Kurt Angle	10.00	25.00
X53	Ric Flair		
X54	Hulk Hogan		
X55	Hulk Hogan		
X56	Hulk Hogan		

2010 TRISTAR TNA Xtreme Autographs Green

*GREEN: .6X TO 1.5X BASIC AUTOS
STATED PRINT RUN 25 SER.#'d SETS

X1	Rob Van Dam		
X2	Rhino	10.00	25.00
X3	Mick Foley		
X4	Tommy Dreamer	10.00	25.00
X5	Sabu	10.00	25.00

X6	Raven		
X7	Stevie Richards	10.00	25.00
X8	Al Snow	12.00	30.00
X9	Kid Kash	8.00	20.00
X10	New Jack	8.00	20.00
X11	P.J. Polaco	8.00	20.00
X12	Tracy Smothers	8.00	20.00
X13	Axl Rotten	8.00	20.00
X14	Too Cold Scorpio	8.00	20.00
X15	Bill Alfonso	8.00	20.00
X16	Tony Luke	8.00	20.00
X17	Blue Tillie	8.00	20.00
X18	Swinger	8.00	20.00
X19	Brother Runt	8.00	20.00
X20	Stephen DeAngelis	8.00	20.00
X21	Simon Diamond	8.00	20.00
X22	Nova	8.00	20.00
X23	Guido Maritato	8.00	20.00
X24	Big Sal	8.00	20.00
X25	Mustafa	8.00	20.00
X26	C.W. Anderson	8.00	20.00
X27	Joel Gertner		
X28	John Rechner		
X29	Taz	8.00	20.00
X30	Brian Kendrick	10.00	25.00
X31	Tara	15.00	30.00
X32	Jason Hervey	10.00	25.00
X33	Mickie James	25.00	50.00
X34	Jeremy Borash	8.00	20.00
X35	Samoa Joe	12.00	30.00
X36	Alex Shelley	8.00	20.00
X37	Shannon Moore	12.00	30.00
X38	Jay Lethal	8.00	20.00
X39	Jeff Hardy		
X40	Chris Sabin	8.00	20.00
X41	Kazarian	8.00	20.00
X42	Mr. Anderson	10.00	25.00
X43	Sting		
X44	Abyss	10.00	25.00
X45	AJ Styles	12.00	30.00
X46	Angelina Love	20.00	40.00
X47	Madison Rayne	20.00	40.00
X48	Velvet Sky	20.00	40.00
X49	Lacey Von Erich	20.00	40.00
X50	Christy Hemme	20.00	40.00
X51	Kevin Nash	20.00	40.00
X52	Kurt Angle	20.00	40.00
X53	Ric Flair		
X54	Hulk Hogan		
X55	Hulk Hogan		
X56	Hulk Hogan		

2010 TRISTAR TNA Xtreme Dual Autographed Memorabilia Gold

STATED PRINT RUN 50 SER.#'d SETS

XA7	RVD/Sabu		
XA8	A.Love/V.Sky	35.00	70.00
XA9	J.Hardy/RVD		

2010 TRISTAR TNA Xtreme Dual Autographs Gold

1	R.Flair/M.Foley		
2	Sting/K.Nash		
3	RVD/Sabu		
4	A.Love/V.Sky	12.00	30.00
5	A.Shelley/C.Sabin	8.00	20.00

6	Max & Jeremy Buck	8.00	20.00
7	J.Neal/S.Moore	12.00	25.00
8	Robbie E/Cookie	12.00	30.00
9	Tommy & Trisa Dreamer	12.00	30.00
10	N.Jack/Mustafa		
11	J.Finegan/M.Kehner		
12	Scorpio/C.Anderson		
13	M.Tenay/Taz		
14	Raven/T.Dreamer		
15	H.Hogan/R.Flair		

2010 TRISTAR TNA Xtreme Dual Memorabilia

*GOLD/50: .5X TO 1.2X BASIC MEM
*GREEN/25: .6X TO 1.5X BASIC MEM
*RED/5: UNPRICED DUE TO SCARCITY
*PURPLE/1: UNPRICED DUE TO SCARCITY
STATED PRINT RUN 199 SER.#'d SETS

X12	Robbie E/Cookie	8.00	20.00
X13	Jeremy & Max Buck	6.00	15.00

2010 TRISTAR TNA Xtreme Dual Memorabilia Gold

*GOLD: .5X TO 1.2X BASIC MEM
STATED PRINT RUN 50 SER.#'d SETS

X12	Robbie E/Cookie	10.00	25.00
X13	Jeremy & Max Buck	8.00	20.00

2010 TRISTAR TNA Xtreme Lovely Locks Hair Autographs Turquoise

*PINK/1: UNPRICED DUE TO SCARCITY
STATED PRINT RUN 3 SER.#'d SETS
UNPRICED DUE TO SCARCITY

LL1 Velvet Sky
LL2 Angelina Love
LL3 SoCal Val
LL4 Christy Hemme

2010 TRISTAR TNA Xtreme Memorabilia

*GOLD/50: .5X TO 1.2X BASIC MEM
*GREEN/10: UNPRICED DUE TO SCARCITY
*RED/5: UNPRICED DUE TO SCARCITY
*PURPLE/1: UNPRICED DUE TO SCARCITY
OVERALL MEMORABILIA ODDS ONE PER HOBBY BOX
STATED PRINT RUN 199 SER.#'d SETS

X1	Hulk Hogan		
X2	Rob Van Dam		
X3	Jeff Hardy		
X4	Mr. Anderson	6.00	15.00
X5	Kurt Angle	6.00	15.00
X6	Mickie James		
X7	AJ Styles		
X8	D'Angelo Dinero		
X9	Sabu	6.00	15.00
X10	Al Snow	6.00	15.00
X11	Brother Runt	6.00	15.00

2010 TRISTAR TNA Xtreme Obak

COMPLETE SET (8)		15.00	40.00

STATED PRINT RUN 310 SER.#'d SETS

X1	Hulk Hogan	8.00	20.00
X2	Jeff Hardy	5.00	12.00
X3	Rob Van Dam	3.00	8.00
X4	Mickie James	6.00	15.00

X5 AJ Styles 3.00 8.00
X6 Tommy Dreamer 1.25 3.00
X7 Jeff Jarrett 3.00 8.00
X8 Sting 5.00 12.00

2010 TRISTAR TNA Xtreme Quad Autographs

*GOLD/99: UNPRICED DUE TO SCARCITY
*GREEN/25: UNPRICED DUE TO SCARCITY
*RED/5: UNPRICED DUE TO SCARCITY
*PURPLE/1: UNPRICED DUE TO SCARCITY
UNPRICED DUE TO SCARCITY

1 Hogan/Flair/Jarrett/Hardy
2 Angle/Sting/Nash/Foley
3 Sky/Love/Rayne/Tara
4 Tommy & Trisa Dreamer/Kimberly/Brianna

2010 TRISTAR TNA Xtreme Quad Memorabilia Gold

*GREEN/10: UNPRICED DUE TO SCARCITY
*RED/5: UNPRICED DUE TO SCARCITY
*PURPLE/1: UNPRICED DUE TO SCARCITY
STATED PRINT RUN 50 SER.#'d SETS

X14 Hogan/Sting/RVD/Hardy
X15 Sky/Love/Von Erich/Rayne
X16 Hogan/Flair/Foley/Sting
X17 Tara/James/Sky/Love
X18 Snow/B.Runt/Scorpio/Tillie 15.00 30.00
X19 Dreamer/RVD/Sabu/Snow 15.00 30.00

2010 TRISTAR TNA Xtreme Six Autographs

*GOLD/99: UNPRICED DUE TO SCARCITY
*GREEN/25: UNPRICED DUE TO SCARCITY
*RED/5: UNPRICED DUE TO SCARCITY
*PURPLE/1: UNPRICED DUE TO SCARCITY
UNPRICED DUE TO SCARCITY

1 Flair/Styles/Storm
Roode/Kazarian/Morgan
2 Hogan/Flair/Hardy
Jarrett/Angle/Sting
3 Dreamer/Foley/Richards
Rhino/Raven/Sabu
4 Smothers/Luke/Maritato
Kash/Diamond/Swinger

2010 TRISTAR TNA Xtreme Six Autographs Gold

STATED PRINT RUN 99 SER. #'d SETS

1 Flair/Styles/Storm
Roode/Kazarian/Morgan
2 Hogan/Flair/Hardy
Jarrett/Angle/Sting
3 Dreamer/Foley/Richards
Rhino/Raven/Sabu
4 Smothers/Luke/Maritato
Kash/Diamond/Swinger

2010 TRISTAR TNA Xtreme Sting Die-Cut Letter Memorabilia Green

STATED PRINT RUN 10 SER.#'d SETS

S1 Sting S 20.00 40.00
S2 Sting T 20.00 40.00
S3 Sting I 20.00 40.00
S4 Sting N 20.00 40.00
S5 Sting G 20.00 40.00

2010 TRISTAR TNA Xtreme Sting Face Paint Red

STATED PRINT RUN 5 SER.#'d SETS
UNPRICED DUE TO SCARCITY

S3 Sting
S4 Sting

2010 TRISTAR TNA Xtreme Triple Autographs Gold

STATED PRINT RUN 99 SER.#'d SETS

1 Hogan/Jarrett/Flair
2 Foley/Angle/Anderson
3 Raven/Dreamer/Foley
4 Richards/Nova/Polaco
5 Rhino/Runt/Snow
6 Ray/Devon/Gertner
7 Sabu/VanDam/Alfonso

2010 TRISTAR TNA Xtreme Velvet Sky Die-Cut Letter Memorabilia Gold

STATED PRINT RUN 50 SER.#'d SETS

VS1 Velvet Sky S 25.00 50.00
VS2 Velvet Sky K 25.00 50.00
VS3 Velvet Sky Y 25.00 50.00

2006 Unilever WWE

NNO Batista 5.00 12.00
NNO Booker T 3.00 8.00
NNO Carlito 5.00 12.00
NNO Hulk Hogan 8.00 20.00
NNO The Hurricane 1.25 3.00
NNO John Cena 8.00 20.00
NNO Kurt Angle 8.00 20.00
NNO Rey Mysterio 5.00 12.00
NNO Stone Cold Steve Austin 8.00 20.00
NNO The Undertaker 6.00 15.00

2021 Upper Deck AEW

COMPLETE SET W/SP (100) 100.00 200.00
COMPLETE SET W/O SP (60) 30.00 75.00
COMMON TT (61-70) .60 1.50
COMMON CREW (71-80) .60 1.50
COMMON MAG (81-100) 1.25 3.00
*GOLD: .5X TO 1.2X BASIC CARDS
*GOLD TT: .5X TO 1.2X BASIC CARDS
*GOLD CREW: .5X TO 1.2X BASIC CARDS
*GOLD MAG: .5X TO 1.2X BASIC CARDS
*PYRO: .6X TO 1.5X BASIC CARDS
*PYRO TT: .6X TO 1.5X BASIC CARDS
*PYRO CREW: .6X TO 1.5X BASIC CARDS
*PYRO MAG: .6X TO 1.5X BASIC CARDS
*EXCLUSIVES/100: 8X TO 20X BASIC CARDS
*HIGH GLOSS/10: UNPRICED DUE TO SCARCITY
*BLACK/1: UNPRICED DUE TO SCARCITY

1 Cody Rhodes 1.00 2.50
2 Kris Statlander .50 1.25
3 Shawn Spears .30 .75
4 Dustin Rhodes .60 1.50
5 Lance Archer 1.25 3.00
6 Penelope Ford .50 1.25
7 Hangman Adam Page 2.00 5.00
8 Scorpio Sky .30 .75
9 Miro .60 1.50
10 QT Marshall .40 1.00
11 Dr. Britt Baker 3.00 8.00
12 Joey Janela .30 .75
13 Jon Moxley .75 2.00
14 Isiah Kassidy .40 1.00
15 Sammy Guevara .75 2.00
16 Kenny Omega 2.00 5.00
17 The Blade .50 1.25
18 John Silver .30 .75
19 Jake Hager .60 1.50
20 Nick Jackson 1.25 3.00
21 PAC .60 1.50
22 Abadon .30 .75
23 Jungle Boy 2.00 5.00
24 Marq Quen .40 1.00
25 RIHO 1.25 3.00
26 Ricky Starks .75 2.00
27 Frankie Kazarian .40 1.00
28 Anna Jay 1.50 4.00
29 Matt Jackson 1.25 3.00
30 Ortiz .50 1.25
31 Cash Wheeler .50 1.25
32 Stu Grayson .30 .75
33 Darby Allin 4.00 10.00
34 Chuck Taylor .40 1.00
35 Trent? .75 2.00
36 Alex Reynolds .30 .75
37 Matt Hardy .60 1.50
38 The Butcher .50 1.25
39 Tay Conti 1.25 3.00
40 Orange Cassidy 2.00 5.00
41 Big Swole .50 1.25
42 Penta el Zero M .75 2.00
43 Kip Sabian .60 1.50
44 Christopher Daniels .50 1.25
45 Brian Cage .40 1.00
46 Luchasaurus 1.00 2.50
47 Colt Cabana .40 1.00
48 The Bunny .75 2.00
49 Wardlow .60 1.50
50 Nyla Rose .60 1.50
51 MJF 3.00 8.00
52 Santana .50 1.25
53 Brandi Rhodes 1.50 4.00
54 Chris Jericho 1.25 3.00
55 Hikaru Shida 1.00 2.50
56 Powerhouse Hobbs .60 1.50
57 Dax Harwood .50 1.25
58 Rey Fenix .75 2.00
59 Evil Uno .60 1.50
60 Mr. Brodie Lee .75 2.00
61 Trent?/Chuck Taylor SP 1.25 3.00
62 The Butcher/The Blade SP .75 2.00
63 Dax Harwood/Cash Wheeler SP .75 2.00
64 Santana/Ortiz SP .75 2.00
65 Jungle Boy/Luchasaurus SP 3.00 8.00
66 Rey Fenix/Penta el Zero M SP 1.25 3.00
67 Evil Uno/Stu Grayson SP 1.00 2.50
68 Marq Quen/Isiah Kassidy SP .60 1.50
69 Frankie Kazarian/Scorpio Sky SP .60 1.50
70 Matt Jackson/Nick Jackson SP 2.00 5.00
71 Arn Anderson SP 1.00 2.50
72 Billy Gunn SP .75 2.00
73 Jake Roberts SP 1.00 2.50
74 Jim Ross SP 1.50 4.00
75 Justin Roberts SP .60 1.50
76 Paul Turner SP .60 1.50
77 Sting SP 1.50 4.00
78 Taz SP .75 2.00
79 Tony Schiavone SP .75 2.00
80 Tully Blanchard SP 1.00 2.50
81 Sting SP 2.50 6.00
82 Brian Cage SP 1.25 3.00
83 Dr. Britt Baker SP 10.00 25.00
84 Chris Jericho SP 4.00 10.00
85 Cody Rhodes SP 3.00 8.00
86 Colt Cabana SP 1.25 3.00
87 Darby Allin SP 12.00 30.00
88 Hikaru Shida SP 3.00 8.00
89 Jon Moxley SP 2.50 6.00
90 Kenny Omega SP 6.00 15.00
91 Lance Archer SP 4.00 10.00
92 Matt Hardy SP 2.00 5.00
93 Matt Jackson SP 4.00 10.00
94 MJF SP 10.00 25.00
95 Mr. Brodie Lee SP 2.50 6.00
96 Nick Jackson SP 4.00 10.00
97 Nyla Rose SP 2.00 5.00
98 Orange Cassidy SP 6.00 15.00
99 Rey Fenix SP 2.50 6.00
100 Sammy Guevara SP 2.50 6.00

2021 Upper Deck AEW Autographs

*PYRO/25: UNPRICED DUE TO SCARCITY
*DYNAMITE/5: UNPRICED DUE TO SCARCITY
*GOLD/1: UNPRICED DUE TO SCARCITY
*P.P.BLACK/1: UNPRICED DUE TO SCARCITY
*P.P.CYAN/1: UNPRICED DUE TO SCARCITY
*P.P.MAGENTA/1: UNPRICED DUE TO SCARCITY
*P.P.YELLOW/1: UNPRICED DUE TO SCARCITY
GROUP A ODDS 1:7,581
GROUP B ODDS 1:1,832
GROUP C ODDS 1:913
GROUP D ODDS 1:464
GROUP E ODDS 1:341
STATED ODDS 1:146 HOBBY/EPACK
STATED ODDS 1:113 BLASTER/FAT PACKS
STATED TT ODDS 1:2,048 HOBBY
STATED TT ODDS 1:1,700 EPACK/BLAST/FAT
STATED CREW ODDS 1:1,024 HOBBY/EPACK
STATED CREW ODDS 1:800 BLASTER/FAT
STATED MAG ODDS 1:768 HOBBY/EPACK
STATED MAG ODDS 1:600 BLASTER/FAT

1 Cody Rhodes B 125.00 250.00
2 Kris Statlander E 100.00 200.00
3 Shawn Spears D 25.00 60.00
4 Dustin Rhodes D 30.00 75.00
5 Lance Archer C 50.00 100.00
6 Penelope Ford E 125.00 300.00
7 Hangman Adam Page D 200.00 400.00
8 Scorpio Sky D 75.00 150.00
9 Miro D 30.00 75.00
10 QT Marshall E 20.00 50.00
11 Dr. Britt Baker C 500.00 1000.00
12 Joey Janela D 15.00 40.00
13 Jon Moxley B

No.	Card	Lo	Hi
14	Isiah Kassidy C		
15	Sammy Guevara C		
16	Kenny Omega B	200.00	400.00
17	The Blade C		
18	John Silver D	25.00	60.00
19	Jake Hager E	20.00	50.00
20	Nick Jackson A	75.00	150.00
21	PAC E	60.00	120.00
22	Abadon E	30.00	75.00
23	Jungle Boy D	200.00	400.00
24	Marq Quen D	8.00	20.00
25	RIHO E	100.00	200.00
26	Ricky Starks D	25.00	60.00
27	Frankie Kazarian C	15.00	40.00
28	Anna Jay E	100.00	200.00
29	Matt Jackson A	100.00	200.00
30	Ortiz D	30.00	75.00
31	Cash Wheeler D	20.00	50.00
32	Stu Grayson D		
33	Darby Allin B	500.00	1000.00
34	Chuck Taylor D	25.00	60.00
35	Trent? D	50.00	100.00
36	Alex Reynolds E	25.00	60.00
37	Matt Hardy B	25.00	60.00
38	The Butcher C	75.00	150.00
39	Tay Conti E	125.00	250.00
40	Orange Cassidy B	200.00	400.00
41	Big Swole E	50.00	100.00
42	Penta el Zero M C		
43	Kip Sabian E	25.00	60.00
44	Christopher Daniels E	20.00	50.00
45	Brian Cage C		
46	Luchasaurus C	125.00	250.00
47	Colt Cabana C	50.00	100.00
48	The Bunny E	75.00	150.00
49	Wardlow E	150.00	300.00
50	Nyla Rose C	60.00	120.00
51	MJF B	300.00	600.00
52	Santana D	50.00	100.00
53	Brandi Rhodes E	60.00	120.00
54	Chris Jericho B	175.00	350.00
55	Hikaru Shida B		
56	Powerhouse Hobbs D		
57	Dax Harwood D	25.00	60.00
58	Rey Fenix A	30.00	75.00
59	Evil Uno D	50.00	100.00
61	Chuck Taylor/Trent? B	60.00	120.00
62	The Butcher/The Blade B	100.00	200.00
63	Dax Harwood/Cash Wheeler B	75.00	150.00
64	Santana/Ortiz B		
65	Jungle Boy/Luchasaurus B	300.00	600.00
66	Rey Fenix/Penta el Zero M B		
67	Evil Uno/Stu Grayson B	75.00	150.00
68	Marq Quen/Isiah Kassidy B		
69	Frankie Kazarian/Scorpio Sky B	60.00	120.00
70	Matt Jackson/Nick Jackson A		
71	Arn Anderson B	30.00	75.00
72	Billy Gunn A	60.00	120.00
73	Jake Roberts B	25.00	60.00
74	Jim Ross B	60.00	120.00
75	Justin Roberts B	30.00	75.00
76	Paul Turner B	15.00	40.00
77	Sting A	250.00	500.00
78	Taz B		
79	Tony Schiavone B	75.00	150.00
80	Tully Blanchard B	75.00	150.00
81	Sting B		
82	Brian Cage C	50.00	100.00
83	Dr. Britt Baker C	500.00	1000.00
84	Chris Jericho A	150.00	300.00
85	Cody Rhodes A	150.00	300.00
86	Colt Cabana C	50.00	100.00
87	Darby Allin C	500.00	1000.00
88	Hikaru Shida C	200.00	400.00
89	Jon Moxley B	100.00	200.00
90	Kenny Omega C	250.00	500.00
91	Lance Archer C	50.00	100.00
92	Matt Hardy C	30.00	75.00
93	Matt Jackson B		
94	MJF C	250.00	500.00
96	Nick Jackson B	60.00	120.00
97	Nyla Rose C	60.00	120.00
98	Orange Cassidy C	150.00	300.00
99	Rey Fenix B	50.00	100.00
100	Sammy Guevara C	125.00	250.00

2021 Upper Deck AEW Canvas

COMPLETE SET W/O SP (30) 125.00 250.00
STATED ODDS 1:5
STATED SP ODDS 1:40

No.	Card	Lo	Hi
C1	Matt Hardy	3.00	8.00
C2	Brian Cage	3.00	8.00
C3	Dustin Rhodes	5.00	12.00
C4	Jungle Boy	8.00	20.00
C5	Brandi Rhodes	5.00	12.00
C6	Darby Allin	12.00	30.00
C7	Dr. Britt Baker	15.00	40.00
C8	Austin Gunn	2.50	6.00
C9	Tay Conti	8.00	20.00
C10	PAC	2.50	6.00
C11	Best Friends	4.00	10.00
C12	Colt Cabana	2.50	6.00
C13	Taz	4.00	10.00
C14	Nyla Rose	2.50	6.00
C15	The Butcher/The Blade	2.50	6.00
C16	Santana/Ortiz	3.00	8.00
C17	Lance Archer	5.00	12.00
C18	Sting	10.00	25.00
C19	Ricky Starks	4.00	10.00
C20	Luchasaurus	6.00	15.00
C21	Scorpio Sky	2.50	6.00
C22	Anna Jay	8.00	20.00
C23	Dax Harwood/Cash Wheeler	4.00	10.00
C24	Jim Ross	5.00	12.00
C25	Big Swole	2.50	6.00
C26	Joey Janela	2.50	6.00
C27	Rey Fenix/Penta el Zero M	6.00	15.00
C28	Tony Schiavone	3.00	8.00
C29	Sammy Guevara	5.00	12.00
C30	Hikaru Shida	10.00	25.00
C31	Cody Rhodes SP	15.00	40.00
C32	Nick Jackson SP	15.00	40.00
C33	Matt Jackson SP	15.00	40.00
C34	Mr. Brodie Lee SP	20.00	50.00
C35	Chris Jericho SP	15.00	40.00
C36	Hangman Adam Page SP	25.00	60.00
C37	Orange Cassidy SP	15.00	40.00
C38	MJF SP	20.00	50.00
C39	Kenny Omega SP	30.00	75.00
C40	Jon Moxley SP	15.00	40.00

2021 Upper Deck AEW The Dotted Line Autographs

STATED ODDS 1:1,536 HOBBY/EPACK
STATED ODDS 1:3,072 BLASTER
STATED ODDS 1:6,144 FAT PACKS

Code	Card	Lo	Hi
DLCJ	Chris Jericho	250.00	400.00
DLCR	Cody Rhodes		
DLDA	Darby Allin		
DLHS	Hikaru Shida		
DLJM	Jon Moxley		
DLKO	Kenny Omega	1500.00	3000.00
DLMF	MJF		
DLMH	Matt Hardy		
DLMJ	Matt Jackson		
DLNJ	Nick Jackson		
DLOC	Orange Cassidy		

2021 Upper Deck AEW Main Features

COMPLETE SET (40) 30.00 75.00
*SILVER: .5X TO 1.2X BASIC CARDS
*GREEN/199: 1.5X TO 4X BASIC CARDS
*RED/50: 2X TO 5X BASIC CARDS
*PURPLE/25: 2.5X TO 6X BASIC CARDS
*BLACK/1: UNPRICED DUE TO SCARCITY
STATED ODDS 1:1

No.	Card	Lo	Hi
MF1	Cody Rhodes	1.25	3.00
MF2	Darby Allin	5.00	12.00
MF3	Lance Archer	1.50	4.00
MF4	Chris Jericho	1.50	4.00
MF5	RIHO	1.50	4.00
MF6	Santana	.60	1.50
MF7	Orange Cassidy	2.50	6.00
MF8	Hikaru Shida	1.25	3.00
MF9	Dax Harwood	.60	1.50
MF10	Kenny Omega	2.50	6.00
MF11	Big Swole	.60	1.50
MF12	Dustin Rhodes	.75	2.00
MF13	Shawn Spears	.40	1.00
MF14	PAC	.75	2.00
MF15	Brandi Rhodes	2.00	5.00
MF16	Cash Wheeler	.60	1.50
MF17	Frankie Kazarian	.50	1.25
MF18	Tay Conti	1.50	4.00
MF19	Nick Jackson	1.50	4.00
MF20	Penta el Zero M	1.00	2.50
MF21	Nyla Rose	.75	2.00
MF22	Brian Cage	.50	1.25
MF23	Sting	1.00	2.50
MF24	Ortiz	.60	1.50
MF25	Hangman Adam Page	2.50	6.00
MF26	Luchasaurus	1.25	3.00
MF27	Scorpio Sky	.40	1.00
MF28	MJF	4.00	10.00
MF29	Jungle Boy	2.50	6.00
MF30	The Blade	.60	1.50
MF31	Matt Jackson	1.50	4.00
MF32	Matt Hardy	.75	2.00
MF33	Colt Cabana	.50	1.25
MF34	Rey Fenix	1.00	2.50
MF35	Dr. Britt Baker	4.00	10.00
MF36	Anna Jay	2.00	5.00
MF37	Ricky Starks	1.00	2.50
MF38	Sammy Guevara	1.00	2.50
MF39	Jake Hager	.75	2.00
MF40	Jon Moxley	1.00	2.50

2021 Upper Deck AEW Memorabilia Gold

*RED/50: .75X TO 2X BASIC MEM
STATED PRINT RUN 199 OR FEWER

No.	Card	Lo	Hi
1	Cody Rhodes	50.00	100.00
2	Kris Statlander	50.00	100.00
3	Shawn Spears	10.00	25.00
4	Dustin Rhodes	12.00	30.00
5	Lance Archer	12.00	30.00
6	Penelope Ford		
7	Hangman Adam Page	75.00	150.00
8	Scorpio Sky	25.00	60.00
9	Miro	15.00	40.00
10	QT Marshall	8.00	20.00
11	Dr. Britt Baker	50.00	100.00
12	Joey Janela	8.00	20.00
13	Jon Moxley		
14	Isiah Kassidy	12.00	30.00
15	Sammy Guevara	20.00	50.00
16	Kenny Omega	75.00	150.00
17	The Blade	8.00	20.00
18	John Silver	10.00	25.00
19	Jake Hager	10.00	25.00
20	Nick Jackson		
21	PAC	10.00	25.00
22	Abadon		
23	Jungle Boy	30.00	75.00
24	Marq Quen	8.00	20.00
26	Ricky Starks	15.00	40.00
27	Frankie Kazarian	12.00	30.00
28	Anna Jay	15.00	40.00
29	Matt Jackson		
30	Ortiz		
31	Cash Wheeler	12.00	30.00
32	Stu Grayson	15.00	40.00
33	Darby Allin	60.00	120.00
34	Chuck Taylor	8.00	20.00
35	Trent?		
36	Alex Reynolds		
37	Matt Hardy	10.00	25.00
38	The Butcher	8.00	20.00
39	Tay Conti	30.00	75.00
40	Orange Cassidy	30.00	75.00
41	Big Swole	12.00	30.00
42	Penta el Zero M	15.00	40.00
43	Kip Sabian	8.00	20.00
44	Christopher Daniels		
45	Brian Cage	12.00	30.00

46	Luchasaurus	25.00	60.00
47	Colt Cabana	12.00	30.00
48	The Bunny	50.00	100.00
49	Wardlow	15.00	40.00
50	Nyla Rose	10.00	25.00
51	MJF	30.00	75.00
52	Santana	10.00	25.00
53	Brandi Rhodes	20.00	50.00
54	Chris Jericho		
55	Hikaru Shida	50.00	100.00
56	Powerhouse Hobbs		
57	Dax Harwood	15.00	40.00
58	Rey Fenix		
59	Evil Uno		
61	Chuck Taylor/Trent?		
62	The Butcher/The Blade		
63	Dax Harwood/Cash Wheeler		
64	Santana/Ortiz		
65	Jungle Boy/Luchasaurus		
66	Rey Fenix/Penta el Zero M		
67	Evil Uno/Stu Grayson		
68	Marq Quen/Isiah Kassidy		
69	Frankie Kazarian/Scorpio Sky		
70	Matt Jackson/Nick Jackson		
71	Arn Anderson	15.00	40.00
72	Billy Gunn		
73	Jake Roberts		
74	Jim Ross		
78	Taz		
80	Tully Blanchard	10.00	25.00

2021 Upper Deck AEW NYCC Promo Sheet

PV1	Cody Rhodes	20.00	50.00
PV2 Miro/PV3 Dr. Britt Baker/PV4 Kenny Omega/NNO Cover Card/PV5 Chris Jericho/PV6 Hikaru Shida/PV7 Sting/PV8 Jon Moxley			

2021 Upper Deck AEW NYCC Promos

NNO	Cover Card	1.50	4.00
PV1	Cody Rhodes	2.00	5.00
PV2	Miro	2.00	5.00
PV3	Dr. Britt Baker	12.00	30.00
PV4	Kenny Omega	8.00	20.00
PV5	Chris Jericho	3.00	8.00
PV6	Hikaru Shida	5.00	12.00
PV7	Sting	6.00	15.00
PV8	Jon Moxley	4.00	10.00

2021 Upper Deck AEW Preview

0	CM Punk	20.00	50.00
PP1	Adam Cole	12.00	30.00
PP2	Bryan Danielson	15.00	40.00

2021 Upper Deck AEW Preview Autograph

0	CM Punk		

2021 Upper Deck AEW Rhodes to Success

COMPLETE SET (10)		15.00	40.00
*SILVER: .5X to 1.2X BASIC CARDS			
*RED/50: 1.5X to 4X BASIC CARDS			
*BLACK/1: UNPRICED DUE TO SCARCITY			
STATED ODDS 1:10 HOBBY/EPACK/BLASTER			
STATED ODDS 1:5 FAT PACKS			
RS1	Cody Rhodes	2.50	6.00
RS2	Cody Rhodes	2.50	6.00
RS3	Cody Rhodes	2.50	6.00
RS4	Cody Rhodes	2.50	6.00
RS5	Cody Rhodes	2.50	6.00
RS6	Cody Rhodes	2.50	6.00
RS7	Cody Rhodes	2.50	6.00
RS8	Cody Rhodes	2.50	6.00
RS9	Cody Rhodes	2.50	6.00
RS10	Cody Rhodes	2.50	6.00

2021 Upper Deck AEW Top Rope

COMPLETE SET (10)		12.00	30.00
*SILVER: .5X to 1.2X BASIC CARDS			
*RED/50: 2X to 5X BASIC CARDS			
*BLACK/1: UNPRICED DUE TO SCARCITY			
STATED ODDS 1:10 HOBBY/EPACK/BLASTER			
STATED ODDS 1:5 FAT PACKS			
TR1	PAC	1.00	2.50
TR2	Darby Allin	6.00	15.00
TR3	Nick Jackson	2.00	5.00
TR4	RIHO	2.00	5.00
TR5	Kenny Omega	3.00	8.00
TR6	Joey Janela	.50	1.25
TR7	Rey Fenix	1.25	3.00
TR8	Hangman Adam Page	3.00	8.00
TR9	Marq Quen	.60	1.50
TR10	Sammy Guevara	1.25	3.00

2021 Upper Deck AEW Wednesday in Action

COMPLETE SET (33)		250.00	500.00
STATED ODDS 1:64			
WIA1	Orange Cassidy	20.00	50.00
WIA2	Luchasaurus	10.00	25.00
WIA3	Chris Jericho	12.00	30.00
WIA4	Anna Jay	15.00	40.00
WIA5	Dax Harwood	5.00	12.00
WIA6	Matt Hardy	6.00	15.00
WIA7	Brian Cage	4.00	10.00
WIA8	Santana	5.00	12.00
WIA9	Jon Moxley	8.00	20.00
WIA10	Hikaru Shida	10.00	25.00
WIA11	Matt Jackson	12.00	30.00
WIA12	Nick Jackson	12.00	30.00
WIA13	Dustin Rhodes	6.00	15.00
WIA14	Ricky Starks	8.00	20.00
WIA15	Dr. Britt Baker	30.00	80.00
WIA16	MJF	30.00	80.00
WIA17	Lance Archer	12.00	30.00
WIA18	Kenny Omega	20.00	50.00
WIA19	Penta el Zero M	8.00	20.00
WIA20	Sammy Guevara	8.00	20.00
WIA21	Ortiz	5.00	12.00
WIA22	Tay Conti	12.00	30.00
WIA23	Cody Rhodes	10.00	25.00
WIA24	Joey Janela	3.00	8.00
WIA25	Scorpio Sky	3.00	8.00
WIA26	Rey Fenix	8.00	20.00
WIA27	Sting	8.00	20.00
WIA28	Brandi Rhodes	15.00	40.00
WIA29	Cash Wheeler	5.00	12.00
WIA30	Christopher Daniels	5.00	12.00
WIA31	Jungle Boy	20.00	50.00
WIA32	Nyla Rose	6.00	15.00
WIA33	Hangman Adam Page	20.00	50.00

2000 Waldenbooks WWF Limited Edition

COMPLETE SET (2)		8.00	20.00
1	Have a Nice Day!	3.00	8.00
2	The Rock Says	6.00	15.00

1993 WCW Magazine Collector's Special 3

10	Steve Austin	75.00	150.00
11	Johnny B. Badd		
12	Cactus Jack		
13	Shane Douglas		
14	Van Hammer		
15	Missy Hyatt	2.50	6.00
16	Jushin Liger		
17	Madusa		
18	Brian Pillman		
19	Dustin Rhodes		
20	Rick Rude	3.00	8.00
21	Ron Simmons		
22	Ricky Steamboat		
23	Sting		
24	Big Van Vader		
25	Erik Watts	3.00	8.00
26	Barry Windham	2.50	6.00
27	Tom Zenk		

1988 Wonderama NWA

COMPLETE SET (343)		300.00	600.00
1	Ric Flair	75.00	150.00
2	Tommy Angel	.40	1.00
3	Dusty Rhodes/Tully Blanchard	2.50	6.00
4	Baby Doll	1.25	3.00
5	Eddie Gilbert	2.00	5.00
6	Rocky King	.75	2.00
7	Lex Luger/Arn Anderson	1.50	4.00
8	Mike Rotunda vs. Ivan Koloff	.60	1.50
9	Barry Windham/Sting	5.00	12.00
10	Ron Simmons	.20	3.00
11	Mighty Wilbur	.40	1.00
12	Skandor Akbar	.60	1.50
13	Precious	1.50	4.00
14	Shaska Whatley vs. Jimmy Valiant	.40	1.00
15	Curtis Thompson	.75	2.00
16	Kendall Windham	2.00	5.00
17	Sting	20.00	50.00
18	Paul Ellering	1.25	3.00
19	Johnny Ace	.75	2.00
20	Kat Leroux w/Linda Dallas	.75	2.00
21	Michael Hayes	1.00	2.50
22	Terry Taylor	.40	1.00
23	Barry Windham	2.50	6.00
24	Johnny Weaver vs. J.J. Dillon	.40	1.00
25	Tully Blanchard	1.00	2.50
26	Dick Murdoch	.75	2.00
27	Stan Lane	.75	2.00
28	Barbarian w/Paul Jones	.40	1.00
29	Linda Dallas w/Misty Blue	.75	2.00
30	Road Warriors	15.00	40.00
31	Stan Lane vs. Sean Royal	.50	1.25
32	Ricky Santana	.40	1.00
33	Jimmy Valiant	1.25	3.00
34	Larry Zbyszko vs. Kendall Windham	.75	2.00
35	Lex Luger	2.00	5.00
36	Shaska Whatley	.40	1.00
37	Warlord	.40	1.00
38	Bobby Eaton	2.00	5.00
39	Dusty Rhodes	2.50	6.00
40	Paul Jones	.40	1.00
41	Eddie Gilbert/Sting	2.00	5.00
42	Butch Miller	.40	1.00
43	Barry Windham/Arn Anderson	3.00	8.00
44	Michael Hayes	1.00	2.50
45	Larry Stephens	.40	1.00
46	Black Bart	.40	1.00
47	Gladiator #2	.40	.30
48	Ric Flair/Sting	3.00	8.00
49	Ivan Koloff	1.25	3.00
50	Jamie West	.40	1.00
51	Larry Zbyszko	.75	2.00
52	Sean Royal vs. Bobby Eaton	.40	1.00
53	Arn Anderson vs. Lex Luger	2.00	5.00
54	Baby Doll	.60	1.50
55	Tim Horner vs. Shaska Whatley	.40	1.00
56	Jimmy Garvin vs. Tully Blanchard	1.00	2.50
57	Kendall Windham vs. Gladiator	.40	1.00
58	Terry Taylor vs. Eddie Gilbert	.75	2.00
59	Dick Murdoch	.50	1.25
60	Stan Lane vs. Sean Royal	.40	.30
61	Magnum T.A.	.75	.75
62	Ricky Santana	.40	.30
63	Luke Williams	.40	.30
64	Robert Gibson	1.50	4.00
65	Ron Garvin	.40	1.00
66	Ivan Koloff	.50	.50
67	Larry Zbyszko vs. Kendall Windham	.50	.50
68a	Butch Miller	1.25	3.00
68b	Ric Flair logo	6.00	15.00
69	Ricky Morton	1.50	4.00
70	Tommy Angel	.40	1.00
71	Stan Lane vs. Sean Royal	.40	.30
72	Kendall Windham	.40	.30
73	Baby Doll	.50	.50
74a	Black Bart		
74b	Barry Windham logo	1.00	2.50
75	Road Warrior Hawk	1.50	4.00
76	Mike Rotunda	.60	1.50
77	Ron Simmons/Arn Anderson	1.00	2.50
78	J.J. Dillon	.40	1.00
79	Shaska Whatley vs. Jimmy Valiant	.60	1.50
80	Kat Leroux	.50	1.25
81	Kendall Windham vs. Larry Zbyszko	.50	1.25
82	Road Warrior Animal	2.00	5.00
83	D.Murdoch/Steve Williams	.50	1.25
84	Tully Blanchard	2.50	6.00
85	Barbarian	.75	2.00
86	Robert Gibson	1.25	3.00
87	Ricky Santana	.40	1.00
88	Jimmy Valiant	.60	1.50
89	Nikita Koloff/Ric Flair	4.00	10.00

#	Card		
90	Kat Leroux vs. Misty Blue	.50	1.25
91	Kevin Sullivan	6.00	15.00
92	Luke Williams	.40	1.00
93	Lex Luger/Arn Anderson	1.00	2.50
94	Big Bubba Rogers	1.25	3.00
95	Bobby Eaton	.60	1.50
96	Paul Jones	.40	1.00
97	Butch Miller	.40	.30
98	Jimmy Garvin w/Precious	1.25	3.00
99a	Warlord vs. Sting	2.00	5.00
99b	Dusty Rhodes logo	3.00	8.00
100	Ivan Koloff	.50	1.25
101	Larry Zbyszko	.50	.50
102	Sting	20.00	50.00
103	Larry Zbyszko/Baby Doll	.60	1.50
104	Eddie Gilbert/Sting	1.00	2.50
105	Dusty Rhodes	2.00	5.00
106	Mighty Wilbur	.40	1.00
107	Michael Hayes/Ric Flair	.60	1.50
108	Brad Armstorng w/Tom Horner	.40	.30
109	Terry Taylor	.40	.30
110	Dick Murdoch	.50	.50
111	Tully Blanchard	.75	2.00
112	Ricky Santana vs. Warlord	.40	1.00
113	Jimmy Valiant	1.25	3.00
114	Kevin Sullivan	.60	1.50
115	Paul Jones	.40	1.00
116	Lex Luger/Sting	8.00	20.00
117	Ivan Koloff	.50	1.25
118	Larry Zbyszko/Barry Windham	.50	.50
119	Italian Stallion	.40	.30
120	Dusty Rhodes	2.00	5.00
121	Tim Horner vs. Chris Champion	.40	1.00
122	Eddie Gilbert/Sting	1.50	4.00
123	Mighty Wilbur vs. Ivan Koloff	.50	1.25
124	Barry Windham	.50	.50
125	Dick Murdoch	.50	1.25
126	Lex Luger	3.00	8.00
127	Dusty Rhodes/Nikita Koloff	1.00	2.50
128	Barbarian/Warlord/Ivan Koloff	.50	1.25
129	Paul Jones	.40	.30
130	Arn Anderson/Barry Windham	.75	2.00
131	Ivan Koloff	.75	2.00
132	Baby Doll/Dusty Rhodes	1.50	4.00
133	Eddie Gilbert w/Terry Taylor	.60	1.50
134	Rocky King w/Kendall Windham	.40	1.00
135	Jimmy Garvin vs. Tully Blanchard	.75	2.00
136a	Ricky Morton vs. Ric Flair	1.50	4.00
136b	Lex Luger logo	1.50	4.00
137	Tim Horner vs. Gladiator	.40	1.00
138	Kendall Windham	.40	.30
139	Magnum T.A.	.75	.75
140	Terry Taylor	.40	.30
141	Dick Murdoch/Steve Williams	.60	.60
142	Barbarian	.40	.30
143	Mad Dog Debbie	.40	.30
144	Dr. Death Steve Williams	.50	.50
145	Italian Stallion	.40	.30
146	Jimmy Valiant	3.00	8.00
147	Kevin Sullivan vs. Jimmy Garvin	.40	1.00
148	Ron Garvin	.40	.30
149	Ricky Morton	1.00	2.50
150	Luke Williams	.40	1.00
151	Paul Jones	.40	.30
152	Butch Miller	.40	.30
153	Warlord/Sting	1.50	4.00
154	Ricky Morton/Ric Flair	1.25	3.00
155	Black Bart	.40	1.00
156	Gladiators 1 & 2	.40	1.00
157	Ivan Koloff	.50	1.25
158	Larry Zbyszko w/Baby Doll	.60	1.50
159	Road Warrior Hawk	1.50	4.00
160	Bobby Eaton vs. Chris Champion	.40	1.00
161	Paul Jones	.40	1.00
162	Ric Flair	10.00	25.00
163	Luke Williams	.40	.30
164	Dick Murdoch/Steve Williams	.50	.50
165	J.J. Dillon	.40	.30
166	Linda Dallas vs. Misty Blue	.50	.50
167	Mike Rotunda	.40	1.00
168	Tommy Angel	.40	.30
169	Baby Doll	.50	.50
170	Animal/I.Koloff	.60	.60
171	Mike Rotunda w/Kevin Sullivan	.40	.30
172	Ron Garvin	.40	.30
173	Ron Simmons	.50	.50
174	Robert Gibson	.40	.30
175	Four Horsemen logo	4.00	10.00
176	Pee Wee Anderson	.40	1.00
177	Tony Schiavone	1.50	4.00
178	Tiger Conway	.40	1.00
179	Nikita Koloff	.75	2.00
180	Chris Champion	.40	1.00
181	Kendall Windham	.40	.30
182	Paul Ellering vs. Paul Jones	.40	.30
183	Lex Luger	1.50	4.00
184	Johnny Ace	.40	1.00
185	Cougar Jay	.40	1.00
186	Missy Hyatt w/Magnum T.A.	.75	.75
187	Precious	1.00	2.50
188	Kat Leroux vs. Misty Blue	.50	1.25
189	Denny Brown w/Nelson Royal	.40	.30
190	Johnny Weaver	.40	.30
191	Sting/Eddie Gilbert	6.00	15.00
192	Dick Murdoch	.50	1.25
193	Ole Anderson	.40	.30
194	Sting	20.00	50.00
195	Barbarian	.40	1.00
196	Road Warrior Animal	2.00	5.00
197	Michael Hayes/Ric Flair	.60	1.50
198	Paul Jones	.40	.30
199	Ricky Santana	.40	.30
200	Ron Garvin	.40	.30
201	Jimmy Valiant	.40	.30
202	Tully Blanchard	.50	.50
203	Shaska Whatley	.40	.30
204	Rock 'N Roll Express	5.00	12.00
205	Brad Armstrong	.40	1.00
206	Misty Blue	.50	.50
207	Road Warriors	5.00	12.00
208	Larry Zbyszko	.50	1.25
209	Bobby Eaton	.40	.30
210	Paul Jones w/Warlord	.40	.30
211	Butch Miller	.40	.30
212	Lex Luger	.75	2.00
213	Larry Stephens	.40	1.00
214	Warlord/Sting	1.25	3.00
215	Dr. Death Steve Williams	.50	1.25
216	Tommy Young	.40	.30
217	Nikita Koloff	.40	.30
218	George South	.40	.30
219	Dusty Rhodes/Ric Flair	3.00	8.00
220	Black Bart	.40	1.00
221	Ivan Koloff	.50	.50
222	Barry Windham	.50	.50
223	Larry Zbyszko	.50	.50
224	Sean Royal	.40	.30
225	Kevin Sullivan vs. Jimmy Garvin	.40	.30
226	Eddie Gilbert	.50	.50
227	Ric Flair/Robert Gibson	2.50	6.00
228	Eddie Gilbert	.50	1.25
229	Rocky King vs. Nelson Royal	.40	.30
230	Mike Rotunda	.40	1.00
231	Arn Anderson	.50	.50
232	Ron Simmons	1.25	3.00
233	Mighty Wilbur	.40	.30
234	Tony Schiavone	1.50	4.00
235	Skandor Akbar	.40	.30
236	Jimmy Garvin vs. Tully Blanchard	.50	.50
237	Jive Tones	.40	.30
238	Tim Horner	.40	.30
239	Arn Anderson	1.25	3.00
240	Ivan Koloff w/Paul Jones	.50	1.25
241	Paul Jones	.40	.30
242	Magnum T.A./Arn Anderson	.75	.75
243	Kevin Sullivan w/Mike Rotunda	.40	.30
244	Ricky Santana	.40	.30
245	Baby Doll	.50	.50
246	Eddie Gilbert/Ron Garvin	.50	.50
247	Dr. Death Steve Williams	.50	.50
248	Mike Rotunda vs. Jimmy Garvin	.40	.30
249	Mighty Wilbur	.40	.30
250	Kevin Sullivan vs. Jimmy Garvin	.40	.30
251	Dick Murdoch	.50	.50
252	Ron Garvin/Ric Flair	.60	1.50
253	Trent Knight	.40	.30
254	Curtis Thompson	.40	.30
255	Mighty Wilbur	.40	.30
256	Luke Williams	.40	.30
257	Ricky Morton/Ric Flair	.60	1.50
258	Missy Hyatt	2.00	5.00
259	Road Warrior Animal	1.50	4.00
260	Nelson Royal	.40	1.00
261	Magnum T.A.	.75	.75
262	Road Warriors	2.00	5.00
263	Johnny Weaver	.40	1.00
264	Precious	.50	1.25
265	Robert Gibson	.40	.30
266	Dick Murdoch	.50	.50
267	Arn Anderson	.50	.50
268	Ole Anderson	.50	.50
269	Barbarian	.40	.30
270	Ric Flair/Ron Garvin	2.00	5.00
271	Linda Dallas vs. Venus	.50	.50
272	Gene Ligon	.40	1.00
273	Ricky Santana	.40	.30
274	Lex Luger/Nikita Koloff	.40	1.00
275	Misty Blue vs. Linda Dallas	.50	.50
276	J.J. Dillon	.40	.30
277	David Isley	.40	.30
278	Teddy Long	.40	1.00
279	Road Warriors	2.00	5.00
280	Kevin Sullivan	.40	1.00
281	Road Warrior Animal	1.25	3.00
282	Luke Williams	.40	.30
283	Big Bubba Rogers	1.25	3.00
284	Jimmy Garvin	.40	.30
285	Denny Brown	.40	.30
286	Bobby Eaton	.40	.30
287	Robert Gibson	.40	.30
288	Paul Jones	.40	.30
289	Butch Miller	.40	.30
290	Warlord vs. Road Warrior Animal	.60	1.50
291	Tommy Young	.40	.30
292	Nikita Koloff	.40	.30
293	Black Bart	.40	.30
294	Gladiator #1	.40	.30
295	Ivan Koloff	.50	.50
296	Ricky Nelson	.40	.30
297	Dr. Death Steve Williams	.50	.50
298	Rick Steiner	.40	1.00
299	Larry Zbyszko	.60	.60
300	Sean Royal	.40	.30
301	Road Warriors	.60	.60
302	Baby Doll	.50	.50
303	J.J. Dillon/Lex Luger	.50	1.25
304	Tim Horner	.40	.30
305	Paul Ellering	.40	.30
306	Lex Luger/Gladiator	.40	1.00
307	J.J. Dillon	.40	.30
308	Midnight Express	.40	.30
309	Sheepherders w/Johnny Ace	.40	.30
310	Jimmy Garvin w/Precious	.40	.30
311	Kat Leroux	.50	.50
312	Jimmy Garvin	.40	.30
313	Road Warriors	.60	.60
314	Ricky Morton	.40	.30
315	Barbarian	.40	.30
316	Linda Dallas	.50	.50
317	Sting/Eddie Gilbert	2.50	6.00
318	Italian Stallion	.40	.30
319	Ricky Santana	.40	.30
320	Jimmy Valiant	.40	.30
321	Shaska Whatley	.40	.30
322	Michael Hayes	.40	.30
323	Misty Blue	.50	.50
324	Magnum T.A.	.75	.75
325	Venus	.40	1.00
326	Luke Williams	.40	.30
327	Road Warrior Animal	1.25	3.00
328	Dr. Death Steve Williams	.50	.50
329	Bobby Eaton	.40	.30
330	Paul Jones	.40	.30
331	Butch Miller	.40	.30
332	Tully Blanchard	1.25	3.00
333	Warlord vs. Road Warrior Hawk	.75	.75
334	Ivan Koloff w/Paul Jones	.50	.50
335	Jamie West	.40	.30
336	Larry Zbyszko/Dusty Rhodes	.75	.75
337	Lex Luger	.40	1.00
338	Sean Royal	.40	.30
339	Four Horsemen	30.00	75.00
340	Jimmy Garvin	.40	.30
341	Road Warriors/Paul Ellering	.60	.60
342	Comrade Orga	.40	.30
343	Magnum T.A.	.75	.75
NNO	Checklist 1	.75	2.00
NNO	Checklist 2	.75	2.00
NNO	Checklist 3	.75	2.00
NNO	Checklist 4	.75	2.00

2019-20 WWE Bray Wyatt Collector's Boxes

Box 1	Firefly Funhouse/500*	125.00	250.00
Box 2	Wyatt Gym/1000*	30.00	75.00
Box 3	The Holidays with Ramblin' Rabbit	30.00	75.00
Box 4	Mercy the Buzzard		

Action Figures & Figurines

2017 Bleacher Creatures WWE

NNO	AJ Styles	12.50	25.00
NNO	Bayley	12.50	25.00
NNO	Braun Strowman		
NNO	Finn Balor	7.50	15.00
NNO	Jeff Hardy		
NNO	Kevin Owens	12.50	25.00
NNO	Seth Rollins	10.00	20.00
NNO	Shinsuke Nakamura		
NNO	Stone Cold Steve Austin		

2013-18 Bleacher Creatures WWE Shop Exclusives

NNO	Hulk Hogan
NNO	John Cena
NNO	Roman Reigns
NNO	Ultimate Warrior

2013 Bleacher Creatures WWE Series 1

NNO	CM Punk
NNO	Daniel Bryan
NNO	John Cena
NNO	Kane
NNO	Ryback
NNO	Sheamus

2013 Bleacher Creatures WWE Series 2

NNO	CM Punk
NNO	John Cena
NNO	Randy Orton

2014 Bleacher Creatures WWE WrestleMania 30

NNO	New Orleans Bear

2010 Burger King WWEKids.com Plush 6-Inch

NNO	John Cena
NNO	Triple H
NNO	Undertaker

2021 Creative Ventures Brawler Ballz

NNO	Lucha Bros.
NNO	Road Warriors
NNO	Rowdy Roddy Piper

2016 Figures Toy Co. Ring of Honor Series 1

NNO	Jay Briscoe
NNO	Jay Lethal
NNO	Kevin Steen
NNO	Mark Briscoe

2016 Figures Toy Co. Ring of Honor Series 1 2-Packs

NNO	Jay & Mark Briscoe
NNO	Kevin Steen & Jay Lethal

2016 Figures Toy Co. Ring of Honor Series 1 4-Pack

NNO	Kevin Steen/Jay Briscoe/Mark Briscoe/Jay Lethal

2017 Figures Toy Co. Ring of Honor Series 2

NNO	Adam Cole
NNO	Bobby Fish
NNO	Delirious
NNO	Kyle O'Reilly

2018 Figures Toy Co. Ring of Honor Series 3

NNO	Hanson
NNO	Nigel McGuinness
NNO	Raymond Rowe
NNO	Roderick Strong

2019 Figures Toy Co. Ring of Honor Series 4

NNO	ACH
NNO	Dalton Castle
NNO	Matt Taven
NNO	Moose

2008 FOCO Bobbleheads WWE

NNO	CM Punk
NNO	Hornswoggle
NNO	Jeff Hardy
NNO	John Cena
NNO	Mr. Kennedy
NNO	Rey Mysterio
NNO	Shawn Michaels
NNO	Stone Cold Steve Austin
NNO	Triple H
NNO	Undertaker

2021 FOCO Bobbleheads WWE

NNO	AJ Styles
NNO	Andre the Giant
NNO	Asuka
NNO	Daniel Bryan (Moment)
NNO	Edge
NNO	Edge vs. Jeff Hardy (Moment)
NNO	Hulk Hogan (red and yellow pose)
NNO	Hulk Hogan nWo
NNO	Kane (Brothers of Destruction)
NNO	Kevin Nash nWo
NNO	Mankind & Undertaker (HIAC)
NNO	Rey Mysterio
NNO	Ric Flair
NNO	Roman Reigns
NNO	Ronda Rousey
NNO	Sasha Banks
NNO	Scott Hall nWo
NNO	Stone Cold Steve Austin
NNO	The Fiend Bray Wyatt
NNO	Triple H
NNO	Ultimate Warrior (Moment)
NNO	Undertaker
NNO	Undertaker (Brothers of Destruction)

2015 Funko Mystery Minis WWE Series 1

COMPLETE SET (15)		55.00	110.00
UNOPENED CASE (12 BOXES)			
UNOPENED BOX (1 MINI)			
NNO	Andre the Giant	3.00	6.00
NNO	Brie Bella	3.00	6.00
NNO	Daniel Bryan	3.00	6.00
NNO	George The Animal Steele	6.00	12.00
NNO	Hacksaw Jim Duggan WM	10.00	20.00
NNO	Hulk Hogan	12.50	25.00
NNO	Iron Sheik	6.00	12.00
NNO	John Cena	3.00	6.00
NNO	Nikki Bella	4.00	8.00
NNO	Randy Savage WM	12.50	25.00
NNO	Ric Flair	12.50	25.00
NNO	Rock	7.50	15.00
NNO	Rowdy Roddy Piper WM	15.00	30.00
NNO	Ultimate Warrior	6.00	12.00
NNO	Undertaker	4.00	8.00

2016 Funko Mystery Minis WWE Series 2

COMPLETE SET (15)		50.00	100.00
UNOPENED CASE (12 BOXES)			
UNOPENED BOX (1 MINI)			
NNO	Bret Hitman Hart	3.00	6.00
NNO	Brock Lesnar	4.00	8.00
NNO	Dusty Rhodes	3.00	6.00
NNO	Goldust	3.00	6.00
NNO	Jake The Snake Roberts TAR	20.00	40.00
NNO	John Cena	4.00	8.00
NNO	Kevin Nash	3.00	6.00
NNO	Million Dollar Man Ted Dibiase	3.00	6.00
NNO	Randy Orton	3.00	6.00
NNO	Razor Ramon TAR	15.00	30.00
NNO	Roman Reigns	3.00	6.00
NNO	Seth Rollins	3.00	6.00
NNO	Sgt. Slaughter TAR	10.00	20.00
NNO	Sting	3.00	6.00
NNO	Stone Cold Steve Austin	6.00	12.00

2017 Funko Pint Size Heroes WWE

COMPLETE SET (19)		75.00	150.00
NNO	Andre the Giant	10.00	20.00
NNO	Big E	4.00	8.00
NNO	Bray Wyatt	4.00	8.00
NNO	Brock Lesnar	3.00	6.00
NNO	Enzo Amore	5.00	10.00
NNO	Finn Balor TRU	10.00	20.00
NNO	John Cena	3.00	6.00
NNO	Kevin Owens	4.00	8.00
NNO	Kofi Kingston	5.00	10.00
NNO	Macho Man Randy Savage	15.00	30.00
NNO	Nikki Bella	4.00	8.00
NNO	Ric Flair TRU	7.50	15.00
NNO	Roman Reigns	4.00	8.00
NNO	Sasha Banks	4.00	8.00
NNO	Seth Rollins	3.00	6.00

NNO	Stone Cold Steve Austin TRU	10.00	20.00
NNO	Ultimate Warrior	7.50	15.00
NNO	Undertaker	4.00	8.00
NNO	Xavier Woods	3.00	6.00

2020-22 Funko Pop Vinyl Art Series

44 The Rock
(2022 Walmart Exclusive)

2011-20 Funko Pop Vinyl Freddy Funko

	COMMON FUNKO POP	12.50	25.00
34A	Hulk Hogan/500* FD	600.00	1200.00
34B	Hulk Hogan Injured /500* FD	500.00	1000.00
52	Sting/500* FD	500.00	750.00

2015-19 Funko Pop Vinyl Pocket Pop Keychains WWE

NNO	Hulk Hogan	7.50	15.00
NNO	John Cena V	7.50	15.00
NNO	John Cena WM DVD	6.00	12.00
NNO	Macho Man WM DVD	6.00	12.00
NNO	The Rock WM DVD	6.00	12.00
NNO	Sting WM DVD	5.00	10.00
NNO	Ultimate Warrior WM DVD	7.50	15.00
NNO	Undertaker WM DVD	10.00	20.00

2011-22 Funko Pop Vinyl WWE

1A	John Cena	25.00	50.00
1B	J.Cena Black Pants WWE.com	250.00	500.00
1C	J.Cena Green-Orange	25.00	50.00
1D	J.Cena Green Hat WWE.com	600.00	1200.00
2A	CM Punk V	150.00	300.00
2B	CM Punk Pink Trunks HT	250.00	500.00
3	The Rock V	50.00	100.00
4	Sheamus V	50.00	100.00
5A	Stone Cold Steve Austin V	40.00	80.00
5B	SC Steve Austin 2K16 GS	30.00	60.00
6A	Rey Mysterio V	150.00	300.00
6B	R.Mysterio Bright Blue 7-11	250.00	500.00
6C	Rey Mysterio Dark SDCC	600.00	1200.00
7A	Daniel Bryan V	60.00	120.00
7B	Daniel Bryan Red Trunks HT/UT	50.00	100.00
7C	Daniel Bryan Patterned WWE.com	300.00	600.00
8	Undertaker	50.00	100.00
9	Triple H V	30.00	60.00
10A	Macho Man Randy Savage V	30.00	75.00
10B	Savage Pink WWE.com	750.00	1500.00
10C	Macho Man Randy Savage Purple FYE	30.00	75.00
11A	Hulk Hogan	40.00	80.00
11B	Hogan Hulk Rules WWE.com	500.00	1000.00
11C	Hollywood Hogan WWE 2K15	100.00	200.00
12	AJ Lee WWE.com	300.00	600.00
13	Brock Lesnar WM	30.00	60.00
14	Brie Bella	20.00	40.00
15	Nikki Bella	15.00	30.00
16	Paige V	30.00	75.00
17	Ric Flair TAR	25.00	50.00
18	Roddy Piper TAR	30.00	60.00
19A	Sting	50.00	100.00
19B	Wolfpac Sting GS	60.00	120.00
20	Ultimate Warrior	40.00	80.00
21	Andre the Giant	20.00	40.00
23	Roman Reigns	30.00	60.00
24A	Seth Rollins V	20.00	40.00
24B	Seth Rollins White Attire FYE	20.00	40.00
25	Bret Hart	20.00	40.00
26	Eva Marie	7.50	15.00
27	Kevin Owens V	20.00	40.00
28	Bray Wyatt V	25.00	50.00
29	Big E	10.00	20.00
30	Xavier Woods	7.50	15.00
31	Kofi Kingston	7.50	15.00
32	Shawn Michaels WG	12.50	25.00
33	Kane WG	25.00	50.00
34A	Finn Balor	15.00	30.00
34B	Finn Balor Demon Mask CH	45.00	90.00
35	Mick Foley	30.00	75.00
36	Goldberg	20.00	40.00
37	AJ Styles	15.00	30.00
38	The Demon Finn Balor FYE	25.00	50.00
39	Bayley TRU	20.00	40.00
40A	Chris Jericho Red	20.00	40.00
40B	Chris Jericho Blue FYE	25.00	50.00
41A	Million Dollar Man Black	10.00	20.00
41B	Million Dollar Man White CH	20.00	40.00
42	Sasha Banks	25.00	50.00
43A	Iron Sheik White	6.00	12.00
43B	Iron Sheik Red CH	20.00	40.00
44A	Zack Ryder NYCC	30.00	75.00
44B	Zack Ryder FCE	20.00	40.00
44C	Zack Ryder Green Tights/500* FHQ	500.00	1000.00
45	Shinsuke Nakamura TRU	20.00	40.00
46A	The Rock	15.00	30.00
46B	The Rock Black Jacket CH	25.00	50.00
46C	The Rock Gold NYCC/TAR	25.00	50.00
46D	The Rock Gold TAR	15.00	30.00
47A	Razor Ramon	12.50	25.00
47B	Razor Ramon nWo Trunks CH	60.00	120.00
48	Braun Strowman	20.00	40.00
49	Alexa Bliss	30.00	60.00
50	Shawn Michaels	20.00	40.00
51A	Jake The Snake Roberts Green	15.00	30.00
51B	Jake The Snake Roberts Blue CH	30.00	60.00
52A	Triple H	7.50	15.00
52B	Triple H Masked CH	30.00	60.00
53A	Mr. McMahon	6.00	12.00
53B	Mr. McMahon Pink Jacket CH	30.00	75.00
54	Sgt. Slaughter	12.50	25.00
55	Kurt Angle	25.00	50.00
56A	Asuka SDCC	30.00	75.00
56B	Asuka SCE	20.00	40.00
56C	Asuka w/Mask WM	25.00	50.00
56D	Asuka w/Mask TAR	25.00	50.00
57	Ric Flair Classic 2K19	30.00	75.00
58	Ronda Rousey	12.50	25.00
59	John Cena Clear AMZ	15.00	30.00
60	Randy Orton	20.00	40.00
61	Batista	10.00	20.00
62A	Charlotte Flair	7.50	15.00
62B	Charlotte Flair Blue Robe FL	15.00	30.00
63	Ric Flair Red Robe	20.00	40.00
64	Andre the Giant 6" WM	20.00	40.00
65	Becky Lynch	7.50	15.00
66	Trish Stratus	7.50	15.00
67	Elias	7.50	15.00
68	Bret Hit Man Hart Pink	15.00	30.00
69A	Undertaker Hooded	15.00	30.00
69B	Undertaker Hooded Purple Translucent AMZ	20.00	40.00
70	Becky Lynch The Man AMZ	25.00	50.00
71	Hulk Hogan Python Power WM	10.00	20.00
72	The Miz	7.50	15.00
73	Mean Gene Okerlund	7.50	15.00
74A	Diesel	6.00	12.00
74B	Kevin Nash CH	30.00	75.00
75A	Naomi	6.00	12.00
75B	Naomi GITD CH	12.50	25.00
76	John Cena Thuganomics	7.50	15.00
77	The Fiend Bray Wyatt AMZ	17.50	35.00
78	The Rock w/Microphone	17.50	35.00
79	Macho Man Randy Savage DC GS	7.50	15.00
80	Mr. T	6.00	12.00
81	Undertaker ABA AMZ	17.50	35.00
82	Ric Flair '92 Royal Rumble GS	17.50	35.00
83	Macho Man Randy Savage Checkered Glasses GS	17.50	35.00
84	Stone Cold Steve Austin w/Belt	7.50	15.00
85	Chyna	7.50	15.00
86	Edge	7.50	15.00
87	Drew McIntyre	12.50	25.00
88	Otis MITB	7.50	15.00
89	Stone Cold Steve Austin 2 Belts 711	15.00	30.00
90	Eddie Guerrero w/Pop Pin GS	15.00	30.00
91	The Rock Bring It Shirt EE	12.50	25.00
92	Xavier Woods Up Up Down Down MET TAR	10.00	20.00
93	Rey Mysterio	10.00	20.00
94	Angelo Dawkins	6.00	12.00
95	Montez Ford	7.50	15.00
96	Asuka	6.00	12.00
97	Jerry Lawler	6.00	12.00
98	Roman Reigns MET AMZ	12.50	25.00
99	Triple H DX GS	25.00	50.00
100	The Fiend Bray Wyatt Santa WM	12.50	25.00
104	Alexa Bliss WM		
105	Cactus Jack GS		
106	Undertaker Coffin GS		
107A	Alexa Bliss		
107B	Alexa Bliss Black Dress CH		
108	Bianca Belair		
109	Dude Love		

1991 Galoob WCW Superstars 14-Inch

NNO	Lex Luger	50.00	100.00
NNO	Ric Flair	60.00	120.00
NNO	Sid Vicious	50.00	100.00
NNO	Sting	100.00	200.00

1991 Galoob WCW Superstars 14-Inch (loose)

NNO	Lex Luger	20.00	40.00
NNO	Ric Flair	30.00	75.00
NNO	Sid Vicious	30.00	75.00
NNO	Sting	30.00	60.00

1991 Galoob WCW Superstars Accessories

NNO	12-Figure Collector's Case	30.00	75.00
NNO	Championship Belt	75.00	150.00
NNO	Slam Action Wrestling Arena	125.00	250.00

1991 Galoob WCW Superstars Series 1

NNO	Arn Anderson	30.00	60.00
NNO	Barry Windham	25.00	50.00
NNO	Brian Pillman	30.00	60.00
NNO	Butch Reed	20.00	40.00
NNO	Lex Luger	15.00	30.00
NNO	Ric Flair	50.00	90.00
NNO	Rick Steiner	20.00	40.00
NNO	Ron Simmons	20.00	40.00
NNO	Scott Steiner	20.00	40.00
NNO	Sid Vicious	30.00	60.00
NNO	Sting/Blue Tights	30.00	60.00
NNO	Sting/Orange Tights	150.00	300.00
NNO	Tom Zenk	20.00	40.00

1991 Galoob WCW Superstars Series 1 (loose)

NNO	Arn Anderson	7.50	15.00
NNO	Barry Windham	7.50	15.00
NNO	Brian Pillman	7.50	15.00
NNO	Butch Reed	10.00	20.00
NNO	Lex Luger	7.50	15.00
NNO	Ric Flair	10.00	20.00
NNO	Rick Steiner	7.50	15.00
NNO	Ron Simmons	7.50	15.00
NNO	Scott Steiner	7.50	15.00
NNO	Sid Vicious	10.00	20.00
NNO	Sting/Blue Tights	12.50	25.00
NNO	Sting/Orange Tights	25.00	50.00
NNO	Tom Zenk	6.00	12.00

1991 Galoob WCW Superstars Series 2

NNO	Arn Anderson/Red Trunks	125.00	250.00
NNO	Barry Windham/Blue Trunks	125.00	250.00
NNO	Brian Pillman/Lt Blue Trunks	100.00	200.00
NNO	Lex Luger/Green Trunks	125.00	250.00
NNO	Ric Flair/Red Trunks	150.00	300.00
NNO	Rick Steiner/Green Tights	100.00	200.00
NNO	Ron Simmons/Blue Tights	25.00	50.00
NNO	Scott Steiner/	125.00	250.00
	Red & Blue Tights		
NNO	Sid Vicious/Pink Tights	100.00	200.00
NNO	Sting/Black Tights	150.00	300.00

1991 Galoob WCW Superstars Series 2 (loose)

NNO	Arn Anderson/Red Trunks	15.00	30.00
NNO	Barry Windham/Blue Trunks	12.50	25.00
NNO	Brian Pillman/Lt Blue Trunks	25.00	50.00
NNO	Lex Luger/Green Trunks	20.00	40.00
NNO	Ric Flair/Red Trunks	15.00	30.00
NNO	Rick Steiner/Green Tights	15.00	30.00
NNO	Ron Simmons/Blue Tights	20.00	40.00
NNO	Scott Steiner/	25.00	50.00
	Red & Blue Tights		
NNO	Sid Vicious/Pink Tights	20.00	40.00
NNO	Sting/Black Tights	20.00	40.00

1991 Galoob WCW Superstars UK

NNO	Big Josh	500.00	1000.00
NNO	Dustin Rhodes	100.00	200.00
NNO	El Gigante	150.00	300.00
NNO	Jimmy Garvin	150.00	300.00
NNO	Lex Luger/Robe		
NNO	Michael Hayes	200.00	350.00
NNO	Sting/Robe	250.00	400.00

1991 Galoob WCW Superstars UK (loose)

NNO	Big Josh	150.00	300.00
NNO	Dustin Rhodes	75.00	150.00
NNO	El Gigante	30.00	75.00
NNO	Jimmy Garvin	20.00	40.00
NNO	Lex Luger/Robe	75.00	150.00
NNO	Michael Hayes	20.00	40.00
NNO	Sting/Robe	60.00	120.00

1991 Galoob WCW Tag Team Superstars UK

NNO	Lex Luger/Sting		
NNO	Michael Haynes/Jimmy Garvin		
NNO	Ric Flair/Arn Anderson		
NNO	Rick & Scott Steiner		

1990 Galoob WCW Tag Team Superstars US

NNO	Lex Luger/Sting	75.00	150.00
NNO	Ric Flair/Arn Anderson	75.00	150.00
NNO	Rick & Scott Steiner	60.00	120.00
NNO	Ron Simmons/Butch Reed	100.00	200.00

1990 Hasbro WWF Series 1

NNO	Akeem	200.00	350.00
NNO	Andre the Giant	150.00	300.00
NNO	Ax	125.00	250.00
NNO	Big Boss Man	75.00	150.00
NNO	Brutus The Barber Beefcake	60.00	120.00
NNO	Hulk Hogan	150.00	300.00
NNO	Jake The Snake Roberts	100.00	200.00
NNO	Macho Man Randy Savage	300.00	600.00
NNO	Million Dollar Man Ted DiBiase	125.00	250.00
NNO	Ravishing Rick Rude	125.00	250.00
NNO	Smash	60.00	120.00
NNO	Ultimate Warrior	200.00	350.00

1990 Hasbro WWF Series 1 (loose)

NNO	Akeem	10.00	20.00
NNO	Andre the Giant	25.00	50.00
NNO	Ax	12.50	25.00
NNO	Big Boss Man	10.00	20.00
NNO	Brutus The Barber Beefcake	12.50	25.00
NNO	Hulk Hogan	15.00	30.00
NNO	Jake The Snake Roberts	12.50	25.00
NNO	Macho Man Randy Savage	20.00	40.00
NNO	Million Dollar Man Ted DiBiase	10.00	20.00
NNO	Ravishing Rick Rude	7.50	15.00
NNO	Smash	7.50	15.00
NNO	Ultimate Warrior	10.00	20.00

1991 Hasbro WWF Series 2

NNO	Dusty Rhodes	600.00	1000.00
NNO	Hacksaw Jim Duggan	75.00	150.00
NNO	Honky Tonk Man	60.00	120.00
NNO	Hulk Hogan	75.00	150.00
NNO	Macho King	150.00	300.00
NNO	Million Dollar Man	75.00	150.00
NNO	Rowdy Roddy Piper	75.00	150.00
NNO	Superfly Jim Snuka	60.00	120.00
NNO	Ultimate Warrior	125.00	250.00

1991 Hasbro WWF Series 2 (loose)

NNO	Dusty Rhodes	50.00	100.00
NNO	Hacksaw Jim Duggan	10.00	20.00
NNO	Honky Tonk Man	15.00	30.00
NNO	Hulk Hogan	12.50	25.00
NNO	Macho King	25.00	50.00
NNO	Million Dollar Man	7.50	15.00
NNO	Rowdy Roddy Piper	7.50	15.00
NNO	Superfly Jim Snuka	7.50	15.00
NNO	Ultimate Warrior	15.00	30.00

1991 Hasbro WWF Series 2 Tag Teams

NNO	The Bushwhackers	60.00	120.00
NNO	Demolition	150.00	300.00
NNO	The Rockers	60.00	120.00

1991 Hasbro WWF Series 2 Tag Teams (loose)

NNO	Butch	12.50	25.00
NNO	Crush	10.00	20.00
NNO	Luke	12.50	25.00
NNO	Marty Janetty	10.00	20.00
NNO	Shawn Michaels	10.00	20.00
NNO	Smash	10.00	20.00

1992 Hasbro WWF Series 3

NNO	Big Boss Man	60.00	120.00
NNO	Brutus Beefcake/Zebra Tights	200.00	400.00
NNO	Earthquake	75.00	150.00
NNO	Greg The Hammer Valentine	50.00	100.00
NNO	Hulk Hogan	100.00	200.00
NNO	Koko B. Ware	75.00	150.00
NNO	Macho Man Randy Savage	90.00	175.00
NNO	Mr. Perfect	60.00	120.00
NNO	Sgt. Slaughter	60.00	120.00
NNO	Texas Tornado	60.00	120.00
NNO	Typhoon	50.00	100.00
NNO	Ultimate Warrior	125.00	250.00

1992 Hasbro WWF Series 3 (loose)

NNO	Big Boss Man	10.00	20.00
NNO	Brutus The Barber Beefcake	30.00	60.00
NNO	Earthquake	12.50	25.00
NNO	Greg The Hammer Valentine	10.00	20.00
NNO	Hulk Hogan	15.00	30.00
NNO	Koko B. Ware	15.00	30.00
NNO	Macho Man Randy Savage	10.00	20.00
NNO	Mr. Perfect	15.00	30.00
NNO	Sgt. Slaughter	15.00	30.00
NNO	Texas Tornado	12.50	25.00
NNO	Typhoon	10.00	20.00
NNO	Ultimate Warrior	25.00	50.00

1992 Hasbro WWF Series 3 Tag Teams

NNO	Legion of Doom	125.00	250.00
NNO	Nasty Boys	125.00	250.00

1992 Hasbro WWF Series 3 Tag Teams (loose)

NNO	Animal	20.00	40.00
NNO	Hawk	20.00	40.00
NNO	Knobbs	10.00	20.00
NNO	Sags	10.00	20.00

1992 Hasbro WWF Series 4

NNO	Bret Hart	200.00	350.00
NNO	British Bulldog	75.00	150.00
NNO	Ricky The Dragon Steamboat	50.00	100.00
NNO	Undertaker	75.00	150.00

1992 Hasbro WWF Series 4 (loose)

NNO	Bret Hart	20.00	40.00
NNO	British Bulldog	12.50	25.00
NNO	Ricky The Dragon Steamboat	12.50	25.00
NNO	Undertaker	20.00	40.00

1993 Hasbro WWF Series 5

NNO	Hulk Hogan	75.00	150.00
NNO	IRS	50.00	100.00
NNO	Jim Neidhart	60.00	120.00
NNO	Macho Man	100.00	200.00
NNO	Mountie	50.00	100.00
NNO	Rick Martel	50.00	100.00
NNO	Sid Justice	60.00	120.00
NNO	Skinner	50.00	100.00
NNO	Virgil	30.00	75.00
NNO	Warlord	60.00	120.00

1993 Hasbro WWF Series 5 (loose)

NNO	Hulk Hogan	12.50	25.00
NNO	IRS	10.00	20.00
NNO	Jim Neidhart	10.00	20.00
NNO	Macho Man	20.00	40.00

NNO	Mountie	20.00	40.00
NNO	Rick Martel	12.50	25.00
NNO	Sid Justice	12.50	25.00
NNO	Skinner	12.50	25.00
NNO	Virgil	10.00	20.00
NNO	Warlord	15.00	30.00

1993 Hasbro WWF Series 6

NNO	Berzerker	75.00	150.00
NNO	El Matador	30.00	75.00
NNO	Papa Shango	75.00	150.00
NNO	Repo Man	60.00	120.00
NNO	Ric Flair	125.00	250.00
NNO	Tatanka	50.00	100.00

1993 Hasbro WWF Series 6 (loose)

NNO	Berzerker	20.00	40.00
NNO	El Matador	12.50	25.00
NNO	Papa Shango	15.00	30.00
NNO	Repo Man	12.50	25.00
NNO	Ric Flair	15.00	30.00
NNO	Tatanka	10.00	20.00

1993 Hasbro WWF Series 7

NNO	Crush	75.00	150.00
NNO	Kamala/Star on Belly	100.00	200.00
NNO	Kamala/Crescent Moon Belly	4000.00	8000.00
NNO	Nailz	125.00	250.00
NNO	Owen Hart	150.00	300.00
NNO	Razor Ramon	75.00	150.00
NNO	Shawn Michaels	75.00	150.00

1993 Hasbro WWF Series 7 (loose)

NNO	Crush	15.00	30.00
NNO	Kamala/Star on Belly	20.00	40.00
NNO	Kamala/Crescent Moon Belly	750.00	1500.00
NNO	Nailz	25.00	50.00
NNO	Owen Hart	25.00	50.00
NNO	Razor Ramon	25.00	50.00
NNO	Shawn Michaels	25.00	50.00

1993 Hasbro WWF Series 8

NNO	Bam Bam Bigelow	125.00	250.00
NNO	Bret Hart	200.00	400.00
NNO	Lex Luger	75.00	150.00
NNO	Mr. Perfect	100.00	200.00
NNO	Undertaker	250.00	500.00
NNO	Yokozuna	100.00	200.00

1993 Hasbro WWF Series 8 (loose)

NNO	Bam Bam Bigelow	25.00	50.00
NNO	Bret Hart	30.00	75.00
NNO	Lex Luger	15.00	30.00
NNO	Mr. Perfect	15.00	30.00
NNO	Undertaker	60.00	120.00
NNO	Yokozuna	30.00	75.00

1993 Hasbro WWF Series 9

NNO	Doink the Clown	100.00	200.00
NNO	Hacksaw Jim Duggan	100.00	200.00
NNO	Million Dollar Man	75.00	150.00
NNO	Rick Steiner	60.00	120.00
NNO	Scott Steiner	50.00	100.00
NNO	Tatanka	60.00	120.00

1993 Hasbro WWF Series 9 (loose)

NNO	Doink the Clown	25.00	50.00
NNO	Hacksaw Jim Duggan	30.00	75.00
NNO	Million Dollar Man	20.00	40.00
NNO	Rick Steiner	20.00	40.00
NNO	Scott Steiner	15.00	30.00

1993 Hasbro WWF Series 10

NNO	Butch	50.00	100.00
NNO	Fatu	50.00	100.00
NNO	Giant Gonzalez	60.00	120.00
NNO	Luke	50.00	100.00
NNO	Marty Jannetty	30.00	75.00
NNO	Razor Ramon/Purple Shorts	125.00	250.00
NNO	Razor Ramon/Red Shorts	150.00	300.00
NNO	Samu	30.00	75.00
NNO	Shawn Michaels/Black Tights	200.00	400.00
NNO	Shawn Michaels/White Tights	150.00	300.00

1993 Hasbro WWF Series 10 (loose)

NNO	Butch	15.00	30.00
NNO	Fatu	10.00	20.00
NNO	Giant Gonzalez	12.50	25.00
NNO	Luke	15.00	30.00
NNO	Marty Jannetty	15.00	30.00
NNO	Razor Ramon/Purple Shorts	50.00	100.00
NNO	Razor Ramon/Red Shorts	15.00	30.00
NNO	Samu	10.00	20.00
NNO	Shawn Michaels/Black Tights	50.00	100.00
NNO	Shawn Michaels/White Tights	10.00	20.00

1994 Hasbro WWF Series 11

NNO	1-2-3 Kid	500.00	1000.00
NNO	Adam Bomb	125.00	250.00
NNO	Bart Gunn	150.00	300.00
NNO	Billy Gunn	150.00	300.00
NNO	Crush	300.00	600.00
NNO	Ludvig Borga	150.00	300.00
NNO	Yokozuna	300.00	600.00

1994 Hasbro WWF Series 11 (loose)

NNO	1-2-3 Kid	200.00	400.00
NNO	Adam Bomb	100.00	200.00
NNO	Bart Gunn	100.00	200.00
NNO	Billy Gunn	125.00	250.00
NNO	Crush	125.00	250.00
NNO	Ludvig Borga	75.00	150.00
NNO	Yokozuna	75.00	150.00

1992 Hasbro WWF Accessories and Playsets

NNO	King of the Ring (yellow)
NNO	Official Wrestling Ring (blue)
NNO	Official Wrestling Ring (sound effects)

1993 Hasbro WWF Magazine Series

NNO	Bret Hart	600.00	1200.00
NNO	Hulk Hogan	600.00	1200.00
NNO	Undertaker	1500.00	2500.00

1993 Hasbro WWF Magazine Series (loose)

NNO	Bret Hart	50.00	100.00
NNO	Hulk Hogan	400.00	800.00
NNO	Undertaker	1000.00	1500.00

1992 Hasbro WWF Mini Wrestlers

NNO	Brutus Beefcake/Butch/Luke/Greg Valentine	30.00	75.00
NNO	Mr. Perfect/Jim Duggan/Roddy Piper/Texas Tornado	30.00	75.00
NNO	Typhoon/Earthquake/Animal/Hawk	25.00	60.00

1992 Hasbro WWF Mini Wrestlers Playset

NNO	Royal Rumble Wrestling Ring (w/Hogan/Slaughter/Roberts/DiBiase/Boss Man/Savage

1992 Hasbro WWF Mini Wrestlers Playset Figures (loose)

NNO	Big Boss Man	10.00	20.00
NNO	Hulk Hogan	20.00	40.00
NNO	Jake The Snake Roberts	15.00	30.00
NNO	Macho Man Randy Savage	20.00	40.00
NNO	Million Dollar Man Ted DiBiase	10.00	20.00
NNO	Sgt. Slaughter	20.00	40.00

2019 HeroClix WWE Series 1 Mixed Match Challenge

107	Charlotte Flair
108	Sasha Banks
109	Finn Balor
110	AJ Styles
111	WWE Ring

2019 HeroClix WWE Series 1 Mixed Match Challenge Maps

M001	WWE Backstage Area
M001	WWE Arena

2019 HeroClix WWE Series 1 Rock 'N Sock Starter Set

101	The Rock
102	Mankind
103	Stone Cold Steve Austin
104	Triple H
105	Ric Flair
106	Shawn Michaels

2019 HeroClix WWE Series 1 Rock 'N Sock Starter Set Maps

M001	WWE Training Center
M002	WWE War Games

1998 The Idea Factory WCW Beanbag Brawlers Series 1

NNO	Bret "Hit Man" Hart/21,000*
NNO	Diamond Dallas Page/28,000*
NNO	Goldberg/35,000*
NNO	Hollywood Hogan/21,000*
NNO	Kevin Nash/28,000*
NNO	Sting/35,000*

1999 The Idea Factory WCW Beanbag Brawlers Series 2

NNO	Booker T/
NNO	Buff Bagwell/
NNO	Goldberg/
NNO	Jeff Jarrett/
NNO	Scott Steiner/
NNO	Sting/
NNO	Vampiro/

2017 Jada Toys WWE Metalfigs 2.5-Inch

M228	John Cena
M229	Brock Lesnar
M230	Triple H
M231	Finn Balor
M232	Paige
M243	Sasha Banks

2017 Jada Toys WWE Metalfigs 4-Inch

M200 Finn Balor
M202 Paige
M203 Brock Lesnar
M205 John Cena
M206 Sami Zayn
M207 Sasha Banks
M210 Seth Rollins
M211 The Rock
M212 Charlotte Flair
M213 Kevin Owens
M218 AJ Styles
M220 The Rock
M242 John Cena
M275 Finn Balor

2017 Jada Toys WWE Metalfigs 6-Inch

M209 Triple H

2017 Jada Toys WWE Nano Metalfigs

W1 John Cena
W2 Triple H
W3 The Rock
W4 Roman Reigns
W5 Charlotte Flair
W6 Bayley
W7 Sami Zayn
W8 Chris Jericho
W9 Dean Ambrose
W10 Macho Man Randy Savage
W11 Sting
W12 Undertaker
W13 AJ Styles
W14 Kevin Owens
W15 Seth Rollins
W16 Finn Balor
W17 Sasha Banks
W18 Brock Lesnar
W19 Becky Lynch
W20 Kalisto
W21 Bray Wyatt
W22 Nikki Bella
W23 Ultimate Warrior
W24 Rowdy Roddy Piper

2017 Jada Toys WWE Nano Metalfigs 20-Pack

NNO Cena/Triple H/Rock/Reigns/Charlotte
Bayley/Zayn/Jericho/Ambrose/Savage/Sting/Undertaker/Styles/Owens/Rollin
s/Balor/Banks/Lesnar/Kalisto/Wyatt/(2017 Toys R Us Exclusive)

2007-08 Jakks Pacific ECW Wrestling Series 1

NNO	CM Punk	20.00	40.00
NNO	Kevin Thorn	25.00	50.00
NNO	Rob Van Dam	15.00	30.00
NNO	Sandman	25.00	50.00
NNO	Tommy Dreamer	25.00	50.00

2007-08 Jakks Pacific ECW Wrestling Series 2

NNO	Ariel	15.00	30.00
NNO	Balls Mahoney	12.50	25.00
NNO	Elijah Burke	25.00	50.00
NNO	Joey Styles	20.00	40.00
NNO	Kelly Kelly	25.00	50.00
NNO	Mike Knox	15.00	30.00

2007-08 Jakks Pacific ECW Wrestling Series 3

NNO	Layla	12.50	25.00
NNO	Marcus Cor Von		
NNO	Matt Striker	7.50	15.00
NNO	Nunzio	6.00	12.00
NNO	Snitsky		
NNO	Stevie Richards		
NNO	Tazz		

2007-08 Jakks Pacific ECW Wrestling Series 4

NNO	Boogeyman		
NNO	CM Punk	7.50	15.00
NNO	Elijah Burke	15.00	30.00
NNO	John Morrison	10.00	20.00
NNO	Matt Striker		
NNO	Tommy Dreamer		

2007-08 Jakks Pacific ECW Wrestling Series 5

NNO	Christian	12.50	25.00
NNO	Evan Bourne		
NNO	Fit Finlay	12.50	25.00
NNO	Jack Swagger		
NNO	Mark Henry		
NNO	Tyson Kidd	6.00	12.00

2010 Jakks Pacific TNA Wrestling Cross the Line Series 1

NNO	James Storm/Bobby Roode	30.00	75.00
NNO	Samoa Joe/Mick Foley	30.00	60.00
NNO	Scott Steiner/Kevin Nash	25.00	50.00

2010 Jakks Pacific TNA Wrestling Cross the Line Series 2

NNO	AJ Styles/Jeff Jarrett		
NNO	Alex Shelley/Chris Sabin	30.00	75.00
NNO	Brother Ray/Brother Devon		

2010 Jakks Pacific TNA Wrestling Cross the Line Series 3

NNO	AJ Styles/Jeff Hardy		
NNO	Kurt Angle/Mr. Anderson	20.00	40.00
NNO	Stevie Richards/Daffney	12.50	25.00

2010 Jakks Pacific TNA Wrestling Cross the Line Series 4

NNO	Eric Young/Kevin Nash	15.00	30.00
NNO	Hulk Hogan/Abyss	30.00	75.00
NNO	Sting/Rob Van Dam	20.00	40.00

2010 Jakks Pacific TNA Wrestling Deluxe Impact Series 1

NNO	AJ Styles/No Stubble		
NNO	AJ Styles/Stubble		
NNO	Jeff Jarrett/Dk Blonde Hair	10.00	20.00
NNO	Jeff Jarrett/Lt Blonde Hair		
NNO	Kurt Angle	10.00	20.00
NNO	Samoa Joe	15.00	30.00
NNO	Sting		
NNO	Suicide		

2010 Jakks Pacific TNA Wrestling Deluxe Impact Series 1 Slammin' Celebration Exclusives

NNO AJ Styles
NNO Jeff Jarrett
NNO Kurt Angle
NNO Samoa Joe
NNO Sting
NNO Suicide

2010 Jakks Pacific TNA Wrestling Deluxe Impact Series 2

NNO	AJ Styles		
NNO	Amazing Red		
NNO	Eric Young		
NNO	Hernandez	25.00	50.00
NNO	Hulk Hogan	40.00	80.00
NNO	Mick Foley		

2010 Jakks Pacific TNA Wrestling Deluxe Impact Series 3

NNO	Jay Lethal	15.00	30.00
NNO	Kevin Nash	12.50	25.00
NNO	Matt Morgan	20.00	40.00
NNO	Shark Boy	15.00	30.00
NNO	Sting		
NNO	Velvet Sky	20.00	40.00

2010 Jakks Pacific TNA Wrestling Deluxe Impact Series 4

NNO	Abyss	50.00	100.00
NNO	D'Angelo Dinero		
NNO	Desmond Wolfe	25.00	50.00
NNO	Hulk Hogan	30.00	60.00
NNO	Jeff Hardy		
NNO	Rob Van Dam		

2010 Jakks Pacific TNA Wrestling Deluxe Impact Series 5

NNO	Angelina Love	20.00	40.00
NNO	Jeff Hardy		
NNO	Mr. Anderson		
NNO	Raven LOTR		
NNO	Rob Terry	10.00	20.00
NNO	Samoa Joe	20.00	40.00

2011 Jakks Pacific TNA Wrestling Deluxe Impact Series 6

NNO	Doug Williams		
NNO	Kazarian	12.50	25.00
NNO	Kurt Angle	15.00	30.00
NNO	Madison Rayne	20.00	40.00
NNO	Sting	15.00	30.00
NNO	Terry Taylor LOTR	17.50	35.00

2012 Jakks Pacific TNA Wrestling Deluxe Impact Series 7

NNO	Bobby Roode	10.00	20.00
NNO	James Storm		
NNO	James Storm/Belt	30.00	75.00
NNO	Jeff Hardy	30.00	60.00
NNO	Mr. Anderson	10.00	20.00
NNO	Velvet Sky	12.50	25.00

2012 Jakks Pacific TNA Wrestling Deluxe Impact Series 8

NNO	AJ Styles		
NNO	Hulk Hogan	30.00	60.00
NNO	Matt Morgan	7.50	15.00
NNO	Rob Van Dam		
NNO	Rob Van Dam/Belt		
NNO	Sting		

2013 Jakks Pacific TNA Wrestling Deluxe Impact Series 9

NNO Austin Aries
NNO Christopher Daniels

NNO Gail Kim
NNO Jeff Hardy
NNO Jeff Hardy/Belt
NNO Magnus

2013 Jakks Pacific TNA Wrestling Deluxe Impact Series 10

NNO Crimson
NNO Kurt Angle
NNO Miss Tessmacher
NNO Rob Terry
NNO Rob Van Dam

2013 Jakks Pacific TNA Wrestling Deluxe Impact Series 11

NNO AJ Styles
NNO Austin Aries
NNO Jeff Hardy
NNO Velvet Sky

2014 Jakks Pacific TNA Wrestling Deluxe Impact Series 12

NNO	Bully Ray	12.50	25.00
NNO	Chris Sabin	20.00	40.00
NNO	Hernandez	12.50	25.00
NNO	Magnus		

2014 Jakks Pacific TNA Wrestling Deluxe Impact Series 13

NNO	Angelina Love	12.50	25.00
NNO	Mr. Anderson	7.50	15.00

2010 Jakks Pacific TNA Wrestling Genesis

NNO AJ Styles
NNO AJ Styles/Belt
NNO Jeff Jarrett
NNO Jeff Jarrett/Belt
NNO Kurt Angle
NNO Kurt Angle/Belt
NNO Samoa Joe
NNO Samoa Joe/Belt
NNO Sting
NNO Sting/Belt
NNO Suicide
NNO Suicide/Belt

2010 Jakks Pacific TNA Wrestling Genesis 3-Packs

NNO AJ Styles/Kurt Angle/Suicide
NNO Jeff Jarrett/Samoa Joe/Sting

2010 Jakks Pacific TNA Wrestling Genesis 4-Packs

NNO AJ Styles/Kurt Angle/
Sting/Suicide
NNO Jeff Jarrett/Kurt Angle/
Samoa Joe/Sting

2010 Jakks Pacific TNA Wrestling Impact Series 1

NNO	Abyss	15.00	30.00
NNO	Jay Lethal	10.00	20.00
NNO	Kevin Nash	7.50	15.00
NNO	Kurt Angle	7.50	15.00
NNO	Sting	12.50	25.00
NNO	Suicide	20.00	40.00

2010 Jakks Pacific TNA Wrestling Legends of the Ring

NNO Hulk Hogan
NNO Jeff Jarrett
NNO Kevin Nash
NNO Kurt Angle
NNO Sting
NNO Sting USA Gear RSC

2010 Jakks Pacific TNA Wrestling Micro Impact Series 1

NNO Abyss/Shark Boy/Suicide
NNO AJ Styles/Jeff Jarrett/Mick Foley
NNO C. Daniels/Creed/Jay Lethal
NNO Kevin Nash/Kurt Angle/Sting

2010 Jakks Pacific TNA Wrestling Micro Impact Series 1 10-Pack

NNO Sting/Shark Boy/Jeff Jarrett/Suicide/Abyss
Jay Lethal/AJ Styles/Mick Foley/Kurt Angle/Kevin Nash

2010 Jakks Pacific TNA Wrestling Micro Impact Series 2

NNO	Abyss/Hulk Hogan/Jeff Hardy		
NNO	Eric Young/Lethal/Nash		
NNO	James Storm/Morgan/Roode	15.00	30.00
NNO	Jeff Jarrett/RVD/Sting		

1998 Jakks Pacific WWF 2 Tuff Series 1

NNO	Chyna/HHH	12.50	25.00
NNO	D.O.A.	7.50	15.00
NNO	Goldust/Marlena	10.00	20.00
NNO	Truth Commission	7.50	15.00

1998 Jakks Pacific WWF 2 Tuff Series 2

NNO	B. Christopher/J. Lawler	7.50	15.00
NNO	Kama Mustafa/D'Lo Brown	10.00	20.00
NNO	Kurrgan/Jackal	7.50	15.00
NNO	Road Dogg/B.A. Billy Gunn	12.50	25.00

1999 Jakks Pacific WWF 2 Tuff Series 3

NNO	Kane/Corporate Mankind	10.00	20.00
NNO	LOD 2000	15.00	30.00
NNO	Steve Austin/Undertaker	12.50	25.00
NNO	The Rock/Owen Hart	15.00	30.00

1999 Jakks Pacific WWF 2 Tuff Series 4

NNO	Big Boss Man vs. Steve Austin	12.50	25.00
NNO	The Rock vs. Mankind	10.00	20.00
NNO	Undertaker vs. Kane	12.50	25.00
NNO	Val Venis vs. B.A. Billy Gunn	7.50	15.00

1999 Jakks Pacific WWF 2 Tuff Series 5

NNO	Billy Gunn vs. Road Dogg	10.00	20.00
NNO	Debra McMichaels vs. Double J	7.50	15.00
NNO	Stone Cold Steve Austin vs. The Rock	12.50	25.00
NNO	Viscera vs. Undertaker	10.00	20.00

2003 Jakks Pacific WWE Adrenaline Series 1

NNO	Big Show/Brock Lesnar	25.00	50.00
NNO	Shawn Michaels/RVD	15.00	30.00
NNO	Tommy Dreamer		
	Jeff Hardy		

2003 Jakks Pacific WWE Adrenaline Series 2

NNO	Johnny Stamboli	15.00	30.00
	Chavo Guerrero		

NNO	Rey Mysterio/Matt Hardy	20.00	40.00
NNO	Test/Stacy Keibler	20.00	40.00

2003 Jakks Pacific WWE Adrenaline Series 3

NNO	Kurt Angle/Brock Lesnar	20.00	40.00
NNO	Shawn Michaels/Y2J		
NNO	Steve Austin/Eric Bischoff	20.00	40.00

2003 Jakks Pacific WWE Adrenaline Series 4

NNO	Billy Gunn/Torrie Wilson	12.50	25.00
NNO	Chris Benoit/Rhyno	17.50	35.00
NNO	Undertaker/John Cena	25.00	50.00

2003 Jakks Pacific WWE Adrenaline Series 5

NNO	Eddie Guerrero	25.00	50.00
	John Cena		
NNO	Rey Mysterio	15.00	30.00
	Billy Kidman		
NNO	Shelton Benjamin	10.00	20.00
	Charlie Haas		

2003 Jakks Pacific WWE Adrenaline Series 6

NNO	Eddie and Chavo Guerrero	15.00	30.00
NNO	Faarooq/Bradshaw	10.00	20.00
NNO	The Hurricane/Rosey	10.00	20.00

2004 Jakks Pacific WWE Adrenaline Series 7

NNO	Batista/Randy Orton	17.50	35.00
NNO	Chris Jericho/Christian		
NNO	Scott Steiner/Test	12.50	25.00

2004 Jakks Pacific WWE Adrenaline Series 8

NNO	Bubba Ray/D-Von Dudley	10.00	20.00
NNO	Rene Dupree	12.50	25.00
	Rob Conway		
NNO	Steven Richards/Victoria	15.00	30.00

2004 Jakks Pacific WWE Adrenaline Series 9

NNO	Charlie Haas/Rico	12.50	25.00
NNO	Eddie Guerrero	20.00	40.00
	John Bradshaw Layfield		
NNO	Matt Hardy/Lita	20.00	40.00

2004 Jakks Pacific WWE Adrenaline Series 10

NNO	Christian/Trish Stratus	20.00	40.00
NNO	Doug and Danny Basham	12.50	25.00
NNO	Triple H/Randy Orton	20.00	40.00

2005 Jakks Pacific WWE Adrenaline Series 11

NNO	Billy Kidman/Paul London	12.50	25.00
NNO	Heidenreich/Paul Heyman	12.50	25.00
NNO	John Cena/Funaki	20.00	40.00

2005 Jakks Pacific WWE Adrenaline Series 12

NNO	Batista/Triple H	15.00	30.00
NNO	JBL/Orlando Jordan	12.50	25.00
NNO	RVD/Rey Mysterio	15.00	30.00

2005 Jakks Pacific WWE Adrenaline Series 13

NNO	Luther Reigns/Kurt Angle	12.50	25.00
NNO	Rey Mysterio/Teddy Long	15.00	30.00
NNO	Rob Conway	12.50	25.00
	Sylvain Grenier		

2005 Jakks Pacific WWE Adrenaline Series 14

NNO	Eddie Guerrero/Booker T	15.00	30.00
NNO	M. Hassan/Daivari	20.00	40.00
NNO	William Regal/Tajiri	12.50	25.00

2005 Jakks Pacific WWE Adrenaline Series 15

NNO	John Cena/JBL	15.00	30.00
NNO	Kane/Edge	20.00	40.00
NNO	Rey Mysterio	25.00	50.00
	Eddie Guerrero		

2005 Jakks Pacific WWE Adrenaline Series 16

NNO	Batista/JBL	15.00	30.00
NNO	Chris Jericho/John Cena	20.00	40.00
NNO	Johnny Nitro	12.50	25.00
	Joey Mercury		

2006 Jakks Pacific WWE Adrenaline Series 17

NNO	John Cena/Kurt Angle	12.50	25.00
NNO	Matt Hardy/Edge	12.50	25.00
NNO	Super Crazy/Psicosis	15.00	30.00

2006 Jakks Pacific WWE Adrenaline Series 18

NNO	Bobby Lashley	17.50	35.00
	Orlando Jordan		
NNO	Lance Cade	15.00	30.00
	Trevor Murdoch		
NNO	Johnny Nitro		
	Road Warrior Animal		

2006 Jakks Pacific WWE Adrenaline Series 19

NNO	John Cena/Edge	15.00	30.00
NNO	Johnny Nitro	10.00	20.00
	Joey Mercury		
NNO	Rey Mysterio/Mark Henry	20.00	40.00

2006 Jakks Pacific WWE Adrenaline Series 20

NNO	Triple H/John Cena		
NNO	Trish Stratus/HBK	15.00	30.00
NNO	William Regal	12.50	25.00
	Paul Burchill		

2006 Jakks Pacific WWE Adrenaline Series 21

NNO	Booker T/Boogeyman	12.50	25.00
NNO	Gymini	12.50	25.00
NNO	Mikey vs. Big Show	15.00	30.00

2006 Jakks Pacific WWE Adrenaline Series 22

NNO	Johnny/Mitch	10.00	20.00
NNO	Psicosis/Super Crazy	15.00	30.00
NNO	Umaga/Armando Estrada	15.00	30.00

2007 Jakks Pacific WWE Adrenaline Series 23

NNO	Booker T vs. Batista	12.50	25.00
NNO	Elijah Burke	15.00	30.00
	Sylvester Terkay		
NNO	Jeff Hardy vs. Johnny Nitro	20.00	40.00

2007 Jakks Pacific WWE Adrenaline Series 24

NNO	Brian Kendrick/Paul London	12.50	25.00
NNO	HHH/Shawn Michaels	17.50	35.00
NNO	Undertaker/Kane	15.00	30.00

2007 Jakks Pacific WWE Adrenaline Series 25

NNO	Charlie Haas/Shelton Benjamin	12.50	25.00
NNO	John Cena vs. The Great Khali	20.00	40.00
NNO	MVP vs. Kane	15.00	30.00

2007 Jakks Pacific WWE Adrenaline Series 26

NNO	Cryme Tyme	12.50	25.00
NNO	The Highlanders	12.50	25.00
NNO	King Booker/Queen Sharmell	15.00	30.00

2007 Jakks Pacific WWE Adrenaline Series 27

NNO	Deuce/Domino	15.00	30.00
NNO	Jeff and Matt Hardy	17.50	35.00
NNO	Lance Cade/Trevor Murdoch	12.50	25.00

2007 Jakks Pacific WWE Adrenaline Series 28

NNO	CM Punk/Elijah Burke	15.00	30.00
NNO	Mr. Kennedy/Edge	12.50	25.00
NNO	Umage/Vince McMahon	12.50	25.00

2008 Jakks Pacific WWE Adrenaline Series 29

NNO	Cody & Dusty Rhodes	12.50	25.00
NNO	Miz/Layla	12.50	25.00
NNO	MVP/Matt Hardy	15.00	30.00

2008 Jakks Pacific WWE Adrenaline Series 30

NNO	Balls Mahoney/Kelly Kelly	20.00	40.00
NNO	HHH/Umaga	15.00	30.00
NNO	Rey Mysterio/Finlay		

2008 Jakks Pacific WWE Adrenaline Series 31

NNO	Big Daddy V/Matt Striker	12.50	25.00
NNO	Chuck Palumbo	15.00	30.00
	Michelle McCool		
NNO	The Highlanders	12.50	25.00

2008 Jakks Pacific WWE Adrenaline Series 32

NNO	Jesse/Festus	10.00	20.00
NNO	John Morrison/The Miz	15.00	30.00
NNO	Santino Marella/Maria	15.00	30.00

2008 Jakks Pacific WWE Adrenaline Series 33

NNO	Chavo Guerrero/Kane	15.00	30.00
NNO	Katie Lea/Paul Burchill	15.00	30.00
NNO	Vickie Guerrero/Edge	20.00	40.00

2008 Jakks Pacific WWE Adrenaline Series 34

NNO	Hornswoggle/Finlay	30.00	60.00
NNO	Randy Orton/JBL		
NNO	Tommy Dreamer	20.00	40.00
	Joey Styles		

2009 Jakks Pacific WWE Adrenaline Series 35

NNO	Cody Rhodes/Ted DiBiase Jr.		
NNO	Curt Hawkins/Zach Ryder	15.00	30.00
NNO	Evan Bourne/Rey Mysterio		

2009 Jakks Pacific WWE Adrenaline Series 36

NNO	Brian Kendrick/Ezekiel Jackson	15.00	30.00
NNO	Mark Henry/Tony Atlas	15.00	30.00
NNO	Shad Gaspard/JTG	20.00	40.00

2009 Jakks Pacific WWE Adrenaline Series 37

NNO	Jeff Hardy/The Undertaker	20.00	40.00
NNO	Million Dollar Man/DiBiase Jr.		
NNO	Triple H/Randy Orton	12.50	25.00

2009 Jakks Pacific WWE Adrenaline Series 38

NNO	Edge vs. Big Show		
NNO	Finlay/Hornswoggle	25.00	50.00
NNO	Jack Swagger vs. Christian		

2009 Jakks Pacific WWE Adrenaline Series 39

NNO	Undertaker/HBK	12.50	25.00
NNO	Triple H/Stephanie		
NNO	Natalya/Tyson Kidd		

2000 Jakks Pacific WWF Back Talkin' Crushers Exclusive

NNO	Stone Cold Steve Austin TF	10.00	20.00

1999 Jakks Pacific WWF Back Talkin' Crushers Series 1

NNO	Big Show	6.00	12.00
NNO	The Rock	7.50	15.00
NNO	Steve Austin	10.00	20.00
NNO	Undertaker	7.50	15.00

2000 Jakks Pacific WWF Back Talkin' Crushers Series 2

NNO	Mankind	7.50	15.00
NNO	Road Dogg	6.00	12.00
NNO	The Rock	10.00	20.00

2000 Jakks Pacific WWF Back Talkin' Crushers Series 3

NNO	Chris Jericho	10.00	20.00
NNO	Steve Austin	10.00	20.00
NNO	Triple H	7.50	15.00

2001 Jakks Pacific WWF Back Talkin' Slammers Series 1

NNO	The Rock	12.50	25.00
NNO	Stone Cold Steve Austin	12.50	25.00
NNO	Triple H	10.00	20.00

2001 Jakks Pacific WWF Back Talkin' Slammers Series 2

NNO	Chris Jericho	10.00	20.00
NNO	Kurt Angle	12.50	25.00
NNO	Undertaker		

2001 Jakks Pacific WWF Back Talkin' Slammers Series 3

NNO	Chris Jericho	10.00	20.00
NNO	Kurt Angle	12.50	25.00
NNO	Stone Cold Steve Austin	10.00	20.00
NNO	The Rock	10.00	20.00
NNO	Triple H	7.50	15.00
NNO	Undertaker		

2002 Jakks Pacific WWF Back Talkin' Slammers Series 4

NNO	Chris Jericho		
NNO	Kurt Angle		
NNO	Triple H		

2000 Jakks Pacific WWF Backlash Series 1

NNO	Al Snow	12.50	25.00
NNO	Kane	6.00	12.00
NNO	Shawn Michaels	15.00	30.00
NNO	Stone Cold Steve Austin	10.00	20.00
NNO	The Rock	12.50	25.00
NNO	Triple H	10.00	20.00
NNO	Undertaker	10.00	20.00
NNO	X-Pac	7.50	15.00

2000 Jakks Pacific WWF Backlash Series 2

NNO	Big Boss Man		
NNO	Edge		
NNO	Hardcore Holly		
NNO	Road Dogg		
NNO	The Rock		
NNO	Stone Cold Steve Austin		

NNO Triple H 7.50 15.00
NNO X-Pac 6.00 12.00

2000 Jakks Pacific WWF Backlash Series 3

NNO Billy Gunn 7.50 15.00
NNO Edge. 10.00 20.00
NNO Kane 7.50 15.00
NNO The Rock
NNO Stone Cold Steve Austin
NNO Test
NNO Triple H
NNO Undertaker

2000 Jakks Pacific WWF Backlash Series 4

NNO Big Boss Man 6.00 12.00
NNO Billy Gunn 7.50 15.00
NNO Edge 10.00 20.00
NNO Kane 10.00 20.00
NNO The Rock
NNO Stone Cold Steve Austin 12.50 25.00
NNO Triple H
NNO Undertaker 15.00 30.00

2000 Jakks Pacific WWF Backlash Series 5

NNO Al Snow
NNO Hardcore Holly 6.00 12.00
NNO Rock
NNO Stone Cold Steve Austin 12.50 25.00
NNO Test
NNO Undertaker 15.00 30.00
NNO Val Venis
NNO X-Pac

2005 Jakks Pacific WWE Backlash Series 7

NNO Batista 12.50 25.00
NNO Chris Benoit 12.50 25.00
NNO Kurt Angle 10.00 20.00
NNO Undertaker 15.00 30.00

2005 Jakks Pacific WWE Backlash Series 8

NNO Batista 12.50 25.00
NNO Edge 10.00 20.00
NNO Kurt Angle 12.50 25.00
NNO Triple H 10.00 20.00

2005 Jakks Pacific WWE Backlash Series 9

NNO Carlito 12.50 25.00
NNO Kurt Angle 20.00 40.00
NNO Randy Orton 7.50 15.00
NNO Rob Van Dam 12.50 25.00
NNO Shawn Michaels
NNO Undertaker

2005 Jakks Pacific WWE Backlash Series 10

NNO Batista 12.50 25.00
NNO Chris Benoit 7.50 15.00
NNO John Cena 12.50 25.00
NNO Rob Van Dam 7.50 15.00
NNO Shawn Michaels 15.00 30.00
NNO Triple H 10.00 20.00

2007 Jakks Pacific WWE Backlash Series 11

NNO Bobby Lashley 12.50 25.00
NNO Edge 15.00 30.00
NNO Finlay 15.00 30.00
NNO Jeff Hardy 15.00 30.00
NNO Rey Mysterio 20.00 40.00
NNO Undertaker 20.00 40.00

2008 Jakks Pacific WWE Backlash Series 12

NNO Kane
NNO Matt Hardy
NNO Miz
NNO Mr. Kennedy
NNO Randy Orton
NNO Triple H

2009 Jakks Pacific WWE Backlash Series 13

NNO Batista
NNO Chavo Guerrero
NNO Chris Jericho
NNO Elijah Burke
NNO John Cena
NNO Nunzio

2009 Jakks Pacific WWE Backlash Series 14

NNO Chavo Guerrero
NNO Cody Rhodes
NNO Matt Hardy 10.00 20.00
NNO Stone Cold Steve Austin
NNO Triple H

2009 Jakks Pacific WWE Backlash Series 15

NNO Chris Jericho 15.00 30.00
NNO CM Punk
NNO John Cena 10.00 20.00
NNO Rey Mysterio 20.00 40.00
NNO Shawn Michaels 12.50 25.00
NNO Triple H 15.00 30.00

2008 Jakks Pacific WWE Best of Classic Superstars

NNO Andre the Giant 20.00 40.00
NNO Bret Hit Man Hart 20.00 40.00
NNO Eddie Guerrero 12.50 25.00
NNO Rowdy Roddy Piper
NNO Shawn Michaels 12.50 25.00

2009 Jakks Pacific WWE Best of Deluxe Aggression

NNO Chris Jericho
NNO John Cena
NNO Randy Orton
NNO Rey Mysterio
NNO Triple H
NNO Undertaker

2006 Jakks Pacific WWE Best of Deluxe Aggression

NNO Batista 7.50 15.00
NNO John Cena 15.00 30.00
NNO Kane 10.00 20.00
NNO Rey Mysterio 10.00 20.00
NNO Triple H 7.50 15.00
NNO Undertaker 20.00 40.00

2008 Jakks Pacific WWE Best of Deluxe Aggression

NNO Chris Jericho 15.00 30.00
NNO CM Punk
NNO John Cena 10.00 20.00
NNO Rey Mysterio 17.50 35.00
NNO Shawn Michaels 12.50 25.00
NNO Undertaker 20.00 40.00

2005 Jakks Pacific WWE Best of ECW

NNO Bubba Ray Dudley 15.00 30.00
NNO D-Von Dudley 12.50 25.00
NNO Rey Mysterio 12.50 25.00
NNO Rhyno 7.50 15.00
NNO Rob Van Dam 15.00 30.00
NNO Stevie Richards 7.50 15.00

2005 Jakks Pacific WWE Best of WCW

NNO Billy Kidman 10.00 20.00
NNO Chris Benoit 15.00 30.00
NNO Chris Jericho 12.50 25.00
NNO Eddie Guerrero 10.00 20.00
NNO Rey Mysterio 15.00 30.00
NNO Ric Flair 20.00 40.00

1998 Jakks Pacific WWF Bone Crunchin' Buddies

NNO Animal
NNO Dude Love
NNO Hawk
NNO Shawn Michaels

1999 Jakks Pacific WWF Bone Crunchin' Buddies

NNO Kane
NNO The Rock
NNO Steve Austin/Ring Gear 20.00 40.00
NNO Steve Austin/Street Clothes
NNO Triple H 20.00 40.00
NNO Undertaker

2001 Jakks Pacific WWF Bone Crunchin' Buddies

NNO Animal
NNO Hawk
NNO The Rock
NNO Stone Cold Steve Austin
NNO Undertaker

1999 Jakks Pacific WWF Break Down In Your House

NNO D'Lo Brown 7.50 15.00
NNO Droz 6.00 12.00
NNO Goldust 6.00 12.00
NNO Mankind 12.50 25.00
NNO Steve Austin 10.00 20.00
NNO X-Pac 6.00 12.00

1999 Jakks Pacific WWF Break Down In Your House Multi-Packs

NNO Steve Austin/D'Lo Brown/Droz BJ
NNO Steve Austin/Droz/Goldust/X-Pac SC
NNO X-Pac/Mankind/Goldust BJ

2003 Jakks Pacific WWE Bring the Noise

NNO Matt Hardy 10.00 20.00
NNO Shawn Michaels 7.50 15.00
NNO The Rock 20.00 40.00
NNO Tommy Dreamer 12.50 25.00
NNO Triple H 12.50 25.00
NNO Undertaker

2008 Jakks Pacific WWE Build N' Brawl Playset

NNO Wrestling Ring
{w/HHH & Orton TRU

2008 Jakks Pacific WWE Build N' Brawl Series 1

NNO Batista
NNO Bobby Lashley

NNO Edge
NNO John Cena
NNO Triple H
NNO Undertaker

2008 Jakks Pacific WWE Build N' Brawl Series 2

NNO Batista
NNO Kane
NNO Mr. Kennedy
NNO Randy Orton
NNO Rey Mysterio
NNO Shawn Michaels

2008 Jakks Pacific WWE Build N' Brawl Series 3

NNO Boogeyman
NNO CM Punk
NNO Jeff Hardy
NNO Matt Hardy
NNO MVP
NNO Umaga

2008 Jakks Pacific WWE Build N' Brawl Series 4

NNO Chris Jericho
NNO Deuce
NNO Domino
NNO The Miz
NNO John Morrison
NNO Stone Cold Steve Austin

2008 Jakks Pacific WWE Build N' Brawl Series 5

NNO Chavo Guerrero
NNO Elijah Burke
NNO Finlay
NNO JBL
NNO Razor Ramon
NNO William Regal

2008 Jakks Pacific WWE Build N' Brawl Series 6

NNO Curt Hawkins
NNO Kofi Kingston
NNO Rey Mysterio
NNO Santino Marella
NNO Sgt. Slaughter
NNO Zack Ryder

2008 Jakks Pacific WWE Build N' Brawl Series 7

NNO Bret Hart
NNO John Cena
NNO Mark Henry
NNO Matt Hardy
NNO Rey Mysterio
NNO Undertaker

2008 Jakks Pacific WWE Build N' Brawl Series 8

NNO Batista
NNO Big Show
NNO Rey Mysterio
NNO The Rock
NNO Roddy Piper
NNO Shawn Michaels

2008 Jakks Pacific WWE Build N' Brawl Series 9

NNO John Cena
NNO Rey Mysterio
NNO Undertaker

2008 Jakks Pacific WWE Build N' Brawl WrestleMania

NNO John Cena		
NNO Rey Mysterio	12.50	25.00
NNO Triple H	10.00	20.00

1999 Jakks Pacific WWF Camo Carnage

NNO B.A. Billy Gunn	6.00	12.00
NNO Billy Gunn SI	7.50	15.00
NNO Billy Gunn w/Gun	7.50	15.00
NNO Chyna	6.00	12.00
NNO Chyna SI	7.50	15.00
NNO Chyna w/Gun	7.50	15.00
NNO HHH	6.00	12.00
NNO HHH SI	7.50	15.00
NNO HHH w/Gun	7.50	15.00
NNO Road Dogg	5.00	10.00
NNO Road Dogg SI	6.00	12.00
NNO Road Dogg w/Gun	6.00	12.00
NNO Stone Cold Steve Austin	7.50	15.00
NNO Steve Austin SI	10.00	20.00
NNO Steve Austin w/Gun	10.00	20.00
NNO X-Pac	5.00	10.00
NNO X-Pac SI	6.00	12.00
NNO X-Pac w/Gun	6.00	12.00

2004 Jakks Pacific WWE Classic Superstars Series 1

NNO Andre the Giant	20.00	40.00
NNO Bret Hart	30.00	75.00
NNO Hunter Hearst Helmsley	10.00	20.00
NNO Shawn Michaels	25.00	50.00
NNO Ultimate Warrior	15.00	30.00
NNO Undertaker	15.00	30.00

2004 Jakks Pacific WWE Classic Superstars Series 2

NNO Big John Studd	12.50	25.00
Chair & Microphone		
NNO Big John Studd	20.00	40.00
Ring Bell & Stretcher		
NNO Dude Love	15.00	30.00
Tye-Dye Wrist Bands		
NNO Dude Love	12.50	25.00
Yellow Wrist Bands		
NNO George The Animal Steele	15.00	30.00
Painted Body Hair		
NNO George The Animal Steele	25.00	50.00
Synthetic Body Hair		
NNO Mankind	20.00	40.00
NNO Ric Flair	20.00	40.00
NNO Sgt. Slaughter/Jacket Off		
NNO Sgt. Slaughter/Jacket On	15.00	30.00

2004 Jakks Pacific WWE Classic Superstars Series 3

NNO Bret Hit Man Hart	15.00	30.00
NNO Jake The Snake Roberts	15.00	30.00
NNO Million Dollar Man Ted DiBiase	25.00	50.00
NNO Superfly Jimmy Snuka	15.00	30.00
NNO Undertaker	12.50	25.00
NNO Ultimate Warrior		

2004 Jakks Pacific WWE Classic Superstars Series 4

NNO Hacksaw Jim Duggan	20.00	40.00
NNO Hillbilly Jim	15.00	30.00

NNO Junkyard Dog	12.50	25.00
NNO Rowdy Roddy Piper	15.00	30.00
NNO Tito Santana	12.50	25.00
NNO Yokozuna		
Smooth Belt Strap		
NNO Yokozuna	20.00	40.00
Textured Belt Strap		

2004 Jakks Pacific WWE Classic Superstars Series 5

NNO Brutus The Barber Beefcake	15.00	30.00
NNO Iron Sheik	15.00	30.00
NNO King Kong Bundy	20.00	40.00
NNO Mr. Wonderful Paul Orndorff	15.00	30.00
NNO Nikolai Volkoff	20.00	40.00
NNO Terry Funk	25.00	50.00

2005 Jakks Pacific WWE Classic Superstars Series 6

NNO Andre the Giant	15.00	30.00
NNO Bobby The Brain Heenan	12.50	25.00
NNO Doink	15.00	30.00
NNO Earthquake	10.00	20.00
Painted Chest Hair		
NNO Earthquake	12.50	25.00
Synthetic Chest Hair		
NNO Koko B. Ware	25.00	50.00
NNO One Man Gang	20.00	40.00
NNO Road Warrior Animal	20.00	40.00
NNO Road Warrior Hawk	15.00	30.00
NNO Shawn Michaels	12.50	25.00

2005 Jakks Pacific WWE Classic Superstars Series 7

NNO Andre the Giant	15.00	30.00
NNO British Bulldog	12.50	25.00
NNO Don Muraco	15.00	30.00
NNO Eddie Guerrero	10.00	20.00
NNO Gorilla Monsoon	12.50	25.00
NNO Jimmy Hart	15.00	30.00
NNO King Harley Race	20.00	40.00
NNO Superstar Billy Graham	12.50	25.00
NNO The Ultimate Warrior	15.00	30.00

2005 Jakks Pacific WWE Classic Superstars Series 8

NNO Bruiser Brody	25.00	50.00
NNO Chief Jay Strongbow	15.00	30.00
NNO Classy Freddie Blassie	10.00	20.00
NNO Cowboy Bob Orton	20.00	40.00
Ace on Boots		
NNO Cowboy Bob Orton	15.00	30.00
Plain Boots		
NNO Hollywood Hogan	20.00	40.00
Large World Title		
NNO Hollywood Hogan	15.00	30.00
Small World Title		
NNO Hulk Hogan/'80s WWF Title	30.00	75.00
NNO Hulk Hogan/'90s WWF Title	20.00	40.00
NNO Jerry The King Lawler	15.00	30.00
NNO Vader	25.00	50.00

2006 Jakks Pacific WWE Classic Superstars Series 9

NNO Akeem	12.50	25.00
NNO Bam Bam Bigelow	25.00	50.00
NNO The Godfather	15.00	30.00

NNO	Kamala	15.00	30.00
NNO	Papa Shango	20.00	40.00
NNO	Paul Bearer/Bow Tie	15.00	30.00
NNO	Paul Bearer/Windsor Tie	15.00	30.00
NNO	Ric Flair/Smooth Wrists	15.00	30.00
NNO	Ric Flair/Taped Wrists	10.00	20.00
NNO	Road Warrior Animal	10.00	20.00
NNO	Road Warrior Hawk	10.00	20.00

2006 Jakks Pacific WWE Classic Superstars
Series 10

NNO	Bruno Sammartino	12.50	25.00
NNO	Dusty Rhodes	20.00	40.00
NNO	Gorilla Monsoon	25.00	50.00
NNO	Greg The Hammer Valentine	20.00	40.00
NNO	Harley Race	15.00	30.00
NNO	Mr. Perfect	15.00	30.00
NNO	Rocky Maivia	20.00	40.00
NNO	Sabu	20.00	40.00

2006 Jakks Pacific WWE Classic Superstars
Series 11

NNO	123 Kid	20.00	40.00
NNO	Barry Windham	10.00	20.00
NNO	Diesel	15.00	30.00
NNO	Fabulous Moolah	10.00	20.00
NNO	Hulk Hogan Black Weightlifting Belt	12.50	25.00
NNO	Hulk Hogan Yellow Weightlifting Belt	20.00	40.00
NNO	Irwin R. Schyster	15.00	30.00
NNO	Ken Shamrock	12.50	25.00
NNO	Rick Steiner	15.00	30.00

2006 Jakks Pacific WWE Classic Superstars
Series 12

NNO	Arn Anderson	12.50	25.00
NNO	Brooklyn Brawler	15.00	30.00
NNO	Captain Lou Albano	15.00	30.00
NNO	Dean Malenko	12.50	25.00
NNO	Handsome Jimmy Valiant	20.00	40.00
NNO	Hollywood Hulk Hogan	30.00	60.00
NNO	Killer Kowalski	12.50	25.00
NNO	Nasty Boy Brian Knobbs	12.50	25.00
NNO	Nasty Boy Jerry Sags	12.50	25.00
NNO	Ultimate Warrior Facing Back	15.00	30.00
NNO	Ultimate Warrior Facing Forward	15.00	30.00

2006 Jakks Pacific WWE Classic Superstars
Series 13

NNO	Al Snow	15.00	30.00
NNO	Bad News Brown	10.00	20.00
NNO	Bret Hit Man Hart	15.00	30.00
NNO	Brother Love	25.00	50.00
NNO	Droz	10.00	20.00
NNO	Dusty Rhodes	15.00	30.00
NNO	Ernie Ladd	15.00	30.00
NNO	Luna Vachon	20.00	40.00
NNO	The Mountie	25.00	50.00
NNO	Mr. Perfect	15.00	30.00
NNO	Ravishing Rick Rude	20.00	40.00
NNO	Undertaker/LJN Style	25.00	50.00

2007 Jakks Pacific WWE Classic Superstars
Series 14

NNO	Abdullah The Butcher	30.00	60.00
NNO	Bob Backlund	20.00	40.00
NNO	Demolition Ax	20.00	40.00
NNO	Demolition Smash	20.00	40.00
NNO	Diamond Dallas Page	20.00	40.00
NNO	Honky Tonk Man	17.50	35.00
NNO	Mean Gene Okerlund	30.00	60.00
NNO	Rick The Model Martel	25.00	50.00
NNO	Sensational Sherri	15.00	30.00
NNO	Steve Austin/LJN Black Card	15.00	30.00
NNO	Steve Austin/LJN Blue Card		
NNO	The Ultimate Warrior	15.00	30.00

2007 Jakks Pacific WWE Classic Superstars
Series 15

NNO	The Genius	20.00	40.00
NNO	Johnny Rodz	12.50	25.00
NNO	Lex Luger	15.00	30.00
NNO	Outlaw Ron Bass	12.50	25.00
NNO	Razor Ramon	20.00	40.00
NNO	The Rock/LJN Style	12.50	25.00
NNO	Shawn Michaels w/Entrance Gear	15.00	30.00
NNO	Shawn Michaels w/o Entrance Gear	15.00	30.00
NNO	Tank Abbott w/Chair+Barbell	15.00	30.00
NNO	Tank Abbott w/Chair	20.00	40.00
NNO	Tully Blanchard	15.00	30.00
NNO	Zeus w/Chain+Pipe	40.00	80.00
NNO	Zeus w/Chain	20.00	40.00

2007 Jakks Pacific WWE Classic Superstars
Series 16

NNO	Barbarian	20.00	40.00
NNO	Giant Gonzalez/Painted Fur	25.00	50.00
NNO	Giant Gonzalez Synthetic Fur/500*	60.00	120.00
NNO	Shawn Michaels/LJN Style	12.50	25.00
NNO	Sycho Sid w/Knee Pads & {WWF Belt by Feet	15.00	30.00
NNO	Sycho Sid w/Knee Pads & {WWF Belt by Waist	20.00	40.00
NNO	Sycho Sid w/o Knee Pads & {WWF Belt by Feet	20.00	40.00
NNO	Sycho Sid w/o Knee Pads & {WWF Belt by Waist	12.50	25.00
NNO	Vince McMahon	20.00	40.00
NNO	Warlord	20.00	40.00
NNO	The Ultimate Warrior	25.00	50.00
NNO	X-Pac/Belt by Feet	12.50	25.00
NNO	X-Pac/Belt by Waist		

2007 Jakks Pacific WWE Classic Superstars
Series 17

NNO	Eddie Guerrero	17.50	35.00
NNO	Ivan Putski	15.00	30.00
NNO	Ken Patera	25.00	50.00
NNO	Repo Man	17.50	35.00
NNO	The Rock	20.00	40.00
NNO	Rocky Johnson	15.00	30.00
NNO	Shane McMahon Centered Jersey Logo	15.00	30.00
NNO	Shane McMahon Off-Centered Jersey Logo		
NNO	Triple H/LJN Style	15.00	30.00
NNO	Typhoon	17.50	35.00

2007 Jakks Pacific WWE Classic Superstars
Series 18

NNO	Honky Tonk Man	15.00	30.00
NNO	Jim Ross	30.00	75.00
NNO	Kane	25.00	50.00
NNO	King Mabel	30.00	75.00
NNO	Mae Young	30.00	60.00
NNO	Ric Flair/LJN Style	15.00	30.00
NNO	Rikishi	15.00	30.00
NNO	Stone Cold Steve Austin	15.00	30.00
NNO	Sunny	20.00	40.00
NNO	Val Venis Cruiserweight Torso		
NNO	Val Venis Heavyweight Torso	20.00	40.00

2008 Jakks Pacific WWE Classic Superstars
Series 19

NNO	Adam Bomb	30.00	75.00
NNO	Cactus Jack	12.50	25.00
NNO	Eddie Guerrero	15.00	30.00
NNO	Evil Doink	20.00	40.00
NNO	Howard Finkel	20.00	40.00
NNO	Kevin Sullivan	15.00	30.00
NNO	Mankind/LJN Style	17.50	35.00
NNO	Nikita Koloff	30.00	60.00
NNO	The Rock	15.00	30.00
NNO	Tatanka	15.00	30.00

2008 Jakks Pacific WWE Classic Superstars
Series 20

NNO	Dynamite Kid	20.00	40.00
NNO	John Cena/LJN Style	12.50	25.00
NNO	Rey Mysterio	17.50	35.00
NNO	Ric Flair	25.00	50.00
NNO	The Rock	15.00	30.00
NNO	Ron Simmons	15.00	30.00
NNO	Tony Atlas	20.00	40.00

2008 Jakks Pacific WWE Classic Superstars
Series 21

NNO	Brian Pillman	12.50	25.00
NNO	Buff Bagwell	30.00	60.00
NNO	Chris Jericho	15.00	30.00
NNO	Jeff Hardy	20.00	40.00
NNO	Jesse The Body Ventura	15.00	30.00
NNO	Rey Mysterio/LJN Style	20.00	40.00
NNO	Tazz	12.50	25.00

2008 Jakks Pacific WWE Classic Superstars
Series 22

NNO	Andy Kaufman	50.00	100.00
NNO	Bob Spark Plugg Holly	15.00	30.00
NNO	Chainsaw Charlie	15.00	30.00
NNO	Earthquake	17.50	35.00
NNO	Eddie Guerrero/LJN Style	15.00	30.00
NNO	Matt Hardy	20.00	40.00
NNO	Mr. McMahon	15.00	30.00
NNO	Stone Cold Steve Austin	25.00	50.00

2009 Jakks Pacific WWE Classic Superstars
Series 23

NNO	The Berzerker	25.00	50.00
NNO	Big Boss Man	30.00	60.00
NNO	Billy Kidman	15.00	30.00
NNO	Lance Storm	25.00	50.00
NNO	Road Warrior Animal	15.00	30.00

NNO Road Warrior Hawk   15.00   30.00
NNO Rob Van Dam   17.50   35.00
NNO Spike Dudley   25.00   50.00
NNO Trish Stratus/LJN Style   25.00   50.00

2009 Jakks Pacific WWE Classic Superstars Series 24

NNO B. Brian Blair   20.00   40.00
NNO Davey Boy Smith   15.00   30.00
NNO Dynamite Kid   15.00   30.00
NNO Hunter-Hearst-Helmsley   15.00   30.00
NNO Jim Brunzell   15.00   30.00
NNO Rey Mysterio   20.00   40.00
NNO Rob Van Dam/LJN Style   15.00   30.00
NNO Stephanie McMahon   15.00   30.00
NNO Trish Stratus   30.00   60.00

2009 Jakks Pacific WWE Classic Superstars Series 25

NNO Bastion Booger   30.00   75.00
NNO Big Boss Man   15.00   30.00
NNO Big Show   15.00   30.00
NNO Goldberg   50.00   100.00
NNO Haku   50.00   100.00
NNO Jack Brisco   30.00   60.00
NNO Jeff Hardy/LJN Style   20.00   40.00
NNO Jerry Brisco   30.00   75.00
NNO Jesse The Body Ventura   40.00   80.00

2009 Jakks Pacific WWE Classic Superstars Series 26

NNO Bret Hit Man Hart   15.00   30.00
NNO Dangerous Danny Davis   20.00   40.00
NNO Dr. Death Steve Williams   30.00   60.00
NNO Giant Machine/Andre   20.00   40.00
NNO The Iron Sheik   20.00   40.00
NNO Junkyard Dog   12.50   25.00
NNO Matt Hardy/LJN Style   12.50   25.00
NNO Meng   15.00   30.00
NNO Mr. Fuji   20.00   40.00
NNO The Sheik   25.00   50.00
NNO The Shockmaster   25.00   50.00

2009 Jakks Pacific WWE Classic Superstars Series 27

NNO The Barbarian   15.00   30.00
NNO Bill Goldberg   50.00   100.00
NNO Evil Doink   15.00   30.00
NNO The Giant
NNO Kona Crush   50.00   100.00
NNO Sgt. Slaughter   15.00   30.00
NNO Steve Blackman   25.00   50.00
NNO The Warlord   15.00   30.00

2009 Jakks Pacific WWE Classic Superstars Series 28

NNO Bret Hit Man Hart   20.00   40.00
NNO Rey Mysterio/LJN Style   30.00   60.00
NNO Rowdy Roddy Piper   20.00   40.00
NNO Shawn Michaels   12.50   25.00
NNO Triple H   12.50   25.00
NNO The Undertaker   25.00   50.00

2004 Jakks Pacific WWE Classic Superstars 2-Packs Series 1

NNO Hart Foundation   75.00   150.00
Black Knee Pads on Bret UK
NNO Hart Foundation   30.00   75.00

Pink Knee Pads
NNO Road Warriors
NNO Rockers   30.00   75.00

2005 Jakks Pacific WWE Classic Superstars 2-Packs Series 2

NNO Jake Roberts/Steve Austin   30.00   75.00
NNO Mankind/Undertaker   30.00   60.00
NNO Roddy Piper/Jimmy Snuka   30.00   60.00

2005 Jakks Pacific WWE Classic Superstars 2-Packs Series 3

NNO Bushwhackers   25.00   50.00
NNO Steve Austin/Roddy Piper   25.00   50.00
NNO Wild Samoans   20.00   40.00

2006 Jakks Pacific WWE Classic Superstars 2-Packs Series 4

NNO Hulk Hogan/Freddie Blassie   25.00   50.00
NNO Sgt. Slaughter/Col. Mustafa   20.00   40.00
NNO Undertaker/Paul Bearer   25.00   50.00

2006 Jakks Pacific WWE Classic Superstars 2-Packs Series 5

NNO Demolition   40.00   80.00
NNO Hulk Hogan/Ultimate Warrior   60.00   120.00
NNO Hulk Hogan/Ultimate Warrior Head Variant
NNO Ted DiBiase/Virgil   20.00   40.00

2007 Jakks Pacific WWE Classic Superstars 2-Packs Series 6

NNO Hollywood Blondes   30.00   60.00
NNO Midnight Express   50.00   75.00
NNO Strike Force   30.00   60.00

2007 Jakks Pacific WWE Classic Superstars 2-Packs Series 7

NNO Arn Anderson/Tully Blanchard   25.00   50.00
NNO Lex Luger/Dean Malenko   25.00   50.00
NNO Ric Flair/Barry Windham   25.00   50.00

2008 Jakks Pacific WWE Classic Superstars 2-Packs Series 8

NNO Giant Gonzales   30.00   75.00
Harvey Wippleman
NNO Jerry Lawler vs.   50.00   100.00
{Andy Kaufman
NNO Killer Bees   40.00   80.00

2008 Jakks Pacific WWE Classic Superstars 2-Packs Series 9

NNO British Bulldogs   75.00   150.00
NNO Ivan & Nikita Koloff   30.00   75.00
NNO Rock 'n Roll Express   60.00   120.00

2009 Jakks Pacific WWE Classic Superstars 2-Packs Series 10

NNO Tony Atlas/Rocky Johnson
NNO Too Cool
NNO Yokozuna vs. Bret Hart   30.00   60.00

2009 Jakks Pacific WWE Classic Superstars 2-Packs Series 11

NNO Jake Roberts vs. Rick Martel
NNO Jake Roberts vs. Rick Martel/Blindfolds
NNO Rob Van Dam vs. Tazz   25.00   50.00
NNO Rowdy Roddy Piper vs. Mr. Fuji   40.00   80.00

2009 Jakks Pacific WWE Classic Superstars 2-Packs Series 12

NNO Cowboy Bob Orton/Randy Orton   30.00   60.00
NNO Jim Neidhart/Natalya   30.00   75.00
NNO Million Dollar Man/DiBiase Jr.   20.00   40.00

2009 Jakks Pacific WWE Classic Superstars 2-Packs Series 13

NNO Steve Austin vs. Rock   30.00   60.00
NNO Triple H/X-Pac   20.00   40.00
NNO Bobby Heenan/Abe Schwartz   30.00   60.00

2004 Jakks Pacific WWE Classic Superstars 3-Packs Series 1

NNO Jake Roberts/Andre Single Strap   150.00   300.00
John Studd
NNO Jake Roberts/Andre Double Strap   30.00   75.00
John Studd

2005 Jakks Pacific WWE Classic Superstars 3-Packs Series 2

NNO Bret Hart/Rock/HBK   30.00   75.00

2005 Jakks Pacific WWE Classic Superstars 3-Packs Series 3

NNO 3 Faces of Undertaker   60.00   120.00
NNO Jim Neidhart/Tito Santana   20.00   40.00
Marty Janetty

2005 Jakks Pacific WWE Classic Superstars 3-Packs Series 4

NNO King Kong Bundy   45.00   90.00
Volkoff & Sheik
NNO Hart Foundation w/J. Hart   30.00   75.00

2006 Jakks Pacific WWE Classic Superstars 3-Packs Series 5

NNO Fabulous Freebirds   30.00   60.00
NNO Fabulous Freebirds
Taped Wrists
NNO Mega-Maniacs   25.00   50.00
w/Jimmy Hart

2006 Jakks Pacific WWE Classic Superstars 3-Packs Series 6

NNO Captain Lou Albano   20.00   40.00
Wild Samoans
NNO Rowdy Roddy Piper/Cowboy Bob Orton/Mr. Wonderful 25.00   50.00

2006 Jakks Pacific WWE Classic Superstars 3-Packs Series 7

NNO Terry Funk/Cactus Jack/Sabu   25.00   50.00
NNO Undertaker/Kane/Paul Bearer   25.00   50.00

2007 Jakks Pacific WWE Classic Superstars 3-Packs Series 8

NNO Jake Roberts/British   40.00   80.00
{Bulldog/Koko B. Ware
NNO Ric Flair/Perfect/Heenan   25.00   50.00

2008 Jakks Pacific WWE Classic Superstars 3-Packs Series 9

NNO Rhythm & Blues   30.00   75.00
{w/Jimmy Hart
NNO Rocky Johnson/Peter Maivia/The Rock   40.00   80.00

2009 WWE Classic Superstars 3-Packs Series 10

NNO	Brainbusters w/Bobby Heenan	25.00	50.00
NNO	Demolition/Ax/ Smash/Crush	75.00	150.00

2009 Jakks Pacific WWE Classic Superstars 3-Packs Series 11

NNO	LOD 2000 w/Sunny	75.00	150.00
NNO	Nasty Boys w/Jimmy Hart	30.00	60.00

2009 Jakks Pacific WWE Classic Superstars 3-Packs Series 12

NNO	Powers of Pain w/Mr. Fuji
NNO	Tito Santana/HBK w/Sherri

1999 Jakks Pacific WWF Deadly Games

NNO	Droz	6.00	12.00
NNO	HHH	6.00	12.00
NNO	Stone Cold Steve Austin	7.50	15.00

2005 Jakks Pacific WWE Deluxe Aggression Series 1

NNO	Batista	20.00	40.00
NNO	Kurt Angle	12.50	25.00
NNO	John Cena	30.00	60.00
NNO	Randy Orton	15.00	30.00
NNO	Rey Mysterio	20.00	40.00
NNO	Triple H	15.00	30.00

2006 Jakks Pacific WWE Deluxe Aggression Series 2

NNO	Booker T	10.00	20.00
NNO	Carlito Cool	10.00	20.00
NNO	Edge	10.00	20.00
NNO	Kane	15.00	30.00
NNO	Rey Mysterio	15.00	30.00
NNO	Undertaker	25.00	50.00

2006 Jakks Pacific WWE Deluxe Aggression Series 3

NNO	Batista	12.50	25.00
NNO	Chris Benoit	15.00	30.00
NNO	John Cena		
NNO	Kurt Angle	12.50	25.00
NNO	Lashley	7.50	15.00
NNO	Shawn Michaels		

2006 Jakks Pacific WWE Deluxe Aggression Series 4

NNO	Boogeyman	12.50	25.00
NNO	Chris Masters	10.00	20.00
NNO	JBL	7.50	15.00
NNO	Mr. Kennedy		
NNO	Randy Orton	10.00	20.00
NNO	Rob Conway	7.50	15.00
NNO	Shelton Benjamin		

2006 Jakks Pacific WWE Deluxe Aggression Series 5

NNO	Batista	10.00	20.00
NNO	Big Show	15.00	30.00
NNO	John Cena	20.00	40.00
NNO	Matt Hardy	10.00	20.00
NNO	Rob Van Dam	10.00	20.00
NNO	Triple H.		

2007 Jakks Pacific WWE Deluxe Aggression Series 6

NNO	Booker T
NNO	Edge
NNO	Finlay
NNO	John Cena
NNO	Kenny
NNO	Rob Van Dam

2007 Jakks Pacific WWE Deluxe Aggression Series 7

NNO	Carlito
NNO	Chris Benoit
NNO	Mr. Kennedy
NNO	Jeff Hardy
NNO	Sabu
NNO	Rey Mysterio

2007 Jakks Pacific WWE Deluxe Aggression Series 8

NNO	Bobby Lashley
NNO	CM Punk
NNO	Sandman
NNO	Gregory Helms
NNO	Undertaker
NNO	Johnny Nitro

2007 Jakks Pacific WWE Deluxe Aggression Series 8 (loose)

NNO	Bobby Lashley
NNO	CM Punk
NNO	Sandman
NNO	Gregory Helms
NNO	Undertaker
NNO	Johnny Nitro

2007 Jakks Pacific WWE Deluxe Aggression Series 9

NNO	Mr. McMahon
NNO	Kenny Dykstra
NNO	Kevin Thorn
NNO	John Cena
NNO	Jimmy Wang Yang
NNO	Tommy Dreamer

2007 Jakks Pacific WWE Deluxe Aggression Series 10

NNO	Batista
NNO	Daivari
NNO	JBL
NNO	Matt Hardy
NNO	Randy Orton
NNO	Shawn Michaels

2007 Jakks Pacific WWE Deluxe Aggression Series 11

NNO	Chavo Guerrero
NNO	Elijah Burke
NNO	John Cena
NNO	MVP
NNO	Snitsky
NNO	William Regal

2007 Jakks Pacific WWE Deluxe Aggression Series 12

NNO	Batista
NNO	Boogeyman

NNO	CM Punk
NNO	Paul London
NNO	Shawn Michaels
NNO	Umaga

2008 Jakks Pacific WWE Deluxe Aggression Series 13

NNO	Cody Rhodes	12.50	25.00
NNO	John Cena	12.50	25.00
NNO	Miz	10.00	20.00
NNO	Rey Mysterio	12.50	25.00
NNO	Stone Cold Steve Austin	15.00	30.00
NNO	Triple H	17.50	35.00

2008 Jakks Pacific WWE Deluxe Aggression Series 14

NNO	John Morrison	20.00	40.00
NNO	Armando Estrada	10.00	20.00
NNO	Brian Kendrick	10.00	20.00
NNO	MVP	10.00	20.00
NNO	Randy Orton	12.50	25.00
NNO	Undertaker	20.00	40.00

2008 Jakks Pacific WWE Deluxe Aggression Series 15

NNO	Chris Jericho		
NNO	Finlay		
NNO	Matt Striker	15.00	30.00
NNO	Mr. Kennedy		
NNO	Tazz		
NNO	Undertaker		

2008 Jakks Pacific WWE Deluxe Aggression Series 16

NNO	Batista		
NNO	Edge	15.00	30.00
NNO	JBL	10.00	20.00
NNO	Nunzio		
NNO	Randy Orton		
NNO	Shelton Benjamin		

2008 Jakks Pacific WWE Deluxe Aggression Series 17

NNO	Curt Hawkins		
NNO	DH Smith	12.50	25.00
NNO	Kofi Kingston	15.00	30.00
NNO	Paul Burchill	10.00	20.00
NNO	Santino Marella	10.00	20.00
NNO	Zack Ryder		

2008 Jakks Pacific WWE Deluxe Aggression Series 18

NNO	Chris Jericho	15.00	30.00
NNO	Festus	10.00	20.00
NNO	Hardcore Holly	10.00	20.00
NNO	Jesse	10.00	20.00
NNO	John Morrison	10.00	20.00
NNO	The Miz		

2009 Jakks Pacific WWE Deluxe Aggression Series 19

NNO	Chris Jericho		
NNO	John Cena	15.00	30.00
NNO	JTG	10.00	20.00
NNO	Matt Hardy	15.00	30.00
NNO	Shad	10.00	20.00
NNO	Ted DiBiase	12.50	25.00

2009 Jakks Pacific WWE Deluxe Aggression Series 20

NNO	Big Show	10.00	20.00
NNO	Evan Bourne		
NNO	Shawn Michaels		
NNO	Stone Cold Steve Austin		
NNO	R-Truth	10.00	20.00
NNO	Rey Mysterio	17.50	35.00

2009 Jakks Pacific WWE Deluxe Aggression Series 21

NNO	Edge	12.50	25.00
NNO	Goldust		
NNO	Jeff Hardy	25.00	50.00
NNO	John Cena	12.50	25.00
NNO	Rey Mysterio	20.00	40.00
NNO	Vladimir Kozlov	10.00	20.00

2009 Jakks Pacific WWE Deluxe Aggression Series 22

NNO	Batista		
NNO	Christian	25.00	50.00
NNO	CM Punk	30.00	60.00
NNO	Jack Swagger	12.50	25.00
NNO	Randy Orton		
NNO	Triple H		

2009 Jakks Pacific WWE Deluxe Aggression Series 23

NNO	Batista		
NNO	Big Show	10.00	20.00
NNO	John Cena	10.00	20.00
NNO	Randy Orton		
NNO	Rey Mysterio		
NNO	Triple H	15.00	30.00

2009 Jakks Pacific WWE Deluxe Aggression Series 24

NNO	Kofi Kingston		
NNO	Matt Hardy		
NNO	MVP		
NNO	Rey Mysterio	15.00	30.00

2007 Jakks Pacific WWE Deluxe Aggression 2-Packs

NNO	Edge/Batista		
NNO	Undertaker/Kane		
NNO	Shawn Michaels/Triple H		

2006 Jakks Pacific WWE Deluxe Aggression 3-Packs Series 1

NNO	Triple H/John Cena/Edge	15.00	30.00
NNO	Rey Mysterio/Randy Orton/Kurt Angle	25.00	50.00

2007 Jakks Pacific WWE Deluxe Aggression 3-Packs Series 2

NNO	DX & The Big Show		
NNO	Rey Mysterio		
	Lashley/Batista		

2007 Jakks Pacific WWE Deluxe Aggression 3-Packs Series 3

NNO	Lashley/Sabu/RVD		
NNO	Randy Orton/Edge/Jeff Hardy		

2008 Jakks Pacific WWE Deluxe Aggression 3-Packs Series 4

NNO	Shawn Michaels/John Cena/Edge		
NNO	Mr. Kennedy/Undertaker/Fit Finlay	20.00	40.00

2008 Jakks Pacific WWE Deluxe Aggression 3-Packs Series 5

NNO	Umaga/Triple H/Randy Orton	25.00	50.00
NNO	Rey Mysterio/Undertaker/Fit Finlay	25.00	50.00

2009 Jakks Pacific WWE Deluxe Aggression 3-Packs Series 6

NNO	Chris Jericho/Kane/Shawn Michaels		
NNO	CM Punk/Edge/Chavo Guerrero		

2006 Jakks Pacific WWE Deluxe Classic Superstars Series 1

NNO	Hulk Hogan	25.00	50.00
NNO	Ric Flair	25.00	50.00
NNO	Rowdy Roddy Piper (black tape)	15.00	30.00
NNO	Rowdy Roddy Piper (gold tape)		
NNO	Stone Cold Steve Austin	15.00	30.00
NNO	The Rock	20.00	40.00

2007 Jakks Pacific WWE Deluxe Classic Superstars Series 2

NNO	Bret Hart		
NNO	British Bulldog		
NNO	Kevin Nash		
NNO	Mr. Perfect		
NNO	Shawn Michaels		

2007 Jakks Pacific WWE Deluxe Classic Superstars Series 3

NNO	Jake The Snake Roberts		
NNO	Lex Luger		
NNO	Ravishing Rick Rude		
NNO	Scott Hall		
NNO	Undertaker		

2007 Jakks Pacific WWE Deluxe Classic Superstars Series 4

NNO	Brutus Beefcake		
NNO	Honky Tonk Man		
NNO	Iron Sheik		
NNO	Million Dollar Man Ted DiBiase		
NNO	Shawn Michaels		

2008 Jakks Pacific WWE Deluxe Classic Superstars Series 5

NNO	Buff Bagwell	12.50	25.00
NNO	Diamond Dallas Page		
NNO	Jim The Anvil Neidhart	20.00	40.00
NNO	Jimmy Superfly Snuka	12.50	25.00

2008 Jakks Pacific WWE Deluxe Classic Superstars Series 6

NNO	Eddie Guerrero	25.00	50.00
NNO	Hillbilly Jim	20.00	40.00
NNO	Kane	30.00	60.00
NNO	Sgt. Slaughter	17.50	35.00
NNO	Triple H	12.50	25.00

2009 Jakks Pacific WWE Deluxe Classic Superstars Series 7

NNO	Bret Hart	20.00	40.00
NNO	Shawn Michaels	15.00	30.00
NNO	The Rock	15.00	30.00
NNO	Tito Santana	12.50	25.00
NNO	Undertaker	20.00	40.00

2009 Jakks Pacific WWE Deluxe Classic Superstars Series 8

NNO	Big John Studd	30.00	40.00
NNO	British Bulldog	12.50	25.00
NNO	Chainsaw Charlie	10.00	20.00
NNO	Dynamite Kid	20.00	40.00
NNO	Stone Cold Steve Austin	25.00	50.00

2000 Jakks Pacific WWF Double Slam Series 1

NNO	Edge/Christian	17.50	35.00
NNO	Kane/X-Pac	10.00	20.00
NNO	Stone Cold Steve Austin	15.00	30.00
	Shane McMahon		
NNO	Vince McMahon/Undertaker	10.00	20.00

2000 Jakks Pacific WWF Double Slam Series 2

NNO	Big Show	12.50	25.00
	Stone Cold Steve Austin		
NNO	HHH/X-Pac		
NNO	The Rock/Billy Gunn	10.00	20.00
NNO	Undertaker/Kane		

2000 Jakks Pacific WWF Double Slam Series 3

NNO	Big Show/Test	7.50	15.00
NNO	Billy Gunn/Hardcore Holly	7.50	15.00
NNO	Debra/Stone Cold Steve Austin	15.00	30.00
NNO	Mankind/Undertaker	15.00	30.00

2000 Jakks Pacific WWF Double Slam Series 4

NNO	Chyna/Chris Jericho	17.50	35.00
NNO	Matt Hardy/Jeff Hardy	17.50	35.00
NNO	Triple H/Billy Gunn	10.00	20.00

2000 Jakks Pacific WWF Double Slam Series 5

NNO	Bradshaw/Faarooq	10.00	20.00
NNO	Edge/Christian	12.50	25.00
NNO	Triple H/The Rock		

1998 Jakks Pacific WWF DTA Tour Series 1

NNO	8-Ball	6.00	12.00
NNO	Chainz	7.50	15.00
NNO	Dude Love	7.50	15.00
NNO	Faarooq	6.00	12.00
NNO	HHH	6.00	12.00
NNO	Kane	12.50	25.00
NNO	Shawn Michaels	10.00	20.00
NNO	Vader	6.00	12.00

1999 Jakks Pacific WWF DTA Tour Series 2

NNO	Double J Jeff Jarrett	6.00	12.00
NNO	Al Snow	6.00	12.00
NNO	Blue Blazer	15.00	30.00
NNO	Edge	7.50	15.00
NNO	Steve Blackman	6.00	12.00
NNO	Undertaker	10.00	20.00

1999 Jakks Pacific WWF DTA Tour Series 3

NNO	Christian	5.00	10.00
NNO	Godfather	5.00	10.00
NNO	HHH	7.50	15.00
NNO	Ken Shamrock	7.50	15.00
NNO	Stone Cold Steve Austin	12.50	25.00
NNO	X-Pac	6.00	12.00

2004 Jakks Pacific WWE Exclusives

NNO Legion of Doom	150.00	300.00
(Ringside Collectibles Exclusive)		
NNO Roddy Piper/100* TFM	1000.00	2000.00
NNO Roddy Piper/1800* RSF	150.00	300.00
NNO Roddy Piper/3000* TFM	75.00	150.00
NNO Ultimate Warrior/100* NYC TF	1500.00	3000.00

2005 Jakks Pacific WWE Exclusives

NNO Hillbilly Jim/5000*	30.00	75.00
RTWM21 TOUR		
NNO Hulk Hogan vs. Shawn Michaels/3000* RSC	75.00	150.00
NNO Mankind vs. Terry Funk KM	25.00	50.00
NNO Sgt. Slaughter/100* TFM	500.00	1000.00
NNO Sgt. Slaughter/3000* TFM	30.00	60.00
NNO Superstar B. Graham/3000* TRU CAN		
NNO Superstar B.Graham		
Blue Jeans/14000* TRU		
NNO Superstar B. Graham		
Green Gear/7000* TRU		
NNO Superstar B. Graham		
Pink Suit/7000 TRU		
NNO Superstar B. Graham		
Red Suit/400* TRU Orland		
NNO Terry Funk/100* NYC TF		

2006 Jakks Pacific WWE Exclusives

NNO Bobby Heenan Weasel/100* NYC TF	300.00	500.00
NNO Bret Hart vs. Shawn Michaels RSF	125.00	250.00
NNO British Bulldog & William Regal	50.00	100.00
Best of British ARGO UK		
NNO Diesel & Shawn Michaels	60.00	120.00
2 Dudes with Attitudes RSC		
NNO Dusty Rhodes/3000* OL	50.00	100.00
NNO Hulk Hogan/Blue Trunks &	30.00	75.00
{White Boots WM CAN		
NNO Hulk Hogan/Blue Trunks &	25.00	60.00
{White Boots WM US		
NNO Hulk Hogan/Tye Dye &		
{Knee Brace WM US		
NNO Hulk Hogan/Tye Dye &	30.00	75.00
{No Knee Brace WM US		
NNO Hulk Hogan/Tye Dye WM CAN		
NNO Hulk Hogan 2-in-1 MANIA TIX	75.00	150.00
NNO Hulk Hogan vs.	60.00	120.00
{Andre the Giant ARGO/BL		
NNO Hulk Hogan/100* TFM	1500.00	3000.00
NNO Hulk Hogan/3000* TFM	60.00	120.00
NNO Jimmy Hart/100* NYC TF	600.00	1200.00
NNO Steve Austin WWE SZ	30.00	75.00
NNO Tazz/Towel Around Waist RSC		
NNO Tazz/Towel in Package RSC	60.00	120.00

2007 Jakks Pacific WWE Exclusives

NNO Bret Hart vs. Jeff Hardy OL	100.00	200.00
NNO Razor Ramon vs. HBK RSC	60.00	120.00
NNO Roddy Piper Deluxe/100* NYC TF	1000.00	2000.00
NNO Scott Hall & Kevin Nash	75.00	150.00
The Outsiders RSC		
NNO Steve Austin vs. Bret Hart RSF	150.00	300.00
NNO Ultimate Warrior Classic		
Superstars Marble Finish/20*		
NNO Ultimate Warrior Classic Superstars	2000.00	3500.00
One Warrior Nation/20*		
NNO Ultimate Warrior Classic		
Superstars Warrior America/5*		
NNO Ultimate Warrior Classic		

Superstars WCW 1998/20*		
NNO Ultimate Warrior Ring Giant	1800.00	3000.00
Warrior America/25*		
NNO Ultimate Warrior Unmatched Fury	4000.00	6000.00
Warrior America Gear/15*		

2008 Jakks Pacific WWE Exclusives

NNO Cactus Jack/3000* TFM	50.00	100.00
NNO D-Generation X RSC	75.00	150.00
NNO Eddie Guerrero vs. Rey Mysterio	400.00	750.00
{Halloween Havoc RSC		
NNO Eddie Guerrero/100* NYC TF	1000.00	2000.00
NNO Hardy Boys RSC		
NNO Hardy Boys WWE SZ		
NNO Hart Foundation PROFIG		
NNO Ric Flair/3000* WWE 24/7	30.00	75.00
NNO Stephanie & Triple H RSC	60.00	120.00
NNO Undertaker vs. Kane RSC	300.00	600.00
NNO Undertaker GITD/100* TFM	1000.00	2000.00
NNO Undertaker/3000* TFM	75.00	150.00

2009 Jakks Pacific WWE Exclusives

NNO Edge/3000* TFM	125.00	250.00
NNO Goldust Shattered RSC	125.00	250.00
NNO Kane vs. Vader OL	30.00	60.00
NNO Rey Mysterio/100* TFM	300.00	600.00
NNO Shawn Michaels/	125.00	250.00
Multi-Belts PROFIG		
NNO Shawn Michaels vs.	75.00	150.00
{Steve Austin WWE SZ		
NNO Shawn Michaels vs.	100.00	200.00
{Undertaker RSC		
NNO Sunny/100* TFM	300.00	500.00
NNO Sunny/3000* TFM	30.00	75.00
NNO Undertaker vs.	100.00	200.00
{Triple H WWE SZ		

2005 Jakks Pacific WWE Face Flippin' Fighters

NNO Batista	12.50	25.00
NNO Chris Benoit	10.00	20.00
NNO Eddie Guerrero	12.50	25.00
NNO John Cena	20.00	40.00
NNO Randy Orton	12.50	25.00
NNO Undertaker	20.00	40.00

2001 Jakks Pacific WWF Famous Scenes Series 1

NNO Jeff Hardy/Matt Hardy	15.00	30.00
NNO Mick Foley/Undertaker	20.00	50.00
NNO The Rock/Triple H	12.50	25.00

2001 Jakks Pacific WWF Famous Scenes Series 2

NNO Chris Benoit/Chris Jericho	12.50	25.00
NNO HHH/Cactus Jack	20.00	40.00
NNO Kurt Angle/Rikishi	15.00	30.00

2001 Jakks Pacific WWF Famous Scenes Series 3

NNO Bubba Ray Dudley/D-Von Dudley	15.00	30.00
NNO Stone Cold Steve Austin		
Vince McMahon		

2001 Jakks Pacific WWF Famous Scenes Series 4

NNO Lita/Test	15.00	30.00
NNO The Rock/Billy Gunn		
NNO Stone Cold Steve Austin	12.50	25.00
Undertaker		

1998 Jakks Pacific WWF Fantasy Warfare

NNO Stone Cold Steve Austin vs. Andre the Giant	12.50	25.00
NNO Undertaker vs. Mankind	15.00	30.00

2002 Jakks Pacific WWF Fatal 4-Way Series 1

NNO Bubba Ray Dudley	6.00	12.00
NNO Edge	10.00	20.00
NNO Jeff Hardy	15.00	30.00
NNO Lita	12.50	25.00

2002 Jakks Pacific WWF Fatal 4-Way Series 2

NNO Chris Jericho	20.00	40.00
NNO Christian	7.50	15.00
NNO Stone Cold Steve Austin	12.50	25.00
NNO Undertaker	20.00	40.00

2002 Jakks Pacific WWF Fatal 4-Way Series 3

NNO Bubba Ray Dudley	6.00	12.00
NNO Chris Jericho	10.00	20.00
NNO Christian	10.00	20.00
NNO Jeff Hardy	12.50	25.00

1999 Jakks Pacific WWF Federation Fighters

NNO Kane		
(two sleeves)		
NNO Stone Cold Steve Austin	15.00	30.00
NNO Steve Austin/Jumpsuit	20.00	40.00

1999 Jakks Pacific WWF Federation Fighters Series 2

NNO Big Show	15.00	30.00
NNO Rock	25.00	50.00
NNO Stone Cold Steve Austin	15.00	30.00
NNO Undertaker	20.00	40.00

2001 Jakks Pacific WWF-WWE Final Count Series 1

NNO Billy Gunn vs. Edge		
Downward Spiral		
NNO Billy Gunn vs. Edge		
Famous-er		
NNO Lita vs. Matt Hardy		
Litacanrana		
NNO Lita vs. Matt Hardy		
Twist of Fate		
NNO Undertaker vs. Steve Austin		
The Last Ride		
NNO Undertaker vs. Steve Austin		
Stone Cold Stunner		

2002 Jakks Pacific WWF-WWE Final Count Series 2

NNO Kane vs. Steve Austin		
NNO Kurt Angle vs. Triple H	12.50	25.00
NNO The Rock vs. Chris Jericho	20.00	40.00

2002 Jakks Pacific WWF-WWE Final Count Series 3

NNO Billy Gunn/Jeff Hardy	12.50	25.00
NNO Chris Jericho/Steve Austin		
NNO Rikishi/Bubba Ray Dudley		

2002 Jakks Pacific WWF-WWE Final Count Series 4

NNO Albert/Scotty Too Hotty		
NNO The Rock/Kurt Angle	15.00	30.00
NNO Test/Christian		

2002 Jakks Pacific WWF-WWE Final Count Series 5

NNO Bradshaw/Undertaker
NNO Jeff Hardy/Trish Stratus — 12.50 — 25.00
NNO Rob Van Dam — 25.00 — 50.00
Eddie Guerrero

2002 Jakks Pacific WWF-WWE Final Count Series 6

NNO Billy vs. Chuck — 10.00 — 20.00
Famous-er
NNO Billy vs. Chuck — 10.00 — 20.00
Jungle Kick
NNO C.Jericho vs. C.Benoit — 15.00 — 30.00
Crippler Crossface
NNO C.Jericho vs. C.Benoit — 15.00 — 30.00
Walls of Jericho
NNO Hulk Hogan vs. HHH — 12.50 — 25.00
Pedigree
NNO Hulk Hogan vs. HHH — 12.50 — 25.00
Running Leg Drop

2002 Jakks Pacific WWF-WWE Final Count Series 7

NNO Batista
NNO Billy Kidman
NNO Hurricane

2001 Jakks Pacific WWF Finishing Moves Series 1

NNO Chris Jericho/Kurt Angle
NNO The Hardy Boyz
NNO Triple H/The Rock

2001 Jakks Pacific WWF Finishing Moves Series 2

NNO Chris Jericho/The Rock
NNO Kane/Undertaker
NNO Rikishi/Triple H

2001 Jakks Pacific WWF Finishing Moves Series 3

NNO Chris Benoit/Chris Jericho
NNO Eddie Guerrero/Billy Gunn
NNO The Hardy Boyz

2001 Jakks Pacific WWF Finishing Moves Series 4

NNO Kane/Edge
NNO Lita/Buh Buh Dudley
NNO The Rock/Stone Cold Steve Austin

2002 Jakks Pacific WWE Flex 'Ems Series 1

NNO Chris Jericho — 7.50 — 15.00
NNO Edge — 7.50 — 15.00
NNO Hulk Hogan — 10.00 — 20.00
NNO Kurt Angle — 7.50 — 15.00
NNO The Rock — 10.00 — 20.00
NNO Triple H — 7.50 — 15.00

2002 Jakks Pacific WWE Flex 'Ems Series 2

NNO Batista — 10.00 — 20.00
NNO Booker T — 7.50 — 15.00
NNO Brock Lesnar — 6.00 — 12.00
NNO Chris Benoit — 6.00 — 12.00
NNO Hurricane — 7.50 — 15.00
NNO Rob Van Dam — 7.50 — 15.00

2002 Jakks Pacific WWE Flex 'Ems Series 3

NNO Batista — 7.50 — 15.00
NNO Chris Benoit — 7.50 — 15.00

NNO Chris Jericho — 7.50 — 15.00
NNO Hurricane — 7.50 — 15.00
NNO Rob Van Dam — 7.50 — 15.00
NNO The Rock — 10.00 — 20.00

2003 Jakks Pacific WWE Flex 'Ems Series 4

NNO Booker T
NNO Kane
NNO Kurt Angle
NNO Rey Mysterio
NNO Triple H
NNO Undertaker

2003 Jakks Pacific WWE Flex 'Ems Series 5

NNO Booker T
NNO Brock Lesnar
NNO Chris Benoit
NNO Chris Jericho
NNO Rey Mysterio
NNO Rob Van Dam

2003 Jakks Pacific WWE Flex 'Ems Series 8

NNO Chris Jericho
NNO Eddie Guerrero
NNO Kurt Angle
NNO Matt Hardy
NNO Randy Orton
NNO Rey Mysterio

2003 Jakks Pacific WWE Flex 'Ems Series 9

NNO Batista
NNO Chris Benoit
NNO Eddie Guerrero
NNO Randy Orton
NNO Rey Mysterio
NNO Rob Van Dam

2003 Jakks Pacific WWE Flex 'Ems Series 10

NNO Batista
NNO Booker T
NNO Chris Benoit
NNO Chris Jericho
NNO Eddie Guerrero
NNO Rey Mysterio

2003 Jakks Pacific WWE Flex 'Ems Series 11

NNO Batista
NNO Kurt Angle
NNO Randy Orton
NNO Rey Mysterio
NNO Triple H
NNO Undertaker

2003 Jakks Pacific WWE Flex 'Ems Series 12

NNO Kane
NNO Rey Mysterio
NNO Shawn Michaels
NNO Triple H

2003 Jakks Pacific WWE Flex 'Ems Series 13

NNO Batista
NNO Chris Benoit
NNO Randy Orton
NNO Rob Van Dam

2003 Jakks Pacific WWE Flex 'Ems Series 14

NNO Rey Mysterio
NNO Shawn Michaels

NNO Chris Jericho — 7.50 — 15.00
NNO Hurricane — 7.50 — 15.00
NNO Rob Van Dam — 7.50 — 15.00
NNO The Rock — 10.00 — 20.00

2003 Jakks Pacific WWE Flex 'Ems Series 4

NNO Booker T
NNO Kane
NNO Kurt Angle
NNO Rey Mysterio
NNO Triple H
NNO Undertaker

NNO Triple H
NNO Undertaker

1998 Jakks Pacific WWF Fully Loaded Series 1

NNO Al Snow — 6.00 — 12.00
NNO B.A. Billy Gunn — 7.50 — 15.00
NNO HHH — 6.00 — 12.00
NNO Kane — 7.50 — 15.00
NNO Road Dogg — 5.00 — 10.00
NNO The Rock — 10.00 — 20.00

1999 Jakks Pacific WWF Fully Loaded Series 2

NNO Road Dogg Jesse James — 6.00 — 12.00
NNO The Rock — 10.00 — 20.00
NNO Shane McMahon — 12.50 — 25.00
NNO Stone Cold Steve Austin — 10.00 — 20.00
NNO Test
NNO X-Pac — 7.50 — 15.00

2003 Jakks Pacific WWE Grudge Brawlers

NNO Christian
NNO Chris Jericho
NNO Kurt Angle
NNO Jeff Hardy — 30.00 — 60.00
NNO Triple H
NNO Undertaker

1997 Jakks Pacific WWF Grudge Match

NNO Bret Hitman Hart vs. Stone Cold Steve Austin — 10.00 — 20.00
NNO Goldust vs. Savio Vega — 6.00 — 12.00
NNO Shawn Michaels vs. Owen Hart — 7.50 — 15.00
NNO Sycho Sid vs. Vader — 10.00 — 20.00
NNO The Undertaker vs. Mankind — 15.00 — 30.00
NNO Yokozuna vs. Ahmed Johnson — 6.00 — 12.00

1998 Jakks Pacific WWF Grudge Match Series 1

NNO HHH vs. Owen Hart — 7.50 — 15.00
NNO Ken Shamrock vs. Dan Severn — 7.50 — 15.00
NNO Luna vs. Sable — 20.00 — 40.00
NNO Marvelous Marc Mero vs. Lethal Weapon Steve Blackman
NNO Stone Cold Steve Austin vs. Shawn Michaels — 10.00 — 20.00
NNO Undertaker vs. Kane — 10.00 — 20.00

1998 Jakks Pacific WWF Grudge Match Series 2

NNO HHH vs. Shawn Michaels — 7.50 — 15.00
NNO Road Dogg Jesse James vs. Al Snow
NNO Stone Cold Steve Austin vs. Vince McMahon — 12.50 — 25.00

1998 Jakks Pacific WWF Grudge Match Series 3

NNO Stone Cold Steve Austin vs. The Rock — 7.50 — 15.00
NNO X-Pac vs. Double J Jeff Jarrett — 10.00 — 20.00

2005 Jakks Pacific WWE Havoc Unleashed Series 1

NNO Booker T — 10.00 — 20.00
NNO Chris Benoit — 7.50 — 15.00
NNO Edge — 7.50 — 15.00
NNO Kurt Angle — 12.50 — 25.00
NNO Scotty 2 Hotty — 10.00 — 20.00
NNO Triple H — 10.00 — 20.00

2006 Jakks Pacific WWE Havoc Unleashed Series 2

NNO Batista — 10.00 — 20.00
NNO JBL — 7.50 — 15.00
NNO RVD — 12.50 — 25.00
NNO Shawn Michaels — 12.50 — 25.00

2007 Jakks Pacific WWE Havoc Unleashed Series 3

NNO Bobby Lashley
NNO Edge
NNO HHH
NNO John Cena
NNO Kane
NNO Matt Hardy

2009 Jakks Pacific WWE Havoc Unleashed Series 4

NNO Batista	10.00	20.00
NNO HHH	6.00	12.00
NNO JBL	7.50	15.00
NNO Matt Hardy	7.50	15.00
NNO Undertaker	10.00	20.00

1997 Jakks Pacific WWF Heroes of Wrestling

NNO Sycho Sid	10.00	20.00
NNO Undertaker	12.50	25.00

2000 Jakks Pacific WWF House of Pain

NNO HHH	7.50	15.00
NNO Rock	12.50	25.00
NNO Stone Cold Steve Austin	12.50	25.00
NNO Tori	7.50	15.00
NNO Undertaker	12.50	25.00
NNO X-Pac	6.00	12.00

2000 Jakks Pacific WWF House of Pain (loose)

NNO HHH
NNO The Rock
NNO Stone Cold Steve Austin
NNO Tori
NNO Undertaker
NNO X-Pac

1998 Jakks Pacific WWF Jakk'd Up

NNO Sable
NNO Stone Cold Steve Austin
NNO Kane
NNO Undertaker

1998 Jakks Pacific WWF Jakk'd Up (loose)

NNO Sable
NNO Stone Cold Steve Austin
NNO Kane
NNO Undertaker

1997 Jakks Pacific WWF Boxed Sets

NNO Championship Title Series
Undertaker/Rocky/Bulldog/Owen
NNO King of the Iron Rungs
Hart/Austin/Ref/Johnson
NNO Nation of Domination
Mason/Faarooq/Vega/Crush
NNO RAW Is War 1
Sunny/Bret Hart/Sid/Vince
NNO Survivor Series 1996
Bearer/Mankind/Undertaker/Executioner
NNO Triple Threat
Johnson/Mero/Yokozuna

1998 Jakks Pacific WWF Boxed Sets

NNO Bad to the Bonz Steve Austin TRU
NNO Badd Blood
Bearer/Undertaker/Kane/Austin WM CAN
NNO DX
HHH/Chyna/Billy/Road Dogg MEI
NNO Go Mental
HHH/Dude Love/Austin/Undertaker SAM
NNO Legends of the Past and Present
Andre/Undertaker/Austin WM
NNO Mankind Grapple KM
NNO No Holds Barred
Kane/Austin/Cactus Jack KB
NNO Off the Mat
Austin/Rock/Billy Gunn/Road Dogg TRU
NNO RAW Is War 2
Austin/Undertaker/Rock/Mankind)
NNO Rock Bottom KM
NNO Shotgun Saturday Night
Austin/Kane/HBK/The Rock
NNO Slammers
Mankind/HBK/Undertaker/Austin
NNO Stone Cold Steve Austin Breakaway Table KM
NNO Stone Cold Steve Austin Grapple KM
NNO Stone Cold Steve Austin Special Collection HILLS
NNO Survivor Series
Undertaker/Kane/Austin/Rock
NNO Undertaker Special Collection HILLS
NNO WrestleMania XV Fully Loaded
Undertaker/Austin/Road Dogg/Billy Gunn
NNO WrestleMania XV Judgment Day
Undertaker/Austin/Vince

1999 Jakks Pacific WWF Boxed Sets

NNO Buried Alive	30.00	75.00
HHH/Vince/Undertaker/Austin		
NNO Championship Title Series	20.00	40.00
Austin/X-Pac/Kane/The Rock TRU		
NNO Hardcore Champions	20.00	40.00
Big Boss Man/Mankind/Al Snow/Hardcore Holly		
NNO Mick Foley's Triple Threat	25.00	50.00
Mankind/Dude Love/Cactus Jack KB		
NNO No Chance	20.00	40.00
Vince/Austin/Paul Wight		
NNO Over the Edge	15.00	30.00
Austin/Rock/HHH/Kane		
NNO Perfect 10		
Austin/Rock/Kane/Undertaker/Mankind/Big Show/X-Pac/HHH/Road Dogg/Billy Gunn TRU		
NNO SummerSlam '99 Camo Carnage	17.50	35.00
HHH/Billy Gunn/Ausin		
NNO SummerSlam Expect No Mercy		
Austin/Rock/Vince/Undertaker		
NNO SummerSlam '99 Last Man Standing	20.00	40.00
Austin/Rock/Vince/Shane		
NNO Survivor Series Mayhem	17.50	35.00
HHH/Rock/Austin		
NNO WWF Attitude	20.00	40.00
HBK/Animal/Austin/Hawk KM		

2001 Jakks Pacific WWF Boxed Sets

NNO 2 Extreme	30.00	75.00
Lita & The Hardys		
NNO Back in the Ring/Undertaker	25.00	50.00
Stone Cold Steve Austin/Mick Foley KM		
NNO Brothers of Destruction		
Austin/Undertaker/Kane TRU		
NNO Cold Day in Dudleyville	30.00	60.00
Rock/D-Von/Buh Buh Ray TRU		
NNO Get in the Groove	50.00	100.00
(Scottie/Rikishi/Sexay MEI		
NNO Insurrextion		
HHH/Austin/Bubba/Edge/Kane/Rock/Test/Jeff Hardy/Y2J/Regal UK		
NNO KOTR Lead Me to My Throne		
D-Von/Edge/Austin/Angle/Hardys		
NNO Picture Perfect	20.00	40.00
Edge/Christian KM		
NNO Renegades		
Raven/Austin/Shane McMahon KM		
NNO Team Extreme	20.00	40.00
Matt & Jeff Hardy/Lita		
NNO Triple Threat	12.50	25.00
Y2J/Rock/HHH		

2002 Jakks Pacific WWE Boxed Sets

NNO nWo Federation Poison	25.00	50.00
Nash/X-Pac/Hall		
NNO RAW Draft		
Bubba Ray/Undertaker/Flair/Austin		
NNO Rock Solid	20.00	40.00
Rock/Scorpion King		
NNO SmackDown Draft		
Y2J/Hogan/Vince/Rock		

2004 Jakks Pacific WWE Employee Gift Exclusives

NNO Ric Flair/25*
NNO Rowdy Roddy Piper/20*
NNO Sgt. Slaughter/20*

2002 Jakks Pacific WWF-WWE King of the Ring Series 1

NNO D-Von Dudley	7.50	15.00
NNO Edge	20.00	40.00
NNO Jeff Hardy	12.50	25.00
NNO Kurt Angle	10.00	20.00
NNO Matt Hardy	7.50	15.00
NNO Stone Cold Steve Austin		

2002 Jakks Pacific WWF-WWE King of the Ring Series 2

NNO Brock Lesnar	15.00	30.00
NNO Chris Jericho	12.50	25.00
NNO Hardcore Holly	12.50	25.00
NNO Rob Van Dam	15.00	30.00
NNO Test	10.00	20.00
NNO X-Pac	10.00	20.00

1998 Jakks Pacific WWF Legends

NNO Andre the Giant	20.00	40.00
NNO Captain Lou Albano	7.50	15.00
NNO Classy Freddie Blassie	7.50	15.00
NNO Jimmy Superfly Snuka	10.00	20.00

1999 Jakks Pacific WWF Live Wire Series 1

NNO Chyna	10.00	20.00
NNO Ken Shamrock	7.50	15.00
NNO Mankind	10.00	20.00
NNO Stone Cold Steve Austin	12.50	25.00
NNO Undertaker	15.00	30.00
NNO Vader	7.50	15.00

1999 Jakks Pacific WWF Live Wire Series 2

NNO Mark Henry	7.50	15.00
NNO Marvelous Marc Mero	6.00	12.00
NNO Rock	10.00	20.00
NNO Shawn Michaels	7.50	15.00
NNO Val Venis	6.00	12.00
NNO X-Pac	7.50	15.00

2003 Jakks Pacific WWE Main Event

NNO	Hulk Hogan	12.50	25.00
NNO	Shawn Michaels		
NNO	Spike Dudley	15.00	30.00
NNO	Stacy Keibler	10.00	20.00
NNO	Tazz		
NNO	Torrie Wilson	10.00	20.00
NNO	Triple H		

1997 Jakks Pacific WWF Managers Series 1

NNO	Bob Backlund/Sultan	12.50	25.00
NNO	Clarence Mason/Crush	10.00	20.00
NNO	Paul Bearer/Mankind	12.50	25.00
NNO	Sable/Marc Mero	10.00	20.00

2002 Jakks Pacific WWE Match Champs

NNO	Booker T	10.00	20.00
NNO	Jeff Hardy	10.00	20.00
NNO	Ric Flair	7.50	15.00
NNO	Rob Van Dam	7.50	15.00
NNO	The Rock	10.00	20.00
NNO	Triple H	7.50	15.00

2002 Jakks Pacific WWF Match Enders

NNO	Billy Gunn/Famous-er		
NNO	Edge/Downward Spiral		
NNO	Lita/Litacanrana		
NNO	Matt Hardy/Twist of Fate		
NNO	Triple H/Pedigree		
NNO	Undertaker/Last Ride	12.50	25.00

2007 Jakks Pacific WWE Maximum Aggression Series 1

NNO	Bobby Lashley
NNO	Carlito
NNO	CM Punk
NNO	Rey Mysterio
NNO	Triple H

2008 Jakks Pacific WWE Maximum Aggression Series 2

NNO	Carlito	20.00	40.00
NNO	Chris Jericho		
NNO	Elijah Burke	25.00	50.00
NNO	Undertaker	20.00	40.00

2008 Jakks Pacific WWE Maximum Aggression Series 3

NNO	Edge	20.00	40.00
NNO	John Cena	15.00	30.00
NNO	John Morrison		
NNO	Randy Orton	15.00	30.00

2008 Jakks Pacific WWE Maximum Aggression Series 4

NNO	Matt Hardy
NNO	Kane
NNO	Mr. Kennedy
NNO	Shelton Benjamin

2009 Jakks Pacific WWE Maximum Aggression Series 5

NNO	CM Punk	15.00	30.00
NNO	John Cena	20.00	40.00
NNO	Matt Hardy		
NNO	Triple H	15.00	30.00

2009 Jakks Pacific WWE Maximum Aggression Series 6

NNO	Rey Mysterio	25.00	50.00
NNO	Shawn Michaels		
NNO	Triple H	15.00	30.00
NNO	Undertaker	20.00	40.00

1999 Jakks Pacific WWF Maximum Sweat Series 1

NNO	Hunter Hearst-Helmsley	6.00	12.00
NNO	Kane/Mask Off	10.00	20.00
NNO	Kane/Mask On	12.50	25.00
NNO	Rock The People's Champion	15.00	30.00
NNO	Shawn Michaels	12.50	25.00
NNO	Stone Cold Steve Austin	10.00	20.00
NNO	Undertaker	15.00	30.00

1999 Jakks Pacific WWF Maximum Sweat Series 2

NNO	B.A. Billy Gunn	10.00	20.00
NNO	Edge	7.50	15.00
NNO	Ken Shamrock	7.50	15.00
NNO	Road Dogg	10.00	20.00
NNO	Stone Cold Steve Austin	12.50	25.00
NNO	Undertaker	10.00	20.00

1999 Jakks Pacific WWF Maximum Sweat Series 3

NNO	Big Show	10.00	20.00
NNO	Gangrel/Blue Shirt		
NNO	Gangrel/Lt. Blue Shirt	12.50	25.00
NNO	Mankind	7.50	15.00
NNO	The Rock	10.00	20.00
NNO	Stone Cold Steve Austin	10.00	20.00

1999 Jakks Pacific WWF Maximum Sweat Series 4

NNO	Billy Gunn	7.50	15.00
NNO	Droz	7.50	15.00
NNO	Kane	7.50	15.00
NNO	Road Dogg	7.50	15.00
NNO	Stone Cold Steve Austin	10.00	20.00
NNO	Undertaker		

1999 Jakks Pacific WWF Maximum Sweat Special Series

NNO	B.A. Billy Gunn
NNO	Edge
NNO	Ken Shamrock
NNO	Road Dogg

2008 Jakks Pacific WWE Micro Aggression 10-Packs

NNO	Batista/Jeff Hardy/HBK/Kennedy/Cena Mysterio/Undertaker/Carlito/HHH/Kane
NNO	John Cena/Kennedy/HBK/CM Punk/Batista Kane/HHH/Carlito/Undertaker/Mysterio
NNO	John Cena/Matt Hardy/Orton/MVP/Primo Kane/HHH/Carlito/Undertaker/Mysterio

2006 Jakks Pacific WWE Micro Aggression Playset

NNO	Crash and Bash Playset	30.00	75.00
	Chris Benoit/Triple H/Kane/Rey Mysterio		

2007 Jakks Pacific WWE Micro Aggression Playset

NNO	Crash and Bash Arena
	w/John Cena/HBK/Lashley/Edge

2008 Jakks Pacific WWE Micro Aggression Playsets

NNO	Crash and Bash Cell	60.00	120.00
	w/Cena/Undertaker/HBK/CM Punk		
NNO	Crash and Bash El. Chamber	30.00	75.00
	w/Cena/Rey Mysterio/Umaga/Kane		

2006 Jakks Pacific WWE Micro Aggression Series 1

NNO	Kane/Undertaker/Chris Benoit	15.00	30.00
NNO	Rey Mysterio/John Cena/Rob Van Dam	12.50	25.00
NNO	Triple H/Shawn Michaels/John Cena	12.50	25.00

2007 Jakks Pacific WWE Micro Aggression Series 2

NNO	Edge/Cena/RVD
NNO	Rey Mysterio/Batista/Hogan
NNO	Triple H/HBK/Orton

2007 Jakks Pacific WWE Micro Aggression Series 3

NNO	Jeff Hardy/Cena/Carlito
NNO	Jimmy Wang Yang/Undertaker/ Kennedy
NNO	Shawn Michaels/CM Punk/ Tommy Dreamer

2007 Jakks Pacific WWE Micro Aggression Series 4

NNO	Batista/Finlay/Rey Mysterio
NNO	CM Punk/Lashley/ Hardcore Holly
NNO	Edge/Cena/Orton

2008 Jakks Pacific WWE Micro Aggression Series 5

NNO	CM Punk/Lashley/T.Dreamer
NNO	Jeff Hardy/Cena/HBK
NNO	Undertaker/Kennedy/Batista

2008 Jakks Pacific WWE Micro Aggression Series 6

NNO	Carlito/King Booker/HHH
NNO	Chris Masters/MVP/Edge
NNO	Hardcore Holly/Burke/ Boogeyman

2008 Jakks Pacific WWE Micro Aggression Series 7

NNO	John Cena/Umaga/Kennedy
NNO	John Morrison/CM Punk/ Tommy Dreamer
NNO	Matt Hardy/Batista/ Rey Mysterio

2008 Jakks Pacific WWE Micro Aggression Series 8

NNO	Edge/Kane/Finlay
NNO	Miz/Boogeyman/Burke
NNO	Triple H/Jeff Hardy/Lashley

2008 Jakks Pacific WWE Micro Aggression Series 9

NNO CM Punk/Finlay/Morrison
NNO Rey Mysterio/MVP/Undertaker
NNO Shawn Michaels/Cena/Kennedy

2008 Jakks Pacific WWE Micro Aggression Series 10

NNO Chris Jericho/John Cena/JBL
NNO CM Punk/Elijah Burke/Domino
NNO Great Khali/Undertaker/Deuce

2008 Jakks Pacific WWE Micro Aggression Series 11

NNO Chavo/Big Daddy V/Benjamin
NNO Edge/Ric Flair/Kane
NNO Triple H/Cody Rhodes/Umaga

2008 Jakks Pacific WWE Micro Aggression Series 12

NNO Carlito/Santino/Orton
NNO Matt Hardy/Ryder/Hawkins
NNO Tommy Dreamer/Kofi/Miz

2009 Jakks Pacific WWE Micro Aggression Series 13

NNO Kane/Mysterio/Cena	10.00	20.00
NNO MVP/Undertaker/Jeff Hardy		
NNO Shawn Michaels/CM Punk/Y2J	12.50	25.00

2009 Jakks Pacific WWE Micro Aggression Series 14

NNO Carlito/Ryder/Hawkins	7.50	15.00
NNO Cody Rhodes/DiBiase/JBL	7.50	15.00
NNO Finlay/Dreamer/Matt Hardy		

2009 Jakks Pacific WWE Micro Aggression Series 15

NNO Cody Rhodes/Mysterio/Cena	10.00	20.00
NNO Edge/Jeff Hardy/HHH	7.50	15.00
NNO MVP/Matt Hardy/Morrison		

Jakks Pacific WWE Micro Aggression Series 16

NNO John Cena/Mysterio/Undertaker	12.50	25.00
NNO Randy Orton/Rhodes/DiBiase		
NNO Triple H/MVP/Edge	10.00	20.00

2009 Jakks Pacific WWE Micro Aggression Series 17

NNO Finlay/Dreamer/Morrison		
NNO John Cena/Mysterio/Kane	12.50	25.00
NNO Undertaker/Hawkins/Ryder		

2001 Jakks Pacific WWF No Way Out Series 1

NNO Chris Jericho	10.00	20.00
NNO Grandmaster Sexay	7.50	15.00
NNO Kurt Angle		
NNO The Rock	15.00	30.00
NNO Scotty 2 Hotty	7.50	15.00
NNO Stone Cold Steve Austin	12.50	25.00

2001 Jakks Pacific WWF No Way Out Series 2

NNO Chris Benoit	15.00	30.00
NNO Chris Jericho	15.00	30.00
NNO Christian	10.00	20.00

NNO Kurt Angle	12.50	25.00
NNO Lita	10.00	20.00
NNO Matt Hardy	12.50	25.00
NNO Raven	10.00	20.00
NNO Undertaker	15.00	30.00

2002 Jakks Pacific WWE nWo

NNO Hulk Hogan/Tights	15.00	30.00
NNO Hulk Hogan/T-Shirt	12.50	25.00
NNO Kevin Nash/Tights	12.50	25.00
NNO Kevin Nash/T-Shirt	10.00	20.00
NNO Scott Hall/Tights	12.50	25.00
NNO Scott Hall/T-Shirt	10.00	20.00

2002 Jakks Pacific WWE nWo 2-Packs

NNO Hulk Hogan vs. The Rock	12.50	25.00
NNO Kane vs. Kevin Nash	20.00	40.00
NNO Steve Austin vs. Scott Hall	20.00	40.00

2002 Jakks Pacific WWE nWo Playset

NNO Metal Match	30.00	60.00

2002 Jakks Pacific WWE Off the Ropes Series 1

NNO Booker T	7.50	15.00
NNO Brock Lesnar	10.00	20.00
NNO Edge	7.50	15.00
NNO Hollywood Hulk Hogan	15.00	30.00
NNO Triple H	10.00	20.00
NNO Trish Stratus	20.00	40.00

2003 Jakks Pacific WWE Off the Ropes Series 2

NNO Chris Benoit	12.50	25.00
NNO Hurricane	15.00	30.00
NNO Kurt Angle	10.00	20.00
NNO Matt Hardy		
NNO Rikishi		

2003 Jakks Pacific WWE Off the Ropes Series 2 (loose)

NNO Brock Lesnar	12.50	25.00
NNO Chris Jericho	10.00	20.00
NNO Christian	10.00	20.00
NNO Rey Mysterio	15.00	30.00

2003 Jakks Pacific WWE Off the Ropes Series 4

NNO Jamie Noble	7.50	15.00
NNO Rob Van Dam	10.00	20.00
NNO Scott Steiner	4.00	15.00
NNO Undertaker		

2003 Jakks Pacific WWE Off the Ropes Series 5

NNO Billy Gunn	10.00	20.00
NNO Brock Lesnar	12.50	25.00
NNO Eddie Guerrero	10.00	20.00
NNO Ric Flair	7.50	15.00
NNO Stone Cold Steve Austin	12.50	25.00
NNO Triple H	10.00	20.00

2003 Jakks Pacific WWE Off the Ropes Series 6

NNO Al Snow	12.50	25.00
NNO A-Train	10.00	20.00
NNO Big Show	7.50	15.00
NNO Spike Dudley	10.00	20.00
NNO Tajiri	12.50	25.00

2004 Jakks Pacific WWE Off the Ropes Series 7

NNO Brock Lesnar	10.00	20.00
NNO Chris Benoit	10.00	20.00
NNO Lance Storm	7.50	15.00
NNO Matt Hardy	12.50	25.00
NNO Rob Van Dam	12.50	25.00
NNO Triple H	10.00	20.00

2004 Jakks Pacific WWE Off the Ropes Series 8

NNO JBL	10.00	20.00
NNO Maven	10.00	20.00
NNO Rob Van Dam	10.00	20.00
NNO The Rock	15.00	30.00
NNO Stacy Keibler	20.00	40.00
NNO Steven Richards	7.50	15.00

2005 Jakks Pacific WWE Off the Ropes Series 9

NNO Chris Benoit	12.50	25.00
NNO Rey Mysterio	10.00	20.00
NNO Triple H	10.00	20.00

2006 Jakks Pacific WWE Off the Ropes Series 10

NNO Batista	7.50	15.00
NNO Chris Masters	7.50	15.00
NNO John Cena	10.00	20.00
NNO Kurt Angle	10.00	20.00
NNO Shawn Michaels	12.50	25.00

2007 Jakks Pacific WWE Off the Ropes Series 11

NNO Boogeyman
NNO JBL
NNO John Cena
NNO Randy Orton
NNO Ric Flair
NNO Shawn Michaels

2007 Jakks Pacific WWE Off the Ropes Series 12

NNO Batista
NNO Elijah Burke
NNO The Great Khali
NNO Jeff Hardy
NNO Mr. Kennedy
NNO Tommy Dreamer

2009 Jakks Pacific WWE Off the Ropes Series 13

NNO Big Show	10.00	20.00
NNO Chris Jericho	15.00	30.00
NNO Festus	7.50	15.00
NNO Hornswoggle		
NNO JBL	7.50	15.00
NNO Kofi Kingston	7.50	15.00

2003 Jakks Pacific WWE Pay Per View Series 1

NNO Booker T	12.50	25.00
NNO Goldberg	20.00	40.00
NNO Ric Flair	10.00	20.00
NNO Scott Steiner	30.00	75.00
NNO Stone Cold Steve Austin		
NNO Triple H		

2003 Jakks Pacific WWE Pay Per View Series 2

NNO Eddie Guerrero
NNO Goldberg
NNO Kurt Angle
NNO Stone Cold Steve Austin
NNO Triple H
NNO Undertaker

2003 Jakks Pacific WWE Pay Per View Series 3

NNO Kane
NNO Kurt Angle
NNO Randy Orton
NNO Eric Bischoff
NNO Goldberg
NNO John Cena

2004 Jakks Pacific WWE Pay Per View Series 4

NNO Chris Benoit	10.00	20.00
NNO Chris Jericho	15.00	30.00
NNO Edge	10.00	20.00
NNO Hurricane	12.50	25.00
NNO Randy Orton	15.00	30.00
NNO Shelton Benjamin	12.50	25.00

2004 Jakks Pacific WWE Pay Per View Series 6

NNO Chris Jericho	10.00	20.00
NNO Edge	15.00	30.00
NNO JBL	10.00	20.00
NNO John Cena	12.50	25.00
NNO Kane	7.50	15.00
NNO Torrie Wilson	20.00	40.00

2004 Jakks Pacific WWE Pay Per View Series 7

NNO Eddie Guerrero	10.00	20.00
NNO Edge	7.50	15.00
NNO JBL	6.00	12.00
NNO Randy Orton	12.50	25.00
NNO Trish Stratus	15.00	30.00
NNO Undertaker	12.50	25.00

2005 Jakks Pacific WWE Pay Per View Series 8

NNO Batista	12.50	25.00
NNO Eugene	10.00	20.00
NNO Kane	15.00	30.00
NNO Maven	7.50	15.00
NNO Shawn Michaels/Ref Gear	15.00	30.00
NNO Triple H	7.50	15.00

2005 Jakks Pacific WWE Pay Per View Series 9

NNO Bubba Ray Dudley	12.50	25.00
NNO D-Von Dudley	10.00	20.00
NNO Eric Bischoff		
NNO JBL	7.50	15.00
NNO Kurt Angle/Referee Gear		
NNO Paul Heyman	10.00	20.00
NNO Rey Mysterio	15.00	30.00
NNO Rob Van Dam	10.00	20.00
NNO Stone Cold Steve Austin		
NNO Tajiri	12.50	25.00
NNO Tazz	7.50	15.00
NNO Tommy Dreamer	15.00	30.00

2006 Jakks Pacific WWE Pay Per View Series 10

NNO Animal	7.50	15.00
NNO Batista	7.50	15.00
NNO JBL/Vest		
NNO Orlando Jordan	12.50	25.00
NNO Rey Mysterio	12.50	25.00
NNO Undertaker	15.00	30.00

2006 Jakks Pacific WWE Pay Per View Series 11

NNO Batista	15.00	30.00
NNO Daivari/Ref Gear		
NNO John Cena		
NNO Kurt Angle	7.50	15.00

NNO Randy Orton	10.00	20.00
NNO Undertaker		

2006 Jakks Pacific WWE Pay Per View Series 12

NNO Gregory Helms	10.00	20.00
NNO Kurt Angle	12.50	25.00
NNO Matt Hardy	12.50	25.00
NNO Randy Orton	15.00	30.00
NNO Rey Mysterio	15.00	30.00
NNO Undertaker	12.50	25.00

2006 Jakks Pacific WWE Pay Per View Series 13

NNO Carlito		
NNO Edge	15.00	30.00
NNO John Cena	20.00	40.00
NNO Ric Flair	12.50	25.00
NNO Rob Van Dam	10.00	20.00
NNO Shawn Michaels		

2007 Jakks Pacific WWE Pay Per View Series 14

NNO Carlito
NNO Eric Bischoff/Ref Gear
NNO Jeff Hardy
NNO John Cena
NNO King Booker
NNO Umaga

2007 Jakks Pacific WWE Pay Per View Series 15

NNO Batista
NNO Brian Kendrick
NNO Finlay
NNO John Cena
NNO Johnny Nitro
NNO Kane

2007 Jakks Pacific WWE Pay Per View Series 16

NNO Bobby Lashley
NNO Deuce
NNO Edge
NNO John Cena
NNO Mark Henry
NNO Matt Hardy

2008 Jakks Pacific WWE Pay Per View Series 17

NNO Batista
NNO CM Punk
NNO Randy Orton
NNO Rey Mysterio
NNO Triple H
NNO Umaga

2008 Jakks Pacific WWE Pay Per View Series 18

NNO Chavo Guerrero
NNO Edge
NNO JBL
NNO John Cena
NNO Triple H
NNO Undertaker

2008 Jakks Pacific WWE Pay Per View Series 19

NNO Batista
NNO Big Show
NNO JBL
NNO Triple H
NNO Umaga
NNO Undertaker

2008 Jakks Pacific WWE Pay Per View Series 20

NNO Batista
NNO Jeff Hardy
NNO Matt Hardy
NNO Rey Mysterio
NNO Triple H
NNO Undertaker

2008 Jakks Pacific WWE Pay Per View Series 21

NNO Edge
NNO Jack Swagger
NNO Randy Orton
NNO Shane McMahon
NNO Shawn Michaels
NNO Triple H

2001 Jakks Pacific WWF Playsets

NNO Attitude Ring	25.00	50.00
NNO Hardcore Action Ring w/Ref/Jim Ross	20.00	40.00
NNO Hardcore Action Ring w/Ref/Jim Ross/Mick Foley	20.00	40.00

2016-17 Jakks Pacific WWE Plush Hangers

NNO AJ Styles
NNO Brock Lesnar
NNO Dean Ambrose
NNO Finn Balor
NNO John Cena
NNO Roman Reigns
NNO Seth Rollins
NNO Undertaker

2000 Jakks Pacific WWF Prop Boxes

NNO Back Alley Street Fight	12.50	25.00
NNO Break Room Brawl		
NNO House of Pain	20.00	40.00

2004 Jakks Pacific WWE Pump 'N Flex Series 1

NNO Chris Benoit	7.50	15.00
NNO Eddie Guerrero	15.00	30.00
NNO John Cena	20.00	40.00
NNO Kane	12.50	25.00
NNO Kurt Angle	10.00	20.00
NNO Triple H	10.00	20.00

2004 Jakks Pacific WWE Pump 'N Flex Series 2

NNO Batista		
NNO Booker T	12.50	25.00
NNO John Cena	12.50	25.00
NNO Randy Orton	7.50	15.00
NNO Rene Dupree		

2003 Jakks Pacific WWE RAW 10th Anniversary

NNO Goldust	10.00	20.00
NNO Jeff Hardy	15.00	30.00
NNO Jerry Lawler	12.50	25.00
NNO Kurt Angle	10.00	20.00
NNO The Rock	15.00	30.00
NNO RVD	12.50	25.00
NNO Shane McMahon	15.00	30.00
NNO Shawn Michaels	12.50	25.00
NNO Steve Austin	20.00	40.00
NNO Triple H	10.00	20.00
NNO Trish Stratus	15.00	30.00
NNO Undertaker	17.50	35.00

2002 Jakks Pacific WWE RAW Draft

1 Undertaker/27,500*	12.50	25.00
2A Kevin Nash/8,750*	12.50	25.00
2B Scott Hall/8,750*	12.50	25.00
2C X-Pac/10,000*	7.50	15.00
3 Kane/25,000*	12.50	25.00
4 Rob Van Dam/21,250*	10.00	20.00
5 Booker T/20,000*	12.50	25.00
6 Big Show/18,750*	10.00	20.00
7 Bubba Ray/18,750*	12.50	25.00
8 Brock Lesnar		
9 William Regal/16,250*	10.00	20.00
10 Lita/16,250*	15.00	30.00
11 Bradshaw/13,750*	7.50	15.00
12 Steven Richards/12,500*		
13 Matt Hardy/11,250*	10.00	20.00
14 Raven/8,750*	12.50	25.00
15 Jeff Hardy/7,500*	20.00	40.00
16 Mr. Perfect		
17 Spike Dudley/5,000*		
18 D'Lo Brown		
19 Shawn Stasiak		
20 Terri		

1999 Jakks Pacific WWF RAW Is War

NNO Mankind	7.50	15.00
NNO The Rock	15.00	30.00
NNO Stone Cold Steve Austin	7.50	15.00
NNO Undertaker	10.00	20.00

2003 Jakks Pacific WWE RAW Uncovered

NNO Jeff Hardy	20.00	40.00
NNO Kane	50.00	100.00
NNO Kurt Angle	15.00	30.00
NNO Matt Hardy	15.00	30.00
NNO Rey Mysterio	20.00	40.00
NNO Rob Van Dam	12.50	25.00

2002 Jakks Pacific WWF Real Reaction R-3 Tech Series 1

NNO Chris Benoit	12.50	25.00
NNO Chris Jericho	10.00	20.00
NNO Kane	15.00	30.00
NNO Matt Hardy	10.00	20.00
NNO The Rock	10.00	20.00
NNO Stone Cold Steve Austin	12.50	25.00

2002 Jakks Pacific WWF Real Reaction R-3 Tech Series 2

NNO Big Show	12.50	25.00
NNO Edge	10.00	20.00
NNO Jeff Hardy	15.00	30.00
NNO Rock	10.00	20.00
NNO Stone Cold Steve Austin	10.00	20.00
NNO Undertaker	15.00	30.00

2002 Jakks Pacific WWF Real Reaction R-3 Tech Series 3

NNO Big Show	12.50	25.00
NNO Jeff Hardy	15.00	30.00
NNO Kane		
NNO Matt Hardy	7.50	15.00
NNO Stone Cold Steve Austin		
NNO Undertaker	10.00	20.00

2002 Jakks Pacific WWF Real Reaction R-3 Tech Series 4

NNO Billy Gunn	7.50	15.00
NNO Chuck Palumbo	7.50	15.00
NNO Kurt Angle	7.50	15.00
NNO Rikishi	7.50	15.00
NNO Test	6.00	12.00
NNO Triple H	12.50	25.00

2002 Jakks Pacific WWF Real Reaction R-3 Tech Series 5

NNO Booker T	7.50	15.00
NNO Chris Benoit	7.50	15.00
NNO Jeff Hardy	10.00	20.00
NNO Kevin Nash	7.50	15.00
NNO Rob Van Dam	6.00	12.00
NNO Undertaker	12.50	25.00

2000 Jakks Pacific WWF Rebellion Series 1

NNO Chris Benoit	10.00	20.00
NNO Chris Jericho	12.50	25.00
NNO Jeff Hardy	7.50	15.00
NNO The Rock	12.50	25.00
NNO Undertaker	15.00	30.00
NNO X-Pac	7.50	15.00

2001 Jakks Pacific WWF Rebellion Series 2

NNO Chris Benoit	10.00	20.00
NNO Chris Jericho	7.50	15.00
NNO Crash Holly	10.00	20.00
NNO Kurt Angle	10.00	20.00
NNO The Rock	15.00	30.00

2001 Jakks Pacific WWF Rebellion Series 3

NNO D-Von Dudley	7.50	15.00
NNO Jeff Hardy	12.50	25.00
NNO Kurt Angle	10.00	20.00
NNO Stone Cold Steve Austin	20.00	40.00
NNO The Rock	12.50	25.00
NNO Triple H	7.50	15.00
NNO Undertaker	12.50	25.00

2001 Jakks Pacific WWF Rebellion Series 4

NNO Billy Gunn	7.50	15.00
NNO Chris Benoit	10.00	20.00
NNO Edge	10.00	20.00
NNO HHH	10.00	20.00
NNO Lita	10.00	20.00
NNO X-Pac	7.50	15.00

2002 Jakks Pacific WWE Relentless

NNO Booker T		
NNO Edge	10.00	20.00
NNO Rob Van Dam	15.00	30.00
NNO Triple H		

2005 Jakks Pacific WWE Ring Giants Classic Series 1

NNO Rowdy Roddy Piper	30.00	60.00
NNO Ted DiBiase	25.00	50.00
NNO Ultimate Warrior	30.00	75.00

2005 Jakks Pacific WWE Ring Giants Series 1

NNO Chris Benoit	20.00	40.00
NNO Eddie Guerrero	15.00	30.00
NNO John Cena	15.00	30.00
NNO Triple H	15.00	30.00

2005 Jakks Pacific WWE Ring Giants Series 2

NNO Batista	12.50	25.00
NNO Booker T	15.00	30.00
NNO Kurt Angle	20.00	40.00
NNO Randy Orton	15.00	30.00

2005 Jakks Pacific WWE Ring Giants Series 3

NNO Carlito/Hair	20.00	40.00
NNO Carlito/No Hair		
NNO Kane	12.50	25.00
NNO Rey Mysterio	30.00	75.00
Red White Blue Pants		
NNO Shawn Michaels	20.00	40.00

2005 Jakks Pacific WWE Ring Giants Series 4

NNO Batista	15.00	30.00
NNO John Cena	20.00	40.00
NNO Rey Mysterio	15.00	30.00
NNO Undertaker	20.00	40.00

2006 Jakks Pacific WWE Ring Giants Series 5

NNO Batista		
NNO John Cena		
NNO Kurt Angle		
NNO Rey Mysterio		

2006 Jakks Pacific WWE Ring Giants Series 6

NNO Bobby Lashley		
NNO Boogeyman		
NNO Kurt Angle		
NNO Rey Mysterio		

2006 Jakks Pacific WWE Ring Giants Series 7

NNO Batista		
NNO Hulk Hogan		
NNO John Cena		
NNO Rob Van Dam		

2007 Jakks Pacific WWE Ring Giants Series 8

NNO Edge		
NNO John Cena		
NNO Rey Mysterio		
NNO Shawn Michaels		

2007 Jakks Pacific WWE Ring Giants Series 9

NNO Carlito		
NNO Shawn Michaels		
NNO Triple H		
NNO Undertaker		

2007 Jakks Pacific WWE Ring Giants Series 10

NNO Batista		
NNO Jeff Hardy		
NNO Mr. Kennedy		
NNO Randy Orton		

2007 Jakks Pacific WWE Ring Giants Series 11

NNO Boogeyman		
NNO Edge		
NNO Fit Finlay		
NNO Matt Hardy		

2007 Jakks Pacific WWE Ring Giants Series 12

NNO Jeff Hardy		
NNO John Cena		
NNO Rey Mysterio		
NNO Triple H		

2007 Jakks Pacific WWE Ring Giants Series 13

NNO Boogeyman
NNO Finlay
NNO Matt Hardy
NNO Randy Orton

1997 Jakks Pacific WWF Ring Masters

NNO Bret Hit Man Hart	10.00	20.00
NNO Goldust	6.00	12.00
NNO Shawn Michaels	10.00	20.00
NNO Sycho Sid	6.00	12.00
NNO Undertaker	7.50	15.00
NNO Yokozuna		

2002 Jakks Pacific WWE Ringleader Collection

NNO Chris Jericho	10.00	20.00
NNO Hollywood Hulk Hogan	17.50	35.00
NNO The Rock	10.00	20.00
NNO Triple H	15.00	30.00
NNO Undertaker	15.00	30.00

2002 Jakks Pacific WWE Ringside Rebels Series 1

NNO The Rock	20.00	40.00
NNO Stone Cold Steve Austin		
NNO Undertaker	25.00	50.00

2002 Jakks Pacific WWE Ringside Rebels Series 2

NNO Chris Jericho	15.00	30.00
NNO The Rock	15.00	30.00
NNO Triple H	12.50	25.00

2002 Jakks Pacific WWE Ringside Rebels Series 3

NNO Booker T	10.00	20.00
NNO Rob Van Dam	15.00	30.00
NNO Triple H	12.50	25.00

2002 Jakks Pacific WWE Ringside Rebels Series 4

NNO Hulk Hogan	20.00	40.00
NNO Jeff Hardy	15.00	30.00

2002 Jakks Pacific WWE Ringside Rivals Fatal Showdown

NNO Chris Jericho vs. Triple H
NNO Jeff Hardy vs. Eddie Guerrero
NNO Undertaker vs. Hollywood Hogan

2002 Jakks Pacific WWE Ringside Rivals Head to Head

NNO Edge vs. Kurt Angle
NNO Rob Van Dam vs. Booker T
NNO Test vs. Tajiri

2002 Jakks Pacific WWE Ringside Rivals New Series

NNO Billy Gunn vs. Chuck Palumbo
NNO Matt Hardy vs. Jeff Hardy
NNO The Rock vs. Brock Lesnar

2002 Jakks Pacific WWE Ringside Rivals Raging Tempers

NNO Rob Van Dam vs. Test
NNO The Rock vs. Booker T
NNO Vince McMahon vs. Ric Flair

2001 Jakks Pacific WWF Ringside Rivals Series 1

NNO Bradshaw vs. Test	10.00	20.00
NNO Father (Vince) vs. Son (Shane)	12.50	25.00
NNO The Rock vs. Stone Cold Steve Austin	15.00	30.00

2001 Jakks Pacific WWF Ringside Rivals Series 2

NNO Edge vs. Christian	25.00	50.00
NNO Kurt Angle vs. Undertaker	15.00	30.00
NNO Matt Hardy vs. Bubba Ray Dudley	12.50	25.00
NNO The Rock vs. Chris Jericho	25.00	50.00
NNO Triple H vs. Stone Cold Steve Austin	20.00	40.00
NNO William Regal vs. Mick Foley	20.00	40.00

2002 Jakks Pacific WWF Ringside Rivals Series 3

NNO D-Von vs. Spike
NNO Edge vs. William Regal
NNO Triple H vs. Kurt Angle

1998 Jakks Pacific WWF Ringside Collection Series 1

NNO Referee	5.00	10.00
NNO Sable	7.50	15.00
NNO Sunny	10.00	20.00
NNO Vince McMahon	6.00	12.00

1998 Jakks Pacific WWF Ringside Collection Series 2

NNO Honky Tonk Man	6.00	12.00
NNO Jim Cornette	15.00	30.00
NNO Jim Ross	12.50	25.00
NNO Referee	5.00	10.00
NNO Sgt. Slaughter	7.50	15.00
NNO Vince McMahon	7.50	15.00

1997 Jakks Pacific WWF Ripped and Ruthless Series 1

NNO Goldust	5.00	10.00
NNO Mankind	7.50	15.00
NNO Stone Cold Steve Austin	10.00	20.00
NNO Undertaker	12.50	25.00

1998 Jakks Pacific WWF Ripped and Ruthless Series 2

NNO Kane	15.00	30.00
NNO Sable	12.50	25.00
NNO Shawn Michaels	10.00	20.00
NNO Triple H	10.00	20.00

1998 Jakks Pacific WWF Ripped and Ruthless 2-Pack

NNO Undertaker/Stone Cold Steve Austin

1999 Jakks Pacific WWF Road Rage

NNO Al Snow	7.50	15.00
NNO Gangrel	7.50	15.00
NNO Godfather	10.00	20.00
NNO Hardcore Holly	6.00	12.00
NNO The Rock	12.50	25.00
NNO Test	6.00	12.00

2002 Jakks Pacific WWF Road to WrestleMania

NNO Bubba Ray Dudley
NNO Chris Benoit
NNO Chris Jericho
NNO D-Von Dudley
NNO Jeff Hardy
NNO Undertaker

2006 Jakks Pacific WWE Road to WrestleMania 22 Gear and Figure Sets

NNO Kane/Glove & Elbow Pad
NNO Rey Mysterio/Mask
NNO Triple H/Crown

2006 Jakks Pacific WWE Road to WrestleMania 22 Series 1

NNO Chris Benoit
NNO Eddie Guerrero
NNO John Cena
NNO Kurt Angle
NNO Rey Mysterio
NNO Shawn Michaels
NNO Shawn Michaels
Hulk Hogan Costume

2006 Jakks Pacific WWE Road to WrestleMania 22 2-Packs Series 1

NNO Batista/JBL
NNO Edge/Matt Hardy
NNO Undertaker/Randy Orton

2006 Jakks Pacific WWE Road to WrestleMania 22 Series 2

NNO Batista
NNO Carlito
NNO Chris Masters
NNO John Cena
NNO Kurt Angle
NNO Shawn Michaels

2006 Jakks Pacific WWE Road to WrestleMania 22 2-Packs Series 2

NNO Kane/Big Show
NNO Rey Mysterio/Matt Hardy
NNO Rob Conway/Tyson Tomko

2006 Jakks Pacific WWE Road to WrestleMania 22 Series 3

NNO Bobby Lashley
NNO Finlay
NNO Matt Hardy
NNO Ric Flair
NNO RVD
NNO Shelton Benjamin

2006 Jakks Pacific WWE Road to WrestleMania 22 2-Packs Series 3

NNO John Cena/Edge
NNO Kurt Angle/Rey Mysterio
NNO Undertaker/Mark Henry

2007 Jakks Pacific WWE Road to WrestleMania 23 Series 1

NNO Batista
NNO King Booker
NNO Rey Mysterio
NNO Ric Flair
NNO Shawn Michaels
NNO Triple H

2007 Jakks Pacific WWE Road to WrestleMania 23 2-Packs Series 1

NNO John Cena/Edge
NNO Randy Orton/Hulk Hogan
NNO Sabu/Big Show

2007 Jakks Pacific WWE Road to WrestleMania 23 Series 2

NNO Batista
NNO Chris Benoit
NNO CM Punk

NNO Ron Simmons
NNO Triple H

2007 Jakks Pacific WWE Road to WrestleMania 23
2-Packs Series 2

NNO Bobby Lashley/John Cena
NNO Matt Hardy/Jeff Hardy
NNO Undertaker/Mr. Kennedy

2007 Jakks Pacific WWE Road to WrestleMania 23
Series 3

NNO CM Punk
NNO Elijah Burke
NNO Jeff Hardy
NNO Matt Hardy
NNO Mr. Kennedy
NNO MVP

2007 Jakks Pacific WWE Road to WrestleMania 23
2-Packs Series 3

NNO Batista/Undertaker
NNO Bobby Lashley/Umaga
NNO John Cena/Shawn Michaels

2008 Jakks Pacific WWE Road to WrestleMania 24
Series 1

NNO Batista
NNO Carlito
NNO CM Punk/Blue Trunks
NNO Kane
NNO Mr. Kennedy
NNO Umaga

2008 Jakks Pacific WWE Road to WrestleMania 24
Series 1 2-Packs

NNO Randy Orton/John Cena
NNO Rey Mysterio/Chavo Guerrero   15.00   30.00
NNO Triple H/Mr. McMahon

2008 Jakks Pacific WWE Road to WrestleMania 24
Series 2

NNO Batista
NNO CM Punk/Red Trunks
NNO Kane
NNO Triple H
NNO Umaga
NNO Undertaker

2008 Jakks Pacific WWE Road to WrestleMania 24
Series 2 2-Packs

NNO Finlay & Mysterio
NNO Mr. Kennedy & Jeff Hardy
NNO Shawn Michaels & Randy Orton

2008 Jakks Pacific WWE Road to WrestleMania 24
Series 3

NNO Chris Jericho
NNO CM Punk/Black Trunks
NNO Finlay
NNO John Cena
NNO Kane
NNO Randy Orton

2008 Jakks Pacific WWE Road to WrestleMania 24
Series 3 2-Packs

NNO Batista & Umaga
NNO Edge & Undertaker
NNO Ric Flair & Shawn Michaels

2008 Jakks Pacific WWE Road to WrestleMania 24
Best of WrestleMania

NNO Batista
NNO John Cena
NNO Kane
NNO Rey Mysterio
NNO Shawn Michaels
NNO Triple H

2008 Jakks Pacific WWE Road to WrestleMania 24
Mask and Figure Sets

NNO Rey Mysterio
Black and Green Pants
NNO Rey Mysterio/Blue Pants
NNO Rey Mysterio/Silver Pants

2002 Jakks Pacific WWE Rollin' Rebels

NNO Hulk Hogan	30.00	75.00
NNO Undertaker	30.00	60.00

2002 Jakks Pacific WWE Royal Rumble

NNO Chris Jericho	7.50	15.00
NNO Referee Earl Hebner	6.00	12.00
NNO Ric Flair	10.00	20.00
NNO Tazz	6.00	12.00
NNO Triple H	7.50	15.00
NNO William Regal	6.00	12.00

2006 Jakks Pacific WWE Royal Rumble

NNO Carlito		
NNO Randy Orton		
NNO Rey Mysterio		
NNO Rob Van Dam	12.50	25.00
NNO Shawn Michaels		
NNO Triple H		

2007 Jakks Pacific WWE Royal Rumble

NNO Batista
NNO Bobby Lashley
NNO John Cena
NNO Mr. Kennedy
NNO Shawn Michaels
NNO Undertaker

2008 Jakks Pacific WWE Royal Rumble

NNO Chris Jericho
NNO Edge
NNO JBL
NNO John Cena
NNO Randy Orton
NNO Ric Flair

2009 Jakks Pacific WWE Royal Rumble

NNO Kane
NNO Mark Henry
NNO Ted DiBiase
NNO Vladimir Kozlov
NNO Cody Rhodes
NNO Great Khali

2008 Jakks Pacific WWE Royal Rumble Playset

NNO Deluxe Ring
{w/Cena/Y2J/Mysterio/Edge}

2000 Jakks Pacific WWF Rulers of the Ring Series 1

NNO Al Snow	6.00	12.00
NNO Buh Buh Ray	7.50	15.00

NNO D-Von	7.50	15.00
NNO Edge	6.00	12.00
NNO Ivory	10.00	20.00
NNO Tazz	10.00	20.00

2000 Jakks Pacific WWF Rulers of the Ring Series 2

NNO Big Boss Man	7.50	15.00
NNO Brian Christopher	7.50	15.00
NNO Crash Holly	6.00	12.00
NNO Rikishi	7.50	15.00
NNO Scotty 2 Hotty	6.00	12.00
NNO Steve Blackman	10.00	20.00

2001 Jakks Pacific WWF Rulers of the Ring Series 3

NNO Eddie Guerrero	12.50	25.00
NNO Perry Saturn	10.00	20.00
NNO Prince Albert	10.00	20.00
NNO Raven	12.50	25.00
NNO Stephanie McMahon-Helmsley	10.00	20.00
NNO Steven Richards	7.50	15.00

2001 Jakks Pacific WWF Rulers of the Ring Series 4

NNO Bob Holly	10.00	20.00
NNO Christian	7.50	15.00
NNO Justin Credible	10.00	20.00
NNO Molly Holly	10.00	20.00
NNO Shane McMahon	15.00	30.00

2003 Jakks Pacific WWE Ruthless Aggression Best of 2003

NNO A-Train
NNO Chavo Guerrero
NNO Eric Bischoff
NNO Goldust
NNO Rey Mysterio
NNO Rico
NNO Scott Steiner

2006 Jakks Pacific WWE Ruthless Aggression Best of 2006

NNO Boogeyman
NNO Carlito
NNO Chris Masters
NNO Edge
NNO John Cena
NNO Kurt Angle
NNO Rey Mysterio
NNO Rob Van Dam
NNO Shawn Michaels

2007 Jakks Pacific WWE Ruthless Aggression Best of 2007

NNO Great Khali	15.00	30.00
NNO John Cena	10.00	20.00
NNO Rey Mysterio	12.50	25.00
NNO Shawn Michaels	10.00	20.00
NNO Umaga		
NNO Undertaker		

2008 Jakks Pacific WWE Ruthless Aggression Best of 2008

NNO Batista		
NNO John Cena	10.00	20.00
NNO Ric Flair	12.50	25.00

NNO	Triple H	10.00	20.00
NNO	Umaga	10.00	20.00
NNO	Undertaker		

2009 Jakks Pacific WWE Ruthless Aggression
Best of 2009

NNO	Batista		
NNO	Hornswoggle		
NNO	John Cena		
NNO	Randy Orton		
NNO	Rey Mysterio	15.00	30.00
NNO	Triple H		

2002 Jakks Pacific WWE Ruthless Aggression
Series 1

NNO	Brock Lesnar	15.00	30.00
NNO	Chavo Guerrero	7.50	15.00
NNO	Eric Bischoff	20.00	40.00
NNO	John Cena	15.00	30.00
NNO	Randy Orton	10.00	20.00
NNO	Rey Mysterio		

2003 Jakks Pacific WWE Ruthless Aggression
Series 2

NNO	Batista	6.00	12.00
NNO	Billy Kidman	7.50	15.00
NNO	Jamie Noble	6.00	12.00
NNO	Rico	6.00	12.00
NNO	Scott Steiner	7.50	15.00
NNO	Tommy Dreamer	15.00	30.00

2003 Jakks Pacific WWE Ruthless Aggression
Series 3

NNO	A-Train		
NNO	Goldust	10.00	20.00
NNO	John Cena	15.00	30.00
NNO	Rey Mysterio	12.50	25.00
NNO	Rob Van Dam	12.50	25.00
NNO	Scott Steiner	25.00	50.00

2003 Jakks Pacific WWE Ruthless Aggression
Series 3.5

NNO	Chavo Guerrero		
NNO	Eric Bischoff	12.50	25.00
NNO	Goldust		
NNO	Rey Mysterio		
NNO	Rico		
NNO	Scott Steiner		

2003 Jakks Pacific WWE Ruthless Aggression
Series 4

NNO	Bill Goldberg	25.00	50.00
NNO	Chris Benoit	15.00	30.00
NNO	Eddie Guerrero	10.00	20.00
NNO	The Hurricane	15.00	30.00
NNO	The Rock	25.00	50.00
NNO	Undertaker	12.50	25.00

2003 Jakks Pacific WWE Ruthless Aggression
Series 5

NNO	Billy Kidman	7.50	15.00
NNO	John Cena	15.00	30.00
NNO	Kane	15.00	30.00
NNO	Kevin Nash	7.50	15.00
NNO	Shawn Michaels	12.50	25.00
NNO	Tajiri	7.50	15.00

2003 Jakks Pacific WWE Ruthless Aggression
Series 6

NNO	Bill Goldberg	30.00	60.00
NNO	Kurt Angle	7.50	15.00
NNO	Maven	6.00	12.00
NNO	Rey Mysterio	12.50	25.00
NNO	Rob Van Dam	6.00	12.00
NNO	Triple H	20.00	40.00

2003 Jakks Pacific WWE Ruthless Aggression
Series 7

NNO	Brock Lesnar	15.00	30.00
NNO	Chris Benoit	25.00	50.00
NNO	Chris Jericho	12.50	25.00
NNO	Kane/Unmasked	10.00	20.00
NNO	Matt Hardy	10.00	20.00
NNO	Randy Orton	10.00	20.00

2003 Jakks Pacific WWE Ruthless Aggression
Series 7.5

NNO	Bill Goldberg		
NNO	Chris Jericho		
NNO	Goldust		
NNO	Rey Mysterio	6.00	12.00
NNO	Rob Van Dam		
NNO	Stone Cold Steve Austin		

2004 Jakks Pacific WWE Ruthless Aggression
Series 8

NNO	Bill Goldberg	30.00	75.00
NNO	Christian (long sleeves)	12.50	25.00
NNO	Christian (short sleeves)		
NNO	Kurt Angle	6.00	12.00
NNO	Test		
NNO	The Rock	15.00	30.00
NNO	Ultimo Dragon	20.00	40.00

2004 Jakks Pacific WWE Ruthless Aggression
Series 8.5

NNO	A-Train		
NNO	Big Show	6.00	12.00
NNO	Eddie Guerrero	7.50	15.00
NNO	John Cena	6.00	12.00
NNO	Rey Mysterio		
NNO	Undertaker		

2004 Jakks Pacific WWE Ruthless Aggression
Series 9

NNO	Booker T SE	15.00	30.00
NNO	Jamie Noble	7.50	15.00
NNO	Kane	10.00	20.00
NNO	Matt Hardy	12.50	25.00
NNO	Matt Morgan	10.00	20.00
NNO	Rob Van Dam	10.00	20.00
NNO	Stone Cold Steve Austin	12.50	25.00

2004 Jakks Pacific WWE Ruthless Aggression
Series 10

NNO	Chris Benoit	10.00	20.00
NNO	Chris Jericho	7.50	15.00
NNO	Edge	15.00	30.00
NNO	Kurt Angle	10.00	20.00
NNO	Rey Mysterio	12.50	25.00
NNO	Ultimo Dragon	12.50	25.00

2004 Jakks Pacific WWE Ruthless Aggression
Series 10.5

NNO	Charlie Haas		
NNO	Jamie Noble	7.50	15.00
NNO	John Bradshaw Layfield		
NNO	Matt Hardy	10.00	20.00
NNO	Shelton Benjamin		
NNO	Tajiri		

2004 Jakks Pacific WWE Ruthless Aggression
Series 11

NNO	Batista	7.50	15.00
NNO	Booker T	12.50	25.00
NNO	Eugene	7.50	15.00
NNO	John Cena	7.50	15.00
NNO	Rene Dupree	6.00	12.00
NNO	Undertaker	10.00	20.00

2004 Jakks Pacific WWE Ruthless Aggression
Series 11.5

NNO	Charlie Haas		
NNO	John Cena		
NNO	Randy Orton	10.00	20.00
NNO	Rene Dupree		
NNO	Rob Conway		
NNO	Shelton Benjamin		

2004 Jakks Pacific WWE Ruthless Aggression
Series 12

NNO	Booker T	7.50	15.00
NNO	Chris Jericho	7.50	15.00
NNO	Eric Bischoff	10.00	20.00
NNO	Kurt Angle	12.50	25.00
NNO	Randy Orton	7.50	15.00
NNO	Rey Mysterio	12.50	25.00

2004 Jakks Pacific WWE Ruthless Aggression
Series 12.5

NNO	Chris Benoit		
NNO	Edge		
NNO	Eric Bischoff		
NNO	Randy Orton		
NNO	Shelton Benjamin		
NNO	Triple H		

2005 Jakks Pacific WWE Ruthless Aggression
Series 13

NNO	Chavo Guerrero	7.50	15.00
NNO	Kurt Angle	10.00	20.00
NNO	Rosey	12.50	25.00
NNO	Shelton Benjamin	10.00	20.00
NNO	Tyson Tomko	7.50	15.00
NNO	William Regal	10.00	20.00

2005 Jakks Pacific WWE Ruthless Aggression
Series 14

NNO	John Cena	15.00	30.00
NNO	Ric Flair	10.00	20.00
NNO	Shelton Benjamin	7.50	15.00
NNO	Triple H	10.00	20.00
NNO	Trish Stratus	12.50	25.00
NNO	Undertaker	7.50	15.00

2005 Jakks Pacific WWE Ruthless Aggression
Series 15

NNO	Big Show	17.50	35.00
NNO	Carlito	7.50	15.00

NNO Christian	12.50	25.00
NNO Gene Snitsky	15.00	30.00
NNO Johnathan Coachman	7.50	15.00
NNO Mark Jindrak	7.50	15.00

2005 Jakks Pacific WWE Ruthless Aggression Series 15.5

NNO Chris Masters
NNO Eric Bischoff
NNO Heidenreich
NNO Scotty 2 Hotty
NNO Shannon Moore
NNO Simon Dean

2005 Jakks Pacific WWE Ruthless Aggression Series 16

NNO Batista	10.00	20.00
NNO Kurt Angle	12.50	25.00
NNO Rey Mysterio	12.50	25.00
NNO Stone Cold Steve Austin	10.00	20.00
NNO Triple H	10.00	20.00
NNO Undertaker	12.50	25.00

2005 Jakks Pacific WWE Ruthless Aggression Series 16.5

NNO Chris Jericho
NNO John Cena
NNO Rob Van Dam
NNO Shawn Michaels
NNO Undertaker

NNO Viscera	15.00	30.00

2005 Jakks Pacific WWE Ruthless Aggression Series 17

NNO Hardcore Holly	10.00	20.00
NNO Nunzio	7.50	15.00
NNO Orlando Jordan	7.50	15.00
NNO Paul London	7.50	15.00
NNO Steven Richards	10.00	20.00
NNO Tajiri	6.00	12.00

2005 Jakks Pacific WWE Ruthless Aggression Series 17.5

NNO Batista	10.00	20.00
NNO The Hurricane	20.00	40.00
NNO John Cena	7.50	15.00
NNO Rey Mysterio	10.00	20.00
NNO Shawn Michaels		
NNO Undertaker		

2006 Jakks Pacific WWE Ruthless Aggression Series 18

NNO Batista

NNO Carlito	20.00	40.00
NNO Eddie Guerrero	10.00	20.00
NNO Heidenreich	12.50	25.00
NNO John Cena	20.00	40.00
NNO Shawn Michaels		

2006 Jakks Pacific WWE Ruthless Aggression Series 18.5

NNO Batista
NNO Chris Benoit
NNO Edge
NNO John Cena
NNO Matt Hardy
NNO Randy Orton

2006 Jakks Pacific WWE Ruthless Aggression Series 19

NNO Chris Benoit
NNO Ken Kennedy

NNO Kurt Angle	15.00	30.00
NNO Randy Orton	7.50	15.00
NNO Rey Mysterio		
NNO Rob Conway		

2006 Jakks Pacific WWE Ruthless Aggression Series 20

NNO Boogeyman	10.00	20.00
NNO Booker T		
NNO Chris Masters	7.50	15.00
NNO Kid Kash		
NNO Ric Flair	15.00	30.00

2006 Jakks Pacific WWE Ruthless Aggression Series 20.5

NNO Batista
NNO Ken Kennedy
NNO Randy Orton
NNO Rey Mysterio
NNO Undertaker

2006 Jakks Pacific WWE Ruthless Aggression Series 21

NNO Carlito
NNO Chavo Guerrero
NNO Edge
NNO John Cena
NNO Rob Van Dam
NNO Triple H

2006 Jakks Pacific WWE Ruthless Aggression Series 22

NNO Kurt Angle	15.00	30.00
NNO Matt Striker	12.50	25.00
NNO Nicky	6.00	12.00
NNO Rey Mysterio		
NNO Torrie Wilson	12.50	25.00
NNO Victoria		20.00

2006 Jakks Pacific WWE Ruthless Aggression Series 22.5

NNO Big Show
NNO Edge
NNO Lita
NNO Psicosis
NNO Rey Mysterio
NNO Shawn Michaels
NNO Undertaker

2006 Jakks Pacific WWE Ruthless Aggression Series 23

NNO John Cena
NNO Paul London

NNO Rey Mysterio	15.00	30.00
NNO Shelton Benjamin		
NNO Tatanka		
NNO Triple H		

2006 Jakks Pacific WWE Ruthless Aggression Series 23.5

NNO Carlito
NNO Chris Masters
NNO Edge

NNO John Cena
NNO Rob Van Dam
NNO Shawn Michaels

2006 Jakks Pacific WWE Ruthless Aggression Series 24

NNO Big Show
NNO Booker T
NNO Kane

NNO Kenny	10.00	20.00
NNO Sabu	15.00	30.00
NNO The Great Khali	20.00	40.00

2006 Jakks Pacific WWE Ruthless Aggression Series 24.5

NNO Batista
NNO John Cena

NNO Paul Heyman	15.00	30.00
NNO Tommy Dreamer		
NNO Triple H		
NNO Undertaker		

2006 Jakks Pacific WWE Ruthless Aggression Series 25

NNO Batista
NNO Brian Kendrick
NNO Carlito

NNO Rey Mysterio	6.00	12.00
NNO Shawn Michaels		
NNO Test		

2007 Jakks Pacific WWE Ruthless Aggression Series 26

NNO Candice Michelle	12.50	25.00
NNO Chris Benoit	15.00	30.00
NNO Finlay	10.00	20.00
NNO Hardcore Holly	7.50	15.00
NNO John Cena	7.50	15.00
NNO William Regal	15.00	30.00

2007 Jakks Pacific WWE Ruthless Aggression Series 27

NNO Batista	6.00	12.00
NNO Bobby Lashley	15.00	30.00
NNO Chris Masters	7.50	15.00
NNO John Cena	6.00	12.00
NNO Mr. Kennedy	7.50	15.00
NNO Rey Mysterio	6.00	12.00

2007 Jakks Pacific WWE Ruthless Aggression Series 28

NNO Kenny Dykstra

NNO Miz	10.00	20.00
NNO Mr. McMahon		
NNO Rey Mysterio	12.50	25.00
NNO Super Crazy	10.00	20.00
NNO Torrie Wilson	20.00	40.00
NNO Victoria	15.00	30.00

2007 Jakks Pacific WWE Ruthless Aggression Series 29

NNO Batista	7.50	15.00
NNO Candice Michelle	12.50	25.00
NNO Edge	12.50	25.00
NNO Ken Kennedy	10.00	20.00
NNO Matt Hardy	12.50	25.00
NNO Melina	15.00	30.00
NNO Shawn Michaels	12.50	25.00

2007 Jakks Pacific WWE Ruthless Aggression Series 30

NNO	Boogeyman	12.50	25.00
NNO	John Cena	7.50	15.00
NNO	Mark Henry	10.00	20.00
NNO	MVP	10.00	20.00
NNO	Sandman	12.50	25.00
NNO	Triple H	10.00	20.00

2007 Jakks Pacific WWE Ruthless Aggression Series 31

NNO	Batista	6.00	12.00
NNO	Jillian Hall	12.50	25.00
NNO	John Cena	7.50	15.00
NNO	John Morrison	10.00	20.00
NNO	Kelly Kelly	12.50	25.00
NNO	Kevin Thorn	10.00	20.00
NNO	Ric Flair	12.50	25.00

2007 Jakks Pacific WWE Ruthless Aggression Series 31.5

NNO	Batista	10.00	20.00
NNO	Boogeyman	10.00	20.00
NNO	CM Punk	12.50	25.00
NNO	John Morrison	10.00	20.00
NNO	Matt Hardy	10.00	20.00
NNO	Randy Orton	12.50	25.00

2007 Jakks Pacific WWE Ruthless Aggression Series 32

NNO	Carlito	12.50	25.00
NNO	John Morrison	12.50	25.00
NNO	Randy Orton	10.00	20.00
NNO	Triple H	10.00	20.00
NNO	Umaga	10.00	20.00
NNO	Undertaker	12.50	25.00

2008 Jakks Pacific WWE Ruthless Aggression Series 33

NNO	Candice Michelle	15.00	30.00
NNO	CM Punk	15.00	30.00
NNO	John Cena	7.50	15.00
NNO	Melina	20.00	40.00
NNO	Randy Orton	7.50	15.00
NNO	Rey Mysterio	15.00	30.00
NNO	Triple H	12.50	25.00

2008 Jakks Pacific WWE Ruthless Aggression Series 34

NNO	Chris Jericho	10.00	20.00
NNO	Funaki	7.50	15.00
NNO	Great Khali		
NNO	Lilian Garcia	12.50	25.00
NNO	Mickie James	15.00	30.00
NNO	Nunzio		
NNO	Shelton Benjamin		

2008 Jakks Pacific WWE Ruthless Aggression Series 34.5

NNO	Batista		
NNO	Cody Rhodes		
NNO	Jamie Noble		
NNO	The Miz		
NNO	Ric Flair	10.00	20.00
NNO	Great Khali		

2008 Jakks Pacific WWE Ruthless Aggression Series 35

NNO	Beth Phoenix	6.00	12.00
NNO	Edge	7.50	15.00
NNO	Hornswoggle	15.00	30.00
NNO	Joey Styles	6.00	12.00
NNO	Rey Mysterio		
NNO	Santino		
NNO	Victoria	15.00	30.00

2008 Jakks Pacific WWE Ruthless Aggression Series 35.5

NNO	Carlito	10.00	20.00
NNO	Edge	7.50	15.00
NNO	Elijah Burke	10.00	20.00
NNO	Matt Hardy	10.00	20.00
NNO	Ken Kennedy		
NNO	Triple H	15.00	30.00

2008 Jakks Pacific WWE Ruthless Aggression Series 36

NNO	Big Show	12.50	25.00
NNO	Charlie Haas	10.00	20.00
NNO	David Hart Smith	15.00	30.00
NNO	Kofi Kingston	15.00	30.00
NNO	Maryse	12.50	25.00
NNO	Mickie James	15.00	30.00
NNO	Umaga	12.50	25.00

2008 Jakks Pacific WWE Ruthless Aggression Series 37

NNO	Cherry	17.50	35.00
NNO	Colin Delaney	15.00	30.00
NNO	Festus	7.50	15.00
NNO	Katie Lee Burchill	20.00	40.00
NNO	MVP		
NNO	Paul Burchill		
NNO	Santino Marella	12.50	25.00

2008 Jakks Pacific WWE Ruthless Aggression Series 38

NNO	Batista	10.00	20.00
NNO	The Brian Kendrick	15.00	30.00
NNO	Hornswoggle	12.50	25.00
NNO	Jesse		
NNO	John Cena	10.00	20.00
NNO	Rey Mysterio	15.00	30.00

2008 Jakks Pacific WWE Ruthless Aggression Series 38.5

NNO	Big Show		
NNO	Chris Jericho		
NNO	Festus	10.00	20.00
NNO	Jesse		
NNO	Kane		
NNO	Kofi Kingston	12.50	25.00

2009 Jakks Pacific WWE Ruthless Aggression Series 39

NNO	Evan Bourne	10.00	20.00
NNO	Jeff Hardy	15.00	30.00
NNO	Mark Henry		
NNO	Rey Mysterio	15.00	30.00
NNO	Ted DiBiase	15.00	30.00
NNO	Vladimir Kozlov	10.00	20.00

2009 Jakks Pacific WWE Ruthless Aggression Series 40

NNO	Chris Jericho	20.00	40.00
NNO	Edge	17.50	35.00
NNO	Matt Hardy	12.50	25.00
NNO	Randy Orton	12.50	25.00
NNO	R-Truth		
NNO	Undertaker	12.50	25.00

2009 Jakks Pacific WWE Ruthless Aggression Series 40.5

NNO	Cody Rhodes	10.00	20.00
NNO	Matt Hardy	10.00	20.00
NNO	Ted DiBiase		
NNO	Triple H	12.50	25.00
NNO	Undertaker	20.00	40.00
NNO	Vladimir Kozlov	10.00	20.00

2009 Jakks Pacific WWE Ruthless Aggression Series 41

NNO	The Brian Kendrick	20.00	40.00
NNO	CM Punk	20.00	40.00
NNO	Goldust	15.00	30.00
NNO	Hornswoggle	25.00	50.00
NNO	John Cena	25.00	50.00
NNO	Rey Mysterio	20.00	40.00

2009 Jakks Pacific WWE Ruthless Aggression Series 42

NNO	Christian	20.00	40.00
NNO	CM Punk	20.00	40.00
NNO	The Great Khali		
NNO	Jack Swagger		
NNO	Shawn Michaels	25.00	50.00
NNO	Triple H	10.00	20.00

2009 Jakks Pacific WWE Ruthless Aggression Series 43

NNO	Batista	15.00	30.00
NNO	John Cena	20.00	40.00
NNO	Randy Orton	20.00	40.00
NNO	Rey Mysterio	25.00	50.00
NNO	Triple H		
NNO	Undertaker		

2009 Jakks Pacific WWE Ruthless Aggression Series 44

NNO	Edge	15.00	30.00
NNO	John Cena	12.50	25.00
NNO	Kane	15.00	30.00
NNO	Matt Hardy		
NNO	MVP		
NNO	Rey Mysterio		

1998 Jakks Pacific WWF Shotgun Saturday Night Series 1

NNO	Animal	7.50	15.00
NNO	Hawk	7.50	15.00
NNO	Henry Godwinn	6.00	12.00
NNO	Phineas Godwinn	6.00	12.00
NNO	Rocky Maivia	12.50	25.00
NNO	Savio Vega	10.00	20.00
NNO	Steve Austin	12.50	25.00
NNO	Undertaker	7.50	15.00
NNO	Stone Cold Steve Austin/Kane		
	Shawn Michaels/Rocky Maivia		

1998 Jakks Pacific WWF Shotgun Saturday Night Series 2

NNO B.A. Billy Gunn	7.50	15.00
NNO Jeff Jarrett	6.00	12.00
NNO Jesse James	7.50	15.00
NNO Kane	10.00	20.00
NNO Sable	7.50	15.00
NNO Shawn Michaels	7.50	15.00

1999 Jakks Pacific WWF Shotgun Saturday Night Series 3

NNO Droz	5.00	10.00
NNO Edge	7.50	15.00
NNO Kurgann	6.00	12.00
NNO Road Dogg Jesse James	6.00	12.00
NNO Stone Cold Steve Austin	10.00	20.00
NNO Triple H	7.50	15.00

1999 Jakks Pacific WWF Shotgun Saturday Night Series 4

NNO Al Snow	6.00	12.00
NNO Gangrel	6.00	12.00
NNO Godfather	6.00	12.00
NNO Hardcore Holly	5.00	10.00
NNO Rock	7.50	15.00
NNO Test		

2001 Jakks Pacific WWF Signature Jams Series 1

NNO Billy Gunn	7.50	15.00
NNO Chris Jericho	12.50	25.00
NNO Jeff Hardy	15.00	30.00
NNO Kurt Angle	7.50	15.00
NNO The Rock	12.50	25.00
NNO Triple H	7.50	15.00

2001 Jakks Pacific WWF Signature Jams Series 2

NNO Chris Benoit		
NNO D-Von Dudley	7.50	15.00
NNO Kane		
NNO Matt Hardy	12.50	25.00
NNO Stone Cold Steve Austin		
NNO Undertaker		

2002 Jakks Pacific WWF Signature Jams Series 3

NNO Kane		
NNO Matt Hardy		
NNO Stone Cold Steve Austin		
NNO Undertaker		

2002 Jakks Pacific WWF Signature Jams Slam Grooves

NNO Billy Gunn		
NNO Jeff Hardy		
NNO Stone Cold Steve Austin		
NNO Undertaker		

1997 Jakks Pacific WWF Signature Series 1

NNO Goldust	7.50	15.00
NNO HHH	6.00	12.00
NNO Mankind	10.00	20.00
NNO Road Warrior Animal	7.50	15.00
NNO Road Warrior Hawk	7.50	15.00
NNO Steve Austin	7.50	15.00

1998 Jakks Pacific WWF Signature Series 2

NNO B.A. Billy Gunn	5.00	10.00
NNO Dude Love	10.00	20.00
NNO Kane	10.00	20.00
NNO Road Dogg	5.00	10.00
NNO Shawn Michaels	7.50	15.00
NNO Undertaker	7.50	15.00

1998 Jakks Pacific WWF Signature Series 3

NNO Edge	6.00	12.00
NNO HHH	7.50	15.00
NNO Jacqueline	10.00	20.00
NNO The Rock	10.00	20.00
NNO Stone Cold Steve Austin	7.50	15.00
NNO Undertaker	12.50	25.00

1999 Jakks Pacific WWF Signature Series 4

NNO Big Show	10.00	20.00
NNO Edge	7.50	15.00
NNO Ken Shamrock	7.50	15.00
NNO Rock	10.00	20.00
NNO Stone Cold Steve Austin	7.50	15.00
NNO X-Pac	6.00	12.00

1999 Jakks Pacific WWF Signature Series 5

NNO Al Snow	7.50	15.00
NNO Big Bossman	6.00	12.00
NNO Billy Gunn	6.00	12.00
NNO Kane	10.00	20.00
NNO Road Dogg	6.00	12.00
NNO Stone Cold Steve Austin	10.00	20.00

1999 Jakks Pacific WWF Signature Series 6

NNO Hardcore Holly	5.00	10.00
NNO HHH	7.50	15.00
NNO Mankind	7.50	15.00
NNO Stone Cold Steve Austin	10.00	20.00
NNO Undertaker	7.50	15.00
NNO Vince McMahon	7.50	15.00

1998 Jakks Pacific WWF Slammers Series 1

NNO Bret Hart	7.50	15.00
NNO Faarooq	6.00	12.00
NNO Goldust	6.00	12.00
NNO Mankind	6.00	12.00
NNO Steve Austin	7.50	15.00
NNO Undertaker	7.50	15.00

1998 Jakks Pacific WWF Slammers Series 2

NNO Brian Pillman	6.00	12.00
NNO Dude Love	7.50	15.00
NNO Kane	7.50	15.00
NNO Patriot	6.00	12.00
NNO Shawn Michaels	7.50	15.00
NNO Taka	6.00	12.00

2002 Jakks Pacific WWE SmackDown Draft

1 The Rock/26,250*	10.00	20.00
2 Kurt Angle/25,000*	12.50	25.00
3 Chris Benoit/23,750*	10.00	20.00
4 Hollywood Hogan/22,500*	15.00	30.00
6 Edge/18,750*	10.00	20.00
7 Rikishi/17,500*		
8 D-Von Dudley/16,250*	12.50	25.00
9 Mark Henry		
10 Maven/15,000*		
11 Billy Kidman		
12 Tajiri/13,750*	15.00	30.00
13 Chris Jericho/11,250*	15.00	30.00
14 Ivory/11,250*	15.00	30.00
15 Albert/8,750*	20.00	40.00
16 The Hurricane/7,500*	25.00	50.00
17 Al Snow/6,250*	12.50	25.00
18 Lance Storm/5,000*	25.00	50.00
19 DDP/3,750*	30.00	75.00
20 Torrie Wilson		
5A Billy/11,250*	15.00	30.00
5B Chuck/11,250*	15.00	30.00

2002 Jakks Pacific WWF Snappin' Bashers

NNO Chris Benoit	12.50	25.00
NNO Chris Jericho		
NNO Jeff Hardy	15.00	30.00
NNO The Rock		
NNO Stone Cold Steve Austin	7.50	15.00
NNO Undertaker		

1997 Jakks Pacific WWF Special Edition Series 1

NNO Ahmed Johnson	6.00	12.00
NNO British Bulldog	6.00	12.00
NNO Rocky Maivia	10.00	20.00
NNO Sunny	7.50	15.00
NNO Undertaker	7.50	15.00
NNO Vader	12.50	25.00
NNO Yokozuna/18000*	15.00	30.00

1998 Jakks Pacific WWF Special Edition Series 2

NNO Faarooq	6.00	12.00
NNO Goldust	6.00	12.00
NNO HHH	7.50	15.00
NNO Sable	10.00	20.00
NNO Savio Vega	6.00	12.00
NNO Stone Cold Steve Austin	7.50	15.00

1998 Jakks Pacific WWF Special Edition Series 3

NNO Animal	10.00	20.00
NNO Dan Severn	12.50	25.00
NNO Hawk	10.00	20.00
NNO Hunter Hearst-Helmsley	7.50	15.00
NNO Marvelous Marc Mero	7.50	15.00
NNO Shamrock	6.00	12.00

1999 Jakks Pacific WWF Special Edition Series 4

NNO B.A. Billy Gunn	7.50	15.00
NNO Chyna	10.00	20.00
NNO Mankind	12.50	25.00
NNO Road Dogg	7.50	15.00
NNO Stone Cold Steve Austin	10.00	20.00
NNO Undertaker		

1999 Jakks Pacific WWF Special Edition Series 5

NNO Al Snow	6.00	12.00
NNO Edge	7.50	15.00
NNO Mark Henry		
NNO Shamrock		
NNO Val Venis	6.00	12.00
NNO X-Pac		

1999 Jakks Pacific WWF Special Edition Series 6

NNO Double J	7.50	15.00
NNO Hardcore Holly	6.00	12.00
NNO HHH	7.50	15.00
NNO Stone Cold Steve Austin	10.00	20.00
NNO Test		
NNO The Rock	10.00	20.00

1997 Jakks Pacific WWF S.T.O.M.P. Series 1

NNO	Ahmed Johnson	7.50	15.00
NNO	Brian Pillman	5.00	10.00
NNO	Crush	6.00	12.00
NNO	Ken Shamrock	7.50	15.00
NNO	Stone Cold Steve Austin	10.00	20.00
NNO	Undertaker	7.50	15.00

1998 Jakks Pacific WWF S.T.O.M.P. Series 2

NNO	Chyna	10.00	20.00
NNO	Headbanger Mosh	7.50	15.00
NNO	Headbanger Thrash	7.50	15.00
NNO	Owen Hart	10.00	20.00
NNO	Rocky Maivia	12.50	25.00
NNO	Stone Cold Steve Austin	10.00	20.00

1998 Jakks Pacific WWF S.T.O.M.P. Series 3

NNO	Animal	7.50	15.00
NNO	Hawk	7.50	15.00
NNO	Kane	7.50	15.00
NNO	Marc Mero	15.00	30.00
NNO	Sable	10.00	20.00
NNO	Undertaker	10.00	20.00

2000 Jakks Pacific WWF S.T.O.M.P. Series 4

NNO	B.A. Billy Gunn		
NNO	Chyna		
NNO	Road Dogg Jesse James		
NNO	Stone Cold Steve Austin		
NNO	Triple H		
NNO	X-Pac		

1997 Jakks Pacific WWF Stretchin'

NNO	Bret Hit Man Hart	12.50	25.00
NNO	Shawn Michaels		
NNO	Sycho Sid	10.00	20.00
NNO	Undertaker	12.50	25.00

2001 Jakks Pacific WWF Stunt Action Superstars Series 1

NNO	Jeff Hardy	12.50	25.00
NNO	Kurt Angle	10.00	20.00
NNO	Rikishi	7.50	15.00
NNO	Stephanie McMahon	15.00	30.00
NNO	Triple H	10.00	20.00
NNO	X-Pac	7.50	15.00

2005 Jakks Pacific WWE SummerSlam Limited Edition

NNO	Chris Benoit		
NNO	Chris Jericho		
NNO	Kane		
NNO	Matt Hardy		
NNO	Stone Cold Steve Austin		
NNO	Test		
NNO	The Rock		
NNO	X-Pac		

1999 Jakks Pacific WWF Sunday Night Heat

NNO	B.A. Billy Gunn	7.50	15.00
NNO	Road Dogg		
NNO	The Rock		
NNO	Sable	7.50	15.00
NNO	Stone Cold Steve Austin		
NNO	Undertaker		

2016-17 Jakks Pacific WWE Superstar Buddies

NNO	AJ Styles		
NNO	John Cena		
NNO	The Rock		

1997 Jakks Pacific WWF Superstars Best of 1997

NNO	Bret Hart		
NNO	British Bulldog	7.50	15.00
NNO	Owen Hart	10.00	20.00

1997 Jakks Pacific WWF Superstars Best of 1997 Tag Teams

NNO	Godwinns	12.50	25.00
NNO	Headbangers	15.00	30.00
NNO	Legion of Doom		
NNO	New Blackjacks	10.00	20.00

1998 Jakks Pacific WWF Superstars Best of 1998 Series 1

NNO	8-Ball	6.00	12.00
NNO	Blackjack Bradshaw	10.00	20.00
NNO	Brian Christopher	6.00	12.00
NNO	Chyna	12.50	25.00
NNO	Shawn Michaels	10.00	20.00
NNO	Skull	6.00	12.00
NNO	Stone Cold Steve Austin	12.50	25.00
NNO	Vader	6.00	12.00

1998 Jakks Pacific WWF Superstars Best of 1998 Series 2

NNO	Dan Severn	5.00	10.00
NNO	Dude Love	6.00	12.00
NNO	HHH	7.50	15.00
NNO	Jeff Jarrett	6.00	12.00
NNO	Ken Shamrock	6.00	12.00
NNO	Mark Henry	6.00	12.00
NNO	Stone Cold Steve Austin	10.00	20.00
NNO	Undertaker	7.50	15.00

1998 Jakks Pacific WWF Superstars Best of 1998 Tag Teams

NNO	Headbangers		
NNO	LOD 2000		
NNO	New Age Outlaws		

1996 Jakks Pacific WWF Superstars Series 1

NNO	Bret Hart	20.00	40.00
NNO	Diesel	15.00	30.00
NNO	Goldust	15.00	30.00
NNO	Razor Ramon	20.00	40.00
NNO	Shawn Michaels	12.50	25.00
NNO	Undertaker	15.00	30.00

1996 Jakks Pacific WWF Superstars Series 2

NNO	Bret Hart	12.50	25.00
NNO	Owen Hart	20.00	40.00
NNO	Shawn Michaels	15.00	30.00
NNO	Ultimate Warrior	20.00	40.00
NNO	Undertaker GITD	25.00	50.00
NNO	Vader	10.00	20.00

1997 Jakks Pacific WWF Superstars Series 3

NNO	Ahmed Johnson	10.00	20.00
NNO	Bret Hart	12.50	25.00
NNO	British Bulldog	7.50	15.00
NNO	Mankind	10.00	20.00
NNO	Shawn Michaels	10.00	20.00
NNO	Sycho Sid	7.50	15.00

1997 Jakks Pacific WWF Superstars Series 4

NNO	Faarooq	5.00	10.00
NNO	Hunter Hearst Helmsley	6.00	12.00
NNO	Jerry Lawler	7.50	15.00
NNO	Justin Hawk Bradshaw	12.50	25.00
NNO	Stone Cold Steve Austin	7.50	15.00
NNO	Vader	7.50	15.00

1997 Jakks Pacific WWF Superstars Series 5

NNO	Flash Funk	10.00	20.00
NNO	Ken Shamrock	6.00	12.00
NNO	Rocky Maivia	12.50	20.00
NNO	Savio Vega	7.50	15.00
NNO	Stone Cold Steve Austin	12.50	25.00
NNO	Sycho Sid	6.00	12.00

1998 Jakks Pacific WWF Superstars Series 6

NNO	Jeff Jarrett	10.00	20.00
NNO	Marc Mero	6.00	12.00
NNO	Mark Henry	7.50	15.00
NNO	Owen Hart	12.50	25.00
NNO	Steve Blackman	12.50	25.00
NNO	Triple H	7.50	15.00

1998 Jakks Pacific WWF Superstars Series 7

NNO	Dr. Death Steve Williams	12.50	25.00
NNO	Edge	7.50	15.00
NNO	Steve Austin	7.50	15.00
NNO	Undertaker	7.50	15.00
NNO	Val Venis	7.50	15.00
NNO	X-Pac	6.00	12.00

1999 Jakks Pacific WWF Superstars Series 8

NNO	Big Boss Man	6.00	12.00
NNO	Kane	7.50	15.00
NNO	Ken Shamrock		
NNO	The Rock	7.50	15.00
NNO	Shane McMahon	7.50	15.00
NNO	Shawn Michaels	7.50	15.00

1999 Jakks Pacific WWF Superstars Series 9

NNO	Bob Holly	6.00	12.00
NNO	Christian	6.00	12.00
NNO	Gangrel	10.00	20.00
NNO	Paul Wight	7.50	15.00
NNO	Undertaker	7.50	15.00
NNO	Vince McMahon	7.50	15.00

2006 Jakks Pacific WWE Superstars Series 1

NNO	Hulk Hogan		
NNO	The Rock		
NNO	Ric Flair		
NNO	Roddy Piper		
	Black Wrist Tape		
NNO	Roddy Piper		
	White Wrist Tape		
NNO	Stone Cold Steve Austin		

2007 Jakks Pacific WWE Superstars Series 2

NNO	Bret Hit Man Hart		
NNO	British Bulldog		
NNO	Kevin Nash		
NNO	Mr. Perfect		
NNO	Shawn Michaels		

2007 Jakks Pacific WWE Superstars Series 3

NNO Jake The Snake Roberts
NNO Lex Luger
NNO Ravishing Rick Rude
NNO Scott Hall
NNO Undertaker

2008 Jakks Pacific WWE Superstars Series 4

NNO Brutus The Barber Beefcake
NNO Honky Tonk Man
NNO Iron Sheik
NNO Million Dollar Man
NNO Shawn Michaels

2008 Jakks Pacific WWE Superstars Series 5

NNO Buff Bagwell
NNO Diamond Dallas Page
NNO Jim The Anvil Neidhart
NNO Superfly Jimmy Snuka

2009 Jakks Pacific WWE Superstars Series 6

NNO Eddie Guerrero
NNO Hillbilly Jim
NNO Hunter Hearst Helmsley
NNO Kane
NNO Sgt. Slaughter

2009 Jakks Pacific WWE Superstars Series 7

NNO Bret Hit Man Hart
NNO Shawn Michaels
NNO El Matador
NNO The Rock
NNO Undertaker

2009 Jakks Pacific WWE Superstars Series 8

NNO Big John Studd
NNO Chainsaw Charlie
NNO Davey Boy Smith
NNO Dynamite Kid
NNO Stone Cold Steve Austin

2003 Jakks Pacific WWE Superstars Uncovered

NNO Hulk Hogan	20.00	40.00
NNO Kurt Angle	12.50	25.00
NNO Rob Van Dam	12.50	25.00
NNO The Rock	30.00	60.00
NNO Triple H	10.00	20.00
NNO Undertaker	15.00	30.00

2004 Jakks Pacific WWE Talkin' Pounders

NNO The Hurricane
NNO John Cena
NNO Randy Orton
NNO Rey Mysterio

1997 Jakks Pacific WWF Talking Undertaker 14-Inch

NNO Undertaker	25.00	50.00

1997 Jakks Pacific WWF Thumb Wrestlers

NNO Bulldog vs. Shamrock	10.00	20.00
NNO HHH vs. Mankind	10.00	20.00
NNO Steve Austin vs. Owen Hart	12.50	25.00
NNO Undertaker vs. HBK	15.00	30.00

1999 Jakks Pacific WWF Titan Tron Live Series 1

NNO Kane	7.50	15.00
NNO Mankind	7.50	15.00
NNO Road Dogg	6.00	12.00
NNO Rock	10.00	20.00
NNO Stone Cold Steve Austin	15.00	30.00
NNO Undertaker	15.00	30.00

2000 Jakks Pacific WWF Titan Tron Live Series 2

NNO Big Show	6.00	12.00
NNO Kane	17.50	35.00
NNO Ken Shamrock	7.50	15.00
NNO The Rock	12.50	25.00
NNO Stone Cold Steve Austin	7.50	15.00
NNO X-Pac	6.00	12.00

2000 Jakks Pacific WWF Titan Tron Live Series 3

NNO Big Boss Man	7.50	15.00
NNO Chris Jericho	7.50	15.00
NNO Chyna	12.50	25.00
NNO The Rock	7.50	15.00
NNO Stone Cold Steve Austin	10.00	20.00
NNO Test	6.00	12.00

2000 Jakks Pacific WWF Titan Tron Live Series 4

NNO Big Show		
NNO Cactus Jack	10.00	20.00
NNO Road Dogg		
NNO The Rock		
NNO Triple H		
NNO X-Pac		

2000 Jakks Pacific WWF Titan Tron Live Series 5

NNO Chris Jericho	6.00	15.00
NNO Kurt Angle	6.00	15.00
NNO The Rock	10.00	20.00
NNO Stone Cold Steve Austin	10.00	20.00
NNO Test	6.00	12.00
NNO Undertaker	10.00	20.00

2000 Jakks Pacific WWF Titan Tron Live Series 6

NNO Big Show
NNO Edge
NNO Jeff Hardy
NNO Rock
NNO Tazz
NNO Triple H

2000 Jakks Pacific WWF Titan Tron Live Series 7

NNO Chris Jericho
NNO Kane
NNO Kurt Angle
NNO Stephanie McMahon
NNO Triple H
NNO Undertaker

2000 Jakks Pacific WWF Titan Tron Live Series 8

NNO Bubba Ray Dudley
NNO Jeff Hardy
NNO Matt Hardy
NNO Rikishi
NNO Road Dogg
NNO The Rock

2001 Jakks Pacific WWF Titan Tron Live Series 9

NNO Chyna
NNO Kurt Angle
NNO Mick Foley
NNO Rikishi
NNO The Rock
NNO Triple H

2001 Jakks Pacific WWF Titan Tron Live Series 10

NNO Billy Gunn	7.50	15.00
NNO Kane	7.50	15.00
NNO Matt Hardy	7.50	15.00
NNO Rikishi	7.50	15.00
NNO Stone Cold Steve Austin	10.00	20.00
NNO Triple H	10.00	20.00

2001 Jakks Pacific WWF Titan Tron Live Series 11

NNO Jeff Hardy	7.50	15.00
NNO Kurt Angle	7.50	15.00
NNO Rikishi	7.50	15.00
NNO Stephanie McMahon	10.00	20.00
NNO Stone Cold Steve Austin	10.00	20.00
NNO Triple H	10.00	20.00

2001 Jakks Pacific WWF Titan Tron Live Series 12

NNO Big Show	6.00	12.00
NNO Chris Jericho	7.50	15.00
NNO Kurt Angle	6.00	12.00
NNO Rock	10.00	20.00
NNO Stone Cold Steve Austin	10.00	20.00
NNO Undertaker	12.50	25.00

2001 Jakks Pacific WWF Titan Tron Live Series 13

NNO Chris Jericho	6.00	12.00
NNO Lita	7.50	15.00
NNO Rock	10.00	20.00
NNO Stone Cold Steve Austin	12.50	25.00
NNO Triple H	7.50	15.00
NNO Undertaker	12.50	25.00

2000 Jakks Pacific WWF ToyFare Exclusives

NNO Big Show	12.50	25.00
NNO Debra	15.00	30.00
NNO The Rock	20.00	40.00

2002 Jakks Pacific WWE Trash Talkin' Champions

NNO Chris Jericho	20.00	40.00
NNO Kurt Angle	10.00	20.00

2005 Jakks Pacific WWE Treacherous Trios Series 1

NNO Kurt Angle/Eddie Guerrero/Big Show		
NNO Triple H/Ric Flair/Batista	12.50	25.00
NNO Undertaker/JBL/Heidenreich	15.00	30.00

2005 Jakks Pacific WWE Treacherous Trios Series 2

NNO Mark Jindrak/Booker T/Kurt Angle	15.00	30.00
NNO Orlando Jordan/Danny Basham/Doug Basham	12.50	25.00
NNO Trish Stratus/Tyson Tomko/Christian	15.00	30.00

2005 Jakks Pacific WWE Treacherous Trios Series 3

NNO Edge/Lita/Matt Hardy	30.00	60.00
NNO Randy Orton/Undertaker	25.00	50.00
Cowboy Bob Orton Jr.		
NNO Rey Mysterio/Chris Benoit/Batista	25.00	50.00

2006 Jakks Pacific WWE Treacherous Trios Series 4

NNO Chris Benoit/Booker T/Randy Orton
NNO Melina/Johnny Nitro/Joey Mercury
NNO Kurt Angle/Daivari/Mark Henry

2007 Jakks Pacific WWE Treacherous Trios Series 5

NNO Randy Orton/Edge/Carlito
NNO Rey Mysterio/Booker T/Chavo
NNO Shawn Michaels/HHH/
Coachman

2007 Jakks Pacific WWE Treacherous Trios Series 6

NNO Batista/Long/Undertaker
NNO Brian Kendrick/Yang/London
NNO Umaga/Cena/Armando Estrada

2008 Jakks Pacific WWE Treacherous Trios Series 7

NNO Elijah Burke/CM Punk/	25.00	50.00
Tommy Dreamer		
NNO Great Khali/Batista/Undertaker		
NNO Randy Orton/John Cena/		
Jonathan Coachman		

2008 Jakks Pacific WWE Treacherous Trios Series 8

NNO Curt Hawkins/Edge/Zack Ryder		
NNO Deuce/Cherry/Domino	30.00	75.00
NNO Triple H/John Cena/Orton	15.00	30.00

2009 Jakks Pacific WWE Treacherous Trios Series 9

NNO Finlay/JBL/Hornswoggle		
NNO JTG/John Cena/Shad	20.00	40.00
NNO Miz/Matt Hardy/Morrison	25.00	50.00

2009 Jakks Pacific WWE Treacherous Trios Series 10

NNO Big Show/Undertaker/Khali
NNO Chris Jericho/Cena/CM Punk
NNO Matt Hardy/Edge/Jeff Hardy

2002 Jakks Pacific WWE Unchained Fury Series 1

NNO Booker T	10.00	20.00
NNO Hurricane Helms	12.50	25.00
NNO Lance Storm	10.00	20.00
NNO Ric Flair	12.50	25.00

2002 Jakks Pacific WWE Unchained Fury Series 1 2-Packs

NNO Booker T/Steve Austin	20.00	40.00
NNO Ric Flair/Vince McMahon	25.00	50.00
NNO Rob Van Dam/Chris Jericho		

2002 Jakks Pacific WWE Unchained Fury Series 2

NNO Booker T	10.00	20.00
NNO Kevin Nash	15.00	30.00
NNO Kurt Angle	10.00	20.00
NNO Rhyno	12.50	25.00
NNO Rob Van Dam	15.00	30.00
NNO Tajiri	10.00	20.00

2002 Jakks Pacific WWE Unchained Fury Series 2 2-Packs

NNO Christian/DDP	12.50	25.00
NNO Chuck Palumbo/Billy Gunn	15.00	30.00
NNO Kurt Angle/Edge	15.00	30.00

2003 Jakks Pacific WWE Unlimited Series 1

NNO Chris Jericho	12.50	25.00
NNO Edge	12.50	25.00
NNO Hulk Hogan	15.00	30.00
NNO Kurt Angle	10.00	20.00
NNO Rob Van Dam	7.50	15.00
NNO The Rock	12.50	25.00

2003 Jakks Pacific WWE Unlimited Series 2

NNO Batista	15.00	30.00
NNO Billy Kidman	10.00	20.00
NNO Booker T	12.50	25.00
NNO Brock Lesnar	15.00	30.00
NNO Eddie Guerrero	12.50	25.00
NNO Triple H	10.00	20.00

2003 Jakks Pacific WWE Unlimited Series 3

NNO Booker T	12.50	25.00
NNO Brock Lesnar	20.00	40.00
NNO Chris Benoit	10.00	20.00
NNO Chris Jericho	10.00	20.00
NNO Hulk Hogan	15.00	30.00
NNO The Rock	15.00	30.00

2003 Jakks Pacific WWE Unlimited Series 4

NNO Chris Benoit		
NNO Kurt Angle		
NNO Rob Van Dam	10.00	20.00
NNO The Rock	15.00	30.00
NNO Triple H	12.50	25.00

2006 Jakks Pacific WWE Unmatched Fury Series 1

NNO Batista
NNO Hulk Hogan
NNO John Cena
NNO Rey Mysterio

2007 Jakks Pacific WWE Unmatched Fury Series 2

NNO Rob Van Dam	20.00	40.00
NNO Shawn Michaels	30.00	60.00
NNO Triple H	12.50	25.00
NNO Undertaker	20.00	40.00
NNO Undertaker GITD	300.00	500.00
100* NYC TF		

2007 Jakks Pacific WWE Unmatched Fury Series 3

NNO Carlito	15.00	30.00
NNO Jeff Hardy	20.00	40.00
NNO John Cena	15.00	30.00
NNO Sabu	15.00	30.00

2007 Jakks Pacific WWE Unmatched Fury Series 4

NNO Ken Kennedy	12.50	25.00
NNO Mr.Perfect	20.00	40.00
NNO Ric Flair	15.00	30.00
NNO Umaga	12.50	25.00

2007 Jakks Pacific WWE Unmatched Fury Series 5

NNO Bobby Lashley	25.00	50.00
NNO Mick Foley	15.00	30.00
NNO The Rock	20.00	40.00
NNO Undertaker		

2007 Jakks Pacific WWE Unmatched Fury Series 6

NNO Eddie Guerrero	15.00	30.00
NNO Kane	12.50	25.00
NNO Randy Orton	25.00	50.00
NNO Rowdy Roddy Piper	30.00	60.00

2008 Jakks Pacific WWE Unmatched Fury Series 7

NNO British Bulldog
NNO Edge
NNO Ravishing Rick Rude
NNO Undertaker

2008 Jakks Pacific WWE Unmatched Fury Series 8

NNO Boogeyman
NNO Iron Sheik
NNO Matt Hardy
NNO Shawn Michaels

2008 Jakks Pacific WWE Unmatched Fury Series 9

NNO Bret Hitman Hart	30.00	60.00
NNO Finlay	12.50	25.00
NNO Hornswoggle	20.00	50.00
NNO Hornswoggle LE	200.00	350.00
{Green/Gold/500*		
NNO Undertaker		

2008 Jakks Pacific WWE Unmatched Fury Series 10

NNO Great Khali
NNO Junk Yard Dog
NNO MVP
NNO Ultimate Warrior

2008 Jakks Pacific WWE Unmatched Fury Series 11

NNO Chris Jericho
NNO CM Punk
NNO Honkytonk Man
NNO Million Dollar Man

2008 Jakks Pacific WWE Unmatched Fury Series 12

NNO Big Show
NNO JBL
NNO Razor Ramon
NNO Undertaker

2009 Jakks Pacific WWE Unmatched Fury Series 14

NNO Bret Hitman Hart	30.00	60.00
NNO Hornswoggle	20.00	40.00
NNO John Cena	15.00	30.00
NNO Rey Mysterio	20.00	40.00

2009 Jakks Pacific WWE Unmatched Fury Series 15

NNO CM Punk	60.00	120.00
NNO Eddie Guerrero	25.00	50.00
NNO Rowdy Roddy Piper	30.00	60.00
NNO Stone Cold Steve Austin	20.00	40.00

2003 Jakks Pacific WWE Unrelenting

NNO Booker T	7.50	15.00
NNO Chris Jericho	10.00	20.00
NNO Edge		
NNO Jeff Hardy		
NNO Rob Van Dam		
NNO Triple H		

2008 Jakks Pacific WWE Vinyl Aggression Exclusive

NNO	Bret Hart RSC	20.00	40.00

2009 Jakks Pacific WWE Vinyl Aggression Exclusive

NNO Jesse Ventura/100* NYC TF

2008 Jakks Pacific WWE Vinyl Aggression Series 1

NNO Carlito
NNO ECW Stylized
NNO Hornswoggle
NNO John Cena
NNO Mankind
NNO Umaga
NNO Undertaker

2008 Jakks Pacific WWE Vinyl Aggression Series 2

NNO Batista
NNO Chris Jericho
NNO CM Punk
NNO DX Stylized
NNO Finlay
NNO Honkytonk Man
NNO Mr. Kennedy
NNO MVP
NNO Rey Mysterio
NNO Rock
NNO Shawn Michaels
NNO Tommy Dreamer
NNO Triple H Stylized

2008 Jakks Pacific WWE Vinyl Aggression Series 3

NNO Batista
NNO Chris Jericho
NNO Shawn Michaels
NNO Rock
NNO Tommy Dreamer
NNO Triple H

2008 Jakks Pacific WWE Vinyl Aggression Series 4

NNO Edge
NNO Jimmy Wang Yang
NNO Miz
NNO Randy Orton
NNO Santino
NNO Ted DiBiase

2008 Jakks Pacific WWE Vinyl Aggression Series 5

NNO Big Show
NNO DX Stylized
NNO Jake Roberts
NNO Kane
NNO Kofi Kingston
NNO Matt Hardy

2008 Jakks Pacific WWE Vinyl Aggression Series 6

NNO Festus
NNO Jesse
NNO John Morrison
NNO JTG

NNO Rowdy Roddy Piper
NNO Shad

2008 Jakks Pacific WWE Vinyl Aggression Series 7

NNO Beth Phoenix
NNO Boogeyman
NNO Great Khali
NNO Kane/Classic Mask
NNO Ricky Ortiz
NNO Triple H

1999 Jakks Pacific WWF White's Exclusives

NNO Sable
NNO Undertaker

1998 Jakks Pacific WWF WrestleMania XIV

NNO	Headbanger Mosh	6.00	12.00
NNO	Headbanger Thrasher	6.00	12.00
NNO	HHH	10.00	20.00
NNO	Rocky Maivia	7.50	15.00
NNO	Shawn Michaels	10.00	20.00
NNO	Stone Cold Steve Austin	7.50	15.00

2001 Jakks Pacific WWF WrestleMania X-7

NNO	Chris Jericho	7.50	15.00
NNO	Chyna	10.00	20.00
NNO	Eddie Guerrero	7.50	15.00
NNO	Edge	7.50	15.00
NNO	Kane	10.00	20.00
NNO	Stone Cold Steve Austin	12.50	25.00

2002 Jakks Pacific WWE WrestleMania X-8

NNO	Billy Gunn	7.50	15.00
NNO	Chuck Palumbo	7.50	15.00
NNO	Diamond Dallas Page	7.50	15.00
NNO	HHH	15.00	30.00
NNO	Maven	7.50	15.00
NNO	Rob Van Dam	12.50	25.00

2002 Jakks Pacific WWE WrestleMania X-8 2-Packs

NNO	Booker T/Edge	15.00	30.00
NNO	Kurt Angle/Kane	12.50	25.00
NNO	The Rock vs. Hollywood Hogan	30.00	60.00
NNO	Undertaker vs. Ric Flair	30.00	75.00

2004 Jakks Pacific WWE WrestleMania 19 Winners

NNO Chris Benoit
NNO Chris Jericho
NNO Kane
NNO Kurt Angle
NNO The Rock

2004 Jakks Pacific WWE WrestleMania 19 Winners 2-Packs

NNO D-Von and Bubba Ray Dudley
NNO La Resistance
Conway/Dupree
NNO Team Angle
Benjamin/Haas

2004 Jakks Pacific WWE WrestleMania 20 Series 1

NNO Edge
NNO Hardcore Holly

NNO Rob Van Dam
NNO Shane McMahon
NNO Stone Cold Steve Austin
NNO Triple H

2004 Jakks Pacific WWE WrestleMania 20 Series 3

NNO Booker T
NNO Chris Benoit
NNO Chris Jericho
NNO Kane
NNO Kurt Angle
NNO The Rock

2004 Jakks Pacific WWE WrestleMania 20 Series 3 2-Packs

NNO Bubba Ray & D-Von
NNO Rob Conway & Rene Dupree
NNO Shelton Benjamin & Charlie Haas

2004 Jakks Pacific WWE WrestleMania 20 Mask and Figure Sets Series 1

NNO Hurricane
NNO Kane
NNO Mankind
NNO Rey Mysterio

2004 Jakks Pacific WWE WrestleMania 20 Mask and Figure Sets Series 2

NNO Rey Mysterio
NNO Rosey
NNO Ultimo Dragon

2004 Jakks Pacific WWE WrestleMania 20 Playset

NNO Stage Entrance and Stunt Ring

2004 Jakks Pacific WWE WrestleMania 20 Times Square Limited Edition

NNO Ric Flair/600*
NNO Triple H/600*

2004 Jakks Pacific WWE WrestleMania 20 Series 2

NNO Chavo Guerrero
NNO Chris Benoit
NNO Christian
NNO Eddie Guerrero
NNO John Cena
NNO Undertaker

2004 Jakks Pacific WWE WrestleMania 20 Series 2 2-Packs

NNO Booker T/Rob Van Dam
NNO Ric Flair/Randy Orton
NNO Rikishi/Scotty 2 Hotty

2004 Jakks Pacific WWE WrestleMania 20 Series 1 2-Packs

NNO Brock Lesnar/Kurt Angle
NNO Edge/Christian
NNO Steve Austin/HBK

2005 Jakks Pacific WWE WrestleMania 21 Series 1

NNO	Eddie Guerrero	12.50	25.00
NNO	Rey Mysterio		
NNO	Triple H		
NNO	Victoria		

2005 Jakks Pacific WWE WrestleMania 21 Series 1 2-Packs

NNO Chris Jericho vs. Shawn Michaels
NNO John Cena vs. Big Show
NNO Kane vs. Kurt Angle

2005 Jakks Pacific WWE WrestleMania 21 Series 2

NNO Batista
NNO Booker T
NNO Charlie Haas
NNO Chris Benoit
NNO Eddie Guerrero   12.50   25.00
NNO Lita

2005 Jakks Pacific WWE WrestleMania 21 Series 2 2-Packs

NNO Maven/Eugene
NNO Rey Mysterio/Rene Dupree
NNO Rob Conway/William Regal

2005 Jakks Pacific WWE WrestleMania 21 Series 3

NNO Booker T
NNO Carlito
NNO Edge
NNO Randy Orton
NNO Stone Cold Steve Austin
NNO Undertaker

2005 Jakks Pacific WWE WrestleMania 21 Series 3 2-Packs

NNO John Cena/John Bradshaw Layfield
NNO Kurt Angle/Shawn Michaels
NNO Triple H/Batista

2005 Jakks Pacific WWE WrestleMania 21 Gear and Figure Sets Series 1

NNO Edge   10.00   20.00
NNO Hurricane
NNO JBL
NNO Kurt Angle
NNO Rey Mysterio   12.50   25.00
NNO Undertaker

2005 Jakks Pacific WWE WrestleMania 21 Gear and Figure Sets Series 2

NNO John Cena
NNO Rey Mysterio   12.50   25.00
NNO Undertaker   10.00   20.00

2005 Jakks Pacific WWE WrestleMania 21 Gear and Figure Sets Series 3

NNO Edge   10.00   20.00
NNO JBL
NNO Kurt Angle

2005 Jakks Pacific WWE WrestleMania 21 Gear and Figure Sets Series 4

NNO Hurricane
NNO John Cena
NNO Rey Mysterio   12.50   25.00

2005 Jakks Pacific WWE WrestleMania 21 Gear and Figure Sets 2-Packs

NNO Rey Mysterio/Rey Mysterio
NNO Rosey/Hurricane

2002 Jakks Pacific WWE Wrestling's Most Wanted

NNO Rock n' Roll Rivals
Edge/Y2J
NNO Ultimate Hardcore Match
RVD/Hardcore Holly
NNO Iron Man Match
HHH/Chris Benoit

2020-21 Jazwares AEW Exclusives

NNO Britt Baker Lights Out
NNO Chris Jericho Bubbly   30.00   75.00
NNO Cody & Dustin Rhodes Blood Brothers 30.00   75.00
NNO Darby Allin Coffin Drop
NNO Jurassic Express   50.00   100.00
NNO Jurassic Express (Package Variant) 75.00   150.00
NNO Kenny Omega & Jon Moxley Death Match

2021 Jazwares AEW Unmatched Series 1

NNO Britt Baker DMD   30.00   75.00
NNO Cody (LJN style)   25.00   50.00
NNO Darby Allin   30.00   75.00
NNO Dustin Rhodes   25.00   50.00
NNO Kenny Omega   30.00   60.00
NNO Miro   30.00   75.00

2021 Jazwares AEW Unmatched Series 2

NNO MJF
NNO Ortiz
NNO Santana
NNO Sting
NNO Tay Conti
NNO Wardlow

2022 Jazwares AEW Unmatched Series 3

NNO Anna Jay
NNO Evil Uno
NNO John Silver
NNO Mr. Brodie Lee
NNO Stu Grayson

2020-21 Jazwares AEW Unrivaled Collection Playsets

NNO Action Ring   30.00   75.00
NNO Action Ring w/Cody UK   75.00   150.00
NNO Authentic Scale Ring (w/Aubrey Edwards)
NNO Authentic Scale Ring (w/Kenny Omega) 100.00 200.00

2020 Jazwares AEW Unrivaled Collection Series 1

NNO Brandi Rhodes   75.00   150.00
NNO Chris Jericho   25.00   50.00
NNO Chris Jericho/1000* CH   250.00   500.00
NNO Cody Rhodes   25.00   50.00
NNO Cody Rhodes/500* CH   600.00 1200.00
NNO Kenny Omega   30.00   75.00
NNO Matt Jackson   20.00   40.00
NNO Nick Jackson   25.00   50.00

2020 Jazwares AEW Unrivaled Collection Series 2

NNO Dustin Rhodes
NNO Hangman Adam Page
NNO Jon Moxley
NNO MJF
NNO MJF
(CHASE)
NNO Pentagon Jr.
NNO Rey Fenix

2021 Jazwares AEW Unrivaled Collection Series 3

NNO Darby Allin   30.00   60.00
NNO Darby Allin   500.00 1000.00
(CHASE)
NNO Matt Jackson   20.00   40.00
NNO Nick Jackson   20.00   40.00
NNO Orange Cassidy   25.00   50.00
NNO Pac   25.00   50.00
NNO Riho   20.00   40.00
NNO Riho   150.00   300.00
(CHASE)

2021 Jazwares AEW Unrivaled Collection Series 4

NNO Cody   25.00   50.00
NNO Cody CH   200.00   400.00
NNO Kenny Omega   30.00   60.00
NNO Matt Hardy   25.00   50.00
NNO Matt Hardy CH
NNO Ortiz   20.00   40.00
NNO Sammy Guevara   30.00   75.00
NNO Santana   30.00   60.00

2021 Jazwares AEW Unrivaled Collection Series 5

NNO Hangman Adam Page   25.00   50.00
NNO Hangman Adam Page (w/chaps)/3,000* R 350.00 700.00
NNO Jon Moxley   30.00   75.00
NNO Jon Moxley (Paradigm Shift)/5,000* 250.00 500.00
(CHASE)
NNO Jungle Boy (black tights)   30.00   60.00
NNO Kazarian   25.00   50.00
NNO Luchasaurus (black tights)   30.00   75.00
NNO Scorpio Sky   25.00   50.00

2021 Jazwares AEW Unrivaled Collection Series 6

NNO Chris Jericho   25.00   50.00
NNO Chris Jericho CH   200.00   400.00
NNO Hikaru Shida   20.00   40.00
NNO Jake Hager   25.00   50.00
NNO Jake Hager CH   150.00   300.00
NNO MJF   20.00   40.00
NNO Pentagon Jr.   30.00   75.00
NNO Rey Fenix   20.00   40.00

2021 Jazwares AEW Unrivaled Collection Series 7

NNO Cash Wheeler
NNO Dax Harwood
NNO Lance Archer
NNO Lance Archer (silver tights)/3,000
(RARE)
NNO Matt Jackson
NNO Nick Jackson
NNO Nyla Rose
NNO Nyla Rose (orange scarf)/5,000
(CHASE)

2021 Jazwares AEW Unrivaled Collection Series 8

NNO Chris Jericho
NNO Chuck Taylor
NNO Jon Moxley
NNO Kris Statlander
NNO Orange Cassidy
NNO Trent?

1990 JusToys WCW Bend-Ems

NNO Arn Anderson   20.00   40.00
NNO Barry Windham   20.00   40.00
NNO Brian Pillman   15.00   30.00

NNO	Butch Reed	15.00	30.00
NNO	Lex Luger	15.00	30.00
NNO	Ric Flair	30.00	60.00
NNO	Rick Steiner	12.50	25.00
NNO	Ron Simmons	15.00	30.00
NNO	Scott Steiner	20.00	40.00
NNO	Sid Vicious	15.00	30.00
NNO	Sting	25.00	50.00
NNO	Tom Zenk	30.00	75.00

1990 JusToys WCW Bend-Ems Challenge 2-Pack

NNO	The Steiner Brothers		

2001 JusToys WWF Bend-Ems Gear

NNO	Chris Jericho		
NNO	Jeff Hardy	20.00	40.00
NNO	Kane	25.00	50.00
NNO	Matt Hardy	20.00	40.00
NNO	Road Dogg	15.00	30.00
NNO	Rock (black & white)	12.50	25.00
NNO	Rock (blue & yellow)	15.00	30.00
NNO	Steve Austin	12.50	25.00
NNO	Triple H	20.00	40.00

1998 JusToys WWF Bend-Ems Playsets

NNO	Super Slam Wrestling Ring (w/Austin & Michaels)		
NNO	Super Slam Wrestling Ring (w/Paul Bearer)	30.00	60.00

1994 JusToys WWF Bend-Ems Series I

NNO	Bret Hitman Hart	12.50	25.00
NNO	Diesel	7.50	15.00
NNO	Doink	7.50	15.00
NNO	Lex Luger	10.00	20.00
NNO	Razor Ramon	10.00	20.00

1995 JusToys WWF Bend-Ems Series II

NNO	1-2-3 Kid	6.00	12.00
NNO	British Bulldog	7.50	15.00
NNO	Mabel	6.00	12.00
NNO	Undertaker	7.50	15.00

1996 JusToys WWF Bend-Ems Series III

NNO	Ahmed Johnson	5.00	10.00
NNO	Goldust	6.00	12.00
NNO	Shawn Michaels	7.50	15.00
NNO	Yokozuna	6.00	12.00

1996 JusToys WWF Bend-Ems Series IV

NNO	Sunny	7.50	15.00
NNO	Sycho Sid	6.00	12.00
NNO	Vader	6.00	12.00
NNO	Wildman Marc Mero	5.00	10.00

1997 JusToys WWF Bend-Ems Series V

NNO	Faarooq	6.00	12.00
NNO	Mankind	10.00	20.00
NNO	Rocky Maivia	12.50	25.00
NNO	Stone Cold Steve Austin	6.00	12.00

1997 JusToys WWF Bend-Ems Series VI

NNO	Animal	6.00	12.00
NNO	Hawk	6.00	12.00
NNO	Hunter Hearts Helmsley	5.00	10.00
NNO	Undertaker	10.00	20.00

1997 JusToys WWF Bend-Ems Series VII

NNO	Crush	7.50	15.00
NNO	Ken Shamrock	7.50	15.00
NNO	Owen Hart	12.50	25.00
NNO	The Patriot	10.00	20.00

1998 JusToys WWF Bend-Ems Series IX

NNO	Brian Christopher	6.00	12.00
NNO	Cactus Jack	7.50	15.00
NNO	Sable	10.00	20.00
NNO	X-Pac	6.00	12.00

1998 JusToys WWF Bend-Ems Series VIII

NNO	Chyna	7.50	15.00
NNO	Jeff Jarrett	6.00	12.00
NNO	Kane	7.50	15.00
NNO	Taka	5.00	10.00

1998 JusToys WWF Bend-Ems Series X

NNO	B.A. Billy Gunn	6.00	12.00
NNO	Edge	7.50	15.00
NNO	Road Dogg	6.00	12.00
NNO	Steve Blackman	5.00	10.00

1999 JusToys WWF Bend-Ems Series XI

NNO	Al Snow	6.00	12.00
NNO	Godfather	7.50	15.00
NNO	Mr. McMahon	7.50	15.00
NNO	Val Venis	5.00	10.00

1999 JusToys WWF Bend-Ems Series XII

NNO	Big Boss Man	5.00	10.00
NNO	Mankind	7.50	15.00
NNO	Paul Wight	5.00	10.00
NNO	Steve Austin	10.00	20.00
NNO	Undertaker	7.50	15.00

1999 JusToys WWF Bend-Ems Series XIII

NNO	Droz	5.00	10.00
NNO	D'Lo Brown	5.00	10.00
NNO	Hardcore Holly	5.00	10.00
NNO	Shane McMahon	6.00	12.00
NNO	Steve Austin	7.50	15.00

2000 JusToys WWF Bend-Ems Series XIV

NNO	Chris Jericho	6.00	12.00
NNO	Jeff Hardy	6.00	12.00
NNO	Matt Hardy	5.00	10.00
NNO	The Rock	7.50	15.00

2001 JusToys WWF Bend-Ems Series XV

NNO	Tazz		
NNO	Grandmaster Sexay		
NNO	Rikishi		
NNO	The Rock/Repack		
NNO	Scotty 2 Hotty		

1994 Kelian AAA Wrestling Figures

NNO	Blue Panther		
NNO	Cien Caras	30.00	60.00
NNO	Fuerza Guerrera		
NNO	Heavy Metal	50.00	100.00
NNO	Hijo Del Santo	60.00	120.00
NNO	Konnan		
NNO	La Parka	60.00	120.00
NNO	Mascara Sagrada		
NNO	Octagon		

NNO	Perro Aguayo	40.00	80.00
NNO	Psicosis		
NNO	Rey Misterio		

1994 Kelian AAA Wrestling Figures (loose)

NNO	Blue Panther		
NNO	Cien Caras	20.00	40.00
NNO	Fuerza Guerrera		
NNO	Heavy Metal		
NNO	Hijo Del Santo		
NNO	Konnan		
NNO	La Parka		
NNO	Mascara Sagrada		
NNO	Octagon	12.50	25.00
NNO	Perro Aguayo		
NNO	Psicosis	30.00	75.00
NNO	Rey Misterio	25.00	60.00

2019 Kidrobot Collectible Vinyl Mini Series WWE

NNO	AJ Styles	6.00	12.00
NNO	Alexa Bliss	7.50	15.00
NNO	Andre the Giant	4.00	8.00
NNO	Charlotte Flair	6.00	12.00
NNO	John Cena	7.50	15.00
NNO	Ric Flair	6.00	12.00
NNO	Roman Reigns	5.00	10.00
NNO	Ronda Rousey	5.00	10.00
NNO	Sasha Banks	7.50	15.00
NNO	Shawn Michaels	5.00	10.00
NNO	The Rock	7.50	15.00
NNO	Triple H Mystery CH		
NNO	Ultimate Warrior	20.00	40.00
NNO	Undertaker	7.50	15.00

1985 LJN WWF Wrestling Superstars 16-Inch

NNO	Hulk Hogan	225.00	450.00
NNO	Rowdy Roddy Piper	175.00	350.00

1985 LJN WWF Wrestling Superstars 16-Inch (loose)

NNO	Hulk Hogan	60.00	120.00
NNO	Rowdy Roddy Piper	75.00	150.00

1985 LJN WWF Wrestling Superstars Bendies

NNO	Andre the Giant	50.00	100.00
NNO	Big John Studd	30.00	75.00
NNO	Bobby Heenan	50.00	100.00
NNO	Brutus Beefcake	20.00	40.00
NNO	Captain Lou Albano	50.00	100.00
NNO	Corporal Kirchner	20.00	40.00
NNO	George Steele	30.00	75.00
NNO	Hillbilly Jim	30.00	75.00
NNO	Hulk Hogan/Blue Knee Pads	25.00	50.00
NNO	Hulk Hogan/Red Knee Pads	25.00	50.00
NNO	Iron Sheik	25.00	60.00
NNO	Jesse Ventura	30.00	60.00
NNO	Junk Yard Dog	30.00	75.00
NNO	King Kong Bundy	20.00	40.00
NNO	Mr. Wonderful	25.00	60.00
NNO	Nikolai Volkoff	25.00	60.00
NNO	Randy Macho Man Savage	75.00	150.00
NNO	Ricky The Dragon Steamboat	30.00	75.00
NNO	Rowdy Roddy Piper	50.00	100.00

1985 LJN WWF Wrestling Superstars Bendies (loose)

NNO	Andre the Giant	10.00	20.00

NNO	Big John Studd	10.00	20.00
NNO	Bobby Heenan	10.00	20.00
NNO	Brutus Beefcake	7.50	15.00
NNO	Captain Lou Albano	12.50	25.00
NNO	Corporal Kirchner	6.00	12.00
NNO	George Steele	7.50	15.00
NNO	Hillbilly Jim	6.00	12.00
NNO	Hulk Hogan/Blue Knee Pads	10.00	20.00
NNO	Hulk Hogan/Red Knee Pads	10.00	20.00
NNO	Iron Sheik	6.00	12.00
NNO	Jesse Ventura	7.50	15.00
NNO	Junk Yard Dog	7.50	15.00
NNO	King Kong Bundy	5.00	10.00
NNO	Mr. Wonderful	7.50	15.00
NNO	Nikolai Volkoff	6.00	12.00
NNO	Randy Macho Man Savage	20.00	40.00
NNO	Ricky The Dragon Steamboat	15.00	30.00
NNO	Rowdy Roddy Piper	15.00	30.00

1985 LJN WWF Wrestling Superstars Bendies Playset

NNO	Cage Match Challenge w/Hogan Blue Knee Pads	150.00	300.00

1985 LJN WWF Wrestling Superstars Bendies Playset (loose)

NNO	Cage Match Challenge	50.00	100.00

1985 LJN WWF Wrestling Superstars Bendies Tag Teams

NNO	Hulk Hogan/Junk Yard Dog		
NNO	Iron Sheik/Nikolai Volkoff	25.00	50.00
NNO	George Steele/Captain Lou Albano	25.00	50.00
NNO	King Kong Bundy/Big John Studd	50.00	100.00
NNO	Randy Savage/Jesse Ventura	50.00	100.00
NNO	Ricky Steamboat/Corporal Kirchner	60.00	120.00

1989 LJN WWF Wrestling Superstars Black Card Re-Release

NNO	Adrian Adonis		
NNO	Bam Bam Bigelow	50.00	100.00
NNO	Big John Studd		
NNO	Bret Hitman Hart		
NNO	Brutus The Barber Beefcake		
NNO	Demolition Ax		
NNO	Elizabeth/Gold Skirt		
NNO	Elizabeth/Purple Skirt		
NNO	Hacksaw Jim Duggan	350.00	500.00
NNO	Honky Tonk Man	450.00	900.00
NNO	Hulk Hogan/Red Shirt		
NNO	Hulk Hogan/White Shirt	1000.00	2000.00
NNO	Jake The Snake Roberts	150.00	300.00
NNO	Randy Macho Man Savage		
NNO	Ted DiBiase		

1984 LJN WWF Wrestling Superstars Series 1

NNO	Andre the Giant/Long Hair	250.00	500.00
NNO	Big John Studd	125.00	250.00
NNO	Hillbilly Jim	150.00	300.00
NNO	Hulk Hogan	350.00	700.00
NNO	Iron Sheik	200.00	400.00
NNO	Jimmy Snuka	125.00	250.00
NNO	Junk Yard Dog/Red Chain	125.00	250.00
NNO	Junk Yard Dog/Silver Chain	150.00	300.00
NNO	Nikolai Volkoff	125.00	250.00
NNO	Rowdy Roddy Piper/Brown Boots		
NNO	Rowdy Roddy Piiper/Red Boots	125.00	250.00

1984 LJN WWF Wrestling Superstars Series 1 (loose)

NNO	Andre the Giant/Long Hair	25.00	50.00
NNO	Big John Studd	15.00	40.00
NNO	Hillbilly Jim	15.00	40.00
NNO	Hulk Hogan	30.00	60.00
NNO	Iron Sheik	15.00	30.00
NNO	Jimmy Snuka	15.00	40.00
NNO	Junk Yard Dog/Red Chain	25.00	50.00
NNO	Junk Yard Dog/Silver Chain	15.00	30.00
NNO	Nikolai Volkoff	15.00	30.00
NNO	Rowdy Roddy Piper/Brown Boots		
NNO	Rowdy Roddy Piper/Red Boots	30.00	60.00

1985 LJN WWF Wrestling Superstars Series 2

NNO	Andre the Giant/Short Hair	300.00	600.00
NNO	Brutus Beefcake	200.00	400.00
NNO	George Steele	100.00	200.00
NNO	Greg Valentine/Dk. Blonde Hair		
NNO	Greg Valentine/Lt. Blonde Hair	100.00	200.00
NNO	King Kong Bundy	100.00	200.00
NNO	Mr. Wonderful	150.00	300.00

1985 LJN WWF Wrestling Superstars Series 2 (loose)

NNO	Andre the Giant/Short Hair	50.00	100.00
NNO	Brutus Beefcake	15.00	30.00
NNO	George Steele	15.00	30.00
NNO	Greg Valentine/Dk Blond Hair	12.50	25.00
NNO	Greg Valentine/Lt. Blonde Hair	10.00	20.00
NNO	King Kong Bundy	20.00	40.00
NNO	Mr. Wonderful	15.00	30.00

1986 LJN WWF Wrestling Superstars Series 3

NNO	Bobby Heenan/No Scrolls		
NNO	Bobby Heenan/Scrolls	75.00	150.00
NNO	Bruno Sammartino	60.00	120.00
NNO	Captain Lou Albano/Red Lapel	50.00	100.00
NNO	Captain Lou Albano/White Lapel	75.00	150.00
NNO	Classy Freddie Blassie	60.00	120.00
NNO	Corporal Kirchner/Beard		
NNO	Corporal Kirchner/No Stubble	60.00	120.00
NNO	Corporal Kirchner/Stubble		
NNO	Don Muraco	100.00	200.00
NNO	Jesse Ventura	125.00	250.00
NNO	Jimmy Hart/Hearts on Megaphone	60.00	120.00
NNO	Jimmy Hart/No Hearts on Megaphone	60.00	120.00
NNO	Randy Savage	300.00	500.00
NNO	Ricky Steamboat	100.00	200.00
NNO	SD Jones/Hawaiian Shirt	75.00	150.00
NNO	SD Jones/Red Shirt	60.00	120.00
NNO	Terry Funk	125.00	250.00
NNO	Tito Santana	100.00	200.00

1986 LJN WWF Wrestling Superstars Series 3 (loose)

NNO	Bobby Heenan/No Scrolls	30.00	60.00
NNO	Bobby Heenan/Scrolls	20.00	50.00
NNO	Bruno Sammartino	20.00	40.00
NNO	Captain Lou Albano/Red Lapel	12.50	25.00
NNO	Captain Lou Albano/White Lapel	15.00	30.00
NNO	Classy Freddie Blassie	30.00	60.00
NNO	Corporal Kirchner/Beard		
NNO	Corporal Kirchner/No Stubble	15.00	30.00
NNO	Corporal Kirchner/Stubble	15.00	30.00
NNO	Don Muraco	20.00	40.00
NNO	Jesse Ventura	20.00	40.00

1986 LJN WWF Wrestling Superstars Series 3 (continued)

NNO	Jimmy Hart/Hearts on Megaphone	20.00	40.00
NNO	Jimmy Hart/No Hearts on Megaphone	10.00	20.00
NNO	Randy Savage	30.00	60.00
NNO	Ricky Steamboat	15.00	30.00
NNO	SD Jones/Hawaiian Shirt	20.00	40.00
NNO	SD Jones/Red Shirt	12.50	25.00
NNO	Terry Funk	30.00	75.00
NNO	Tito Santana	20.00	40.00

1987 LJN WWF Wrestling Superstars Series 4

NNO	Adrian Adonis	75.00	150.00
NNO	Billy Jack Haynes	200.00	350.00
NNO	Bret Hart/Pink Tights	300.00	600.00
NNO	Bret Hart/Purple Tights		
NNO	Brian Blair/Non-Tan	75.00	150.00
NNO	Brian Blair/Tan	125.00	250.00
NNO	Cowboy Bob Orton	100.00	200.00
NNO	Elizabeth/Gold Skirt	125.00	250.00
NNO	Elizabeth/Purple Skirt	1200.00	1800.00
NNO	Hercules Hernandez	100.00	200.00
NNO	Jake the Snake Roberts	200.00	400.00
NNO	Jim Brunzell/Non-Tan	125.00	250.00
NNO	Jim Brunzell/Tan	150.00	300.00
NNO	Jim Neidhart/Pink Tights	300.00	600.00
NNO	Jim Neidhart/Purple Tights		
NNO	Kamala	150.00	300.00
NNO	King Harley Race	300.00	500.00
NNO	Koko B. Ware	200.00	350.00
NNO	Mean Gene Okerlund	100.00	200.00
NNO	Mr. Fuji	125.00	250.00
NNO	Outback Jack	100.00	200.00
NNO	Ted Arcidi	150.00	300.00

1987 LJN WWF Wrestling Superstars Series 4 (loose)

NNO	Adrian Adonis	25.00	50.00
NNO	Billy Jack Haynes	50.00	100.00
NNO	Bret Hart/Pink Tights	50.00	100.00
NNO	Bret Hart/Purple Tights		
NNO	Brian Blair/Non-Tan	20.00	40.00
NNO	Brian Blair/Tan		
NNO	Cowboy Bob Orton	30.00	60.00
NNO	Elizabeth/Gold Skirt	50.00	100.00
NNO	Elizabeth/Purple Skirt	200.00	350.00
NNO	Hercules Hernandez	20.00	40.00
NNO	Jake the Snake Roberts	50.00	100.00
NNO	Jim Brunzell/Non-Tan	15.00	30.00
NNO	Jim Brunzell/Tan		
NNO	Jim Neidhart/Pink Tights	30.00	75.00
NNO	Jim Neidhart/Purple Tights		
NNO	Kamala	30.00	60.00
NNO	King Harley Race	60.00	120.00
NNO	Koko B. Ware	30.00	75.00
NNO	Mean Gene Okerlund	20.00	40.00
NNO	Mr. Fuji	30.00	60.00
NNO	Outback Jack	30.00	75.00
NNO	Ted Arcidi	20.00	40.00

1988 LJN WWF Wrestling Superstars Series 5

NNO	Ax	300.00	600.00
NNO	Bam Bam Bigelow	200.00	400.00
NNO	Hacksaw Jim Duggan	300.00	450.00
NNO	Honky Tonk Man	300.00	500.00
NNO	Hulk Hogan/Red Shirt		
NNO	Hulk Hogan/White Shirt		
NNO	Johnny V	90.00	175.00
NNO	Ken Patera	150.00	300.00
NNO	One Man Gang	200.00	400.00

NNO	Referee/Blue Shirt	200.00	400.00
NNO	Referee/White Shirt	400.00	750.00
NNO	Rick Martel	300.00	600.00
NNO	Slick	150.00	300.00
NNO	Ted Dibiase	300.00	500.00
NNO	Tito Santana/White Trunks	200.00	350.00
NNO	Vince McMahon	150.00	300.00

1988 LJN WWF Wrestling Superstars Series 5 (loose)

NNO	Ax	50.00	100.00
NNO	Bam Bam Bigelow	50.00	100.00
NNO	Hacksaw Jim Duggan	100.00	200.00
NNO	Honky Tonk Man	50.00	100.00
NNO	Hulk Hogan/Red Shirt	125.00	250.00
NNO	Hulk Hogan/White Shirt	125.00	250.00
NNO	Johnny V	20.00	40.00
NNO	Ken Patera	30.00	60.00
NNO	One Man Gang	30.00	75.00
NNO	Referee/Blue Shirt	50.00	100.00
NNO	Referee/White Shirt	60.00	120.00
NNO	Rick Martel	30.00	60.00
NNO	Slick	30.00	75.00
NNO	Ted Dibiase	60.00	120.00
NNO	Tito Santana	25.00	50.00
NNO	Vince McMahon	60.00	120.00

1989 LJN WWF Wrestling Superstars Series 6

NNO	Andre the Giant	2000.00	4000.00
NNO	Big Boss Man	1250.00	2500.00
NNO	Haku	500.00	1000.00
NNO	Rick Rude	500.00	1000.00
NNO	Ultimate Warrior	3000.00	6000.00
NNO	Warlord	1500.00	3000.00

1984 LJN WWF Wrestling Superstars Accessories

NNO	Hulkamania Barbell Workout Set		
NNO	Hulkamania Deluxe Workout Set	300.00	600.00

1986 LJN WWF Wrestling Superstars Stretch Wrestlers

NNO	George The Animal Steele	125.00	250.00
NNO	Hulk Hogan	300.00	600.00
NNO	Junkyard Dog	125.00	250.00
NNO	King Kong Bundy	125.00	250.00
NNO	Macho Man Randy Savage	250.00	400.00
NNO	Mr. Wonderful Paul Orndorff	75.00	150.00
NNO	Ricky The Dragon Steamboat	150.00	300.00
NNO	Rowdy Roddy Piper	250.00	500.00

1985 LJN WWF Wrestling Superstars Tag Teams

NNO	British Bulldogs	400.00	800.00
NNO	Greg Valentine & Brutus Beefcake	200.00	400.00
NNO	Hart Foundation	1000.00	1500.00
NNO	Hillbilly Jim & Hulk Hogan	250.00	500.00
NNO	Iron Sheik & Nikolai Volkoff	150.00	300.00
NNO	Killer Bees	200.00	400.00
NNO	Strike Force	300.00	500.00

1986 LJN WWF Wrestling Superstars Thumb Wrestlers

NNO	Hillbilly Jim/Big John Studd	75.00	150.00
NNO	Hillbilly Jim/Macho Man Randy Savage	15.00	30.00
NNO	Hillbilly Jim/Nikolai Volkoff	12.50	25.00
NNO	Hillbilly Jim/Rowdy Roddy Piper	30.00	60.00
NNO	Hillbilly Jim/The Iron Sheik	30.00	75.00
NNO	Hulk Hogan/Big John Studd	25.00	50.00

NNO	Hulk Hogan/Jake The Snake Roberts	30.00	75.00
NNO	Hulk Hogan/King Kong Bundy	20.00	40.00
NNO	Hulk Hogan/Macho Man Randy Savage	25.00	50.00
NNO	Hulk Hogan/Nikolai Volkoff	30.00	75.00
NNO	Hulk Hogan/Rowdy Roddy Piper	60.00	120.00
NNO	Hulk Hogan/The Iron Sheik	20.00	40.00
NNO	Junkyard Dog/Big John Studd	15.00	30.00
NNO	Junkyard Dog/Nikolai Volkoff	30.00	75.00
NNO	Junkyard Dog/Rowdy Roddy Piper	100.00	200.00
NNO	Junkyard Dog/The Iron Sheik	15.00	30.00
NNO	Mr. Wonderful Paul Orndorff/Big John Studd	30.00	75.00
NNO	Mr. Wonderful Paul Orndorff/King Kong Bundy	15.00	30.00
NNO	Mr. Wonderful Paul Orndorff/Rowdy Roddy Piper	50.00	100.00
NNO	Ricky The Dragon Steamboat/Jake The Snake Roberts	30.00	75.00
NNO	Ricky The Dragon Steamboat Macho Man Randy Savage	25.00	50.00
NNO	Ricky The Dragon Steamboat/Nikolai Volkoff	12.50	25.00
NNO	Ricky The Dragon Steamboat/Rowdy Roddy Piper	15.00	30.00

1986 LJN WWF Wrestling Superstars Thumb Wrestlers (loose)

NNO	Big John Studd	5.00	10.00
NNO	Hillbilly Jim	5.00	10.00
NNO	Hulk Hogan	7.50	15.00
NNO	Iron Sheik	3.00	8.00
NNO	Jake The Snake Roberts	5.00	10.00
NNO	Junkyard Dog	3.00	8.00
NNO	King Kong Bundy	6.00	12.00
NNO	Macho Man Randy Savage	7.50	15.00
NNO	Mr. Wonderful Paul Orndorff	3.00	8.00
NNO	Nikolai Volkoff	3.00	8.00
NNO	Ricky The Dragon Steamboat	5.00	10.00
NNO	Rowdy Roddy Piper	6.00	12.00

2018 The Loyal Subjects Action Vinyls WWE

NNO	AJ Styles		
NNO	Brock Lesnar	10.00	20.00
NNO	Demon King Finn Balor	12.50	25.00
NNO	Demon King Finn Balor Black and White		
NNO	Finn Balor/Blue Trunks	30.00	75.00
NNO	John Cena	7.50	15.00
NNO	Macho Man Randy Savage/Gold/2*		
NNO	Macho Man Randy Savage	12.50	25.00
NNO	Macho Man Randy Savage/American Flag	30.00	75.00
NNO	Referee		
NNO	Referee/GITD		
NNO	Roman Reigns	10.00	20.00
NNO	Sasha Banks CH	40.00	80.00
NNO	Shinsuke Nakamura	7.50	15.00
NNO	Shinsuke Nakamura/Black Pants	15.00	30.00
NNO	Sting	15.00	30.00
NNO	Undertaker	12.50	25.00
NNO	RAW Ring/Bottom Left	10.00	20.00
NNO	RAW Ring/Bottom Right	10.00	20.00
NNO	RAW Ring/Top Left	10.00	20.00
NNO	RAW Ring/Top Right	10.00	20.00

2018 The Loyal Subjects Action Vinyls WWE SDCC Exclusives

NNO	AJ Styles vs. Shinsuke Nakamura	20.00	40.00
NNO	Brock Lesnar vs. Roman Reigns	12.50	25.00
NNO	John Cena vs. Undertaker	30.00	75.00

2020 Major Wrestling Figure Podcast Ringside Collectibles Exclusives

NNO	Zack Ryder/Curt Hawkins/500		
NNO	Zack Ryder/Curt Hawkins (NY Mets colors)/250		

2015 Mattel Create A WWE Superstar Series 1

NNO	Bray Wyatt	10.00	20.00
NNO	Hulk Hogan	20.00	40.00
NNO	John Cena	12.50	25.00
NNO	The Rock	15.00	30.00

2015 Mattel Create A WWE Superstar Series 1 Sets

NNO	Gladiator Set	10.00	20.00
NNO	Lucha Set	10.00	20.00
NNO	Rocker Set	10.00	20.00

2015 Mattel Create A WWE Superstar Series 2

NNO	Kane	12.50	25.00
NNO	Randy Orton	10.00	20.00
NNO	Sheamus	10.00	20.00
NNO	Stone Cold Steve Austin		

2015 Mattel Create A WWE Superstar Series 2 Sets

NNO	Samurai Set		
NNO	Special Ops Set	20.00	40.00
NNO	Zombie Set	15.00	30.00

2015 Mattel Create A WWE Superstar Series 3

NNO	Goldust	25.00	50.00
NNO	John Cena	15.00	30.00
NNO	Rusev		
NNO	Triple H		
NNO	Ultimate Warrior	12.50	25.00

2015 Mattel Create A WWE Superstar Series 3 Sets

NNO	Enforcer Set	10.00	20.00
NNO	Hip Hop Set	10.00	20.00
NNO	Vigilante Set	15.00	30.00

2015 Mattel Create A WWE Superstar Series Playset

NNO	Ring Builder	30.00	75.00

2019 Mattel Masters of the WWE Universe

NNO	Finn Balor	20.00	40.00
NNO	Sting	30.00	60.00
NNO	Triple H	20.00	40.00
NNO	Ultimate Warrior	15.00	30.00

2019 Mattel Masters of the WWE Universe Playsets

NNO	Grayskull Mania (w/John Cena & Terror Claws Triple H)	25.00	50.00
NNO	Grayskull Ring	20.00	40.00

2020 Mattel Masters of the WWE Universe Wave 2

NNO	Macho Man	20.00	40.00
NNO	John Cena	15.00	30.00
NNO	Roman Reigns	20.00	40.00
NNO	Rey Mysterio	25.00	50.00

2020 Mattel Masters of the WWE Universe Wave 3

NNO	Braun Strowman	25.00	50.00
NNO	The New Day	30.00	75.00
NNO	The Rock	30.00	75.00
NNO	Undertaker	50.00	100.00

2020 Mattel Masters of the WWE Universe Wave 4

NNO	The Fiend Bray Wyatt	30.00	60.00
NNO	Jake "The Snake" Roberts	25.00	50.00
NNO	Mr. T	45.00	90.00
NNO	Seth Rollins	25.00	50.00

2020 Mattel Masters of the WWE Universe Wave 5

NNO	Becky Lynch	15.00	30.00
NNO	Macho Man Randy Savage	20.00	40.00
NNO	Ricky "The Dragon" Steamboat	15.00	30.00
NNO	Rowdy Roddy Piper	15.00	30.00

2020 Mattel Masters of the WWE Universe Wave 6

NNO	Goldberg	12.50	25.00
NNO	Kane	12.50	25.00
NNO	Stephanie McMahon	10.00	20.00
NNO	Ultimate Warrior	12.50	25.00

2021 Mattel Masters of the WWE Universe Wave 7

NNO	Bret "Hit Man" Hart	20.00	40.00
NNO	Andre the Giant	30.00	75.00
NNO	Junkyard Dog	20.00	40.00
NNO	Sgt. Slaughter	20.00	40.00

2021 Mattel Masters of the WWE Universe Wave 8

NNO	Chyna	20.00	40.00
NNO	Rey Mysterio	20.00	40.00
NNO	Stone Cold Steve Austin	15.00	30.00

2010 Mattel WWE Battle Packs Series 1

NNO	Santino/Beth Phoenix	15.00	30.00
NNO	Shawn Michaels vs. {Chris Jericho	20.00	40.00
NNO	Ted DiBiase/Cody Rhodes	30.00	75.00

2010 Mattel WWE Battle Packs Series 2

NNO	Carlito/Primo	12.50	25.00
NNO	Finlay/Hornswoggle	20.00	40.00
NNO	John Morrison/The Miz	15.00	30.00

2010 Mattel WWE Battle Packs Series 3

NNO	Edge/Big Show		
NNO	Rey Mysterio/Evan Bourne	25.00	50.00
NNO	Shad/JTG	30.00	60.00

2010 Mattel WWE Battle Packs Series 4

NNO	Chavo vs. Hornswoggle	7.50	15.00
NNO	Christian/Tommy Dreamer	40.00	80.00
NNO	Hart Dynasty	20.00	40.00

2010 Mattel WWE Battle Packs Series 5

NNO	Carlito/Primo	20.00	40.00
NNO	D-Generation X	25.00	50.00
NNO	Ricky Steamboat vs. Y2J	15.00	30.00

2010 Mattel WWE Battle Packs Series 6

NNO	Mark Henry & MVP		
NNO	Undertaker vs. Batista		
NNO	Vladimir Kozlov & Ezekiel Jackson	7.50	15.00

2010 Mattel WWE Battle Packs Series 7

NNO	CM Punk & Luke Gallows	20.00	40.00
NNO	Dolph Ziggler vs. John Morrison		
NNO	The Miz & Big Show		

2011 Mattel WWE Battle Packs Series 8

NNO	John Cena vs. Randy Orton		
NNO	Matt Hardy/Great Khali		
NNO	Ted DiBiase/Cody Rhodes		

2011 Mattel WWE Battle Packs Series 9

NNO	Christian/Heath Slater	7.50	15.00
NNO	Hart Dynasty	15.00	30.00
NNO	Sheamus/Triple H	12.50	25.00

2011 Mattel WWE Battle Packs Series 10

NNO	Darren Young/Justin Gabriel	15.00	30.00
NNO	David Otunga/ Michael Tarver	15.00	30.00
NNO	Randy Orton vs. Edge	40.00	80.00

2011 Mattel WWE Battle Packs Series 11

NNO	Drew McIntyre/ Cody Rhodes	75.00	150.00
NNO	Jimmy Uso/Jey Uso	25.00	50.00
NNO	Undertaker/Kane	30.00	75.00

2011 Mattel WWE Battle Packs Series 13

NNO	John Cena vs. R-Truth	15.00	30.00
NNO	The Miz vs. Alex Riley	20.00	40.00
NNO	Rey Mysterio vs. Cody Rhodes	30.00	60.00

2012 Mattel WWE Battle Packs Series 14

NNO	Heath Slater/Justin Gabriel	12.50	25.00
NNO	Macho Man Randy Savage vs. CM Punk	25.00	50.00
NNO	Randy Orton vs. Mason Ryan	12.50	25.00

2012 Mattel WWE Battle Packs Series 15

NNO	Brie Bella/Nikki Bella	30.00	60.00
NNO	Sin Cara vs. Daniel Bryan	25.00	50.00
NNO	The Rock vs. John Cena	12.50	25.00

2012 Mattel WWE Battle Packs Series 16

NNO	Alberto Del Rio vs. Big Show		
NNO	David Otunga/ Michael McGillicutty	12.50	25.00
NNO	Randy Orton vs. Christian	15.00	30.00

2012 Mattel WWE Battle Packs Series 17

NNO	John Cena vs. CM Punk	15.00	30.00
NNO	Mark Henry vs. Trent Barreta	15.00	30.00
NNO	Rey Mysterio vs. The Miz	25.00	50.00

2012 Mattel WWE Battle Packs Series 18

NNO	CM Punk vs. Triple H	20.00	40.00
NNO	Randy Orton vs. Wade Barrett		
NNO	Zack Ryder vs. Dolph Ziggler	15.00	30.00

2012 Mattel WWE Battle Packs Series 19

NNO	Daniel Bryan vs. Big Show	15.00	30.00
NNO	Epico/Primo	25.00	50.00
NNO	John Cena vs. Kane		

2013 Mattel WWE Battle Packs Series 20

NNO	Brock Lesnar vs. Triple H	15.00	30.00
NNO	Brodus Clay vs. Curt Hawkins	10.00	20.00
NNO	Kofi Kingston/R-Truth	15.00	30.00

2013 Mattel WWE Battle Packs Series 21

NNO	Darren Young/Titus O'Neil	12.50	25.00
NNO	Kane vs. Daniel Bryan	20.00	40.00
NNO	Sheamus vs. Randy Orton	15.00	30.00

2013 Mattel WWE Battle Packs Series 22

NNO	Dolph Ziggler/ Vickie Guerrero	12.50	25.00
NNO	Ryback vs. Jinder Mahal	12.50	25.00
NNO	Sin Cara/Rey Mysterio	7.50	15.00

2013 Mattel WWE Battle Packs Series 23

NNO	CM Punk vs. Mr. McMahon	20.00	40.00
NNO	Rey Mysterio vs. Kofi Kingston	15.00	30.00
NNO	Sin Cara vs. Cody Rhodes	15.00	30.00

2013 Mattel WWE Battle Packs Series 24

NNO	Naomi/Cameron	20.00	40.00
NNO	The Rock vs. John Cena	17.50	35.00
NNO	Seth Rollins/Roman Reigns	15.00	30.00

2013 Mattel WWE Battle Packs Series 25

NNO	Brock Lesnar/Paul Heyman	15.00	30.00
NNO	CM Punk vs. Undertaker	25.00	50.00
NNO	Mark Henry vs. Ryback	20.00	40.00

2014 Mattel WWE Battle Packs Series 26

NNO	Nikki Bella/Brie Bella	20.00	40.00
NNO	Seth Rollins/Dean Ambrose	15.00	30.00
NNO	Triple H vs. Curtis Axel	12.50	25.00

2014 Mattel WWE Battle Packs Series 27

NNO	Big Show/Mark Henry	12.50	25.00
NNO	Brodus Clay/Tensai	10.00	20.00
NNO	Daniel Bryan/Randy Orton	12.50	25.00

2014 Mattel WWE Battle Packs Series 28

NNO	Big E/AJ Lee	20.00	40.00
NNO	Jimmy Uso/Jey Uso	10.00	20.00
NNO	Luke Harper/Erick Rowan	15.00	30.00

2014 Mattel WWE Battle Packs Series 29

NNO	CM Punk vs. Ryback	25.00	50.00
NNO	Goldust/Cody Rhodes	20.00	40.00
NNO	Los Matadores	12.50	25.00

2014 Mattel WWE Battle Packs Series 30

NNO	Brock Lesnar vs. Undertaker	15.00	30.00
NNO	Jake Roberts/Dean Ambrose	15.00	30.00
NNO	Xavier Woods/R-Truth	12.50	25.00

2014 Mattel WWE Battle Packs Series 31

NNO	John Cena/Ultimate Warrior	12.50	25.00
NNO	Luke Harper/Erick Rowan	12.50	30.00
NNO	Sin Cara/Alberto Del Rio	10.00	20.00

2015 Mattel WWE Battle Packs Series 32

NNO	Daniel Bryan/Triple H	15.00	30.00
NNO	Jimmy Uso/Jey Uso	20.00	40.00
NNO	Road Dogg/Billy Gunn	15.00	30.00

2015 Mattel WWE Battle Packs Series 33

NNO	Andre the Giant/Big Show	25.00	50.00
NNO	Rey Mysterio/RVD	15.00	30.00
NNO	Shawn Michaels/Undertaker	7.50	15.00

2015 Mattel WWE Battle Packs Series 34

NNO	Animal/Hawk	30.00	75.00
NNO	Hornswoggle/El Torito	30.00	60.00
NNO	Lana/Rusev	15.00	30.00

2015 Mattel WWE Battle Packs Series 35

NNO	Kane/Roman Reigns	12.50	25.00
NNO	Ryback/Curtis Axel	15.00	30.00
NNO	Zeb Colter/Jack Swagger	12.50	25.00

2015 Mattel WWE Battle Packs Series 36

NNO	Big E/Kofi Kingston	15.00	30.00
NNO	Dean Ambrose/Seth Rollins	10.00	20.00
NNO	Kevin Nash/Scott Hall	15.00	30.00

2015 Mattel WWE Battle Packs Series 37

NNO	Jamie Noble/Joey Mercury	12.50	25.00
NNO	Jey Uso/Jimmy Uso	12.50	25.00
NNO	Konnor/Viktor	10.00	20.00

2015 Mattel WWE Battle Packs Series 38

NNO	Adam Rose/Bunny	10.00	20.00
NNO	Bray Wyatt/Undertaker	15.00	30.00
NNO	Nikki Bella/Brie Bella	20.00	40.00

2016 Mattel WWE Battle Packs Series 39

NNO	Darren Young/Titus O'Neill	10.00	20.00
NNO	John Cena/Kevin Owens	7.50	15.00
NNO	Tyson Kidd/Cesaro	7.50	15.00

2016 Mattel WWE Battle Packs Series 40

NNO	Bushwhackers	10.00	20.00
NNO	Enzo Amore/Big Cass	15.00	30.00
NNO	Steve Austin/Mr. McMahon	15.00	30.00

2016 Mattel WWE Battle Packs Series 41

NNO	Bubba Ray/Devon Dudley	15.00	30.00
NNO	Charlotte/Ric Flair	12.50	25.00
NNO	Simon Gotch/Aiden English		

2016 Mattel WWE Battle Packs Series 42

NNO	Edge/Christian	10.00	20.00
NNO	Sin Cara/Kalisto	15.00	30.00
NNO	Triple H/Stephanie	12.50	25.00

2016 Mattel WWE Battle Packs Series 43A

NNO	Big E/Kofi Kingston	15.00	30.00
NNO	Nikki Bella/Brie Bella	20.00	40.00
NNO	Undertaker/Kane	12.50	25.00

2016 Mattel WWE Battle Packs Series 43B

NNO	Dean Ambrose/Brock Lesnar	12.50	25.00
NNO	Finn Balor/Samoa Joe	20.00	40.00
NNO	John Cena/Seth Rollins	10.00	20.00
NNO	Roman Reigns/Sheamus	12.50	25.00

2016 Mattel WWE Battle Packs Series 44

NNO	American Alpha	10.00	20.00
NNO	Sami Zayn/Kevin Owens	12.50	25.00
NNO	The Usos	15.00	30.00

2017 Mattel WWE Battle Packs Series 45

NNO	AJ Styles/Roman Reigns	15.00	30.00
NNO	Enzo Amore/Big Cass	20.00	40.00
NNO	Scott Dawson/Dash Wilder	15.00	30.00
NNO	Triple H/Road Dogg	15.00	30.00

2017 Mattel WWE Battle Packs Series 46

NNO	Dean Ambrose/Shane McMahon	15.00	30.00
NNO	Karl Anderson/Luke Gallows	25.00	50.00
NNO	The Miz & Maryse	15.00	30.00
NNO	The New Day (Kingston/Woods)	15.00	30.00

2017 Mattel WWE Battle Packs Series 47

NNO	Bray Wyatt/Luke Harper	12.50	25.00
NNO	The Hart Foundation	12.50	25.00
NNO	Roman Reigns vs. Rusev	12.50	25.00
NNO	Sasha Banks vs. Charlotte Flair	15.00	30.00

2017 Mattel WWE Battle Packs Series 48

NNO	American Alpha	12.50	25.00
NNO	Hype Bros.	10.00	20.00
NNO	Shawn Michaels/Diesel	12.50	25.00

2017 Mattel WWE Battle Packs Series 49

NNO	Daniel Bryan/The Miz	12.50	25.00
NNO	Sheamus/Cesaro	12.50	25.00
NNO	Stephanie McMahon/Mick Foley	10.00	20.00

2017 Mattel WWE Battle Packs Series 50

NNO	Konnor/Viktor	10.00	20.00
NNO	Luke Gallows/Karl Anderson	20.00	40.00
NNO	Randy Orton/Bray Wyatt	12.50	25.00

2017 Mattel WWE Battle Packs Series 51

NNO	Big E/Xavier Woods	12.50	25.00
NNO	The Miz/Maryse	10.00	20.00
NNO	Scott Dawson/Dash Wilder	15.00	30.00

2018 Mattel WWE Battle Packs Series 52

NNO	Jey Uso/Jimmy Uso	30.00	60.00
NNO	Roman Reigns/Brock Lesnar	12.50	25.00
NNO	Sheamus/Cesaro	15.00	30.00

2018 Mattel WWE Battle Packs Series 53

NNO	Carmella/James Ellsworth	12.50	25.00
NNO	Matt Hardy/Jeff Hardy	25.00	50.00
NNO	S. Nakamura/D. Ziggler	12.50	25.00

2018 Mattel WWE Battle Packs Series 54

NNO	B. Strowman/R. Reigns	15.00	30.00
NNO	Bray Wyatt/Finn Balor	12.50	25.00
NNO	Nia Jax/Alexa Bliss	25.00	50.00
NNO	Tyler Breeze/Fandango	10.00	20.00

2018 Mattel WWE Battle Packs Series 55

NNO	Big Show/Big Cass	17.50	35.00
NNO	Charlotte Flair/Becky Lynch	20.00	40.00
NNO	Seth Rollins/Dean Ambrose	15.00	30.00

2018 Mattel WWE Battle Packs Series 56

NNO	Miztourage		
NNO	Roman Reigns vs. John Cena		
NNO	Kurt Angle/Jason Jordan		

2019 Mattel WWE Battle Packs Series 57

NNO	Braun Strowman vs. Kane		
NNO	Sunil &Samir Singh		
NNO	Finn Balor vs. Shinsuke Nakamura		

2019 Mattel WWE Battle Packs Series 58

NNO	Kevin Owens/Sami Zayn		
NNO	S. Benjamin/C. Gable		
NNO	Triple H/HBK		

2019 Mattel WWE Battle Packs Series 59

NNO	The Hardy Boyz		
NNO	Jinder Mahal vs. AJ Styles		
NNO	The Shield (Ambrose/Rollins)		

2019 Mattel WWE Battle Packs Series 60

NNO	The Bar (Cesaro/Sheamus)		
NNO	Goldberg vs. Stone Cold Steve Austin		
NNO	Sasha Banks vs. Alexa Bliss		

2019 Mattel WWE Battle Packs Series 61

NNO	AJ Styles/Daniel Bryan		
NNO	The Ilconics (Billie Kay/Peyton Royce)		
NNO	Jimmy and Jey Uso		

2019 Mattel WWE Battle Packs Series 62

NNO	Akam & Rezar		
NNO	Andrade/Zelina Vega		
NNO	Rey Mysterio/Shinsuke Nakamura		

2019 Mattel WWE Battle Packs Series 63

NNO	Bobby Lashley vs. Finn Balor		
NNO	The New Day (Big E/Xavier Woods)		
NNO	Seth Rollins vs. Brock Lesnar		

2020 Mattel WWE Battle Packs Series 64

NNO	Daniel Bryan vs. AJ Styles	15.00	30.00
NNO	Lita & Trish Stratus	30.00	75.00
NNO	The Usos	60.00	120.00

2020 Mattel WWE Battle Packs Series 65

NNO	Ali & Kevin Owens	20.00	40.00
NNO	The Hardy Boyz	25.00	50.00
NNO	Ricochet & Velveteen	20.00	40.00

2020 Mattel WWE Battle Packs Series 66

NNO	Seth Rollins & Becky Lynch	25.00	50.00
NNO	Roman Reigns & Undertaker	30.00	60.00
NNO	Shane McMahon & Drew McIntyre	15.00	30.00

2016 Mattel WWE Battle Packs SummerSlam Heritage

NNO	John Cena/Brock Lesnar	12.50	25.00
NNO	Roman Reigns/Dean Ambrose	10.00	20.00

2017 Mattel WWE Battle Packs SummerSlam Heritage

NNO	Brock Lesnar/Randy Orton	15.00	30.00
NNO	Ultimate Warrior/Honkytonk Man	15.00	30.00

2016 Mattel WWE Battle Packs Then Now Forever

NNO	Dean Ambrose/Brian Pillman	10.00	20.00
NNO	John Cena/Steve Austin	15.00	30.00
NNO	Ultimate Warrior/Sting	12.50	25.00

2010 Mattel WWE Battle Packs WrestleMania 26

NNO	John Cena/Batista		
NNO	The Miz/Big Show	20.00	40.00
NNO	R-Truth/John Morrison		

2014 Mattel WWE Battle Packs WrestleMania 30 Heritage

NNO	Batista vs. Brock Lesnar	15.00	30.00
NNO	Sheamus vs. Ultimate Warrior	12.50	25.00

2015 Mattel WWE Battle Packs WrestleMania 31 Heritage

NNO	Daniel Bryan vs. Rey Mysterio	20.00	40.00
NNO	Triple H vs. Roman Reigns	20.00	40.00

2016 Mattel WWE Battle Packs WrestleMania 32 Heritage

NNO	Bret Hart & Steve Austin	15.00	30.00
NNO	Ric Flair & The Rock	12.50	25.00

2016 Mattel WWE Battle Packs WrestleMania 33 Heritage

NNO	Andre the Giant/ Ted DiBiase	10.00	20.00
NNO	The Rock/John Cena	12.50	25.00

2018 Mattel WWE Battle Packs WrestleMania 34 Heritage

NNO	Sting/Triple H	10.00	20.00
NNO	John Cena/Nikki Bella	15.00	30.00
NNO	Roman Reigns/Undertaker	12.50	25.00

2018 Mattel WWE Battle Packs WrestleMania 35 Heritage

NNO	AJ Styles vs. Shinsuke Nakamura	15.00	30.00
NNO	Jeff Hardy vs. Edge	15.00	30.00
NNO	The Miz vs. Seth Rollins	12.50	25.00

2020 Mattel WWE Beast Mode

NNO	AJ Styles	7.50	15.00
NNO	Becky Lynch	7.50	15.00
NNO	Braun Strowman	5.00	10.00
NNO	Daniel Bryan	6.00	12.00
NNO	Finn Balor	7.50	15.00
NNO	The Rock	5.00	10.00
NNO	Roman Reigns	10.00	20.00
NNO	Triple H	7.50	15.00

2021 Mattel WWE Beast Mode

NNO	Becky Lynch
NNO	Big E
NNO	Bray Wyatt
NNO	Kofi Kingston
NNO	Seth Rollins
NNO	The Rock
NNO	Undertaker
NNO	Xavier Woods

2022 Mattel WWE Bend 'N Bash Series 1

NNO	John Cena
NNO	Rey Mysterio
NNO	The Rock
NNO	Roman Reigns

2022 Mattel WWE Bend 'N Bash Series 2

NNO	Bobby Lashley
NNO	Drew McIntyre
NNO	Kofi Kingston
NNO	Undertaker

2010 Mattel WWE Best of 2010

NNO	Batista	12.50	25.00
NNO	Evan Bourne	7.50	15.00
NNO	Hornswoggle	20.00	40.00
NNO	John Cena	10.00	20.00
NNO	Mark Henry	7.50	15.00
NNO	Rey Mysterio	12.50	25.00

2011 Mattel WWE Best of 2011

NNO	Big Show	12.50	25.00
NNO	John Cena	6.00	12.00
NNO	Kofi Kingston		

NNO	Randy Orton	7.50	15.00
NNO	Rey Mysterio	25.00	50.00
NNO	Santino Marella	7.50	15.00

2012 Mattel WWE Best of 2012

NNO	Alberto Del Rio		
NNO	Brodus Clay		
NNO	Daniel Bryan	15.00	30.00
NNO	Great Khali	40.00	80.00
NNO	Rey Mysterio	12.50	25.00
NNO	Sin Cara	25.00	50.00

2013 Mattel WWE Best of 2013

NNO	Brock Lesnar
NNO	Great Khali
NNO	Kaitlyn
NNO	Rey Mysterio
NNO	Tensai
NNO	Undertaker

2014 Mattel WWE Best of 2014

NNO	Cesaro	7.50	15.00
NNO	El Torito	12.50	25.00
NNO	John Cena	10.00	20.00
NNO	Roman Reigns	20.00	40.00
NNO	Sin Cara	25.00	50.00
NNO	Undertaker	10.00	20.00

2012 Mattel WWE Best of PPV Series 1

NNO	Christian		
NNO	John Cena		
NNO	Mark Henry		
NNO	Rey Mysterio	30.00	75.00

2012 Mattel WWE Best of PPV Series 2

NNO	John Cena
NNO	The Rock
NNO	Sheamus
NNO	Triple H

2013 Mattel WWE Best of PPV Series 3

NNO	Alberto Del Rio
NNO	John Cena
NNO	Mark Henry
NNO	Rey Mysterio

2013 Mattel WWE Best of PPV Series 4

NNO	Alberto Del Rio	7.50	15.00
NNO	Sheamus	7.50	15.00
NNO	The Rock	12.50	25.00
NNO	Undertaker	10.00	20.00

2014 Mattel WWE Best of PPV Series 5

NNO	Damien Sandow
NNO	Daniel Bryan
NNO	Dolph Ziggler
NNO	Kofi Kingston

2016 Mattel WWE Best of PPV

NNO	Chris Jericho	10.00	20.00
NNO	Neville		
NNO	Rusev		
NNO	Undertaker		

2015 Mattel WWE Big Reveal 12-Inch

NNO	Rey Mysterio
NNO	Triple H

NNO	Ultimate Warrior
NNO	Undertaker

2012 Mattel WWE Brawlin' Buddies

NNO	John Cena
NNO	Randy Orton
NNO	Rey Mysterio
NNO	Sheamus

2013 Mattel WWE Brawlin' Buddies

NNO	John Cena
NNO	Kofi Kingston
NNO	Rey Mysterio
NNO	Zack Ryder

2012 Mattel WWE Brawlin' Buddies 2-Pack

NNO Rey Mysterio/John Cena
(Toys R Us Exclusive)

2013 Mattel WWE Brawlin' Buddies Championship Buddies

NNO	Brodus Clay
NNO	John Cena
NNO	The Rock
NNO	Sheamus

2014 Mattel WWE Dollar Store Series 1

NNO	CM Punk
NNO	John Cena
NNO	Kane
NNO	Randy Orton
NNO	Rey Mysterio
NNO	Sheamus

2014 Mattel WWE Dollar Store Series 2

NNO	Alberto Del Rio
NNO	Big Show
NNO	Brodus Clay
NNO	Daniel Bryan
NNO	John Cena
NNO	Undertaker

2017 Mattel WWE Dollar Store

NNO	Brock Lesnar
NNO	John Cena
NNO	Roman Reigns
NNO	Undertaker

2019 Mattel WWE Dollar Store

NNO	AJ Styles
NNO	Finn Balor
NNO	John Cena
NNO	The Rock
NNO	Roman Reigns

2019 Mattel WWE Dollar Store 5-Pack

NNO Cena/Rock/Styles/Balor/Reigns

2020 Mattel WWE Elite Collection 2-Packs

NNO	Bret "Hit Man" Hart & Goldberg	30.00	75.00
NNO	Brood Hardy Boyz	50.00	100.00
(Ringside Exclusive)			
NNO	Chyna & Triple H	30.00	75.00
NNO	Mr. T & "Rowdy" Roddy Piper	60.00	120.00

2021 Mattel WWE Elite Collection 2-Packs

NNO	Jeff Hardy vs. Triple H	25.00	50.00
NNO	The Rock & Mankind (Rock 'N' Sock Connection)	50.00	100.00

2010 Mattel WWE Elite Collection Best of 2010

NNO	John Cena	20.00	40.00
NNO	Kane	50.00	100.00
NNO	Randy Orton	50.00	90.00
NNO	Rey Mysterio	60.00	120.00
NNO	Triple H	25.00	50.00
NNO	Undertaker	30.00	60.00

2011 Mattel WWE Elite Collection Best of 2011

NNO	John Cena	25.00	50.00
NNO	John Morrison	60.00	120.00
NNO	Randy Orton	20.00	40.00
NNO	Rey Mysterio	30.00	75.00
NNO	Sheamus		

2018 Mattel WWE Elite Collection Best of Attitude Era

NNO	Chris Jericho	10.00	20.00
NNO	The Rock	20.00	40.00
NNO	Stone Cold Steve Austin	20.00	40.00
NNO	Triple H	12.50	25.00

2012 Mattel WWE Elite Collection Best of PPV Series 1

NNO	Bret Hart
NNO	Daniel Bryan
NNO	John Cena
NNO	Triple H

2012 Mattel WWE Elite Collection Best of PPV Series 2

NNO	Big Show
NNO	CM Punk
NNO	The Miz
NNO	Shawn Michaels
NNO	Undertaker EXCL

2013 Mattel WWE Elite Collection Best of PPV Series 3

NNO	Christian	60.00	120.00
NNO	John Cena	25.00	50.00
NNO	Sheamus	15.00	30.00
NNO	Sin Cara	30.00	75.00

2013 Mattel WWE Elite Collection Best of PPV Series 4

NNO	Brock Lesnar	15.00	30.00
NNO	CM Punk	30.00	60.00
NNO	Daniel Bryan	15.00	30.00
NNO	John Cena	12.50	25.00

2014 Mattel WWE Elite Collection Best of PPV Series 5

NNO	Alberto Del Rio	20.00	40.00
NNO	CM Punk	30.00	60.00
NNO	Curtis Axel	25.00	50.00
NNO	Paul Bearer	15.00	30.00
NNO	Randy Orton	17.50	35.00

2014 Mattel WWE Elite Collection Best of PPV Series 6

NNO	Bray Wyatt	12.50	25.00
NNO	Daniel Bryan	20.00	40.00

NNO	John Cena	12.50	25.00
NNO	Undertaker	20.00	40.00

2017 Mattel WWE Elite Collection Booty-O's 3-Pack

NNO	The New Day	25.00	50.00

2011 Mattel WWE Elite Collection Defining Moments Series 1

NNO	Macho Man Randy Savage	50.00	100.00
NNO	Shawn Michaels	75.00	150.00

2011 Mattel WWE Elite Collection Defining Moments Series 2

NNO	The Rock	100.00	200.00
NNO	Ultimate Warrior	60.00	120.00

2011 Mattel WWE Elite Collection Defining Moments Series 3

NNO	Ricky Steamboat	40.00	80.00
NNO	Triple H	125.00	250.00

2011 Mattel WWE Elite Collection Defining Moments Series 4

NNO	Stone Cold Steve Austin	40.00	80.00
NNO	Undertaker	100.00	200.00

2011 Mattel WWE Elite Collection Defining Moments Series 5

NNO	Bret Hart	100.00	200.00
NNO	John Cena	30.00	60.00

2014 Mattel WWE Elite Collection Defining Moments Series 6

NNO	Hulk Hogan	30.00	75.00
NNO	Ric Flair	40.00	80.00

2015 Mattel WWE Elite Collection Defining Moments Series 7

NNO	Hulk Hogan
NNO	Razor Ramon
NNO	Sting
NNO	Undertaker

2016 Mattel WWE Elite Collection Defining Moments Series 8

NNO	John Cena
NNO	Ric Flair/Retirement
NNO	Stone Cold Steve Austin
NNO	Sting/Surfer Gear
NNO	Ultimate Warrior

2017 Mattel WWE Elite Collection Defining Moments Series 9

NNO	Chris Jericho	15.00	30.00
NNO	Macho Man Randy Savage	20.00	40.00
NNO	Shinsuke Nakamura	20.00	40.00

2018 Mattel WWE Elite Collection Entrance Greats

NNO	Bobby Roode	20.00	40.00
NNO	Elias		
NNO	Finn Balor		
NNO	Goldberg	25.00	50.00
NNO	Jeff Hardy	30.00	60.00
NNO	Kurt Angle		

2010 Mattel WWE Elite Collection Entrance Greats Series 1

NNO	Rey Mysterio	50.00	100.00
NNO	Shawn Michaels	25.00	50.00
NNO	Triple H	20.00	40.00

2010 Mattel WWE Elite Collection Entrance Greats Series 2

NNO	Chris Jericho	30.00	60.00
NNO	Million Dollar Man	20.00	40.00
NNO	Rowdy Roddy Piper	25.00	50.00

2010 Mattel WWE Elite Collection Entrance Greats Series 3

NNO	The Rock	30.00	75.00
NNO	Undertaker	50.00	100.00

2018 Mattel WWE Elite Collection Epic Moments

NNO	Festival of Friendship Chris Jericho/Kevin Owens	30.00	75.00
NNO	Milk-O-Mania Kurt Angle/Stone Cold Steve Austin/Stephanie McMahon	25.00	50.00
NNO	Shield Reunion Seth Rollins/Roman Reigns/Dean Ambrose	50.00	100.00
NNO	Team Xtreme Matt & Jeff Hardy	30.00	60.00
NNO	Undisputed Era Adam Cole/Bobby Fish/Kyle O'Reilly	60.00	120.00

2010 Mattel WWE Elite Collection Exclusives

NNO	Rey Mysterio Flash RSC	150.00	300.00

2011 Mattel WWE Elite Collection Exclusives

NNO	Bret Hart P&B Attack RSC	150.00	300.00
NNO	CM Punk Straight Edge RSC	200.00	350.00
NNO	Macho King RSC	150.00	300.00
NNO	Undertaker SDCC	75.00	150.00
NNO	Vince McMahon MA	60.00	120.00

2012 Mattel WWE Elite Collection Exclusives

NNO	Macho Man nWo RSC	75.00	150.00
NNO	Steve Austin Rattlesnake RSC		
NNO	Triple H COO MA	20.00	40.00

2013 Mattel WWE Elite Collection Exclusives

NNO	Brock Lesnar Pain RSC	30.00	75.00
NNO	Cactus Jack Bang RSC	30.00	60.00
NNO	Undertaker 21-0 TRU		

2014 Mattel WWE Elite Collection Exclusives

NNO	CM Punk ECW (Flashback RSC	60.00	120.00
NNO	Edge Rated R RSC	100.00	200.00
NNO	Kane Hardcore RSC	125.00	250.00
NNO	Kane Unmasked RSC		
NNO	The Rock IC Champ RSC	25.00	50.00
NNO	Mankind AMZ	25.00	50.00
NNO	Rocky Maivia TAR	30.00	75.00
NNO	Brock Lesnar 21-1 TRU	25.00	50.00

2015 Mattel WWE Elite Collection Exclusives

NNO	Hulk Hogan American RSC	60.00	120.00
NNO	John Cena TRU	50.00	100.00
NNO	Scott Hall nWo RSC	50.00	100.00
NNO	Seth Rollins TRU	30.00	60.00
NNO	Shawn Michaels DX SE WG	30.00	60.00
NNO	Shawn Michaels SS RSC	50.00	100.00

NNO	Triple H DX SE WG	30.00	60.00
NNO	Virgil Convention Sign	30.00	60.00

2016 Mattel WWE Elite Collection Exclusives

NNO	Chris Jericho WM XIX RSC	25.00	50.00
NNO	Finn Balor Balor Club RSC	30.00	75.00
NNO	Kevin Nash nWo RSC	75.00	150.00
NNO	Nation of Domination KM OL	60.00	120.00
NNO	Sting nWo Wolfpac RSC	60.00	120.00
NNO	Brock Lesnar/	25.00	50.00
	WWE 2K17 GS		
NNO	Shockmaster SDCC	60.00	120.00

2017 Mattel WWE Elite Collection Exclusives

NNO	AJ Styles WRMS	25.00	50.00
NNO	Andre the Giant AMZ	30.00	75.00
NNO	Becky Lynch WG	20.00	40.00
NNO	Bret Hit Man Hart KOTR RSC	60.00	120.00
NNO	Chris Jericho List GS	30.00	75.00
NNO	Hardy Boyz WWE SZ		
NNO	Isaac Yankem DDS TRU	60.00	120.00
NNO	Macho Man Wolfpack RSC	75.00	150.00
NNO	Maryse WG	20.00	40.00
NNO	Samoa Joe GS	20.00	40.00
NNO	Sasha Banks Title WG	25.00	50.00
NNO	Shano Mac RSC	30.00	75.00

2018 Mattel WWE Elite Collection Exclusives

NNO	AJ Styles TRU	25.00	50.00
NNO	The Brian Kendrick RSC	20.00	40.00
NNO	Hardy Boyz Brood RSC	50.00	100.00
NNO	Kurt Angle Shield RSC	15.00	30.00
NNO	Matt Hardy ECW RSC	25.00	50.00
NNO	Pete Dunne	30.00	75.00
NNO	The Shark SDCC	20.00	40.00

2019 Mattel WWE Elite Collection Exclusives

NNO	Alexa Bliss WG	25.00	50.00
NNO	Alexander Wolfe TAR	20.00	40.00
NNO	Andrade Cien Almas (NXT TakeOver) RSC	30.00	60.00
NNO	Bob Backlund WM	20.00	40.00
NNO	Gorilla Monsoon WM	60.00	120.00
NNO	Kassius Ohno TAR	75.00	150.00
NNO	Liv Morgan TAR	60.00	120.00
NNO	Macho Man Randy Savage (Slim Jim) SDCC	75.00	150.00
NNO	Paige TAR	50.00	100.00
NNO	Pat Patterson WM	20.00	40.00
NNO	Red Rooster TAR	50.00	100.00
NNO	Rock (SmackDown Live) WM	20.00	40.00
NNO	Sensational Sherri WG	20.00	40.00
NNO	Sonya Deville TAR	30.00	60.00
NNO	Tyler Bate (UK Champion)	25.00	50.00
NNO	Undertaker as Kane (Deadman's Revenge) RSC	30.00	60.00

2020 Mattel WWE Elite Collection Exclusives

NNO	Finn Balor/AJ Styles	30.00	75.00
NNO	Rey Mysterio/Samoa Joe (WrestleMania Moment)	60.00	120.00

2021 Mattel WWE Elite Collection Exclusives

NNO	Bray Wyatt Firefly Funhouse RSC	30.00	75.00
NNO	Cactus Jack ECW RSC	25.00	50.00
NNO	John Cena nWo RSC	30.00	60.00
NNO	Ultimate Warrior WrestleMania 12 RSC	20.00	40.00
NNO	Undertaker Tag Champ RSC		
NNO	Walter RSC	25.00	50.00

2018 Mattel WWE Elite Collection Fan Central

NNO	Carmella	25.00	50.00

2019 Mattel WWE Elite Collection Fan Central

NNO	Akira Tozawa	20.00	40.00
NNO	Big Show	25.00	50.00
NNO	Bobby The Brain Heenan	20.00	40.00
NNO	Daniel Bryan	15.00	30.00
NNO	Mark Henry	25.00	50.00
NNO	Mojo Rawley	15.00	30.00
NNO	Triple H	15.00	30.00

2018 Mattel WWE Elite Collection Flashback Series 1

NNO	Mean Gene Okerlund	30.00	75.00
NNO	Syxx	25.00	50.00
NNO	Ultimate Warrior	25.00	50.00
NNO	Yokozuna	20.00	40.00

2018 Mattel WWE Elite Collection Flashback Series 2

NNO	Alundra Blayze	15.00	30.00
NNO	Razor Ramon	15.00	30.00
NNO	Shawn Michaels	20.00	40.00

2018 Mattel WWE Elite Collection Hall of Champions Series 3

NNO	Billy Gunn	15.00	30.00
NNO	Paul Bearer	25.00	50.00
NNO	Road Dogg	15.00	30.00
NNO	Ultimate Warrior	25.00	50.00

2016 Mattel WWE Elite Collection Hall of Fame 2-Packs

NNO	Papa Shango/Ultimate Warrior	25.00	50.00
NNO	Wild Samoans	20.00	40.00

2017 Mattel WWE Elite Collection Hall of Fame 4-Pack

NNO	Eddie Guerrero/Kevin Nash/ Scott Hall/Larry Zybysko	25.00	50.00

2015 Mattel WWE Elite Collection Hall of Fame Four Horsemen 4-Pack

NNO	Ric Flair/Arn Anderson/Barry Windham/Tully Blanchard	30.00	75.00

2015 Mattel WWE Elite Collection Hall of Fame Series 1

NNO	Sgt. Slaughter	20.00	40.00
NNO	Stone Cold Steve Austin	25.00	50.00
NNO	Trish Stratus	25.00	50.00
NNO	Ultimate Warrior	20.00	40.00

2015 Mattel WWE Elite Collection Hall of Fame Series 2

NNO	Eddie Guerrero	15.00	30.00
NNO	Hulk Hogan	25.00	50.00
NNO	Tito Santana	10.00	20.00
NNO	Yokozuna	20.00	40.00

2016 Mattel WWE Elite Collection Hall of Fame Series 3

NNO	Jimmy Hart	20.00	40.00
NNO	Macho Man Randy Savage	25.00	50.00
NNO	Million Dollar Man Ted DiBiase	17.50	35.00

2016 Mattel WWE Elite Collection Hall of Fame Series 4

NNO	Edge	25.00	50.00
NNO	Jerry Lawler	15.00	30.00
NNO	King Booker	20.00	40.00
NNO	Sting	20.00	40.00

2017 Mattel WWE Elite Collection Hall of Fame Series 5

NNO	Diesel	17.50	35.00
NNO	George The Animal Steele		
NNO	Jake Roberts	12.50	25.00
NNO	Roddy Piper	12.50	25.00

2019 Mattel WWE Elite Collection Ghostbusters

NNO	John Cena	12.50	25.00
NNO	The Rock	15.00	30.00
NNO	Shawn Michaels	12.50	25.00
NNO	Stone Cold Steve Austin	12.50	25.00
NNO	Undertaker	15.00	30.00

2010 Mattel WWE Elite Collection Legends Hall of Fame Series

NNO	Am. Dream Dusty Rhodes	25.00	50.00
NNO	Jimmy Superfly Snuka	25.00	50.00
NNO	Ricky Steamboat	30.00	75.00
NNO	Sgt. Slaughter		
NNO	Stone Cold Steve Austin	50.00	100.00
NNO	Terry Funk	25.00	50.00

2010 Mattel WWE Elite Collection Legends Series 1

NNO	Am. Dream Dusty Rhodes	30.00	75.00
NNO	Ricky Steamboat	30.00	75.00
NNO	Road Warrior Animal	50.00	100.00
NNO	Road Warrior Hawk	50.00	100.00
NNO	Sgt. Slaughter	25.00	50.00
NNO	Stone Cold Steve Austin	40.00	80.00

2010 Mattel WWE Elite Collection Legends Series 1 2-Packs

NNO	Bushwhackers	30.00	75.00
NNO	Iron Sheik/Nikolai Volkoff	50.00	100.00
NNO	Rowdy Roddy Piper/Cowboy Bob Orton	50.00	100.00

2010 Mattel WWE Elite Collection Legends Series 2

NNO	Iron Sheik	30.00	60.00
NNO	Jake The Snake Roberts	30.00	60.00
NNO	Jimmy Superfly Snuka	50.00	100.00
NNO	Kamala	20.00	40.00
NNO	Ravishing Rick Rude	30.00	75.00
NNO	Terry Funk	20.00	40.00

2010 Mattel WWE Elite Collection Legends Series 2 2-Packs

NNO	Kerry and Kevin Von Erich		
NNO	Marty Jannetty/HBK		

2010 Mattel WWE Elite Collection Legends Series 3

NNO	Brian Pillman	60.00	120.00
NNO	British Bulldog	30.00	75.00
NNO	Hacksaw Jim Duggan	50.00	100.00
NNO	Mr. Perfect	30.00	75.00
NNO	The Rock	25.00	50.00

NNO Vader/Black Mask	75.00	150.00
NNO Vader/Red Mask	50.00	100.00

2011 Mattel WWE Elite Collection Legends Series 4

NNO Ax	60.00	120.00
NNO George The Animal Steele	30.00	60.00
NNO Hillbilly Jim	30.00	75.00
NNO Paul Orndorff	75.00	150.00
NNO Smash	60.00	120.00
NNO Ultimate Warrior	30.00	60.00

2011 Mattel WWE Elite Collection Legends Series 5

NNO Akeem	100.00	200.00
NNO Bam Bam Bigelow	30.00	60.00
NNO Macho Man Randy Savage	30.00	75.00
NNO Rick Martel	100.00	200.00

2011 Mattel WWE Elite Collection Legends Series 6

NNO Eddie Guerrero	75.00	150.00
NNO Kerry Von Erich	100.00	200.00
NNO Kevin Von Erich	125.00	250.00
NNO Texas Tornado	75.00	150.00
NNO Ultimate Warrior	30.00	75.00

2015 Mattel WWE Elite Collection Network Spotlight

NNO The Ringmaster Steve Austin	15.00	30.00
NNO Big Boss Man	20.00	40.00
NNO Hunter Hearst Helmsley	15.00	30.00

2016 Mattel WWE Elite Collection Network Spotlight

NNO Bayley	17.50	35.00
NNO Roman Reigns	20.00	40.00
NNO Shawn Michaels	25.00	50.00

2017 Mattel WWE Elite Collection Network Spotlight

NNO Dean Ambrose	17.50	35.00
NNO Finn Balor	20.00	40.00
NNO TJ Perkins	25.00	50.00
NNO Undertaker	25.00	50.00
NNO Vince McMahon	15.00	30.00

2019 Mattel WWE Elite Collection Network Spotlight

NNO Asuka	20.00	40.00
NNO Diesel	17.50	35.00
NNO Jinder Mahal	15.00	30.00
NNO Rey Mysterio	25.00	50.00

2020 Mattel WWE Elite Collection Network Spotlight

NNO Kurt Angle	25.00	50.00
NNO Matt Hardy	20.00	40.00
NNO Ricochet	20.00	40.00
NNO Wendi Richter	12.50	25.00

2017 Mattel WWE Elite Collection NXT Series 1

NNO Austin Aries	20.00	40.00
NNO No Way Jose	30.00	60.00
NNO Seth Rollins	20.00	40.00

2017 Mattel WWE Elite Collection NXT Series 2

NNO Asuka	25.00	50.00
NNO Dash Wilder	17.50	35.00
NNO Scott Dawson	17.50	35.00
NNO Shinsuke Nakamura	15.00	30.00

2018 Mattel WWE Elite Collection NXT Series 3

NNO Alexander Rusev	15.00	30.00
NNO Bobby Roode	20.00	40.00
NNO Ember Moon	20.00	40.00
NNO Roman Reigns	20.00	40.00

2021 Mattel WWE Elite Collection Royal Rumble 2021

NNO Stone Cold Steve Austin	20.00	40.00
NNO Titus O'Neil	15.00	30.00
NNO Ultimate Warrior	30.00	60.00
NNO Umaga	20.00	40.00

2010 Mattel WWE Elite Collection Series 1

NNO CM Punk	75.00	150.00
NNO Edge	30.00	75.00
NNO MVP		
NNO Rey Mysterio	75.00	150.00
NNO Undertaker	50.00	100.00

2010 Mattel WWE Elite Collection Series 2

NNO Batista		
NNO Matt Hardy		
NNO R-Truth	30.00	75.00
NNO Randy Orton	60.00	120.00
NNO Ted Dibiase	40.00	80.00
NNO Triple H	30.00	75.00
NNO Triple H (bottle pack)		

2010 Mattel WWE Elite Collection Series 3

NNO Christian	60.00	120.00
NNO Cody Rhodes	30.00	60.00
NNO John Cena	40.00	80.00
NNO The Miz	25.00	50.00
NNO Santino Marella		
NNO Shawn Michaels	60.00	120.00

2010 Mattel WWE Elite Collection Series 4

NNO Big Show	25.00	50.00
NNO Chris Jericho/Blue Gear	40.00	80.00
NNO Chris Jericho/Purple Gear	50.00	100.00
NNO Finlay		
NNO John Morrison/ Bright Red Robe		
NNO John Morrison/ Dk Red Robe	125.00	250.00
NNO Kane	60.00	120.00
NNO Kofi Kingston		

2010 Mattel WWE Elite Collection Series 5

NNO Chavo Guerrero	25.00	50.00
NNO Dolph Ziggler	20.00	40.00
NNO Jack Swagger/No Singlet	20.00	40.00
NNO Jack Swagger/Singlet	30.00	60.00
NNO Mark Henry	20.00	40.00
NNO Rey Mysterio	75.00	150.00
NNO Vladimir Kozlov/ Jacket Sleeves		
NNO Vladimir Kozlov/ No Jacket Sleeves		

2010 Mattel WWE Elite Collection Series 6

NNO Batista	50.00	100.00
NNO CM Punk	60.00	120.00
NNO Goldust	30.00	75.00
NNO JTG	45.00	90.00
NNO Matt Hardy	50.00	100.00
NNO Shad	45.00	90.00

2011 Mattel WWE Elite Collection Series 7

NNO David Hart Smith	25.00	50.00
NNO Hornswoggle	60.00	120.00
NNO John Cena	30.00	75.00
NNO Shawn Michaels	75.00	150.00
NNO Triple H	30.00	75.00
NNO Tyson Kidd	25.00	50.00

2011 Mattel WWE Elite Collection Series 8

NNO Drew McIntyre	30.00	60.00
NNO Edge	30.00	75.00
NNO Evan Bourne	50.00	100.00
NNO Sheamus	25.00	50.00
NNO Undertaker	30.00	60.00
NNO William Regal	40.00	80.00

2011 Mattel WWE Elite Collection Series 9

NNO Kofi Kingston		
NNO Luke Gallows	25.00	50.00
NNO The Miz	30.00	75.00
NNO MVP	60.00	120.00
NNO Randy Orton	25.00	50.00
NNO Zack Ryder	25.00	50.00

2011 Mattel WWE Elite Collection Series 10

NNO Big Show	30.00	75.00
NNO John Morrison	50.00	100.00
NNO Kane	50.00	100.00
NNO R-Truth	25.00	50.00
NNO Ted Dibiase	30.00	60.00
NNO Yoshi Tatsu	30.00	75.00

2011 Mattel WWE Elite Collection Series 11

NNO Christian	30.00	60.00
NNO CM Punk	50.00	100.00
NNO John Cena		
NNO The Miz	40.00	80.00
NNO Rey Mysterio	60.00	120.00
NNO Wade Barrett	40.00	80.00

2011 Mattel WWE Elite Collection Series 12

NNO Alberto Del Rio	15.00	30.00
NNO Daniel Bryan	20.00	40.00
NNO Justin Gabriel	30.00	60.00
NNO Kane FB	50.00	100.00
NNO Papa Shango FB	25.00	50.00
NNO Randy Orton	20.00	40.00

2012 Mattel WWE Elite Collection Series 13

NNO Big Show	25.00	50.00
NNO Cody Rhodes	45.00	90.00
NNO Dolph Ziggler	20.00	40.00
NNO Edge FB	30.00	75.00
NNO Rey Mysterio	75.00	150.00
NNO Sheamus	20.00	40.00

2012 Mattel WWE Elite Collection Series 14

NNO Alberto Del Rio	20.00	40.00
NNO Big Boss Man FB	30.00	75.00

NNO	John Cena	30.00	75.00
NNO	King Booker FB	25.00	50.00
NNO	The Rock	20.00	40.00
NNO	Undertaker	30.00	60.00

2012 Mattel WWE Elite Collection Series 15

NNO	Evan Bourne	30.00	75.00
NNO	Mark Henry	25.00	50.00
NNO	R-Truth	30.00	75.00
NNO	Rey Mysterio		
NNO	Sin Cara	30.00	60.00
NNO	Yokozuna FB	20.00	40.00

2012 Mattel WWE Elite Collection Series 16

NNO	CM Punk	50.00	100.00
NNO	Diesel FB	30.00	60.00
NNO	Ezekiel Jackson	30.00	75.00
NNO	Heath Slater	20.00	40.00
NNO	Kevin Nash FB	60.00	120.00
NNO	Randy Orton	15.00	30.00
NNO	The Rock	30.00	60.00

2012 Mattel WWE Elite Collection Series 17

NNO	John Cena	20.00	40.00
NNO	Kelly Kelly	30.00	60.00
NNO	Kofi Kingston	20.00	40.00
NNO	Mankind FB	30.00	75.00
NNO	Sheamus	15.00	30.00
NNO	Zack Ryder	30.00	60.00

2012 Mattel WWE Elite Collection Series 18

NNO	Brodus Clay	10.00	20.00
NNO	Jerry Lawler FB	15.00	30.00
NNO	Rey Mysterio	50.00	100.00
NNO	Sin Cara	75.00	150.00
NNO	Undertaker FB	30.00	75.00
NNO	Wade Barrett	15.00	30.00

2013 Mattel WWE Elite Collection Series 19

NNO	Brock Lesnar	20.00	40.00
NNO	Daniel Bryan	20.00	40.00
NNO	Dolph Ziggler	15.00	30.00
NNO	Kane	30.00	60.00
NNO	Miss Elizabeth FB	20.00	40.00
NNO	Shawn Michaels	20.00	40.00

2013 Mattel WWE Elite Collection Series 20

NNO	Chris Jericho	20.00	40.00
NNO	Christian FB	30.00	60.00
NNO	CM Punk	50.00	100.00
NNO	Cody Rhodes	20.00	40.00
NNO	John Cena	25.00	50.00
NNO	Santino Morella	30.00	75.00

2013 Mattel WWE Elite Collection Series 21

NNO	AJ Lee	25.00	50.00
NNO	Alberto Del Rio	15.00	30.00
NNO	Honky Tonk Man FB	25.00	50.00
NNO	Randy Orton	17.50	35.00
NNO	Rey Mysterio	60.00	120.00
NNO	Ryback	15.00	30.00

2013 Mattel WWE Elite Collection Series 22

NNO	Big Show	25.00	50.00
NNO	Damien Sandow	12.50	25.00
NNO	The Giant FB	50.00	100.00
NNO	Kane	20.00	40.00

NNO	The Rock	30.00	60.00
NNO	Tensai	15.00	30.00

2013 Mattel WWE Elite Collection Series 23

NNO	Antonio Cesaro	15.00	30.00
NNO	JBL FB	25.00	50.00
NNO	John Cena	20.00	40.00
NNO	Macho Man Randy Savage	25.00	50.00
NNO	Triple H FB	15.00	30.00
NNO	Undertaker FB	20.00	40.00

2013 Mattel WWE Elite Collection Series 24

NNO	Dolph Ziggler	20.00	40.00
NNO	The Miz	12.50	25.00
NNO	Rey Mysterio	30.00	75.00
NNO	Ryback	15.00	30.00
NNO	Trish Stratus FB	30.00	75.00
NNO	Wade Barrett	15.00	30.00

2013 Mattel WWE Elite Collection Series 25

NNO	Brodus Clay	12.50	25.00
NNO	Bruno Sammartino FB	30.00	60.00
NNO	Dean Ambrose	20.00	40.00
NNO	Seth Rollins	20.00	40.00
NNO	Sheamus	15.00	30.00
NNO	Sin Cara	25.00	50.00

2014 Mattel WWE Elite Collection Series 26

NNO	Big E Langston	12.50	25.00
NNO	Jack Swagger	25.00	50.00
NNO	Mark Henry	20.00	40.00
NNO	Road Dogg FB	25.00	50.00
NNO	Roman Reigns	20.00	40.00
NNO	Ultimate Warrior FB	15.00	30.00

2014 Mattel WWE Elite Collection Series 27

NNO	Billy Gunn FB	25.00	50.00
NNO	Fandango	12.50	25.00
NNO	Kofi Kingston	12.50	25.00
NNO	Rikishi FB/Gear on Side	25.00	50.00
NNO	Rikishi FB/Wearing Gear	20.00	40.00
NNO	Rob Van Dam	30.00	75.00
NNO	Undertaker	20.00	40.00

2014 Mattel WWE Elite Collection Series 28

NNO	Big Show	20.00	40.00
NNO	Bray Wyatt	20.00	40.00
NNO	Daniel Bryan	20.00	40.00
NNO	Demolition Crush FB	20.00	50.00
NNO	John Cena	20.00	40.00
NNO	Triple H	15.00	30.00

2014 Mattel WWE Elite Collection Series 29

NNO	Andre the Giant FB	30.00	60.00
NNO	CM Punk	30.00	75.00
NNO	Damien Sandow	15.00	30.00
NNO	Erick Rowan	20.00	40.00
NNO	Goldust	15.00	30.00
NNO	Luke Harper	20.00	40.00

2014 Mattel WWE Elite Collection Series 30

NNO	Batista	20.00	40.00
NNO	Brock Lesnar	15.00	30.00
NNO	Lex Luger FB	20.00	40.00
NNO	Road Warrior Animal FB	60.00	120.00
NNO	Road Warrior Hawk FB	60.00	120.00
NNO	Ryback	15.00	30.00

2014 Mattel WWE Elite Collection Series 31

NNO	Dean Ambrose	25.00	50.00
NNO	Jey Uso	15.00	30.00
NNO	Jimmy Uso	15.00	30.00
NNO	Kane	30.00	75.00
NNO	The Rock FB	25.00	50.00
NNO	Vader FB	50.00	100.00

2014 Mattel WWE Elite Collection Series 32

NNO	Big E Langston	12.50	25.00
NNO	Cody Rhodes	25.00	50.00
NNO	Daniel Bryan	17.50	35.00
NNO	Mark Henry	20.00	40.00
NNO	Rey Mysterio FB	50.00	100.00
NNO	Sin Cara	40.00	80.00

2015 Mattel WWE Elite Collection Series 33

NNO	Batista	25.00	50.00
NNO	Cesaro	12.50	25.00
NNO	Junkyard Dog FB	15.00	30.00
NNO	Roman Reigns	15.00	30.00
NNO	Seth Rollins	12.50	25.00
NNO	X-Pac FB	20.00	40.00

2015 Mattel WWE Elite Collection Series 34

NNO	Bad News Barrett	12.50	25.00
NNO	Doink the Clown FB	20.00	40.00
NNO	Hulk Hogan	25.00	50.00
NNO	John Cena	20.00	40.00
NNO	Paige	25.00	50.00
NNO	Rusev	12.50	25.00

2015 Mattel WWE Elite Collection Series 35

NNO	Diego	10.00	20.00
NNO	Earthquake FB	17.50	35.00
NNO	Fernando	15.00	30.00
NNO	Luke Harper	20.00	40.00
NNO	Randy Orton	15.00	30.00
NNO	Triple H	12.50	25.00

2015 Mattel WWE Elite Collection Series 36

NNO	Bo Dallas	12.50	25.00
NNO	Bray Wyatt	12.50	25.00
NNO	Dean Ambrose	15.00	30.00
NNO	DDP FB	25.00	50.00
NNO	Goldust	17.50	35.00
NNO	Stardust	20.00	40.00

2015 Mattel WWE Elite Collection Series 37

NNO	Brock Lesnar	15.00	30.00
NNO	Dean Malenko FB	17.50	35.00
NNO	John Cena	15.00	30.00
NNO	The Miz	12.50	25.00
NNO	Seth Rollins	25.00	50.00
NNO	Stephanie McMahon	12.50	25.00

2015 Mattel WWE Elite Collection Series 38

NNO	Adam Rose	10.00	20.00
NNO	Bradshaw FB	15.00	30.00
NNO	Daniel Bryan	30.00	60.00
NNO	Faarooq FB	15.00	30.00
NNO	Macho Man Randy Savage FB	15.00	30.00
NNO	Roman Reigns	20.00	40.00

2015 Mattel WWE Elite Collection Series 39

NNO	British Bulldog FB	15.00	30.00
NNO	Damien Mizdow	10.00	20.00

NNO	Dolph Ziggler	25.00	50.00
NNO	Godfather FB	15.00	30.00
NNO	Sting	20.00	40.00
NNO	Sycho Sid FB	12.50	25.00

2016 Mattel WWE Elite Collection Series 40

NNO	Irwin R. Schyster FB	10.00	20.00
NNO	John Cena	25.00	50.00
NNO	Ravishing Rick Rude FB	15.00	30.00
NNO	Sami Zayn	10.00	20.00
NNO	Tyson Kidd	12.50	25.00
NNO	Umaga FB	12.50	25.00

2016 Mattel WWE Elite Collection Series 41

NNO	123 Kid FB	15.00	30.00
NNO	Dean Ambrose	15.00	30.00
NNO	Finn Balor	15.00	30.00
NNO	Lita FB	12.50	25.00
NNO	Ryback	15.00	30.00
NNO	Terry Funk FB	20.00	40.00

2016 Mattel WWE Elite Collection Series 42

NNO	Kalisto	20.00	40.00
NNO	Nasty Boy Brian Knobbs FB	12.50	25.00
NNO	Nasty Boy Jerry Sags FB	12.50	25.00
NNO	Neville	10.00	20.00
NNO	Triple H	12.50	25.00
NNO	Xavier Woods	10.00	20.00

2016 Mattel WWE Elite Collection Series 43

NNO	Alberto Del Rio	7.50	15.00
NNO	Bret Hart FB	25.00	50.00
NNO	Jim Neidhart FB	12.50	25.00
NNO	Kevin Owens	10.00	20.00
NNO	Kofi Kingston	10.00	20.00
NNO	Samoa Joe	10.00	20.00

2016 Mattel WWE Elite Collection Series 44

NNO	Big E	10.00	20.00
NNO	Braun Strowman	20.00	40.00
NNO	Randy Savage FB	15.00	30.00
NNO	Sasha Banks	15.00	30.00
NNO	Sin Cara	30.00	75.00
NNO	Tugboat FB	10.00	20.00

2016 Mattel WWE Elite Collection Series 45

NNO	Bubba Ray Dudley	25.00	50.00
NNO	D-Von Dudley	25.00	50.00
NNO	Lord Steven Regal FB	12.50	25.00
NNO	Narcissist Lex Luger FB	10.00	20.00
NNO	Roman Reigns	15.00	30.00
NNO	Seth Rollins	20.00	40.00

2016 Mattel WWE Elite Collection Series 46

NNO	Booker T FB	15.00	30.00
NNO	Finn Balor	12.50	25.00
NNO	John Cena	12.50	25.00
NNO	Rusev	10.00	20.00
NNO	Sheamus	10.00	20.00
NNO	Stevie Ray FB	12.50	25.00

2016 Mattel WWE Elite Collection Series 47A

NNO	AJ Styles	15.00	30.00
NNO	Asuka	20.00	40.00
NNO	Big Boss Man FB	12.50	25.00
NNO	Cesaro	15.00	30.00

NNO	Kevin Owens	10.00	20.00
NNO	Tatanka FB	12.50	25.00

2016 Mattel WWE Elite Collection Series 47B

NNO	Brian Pillman FB		
NNO	Demon Kane		
NNO	Goldust FB		
NNO	Konnor		
NNO	The Rock FB		
NNO	Viktor		

2017 Mattel WWE Elite Collection Series 48

NNO	Boogeyman FB	25.00	50.00
NNO	Cactus Jack FB	25.00	50.00
NNO	Dean Ambrose	20.00	40.00
NNO	Dolph Ziggler	20.00	40.00
NNO	Erick Rowan	15.00	30.00
NNO	Kalisto	25.00	50.00

2017 Mattel WWE Elite Collection Series 49

NNO	Apollo Crews	15.00	30.00
NNO	Becky Lynch	12.50	25.00
NNO	Big Cass	10.00	20.00
NNO	Brutus Beefcake FB	10.00	20.00
NNO	Enzo Amore	10.00	20.00
NNO	Randy Orton FB	20.00	40.00

2017 Mattel WWE Elite Collection Series 50

NNO	Baron Corbin	7.50	15.00
NNO	John Cena	12.50	25.00
NNO	Rhyno	10.00	20.00
NNO	Shane McMahon	15.00	30.00
NNO	Stephanie McMahon	15.00	30.00
NNO	Warlord FB	12.50	25.00

2017 Mattel WWE Elite Collection Series 51

NNO	AJ Styles	12.50	25.00
NNO	Berzerker FB	7.50	15.00
NNO	Mankind FB	12.50	25.00
NNO	Roman Reigns	12.50	25.00
NNO	Sami Zayn	7.50	15.00
NNO	Scott Hall FB	12.50	25.00

2017 Mattel WWE Elite Collection Series 52

NNO	Braun Strowman	20.00	40.00
NNO	D'Lo Brown FB	12.50	25.00
NNO	Ken Shamrock FB	12.50	25.00
NNO	Kofi Kingston	10.00	20.00
NNO	Seth Rollins	12.50	25.00
NNO	Xavier Woods	7.50	15.00

2017 Mattel WWE Elite Collection Series 53

NNO	Alexa Bliss	15.00	30.00
NNO	Big E	10.00	20.00
NNO	Chris Jericho	10.00	20.00
NNO	Heath Slater	12.50	25.00
NNO	Kevin Owens	10.00	20.00
NNO	The Miz	10.00	20.00

2017 Mattel WWE Elite Collection Series 54

NNO	Bray Wyatt	15.00	30.00
NNO	Charlotte Flair	15.00	30.00
NNO	Jey Uso	12.50	25.00
NNO	Jimmy Uso	12.50	25.00
NNO	John Cena	15.00	30.00
NNO	Rich Swann	15.00	30.00

2017 Mattel WWE Elite Collection Series 55

NNO	Big Cass	10.00	20.00
NNO	Brock Lesnar	25.00	50.00
NNO	Enzo Amore	30.00	60.00
NNO	James Ellsworth	15.00	30.00
NNO	Neville FB	25.00	50.00
NNO	Undertaker	25.00	50.00

2017 Mattel WWE Elite Collection Series 56

NNO	AJ Styles	15.00	30.00
NNO	Jack Gallagher	10.00	20.00
NNO	Karl Anderson	15.00	30.00
NNO	Luke Gallows	15.00	30.00
NNO	Roman Reigns	20.00	40.00
NNO	Samoa Joe	10.00	20.00

2017 Mattel WWE Elite Collection Series 57

NNO	Baron Corbin	10.00	20.00
NNO	Jeff Hardy	30.00	75.00
NNO	Scotty 2 Hotty	12.50	25.00
NNO	Seth Rollins	15.00	30.00
NNO	Shinsuke Nakamura	15.00	30.00
NNO	Tye Dillinger	15.00	30.00

2017 Mattel WWE Elite Collection Series 58

NNO	Braun Strowman	15.00	30.00
NNO	Cesaro	12.50	25.00
NNO	Dean Ambrose	12.50	25.00
NNO	Matt Hardy	25.00	50.00
NNO	Mickie James	17.50	35.00
NNO	Sheamus	12.50	25.00

2017 Mattel WWE Elite Collection Series 59

NNO	Chad Gable	15.00	30.00
NNO	Finn Balor	15.00	30.00
NNO	Jason Jordan	15.00	30.00
NNO	Kurt Angle	12.50	25.00
NNO	The Miz	12.50	25.00
NNO	Zack Ryder	10.00	20.00

2017 Mattel WWE Elite Collection Series 60

NNO	Andre/Giant Machine	20.00	40.00
NNO	Elias	20.00	40.00
NNO	John Cena	15.00	30.00
NNO	Kofi Kingston	12.50	25.00
NNO	Triple H	20.00	40.00
NNO	Xavier Woods	12.50	25.00

2018 Mattel WWE Elite Collection Series 61

NNO	AJ Styles	15.00	30.00
NNO	Big E	12.50	25.00
NNO	Fandango	12.50	25.00
NNO	Kevin Owens	12.50	25.00
NNO	Shane McMahon	15.00	30.00
NNO	Tyler Breeze	12.50	25.00

2018 Mattel WWE Elite Collection Series 62

NNO	Roman Reigns	17.50	35.00
NNO	Braun Strowman	20.00	40.00
NNO	Dude Love	15.00	30.00
NNO	Akam	12.50	25.00
NNO	Rezar	12.50	25.00
NNO	Sting/Surfer Gear	17.50	35.00

2018 Mattel WWE Elite Collection Series 63

NNO	Dean Ambrose	12.50	25.00
NNO	Dusty Rhodes	17.50	35.00

NNO Kane	12.50	25.00
NNO Sami Zayn	12.50	25.00
NNO Shelton Benjamin	20.00	40.00
NNO Shelton Benjamin Gold Tights CH		
NNO Shinsuke Nakamura	12.50	25.00

2018 Mattel WWE Elite Collection Series 64

NNO Curt Hawkins	25.00	50.00
NNO Curt Hawkins Black Gear CH		
NNO Jey Uso	15.00	30.00
NNO Jimmy Uso	15.00	30.00
NNO John Cena	20.00	40.00
NNO Samoa Joe	20.00	40.00
NNO Seth Rollins	25.00	50.00

2018 Mattel WWE Elite Collection Series 65

NNO Aiden English		
NNO Aiden English Black Scarf CH		
NNO Eric Young	17.50	35.00
NNO Nia Jax	15.00	30.00
NNO Roman Reigns	15.00	30.00
NNO Ronda Rousey	20.00	40.00
NNO Rusev		

2018 Mattel WWE Elite Collection Series 66

NNO AJ Styles	20.00	40.00
NNO Erick Rowan	15.00	30.00
NNO Kevin Owens	10.00	20.00
NNO Kevin Owens (KO Mania) (CHASE)		
NNO Kurt Angle	15.00	30.00
NNO Luke Harper	15.00	30.00
NNO Nikki Cross	25.00	50.00

2019 Mattel WWE Elite Collection Series 67

NNO Cedric Alexander FP	12.50	25.00
NNO Jeff Hardy	12.50	25.00
NNO Jeff Hardy USA Face Paint CH		
NNO Randy Orton	10.00	20.00
NNO Rey Mysterio	15.00	30.00
NNO Shayna Baszler FP	15.00	30.00
NNO Velveteen Dream FP	12.50	25.00

2019 Mattel WWE Elite Collection Series 68

NNO Braun Strowman	12.50	25.00
NNO Brie Bella	12.50	25.00
NNO Daniel Bryan	12.50	25.00
NNO King Mabel FP	10.00	20.00
NNO King Mabel FP Lightning CH		
NNO Roman Reigns	12.50	25.00
NNO Undertaker	20.00	40.00

2019 Mattel WWE Elite Collection Series 69

NNO Bobby Lashley	10.00	20.00
NNO Miz	10.00	20.00
NNO Mustafa Ali	12.50	25.00
NNO Mustafa Ali (orange pants) (CHASE)		
NNO Rey Mysterio	12.50	25.00
NNO Ricochet	15.00	30.00
NNO Tommaso Ciampa	12.50	25.00

2019 Mattel WWE Elite Collection Series 70

NNO Demon Finn Balor	15.00	30.00
NNO Dolph Ziggler	12.50	25.00
NNO Dolph Ziggler Pink CH	25.00	50.00
NNO EC3	10.00	20.00

NNO Johnny Gargano	15.00	30.00
NNO Seth Rollins/Shield Fatigues	15.00	30.00
NNO Vince McMahon	15.00	30.00

2019 Mattel WWE Elite Collection Series 71

NNO Adam Cole		
NNO Big Show		
NNO Drew McIntyre		
NNO Jeff Hardy		
NNO John Cena		
NNO Nikki Bella		
NNO Nikki Bella Red Gear CH		

2019 Mattel WWE Elite Collection Series 72

NNO Batista		
NNO Becky Lynch		
NNO Buddy Murphy		
NNO Buddy Murphy Black Shorts CH		
NNO Rey Mysterio		
NNO Roderick Strong		
NNO Velveteen Dream		

2019 Mattel WWE Elite Collection Series 73

NNO Aleister Black		
NNO Daniel Bryan		
NNO Elias		
NNO Gran Metalik		
NNO Gran Metalik Black Shirt CH		
NNO Kairi Sane		
NNO Triple H		

2019 Mattel WWE Elite Collection Series 74

NNO AJ Styles		
NNO Andrade		
NNO Finn Balor		
NNO Goldberg		
NNO Lince Dorado		
NNO Lince Dorado Gold CH		
NNO Natalya		

2020 Mattel WWE Elite Collection Series 75

NNO Hurricane	20.00	40.00
NNO Hurricane White Boots CH	30.00	60.00
NNO Jeff Hardy	15.00	30.00
NNO Kalisto	30.00	60.00
NNO Mandy Rose	20.00	40.00
NNO Pete Dunne	20.00	40.00
NNO Seth Rollins	20.00	40.00

2020 Mattel WWE Elite Collection Series 76

NNO Braun Strowman	20.00	40.00
NNO Christian Black Shirt CH	20.00	40.00
NNO Christian White Shirt	20.00	40.00
NNO John Cena	25.00	50.00
NNO Lacey Evans	20.00	40.00
NNO Tucker	15.00	30.00

2020 Mattel WWE Elite Collection Series 77

NNO AJ Styles	20.00	40.00
NNO Classy Freddie Blassie RSC	30.00	60.00
NNO The Fiend Bray Wyatt	25.00	50.00
NNO Miss Elizabeth	20.00	40.00
NNO Ravishing Rick Rude Ult. Warrior Tights	20.00	40.00
NNO Ravishing Rick Rude Yellow Tights CH	30.00	60.00
NNO Ronda Rousey	15.00	30.00
NNO Viscera	20.00	40.00

2020 Mattel WWE Elite Collection Series 78

NNO Drake Maverick	15.00	30.00
NNO Kofi Kingston	20.00	40.00
NNO Matt Riddle	25.00	50.00
NNO Naomi	15.00	30.00
NNO Naomi Glow CH	20.00	40.00
NNO Randy Orton	25.00	50.00
NNO R-Truth	15.00	30.00
NNO Superstar Billy Graham TAR	20.00	40.00

2020 Mattel WWE Elite Collection Series 79

NNO Big E	15.00	30.00
NNO Bobby Fish	20.00	40.00
NNO Bobby Fish Black Gear CH	25.00	50.00
NNO Daniel Bryan	15.00	30.00
NNO Io Shirai	20.00	40.00
NNO Roman Reigns	15.00	30.00
NNO Xavier Woods	15.00	30.00

2020 Mattel WWE Elite Collection Series 80

NNO Bayley	25.00	50.00
NNO Erik	15.00	30.00
NNO Ivar	15.00	30.00
NNO Kevin Owens	20.00	40.00
NNO Kyle O'Reilly	20.00	40.00
NNO Kyle O'Reilly Black Gear CH	25.00	50.00
NNO Ricochet	15.00	30.00
NNO Rocky Johnson TAR	20.00	40.00

2020 Mattel WWE Elite Collection Series 81

NNO Angelo Dawkins	15.00	30.00
NNO Bianca Belair	30.00	60.00
NNO Mae Young WM	25.00	50.00
NNO Montez Ford	15.00	30.00
NNO The Rock	20.00	40.00
NNO Shinsuke Nakamura	20.00	40.00
NNO S.Nakamura Black CH	25.00	50.00
NNO Stunning Steve Austin	25.00	50.00

2021 Mattel WWE Elite Collection Series 82

NNO Alexa Bliss	20.00	40.00
NNO Finn Balor	15.00	30.00
NNO Jerry The King Lawler	15.00	30.00
NNO John Morrison	15.00	30.00
NNO Keith Lee	15.00	30.00
NNO Keith Lee White Gear CH	20.00	40.00
NNO Rob Gronkowski	40.00	80.00

2021 Mattel WWE Elite Collection Series 83

NNO Drew McIntyre	15.00	30.00
NNO Dusty Rhodes	15.00	30.00
NNO Edge	20.00	40.00
NNO Edge Black Gear CH	20.00	40.00
NNO King Baron Corbin	15.00	30.00
NNO Michael PS Hayes TAR	20.00	40.00
NNO Sasha Banks	20.00	40.00

2021 Mattel WWE Elite Collection Series 84

NNO Angel Garza	15.00	30.00
NNO Jeff Hardy	15.00	30.00
NNO Jeff Hardy CH	20.00	40.00
NNO Murphy	15.00	30.00
NNO Rhea Ripley	15.00	30.00
NNO Roman Reigns	25.00	50.00
NNO Sheamus	15.00	30.00

2021 Mattel WWE Elite Collection Series 85

NNO	Aleister Black	15.00	30.00
NNO	Aleister Black CH	30.00	60.00
NNO	Becky Lynch	15.00	30.00
NNO	Bray Wyatt	20.00	40.00
NNO	Karrion Kross	25.00	50.00
NNO	Liv Morgan	20.00	40.00
NNO	Undertaker	25.00	50.00

2021 Mattel WWE Elite Collection Series 86

NNO	Carmella	20.00	40.00
NNO	The Fiend Bray Wyatt	25.00	50.00
NNO	The Miz	20.00	40.00
NNO	Seth Rollins	20.00	40.00
NNO	Sid Justice	20.00	40.00
NNO	Triple H Purple	15.00	30.00
NNO	Triple H Red CH	20.00	40.00

2021 Mattel WWE Elite Collection Series 87

NNO	Apollo Crews (blue trunks)	15.00	30.00
NNO	Apollo Crews (white trunks) (CHASE)	20.00	40.00
NNO	Asuka	15.00	30.00
NNO	Braun Strowman	15.00	30.00
NNO	Candice LeRae	15.00	30.00
NNO	Otis	12.50	25.00
NNO	Santos Escobar	12.50	25.00

2021 Mattel WWE Elite Collection Series 88

NNO	Kushida	12.50	25.00
NNO	Matt Riddle	25.00	50.00
NNO	MVP	20.00	40.00
NNO	Rey Mysterio	20.00	40.00
NNO	Trish Stratus	15.00	30.00
NNO	Trish Stratus (Canadian gear) (CHASE)	25.00	50.00

2021 Mattel WWE Elite Collection Series 89

NNO	Bobby Lashley	15.00	30.00
NNO	Damian Priest	20.00	40.00
NNO	Dominik Mysterio	30.00	60.00
NNO	Drew McIntyre	15.00	30.00
NNO	Nia Jax	12.50	25.00
NNO	Nia Jax (purple gear) (CHASE)	15.00	30.00
NNO	Sgt. Slaughter	20.00	40.00

2021 Mattel WWE Elite Collection Series 90

NNO	Big Bossman	15.00	30.00
NNO	Big Bossman (black gear) (CHASE)	25.00	50.00
NNO	Bronson Reed	12.50	25.00
NNO	Jey Uso	17.50	35.00
NNO	Mustafa Ali	15.00	30.00
NNO	Randy Orton	15.00	30.00

2022 Mattel WWE Elite Collection Series 91

NNO	Austin Theory		
NNO	Bianca Belair		
NNO	Hulk Hogan		
NNO	Kevin Owens		
NNO	Rob Van Dam		
NNO	Rob Van Dam (CHASE)		
NNO	Sami Zayn		

2022 Mattel WWE Elite Collection Series 92

NNO	Adam Cole		
NNO	Adam Cole (camo trunks) (CHASE)		
NNO	Burnt Fiend		
NNO	Charlotte Flair		
NNO	Rey Mysterio		
NNO	Ric Flair		
NNO	Scarlett		

2022 Mattel WWE Elite Collection Series 93

NNO	Cesaro		
NNO	Karrion Kross		
NNO	Raquel Gonzalez		
NNO	Ricky Steamboat (white gear)		
NNO	Ricky Steamboat (yellow year) (CHASE)		
NNO	Seth Rollins		
NNO	T-Bar		

2018 Mattel WWE Elite Collection SummerSlam 2018

NNO	Dean Ambrose	20.00	40.00
NNO	Edge	12.50	25.00
NNO	Matt Hardy	10.00	20.00
NNO	Seth Rollins	15.00	30.00

2019 Mattel WWE Elite Collection Survivor Series

NNO	Alicia Fox		
NNO	Don Muraco		
NNO	Jeff Hardy		
NNO	Shinsuke Nakamura		

2021 Mattel WWE Elite Collection Survivor Series 2021

NNO	Bayley	20.00	40.00
NNO	Bret "Hit Man" Hart	25.00	50.00
NNO	Hulk Hogan	25.00	50.00
NNO	Keith Lee	20.00	40.00

2017 Mattel WWE Elite Collection Then Now Forever 3-Packs

NNO	Lex Luger/Randy Savage/Sting	30.00	60.00
NNO	The Shield - Seth Rollins Dean Ambrose/Roman Reigns	75.00	150.00

2016 Mattel WWE Elite Collection Then Now Forever Series 1

NNO	Bam Bam Bigelow FB	25.00	50.00
NNO	Rusev	15.00	30.00
NNO	The Rock FB	20.00	40.00
NNO	Tyler Breeze	15.00	30.00

2017 Mattel WWE Elite Collection Then Now Forever Series 2

NNO	Earthquake FB	15.00	30.00
NNO	Macho Man Randy Savage FB	17.50	35.00
NNO	Sami Zayn	7.50	15.00
NNO	Typhoon FB	15.00	30.00

2017 Mattel WWE Elite Collection Then Now Forever Series 3

NNO	Chad Gable	12.50	25.00
NNO	Jason Jordan	10.00	20.00
NNO	Miss Elizabeth	15.00	30.00
NNO	Seth Rollins	12.50	25.00

2020 Mattel WWE Elite Collection Top Picks 2020

NNO	Braun Strowman	20.00	40.00
NNO	Ricochet	20.00	40.00
NNO	Roman Reigns	20.00	40.00
NNO	Seth Rollins	20.00	40.00

2021 Mattel WWE Elite Collection Top Picks 2021

NNO	Drew McIntyre	15.00	30.00
NNO	The Fiend Bray Wyatt	20.00	40.00
NNO	Kofi Kingston	12.50	25.00
NNO	Roman Reigns	12.50	25.00

2021 Mattel WWE Elite Collection Top Picks 2022

NNO	Drew McIntyre	15.00	30.00
NNO	John Cena	17.50	35.00
NNO	Rey Mysterio	25.00	50.00
NNO	Roman Reigns	15.00	30.00

2021 Mattel WWE Elite Collection Top Picks 2023

NNO	Rey Mysterio		
NNO	The Rock		
NNO	Undertaker		

2018 Mattel WWE Elite Collection Top Talent 2018

NNO	AJ Styles	20.00	40.00
NNO	Braun Strowman	15.00	30.00
NNO	Finn Balor	15.00	30.00
NNO	Seth Rollins	15.00	30.00

2019 Mattel WWE Elite Collection Top Talent 2019

NNO	AJ Styles	15.00	30.00
NNO	Braun Strowman	12.50	25.00
NNO	Finn Balor	12.50	25.00
NNO	Seth Rollins	10.00	20.00

2021 Mattel WWE Elite Collection Top Talent 2022

NNO	Goldberg		
NNO	Jeff Hardy		
NNO	Roman Reigns		

2017 Mattel WWE Elite Collection Women's Division

NNO	Alexa Bliss	20.00	40.00
NNO	Becky Lynch	20.00	40.00
NNO	Maryse	15.00	30.00
NNO	Sasha Banks	17.50	35.00

2010 Mattel WWE Elite Collection WrestleMania 26

NNO	Jack Swagger	25.00	50.00
NNO	Rey Mysterio	30.00	60.00
NNO	Triple H		
NNO	Undertaker	30.00	60.00

2011 Mattel WWE Elite Collection WrestleMania 27

NNO	Kofi Kingston	17.50	35.00
NNO	The Miz	20.00	40.00
NNO	The Rock	30.00	75.00
NNO	Stone Cold Steve Austin	30.00	60.00
NNO	Undertaker	30.00	75.00

2014 Mattel WWE Elite Collection WrestleMania 30 Heritage

NNO	Bret Hart	25.00	50.00
NNO	Shawn Michaels	30.00	60.00

2015 Mattel WWE Elite Collection WrestleMania 31 Heritage

NNO	Kane	30.00	75.00
NNO	Undertaker	25.00	50.00

2016 Mattel WWE Elite Collection WrestleMania 32 Heritage

NNO	Brock Lesnar	20.00	40.00
NNO	Undertaker	20.00	40.00

2017 Mattel WWE Elite Collection WrestleMania 33 Heritage

NNO	Shawn Michaels	25.00	50.00
NNO	Triple H	15.00	30.00

2018 Mattel WWE Elite Collection WrestleMania 34 Heritage

NNO	Brutus Beefcake FB	7.50	15.00
NNO	John Cena	12.50	25.00
NNO	Kevin Owens	10.00	20.00
NNO	Randy Orton	20.00	40.00

2018 Mattel WWE Elite Collection WrestleMania 35 Heritage

NNO	Sasha Banks	15.00	30.00
NNO	Scott Hall	15.00	30.00
NNO	Triple H	12.50	25.00
NNO	Undertaker	17.50	35.00

2020 Mattel WWE Elite Collection WrestleMania 36 Heritage

NNO	Booker T	20.00	40.00
NNO	Kofi Kingston	15.00	30.00
NNO	Mick Foley	20.00	40.00
NNO	Woken Matt Hardy	12.50	25.00

2021 Mattel WWE Elite Collection WrestleMania 37 Heritage

NNO	Chyna	12.50	25.00
NNO	Edge	20.00	40.00
NNO	Goldberg	15.00	30.00
NNO	Shawn Michaels	30.00	60.00

2021 Mattel WWE Elite Collection WrestleMania 37 Heritage (loose)

NNO Paul Ellering w/Rocco
(Build-A-Figure)

2021 Mattel WWE Elite Collection WrestleMania 38 Heritage

NNO	AJ Styles	15.00	30.00
NNO	Bret "Hit Man" Hart	15.00	30.00
NNO	Shawn Michaels	12.50	25.00
NNO	Stone Cold Steve Austin	15.00	30.00

2021 Mattel WWE Elite Collection WrestleMania 38 Heritage (loose)

NNO Vince McMahon
(Build-A-Figure)

2011 Mattel WWE Elite Collection WWE All-Stars 2-Packs

NNO	Jake The Snake Roberts vs. Randy Orton	60.00	120.00
NNO	Macho Man Randy Savage vs. John Morrison	50.00	100.00
NNO	Stone Cold Steve Austin vs. CM Punk	125.00	250.00

2012 Mattel WWE Fan Central

NNO Big Show
NNO John Cena
NNO Kane
NNO Kofi Kingston

2014 Mattel WWE Fan Central

NNO	Daniel Bryan	30.00	60.00
NNO	The Rock		

2014-15 Mattel WWE Fan Central

NNO	Dean Ambrose	12.50	25.00
NNO	John Cena	10.00	20.00
NNO	Randy Orton	10.00	20.00

2015 Mattel WWE Fan Central

NNO Bad News Barrett
NNO Daniel Bryan
NNO Ultimate Warrior

2016 Mattel WWE Fan Central

NNO	Finn Balor	10.00	20.00
NNO	John Cena	7.50	15.00
NNO	Ryback	7.50	15.00
NNO	Triple H	6.00	12.00

2018 Mattel WWE Fan Central

NNO	Finn Balor	12.50	25.00
NNO	Kevin Nash	15.00	30.00
NNO	Randy Orton	10.00	20.00
NNO	Rusev	7.50	15.00

2018 Mattel WWE Flashback Series 1

NNO	Cowboy Bob Orton	7.50	15.00
NNO	The Million Dollar Man	7.50	15.00
NNO	Ravishing Rick Rude	7.50	15.00
NNO	Sgt. Slaughter	10.00	20.00

2018 Mattel WWE Flashback Series 2

NNO	Booker T	12.50	25.00
NNO	Lex Luger	10.00	20.00
NNO	Ric Flair	12.50	25.00
NNO	Sting	15.00	30.00

2010-11 Mattel WWE Flex Force

NNO Batista
NNO Big Show
NNO Big Show
(card variant)
NNO Chris Jericho
NNO CM Punk (back flippin')
NNO CM Punk (hook throwin' w/belt)
(Toys R Us Exclusive)
NNO CM Punk (hook throwin')
NNO CM Punk (super jumpin')
NNO Edge
NNO Evan Bourne (back flippin')
NNO Evan Bourne (flip kickin')
NNO Jack Swagger
NNO John Cena (body slammin')
NNO John Cena (fist poundin' w/belt)
(Toys R Us Exclusive)
NNO John Cena (fist poundin')
NNO John Cena (hook throwin')
NNO John Cena (hook throwin')
(card variant)
NNO John Morrison (flip kickin')

NNO John Morrison (super jumpin')
NNO Kane
NNO Kofi Kingston
NNO Matt Hardy
NNO Matt Hardy (w/belt)
(Toys R Us Exclusive)
NNO Miz (back flippin')
NNO Miz (hook throwin')
NNO Randy Orton (fist poundin')
NNO Randy Orton (flip kickin')
NNO Randy Orton (hook throwin')
NNO Rey Mysterio (fist poundin')
NNO Rey Mysterio (flip kickin' green)
NNO Rey Mysterio (flip kickin' red)
NNO Rey Mysterio (flip kickin' yellow w/belt)
(Toys R Us Exclusive)
NNO Rey Mysterio (flip kickin' yellow)
NNO Rey Mysterio (super jumpin')
NNO R-Truth
NNO Shawn Michaels (flip kickin')
NNO Shawn Michaels (hook throwin')
NNO Sheamus
NNO Triple H
NNO Undertaker (fist poundin' w/belt)
(Toys R Us Exclusive)
NNO Undertaker (fist poundin')
NNO Undertaker (fist poundin')
(card variant)

2011-12 Mattel WWE Flex Force

NNO Alberto Del Rio
NNO Big Show
NNO Christian
NNO Evan Bourne
NNO John Cena (body slammin')
NNO John Cena (hook throwin')
NNO Kofi Kingston
NNO Randy Orton (flip kickin')
NNO Randy Orton (scissor kickin')
NNO Rey Mysterio (super jumpin')
NNO Rey Mysterio (swing kickin')
NNO The Rock
NNO Sheamus
NNO Sin Cara
NNO Wade Barrett

2010 Mattel WWE Flex Force Big Talkin'

NNO CM Punk
NNO MVP
NNO Randy Orton
NNO Triple H

2011 Mattel WWE Flex Force Champions Series 1

NNO John Cena vs. Sheamus
NNO The Miz vs. R-Truth
NNO Randy Orton vs. Rey Mysterio

2012 Mattel WWE Flex Force Champions Series 2

NNO Alberto Del Rio vs. Rey Mysterio
NNO John Cena vs. Undertaker
NNO Randy Orton vs. Kane
NNO Sheamus vs. Kofi Kingston

2010 Mattel WWE Flex Force Deluxe

NNO CM Punk
NNO John Cena
NNO Matt Hardy
NNO Rey Mysterio
NNO Undertaker

2010 Mattel WWE Flex Force DVD Heroes

NNO CM Punk
NNO John Cena
NNO John Morrison
NNO Rey Mysterio

2011-12 Mattel WWE Flex Force Lightning

NNO Big Show
NNO Evan Bourne
NNO John Cena (fist poundin')
NNO John Cena (hook throwin')
NNO Kane
NNO Kofi Kingston
NNO The Miz
NNO Randy Orton
NNO Rey Mysterio (blue)
NNO Rey Mysterio (red)
NNO Sheamus
NNO Sin Cara

2010 Mattel WWE Flex Force Playsets

NNO Breakdown Brawl Ring
NNO Breakdown Brawl Ring (w/Big Show)
(Walmart Exclusive)
NNO Colossal Crashdown Arena
NNO Launchin' Entrance Ring

2011 Mattel WWE Flex Force Playsets

NNO High Flyin' Fury
NNO Money in the Bank Ring

2012 Mattel WWE Flex Force Playsets

NNO Tornado Takedown Ring

2010 Mattel WWE Flex Force Smash Scenes

NNO CM Punk
NNO John Cena (body slammin')
NNO John Cena (fist poundin')
NNO Matt Hardy
NNO Randy Orton
NNO Rey Mysterio

2018 Mattel WWE Flextremes

NNO Finn Balor
NNO John Cena
NNO The Rock
NNO Roman Reigns

2018 Mattel WWE Flextremes 4-Pack

NNO Cena/Rock/Balor/Reigns	15.00	30.00

2011 Mattel WWE Heritage Series

NNO CM Punk
NNO John Cena
NNO Kane
NNO Melina
NNO Randy Orton
NNO Triple H

2011-12 Mattel WWE Legends Mattyshop Exclusives

NNO Andre the Giant	125.00	250.00
NNO Arn Anderson	100.00	200.00
NNO Diamond Dallas Page	60.00	120.00
NNO King Kong Bundy	125.00	250.00
NNO The Rockers (Jannetty/Michaels)	200.00	350.00
NNO Tully Blanchard	100.00	200.00

2017 Mattel WWE Make-A-Wish Foundation

NNO John Cena	15.00	30.00

2015 Mattel WWE Mighty Minis Series 1

NNO Bret Hart (blue)		
NNO Bret Hart (pink)		
NNO Daniel Bryan	2.50	5.00
NNO Dolph Ziggler	2.00	4.00
NNO John Cena	3.00	6.00
NNO Roman Reigns	2.00	4.00
NNO Rusev	2.50	5.00
NNO Seth Rollins	2.00	4.00
NNO Ted DiBiase	2.00	4.00
NNO Undertaker	3.00	6.00

2015 Mattel WWE Mighty Minis Series 2

NNO Brock Lesnar		
NNO Dean Ambrose		
NNO Goldust		
NNO John Cena		
NNO Kane	2.00	4.00
NNO The Rock	4.00	8.00
NNO Stone Cold Steve Austin		
NNO Triple H		
NNO Ultimate Warrior (orange)		
NNO Ultimate Warrior (white)		

2016 Mattel WWE Mighty Minis SDCC Exclusive

NNO Dean Ambrose	5.00	10.00

2017 Mattel WWE Monsters

NNO Asuka as The Phantom	7.50	15.00
NNO Braun Strowman as Frankenstein	12.50	25.00
NNO Chris Jericho as The Mummy	7.50	15.00
NNO Jake Roberts as The Creature	12.50	25.00
NNO Roman Reigns as The Werewolf	10.00	20.00
NNO Undertaker as The Vampire	12.50	25.00

2018 Mattel WWE M.U.S.C.L.E. SDCC Exclusives

NNO Andre the Giant
NNO Hacksaw Jim Duggan
NNO Iron Sheik
NNO Jake The Snake Roberts
NNO Junkyard Dog
NNO Macho Man Randy Savage
NNO Mean Gene Okerlund
NNO Million Dollar Man
NNO Ric Flair
NNO Rowdy Roddy Piper
NNO Sgt. Slaughter
NNO Ultimate Warrior

2018 Mattel WWE M.U.S.C.L.E. SDCC Exclusives 3-Pack

NNO WWE Figurines	3.00	6.00

2016 Mattel WWE Mutants

NNO Bray Wyatt	6.00	12.00
NNO Brock Lesnar	20.00	40.00
NNO Finn Balor	12.50	25.00
NNO John Cena	7.50	15.00
NNO Stardust	6.00	12.00
NNO Sting	7.50	15.00

2017 Mattel WWE Network Spotlight

NNO Big Cass	6.00	12.00
NNO Brock Lesnar	7.50	15.00

NNO Enzo Amore	12.50	25.00
NNO Sting Surfer Gear FB	10.00	20.00

2017 Mattel WWE NXT Series 1

NNO Andrade Cien Almas	15.00	30.00
NNO Hideo Itami	7.50	15.00
NNO Kevin Owens	6.00	12.00
NNO Sami Zayn	6.00	12.00
NNO Samoa Joe	7.50	15.00
NNO Tye Dillinger	6.00	12.00

2017 Mattel WWE NXT Series 2

NNO Akam	12.50	25.00
NNO Bobby Roode	10.00	20.00
NNO Eva Marie	20.00	40.00
NNO Johnny Gargano		
NNO Rezar	12.50	25.00
NNO Tommaso Ciampa		

2017 Mattel WWE NXT Series 3

NNO Johnny Gargano	15.00	30.00
NNO Tommaso Ciampa	15.00	30.00

2018 Mattel WWE NXT Series 4

NNO Billie Kay
NNO Paige
NNO Roderick Strong
NNO Triple H
NNO Xavier Woods

2012 Mattel WWE Power Slammers

NNO Brodus Clay	10.00	20.00
NNO John Cena		
NNO Kofi Kingston		
NNO Rey Mysterio	12.50	25.00
NNO Sheamus		
NNO The Miz		
NNO Zack Ryder		

2010 Mattel WWE PPV Series 1

NNO Batista
NNO Edge
NNO John Cena
NNO Randy Orton
NNO Steve Austin
NNO Undertaker

2010 Mattel WWE PPV Series 2

NNO John Cena
NNO John Morrison
NNO Kofi Kingston
NNO The Miz
NNO Rey Mysterio
NNO Undertaker

2010 Mattel WWE PPV Series 3

NNO Beth Phoenix
NNO Chris Jericho
NNO CM Punk
NNO Cody Rhodes
NNO Edge
NNO Triple H

2010 Mattel WWE PPV Series 4

NNO Batista
NNO Chris Jericho
NNO Drew McIntyre

NNO John Cena
NNO Rey Mysterio
NNO Undertaker

2010 Mattel WWE PPV Series 5

NNO Big Show
NNO CM Punk
NNO Jack Swagger
NNO John Cena
NNO Rey Mysterio
NNO R-Truth

2010 Mattel WWE PPV Series 6

NNO Christian
NNO John Cena
NNO Randy Orton
NNO Rey Mysterio
NNO Sheamus
NNO Undertaker

2011 Mattel WWE PPV Series 7

NNO CM Punk
NNO John Cena
NNO Kane
NNO Melina
NNO Randy Orton
NNO Triple H

2011 Mattel WWE PPV Series 8

NNO Edge		
NNO John Cena	20.00	40.00
NNO John Morrison		
NNO Rey Mysterio		
NNO Sheamus		
NNO Wade Barrett		

2011 Mattel WWE PPV Series 9

NNO Edge	15.00	30.00
NNO Great Khali	20.00	40.00
NNO John Cena		
NNO Randy Orton		
NNO Rey Mysterio		
NNO Triple H		

2011 Mattel WWE PPV Series 10

NNO Alberto Del Rio
NNO Christian
NNO John Cena
NNO Rey Mysterio
NNO R-Truth
NNO Sheamus

2011 Mattel WWE PPV Series 11

NNO Big Show
NNO Chris Masters
NNO Evan Bourne
NNO John Cena
NNO The Rock
NNO Sheamus

2016 Mattel WWE Retro Series 1

NNO Brock Lesnar	15.00	30.00
NNO John Cena	20.00	40.00
NNO Kevin Owens	20.00	40.00
NNO Roman Reigns	75.00	150.00
NNO Ultimate Warrior	15.00	30.00
NNO Undertaker	25.00	50.00

2017 Mattel WWE Retro Series 2

NNO Kane	20.00	40.00
NNO Mankind	20.00	40.00
NNO The Rock	12.50	25.00
NNO Sting	15.00	30.00
NNO Stone Cold Steve Austin	15.00	30.00
NNO Triple H	15.00	30.00

2017 Mattel WWE Retro Series 3

NNO AJ Styles	6.00	12.00
NNO Dean Ambrose	7.50	15.00
NNO Goldberg	6.00	12.00
NNO Seth Rollins	10.00	20.00

2017 Mattel WWE Retro Series 4

NNO Finn Balor	15.00	30.00
NNO Kevin Owens	10.00	20.00
NNO Ric Flair	30.00	60.00
NNO Sami Zayn	7.50	15.00

2017 Mattel WWE Retro Series 5

NNO Big E	7.50	15.00
NNO Kofi Kingston	10.00	20.00
NNO Macho Man Randy Savage	12.50	25.00
NNO Macho Man/Arms Down	12.50	25.00
NNO Xavier Woods	6.00	12.00

2018 Mattel WWE Retro Series 6

NNO Bray Wyatt	7.50	15.00
NNO Daniel Bryan	10.00	20.00
NNO Shinsuke Nakamura	7.50	15.00
NNO Sting/Wolfpac	12.50	25.00

2018 Mattel WWE Retro Series 7

NNO Chris Jericho	7.50	15.00
NNO Kurt Angle	7.50	15.00
NNO Shawn Michaels	10.00	20.00
NNO Sheamus	7.50	15.00

2019 Mattel WWE Retro Series 8

NNO Braun Strowman	7.50	15.00
NNO Iron Sheik	7.50	15.00
NNO Jeff Hardy	7.50	15.00
NNO Zack Ryder	7.50	15.00

2019 Mattel WWE Retro Series 9

NNO Goldust	7.50	15.00
NNO Macho Man Randy Savage	12.50	25.00
NNO Randy Orton	7.50	15.00
NNO Samoa Joe	12.50	25.00

2019 Mattel WWE Retro Series 10

NNO Diesel	10.00	20.00
NNO Elias	7.50	15.00
NNO Junkyard Dog	15.00	30.00
NNO Matt Hardy	6.00	12.00

2018 Mattel WWE Retro Series Playset

NNO Collectible Retro Ring

2018-19 Mattel WWE Retrofest

NNO Hacksaw Jim Duggan	10.00	20.00
NNO Honky Tonk Man	10.00	20.00
NNO Macho Man Randy Savage	12.50	25.00
NNO Mr. Perfect	15.00	30.00
NNO Ric Flair	10.00	20.00
NNO Shawn Michaels	12.50	25.00

2010 Mattel WWE Series 1

NNO Batista
NNO Batista w/Title Belt/1000
NNO Big Show
NNO Big Show w/Title Belt/1000
NNO Evan Bourne
NNO Evan Bourne w/Title Belt/1000
NNO John Cena
NNO John Cena w/Title Belt/1000
NNO Kofi Kingston
NNO Kofi Kingston w/Title Belt/1000
NNO Triple H
NNO Triple H w/Title Belt/1000

2010 Mattel WWE Series 2

NNO CM Punk		
NNO CM Punk w/Title Belt/1000		
NNO Jack Swagger		
NNO Jack Swagger w/Title Belt/1000		
NNO Kane		
NNO Kane w/Title Belt/1000		
NNO Mark Henry	10.00	20.00
NNO Mark Henry w/Title Belt/1000		
NNO Rey Mysterio/Dk Blue		
NNO Rey Mysterio (light blue w/title belt)/1000		
NNO Rey Mysterio/Lt Blue	25.00	50.00
NNO Vladimir Kozlov		
NNO Vladimir Kozlov w/Title Belt/1000		

2010 Mattel WWE Series 3

NNO Chris Jericho	10.00	20.00
NNO Chris Jericho w/Title Belt/1000		
NNO Great Khali		
NNO Great Khali w/Title Belt/1000		
NNO Mickie James	12.50	25.00
NNO Mickie James w/Title Belt/1000		
NNO Randy Orton		
NNO Shelton Benjamin		
NNO Shelton Benjamin w/Title Belt/1000		
NNO Undertaker		
NNO Undertaker w/Title Belt/1000		

2010 Mattel WWE Series 4

NNO Dolph Ziggler	12.50	25.00
NNO Dolph Ziggler w/Title Belt/1000		
NNO Goldust	12.50	25.00
NNO Goldust w/Title Belt/1000		
NNO Matt Hardy	12.50	25.00
NNO Matt Hardy w/Title Belt/1000		
NNO MVP	15.00	30.00
NNO MVP w/Title Belt/1000		
NNO Shawn Michaels	17.50	35.00
NNO Shawn Michaels w/Title Belt/1000		
NNO William Regal	10.00	20.00
NNO William Regal w/Title Belt/1000		

2010 Mattel WWE Series 5

NNO Batista	12.50	25.00
NNO Hurricane	12.50	25.00
NNO Hurricane w/Title Belt/1000		
NNO John Cena	10.00	20.00
NNO Melina	20.00	40.00
NNO Melina w/Title Belt/1000		
NNO Mike Knox	25.00	50.00
NNO Mike Knox w/Title Belt/1000		
NNO R-Truth		
NNO R-Truth w/Title Belt/1000		

2010 Mattel WWE Series 6

NNO	Big Show	10.00	20.00
NNO	Drew McIntyre	15.00	30.00
NNO	Edge		
NNO	Kelly Kelly	20.00	40.00
NNO	The Miz		
NNO	Ted DiBiase	12.50	25.00

2010 Mattel WWE Series 7

NNO	Kofi Kingston		
NNO	Michelle McCool	25.00	50.00
NNO	Rey Mysterio	25.00	50.00
NNO	Sheamus		
NNO	Undertaker		
NNO	Yoshi Tatsu	12.50	25.00
NNO	Yoshi Tatsu w/Title Belt/1000		
NNO	Sheamus w/Title Belt/1000		
NNO	Michelle McCool w/Title Belt/1000		

2011 Mattel WWE Series 8

NNO	Chris Masters	15.00	30.00
NNO	Christian	10.00	20.00
NNO	Finlay	12.50	25.00
NNO	Kane	12.50	25.00
NNO	Kofi Kingston	15.00	30.00
NNO	Maryse	30.00	60.00

2011 Mattel WWE Series 9

NNO	Evan Bourne	7.50	15.00
NNO	Jack Swagger	6.00	12.00
NNO	JTG	10.00	20.00
NNO	Mark Henry		
NNO	Natalya	20.00	40.00
NNO	Rey Mysterio		

2011 Mattel WWE Series 10

NNO	Dolph Ziggler	10.00	20.00
NNO	John Cena	12.50	25.00
NNO	Kofi Kingston	10.00	20.00
NNO	Triple H		
NNO	Wade Barrett	7.50	15.00
NNO	Zack Ryder	10.00	20.00

2011 Mattel WWE Series 11

NNO	Big Show	12.50	25.00
NNO	Daniel Bryan	7.50	15.00
NNO	Eve	12.50	25.00
NNO	Sheamus	6.00	12.00
NNO	Skip Sheffield	12.50	25.00

2011 Mattel WWE Series 12

NNO	Alberto Del Rio	7.50	15.00
NNO	Evan Bourne	7.50	15.00
NNO	John Morrison		
NNO	Randy Orton	7.50	15.00
NNO	Rey Mysterio		
NNO	Wade Barrett	7.50	15.00

2012 Mattel WWE Series 13

1	Rey Mysterio		
2	Vickie Guerrero	15.00	30.00
3	John Morrison		
4	R-Truth	15.00	30.00
5	Ezekiel Jackson		
6	Undertaker		

2012 Mattel WWE Series 14

7	Bret Hit Man Hart		
8	Shawn Michaels		
9	Goldust		
10	Rey Mysterio		
11	John Morrison		
12	Alberto Del Rio		

2012 Mattel WWE Series 15

13	Layla	30.00	75.00
14	Kofi Kingston	15.00	30.00
15	John Cena	7.50	15.00
16	Wade Barrett	20.00	40.00
17	Brodus Clay		
18	Kane		

2012 Mattel WWE Series 16

19	Ultimate Warrior	15.00	30.00
20	John Cena	10.00	20.00
21	Eddie Guerrero	17.50	35.00
22	Triple H		
23	Undertaker		
24	Jack Swagger	7.50	15.00

2012 Mattel WWE Series 17

25	Rey Mysterio	15.00	30.00
26	Dolph Ziggler	10.00	20.00
27	Zack Ryder	10.00	20.00
28	The Miz	7.50	15.00
29	Alex Riley	7.50	15.00
30	Mark Henry	10.00	20.00

2012 Mattel WWE Series 18

31	Kelly Kelly	12.50	25.00
32	Sin Cara		
33	Hunico	15.00	30.00
34	CM Punk	10.00	20.00
35	John Cena	7.50	15.00
36	Cody Rhodes		

2012 Mattel WWE Series 19

37	Hornswoggle		
38	Evan Bourne	10.00	20.00
39	Kofi Kingston	7.50	15.00
40	Justin Gabriel	6.00	12.00
41	Jinder Mahal	7.50	15.00
42	Randy Orton	7.50	15.00

2012 Mattel WWE Series 20

43	Natalya		
44	Rey Mysterio		
45	Yoshi Tatsu	7.50	15.00
46	John Cena	7.50	15.00
47	Sheamus	10.00	20.00
48	Wade Barrett		

2012 Mattel WWE Series 21

49	Beth Phoenix	25.00	50.00
50	R-Truth		
51	The Miz		
52	Mason Ryan		
53	Jack Swagger		
54	Big Show		

2012 Mattel WWE Series 22

55	Booker T	12.50	25.00
56	Mark Henry		
57	Chris Jericho	6.00	12.00
58	Christian	10.00	20.00
59	John Cena	7.50	15.00
60	Zack Ryder	7.50	15.00

2012 Mattel WWE Series 23

61	Rey Mysterio	15.00	30.00
62	Alicia Fox	15.00	30.00
63	Hunico	10.00	20.00
64	Santino Marella	7.50	15.00
65	Triple H		
66	Kane		

2013 Mattel WWE Series 24

1	John Cena		
2	CM Punk		
3	Zack Ryder	15.00	30.00
4	Drew McIntyre	15.00	30.00
5	Sheamus		
6	AJ	20.00	40.00

2013 Mattel WWE Series 25

7	Big Show		
8	Brock Lesnar		
9	Randy Orton		
10	The Miz	12.50	25.00
11	Eve	20.00	40.00
12	David Otunga	10.00	20.00

2013 Mattel WWE Series 26

13	Macho Man Randy Savage	12.50	25.00
14	Shawn Michaels	12.50	25.00
15	Undertaker	10.00	20.00
16	Kane	25.00	50.00
17	Mark Henry		
18	Daniel Bryan	10.00	20.00

2013 Mattel WWE Series 27

19	Cody Rhodes		
20	Kofi Kingston		
21	Wade Barrett		
22	Ryback	12.50	25.00
23	Brodus Clay		
24	Antonio Cesaro	10.00	20.00

2013 Mattel WWE Series 28

25	Rey Mysterio		
26	R-Truth	10.00	20.00
27	Heath Slater	10.00	20.00
28	Sin Cara	20.00	50.00
29	Tensai	7.50	15.00
30	Damien Sandow	7.50	15.00

2013 Mattel WWE Series 29

31	Ultimate Warrior		
32	Eddie Guerrero	15.00	30.00
33	Stone Cold Steve Austin		
34	Big Show		
35	John Cena	7.50	15.00
36	CM Punk		

2013 Mattel WWE Series 30

37	The Miz		
38	Hornswoggle	30.00	60.00
39	Santino Marella		
40	Sheamus	10.00	20.00
41	Daniel Bryan	10.00	20.00
42	AJ Lee	20.00	40.00

2013 Mattel WWE Series 31

43 Kane		
44 R-Truth	10.00	20.00
45 Zack Ryder		
46 Rosa Mendes	10.00	20.00
47 Wade Barrett	7.50	15.00
48 Alberto Del Rio	7.50	15.00

2013 Mattel WWE Series 32

49 Chris Jericho	10.00	20.00
50 The Rock	12.50	25.00
51 Randy Orton	12.50	25.00
52 John Cena	7.50	15.00
53 Ryback		
54 Antonio Cesaro	7.50	15.00

2013 Mattel WWE Series 33

55 Big Show		
56 Dolph Ziggler	10.00	20.00
57 Great Khali		
58 CM Punk	12.50	25.00
59 Tamina Snuka	10.00	20.00
60 Dean Ambrose		

2013 Mattel WWE Series 34

61 John Cena	7.50	15.00
62 The Miz		
63 Rey Mysterio		
64 Sin Cara	20.00	40.00
65 Ricardo Rodriguez	12.50	25.00
66 Brodus Clay	7.50	15.00

2014 Mattel WWE Series 35

1 Kane		
2 Damien Sandow	7.50	15.00
3 Daniel Bryan	17.50	35.00
4 Triple H		
5 Cody Rhodes	7.50	15.00
6 Jinder Mahal	10.00	20.00

2014 Mattel WWE Series 36

7 CM Punk	15.00	30.00
8 Big E Langston	7.50	15.00
9 Christian		
10 Jack Swagger		
11 Fandango		
12 Kaitlyn	12.50	25.00

2014 Mattel WWE Series 37

13 Mr. Perfect		
14 Batista		
15 Roman Reigns		
16 Ryback		
17 Zeb Colter		
18 Randy Orton		

2014 Mattel WWE Series 38

19 Chris Jericho		
20 Dolph Ziggler	7.50	15.00
21 Vickie Guerrero	10.00	20.00
22 Sheamus		
23 The Miz		
24 Kofi Kingston	7.50	15.00

2014 Mattel WWE Series 39

25 Bray Wyatt	7.50	15.00
26 Rob Van Dam	12.50	25.00

27 Justin Gabriel	10.00	20.00
28 John Cena		
29 Christian		
30 Heath Slater	10.00	20.00

2014 Mattel WWE Series 40

31 CM Punk	17.50	35.00
32 Alberto Del Rio	7.50	15.00
33 Rey Mysterio		
34 The Great Khali		
35 Zack Ryder	7.50	15.00
36 Edge	12.50	25.00

2014 Mattel WWE Series 41

37 Daniel Bryan	10.00	20.00
38 Santino Marella		
39 Cesaro		
40 Drew McIntyre		
41 Bray Wyatt		
42 Fandango		

2014 Mattel WWE Series 42

43 Natalya	12.50	25.00
44 Batista		
45 El Torito	10.00	20.00
46 Big Show		
47 Roman Reigns	10.00	20.00
48 Sin Cara		

2014 Mattel WWE Series 43

49 Mark Henry		
50 Eva Marie	10.00	20.00
51 Rob Van Dam	17.50	35.00
52 John Cena	7.50	15.00
54 Dolph Ziggler	7.50	15.00
55 Rey Mysterio		

2014 Mattel WWE Series 44

53 Kane	20.00	40.00
56 Big E		
57 Randy Orton		
58 Seth Rollins	10.00	20.00
59 Titus O'Neil		
60 Goldust	10.00	20.00

2015 Mattel WWE Series 45

1 Triple H	6.00	12.00
2 Chris Jericho	10.00	20.00
3 Mankind	10.00	20.00
4 The Miz	7.50	15.00
5 Ricky The Dragon Steamboat	10.00	20.00
6 Daniel Bryan	15.00	30.00

2015 Mattel WWE Series 46

8 Big Show	12.50	25.00
9 Kofi Kingston	10.00	20.00
10 Bad News Barrett	7.50	15.00
11 Jerry The King Lawler	20.00	40.00
12 Batista	17.50	35.00

2015 Mattel WWE Series 47

13 Alicia Fox	7.50	15.00
14 Rusev	6.00	12.00
15 Brock Lesnar	10.00	20.00
16 Kane	20.00	40.00
17 Christian	10.00	20.00
18 Cesaro	10.00	20.00

2015 Mattel WWE Series 48

19 Ric Flair	10.00	20.00
20 Hulk Hogan	12.50	25.00
21 Brie Bella	10.00	20.00
22 John Cena	7.50	15.00
23 Booker T	15.00	30.00
24 Randy Orton		

2015 Mattel WWE Series 49

25 Ryback		
26 Bray Wyatt	7.50	15.00
27 Roman Reigns	10.00	20.00
28 Bret Hart	12.50	25.00
29 Bo Dallas	7.50	15.00
30A Emma FP	12.50	25.00
30B Emma FP/Legs Variant		

2015 Mattel WWE Series 50

31 Daniel Bryan	10.00	20.00
32 Adam Rose	6.00	12.00
33 Seth Rollins	7.50	15.00
34 Goldust	10.00	20.00
35 Summer Rae FP	15.00	30.00
36 Sami Zayn FP	6.00	12.00

2015 Mattel WWE Series 51

37 Dolph Ziggler	7.50	15.00
38 Dean Ambrose	10.00	20.00
39 Stardust	25.00	50.00
40 Stephanie McMahon	10.00	20.00
41 Stone Cold Steve Austin FB	12.50	25.00
42 Heath Slater	7.50	15.00

2015 Mattel WWE Series 52

43 John Cena		
44 Chris Jericho	6.00	12.00
45 The Miz	7.50	15.00
46 Nikki Bella	7.50	15.00
47 Mark Henry		
48 Adrian Neville FP	10.00	20.00

2015 Mattel WWE Series 53

49 Brock Lesnar	7.50	15.00
50 The Rock	10.00	20.00
51 Triple H	7.50	15.00
52 Damien Mizdow	6.00	12.00
53 AJ Lee	30.00	75.00
54 Tyler Breeze FP	6.00	12.00

2015 Mattel WWE Series 54

55 Roman Reigns	10.00	20.00
56 The Rock	10.00	20.00
57 Rusev	6.00	12.00
58 Big Show	12.50	25.00
59 Dolph Ziggler	7.50	15.00
60 Tyson Kidd	6.00	12.00

2015 Mattel WWE Series 55

60 Sting FB	10.00	20.00
61 John Cena	7.50	15.00
62 El Torito	20.00	40.00
63 Kane	7.50	15.00
64 Randy Orton	10.00	20.00
65 Bray Wyatt	10.00	20.00
66 Undertaker	12.50	25.00
67 Charlotte FP	15.00	30.00

2015 Mattel WWE Series 56

NNO Dean Ambrose	7.50	15.00
NNO Dean Ambrose/WWE Title		
NNO Hideo Itami FP	6.00	12.00
NNO John Cena	10.00	20.00
NNO John Cena/WWE Title	15.00	30.00
NNO Naomi	7.50	15.00
NNO Naomi/WWE Title	12.50	25.00
NNO Ultimate Warrior FB	12.50	25.00
NNO Ultimate Warrior FB/WWE Title		
NNO Xavier Woods	6.00	12.00
NNO Xavier Woods/WWE Title		

2015 Mattel WWE Series 57

NNO Big Show		
NNO Big Show/WWE Title	15.00	30.00
NNO Daniel Bryan	7.50	15.00
NNO Daniel Bryan/WWE Title	12.50	25.00
NNO Erick Rowan	6.00	12.00
NNO Erick Rowan/WWE Title	10.00	20.00
NNO Finn Balor FP	10.00	20.00
NNO Paige	12.50	25.00
NNO Paige/WWE Title	20.00	40.00
NNO Ryback	6.00	12.00
NNO Ryback/WWE Title		

2015 Mattel WWE Series 58

NNO Bad News Barrett	7.50	15.00
NNO Bad News Barrett/WWE Title		
NNO Bayley	10.00	20.00
NNO Bayley/WWE Title		
NNO Edge FB	7.50	15.00
NNO Edge FB/WWE Title		
NNO Fandango	6.00	12.00
NNO Fandango/WWE Title		
NNO Kevin Owens	7.50	15.00
NNO Kevin Owens/WWE Title		
NNO Lana	7.50	15.00
NNO Lana/WWE Title	15.00	30.00
NNO Paul Orndorff FB	7.50	15.00
NNO Paul Orndorff FB/WWE Title		
NNO Stardust	10.00	20.00
NNO Stardust/WWE Title		
NNO Undertaker	12.50	25.00
NNO Undertaker/WWE Title	20.00	40.00

2016 Mattel WWE Series 59

NNO Bray Wyatt	7.50	15.00
NNO Bray Wyatt/WWE Title		
NNO Eva Marie	10.00	20.00
NNO Eva Marie/WWE Title	12.50	25.00
NNO Honky Tonk Man FB	6.00	12.00
NNO Honky Tonk Man FB/WWE Title		
NNO Iron Sheik FB	10.00	20.00
NNO Iron Sheik FB/WWE Title		
NNO R-Truth	12.50	25.00
NNO R-Truth/WWE Title		
NNO Sasha Banks FP	10.00	20.00
NNO Sasha Banks FP/WWE Title		
NNO Sheamus	6.00	12.00
NNO Sheamus/WWE Title	7.50	15.00
NNO Triple H	6.00	12.00
NNO Triple H/WWE Title		

2016 Mattel WWE Series 60

NNO Brock Lesnar	7.50	15.00
NNO Brock Lesnar/WWE Title		
NNO John Cena	10.00	20.00
NNO John Cena/WWE Title		
NNO Kalisto FP	12.50	25.00
NNO Kalisto FP/WWE Title		
NNO Kofi Kingston	7.50	15.00
NNO Kofi Kingston/WWE Title		
NNO Luke Harper	6.00	12.00
NNO Luke Harper/WWE Title		
NNO Randy Orton	7.50	15.00
NNO Randy Orton/WWE Title		
NNO Renee Young	7.50	15.00
NNO Renee Young/WWE Title	10.00	20.00
NNO Seth Rollins	7.50	15.00
NNO Seth Rollins/WWE Title		

2016 Mattel WWE Series 61

NNO Big E	7.50	15.00
NNO Dean Ambrose	6.00	12.00
NNO Dolph Ziggler	7.50	15.00
NNO Finn Balor	10.00	20.00
NNO John Cena	7.50	15.00
NNO Natalya	10.00	20.00
NNO Neville	6.00	12.00
NNO Sami Zayn	6.00	12.00
NNO Zack Ryder	7.50	15.00

2016 Mattel WWE Series 62

NNO Becky Lynch FP	20.00	40.00
NNO The Miz	7.50	15.00
NNO Roman Reigns	10.00	20.00
NNO Sin Cara	20.00	40.00
NNO Sting FB	15.00	30.00

2016 Mattel WWE Series 63

NNO Alberto Del Rio	10.00	20.00
NNO Baron Corbin FP	7.50	15.00
NNO Paul Heyman	12.50	25.00
NNO Rusev	10.00	20.00
NNO Ryback	10.00	20.00
NNO Seth Rollins	7.50	15.00
NNO Sid Justice FB	10.00	20.00
NNO Undertaker	12.50	25.00

2016 Mattel WWE Series 64

NNO Apollo Crews FP	10.00	20.00
NNO Braun Strowman	15.00	30.00
NNO Brock Lesnar	12.50	25.00
NNO Dolph Ziggler	7.50	15.00
NNO John Cena	7.50	15.00
NNO Lana	10.00	20.00
NNO Xavier Woods	6.00	12.00

2016 Mattel WWE Series 65

NNO Emma	10.00	20.00
NNO Kane	10.00	20.00
NNO Kevin Owens	7.50	15.00
NNO The Rock	12.50	25.00
NNO Roman Reigns	7.50	15.00
NNO Samoa Joe	7.50	15.00
NNO Sheamus	7.50	15.00

2016 Mattel WWE Series 66

NNO Alberto Del Rio	7.50	15.00
NNO Big Show		
NNO Daniel Bryan	12.50	25.00
NNO Dean Ambrose	7.50	15.00
NNO Paige	15.00	30.00

2016 Mattel WWE Series 67 (continued)

NNO Roman Reigns	12.50	25.00
NNO Tyler Breeze	6.00	12.00

2016 Mattel WWE Series 67

NNO Cesaro	6.00	12.00
NNO Cesaro/Slammy		
NNO Goldust	10.00	20.00
NNO Goldust/Slammy	12.50	25.00
NNO JBL	7.50	15.00
NNO JBL/Slammy		
NNO John Cena	7.50	15.00
NNO John Cena/Slammy	12.50	25.00
NNO Luke Harper	7.50	15.00
NNO Luke Harper/Slammy	7.50	15.00
NNO Naomi	10.00	20.00
NNO Naomi/Slammy	7.50	15.00
NNO Randy Orton	7.50	15.00
NNO Randy Orton/Slammy	12.50	25.00
NNO Xavier Woods	7.50	15.00
NNO Xavier Woods/Slammy		

2016 Mattel WWE Series 68A

NNO Bo Dallas	7.50	15.00
NNO Bo Dallas/Slammy	7.50	15.00
NNO Dana Brooke	12.50	25.00
NNO Dana Brooke/Slammy	7.50	15.00
NNO DDP FB	10.00	20.00
NNO Diamond Dallas Page/Slammy	7.50	15.00
NNO Finn Balor	7.50	15.00
NNO Finn Balor/Slammy	7.50	15.00
NNO Kalisto	15.00	30.00
NNO Kalisto/Slammy	12.50	25.00
NNO Neville	6.00	12.00
NNO Neville/Slammy	6.00	12.00

2016 Mattel WWE Series 68B

NNO AJ Styles	6.00	12.00
NNO AJ Styles/Slammy	6.00	12.00
NNO Alexa Bliss FP	20.00	40.00
NNO Alexa Bliss FP/Slammy	12.50	25.00
NNO Chris Jericho	7.50	15.00
NNO Chris Jericho/Slammy	7.50	15.00
NNO The Rock	10.00	20.00
NNO The Rock/Slammy	15.00	30.00
NNO Seth Rollins	7.50	15.00
NNO Seth Rollins/Slammy	7.50	15.00
NNO Sting FB	7.50	15.00
NNO Sting FB/Slammy		

2016 Mattel WWE Series 69

NNO Bray Wyatt	7.50	15.00
NNO Bray Wyatt/Slammy	10.00	20.00
NNO John Cena	6.00	12.00
NNO John Cena/Slammy	7.50	15.00
NNO Sami Zayn	6.00	12.00
NNO Sami Zayn/Slammy	6.00	12.00
NNO Sgt. Slaughter FB	6.00	12.00
NNO Sgt. Slaughter FB/Slammy	10.00	20.00
NNO Tamina	7.50	15.00
NNO Tamina/Slammy	7.50	15.00
NNO Triple H	7.50	15.00
NNO Triple H/Slammy	7.50	15.00

2017 Mattel WWE Series 70

NNO Apollo Crews	7.50	15.00
NNO Brie Bella	10.00	20.00
NNO Carmella FP	12.50	25.00
NNO Ric Flair	7.50	15.00

NNO	The Rock FB	12.50	25.00
NNO	Roman Reigns	10.00	20.00
NNO	Samoa Joe	12.50	25.00
NNO	Ultimate Warrior	15.00	30.00

2017 Mattel WWE Series 71

NNO	Austin Aries FP	6.00	12.00
NNO	Baron Corbin	6.00	12.00
NNO	Charlotte Flair	10.00	20.00
NNO	Finn Balor	12.50	25.00
NNO	John Cena	7.50	15.00
NNO	Seth Rollins	7.50	15.00
NNO	Undertaker	20.00	40.00

2017 Mattel WWE Series 72

NNO	Dean Ambrose	10.00	20.00
NNO	Dolph Ziggler	7.50	15.00
NNO	Nia Jax FP	7.50	15.00
NNO	Sheamus	10.00	20.00
NNO	Shinsuke Nakamura	7.50	15.00
NNO	Zack Ryder	10.00	20.00

2017 Mattel WWE Series 73

NNO	AJ Styles	10.00	20.00
NNO	Big E	10.00	20.00
NNO	Cesaro	7.50	15.00
NNO	Kevin Owens	10.00	20.00
NNO	Seth Rollins	7.50	15.00
NNO	Triple H	6.00	12.00

2017 Mattel WWE Series 74

NNO	Bayley	10.00	20.00
NNO	John Cena	7.50	15.00
NNO	Kane	20.00	40.00
NNO	Neville	7.50	15.00
NNO	Roman Reigns	7.50	15.00
NNO	Samoa Joe	10.00	20.00

2017 Mattel WWE Series 75

NNO	Braun Strowman	12.50	25.00
NNO	Brock Lesnar	10.00	20.00
NNO	Chris Jericho	6.00	12.00
NNO	Finn Balor	6.00	12.00
NNO	Lana	7.50	15.00
NNO	Randy Orton	15.00	30.00

2017 Mattel WWE Series 76

NNO	AJ Styles	6.00	12.00
NNO	Dolph Ziggler	7.50	15.00
NNO	John Cena	7.50	15.00
NNO	Macho King Randy Savage FB	10.00	20.00
NNO	The Rock FB	12.50	25.00
NNO	Sami Zayn	6.00	12.00

2017 Mattel WWE Series 77

NNO	Corey Graves	6.00	12.00
NNO	Dean Ambrose	6.00	12.00
NNO	Finn Balor	10.00	20.00
NNO	Roman Reigns	10.00	20.00
NNO	Seth Rollins	12.50	25.00

2017 Mattel WWE Series 78

NNO	AJ Styles	10.00	20.00
NNO	AJ Styles/Case	7.50	15.00
NNO	Braun Strowman	20.00	40.00
NNO	Braun Strowman/Case		
NNO	Kevin Owens	7.50	15.00

NNO	Kevin Owens/Case		
NNO	Natalya	10.00	20.00
NNO	Natalya/Case	7.50	15.00
NNO	The Rock FB	12.50	25.00
NNO	The Rock FB/Case	12.50	25.00
NNO	Shane McMahon	10.00	20.00
NNO	Shane McMahon/Case	10.00	20.00

2017 Mattel WWE Series 79

NNO	Baron Corbin	7.50	15.00
NNO	Baron Corbin/Case	7.50	15.00
NNO	Neville	7.50	15.00
NNO	Neville/Case		
NNO	Nia Jax	7.50	15.00
NNO	Nia Jax/Case	7.50	15.00
NNO	Samoa Joe	7.50	15.00
NNO	Samoa Joe/Case	10.00	20.00
NNO	Stone Cold Steve Austin	10.00	20.00
NNO	Steve Austin/Case	15.00	30.00
NNO	TJ Perkins	10.00	20.00
NNO	TJ Perkins/Case		

2017 Mattel WWE Series 80

NNO	Brock Lesnar	7.50	15.00
NNO	Chris Jericho	7.50	15.00
NNO	Chris Jericho/Case	7.50	15.00
NNO	Rich Swann	6.00	12.00
NNO	Rich Swann/Case	6.00	12.00
NNO	Roman Reigns	7.50	15.00
NNO	Roman Reigns/Case	10.00	20.00
NNO	Sasha Banks	10.00	20.00
NNO	Sasha Banks/Case	12.50	25.00

2017 Mattel WWE Series 81

NNO	Dana Brooke	7.50	15.00
NNO	Dana Brooke/Case	7.50	15.00
NNO	Kofi Kingston	7.50	15.00
NNO	Kofi Kingston/Case	7.50	15.00
NNO	Rhyno	10.00	20.00
NNO	Rhyno/Case	10.00	20.00
NNO	Sami Zayn	7.50	15.00
NNO	Sami Zayn/Case	7.50	15.00
NNO	Seth Rollins	7.50	15.00
NNO	Seth Rollins/Case	7.50	15.00

2017 Mattel WWE Series 82

NNO	AJ Styles	10.00	20.00
NNO	AJ Styles/Case	10.00	20.00
NNO	Becky Lynch	15.00	30.00
NNO	Becky Lynch/Case	10.00	20.00
NNO	John Cena	6.00	12.00
NNO	John Cena/Case	6.00	12.00
NNO	Luke Harper	7.50	15.00
NNO	Luke Harper/Case	7.50	15.00
NNO	Shinsuke Nakamura	7.50	15.00
NNO	Shinsuke Nakaura/Case		

2017 Mattel WWE Series 83

NNO	Alicia Fox	7.50	15.00
NNO	Alicia Fox/Case	7.50	15.00
NNO	Kurt Angle	7.50	15.00
NNO	Kurt Angle/Case	7.50	15.00
NNO	Randy Orton	12.50	25.00
NNO	Randy Orton/Case	10.00	20.00
NNO	Triple H	7.50	15.00
NNO	Triple H/Case	7.50	15.00
NNO	Tye Dillinger	6.00	12.00
NNO	Tye Dillinger/Case	7.50	15.00

2017 Mattel WWE Series 84

NNO	Dean Ambrose	7.50	15.00
NNO	Dean Ambrose/Case	7.50	15.00
NNO	Finn Balor	7.50	15.00
NNO	Finn Balor/Case	10.00	20.00
NNO	Kevin Owens	10.00	20.00
NNO	Kevin Owens/Case		
NNO	Naomi	7.50	15.00
NNO	Naomi/Case		
NNO	Rusev	7.50	15.00
NNO	Rusev/Case		

2017 Mattel WWE Series 85

NNO	AJ Styles	10.00	20.00
NNO	AJ Styles/Case	10.00	20.00
NNO	Alexa Bliss	10.00	30.00
NNO	Alexa Bliss/Case		
NNO	Bobby Roode	12.50	25.00
NNO	Bobby Roode/Case		
NNO	John Cena	7.50	15.00
NNO	John Cena/Case	7.50	15.00
NNO	Seth Rollins	10.00	20.00
NNO	Seth Rollins/Case	10.00	20.00

2018 Mattel WWE Series 86

NNO	Akira Tozawa	6.00	12.00
NNO	Charlotte Flair	7.50	15.00
NNO	Dolph Ziggler	12.50	25.00
NNO	The Rock	15.00	30.00
NNO	Roman Reigns	12.50	25.00

2018 Mattel WWE Series 87

NNO	AJ Styles	10.00	20.00
NNO	Bayley	7.50	15.00
NNO	Dean Ambrose	10.00	20.00
NNO	Jason Jordan	6.00	12.00
NNO	The Miz	7.50	15.00

2018 Mattel WWE Series 88

NNO	Baron Corbin	7.50	15.00
NNO	Chad Gable	6.00	12.00
NNO	Elias	7.50	15.00
NNO	John Cena	7.50	15.00
NNO	Sasha Banks	10.00	20.00

2018 Mattel WWE Series 89

NNO	Carmella	10.00	20.00
NNO	Cesaro	6.00	12.00
NNO	Kalisto	12.50	25.00
NNO	Kurt Angle	7.50	15.00
NNO	Sheamus	10.00	20.00

2018 Mattel WWE Series 90

NNO	Aiden English	6.00	12.00
NNO	Kane	12.50	25.00
NNO	The Miz	7.50	15.00
NNO	Roman Reigns	7.50	15.00
NNO	Roman Reigns/Shield Shirt	10.00	20.00
NNO	Ronda Rousey	15.00	30.00

2018 Mattel WWE Series 91

NNO	Alexa Bliss	10.00	20.00
NNO	Dean Ambrose	7.50	15.00
NNO	Dean Ambrose/Shield Shirt		
NNO	Drew Gulak	10.00	20.00
NNO	Finn Balor	7.50	15.00
NNO	Shinsuke Nakamura	7.50	15.00

2018 Mattel WWE Series 92

NNO	Jeff Hardy	10.00	20.00
NNO	John Cena	7.50	15.00
NNO	Mandy Rose	15.00	30.00
NNO	Samoa Joe	12.50	25.00
NNO	Seth Rollins	6.00	12.00
NNO	Seth Rollins/Shield Shirt		

2019 Mattel WWE Series 93

NNO	Bayley	7.50	15.00
NNO	Jinder Mahal	6.00	12.00
NNO	Macho Man Randy Savage	7.50	15.00
NNO	Macho Man/White Lightning CH	12.50	25.00
NNO	Triple H	6.00	12.00
NNO	Undertaker	7.50	15.00

2019 Mattel WWE Series 94

NNO	Big E	6.00	12.00
NNO	Kofi Kingston	10.00	20.00
NNO	Matt Hardy	6.00	12.00
NNO	Matt Hardy Mower of Lawn CH	12.50	25.00
NNO	Randy Orton		
NNO	Xavier Woods	6.00	12.00

2019 Mattel WWE Series 95

NNO	AJ Styles		
NNO	Bray Wyatt	7.50	15.00
NNO	Kurt Angle	7.50	15.00
NNO	Rusev	6.00	12.00
NNO	Sonya Deville	6.00	12.00
NNO	Sonya Deville Black Attire CH	10.00	20.00

2019 Mattel WWE Series 96

NNO	Bobby Roode		
NNO	Daniel Bryan	7.50	15.00
NNO	Kevin Owens	6.00	12.00
NNO	Sami Zayn	6.00	12.00
NNO	Sami Zayn Arabic CH		
NNO	Sasha Banks	10.00	20.00

2019 Mattel WWE Series 97

NNO	AJ Styles	7.50	15.00
NNO	Bret Hitman Hart	7.50	15.00
NNO	Jeff Hardy	7.50	15.00
NNO	Miz White Trunks	6.00	12.00
NNO	Miz Black Trunks CH	10.00	20.00
NNO	Razor Ramon	7.50	15.00

2019 Mattel WWE Series 98

NNO	Finn Balor	10.00	20.00
NNO	Elias	6.00	12.00
NNO	Ruby Riott	10.00	20.00
NNO	Tony Nese White Tights FP	7.50	15.00
NNO	Tony Nese Gray Tights FP CH	12.50	25.00
NNO	Ultimate Warrior	7.50	15.00

2019 Mattel WWE Series 99

NNO	Ariya Daivari White Tights CH	6.00	12.00
NNO	Ariya Daivari Black Tights CH	7.50	15.00
NNO	Becky Lynch	10.00	20.00
NNO	Drew McIntyre	10.00	20.00
NNO	Rey Mysterio	7.50	15.00
NNO	Shinsuke Nakamura	10.00	20.00

2019 Mattel WWE Series 100

NNO	John Cena	10.00	20.00
NNO	The Rock	10.00	20.00

NNO	Stone Cold Steve Austin	12.50	25.00
NNO	Shawn Michaels	10.00	20.00
NNO	Shawn Michaels Red & White CH	20.00	40.00
NNO	Undertaker	12.50	25.00

2019 Mattel WWE Series 101

NNO	AJ Styles		
NNO	Bobby Lashley		
NNO	Ali		
NNO	Ali Green Tights CH		
NNO	Ronda Rousey		
NNO	Sarah Logan		

2019 Mattel WWE Series 102

NNO	Constable Baron Corbin		
NNO	Drake Maverick		
NNO	Drake Maverick (black gear) (CHASE)		
NNO	Jeff Hardy		
NNO	The Miz		
NNO	Seth Rollins		

2019 Mattel WWE Series 103

NNO	AJ Styles		
NNO	Becky Lynch		
NNO	Becky Lynch Orange Shirt CH		
NNO	Brock Lesnar		
NNO	Kofi Kingston		
NNO	Matt Riddle		

2019 Mattel WWE Series 104

NNO	Alexa Bliss		
NNO	Daniel Bryan		
NNO	Keith Lee		
NNO	Keith Lee Black Tights CH		
NNO	Randy Orton		
NNO	Rey Mysterio		

2019 Mattel WWE Series 105

NNO	John Cena		
NNO	Lars Sullivan		
NNO	Paige GM		
NNO	Roman Reigns		
NNO	Ronda Rousey		
NNO	Ronda Rousey (CHASE)		

2020 Mattel WWE Series 106

NNO	Carmella	15.00	30.00
NNO	Carmella Orange/Purple CH	15.00	30.00
NNO	Finn Balor	7.50	15.00
NNO	Johnny Gargano	10.00	20.00
NNO	R-Truth	10.00	20.00
NNO	Triple H	7.50	15.00

2020 Mattel WWE Series 107

NNO	Bianca Belair	10.00	20.00
NNO	Braun Strowman	12.50	25.00
NNO	EC3	12.50	25.00
NNO	The Rock	15.00	30.00
NNO	Shinsuke Nakamura Black Gear	7.50	15.00
NNO	Shinsuke Nakamura Blue Gear CH	12.50	25.00

2020 Mattel WWE Series 108

NNO	AJ Styles Red/Gray	15.00	30.00
NNO	AJ Styles White/Gold CH	25.00	50.00
NNO	Aleister Black	12.50	25.00

NNO	Angelo Dawkins		
NNO	Montez Ford	7.50	15.00
NNO	Roman Reigns	15.00	30.00

2020 Mattel WWE Series 109

NNO	Becky Lynch	10.00	20.00
NNO	Lana Blue Gear CH	12.50	25.00
NNO	Lana Red Gear	7.50	15.00
NNO	Ricochet	10.00	20.00
NNO	Seth Rollins	7.50	15.00
NNO	Undertaker	12.50	25.00

2020 Mattel WWE Series 110

NNO	Finn Balor	7.50	15.00
NNO	John Cena	10.00	20.00
NNO	Kofi Kingston	7.50	15.00
NNO	Liv Morgan	15.00	30.00
NNO	Mike Kanellis Barbed Wire Tights	7.50	15.00
NNO	Mike Kanellis Name on Tights CH	12.50	25.00

2020 Mattel WWE Series 111

NNO	Bray Wyatt	12.50	25.00
NNO	Erick Rowan	7.50	15.00
NNO	Jeff Hardy	10.00	20.00
NNO	Kevin Owens	12.50	25.00
NNO	Nikki Cross	10.00	20.00
NNO	Nikki Cross Gray Pants CH	12.50	25.00

2020 Mattel WWE Series 112

NNO	Adam Cole	10.00	20.00
NNO	Bobby Lashley	10.00	20.00
NNO	Bobby Lashley Red CH	12.50	25.00
NNO	Braun Strowman	12.50	25.00
NNO	Sasha Banks	20.00	40.00
NNO	Seth Rollins	10.00	20.00

2020 Mattel WWE Series 113

NNO	Buddy Murphy	15.00	30.00
NNO	Drew McIntyre	15.00	30.00
NNO	Edge	12.50	25.00
NNO	Edge Silver Boots CH	15.00	30.00
NNO	John Cena	12.50	25.00
NNO	Mia Yim	15.00	30.00

2020 Mattel WWE Series 114

NNO	The Fiend Bray Wyatt	20.00	40.00
NNO	Kofi Kingston	7.50	15.00
NNO	Rhea Ripley	15.00	30.00
NNO	Ricochet	10.00	20.00
NNO	Ricochet (yellow gear) (CHASE)	12.50	25.00
NNO	Shorty G	7.50	15.00

2021 Mattel WWE Series 115

NNO	Becky Lynch	12.50	25.00
NNO	Big E	6.00	12.00
NNO	Braun Strowman	10.00	20.00
NNO	Humberto Carrillo	7.50	15.00
NNO	Humberto Carrillo Blue/White CH	12.50	25.00
NNO	Tegan Nox	10.00	20.00

2021 Mattel WWE Series 116

NNO	Dakota Kai	15.00	30.00
NNO	Kevin Owens	12.50	25.00
NNO	Roderick Strong	10.00	20.00
NNO	Roderick Strong Black Gear CH	12.50	25.00
NNO	Seth Rollins	12.50	25.00
NNO	Sheamus	7.50	15.00

2021 Mattel WWE Series 117

NNO	Otis	10.00	20.00
NNO	Roman Reigns	10.00	20.00
NNO	Toni Storm	20.00	40.00
NNO	Toni Storm Red Gear CH	25.00	50.00
NNO	Tucker		
NNO	Undertaker	15.00	30.00

2021 Mattel WWE Series 118

NNO	Austin Theory	7.50	15.00
NNO	Austin Theory Red Tights CH	10.00	20.00
NNO	Erik	10.00	20.00
NNO	Finn Balor	7.50	15.00
NNO	Ivar	7.50	15.00
NNO	Jeff Hardy	7.50	15.00

2021 Mattel WWE Series 119

NNO	Dominik Dijakovic	7.50	15.00
NNO	John Cena	12.50	25.00
NNO	Lacey Evans Red CH	12.50	25.00
NNO	Lacey Evans Yellow	6.00	12.00
NNO	Randy Orton	12.50	25.00
NNO	Triple H	7.50	15.00

2021 Mattel WWE Series 120

NNO	Edge	10.00	20.00
NNO	Karrion Kross	10.00	20.00
NNO	Pete Dunne	12.50	25.00
NNO	Scarlett (trunks and top)) (CHASE)	15.00	30.00
NNO	Scarlett (body suit)	12.50	25.00
NNO	Shawn Michaels	7.50	15.00

2021 Mattel WWE Series 121

NNO	Apollo Crews (black trunks) (CHASE)	12.50	25.00
NNO	Apollo Crews (gray trunks)	7.50	15.00
NNO	Bayley	6.00	12.00
NNO	Kane	12.50	25.00
NNO	Rey Mysterio	10.00	20.00
NNO	Roman Reigns	7.50	15.00

2021 Mattel WWE Series 122

NNO	Charlotte Flair	10.00	20.00
NNO	Drew McIntyre	7.50	15.00
NNO	Chelsea Green (black gear) (CHASE)	15.00	30.00
NNO	Chelsea Green (purple gear)	12.50	25.00
NNO	Damian Priest	7.50	15.00

2021 Mattel WWE Series 123

NNO	Bobby Lashley	12.50	25.00
NNO	Braun Strowman	7.50	15.00
NNO	Dexter Lumis	10.00	20.00
NNO	Jake Atlas	7.50	15.00
NNO	Jake Atlas (white gear) (CHASE)	12.50	25.00
NNO	Otis	6.00	12.00

2021 Mattel WWE Series 124

NNO	Angel Garza	7.50	15.00
NNO	Angel Garza (green gear) (CHASE)	12.50	25.00
NNO	Io Shirai	10.00	20.00
NNO	Kyle O'Reilly	10.00	20.00
NNO	Rey Mysterio	10.00	20.00
NNO	Seth Rollins	7.50	15.00

2021 Mattel WWE Series 125

NNO	Elias	6.00	12.00
NNO	Ember Moon	12.50	25.00
NNO	Isaiah Swerve Scott	10.00	20.00
NNO	Isaiah Swerve Scott (red shorts) (CHASE)	15.00	30.00
NNO	Jeff Hardy	12.50	25.00
NNO	The Rock	12.50	25.00

2021 Mattel WWE Series 126

NNO	Bobby Fish	15.00	30.00
NNO	Drew McIntyre		
NNO	Macho Man Randy Savage	12.50	25.00
NNO	Mandy Rose	15.00	30.00
NNO	Mandy Rose (pink gear) (CHASE)	20.00	40.00
NNO	Seth Rollins	10.00	20.00

2021 Mattel WWE Series 127

NNO	Joaquin Wilde	10.00	20.00
NNO	Joaquin Wilde (no face paint) (CHASE)	15.00	30.00
NNO	Keith Lee	12.50	25.00
NNO	Rey Mysterio		
NNO	Santos Escobar	7.50	15.00
NNO	Shayna Baszler	12.50	25.00

2021 Mattel WWE Series 128

NNO	Big E
NNO	Edge
NNO	MVP
NNO	Raul Mendoza
NNO	Raul Mendoza (w/face paint) (CHASE)
NNO	Sasha Banks

2022 Mattel WWE Series 129

NNO	Carmella
NNO	Dominik Mysterio
NNO	The Miz
NNO	Noam Dar
NNO	Roman Reigns

2022 Mattel WWE Series 130

NNO	AJ Styles
NNO	Gran Metalik
NNO	John Cena
NNO	Johnny Gargano (black & red gear) (CHASE)
NNO	Johnny Gargano (The Way)
NNO	Omos

2020 Mattel WWE Showdown 2-Packs Series 1

NNO	Roman Reigns vs. Finn Balor	15.00	30.00
NNO	Sasha Banks vs. Alexa Bliss	25.00	50.00
NNO	Undertaker vs. Jeff Hardy	20.00	40.00

2020 Mattel WWE Showdown 2-Packs Series 2

NNO	Bobby Lashley vs. King Booker	20.00	40.00
NNO	Randy Orton vs. John Cena	25.00	50.00
NNO	The Rock vs. Triple H	20.00	40.00

2020 Mattel WWE Showdown 2-Packs Series 3

NNO	The Fiend Bray Wyatt vs. Daniel Bryan
NNO	The Giant vs. Ric Flair
NNO	Kane vs. Edge

2021 Mattel WWE Showdown 2-Packs Series 4

NNO	Drew McIntyre vs. Seth Rollins	15.00	30.00
NNO	John Morrison vs. Kofi Kingston	15.00	30.00
NNO	Riddle vs. AJ Styles	20.00	40.00

2021 Mattel WWE Showdown 2-Packs Series 5

NNO	Mankind vs. Stone Cold Steve Austin	15.00	30.00
NNO	British Bulldog vs. Big Boss Man	17.50	35.00
NNO	Chyna vs. Trish Stratus	15.00	30.00

2021 Mattel WWE Showdown 2-Packs Series 6

NNO	Angelo Dawkins & Montez Ford	20.00	40.00
NNO	Shawn Michaels & John Cena	17.50	35.00
NNO	The Usos	30.00	75.00

2021 Mattel WWE Showdown 2-Packs Series 7

NNO	Cesaro vs. Roman Reigns	20.00	40.00
NNO	Kane vs. "Stone Cold" Steve Austin	15.00	30.00
NNO	Rhea Ripley vs. Charlotte Flair	12.50	25.00

2021 Mattel WWE Showdown 2-Packs Series 8

NNO	Bret "Hit Man" Hart vs. Undertaker	25.00	50.00
NNO	Goldberg vs. Drew McIntyre		
NNO	Street Profits		

2022 Mattel WWE Showdown 2-Packs Series 9

NNO	Bayley vs. Sasha Banks
NNO	The Rock vs. John Cena
NNO	Sheamus vs. Ricochet

2010 Mattel WWE Signature Series

NNO	Chris Jericho		
NNO	Dave Batista	12.50	25.00
NNO	John Cena	10.00	20.00
NNO	Shawn Michaels		

2011 Mattel WWE Signature Series

NNO	Edge		
NNO	Edge/Black		
NNO	John Cena	7.50	15.00
NNO	Randy Orton	10.00	20.00
NNO	Rey Mysterio	7.50	15.00
NNO	Triple H		
NNO	Undertaker		

2012 Mattel WWE Signature Series

NNO	Big Show
NNO	CM Punk
NNO	John Cena/Dk Shorts
NNO	John Cena/ Green Wristbands
NNO	John Cena/Lt Shorts
NNO	Kane
NNO	Randy Orton
NNO	Rey Mysterio/Gray
NNO	Rey Mysterio Red and White
NNO	Rey Mysterio/Red
NNO	Sheamus
NNO	Sin Cara
NNO	The Miz
NNO	The Rock

2015 Mattel WWE Signature Series

NNO	Bray Wyatt	7.50	15.00
NNO	Daniel Bryan	15.00	30.00
NNO	Dave Batista	7.50	15.00

NNO Dean Ambrose	7.50	15.00
NNO Hulk Hogan	15.00	30.00
NNO John Cena	7.50	15.00

2013 Mattel WWE Slam City Series 1

NNO Alberto Del Rio		
NNO Big Show	15.00	30.00
NNO Brock Lesnar		
NNO John Cena	7.50	15.00
NNO Kane	20.00	40.00
NNO Rey Mysterio	15.00	30.00

2018 Mattel WWE Sound Slammers Playset

NNO Destruction Zone	50.00	100.00

2018 Mattel WWE Sound Slammers Series 1

NNO Dean Ambrose	12.50	25.00
NNO John Cena	20.00	40.00
NNO Kevin Owens	12.50	25.00
NNO Roman Reigns	12.50	25.00
NNO Seth Rollins	12.50	25.00

2018 Mattel WWE Sound Slammers Series 2

NNO AJ Styles	10.00	20.00
NNO Bobby Roode	10.00	20.00
NNO Finn Balor	20.00	40.00
NNO Kurt Angle	10.00	20.00
NNO The Miz	10.00	20.00

2018 Mattel WWE SummerSlam Heritage

NNO John Cena	6.00	12.00
NNO Kurt Angle	6.00	12.00
NNO Ric Flair	7.50	15.00
NNO Roman Reigns	7.50	15.00
NNO Shane McMahon	7.50	15.00
NNO Shinsuke Nakamura	12.50	25.00

2014 Mattel WWE SummerSlam Heritage

NNO CM Punk	15.00	30.00
NNO Million Dollar Man Ted DiBiase	12.50	25.00
NNO Rey Mysterio		
NNO Shawn Michaels	12.50	25.00
NNO Triple H	10.00	20.00
NNO Undertaker	12.50	25.00

2016 Mattel WWE SummerSlam Heritage

NNO British Bulldog FB	6.00	12.00
NNO Dave Batista FB	6.00	12.00
NNO Jim Duggan FB	7.50	15.00
NNO Undertaker FB	12.50	25.00

2017 Mattel WWE SummerSlam Heritage

NNO Dusty Rhodes FB	7.50	15.00
NNO Nikki Bella	12.50	25.00
NNO The Rock FB	10.00	20.00
NNO Seth Rollins	7.50	15.00

2013 Mattel WWE Super Strikers

NNO Alberto Del Rio		
NNO Big Show	7.50	15.00
NNO Brock Lesnar		
NNO CM Punk	10.00	20.00
NNO Daniel Bryan	12.50	25.00
NNO Dolph Ziggler		
NNO John Cena		
NNO Kofi Kingston	7.50	15.00
NNO The Miz		

NNO Randy Orton	10.00	20.00
NNO The Rock		
NNO Roman Reigns	15.00	30.00
NNO Ryback		
NNO Sheamus	10.00	20.00
NNO Undertaker	12.50	25.00

2012 Mattel WWE Superstar Entrances Series 1

NNO CM Punk	20.00	40.00
NNO Dolph Ziggler		
NNO John Cena	12.50	25.00
NNO The Miz	7.50	15.00
NNO R-Truth	7.50	15.00
NNO Randy Orton	12.50	25.00
NNO Triple H	10.00	20.00

2013 Mattel WWE Superstar Entrances Series 2

NNO Daniel Bryan	15.00	30.00
NNO John Cena	10.00	20.00
NNO Ryback		
NNO Santino Marella		
NNO The Rock	10.00	20.00
NNO Zack Ryder		

2014 Mattel WWE Superstar Entrances Series 3

NNO Brock Lesnar	10.00	20.00
NNO CM Punk	20.00	40.00
NNO Cody Rhodes	15.00	30.00
NNO John Cena	10.00	20.00
NNO Macho Man Randy Savage	15.00	30.00
NNO Sheamus	10.00	20.00
NNO The Rock	10.00	20.00

2014 Mattel WWE Superstar Entrances Series 4

NNO AJ Lee	30.00	60.00
NNO Daniel Bryan	15.00	30.00
NNO Dolph Ziggler		
NNO John Cena	10.00	20.00
NNO Rob Van Dam	15.00	30.00
NNO The Rock	7.50	15.00

2015 Mattel WWE Superstar Entrances Series 5

NNO Daniel Bryan	15.00	30.00
NNO John Cena	10.00	20.00
NNO Randy Orton	10.00	20.00
NNO Rowdy Roddy Piper	15.00	30.00
NNO Triple H	7.50	15.00

2015 Mattel WWE Superstar Entrances Series 6

NNO Bo Dallas	7.50	15.00
NNO Hulk Hogan	20.00	40.00
NNO John Cena	10.00	20.00
NNO Kofi Kingston	7.50	15.00
NNO Wade Barrett	6.00	12.00

2011 Mattel WWE Superstar Matchups Series 4

NNO Rey Mysterio/		
Blue and White		
NNO Rey Mysterio/Black and Blue		
NNO Sin Cara		

2017 Mattel WWE Superstars Dolls 12-Inch

NNO Alicia Fox		
NNO Asuka		
NNO Bayley		
NNO Becky Lynch	15.00	30.00
NNO Carmella		

NNO Charlotte Flair	12.50	25.00
NNO Eva Marie	10.00	20.00
NNO Lana		
NNO Natalya		

2017 Mattel WWE Superstars Dolls 12-Inch Fashions

NNO Alexa Bliss		
NNO Bayley		
NNO Becky Lynch		
NNO Brie Bella	12.50	25.00
NNO Natalya	12.50	25.00
NNO Nikki Bella	15.00	30.00
NNO Sasha Banks	12.50	25.00

2017 Mattel WWE Superstars Dolls 12-Inch Multi-Packs

NNO Charlotte Flair/Sasha Banks SDCC		
NNO Natalya/Becky Lynch/Sasha Banks/Bellas		

2017 Mattel WWE Superstars Dolls Action Figures Playset

NNO Ultimate Entrance Playset (w/Nikki Bella)		

2017 Mattel WWE Superstars Dolls Action Figures Series 1

NNO Brie Bella		
NNO Charlotte Flair		
NNO Nikki Bella		

2017 Mattel WWE Superstars Dolls Action Figures Series 2

NNO Alexa Bliss		
NNO Brie Bella		
NNO Natalya		
NNO Nikki Bella		

2017 Mattel WWE Superstars Dolls Action Figures Ultimate Fan Packs

NNO Bayley		
NNO Charlotte Flair		
NNO Sasha Banks		

2017 Mattel WWE Surf's Up 2 WaveMania Action Figure DVD Combo

NNO Batista		
NNO Big Show		
NNO Bray Wyatt		
NNO Daniel Bryan		
NNO Dean Ambrose (black shirt)		
NNO Dean Ambrose (white shirt)		
NNO Dolph Ziggler		
NNO El Torito		
NNO Goldust		
NNO John Cena (black shorts)		
NNO John Cena (blue shorts)		
NNO John Cena (green shorts)		
NNO John Cena (tan shorts/blue armband)		
NNO John Cena (tan shorts/red armband)		
NNO Justin Gabriel		
NNO Kane		
NNO Mankind		
NNO Miz		
NNO Randy Orton		
NNO Rey Mysterio		
NNO Ric Flair		
NNO Ricky "The Dragon" Steamboat		

NNO Roman Reigns
NNO Rusev
NNO Ryback
NNO Santino Marella
NNO Seth Rollins
NNO Titus O'Neill
NNO Triple H

2013 Mattel WWE Survivor Series 2013

NNO CM Punk
NNO Ryback

2019 Mattel WWE Tag Team Buddies Plush Dolls 14"

NNO Bayley
NNO Becky Lynch
NNO Sasha Banks

2016 Mattel WWE Teenage Mutant Ninja Turtles Ninja Superstars Series 1

NNO Donatello as Undertaker	15.00	30.00
NNO Leonardo as John Cena	10.00	20.00
NNO Michelangelo as Macho Man Randy Savage	12.50	25.00
NNO Raphael as Sting	12.50	25.00

2017 Mattel WWE Teenage Mutant Ninja Turtles Ninja Superstars Series 2

NNO Donatello as Ultimate Warrior	12.50	25.00
NNO Leonardo as Finn Balor	10.00	20.00
NNO Michelangelo as Rowdy Roddy Piper	7.50	15.00
NNO Raphael as The Rock	15.00	30.00

2016 Mattel WWE Then Now Forever Series 1

NNO Chris Jericho	6.00	12.00
NNO Seth Rollins	10.00	20.00
NNO Sin Cara	40.00	80.00
NNO Undertaker	15.00	30.00

2017 Mattel WWE Then Now Forever Series 2

NNO Neville	6.00	12.00
NNO Sheamus	10.00	20.00
NNO Stone Cold Steve Austin FB	10.00	20.00
NNO Ultimate Warrior FB	12.50	25.00

2017 Mattel WWE Then Now Forever Series 3

NNO Bray Wyatt	7.50	15.00
NNO Kevin Owens	6.00	12.00
NNO Seth Rollins	10.00	20.00
NNO Triple H	12.50	25.00
NNO X-Pac	12.50	25.00

2013 Mattel WWE TLC 2013

NNO Alberto Del Rio
NNO Kofi Kingston
NNO Mark Henry
NNO Sheamus

2020 Mattel WWE Top Picks 2020

NNO John Cena	15.00	30.00
NNO Kofi Kingston	15.00	30.00
NNO The Rock	20.00	40.00
NNO Roman Reigns	12.50	25.00

2021 Mattel WWE Top Picks 2021

NNO Braun Strowman
NNO John Cena
NNO The Rock
NNO Roman Reigns

2021 Mattel WWE Top Picks 2022

NNO Drew McIntyre
NNO The Fiend Bray Wyatt
NNO John Cena
NNO The Rock

2021 Mattel WWE Top Picks 2023

NNO Bray Wyatt
NNO Roman Reigns
NNO Undertaker

2018 Mattel WWE Top Talent 2018

NNO AJ Styles	15.00	20.00
NNO John Cena	7.50	15.00
NNO Roman Reigns	7.50	15.00
NNO Seth Rollins	6.00	12.00

2019 Mattel WWE Top Talent 2019

NNO AJ Styles		
NNO Jeff Hardy	7.50	15.00
NNO John Cena	12.50	25.00
NNO Seth Rollins	7.50	15.00

2020 Mattel WWE Top Talent 2020

NNO AJ Styles		
NNO Braun Strowman	15.00	30.00
NNO Finn Balor		
NNO John Cena	12.50	25.00

2021 Mattel WWE Top Talent 2022

NNO John Cena
NNO The Rock
NNO Roman Reigns

2017 Mattel WWE Tough Talkers Series 1

NNO Bray Wyatt	15.00	30.00
NNO Dean Ambrose	12.50	25.00
NNO John Cena	15.00	30.00
NNO Kevin Owens	10.00	20.00
NNO Roman Reigns	12.50	25.00
NNO Seth Rollins	12.50	25.00

2017 Mattel WWE Tough Talkers Series 2

NNO Big E	7.50	15.00
NNO Brock Lesnar	12.50	25.00
NNO Dean Ambrose	12.50	25.00
NNO John Cena	20.00	40.00
NNO Kofi Kingston	10.00	20.00
NNO Xavier Woods	10.00	20.00

2017 Mattel WWE Tough Talkers 2-Packs Series 1

NNO The Rock/Stone Cold Steve Austin	25.00	50.00
NNO Undertaker/Brock Lesnar	25.00	50.00

2017 Mattel WWE Tough Talkers 2-Packs Series 2

NNO AJ Styles/Seth Rollins	20.00	40.00
NNO Triple H/Roman Reigns	17.50	35.00

2017 Mattel WWE Tough Talkers Hall of Fame Series

NNO Macho Man Randy Savage	12.50	25.00
NNO Ric Flair	12.50	25.00
NNO Rowdy Roddy Piper	12.50	25.00

2017 Mattel WWE Tough Talkers Total Tag Team

NNO AJ Styles	15.00	30.00
NNO Randy Orton	12.50	25.00

NNO Sting	12.50	25.00
NNO Xavier Woods	10.00	20.00

2017 Mattel WWE Tough Talkers Total Tag Team 2-Packs

NNO Big E/Kofi Kingston	17.50	35.00
NNO Kevin Owens & Chris Jericho	15.00	30.00

2012 Mattel WWE Tribute to the Troops

NNO Big Show/Brown Hat		
NNO Big Show/Green Hat		
NNO John Cena	12.50	25.00
NNO Randy Orton/Brown Vest	10.00	20.00
NNO Randy Orton/Green Vest	10.00	20.00
NNO Rey Mysterio	20.00	40.00

2010 Mattel WWE Triple Threat 3-Packs

NNO Evan Bourne/Swagger/Kozlov
NNO John Cena/Batista/Y2J
NNO Kane/John Cena/Big Show
NNO Kane/Triple H/Great Khali
NNO Sheamus/John Cena/Triple H

2018 Mattel WWE True Moves 12-Inch

NNO AJ Styles	12.50	25.00
NNO Kane	10.00	20.00
NNO Randy Orton	10.00	20.00
NNO Kevin Owens	12.50	25.00
NNO Kurt Angle	10.00	20.00
NNO Kalisto	15.00	30.00
NNO Seth Rollins	12.50	25.00

2019 Mattel WWE Ultimate Edition Series 1

NNO Ultimate Warrior	20.00	40.00
NNO Ronda Rousey	25.00	50.00

2019 Mattel WWE Ultimate Edition Series 2

NNO Bret "Hitman" Hart	25.00	50.00
NNO Shinsuke Nakamura	20.00	40.00

2019 Mattel WWE Ultimate Edition Series 3

NNO Finn Balor
NNO Triple H

2020 Mattel WWE Ultimate Edition Series 4

NNO Brock Lesnar	30.00	60.00
NNO Shawn Michaels	60.00	120.00

2020 Mattel WWE Ultimate Edition Series 5

NNO Becky Lynch	30.00	60.00
NNO John Cena	40.00	80.00

2020 Mattel WWE Ultimate Edition Series 6

NNO Charlotte Flair	30.00	60.00
NNO The Rock	60.00	120.00
(Amazon Exclusive)		

2020 Mattel WWE Ultimate Edition Series 7

NNO The Fiend Bray Wyatt	30.00	75.00
NNO Hollywood Hulk Hogan	50.00	100.00

2021 Mattel WWE Ultimate Edition Series 8

NNO Edge	25.00	50.00
NNO Macho Man Randy Savage	25.00	50.00

2021 Mattel WWE Ultimate Edition Series 9

NNO	Stone Cold Steve Austin	30.00	60.00
NNO	Ric Flair	30.00	75.00

2021 Mattel WWE Ultimate Edition Series 10

NNO	John Cena	20.00	40.00
NNO	The Rock	25.00	50.00

2021 Mattel WWE Ultimate Edition Series 11

NNO	Kane	30.00	60.00
NNO	Undertaker	30.00	60.00

2022 Mattel WWE Ultimate Edition Series 12

NNO	Alexa Bliss
NNO	The Fiend Bray Wyatt

2017 Mattel WWE Undertaker 5-Pack

NNO	1990/1994/1998/2014/2016	30.00	75.00

2019 Mattel WWE Wrekkin' Playsets

NNO	Entrance Stage Playset	40.00	80.00
NNO	Performance Center Playset	30.00	75.00
NNO	Slam Mobile (w/Braun Strowman)	20.00	40.00

2019 Mattel WWE Wrekkin' Series 1

NNO	AJ Styles	10.00	20.00
NNO	John Cena	12.50	25.00
NNO	Seth Rollins	10.00	20.00
NNO	Undertaker	15.00	30.00

2019 Mattel WWE Wrekkin' Series 2

NNO	Miz
NNO	Woken Matt Hardy

2019 Mattel WWE Wrekkin' Series 3

NNO	Daniel Bryan
NNO	Rey Mysterio

2020 Mattel WWE Wrekkin' Playsets

NNO	Collision Cage	60.00	120.00
NNO	Slambulance	50.00	100.00
NNO	Slamcycle (w/Drew McIntyre)	30.00	60.00
NNO	Slamcycle (w/Undertaker)	30.00	60.00

2020 Mattel WWE Wrekkin' Series 4

NNO	Elias	20.00	40.00
NNO	Roman Reigns	25.00	50.00

2010 Mattel WWE WrestleMania 26

NNO	Chris Jericho		
NNO	Christian	15.00	30.00
NNO	Drew McIntyre	12.50	25.00
NNO	Kane		
NNO	Matt Hardy		
NNO	Shawn Michaels		
NNO	Shelton Benjamin		

2011 Mattel WWE WrestleMania 27

NNO	Alberto Del Rio	6.00	12.00
NNO	Christian	20.00	40.00
NNO	John Cena	12.50	25.00
NNO	John Morrison	10.00	20.00
NNO	Randy Orton	10.00	20.00
NNO	Triple H	12.50	25.00

2021 Mattel WWE WrestleMania 37 Celebration

NNO	Andre the Giant	20.00	40.00
NNO	Macho Man Randy Savage	20.00	40.00

2014 Mattel WWE WrestleMania 30 Heritage

NNO	Brock Lesnar		
NNO	John Cena	12.50	25.00
NNO	The Rock	12.50	25.00
NNO	Undertaker	10.00	20.00

2015 Mattel WWE WrestleMania 31 Heritage

NNO	Hulk Hogan	15.00	30.00
NNO	John Cena		
NNO	The Rock	12.50	25.00
NNO	Shawn Michaels	10.00	20.00

2016 Mattel WWE WrestleMania 32 Heritage

NNO	Cesaro	6.00	12.00
NNO	Eddie Guerrero	10.00	20.00
NNO	Razor Ramon	17.50	35.00
NNO	Roman Reigns	7.50	15.00

2017 Mattel WWE WrestleMania 33 Heritage

NNO	Chris Jericho	12.50	25.00
NNO	Roman Reigns	15.00	30.00
NNO	Stone Cold Steve Austin	10.00	20.00
NNO	Undertaker	15.00	30.00

2018 Mattel WWE WrestleMania 34 Heritage

NNO	AJ Styles	7.50	15.00
NNO	Bayley	7.50	15.00
NNO	Big Show	20.00	40.00
NNO	Dean Ambrose	7.50	15.00
NNO	Mojo Rawley	6.00	12.00
NNO	Seth Rollins	7.50	15.00

2018 Mattel WWE WrestleMania 35 Heritage

NNO	Charlotte Flair	12.50	25.00
NNO	Elias	7.50	15.00
NNO	John Cena		
NNO	Kevin Nash	10.00	20.00
NNO	Matt Hardy	7.50	15.00
NNO	Trish Stratus	12.50	25.00

2020 Mattel WWE WrestleMania 36 Heritage

NNO	Batista	20.00	40.00
NNO	Becky Lynch	12.50	25.00
NNO	The Rock	15.00	30.00
NNO	Seth Rollins	10.00	20.00
NNO	Shane McMahon	15.00	30.00
NNO	Stephanie McMahon	12.50	25.00

2021 Mattel WWE WrestleMania 37 Heritage

NNO	Andrade	6.00	12.00
NNO	Drew McIntyre	12.50	25.00
NNO	The Fiend Bray Wyatt	12.50	25.00
NNO	Ricochet	6.00	12.00

2021 Mattel WWE WrestleMania 38 Heritage

NNO	Bianca Belair
NNO	Hulk Hogan
NNO	Seth Rollins
NNO	Sheamus

2016 Mattel WWE Zombies Series 1

NNO	Bray Wyatt	7.50	15.00
NNO	Dean Ambrose	15.00	30.00
NNO	John Cena	15.00	30.00
NNO	Paige	7.50	15.00
NNO	The Rock	12.50	25.00
NNO	Roman Reigns	12.50	25.00

(continued)

NNO	Triple H	7.50	15.00
NNO	Undertaker	12.50	25.00

2017 Mattel WWE Zombies Series 2

NNO	Stone Cold Steve Austin	12.50	25.00
NNO	AJ Styles	7.50	15.00
NNO	Brock Lesnar	7.50	15.00
NNO	Kevin Owens	6.00	12.00
NNO	Sasha Banks	12.50	25.00
NNO	Seth Rollins	7.50	15.00

2018 Mattel WWE Zombies Series 3

NNO	Charlotte Flair	10.00	20.00
NNO	Finn Balor	12.50	25.00
NNO	Jeff Hardy	10.00	20.00
NNO	Kane	20.00	40.00
NNO	Matt Hardy	10.00	20.00
NNO	Shinsuke Nakamura	10.00	20.00

1990 Multi Toys WWF Power Grip Squirts

NNO	Big Boss Man
NNO	Hulk Hogan
NNO	Jake The Snake Roberts
NNO	Macho King Randy Savage
NNO	Million Dollar Man Ted Dibiase
NNO	Ultimate Warrior

1990 Multi Toys WWF Power Grip Squirts Tag Teams

NNO	Bushwhackers
NNO	Legion of Doom
NNO	The Rockers

1990 Multi Toys WWF Squirt Heads

NNO	Big Boss Man
NNO	Hulk Hogan
NNO	Jake The Snake Roberts
NNO	Macho King Randy Savage
NNO	Million Dollar Man Ted Dibiase
NNO	Ultimate Warrior

2017 Ooshies WWE Series 1

NNO	Asuka R
NNO	Booker T R
NNO	Booker T Black Trunks R
NNO	Bray Wyatt C
NNO	Brie Bella R
NNO	Brock Lesnar C
NNO	Cesaro C
NNO	Charlotte Flair R
NNO	Dean Ambrose C
NNO	Dolph Ziggler C
NNO	Finn Balor R
NNO	Finn Balor (hologram) LE
NNO	Jey Uso R
NNO	Jimmy Uso R
NNO	John Cena C
NNO	John Cena Never Give Up R
NNO	Junkyard Dog R
NNO	Kalisto R
NNO	Kalisto (golden) LE
NNO	Kane R
NNO	Kevin Owens C
NNO	Kofi Kingston R
NNO	Kofi Kingston Green Tights R
NNO	Macho Man Randy Savage C
NNO	Macho Man Randy Savage (glow-in-the-dark) R

NNO	The Miz C	
NNO	Nikki Bella R	
NNO	Randy Orton C	
NNO	Randy Orton (glow-in-the-dark) R	
NNO	The Rock C	
NNO	The Rock (glow-in-the-dark) R	
NNO	Roman Reigns C	
NNO	Seth Rollins C	
NNO	Sheamus C	
NNO	Sting R	
NNO	Sting Wolfpack LE	
NNO	Stone Cold Steve Austin C	
NNO	Ultimate Warrior C	
NNO	Ultimate Warrior (glow-in-the-dark) R	
NNO	Undertaker R	

1991 Original San Francisco Toymakers CMLL Luchadores

NNO	Atlantis	25.00	50.00
NNO	Lizmark	30.00	75.00
NNO	Pierroth		
NNO	Rayo de Jalisco		
NNO	Ultimo Dragon	50.00	100.00
NNO	Vampiro Canadiense	60.00	120.00

1999-00 Original San Francisco Toymakers ECW Wrestling Accessories

NNO	Hardcore Grapple Gear
NNO	Wrestling Ring Gift Set (w/Rob Van Dam & Sabu)
(Toys R Us Exclusive)	

1999-00 Original San Francisco Toymakers ECW Wrestling Series 1

NNO	Chris Candido	25.00	50.00
NNO	Justin Credible	15.00	30.00
NNO	Rob Van Dam	30.00	60.00
NNO	Sabu	20.00	40.00
NNO	Shane Douglas	15.00	30.00
NNO	Taz	25.00	50.00

1999-00 Original San Francisco Toymakers ECW Wrestling Series 2

NNO	Buh Buh Ray Dudley	20.00	40.00
NNO	D-Von Dudley	20.00	40.00
NNO	Lance Storm	15.00	30.00
NNO	New Jack	30.00	75.00
NNO	Tommy Dreamer	15.00	30.00

1999-00 Original San Francisco Toymakers ECW Wrestling Series 3

NNO	Justin Credible
NNO	New Jack
NNO	Taz

1999-00 Original San Francisco Toymakers ECW Wrestling Series 4

NNO	Axl Rotten	20.00	40.00
NNO	Balls Mahoney	20.00	40.00
NNO	Jerry Lynn	30.00	75.00
NNO	Raven	25.00	50.00
NNO	Rhino	30.00	60.00
NNO	Rob Van Dam	30.00	60.00
NNO	Taz	20.00	40.00
NNO	Yoshihiro Tajiri	30.00	60.00

1999-00 Original San Francisco Toymakers ECW Wrestling Series 5

NNO	Justin Credible	15.00	30.00
NNO	Little Guido		
NNO	Mike Awesome	60.00	120.00
NNO	Nova	25.00	50.00
NNO	Sabu	30.00	60.00
NNO	Sandman	30.00	75.00
NNO	Steve Corino		
NNO	Super Crazy		

1999-00 Original San Francisco Toymakers ECW Wrestling Series 6

NNO	Balls Mahoney	25.00	50.00
NNO	Chris Candido	30.00	60.00
NNO	Lance Storm	20.00	40.00
NNO	New Jack	30.00	75.00
NNO	Raven	30.00	75.00
NNO	Rhino	50.00	100.00
NNO	Rob Van Dam	30.00	60.00
NNO	Tommy Dreamer	20.00	40.00

1998 Original San Francisco Toymakers WCW

NNO	Bret Hart	10.00	20.00
NNO	Chris Benoit	12.50	25.00
NNO	Diamond Dallas Page	20.00	40.00
NNO	Goldberg	15.00	30.00
NNO	Raven	7.50	15.00
NNO	Rey Mysterio	12.50	25.00
NNO	Ric Flair	10.00	20.00
NNO	Sting	10.00	20.00

1998 Original San Francisco Toymakers WCW 12-Inch

NNO	Bill Goldberg	20.00	40.00
NNO	Hollywood Hulk Hogan	15.00	30.00
NNO	Macho Man Randy Savage	20.00	40.00
NNO	Sting/Black & White	15.00	30.00
NNO	Sting/Red & Black	12.50	25.00

1998 Original San Francisco Toymakers WCW 4.5-Inch

NNO	Goldberg	7.50	15.00
NNO	Ric Flair	7.50	15.00
NNO	Rick Steiner	6.00	12.00
NNO	Sting	7.50	15.00

1997-98 Original San Francisco Toymakers WCW Boxed Sets

NNO	Clash of the Champions	25.00	50.00
	Lex Luger/Scott Hall		
NNO	Fall Brawl	10.00	20.00
	Sting/Giant		
NNO	Fearsome Foursome	20.00	40.00
	Goldberg/Flair/DDP/Chris Benoit		
NNO	Halloween Havoc	20.00	40.00
	Giant/Savage		
NNO	Live on Forever	30.00	75.00
	Hogan/Bagwell/Giant/Scott Steiner		
NNO	No Retreat No Surrender	25.00	50.00
	Nash/Sting/Savage/Luger		
NNO	Starrcade	20.00	40.00
	Hogan/Sting		
NNO	We Are the Champions	25.00	50.00
	Goldberg/Giant/Hall/Hart		
NNO	World War 3	12.50	25.00
	Page/Nash		

1997 Original San Francisco Toymakers WCW Fly Buddies

NNO	Giant	10.00	20.00
NNO	Hollywood Hulk Hogan	15.00	30.00
NNO	Sting	10.00	20.00

1998 Original San Francisco Toymakers WCW nWo 4.5-Inch

NNO	Giant	5.00	10.00
NNO	Hollywood Hogan	6.00	12.00
NNO	Kevin Nash	5.00	10.00
NNO	Lex Luger	3.00	8.00
NNO	Macho Man Randy Savage	5.00	10.00
NNO	Scott Hall	5.00	10.00
NNO	Scott Steiner	3.00	8.00

1998 Original San Francisco Toymakers WCW nWo Series

NNO	Curt Henning UER	6.00	12.00
NNO	The Giant	6.00	12.00
NNO	Hollywood Hogan	7.50	15.00
NNO	Kevin Nash	6.00	12.00
NNO	Lex Luger	5.00	10.00
NNO	Macho Man Randy Savage	7.50	15.00
NNO	Marcus Bagwell	3.00	8.00
NNO	Scott Hall	6.00	12.00
NNO	Scott Steiner	5.00	10.00
NNO	Sting	6.00	12.00

1995 Original San Francisco Toymakers WCW Playsets

NNO	Wrestling Ring & Cage	25.00	50.00

1998 Original San Francisco Toymakers WCW Playsets

NNO	Battle Royal Wrestling Ring & Cage		
	Hogan/Nash/Savage/Sting/Rick Steiner/Luger		
NNO	Thunder Wrestling Ring & Cage	30.00	60.00
	Nash/Giant/Luger/Sting		
NNO	Wrestling Ring & Cage w/Action Sounds	20.00	40.00
NNO	Wrestling Ring & Cage w/Giant/Luger	30.00	75.00
NNO	Wrestling Ring & Cage w/Sting KMART		
NNO	Wrestling Ring & Cage	20.00	40.00
	Hogan/Rick Steiner/Savage/Sting		

1995 Original San Francisco Toymakers WCW Series 1

1	Brian Knobbs	12.50	25.00
2	Hulk Hogan	30.00	75.00
3	Jerry Sags	10.00	20.00
4	Jimmy Hart ERR/Dk. Skin	150.00	300.00
5	Jimmy Hart/Lt. Skin	12.50	25.00
6	Johnny B. Badd	20.00	40.00
7	Kevin Sullivan	12.50	25.00
8	Ric Flair/Blue Tights	15.00	30.00
9	Ric Flair/Purple Tights	15.00	30.00
10	Sting	25.00	50.00
11	Vader	20.00	40.00

1995 Original San Francisco Toymakers WCW Series 1 (loose)

NNO	Brian Knobbs
NNO	Hulk Hogan
NNO	Jerry Sags
NNO	Jimmy Hart
NNO	Johnny B. Badd
NNO	Kevin Sullivan

NNO Ric Flair/Blue Tights
NNO Ric Flair/Purple Tights
NNO Sting
NNO Vader

1996 Original San Francisco Toymakers WCW Series 2

NNO Hulk Hogan	20.00	40.00
NNO Jimmy Hart	12.50	25.00
NNO Johnny B. Badd	15.00	30.00
NNO Kevin Sullivan	10.00	20.00
NNO Macho Man Randy Savage	50.00	100.00
NNO Ric Flair/Green Tights	15.00	30.00
NNO Ric Flair/Purple Tights	15.00	30.00
NNO Sting	20.00	40.00
NNO Vader	25.00	50.00

1996 Original San Francisco Toymakers WCW Series 3

NNO Alex Wright	12.50	25.00
NNO Big Bubba Rogers	10.00	20.00
NNO Booker T	7.50	15.00
NNO Craig Pittman	7.50	15.00
NNO Giant	12.50	25.00
NNO Hulk Hogan	15.00	30.00
NNO Macho Man Randy Savage	15.00	30.00
NNO Ric Flair	12.50	25.00
NNO Stevie Ray	10.00	20.00
NNO Sting	15.00	30.00

1998 Original San Francisco Toymakers WCW Special Edition

NNO Sting/Diamond Dallas Page		
NNO Diamond Dallas Page		
NNO nWo Wolfpack Sting		
NNO Sting/nWo Wolfpack Sting		
NNO Sting	15.00	30.00

1995 Original San Francisco Toymakers WCW Tag Teams Series 1

NNO Harlem Heat	25.00	50.00
NNO Hulk Hogan/Sting	60.00	120.00
NNO Nasty Boys/Black	15.00	30.00
NNO Nasty Boys/Green	75.00	150.00

1995 Original San Francisco Toymakers WCW Tag Teams Series 1 (loose)

NNO Booker T
NNO Brian Knobbs/Black
NNO Brian Knobbs/Green
NNO Hulk Hogan
NNO Jerry Sags/Black
NNO Jerry Sags/Green
NNO Stevie Ray
NNO Sting

1996 Original San Francisco Toymakers WCW Tag Teams Series 2

NNO Harlem Heat	30.00	60.00
NNO Hulk Hogan/Sting	75.00	150.00
NNO Nasty Boys	25.00	50.00

1996 Original San Francisco Toymakers WCW Tag Teams Series 3

NNO Blue Bloods	25.00	50.00
NNO Harlem Heat	20.00	40.00
NNO Hollywood Hogan/Macho Man	20.00	40.00

1997 Original San Francisco Toymakers WCW Vibrating Action Figures

NNO Chris Benoit	7.50	15.00
NNO Giant	7.50	15.00
NNO Hollywood Hulk Hogan	12.50	25.00
NNO Lex Luger	6.00	12.00
NNO Scott Hall	7.50	15.00
NNO Sting	10.00	20.00
NNO Taskmaster Kevin Sullivan	6.00	12.00

1999 Planet Toys WWF Head Crushers

NNO Mankind
NNO The Rock
NNO Stone Cold Steve Austin

2010 Playmates Lucha Libre Masked Warriors

NNO Charly Malice
NNO Lizmark Jr.
NNO Marco Corleone
NNO Super Nova
NNO Sydistiko
NNO Tinieblas Jr.

2010 Playmates Lucha Libre Masked Warriors Accessories

NNO Hexalateral Wrestling Ring

2010 Playmates Lucha Libre Masked Warriors Combo Packs

NNO Super Nova
NNO Tinieblas Jr.

2010 Playmates Lucha Libre Masked Warriors Masks

NNO Super Nova
NNO Tinieblas Jr.

2016 Playmates WWE Nitro Machines

NNO Dean Ambrose	3.00	8.00
NNO John Cena	6.00	12.00
NNO The Rock	7.50	15.00
NNO Undertaker	7.50	15.00

2016 Playmates WWE Nitro Machines (loose)

NNO Brock Lesnar	7.50	15.00
NNO John Cena	7.50	15.00
NNO The Rock	10.00	20.00
NNO Undertaker	7.50	15.00

2021 Pro Wrestling Tees Micro Brawlers AEW Wave 1

NNO Brodie Lee	20.00	40.00
NNO Chris Jericho	25.00	50.00
NNO Darby Allin	20.00	40.00
NNO Dr. Britt Baker, DMD	30.00	60.00
NNO Hikaru Shida	25.00	50.00
NNO Jon Moxley	25.00	50.00
NNO Orange Cassidy	30.00	75.00

2021-22 Pro Wrestling Tees Micro Brawlers AEW Crate Exclusive

NNO Sting	30.00	75.00
NNO Nyla Rose	15.00	30.00

2021-22 Pro Wrestling Tees Micro Brawlers AEW Limited Edition

NNO Christian Cage	25.00	50.00

NNO Sting (retro blue and orange)
NNO Sting (retro black and green chase)

2017 Pro Wrestling Tees Micro Brawlers Crate Exclusives

NNO Big Van Vader	20.00	40.00
NNO CM Punk	30.00	75.00
NNO Colt Cabana	15.00	30.00
NNO Joey Ryan	12.50	25.00
NNO Kenny Omega	20.00	40.00
NNO Matt Jackson		
NNO Nick Jackson		
NNO Penta El Zero M	30.00	60.00
NNO Taz	75.00	150.00
NNO :Villain" Marty Scurll	15.00	30.00

2018 Pro Wrestling Tees Micro Brawlers Crate Exclusives

NNO American Nightmare Cody	15.00	30.00
NNO Andre the Giant	25.00	50.00
NNO Bad Boy Tama Tonga	12.50	25.00
NNO Candice LeRae	10.00	20.00
NNO Eddie Guerrero	20.00	40.00
NNO Hangman Adam Page	25.00	50.00
NNO Kazuchika Okada	20.00	40.00
NNO Papa Shango	15.00	30.00
NNO Road Warrior Animal	30.00	60.00
NNO Road Warrior Hawk	25.00	50.00
NNO Tetsuya Naito	20.00	40.00
NNO ZSJ Zack Sabre Jr.	10.00	20.00

2019 Pro Wrestling Tees Micro Brawlers Crate Exclusives

NNO Bruiser Brody	20.00	40.00
NNO Brutus "The Barber" Beefcake	10.00	20.00
NNO Demolition Ax	15.00	30.00
NNO Demolition Smash	20.00	40.00
NNO Jeff Cobb	7.50	15.00
NNO Jim Ross	12.50	25.00
NNO Kota Ibushi	12.50	25.00
NNO Macho Man Randy Savage	30.00	60.00
NNO MJF	12.50	25.00
NNO Raven	20.00	40.00
NNO Rey Fenix	15.00	30.00
NNO Warrior	25.00	50.00

2020 Pro Wrestling Tees Micro Brawlers Crate Exclusives

NNO The Boogeyman	10.00	20.00
NNO Bret "The Hitman" Hart	20.00	40.00
NNO Brian Meyers		
NNO Chris Hero	7.50	15.00
NNO El Generico	12.50	25.00
NNO Hacksaw Jim Duggan	10.00	20.00
NNO Honky Tonk Man	10.00	20.00
NNO Kamala	10.00	20.00
NNO Koko B. Ware	15.00	30.00
NNO Matt Cardona	15.00	30.00
NNO Tatanka	7.50	15.00
NNO Tommy Dreamer	15.00	30.00

2021 Pro Wrestling Tees Micro Brawlers Crate Exclusives

NNO Jake "The Snake" Roberts (blue and yellow tights)	15.00	30.00
NNO Jake "The Snake" Roberts (black and yellow tights chase)		

NNO Owen Hart (blue tights)	12.50	25.00
NNO Owen Hart (red tights chase)		
NNO Kevin Nash (Super Shredder) (black tights)	15.00	30.00
NNO Kevin Nash (Super Shredder) (purple tights chase)	15.00	30.00
NNO Tanga Loa (camo tights)	15.00	30.00
NNO Tanga Loa (black camo tights chase)	30.00	75.00
NNO Iron Sheik (red and black boots)		
NNO Iron Sheik (yellow boots chase)		
NNO Bully Ray (black and white attire)	15.00	30.00
NNO Bully Ray (black and red attire chase)	25.00	50.00
NNO Flyin' Brian Pillman (tiger print tights)	10.00	20.00
NNO Flyin' Brian Pillman (blue tights chase)	30.00	60.00
NNO Lex Luger (red white and blue tights)	12.50	25.00
NNO Lex Luger (red white and blue tights chase)	30.00	75.00
NNO Adam Bomb (red and yellow tights)	12.50	25.00
NNO Adam Bomb (orange and yellow tights chase)	50.00	100.00
NNO Shane Helms (brown hair)	15.00	30.00
NNO Shane Helms (green hair chase)	50.00	100.00
NNO Virgil	10.00	20.00
NNO Virgil (chase)	30.00	60.00
NNO Glacier (blue and white)	15.00	30.00
NNO Glacier (light blue and white chase)	30.00	75.00

2020-21 Pro Wrestling Tees Micro Brawlers Limited Edition

NNO Big Van Vader		
NNO Brian Knobs/350*	20.00	40.00
NNO Dragon Lee (Online Exclusive)	20.00	40.00
NNO Dynamite Kid	25.00	50.00
NNO Francine/300*	50.00	100.00
NNO Frank the Clown/300*	20.00	40.00
NNO Iron Sheik/150*	75.00	150.00
NNO Jerry Sags/350*	20.00	40.00
NNO Jonathan Gresham	15.00	30.00
NNO Josh Mathews		
NNO Kevin Nash/350*	30.00	75.00
NNO Kurt Angle/150*	100.00	200.00
NNO Loose Cannon Brian Pillman (Online Exclusive)	20.00	40.00
NNO Luna Vachon	25.00	50.00
NNO Macho Man (black & white) (Online Exclusive)	20.00	40.00
NNO Macho Man (classic orange) (Online Exclusive)	15.00	30.00
NNO Macho Man (classic pink) (Online Exclusive)	12.50	25.00

NNO Macho Man (lime green) (Online Exclusive)	10.00	20.00
NNO Macho Man (Mega Powers) (Online Exclusive)	20.00	40.00
NNO Macho Man (USA Edition) (Online Exclusive)	25.00	50.00
NNO New Jack (Online Exclusive)	20.00	40.00
NNO Owen Hart (Japanese Tour) (Online Exclusive)	20.00	40.00
NNO Owen Hart/150*	100.00	200.00
NNO Psychosis (Online Exclusive)	20.00	40.00
NNO Rob Van Dam (green tights) (Online Exclusive chase)	125.00	250.00
NNO Rob Van Dam (Online Exclusive)	30.00	60.00
NNO Sabu (Online Exclusive)	20.00	40.00
NNO Sandman (Online Exclusive)	20.00	40.00
NNO Sommarhausen (Online Exclusive)	30.00	60.00
NNO Terry Funk		

2022 Pro Wrestling Tees Micro Brawlers Limited Edition

NNO Andre the Giant		
NNO British Bulldog		

2021 Pro Wrestling Tees Micro Brawlers MLW Exclusives

NNO Alexander Hammerstone	30.00	60.00
NNO LA Park	60.00	120.00
NNO Richard Holliday	30.00	60.00

2020-21 Pro Wrestling Tees Micro Brawlers ROH Exclusives

NNO Angelina Love	20.00	40.00
NNO Danhausen	30.00	75.00
NNO Jonathan Gresham		
NNO Session Moth Martina	10.00	20.00
NNO Shane Taylor	15.00	30.00

2021 Pro Wrestling Tees Micro Brawlers Staff Edition Exclusives

NNO Barracuda Mailbox Bomber/150*	75.00	150.00
NNO Marvelous Matt Knicks/150*	20.00	40.00

2022 Pro Wrestling Tees Micro Brawlers Talk 'N Shop-a-Mania

NNO Sex Ferguson		
NNO Chico El Luchador		
NNO Chad 2 Badd		

2018 Pro Wrestling Tees Micro Brawlers Wave 1

NNO British Bulldog		
NNO Brooklyn Brawler		
NNO Burnard the Business Bear	30.00	60.00
NNO Cheesburger		
NNO Chris Hero	7.50	15.00
NNO Cody	12.50	25.00
NNO Dalton Castle		
NNO Jay Lethal		
NNO Jay White	20.00	40.00
NNO Kenny Omega	25.00	50.00
NNO Ricky The Dragon Steamboat		

NNO Rosemary		
NNO Rowdy Roddy Piper	300.00	500.00
NNO Sami Callihan		
NNO Swoggle		
NNO Tenille Dashwood		
NNO Vickie Guerrero	15.00	30.00
NNO Villain Marty Scurll	17.50	35.00

2018 Pro Wrestling Tees Micro Brawlers Wave 1 Limited Edition Tag Team 2-Packs

NNO The Briscoes		
NNO The Young Bucks		

2019 Pro Wrestling Tees Micro Brawlers Wave 2

NNO Badd Ass Billy Gunn		
NNO Brandi Rhodes		
NNO Bushi		
NNO Christopher Daniels		
NNO Evil	10.00	20.00
NNO Flip Gordon		
NNO Frankie Kazarian	17.50	35.00
NNO Hiromu Takahashi	20.00	40.00
NNO Joey Ryan	15.00	30.00
NNO Sanada	20.00	40.00
NNO Scorpio Sky		
NNO Tetsuya Naito	15.00	30.00
NNO Xpac		

2019 Pro Wrestling Tees Micro Brawlers Wave 3

NNO Blue Meanie		
NNO Brian Cage		
NNO Colt Cabana	12.50	25.00
NNO Fat Ass Masa	50.00	100.00
NNO Hiroshi Tanahashi/250*	25.00	50.00
NNO Hot Mess Chelsea Green	30.00	60.00
NNO Johnny Gimmick Name	25.00	50.00
NNO King Kong Bundy		
NNO Mandy Leon	30.00	75.00
NNO Villain Marty Scurll		

2019 Pro Wrestling Tees Micro Brawlers Wave 4

NNO Bandido	15.00	30.00
NNO Big Poppa Pump Scott Steiner	30.00	75.00
NNO Bone Soldier Taiji Ishimora		
NNO Flamboyant Juice Robinson	25.00	50.00
NNO Penta El Zero M		
NNO Rush	7.50	15.00
NNO Tomohiro Ishii		

2019 Pro Wrestling Tees Micro Brawlers Wave 4 Limited Edition Multi-Packs

NNO The Kingdom 3-Pack	30.00	75.00
NNO The Road Warriors 2-Pack		

2020 Pro Wrestling Tees Micro Brawlers Wave 5

NNO Crown Jewel Chase Owens		
NNO Dustin Rhodes		
NNO Kazuchika Okada	20.00	40.00
NNO Terry Funk	25.00	50.00
NNO The Enforcer Arn Anderson		
NNO Underboss Bad Luck Fale	20.00	40.00

2020 Pro Wrestling Tees Micro Brawlers Wave 6

NNO Brody King	20.00	40.00
NNO Ian Riccaboni	15.00	30.00
NNO PCO		
NNO Rhino	25.00	50.00

NNO Taya Valkyrie		
NNO Undeniable Tessa B	20.00	40.00

1985 Remco AWA Wrestling Accessories and Playsets

NNO Battle Royal Playset (w/7 figures)	400.00	600.00
NNO Battle Royal Playset 2 (w/7 figures)	500.00	800.00
NNO Championship Belt Figure Holder	200.00	400.00
NNO Regular Ring Playset	125.00	200.00
NNO Steel Cage Match	300.00	600.00

1986 Remco AWA Wrestling Mini-Mashers

NNO Animal
NNO Barbarian
NNO Boris Zhukov
NNO Curt Henning
NNO Hawk
NNO Larry Zbyszko
NNO Marty Jannetty
NNO Nick Bockwinkel
NNO Ric Flair
NNO Scott Hall
NNO Shawn Michaels
NNO Stan Hansen

1986 Remco AWA Wrestling Mini-Mashers Green

NNO Animal
NNO Barbarian
NNO Boris Zhukov
NNO Curt Henning
NNO Hawk
NNO Larry Zbyszko
NNO Marty Jannetty
NNO Nick Bockwinkel
NNO Ric Flair
NNO Scott Hall
NNO Shawn Michaels
NNO Stan Hansen

1986 Remco AWA Wrestling Mini-Mashers Packs

NNO 4-Pack	25.00	50.00
NNO 8-Pack	50.00	100.00
NNO 12-Pack	60.00	120.00

1986 Remco AWA Wrestling Mini-Mashers Purple

NNO Animal
NNO Barbarian
NNO Boris Zhukov
NNO Curt Henning
NNO Hawk
NNO Larry Zbyszko
NNO Marty Jannetty
NNO Nick Bockwinkel
NNO Ric Flair
NNO Scott Hall
NNO Shawn Michaels
NNO Stan Hansen

1986 Remco AWA Wrestling Mini-Mashers Red

NNO Animal
NNO Barbarian
NNO Boris Zhukov
NNO Curt Henning
NNO Hawk
NNO Larry Zbyszko
NNO Marty Jannetty
NNO Nick Bockwinkel
NNO Ric Flair
NNO Scott Hall
NNO Shawn Michaels
NNO Stan Hansen

1985 Remco AWA Wrestling Series 1

NNO Fabulous Ones	100.00	200.00
Steve Keirn/Stan Lane		
NNO High Flyers	100.00	200.00
Greg Gagne/Jim Brunzell		
NNO Ric Flair/Larry Zbyszko	125.00	250.00
NNO Rick Martel/Baron von Raschke w/AWA Ring	125.00	250.00
NNO Rick Martel/Baron von Raschke w/AWA Sticker	75.00	150.00
NNO Road Warriors	200.00	400.00
Animal/Hawk No Belts		
NNO Road Warriors	150.00	300.00
Animal/Hawk w/Belts		

1985 Remco AWA Wrestling Series 1 (loose)

NNO Animal	6.00	12.00
NNO Baron von Raschke	7.50	15.00
NNO Greg Gagne	7.50	15.00
NNO Hawk	6.00	12.00
NNO Jim Brunzell	6.00	12.00
NNO Larry Zbyszko	6.00	12.00
NNO Ric Flair	15.00	30.00
NNO Rick Martel	12.50	25.00
NNO Stan Lane	6.00	15.00
NNO Steve Keirn	6.00	12.00

1985 Remco AWA Wrestling Series 2

NNO Fabulous Freebirds	100.00	200.00
Buddy Roberts/Terry Gordy/Michael Hayes		
NNO Gagne's Raiders	125.00	250.00
Greg Gagne/Curt Henning		
NNO Jimmy Garvin/Precious/Steve Regal	75.00	150.00
NNO Long Riders	100.00	200.00
Wild Bill Irwin/Scott Hog Irwin		
NNO Road Warriors	150.00	300.00
Animal/Hawk/Paul Ellering		

1985 Remco AWA Wrestling Series 2 (loose)

NNO Animal	10.00	20.00
NNO Buddy Roberts	12.50	25.00
NNO Curt Henning	10.00	20.00
NNO Greg Gagne	6.00	12.00
NNO Hawk	10.00	20.00
NNO Jimmy Garvin	10.00	20.00
NNO Michael Hayes	12.50	25.00
NNO Paul Ellering	12.50	25.00
NNO Precious	10.00	20.00
NNO Scott Hog Irwin	7.50	15.00
NNO Steve Regal	6.00	12.00
NNO Terry Gordy	12.50	25.00
NNO Wild Bill Irwin	7.50	15.00

1985 Remco AWA Wrestling Series 2 Fight to the Finish 2-Pack

NNO Steve Regal vs. Curt Hennig (w/VHS Tape)	50.00	100.00

1985 Remco AWA Wrestling Series 3

NNO Nick Bockwinkel vs. Larry Zbyszko	150.00	300.00
NNO Scott Hall vs. Gorgeous Jimmy Garvin	150.00	300.00
NNO Stan Hansen vs. Jerry Blackwell	100.00	200.00
NNO Carlos Colon vs. Abdullah the Butcher	150.00	300.00

1985 Remco AWA Wrestling Series 3 (loose)

NNO Abdullah the Butcher	20.00	40.00
NNO Carlos Colon	7.50	15.00
NNO Gorgeous Jimmy Garvin	5.00	10.00
NNO Jerry Blackwell	10.00	20.00
NNO Larry Zbyszko	15.00	30.00
NNO Nick Bockwinkel	20.00	40.00
NNO Referee Curley Brown	12.50	25.00
NNO Referee Nasty Ned	15.00	30.00
NNO Scott Hall	30.00	75.00
NNO Stan Hansen	20.00	40.00

1986 Remco AWA Wrestling Series 4

NNO Boris Zhukov	300.00	600.00
NNO Buddy Rose	250.00	500.00
NNO Doug Somers	200.00	400.00
NNO Marty Jannetty	400.00	800.00
NNO Nick Bockwinkel		
NNO Nord the Barbarian	250.00	500.00
NNO Paul Ellering		
NNO Referee Dick Woehrle	200.00	350.00
NNO Ric Flair	500.00	1000.00
NNO Shawn Michaels	750.00	1500.00
NNO Sheik Adnan Al-Kaissie	200.00	400.00

1986 Remco AWA Wrestling Series 4 (loose)

NNO Boris Zhukov	125.00	250.00
NNO Buddy Rose	125.00	250.00
NNO Doug Somers	100.00	200.00
NNO Marty Jannetty	150.00	300.00
NNO Nord the Barbarian	150.00	300.00
NNO Referee Dick Woehrle	60.00	120.00
NNO Shawn Michaels	250.00	400.00
NNO Sheik Adnan Al-Kaissie	250.00	500.00

1985 Remco AWA Wrestling Thumbsters

NNO Greg Gagne vs. Hawk	30.00	75.00
NNO Ric Flair vs. Larry Zbyszko	50.00	100.00
NNO Rick Martel vs. Animal	30.00	75.00

1985 Remco AWA Wrestling Thumbsters (loose)

NNO Animal	7.50	15.00
NNO Greg Gagne	5.00	10.00
NNO Hawk	7.50	15.00
NNO Larry Zbyszko	5.00	10.00
NNO Ric Flair	10.00	20.00
NNO Rick Martel	7.50	15.00

1998 Ringside Supplies WWF Squirt Heads Cellophane Package

NNO The Rock
NNO Stone Cold Steve Austin
NNO Undertaker

1998 Ringside Supplies WWF Squirt Heads Mesh Package

NNO The Rock
NNO Stone Cold Steve Austin
NNO Undertaker

2017 S.H. Figuarts WWE

NNO Kane	30.00	75.00
NNO The Rock	30.00	60.00
NNO Stone Cold Steve Austin	20.00	40.00
NNO Triple H	12.50	25.00
NNO Undertaker	30.00	75.00
NNO Vince McMahon		

1990 Spectra Star WWF Rad Rollers Collection

NNO Hulk Hogan/Jake The Snake Roberts/Macho King Randy Savage
Big Boss Man/Million Dollar Man Ted DiBiase/Ultimate Warrior

1990 Spectra Star WWF Rad Rollers Collection (loose)

NNO Big Boss Man
NNO Hulk Hogan
NNO Jake The Snake Roberts
NNO Macho King Randy Savage
NNO Million Dollar Man Ted DiBiase
NNO Ultimate Warrior

1990 Spectra Star WWF Superstars Radical Flying Discs

NNO Ultimate Warrior (green)
NNO Ultimate Warrior (pink)

1991 Spectra Star WWF Superstars Radical Flying Discs

NNO Hulk Hogan

2019 Super 7 ReAction Wrestling Figures

NNO Andre the Giant (singlet)
NNO Andre the Giant (w/vest)

2021 Super 7 Ultimate Wrestling Figures

NNO Brian Meyers
NNO Doc Gallows
NNO Karl Anderson
NNO Matt Cardona

2017 TeenyMates WWE Collector Sets

NNO WWE Hall of Fame Inductees
NNO WWE Superstars (w/Andre the Giant GITD)

2016 TeenyMates WWE Series 1

NNO Big Show C
NNO Bray Wyatt C
NNO Bret Hart C
NNO Brie Bella C
NNO Brock Lesnar C
NNO Daniel Bryan C
NNO Dean Ambrose C
NNO Dolph Ziggler C
NNO Goldust C
NNO Jey Uso C
NNO Jimmy Uso C
NNO John Cena (crystal clear) R
NNO John Cena C
NNO Kane C
NNO Kofi Kingston C
NNO Macho Man Randy Savage (orange) C
NNO Macho Man Randy Savage (glow-in-the-dark) R
(Collector Tin Exclusive)
NNO Macho Man Randy Savage (purple) R
NNO Nikki Bella C
NNO Randy Orton C
NNO The Rock C
NNO The Rock (metallic gold) UR
NNO Roman Reigns C
NNO Seth Rollins C
NNO Sheamus C
NNO Sin Cara C
NNO Stardust C
NNO Sting C
NNO Stone Cold Steve Austin C

NNO Triple H C
NNO Ultimate Warrior C
NNO Undertaker (glow-in-the-dark) R
NNO Undertaker C

2017 TeenyMates WWE Series 2

NNO AJ Styles C
NNO Andre the Giant C
NNO Andre the Giant (glow-in-the-dark) R
(Collector's Set Exclusive)
NNO Becky Lynch C
NNO Big E C
NNO Bray Wyatt C
NNO Brock Lesnar C
NNO Chris Jericho C
NNO Dean Ambrose C
NNO Finn Balor C
NNO Finn Balor (glow-in-the-dark) R
NNO Jake the Snake Roberts C
NNO John Cena (ice blue) R
NNO John Cena C
NNO Kane C
NNO Kevin Owens C
NNO Kofi Kingston C
NNO Macho Man Randy Savage C
NNO Mankind C
NNO Ric Flair (blue robe) UR
NNO Ric Flair (pink robe) C
NNO The Rock C
NNO Roman Reigns C
NNO Rowdy Roddy Piper C
NNO Sasha Banks C
NNO Seth Rollins C
NNO Sgt. Slaughter R
NNO Shawn Michaels C
NNO Sting C
NNO Triple H C
NNO Ultimate Warrior C
NNO Ultimate Warrior (metallic gold) UR
NNO Xavier Woods C

2019 Tomy WWE Blitz Brawlers

NNO AJ Styles
NNO John Cena

1990 Tonka WWF Wrestling Buddies

NNO Big Boss Man	100.00	200.00
NNO Hulk Hogan	250.00	500.00
NNO Jake "The Snake" Roberts	325.00	650.00
NNO Macho King Randy Savage	150.00	300.00
NNO Million Dollar Man Ted DiBiase	400.00	800.00
NNO Ultimate Warrior	250.00	500.00

1990 Tonka WWF Wrestling Buddies (loose)

NNO Animal (Legion of Doom)
NNO Big Boss Man
NNO Hawk (Legion of Doom)
NNO Hulk Hogan
NNO Jake "The Snake" Roberts
NNO Macho King Randy Savage
NNO Million Dollar Man Ted DiBiase
NNO Ultimate Warrior

1990 Tonka WWF Wrestling Buddies Tag Team

NNO Legion of Doom

2005 Toy Biz Best of TNA Series 1

NNO AJ Styles
NNO Elix Skipper
NNO Jeff Hardy
NNO Ron Killings

2006 Toy Biz Best of TNA Series 2

NNO AJ Styles
NNO Chris Sabin
NNO Jeff Hardy
NNO Monty Brown
NNO Raven
NNO Ron Killings

2005 Toy Biz TNA Wrestling 2-Packs Series 1

NNO BG James/Konnan	15.00	30.00
NNO Elix Skipper/C. Daniels	12.50	25.00
NNO James Storm/Chris Harris	30.00	75.00

2006 Toy Biz TNA Wrestling 2-Packs Series 2

NNO AJ Styles vs. Samoa Joe	20.00	40.00
NNO Jeff Hardy vs. Abyss	50.00	100.00
NNO Jeff Jarrett vs. Monty Brown	20.00	40.00

2006 Toy Biz TNA Wrestling 2-Packs Series 3

NNO BG James/Kip James	20.00	40.00
NNO Raven vs. Sabu	30.00	75.00
NNO Sting vs. Jeff Jarrett	25.00	50.00

2007 Toy Biz TNA Wrestling 2-Packs Series 4

NNO Christian Cage/Rhyno	20.00	40.00
NNO Christopher Daniels	15.00	30.00
Homicide		
NNO Kevin Nash/Chris Sabin	20.00	40.00

2007 TNA Wrestling Bashin' Brawlers Series 1

NNO Samoa Joe	12.50	25.00
NNO Sting	15.00	30.00

2007 TNA Wrestling Bashin' Brawlers Series 2

NNO Christian Cage	10.00	20.00
NNO Kevin Nash	10.00	20.00

2007 Toy Biz TNA Wrestling Collector's Edition 12-Inch Series 1

NNO AJ Styles	30.00	60.00
NNO Sting	30.00	75.00

2007 Toy Biz TNA Wrestling Collector's Edition 12-Inch Series 2

NNO Christopher Daniels	15.00	30.00
NNO Kurt Angle	25.00	50.00

2006 Toy Biz TNA Wrestling Masked Fury

NNO Abyss	20.00	40.00
NNO Shark Boy	20.00	40.00
NNO Sting	25.00	50.00

2005 Toy Biz TNA Wrestling Playsets

NNO 6-Sided Wrestling Ring	75.00	150.00
w/AJ Styles		

2006 Toy Biz TNA Wrestling Playsets

NNO Lockdown Six Sides of Steel
w/Christian Cage
NNO Champion X Ring
w/AJ Styles

NNO Championship Belt
w/AJ Styles & Jeff Jarrett/Blue Package
NNO Championship Belt
w/AJ Styles & Jeff Jarrett/Red Package

2007 Toy Biz TNA Wrestling Playsets

NNO	Ultimate X Ring	50.00	100.00
	w/Christopher Daniels		

2005 Toy Biz TNA Wrestling Series 1

NNO	Abyss	15.00	30.00
NNO	AJ Styles	20.00	40.00
NNO	Jeff Jarrett	12.50	25.00
NNO	Raven	12.50	25.00

2005 Toy Biz TNA Wrestling Series 2

NNO	Christopher Daniels	12.50	25.00
NNO	Jeff Hardy	20.00	40.00
NNO	Ron The Truth Killings	15.00	30.00
NNO	Shark Boy	12.50	25.00

2005 Toy Biz TNA Wrestling Series 3

NNO	AJ Styles	15.00	30.00
NNO	Alpha Male Monty Brown	20.00	40.00
NNO	Chris Sabin	20.00	40.00
NNO	Raven/Straight Jacket	12.50	25.00

2006 Toy Biz TNA Wrestling Series 4

NNO	Kevin Nash		
NNO	Petey Williams	12.50	25.00
NNO	Rhino	20.00	40.00
NNO	Wildcat Chris Harris	7.50	15.00
	Mustache		
NNO	Wildcat Chris Harris		
	No Mustache		

2006 Toy Biz TNA Wrestling Series 5

NNO	James Cowboy Storm	10.00	20.00
NNO	Kip James	10.00	20.00
NNO	Kip James/Black Trunks		
NNO	Lance Hoyt	15.00	30.00
NNO	Lance Hoyt/White Pants		
NNO	Samoa Joe	12.50	25.00
NNO	Samoa Joe		
	Blue and Black Trunks		
NNO	Sting	15.00	30.00

2007 Toy Biz TNA Wrestling Series 6

NNO	Alex Shelley	10.00	20.00
NNO	Alex Shelley		
	Green on Shorts		
NNO	Christian Cage	12.50	25.00
NNO	Jay Lethal	12.50	25.00
NNO	Jay Lethal/Green Gear		
NNO	Sonjay Dutt	7.50	15.00
NNO	Sonjay Dutt/Green Gear		

2007 Toy Biz TNA Wrestling Series 7

NNO	Brother Devon	10.00	20.00
NNO	Matt Bentley	10.00	20.00
NNO	Robert Roode	12.50	25.00
NNO	Robert Roode/Team Canada		
NNO	Scott Steiner	15.00	30.00
NNO	Scott Steiner/Black Pants		

2007 Toy Biz TNA Wrestling Series 8

NNO	Chase Stevens	15.00	30.00
NNO	Chase Stevens		
	Headband and Jacket		
NNO	Eric Young	12.50	25.00
NNO	Eric Young/Team Canada	20.00	40.00
NNO	James Mitchell CH	20.00	40.00
NNO	Kurt Angle	10.00	20.00
NNO	Senshi	20.00	40.00
NNO	Senshi/Black Pants	25.00	50.00

2000 Toy Biz WCW Bash at the Beach

NNO	Bret Hitman Hart		
NNO	Diamond Dallas Page		
NNO	Goldberg	10.00	20.00
NNO	Lex Luger	6.00	12.00
NNO	Sting		

1998 Toy Biz WCW Bashin' Brawlers

NNO	Big Poppa Pump Scott Steiner		
NNO	Diamond Dallas Page	30.00	75.00
NNO	Goldberg	60.00	120.00
NNO	Hollywood Hogan	75.00	150.00
NNO	Kevin Nash		
NNO	Macho Man Randy Savage	50.00	100.00
NNO	Sting	60.00	120.00
NNO	Sting (Wolfpac)		

2000 Toy Biz WCW Battle Arms

NNO	Sting	12.50	25.00
NNO	Goldberg	15.00	30.00
NNO	Bret Hitman Hart	12.50	25.00

1999 Toy Biz WCW Bend 'N Flex

NNO	Booker T	7.50	15.00
NNO	Bret Hart	6.00	12.00
NNO	Diamond Dallas Page	6.00	12.00
NNO	Goldberg	10.00	20.00
NNO	Kevin Nash	12.50	25.00
NNO	Scott Hall	7.50	15.00
NNO	Scott Steiner	6.00	12.00
NNO	Sting	7.50	15.00

1999 Toy Biz WCW Bend 'N Flex 6-Pack

NNO	Sting/Goldberg/DDP	25.00	50.00
	Hall/Steiner/Nash		

1999 Toy Biz WCW Boxed Sets

NNO	Heavyweight Champions	30.00	75.00
	Hogan/Goldberg/Sting		
NNO	IV Horsemen	15.00	30.00
	Flair/Benoit/Malenko/Mongo		
NNO	Red & Black Attack	30.00	60.00
	Hogan/Bischoff/Nash		

1999 Toy Biz WCW Brawlin' Bikers

NNO	DDP		
NNO	Goldberg	7.50	15.00
NNO	Hulk Hogan	20.00	40.00
NNO	Sting	10.00	20.00

2001 Toy Biz WCW Bruisers

NNO	Bam Bam Bigelow	7.50	15.00
NNO	DDP	12.50	25.00
NNO	Disco Inferno	10.00	20.00
NNO	Goldberg	20.00	40.00
NNO	Kevin Nash	10.00	20.00

NNO	Kidman	10.00	20.00
NNO	Randy Macho Man Savage	12.50	25.00
NNO	Raven	7.50	15.00
NNO	Rey Mysterio Jr.	15.00	30.00
NNO	Stevie Ray	10.00	20.00
NNO	Sting	15.00	30.00
NNO	Wrath	7.50	15.00

1999 Toy Biz WCW Collector's Edition 8-Inch Figures

NNO	Hollywood Hogan TAR	
NNO	Kevin Nash TAR	
NNO	Sting KB	

2000 Toy Biz WCW Grip 'N Flip Series 2

NNO	Kevin Nash vs. Konnan	10.00	20.00
NNO	Scott Steiner vs. Rick Steiner	7.50	15.00
NNO	Sting vs. Buff Bagwell	7.50	15.00

2000 Toy Biz WCW Gross-Out Wrestlers

NNO	Goldberg	30.00	75.00
NNO	Sid Vicious	25.00	50.00
NNO	Sting	50.00	100.00

1999 Toy Biz WCW Head Ringers

NNO	Bret Hart	
NNO	Buff Bagwell	
NNO	Diamond Dallas Page	
NNO	Goldberg	
NNO	Hulk Hogan	
NNO	Kevin Nash	
NNO	Konnan	
NNO	Sting	

1999 Toy Biz WCW Head Ringers (loose)

NNO	Bret Hart	
NNO	Buff Bagwell	
NNO	Diamond Dallas Page	
NNO	Goldberg	
NNO	Hulk Hogan	
NNO	Kevin Nash	
NNO	Konnan	
NNO	Sting	

2000 Toy Biz WCW Main Event 2-Packs

NNO	Goldberg/Sid Vicious		
NNO	Hulk Hogan/Ric Flair	40.00	80.00
NNO	Sting/The Total Package	30.00	60.00

2000 Toy Biz WCW Nitro Active Wrestlers

NNO	Buff Bagwell/Black Pants	
NNO	Buff Bagwell/Red Pants	
NNO	Goldberg	
NNO	Jeff Jarrett	
NNO	Kevin Nash	

1999 Toy Biz WCW Playset

NNO	Electronic Monday Nitro Arena	125.00	250.00

2000 Toy Biz WCW Power Slam

NNO	Buff Bagwell	7.50	15.00
NNO	Dennis Rodman/Blue Hair	10.00	20.00
NNO	Dennis Rodman/Green Hair		
NNO	Dennis Rodman/Orange Hair	15.00	30.00
NNO	Goldberg	25.00	50.00
NNO	Hak	15.00	30.00
NNO	Hollywood Hogan	12.50	25.00

NNO	Hulk Hogan	12.50	25.00
NNO	Kanyon	6.00	12.00
NNO	Kevin Nash	10.00	20.00
NNO	Rowdy Roddy Piper	10.00	20.00
NNO	Sid Vicious	7.50	15.00
NNO	Sting	7.50	15.00

1999 Toy Biz WCW Ring Announcers

NNO	Mean Gene	30.00	60.00
	{w/Nash & Goldberg		
NNO	Michael Buffer	15.00	30.00
	{w/Scott Steiner & DDP		

2001 Toy Biz WCW Ring Fighters

NNO	Booker T/Dk Tights	12.50	25.00
NNO	Booker T/White Tights	10.00	20.00
NNO	Bret Hart	7.50	15.00
NNO	Chris Benoit/Red Tights	7.50	15.00
NNO	Chris Benoit/Blue Tights	10.00	20.00
NNO	Goldberg	10.00	20.00
NNO	Scott Steiner/Black Tights		
NNO	Scott Steiner/White Tights	10.00	20.00
NNO	Sting	12.50	25.00

1999 Toy Biz WCW Ring Masters

NNO	Bret Hart	10.00	20.00
NNO	Chris Jericho	10.00	20.00
NNO	Goldberg	15.00	30.00
NNO	Hulk Hogan	12.50	25.00
NNO	Lex Luger	7.50	15.00
NNO	Rick Steiner	10.00	20.00

2000 Toy Biz WCW Road Rebels

NNO	Goldberg		
NNO	Hulk Hogan		
NNO	Sting		

1999 Toy Biz WCW Road Wild Wrestlers

NNO	Goldberg	25.00	50.00
NNO	Hollywood Hogan	30.00	60.00
NNO	Kevin Nash	15.00	30.00
NNO	Sting	20.00	40.00

1999 Toy Biz WCW Rumble 'N Roar

NNO	Goldberg	25.00	50.00
NNO	Sting	30.00	60.00

1999 Toy Biz WCW Slam 'N Crunch

NNO	Buff Bagwell	10.00	20.00
NNO	Goldberg	15.00	30.00
NNO	Kevin Nash	10.00	20.00
NNO	Konnan	15.00	30.00
NNO	Saturn		
NNO	Sting	12.50	25.00

2001 Toy Biz WCW Slam Force

NNO	Bret Hart	20.00	40.00
NNO	Goldberg		
NNO	Hollywood Hogan		
NNO	Kevin Nash	12.50	25.00
NNO	Lex Luger		

1999 Toy Biz WCW Smash 'N Slam

NNO	DDP/No Vest	12.50	25.00
NNO	DDP/Vest	6.00	12.00
NNO	Giant w/Luchadore	10.00	20.00
NNO	Goldberg KB		

NNO	Goldberg w/Blue	10.00	20.00
	{Masked Lucha		
NNO	Goldberg w/Red	15.00	30.00
	Masked Lucha		
NNO	Hollywood Hogan/	10.00	20.00
	No Tank Top		
NNO	Hollywood Hogan/	12.50	25.00
	Tank Top		
NNO	Kevin Nash w/Referee/	7.50	15.00
	No Red Pants		
NNO	Kevin Nash w/Referee/	7.50	15.00
	Red Pants		
NNO	Lex Luger/No Shirt	6.00	12.00
NNO	Lex Luger/Shirt	12.50	25.00
NNO	Macho Man/Black and Red	15.00	30.00
NNO	Macho Man/Black and White	10.00	20.00
NNO	Scott Hall/Black and Red	12.50	25.00
NNO	Scott Hall/Black and White	12.50	25.00
NNO	Sting/Black and Red	10.00	20.00
NNO	Sting/Black and White	15.00	30.00

1999 Toy Biz WCW Smash 'N Slam 2-Packs

NNO	The Giant/Kevin Nash		
NNO	Macho Man/Miss Elizabeth		
NNO	Sting/Hulk Hogan	15.00	30.00

2001 Toy Biz WCW Target Exclusives

NNO	Hollywood Hogan	20.00	40.00
NNO	Kevin Nash	12.50	25.00

2000 Toy Biz WCW Thunder Slam

NNO	Bagwell/Jarrett/Vampiro		
NNO	Goldberg/Bam Bam Bigelow	10.00	20.00
NNO	Scott Hall/KevinNash	20.00	40.00
NNO	Sting/Bret Hart	10.00	20.00

2001 Toy Biz WCW TNT

NNO	Goldberg	17.50	35.00
NNO	Jeff Jarrett	12.50	25.00
NNO	Scott Steiner	15.00	30.00
NNO	Vampiro	12.50	25.00

2000 Toy Biz WCW Tuff Talkin' Wrestlers

NNO	Scott Steiner	15.00	30.00
NNO	Buff Bagwell	15.00	30.00
NNO	Macho Man Randy Savage	25.00	50.00
NNO	Konnan	12.50	25.00

2000 Toy Biz WCW Tuff Talkin' Wrestlers 2-Packs

NNO	Goldberg/Kevin Nash	30.00	75.00
NNO	Sting/Diamond Dallas Page	30.00	60.00

2000 Toy Biz WCW Unleashed

NNO	Franchise (Shane Douglas)	15.00	30.00
NNO	Kidman	15.00	30.00
NNO	Mike Awesome	10.00	20.00
NNO	Vampiro	12.50	25.00

2000 Toy Biz WCW Whiplashers

NNO	Kidman vs. Rey Mysterio		
NNO	Scott Steiner vs. Buff Bagwell		
NNO	Sting vs. Goldberg		

2000 Toy Biz WCW Window Crashers

NNO	Goldberg		
NNO	Hulk Hogan		

NNO	Kevin Nash		
NNO	Sting		

1991 Toymax WCW Finger Fighters

NNO	Lex Luger & Sid Vicious		
NNO	Sting & Ric Flair		

1991 Toymax WCW Wrestling Champs

NNO	Lex Luger		
NNO	Ric Flair		
NNO	Rick Steiner		
NNO	Sid Vicious		
NNO	Sting		

2014 Wicked Cool Toys WWE Bobblestars

NNO	CM Punk		
NNO	Daniel Bryan		
NNO	John Cena		
NNO	Rey Mysterio		
NNO	Road Warrior Animal		
NNO	Road Warrior Hawk		
NNO	Undertaker		

2019 Wicked Cool Toys WWE Micro Maniax Battle Game On!

NNO	Wrestling Ring		

2019 Wicked Cool Toys WWE Micro Maniax Series 1

NNO	Alexa Bliss		
NNO	Braun Strowman		
NNO	Daniel Bryan		
NNO	Finn Balor		
NNO	John Cena		
NNO	Macho Man Randy Savage		
NNO	Roman Reigns		
NNO	Ronda Rousey		

1985 Winston Toys WWF Hulk Hogan Rock 'n' Wrestling Figurine Erasers

NNO	Hulk Hogan	75.00	150.00
NNO	Iron Sheik	100.00	200.00
NNO	Jimmy "Superfly" Snuka	30.00	75.00
NNO	Junkyard Dog		
NNO	Rowdy Roddy Piper		
NNO	Wendi Richter		

1985 Winston Toys WWF Hulk Hogan Rock 'n' Wrestling Figurine Erasers (loose)

NNO	Hulk Hogan		
NNO	Iron Sheik		
NNO	Jimmy "Superfly" Snuka		
NNO	Junkyard Dog		
NNO	Rowdy Roddy Piper		
NNO	Wendi Richter		

2019 Zag Toys Domez WWE

NNO	Andre the Giant		
NNO	Jake The Snake Roberts		
NNO	Macho Man Randy Savage		
NNO	Ric Flair		
NNO	Rowdy Roddy Piper		
NNO	Sting		
NNO	Stone Cold Steve Austin		
NNO	Undertaker		
NNO	Undertaker Clear CH		